W9-CTW-422

FOR REFERENCE

Do Not Take From This Room

Contemporary
Literary Criticism

Guide to Gale Literary Criticism Series

When you need to review criticism of literary works, these are the Gale series to use:

If the author's death date is: **You should turn to:**

After Dec. 31, 1959
(or author is still living)

CONTEMPORARY LITERARY CRITICISM

for example: Jorge Luis Borges, Anthony Burgess,
William Faulkner, Mary Gordon,
Ernest Hemingway, Iris Murdoch

1900 through 1959

TWENTIETH-CENTURY LITERARY CRITICISM

for example: Willa Cather, F. Scott Fitzgerald,
Henry James, Mark Twain, Virginia Woolf

1800 through 1899

NINETEENTH-CENTURY LITERATURE CRITICISM

for example: Fedor Dostoevski, Nathaniel Hawthorne,
George Sand, William Wordsworth

1400 through 1799

LITERATURE CRITICISM FROM 1400 TO 1800
(excluding Shakespeare)

for example: Anne Bradstreet, Daniel Defoe,
Alexander Pope, François Rabelais,
Jonathan Swift, Phillis Wheatley

SHAKESPEAREAN CRITICISM

Shakespeare's plays and poetry

Antiquity through 1399

CLASSICAL AND MEDIEVAL LITERATURE CRITICISM

for example: Dante, Homer, Plato, Sophocles, Vergil,
the Beowulf Poet

Gale also publishes related criticism series:

BLACK LITERATURE CRITICISM

This three-volume series presents criticism of works by major black writers of the past two hundred years.

CHILDREN'S LITERATURE REVIEW

This series covers authors of all eras who have written for the preschool through high school audience.

DRAMA CRITICISM

This series covers playwrights of all nationalities and periods of literary history.

POETRY CRITICISM

This series covers poets of all nationalities, movements, and periods of literary history.

SHORT STORY CRITICISM

This series covers the major short fiction writers of all nationalities and periods of literary history.

ISSN 0091-3421

Volume 72

Contemporary Literary Criticism

Excerpts from Criticism of the
Works of Today's Novelists, Poets,
Playwrights, Short Story Writers, Scriptwriters,
and Other Creative Writers

Thomas Votteler
EDITOR

Elizabeth Henry
Marie Lazzari
Thomas Ligotti
Sean René Pollock
David Segal
Bridget Travers
Janet M. Witalec
Robyn Young
ASSOCIATE EDITORS

Gale Research Inc. · DETROIT · LONDON

Riverside Community College
Library
4800 Magnolia Avenue
Riverside, California 92506

NOV '92

STAFF

Thomas Votteler, *Editor*

Elizabeth Henry, Marie Lazzari, Sean René Pollock, Bridget Travers,
Janet M. Witalec, Robyn Young, *Associate Editors*

Jennifer Brostrom, Ian A. Goodhall, Christopher Giroux, Kyung-Sun Lim, Dale R. Miller, Brigham Narins,
Kristin Palm, Alexander C. Sweda, *Assistant Editors*

Jeanne A. Gough, *Production & Permissions Manager*
Linda M. Pugliese, *Production Supervisor*
Paul Lewon, Maureen A. Puhl, Camille P. Robinson, Jennifer VanSickle, *Editorial Associates*
Donna Craft, Rosita D'Souza, Sheila Walencewicz, *Editorial Assistants*

Sandra C. Davis, *Permissions Supervisor (Text)*
Maria L. Franklin, Josephine M. Keene, Michele Lonoconus, Denise M. Singleton,
Kimberly F. Smilay, *Permissions Associates*
Brandy C. Johnson, Shelly Rakoczy, Shalice Shah, *Permissions Assistants*

Margaret A. Chamberlain, *Permissions Supervisor (Pictures)*
Pamela A. Hayes, *Permissions Associate*
Amy Lynn Emrich, Karla Kulkis, Nancy Rattenbury, Keith Reed, *Permissions Assistants*

Victoria B. Cariappa, *Research Manager*
Maureen Richards, *Research Supervisor*
Mary Beth McElmeel, Tamara C. Nott, *Editorial Associates*
Andrea B. Ghorai, Daniel Jankowski, Julie Karmazin, Robert S. Lazich, *Editorial Assistants*

Mary Beth Trimper, *Production Director*
Shanna Heilveil, *Production Assistant*

Cynthia Baldwin, *Art Director*
Nick Jakubiak, C. J. Jonik, *Keyliners*

Since this page cannot legibly accommodate all the copyright notices, the Acknowledgments section constitutes an extension of the copyright notice.

While every effort has been made to ensure the reliability of the information presented in this publication, Gale Research Inc. does not guarantee the accuracy of the data contained herein. Gale accepts no payment for listing; and inclusion in the publication of any organization, agency, institution, publication, service, or individual does not imply endorsement of the editors or publisher.

Errors brought to the attention of the publisher and verified to the satisfaction of the publisher will be corrected in future editions.

The paper used in this publication meets the minimum requirements of American National Standard for Information Sciences—Permanence Paper for Printed Library Materials, ANSI Z39.48-1984. ∞™

This publication is a creative work copyrighted by Gale Research Inc. and fully protected by all applicable copyright laws, as well as by misappropriation, trade secret, unfair competition, and other applicable laws. The authors and editors of this work have added value to the underlying factual material herein through one or more of the following: unique and original selection, coordination, expression, arrangement, and classification of the information.

Gale Research Inc. will vigorously defend all of its rights in this publication.

Copyright © 1992 by Gale Research Inc.
835 Penobscot Building
Detroit, MI 48226

All rights reserved including the right of reproduction in whole or in part in any form.

Library of Congress Catalog Card Number 76-38938
ISBN 0-8103-4976-0
ISSN 0091-3421

Printed in the United States of America

Published simultaneously in the United Kingdom
by Gale Research International Limited
(An affiliated company of Gale Research Inc.)
10 9 8 7 6 5 4 3 2 1

Contents

Preface   vii

Acknowledgments ix

Russell Banks 1940-..1
  American novelist

Ingmar Bergman 1918-..25
  Swedish scriptwriter

Heinrich Böll 1917-1985...65
  German short story writer

Philip K. Dick 1928-1982 103
  American novelist

Eduardo Galeano 1940-..126
  Uruguayan novelist

Graham Greene 1904-1991 146
  English novelist

Marilyn Hacker 1942-...181
  American poet

Susan Howe 1937-...194
  Irish-born American poet

Paule Marshall 1929-...210
  American novelist

Paul Muldoon 1951-...263
  Irish poet

Raymond Mungo 1946-..285
  American nonfiction writer

Thomas Pynchon 1937-...294
  American novelist; entry devoted to The Crying of Lot 49

Jack Spicer 1925-1965 343
  American poet

Bruce Sterling 1954-...367
  American novelist

Gore Vidal 1925-...375
  American novelist

Literary Criticism Series Cumulative Author Index   411

CLC Cumulative Nationality Index   465

CLC-72 Title Index   479

Preface

Named "one of the twenty-five most distinguished reference titles published during the past twenty-five years" by *Reference Quarterly,* the *Contemporary Literary Criticism (CLC)* series provides readers with critical commentary and general information on more than 2,000 authors now living or who died after December 31, 1959. Previous to the publication of the first volume of *CLC* in 1973, there was no ongoing digest monitoring scholarly and popular sources of critical opinion and explication of modern literature. *CLC,* therefore, has fulfilled an essential need, particularly since the complexity and variety of contemporary literature makes the function of criticism especially important to today's reader.

Scope of the Series

CLC presents significant passages from published criticism of works by creative writers. Since many of the authors covered by *CLC* inspire continual critical commentary, writers are often represented in more than one volume. There is, of course, no duplication of reprinted criticism.

Authors are selected for inclusion for a variety of reasons, among them the publication or dramatic production of a critically acclaimed new work, the reception of a major literary award, revival of interest in past writings, or the adaptation of a literary work to film or television.

Attention is also given to several other groups of writers—authors of considerable public interest—about whose work criticism is often difficult to locate. These include mystery and science fiction writers, literary and social critics, foreign writers, and authors who represent particular ethnic groups within the United States.

Format of the Book

Each *CLC* volume contains about 500 individual excerpts—with approximately seventeen excerpts per author—taken from hundreds of book review periodicals, general magazines, scholarly journals, monographs, and books. Entries include critical evaluations spanning from the beginning of an author's career to the most current commentary. Interviews, feature articles, and other published writings that offer insight into the author's works are also presented. Students, teachers, librarians, and researchers will find that the generous excerpts and supplementary material in *CLC* provide them with vital information needed to write a term paper, analyze a poem, or lead a book discussion group. In addition, complete bibliographical citations note the original source and all of the information necessary for a term paper footnote or bibliography.

Features

A *CLC* author entry consists of the following elements:

• The **author heading** cites the form under which the author has most commonly published, followed by birth date, and death date when applicable. Uncertainty as to a birth or death date is indicated by a question mark.

• A **portrait** of the author is included when available.

• A brief **biographical and critical introduction** to the author and his or her work precedes the excerpted criticism. The first line of the introduction provides the author's full name, pseudonyms (if applicable), nationality, and a listing of genres in which the author has written. Since *CLC* is not intended to be a definitive biographical source, cross-references have been included to direct readers to these useful sources published by Gale Research: *Short Story Criticism* and *Children's Literature Review, Contemporary Authors, Something about the Author, Dictionary of Literary Biography,* and *Contemporary Authors Autobiography Series* and *Something about the Author Autobiography Series.* Previous volumes of *CLC* in which the author has been featured are also listed in the introduction.

• A list of **principal works,** usually divided into genre categories, notes the most important works by the author.

• The **excerpted criticism** represents various kinds of critical writing, ranging in form from the brief review to the scholarly exegesis. Essays are selected by the editors to reflect the spectrum of opinion about a specific work or about an author's literary career in general. The excerpts are presented chronologically, adding a useful perspective to the entry. All titles by the author featured in the entry are printed in boldface type, which enables the reader to easily identify the works being discussed. Publication information (such as publisher names and book prices) and parenthetical numerical references (such as footnotes or page and line references to specific editions of a work) have been deleted at the editor's discretion to provide smoother reading of the text.

• A complete **bibliographical citation** designed to help the user find the original essay or book follows each excerpt.

• A concise **further reading** section appears at the end of entries on authors for whom a significant amount of criticism exists in addition to the pieces reprinted in *CLC*. In some cases, this annotated bibliography includes references to material for which the editors could not obtain reprint rights.

Other Features

• An **Acknowledgments** section lists the copyright holders who have granted permission to reprint material in this volume of *CLC*. It does not, however, list every book or periodical reprinted or consulted during the preparation of the volume.

• A **Cumulative Author Index** lists all the authors who have appeared in the various literary criticism series published by Gale Research, with cross-references to Gale's biographical and autobiographical series. A full listing of the series referenced there appears on the first page of the indexes of this volume. Readers will welcome this cumulated author index as a useful tool for locating an author within the various series. The index, which lists birth and death dates when available, will be particularly valuable for those authors who are identified with a certain period but whose death date causes them to be placed in another, or for those authors whose careers span two periods. For example, Ernest Hemingway is found in *CLC*, yet a writer often associated with him, F. Scott Fitzgerald, is found in *Twentieth-Century Literary Criticism*.

• A **Cumulative Nationality Index** alphabetically lists all authors featured in *CLC* by nationality, followed by numbers corresponding to the volumes in which they appear.

• A **Title Index** alphabetically lists all titles reviewed in the current volume of *CLC*. Listings are followed by the author's name and the corresponding page numbers where the titles are discussed. English translations of foreign titles and variations of titles are cross-referenced to the title under which a work was originally published. Titles of novels, novellas, dramas, films, record albums, and poetry, short story, and essay collections are printed in italics, while all individual poems, short stories, essays, and songs are printed in roman type within quotation marks; when published separately (e.g., T.S. Eliot's poem *The Waste Land*), the titles of long poems are printed in italics.

• In response to numerous suggestions from librarians, Gale has also produced a **special paperbound edition** of the *CLC* title index. This annual cumulation, which alphabetically lists all titles reviewed in the series, is available to all customers and will be published with the first volume of *CLC* issued in each calendar year. Additional copies of the index are available upon request. Librarians and patrons will welcome this separate index: it saves shelf space, is easy to use, and is disposable upon receipt of the following year's cumulation.

A Note to the Reader

When writing papers, students who quote directly from any volume in the Literary Criticism Series may use the following general forms to footnote reprinted criticism. The first example pertains to material drawn from periodicals, the second to material reprinted from books:

[1]Anne Tyler, "Manic Monologue," *The New Republic* 200 (April 17, 1989), 44-6; excerpted and reprinted in *Contemporary Literary Criticism,* Vol. 58, ed. Roger Matuz (Detroit: Gale Research Inc., 1990), p. 325.

[2]Patrick Reilly, *The Literature of Guilt: From 'Gulliver' to Golding* (University of Iowa Press, 1988); excerpted and reprinted in *Contemporary Literary Criticism,* Vol. 58, ed. Roger Matuz (Detroit: Gale Research Inc., 1990), pp. 206-12.

Suggestions Are Welcome

The editors welcome the comments and suggestions of readers to expand the coverage and enhance the usefulness of the series.

Acknowledgments

The editors wish to thank the copyright holders of the excerpted criticism included in this volume, the permissions managers of many book and magazine publishing companies for assisting us in securing reprint rights, and Anthony Bogucki for assistance with copyright research. We are also grateful to the staffs of the Detroit Public Library, the Library of Congress, the University of Detroit Library, Wayne State University Purdy/Kresge Library Complex, and the University of Michigan Libraries for making their resources available to us. Following is a list of the copyright holders who granted us permission to reprint material in this volume of *CLC*. Every effort has been made to trace copyright, but if omissions have been made, please let us know.

COPYRIGHTED EXCERPTS IN *CLC*, VOLUME 72, WERE REPRINTED FROM THE FOLLOWING PERIODICALS:

American Film, v. XIV, October, 1988. Copyright 1988 by *American Film.—American Forests,* v. 77, March, 1971. Copyright © 1971 by The American Forestry Association.—*American Poetry Review,* v. 15, July-August, 1986 for "Recharging the Canon: Some Reflections on Feminist Poetics and the Avant-Garde" by Marjorie Perloff. Copyright © 1986 by World Poetry, Inc. Reprinted by permission of the author.—*Analog Science Fiction/Science Fact,* v. CVIII, December, 1988 for "Islands in the Net" by Tom Easton. © 1988 by Davis Publications, Inc. Reprinted by permission of the author.—*Anglo-Welsh Review,* 1981.—*Isaac Asimov's Science Fiction Magazine,* 1986 for "The Neuromantics" by Norman Spinrad. Copyright © 1986 by Norman Spinrad. Reprinted by permission of the author.—*Belles Lettres: A Review of Books by Women,* v. 7, Winter, 1991-92. Reprinted by permission of the publisher.—*Best Sellers,* v. 45, August, 1985. Copyright © 1985 Helen Dwight Reid Educational Foundation. Reprinted by permission of the publisher.—*The Bloomsbury Review,* v. 9, November-December, 1989 for a review of "Affliction" by Robert F. Gish; v. 11, April-May, 1991, for a review of "Beyond the Revolution" by Phil Woods; v. 11, December, 1991 for a review of "The Book of Embraces" by Bronwyn Mills; v. 11, December, 1991 for an interview with Eduardo Galeano and Bronwyn Mills. Copyright © by Owaissa Communications Company, Inc. 1989, 1991. All reprinted by permission of the respective authors.—*Book World—The Washington Post,* April 5, 1987 for "History as Fable: An American Mosaic" by Robert Cox; May 22, 1988 for "Sambas, Saints and Superstitions" by Pat Aufderheide; July 7, 1991 for "The Dream World of Eduardo Galeano." © 1987, 1988, 1991, *The Washington Post.* All reprinted by permission of the respective authors./ November 22, 1970. © 1970 Postrib Corp. Reprinted by courtesy of the *Chicago Tribune* and *The Washington Post.*/ June 30, 1985; June 26, 1988; August 27, 1989. © 1985, 1988, 1989, *The Washington Post.* All reprinted by permission of the publisher.—*Books Abroad,* v. 47, Autumn, 1973. Copyright 1973 by the University of Oklahoma Press. Reprinted by permission of the publisher.—*Boston Review,* v. XI, August, 1986 for a review of "Success Stories" by John Domini. Copyright © 1986 by the Boston Critic, Inc. Reprinted by permission of the author.—*boundary 2,* v. VI, Fall, 1977; v. IX, Winter, 1981. Copyright © *boundary 2,* 1977, 1981. Both reprinted by permission of the publisher.—*Callaloo,* v. 6, Spring-Summer, 1983 for "Paltry Things: Immigrants and Marginal Men in Paule Marshall's Short Fiction" by Marilyn Nelson Waniek. Copyright © 1983 by Charles H. Rowell. All rights reserved. Reprinted by permission of the author.—*Chicago Review,* v. 35, Autumn, 1985. Copyright © 1985 by *Chicago Review.* Reprinted by permission of the publisher.—*Chicago Tribune—Books,* June 30, 1991 for "A Tragic Continent's Fantasies and Dreams" by Rockwell Gray; October 6, 1991 for "Caribbean Voices" by Jane Smiley. © copyrighted 1991, Chicago Tribune Company. All rights reserved. Both reprinted by permission of the respective authors.—*The Christian Science Monitor,* April 30, 1970; July 25, 1984; July 20, 1987. © 1970, 1984, 1987 The Christian Science Publishing Society. All rights reserved. All reprinted by permission from *The Christian Science Monitor.*—*College Literature,* v. XII, Winter, 1985. Copyright © 1985 by West Chester University. Reprinted by permission of the publisher.—*Commonweal,* v. LXXX, July 8, 1966; v. C, May 10, 1974. Copyright © 1974 Commonweal Publishing Co., Inc. Reprinted by permission of Commonweal Foundation.—*Conjunctions,* v. 11, 1987. Reprinted by permission of the publisher.—*Contemporary Literature,* v. 26, Winter, 1985; v. 30, Winter, 1989. © 1985, 1989 by the Board of Regents of the University of Wisconsin System. Both reprinted by permission of The University of Wisconsin Press.—*Criticism: A Quarterly for Literature and the Arts,* v. XXIX, Winter, 1987 for "Bergman's 'Fanny and Alexander': Family Romance or Artistic Allegory?" by Lynda K. Bundtzen. Reprinted by permission of Wayne State University Press and the author.—*Critique: Studies in Modern Fiction,* v. XVI, 1974. Copyright © 1974 Helen Dwight Reid Educational Foundation. Reprinted with permission of the Helen Dwight Reid Educational Foundation, published by Heldref Publications, 1319 18th Street, NW, Washington DC 20036-1802.—*The Denver Quarterly,* v. 20, Summer, 1985 for "Studying Interior Architecture by Keyhole: Four Poets" by Reg Saner. Copyright © 1985 by the University of Denver. Reprinted by permission of the author.—*Éire-Ireland,* v. XXIV, Spring, 1989 for "Paul Muldoon's 'Juggling a Red-Hot Half-Brick in an Old Sock': Poets in Ireland Renovate the English-Language Sonnet" by Ronald Marken. Copyright © 1989 Irish American Cultural Institute, 2115 Summit Ave., No. 5026, St. Paul, MN 55105. Reprinted by permission of the publisher and the author.—*Essays in Literature,* v. 1, Spring, 1974. Copyright 1974 by Western Illinois University. Reprinted by permission of the publisher.—*Film Comment,* v. 14, January-February, 1978 for "Responsibilities of a Gay Film Critic" by Robin Wood. Copyright © 1978 by the author. Reprinted by permission of the author./ v. 3, Spring, 1965. Copyright © 1965 by Lorien Productions, Inc.; Summer, 1970. Copyright © 1970 by Film Comment Publishing Corporation. All rights reserved. Both reprinted by permission of the publisher.—*The German Quarterly,* v. XLV, May, 1972. Copyright © 1972 by the American Association of Teachers of German. Reprinted by permission of the publisher.—*The Germanic Review,* v. LIX, Summer, 1984 for "Heinrich Böll's 'Nicht nur zur Weihnachtszeit': A Satire for All Ages" by Robert C. Conrad. Copyright 1984 by Helen Dwight Reid Educational Foundation. Reprinted by permission of the author.—*Ironwood,* v. 14, Fall, 1986. Copyright © 1986 by Ironwood Press. Reprinted by permission of the publisher.—*Journal of Black Studies,* v. 1, December, 1970. Copyright © 1970 by Sage Publications, Inc. Reprinted with permission of Sage Publications, Inc.—*The Kenyon Review,* v. X, Summer, 1988 for "Formal Allegiances: Selected Poems × 6″" by Dave Smith. Copyright 1988 by Kenyon College. All rights reserved. Reprinted by permission of the author.—*The Listener,* v. 118, December 17-24, 1987 for "Remember Pound" by Stephen Fender. © British Broadcasting Corp. 1987. Reprinted by permission of the author.—*Literature/Film Quarterly,* v. 12, 1984. © copyright 1984 Salisbury State College. Reprinted by permission of the publisher.—*Locus,* v. 23, September, 1989 for a review of "Crystal Express" by Dan Chow. © 1989 Dan Chow. Reprinted by permission of the publisher and the author.—*London Review of Books,* v. 9, 1987 for "Out of the Blue" by Mark Ford; v. 12, December 20, 1990 for "Muldoon—A Mystery" by Michael Hofmann; v. 13, August 29, 1991 for "Voyage to Uchronia" by Paul Delany. All appear here by permission of the *London Review of Books* and the authors.—*Los Angeles Times Book Review,* April 10, 1983; June 22, 1986; March 15, 1987; May 24, 1987; July 17, 1988; December 16, 1990; September 1, 1991. Copyright, 1983, 1986, 1987, 1988, 1990, 1991, *Los Angeles Times.* All reprinted by permission of the publisher.—*The Nation,* New York, v. 236, June 25, 1983; v. 240, April 27, 1985; v. 243, September 13, 1986; v. 243, November 1, 1986; v. 253, December 16, 1991. Copyright 1983, 1985, 1986, 1991 *The Nation* magazine/The Nation Company, Inc. All reprinted by permission of the publisher.—*The New Criterion,* v. 8, November, 1989 for "Graham Greene: The Politics" by Bruce Bawer. Copyright © 1989 by The Foundation for Cultural Review. Reprinted by permission of the author.—*New England Review and Bread Loaf Quarterly,* v. XII, Winter, 1989. Copyright © 1989 by Kenyon Hill Publications, Inc. Reprinted by permission of the publisher.—*New Letters,* v. 40, October, 1973 for "Paule Marshall's Timeless People" by Peter Nazareth. © copyright 1973 The Curators of the University of Missouri. Reprinted by permission of the publisher and the author./ v. 53, Spring, 1987 for an interview with Russell Banks and Trish Reeves. Reprinted by permission of the publisher, Russell Banks and Trish Reeves.—*The New Republic,* v. 154, May 14, 1966; v. 155, November 12, 1966; v. 194, April 7, 1986; v. 201, September, 1989. © 1966, 1986, 1989 The New Republic, Inc. All reprinted by permission of *The New Republic.*—*New Statesman,* v. 3, June 13, 1986. © 1986 The Statesman & Nation Publishing Co. Ltd. Reprinted by permission of the publisher.—*New Statesman & Society,* v. 49, May 12, 1989; v. 2, November 3, 1989. © 1989 Statesman & Nation Publishing Company Limited. Both reprinted by permission of the publisher.—*The New York Review of Books,* v. XIV, March 26, 1970; v. XXXI, July 19, 1984; v. XXXVI, December 7, 1989; v. XXXVII, March 29, 1990; v. XXXVII, August 16, 1990; v. XXXVIII, May 30, 1991. Copyright © 1970, 1984, 1989, 1990, 1991 Nyrev, Inc. Reprinted by permission from *The New York Review of Books.*—*The New York Times,* June 11, 1987. Copyright © 1987 by The New York Times Company. All reprinted by permission of the publisher.—*The New York Times Book Review,* May 1, 1966; June 28, 1970; November 15, 1970; September 7, 1975; April 13, 1980; May 26, 1985; October 27, 1985; June 22, 1986; June 14, 1987; September 18, 1988; January 21, 1990; April 21, 1991; September 15, 1991; October 27, 1991; November 3, 1991. Copyright © 1966, 1970, 1975, 1980, 1985, 1986, 1987, 1988, 1990, 1991 by The New York Times Company. All reprinted by permission of the publisher.—*Newsweek,* v. LXXVI, August 10, 1970. Copyright 1970, by Newsweek, Inc. All rights reserved. Reprinted by permission of the publisher.—*Northwest Review,* v. XXIV, 1986. Copyright © 1986 by *Northwest Review.* Reprinted by permission of the publisher.—*Novel: A Forum on Fiction,* v. 22, Fall, 1988. Copyright © Novel Corp., 1988. Reprinted by permission of the publisher.—*The Observer,* November 22, 1987; November 5, 1989. Both reprinted by permission of The Observer Limited, London.—*Pacific Historical Review,* v. XLIV, November, 1975 for "Open Veins of Latin America: Five Centuries of the Pillage of a Continent" by Ramon Eduardo Ruiz. © 1975 by the Pacific Coast Branch, American Historical Association. Reprinted by permission of The Branch and the author.—*Parnassus: Poetry in Review,* v. 14, 1988. Copyright © 1988 Poetry in Review Foundation, NY. Reprinted by permission of the publisher.—*Poetry,* December, 1985 for a review of "Assumptions" by Sandra M. Gilbert. © 1985 by the Modern Poetry Association. Reprinted by permission of the Editor of *Poetry* and the author.—*Prairie Schooner,* v. 61, Winter, 1987 for "Love, Death and the Changing of the Seasons" by Kathleene West. © 1987 by University of Nebraska Press. Reprinted from *Prairie Schooner* by permission of the University of Nebraska Press and the author.—*SAGE: A Scholarly Journal on Black Women,* v. III, Fall, 1986. Copyright © 1986 by The Sage Women's Educational Press, Inc. All rights reserved. Reprinted by permission of the publisher.—*Saturday Review,* v. XLIII, August 27, 1960. © 1960 *Saturday Review* magazine.—*Science and Society,* v. XXXIX, Winter, 1975-76. Copyright 1976 by S & S Quarterly, Inc. Reprinted by permission of the publisher.—*Science-Fiction Studies,* v. 11, March, 1984; v. 15, July, 1988. Copyright © 1984, 1988 by SFS Publications. Reprinted by permission of the publisher.—*Seminar,* v. XX, November, 1984. © The Canadian Association of University Teachers of German 1984. Reprinted by permission of the publisher.—*The Southern Humanities Review,* v. XVII, Winter 1983 for "Who Bids for Tristero? The Conversion of Pynchon's Oedipa Maas" by Robert

N. Watson. Reprinted by permission of the author.—*The Spectator,* v. 263, November 4, 1989. © 1989 by *The Spectator.* Reprinted by permission of *The Spectator.*—*The Threepenny Review,* v. V, Spring, 1983. © copyright 1983 by *The Threepenny Review.* Reprinted by permission of the publisher.—*The Times Literary Supplement,* n. 3711, April 20, 1973; n. 3855, January 30, 1976; n. 3929, July 1, 1977; n. 4050, November 14, 1980. © The Times Literary Supplements Limited 1973, 1976, 1977, 1980. All reproduced from *The Times Literary Supplement* by permission.—*TriQuarterly 20,* n. 20, Winter, 1971. © 1971 by *TriQuarterly,* Northwestern University.—*The Village Voice,* v. XXXII, October 6, 1987 for "His Country, Right or Wrong" by Tom Carson; v. XXXVI, July 2, 1991 for "Fond Embraces" by Alan West. Copyright © News Group Publications, Inc., 1987, 1991. Both reprinted by permission of *The Village Voice* and the respective authors.—*VLS,* n. 54, April, 1987. Copyright © 1987 News Group Publications, Inc./ n. 15, March, 1983 for a review of "Days and Nights of Love and War" by Eve Ottenberg; n. 25, April, 1984 for "Meaningless Relationships" by Geoffrey O'Brien; n. 78, September, 1989 for "Head of the Class" by Fred Pfeil; n. 84, April, 1990 for a review of "Going Back to the River" by Elizabeth Alexander; n. 91, December, 1990 for "The Way We Word" by Geoffrey O'Brien. Copyright © 1983, 1984, 1989, 1990 News Group Publications, Inc. All reprinted by permission of *The Village Voice* and the respective authors.—*The Western Journal of Black Studies,* v. 10, Fall, 1986. Reprinted by permission of the publisher.—*The Women's Review of Books,* v. VII, April, 1990 for "The Roots of Rage" by Carol Ascher; v. VII, July, 1990 for "Feminist Formalist" by Judith Barrington; v. VIII, July, 1991 for an interview with Paule Marshall by Sylvia Baer; v. IX, November, 1991 for "Compromised Lives" by Carol Ascher. Copyright © 1990, 1991. All rights reserved. All reprinted by permission of the respective authors.

COPYRIGHTED EXCERPTS IN *CLC,* VOLUME 72, WERE REPRINTED FROM THE FOLLOWING BOOKS:

Busia, Abena P. A. From "What Is Your Nation?: Reconnecting Africa and Her Diaspora through Paule Marshall's 'Praisesong for the Widow'," in *Changing Our Own Words: Essays on Criticism, Theory, and Writing by Black Women.* Edited by Cheryl A. Wall. Rutgers University Press, 1989. Copyright © 1989 by Rutgers, The State University. All rights reserved. Reprinted by permission of the publisher.—Christol, Hélène. From "Paule Marshall's Bajan Women in 'Brown Girl, Brownstones'," in *Women and War: The Changing Status of American Women from the 1930's to the 1950's.* Edited by Maria Diedrich and Dorothea Fischer-Hornung. Berg, 1990. All rights reserved. Reprinted by permission of Berg Publishers Ltd.—Galeano, Eduardo. From *Days and Nights of Love and War.* Translated by Judith Brister. Monthly Review Press, 1983. Copyright © 1983 by Monthly Review Press. All rights reserved.—Ghurye, Charlotte W. From *The Writer and Society: Studies in the Fiction of Günter Grass and Heinrich Böll.* Herbert Lang, 1976. © Herbert Lang & Co. Ltd., Bern and Peter Lang Ltd., Frankfurt/M 1976. Reprinted by permission of the publisher.—Johnstone, Richard. From *The Will to Believe: Novelists of the Nineteen-thirties.* Oxford University Press, Oxford, 1982. © Richard Johnstone, 1982. Reprinted by permission of Oxford University Press.—Kelly, Richard. From *Graham Greene.* Frederick Ungar Publishing Co., 1984. Copyright © 1984 by The Ungar Publishing Company. Reprinted by permission of the publisher.—Kiernan, Robert F. From *Gore Vidal.* Frederick Ungar Publishing Co., 1982. Copyright © 1982 by The Ungar Publishing Company. Reprinted by permission of the publisher.—Mauriac, François. From *Men I Hold Great.* Translated by Elsie Pell. Philosophical Library, 1951. Copyright, 1951, by Philosophical Library. Reprinted by permission of the publisher.—Mendelson, Edward. From "The Sacred, the Profane, and 'The Crying of Lot 49'," in *Individual and Community: Variations on a Theme in American Fiction.* Edited by Kenneth H. Baldwin and David K. Kirby. Duke University Press, 1975. Copyright © 1975 by Duke University Press, Durham, NC. Reprinted by permission of the publisher.—Mungo, Raymond. From *Mungobus.* Avon Books, 1979. Copyright © 1970, 1975 by Raymond Mungo. All rights reserved.—Olsen, Lance. From *Ellipse of Uncertainty: An Introduction to Postmodern Fantasy.* Greenwood Press, 1987. Copyright © 1987 by Lance Olsen. All rights reserved. Reprinted by permissions of Greenwood Publishing Group, Inc., Westport, CT.—Pierce, Hazel. From "Philip K. Dick's Political Dreams," in *Philip K. Dick.* Edited by Martin Harry Greenberg and Joseph D. Olander. Taplinger Publishing Company, Inc., 1983. Copyright © 1983 by Martin Harry Greenberg and Joseph D. Olander. All rights reserved.—Prichett, V. S. From *The Tale Bearers: Literary Essays.* Random House, 1980. Published in England as *The Tale Bearers: Essays on English, American, and Other Writers.* Chatto & Windus, 1980. Copyright © 1980 by V. S. Pritchett. All rights reserved. Reprinted by permission of Random House, Inc. In Canada by the author and Chatto & Windus.—Pynchon, Thomas. From *The Crying of Lot 49.* Lippincott, 1966. Copyright © 1966, 1965 by Thomas Pynchon. All rights reserved.—Rea, Paul W. From "Individual and Societal Encounters with Darkness and the Shadow in 'The Third Man'," in *Film and Literature: A Comparative Approach to Adaption.* Edited by Wendell Aycock and Michael Schoenecke. Texas Tech University Press, 1988. Copyright 1988 Texas Tech University Press. All rights reserved. Reprinted by permission of the publisher and the author.—Reid, James Henderson. From *Heinrich Böll: Withdrawal and Re-emergence.* Wolff, 1973. © 1973 Oswald Wolff (Publishers) Limited. Reprinted by permission of Berg Publishers Ltd.—Reyes, Angelita. From "Politics and Metaphors of Materialism in Paule Marshall's 'Praisesong for the Widow' and Toni Morrison's 'Tar Baby'," in *Politics and the Muse: Studies in the Politics of Recent American Literature.* Edited by Adam J. Sorkin. Bowling Green State University Popular Press, 1989. Copyright © 1989 by Bowling Green State University Popular Press. Reprinted by permission of the publisher.—Rhode, Eric. From *A History of the Cinema from Its Origins to 1970.* Hill and Wang, 1976. Copyright © 1976 by Eric Rhode. All rights reserved. Reprinted by permission of Hill and Wang, a division of Farrar, Straus and Giroux, Inc.—Samuels, Charles Thomas.

From an interview in *Encountering Directors.* By Charles Thomas Samuels. G. P. Putnam's Sons, 1972. Copyright © 1972 by Charles Thomas Samuels. All rights reserved. Reprinted by permission of The Putnam Publishing Group.—Schaub, Thomas H. From *Pynchon: The Voice of Ambiquity.* University of Illinois Press, 1981. © 1981 by the Board of Trustees of the University of Illinois. Reprinted by permission of the publisher and the author.— Scholes, Robert, and Eric S. Rabkin. From *Science Fiction: History, Science, Vision.* Oxford University Press, 1977. Copyright © 1977 by Oxford University Press, Inc. Reprinted by permission of the publisher—Schwarz, Wilhelm Johannes. From *Heinrich Böll, Teller of Tales: A Study of His Works and Characters.* Translated by Alexander Henderson and Elizabeth Henderson. Frederick Ungar Publishing Co., 1969. Copyright © 1969 by The Ungar Publishing Company. Reprinted by permission of the publisher.—Spinrad, Norman. From *Science Fiction in the Real World.* Southern Illinois University Press, 1990. Copyright © 1990 by Norman Spinrad. All rights reserved. Reprinted by permission of the publisher.—Tanner, Tony. From *Thomas Pynchon.* Methuen & Co. Ltd., 1982. © 1982 Tony Tanner. All rights reserved. Reprinted by permission of the publisher.—Warrick, Patricia S. From *Mind in Motion: The Fiction of Philip K. Dick.* Southern Illinois University Press, 1987. Copyright © 1987 by the Board of Trustees, Southern Illinois University. All rights reserved. Reprinted by permission of the publisher.—Washington, Mary Helen. From an afterword to *Brown Girl, Brownstones.* By Paule Marshall. The Feminist Press, 1981. Afterword Copyright © 1981, by Mary Helen Washington. All rights reserved.—Wood, Robin. From *Ingmar Bergman.* Praeger, 1969. © 1969 by Movie Magazine Limited. All rights reserved. Reprinted by permission of the author.

PHOTOGRAPHS AND ILLUSTRATIONS APPEARING IN *CLC,* VOLUME 72, WERE RECEIVED FROM THE FOLLOWING SOURCES:

© Jerry Bauer: **pp. 1, 126, 210, 375;** Courtesy of Svensk Filmindustri: **p. 25;** AB Svensk Filmindustri: **pp. 32, 40, 60;** The Granger Collection, New York: **p. 65;** The Bettmann Archive: **p. 146;** Topham/The Image Works: **p. 164;** Photograph by Layle Silbert: **p. 181;** Photograph by Janet Chalmers: **p. 194** Jacket of *Brown Girl, Brownstones: A Novel,* by Paule Marshall. Random House, 1959: **p. 239;** Courtesy of Bernard Stone, The Turret Book Shop: **p. 263;** Cover of *Why Browlee Left,* by Paul Muldoon. Faber & Faber, 1980. Reprinted by permission of Faber & Faber Limited: **p. 272;** Cover of *The Crying of Lot 49,* by Thomas Pynchon. Copyright © 1966, 1965 by Thomas Pynchon. Cover design by Suzanne Noli. Cover illustration © 1990 by Mark Penberthy. Reprinted by permission of HarperCollins Publishers, Inc.: **p. 307;** Senor Walter Gruen, The Estate of Remedios Varo: **p. 317;** Cover of *Book of Magazine Verse,* by Jack Spicer. White Rabbit Press, 1966: **p. 354;** Courtesy of Bruce Sterling: **p. 367.**

Russell Banks

1940-

American novelist, short story writer, and editor.

This entry focuses on Banks's works published between 1986 and 1991. For further information on his life and career, see *CLC,* Volume 37.

INTRODUCTION

Banks is best known as a naturalistic writer whose works address the psychological effects of poverty, child abuse, and alcoholism on working-class individuals. He has earned praise for his candid prose and trenchant evocations of the anxiety and hopelessness associated with life in economically depressed regions of the United States. Attempting to circumvent what he considers the artifice and didacticism of omniscient narration, Banks employs narrators who speak directly and intimately to the reader. He asserts that his primary goal is to realistically portray the pathos of human life: "As a writer I'm not so much interested in change . . . , really, as in pointing at and revealing pain. I'm horrified by pain. I'm sensitized, I suppose, to people who are in pain because of political and social reasons, oppression of one form or another, power; they're at the bottom, the weak side of a power relationship. And so I write about that, I try to portray that."

The eldest of four children born to working-class parents, Banks was raised in Barnstead, New Hampshire. As a youth he endured many hardships, including living on the brink of poverty and his parents' divorce. Banks enrolled at Colgate College in 1958, but left after only eight weeks because he felt like "a poor kid" among "the sons of the captains of American industry." After this experience, Banks decided to join Fidel Castro's revolutionary army in Cuba. His funds took him only as far St. Petersburg, Florida, however, where he lived in a trailer park, worked a variety of odd jobs, and began writing short fiction. Banks left Florida in the mid-1960s and traveled to the Yucatán and Jamaica, experiences he would later incorporate into his works. Deciding to continue his education, Banks earned an English degree from the University of North Carolina in 1967. He has since taught literature at such institutions as Sarah Lawrence College and Princeton University.

In his early works, Banks experimented with a variety of literary forms and techniques, revealing a talent for blending fantasy into realistically detailed stories. His first novel, *Family Life,* is constructed as a fable and satirizes conventional family histories by replacing the traditional roles of father, mother, and son with those of king, queen, and prince. In *Hamilton Stark,* whose protagonist is alternately presented as a violent alcoholic and as a benevolent man, Banks parodies such literary genres as the mystery,

the memoir, and biography. In the short story collections *Searching for Survivors* and *The New World,* Banks subtly merges extraordinary elements with ordinary ones. For example, in the story "The Conversion," included in *The New World,* Banks introduces a vision of Jesus Christ into his portrait of an emotionally confused adolescent. *The Relation of My Imprisonment* also evidences Banks's penchant for fictional experiments. This work, in which a prisoner publicly recants his sins against God and the religious community, is an allegorical tale modeled after a seventeenth-century literary genre popular among the Puritans known as the "Relation."

In the early 1980s, Banks began to focus on social problems, including poverty and racial and class discrimination, in his fiction. *The Book of Jamaica* chronicles the experiences of a New Hampshire college professor who travels to Jamaica to write a novel and is appalled at the destitution of the country's native inhabitants. The professor eventually befriends the Maroons, descendants of renegade African slaves who fight to preserve their way of life. In the short story collection *Trailerpark,* a work comprising thirteen interrelated stories, Banks examines how the poor, uneducated residents of a trailer park community in

New Hampshire contend with alcoholism, greed, and loneliness. Banks's fifth novel, *Continental Drift,* was the first of his works to attain critical and commercial success. Regarded as one of Banks's most naturalistic novels, the plot of *Continental Drift* shifts between Bob Dubois, a furnace repairman from New Hampshire, and Vanise Dorinville, a Haitian woman who suffers numerous abuses as she flees her country for the United States. After separately attempting to better their lives, Bob and Vanise accidentally meet in a squalid region of Southern Florida where they are both manipulated and betrayed. Critics praised Banks's realistic investigations into the oppression, alienation, and hopelessness often associated with modern American life. James Atlas asserted: "*Continental Drift* is the most convincing portrait I know of contemporary America: its greed, its uprootedness, its indifference to the past. This is a novel about the way we live now."

In the short fiction collection, *Success Stories,* Banks reveals the anxiety and despair of life in a small, working-class town. In one story, a twelve-year-old boy desperately writes letters to a television program called "Queen for a Day," hoping to secure a place on the show for his mother, who has been emotionally and physically mistreated by the boy's father. The novel *Affliction,* whose protagonist is a middle-aged man who was abused as a child, addresses the profound influence of childhood memories on adult life, the cyclical nature of familial violence, and the devastating effects of alcoholism. Banks further explores how people respond to hardships in his seventh novel, *The Sweet Hereafter.* This work differs, however, from his earlier novels in that it delves into the motivations and behaviors of an entire community. Tracing a small town's reaction to a school bus accident in which ten children are killed and many others are severely injured, *The Sweet Hereafter* examines the dynamics of grief, guilt, resentment, and recovery. Most critics concur that by introducing four narrators—the school bus driver, a man whose twin daughters died in the accident, a popular teenager who was paralyzed, and a lawyer determined to find someone to blame—Banks pervasively and poignantly depicts the complex and conflicting feelings that arise in the aftermath of tragedy.

PRINCIPAL WORKS

NOVELS

Family Life   1975
Hamilton Stark   1978
The Book of Jamaica   1980
The Relation of My Imprisonment   1984
Continental Drift   1985
Affliction   1989
The Sweet Hereafter   1991

SHORT FICTION

Searching for Survivors   1975
The New World   1978
Trailerpark   1981
Success Stories   1986

CRITICISM

Richard Eder

Quite steadily, and often powerfully, Russell Banks has been devising fictional varieties of the "this is poison" labels on cigarette advertisements.

Our society's promise of an affable world of clean microdots and expanding consumption—the equivalent of the pool-side set blithely puffing away—has lethal side effects, he tells us. Unlike cigarette ads, this easygoing social gospel comes without warnings; so here is Banks.

He is not much concerned with the sensibility class, those who can afford cocaine, condos and foreign cars with domestic exhaust. He writes about people a notch or two down: blue-collar workers looking for something better, the young unprivileged trying to make it, migrants and emigrants; in short, all those who seek to acquire the kind of bed in which you can dream the American dream. The search is active and forlorn; and because it means muscling in on what is already taken, it can be deadly.

Banks' *Continental Drift* was a fierce novel about two sorts of underclass colliding fatally, as both try to seize what seems to be promised in 1980s America. A New Hampshire repairman, lured by the advertised ease and easy wealth of south Florida, crosses bloody paths with a group of Haitian boat people fleeing their own infinitely tighter constriction for an even more illusory future.

There was a [Theodore] Dreiser-like anger in *Continental Drift,* and there is some of the same kind of social protest in *Success Stories,* along with a predilection for rough irony—as in the title—and a flat correlation of the internal state of his people with what happens to them outside.

Five of the 12 stories in *Success Stories* are linked, giving us glimpses of the partial rise of a boy named Earl Painter out of an old kind of American bleakness into a newer kind. They repeat, dolefully instead of tragically, the theme of imaginary betterment contained in *Continental Drift.*

In the first story, Earl is a child, living in a depressed New Hampshire town with his impoverished mother and a younger brother and sister. Their father has left them for another woman. Feeling himself the man in the family, Earl latches on to the first of a series of social delusions. A local broadcaster runs a queen for a day program; the award—purely symbolic—going to the woman with the hardest-luck story. Earl writes three increasingly pitiable letters about his mother, but never gets an answer.

Over the next three stories, he leaves college, after a semester on a scholarship, and goes to Florida. He works at a menial job and, eventually, a series of better ones decorating store windows. He becomes engaged, as well; but none of these forms of "success" does much for him. Marriage and window-designing stretch ahead as a higher form of servitude; and in a final story, years later, he is back in New Hampshire, divorced and not doing much.

Banks tells the Painter stories with a deliberate lightness and at a deliberate distance. In a way, they are ordinary; but in a way, that is the point. Dryly he suggests the sterility and solitude of middling success, without ever making Earl seem in the least self-pitying or soft. He is no repiner; he goes after things, but they aren't much good.

Some of the stories depart from realism and make their points in fablelike fashion. In **"The Fish,"** a giant fish is discovered in a pond in the Vietnam countryside. At first, the local commandant—this is before the communist victory—tries to destroy it. It simply grows larger, though, and attracts pilgrims. So the commander sells them bottles of pond water. Tank trucks come up from Saigon as the trade grows; and eventually, the water is exhausted and the fish dies. Capitalism, the message goes, can be more lethal than warfare.

Banks has the morals for fables, but sometimes, as here, he lacks the delicacy. On the other hand, he achieves a hallucinatory power in **"Hostage."** Guerrillas in some Third World country kidnap the German ambassador. As the army charges in, disastrously, the ambassador imagines five increasingly outlandish escapes. The effect is to evoke and explore the strange, cut-off world of hostages and captors, where values and emotions are so oddly set askew.

The strongest story in the collection, in fact, is a mixture of fable and realism. In **"Sarah Cole: A Type of Love Story,"** the narrator, a prosperous yuppie, meets an older woman in a New Hampshire bar. She is divorced, has three children and works at a low-paying job in a printing factory. They belong to different classes. But not only in the social and economic sense: He is remarkably handsome; she is extraordinarily ugly.

They fall in love, nonetheless. We are in a parable, yet Banks powerfully underpins it by his absolute feeling for place and person. The unconventional affair continues until Sarah demands that her lover meet her friends and children; in short, acknowledge her publicly. He tries, but it is too much for him. In a fearful scene, he throws her out and reviles her for her ugliness. Suddenly, she seems beautiful.

It is the truth, but unachievable. For a while, the couple had lived out the old-fashioned adage: "Beauty is only skin deep." And then the narrator loses his nerve and retreats back into present-day America, where the adage has been changed to: "Beauty *is* skin deep."

In Banks' work, society, as much as character, is fate. "It is time to stop worrying only about how the bruise makes us feel," I can imagine the author addressing some of his most talented fellow writers. "I want to tell how it got there." (pp. 3, 10)

> *Richard Eder, in a review of "Success Stories,"
> in* Los Angeles Times Book Review, *June 22,
> 1986, pp. 3, 10.*

John W. Aldridge

With his new collection, ***Success Stories,*** Russell Banks has published nine books of fiction—five novels and four volumes of stories—in the past 20 years. Yet until the appearance last year of ***Continental Drift,*** the first of his novels to win relatively large attention, he seemed destined to become a permanent member of that considerable company of American writers, many of them clearly gifted, who publish regularly but are reviewed sparsely if at all, and so remain little known even to the sophisticated reading public.

Part of Mr. Banks's problem is that his work has seemed dramatically out of phase with the most influential developments in postwar American fiction. Where Joseph Heller, John Barth, Thomas Pynchon, John Updike, Saul Bellow and others in the literary establishment have produced a fiction—often in the form of black humor or parodic fabulation—that is primarily concerned with the manifold anxieties and absurdities of affluent middle-class life, Mr. Banks is in no sense innovative or experimental, and he has shown no interest in the expensive tribulations of the urban world.

As we can see again in ***Success Stories,*** he writes a fine, clear prose—some of the best, in fact, now being written by anyone—and his methods and materials derive from the most comfortable conventions of old-style literary realism. His favorite fictional setting is the small, economically depressed New England town, while his characters are nearly always average working-class people of the kind long ago made familiar by Theodore Dreiser, James T. Farrell and John Steinbeck and recently restored to literary fashion by, among others, William Kennedy, Bobbie Ann Mason and Louise Erdrich.

In fact, the rise of blue-collar literary chic may very well help Mr. Banks achieve a more receptive audience for his work, and it may already have been responsible for the greater attention accorded ***Continental Drift.*** But viewed quite apart from the question of whether the working class is the trendy new subject for fiction, ***Continental Drift*** is clearly a compelling and richly detailed novel that is made especially attractive by the fact that it represents a contemporary version of the great classic story of naturalist realism, the tragedy of a typical workingman whose fantasies of the good life have been formed on the sleazy values of the consumer culture and who leaves his small-time futureless job in New Hampshire to seek happiness elsewhere, in this case in Florida. What he experiences there is deepening frustration, the disintegration of his marriage and a fatal involvement in the smuggling of drugs and aliens.

Mr. Banks weights this very grim narrative with a heavy documentation of facts that reveals with absolute clarity the tawdriness of the working-class world and of American materialistic aspirations in general. Yet he is unable to trust his facts to convey the full implications of his theme. Curiously and rather ominously, he from time to time assumes the role of authorial lecturer explaining to his readers exactly what the central action is supposed to signify. It is as if he suspected that the realistic method of cumulative documentation was proving to be an inadequate means for displaying more than the physical and environmental externals of the story he had to tell. And unfortunately, his suspicion turns out to be entirely correct. For beneath the thick layers of factual data, one senses a void where interpretive characterization should begin and does not, and the reason appears to be that Mr. Banks cannot possess imaginatively what cannot be documented, which in this case is the human significance of his story.

This same deficiency seriously weakened two of Mr. Banks's earlier novels, *Hamilton Stark* and *The Book of Jamaica.* But it is in the short story, where, because of the greater concentration of the form, everything depends on the attainment of some climactic moment of meaningful illumination, that his problem becomes crucial. In story after story in his three previous collections, *Searching for Survivors, The New World* and *Trailerpark,* as well as in *Success Stories,* the stage is portentously set for some revelation that is surely at hand. The dramatic situation is expertly choreographed; the prose is invariably excellent; people and places are described in great realistic detail. Mr. Banks's characters, nearly all of whom are working class, are typically presented—as they are in his novels—against a background of the consummate tackiness of New England towns that are dying and cheap trailer parks where they yearn after the symbols of success huckstered at them by television. These situations of human failure and futility have considerable poignancy mainly because they are circumstantial rather than dependent upon the intricacies of human relationship.

In one of the new stories the 12-year-old son of a New Hampshire carpenter, who has taken to drink and abandoned his family, writes letters to the emcees of the television program "Queen for a Day," offering his distraught mother as a candidate who is particularly deserving because she has suffered easily as much as any of the past contestants. The story is a moving depiction of misery and of the boy's vain effort to find in the media world of instant salvation some magical escape from it. But finally it is a study in stoical endurance, one that provides recognition but not insight.

In another of the pieces in *Success Stories*—"Sarah Cole: A Type of Love Story"—the narrator describes himself as an extremely handsome man, and because he is, he finds a certain satanic drama in the idea of having an affair with the homeliest woman he has ever known. He tells us that during the relationship he was at first amused and then embarrassed by the grotesque disparity between their physical appearances, but that after he cruelly sends her away and much later learns that she is dead, he realizes that he loved her.

The problem here is that the narrator's attraction to Sarah Cole is entirely theatrical. It is based on the fact of her extreme ugliness, and we are given no evidence whatever of the existence beyond that of any emotional attachment to her. In fact, her personality and her appearance as described make her seem powerfully unlovable, so that the narrator's relationship with her can only be interpreted as inexcusably perverse and exploitative. Yet one cannot be sure that this is the effect intended, for the tone through-

out is so coolly detached, so fastidiously disinclined to direct the reader's response in any way, that it is impossible to decide whether the author wants us to see the narrator as the moral monster he seems to be or, if he does, what are the implications of the fact, what, after all, do we know about him that would give this knowledge significance?

Nearly all of *Success Stories* is like that—precise and coldly objective delineations of reality, black-and-white prose photographs with virtually no shading or dramatic emphasis. Perhaps Mr. Banks is trying to say that life is simply like that, and of course we know it is. But it is the responsibility of the writer to give form and meaning to the actual, and this he too seldom does. If he is so far largely unknown, that may well be one of the major reasons.

John W. Aldridge, "Blue-Collar Enigmas," in
The New York Times Book Review, *June 22,*
1986, p. 22.

John Domini

Russell Banks is the square peg that won't be fit into the ever-narrowing categories of American fiction. Thus far the apogee of his quirky career has been the 1985 novel *Continental Drift.* This nightmare of worlds in collision (declining white-collar New England, rising no-collar Jamaica) was a terrific accomplishment, and with *Drift* looming so large in the background, *Success Stories* might be mistaken for a publisher's holding action—keeping the author's name before the public while he prepares his next big event. Happily, the book outfoxes such thinking. Bank's fourth collection of stories proves an idiosyncratic triumph, strictly arranged and narrowing in on an essential tragedy. Indeed, *Success Stories* offers insight into the writer's entire body of work.

The book contains two different sorts of stories, and the mix would seem unlikely. One grouping is realistic, full of sympathy, richly meditative about its characters' political and economic circumstances. These stories are contiguous; each concerns Earl, who grows up poor in New Hampshire after his father abandons the family, and who subsequently runs away himself, to the Gold Coast of Florida. There Earl achieves a tentative adulthood, though the last two stories see him back in New Hampshire and still prey to the dislocations of his impoverished youth. Alternating with the chapters of this *Bildungsroman,* however, are five tales that border on the surreal. Their settings are stylized—a hoodoo-haunted military regime, a suburb frightened of its own children. Some attempt parable, others offer formal experiment. All avoid the sympathy which distinguishes Earl's initiations.

Banks has worked this mixture since the beginning of his career. His *Searching for Survivors* (1975) clearly owed a debt to the prevailing fashion for Postmodernism, yet the best piece in the book was **"The Defenseman,"** Banks's long closing elegy to a shattered New Hampshire family. And his 1981 collection *Trailerpark,* though grounded in the sort of blue-collar realism its title suggests, made room for **"The Child Screams and Looks Back at You,"** a fable about a youngster's death no less chilling for its counterpoint of third- and second-person. What allows Banks such freedom?

His unusual narrative voice provides part of the answer. Banks is neither heartlessly flashy like the Postmodernists, nor tamped down and minimalist in keeping with the current tulip craze. In **"Adultery,"** here, he provides a glimpse of the affect he strives for, while describing the difference between Earl's New Hampshire flatness and his girlfriend's Florida drawl:

> My talk was merely that, talk, or so it seemed to me—ideas made over into sounds, feelings translated into symbols and emblems. Hers, though, was the thing itself—feelings and sunlight and rest.

Banks refuses to hurry. His declarations troll the waters with commas and dashes and conversational fill like "or so it seemed to me," and with lists, like the magnificent tabulation of how the day's first vodka goes down in **"Firewood."** Such methods of modulation allow him enormous flexibility. His lines are both stretched with "feelings translated into symbols" and weighted with "the thing itself." His more surreal pieces work the same combination—though it must be said that their terrors can't match those of Earl, his heart steeped in American poverty and the guilt that comes with it.

What finally sets Banks apart, though, isn't voice; his omnivorousness can be sloppy. Rather, his great gift is his insistence on naming sources, reasons, first causes. The world here is one that too few writers ever consider, granted. But sympathy for the downtrodden can lead to blindness; and that **Success Stories** never allows. Earl proves as much of a manipulator as any of the better-born, and out of many of the same desires and fears. Banks identifies differences of class not just to shame us with them, but because it is only once those differences are tagged and out of the way that we can understand what the true "thing itself" consists of—what humanity itself consists of. The best piece here, **"Sarah Coles: A Type of Love Story,"** climaxes with just such a stripping-down. The point of view is another strange one, retrospective first- and third-person, and yet the protagonist/narrator is clearly Earl. By now he's a professional man, good-looking and single—a success. But he falls for a woman far beneath his newly achieved station, the ugly divorcée Sarah. And when at last the clothes come off, in spite of their differences these two rise to something near the level of the Ideal:

> . . .two naked members of the same species, a male and a female, . . . both individuals standing slackly, as if a great, protracted tension between them had at last been released.
>
> (pp. 27-8)

John Domini, in a review of "Success Stories," in Boston Review, *Vol. XI, No. 4, August, 1986, pp. 27-8.*

Fred Pfeil

[No one] will ever accuse Russell Banks of gorgeous writing: his prose has the precise force of a steady, measured outrage. Which is not to say he is not skilled—only that the craft he was honing through the 1970s in **Searching for Survivors** and **Hamilton Stark** has now been placed at the service of a terrible probity.

In his last book, **Continental Drift,** Banks crosscut the story of Bob DuBois, a working-class white man trying to hustle up some luck in Florida, with the tale of Vanise Dorsinville, a Haitian woman trying to get to the United States with only the loa of voodoo for protection. The result was a powerful if not perfect book: at once a celebration of both Vanise's doomed heroism and Bob's pathetically inadequate goodness, and a howl against what the free market system makes out of the world. A similar project is evident in Banks's new collection, **Success Stories,** whose pieces both compose a loose *Bildungsroman* of another New England working-class boy, Earl Painter, and play off the exemplary story of his betrayal and self-betrayal against a group of parabolic tales of power, many of them set in the Third World. The risk taken in **Continental Drift**—that the more distanced Third World drama will not be able to stand up against the power of Banks's more immediate account of what it means to be an American working-class white man—becomes the manifest weakness of **Success Stories.** The problem is not simply that the Third World and/or political fables (**"The Fish," "The Gully," "Hostages"**) are so much thinner than the tale of Earl Painter trying and failing to find the happiness his culture dreams for him, but that the effect of such disproportion is to render the Third World stories little more than allegorical pendants to the "real" story—the story of the white man's life.

Still, that tale, as in **Continental Drift,** is far more than another wallow in the strange sad weirdness of it all. Indeed, from **"Queen for a Day"** to the closing story, **"Firewood,"** the Painter chronicle is more than worth the price of the book. Banks has put in enough time in working-class America to have an exact sense of what its dreams and betrayals feel like and how they work. What's more, he has constructed a detached narrative style that reminds us of the frightening typicality of Earl Painter's life, and of the lives of those he tries to love. That ability and power are most impressively evident within this collection in **"Sarah Cole: A Type of Love Story,"** in which a man who calls himself Ron, but who could just as easily be a grown-up Earl Painter, recounts the story of a brief affair he had with an ugly woman, and finds he can only do so by continually stepping back and starting again:

> I'm still the man in this story, and Sarah is still the woman, but I'm telling it this way because what I have to tell you now confuses me, embarrasses me and makes me sad, and consequently I'm likely to tell it falsely. I'm likely to cover the truth by making Sarah a better woman than she actually was, while making me appear worse than I actually was or am; or else I'll do the opposite, make Sarah worse than she was and me better. The truth is, I was pretty, extremely so, and she was not, extremely so, and I knew it and she knew it. She walked out the door of Osgood's determined to make love to a man much prettier than any she had seen up close before, and I

walked out determined to make love to a woman much homelier than I had made love to before. We were, in a sense, equals.

No, that's not exactly true . . .

(pp. 227–28)

[These] relentlessly qualifying, additive sentences take us back to Dreiser in their urge to expose and name the everyday crime. Yet Banks writes with a more merciless exactitude than Dreiser ever had, and with far greater and more self-conscious skill. If American "quality fiction" were to abandon its minimalist chic, its obsession with purely private lives, in favor of some larger and more social quest, these are two writers we would have to thank for their part in the change. (p. 228)

> Fred Pfeil, *"More Than Zero," in* The Nation, *New York, Vol. 243, No. 7, September 13, 1986, pp. 226-28.*

Banks on being a writer:

Writing isn't one of those things, in a literate culture, like music or painting, where the gift is obvious at a young age. My obvious gift as a young boy was in painting. I could draw well; I had the gift genetically. I didn't know whether I had any particular writing talent at all. I set out to be a painter in my late teens and gradually discovered that I was writing, as one discovers one is breathing—and so you feel you must be alive! The discovery, the definition, came after the activity.

> *Russell Banks, in an interview in* Publishers Weekly, *March 15, 1985.*

Russell Banks [Interview with Trish Reeves]

[Reeves]: Why do you write?

[Banks]: Not to demean the question, but it's a very hard question to answer the same way twice, probably because one doesn't write for the same reasons twice. So, whenever you answer it you're thinking, why did I write the last time? I think that I began to write for reasons that had to do with the simple desire to be a writer; I had fallen in love with literature. I think Flannery O'Connor said, "Literature attracts literature." I wanted to be one of those people who thrilled me so. I want to thrill others the same way, which is in some important way, perhaps, the wrong reason to write. If that's all you want and that's the only reason you want to write you don't do it for very long. But we always seem to start things for the wrong reasons and then later on we'll straighten out what our reasons are for doing it.

As time went by, I continued to write simply because it seemed I had to write in order to maintain my own clarity, such as it was, in the world. Whatever degree of clarity I could have, whatever knowledge I could have about the world of fact and value, I could only seem to get through writing, through the discipline and rigors of writing fiction

particularly. So it goes on for, I suppose, those reasons, because it's how I have learned to know anything of importance to me about the world. One writes a particular story or novel or whatever for different kinds of reasons on the surface of the work—as presented to you in a dream or a newspaper clipping or an anecdote or a memory. You start to unravel it and pull at it the way you pull a thread out and pretty soon you've got a sweater in your lap. But that kind of thing is a different level of reason for writing. The deeper causes, the deeper compulsions come from, finally, the trust in the process as an access route to knowledge; it's epistemological in the end for me. I certainly don't write for money or fame. I'm 46 now and I've been at it almost 25 years, and it's only in the last year where I could say that I am making more money from this than I am making from anything else I am doing. I'm making now about what a cop makes.

The same thing with fame; you're known to a very small number of people who happen to take contemporary-American fiction very seriously. You'd be better off designing shoes if fame is what you're after.

Your first two published books were poetry. Do you still write poetry?

No. Well, I doodle at it and noodle at it. I'm not really able to write poetry that seems very good or interesting to me. So I keep going back to it hoping some door will open, and I'll fall through into this room where all the poets stand or sit and work. I'm like most fiction writers in that we secretly feel that poetry is the queen of the arts in some way and that if we could only be a poet we wouldn't be a failed poet. Faulkner said all fiction writers are failed poets, and he was speaking of himself. But I think he was also speaking of many of us as well. I suppose it's an easy analogy, but I think that poets feel like pitchers. They know they can't hit but they feel it's not an important part of the game. And most novelists feel like hitters. We know we can hit, and we secretly think we can pitch if they'd just give us a chance to get in the game.

After reading your work, I think of you as someone who focuses his writing on lives and situations that cause a reader to wish for social change. How much of an activist are you?

I'm not a political activist beyond my writing. And I don't think of my writing as political activism. There was a period in my life, in my twenties and early thirties, when I was a political activist and was involved in the civil-rights movement and the protest against the Viet Nam war. But they were very specific events and it wasn't anything I could follow along as a way of life. So my relation to that kind of activity is really marginal. I naturally support specific and particular causes and occasionally even send money for them, sign letters and do the rest of it. But not as a writer, just as John Citizen. As a writer I'm not so much interested in change, as you said, really, as in pointing at and revealing pain. I'm horrified by pain. I'm sensitized, I suppose, to people who are in pain because of political or social reasons, oppression of one form or another, power; they're at the bottom, the weak side of a power relationship. And so I write about that, I try to portray that. All I can do is point at it.

Do you think this pointing will perhaps bring about change?

Well, yes, I hope so. I'm not a nihilist; I have faith in humanity that if we only open our eyes and see, then we will alter how we treat people. If we can only imagine what it's like to be somebody else, then we will treat others better. I really believe that.

I was going to ask you what possible hope we could have, at the end of **Continental Drift,** *for alleviating pain after that bleak portrayal. Awareness?*

Yeah. If we're aware that a man like Bob Dubois or a woman like Vanise the Haitian woman, if we can somehow know through a book like that—that that kind of person has as complex an inner life as we have—we who subscribe to *The New Yorker,* we who have Quality Paperback Book Club subscriptions and so forth, we who live in this upper-middle class world—then we can respect them and respect their inner life in a way that we might not otherwise. And yeah, we'll treat them better. I suppose in that sense if the book works, it works that way. I don't expect to affect immigration legislation or the Reagan budget or anything like that. I'm much more interested in humanity on a larger scale and humanity on the one-to-one scale; nothing in-between seems to be able to engage my imagination. And so I have to deal with it that way. Also, I don't think it's that bleak really, *Continental Drift* itself. Certainly Bob Dubois dies, but there's a dramatic necessity for that. Bob is a man whose life is determined so many ways by a failure of imagination. He doesn't imagine his own relation to the larger economy. Bob's substitute for a sense of community is a sense of himself as a consumer; he's victimized, but he participates in his own victimization. And the opportunities that he has to escape, when they present themselves, he declines to really imagine his life and take hold of it and change it. He doesn't have very *many* options. But his wife has more imagination than he has. She knows where she stands in relation to the rest of the world. She doesn't have this kind of macho hang-up on success and on getting ahead and on being somebody. So she's not as easily manipulated as he is. She knows she's somebody already, so she can't be as easily manipulated.

But then there's the other half of the story, the Haitian culture where death was beside the point, almost.

For Vanise. Yeah. They survive as they do because they have a connection to the spiritual world that Bob doesn't have, which allows them to endure things that Bob, under his circumstances, couldn't begin to endure. But their world is much harsher and crueler than his.

That's partly what I was thinking of when I referred to the "bleakness."

Oh yes. The other culture is in the classic position of the working class immigrant: One generation literally sacrifices itself for the benefit of the next. There is a real act of sacrifice there, an engagement on a biological, historical level. That's what they're going through. Bob is two generations after that, and so his relation to the economy and to the institutionalized world, the United States, is quite different. He's more involved and engaged in his own victimization.

You talked of Bob's wife being ahead of him in this. Do you see his maleness as being part of the problem in the culture?

Sure. He's manipulated by his own macho self-image; I mean who benefits from that kind of a man, that kind of a man's delusions? Only his employers, only the people who sell things benefit from those delusions.

You once said that sometimes your stories have a way of choosing you. Could you expand on that?

I think that most of us sort of start out writing about one thing and as you get into it the story starts to appear on the page in front of your eyes, almost despite you. You thought you were writing about a mother and son but in fact you're writing about a father and his sister or something like that. It unfolds before you the way a painting unfolds; you think you're making a picture of a mountain and it turns out you're making a picture of a tunnel or a hole in the ground. The field reverses itself. And this happens more often than not, I think, for most writers: We discover in the process of writing what it is that wants to be written about.

So, could you say what poets often say, that they really don't have a poem until they've surprised themselves?

Yeah, I don't know how my stories are going to end until the end, until I get there; and then when I know, I stop writing. You discover it in the process. And so in that sense a story's choosing you, you're not choosing it. You just make yourself open, you clear your mind in the act of writing. Some of us do it differently. Some of us take drugs and some of us drink and some of us do this or that to get there; meditation, yoga, sharpen pencils, write letters. But the point is to get there, to where the story can take place through you. I like and try to cultivate, as much as possible, that sense of myself as a vehicle for expression since I'm not truly finally, in the end, interested in *self-*expression or memoirs or any kind of self-portraiture or anything of the sort. Therefore I have to try to make myself as available as possible to be a vehicle for stories to get told through me rather than for me to make them up or tell them.

Do you think writers should be more vocal in support of various causes, in today's world, especially North American writers who are so often accused of being drawn to the insignificant?

There's no reason for writers to be more or less drawn to identify with or support particular causes or issues. What I think depresses me sometimes about American writers is our mistrust of history and our unwillingness to discover and apply to our own work and to the world around us any sense of history. Most of us abandon all hope, in a way, of having an historical perspective, so we tend to write about the domestic most deliberately and pointedly. Only a few writers, like Ed Doctorow, Robert Stone or one or two others stick right out because they do have a sense of history, a particular view of American history, particularly. They are free and in fact they are obliged to write about different things, not *just* the family, not *just* divorce.

Sure, divorce is present in their work, but the scope is much larger, and they end up writing what some of us in our shortsightedness tend to call political fiction; but it's much more than political fiction, it's fiction with a sense of history—and a willingness to fight their way through this maze of histories. I mean, America is a country that is always trying to invent itself over again and pretend it has no history, and so our writers tend to go along with that myth.

I guess there's a big difference between us and most European and Latin American writers who are very conscious of their history and feel strongly that a writer has an obligation to understand the history of his or her society and not just the history of his or her family, which is what we're more inclined to do. A vision of the history of our country is crucial to our understanding of ourselves. This kind of obligation is Homeric. That's what writers have always done: told us who we were, where we came from, where the ends of our lands were, that sort of thing. That's why you brought the bards in from the cold and let them sit around the fires. We've given that function off to the academic specialists, but fiction writers and poets have historically always played that role. And it's only in this country, where we're so terrified of our history, that we seem to have abdicated that in recent times. Our tradition is very much historically preoccupied: Whitman and Melville and Hawthorne and Crane and Twain and so on. And I couldn't say for sure why we seem to have abandoned that. I think it's a temporary aberration.

An awful lot of writers of my generation, those who are now entering maturity as writers, were in adolescence and young adulthood in the sixties. Most of them that I know were very involved in political events of that time. So *their* idea of a meaningful event is one that takes place in a public way, that has to do with society in a larger way than simply the immediate present. Writers such as Stone, Don DeLillo, John Edgar Wideman or Rosellen Brown or a whole range of American writers in their early forties, middle forties, are really writing some wonderful books that we mistakenly call, because they seem unusual, political fiction. But in fact it's just writers returning to the old obligations.

When you were talking about that, I thought about your **The Relation Of My Imprisonment,** *which is almost a global history rather than one country's history.*

Yeah. I don't know what I think about that book; it kind of came as a gift. I wrote it in a very short time. The voice appeared in my ears and almost dictated it, that strange kind of 17th-century English voice or New English voice or whatever it is. Every day I would just go out and sort of tune in a radio station and get it right, and then I would start to transcribe. It was a marvelous event, and one longs for those sort of automatic writing events. They're rare.

Do you think any good came from the much publicized 1986 International Conference?

I'm not sure. I think it was probably disillusioning for many European and Latin American writers because I think they saw American writers at their worst, at their most parochial and most self-absorbed and most distract-

ed by local quarrels. I think that the bad consequences are that in some way we're not taken as seriously as we probably should be by foreign writers; it helps them not take us seriously. And I would rather that didn't happen. Many good things, I think, did come out of it; it depends upon the individual writer of course. But for me, and I think that my response was typical of many others, it was wonderful and enlightening and very reassuring to meet and hear, talk with writers such as Nadine Gordimer, Gunter Grass or dozens of others whose sense of the task and of the pleasure of writing was very much close to mine. I felt much closer to them than I feel, say, to writers of the ilk of John Updike or Saul Bellow or most of the American writers who were there. I felt reaffirmed in my own work and commitment. Which is not to compare my work to theirs, but just the way I think about the act seemed much closer to the way they describe their work. So I didn't feel quite as lonely and crazy.

Sometimes you can feel really isolated and a little awed and you say, I just don't understand why what I'm doing doesn't make sense to other people. Then you realize, well, I'm looking at the world from a very small vantage point, I'm looking at it from inside New York, say from 14th Street to 57th Street, between three avenues. I love that wonderful story of Donald Barthelme's called "Balloon," that area is sort of covered by the balloon in his story—from 14th to 57th, I think, and from Lexington to 6th Avenue—right over the publishing center. So the conference was very reaffirming in that sense, I think for a lot of writers it was terrific in that sense. And it's good to see writers have bodies. I like finding out how big they are, how little they are, that Gunter Grass smells like pipe smoke. Just to get that sense of the physical back onto a name is great, it takes them out of this bloodless world and makes them human beings.

Much of your more recent work uses a narrator who speaks directly to the reader. There aren't so many quotation marks, in more than the literal sense. I think this is at odds with most short stories today, which are mostly dialogue; your style seems both old fashioned and quite new. I was shocked by this technique because it seemed a tremendous risk that worked and was moving in the way that it worked. What about the evolution of your fiction, in technique as well as subject matter, and your thinking on this intrusive narrator approach?

OK, I'll try to talk about that particular aspect of my work, because that's a consciously worked out program, in that I set out some years ago to do what for me was an important thing. I wanted to invent a narrator. I wanted to have a narrator who could tell stories, who played no part in the story itself, but who took responsibility for what was being described. I did not want the story to be about the narrator in any way. To do that, I had to go back over the head of realism, naturalism and Flaubert, back over to the 18th-Century kind of narrator almost, where there was a different sense of the relationship between the author and the reader so you could in a sense address the reader, Dear Reader. The narrator could in fact come forward and present herself or himself to the reader in that intimate way and say, Dear Reader, I'm going to tell you about something that is going to amaze you, amuse you, enlighten you and so forth.

To do that without irony was a goal for me, and it wasn't just an abstract or a theoretical goal, it grew out of a kind of frustration that I felt with the realistic convention of the author as merely a window into the world—a kind of Flaubertian presentation of the experience with the author out somewhere behind the clouds paring his nails so that there is this illusion of reality in front of you. And it *is* merely an illusion; you're aware of that as soon as one starts to write. Then it's in some sense an embarassment, at least it was to me when I was a young writer first starting—I always felt embarrassed. And I mean it the way Emily Dickinson means embarrassed: exposed, and exposed for being false. And I felt uncomfortable in that relation to the reader and in that relation to language. This is all artifice, folks, I wanted to say, on the one hand; but I still want to tell you something, I still want to tell a story. I don't want to simply comment on the artifice and reveal the artifice, which seems boring after a point, and obvious and redundant, so why bother? So I did set out to kind of reinvent, for myself anyhow, a narrator that I could trust and that the reader could trust. It meant that I had to risk being didactic and pompous on the one hand or ironic and wry on the other hand and try to find something else in-between that I could be comfortable with. Each book has struggled with it in one way or the other and I think each has gotten closer and closer to a comfortable kind of narrator. *Continental Drift* probably comes as close as anything of mine published so far that has that presence in the book that I feel is not me but is a storyteller. And one that the reader relates to and trusts or doesn't trust, but deals with, and who is also not part of the story.

It's an invention; I have invented a narrator, in a sense, a person almost. A good metaphor for it occurred to me some years ago, a literal metaphor when I was in Jamaica and spending a lot of time in the back country with the Maroons, who are descendants of escaped slaves in the 17th and 18th century who set up villages there and retain many of the old ways of West African culture. Several of these villages, but one in particular, had a rather rigidly, effectively instituted and marvelous set-up: The chief had a person he called his mouth-man. And the mouth-man was very intelligent and articulate and had an extraordinary presence in public. The chief could be sort of dim and inarticulate and shy, but he had all the power. And the mouth-man had all the responsibility to speak. The chief could always fire the mouth-man if he wanted to or he could blame the mouth-man, sort of like our president's press secretary. The chief could let the mouth-man go, the mouth-man could rap on for hours and the chief was often as amused by him as everybody else. He was a rapper. I loved the idea. I thought, now that's what I want; I want a mouth-man, I want to be free to be sort of dim and shy in the background and yet have someone out there in the page taking responsibility for the story. So I *have* tried to do that, and I've taken some raps for it among readers who don't see the need for that kind of artifice, who are perfectly happy with "realism," and language as a window onto reality rather than language as a creator of reality. They have accused me of somehow having this intrusive narra-

tor, as if I weren't conscious of having an intrusive narrator or hadn't intended to have one in the first place. Or they've accused me of being didactic. He's not that didactic. He's an explainer.

Storyteller is what I kept thinking, the original meaning of storyteller.

Yeah, it's very much a part of **Trailer Park,** it's a more artificial part of it than it is in **Continental Drift.** In **Trailer Park,** if you ever sit down and make a map of the trailer park you can see that there's one trailer that's never named or numbered. There are twelve trailers and one of them is never identified as having a resident, and that's where, presumably, the narrator lives—'cause he knows everything about everybody, the way he would only know if he had lived in the trailer park. He can tell the history of the trailer park back and forward in time, and he can tell all of their stories. He has no story of his own to tell, and you don't miss him. You don't miss his story or anything else. You don't miss his life. But he knows everything. So that's an artificial way of doing it. I was sort of happy with it but I felt it was a little tricky.

With **Continental Drift** I said, OK, I'll invoke a narrator the way you invoke a loa in Haitian Voudon. Which is to say, I'll allow myself, if I can, to be in a sense possessed; I'll let this voice speak through me, and it'll be of a specific character—the loa will be Legba who has the specific character of protector of children, guardian of the crossroads, figure that sees forward and backward in time, and so forth. This sort of fitted the needs I had for a narrator, and so that opening invocation is literally an invocation to bring into existence, into the book the loa Legba to speak for me, Russell Banks, through the book. That, too, has a certain amount of artifice and, well, it somehow frustrates me; I don't feel that's quite there yet either. But this book of short stories, (**Success Stories**) seems to do it differently.

I was going to say that. In "**Adultery,**" *the way it works at the end of that story is wonderful.*

Good, good. Yeah, it's somewhat different now. Each book does evolve in terms of formally trying to make this narrator more readily available to me and to the point where I can forget about it at some point, I can just do it. Just go out there and write the story, that's all I want to do. Just let the narrator tell it like that chieftain sitting back, let my mouth-man tell the story. That might come, too, from a kind of family background that essentially mistrusts language: rural New Englanders, working class. We weren't French or Italian or anything like that; we were these up-tight Yankees. My father was a grim and reticent, depressed man and my mother was a slightly hysterical woman—both of them had basically the same mistrust of language. Neither one of them believed anything useful could be said. Coming out of that background, there's an essential mistrust of the act of speech for myself, too, so that I have to create perhaps a stand-in for myself.

Speaking of New England, there's often a character in your stories who is the wizard, a disguised wizard. And the wizard is usually extreme in what he says, or he's contrary or he's very ironic. My understanding is that wizards abound in New England, but I wonder if there was someone in your background who taught you this trait in a sense?

No no. There isn't any one person in my background, my childhood, or anything like that—and I don't think wizards are found in New England, I never found any anyhow.

I meant that manner, that way of speaking.

I understand. Yes, the wizard figure appears over and over. He's usually a man, an elderly man, out of a longing on my part for there to be such a thing as wisdom. I want to believe that there is wisdom, and so I try to evoke it in my work. And hope that I can make it available through the work, through a character. I can evoke a character who is a wise man. I like to believe in that, I want to believe in that. And to some limited degree I think that I've been able to evoke characters who prove the existence of a wizard. I've searched for wizards since I was a boy, and I've met a couple of individuals who somehow made me feel the search was not an utterly irrational one. They were figures who essentially, like the wizards in my work, I guess, saw clarity through paradox, could embrace contradictions, and had a language that would permit them to demonstrate that. So that's why, I think, they exist on the personal level. And also, they create in the work, I hope, a kind of tension, a kind of intellectual and spiritual tension in work that might otherwise be overtaken by a bleak materialism that I don't feel all that comfortable with. Even though I very much live in a material world and write about a material world, still, it's a material world that's always longing to exchange itself for a transcendent world.

You've been writing for 25, publishing for 20 years now, often concentrating on the American concept of success and the problems with that concept, the false promises. You are now what would have to be called a successful American author. How does that kind of success strike you?

Like the man who ate his hat. I guess at several different levels, I'm not aware of it as success. Of course I'm not naive about it either. My life is not radically changed, not on a day-to-day basis; in fact, it's not changed much at all. I still do exactly what I seem to have been doing for the last couple of decades. It's more affected, by a long-shot, by my children having become teenagers and young women than it has by anything else. It's made me, I suppose, more careful, I necessarily have to be more careful about what I say and do, but not in any big way. Nobody pays that much attention to anybody. It's interesting to me because it's dramatized in my own life what has been a theme throughout my work, which is that I still view myself in the larger world the way I did when I was an adolescent. My view of myself in relation to the larger world is that of a working class family: powerless people who look from below up. I'm unable to escape that. I guess one of my recurrent themes in the work is that one can't escape that—how one views oneself in the larger structure is determined at an extremely early age. The great delusion is that if you only can get success then you will shift your view of yourself, you will no longer look at the world from the bottom, you will look at it from the top, you will be-

come a different person. That's the longing, for success is really not necessarily material goods, but in fact to become a whole new person, not to look at yourself in the same way. The *delusion* is that you can change through success, success will change you—it's the American dream—you can kill the old person and become a new one. In my own life I can see now, if I needed any further proof, that in fact I haven't become another person. I'm still stuck with and still view myself very much the way I did as a boy. Success can fool you into thinking that you're changed, of course, and one has to be on guard against that. I feel that it's been good for my work in that it's brought my work back into print—I like as large an audience as I can have. Why should I not want a large audience? Whether they like me or not, or understand the work or not doesn't matter to me. Give everybody a chance. I'm not sure I understand it or like it myself. But to get back to the point, it hasn't really changed me, to my knowledge, at all. I should hope not.

You may still write some stories about people who want to succeed, to become adults, who are already adults?

Oh, yeah. Isn't that wild. All of us, we're all groaning over that, if only I could become an adult. And then finally you discover like Bob Dubois, there's no such thing as adults. But if there's no such thing as adults, then there's no such thing as children either, really. Human beings are creatures who're different from either children or adults. (pp. 45-59)

Russell Banks and Trish Reeves, in an interview in New Letters, *Vol. 53, No. 3, Spring, 1987, pp. 45-59.*

Fred Pfeil

It is, you might say, a notorious mystery, the secret everyone knows: that there are millions of people in this country working lousy, boring, low-end jobs, and jostling for shreds of dignity against the self-loathing they're invited to adopt. But if you weren't one of these people, and wanted to know what their lives are like, contemporary American fiction is the last place you'd go to find out. It's an obvious fact about the lit-business today—obvious, that is, to anyone who cares to look. We can have a certain limited number of feminist writers and novels around now; and there remains a smaller, but equally distinct quota for "minority voices." But virtually no one within the institutions of literature-land who is in a position to promote, publish, and affirm or canonize "quality fiction" gives a shit about narratives focused on the pathologies and resistances that result from the violence we neutrally call "social class."

So the writer who would make narratives out of working-class (or poor people's) experience tends to find him- or herself in a tightening box from which there are not many exits. One might, like Raymond Carver in his earliest and best work, write so obliquely and sparely of such marginalized and exploited lives that the social location of their angst gradually disappears, and the trauma at its core can be consumed instead as a bleak, existential metaphysic. Or one might, like Bobbie Ann Mason, write about such lives in an idiom whose relentlessly bouncy present-tense simplicity, combined with regular doses of pop-culture cues, allows upscale readers to relish the narration as a virtual transcript of likeable, down-home stupidity. One might take up these strategies without being fully conscious of them as ways of "getting over" to an audience from another class, but rather as ways of dealing with the pain and anger within oneself—or as the results of a desperate striving to get published, to be read and heard. One might, indeed, be required *not* to know or understand what one's work means (as Carver, by his own admission, did not), or how easily and with what patronizing voyeuristic pleasure any Mason story nestled in *The New Yorker,* across from the Tiffany ads, can be misread. Or one might, with the same not-quite consciousness, merely learn to write about some other subject; or learn not to write at all.

I sketch this stunted landscape and its dim possibilities not to lament them, but to celebrate Russell Banks's achievements against the dismal odds. For beginning with *Trailerpark* in 1981, and continuing through his ambitious *Continental Drift* (1985), the collection *Success Stories* (1986), and this new novel, [*Affliction*], he has ever more clearly emerged as a writer from the white working class, writing directly about the rage and damage, the capitulations, self-corruptions, and small resistances of subordinated lives. *Affliction* tells the story of the final two weeks of self-and-other destruction in the life of Wade Whitehouse, a 41-year-old well-driller, snow-plower, and small-town cop in his decrepit hometown of Lawford, New Hampshire. There the mill that once justified the town's existence is long since shut down, leaving Wade's father, Glenn, to early retirement back at the dilapidated family homestead with Wade's faded mother and a secret stash of Canadian Club bottles tucked throughout the house and barn. Wade, however, doesn't get by to see the folks that often. His work life is spent in resentful double fealty to Gordon LaRiviere, Lawford's only success story, a beefy, sleazy entrepreneur and town select-man to whom Wade is indebted as both employee and town cop. His life outside work is a smear of alcohol, depression, and rage that stretches from his trailer south of town through the bars and back roads to the sad but amiable bed of divorced diner waitress Margie Fogg, and all the way down to Concord, where his scornful ex-wife, Lillian, lives in her middle-class home with her middle-class husband and Wade's daughter, Jill, who doesn't want to see him any more.

At 41, in other words, Wade's real daily work is the management of an unstable and ever-enlarging fund of pain and fear. He has lost the woman he loved, who once loved him; he has lost his youth, the promise of a better job, perhaps a state trooper's, one with more respect; he is now losing his child. Worst and most frightening of all, however, is the constant sense of "this particular kind of fragility" in every encounter, even something as simple as a stop for coffee at the local diner, whenever he is reminded of his own failure to connect with or understand the world:

> One minute he was moving securely through time and space, in perfect coordination with other people; then, with no warning, he was out of step, was somehow removed from everyone else's sense of time and place, so that the sligh-

test movement, word, facial expression or gesture contained enormous significance. The room filled with coded messages that he could not decode, and he slipped quickly into barely controlled hysteria.

And, behind all such fears and doubts and dislocations, at their base and as their horizon line, there is always the child who is being beaten, the *Ur*-spectre of Wade's drunken, crazy-mean father fissuring into violence, punching the mother, smacking the boy down onto the floor until finally the mother calms him, waits for him to start whining " 'When I say do something, goddammit, I mean it,' " then soothes him and leads him off to bed.

Affliction is most centrally a representation of that terrible cycle in subaltern lives in which powerlessness breeds self-loathing breeds hysterical violence, and the beaten child is not only father to but identical with the beaten, beating man. Banks avoids the twin dangers of a mere "sociological" accuracy on the one hand and a voyeuristic sensationalism on the other, through a wise combination of elevating and distancing techniques. For one thing, he has constructed a plot for this novel which is as tragic as the plot of *Oedipus Rex,* and in the same way. Wade Whitehouse, like the old original child-man, does not simply suffer his fate but rather fulfills it precisely in the attempt to transcend it and transform himself. In the various plot lines braided through the book, Whitehouse tries to win his daughter back, to bury his mourning for his marriage and make a new life with Margie, to reconcile with his father in the aftermath of his mother's pathetic death, and to find justice and punishment in the public realm for LaRiviere and his cohort, the rich union official whose father-in-law Wade believes they have killed to increase their own corrupt power and wealth. But all these efforts only result in that nightmarish moment in which, out of work, utterly discredited and desperate, he strikes his daughter, draws blood, and receives at last the terrible blessing of the father looking on,

> triumphant athlete, warrior, thief, a man who had come through harrowing adversity and risk with his bitterness not only intact but confirmed, for it was the bitterness that had got him through, and the grin and the crackled laughter was for the confirmation, a defiant thanksgiving gloat. The son finally had turned out to be a man just like the father.

Thus the novel's title, taken from a Simone Weil quote distinguishing between "suffering" and "affliction," between the hard-wired contradictions which we must endure, and the constructed fate—constructed by the gods in one era, by history and society in our own—against which we struggle and by which we are struck down.

This same distinction is, from a different angle, that between melodrama, which provokes our complicit tears, and tragedy, which invites us to draw conclusions, imagine alternatives, to think (and, just possibly, act) otherwise. I'm talking Brecht here, not Aristotle—or, rather, not the standard bourgeois purgation-catharsis model of Aristotle that gets peddled in Drama 101. And so is Banks, knowingly or not, whenever he pulls one of the distancing maneuvers that do so much to heighten and enlarge *Affliction* beyond case study or grotesquerie. To tell Wade Whitehouse's story (and Bob DuBois's, in the half of *Continental Drift* that belongs to him), Banks elects a studiously detached point of view, the expository near-omniscience you can see at work in the quotes above, which follow easily from the middle of dramatic scenes which they then as easily rejoin. He has made a style, in other words, that openly "tells" as much as it "shows," against the pinched advice of every creative-writing primer and 95 per cent of all the "quality fiction" published in this country over the past 40 years. A style which, moreover, largely works by eschewing style as it is ordinarily conceived, in favor of the steady-sighted, straightforward additive sentence, scrupulously naming as it goes, growing not more excited but merely somewhat longer when thoughts and feelings get busy and/or the action heats up—as here, in the middle of a passage about Wade's ex-wife Lillian's feelings, as a young woman, toward her dead alcoholic working class dad:

> Her father was weak and sweet, and he had not frightened a soul. The most alarming moments she had endured with her father came on those rare occasions when she realized that, if he was not drunk, he was thinking about getting drunk and so was not in fact present to her, did not actually see or hear her in the room. Those moments made her feel as if she did not exist and so lonely that she got dizzy and had to sit down and babble to him, make him lift his head and smile benignly at her, a big sleepy horse of a man, while she chattered on about school, about her sisters and her mother, making up events and whole conversations with neighbors, teachers, friends, madly filling with words the hole in the universe that he made with his presence, until, at last, her father rose from the kitchen table, patted her on the head and said, "I love you a whole lot, Lily, a whole lot," and went out the door, leaving her alone in the kitchen, a speck of bright matter, whirling through a dark turbulent sky. And now her father was dead, and she believed that she did not feel that pain anymore, because she missed him so.

Banks's depiction of his female characters is not always up to this mark; the women in his novels are at times more uncertainly observed than understood—as with *Affliction*'s somewhat sentimentalized Margie Fogg. Yet in this passage the timing is as unobtrusively precise as the words themselves. By choosing recounting over representation, sober translation over the standard mimetic attempt to "reproduce" the character's "voice," Banks evinces his respect for his working-class characters, and his sensitivity to the problem of representing them to an alien readership from another class. He also gains an enormous freedom to *move,* from character to character, across an array of splendidly sketched small-town types, between the present and the past, and from individual experience to the wider net of social and material circumstances. Thanks to its steady detachment, Banks's narration is capable of delivering the geologic and social history of the region in which Wade Whitehouse makes and meets his fate, or halting the plot to describe the savage and demotic mysteries of the annual deerhunting ritual, which this year includes the

shooting death, by design or accident, that propels Wade's overdetermined rage for justice. Banks accomplishes all this without ever making us feel that we are wading through yet another intrusive digression. What we get, rather, is a demonstration of the truth of a Marxist insight no American novelist has transmitted with such clarity before: that "Men [sic] make their history; but they do not make it just as they please; they do not make it under circumstances chosen by themselves, but under circumstances directly encountered, given and transmitted by the past." And we also get the revolutionary lesson Marx draws from this principle—that for the sake of human freedom, those circumstances themselves must be changed. To this novel, too, we might properly attach the wish with which Banks ended *Continental Drift,* in all revolutionary seriousness: "Go, my book, and help destroy the world as it is."

How it is that Russell Banks has taken this stance, and attained commercial success with it, would probably make an instructive story in itself. I remember reading some of his early work (*Searching for Survivors,* or perhaps *The New World*) back in the '70s, and finding it oblique in its concerns and pointlessly obsessed with narrational experiment. Yet it may be that those same works, formalistically hollow as they seemed, were actually groping toward that Brechtian combination of directness and estrangement he now employs with such triumphant success—and that the commendation those early works received gave him a position within the quality-lit marketplace which now ensures that works like *Affliction* must be taken seriously. But whatever ruses of authorial and institutional history produced such work and ensured its publicity, Banks has now become, I think, the most important living white male American on the official literary map, a writer we, as readers *and* writers, can actually learn from, whose books help and urge us to change.

All this said, however, I still have to cop to a few dissatisfactions with this new work, chief among them one large and, to me, inexplicable choice. In *Affliction* Banks has decided to try and convince us that all his narration actually issues from one of the novel's characters, Wade's younger brother Rolfe, an escapee from Lawford, New Hampshire, and to some extent—he's a history teacher now, down in the Boston suburbs—from his class fate. The problem is that I simply never believe Rolfe can know all he's saying, nor do I believe in or care about him as a character whenever he is brought into the plot. In fact, *Affliction*'s only systematic lapses occur at those points, usually at the opening of a chapter, when Banks has to reintroduce him (since for the most part, thankfully, we can forget he's supposed to be the source of what we read). There, suddenly, the distanced precision of the rest of the novel collapses into portentous, unpersuasive flailing, including, at worst, swatches of the very self-pity that underlies so much white male writing in this postfeminist age, and that it is otherwise part of *Affliction*'s greatness to refuse—as when Rolfe announces that he is telling us all this because

> finally I could stand the displacement no longer and determined to open my mouth and speak, to let the secrets emerge, regardless of the cost to

me or anyone else. I have done this for no particular social good but simply to be free. Perhaps
then, I thought, my own story and, at last, not
Wade's will start to fill me, and this time it will
be different. . . . Will I marry then? Will I
make a family of my own? Will I become a member of a tribe? Oh, Lord, I pray that I will do
those things and that I will be that man.

The best that can be said of such passages is that they are
mercifully self-contained, and utterly inimical to the rest
of the book. We can easily do as we read what Banks
should have done as he wrote, and excise whiney Rolfe
from the text.

The other problem I have with **Affliction** is more fleeting
but more troublesome; it is with those few, yet central moments in the novel when Banks's painstakingly detailed
account of the historical determinations in class and gender of Wade's working-class masculinity give way to a
revved-up rhetoric that portrays the roots of the syndrome
in terms of a ghastly, ahistorical mythology. Appropriately enough, Rolfe himself pushes this wrongheaded point
most explicitly near the end of the book, when he describes
the ruin that has been Wade's life as "a paradigm, ancient
and ongoing." But the same slippage from history to myth
occurs shortly afterward, in Banks's own depiction of that
climatic moment when, having lost everything, Wade is
down on the ground looking up at his terrifying, vengeful,
drunken father,

> a man compelled to perform a not especially
> pleasant task, the decision to do it having been
> made long ago in forgotten time by a forgotten
> matter, the piece of iron pipe in his meaty hands
> a mighty war club, a basher, an avenging jaw-
> bone of an ass, a cudgel, bludgeon, armor-
> breaking mace, tomahawk, pick, maul, lifted
> slowly, raised like a guillotine blade, sledgeham-
> mer, wooden mallet to pound a circus tent stake
> into the ground, to slam the gong that tests a
> man's strength, to split the log for a house, to
> drive the spike into the tie with one stroke, to
> stun the ox, to break the lump of stone, to smash
> the serpent's head, to destroy the abomination
> in the face of the Lord.

Such a passage has its own power, a persuasiveness based
in the persistence of patriarchy and male violence through
many long epochs and across many cultures. Yet that is
all the more reason why we should resist the urge to collapse their various manifestations into one intractable
mythic image, and insist instead on their determinations
in the here and now. **Affliction** at its best does exactly that,
names the parts and shows how they function with a compassionate detachment that will not yield to the despairing
comfort of myth. Here, for example, against the passage
just quoted, is Banks's quite different description of
Wade's first beating at the hands of his old man:

> There was no time to hide from the blow, no
> time to protect himself with his arms or even to
> turn away. Pop's huge fist descended and collid-
> ed with the boy's cheekbone. Wade felt a terrible
> slow warmth wash thickly across his face, and
> then he felt nothing at all. He was lying on his
> side, his face slammed against the couch, which

smelled like cigarette smoke and sour milk,
when there came a second blow, this one low on
his back, and he heard his mother shout,
"Glenn! Stop!" His body was behind him somewhere and felt hot and soft and bright, as if it
had burst into flame. There was nothing before
his eyes but blackness, and he realized that he
was burrowing his face into the couch, showing
his father his backside as he dug with his paws
like a terrified animal into the earth. He felt his
father's rigid hands reach under his belly like
claws and yank him back, flinging him to his
feet, and when he opened his eyes he saw the
man standing before him with his hand cocked
in a fist, his face twisted in disgust and resignation, as if he were performing a necessary but extremely unpleasant task for a boss.

For all its flaws, **Affliction** is full of such passages, and
such knowledge. However Banks has survived and grown
to write it, and however it has been published, we should
read this work, forgive its failings—and be thankful, even
astonished, that it exists. (pp. 25-6)

Fred Pfeil, "Head of the Class," in VLS, *No.
78, September, 1989, pp. 25-6.*

Banks on his narrative style:

I'm really interested in re-inventing the narrator. . . . It's
a convention that went out the window in the 20th century.
I want to feel I have my arm around a shoulder of this reader and I'm explaining, narrating, telling a wonderful story
to this person that I've stopped, like the wedding guest in
Coleridge's *The Ancient Mariner.* I'm like the ancient mariner stopping the wedding guest in his rush to tell this wonder to him. And I want to have that sense of intimacy, a
face-to-face, arm-around-the-shoulder contact.

Russell Banks, in an interview in Publishers
Weekly, *March 15, 1985.*

Sven Birkerts

Bit by bit the inventory of the soul's dark holdings proceeds, if not in our sciences, then in our arts. We need look
no further than the one-word titles of some of our novels:
Sartre's *Nausea,* Robbe-Grillet's *Jealousy,* Rushdie's
Shame, Nabokov's *Despair,* and Olesha's *Envy.* Each title
is, in effect, the first word of its book; each seems to promise that we will find between the covers the last word on
the subject. The draw is powerful; we want our darkness
objectified in figures and situations and lit by the artist's
understanding. Our happier selves concern us less in fiction—works about *Joy, Satisfaction, Contentment, Ease,*
or *Bliss* are generally reserved for the how-to shelves.

To the remarkable former list we should now add Russell
Banks's **Affliction,** the most sweepingly bleak label of all.
It is Banks's intent to fix his sites on a place at the core
of human unhappiness, and to trace the radial extensions
from that core through the web of a single family. At the
center of that web is Wade Whitehouse, in whom are gath-

ered the various soul ailments itemized above, and a few others besides.

Wade Whitehouse's fictional lineage is a simple one. He is the son of Glenn and Sally Whitehouse, born and raised in the scrubby up-country of New Hampshire. His town is Catamount, which also happened to be the starting place of Bob Dubois, the protagonist of Banks's novel *Continental Drift,* which appeared in 1985. But if Wade's fictional origins are straightforward, the path leading to his creation is not. It has taken Banks a good long time to find the fusion of matter and manner that declares itself so forcefully here. His nine previous novels and story collections can be viewed as a painstaking—and in places, a very successful—progress toward *Affliction.*

Banks started out writing stories with one hand and novels with the other. His first novel, *Family Life* (1974), and his first collection, *Searching For Survivors* (1975), reflect a sensibility divided between the claim of the common life and the claim of the experimental or "artistic." An inclination toward the former often comes refracted through the aspiration toward the latter. In *Searching For Survivors,* for example, the stories of simple people are worked up in a variety of forms, many using oblique narration and unexpected elisions; and *Family Life* plays with its materials using fairy-tale conceits and a deliberately simplistic style. These works, skillful as they are in execution, share a kind of writerly self-consciousness that is the almost inevitable curse of the young writer with large ambitions. We feel the lives as fiction before we feel the lives themselves. The writer is still courting his subject matter from a distance.

With the stories in *The New World* (1978) and the novel *The Book of Jamaica* (1980), Banks veered resolutely onto the high road of naturalistic narrative. *The Book of Jamaica* is a carefully written, almost documentarily faithful rendering of the stages of one man's immersion into the wholly alien culture of the Jamaican Maroons, descendents of African slaves brought to the island by the British colonists. Banks himself spent some time traveling and living in Jamaica, and the local detailings reflect an eye training itself to precise observation. Perhaps too much so: the book lags through long passages of description and historical documentation.

Still, Banks's next book, the novel/story-cycle *Trailerpark* (1981), plants us squarely in the country of his surest inspiration. In a sequence of 13 linked stories, Banks unfolds the lives and relationships of the occupants of a gone-to-seed trailerpark in northern New Hampshire. The prose is vibrant, spirited; Banks has a natural way of presenting the peculiar and twisting drives of his characters, a drifter-druggie, a Jesus fanatic, a woman whose trailer (and life) gets overrun by the guinea pigs she keeps. These people are, in Nelson Algren's phrase, "lonesome monsters," and Banks knows their thoughts and doings, the scope of their daily concern and the erratic inflation of their fantasy lives. If anything is missing from this book, it is perhaps some countervailing sense of normalcy, at very least the pretend normalcy that surrounds us in our day-to-day commerce.

Continental Drift was generally perceived to be Banks's breakthrough. Ambitious in reach, powered by the rage released from pent-up lives, the prose showed that Banks was ready to take up big themes and conflicts. *Continental Drift* was assertively complex in both its formal structure and its plot dynamics. Banks engineered the convergence of two very different lives: Bob Dubois, a refugee from dead-end Catamount, who winds up running a smuggling boat in Florida, and Vanise Dorsinville, a Haitian woman bent upon escaping the privations of her island life. In the catastrophic intersection of their fates we can read the legend of larger cultural forces, forces that drive the characters into actions that they blindly believe themselves to be choosing.

The book remains one of the more powerful achievements in recent American fiction. And one hesitates to quarrel over flaws and weaknesses where so much has been attempted, and with such success. God knows, our literature has little enough that reaches beyond the bedroom or nightclub wall. But it must be said that *Continental Drift* suffered from lopsidedness. The episodes featuring Bob Dubois are rendered with a confidence, a rightness of the kind we acknowledge when we say that a character is "inhabited"; the passages with Vanise, while sharply etched and outwardly penetrating, nonetheless lack this quality. The book belonged to its male lead, and the force of its final encounter is somewhat dissipated by the imbalance.

In many ways, *Affliction* pulls the concerns of *Continental Drift* inside out. Where Banks's earlier novel charted a grand scheme of cultural migration, seeking to isolate the larger as well as the human-sized circulations of malaise, *Affliction* stays rooted in place, hews to a single scale. Its study is the deeper ramifications of blood and kinship; it roots in to find the wellsprings of the will to violence.

The novel maps the flare-up of fate, tragic fate, in the life of Wade Whitehouse. We are told as much in the first sentence. "This," writes Rolfe Whitehouse, the narrator, "is the story of my older brother's strange criminal behavior and his disappearance." Rolfe is a history teacher living in Boston. He has long since fled family and place, and he soon convinces us that it is only the pressure of these extraordinary and sad events that brings him to speak. He has, he claims, pieced his account together from a great many sources, not least from Wade's own drunken telephone calls. The time frame is not large, given the extremity of the change in Wade. "Everything of importance," Rolfe informs us, "—that is, everything that gives rise to the telling of this story—occurred during a single deer-hunting season . . . "

Wade, as we meet him in the opening pages of his brother's narration, is an explosion waiting to happen. He is not different in kind from the other working people in Catamount, but the degrees of temperament and circumstance mark him as a man to be wary of. Wade is 41, divorced, living alone in the shambles of a trailer on the outskirts of town. His ex-wife, Lillian, and his daughter, Jill, are several hours away in Concord, where Lillian has remarried. Wade works two jobs, one as well-digger for Gordon LaRiviere, the town's one entrepreneur, the other as part-time policeman-crossing guard. He spends some of his nights with Margie, a waitress at the local diner, but most of his off-time is passed in bars or in solitary drinking bouts in his trailer. People tend to steer wide of Wade when he has been drinking; they recognize the intensity of the rage he has repressed, even if they don't understand its source.

Rolfe does not unfold Wade's tale as a causal sequence. Rather, he shows how disparate events come sheaving his way, moving him almost irresistibly onto his appointed track. Rolfe knows, too, that there are twists and turns of private circumstance that elude him, but he sets out with patient strokes the incidents he knows about. First, there is the unhappy night of Halloween. Jill has been sent against her wishes to spend the weekend with her father. Wade is awkward with her, his good intentions skewed by guilt and remorse. When he brings Jill to the town Halloween party, he pushes her to take part in the costume contest in progress. The abyss between them is immediately obvious, as is the volatility of the hurt Wade carries:

> The girl took a single step forward and stopped. Wade nudged her a second time. "Go on, Jill. Some of those kids you know." He looked down at the tiger's tail drooping to the floor and the child's blue sneakers peeking out from under the cuffs of the pathetic costume. Then he looked at the back of her head, her flax-colored hair creased by the string from the mask, and he suddenly wanted to weep.

Rolfe does not need to tell much more for us to know that Wade is not at heart a bad or callous man, and that we should consider closely the forces pressing at him. But Jill is miserable. She slips away during the party and calls her mother, who sets out immediately to bring her home. And several hours later, in the parking lot, Wade is made to suffer again the humiliation of his failure as a husband and a father. He vows at that moment to take legal steps to regain custody of Jill.

Other events press in. Late that same night Wade goes for a ride with his young co-worker Jack Hewitt, who brags to him that their boss LaRiviere has asked him to take an out-of-state union official deer hunting. The very next day the man is found shot to death in the woods—a victim, apparently, of a rifle accident. But Wade cannot rest with that explanation. He becomes obsessed with what he sees as the mystery of a backwoods murder. He is convinced of a setup. And for days he can think of little else. He replays the possibilities in his mind in every conceivable variation; he starts making late-night calls to Rolfe to air his theories. It is almost as if he believes that if he can solve the other man's death then he can solve his own life as well.

As the novel gathers its first momentum, the reader has every reason to expect that the mystery of the shooting will form the propulsion, the core, of interest. But once he has planted this obsession in Wade, and, to an extent, in the reader, Banks steers away. While these circumstances will ultimately figure in Wade's tragedy, they will not be the main precipitants. Other factors—having to do with family bonds, and the warping of character through brutality—prove more important. These emerge as Banks begins to peel away at the carapace with which Wade has shielded himself for so many years.

Tracking Wade's movements over the next few days—his workday trials, his consultation with a lawyer—Rolfe also starts to incorporate pieces of the background story. We get an inkling of how Wade came to be in his present situation. And with each bit of information, our picture of the man shifts; the closer Wade is brought to what will look to the outsider as senseless violence, the more we are able to see where the sense of it lies. As we learn the story of Wade and Lillian and Wade's father, we have to shed the preconceptions we were initially encouraged to hold.

As Auden wrote, "I and the public know / What all schoolchildren learn, / Those to whom evil is done / Do evil in return." This physics of evil is what *Affliction* is finally about. For no person, of course, is born bearing hopelessness and rage; we are molded to shape by the people around us. Wade as a young man was very different from the scarred being we have beheld. He had plans; he had a powerful love for Lillian; he had a chance for sane happiness. In the beginning of their relationship, it seems, Lillian was a kind of angel for Wade, all tenderness and encouragement. "Without Lillian," Rolfe writes, "without her recognition and protection, Wade would have been forced to regard himself as no different from the boys and men who surrounded him. . . . "

Alas, her gift was not enough. For night after night Wade had to come home to a vicious, drunken father and a family scene of such helpless terror that damage was inevitable. "Pop" Whitehouse finds Wade's attempts at self-assertion a trigger to his fury. He tries to beat every last shred of independence out of him. Banks is very good at capturing the dulling repetition of these scenes, the rhythms of their intensification, the empty roaring of the aftermath. But what we register most keenly—it is impossible not to flinch—is the pitch of a young man's terror:

> There was no time to hide from the blow, no time to protect himself with his arms or even to turn away. Pop's huge fist descended and collided with the boy's cheekbone. Wade felt a terrible slow warmth wash thickly across his face, and then he felt nothing at all. He was lying on his side, his face slammed against the couch, which smelled like cigarette smoke and sour milk, when there came a second blow, this one low on his back, and he heard his mother shout, "Glenn! Stop!" His body was behind him somewhere and felt hot and soft and bright, as if it had burst into flame. There was nothing before his eyes but blackness, and he realized that he was burrowing his face into the couch, showing his father his backside as he dug with his paws like a terrified animal into the earth.

Here is the root of damage, the source of the evil that later comes spilling forth from the boy grown up. When we learn that Wade may have beaten Lillian during their marriage, we are not surprised. When we see how he greets the oppressions in his life with fists, and alcoholic outbursts, and finally rifle fire, we are confirmed. It is the law of human nature that what enters as experience exits as behavior.

One Sunday, midway through the novel, Wade and Margie pay a visit to Wade's family and find Pop sitting in the kitchen in an alcoholic stupor. The stove has gone out, and Wade's mother is nowhere to be seen. Pop mumbles incoherent answers to their questions. They wait. But as the dreadful silence continues, Wade and Margie start exchanging glances. Finally they push into the bedroom, where they find that Wade's mother has frozen to death under the covers. Pop is too drunk to know what has happened; he is also too abject to draw down Wade's fury. There is no release, no explosion. The scene is as bleakly futile as any in modern literature.

From the time of the funeral on, Wade is in the grip of forces that he cannot command. He continues at his jobs, but he feels disengaged, as though he is walking in his sleep. He and Margie attempt to set up housekeeping with Pop, reckoning that he can no longer take care of himself. But Wade cannot begin to settle in. The atmospheric pressure around him intensifies by the hour. He cannot shake free of thinking about Evan Twombley, the union official. His paranoia is further fueled when he learns that LaRiviere is trying to buy Pop's land, that he has been covertly buying up every parcel on the mountain. Wade cannot figure out the connections, but he is sure they exist. On top of everything else, he has a rotting tooth that starts tormenting him to the point of madness.

I leave it to the reader to follow the skein of events that bring Wade to his final actions. The drive of the plot is intense through the final pages. Perhaps the last moment of any control that Wade has is when he lurches to the upstairs bathroom with a bottle of whiskey and a rusted pair of pliers. The pulpy horror of his tooth can be dealt with, even if the roots of his misery are too deep to be reached. Wade is finally without recourse; he cannot avoid the pull to violence.

This man's story is a tragedy in the Greek sense: at some point he surrendered a possible destiny and accepted a fate instead. Where the Greek heroes were driven to their ends by the implacable will of the gods, Wade is driven by the no less implacable imperatives of his misshapen character. Once that character has been formed, pressed out by blows and kicks, there is little hope that disaster will be averted. The reader's heart fills with pity and terror.

Banks controls the rush of his narrative with practiced skill. His device of refracting the story through Rolfe is a canny one, and it carries an added significance that occurs to us only later. Initially it seems a bit odd. Though Rolfe is giving us a scene-by-scene account of events he did not himself witness, he adopts the novelist's freedom to reconstruct these scenes down to the last detail and to enter into his brother's thoughts and feelings. Objectively, this is presumptuous, even though he claims to have interviewed everyone involved and to have listened for hours to Wade's drunken meanderings. But in fact we soon forget that Rolfe is doing the telling. We come to regard him as a stand-in novelist, a transparent screen through which we peer at the stages of the action. But there is a higher logic to Banks's setup. For Rolfe, too, is a Whitehouse. The novel is about blood ties and the handing on of legacies, and the blood that runs in his veins is Whitehouse blood.

He knows the town, the country; he lived through the tension of those horrifying nights. And he is forced to write because of this—because he recognizes that he is, except by the grace of whatever powers, himself capable of every last dark deed. This echo of kinship within the book amplifies the message more persuasively than any of the chilling turns of the plot.

Banks began his career divided between a common life subject matter and an experimental style. Subject has obviously won out, and Banks's liberated energies have gone into the forging of a straight-on technique. Banks's idiom is now vigorous and gritty, perfectly suited to the life of his characters and place. With his last few books, but with *Affliction* especially, he joins that group of small-town realists—writers like William Kennedy, Andre Dubus, and Larry Woiwode—who have worked to sustain what may in time be seen as our dominant tradition. Like them, Banks unfolds the sufferings of the ordinary life, of those who must worry, who can't be happy. (pp. 38-41)

Sven Birkerts, "Bleak House," in The New Republic, *Vol. 201, No. 11, September 11, 1989, pp. 38-41.*

Robert F. Gish

Russell Banks is one of a handful of contemporary novelists able to get at the essences of the American male's continuing quest for manhood. There is no such thing, of course, as "THE" American male, anymore than there is one definition of "THE" American hero—in fiction or in life.

American maleness is as multitudinous and complicated as the times and cultural contexts which determine the defining. And in the errant eighties, when androgyny and homosexuality blur easy distinctions, establishing one male ideal calls for special caution. In a novel like *Affliction,* and in its predecessor, *Continental Drift* (1986), Banks does not so much establish an ideal or argue for a prototype as he does explain one: the blue-collar, hardworking, middle-class male whose ideas of power and force are determined more by physical violence and tough-guy action rather than aristocratic bloodline, money, name, and formal education.

Insofar as the oversimplified division of American writers and their novelistic counterparts into palefaces and redskins still applies, Banks is very much in the redskin tradition of Cooper, Twain, and Hemingway. No drawingroom fripperies and fineries for Banks and his hue. His protagonists, like those of Mailer, McGuane, Harrison, and company, find that holding a life together—a job, a home, a family—means a fight for recognition and respect, for a sense of self-worth.

This is not to say that Banks, through his male protagonists, reduces contemporary maleness and the search for American masculinity to a beer, a brawl, and a broad, or to the comic quirks of Rodney Dangerfield. What Banks tries to do—and succeeds in doing with empathy but not sentimentality—is understand why an ordinary guy, a guy like Wade Whitehouse, part-time cop, snowplow operator, and well-digger, goes berserk one cold November day and at the age of forty-one does something terrible, something so cruel and violent and criminal that all he has worked for, all that he himself represents and thinks he "is," disappears into the thin-air statistics of fugitives, a man on the lam ironically "wanted" for reasons never anticipated.

Wade Whitehouse's "affliction" takes many forms. He wants to be a good man, tries hard to be. But his whole Lawford, New Hampshire, world falls away in a matter of climactic days during deer hunting season.

A union leader is shot while hunting. Wade suspects foul play and in trying to prove his suspicions crosses his family, his friends, his boss, and most of Lawford's citizenry. He almost solves the "crime"; almost outsmarts his former wife, Lillian; almost regains custody of his daughter, Jill; almost reconciles himself with his abusive and alcoholic father, Glenn; almost remarries a kind and caring woman, Margie Fogg. But in keeping with the relentless ways of naturalistic novels such as Banks is so adept at crafting, afflictions crowd out remedies and Wade succumbs to anger and depression and pain (symbolized by his rotting, aching tooth), lashes out at his best friend, Jack Hewitt, and most monstrously of all, at his diabolical father. Not since *McTeague* has a tooth figured so prominently in American literary naturalism.

Banks chooses as his narrator Wade's school-teacher brother, Rolfe, very much at once the double and foil, who has spent years trying to re-create the facts and the motives of Wade's story through interviews and letters and imaginings. As with all such tellings, *Affliction* is also the narrator's story, for in his effeminate, loquacious way he defines an alternative side of Wade's more virile maleness.

What Robert Bly does in his poetry about men in search of maleness, and what James Welch does so eloquently and powerfully in *Winter in the Blood* and *The Death of Jim Loney,* novels concerned with contemporary Native American alienation and marginality out West, Russell Banks does in *Affliction*—the tale of an all-American man resolved on being a good man, but doomed to violent destruction and New England perdition.

In a time when machismo is reduced to Ramboesque and World Wrestling Federation, Randy (Macho-Man) Savage stereotypes, Banks' accounting of why, in America, a good man is hard to be as well as find needs reading and respect. (pp. 7, 16)

> *Robert F. Gish, in a review of "Affliction," in The Bloomsbury Review, Vol. 9, No. 6, November-December, 1989, pp. 7, 16.*

Robert Towers

Russell Banks is one of a group of American realists concerned with the latter-day condition of some "non-ethnic" Americans of very old stock, whose ancestors (some of them) settled in North America as long ago as the seventeenth century. But far from living in Federal houses or belonging to suburban country clubs, these particular "old" Americans are the ones who have stayed behind in decaying villages or hardscrabble farms, or else have drifted to the Sunbelt or the West, where they are likely to live rootlessly in trailers or "ranchettes," hang out at bars, and work at odd jobs. Whether they have stayed put or moved on, they have, many of them, embraced, or inherited, failure, and they tend to ease their disappointment with hard drinking and activities that go with it, particularly deer hunting and beating up their wives and children. Banks's turf, so to speak, is small-town New Hampshire, where he set the stories of *Trailerpark,* and from which Bob Dubois, the main character of the much celebrated *Continental Drift,* escaped to a life of increasing desperation and criminality in Florida.

Affliction takes place in Lawford, New Hampshire (population 750), in the cold belt of the state north of Keene and Concord, where in the narrow valleys and abrupt hillsides, "life has been characterized by winter, not summer":

> What is normal is snow from early November well into May; normal is week after week of low zinc-gray overcast skies; is ice that cracks and booms as, closer every night to the bottom of the lake, a new layer of water cools, contracts and freezes beneath the layer of old ice above it.

Lawford is the kind of place from which ambitious young people flee as soon as they can, leaving behind an aging population and a residue of younger inhabitants who are regarded by their parents as failures and who behave accordingly. One of those who have fled is the narrator of the novel, Rolfe Whitehouse, who has escaped to a university and now teaches high school in a suburb of Boston. His task—a task of exorcism—is to account for the "strange criminal behavior" and disappearance of his older brother, Wade, one of those who stayed.

Wade is a well-digger and part-time cop, a divorced man of forty-one, gloomy, hard-drinking, full of "dumb belligerence." We first encounter him on Halloween, the night before the deer hunting season begins, when he is taking his reluctant daughter, Jill, to a costume party in Lawford's town hall in the doomed hope that the child, who lives with her mother in Concord, will have a good time, perhaps win a prize for her tiger costume, and gratefully respond to her father's love for her. We then follow Wade for two eventful weeks during which his already damaged life unravels to the point where he goes on a mad and murderous rampage, with which the novel ends.

Banks is particularly concerned with two dilemmas, the first to do with the consequences of a deer-hunting accident in which an obnoxious union official apparently stumbles and shoots himself while out in the woods with his guide, a local young man named Jack Hewitt. Wade, who is more than a little paranoid, convinces himself that Hewitt has murdered the union official at the instigation of Wade's boss and the union man's son-in-law who have been quietly buying up all the available property around Lawford. The other involves Wade's clumsy attempts to reclaim the love of his estranged daughter and his decision to bring a custody suit against his embittered former wife. But these are only the main lines in a novel crowded—perhaps too crowded—with a great many other matters.

Beyond the events of those two weeks are a number of episodes from the past which Rolfe recreates in his determination to make sense of Wade's condition. What has mattered most, we are led to believe, are the brutal beatings that Wade as a boy suffered at the hands of his father—sexually charged beatings that permanently affected Wade's sense of himself as a man and led to uncontrolled and usually inappropriate outbursts of violence. . . .

While the younger brother can be fairly subtle about the psychological effects of such brutality on Wade, he can also be annoyingly obtrusive in his lengthy explanations of his own part in the story. Furthermore, Banks allows certain suspicions to arise concerning Rolfe's reliability as a narrator and commentator. Are these convolutions necessary, the reader may well ask, perhaps longing for a return to the convention of the omniscient narrator, who is free to invent and comment as much as he likes without fuss or apology.

When Banks drops the guise of the younger brother and simply presents his material directly and dramatically, he reveals himself as a powerful and sometimes poetic writer who knows the texture of the things he describes. Here is a passage from the scene of Wade's crazed pursuit of Jack Hewitt through a rugged wintry landscape:

> Then, unexpectedly, the ground leveled off, and the trucks were running alongside a shallow beaver pond, with sumac and chokecherry flashing past. At the far end of the pond, the trail swerved left, . . . too abruptly for Jack to make the turn, and his truck crashed through a stand of skinny birches straight onto the pond, its momentum carrying it swiftly over the surface of the thick ice, its headlights sending huge pale swirls out ahead of it. Wade pulled up at the shore, and he watched Jack's truck slide across the ice like a leaf on a slow-moving river, until it came to a stop halfway across the pond, facing Wade's truck, with its headlights gazing back over the snow-covered surface of the glass-smooth ice. Wade dropped his truck into first gear, edged it to the shore, then down onto the ice, and slowly he drove directly into the glare of Jack's headlights, drawing carefully closer as if toward a fire, until finally the vehicles were face to face, plow blade to plow blade.

For me the most extraordinary scene in the novel occurs when Wade and his undemanding girlfriend, Margie, with whom he hopes to have a new life which will include his daughter, go to his parents' freezing house. There they find that Wade's mother has died of hypothermia, huddled in her bed while his father wandered about the house, too drunk and dazed to call someone in to fix the furnace.

> Stepping carefully away from the thing [an electric heater], [Wade] crossed to the head of the bed, where he could see the woman clearly. Beneath a mound of blankets and afghans, she wore her wool coat over her flannel nightgown and lay curled on her side like a child, with her tiny hands in mittens fisted near her throat, as if in enraged prayer. Her eyes were closed, and her mouth was open slightly. Her skin was chalk white and dry-looking, almost powdery, as if her

face would crumble to the touch. Her body resembled a feather-light husk more than an actual human body, and it seemed incapable of holding up the weight of the blankets that covered her to the shoulders and wrists. "Oh, Lord," Wade whispered. "Oh, Lord." He came forward and sat down on the floor, cross-legged, like a small boy, facing her.

Like the scrubby, screen-filled landscape in which much of it takes place, *Affliction* is almost unremittingly grim; the passages of grotesque comedy are shot through with pain. Yet the grimness is redeemed, if only partly relieved, by the sympathetic insight which the author brings to the hapless Wade, so that the reader in turn is made to care for an unlikable man and to believe that others have loved him. Banks's dour vision is realized intensely and impressively in this novel, and it should strengthen the reputation he earned with *Continental Drift.* (p. 46)

Robert Towers, "You Can Go Home Again," in The New York Review of Books, *Vol. XXXVI, No. 19, December 7, 1989, pp. 46-7.*

Carol Ascher

Picture a square-faced man hunched over a large metal wheel in the painfully cold, windblown, canvas cab of the blue grader he is using to plow the difficult roads of his northern New Hampshire mill town. Forward ten feet, then ten feet back, he makes a "short half turn to the right, short half turn to the left, wrenching that huge steering wheel like the captain of a ship trying to avoid an iceberg." The man, Wade Whitehouse, is the protagonist of [*Affliction*], this gripping, most beautiful, grim and wide-sweeping novel. The book is a requiem for a working-class manhood, no longer viable if it ever had been, that careens between decency, even sweetness, and brutal violence.

Wade seems perilously on the down skid. After building a house for his wife and daughter (they have left him because of his violent drinking bouts), he now lives alone in a trailer at the edge of town. He is not far in miles or consciousness from his childhood farmhouse, where he, his siblings and mother were all battered during their father's binges, and where the old couple now live in precarious isolation. From Wade's early morning hour of respectability as town policeman—holding back traffic as the buses roll into the elementary-school yard—he rushes to his day job as foreman driller for Lariviere Co.; except that when the earth freezes, as it does starting in early November, Wade's boss, who has the town roads contract, sends him out in the company vehicles to clear the snow.

Wade doesn't think of himself as depressed, but he knows he is drinking too much, that he has a chronic toothache for which he can't seem to get to a dentist, and that his ten-year-old daughter is becoming estranged from him. Like too many men, Wade is helpless in the face of a relationship that needs talking through. Still a romantic, he disparages his present affair with a local waitress, Margie Fogg, by comparison with the "perfect love" he and his wife shared as schoolmates and in their early twenties, and the diminishment of his life makes him rageful, envious at the young, and full of sorrow.

Affliction takes place during that early November deer-hunting season which embodies traditional manhood, and the build-up of Wade's paranoia and impotent rage is told retrospectively in the intelligent, passionate and grief-stricken voice of Wade's younger brother. Now a high-school history teacher in Boston, Rolfe has learned different lessons from his father's violence. For while he is not violent, he is alone, afraid of bonds. On the basis of his brother's drunken late-night phone calls and a couple of visits to the town, he pieces together the tragedy of Wade's crimes to free himself of the family's violent heritage. Then, he believes,

> my own story and, at last, not Wade's will start to fill me, and this time it will be different: this time I will truly have left that family and that town. Will I marry then? Will I make a family of my own? Will I become a member of a tribe? Oh, Lord, I pray that I will do those things and that I will be that man.

Though the plot focuses on Wade, *Affliction* is also about his father, Rolfe, two other brothers who were killed in Vietnam, and the New England outdoorsmen whose masculinity seems at once well-known and wonderfully specific. The type, as described by Rolfe, "evolved over tens of thousands of years of holding the reins of another man's horse in the cold rain while the horseman does business inside by the fire." There is a dogged patience as well as an equally dogged anger that is unimaginative, physical, cruel and self-destructive. Like Wade's huge grader, this masculinity often seems blind, and insufficiently agile for the day's more subtle demands.

Why take up the space which might be used to give attention to a book by a woman to review this novel? Besides my conviction that there are few such splendid works of contemporary fiction, and that it deserves to be announced wherever possible, *Affliction* seems deeply informed by feminism. The old Mrs. Whitehouse dies as she lived, a classic country woman, alternately ignored and brutalized (her death is one of the great scenes of the novel), yet when Wade skids into raging violence soon after her funeral, his girlfriend Margie instantly grasps the situation and packs her things. The women who are Wade's contemporaries have seen enough male violence to know they don't like it and they have the economic independence and self-respect to get out of its way. This means that the cycle is partly broken, but also that the men who haven't resolved their violent legacy are now alone.

Yet if one is inclined to think that escape heralds a more contented and likeable generation, Banks doesn't offer much. It is as if, without indissoluble marriages, which kept women like Wade's mother dutifully chained to their vicious husbands, no one really knows how or why to remain in a union. Out on her own again, Margie takes the classic step of those women of middling age who despair of a relationship with a man: she decides to adopt a Latin American baby. Although Wade's former wife Lillian is safely remarried to a white-collar man, she apparently feels both bored and safe enough three years into the mar-

riage to be having an affair. As for Rolfe, having told his story, Wade's story, will he know himself enough to be able to move along the fragile web of nonviolent intimacy with a woman?

Affliction is an old-fashioned novel in a number of ways for which I find myself grateful. With ambitious and certain strokes, Banks paints in a community that one feels one could draw on a map or walk through, nodding a friendly hello to its citizens, easily spotting the trailer park, the school, Margie's restaurant with its "home made cooking" sign, or the old homes that now double as insurance, real estate, guns 'n ammo and haircutting businesses.

Affliction is also old-fashioned in its deep respect for human tragedy. Unlike much current art, which glories in meaningless violence, Banks has written a novel whose goal is to make at least subjective sense out of a man's violent acts. Taken from Simone Weil's statement, "The great enigma of human life is not suffering but affliction," he has crafted a deeply moving work in his attempt to understand the cause-effect sequence that led to one family's and community's tragedy.

> Carol Ascher, "The Roots of Rage," in The Women's Review of Books, *Vol. VII, No. 7, April, 1990, p. 21.*

Banks on writing about working-class life:

I grew up in a working-class family. . . . I have a less obstructed path as a writer to get to the center of their lives. Part of the challenge of what I write is uncovering the resiliency of that kind of life, and part is in demonstrating that even the quietest lives can be as complex and rich, as joyous, conflicted and anguished, as other, seemingly more dramatic lives.

> Russell Banks, in an interview in The New York Times Book Review, *September 15, 1991.*

Richard Eder

Russell Banks has used a small town's response to tragedy to write a novel of compelling moral suspense.

On a snowy morning, the school bus serving Sam Dent, a community at the edge of the Adirondack Mountains, skids off the highway, tumbles down an incline and plunges into the water of an abandoned quarry. Ten children die; others are severely injured. The driver, Dolores Driscoll—a sturdy, compassionate woman who drives to support herself and her crippled husband—had swerved to avoid the sudden appearance of what may have been a child, a small animal or even a snow-fogged trick of vision.

"A town needs its children," says Dolores, who survives. That is part of the theme of Banks' superb book, *The Sweet Hereafter.* The main part goes deeper. Communities form to contain and manage the larger kinds of catastrophe. Unmanageable catastrophe can kill or cripple them. Sam Dent survives, but some of its belief in itself is torn away.

Banks relates the erratic lines of destruction, the unpredictable shifts and displacements of the shock wave that radiates from the tragedy. He uses four voices. They belong to Dolores; to Billy Ansel, a widower garage-owner whose two daughters perish; to Nichole, a bright and popular teen-ager who is permanently paralyzed with a broken back, and to Mitchell Stevens, a New York City negligence lawyer who speeds north and camps for months in Sam Dent's only motel.

He is prompt as Nemesis, this raging, sharp-tongued zealot. Sam Dent is numb with shock; its instinct is to huddle together, to console, to bow its head and move on. Mitchell won't allow it; somebody must pay.

"There are no accidents" is his creed. This termagant, who boasts that negligence lawyers are "the proctologists of the profession," makes money, but he also has a cause. The institutions of our society—government and business—operate a cold balance of risk, a calculation that sets the certain cost of better brakes or stronger guard-rails against the possible cost of being sued. Mitchell's mission, he asserts, is "to make it cheaper to build the bus with that extra bolt."

He is not after Dolores; on the contrary. She is a gutsy, admired member of the community; she is known for devotion to her charges and for her scrupulous driving and maintenance of the bus. And, of course, she has no money. Nobody questions—at this point—her estimate that she was traveling at a safe speed. And Billy Ansel, numb with loss, backs her up. That morning, he had followed his usual routine of driving into town behind the bus, after putting his daughters on board.

Dolores, then, in her anguish, is another victim; and Mitchell tries but fails to add her to his list of parents willing to sue the sueable; the town, county and state. It is a shorter list than he had expected. Mitchell may be after justice, but it is a destructive, rending justice. Banks' moral questions battle each other with the savagery and flair of a bullfight. The town, after all, is the town. To the bereaved, it is both *them* and *us*.

Among those who sign up are the parents of Nichole, whose bright prospects will forever be bound to a wheelchair. Dolores' refusal remains passive; the two principal opponents to Mitchell and his lawsuits are Billy—and Nichole herself.

Billy is aghast at what is happening to his community. People have gone suit-crazy, he rages. Lawyers are suing each other for stealing clients. The school authorities are being sued for their choice of how to spend the contributions that flood in. There is talk of suing the rescue squad for failing to save more children.

Nichole's motives are more complex. She is idealistic and she is angry. Why should she, who is only crippled, make money off a tragedy that has killed her friends? But there is a darker story. Her father is a mild man who had sexually abused her for years.

Realizing she has the power to wreck his case and his expectations of money, Nichole does so. It is a startling and moving act, not only reprisal but liberation as well. From her seat behind Dolores, she had had a clear view of the speedometer. And, she testifies in a pretrial deposition, it showed the bus traveling at 20 m.p.h. over the speed limit. The lawsuits promptly collapsed. Mitchell retreats to New York, and Nichole, who lets her father know just what she has on him, has won freedom. Compared to abuse, a wheelchair confines far more lightly.

If this were all, Banks would have written a remarkable book, a sardonic and compassionate account of a community and its people, and of a catastrophe that vividly characterizes them even as it brutally acts upon them. His portrait of the small northern town is complex and spare at the same time; every detail stands out. None of the principal characters is simple. Mitchell is a second catastrophe following the first; yet his argument is lucid and compelling. Nichole is arrogant as well as innocent, and her act of liberation has an awful ambiguity to it. Billy, more human and less specifically focused, is a mixture of saintliness and weakness.

If this were all—but it's not. What about Dolores? Nichole's testimony seems to expose her, not as wicked but as pitiable. And this creates a disquieting puzzlement. Surely, she is the same person who in her first narrative, which opens the book, seemed so warm, so observant, so shrewd and, in a rough-hewn way, so strong. All these qualities suddenly feel contaminated.

In her second narrative, which comes at the end, our disquiet is dispelled—not smoothly but with powerful tension—and our admiration flowers. For her—and I can't say more without revealing the story's crucial puzzle—and for Banks. He has told us the real story all along while, without the least trickery, managing to conceal it. He also has written an extraordinary fictional character and revealed her to us in a fashion that is theater as much as fiction.

Dolores, finally, will serve as scapegoat. Mitchell was right, in a way; the town needed one. Instead of suing—and, in a way, blaming themselves—the Sam Denters are able to turn their anguish onto a single person. When she goes, one by one, to the funerals of the dead children, no one speaks to her and she respects the silence, even while suffering from it.

Her discourse emerges as the bitten-off, self-taught poetic current that makes *The Sweet Hereafter* much more than the sum of its excellent parts. Stoic and perceptive, capable of a beautifully colored phrase side-by-side with a resigned commonplace, Dolores ends as an exile to everything but her valiant and expanding spirit. There are one or two rough passages, but Banks, one of our strongest writers, has touched his unglamorous small-town Americans with light, and written, I think, his best book. (pp. 3, 8)

Richard Eder, "A Small Town Copes with Tragedy," in Los Angeles Times Book Review, September 1, 1991, pp. 3, 8.

Roger Rosenblatt

You are likely not to have forgotten that heartbreaking accident in East Coldenham, N.Y., in November 1989, when a sudden blast of wind collapsed a wall of an elementary school, killing nine young children. Such a memory is evoked by Russell Banks in *The Sweet Hereafter*—not only the circumstance of the accidental death of children, but also the tormenting helplessness of townspeople who must try to reach a rational understanding of an inexplicable calamity. In this novel the effort to rationalize takes the form of assigning blame, which brings the townspeople as much pain as do the deaths of the children.

This effort to rationalize through blame, which is the modern effort in all things, is Russell Banks's theme. It is a theme hard to find in a novel these days. The assignment of blame makes disorderly occurrences orderly, sets them within our control again. Blame is especially useful in situations in which there is no apparent villain—those moments that prove, despite our advancement of learning, how susceptible we are to high winds and wet roads.

Dolores Driscoll has been the school bus driver in the upstate New York town of Sam Dent since 1968. She and her husband, Abbott, who has had to use a wheelchair since his stroke several years ago, have lived in no other place. In July and August, Sam Dent belongs to the summer people. The remainder of the time it is populated by ordinary people who drive pickup trucks, keep neat woodpiles and live in houses with "flapping plastic over the windows and sagging porches." The local roads, with their "boarded-up roadside diners and dilapidated motels," run among dark mountains. Dolores knows the roads of Sam Dent, "which is one of the reasons I was given this job in 1968 and rehired every year since—the other being my considerable ability as a driver, pure and simple, and my reliability and punctuality."

Those assets are called into question after one snowy morning when, with the straight part of the road shooting before her and her bus filled with children talking quietly among themselves, Dolores sees a dog move into the road, or thinks she does. She swerves right and jams the brakes, and the bus rolls downhill into an icy pond. Fourteen of the children die.

From that terrible moment the lives of the people of Sam Dent are never the same. "For us," says Billy Ansel, a former hero of the Vietnam War who now runs the town garage—and whose children die in the accident—

> there was life, true life, real life, no matter how bad it had seemed, before the accident, and nothing that came after the accident resembled it in any important way. . . . For us, it was as if we, too, had died when the bus went over the embankment and tumbled down into the frozen water-filled sandpit, and now we were lodged temporarily in a kind of purgatory, waiting to be moved to wherever the other dead ones had gone.

The absence of the town's children draws couples apart, drives people to drink and loneliness, makes enemies of friends and creates a void that is soon filled by the need to blame.

Someone, something, has to be held accountable for the deaths of the children. Dolores? The bus? The seat belts? The snowfall? The roads of the state of New York?

Into the void strides Mitchell Stephens, a lawyer from New York City who specializes in accidents. To Mitchell, all accidents are the result of negligence, and he goes around Sam Dent trying to find where the responsibility lies. His job, his mission, is, he says, "to represent *anger.*" For a while he cannot find any anger in Sam Dent. Then he half discovers, half creates a client in Nichole Burnell, a teen-age girl who was partly paralyzed in the crash, and who agrees to pin the blame on Dolores for speeding. Nichole's motive is personal, entirely unrelated to Dolores or to the facts of the accident.

At first the townspeople want nothing to do with her lawsuit. Then they grow excited about the idea, not for the money to be gained or as a concession to the modern litigious disease but because a lawsuit is a blaming instrument. However inaccurately or inadequately, it proclaims in a public arena that an outrageous, impossible event has been understood, that it has been put in a recognizable box, that it is tamed, not mystifying, not out of human control. In a way, modernity is defined by the extent to which life has been brought under human control.

Not only Mitchell Stephens—who is not a bad guy, merely a champion of his age—but the whole town of Sam Dent wants the bus accident brought under human control. Even Dolores wants that. When she learns that she has been blamed for the children's deaths, she is actually relieved: "I felt as if a great weight that I had been lugging around for eight or nine months, since the day of the accident, had been lifted from me," she says. It is less important to her that she has been wrongly accused than that she can at last name her anguish.

But the truth of the situation—the true story of the bus accident and of the wider experience it represents—is that its cause is bewilderingly *out of* human control, just as much of modern experience is bewilderingly out of our control. At the very least the essentials, life and death, are out of our control. Not that this is really a secret; we know how helpless we can be. Yet the knowledge is resisted because it is antimodern, superstitious, a suggestion that there are certain unconquerable forces working against progress.

See the way earthquakes and hurricanes are depicted in the news. The accounts are always made in terms of the number of dead, the number of injured, the dollar amounts of the damage. To quantify is to command the event, to make the disaster less natural. Let it never be reported that a terrible fist came out of nowhere, knocked the stuffing out of us for as long as it pleased and left us naked in the streets.

If we are not in control of our catastrophes, after all, we can only sit back and scrutinize divine justice. We can ask Job's question or ponder the suffering of the innocent or think in circles about God's plots and errors. That, too, is an effort to rationalize, but it is not as satisfying as the assignment of blame, which is reassuring and affirms free will.

What Russell Banks is saying, I think, is that our deeper satisfaction lies elsewhere: that the force of things unrationalized is the source not only of the terror but of the beauty in our lives. Instead of being humbled by the inexplicable, we can be saved by accepting it. By accepting the inexplicable we are thrown toward one another. We may even learn to sympathize with one another for the susceptibility to suffering we have in common.

Mr. Banks is too able a writer to state such things outright. But in the final scene of his novel the town rises to an acceptance of the catastrophe on its own mysterious terms.

Everyone is gathered in the grandstand to watch the last event of the annual Sam Dent Country Fair, the demolition derby. One of the entrants is Boomer, a station wagon once owned by Dolores Driscoll. The crowd cheers wildly every time Boomer takes a hit; the car is being punished as a stand-in for Dolores. Yet it continues running. One by one all the other cars and trucks drop out of the competition, but Boomer, smashed on every side, survives.

Suddenly the crowd starts chanting "Boomer! Boo-mer!" In the end the station wagon is the only vehicle left in the arena; it wins simply by going on. And the crowd rejoices. The townspeople, though they can never say why, are happy.

In *The Lives of a Cell*, Lewis Thomas wrote, "All of the life of the earth dies, all the time, in the same volume as the new life that dazzles us each morning, each spring." I don't know if that is a scientific observation or a religious one, but it is a great consolation in any case. Fourteen of the children in Sam Dent die, but within eight or nine months, the gestation period of Dolores Driscoll's grief, other children will be born. Things will never be the same after the accident, but they will always be the same, too, and eventually the abiding love of the people for one another will crack through the isolation of winter and create life, true life, real life again.

That also is not to be rationalized or controlled. It is the way things are in the world, and in Russell Banks's cold and merciful eye. (pp. 1, 29)

> Roger Rosenblatt, "*An Inescapable Need to Blame,*" in The New York Times Book Review, *September 15, 1991, pp. 1, 29.*

Banks on *The Sweet Hereafter*:

I wanted to write a novel in which the community was the hero, rather than any single individual. I wanted to explore how a community is both disrupted and unified by a tragedy.

> Russell Banks, *in an interview in* The New York Times Book Review, *September 15, 1991.*

Chuck Wachtel

Because *The Sweet Hereafter* is smaller in both scope and page count than *Continental Drift* and *Affliction,* Russell Banks's last two novels, it offers an opportunity to see more easily what is central to the power and importance in his work: the ability to write about ordinary people (most of us) without accepting much apparent guidance or influence from the existing literary manners of doing so, or from the common assumptions of our times.

If not for the effects of the failing national economy, the tentacles of mass media and the upscale vacationers who drive north from the city, the small, upstate New York town of Sam Dent, setting of *The Sweet Hereafter,* would otherwise remain isolated in its own particular late-twentieth-century solitude. On a recent winter morning a schoolbus skids off the road, tumbles down an embankment and into a water-filled sand pit. Fourteen of the town's children are killed. The fabric of order in Sam Dent is suddenly torn apart. The novel does not present this in public acts of mourning or violence; there are few overt acts of vengeance or compensation. Rather, we experience the horror, the uncontainable pain, in the voices of the novel's four narrators, who in the aftermath of the accident present to us not only themselves and the facts as they know them; they also present to us the mysterious and inevitable continuance of their lives.

For the most part, their stories remain inside the perimeters of local, more immediate circumstances. As they tell those stories, increasing our access to their inner lives, the characters do not readily give themselves over to larger, universalizing proportions: We must first experience them in their own terms—their ordinary moments, their revelations—before we respond with the secondary wave of *our* understanding. Lionel Trilling has given us a still very serviceable phrase for what realism in fiction does, or should do: *reveal the human fact in the veil of circumstance.* Central to the power of nearly all of Banks's work is that he is first influenced by his subject matter, the people he writes about. In their context the larger issues become less abstracted, less the possession of idea—more theirs, more ours.

Early in *Continental Drift,* for example, its two main characters, a New Hampshire furnace repairman and a poor, young Haitian woman, escape the lives they were born to and begin separate, haphazard, perilous migrations toward more viable, safer, more comprehendable lives. Although the narration remains centered in the movements of these two characters, it expands in size to encompass the unnavigated drift that seems to be so much of life at the end of this half-millennium we might remember as Columbian America. *Affliction,* set in New Hampshire, is the story of the events leading up to a murder and the disappearance of the man who commits it. It is also a story about the legacy of male anger—from its untraceable beginnings in a time long before the world that this novel occurs in was ever dreamed of—and its effects on family, community and the culture at large. If it is possible for writers to contain such vast thematic centers in their stories, and if readers are still willing even to attempt to accept delivery of them—in short, if this is to work at all—

what is needed is precisely what Banks provides: characters who can be perceived as wholly separate from the conditions their stories make manifest.

As Dolores Driscoll, the bus driver and narrator of the first and last of *The Sweet Hereafter*'s five sections, begins telling her story, the circumstances begin to narrow, to close in around her like a reversal of the circular eddies caused by a stone dropped in water. Dolores has driven the children of Sam Dent to school since 1968, when the bus was her own Dodge station wagon and her own two sons were among the passengers. In the nearly two decades that follow, her husband and companion, Abbott, becomes confined to a wheelchair due to a stroke, making her driver's income the household income; her sons grow up and move on; and the station wagon, which she and the children had named Boomer, is replaced first by a GMC twenty-four seater and, in 1987, "to handle the baby boomers' babies, I'd guess you'd call them, the district had to get me the International fifty-seater."

The second narrator, Billy Ansel, is already widowed when the accident occurs, taking the lives of his two children. A Vietnam vet, owner of a garage, he is a man possessed of a quiet and isolate integrity. He tells us that people who have lost their children "twist themselves into all kinds of weird shapes in order to deny what has happened. Not because of the pain of losing a person they loved—we lose parents and mates and friends, and no matter how painful, it's not the same—but because what has happened is so wickedly unnatural, so profoundly against the necessary order of things, that we cannot accept it."

Mitchell Stephens, Esq., a lawyer who comes up from New York City hoping to represent the families and survivors, is the book's third narrator. Angry, sophisticated, observant, he provides an outsider's view of the other characters and of Sam Dent. In telling us of his own life, particularly as the father of a hopelessly drug-addicted daughter, he places the novel, the accident itself, in the larger, darker context of our times. He tells us we are all losing our children: "I don't know if it was the Vietnam war, or the sexual colonization of kids by industry, or drugs, or TV, or divorce, or what the hell it was; I don't know what are causes and what are effects; but the children are gone. . . . So that trying to protect them is little more than an exercise in denial."

Young Nichole Burnell, a survivor of the accident, has already been forcibly extracted from the fabric of her teenage life by her father, who victimizes her through incest. Outwardly a pretty, popular eighth grader, she lives isolated in an inexpressible silence. The accident, condemning her to a wheelchair for life, completes the process: When we meet her all the connections—to family and friends, to the series of events she had expected to carry her into the future—have already been severed. Nichole is the book's fourth narrator, both a child and a prophet. Hers is perhaps the deepest, clearest view we get into the inner life of Sam Dent.

As readers, caught up in the life of the novel, we make a leap from our burdened and mysterious real lives to something we perceive in the heart of its characters. We seek, and perhaps find, a kind of communion with something larger. Yet since a character is, after all, simply a construct of crafted language, most of what we find there, as in a dream, has to have been ours in the first place. What we seek is ourselves. Yet the life we live and the lives we read about in so many contemporary novels seem to have less and less in common.

In explaining why the storyteller has become a thing of the past, Walter Benjamin told us, "One reason for this phenomenon is obvious: experience has fallen in value." Since he wrote this, the trend has accelerated. Even the complex technologies of fiction we've been steadily evolving since Chekhov cannot keep apace of this devaluation. I see in much of Banks's work a refusal to find this acceptable. Whether vast or local in scope, the foundation for his fiction is experience in its most familiar and simultaneously mysterious circumstance: as we know it, *be* it, before it is crafted into the larger, rarefied context of fictional narrative. We can find it there.

This realism exemplified by Russell Banks is both old-fashioned and new. New because his characters feel as if he first discovered them outside of fiction, not from pre-existing literary or cultural models. Old-fashioned because his work is dedicated to what Cynthia Ozick has called (in a wonderful brief essay, "A Short Note on 'Chekhovian' ") "explicit and definitive portraiture and the muscular trajectory of whole lives."

In the final section of *The Sweet Hereafter,* Dolores Driscoll is watching the demolition derby at the Sam Dent County Fair. The town has shunned her since the accident six months ago. On one side of her, her husband sits in his wheelchair; on the other is Billy Ansel, drunk, the state he has most often been in since the accident. Boomer, now the possession of one of the town's young men, is one of the entries. The crowd cheers each time Boomer is hit. The other drivers, understanding the town's desire to punish the car, to punish Dolores, attack with fury. Even so, the old car prevails. As, one by one, the other cars are eliminated and the process intensifies, the crowd begins chanting "Boomer! Boomer!" The whole town has crossed an invisible border. Although things will never be the same, its inhabitants have touched, perhaps only briefly, some source of their collective lives, one that was there before the accident and, through this time of grief and anger, has somehow remained intact. There is, however, no consolation for Dolores Driscoll, no going back:

> Nichole, I, the children who survived the accident, and the children who did not—it was as if we were the citizens of a wholly different town now, as if we were a town of solitaries living in a sweet hereafter, and no matter how the people of Sam Dent treated us, whether they memorialized us or despised us, whether they cheered for our destruction or applauded our victory over adversity, they did it to meet their needs, not ours. Which, since it could be no other way, was exactly as it should be.

The book's narrative does not go beyond this dark, grim time in the life of its characters, yet it offers us a healing clarity. I think this is because these characters, or the human facts they represent outside of fiction, are the first measure of the story's size and shape. And it seems only after taking that initial measurement that Russell Banks, in *The Sweet Hereafter,* brings his passionate and profoundly exact craft to bear. (pp. 786-88)

Chuck Wachtel, "Character Witness," in The Nation, *New York, Vol. 253, No. 21, December 16, 1991, pp. 786-88.*

Additional coverage of Bank's life and career is contained in the following sources published by Gale Research: *Contemporary Authors,* **Vols. 65-68;** *Contemporary Authors New Revision Series,* **Vol. 19; and** *Contemporary Literary Criticism,* **Vol. 37.**

Ingmar Bergman

1918-

(Full name Ingmar Ernst Bergman) Swedish film and stage director, screenwriter, playwright, and autobiographer

The following entry provides an overview of Bergman's career. For further information on his life and works, see *CLC,* Volume 16.

INTRODUCTION

Throughout the five decades of his career Bergman has written and directed some of the most highly acclaimed films of the postwar period. Many critics have listed *Det sjunde inseglet* (*The Seventh Seal*) and *Smultronstället* (*Wild Strawberries*) among the ten best films of all time, and *Nattvardsgästerna* (*Winter Light*), *Persona, Scener ur ett äktenskap* (*Scenes from a Marriage*), and *Fanny och Alexander* (*Fanny and Alexander*), like all of Bergman's major works, continue to draw the attention of filmmakers, critics, and audiences all over the world. While Bergman's films tend to be confessional and are dominated by religious, philosophical, and psychosexual themes, most of them include moments of humor and gaiety, and he has written and directed several comedies.

Bergman was born in Uppsala, near Stockholm. His father, a Lutheran pastor to the Swedish royal court, and his mother subscribed to strict ideals of child-rearing: discipline, devotion, fear of God, and dispassionately delivered, humiliating punishment. It was not uncommon for them to lock one of their children in a "prayer closet," and Bergman was once made to wear a dress in atonement for disobedience. Bergman has remarked that his greatest pleasures as a child were performing with his puppet theater, playing with his magic lantern (a primitive slide projector and an ancestor of the motion picture camera) and exploring his grandmother's spacious apartment in Uppsala. Each of these activities provided a form of imaginative escape from an otherwise dour routine. In the summer of 1934, Bergman traveled to Germany as an exchange student and lived with a family near Weimar. His hosts, like his friends and most Germans at the time, were ardent supporters of Adolph Hitler. Bergman has admitted that as a teenager he idolized Hitler, and that he and his family supported the Nazis for a number of years, even during the war. When photographs exposing the horrors of the German concentration camps became available, Bergman vowed never again to engage in political activity; nevertheless, his production of *Macbeth* in 1944, one of his first major theatrical works, is remembered as being strongly anti-Nazi.

Bergman's theatrical career began in college with student and amateur groups which performed works by August

Strindberg, Henrik Ibsen, and Shakespeare. During this time Bergman also wrote his own plays, and on the strength of *Kaspers död* (*The Death of Punch*), his first play to be produced, he was offered a job as a reader in the screenplay department at Svensk Filmindustri, the state-supported film company of Sweden. In 1944 Bergman's screenplay *Hets* (*Frenzy*) was filmed by director Alf Sjöberg, a prominent figure in Swedish cinema and theater. The following year Bergman directed his first film, *Kris* (*Crisis*), and in 1948 he began production on *Fängelse* (*Prison*), which many critics consider Bergman's first mature work. In the next five years he made several films, maintained an active schedule of theater and radio production, and earned a national reputation in Sweden. When *Sommarnattens leende* (*Smiles of a Summer Night*) won the Special Jury Prize at the 1956 Cannes Film Festival, Bergman became internationally famous. His next two films, *The Seventh Seal* and *Wild Strawberries,* secured his position at the forefront of contemporary cinema. Throughout the 1960s and 1970s Bergman's career continued successfully with such critically acclaimed films as *Winter Light, Persona,* and *Viskningar och rop* (*Cries and Whispers*). Like a number of prominent filmmakers, Bergman established a troupe of actors and technicians with whom he worked regularly; this group included, most notably, Max von Sydow, Bibi Andersson, Liv Ullmann, Erland Josephson, and the Academy Award-winning cinematographer Sven Nykvist. In 1976 the Swedish government arrested Bergman for tax evasion. The charge was eventually proven groundless and Bergman completely exonerated, but because he was arrested in public and forced to spend a humiliating night in jail, Bergman felt compelled to exile himself. He settled in Germany where he continued to direct plays and films. His films of this period, including *Ansikte mot ansikte* (*Face to Face*) and *Ormen's ägg* (*The Serpent's Egg*), are widely considered the weakest of his mature works. In 1982, at the age of sixty-four, Bergman announced his retirement from the cinema. Since his retirement he has directed a number of films for Swedish television, published an autobiography, *Lanterna Magica* (*The Magic Lantern*), and in 1991 directed Sweden's Royal Dramatic Theater during its tour of the United States.

Critics generally discern in Bergman's films a set of core subjects: loneliness, God's seeming remoteness from human affairs, the nature of the artist, and intimate, often destructive, relationships. These concerns are usually attributed to Bergman's strict religious upbringing. Aesthetically and thematically, critics cite the influence of Strindberg and Ibsen: the former for his unique combination of naturalism and religious concerns, and the latter for his psychological insight and complex symbolism. In the practical matters of filmmaking, Bergman's mentor was director Alf Sjöberg, who was able to suggest ways of translating to the screen those literary aspects and psychological insights that attracted Bergman to the plays of Strindberg and Ibsen. Critics tend to differ on the ultimate quality of these early films; some see them as little more than pretty pictures and melodrama, while others consider them the early sketches of a master. After establishing his reputation and his principal themes and subjects with *Smiles of a Summer Night, The Seventh Seal,* and *Wild Strawberries,* Bergman made two trilogies in the sixties that many consider the high points of his career. The first, or "religious," trilogy comprises *Såsom i en spegel* (*Through a Glass Darkly*), *Winter Light,* and *Tystnaden* (*The Silence*). These films are stark, unrelenting examinations of the religious and psychosexual themes that Bergman first approached in *The Seventh Seal* and *Gycklarnas afton* (*Sawdust and Tinsel*). *Through a Glass Darkly* portrays a father's perversely dispassionate observation of his daughter's descent into madness and, despite having won the 1962 Academy Award for Best Foreign Language Film, is generally considered the weakest of the three; *Winter Light,* the bleak story of a pastor's loss of faith, and *The Silence,* an allegorical, sexually charged tale about isolation and the indifference of God, are widely considered to be masterpieces. Bergman's second trilogy comprises the films *Persona, Vargtimmen* (*Hour of the Wolf*), and *Skammen* (*Shame*). Critics point out that these films employ many of the filmic techniques pioneered by the more experimental avant garde filmmakers in Italy and France; for example, the flouting of classical narrative conventions in *Persona* and the character's direct address to the camera (and therefore the audience) in *Hour of the Wolf* are clearly based on the aggressive approach to film form taken by Federico Fellini and Jean-Luc Godard. Critics have suggested that Bergman's change in style, in

the words of David A. Cook, "signaled a new thematic concern with the nature of human psychology, perception, and identity." It has been further noted that with a more secular thematic emphasis, Bergman's films of the late 1960s began to incorporate political themes and images. In a famous scene in *Persona* an actress, who has refused to speak after suffering a psychological crisis, watches in horror as newsreel footage depicts a Cambodian monk immolating himself. *Shame* details the disintegration of the social order and human relationships during war, and although *Hour of the Wolf* does not have an overtly political theme, it does deal with, in symbolic and dreamlike terms, the artist's relationship with society. In each film, the world beyond the insular lives of the main characters is depicted as inherently malevolent and inimical to constructive, meaningful human activity.

Bergman's two great trilogies of the 1960s contain few moments of humor or optimism. Nonetheless, such positive sentiments are the mainstay of Bergman's comedies, the most famous of which, *Smiles of a Summer Night,* is a warm-hearted bedroom farce that pokes fun at pretension and self-seriousness and extols the joys of romantic love. Furthermore, in his last work for the cinema, *Fanny and Alexander,* he expresses his love of the theater and clearly recalls his fondest childhood memories of unfettered imagination. While Bergman has never been included with such directors as Orson Welles and Jean-Luc Godard as a great innovator in narrative form, he is regarded as one of the finest directors of actors in the history of film and is recognized as a master in the use of the close-up. As Cook concludes: "Ingmar Bergman is an artist of great moral integrity and spiritual courage whose long and productive career continues to affirm the necessity of being human in the face of death, disorder, and despair."

PRINCIPAL WORKS

SCREENPLAYS

Hets   1944
   [*Torment,* 1944; also released as *Frenzy*]
Kris   1946
   [*Crisis,* 1946]
Kvinna utan ansikte   1947
   [*Woman without a Face,* 1947]
Fängelse   1949
   [*Prison,* 1949; also released as *The Devil's Wanton*]
Sommarlek   1950
   [*Summer Interlude,* 1950; also released as *Illicit Interlude*]
Kvinnors vantan   1952
   [*Secrets of Women,* 1952; also released as *Waiting Women*]
Sommaren med Monika   1952
   [*Summer with Monika,* 1952; also released as *Monika*]
Gycklarnas afton   1953
   [*The Naked Night,* 1953; also released as *Sawdust and Tinsel*]
Kvinnodröm   1955
   [*Dreams,* 1955; also released as *Journey into Autumn*]
Sommarnattens leende   1955

[*Smiles of a Summer Night*, 1955]
Sista paret ut 1956
  [*Last Couple Out*, 1956]
Det sjunde inseglet 1957
  [*The Seventh Seal*, 1957]
Smultronstället 1957
  [*Wild Strawberries*, 1957]
Ansiktet 1958
  [*The Magician*, 1958; also released as *The Face*]
Såsom i en spegel 1961
  [*Through a Glass Darkly*, 1961]
Nattvardsgästerna 1962
  [*Winter Light*, 1962; also released as *The Communicants*]
Tystnaden 1963
  [*The Silence*, 1963]
För att ente tala om alla dessa kvinnor 1964
  [*Now About These Women*; with Erland Josephson under the joint pseudonym Buntel Eriksson, 1968]
Persona 1966
Vargtimmen 1968
  [*Hour of the Wolf*, 1968]
Skammen 1968
  [*Shame*, 1968]
Riten 1969
  [*The Ritual*, 1969; also released as *The Rite*]
En Passion 1969
  [*The Passion of Anna*, 1969; also released as *A Passion*]
Beröringen 1970
  [*The Touch*, 1970]
Viskningar och rop 1972
  [*Cries and Whispers*, 1972]
Scener ur ett äktenskap 1974
  [*Scenes from a Marriage*, 1974]
Trollflöjten 1975
  [*The Magic Flute*, 1975]
Ansikte mot ansikte 1976
  [*Face to Face*, 1976]
Ormen's ägg 1977
  [*The Serpent's Egg*, 1977]
Höstsonaten 1978
  [*Autumn Sonata*, 1978]
Fanny och Alexander 1981
  [*Fanny and Alexander*, 1981]

OTHER

Wood Painting: A Morality Play (play) 1972
Bergman on Bergman (interviews) 1973
Four Stories by Ingmar Bergman (short stories) 1977
Lanterna Magica (autobiography) 1988
  [*The Magic Lantern*, 1988]

*This work was directed but not written by Bergman.

CRITICISM

Andrew Sarris

And when he had opened the seventh seal, there was silence in heaven about the space of half an hour.

"Revelation"

A free mind, like a creative imagination, rejoices at the harmonies it can find or make between man and nature; and where it finds none, it solves the conflict so far as it may and then notes and endures it with a shudder.

George Santayana, "Art and Happiness"

Although Ingmar Bergman's ***The Seventh Seal*** is set in medieval Sweden, nothing could be more modern than its author's conception of death as the crucial reality of man's existence. Appearing at a time when the anguished self-consciousness of Kierkegaard and Nietzsche has come back into favor as a statement of the human condition, ***The Seventh Seal*** is perhaps the first genuinely existential film. The plight of the individual in an indifferent universe would have seemed a fatuous subject for an artist a generation ago when human objectives barely extended to the next bread line, and when, it now seems ages ago, Edmund Wilson could reasonably denounce Thornton Wilder's metaphysical concerns in *The Bridge of San Luis Rey* as socially irresponsible. Liberal reform, Marxist determinism and the Social Gospel of Christianity were variously hailed as the formulas of a blissful world, but something went wrong with these collective panaceas partly because thinking men discovered that endless problem-solving reduced life to its one insoluble problem, death, and partly because population explosions, the hydrogen bomb and the Cold War scuttled the idea of Progress as a cause for rejoicing. Quite obviously, the time has come to talk of other things beside the glories of social reconstruction.

Ingmar Bergman, the son of a clergyman, is aware of the decline of religious faith in the modern world, but unlike Dreyer, he refuses to reconstruct mystic consolations from the dead past. If modern man must live without the faith which makes death meaningful, he can at least endure life with the aid of certain necessary illusions. This is what Bergman seems to be saying in ***The Seventh Seal***, a remarkably intricate film with many layers of meaning.

The Biblical context of ***The Seventh Seal*** is never fully retold on the screen, but enough excerpts are provided to keynote the theme of the Last Judgment. A hawk suspended in flight opens the film with a striking image of foreboding against a rising chorale of exultant faith. After ten years on a Crusade to the Holy Land, a knight and his squire return disillusioned to Sweden. Riding north to the knight's castle further and further away from Christianity's birthplace where God has died in their hearts, the knight and the squire are cast allegorically into the void of modern disbelief.

They first appear on a lonely beach, the knight seated by his chessboard, the squire flung awkwardly in a lackey's sleep. The two horses prance against the rushing waves as sun, sky and sea converge on the distant horizon. In the midst of a dazzling progression of sun-setting dissolves, the black-hooded figure of Death confronts the blond knight. Bergman's editing is ambiguous here for one cannot be sure that Death has actually materialized out of space. Nor is there any camera trickery involved in Death's subsequent manifestations. Death is presumably too real for magic lantern effects.

The knight challenges Death to a game of chess, the knight's life to be staked on the outcome. As the game begins with Death taking the black pieces, Bergman composes the first of his many tableaux inspired by medieval church murals. Death and the knight resume their match at fixed dramatic intervals later in the film. Bergman's fable is shaped by this chess game, not so much in the symbolism of the moves, most notably Death takes knight, but in the expanding meanings and ambiguities of the two players. While seeking God in the world of men, the knight relentlessly pursues the enigma of his antagonist.

As the knight and the squire continue their homeward journey, towering overhead shots of the two riders alternate with pulsating images of the sun. This cosmic technique would be pretentious for a lesser theme, but here in the beginning, Bergman is suggesting the dimensions of the universe in which his drama will unfold. Once the philosophical size of the film is established, Bergman's camera probes more intimately into his characters.

The fact that the squire does not share the knight's first encounter with Death is consistent with Bergman's conception of the knight's solitude in his quest for God. Since the squire is a confirmed atheist, the knight cannot seek consolation in that quarter. Indeed, the squire's bawdy songs and low comedy grimaces stamp him as the knight's Sancho Panza until a startling incident transforms him into a co-protagonist. Dismounting to ask a hooded stranger the way to the next town, the squire lifts the hood and beholds the death skull of a plague victim. The squire's reaction is that of a forceful intelligence, and he displays an unexpected flair for irony when he tells the unsuspecting knight that the stranger said nothing but was quite eloquent. Bergman achieves his shock effect here with the aid of a dog frisking about its dead master before the squire lifts the man's hood. This is more than a trick, however, and Bergman later develops the flickering idea involved here.

Bergman adds to his chess pieces as the knight and the squire ride past a carnival wagon in which an actor, a juggler, the juggler's wife and their infant son are asleep. Emerging from the wagon into a sunlit world less intensely illuminated than the world of the knight and the squire, the juggler is awed by a vision of the Virgin Mary walking the Christ Child. He calls his wife to describe this latest miracle of his imaginative existence, and as always, she is kind but skeptical. (Bergman has a priceless talent for establishing states of being in quick scenes.) The juggler and his wife are suggestively named Jof and Mia at slight variance from an explicit identification with Christ's parents. They are never quite that, but when Joseph observes wistfully that his son, Michael, will perform the one impossi-

ble juggling trick, the screen vibrates with Bergman's first intimations of immortality.

Bergman returns to his central theme as the actor steps out of the wagon to announce that he will play Death in the religious pageant at Elsinore. Donning a death mask, he asks (vanity of vanities!) if the women will still admire him in that disguise. As the pompous director of the troupe, he orders Joseph to portray the Soul of Man, a part Joseph dislikes for theatrical reasons. When the actor returns to the wagon, hanging the death skull on a pole outside, the camera lingers on this symbol long enough for the sound track to record the pleasant laughter of Jof and Mia before cutting back to the couple whose merriment operates both as a conscious reaction to the departing actor and as the director's expression of their irreverent attitude towards death. In all this symbolic by-play, Jof and Mia convey a wondrous innocence, and the scene ends on a note of emotional recollection as Mia's avowal of her love for her husband is underscored by the same musical motif which accompanied Jof's vision of the Madonna.

Bergman shifts from the sunlit innocence of the carnival wagon to the ominous atmosphere of a medieval church. While the knight pursues his quest for God at the altar of Christ, the squire exchanges blasphemies with a morbidly cynical church painter whose fearsome murals of the Dance of Death, the Black Plague and religious flagellations are the visual inspiration of *The Seventh Seal.* This circular recognition of a predecessor typifies Bergman's concern with the role of art in transcending the existential limits of human life.

Unable to find solace at the altar, the knight advances towards a hooded figure in the confessional chamber. The knight's unrecognized confessor is Death, and in an electrifying passage of self-revelation, the knight confesses all the agony of a mortal man seeking God while unwilling to embrace a religion of fear. Death, the confessor, offers no consolation, no guarantees, no answers, and in his tactical role, lures the knight into revealing his chess strategy.

The knight's outrage when he discovers the deception may well be shared by the audience. Why should Death cheat on certainties? It is possible that Bergman is intensifying the horror of life by suggesting ultimate nothingness with intermediate stages of accident and caprice. Since Death's timing follows no logical pattern, he might as well indulge in masquerades and linger over interesting chess games. Bergman suggests also that Death is everywhere—the church, the confessional chamber, perhaps even on the Cross.

The knight achieves heroic stature in his reaction to Death's hoax. Extending his hands before him to feel the blood pulsing in his veins, noting the sun still at its zenith, the suddenly exultant knight proclaims to his hitherto uncertain self the one certainty of an appointment to play chess with Death. Almost any other director would have sustained this great cinematic moment with either an immense closeup or a receding tracking shot to the ceiling of the church looking down upon mortal man in his fullest affirmation. Instead, Bergman truncates his effect with a quick cut to the squire entertaining the church painter with a Rabelaisian account of the Crusade. This abrupt transition from sublimity to ridicule is characteristic of Bergman's balanced treatment of the high-low dualism of human life.

From this point on, the fear-ridden world impinges upon the knight and the squire. The Black Plague is now seen sweeping across Sweden on a trail of hysteria, witch-burnings and religious flagellations. The knight asks a young woman condemned for witchcraft to lead him to the Devil, who might confirm the existence of God. The knight is answered only by a piteous wail which evokes the callous inhumanity of the period. The squire rescues a silent girl from a renegade priest who has degenerated into a robber of the dead. Ironically, this same priest, the closest human equivalent of evil in *The Seventh Seal,* once shamed the knight into embarking on the Crusade.

The various threads of the plot are woven together into the fabric of a town which represents for Bergman many of the evils of society. Art reappears in a musical pantomime of cuckoldry presented by Jof, Mia and the preening actor. The medieval approximation which Bergman attempts in this performance is carried over into the actor's flamboyant affair with a flirtatious blacksmith's wife. With dainty steps and cock-robin flourishes, the seduction in the nearby forest derives its tempo from a bawdy nonsense song rendered in the town by Jof and Mia, their faces gaily painted, their manner joyously abandoned. Their performance is meaningfully interrupted by the wailing of flagellants bearing Christ on the Cross. Bergman cuts with brilliant deliberation back and forth between the painful detail of the incense-shrouded procession and tracking shots of the soldiers and townspeople kneeling reverently in turn as the Cross goes past. The same soldiers who threw fruit at the actors (art) now kneel to their Saviour (fear).

The brutalization of a fear-crazed society reaches its climax in an inn where the patrons suspend their discourses on the End of the World to laugh sadistically at Jof's grotesque dance on a table while the renegade priest brandishes a torch at the juggler's feet. (The ordeal of a performer deprived of his mask and the sanctuary of his stage is more fully explored in Bergman's *The Naked Night.*) Joseph escapes only because of the intervention of the squire, who slashes the priest's face. In a film drenched with death, this is the only instance in which blood is drawn.

Withdrawing from the discord of the town, the knight is moved by the innocent contentment of Jof and Mia to offer them his protection and the sanctuary of his castle. The knight, the squire and the silent girl share with the juggler's family an interlude of resignation. The knight consecrates this moment in his memory with sacramental bowls of milk and wild strawberries, Bergman's personal symbols of the bread and wine of human redemption. The final movement of *The Seventh Seal* is then performed in a forest of unearthly calm and tempest, and a castle of last judgement.

The knight's caravan takes on the spiritual contours of an Ark in a drowning world. Having assumed responsibility for Jof's family, the knight is now engaged in a selfless cause. The squire's instinctive humanism has gained him the loyalty of the silent girl he has rescued and the friendship of the cuckolded blacksmith he has pitied. Yet, the growing intimacy of the characters is itself an ominous portent of Death.

The rising tension is checked momentarily by an encounter with the errant blacksmith's wife and the actor. Here Bergman provides the last bawdy counterpoint to his major theme as the blacksmith is reconciled to his wife while the actor feigns suicide with a stage dagger. This apparently gratuitous scene is a fitting prelude to Death's manifestation in the forest. When the actor climbs a tree to be safe from the wood animals during the night only to see Death saw down this medieval tree of life, the dark comedy of the incident confirms Bergman's sense of structure. The buffoonery of actor-blacksmith-wife is the film's last semblance of life unconcerned with death, and it is required for Bergman's graded shocks. However, one is suspended between horror and humor as the tree comes down with the actor screaming soundlessly and a squirrel hopping on to the stump chirping loudly. This image of animal life in the presence of human death expands the notion of individual mortality which Bergman touched upon in his earlier conjunction of the dog and the plague victim.

The caravan next encounters the witch, who is to be burned in the forest. Still searching for God, the knight asks her once more for the whereabouts of the Devil. The girl raves that the Devil is in her eyes, but the knight perceives only the reflection of her terror. When he asks an attending monk why the girl's hands have been broken, the monk who turns his face is Death, now cynically inquiring when the knight will stop asking questions. In this stunning moment of recognition, the knight's destiny is revealed. He must continue his quest despite its futility.

Although the knight has given the witch a drug to ease her pain, her last moments on the stake are filled with wild despair as she realizes that the Devil is not going to claim her from the emptiness which lies beyond the flames. The squire confronts the knight for the first time with evidence (?) of the void, but the knight refuses to abandon hope. One would lose all sympathy for Bergman's characters if they treated the witch's ordeal as merely a test of God's existence. Fortunately, Bergman never loses his human perspective on death even when the renegade priest is stricken by the Plague. The silent girl he once menaced rushes towards him until the squire restrains her, virtually pleading that any help would be futile. Dying never becomes a casual process for Bergman. The actor, the witch, the renegade priest all achieve a form of moral purgation in the inescapable self-pity they arouse in their audiences, both real and fictitious.

When Death confronts the knight for the final moves on the chessboard, the once stark tonal contrasts between the two antagonists have merged into relativistic grayness. Gone is the sun and the sea and the sky. Death has enveloped the forest and no longer makes striking entrances with his black cloak. Jof "sees" Death at the chessboard and takes flight with Mia and Michael. Fearing Death's intervention, the knight knocks over the pieces to allow Jof and his family to escape. Inscrutable to the end, Death does not indicate whether he has been taken in by this diversion, or whether he is tolerant or indifferent, or whether, after all, he *is* actually controlled by a Higher Power. Once Death has achieved checkmate and has claimed the knight and his friends at the next meeting, he still denies he possesses any secrets of the after-life, and in a dissolving close-up, his face is slowly and memorably transformed into a hollow mask.

While Jof and Mia are fleeing Death's storm in the forest, the knight leads his remaining companions into his castle where the knight's wife waits alone, a medieval Penelope who seems as weary of life as does her tortured husband. Here Bergman resists the beguiling temptation to sentimentalize the knight's attitude towards death. Having performed a noble service for Jof and Mia and having retained his wife's love for the ten years sacrificed in a futile search for God, the knight might be allowed to meet Death with the lofty grandeur with which most doomed film heroes crash into oblivion. Instead, when Death appears at the long banquet table to claim the knight and his guests, the knight prays hopelessly and, at last, unconditionally, to a God who must exist if life is not to end in senseless terror. The squire remains true to his own colors as he scoffs at the knight's quest for God. Accepting Death under protest, the squire acclaims his life without God, but significantly the last words are spoken by the silent girl: "It is done."

This elliptical declaration of awareness, perhaps miraculously extracted from the text of Revelation, is less meaningful than the glowing expression in her eyes as she awaits the end of her earthly servitude. The silent girl, more than any of the other characters, has been defeated by life, and in her defeat, has embraced the prospect of death. When we first see her, she is about to be raped and murdered. She passively accepts her role as the squire's housekeeper, and is always seen either bearing some burden or accepting the squire's protection. One almost suspects Bergman of a class statement in his conception of this memorable, yet elusive, character.

Yet, all of Death's victims in the forest and the castle have failed in some way. The actor is impaled on his vanity; the witch deluded into a pointless martyrdom by the ignorance of society; the renegade priest stripped of the last vestiges of self-induced consolation; the knight tortured by endless doubt; the squire limited to the easy wisdom and cynicism of the world; the blacksmith and his wife enmeshed in trivialities; the knight's wife deprived of the passion which might once have resisted Death. Strangely, there is little sense of regret. None of Death's victims ever suggest that they would have lived their lives differently if they had another chance. The knight is not even sorry that he embarked on the Crusade. One hesitates to suggest predestination in such an agnostic context, but it is difficult to recall significant opportunities for moral choice in any of Bergman's films released thus far in America.

When Jof and Mia emerge once more into the sunlight, the Black Cloud of Death is safely past. (Some critics have translated this cloud into the H-bomb, but the analogy is both labored and unnecessary. More substantial social parallels can be derived from the scenes of fear and doubt; the squire's description of his outlook as "modern" is deli-

ciously ironic.) Against the distant sky, Jof sees the Dance of Death, Bergman's majestic summation of medieval imagery. As Death leads his six victims, hand to hand, in the fierce merriment of their last revels, *The Seventh Seal* soars to the heights of imaginative cinema.

It is not until Jof describes the Dance of Death that we realize that his vision is inspired by a creative imagination rather than a Divine Revelation. The people he identifies in the Dance of Death—Death, the knight, the squire, the actor, the blacksmith and his wife, and the renegade priest—are not entirely the same people Death confronts in the castle. Jof has never seen the knight's wife, and her absence from his vision is quite logical. The omission of the silent girl is more puzzling. At least two interesting theories suggest themselves. The silent girl's final expression of acceptance slowly dissolves into the watchful expression of Mia. The two women look very much alike, and whatever this means—Jof developing a mental block in imagining death for someone resembling Mia, Jof unconsciously admiring the silent girl, Jof even absent-mindedly overlooking the existence of this girl—a clear link has been established between these two archetypes of woman.

The second theory is almost frighteningly intellectual. Since Jof calls off the names of the Dancers, it is possible that the unnamed silent girl cannot operate in Jof's artistic imagination. Except for the witch, all the other recurring characters are assigned proper names, but the silent girl, like the witch, remains an abstract being beyond Jof's ability to recall in his creations. This theory raises the question of Bergman's immersion in the technical philosophies of logical and linguistic analysis, a question which can be answered ultimately only by Bergman himself. Yet, it is quite clear from his interviews and his past films that he has been influenced by the irrational ideas of illusion and existence expressed in the works of Camus, Sartre, Anouilh, Strindberg and Pirandello.

If Jof and Mia represent the continuity of man, they do so because of certain transcendent illusions—love, art, contentment and the future of their child. These futile distractions from imminent death make life endurable if not justifiable. Yet, the knight and the squire are also aspects of man, the knight as the questing mystic, the squire as the earthbound philosopher. It is possible to identify Bergman in some measure with all three characters since *The Seventh Seal* is a unique amalgam of beauty, mysticism and rational logic. What is most remarkable about Bergman's achievement is that he projects the most pessimistic view of human existence with an extraordinary vitality. Conceding that life is hell and death is nothingness, he still imparts to the screen a sense of joy in the very futility of man's illusions.

For all its intellectual complexity, *The Seventh Seal* is remarkably entertaining. In the high level of acting we have come to expect in Bergman films, Gunnar Bjornstrand as the squire, and Bengt Ekerot as Death, provide truly remarkable performances. Bjornstrand, previously seen here in *The Naked Night* and *Smiles of a Summer Night,* displays classic range in the sublety and force of his widely dissimilar characterizations. Bengt Ekerot's playing of

Death is so uncanny that it is difficult to imagine this unfamiliar actor in any other role. Max von Sydow has the most difficult part as the mystical knight who must communicate from the depths of his soul, but in his dramatic scenes, he fully captures the tortured nobility of his character. Nils Poppe, Sweden's leading comedian, is very moving as Jof through the counterpoint of his comic personality and his cosmic problems. Bibi Andersson as Mia heads a gallery of unaffectedly beautiful women which includes anonymous faces in Bergman's crowd scenes.

Bergman's camera technique is fully equal to his theme. Except for a glaring process shot in the opening scene, his medieval images are clear and solid in the best tradition of realistic cinematography. Bergman is at his best in intimate scenes where his unobtrusively moving camera builds up tensions before his editing exploits them. One is always aware of the meaningful texture of faces as they react to the uncertainties they confront. Bergman indulges in the sun dissolves endemic to Swedish cinema, and the reverse cloak opening of a frame which Hitchcock invented, but which Bergman gives a special flourish in many of his films. In this instance, Death's black cloak must have been irresistible.

Bergman's overall editing maintains a steady flow of images to create visual progressions for each successive plot development. The plastic symbol of the death skull reappears in each shot at a different expressive angle, and Death himself never repeats the choreography of his comings and goings. Bergman's economy of expression actually makes it difficult to absorb all the meanings in each scene. Instead of fully developing his ideas in long, obligatory confrontations of characters, Bergman distributes fragments of what he is saying into every incident. Yet, a great deal that is implied is left unsaid, and it is possible that *The Seventh Seal* will be a source of controversy for years to come, and that like all classics of the mind, its interpretations will vary with the minds and times of its critics. (pp. 51-61)

> *Andrew Sarris, "The Seventh Seal," in* Film Culture, *No. 19, 1959, pp. 51-61.*

Hollis Alpert

Published screenplays have seldom caused any particular excitement in literary circles. For one thing, they are scarcely very readable, interlarded as they are with *CUT TO*s, *EXT*s, *FADE IN*s, and *CLOSE SHOT*s; and even when these directions are left out of the published versions, screenplays are difficult going (although an exception might be made in the screenplays of Joseph L. Mankiewicz, mainly because of his exceptional ability with dialogue).

Later this year, however, we are undoubtedly going to be in for a change; Simon & Schuster are bringing out a collection of four of Ingmar Bergman's screenplays in translation. Through the kindly offices of Elizabeth Sutherland, the S&S editor who has seen the book through from start to finish, I have been given an advance look at the proofs, and have found myself caught up in the reading of the scripts of *Smiles of a Summer Night, The Seventh Seal,*

Wild Strawberries, and *The Magician,* which will appear in a volume titled *Four Screenplays of Ingmar Bergman.*

Bergman is a phenomenon that has hardly gone unnoticed in the last year or two. It seems to be established that he is the pre-eminent film-maker in the world today, but it is as director rather than writer that he has come to be honored. Indeed, Miss Sutherland informs me that Bergman was reluctant to have his screenplays published. In his introduction he writes,

> I have never had any ambition to be an author. I do not want to write novels, short stories, essays, biographies, or even plays for the theatre. I only want to make films—films about conditions, tensions, pictures, rhythms, and characters which are in one way or another important to me. The motion picture, with its complicated process of birth, is my method of saying what I want to my fellow men. I am a film-maker, not an author.

But whether or not Bergman is, technically speaking, an author, he is certainly a writer and a creative personality of a very high order. Divorced from the screen images, the stories he tells hold one through their narrative power alone, and they are written in a manner that is a combination of narrative fiction and the printed play. There are no technical directions whatsoever. Bergman does not break up his screenplays into the Chinese puzzle of cuts and dissolves and cross-cuts that are the so dearly beloved of the scholarly film specialists. Montages there are in his films, clever, startling uses of all the technical tricks of the cinema; but there is not a sign of these in what he has written. Miss Sutherland, fascinated by what appeared to be a revolutionary kind of screen-writing, made a check to see whether Bergman used a shooting script—that is, a further development of the original screenplay. What she discovered was that these screenplays are exactly what Bergman uses. He has them mimeographed for cast and technicians, and uses one of the mimeographed copies to make notes on as he proceeds. It would seem, then, that for Bergman the technical means of movie-making serve the ideas, rather than the other way around.

One might even go so far as to assume that Bergman takes the technical language of film for granted. Having been developed, it now exists to be used as one forceful method—if not the most forceful—of telling stories. If his practice should spread, he may very well put a lot of film theorists out of jobs, or at least prevent them from indulging in the jargon of their trade—sometimes known as montagemanship.

The reader of Bergman's screenplays will therefore be lucky. He will be able to notice how well Bergman uses words (the translations by Lars Malmstrom and David Kushner beautifully bridge the language difference) and how immaculate is his sense of form. *Smiles of a Summer Night* emerges as an elegant comedy in an area of its own somewhere between an English comedy of manners and a French farce. Fredrik, the middle-aged lawyer, is saddened by the lack of sexual interest in his teen-age wife, and at the same time attracted by the mature charms of an actress who was once his mistress. The characters do

Death (Bengt Ekerot) on his ceaseless round.

not so much play a game of romantic intrigue as they work out a pattern of romantic determinism. The conception would be equally at home in film, on stage, or in a short novel. The detail, on the other hand, is all visual and cinematic.

The detail of *Wild Strawberries* would seem less congenial to film, were it not for the fact that it is Bergman's best motion picture to date. The form of the screenplay is that of a first-person narrative by a doctor of seventy-six, who chronicles what turns out to be the most meaningful day of his life. It is a day of dream and revery, of the present opening doors into the past, of honors for achievement turning ironically into a self-indictment. Here is a sample of Bergman's writing:

> We drove for a while in silence. The sun stood high in the sky and the road was brilliantly white. Suddenly I had an impulse. I slowed down and swung the car into a small side road on the left, leading down to the sea. It was a twisting, forest road, bordered by piles of newly cut timber which smelled strongly in the heat of the sun. . . .

It may be noticed that Bergman has even included an ol-

factory detail. What he has not done is to break the scene down to a series of cuts, although they are there implicitly. Anyone who has spent a year in film production would know exactly what to do, so far as camera set-ups and angles are concerned. It is in Bergman's mind that the important work is done. "The script," he writes, "is a very imperfect *technical* basis for a film." The shades and tones of his vision are what he is after, and these, he has realized, cannot be put down on paper.

His vision of the good knight in *The Seventh Seal* (that most astoundingly original of movies), seeking the meaning of his life as it is about to end, might have been taken from a medieval tapestry. "The night had brought little relief from the heat, and at dawn a hot gust of wind blows across the colorless sea." So the story begins. We meet the hooded figure of Death, a procession of religious flagellants, a young girl bound to a cross that will topple her into a pyre, a company of minstrels, a man of evil, a fool, and a dance of death outlined against "the dark, retreating sky where summer lightning glitters like silver needles over the horizon." This is a vision first written and then turned into film, labored over so that the clumsy apparatus that produces the motion picture will at least approximate what was glimpsed in the mind's eye.

It is this method of creating that has made Bergman unique, the recognition that film can be magic, if the imagination is given sway. In *The Magician* he has looked into the realm of illusion, and has noticed that the prestiditator, the mesmerist, the mindreader, mountebank though he may be, is also in touch with powerful forces of the imagination, of the mind, and the will. The artist, too, is mountebank, Bergman seems to be telling us, but he also seems to suggest that he oughtn't to be underrated, for his too is a method of getting at the truth. Bergman, then, is essentially the artist, as much writer as he is a film-maker. His movies begin in what he calls a mental state. An idea, he says, "is a brightly colored thread sticking out of the dark sack of the unconscious. If I begin to wind up this thread, and do it carefully, a complete film will emerge." What? No montage? No juxtaposition of shots? What on earth would the Screenwriters Guild say! (pp. 22-3)

Hollis Alpert, "Bergman as Writer," in Saturday Review, *Vol. XLIII, No. 35, August 27, 1960, pp. 22-3.*

Birgitta Steene

In each of the four films that form the nucleus of of this essay—*The Seventh Seal, Wild Strawberries, Through a Glass Darkly* and *Winter Light*—Ingmar Bergman depicts as his protagonist a man dwelling in a self-contained world, cut off from life around him. Such detachment is not completely self-willed; yet, it becomes a curse for the man and condemns him as a human being. To be cut off from mankind is to be cut off from love, i.e., from God; is, in fact, to become like Satan.

To dramatize what amounts to the emergence of the devil-image into the mind of the central character, Bergman resorts to actions that might be called variations on the myth of the Fall and of the Faust legend. Bergman's scripts are not strict allegories, of course, although we find in them allegorical elements, such as the figure of Death and the characters of Jof and Mia (Joseph and Mary) in *The Seventh Seal.*

Bergman's action always takes place in realistic settings. Yet we realize that these settings are stylized rather than socially and geographically concrete.

The films under consideration achieve a degree of stylization through historical distance—*The Seventh Seal,* dream interpolations—*Wild Strawberries,* isolation of locale—*Through a Glass Darkly,* and Christian ritual—*Winter Light.* Such stylization makes us aware of the archetypal substructure beneath the literal narrative level of the story.

The Seventh Seal (*Det Sjunde Inseglet*), Bergman's first major film (1954), is an attempt to present on the screen the mythic reality of the medieval church paintings he had observed as a child. Apropos this film, Bergman has offered the following reminiscence (Svensky Filmindustri, programblad, 1957):

> As a child I was sometimes allowed to accompany my father when he travelled about to preach in the small country churches. . . . While Fa-

ther preached away I devoted my interest to the church's mysterious world of low arches, thick walls, the smell of eternity, the strangest medieval paintings and carved figures on ceilings and walls. In a wood sat Death, playing chess with the Crusader. Clutching the branch of a tree was a naked man with staring eyes, while down below stood Death, sawing away to his heart's content. Across gentle hills Death led the final dance toward the dark lands.

> But in the other arch the Holy Virgin was walking in a rosegarden, supporting the Child's faltering steps, and her hands were those of a peasant woman.

As Bergman grew up and developed into an artist, this simple mythic formula provided him with the medium of inquiry into basic existential riddles and enabled him to divorce his creative thought from much of the rationale of the modern sophisticated metaphysician.

Further relevant to *The Seventh Seal* are Bergman's comments on the Devil, in his Introduction, *Four Screenplays by Ingmar Bergman,* Simon and Schuster, New York, 1960, page xiv:

> A child who is born and brought up in a vicarage, acquires an early familiarity with life and death behind the scenes. Father performed funerals, marriages, baptisms, gave advice and prepared sermons. The devil was an early acquaintance, and in the child's mind there was a need to personify him. This is where my magic lantern came in. It consisted of a small metal box with a carbide lamp—I can still remember the smell of the hot metal—and colored glass slides: Red Riding Hood and the Wolf, and all the others. And the Wolf was the Devil, without horns but with a tail and a gaping red mouth, strangely real yet incomprehensible, a picture of wickedness and temptation on the flowered wall of the nursery.

This reminiscence from Bergman's childhood is of general interest to us in terms of his later work in film and also because it may point towards specific scenes in his films; e.g., in *Through a Glass Darkly,* Karin's satanic spider-god appears to her hallucinatory mind against the playing shadows of light and dark on the papered wall of an attic, a room that, like the nursery Bergman mentions above, serves as a refuge from adult reality. But the passage above is especially interesting because it indicates how a mythic Christian conception of reality formed an early core of Bergman's personality. The fairy tales of his childhood were recast in his mind to conform to Christian symbolism; i.e., the world of the imagination became governed by the Devil as the archetype of all things evil and wicked.

The quotation above is illuminating also in that no transition is made between the memory of the father, performing his ministerial rites, and mention of the devil, who occupies the major part of the statement. As we shall see, the father-figure in Bergman's basically patriarchal world sometimes takes on diabolic features; at the same time, the paternal image often fuses with the divine. Hence, in the passage above, we may have either an unconscious identification of the father and the devil, or an implied structural dichotomy between God and Satan.

The Seventh Seal, set in medieval Sweden, tells of a Crusader's quest for God. Weary and disillusioned, Antonius Block has returned from the Holy Land. On the shore of Sweden, a country ravaged by bubonic plague (a historical metaphor, Bergman states, for a world threatened by atomic destruction), the protagonist meets Death, come to claim him. The Crusader delays Death by challenging him to a game of chess: so long as the game goes on, the Crusader is free to continue his quest for knowledge of God.

The Crusader's mind is not what we associate with the conventional medieval man; he is closer to a modern sceptic whose burning need of faith cannot be fulfilled because he refuses to accept a god who does not give intellectual proof of his existence. Without such a proof, "to believe in god is to love someone in the dark who never answers," i.e., to believe hopelessly, meaninglessly.

Although God will not (or cannot) manifest himself to the Crusader on any rationalist grounds, He remains an ever-present force in the film. ***The Seventh Seal*** sets up a dichotomy, to remain basic in Bergman's production, between a god who is a silent monster and torturer of man, and a god who is a lover of life. Neither image of god is objectified, but both exist as fundamental attitudes in Bergman's characters.

Hence a man's experiencing of God will, in its wider psychological ramifications, be a reflection of his relationship with human beings. A rapport with God, i.e., an intuitive apprehension of God as love, will enable man to function in a meaningful social context; a lack of rapport with God will turn man into the cold monster that he accuses or conceives God to be. Such a man does not feel loved but merely haunted by God. The Crusader belongs to this group, and so do the religious fanatics whom he meets during his travel through Sweden. They are beings for whom God has become only a scourge. In a series of powerful images, Bergman projects on the screen people for whom religion means cruelty, persecution and self-torture. Although these images are related to medieval life and depict a time when Catholicism was still the religion in Scandinavia—we see monks lashing one another and struggling under the weight of huge crosses and driving on children who wear crowns of thorn—although these images have some Catholic reference, the total impression of the god worshipped is closer to the god of Bergman's childhood, to the same god over whom Ibsen and Strindberg fought a long and uneven battle: the god of pietism who is a hater of life. One of the monks, rising from his knees with glittering eyes, defines in a voice full of impotent scorn the essence of the revivalist god:

> God has sentenced you to punishment. We shall all perish in the black death. You, standing there like gaping cattle, you who sit there in your glutted complacency, do you know that this may be your last hour? Death stands right behind you. . . . You there, who stand staring like a goat, will your mouth be twisted into the last unfinished gasp before nightfall? And you, woman, who bloom with life and self-satisfaction, will

you pale and become extinguished before the morning dawns? You back there, with your swollen nose and stupid grin, do you have another year left to dirty the earth with your refuse? Do you know, you insensible fools, that you shall die today or tomorrow, or the next day, because all of you have been sentenced? Do you hear what I say? Do you hear the word? You have been sentenced, sentenced!

But God is not only the old Jehovah; he is also the God of Love, and the Crusader meets him for a brief moment in the young couple, Jof and Mia, the visionary man and the maternal woman fleeing the plague with their infant son who one day "will perform the impossible trick of making a ball stand still in the air," i.e., like Christ, will transcend nature.

The traditional function of the Crusader, as seen in medieval art, was not to colonize the Holy Land but to protect the Holy Family. Bergman's knight performs the same service: he leads Jof and Mia and their child through the forest, and when they meet Death, Antonius Block gives Jof and his family a chance to escape. In the game of chess that he plays with Death, Block knocks over the chessmen and distracts Death's attention from Jof and Mia. But, at the same time, the Crusader has given Death a chance to cheat and win. Hence, by losing the game, the knight saves Jof and Mia but gives his life for them. It is, as so often in Bergman, a situation of ironic blasphemy: Man redeems Christ. On the other hand, it is an act made possible only because the Crusader has caught a glimpse of love in his relationship with Jof and Mia. Perhaps the most crucial scene in the film—one that anticipates Bergman's next film, ***Wild Strawberries***—is a low-keyed scene played on a sunny hillside, an idyllic picture of the knight as he is being offered milk and wild strawberries by Mia. Milk and wild strawberries are private symbols in Bergman's world, the Eucharist in a communion between human beings.

It is upon this occasion that the knight vows: "I shall remember this moment. . . . I'll carry this memory between my hands as carefully as if it were a bowl filled to the brim with fresh milk." He turns his face and looks toward the sea and the colorless gray sky. "And it will be an adequate sign—it will be enough for me." In filming the sea and the sky at the opening of the film, Bergman emphasizes their infinite but lifeless aspects; they are part of the mystery the Crusader wants to penetrate, a primordial reality that can be reached only through death or spiritual rebirth.

But the Crusader does not keep his vow for long. The riddle of God continues to haunt him, and he is compelled to go on with his questioning. By now we realize that the search has become his *raison d'être*. It is, in a sense, his clubfoot: without it he could not walk at all; but with it his movements are mutilated and deformed. At one time it had brought about his fall from "paradise," his self-expulsion from a happy marriage. He tells Mia of this loss of innocence: "We [he and his wife] were newly married and we played together. We laughed a great deal. I wrote songs to her eyes, to her nose, to her beautiful little ears. We went hunting together and at night we danced. The house was full of life." But from this idyllic life the Crusader has broken away, and now his constant companion is not a loving woman but a cynical squire, a rationalist who, within the thematic context of the film, functions as a foil to the crusader's own abstractly questioning and ultimately nihilistic nature.

The Crusader's search for God is destined to be not only fruitless but also blasphemous, for as in the archetypal legend of the Fall, a desire for ultimate knowledge is treason against God. Bergman has fully grasped the paradoxical implications of the old myth: living man cannot seek full intellectual cognizance of God without disobeying God; the more he tries to understand the nature of God, the further he removes himself from God. Bergman illustrates this gradual alienation of man from God and paradise by depicting in the Crusader a human being at first engaged in a holy enterprise but at last willing to sell his soul to the devil—could he only find him! For the devil, Block argues with insane logic, must know of God because he exists only in his opposition to God.

In the most brutal scene of the film, staged as a kind of exorcism, the Crusader speaks to Tyan, a young girl about to burn as a witch:

> KNIGHT. They say that you have been in league with the Devil.
>
> TYAN. Why do you ask?
>
> KNIGHT. Not out of curiosity, but for very personal reasons. I too want to meet him.
>
> TYAN. Why?
>
> KNIGHT. I want to ask him about God. He, if anyone, must know.
>
> TYAN. You can see him any time.

But the devil as objectified reality remains as invisible and silent to the Crusader as does God. Block fails to perceive the message implied in the film, that transcendental truth dwells in man himself, not as rational proof but as potentialities for good and evil, of love and denial of love. The negative aspect of the Crusader's quest becomes evident in his reunion with his wife. It is a strangely cold and detached meeting. The wife, whom we see for the first time, is a woman of ascetic features. It is she who, at the end of the film, officiates at a last supper during which, significantly, every sacramental element of redemption and salvation is absent, and only a mood of impending doom prevails. As Death knocks at the castle door, the wife intones the words from the Book of Revelations.

Through his quest the Crusader has come to deny his wife and, by implication, life itself. In a way that seems unknowing, yet deliberate, the Crusader has become his own devil, responsible not only for his own but for his bride's loss of *joie-de-vivre*. But his actions are dictated by compulsion rather than temptation. Nowhere do we sense the modern temper of *The Seventh Seal* more strongly than in the realization that moral will has given way to psychological needs—which exclude a possibility of choice.

Modern psychology is another important part of Bergman's thinking. "Philosophically," he writes, in his Introduction, *Four Screenplays,* page xxl, "there is a book

which was a tremendous experience for me: Eiono Kaila's *Psychology of The Personality.* His thesis that man lives strictly according to his needs—negative and positive—was shattering to me, but terribly true. I built on this ground."

As a dramatic character, the Crusader is not perceived as a moral agent, and in this ambivalence Bergman establishes his affinity with the modern existential world in which we, according to Sartre, must live *as though* we had a free will. The insoluble dilemma dramatized by Bergman points also to one of Ibsen's central themes: the curse (i.e., moral judgment) that falls upon a man who *must* follow his calling.

One final question haunts us in *The Seventh Seal:* Can man achieve salvation, or, in psychological terms, peace of mind? Some of the tentative answers that Bergman gives are deeply ironic. People like the religious fanatics seek redemption by re-enacting the sufferings of Christ, behaviour which, in anyone but Christ, must be termed excessively proud and blasphemous. It is also the monks' god that leads them to burn Tyan as a witch and turns them into murderers. To Tyan, who finally dies without agony, "salvation" comes through her faith in the devil. Hence, in terms of salvation, God emerges as a satanic force, and the devil as the redeemer. Only in Mia and Jof does Bergman depict people who know how to live with a god who is *deus caritatis.* It is their voice, but without any direct reference to God, that is heard in Bergman's next film, ***Wild Strawberries (Smultronstallet,*** 1957).

In this work, the religious aspect of the Crusader's quest is reduced to a quibble between two students, one a prospective doctor (the conventional atheist in fiction) and the other a young boy preparing for the ministry. It is a debate that can have no end, and Bergman leaves it at a first fight between the two boys, which is interrupted while still unsettled (although each antagonist claims he has "won").

Although ***Wild Strawberries*** does not treat any problem of faith, it is conceived as a moral, with pilgrimage as a form of penance. The subject is happiness, and the emphasis is no longer on the essence of God. The central character, Isak Borg, explores the possibility of love and fellowship between human beings. Bergman's basic credo is that dramatized as Jof's and Mia's belief, that God is love and love is God. There is much of Bergman's work a modern Christian ethic from which God can be completely omitted, and ***Wild Strawberries*** is a good example of this.

Wild Strawberries is set in our time. The central character, Isak Borg, is a 76-year-old physician who, when the film begins, is about to receive an honorary doctor's degree, a tribute to his achievement as a scientist, a man of the mind. Isak personifies the death of the heart. Throughout his life, Isak has remained aloof from other people, a spectator, raising abstract questions and watching the love-making of others but never himself a lover. Like the Crusader, Isak can say: "I believe at times that to ask questions is the most important thing."

In his totally scientific preoccupation with life, Isak is Bergman's most clear-cut version of a cinematic Faust.

But Bergman lets us know that, although Isak's withdrawal from the world is a Faustian search for control over life, it is not caused by a desire for omnipotence but is, in effect, an escape from pain. Isak's isolation is the self-created, "secure" world of a man who has been unable to accept adulthood as a loss of the autonomous world of the child and, in erotic terms, as a loss of separateness. Young Isak lost his sweetheart, Sara, because he could not give of himself. But in his inability, there was as much fear as love of self.

As in *The Seventh Seal*, the psychological implications of the story do not exclude a moral evaluation of the protagonist. But in *Wild Strawberries*, Bergman is compelled to utilize a structural device that savors of the therapeutic consulting room: the mythic images that torture the dreams of spiritually distraught patients. Yet, this technique has an organic necessity. Because the conflict is resolved in the conscience of Isak, Bergman requires an idiom to communicate this experience. But of greater importance is the fact that Isak's destiny is not only that of an individual man but to a greater or lesser degree the destiny of all mankind. On the one hand, the dreams are applicable to Isak's personal problem. But on the other hand, their total impact is that of a moral archetype. The images that occur in Isak's dreams are understandable beyond the literal context of the story, and Bergman seems here to be dramatizing the pronouncements of Carl Jung, who claimed that each mythic image in our dreams "contains a piece of human psychology and human destiny, a relic of suffering and delight that has happened countless times in our ancestral story." (*Contributions to Analytical Psychology*.)

The film opens with one of Isak's dreams: on a deserted street Isak walks alone. The scenery is a fitting reflection of the desert landscape of his soul. Isak is a man who communicates with no one. He is also an old man feeling the approach of death, and so in his dream he sees a clock without hands, a symbol of timeless reality, of death. Next, he discovers a man in black who turns out to be a bag-of-blood man without a face. Then Isak catches sight of a hearse that screeches down the narrow cobblestone street and topples over like a baby carriage. A dead arm falls out of the coffin and tries to pull Isak down. This nightmare expresses Isak's fear of death and also his evaluation of himself: he is beginning to realize that, at 76, he is a man without identity, without a face.

One is reminded of a scene in Act I of Stig Dagerman's *The Condemned*. Petus, the dying lawyer, relates a frightening experience he has just undergone in a park, where he met an ominous old man pushing a wheelbarrow, from which dangled the limp arm of a dead man. Petrus felt compelled to pursue it.

As Isak continues his inward search, his initial fear of death subsides and his dreams become self-explorations, classical examination dreams that could be taken right out of Freud's *Traumdeutung*: Isak looks into the microscope of scientific knowledge but sees only himself; he diagnoses a person as dead but she is alive. Such dreams reveal his professional self-absorption and his indifference to others, who are "dead" to him.

In Bergman's works, travelling is often a release for the conflicts of the soul, and in *Wild Strawberries* Isak's search takes the outer form of a journey through Sweden. While the Crusader's quest for meaning took him on horseback through Sweden, Isak travels in a coffin-like black car.

Nathaniel Hawthorne, in his many stories with Faustian implications (e.g., "Ethan Brand," "The Minister's Black Veil," "Rappaccini's Daughter") often depicted the heart of his protagonist, the self-sufficient egotist, as a cave, a dungeon, a prison, and he made these descriptions function within his artistic framework as metaphors of the restricted but deathlike world in which a man of pure intellect dwells. In a similar way, Bergman uses Isak's box-like black car to suggest his withdrawal from the world. Every time Isak steps out of the car, he in a sense steps out into life.

Time—symbolized in one of Isak's dreams as the ticking of the heart—plays an essential part in the film. Most simply, time stands for life, just as the clock without hands stands for death. The whole film is built around a complicated time-table, and we are constantly reminded that time is short for Isak. Throughout his trip Isak keeps looking at his watch; decides he has time for lunch, time to visit his childhood home, time to see his old mother.

Isak's journey through Sweden, accompanied by his daughter-in-law, becomes a journey back in time—not into historical time but into personal time. Isak visits his childhood home, dreams of his sweetheart, Sara, who rejected him for his sensual brother. He stops to see his old mother, who sits at her table like an old frozen relic from the past, absorbed in her bitterness, cut off from a family so large it could stand for humanity itself. Finally, Isak has visions of his dead wife seeking elsewhere the love he was not able to give her. But, as this past unfolds, it becomes part of the present: Sara, the sweetheart, returns as a young hitchhiker; the tortuous relationship between Isak and his wife is reflected in a miserable married couple whose car collides with Isak's; and the coldness of the heart lives on in Isak's son who refuses to have children and demands that his pregnant wife have an abortion.

Isak's experience during his trip from Stockholm to southern Sweden, of which his dreams form an important part, dramatize the existentialist view that is the film's philosophical core: that life is not a matter of spectatorship or cold analysis. In learning that man cannot avoid the claims of life, Isak begins to accept life. His journey—unlike the Crusader's—becomes not so much a journey towards the land of death as an initiation into life, a form of rebirth.

That Bergman wants the redemptive aspect of the journey emphasized seems corroborated by the fact that he omitted from the film a scene in the original manuscript where the academic procession in Lund was to meet a funeral procession. Likewise cut was a conversation in the university hall between Isak and an old schoolmate, during which Isak refers to his friend as an "old corpse." (Information obtained from *The Personal Vision of Ingmar Bergman*, by Jorn Donner.)

Woman plays a key role in the transformation of Isak Borg, for woman is, as the heartbeat in one of Isak's dreams, the living measure of existence. Both Marianne, the daughter-in-law who travels with Isak, and Sara, the hitchhiker, work as catalysts. Psychologically, the film is a series of confrontations between Marianne and Isak. At first there is nothing but coldness and wondrous fright (on Marianne's part) between them. Later, they exchange a hesitant confidence: Isak tries vaguely to recount to Marianne his examination dream, and she tells him of her marriage to his son, Evald, whose need is "to be dead, absolutely, immovably dead." Although Marianne answers in the negative an offer from Isak to help, we no longer sense an awful distance between the two. Mutual confidence has created a certain rapport, and Isak has become involved in his surroundings. The film ends with a warm reconciliation between the old physician and his daughter-in-law. Isak's changing attitude towards Marianne is, then, a measure of his development from atrophy and egotism to love and sympathy.

Isak learns not only to be a human being but, more specifically, to be a parent confronted by children. He learns to care about his son and daughter-in-law, and he learns to love young Sara, who is a child to him. In accepting parenthood, Isak can at last look back on his youth without bitterness. In his final dream, filled with nostalgia rather than nightmarish pain, Isak returns to the strawberry patch of his childhood. But now he no longer watches in self-pity how Sara drops her basket full of fresh strawberries as she loses her innocence to Isak's brother. Instead, young Sara takes old Isak by the hand and brings him to a nearby lake where Isak sees his parents as they sit fishing in placid contentment, wearing the clothes from his childhood. They wave to him, and, in responding to their gesture, old Isak takes the last step out of a world in which human beings were reduced to distant objects. Through the love and peace he sees between his parents, he recognizes the pure compassion that lies in parenthood. He has retrieved his innocence but he has also become an adult.

The inability to accept adulthood, i.e., parenthood, as a "lesson in love," and a self-absorbed father's lack of communication with his children, form the major theme in *Through a Glass Darkly* (*Sa Som I En Spegel*—1961). The setting—a barren island in the Baltic—is a reflection of the emotional sterility of the focal character, David, a mediocre novelist and father of two children, Karin and Minus.

Many regard Karin as the central character in *Through a Glass Darkly,* but her position is similar to those of Oswald Alving in [Henrik Ibsen's] *Ghosts* and Laura Wingfield in *The Glass Menagerie.* Although dramatically intense, Karin's characterization shows little change and development. In contrast, vital insight takes place in David (as it does in Mrs. Alving and Tom Wingfield). The faulty recognition of the relative importance of these characters arises from a tendency in the artists involved—Bergman, Ibsen and Williams—to allow the central character to remain psychologically passive, an onlooker and spectator rather than an active participant.

As the film begins, we see David and Martin, Karin's husband, put out their nets while brother and sister go to fetch the milk. David has just returned from Switzerland where he has been working on his latest novel. Later that evening his homecoming is celebrated with a dinner. Gathering his *dramatis personae* for a meal is part of a ritual pattern in Bergman, a testing point in communication. In *Through a Glass Darkly,* David uses the occasion to present gifts, but they are the wrong kind of gifts, and he further widens the gap between himself and his family by announcing that he will soon leave them again, this time for Yugoslavia. We find here the same conflict between the happiness of family life and professional success that haunted Isak Borg in *Wild Strawberries.* David exists entirely for his own ambition, and he wants nothing to interfere with it. He tells Karin: "When mother became ill, I went away and left you with grandmother. I had my novel to think of. When mother died I had my first big breakthrough. I had arrived, and that meant more to me than her death."

Yet David's search for artistic perfection turns out to be as futile as the Crusader's search for God. Both, in a sense, try to become like God—the one all-creative, the other omniscient. Both are doomed to fail. But David's guilt is more obvious than Antonius Block's, for he not only neglects others; he uses them and in so doing he destroys the life of his child. Bergman hints that David's behavior is the fundamental reason for Karin's defeat in life. Karin feels closer to her father than to her husband. What destroys her last shred of mental equilibrium is her discovery of her father's diary, in which he has written: "Her illness is hopeless, but with occasional periods of lucidity. I have long surmised it, but the certainly nevertheless is almost insufferable. To my horror I discover my curiosity. The compulsion to register the progress, concisely to note her gradual dissolution. To utilize her."

The scientific detachment revealed in this passage puts David in the same category as Isak Borg: he is a spectator in life, a curious but uninvolved observer. But David is also conceived as a far more complex and ambiguous character than Isak, for he emerges also as a deputy for Bergman's two gods from *The Seventh Seal.* In a crucial scene in the attic, when Karin has one of her visions: she sees God as an enormous spider at a moment when her father enters the room. The spider image is reinforced by the spindly form of a helicopter—indeed, a *deus ex machina*—that descends at the same moment to fetch Karin away to an asylum. Considerably shaken by Karin's experience, David is at last able to reach Minus. He breaks his long silence with his son to tell him that in spite of all the horror, God exists as a power of love: "God is love and love is God." Minus, who has the closing lines of the film, reacts to this message, a starry-eyed look on his face, with the words: "Daddy spoke to me," which could read "God spoke to me." From the children's point of view, the father has become connected, if not identified, with their image of God. David has refused to be a parent to Karin, has refused to give her love and security. In her mind, she conceives an image of God that corresponds to that of her father: God becomes a spider feeding upon those that fall into his net, much the same as David in his diary fed upon Karin's illness. For Minus, on the other hand, God is not a silent monster but a sign of forgiveness (Minus is haunted by a feeling of guilt after an incestuous relationship with Karin), just as David is not a threat to him or a severe judge but a parent communicating a message of love.

Yet, God-as-Love remains only a message in *Through a Glass Darkly,* a mere supposition. Perhaps this is all God can be, Bergman seems to say, for those who are to remain in the world. For Karin, who departs for a life-in-death, God can show his face: "For now we see through a glass, darkly; but then face to face: now I know in part; but then I shall know even as also I am known." These words from Paul's first epistle to the Corinthians, which give the film its name, refer to the meeting with God that is the moment of death.

From an artistic point of view, the verbalized ending of *Through a Glass Darkly* is dissatisfying and mars a work that is otherwise unequalled in Bergman's production in terms of dramatic intensity. But this flaw in the film may be somewhat redeemed when evaluated with the next film in the Bergman canon, *Winter Light (Nattvardsgasterna*—1963). It could be said that the closing dialogue between father and son in *Through a Glass Darkly* forms the nucleus from which Bergman develops the central theme of *Winter Light:* although man preaches that "God is love and love is God," his life shows that he cannot live up to that gospel, and his actions tell only of the disintegration of a metaphysical reality that he desires to reach but experiences only as an abstraction.

The central character in *Winter Light* is a Lutheran minister, the widower Tomas Ericsson. Tomas is officiant at a communion in Mittsunda medieval church in Northern Sweden. The time of the year is early winter. Dusk has begun to fall over the plain, and "there is a strong, cold wind blowing raw, moist air from the marshlands to the east." The spectator experiences the same feeling of coldness, sterility and confinement as in the setting of *Through a Glass Darkly.*

Only half a dozen people are present at the communion, a ritual that, like the last supper in *The Seventh Seal,* seems to offer no release, no sense of rebirth, but only an anticipation of death and final judgment. Yet, to Tomas Ericsson, the communion group represents the outside world, to which he must relate himself and through which he will finally be evaluated as a human being. As in Bergman's previous films, we have in *Winter Light* a postulation of an outer and an inner authority. Custom, mores and conventions dictate the norms of the outward behavior of the individual: the Crusader goes on a pilgrimage to the Holy Land; Isak Borg journeys to a formal honorary ceremony in Lund; David brings homecoming gifts to his children and participates in the simple rituals of the day: fishing, eating, etc.; Tomas, finally, administers a sacramental rite. But this outward behavior is often reduced to a meaningless gesture, not in order to disclose any Ibsenite ghosts in society but to bring out in sharper relief the arid soul of the protagonist, his lack of rapport with a world outside of self. It helps carry the spectator into Bergman's other dramatic center: the internal world of man.

In *Winter Light* this internal world is an absolute spiritual vacuum. Yet, as in Bergman's earlier works, this film is not only a study in individual despair but also a study of its repercussions on the surroundings. Man may be an island to himself, but he is still responsible to life on the mainland. Critics who upbraid Bergman for his lack of social conscience apparently fail to see that in its broadest possible ramifications a Bergman conflict is a social conflict, a tension between life in isolation and life in communion with others. The effect upon his congregation of Tomas' paralysis-of-self is dramatized in the encounter after the service between the minister and a couple of his parishioners, the fisherman Persson and his pregnant wife. The husband is worried about the prospect of nuclear war and the destruction of mankind; he wants to have reassurance from Tomas. But all Tomas has to offer Persson is his own fear and insecurity. Their conversation turns into a confessional monologue by Tomas, in which he tries to console himself rather than his parishioners. He talks about his God whom he can only perceive as a destructive force. He calls him a spider god—a verbal repetition of Karin's vision in *Through a Glass Darkly.* Once more, God emerges as a satanic power cutting man off from humanity:

> I was like a little child when I was ordained. Then everything came all at once. I became by chance a seamen's chaplain in Lisbon. This was during the Spanish civil war, and we had a front row seat. I refused to see and understand. I refused to accept reality. I and my God lived in a world, a special world, where everything tallied. All around us the bloody real life was in the throes of agony. But I didn't see it. I turned my eyes to my God.

In *Through a Glass Darkly,* David functioned as a divine image for his children. As a minister, Tomas Ericsson is to serve as a father—God-as-Love substitute, a link between God and His children. But lacking faith in God-as-Love, Tomas is unable to save those who seek God's help. Instead of communicating God to his congregation, the minister can only let them partake of his own despair and doubt. Instead of receiving their problems into his heart, he can only pour out his venomous questioning, and in so doing he destroys not only himself but becomes responsible for the ensuing suicide of fisherman Persson.

In the films discussed here, Bergman presents us with four variations of one character who dwells in a hellish pit of despair. Passionate in their preoccupation with deeply personal, metaphysical problems but cold in their response to the outside world, these are men burning, like the devil archetype, in ice. They emerge also as twentieth-century versions of Faust. Isak Borg, the scientist, becomes—regardless of where the guilt lies—an egotist absorbed in his research. David, the novelist, is a failure as a human being because of his Keatsean "negative capability." Antonius Block, the Crusader, is engaged in a self-centered quest. And Tomas Ericsson, the man of the church, chained to himself in doubt, fear and despair, denies the world he is supposed to serve.

It is interesting to note that in his variations of this single dramatic type, Bergman relates him both to the original Faust figure as well as to the nineteenth-century transformation of the old scholar into a man of artistic genius, (e.g., Ibsen's Rubek) and into a man of the frock, (e.g., Ibsen's Brand, Hawthorne's minister with the black veil, and Selma Lagerlof's Gösta Berling).

In Goethe's as well as in Ibsen's version of Faust, salvation remains a potential hope wrought by a woman's love. Goethe's Gretchen, Agnes in Ibsen's "Brand," and Irene in "When We Dead Awaken" have their counterparts in our four Bergman films. We see the possibility of redemption through Mia in *The Seventh Seal,* and through Sara and Marianne in *Wild Strawberries.* In *Through a Glass Darkly,* Karin's sacrifice opens her father's eyes, however unconvincingly this new awareness is portrayed by Gunnar Björnstrand, as David. But it is a further indication of the pervasive gloom of *Winter Light* that the efforts made by the character embodying a redemptive potential are completely futile: Märta Lundblad, a myopic schoolteacher, presented as a Christ figure with eczema where stigmata occur, is in love with Tomas Ericcson. She comes to plead with him to use her ("take me and use me"), a remark that reinforces the legendary sacrificial role of the redeemer. Her name also has biblical "servant" connotations. Märta-Martha.

But Märta Lundblad fails. Tomas has no use for her, although at one point he seems on his way towards a rapport with her. During a trip in the car he begins to confide in her, as Isak confided in Marianne in *Wild Strawberries.* But as Tomas starts to talk, a train goes by and the noise drowns his voice. The train may seem a superficial and accidental obstacle in his attempt to communicate, but it is a symbolic commentary on Tomas' failure to transmit his inner voice to a world that could perhaps offer him love.

The reason for Märta's failure to save Tomas seems to lie in her insistence on being a companion in love, a sexual mate. What Tomas is seeking—like all Bergman characters—is parental, not erotic, love. Tomas has known his parents only as an authority that has pushed him into his present situation. For this reason, Bergman implies, it is impossible for Tomas to experience God-as-Love; he is unable to disseminate such an image of God because he himself has never experienced love.

We see again how the family microcosm in Bergman's world reflects on and encompasses man's whole existence, including man's experience of a transcendental experience reality. *Winter Light* is constructed as a psychological chain-reaction in the failure of parenthood: Tomas' parents fail him = God fails Tomas = Tomas fails his congregation (fisherman Persson) = fisherman Persson fails his wife and unborn child.

Tomas is torn between a desire to revolt against a hateful God-parent and a need to seek security and proof of love. But the proof must come from the parent. Märta wants to be his wife, not his mother. Without knowing it, she thereby destroys her only chance of getting close to Tomas, of rescuing him from self-destruction. Like the Crusader's wife, Märta will never face a life with the man she loves. Fittingly, the film ends as she and Tomas stand along in the empty church. The bells have stopped ringing, calling the worshippers to the evening service, but no one has shown up. Tomas decides to defy the empty church: he gets up to praise a God he cannot find.

Some critics have found this ending "hopeful," but it is difficult to see the scene as anything but an act of ultimate despair. Like the Crusader, Tomas has drawn the woman who loves him into a death-like world cut off from God and people alike. All he has to offer is a cry that receives no answer. In so doing, he perpetuates his own isolation. For Tomas, God can only be a curse. The structure of the film is that of a vicious circle: a selfish and personal need, a withdrawal into self, and, hence, a curse that shuts him off from all life.

It is worthy of note that the development from the Crusader's confrontation with Tyan in *The Seventh Seal* to Tomas' insistence upon the worship of a silent satanic god is an extended dramatization of a brief scene in an early Bergman film, *The Devil's Wanton,* not discussed here. The scene illustrates the thematic progression of Bergman's work as a kind of spiral. In *The Devil's Wanton,* a preacher convinces a young girl that God exists: because the Devil exists, God also must exist. But, by the end of the film, the preacher confesses: "I am convinced that God is dead and that the Devil is the absolute ruler of the world. I receive no answers to my prayers, and I am mute inside. But you see, that is just why I must believe." (pp. 69-78)

Birgitta Steene, "The Isolated Hero of Ingmar Bergman," in Film Comment, *Vol. 3, No. 2, Spring, 1965, pp. 68-78.*

Robin Wood

The first mental images that the name Ingmar Bergman conjures up are probably of the bizarre, the outlandish, the extreme, the abnormal, the picturesque: the apparitions of Death, the chess game, the flagellants, the witch-burning in *The Seventh Seal;* the dream sequences of *Wild Strawberries;* the horribly detailed rape and revenge of *The Virgin Spring;* Harriet Andersson's vision of God as spider in *Through a Glass Darkly;* masturbation, sodomy and dwarfs in *The Silence.* Certainly Bergman has given us some of the most startling images in the history of the cinema. From this has arisen a composite image of the director: morbid, sensational, neurotically obsessed with cruelty, horror and abnormality, but with a certain intensity and power and a gift for striking compositions. Except for those who think that cinema is a matter of picturesque images, or those who think the ability to create a coherent personal world is sufficient to make anyone a great artist, this is a terribly limiting description; it is also a travesty.

The presence of the extreme, the bizarre, the horrific in an artist's work does not necessarily mean that he is not centrally concerned with universal human experience: it would be easy to find as many 'sensational' situations and images (both dramatic and verbal) in Shakespeare's plays as in Bergman's films; there are scenes in *King Lear* that are at least as outlandish and, by rational standards, as overburdened as anything in Bergman. What matter are the quality and nature of the experience we feel has provoked the images.

One can easily demonstrate that most of Bergman's films deal with themes or concerns absolutely central to human experience: themes that are either the most fundamental or the most banal, depending on the artist's response to them: transience and mortality (*Summer Interlude*); marriage and family (*A Lesson in Love*); the varieties of love (*Smiles of a Summer Night*); the shadow of death (*The Seventh Seal*); old age and the need for self-knowledge (*Wild Strawberries*). And Bergman's recent work, especially *The Silence, Persona* and *Shame,* seems to me to be among the most *essential* investigations in any art form of the contemporary condition—of what it really feels like to be alive today.

In attempting to define the real nature of Bergman's art I want to begin by considering, at risk of obviousness, certain general characteristics. Thinking back over the films, one is struck by how seldom one sees Bergman's characters in their permanent homes. Mai-Britt Nilsson, the ballet-dancer of *Summer Interlude,* is seen only in the theatre and in the summer-house she revisits in order to re-live the past. The women of *Waiting Women* are in their summer-house awaiting their husbands' arrival from the city. The first episode is also set in the summer-house. In the second, Mai-Britt Nilsson is seen briefly in her apartment where, pregnant and unmarried, she lives alone with a cat; most of the episode deals with her temporary stay in Paris, which is shown in flashbacks from the hospital where she gives birth to her child. In the third episode we see Gunnar Bjornstrand and Eva Dahlbeck briefly in their home (they get no further than the hallway); most of it takes place in a lift stuck between floors. In *Summer with Monika,* which was adapted from a novel, we untypically see the characters in their homes quite a bit; but home there is merely something to escape from, and the main body of the film concerns the couple's escape to the islands. The characters of *Sawdust and Tinsel* and *The Face,* and the travelling actors of *The Seventh Seal,* have no permanent homes, living in caravans and moving continually from place to place. The Knight in *The Seventh Seal* reaches his home only at the very end of the film: a dark, cold, almost empty castle. Victor Sjöström in *Wild Strawberries* is seen in his apartment only for the first few minutes. Neither *So Close to Life* nor *The Virgin Spring* was written by Bergman, so we need not expect them to conform to these generalisations, and the latter doesn't; *So Close to Life* is set exclusively in a maternity ward. There is a home and a family in *The Devil's Eye,* but the central character, and very much the film's emotional centre, is Don Juan, whose only home is Hell. We see the characters of *Through a Glass Darkly* only in their summer holiday house on an island. We never see where the Priest in *Winter Light* lives, and we see the schoolmistress only in her kitchen (it's her aunt's house, anyway). In *The Silence* the two sisters are stranded in a foreign city; in *Persona* the two women are staying in somebody else's summer-house. The couple in *Hour of the Wolf* are also seen only in their summer cottage. The case of *A Lesson in Love* is especially interesting, as it is centrally concerned with family relationships—with the family as a unit—yet at no point do we see the central characters in their own home, but only in the doctor-husband's consulting-room and laboratory. Hence Bergman's protagonists seem continually suspend-

ed, without permanent roots, often in the process of movement not only from place to place but from one condition to another.

The importance of journeys in Bergman follows from this. I am not of course claiming that this feature is peculiar to him, or even very unusual: one has only to think of Alfred Hitchcock, the central figures of whose last five films either have no fixed homes or are never seen in them (with the exception of poor Norman Bates), and in whose work journeys have an extreme prominence; or of Westerns. Nonetheless, journeys play leading parts in nearly all Bergman's mature films, and determine the structure of several of his finest. Interestingly, the prominent exceptions are his two retrospective comedies, *Smiles of a Summer Night* and *Now About These Women,* where the comparative stability of the action contributes greatly to one's impression that in them Bergman was more (in the later) or less (in the earlier) deliberately pausing, surveying, consolidating. Several films are based on interrupted journeys, where important new developments and spiritual decisions in the characters' lives are precipitated during the hiatus in their travelling: *Sawdust and Tinsel, The Face* and *The Silence.* One of Bergman's favourite narrative forms is that of a journey during which present events and memories of the past combine to steer the protagonist to a point of self-confrontation, provoking in him or her a radical change in attitude to life, a new orientation with regard to the future. A synopsis suggests that this is at least adumbrated in *Thirst,* the second of Bergman's films to be made from an original screenplay. In its mature form it is the basis of four marvellous films. The main action of *Summer Interlude* (framed by the scenes in the theatre) has Mai-Britt Nilsson returning to the summer-house where she used to stay, where she re-lives in memory the love affair that has been crucial to her experience and whose tragic outcome has arrested her further development, preventing her from accepting the possibilities life still offers. *A Lesson in Love* shows the resolution of a marriage problem during a journey from Mjölby (in central southern Sweden) to Copenhagen, with complicated flashbacks for both husband and wife and various encounters that directly or indirectly affect the outcome. *Wild Strawberries* takes place mostly during a journey from

The Seventh Seal: *Mia (Bibi Andersson) and Jof (Nils Poppe) share a moment of sweetness and light.*

Stockholm to Lund, during which the central figure revisits the people and places of his past, and sees different aspects of his own life reflected in people he meets. The basis of *Winter Light* is the priest's progress from morning service at one church to evening service at another, again with memories and actual events and confrontations interacting to bring about a crisis and partial resolution in his life. The importance of this structure to Bergman is suggested by its recurrence at such different stages of his development, in four films so distinct in tone and mood which also happen to be among his most satisfying.

These four films have another structural feature in common: the strict time-unity within which the past (in the shape of flashbacks) is contained. The sense of tautness and compression that unity of time and place gives is clearly very important to Bergman, and often appears in his work, especially the later work, in a rigorously pure form, without recourse to flashbacks. The Ulla Isaakson-scripted *So Close to Life* is an obvious example of this, and among Bergman's own scripts there are *The Face, Through a Glass Darkly* and *The Silence.* The journey structure prohibits unity of place, obviously, but Bergman preserves strict unity of time in *Journey into Autumn* and the other Isaakson film *The Virgin Spring.* But some of the richest of Bergman's films are those in which the past is felt as a continuing presence, with the characters' re-living and revaluation of it playing a crucial role in their development: the films where strict time-unity in the 'present' narrative is counterpointed with extreme time-freedom in the flashbacks it contains. *Wild Strawberries* is the most obvious because the most elaborate example; but in *Winter Light,* which contains only one brief flashback, the central figure's past is very strongly felt. This presence-of-the-past is also particularly important not only in the other two films built largely on flashbacks, *Summer Interlude* and *A Lesson in Love,* but in *Sawdust and Tinsel* (not only in the introductory Frost-Alma flashback) and *Hour of the Wolf.*

Our sense of the characters' suspension; the presence of the past; a brief, often twenty-four hour, but crucial period wherein a turning-point is reached and the course of the future decided; the importance of journeys: these points take us some way, I think, towards defining the essential nature of Bergman's art. One finds similar characteristics in the work of Antonioni, and comparison seems to me instructive. The characteristic structure of Antonioni's films bears some resemblance to that of Bergman's: for the traditional plot-and-action narrative the two directors tend to substitute a thematic narrative, wherein a character passes through a series of apparently random events and encounters that all contribute to bringing about a self-confrontation. The essential difference between the two directors can be seen in the different use they make of journeys. In Bergman a journey always has a definite purpose and the purpose is usually fulfilled. Occasionally the purpose is consciously related to the characters' inner development: thus in *A Lesson in Love,* Gunnar Björnstrand goes to Copenhagen deliberately to retrieve his wife from her lover, and to re-establish his marriage and the family group on a new and securer footing. More usually the ostensible purpose of the journey is not *directly* related to the

inner development, and often an ironic contrast arises between ostensible purpose and inner discovery: one thinks of Victor Sjöström's journey to Lund to receive his honorary doctorate in *Wild Strawberries,* and of Gunnar Björnstrand's journey to Frostnäs in *Winter Light* to take the evening service. In Antonioni, on the other hand, journeys tend to be a haphazard and goal-less wandering: those of Steve Cochran in *Il Grido* and Jeanne Moreau in *La Notte* are the clearest instances. When there *is* a purpose, it tends to get lost from sight, or the characters allow themselves to be diverted from it: think of the search for Anna in *L'Avventura* or of the repeated deflecting of Thomas in *Blow Up.* Underlying the frequently episodic structure of a Bergman film one can always detect a progress in a straight line, and this dynamic characteristic of the films is also a quality common to their characters. Antonioni's characters, on the other hand, tend to be helpless, allowing things to drift, allowing their destinies to be shaped by their own abdication from responsibility. The contrast is strikingly apparent if one juxtaposes the two directors' films about crises in mentally and emotionally disturbed women. Monica Vitti in *Deserto Rosso* mostly drifts; if she takes positive action, like going to Richard Harris in his hotel, she has to be driven to it by an overwhelming pressure of events upon her, so that it is little more than a reflex action or a plea for help. Harriet Andersson in *Through a Glass Darkly* takes her fate in her own hands and precipitates, at least half-deliberately, her own final breakdown. The characteristic movement of an Antonioni film is towards a defeat that has something in it of self-indulgence, so little energy is summoned up to combat it; that of a Bergman film is a dynamic drive from sickness and imprisonment towards a health and freedom not necessarily reached but passionately sought. (pp. 7-13)

> *Robin Wood, in his* Ingmar Bergman, *Praeger, 1969, 191 p.*

Ingmar Bergman

Experience should be gained before one reaches forty, so a wise man has said. After forty it is permissible for one to comment.

I venture to say that the reverse might apply in my case. No one under forty was more certain of his theories and no one more willing to elucidate them than I was. No one knew better or could visualize more.

But now that I am somewhat older I have become rather more cautious. The experience that I have gained, and which I am still sorting out, is of such a kind that I am unwilling to express myself on the art of the filmmaker. I know for a fact that my work involves technical skill and mental ability, but I know, too, that even my greatest experience will be uninteresting to others, except perhaps to the potential filmmaker.

Moreover, it is my opinion that an artist's work is the only real contribution that he can make to a critical discussion of art. Thus I find it rather unseemly to get involved in such discussion, even with explanations or excuses.

No, the fact that the artist remained unknown was a good

thing in former times. His relative anonymity was a guarantee against irrelevant outside influences, material considerations and the prostitution of his talents. He brought forth his work in spirit and truth as he saw it, and he left the judgment to the Lord. Thus he lived and died without being more or less important than any other artisan. *Eternal values, immortality* and *masterpieces* were terms not applicable in his case.

His work was to the glory of God. The ability to create was a gift and an accomplishment. In such a world there flourished natural assurance and invulnerable humility—two qualities that are the finest hallmarks of art.

But in life to-day the position of the artist has become more and more precarious: the artist has become a curious figure, a kind of performer or athlete who chases from job to job. His isolation, his now almost holy individualism, his artistic subjectivity, can all too easily cause ulcers and neurosis. Exclusiveness becomes a curse that he eulogises. The unusual is both his pain and his satisfaction.

It is possible that I have made a general rule from my own idiosyncrasies. But it is also possible that the conflict of responsibility has been intensified and the moral problems made so difficult because of dependence on popular support and also due to unreasonable economic burdens.

Anyway, I now find that I need to clarify what I have been thinking, what my standards are and what constitutes my position. This will be a personal and not an authoritative pronouncement on film art, with some quite subjective notes on the technical and ethical problems of the filmmaker.

Often [the script] begins with something very hazy and indefinite—a chance remark or a quick change of phrase, a dim but pleasant event, yet one that is not specifically related to the actual situation. It can be a few bars of music, a shaft of light across the street. It has happened in my theatrical work that I have seen performers in fresh make-up in yet unplayed roles.

All in all these seem to be split-second impressions that disappear as quickly as they come, yet nevertheless leave an impression behind just like a pleasant dream.

Most of all they are a brightly coloured thread sticking out of the dark sack of the unconscious. If I begin to wind up this thread and do it carefully, a complete film will emerge.

I would like to say that this is not a case of Pallas Athene in the mind of Zeus, but an unconnected phenomenon, more a mental state than an actual story, but for all that abounding with fertile associations and images.

All this is brought out with pulse-beats and rhythms that are very special and characteristic of the different films. Through these rhythms the picture sequences take a separate pattern, according to the way they were born and mastered by the motive.

This primitive life-cell strives from the beginning to achieve form, but its movements may be lazy and perhaps even a little drowsy. If in this primitive state it shows itself

to have enough strength to transform itself into a film, I then decide to give it life, and I begin work on the script.

The feeling of failure occurs mostly before the writing begins. The dreams become merely cobwebs, the visions fade and become grey and insignificant, the pulse-beat is silent: feelings become small, tired fancies without strength and reality.

I have thus decided to make a certain film, and now begins the complicated and difficult mastered work—to transfer rhythms, moods, atmosphere, tensions, sequences, tones and scents into words and sentences in a readable or at least understandable script.

This is difficult but not impossible.

The vital thing is the dialogue, but dialogue is a sensitive matter that can offer resistance. We have learned (or should have learned) that the written dialogue of the theater is like a score that is almost incomprehensible to the ordinary person. Interpretation of theatrical dialogue demands a technical skill and a certain amount of imagination and feeling, qualities so often lacking in the theatrical profession.

One can write dialogue, but the directions on how the dialogue should be handled, the rhythms and the tempo, the speed at which it is to be taken, and what is to take place between the lines—all that must for practical reasons be left out because a script containing so much detail would be unreadable.

I can squeeze directions and locations, characterisations and atmosphere into my film-scripts in understandable terms, provided I am a tolerable writer and the reader has a fair reading ability, which is not always the case.

However, I now come to essentials, by which I mean montage, rhythm and the relation of one picture to the other—the vital "third dimension" without which the film is merely a dead product of a factory. Here I cannot give "keys" or an adequate indication of the empos of the complexes involved, and it is quite impossible to give a comprehensible idea of what gives life to a work of art. I have often sought a kind of notation that would give me a chance of recording the shades and tones of the ideas and the inner structure of the picture.

(Thus let us state once and for all that the film-script *is a very imperfect technical basis for a film.*)

In this connection I should draw attention to another fact that is often overlooked. Film is not the same thing as literature. As often as not the character and substance of the two art forms are in conflict. What this difference really depends on is hard to define but it probably has to do with the self-responsive process. The written word is read and assimilated by a conscious act and in connection with the intellect, and little by little it plays on the imagination or feelings. It is completely different with the motion picture. When we see a film in a cinema we are conscious that an illusion has been prepared for us, and we relax and accept it with our will and intellect. We prepare the way into our imagination. The sequence of pictures plays directly on our feelings without touching the mind. There are many reasons why we ought to avoid filming existing literature but the most important is that the irrational dimension, which is the heart of a literary work, is often untranslatable, and that in its turn kills the special dimension of the film. If, despite this, we wish to translate something literary into filmic terms, we are obliged to make an infinite number of complicated transformations—which most often give limited or no result in relation to the efforts expended.

I know what I am talking about because I have been subjected to so-called literary judgment. This is about as intelligent as letting a music critic judge an exhibition of paintings or a football reporter criticize a new play.

The only reason for any and everyone believing himself capable of pronouncing a valid judgment on motion pictures is the inability of the film to assert itself as an art form, its need of a definite artistic vocabulary, its extreme youth in relation to the other arts, its obvious ties with economic realities, its direct appeal to the feelings. All these factors cause the motion picture to be regarded with disdain. The directness of expression of the motion picture makes it suspect in certain eyes, and as a result any and everyone thinks himself competent to say anything he likes in whatever way he likes on film art.

I myself have never had ambitions to be an author. I do not wish to write novels, short stories, essays, biographies or treatises on special subjects. I certainly do not want to write plays for the theater. Film-making is what interests me. I want to make films about conditions, tensions, pictures, rhythms and characters within me and that in one way or another interest me. I am a film-maker, not an author. The motion picture is my medium of expression, not the written word. The motion picture and its complicated process of birth are my methods of saying what I want to my fellow men. I find it humiliating for my work to be judged as a book when it is a film. It is like calling a bird a fish, and fire, water.

Consequently the writing of the script is a difficult period, but it is a useful one as it compels me to prove logically the validity of my ideas. While this is taking place I am caught in the difficult conflict of situations. There is a conflict between my need to find a way of filming a complicated situation and my desire for complete simplicity. As I do not intend my works to be solely for the edification of myself or for the few but instead for the public in general, the demands of the public are imperative. Sometimes I try a daring alternative, and it has been shown that the public can appreciate the most advanced and complicated developments.

For a very long time I have wanted to use the film medium for story-telling. This does not mean that I find the narrative form itself faulty, but that I consider the motion picture ideally suited to the epic and the dramatic.

I know, of course, that by using film we can bring in previously unknown worlds, realities beyond reality.

It is of great importance for our long-suffering industry to produce fine dreams, light frolics, germs of ideas, brilliant dazzling bubbles.

I do not say that these things never materialize, only that they are all too infrequent and all too half-hearted.

It happens when I stand there in the half-light of the film studio with its noise and throng, the dirt and wretched atmosphere. I seriously wonder why I am engaged in this most difficult form of artistic creation.

The rules are many and burdensome. I must have three minutes of usable film "in the can" every day. I must keep to the shooting schedule, which is so tight that it excludes almost everything but essentials. I am surrounded by technical equipment that with fiendish cunning tries to sabotage my best intentions. Constantly I am on edge. I am compelled to live the collective life of the studio. Amidst all this must take place a process that is sensitive and that really demands quietness, concentration and confidence.

I mean: working with actors and actresses.

There are many directors who forget that our work in films begins with the human face. We can certainly become completely absorbed in the aesthetics of montage, we can bring together objects and still-life into a wonderful rhythm, we can make nature studies of astounding beauty—but the approach to the human face is without doubt the hallmark and the distinguishing quality of film. From this we might conclude that the film star is our most expensive instrument and that the camera merely registers the reactions of this instrument. In many cases the opposite can be seen: the position and movement of the camera is considered more important than the player, and the picture becomes an end in itself. But this can never do anything but destroy illusions and be artistically devastating.

In order to give the greatest possible strength to the actor's expression, the camera movement must be simple, free and completely synchronised with the action. The camera must be a completely objective observer and only on rare occasions may it participate in the action.

We should realize that the best means of expression the actor has at his command is his appearance. The close-up, if objectively composed, perfectly directed and played, is the most forcible means at the disposal of the film director, while at the same time it is the most certain proof of his competence or incompetence. The lack or abundance of close-ups shows in an uncompromising way the nature of the film director and the extent of his interest in people.

Simplicity, concentration, full knowledge, technical perfection must be the pillars supporting each scene and sequence.

However, in themselves they are not enough.

All these factors exist—and it is necessary for them to do so—but still the one most important element is lacking, the spark that brings the whole thing to life. This intimate spark of life appears or fails to appear, according to its will. This spark of life is crucial and indomitable.

For instance, I well know that everything for a scene must be prepared down to the last detail, each branch of the collective organization must know exactly what it is to do. The entire mechanism must be free from fault as a matter of course. These preliminaries may or may not take a long time, but they should not be dragged out and tire those participating. Rehearsals for the take must be carried out with technical precision, with everyone knowing exactly what he is to do.

Then comes the take. From experience I know that the first take is often the happiest as it is the most natural. This is because with the first take the actors are trying to create something: this creative urge provides a spark of life and comes from natural identification. The camera registers this inner act of creation, which is hardly perceptible to the untrained eye or ear but which is recorded and preserved on the sensitive photographic film and on the sound-track.

I believe it is precisely this sudden act of creation by an actor that keeps me in films and holds me fascinated with the medium. The development and retention of a sudden burst of life gives me ample reward for the thousands of hours of grey gloom, trial and tribulation.

The actor must unconditionally identify himself with his part. This identification should be like a costume that is slipped on. Lengthy concentration, continuous control of feelings and high-pressure working are completely out. The actor must be able in the purely technical sense (and if possible with the director's help) to take on and take off the character he is playing. Mental tensions and lengthy exertions are fatal to all filmic expression.

The director should not deluge the actor with instructions like autumn rain, but rather he should make his points at the right moments. His words should be too few rather than too many. For his performance the actor is little helped by the director's intellectual analysis. What the actor wants are exact instructions at the moment and certain technical corrections without embellishments and digressions. I know that an intonation, a look or a smile from the director can often do far more good to the actor than the most penetrating analysis. This mode of directing sounds like witchcraft, but it is nothing of the sort; it is only a quiet and effective method of control over the actor by his director. Indeed, the fewer the discussions, talks and explanations, the more the affinity, silence, mutual understanding, natural loyalty and confidence.

Many imagine that a commercial film industry lacks morality or that its practices are so definitely based on immorality that an artistically ethical standpoint cannot be maintained. Our films are assigned to businessmen, who at times regard them with apprehension, as motion pictures have to do with something as unreliable as art.

If many may regard our activity as dubious, I must emphasize that its morality is as good as any and so absolute that it could almost cause us embarrassment. However, I have found that I am like the Englishman in the tropics who shaves and dresses for dinner every day. He does not do this to please the wild animals but for his own sake. If he gives up his discipline then the jungle has beaten him.

I know that I shall have lost to the jungle if I take a weak moral standpoint or relax my mental punctiliousness. I have, therefore, come to a certain belief that is based on three powerfully effective commandments. Briefly, I shall state their wording and their meaning. These have become the very fundamentals of my activity in the film world.

The first may sound indecent but really is highly moral. It runs:

THOU SHALT BE ENTERTAINING AT ALL TIMES.

This means that the public that sees my films and thus provides my bread and butter has the right to expect entertainment, a thrill, a joy, a spirited experience. I am responsible for providing that experience. That is the only justification for my activity.

However, this does not mean that I must debase my talents, at least not in any and every way, because then I would break the second commandment, which runs:

THOU SHALT OBEY THY ARTISTIC CONSCIENCE AT ALL TIMES.

This is a very tricky commandment because it obviously forbids me to steal, lie, prostitute my talents, kill or falsify. However, I will say that I am allowed to falsify if it is artistically justified, I may also lie if it is a beautiful lie, I could also kill my friends or myself or anyone else if it would help my art, it may also be permissible to prostitute my talents if it will further my cause, and I should indeed steal if there were no other way out.

If one obeyed one's artistic conscience to the full in every respect then one would find oneself doing a balancing act on a tight-rope, and one would become so dizzy that at any moment one could fall down and break one's neck. Then all the prudent and moral bystanders would say: "Look, there lies the thief, the murderer, the lecher, the liar. Serves him right." Not a thought that all means are allowed except those which lead to a fiasco, and that the most dangerous ways are the only ones that are passable, and that compulsion and dizziness are two necessary parts of our activity. Not a thought that the joy of creation, which is a thing of beauty and a joy forever, is bound up with the necessary fear of creation.

One can incant as often as one desires, magnify one's humility and diminish one's pride to one's heart's content, but the fact still remains that to follow one's artistic conscience is a perversity of the flesh as a result of years and years of mortification and radiant moments of clear asceticism and resistance. In the long run it is the same, however we reckon. First, on the point of fusion, comes the area between belief and submission, which can be called the artistic obvious. I wish to assert at this point that this is by no means my only goal, but merely that I try to keep to the compass as well as I can.

In order to strengthen my will so that I do not slip off the narrow path into the ditch, I have a third good and juicy commandment, which runs: THOU SHALT MAKE EACH FILM AS IF IT WERE THY LAST.

Some may imagine that this commandment is an amusing twist of word-play or a pointless aphorism or perhaps simply a beautiful phrase about the complete vanity of everything. However, that is not the case.

It is reality.

In Sweden film production was interrupted for a whole year some years ago. During my enforced inactivity, I learned that because of commercial complications, and through no fault of my own, I could be out on the street before I knew it.

I do not complain about it, neither am I afraid or bitter: I have merely drawn a logical and highly moral conclusion from the situation: that each film is my last.

For me there is only one loyalty—that is my loyalty to the film on which I am working. What comes (or fails to come) after is insignificant and causes neither anxiety nor longing. This attitude gives me assurance and artistic confidence. The material assurance is apparently limited but I find that artistic integrity is infinitely more important. Therefore I follow the principle: each film is my last.

This conviction gives me strength in another way. I have seen all too many film workers burdened down with anxiety, yet carrying out to the full their necessary duties. Worn out, bored to death and without pleasure, they have fulfilled their work. They have suffered humiliation and affronts from producers, the critics and the public without flinching, without giving up, without leaving the profession. With a tired shrug of the shoulders, they have made their artistic contributions until they went down or were thrown out.

I do not know but perhaps the day will come when I shall be received indifferently by the public, perhaps together with a feeling of disgust in myself. Fatigue and emptiness will descend upon me like a dirty grey sack, and fear will stifle everything. Emptiness will stare me in the face.

When this happens I shall put down my tools and leave the scene, of my own free will, without bitterness and without brooding whether or not the work has been useful and truthful from the viewpoint of eternity.

Bergman on the best directors:

When film is not a document, it is dream. That is why Tarkovsky is the greatest of them all. He moves with such naturalness in the room of dreams. He doesn't explain. What should he explain anyhow? He is a spectator, capable of staging his visions in the most unwieldy but, in a way, the most willing of media. All my life I have hammered on the doors of the rooms in which he moves so naturally. Only a few times have I managed to creep inside. Most of my conscious efforts have ended in embarrassing failure—*The Serpent's Egg, The Touch, Face to Face* and so on.

Fellini, Kurosawa and Buñuel move in the same fields as Tarkovsky. Antonioni was on his way, but expired, suffocated by his own tediousness. Méliès was always there without having to think about it. He was a magician by profession.

Ingmar Bergman, in his The Magic Lantern, *translated by Joan Tate, Hamish Hamilton, 1988.*

Wise and far-sighted men in the Middle Ages used to spend nights in their coffins in order never to forget the tremendous importance of every moment and the transient nature of life itself.

Without taking such drastic and uncomfortable measures, I harden myself to the seeming futility and the fickle cruelty of film-making, with the earnest conviction that each film is my last. (pp. 9-12)

Ingmar Bergman, "My Three Powerfully Effective Commandments," translated by P. E. Burke and Lennart Swahn, in Film Comment, *Vol. 6, No. 2, Summer, 1970, pp. 9-12.*

Ingmar Bergman   [Interview with Charles Thomas Samuels]

[*Samuels*]: *Mr. Bergman, I'd like to start with a rather general question: If I were asked to cite a single reason for your preeminence among film directors, I would point to your creation of a special world—the sort of thing we are accustomed to with great creative figures in the other arts, but rarely in film, and never to your degree. You are, in fact, very much like a writer. Why didn't you become one?*

[Bergman]: When I was a child, I suffered from an almost complete lack of words. My education was very rigid; my father was a priest. As a result, I lived in a private world of my own dreams. I played with my puppet theater.

And—

Excuse me. I had very few contacts with reality or channels to it. I was afraid of my father, my mother, my elder brother—everything. Playing with this puppet theater and a projection device I had was my only form of self-expression. I had great difficulty with fiction and reality; as a small child I mixed them so much that my family always said I was a liar. Even when I grew up, I felt blocked. I had enormous difficulty speaking to others and—

I want to interrupt you for just a moment. This description of your childhood resembles one classic description of the genesis of a writer. Was it only the accident of the puppet theater that sent you the way of theater rather than of books?

No. I remember that during my eighteenth summer, when I had just finished school, suddenly I wrote a novel. And in school, when we had to write compositions, I liked it very much. But I never felt that writing was my cup of tea. I put the novel in my desk and forgot it. But in 1940, suddenly—in the summer—I started writing and wrote twelve—

Plays.

Yes. It was a sudden eruption.

May I offer an hypothesis about this so that you can react to it? Your skill as a writer and your need to express yourself in words are fulfilled more in the theater and cinema because in these arts one also embodies his words and even sees the audience's response to them.

My beginning was otherwise, because when I began writing, I was suspicious of words. And I always lacked words;

it has always been very difficult for me to find the word I want.

Is this suspicion of words one of the reasons why Alma makes Elisabeth say "nothing" in **Persona?**

No. Yes. In a way. But that wasn't conscious on my part.

Because "nothing" is the truest word, one that asserts least.

I don't know. I have always felt suspicious both of what I say and of what others say to me. Always I feel something has been left out. When I read a book, I read very slowly. It takes a lot of time for me to read a play.

Do you direct it in your head?

In a way. I have to translate the words into speeches, movements, flesh and blood. I have an enormous need for contact with an audience, with other people. For me, words are not satisfying.

With a book, the reader is elsewhere.

When you read, words have to pass through your conscious mind to reach your emotions and your soul. In film and theater, things go directly to the emotions. What I need is to come in contact with others.

I see that, but it raises a problem I'm sure you've often discussed. Your films have emotional impact, but since they are also the most intellectually difficult of contemporary films, isn't there sometimes a contradiction between the two effects? Let me give you a specific example. How do you react when I say that while I watched **The Rite,** *my feelings were interfered with by my baffled effort at comprehension?*

Your approach is wrong. I never asked you to understand; I ask only that you feel.

You *haven't asked me anything. I don't see you: I only see the film.*

Yes, but—

And the film asks me to understand. Here are three performers under investigation for a spectacle that the authorities find obscene. The film continuously makes us wonder what the spectacle means, why the authorities want to suppress it, etc. These questions sit next to me. More and more, I feel them grab me by the throat—better, the head—so that I can't feel anything but puzzlement.

But that's you.

It's not the film?

No. **The Rite** merely expresses my resentment against the critics, audience, and government, with which I was in constant battle while I ran the [Royal Dramatic] theater. A year after my resignation from the post, I sat down and wrote this script in five days. I did it merely to free myself.

But then—

Excuse please. The picture is just a game, a way of kicking everyone's—not understanding—intellectual—

To puzzle the audience?

Exactly. I liked very much to write it and even more to make it. We had a lot of fun while we were shooting. My purpose was just to amuse myself and the audience which liked it. Do you understand what I mean?

I understand but—

You must realize—this is very important!—I never ask people to understand what I have made. Stravinsky once said, "I have never understood a piece of music in my life. I always only feel."

But Stravinsky was a composer. By its nature, music is non-discursive; we don't have to understand it. Films, plays, poems, novels all make propositions or observations, embody ideas or beliefs, and we go to these forms—

But you must understand that you are perverted. You belong to a small minority that tries to understand. Ordinary people—and me, too. . . . Look, I have exactly the same feeling when I see a play. It is as if I were hearing a string quartet by Bartok. I never try to understand. I, too, am a little perverted, so I, too, on one level, control myself. Because I am a man of the theater, a professional, and this can—

Destroy spontaneous response?

Exactly. But it never does, because I feel that especially film. . . . You know, they always talk about Brecht's being so intellectual.

Whereas he's very emotional.

Yes. His own comments and those of his commentators come between us and the plays. Music, films, plays always work directly on the emotions.

I must disagree. My two favorites among your films— though there are about ten that I think excellent—are **Persona** *and* **Winter Light.** *Each of these films works as you say a film should, but neither is like* **The Rite.** *I'd therefore like to compare them so as to explore the problem of a film that is too puzzling to be evocative. Let me start with* **Winter Light,** *which I think your purest film. By the way, do you like it?*

Yes.

Although the film raises questions about what the hero thinks and about what he and his mistress represent as different ways of life, the drama is so compelling, the images so powerful that we don't sit there—I didn't sit there, perverted though I am—and say, "What does this mean?" I was caught. **Winter Light** *typifies one of the ways you are at your best; in it, the audience's concern for the fate of the characters is more intense than any puzzlement about their significance. Do you see what I mean?*

Yes. But I think you are wrong.

Why?

Because . . . because . . . when you say, "I like *Winter Light* and *Persona,* and I think these are two of the best you have made," then you say "we," and then you confuse "I" and "we," and you make generalizations, whereas for everyone, *Persona* and *Winter Light* are, I think, my most difficult pictures. So it is impossible for you to take this point of view.

I'll stop mixing "I" and "we"—

I must tell you, I must tell you before we go onto more complicated things: I make my pictures for use! They are not made *sub specie aeternitatis;* they are made for now and for use. They are like a table, or mineral water, or a flower, or a lamp, or anything that is made for someone who wants to use it. Also, they are made to put me in contact with other human beings, to whom I give them and say, "Please use them. Take what you want and throw the rest away. I will come back and make other new and beautiful things. If this was not successful, it doesn't matter." My impulse has nothing to do with intellect or symbolism; it has only to do with dreams and longing, with hope and desire, with passion. Do you understand what I mean? So when you say that a film of mine is intellectually complicated, I have the feeling that you don't talk about one of my pictures. Let us talk about the pictures, not as one of the best, or the most disgusting, or one of the stinking ones; let us talk about attempts to come in contact with other people.

I'm afraid I didn't make myself clear. We started with **The Rite,** *and I said, "This is a film that I think. . . . "*

I'm not interested in what you think! If you like, ask me questions! But I'm not interested in hearing what you think!

I'm not trying to tell you what I like or dislike for the purpose of giving you my opinion but for the purpose of raising questions. I won't say "I" anymore. Let's name a man X; I'll ask you about what X might want to know. Let's say that while watching **The Rite,** *X isn't as emotionally—*

No! It's clear! This is completely uninteresting! *The Rite* has been seen by millions of people who think. . . . It's completely uninteresting if one doesn't like. . . . You know, I live on a small island. The day after *The Rite* was shown on Swedish television, a man came to me on the ferryboat going to the island and said, "It was a nice play. Don't you think it was a nice play? My wife and I, we laughed and laughed, and we had a tremendous evening together." I was completely confused; as we would judge it, he had completely misunderstood the play. But he enjoyed himself! Perhaps he had been drunk; perhaps he had gone to bed with the old girl; perhaps he was being ironic. But he enjoyed coming to me and saying it was nice. Do you understand? So we must find some way of communicating. It's very important. If we continue this way, we will get nothing. We must find some sort of human communication, because if we don't, you only make me irritated and I just want to finish. You know, I can sit down here and discuss everything in an intellectual way. I can say the most astonishing things because I am perfect at giving interviews. But I think we could find another way—do you understand—a sort of human—

Haven't you noticed that I've ignored all my prepared questions?

Yes.

I have been trying to respond to what you say as you say it. I have been trying to communicate. Please, by all means, tell me when I seem to be going astray. But, my God, Mr.

Bergman, I've told you. . . . Look, I have a job: interviewing and writing about you. You've done the most important job already: You've made the films. But despite what you've said, I think there are people who would like help in understanding your films. I want, to the best of my abilities, with whatever aid you'll give me, to work for those people.

Of course. I understand very well that you're trying to reach contact, but this way you've started will only keep us sitting like two puppets discussing absolute nonsense— to me, it is completely uninteresting and, to everybody, completely uninteresting. Please let's try—

Let me suggest two alternatives, and you say which you'd prefer.

No! Go on!

No! I want to make human contact also. Here are the two ways: A few moments ago, you said you met this man who liked **The Rite,** *yet you were surprised because—*

He didn't say he liked it; he said he had a nice evening. Perhaps he was being ironic. But I liked his way of approaching, you know. . . . It was sort of. . . . He used my play. He used it.

Wouldn't you care to know why he found it useful?

That is irrelevant. He used it! Why and how people use are interesting to hear—as with **The Touch,** which got extreme responses: People either liked it or hated it. I like to hear about **The Touch** because it was not the picture I intended to make—for many reasons—especially the actors. You know that actors often change a film, for better or worse.

May I ask you how the film differs from the one you intended?

I intended to paint the portrait of an ordinary woman, in which everything around her would be a reflection. I wanted her in close-up and the surroundings clear only when near her. I wanted the portrait to be very detailed and very lovely and true. But when I joined the actors, they liked the plot more than I did, and I think they seduced me away from my original plan. I can't say if the result is better or worse, but it is different. Bibi Andersson is a close friend of mine—a lovely and extremely talented actress. She is totally oriented toward reality, always needing motives for what she does. She is a warm, fantastic woman. To her, everything is important, so she asked that what I wanted out of focus or shadowed be made utterly clear. I'm not criticizing her; I admire and love her. But she changed the film. When I give an actor a part, I always hope that he will join in the creating by adding something I didn't intend. We collaborate. What Bibi Andersson did made the film more comprehensible for common people and more immediately powerful. I agreed with all her changes.

May I ask about a moment in the film that—I think—is very good? It sounds, from what you say, as if Bibi Andersson was behind it. Karin is giving breakfast to her family; everything is close-up, light, warm, gay. Suddenly, there is a jump cut to a long shot of her alone, drinking coffee, in an utterly quiet, utterly empty kitchen. This is a case in which the clarity of the surroundings immediately makes us understand her. Now we know why she goes to David.

I think this scene is mine, because the film was made about a woman I actually know. This transition from warmth to complete loneliness is typical of her whole life—and of every woman's life. That is why every woman laughs while watching that part of the film.

Do you ever do more than change a film for one of your actresses? Do you ever actually conceive of one to give her a chance to change? Let me give you an example. In **The Naked Night** *Harriet Andersson plays a woman who epitomizes the power of sex. Then the next film you made.* **A Lesson in Love,** *casts her in the role of a tomboy who is afraid of sex. Did you make the later film at all to reverse her performance in* **The Naked Night?**

I know my actors well. We all are closely involved with each other. I know how many parts each carries within him. One day I write one of the parts the actor can play but never has. Sometimes the actors themselves don't know that they can play it. But without actually telling me, they show me the parts they contain.

So it is possible for you to write a script because you realize that a particular actress is now ready to play a particular part.

Exactly. It's fantastic to be surrounded by so many actors, by so many unwritten parts. All the time the actors are giving you material; through their faces, through their movements, their inflections.

Do you sometimes reverse not only the actor but a whole film in the next one you make?

I think only a little bit in the relationship between *Through a Glass Darkly* and *Winter Light.*

Yes, that's a very interesting case. At the end of **Through a Glass Darkly,** *Björnstrand communicates with his son, who had been longing for such an occurrence. The next year we go back to the movie house, and there is Björnstrand playing, in a sense, his own son, only now more desperately in search of communication with a father (God), who will not or cannot answer him.*

I think that is fascinating, but I never had it in mind. You are right, but what you say astonishes me.

I'm not crazy?

No. No. No. You are completely right.

If you don't mind then, I'd like to get back to **Winter Light.** *I want to ask you—ask you—something to see if I'm right. Isn't it true that whereas you are frequently concerned with the impossibility of attaining corroboration for one's faith, in* **Winter Light** *you show that the search for corroboration is itself the cause of harm?*

All the time that I treated the questions of God and ultimate faith. I felt very unhappy. When I left them behind, and also abandoned my enormous desire to make the best film in the world—

To be God.

Yes . . . to . . . to—

Make the perfect creation.

Yes. To make the perfect creation. As soon as I said, here are my limits, which I see very clearly and which I will not jump over but only try to open up—technically—then I became unneurotic—

Like a research scientist?

Yes.

Isn't that how the drama operates in **Persona?** *After the credit sequence, the film begins realistically. There is a woman in a hospital, suffering a sort of catatonic withdrawal. She is tended by a nurse. Then, as the film progresses, this realistic drama starts to break from inside (at one moment, the film itself shatters). Is it true that like a research scientist, you were investigating in* **Persona** *the limits that exist for an artist who wants his imitation of reality to be as true and as complex as reality itself? Don't you say, "Therefore, I will show where the limits are by declaring the artificialities that are my art and by showing them break down or break open at the point where they come closest to touching the truth?"*

That's very interesting, but it's not what I intended. It's very simple: *Persona* is a creation that saved its creator. Before making it, I was ill, having twice had pneumonia and antibiotic poisoning. I lost my balance for three months. The summer before, I had written a script, but I told everyone it would be canceled because it was a complicated picture and I didn't feel up to it. I was going to Hamburg then to stage *The Magic Flute,* and I had to cancel that, too. I remember sitting in my hospital bed, looking directly in front of me at a black spot—because if I turned my head at all, the whole room began to spin. I thought to myself that I would never create anything anymore; I was completely empty, almost dead. The montage at the beginning of the film is just a poem about that personal situation.

With cuts from earlier Bergman films.

Because whenever I thought about making a new film, silly pictures from my old ones came into my head. Suddenly, one day I started thinking of two women sitting next to each other and comparing hands. This was a single scene, which, after an enormous effort, I was able to write down. Then, I thought that if I could make a very small picture—perhaps in 16 mm—about two women, one talking, the other not (thus an enormous monologue), it would not be too hard for me. Every day I wrote a little bit. I had as yet no idea about making a regular film, because I was so sick, but I trained myself for it. Each morning at ten I moved from the bed to the writing table, sat down, and sometimes wrote and at other times couldn't. After I left the hospital, I went to the seaside, where I finished the script, although I was still sick. Nevertheless, we decided to go ahead. The producer was very, very understanding. He kept telling me to go on, that we could throw it away if it was bad because it wasn't an expensive project. In the middle of July I started shooting, still so sick that when I stood up I became dizzy. Throughout the first week the results were terrible.

What did you shoot that week?

We started with the first scene in the hospital.

But not with the precredit sequence?

No, that came afterward. I wanted to give things up, but
the producer kept encouraging me, finally telling me to
move the company to my island. When we got there, slowly things picked up. The actresses and Sven Nykvist were
fantastic; it was a fantastic collaboration. One day we
made a scene that we all felt was good. That gave me courage. Then the next day, another scene; then many scenes.
It grew, and we began to reshoot what hadn't worked. Exactly what happened and why it happened I don't know.

*Here's a film you make immediately after thinking you'll
never make another film again. You come back to life as
an artist, step by step, growing in courage until you can
face—utterly without fear—the problems, absurdities, and
impossibilities of art itself. And you select as a surrogate an
artist who suffers what you suffered, except that Elisabeth
wills it; she chooses to stop being an artist.*

Yes, because she is not sick.

*Let me get at my point another way. When Elisabeth looks
at television and sees a Buddhist monk immolating himself
in Vietnam, several critics wanted to take this as an uncharacteristic expression of your interest in politics. But I think
it must be related to the later scene—in her bedroom—
when she studies the Cartier-Bresson photograph of the
Jews being led out of the Warsaw ghetto. Both scenes dramatize the awe inspired in the artist when he faces true suffering—which, however, cannot escape some involvement with
art, since both the monk and the Jews reach our consciousness through the art of the photographer.*

Let me explain exactly what I tried to express in the first
scene. The monk scares her because his conviction is so
enormous he is willing to die for it. The photograph represents real suffering.

*But it is, paradoxically, also art. And I find it suggestive
that during the great scene in **Shame** when you show the
people being herded in and out of buildings by the soldiers,
you yourself recall the composition of Cartier-Bresson's
great photograph. Didn't you feel the recollection?*

In a way, yes. But I never thought of it. The scene you
mention represents humiliation, which is the subject of
Shame. The film isn't about enormous brutality, but only
meanness. It is exactly like what has happened to the
Czechs. They defended their rights, and now, slowly, they
are being submitted to a tactic of brutalization that wears
them down. ***Shame*** is not about the bombs; it is about the
gradual infiltration of fear.

*So that the low budget and consequent lack of large war
scenes precisely reflect your theme.*

Yes, but ***Shame*** is not precise enough. My original idea
was to show only a single day before the war had broken
out. But then I wrote things, and it all went wrong—I
don't know why. I haven't seen ***Shame*** recently, and I'm
a little afraid to do so. When you make such a picture, you
have to be very hard on yourself. It's a moral question.

Why?

Certain things in life are impossible to represent—like a
concentration camp.

Because the reality is too terrible?

Exactly. It is almost the same with war as with murder or
death. You must be a hundred percent morally conscious
in treating these things.

You must not simply shock.

Exactly. To see someone dying is false—

When we know he will get up after the performance.

In the theater it's not so bad because we accept all these
conventions, but film is different.

*Still, you are more successful in **Shame** than you acknowledge, for example, I think that the interview scene creates
the horror of war without any false killings. Who are these
soldiers? What do they want? How dare they televise their
brutalization? How dare they humiliate other human beings in this way: Life goes to the end of Western civilization?
[Bergman laughs heartily.] Where did you get the idea for
this scene?*

I don't know.

It was in the script? You didn't improvise?

It was in the script.

Do you improvise much at other times?

No. I improvise only when I have a plan. Improvising for
itself is impossible.

*Didn't you improvise the interviews with the actors in **The
Passion of Anna**?*

I'm sorry to say that those are very unsuccessful. I just
wanted to have a break in the film and to let the actors express themselves. Bibi Andersson and Liv Ullman improvised their interviews, but Max von Sydow and Erland
Josephson had no idea what to say, so they said what I told
them to. This led to two different films, and I no longer
understand why I left the whole batch in, because I always
realized that they wouldn't work. But I like *coups de theatre,* things that make people wake up and rejoin the film.
This time, however, it wasn't successful.

*There are no coups in **Winter Light**; the rhythm is even.
I want to ask another question about that film. When Von
Sydow's drowned body is discovered, why is the shot so dis-
tant?*

Because I always feel that something is more terrifying at
a distance. Thus, in ***Shame,*** when Max shoots Björnstrand, we are far away, and I place the crime behind a
wagon.

*But we are close to Elisabeth when she sucks Alma's blood
in **Persona**.*

Because that isn't real.

It's an expression of their relationship rather than an event?

Exactly. It's not meant to be terrifying.

This brings me to a more general area. Do you exercise total control over camera placement and editing?

Yes. When I shoot, I know almost exactly how long a scene will take because I have a sort of rhythm inside that I try to re-create.

Do you ever shoot out of sequence, knowing how things will be put together?

I only do that when contingencies make it necessary. I always try to start at the beginning, shoot forward, and then reshoot later. I always reshoot the first day's work.

There are several possible explanations for Elisabeth's refusal to speak in **Persona.** *It is an act of great honesty; since she only imitates the real suffering in the world, she decides not to get onstage night after night and mock reality with her stage grief. It is also an act of aggression against other people; her silence renders them helpless.*

It is as the doctor in the films says, "Silence too is a role." Elisabeth lacks a sense of humor. Anyone who works in this profession must keep from taking the theater too seriously; it is all a game.

Is that why you call **The Magician** *a comedy?*

Yes.

Because it is about the game of being an artist?

We artists represent the most serious things—life and death—but it is all a game.

In **Persona,** *why do you repeat the scene when Alma analyzes Elisabeth once with Alma on camera and again with Elisabeth on camera, reacting?*

Because both actresses are wonderful. First, I cut it in reverse shots, but I felt that something was missing. I felt that a whole dimension was added by repeating the scene with the other woman on camera.

Why does Alma break down and speak nonsense syllables before she leaves the island?

She has been driven nearly insane by her resentments so that words, which are no longer useful, can no longer be put together by her. But it is not a matter of psychology. Rather, this comes at the point inside the movement of the film itself where words can no longer have any meaning.

Do you think that Elisabeth deliberately sent Alma off with the letter [in which she discusses how she is using the nurse] in order that the girl may read it?

I never thought about that. Perhaps.

Something like that happens often in your films. In **Through a Glass Darkly,** *for example, Karin learns how her father has been studying her when she finds his diary. In* **The Passion of Anna,** *Andreas learns about Anna's lie by finding the letter she left in her purse. Etc. Many of your characters leave evidence about themselves for the very person who must not see it.*

Letters and diaries are very tempting. I'm extremely, passionately interested in human beings. Anything written or left behind tempts me so much that I'd read it if I could.

When my mother died—four years ago—we discovered a diary that we had not known she was keeping daily since 1916! It was a fantastic act to read it because she wrote in a microscopically small script, with many abbreviations. But suddenly we discovered an unknown woman—intelligent, impatient, furious, rebellious—who had lived under this disciplined perfect housewife.

I wouldn't dare to discuss your mother, but the characters in your films who leave evidence behind may, in a sense, be lying. After all, you yourself admit that words must arouse suspicion; the self we write about is an artistic construction.

Words . . . are . . . always . . . difficult. Now we're back to the beginning. The musician writes notes on a score, which are the most perfect signs that exist between creator and performer. But words are a very very bad channel between writer and performer.

And audience.

Yes, so I'm always suspicious of words.

Interesting fact, though: You use music less and less in your films. Why?

Because I think that film itself is music, and I can't put music in music.

Why did it take you so long to discover that?

Because I've been ambivalent.

In **The Touch** *isn't the buzz saw that we hear when Karin comes to David's apartment and finds him gone your new way to use music?*

I think everything on the sound track must complement the image—voices, noises, music; all are equal. Sometimes I feel very unhappy because I have still not found the solution to the problem of sound.

Isn't it true, however, that you use commentative sound more frequently now than in your earlier films?

Yes, it's true.

Another good example of this new use of the sound track is the fog horn in **Persona** *that signals a movement out of the real world. One last question about that film: When Alma leaves, you hold for a moment on the wooden statue of a woman which we see again in* **Shame, The Passion of Anna,** *and* **The Touch.** *Why?*

It's the figurehead from a ship. On the island where I live, I have her outside my house. She's a friend of mine, and I like her because she is made of hardwood. She represents something to me, for personal reasons.

How do you respond to the viewer who has caught such personal references—the reappearing figurehead, all the Voglers and Andreases, the discovered diaries and letters, the personal fear of birds that creates the climax of **Hour of the Wolf** *but must be invoked even to explain small moments (like the bird dashing itself against the window in* **The Passion of Anna?** *What do you say to the person who keeps seeing these things but doesn't understand their significance? Bergman is sending messages, he thinks, but what are they and why?*

Perhaps these things that mean so much to me also mean something to someone else.

You have no specific intention in repeating them?

No.

But do you see what this does to a spectator who follows you as if you were a writer? This problem has been brought on you by your own genius for creating a unique world that others wish to chart. And it's not a playful world either, like Truffaut's, with all his joking references to favorite directors and his playful casting of friends in minor roles. You don't joke in that way; even in your lightest comedy, the spectator never doubts that serious and typical issues are involved. Your admirers want to understand the layout of your world, to know the names and properties and even the importance of all these lakes, islands, rocks. What advice do you give us?

It's irrelevant. All these things are dreams—not necessarily ones that I have dreamed; rather fantasies. When you are dreaming. . . . Perhaps you remember your dreams?

Hardly ever.

But you know that you dream?

Of course. Otherwise I wouldn't sleep.

If you didn't dream, you would go mad.

Yes.

Every night you enter a world of people, colors, furniture, islands, lakes, landscapes, buildings—everything—that belongs to you alone. But if you remember your dreams and start telling them to other people, then maybe the other people will start to know you better.

Then it doesn't bother you when critics interpret you through these items?

Not at all. Not at all. And let me tell you, I learn more from critics who honestly criticize my pictures than from those who are devout.

Why then, very early in our interview, did you insist, "I don't care what you think"?

Because I had the feeling that we started with you trying to stress yourself. . . .

To make myself the subject of the interview?

No. You were so hidden. . . . I saw you had prepared very well, and you remained locked in your preparation. You knew we had little time; you wanted to start in a hurry. So you began to talk to me in a way that was very hard for me to understand. Then I just said anything to break through. Now I think we are in perfect communication. Perhaps our discussion is a little tumultuous, but I like it that way. Now we sit down as two human beings, discussing things in a simple way. When I was impolite and said, "I don't care what you think," I meant it—because all the people who are important to me. . . . Buñuel once said a wonderful thing: "I make pictures only for my friends." And they influence me. They interfere, and I listen to them, and they help me change things. But, you know, I hate the intellectual way of handling things

that are very sensual, very personal to me. Do you understand what I mean? So I just said anything that would cut us down to a level where we could communicate. I myself can't say that ***Persona*** is my best picture. . . . Ten times a month people ask me, "Which is your best picture?" but that is irrelevant to me because some of my pictures are closer to my heart than others. When we meet and you say, "This is good, and this is bad," I can't stand it, but if you say, "This is closer to my heart; I feel this; I don't feel that," then I can understand you. (pp. 181-92)

Ingmar Bergman and Charles Thomas Samuels, in an interview in Encountering Directors *by Charles Thomas Samuels, G. P. Putnam's Sons, 1972, pp. 181-92.*

Eric Rhode

During the thirties the Swedish film industry had, relatively speaking, entered the doldrums: there was no one to match the brilliance of [Mauritz] Stiller or the visionary intensity of [Victor] Sjöström. And then, in 1944, Alf Sjöberg directed ***Frenzy***. Well known at home as a stage producer and actor—his first film had been *The Stronger* (1929)—Sjöberg was an eclectic in his range of film styles and strove too hard to win international attention (an attention necessary to the Swedish film industry, though, which relies on the money made by foreign distribution). But on one occasion at least his theatricality was to marry harmoniously with his subject-matter, a screen adaptation (1951) of Strindberg's play *Miss Julie*. Sjöberg is at his best in ***Frenzy*** when his sense of style is least obtrusive, as during the moments when he builds up the atmosphere in his school location—an atmosphere more appropriate to a nineteenth-century Prussian academy, maybe, than to a Swedish school in the mid twentieth century—or choreographs scenes of bustle and conversation on the school stairs; at his worst when he resorts to a shorthand of swaying lamps and fearful shadows to suggest the terrorizing and death of a shop-girl (Mai Zetterling). In fact, the vitality of ***Frenzy*** arises from other sources: partly from Sjöberg's gift for eliciting exceptional performances from his actors—in this case from Stig Jarrel as the sadistic schoolmaster who drives the shop-girl to her death—and partly from the intensity of a screenplay dominated by the idea of an omnipresent evil. The writer of this screenplay, a young drama student, had only a marginal influence on the film; but in the light of Ingmar Bergman's later output, this influence now appears important. It is possible to surmise that Sjöberg provided the technique and much of the accomplishment of the final effect, Bergman the semi-autobiographical record of adolescent perplexity. The same kind of allocation of responsibility can be ascribed to ***The Woman without a Face*** (1947), scripted by Bergman and directed by the veteran Gustav Molander. Once again a fluent narrative style embodies a recollection of adolescent passion, naïve in statement, lacking in proportion, yet rawly, even hysterically felt. Both screenplays imply a struggle to differentiate feelings of affection from desires of a more cruel kind.

Of his first films as a director, beginning with *Crisis* (1945), Bergman has said that he prefers that they should be forgotten; and on the evidence of *Port of Call* (1948) and *Prison* (1949), his wish deserves to be respected. Picturesque views of docks and moored ships apart, they offer little more than an attempt to contain melodramatic happenings within a naturalistic, even drab framework. But in the same year as *Prison,* Bergman embarked on *Thirst,* and from almost its opening moments reveals the assurance that typifies his later work. At this stage in his development his distinction lies less in the working out of content (a complicated story that never quite knits together either thematically or as a plot) than in his ability to use the camera both in close-up and in some inventively managed two-shots to hint at the unspoken thoughts of his characters. In effect, Bergman had already discovered the secret of sustaining such tension in a sequence that he could hold a shot long beyond the spectator's natural expectation. His accurate sense of camera placement and his sense of timing (both of action within the frame and in editing) had already begun to mark him out as a distinct talent.

During the fifties it became plain that Bergman had an unusual gift for finding fictions, of a widely varied kind, that could act as vehicles for his own conflicts. His freedom to pursue this semi-autobiographical direction speaks admirably for the policy at Svensk Filmindustri. Even so, the invention with which he converted his narrow, often monotonous interests into such richly dramatic plots and images is entirely his own. His mastery of tragic idyll (*Summer with Monica,* 1953), modern comedy (*A Lesson in Love,* 1954), period comedy in the lavish and witty manner of Stiller (*Smiles of a Summer Night,* 1955), medieval allegory (*The Seventh Seal,* 1957) or introspective realism (*Wild Strawberries,* 1957) demonstrates a scope that other directors may have equalled, perhaps, but none with the same emotional commitment to certain themes and symbols: a corpus of meaning (in the main accreting around the problems facing one devil-haunted artist in particular, i.e. Ingmar Bergman) steadily to be worked on through many genres. This sense of a governing intelligence involved in the process of self-discovery was heightened by Bergman's custom of employing the same group of actors—among the more notable being Naima Wifstrand, Eva Dahlbeck, Bibi Andersson, Harriet Andersson, Ingrid Thulin, Liv Ullmann, Gunnar Björnstrand, Max von Sydow and Anders Ek—and of restricting himself to the service of two great cameramen, Gunnar Fischer and Sven Nykvist.

Bergman was eventually to put aside this symphonic virtuosity for a more austere approach, in style not unlike certain kinds of chamber music—a musical analogy appropriate to so musical a talent. As it appeared in his so-called trilogy (*Through a Glass Darkly,* 1961, *Winter Light,* 1963, and *The Silence,* 1963), the new discipline tended at first to lead to an edgy stiffness. But as the decade went on, Bergman managed to modulate his new technique so that a story containing two or three relationships at most could subtly reflect issues of a general nature—such as the theme of war in *Shame* (1968). There was still a tendency to lose problems in over-emphasis, as in the otherwise fine *Persona* (1966), and *Hour of the Wolf* (1968), but on the whole Bergman moved into the

quieter accent. He continued to refine on his mastery of the close-up—and he was to remain incomparable when filming the barely observable fleeting expression. His sense of time grew even more precise; not so much time as it passes as time felt on the pulse.

The limitations of his career would appear to be twofold. Unconsciously, perhaps, he subscribes to a notion of culture as something Olympian, cold and selfconscious in its symbolism: the kind of *Kultur* once represented by Thomas Mann, whom Bergman admires, and which no longer obtains in most countries in the West. Working within the assumptions of this kind of culture allows him easily to refer to art with a capital A (as in the lecture on Mozart's Tamino in *Hour of the Wolf*), to make metaphysical statements and to produce cross-word-puzzle type allegories that most film-makers elsewhere would find unmanageable, thinking these references either pretentious or irrelevant to their experience. Not so Bergman. A culturally isolated society allows him this kind of symbolism; yet even he cannot avoid the impression, sometimes, of having built his plots out of a pack of intellectual cards.

The other limitation is that he appears not only to dislike the majority of his characters but to feel distaste for humanity itself. So often when he slips into over-elaboration or into morbid gloating he conveys the sense that in rejecting the bad he rejects the good also. So often he directs his most lacerating attacks on good yet defenceless people. In the very considerable *Cries and Whispers* (1973) he made these difficulties into his theme, contrasting two kinds of pain: the involuntary suffering of Agnes (Harriet Andersson), who is dying from some appalling illness, and the masochistic self-inflicted pain of her sister Karin (Ingrid Thulin). But although he wishes to distinguish these two kinds of pain, Bergman continues to confuse them, and he films Agnes's death in a manner more suitable to *grand guignol* than to tragedy. He has a flair for *grand guignol* and, at moments, an awareness of the tragic: but—and it is a big 'but' that echoes throughout his career—a fascination with the destructive has often tempted him to confuse the two. (pp. 483-87)

> *Eric Rhode, "Internationalism," in his* History of the Cinema from Its Origins to 1970, *1976. Reprint by Da Capo Press, 1985, pp. 483-524.*

Robin Wood

[The following excerpt is from an essay originally published in 1978.]

If I were to rewrite my early books now, the one on Bergman (published in 1969) would certainly cause me the greatest problems, and be the one in need of the most drastic revision. When I wrote it, my sense of identification with its subject was extraordinarily intense. Beneath the apparently happy surface of a firmly traditional marriage-and-family situation, I was experiencing the sort of anguish and desperation that Bergman's films so compellingly communicate, and accepting it as unchangeable, as "the human condition." Now, it is precisely this tendency of the films to impose themselves as "the human condition" that most worries me. In a supremely revealing moment of the interview-book *Bergman on Bergman,* the film-maker asserts his innocence of any ideology, a substance by which his films are apparently completely uncontaminated. He seems to be using the term in a sense somewhat different from that in which it is usually employed in current film criticism; he means by it a *conscious* structure of social-political ideas. Yet the innocence clearly extends beyond that. There is no awareness that an ideology might exist in one's work, and centrally structure and determine it, without one's being conscious of it. The lack of an explicit social-political dimension to Bergman's work has often been noted; ten years ago I quite failed to see the force of such an objection, my own work as a critic having precisely the same lack.

Another, related way of considering the limitations of Bergman's work is via Andrew Sarris's objection that the films are repeatedly flawed by eruptions of "undigested clinical material." The obstinate recurrence of certain narrative and relationship structures in Bergman's work (structures which, I have argued elsewhere, are basically psychological, the characters representing projections of the artist's inner tensions) is plainly neurotic, and testifies to that central principle of neurosis: resistance wherein the neurosis defends itself against cure. What the films repeatedly assert, with impressive intensity and conviction, is that life under the conditions in which it is lived is intolerable, therefore . . . At which point a shutter comes down. The "therefore" should continue: "therefore we must strive to change the conditions." The shutter asserts, "the conditions are something called 'the human predicament'; they can't be changed."

In Bergman's films, neurotic resistance goes hand in hand with the resistance to any concept of ideology. Since I wrote my book he has made what I consider two of his finest films, **The Passion of Anna** and **The Touch**—though neither seems to be in general very highly regarded, and my admiration for them is not without reservations. Both films contain important elements, both in style and narrative structure, that suggest a desire on Bergman's part to open out his work, to pass beyond the stalemate in which it constantly threatens to get trapped. An extended analysis of these films would take the form of examining the conflict between these innovative elements and the resistance to them. More briefly, one can assert that nowhere more than in **Passion** has the intolerability of possessive relationships—the lies, subterfuges, resentments, frustrations, jealousies, eruptions of "psychic and physical violence," the ultimate mutual destructiveness—been more ruthlessly or vividly analyzed. Yet the films continue, doggedly, to assert all this as a fact of life, as the human condition, rather than as ideologically determined. Even **Passion,** with its relatively open structure and its excitingly spontaneous, exploratory style, can never seriously envisage the possibility that things might be changed.

In any assessment of Bergman's work I would not wish to give much prominence to **Face to Face,** which seems to me one of his very worst films, actively offensive in its self-indulgence. If I focus on it here, it is because it is his first work to deal openly with gayness, and because its treatment of gays provides so precise an index of the limitations of Bergman's work.

Near the beginning of a film devoted to portraying the inner anguish of an individual, defined in terms of personal psychology, the notion of "world revolution" is reduced in passing to a game for 14-year-olds; no possible connection is suggested between the two. Of the three gay characters, two are presented as stereotypical. (The treatment of the actor, Michael Stromberg, is more detailed and sympathetic in the published script, which one might read as a sign that Bergman was actually repressing his own sense of other possibilities in the finished film; the sympatheticness, however, takes the form of suggesting that the character shares in the general anguish.) The third, the character portrayed by Erland Josephsson, is presented favorably by Bergman, the penalty for which is that his gayness is essentially monogamous—a minimal adaptation of the dominant sexual ideology—and that he suffers. Any possible alternative to the dominant ideological assumptions about relationships is firmly put down. We are left with the familiar Bergman pattern: the heroine, tormented in adulthood by her experiences as a child, moves toward forgiveness and reconciliation across the generations. In Bergman's world, as nothing can be changed, all that people can hope for is to learn to forgive each other for the pain they inflict. (pp. 657-58)

Robin Wood, "Responsibilities of a Gay Film Critic," in Movies and Methods: An Anthology, *Vol. II, edited by Bill Nichols, University of California Press, 1985, pp. 649-60.*

Birgitta Ingemanson

Ingmar Bergman's screenplays are remarkable for their extraordinary vitality and curiously suggestive atmosphere. Reading like short stories and plays, their extensive stage directions are replete with qualitative adjectives and verbs, metaphors, similes, examples of personification, interior monologues, and other non-cinematic features which are not normally found in a genre noted mostly for its terse language, technical information, and line-by-line dialogue. While most directors use cinematic tools such as lighting, camera angle, and soundtrack as a matter of course to emphasize the points of view in their films, Bergman's screenplays, with their exact language and original verbal images, offer an additional, new angle from which to observe his work. Unless the carefully chosen words and phrases of the stage directions are injected into the dialogue of the films, only the reading public will benefit from their information. Therefore, the Bergman film viewer who is also armed with his screenplays may be better alerted to the precise tone and message of the work than the film viewer alone.

The fact that a visual artist like Ingmar Bergman spends much creative energy on literary descriptions which will rarely be transferred to the screen raises some intriguing questions about his working methods. Why is the literary aspect of Bergman's work of such great importance to him that he embellishes the screenplays at length and in astonishing detail, even though the writing causes him much agony? What is the function of this type of dramatic literature, and how has it arisen? After an outline of Bergman's use of personification and olfactory detail outside of the dialogue, and a discussion of the development of his screenplays over the years, my analysis will focus on two factors which can explain the raison d'être for this unusual kind of screenplay: Bergman's close relationship with his actors, and his philosophy of films as "consumer articles."

Two non-visual devices favored by Bergman, yet largely unobserved by the critics, are personification and olfactory information. By endowing nature and objects with human qualities and by specifying the scents that surround many situations, Bergman's screenplays manage to create a haunting atmosphere that exactly reflects the psychological dilemmas of the characters and the oppressive nature of various parts of their lives. The characters and their surroundings appear to be tragically interconnected in suffering and pain, a mutual dependency fed by the sadly human characteristics of objects and by the melancholy fragrance of nature and rooms. The reader is confronted with an enormously persuasive, sometimes tragicomic, portrayal of an ailing universe where human beings, by necessity, must be unwell too.

Bergman's personifications can be divided into two major areas. First, there is nature personified, such as the sun and moon, forests, the sea, and the sky. Nature in Bergman's screenplays is a somber backdrop, heaving and sighing in sorrow, bellowing and moaning gloomily, all the while displaying the same pain and cares as the protagonists. The sea becomes an enormous living entity, muttering, mumbling, and trembling; trees whisper and moan; clouds are meekly silent or obstinately marching forward. In *The Seventh Seal*, introducing the knight Antonius Block's harrowing religious quest, the sun "wallows up from the misty sea like some bloated, dying fish," while the forest "sighs and stirs ponderously." The sun in *The Silence* "roars over walls, steel, and window-panes," stressing the nervous pitch in the two sisters' emotional tug of war. The wind, in *Winter Light,* competing with Pastor Eriksson's flu for effect, "presses out a pained sound," and the winter day in *The Touch* "sinks, roving uneasily," parallelling the uneasiness of Karin and David's relationship and foreshadowing its imminent breakup. In *Smiles of a Summer Night* the trees "stand quiet and waiting," showing calm suspense in expectation of the conjugal regroupings.

The second group of personifications includes objects, frequently domestic ones such as houses, cars, different kinds of furniture, and small decorations, and they are also linked with the people around them in melancholy fates of illness and suffering. Bergman himself points out this close relationship, saying of quietly disintegrating Jan Rosenberg, the former violinist in *The Shame,* that "in some way the man is bound to his instrument. At the moment that his instrument is broken, along with all of his concepts, he is transformed." The violin has become a symbol of life in peacetime, and when the civil war destroys all semblance of creative possibility, Jan's final destruction is also sealed. Houses parallel their inhabitants' illnesses (as in *Through a Glass Darkly,* where Karin struggles against her approaching breakdown), bracing themselves against falling, while sighing and moaning. They seem to be on the verge of lapsing into unconsciousness: "The old house is clicking and creaking, as if it were moving quite cautiously in its sleep." The furniture is sickly, too, oozing an indifference and withering of the will which inevitably underscores Karin's apathy and mental disturbance:

> The enormous grandfather clock leans pensively against the wall, and the iron wood-stove turns away in rusty self-pity, while a bulky sofa in the heavy style of *art nouveau* is stretching in the floating diffuse light. . . . [C]uriously formed furniture monsters are asleep . . . under white protective sheets, like snowed-in prehistoric animals dead long ago.

The organ in *Winter Light* "groans," perhaps in sympathy with its tormented pastor, and Erik's dispirited visit to his wife Jenny's hospital room after her suicide attempt in *Face to Face* is accompanied by the door's opening "with a little sigh." Not only the interior in *Cries and Whispers,* where Agnes is awaiting death, but the whole landscape is infused with a sickly vagueness that attests to fading life: "the kerosene lamp blinks and sighs, [and] the eyes of the family portraits stare round and indifferent at the new day, which approaches hesitantly between the autumnal trees of the park."

Cars also take on the personalities and ailments of their owners. Machines are unwilling to start and ambivalent about stopping, deliberately (it seems) mirroring the twists and turns of the ongoing human drama. Cars bump, rattle, tremble, and creak, and their movement is cautious and full of effort: "Friberg's car [in *Winter Light*] comes slowly shuffling along down the hill." The train in the same story "fills the air with smoke and violent wheezing," as the pastor and his rejected fiancée are on their way towards a final dénouement:

> The train wallows by, thundering regally, in a haze of steam and swirling snow. Buffers and couplings clink, brakes and axles squeak. The whole train leans and creaks in the curve, [as] the switches bang away, and then it screeches its way up to the station at Frostnäs, where it stops panting and puffing.

Clocks and kerosene lamps with their natural motions of ticking and flickering seem particularly to reflect the restlessness of the human souls in their midst. Bergman pointedly writes in *Winter Light:* "The wall clock creaks; it has its own mysterious life over there in the corner." The very first lines of *Cries and Whispers* after the preface read: "The clocks in the grey dawn. They all have their personalities, their voices." These voices, continuously whispering their way through Bergman's screenplays, are described in a veritable symphony of tones: conversing with soft voices and receiving answers from one another, ticking eagerly and without remorse, morbidly counting down the seconds and years of human time. Most often they are unwell—hesitating and sighing, wobbling and creaking: "The old wall clock [in *Winter Light*] is limping, hesitating, clearing its throat."

The olfactory detail in Bergman's screenplays is no less descriptive and tantalizing than the personifications, perhaps because scent is one of the kinds of sensory impressions that Bergman retains particularly vividly. Enveloping nature, people, and interiors of houses, tending to reflect the internal condition of the given situation or characters, Bergman's carefully described smells help conjure up a specific mood and meaning. Nature around the dying Johan at the end of *The Hour of the Wolf* is also decaying: "A stench of rotting water is rising from the swamp." More characteristically, nature is full of the melancholy sweetness and longing of the short Swedish summer, underscoring the brief moments of human happiness. We read in *Persona:* "Somewhere a window is open, bringing in a cool fragrance of salt and seaweed, wet wood and rain-soaked juniper bushes," and in *Through a Glass Darkly:* "scents of ever-green forests and algae." The beginning and end of summer have their own special fragrances and meaning. *Smiles of a Summer Night* starts in late spring, and there is an expectant "smell of bird-cherry blossoms" in the Egerman household, perhaps foreshadowing the sweetness of Anne's and Henrik's love. *The Touch,* on the contrary, begins in early fall, the first dinner taking place on "a mild Sunday afternoon with a scent of lingering summer," hinting at the same leftover warmth and impossibility of sustained sunshine as in the relationship between Karin and David.

The domestic smells usually reflect dissatisfaction, perhaps caused by the sadness associated with parting, loneliness, or a lack of belonging. The hallway in *Through a Glass Darkly* gives out "a musty scent of old wood and a dying house," a fitting background for the disjointed atmosphere of Karin's life. The theme of illness in *The Silence* affects the furniture too, sofas and rugs smelling stuffy and full of dust: "The heat is stifling; there is a smell of dust and old wood." Jenny's nightmares in *Face to Face* are suffused with smells of "musty, damp cold," and Manuela's depressing workplace in *The Serpent's Egg,* the cabaret, stinks of "cabbage soup and dead rats." In *Cries and Whispers,* after the funeral, the house is full of "whispering voices and a smell of coffee," and the final picture of Anna alone includes the following sad image: "The scent of withering flowers is mixed with the cigar smoke and the smell of strangers." The debilitating mood of strange presences in a house recently the site of sickness, death, and a funeral is aggravated by the certain decay of everything that has once blossomed.

Sometimes Bergman uses smells of interiors to contrast rather than to agree with the characters' lives. While the old church in *The Touch* sadly "exudes a fragrance of rotten wood and quiet decay" before the restoration, when Karin and David visit it and their love begins to blossom, it is enveloped in smells of healthy "fresh paint and new timber" half a year later, when they meet there to say goodbye. The scents of the little church (which is David's workplace) are musty and forlorn when their life together begins, but when comfort and health have been restored to the old building, the relationship must end.

Unpleasant smells around the characters indicate not only carelessness about outward appearance but a deep psychological imbalance as well. The rapist in *Face to Face* reeks of "sweat and nicotine and dirt," and David in *The Touch* smells of liquor: "The room is stuffy and stinks of cold cigarette smoke. He is only half dressed, has not shaved, and smells of liquor and nocturnal anxiety."

Use of personification and olfactory information to indicate atmospheres of gloom, despondency, and sadness is not an unusual phenomenon in literature, and Bergman's examples are reminiscent of those of countless writers before him. But Bergman is a film director writing for the cinema, and herein lies a significant difference. Whereas works of literature such as novels and short stories are intended for the essentially intellectual purpose of being read, screenplays are ultimately designed for an audio-visual medium where verbal images, if included at all, must be expressed in the dialogue and where scents can be rendered only by deduction. The film viewer reading Bergman's screenplays and noticing their strongly literary nature may go back to the films eagerly searching for some kind of visual transformation of the rich material. Perhaps the literary images in the poignantly descriptive stage directions are meant to be transformed into cinematic language on the screen?

Surprisingly, there is little evidence in the films of an effort on Bergman's part to portray personification (or any other literary features) and olfactory detail cinematically. There is no innovative use of camera angle, sound, or lighting to re-create the literary qualities of the screenplays. In fact, a comparative examination of the texts and the finished films is disappointing in this respect. Personifications become photographed still lifes of natural backgrounds and pieces of furniture that must speak for themselves, as for example the park trees hovering in the background of *Smiles of a Summer Night* and the madonna picture in *The Touch.* In *Winter Light,* the screenplay's many exciting examples of personification have been reduced to flat pictures of the stove, the organ, and the cars. The scene with the lumbering train, although achieving a certain grimness with its coffin-like cars, is void of the turbulent inner life that the screenplay describes. Smells, if not completely ignored, can be expressed only by strong reaction, such as that of Jöns in the "witch's" presence outside the church in *The Seventh Seal.* In *Face to Face,* Jenny has to use the dialogue to inform the audience of the musty smells of mold and snow in her dreams. But her utterances never equal the sinister images of the screenplay, when in the hospital room she again sinks into her nightmares: "[She] disappears out of the world of the living and leaves Tomas on the sunlit shore. *She* returns to the land where the light is like thin ashes and the air a musty damp cold." Only in the case of clocks does Bergman retain the external signs of life in all his films: eternally, his clocks tick eagerly and sigh worriedly in rhythm with the story. But however noteworthy Bergman's obsession with clocks, by far most of his personifications and smells do not reach the screen in any form.

If the carefully worded examples of personification and olfactory detail thus have no equivalent in the films themselves, for whom are they intended? To whose advantage is it to know that the furniture is weary and the summer scents sad? The reason for the haunting animation in

Bergman's screenplays is to be found in the important and unusually creative role they play in Bergman's work with his actors, and at the same time in his strangely ambivalent feelings about that very role. Curious as it may sound, the special nature of Bergman's screenplays seems to be borne directly out of the apparent conflict between his extreme distrust of words and verbal communication on the one hand, and his nevertheless persistent need to communicate with other people on the other. In bridging this gap and as a service to himself, to his film crew, and ultimately to the general audience, Bergman proves himself an almost Taoistic master at unifying conflicting realities for a creative purpose. The direct result is his unusual kind of screenplay with its extensive stage directions and abundant use of literary images.

Bergman, like many of the characters in his films, is frustrated by extreme feelings of inadequacy in his attempts at verbal expression. Although an avid reader and a great admirer of Swedish playwright August Strindberg, Bergman has often stated that his own screenplays are not literature but mere skeletons for the visual and emotional substance of the films-to-be, simply "account[s] of moods" too bare and static to be understood or appreciated by anyone not connected with the film crew. By contrast, he considers cinema an extremely important art form, because it has immediate impact. The visual directness of the film images produces, in his view, instant reactions and through these the instant, sensory communication that is his sole artistic goal, for he desires to banish distance and isolation between people and to touch the feelings and hearts of his audience, "to come into contact, to drive a wedge into people's indifference or passivity." Under such circumstances, the written word becomes a cumbersome and unnecessary detour via the intellect, and the sign of a "correctly made" film is merely that "people have a possibility to experience the film emotionally—I don't mean intellectually." Whether the viewers laugh or cry, become angry or inspired is of no importance as long as they are not indifferent. Consequently, the meaning of each film lies in the individual viewer's own response.

[The critic adds in a Footnote: " . . . I would like to point out Bergman's seemingly intuitive understanding of the concept of 'compact' versus 'differentiated' symbols, as worked out by philosopher Ernst Cassirer. According to his tenets, human experience is communicated either through the analytical sciences (the differentiated symbols), or in art, mythology, and religion, which are more synthetic forms of expression (the compact symbols). Bergman's constant appeal to the heart and feelings demonstrates an unstated wish to let his films remain unanalyzed compact symbols."]

To illustrate this unconventional philosophy of art, Bergman cites the example of a simple man on the island of Faro who responded to a Bergman TV film according to his heart and emotions, and, disdaining all intellectual grapplings with meaning, proclaimed himself genuinely, albeit oddly, moved:

> You know [says Bergman], I live on a small island. The day after *The Rite* was shown on Swedish television, a man came to me on the fer-

ryboat going to the island and said, "It was a nice play. Don't you think it was a nice play? My wife and I, we laughed and laughed, and we had a tremendous evening together." I was completely confused; as we would judge it, he had completely misunderstood the play. But he enjoyed himself! Perhaps he had been drunk; perhaps he had gone to bed with the old girl; perhaps he was being ironic. But he enjoyed coming to me and saying it was nice. Do you understand? So we must find some way of communicating. It's very important.

The screenplay is the first physical sign of a new project, and it must be written in such a way that it perfectly communicates to the actors the desired emotional mood of the story, its vital inner "feel." To unify the seemingly irreconcilable sides of the conflict between the paucity of words and the need to communicate, Bergman overcomes his misgivings and develops a pragmatic and highly descriptive kind of screenplay. While his ultimate goal is to influence through the emotions in order to reach the senses, on the way to doing so he does find himself obliged to use the tool of the intellect—words. But what may seem like a victory of the intellect over the heart is only a partial and temporary delusion, for Bergman's language is geared to rendering the emotional atmosphere of the settings and the mood of the inner lives of the characters. Thus, conversely, the tools of the intellect come to serve the purposes of the heart. To achieve this, Bergman experiments with his screenplays until they virtually tingle with atmosphere: when the sensory background is made explicit and tangible, the direct, sensual communication that he craves becomes possible.

Bergman sees his main task in the filming as providing the tone for a project and offering the emotional stimulus and professional stability for the actors to capture it, "to create an atmosphere around the actors of security and confidence." He often leaves significant decisions about the story and the characters up to them, trusting that they will be as immersed in the film's inner mood as he is. During the perhaps most successfully productive period from the mid-1960s to the mid-70s, his film crew is a well-functioning collective where all members participate in shaping the material. By tailoring the roles for specific actors and expanding the stage directions into perfectly illustrated vignettes of mood, Bergman provides the secure emotional framework for a story or scene. Against this background, actors such as Bibi Andersson, Gunnar Björnstrand, Max von Sydow, Ingrid Thulin, and Liv Ullman are increasingly encouraged to work out the dialogue in given situations according to their own sense and artistic sensitivity, while actors less experienced with Bergman's methods, such as those playing the Grandma and daughter in *Face to Face,* are not given the same freedom.

This unusually democratic approach to filmmaking has not occurred overnight. As the director-actor relationship between Bergman and his team has evolved over the years, so its changes have been reflected in the format of the screenplays. *The Seventh Seal* (1957) looks like a play and is conventionally ordered in terms of dialogue and intervening (sometimes lengthy) stage directions. The actors learn their lines by heart and make few changes in the text.

Although the dialogue is still included in *Through a Glass Darkly* less than five years later, the stage directions have now begun to play a more important role, constituting a large and integral component of the story, where much inner information is contained. By 1970, Bergman says in an interview that his writing style has changed completely: "Nowadays I do not write out the dialogue but I write a suggestion for a dialogue. The screenplay is a collection of motifs which I then work out together with the actors while the filming proceeds." The films that have come out of these "tumultuarious" screenplays, as Bergman calls them, are for example *The Shame, The Passion of Anna, The Touch,* and *Cries and Whispers.* This is the most literary period of Bergman's writing thus far, where non-cinematic imagery is particularly prevalent. Indeed, these screenplays resemble short stories: dialogue is often rendered as indirect speech, and the conventional instructions concerning settings, emotions, and manner of actions swell into veritable prose tales. These expanded stage directions, full of literary devices such as personification, furnish considerable explanatory background to (and commentary on) the story. It is possible to speculate that Bergman's exile to an unfamiliar work situation in Munich in 1976 hastens the return to the more conventional screenplays that had begun a few years earlier with the film originally written not for the cinema but for TV, *Scenes from a Marriage.* Here, as in *The Serpent's Egg, Autumn Sonata,* and to some extent in *Face to Face,* Bergman is gradually reverting to the pre-established dialogue and fewer stage directions. The text of *Autumn Sonata* closely resembles a conventional play and is unique in that it contains virtually no inner commentary by the author.

The information contained in the lengthy descriptive passages of Bergman's screenplays, although intended primarily for the actors, can be of immeasurable value to the general public too. In accordance with Bergman's view of films as consumer articles (*bruksvaror*) much like tables, chairs, lamps, and stoves, the screenplays can be considered the *directions for use* (*bruksanvisningar*) of the films. To play a symphony without a score or repair a machine without its manual is not normally possible at the first attempt. Likewise, the film viewer will appreciate background information to be able to use the films in the best possible manner, and the screenplays provide just such a commentary by the author. Through it the work can be observed more closely and perhaps understood better. Bergman actually hints at such an approach in a passage directed to the reader in the screenplay of *Cries and Whispers,* and in the preface to *Persona,* he urges the public to use his texts in this way: "[I invite] the imagination of the reader or viewer to make free use of the material that I have made available."

The unconventional and interesting format of Bergman's screenplays is a result of their status as catalogues of moods for the films. Although written for himself and the actors, the general film viewer as well as the scholar are also justified in using them as the films' written manuals. Bergman's opposition to such a self-conscious and unspontaneous approach may be imagined; but his screenplays are carefully honed into sensitive psychological instruments containing inner clues which are too eloquent

to ignore. The texts are central to an understanding of the films, offering the public as well as the actors access to the earliest manifestation of his vision. Neither a finished product in themselves nor a goal per se, the screenplays of Ingmar Bergman provide an excellent means to illuminate the films and are as a body a well-written and innovative contribution to the genre of screenwriting. (pp. 26-32)

Birgitta Ingemanson, "The Screenplays of Ingmar Bergman: Personification and Olfactory Detail," in Literature/Film Quarterly, *Vol. 12, No. 1, 1984, pp. 26-33.*

Lynda K. Bundtzen

Fanny and Alexander, Bergman's "farewell" to filmmaking, received mixed reviews when it was released in 1983. On the one hand, the public loved it, and many reviewers supported this popular success by emphasizing the film's appeal as a family romance. Richard Hatch, for example, calls *Fanny and Alexander* an "earthy tale of fabulous beauty": "The story ebbs and flows like the seasons that pass across the screen. It contains death and birth, terror, hope and triumph. It is infectiously comic and repellently brutal. Bergman shows men and women at their worst and at their best; he has mercy for wickedness, compassion for weakness, and he rejoices in virtue." On the other hand, critics like Vernon Young, John Simon, and Stanley Kauffmann, who might be deemed experts on Bergman's *oeuvre,* who have, in the past, been responsible for calling Bergman's work to public attention, explicating its difficulties, dissecting its virtues and flaws—in brief, critics responsible for canonizing Bergman as an *auteur*—are uniform in their detestation of *Fanny and Alexander.* Young despises everything about the film, but seems especially irritated by its biographical allusions ("Narcissus endures," Young sneers). The more generous Kauffmann feels Bergman is trying too hard, and against his own artistic instincts, to be jolly: "the uplift . . . seems fabricated, unsettling . . . like an unskillful and therefore insistent falsehood." And John Simon, perhaps Bergman's greatest supporter and most rigorous analyst, generalizes his despair: "Few things are sadder than the attempt of a great artist, hitherto fully appreciated only by a minority, to reach the masses—regardless of whether or not the attempt succeeds." Implicitly, great art and great artists are "fully appreciated [and comprehended] only by a minority" of discerning viewers, and Bergman has prostituted his genius to win public approval. As might be expected, this is precisely what Pauline Kael, the lover of popular movies over snobby films, approves in *Fanny and Alexander*—at last Bergman has made a movie everyone can enjoy. Strangely, though, Kael is unable, she says, to "abandon" herself to the charms she extolls. She ends her review by separating herself from the pleasures the film affords: "It's as if Bergman's neuroses had been tormenting him for so long that he cut them off and went sprinting back to Victorian health and domesticity. The picture is an almost sustained flight of Victorian fantasy, and it may win Ingmar Bergman his greatest public acceptance. Coming from Bergman, banality is bound to seem deeply satisfying—wholesome. It can pass for the wisdom of maturity." So

Kael, too, shares an intellectual discomfort with the film's sentimental depiction of family life and damns the film for its cheerful accessibility.

What I find surprising in all of these usually astute reviewers is, first, the presumption that *Fanny and Alexander* truly and only is a sprawling soap opera—an old-fashioned costume drama suited for the popular taste and utterly and disappointingly eccentric to Bergman's career. All of these critics, in one way or another, express dismay at Bergman's repudiation of the small-scale "chamber" film and his favored topics: alienation, loss of faith, inability to communicate, and psycho-sexual pathology. Second, they all remark on the film's self-referential nature, but treat Bergman's allusions to his life and past films as tangential to the film's narrative design or merely self-congratulatory. *Fanny and Alexander*'s youthful hero with his puppet theater, *lanterna magica,* and proclivities for fantasizing is clearly a version of Bergman's boyish self; the provincial town where the Ekdahls live feels like Uppsala, home of Bergman's maternal grandmother; Bishop Vergerus both recalls Bergman's clergyman father and belongs to a whole class of Vergerus characters in Bergman's films; and finally, perhaps most important, Bergman boldly intrudes magic to change the direction of the plot in this ostensibly "realistic" nineteenth-century fiction. In brief, he flamboyantly tampers with what these critics describe as an untampered, self-contained world, repeatedly calling attention to himself as the film's creator. Kael dismisses Bergman's directorial intrusions as part of a "male fantasy," thereby exempting her feminine sensibility from sympathy or comprehension, while Simon, Kauffmann, and Young are alternately irritated and baffled, deriding Bergman's mystification and "hocus-pocus." They are absolutely unwilling to attempt an explanation for Bergman's assertive moments in the film, although they are some of the best-qualified commentators to do so.

My argument, first of all, is that no one (even Vernon Young) is less persuaded by the happy family, happy ending fiction of the Ekdahls than Bergman himself. There are several fissures in their portrayal as a comic ideal and these are quite evidently intended by Bergman. Second, . . . the film's underlying structure is a portrait of the artist as a young man, an open-ended odyssey moving the youthful Alexander through a series of significant confrontations and tableaux with symbolic import. It is closer to allegory than family romance, and this may account for the many lapses noted by critics in characters' psychological realism. Alexander's maturation from a childish dreamer to a responsible artist-figure is . . . Bergman's central concern in *Fanny and Alexander.* When Alexander is forced from the Ekdahl to the Vergerus household, he learns how to be a successful liar; and when he arrives at Isak's cluttered curio shop and apartment, a prop-room for the imagination, he confronts in the wild man Ismael his potential powers as an artist-liar, capable of projecting his fantasies into reality. Each of these environs (Ekdahl home; Vergerus palace; Isak's shop and apartment) is rendered cinematically distinct, with its own color, lighting, sounds, framing, and camera movements, resulting in provocative disharmonies that comment on

Alexander's development. These separate worlds, separate treatments, are, I believe, cinematic tropes for the violent, abrupt shifts in sexual, social, moral, and aesthetic values associated with each place Alexander stays. These values clash with one another: Vergerus and his God of truth, his asceticism, his "strong and harsh love," contradict the easy lies, the sensual excesses, the sentimental role-playing of the Ekdahls; in turn, Isak's magic foils Vergerus's self-righteousness and faith in the absolute power of a Christian God, replacing it with a reality manipulable by desire and imagination—divinity's human form.

It would be convenient—and neat—to argue that each new world Alexander enters transcends the last. Such an argument would probably soothe critics' discomfort with Bergman's exaggerations: the "warm gingerbreading" of the Ekdahls, the Gothic nightmare of a family at the Vergerus palace, the "hocus-pocus" of Isak and his weird, seemingly homoerotic nephews, Aron and Ismael. But Bergman's portrait of the artist refuses to repudiate any of these extremes in his own nature. If the film is an affirmation, it praises the artist as a creature of excess: a child with ungovernable sensuous appetites; a self-tormentor who always worries whether he is a charlatan or priest, whether his fictions are fraudulent or potentially useful truths; and finally, a wild man, subject to terrors, superstitions, dreams, and unfit at times for normal human society. Bergman refuses to resolve the conflicts between these various worlds by preferring one over another, and leaves Alexander suspended precariously between them. He also thereby permits his audience considerable latitude in their perception and response to *Fanny and Alexander*'s story, variously described as comic family romance (the happy reunion of the Ekdahls); Gothic melodrama (the foiling of the villain Vergerus); and fairy tale-fantasy (Alexander's initiation as magus). That Bergman has attempted to mingle such disparate narrative strands is in itself daring; but that he blends them often with superb irony and control is . . . testimony to his greatness as a film director. (pp. 89-92)

Lynda K. Bundtzen, "Bergman's 'Fanny and Alexander': Family Romance or Artistic Allegory?" in Criticism: A Quarterly for Literature and the Arts, *Vol. XXIX, No. 1, Winter, 1987, pp. 89-117.*

Woody Allen

The voice of genius!

"Day after day I was dragged or carried, screaming with anguish, into the classroom. I vomited over everything I saw, fainted and lost my sense of balance."

On mother: "I tried to embrace her and kiss her, but she pushed me away and slapped my face."

Father: "Brutal flogging was a recurrent argument." "He hit me and I hit him back. He staggered and ended up sitting on the floor." "Father had been taken to hospital and was to be operated on for a malignant tumour in his gullet. [Mother] wanted me to go to see him. I told her that I had neither time nor desire to do so."

On his brother: "My brother had scarlet fever. . . . (Naturally I hoped he would die. The disease was dangerous in those days.)" "When my brother opened the door, I crashed the carafe down on his head. The carafe shattered, my brother fell with blood pouring out of a gaping wound. A month or so later, he attacked me without warning and knocked out two of my front teeth. I responded by setting light to his bed when he was asleep."

Sister: "My elder brother and I, usually mortal enemies, made peace and planned various ways of killing this repulsive wretch."

On himself: "I have once or twice in my life toyed with the idea of committing suicide."

A religious household: "Most of our upbringing was based on such concepts as sin, confession, punishment, forgiveness and grace. . . . This fact may well have contributed to our astonishing acceptance of Nazism."

And finally, summing up life: "You were born without purpose, you live without meaning. . . . When you die, you are extinguished."

With this kind of background one is forced to be a genius. Either that or you wind up giggling behind locked doors in a room the walls of which have been thickly upholstered by the state. (pp. 1, 29)

The Seventh Seal was always my favorite film, and I remember seeing it with a small audience at the old New Yorker Theater. Who would have thought that that subject matter could yield such a pleasurable experience? If I described the story and tried to persuade a friend to watch it with me, how far would I get? "Well," I'd say, "it takes place in plague-ridden medieval Sweden and explores the limits of faith and reason based on Danish—and some German—philosophical concepts." Now this is hardly anyone's idea of a good time, and yet it's all dealt off with such stupendous imagination, suspense and flair that one sits riveted like a child at a harrowing fairy tale. Suddenly the black figure of Death appears on the seashore to claim his victim, and the Knight of Reason challenges him to a chess game, trying to stall for time and discover some meaning to life. The tale engages and stalks forward with sinister inevitability. Again, the images are breathtaking! The flagellants, the burning of the witch (worthy of Carl Dreyer) and the finale, as Death dances off with all the doomed people to the nether lands in one of the most memorable shots in all movies.

Bergman is prolific, and the films that followed these early works were rich and varied, as his obsession moved from God's silence to the tortured relations between anguished souls trying to make sense of their feelings. (Actually, the films described were not really early but middle works because he had directed a number of movies, not seen here until after his style and reputation caught on. These earlier films are very good but surprisingly conventional, given where he was going.) His influences by the 50's had become well assimilated as his own genius took command. The Germans still impressed him. I see Fritz Lang in his work, and Carl Dreyer, the Dane. Also Chekhov, Strindberg and Kafka. I divide his movies into ones that are

merely superb (*Through a Glass Darkly, Winter Light, The Silence, The Virgin Spring, The Passion of Anna,* to name only some) and the truly remarkable masterpieces (*Persona, Cries and Whispers* and *Scenes From a Marriage.* There are atypical ones like *Shame* and *Fanny and Alexander,* which provide their own special pleasures, and even an occasional stumble like *The Serpent's Egg* or *Face to Face.*

Yet always in Bergman's less successful experiments there are memorable moments. Examples: the sound of a buzz saw whining shrilly outside the window during an intimate scene between the adulterous lovers in *The Touch,* and the moment when Ingrid Bergman shows her pathetic daughter just how a particular prelude should be played on the piano in *Autumn Sonata.* His misses are frequently more interesting than most people's scores. I'm thinking now of *From the Life of the Marionettes* and *After the Rehearsal.*

A digression here about style. The predominant arena for conflict in motion pictures has usually been the external, physical world. Certainly that was true for many years. Witness the staples of slapstick and westerns, war films and chases and gangster movies and musicals. As the Freudian revolution sank in, however, the most fascinating arena of conflict shifted to the interior, and films were faced with a problem. The psyche is not visible. If the most interesting fights are being waged in the heart and mind, what to do? Bergman evolved a style to deal with the human interior, and he alone among directors has explored the soul's battlefield to the fullest. With impunity he put his camera on faces for unconscionable periods of time while actors and actresses wrestled with their anguish. One saw great performers in extreme close-ups that lingered beyond where the textbooks say is good movie form. Faces were everything for him. Close-ups. More close-ups. Extreme close-ups. He created dreams and fantasies and so deftly mingled them with reality that gradually a sense of the human interior emerged. He used huge silences with tremendous effectiveness. The terrain of Bergman films is different from his contemporaries'. It matches the bleak beaches of the rocky island he lives on. He has found a way to show the soul's landscape. (He said he viewed the soul as a membrane, a red membrane, and showed it as such in *Cries and Whispers.*) By rejecting cinema's standard demand for conventional action, he has allowed wars to rage inside characters that are as acutely visual as the movement of armies. See *Persona.*

All this, ladies and gentlemen, and he also works cheaply. He's fast; the films cost very little, and his tiny band of regulars can slap together a major work of art in half the time and for a tenth the price of what most take to mount some glitzy waste of celluloid. Plus he writes the scripts himself. What else could you ask for? Meaning, profundity, style, images, visual beauty, tension, storytelling flair, speed, economy, fecundity, innovation, an actor's director nonpareil. That's what I meant by the best, pound for pound. Perhaps other directors excel him in single areas, but nobody is as complete an artist in films. (pp. 29-30, 34)

Woody Allen, "Through a Life Darkly," in

The Seventh Seal: *Death leads the last dance.*

The New York Times Book Review, *September 18, 1988, pp. 1, 29-30, 34.*

Mark Horowitz

Ingmar Bergman stopped producing films, but that doesn't mean he stopped being productive. At seventy, he is still very much with us. Last fall in Los Angeles there was a production of *Miss Julie,* his first stage production ever to cross the Atlantic. This spring, New York saw his staging of *Hamlet.* Meanwhile, back in Stockholm, there's a new production of O'Neill's *Long Day's Journey Into Night.* And this fall, we have a new autobiography, **The Magic Lantern.**

Much of the new book is devoted to Bergman's life in the theater, which may come as a surprise to those who only know him as a film director. In 1979 he said that feature filmmaking was too physically exhausting for an old man. But theater was another matter: "I hope I will have the chance to work with the theater until they carry me out." He once described film as a mistress, but theater as a loyal wife. He has made over forty films, but since 1938 he has directed at least one hundred stage productions. He has

been the artistic director of several important theaters, including the Royal Dramatic Theater in Stockholm, and, for a time, he was associated with Residenztheater in Munich. His productions of Strindberg's *A Dream Play* and Ibsen's *Hedda Gabler* are legendary. In an odd twist, he even adapted his television miniseries, **Scenes from a Marriage,** and produced it as a stage play in 1981.

Bergman's career in film is certainly more familiar to us. Once he hit the international scene with **Smiles of a Summer Night** (1955) and **The Seventh Seal** (1957) he quickly became the embodiment of the European "art" filmmaker for American audiences, with his brooding black-and-white meditations on God and meaninglessness. Naturally, such a long career had its critical ups and downs. Starting in the late sixties there was a strong anti-Bergman backlash: his films were too stagey, too mannered, too pretentious, and his agony was too forced. He made a strong comeback, however, with the popular success of **Scenes from a Marriage.** By the time of **Fanny and Alexander,** a film of unexpected warmth and sentiment, nearly all was forgiven.

With the publication of **The Magic Lantern,** Bergman-watchers have another "text" to chew on and digest. The most remarkable aspect of the book is how much it reads like a script to another Bergman film. It fits neatly on the shelf alongside his last two retrospective works, *Fanny and Alexander* and *After the Rehearsal,* which is not surprising, since he always used his own life as material for his films. One can't help wondering, though, if he resisted the impulse to "improve" on the material once again. After all, the title is still *The Magic Lantern*—a movie, an illusion.

The book confirms what anyone who's familiar with *Scenes from a Marriage* and *Face to Face* already knows: Ingmar Bergman is not an easy fellow to live with. Yet for such a self-revealing filmmaker, his autobiography can be quite coy. What he avoids is almost as interesting as what he includes. His primary concern is relationships: with special emphasis on man-wife and parent-child. However, it's a strange autobiography that leaves the reader uncertain how many actual wives and children he's had. (By one count there were at least eight of each.)

He describes his childhood, particularly his tumultuous adolescent sexual awakening, in explicit detail. But Bergman speaks of his own children infrequently, and only to admit, without explanation, that he is estranged from nearly all of them. It's a sad and significant omission, since one of the themes of the book, if not its very purpose, is to come to terms with the ghosts of the author's own parents, from whom he was estranged for most of his own life.

One youngster, however, is always present, the child Ingmar, for whom fantasy, illusion, and lies are the chosen escape from an unhappy and oppressive family environment. The book shuttles, without regard to chronology, between two poles: Bergman's relatively happy adult life in the bosom of his theater family (where *he* gets to be the father) and his unhappy life as a child in the bosom of his real family. It appears that, as an adult, Bergman duplicated many of his father's alleged failures as a family man.

In some respects, all of *The Magic Lantern* can be read as a companion to *Fanny and Alexander.* The film's cruel stepfather, Bishop Vergerus, corresponds to Bergman's own true father, a Protestant minister, while the film's warm, theatrical Ekdahl clan turns out to be based on a fantasy. As an example of his childhood habit of compulsively lying, he reports telling a playmate

> that my father was not my real father, but I was the son of a famous actor called Anders de Wahl. Pastor Bergman hated and persecuted me, which was quite understandable. My mother still loved Anders de Wahl. . . . I had been allowed to meet him once outside the theater. He had looked at me with tears in his eyes and kissed me on the forehead.

The story may be a lie, but over forty years later Bergman makes it come true by "giving" himself the childhood he always wanted—on film.

The publication of his autobiography, the recent theater productions, and the release over the last few years of nearly all of his films on videocassette, are a perfect excuse for a "reevaluation" of his career, another critical reappraisal, another "comeback." But what else is there left to look at that hasn't already been over-exposed?

There *is* one area that is often overlooked by even some of Bergman's staunchest admirers: the films he made before *Smiles of a Summer Night,* his first international success, released in 1955. In fact, America's unfamiliarity with Bergman's theater work is almost equalled by our ignorance of his early film career. He wrote or directed *twenty films* by 1955.

The earlier films are usually dismissed by critics (or damned with light praise) as melodramatic and artificial. They may have foreshadowed his future greatness, but they were too literary, not cinematic enough. Worst of all, they were old-fashioned. Bergman himself may have contributed to this view when, in a 1968 interview, he called the early films mere "constructions," too tightly controlled and too dependent on theatrical conventions for his tastes. But that was twenty years ago. His last films, *Fanny and Alexander* and *After the Rehearsal,* both highly "theatrical" films, and now *The Magic Lantern,* with its strong emphasis on theater, hint at a change of heart.

Perhaps it's just that these are conservative times, but Bergman's early films look pretty good today, even on videocassette. One man's old-fashioned "filmed play" may be another's classic chamber film. They are all small, intense, intimate dramas with only a handful of characters whose problems are treated in a cool, objective style. In form, they presage Eric Rohmer's films, or some of Fassbinder's. And they lose little of their strength when seen on the small screen: in fact, their style seems ideally suited to the "cool" medium.

Bergman's taste for intimate dramas and his background in theater (like Fassbinder's) led him naturally to the television format. *The Rite, Scenes from a Marriage, Face to Face, The Magic Flute, From the Life of the Marionettes, Fanny and Alexander,* and *After the Rehearsal* were all originally made for television.

Bergman's career, seen from one angle, may constitute a sophisticated experiment in creating new television forms, rather than cinematic ones. And looking at his small, low-budget films of the early fifties, with their simple dramatic situations, intimate visual style, and a lot of great writing, it's possible to see where it all began. Nine early Bergman films, rarely seen in repertory theaters even when there *were* repertory theaters, are now available on videocassette from Nelson Entertainment. It is at first a shock to discover a Bergman who uses melodrama and comedy to get his points across; less of a shock, though, in light of his last films. What follows is a short guide to some of *Fanny and Alexander*'s ancestors.

[In *Torment* (1944)] a romantic student confronts his sadistic teacher over the girl who sells cigars in a store across from the school. A lurid melodrama, notable now for historical reasons only. Directed by Alf Sjöberg, Sweden's leading director of the time, who was unaware that he would soon be displaced by the film's first-time screenwriter, twenty-six-year-old Ingmar Bergman. A line of Bergman's first screenplay sets the tone for the next forty years: "What crime has this miserable sinner committed?"

[*Port of Call* (1948) is] the earliest film directed by Bergman currently available on videocassette, but actually his fifth effort. Adapted from a novel, this unsentimental, unmelodramatic portrait of a difficult love affair between a dockworker and a reform-school girl was heavily influenced by Italian neorealism. Studio sets are skillfully blended with actual dock and factory locations by Gunnar Fischer, Bergman's cameraman during the fifties. The sexual frankness of this 1948 film, and all of the others mentioned here, is still quite a shock, given what we're normally used to for the period. Sweden was not America. Sex is treated as an ordinary fact of life, not as a lurid secret.

Released when Bergman was thirty-one, [*To Joy* (1950)] still feels like a first or second film by a young director, even though it was the eighth film he directed and the ninth he'd written. The analysis of a relationship: scenes from the marriage of two musicians told through flashbacks. In the opening scene set in a rehearsal hall, a gruesomely melodramatic tragedy occurs—a man is informed by telephone of the accidental death of his wife, which forces him to look back over his short life with her to discover why his selfishness and ambition nearly destroyed what little happiness he had. He has to figure out how to carry on. Bergman's tough-minded theme, one that recurs throughout his career, is restated in *The Magic Lantern* where he writes, "Life has precisely the value one puts on it. . . . Living is its own meaning."

[*Summer Interlude* (1951) is] a revelation. It's surprising to find a film, so early in his career, and so long before his reputation went international, that is so fresh and beautiful. It doesn't feel a bit dated today, particularly if compared to a typical American film of 1951.

Another young love affair cut short by death. It also begins at a rehearsal, though this time the main character is Marie, a young ballerina, and the flashback is triggered by the mysterious arrival of a diary that belonged to a dead lover from her past. Though she's thirtyish, that's old for a ballerina, so the flashback to an idyllic summer of love ten years before has all the poignancy and pull of lost youth. Her trip down memory lane enables her to recover some of her lost innocence, and with it her ability to love again. The warm summer photography by Fischer is exquisite.

[*Secrets of Women* (1952) unfolds as] three separate stories told by three wives as they wait together for their husbands to arrive at a summer house. Each one is a bittersweet tale of infidelity or lost love. The most enjoyable is the third, a comic turn featuring middle-class husband and wife, played by Eva Dahlbeck and Gunnar Björnstrand, who get trapped in an elevator overnight. The wife reveals a past infidelity. But after the husband feels free to reveal his own, the wife retracts her original story. She says she made it up to get him to talk. But he'll never know for sure. This new, unexpected uncertainty arouses them both and when they're rescued the next morning—they're still married.

[*Sawdust and Tinsel* (1953) is] nonstop sadism, infidelity, humiliation, and pain—all with a circus backdrop. This grim nightmare belongs with the gloomy, God-forsaken films of the sixties—*Through a Glass Darkly, The Silence, Hour of the Wolf*—films that are best appreciated when in the grip of a bone-crushing depression.

[*A Lesson in Love* (1954)]: Truffaut discerned the influence of Lubitsch in these "old films about marriage by Ingmar Bergman." This peculiar notion, a "Bergman Comedy," is made possible by the miracle of Eva Dahlbeck, an actress he worked with throughout this period, usually teamed with Gunnar Björnstrand. She embodies all the depth and passion his heroines require but also injects an extra touch of humor that we never find again in Bergman films. She is one of the great pleasures to be discovered in these early films. In his autobiography Bergman calls her "incomparable" and he refers to her "indomitable femininity." Before there was Liv Ullmann or Bibi Andersson or Ingrid Thulin—all quintessential Bergman women—there was Eva Dahlbeck.

A Lesson in Love is a direct outgrowth of the elevator sequence in *Secrets of Women.* Bergman wanted to give Dahlbeck and Gunnar Björnstrand the chance to grapple with each other for the length of an entire film. The result is a brilliant portrait, at times both touching and comic, of a marriage hanging by a thread. All the usual Bergman elements are here. There's the philandering husband, the rebellious wife, the flashbacks, the train trips, the breakups, the reconciliations. In short—the works.

A train journey starts the ball rolling [in *Dreams* (1955)]. Eva Dahlbeck, a former model turned photographer and a younger model (Harriet Andersson) are on their way to Gothenburg for a fashion shoot. They arrive early, so Dahlbeck visits a former lover, a married man, in hopes of rekindling their relationship but the arrival of his wife brings her up short. Meanwhile, Andersson is picked up by a dashing and debonair older man (Gunnar Björnstrand) who seems to be trying to recover his own lost youth through her. The two interlocking stories move delicately between the dreams of youth and the disillusionment of age.

If [the] delicious sex comedy [*Smiles of a Summer Night* (1955)] is the only "early" Bergman film one sees, then it hardly seems possible that the director of *Cries and Whispers* could have made it. But viewed in the light of what came before, it makes perfect sense. Bergman was influenced by Molnar, Marivaux, Lubitsch, and Renoir; in turn, he influenced, among others, Sondheim and Woody Allen (both of whom remade their own versions of this film, *A Little Night Music* and *A Midsummer Night's Sex Comedy,* respectively). *Smiles* is the model chamber movie, the kind of "filmed play" that you could never find on any stage. (pp. 55-7)

Mark Horowitz, "Scenes from a Life," in American Film, *Vol. XIV, No. 1, October, 1988, pp. 55-7.*

FURTHER READING

Bibliography

Steene, Birgitta. In her *Ingmar Bergman: A Guide to References and Resources,* G. K. Hall & Co., 1987.
> Filmography and guide to secondary sources. In an introductory essay Steene discusses the relationship between Bergman's life and work.

Criticism

Armes, Roy. "Ingmar Bergman: The Disintegrated Artist." In his *Ambiguous Image: Narrative Style in Modern European Cinema,* pp. 95-107. Bloomington: Indiana University Press, 1976.
> Suggests that *The Magician* and *Persona* represent Bergman's attempts to come to terms with his role as an artist.

Baldwin, James. "The Precarious Vogue of Ingmar Bergman." *Esquire* LIII, No. 4 (April 1960): 128-32.
> Baldwin's account of meeting Bergman for the first time. Baldwin describes him as "an evangelist . . . who, for all his inflations, errors, and limits, keeps insisting that men are responsible for what is happening to men."

Brustein, Robert. "The Dreams of Ingmar Bergman." *The New Republic* 205, No. 5 (29 July 1991): 29-31.
> Positively reviews productions of August Strindberg's *Miss Julie* and Eugene O'Neill's *A Long Day's Journey Into Night,* which were directed by Bergman and performed by the Royal Dramatic Theater of Sweden.

Burch, Noël. "Fictional Subjects." In his *Theory of Film Practice,* pp. 139-55. Princeton: Princeton University Press, 1981.
> Argues that *Persona* is "a kind of synthesis of the approaches [to narrative subject matter] embodied in *Last Year at Marienbad* and *Pierrot le fou*" and suggests that one should not "interpret" Bergman: his films should be "experienced" much like a John Ford western or a Raoul Walsh crime drama.

Cavell, Stanley. "On Makavajev On Bergman." *Critical Inquiry* 6, No. 3 (Winter 1979): 305-30.
> Examination of filmmaker Dušan Makavejev's experiment in which he combined extended silent passages from various Bergman films and then discussed the results with various audiences.

Coates, Paul. "Bergman, Rymkiewicz, and Von Trotta: Women and Children as Doubles." In his *The Gorgon's Gaze: German Cinema, Expressionism, and the Image of Horror,* pp. 193-213. Cambridge: Cambridge University Press, 1991.
> Intricate analysis of *Persona* and the theme of the humiliated artist in Bergman. Coates concludes that "for [Bergman]—as has often been the case for other directors—the self-reflexive work marked a crisis and watershed in his career. The whole of the rest of that career can be read as a flight from, and repression of, *Persona,* whose exemplary clarity he would never again recover—toward the self-delusive self-absolution of *Fanny and Alexander.*"

Cook, David A. "European Renaissance: Ingmar Bergman." In his *A History of Narrative Film,* pp. 518-25. New York: W. W. Norton & Co., 1981.
> Survey of Bergman's career that pays particular attention to the two trilogies of the 1960s.

Corliss, Richard, and Hoops, Jonathan. Review of Bergman's *Hour of the Wolf. Film Quarterly* XXI, No. 4 (Summer 1968): 33-40.
> Detailed review of the film in which the authors also comment briefly on the history of Bergman's critical reception outside of Sweden.

Dawson, Jan. "Ingmar Bergman." In *Cinema: A Critical Dictionary, Volume One: Aldrich to King,* edited by Richard Roud, pp. 111-21. New York: The Viking Press, 1980.
> Survey that pays particular attention to how the theater—as a set of images and a set of themes—operates in Bergman's film work.

Donohoe, Joseph. "Cultivating Bergman's Strawberry Patch: The Emergence of a Cinematic Idea." *Wide Angle* 2, No. 2 (1977): 26-30.
> Argues that the primary thematic motif in Bergman's *Wild Strawberries*—the remembrance of things past caused by the eating or smelling of strawberries—has its origins in his *Summer Interlude* and *The Seventh Seal.*

Farber, Manny. "Carbonated Dyspepsia" and "One-to-One." In his *Negative Space: Manny Farber on the Movies,* pp. 188-94, pp. 195-99. New York: Praeger, 1970.
> First essay discusses alienation themes in films of the late sixties, including *Persona,* in which Farber is critical of the fashionable torpor of the characters but finds value in the uniquely cinematic means of its representation. The second essay discusses *Persona* and other films characterized by cinematically dynamic representations of "angst at its most enervated."

Gianvito, John. "Bergman's *Magic Lantern:* 'Living Is Its Own Meaning'." *Literature/Film Quarterly* 17, No. 2 (1989): 138-40.
> Mixed review of Bergman's autobiography, *The Magic Lantern.*

Glassco, David. "Films Out of Books: Bergman, Visconti and Mann." *Mosaic* XVI, Nos. 1-2 (Winter-Spring 1983): 165-73.
> Refutes Bergman's contention that cinema and literature are inherently incompatible. Bergman provides only the theoretical background for Glassco's argument; the texts under consideration are provided by Thomas Mann and Luchino Visconti: the former's *Death in Venice* and the latter's "banal and silly" film version of it.

Godard, Jean-Luc. "Bergmanorama," "*Summer with Monika,*" and "Telegram from Berlin." In *Godard on Godard,* edited and translated by Tom Milne, pp. 75-80, pp. 84-5, pp. 89-90. New York: Da Capo Press, 1972.
> Reviews and analyses of Bergman's work and career written for *Cahiers du cinéma* in the late 1950s.

Insdorf, Annette. In her *Indelible Shadows: Film and the Holocaust,* pp. 45-50. New York: Cambridge University Press, 1983.
> Focuses on *The Serpent's Egg*—a film not well received by most critics—and praises it for its "distanciation effects," which, as Bertolt Brecht advocated in his essays and practiced in his plays, force the spectator into a more critical, self-reflective awareness of the work, a perspective appropriate to films which deal with the

often exploited images of suffering associated with the Holocaust.

Sitney, P. Adams. "Color and Myth in *Cries and Whispers.*" *Film Criticism* XIII, No. 3 (Spring 1989): 37-41.
    Careful analysis of Bergman's use of color and a "fairy tale" narrative structure in *Cries and Whispers.*

Steene, Birgitta. "About Bergman: Some Critical Responses to His Films." *Cinema Journal* XIII, No. 2 (Spring 1974): 1-10.
    Summarizes the major Bergman criticism, finding most of it inadequate.

Wolf, William. "God, Sex, and Ingmar Bergman." *Film Comment* 19, No. 3 (May-June 1983): 13-7.
    Discusses *Fanny and Alexander* and its place within Bergman's body of work. In a brief discussion of contemporary Scandinavian cinema, Wolf also addresses the significance of Bergman's decision to retire from filmmaking.

Wood, Robin. "Images of Childhood." In his *Personal Views: Explorations in Film,* pp. 156-60. London: Gordon Fraser, 1976.
    Brief discussion of Bergman's major films that focuses on the symbolic role of "the Child" and its gradually changing importance in the structure of Bergman's Strindbergian "psychodramas."

Additional coverage of Bergman's life and career is contained in the following sources published by Gale Research: *Contemporary Authors,* Vols. 81-84; *Contemporary Authors New Revision Series,* Vol. 33; and *Contemporary Literary Criticism,* Vol. 16.

Heinrich Böll

1917-1985

(Full name Heinrich Theodor Böll; also transliterated as Boell) German novelist, short fiction writer, playwright, translator, essayist, poet, and editor.

The following entry focuses on Böll's short fiction. For further discussion of the author's life and works, see *CLC,* Volumes 2, 3, 6, 9, 11, 15, 27, and 39.

INTRODUCTION

A recipient of the Nobel Prize for Literature who has often been deemed "the conscience of the German nation," Böll is best known for satires and moral tales in which he delineates the problems of post-World War II German society. Noted for their concise and simple style, varied narrative voices, and nonconformist themes, Böll's works marked an abrupt departure from the propagandist fiction of Nazi Germany. His short stories, like his novels, are usually set during and after World War II and dramatize the plight of the victim in order to stress the need for compassion, tolerance, and social reform. Victor Lange noted that Böll's "fiction combines a sharply localized, vivid sort of reporting with that mixture of involvement and spectatorial reserve with which the experiences of the past . . . are viewed by many Germans who have remained emotionally entangled in their aftermath."

Böll was born in Cologne into a family of devout Catholics. Because Cologne was the site of numerous Nazi demonstrations in the 1920s and 1930s, Böll grew up with a strong dislike of Germany's new political structure; when asked to join Adolf Hitler's Youth Corps, he refused. After graduating from a local secondary school in 1937, Böll became apprenticed to a bookseller in Bonn and then served in Hitler's compulsory labor program. He enrolled in the University of Cologne in 1939 intending to study philology and literature, but his studies were interrupted when he was drafted into the German army. Forced to serve on the French and Russian fronts, Böll grew resentful and quickly became an outspoken critic of the German military. In 1945 he deserted from the German army and was later interred in an Allied prisoner-of-war camp. Upon being released, Böll returned to Cologne in West Germany to resume his writing career, only to discover that his early writings, including drafts of six novels, had been destroyed. Returning to writing, he published his first short story, "Die Botschaft" ("Breaking the News"), in 1947 and his first novella, *Der Zug war pünktlich* (*The Train Was on Time*), in 1949.

Böll received numerous honors in his lifetime in addition to the Nobel Prize: he was recognized by the prominent German literary organization *Gruppe 47* and became the first German president of P.E.N., the International Asso-

ciation of Poets, Playwrights, Editors, Essayists, and Novelists. A democratic socialist, Böll was also actively involved in politics, denouncing German rearmament in the 1950s as well as capitalism and calling for a social system that valued and protected basic human rights. Because his political views often contradicted government policy—in 1972, for example, he defended the terrorist Baader-Meinhof group on the grounds that its members had been denied a fair trial—he was asked to resign from his position as the president of P.E.N. and was frequently placed under police surveillance after 1974. He died in 1985.

Böll's earliest works are set during World War II and often focus on individuals who are confronted with an awareness of their own mortality and the senselessness of war. In *The Train Was on Time,* a soldier dreams of his death and seeks to validate his existence while on a three-day leave. Reminiscing about the simple pleasures of life, he realizes: "I have been ungrateful to Providence. I have denied the existence of human happiness." The ironic title work of Böll's first short story collection, *Wanderer, kommst du nach Spa . . .* (*Traveller, If You Come to Spa*), similarly details the last hours of a fatally wounded German soldier. While lying inside a schoolhouse that now serves as a makeshift hospital, the first-person narrator slowly begins to notice the artwork hanging on the walls in honor of famous military heroes. As he nears death, he recognizes that he is in the school he attended as a student only three months earlier. Many scholars have classified Böll's story as a critique of humanity's tendency to glorify war and thereby justify death and destruction, noting that "Traveler, If You Come to Spa" alludes to Friedrich Schiller's poem "Der Spazierengang," an elegy honoring the victims of war and advocating a return to nature.

Although Böll's first published story, "Breaking the News," is also set during the war, this piece introduces themes that would preoccupy Böll in his later works, particularly the sense of loss and guilt experienced by the German people following the war. "Breaking the News," which dramatizes the dilemma faced by a soldier who must inform his comrade's wife that her husband has been killed, ends with the protagonist's realization that "the war would never be finished, never as long as somewhere a wound was bleeding that it had caused." "Nicht nur zur Weihnachtzeit" ("Christmas Every Day"), a satirical story often considered a classic work of postwar German literature, similarly focuses on the problem of guilt in the postwar era, specifically the attempts of many Germans to deny that atrocities were committed during World War II. Rather than admit her share of responsibility, Aunt Milla pretends that every day is Christmas—a day she associates with joy, goodwill, and gift-giving. Although Aunt Milla's relatives buy Christmas trees and presents daily to humor her, they realize the futility of her actions and themselves explore other ways of coming to terms with the past, such as emigration and political activism.

Much of Böll's short fiction also chronicles Germany's attempts to rebuild in the years after the war. In such stories as "Der Wegwerfer" ("The Thrower-Away") and "An der Brücke"—which lampoon capitalism, the work ethic, and Germany's *Wirtschaftwunder,* or economic miracle—the government creates inane jobs for its citizens in order to curb unemployment. For example, the crippled protagonist of "An der Brücke" keeps count of the number of people who cross a local bridge, and although he usually falsifies his records, he is promoted for providing what his superiors assume to be accurate accounts. The novella *Das Brot der frühen Jahre (The Bread of Our Early Years)* examines a day in the life of a teacher who can only find work as a washing-machine repairman. Through his stark depiction of the economic hardships of postwar Germany, Böll implies that individuals who are accustomed to being deprived of food, drink, and shelter are unable to move beyond their physical needs and engage in meaningful relationships.

Although the majority of Böll's stories are concerned with World War II and its aftermath, "Die Waage der Baleks" ("The Balek Scales") and *Die verlorene Ehre der Katharina Blum; oder, Wie Gewalt entstehen und wohin sie führen kann (The Lost Honor of Katharina Blum: How Violence Develops and Where It Can Lead)* examine universal forms of persecution. "The Balek Scales" focuses on a small turn-of-the-century agricultural community whose inhabitants work for the powerful Balek family.

After one of the peasants, Franz Brücher, protests that the scale which the Baleks use to weigh the villagers' produce is inaccurate, the Baleks exert their authority—Brücher's sister is killed and his family exiled from the community. Critics note that in addition to being a tale of socioeconomic injustice, this story is a philosophical examination of humanity's inability to create a just legal system. In *The Lost Honor of Katharina Blum,* a novella based on the trial of the Baader-Meinhof group, Böll examines how the media's manipulation of public opinion may lead to violence. Katharina Blum, a housekeeper, is charged with treason after her boyfriend, a political activist, is labelled a terrorist. Since her case is tried in the newspapers rather than in the courtroom, she is forced to take matters into her own hands and to kill the reporter who is responsible for defaming her.

Like his short stories, Böll's novels often focus on postwar German society. *Und sagte kein einziges Wort (Acquainted with the Night)*, which established Böll as a master storyteller, is the tragic story of a man's inability to adjust to civilian life. *Haus ohne Hüter (Tomorrow and Yesterday)* recounts the struggle of two fatherless boys to survive in a war-torn city. Böll's novels of the 1960s and 1970s examine Germany's attempts to construct a new identity out of its Nazi past. In *Ansichten eines Clowns (The Clown)*, an alienated entertainer exposes the hypocrisy of affluent Germans, including those within his own family and the Roman Catholic church, who altered their political and moral stance for opportunistic reasons. *Gruppenbild mit Dame (Group Portrait with Lady)*, one of Böll's most accomplished and critically acclaimed works, centers around Leni Pfeiffer's attempts to defy the doctrines of a capitalistic society. *Fursorgliche Belagerung (The Safety Net)* and *Frauen vor Flußlandschaft: Roman in Dialogen und Selbstgesprächen* both focus on political unrest and disillusionment.

Because Böll was of Catholic ancestry and his fiction advocates individual rights and a return to Christian ethics, some critics have described him as a Catholic writer. Böll disliked the term, however, since the Roman Catholic church in Germany often denied human rights and even supported the policies of the Nazi government during World War II. Nevertheless, Peter Prochnik observed that Böll's "strong appeal is unquestionably rooted in the ability of Böll's readers to identify easily with his insistent claims for the rights of the individual and for a return to humane values. Essentially Böll is concerned with the dispossessed, whom he tries to save from extinction by dignifying and giving meaning to their bleak and seemingly purposeless lives."

PRINCIPAL WORKS

SHORT FICTION

Der Zug war pünktlich (novella) 1949
   [*The Train Was on Time,* 1956; also published in *Adam and the Train: Two Novels,* 1970]
Wanderer, kommst du nach Spa . . . 1950
   [*Traveller, If You Come to Spa,* 1956]
Nicht nur zur Weihnachtzeit 1952; also published in

Nicht nur zur Weihnachtzeit. Der Mann mit den Messern, 1959

Das Brot der frühen Jahre (novella) 1955
  [*The Bread of Our Early Years,* 1957; also published as *The Bread of Those Early Years,* 1976]

So ward Abend und Morgen 1955

Unberechenbare Gäste 1956

Abenteuer eines Brotbeutels, und andere Geschichten 1957

Doktor Murkes gesammeltes Schweigen, und andere Satiren 1958

Der Bahnhof von Zimpren 1959

Nicht nur zur Weihnachtzeit. Der Mann mit den Messern 1959

Die Waage der Baleks, und andere Erzählungen 1959

Als der Krieg ausbrach (novellas) 1956; also published in *Als der Kriegausbrach; Als der Krieg zu Ende war: Zwei Erzählungen,* 1962
  [*Enter and Exit* published in *Absent without Leave: Two Novellas,* 1965; also published in *Absent without Leave, and Other Stories,* 1967]

Die Essenholer, und andere Erzählungen 1963

1947 bis 1951 1963

Entfernung von der Truppe (novella) 1964
  [*Absent without Leave* published in *Absent without Leave: Two Novellas,* 1965; also published in *Absent without Leave, and Other Stories,* 1967]

18 Stories 1966

Ende einer Dienstfahrt (novella) 1966
  [*End of a Mission,* 1967]

Children Are Civilians, Too 1970

Erzählungen, 1950-1970 1972

Die verlorene Ehre der Katharina Blum; oder, Wie Gewalt entstehen und wohin sie führen kann (novella) 1974
  [*The Lost Honor of Katharina Blum: How Violence Develops and Where It Can Lead,* 1975]

Du fährst zu oft nach Heidelberg, und andere Erzählungen 1979

Gesammelte Erzählungen. 2 vols. 1981

Der Angriff: Erzählungen, 1947-1949 1983

Die schwarzen Schafe: Erzählungen, 1950-1952 1983

Die Verwundung, und andere frühe Erzählungen 1983
  [*The Casualty,* 1986]

Veränderungen in Staech: Erzählungen, 1962-1980 1984

The Stories of Heinrich Böll 1986

NOVELS

Wo warst du, Adam? 1951
  [*Adam, Where Art Thou?,* 1955; also published as *And Where Were You, Adam?* in *Adam and the Train: Two Novels,* 1970]

Und sagte kein einziges Wort 1953
  [*Acquainted with the Night,* 1954; also published as *And Never Said a Word,* 1978]

Haus ohne Hüter 1954
  [*Tomorrow and Yesterday,* 1957; also published as *The Unguarded House,* 1957]

Billard um halb zehn 1959
  [*Billiards at Half-past Nine,* 1961]

Ansichten eines Clowns 1963
  [*The Clown,* 1965]

Gruppenbild mit Dame 1971
  [*Group Portrait with Lady,* 1973]

Fürsorgliche Belagerung 1979
  [*The Safety Net,* 1981]

**Der Vermächtnis* 1982
  [*A Soldier's Legacy,* 1985]

Frauen vor Flußlandschaft: Roman in Dialogen und Selbstgesprächen 1985

OTHER

Irisches Tagebuch (travelogue) 1957
  [*Irish Journal,* 1967]

Ein Schluck Erde (drama) 1962

Missing Persons, and Other Essays (essays) 1977

Werke: Romane und Erzählungen. 5 vols. (novels, novellas, and short stories) 1977

Was soll aus dem Jungen bloß werden?; oder, Irgendwas mit Büchern (autobiography) 1981
  [*What's to Become of the Boy? or, Something to Do with Books,* 1984]

Heinrich Böll als Lyriker (poetry) 1985

*This work was written in 1948.

CRITICISM

Edward Grossman

[In *18 Stories*], Heinrich Böll begins a short story about the moral price-tag on prosperity this way:

> That evening we had invited the Zumpens over for dinner, nice people; it was through my father-in-law that we had got to know them: ever since we have been married he has helped me to meet people who can be useful to me in business, and Zumpen can be useful: he is chairman of a committee which places contracts for large housing projects, and I have married into the excavating business.

At least two-thirds of the stories here (admirably translated by Leila Vennewitz) sustain this dry, suggestive voice. In them Böll is convincing: he is in control of his language, of his goal, of the reader, and most pleasing of all, his clear eye for a multitude of mundane villainies does not keep him from sympathizing with his protagonists. They are spiritual outsiders to the *Wirtschaftswunder* but hardly able to act significantly against it. In **"The Thrower-away,"** a functionary is making a comfortable living simply unwrapping and disposing of junk mail for a corporation. Subconsciously despising himself for this non-work which flush times have given him, he seeks to rescue his esteem with self-imposed "research" in his field:

> I am making an intensive study of a young man from my neighborhood who earned his living as a book reviewer but at times was unable to practice his profession because he found it impossible

to undo the twisted wire tied around the parcel, and even when he did find himself equal to this physical exertion, he was incapable of penetrating the massive layer of gummed paper with which the corrugated paper is stuck together. The man appears deeply disturbed and has now gone over to reviewing the books unread and placing the parcels on his bookshelves without unwrapping them. I leave it to the reader's imagination to depict for himself the effect of such a case on our intellectual life.

What can mar a Böll story—and a handful here are imperfect—is when his sympathy goes over into pathos, as in **"The Death of Elsa Baskoleit,"** an elegy to the memory of a little girl killed in the war. The two novels for which Böll is known in this country, *Billiards at Half-Past Nine* and *The Clown,* though they stand among the best work to come out of Germany since the war, are sporadically hurt by the same kind of too-vivid identification of the author with sensitive misfits who find themselves separated from the dominant strain of callous, optimistic Teutonism. This sentimentality is curious in a writer who can be as viciously anti-sentimental as Böll is in his rendering of a lady-listener's letter to the PR man at the state radio station:

> The way the canine soul is being neglected in radio is gradually becoming a disgrace. And you call that humanism. I am sure Hitler had his bad points: if one is to believe all one hears, he was a dreadful man, but one thing he did have: a real affection for dogs, and he did a lot for them. When are dogs going to come into their own again in German radio?

I prefer Böll when he is in this frame of mind to when he is over-drawing his humanity, which is considerable to begin with—especially in comparison to the rougher and more inventive Gunter Grass. Within the form of a short story Böll is often able to strike a fine balance between his twin tendencies. The result is gratifying to read and sometimes quite funny. (pp. 33, 35)

> *Edward Grossman, "Price Tags on Prosperity," in* The New Republic, *Vol. 155, No. 20, November 12, 1966, pp. 33, 35.*

The Times Literary Supplement

The discovery that *Absent Without Leave*—a generous offering of two novellas and sundry short stories—is only the third of Heinrich Böll's works to have scaled the language barrier comes as something of a shock. Heinrich Böll is after all—despite his comparative youth—a Grand Old Man of the literature that has grown up in Germany since the Year Zero.

Appropriately enough a fair slice of this collection deals with events of the Year Zero and the preceding minus timescale. The title story [**"Absent Without Leave"**] is a recollection—in broken-backed tranquility—of an all-too-brief wartime interlude of happiness; in the telling of it past and present interweave apparently at random—until a sudden convergence of images establishes in painfully

sharp focus the narrator's hysteria-tinged sense of irreplaceable loss.

Not every wartime tale in the volume conceals the same emotional depth charge, although they all share a pervasive mood of vulnerability as if the characters in them moved through situations without skin on their bodies. Sardonic humour surfaces in unexpected places: an earnest POW entrained for home talks endlessly about Tucholski, Karl Kraus and Germany's spiritual rebirth while sewing on the ensign's piping around the shoulder-straps of his redundant uniform.

Even more sardonic—and vaguely evocative of Kraus in its outraged hilarity—is a phantasmagoria called **"Bonn Diary"** in which a group of aristocratic officers bring about the posthumous exoneration of their former commander by producing proof that he was responsible for the death of far more men than had previously been estimated.

Complementing the war stories are evocations of peace—only in Herr Böll's world is peace not so much the antithesis of war as its transcription into a minor key. "Economic miracle" vignettes read like front-line reports on a peace that passeth understanding; a well-primed applicant for a job avers, "I no longer acknowledge the term free time—on my fifteenth birthday I eliminated it from my vocabulary, for in the beginning was the act", and a chair-borne business executive exhibits dynamic adaptability by simultaneously conducting conversations through two telephones, taking notes with a pen gripped between his teeth and operating a knitting machine under his desk with bare feet.

For the reader's bemused edification Herr Böll also displays species of economic man farther from the mainstream—the throwaway expert, whom destruction fills with creative frenzy, and the professional laugher whose home resembles a morgue. The introvert laughing for a livelihood is brother under the skin to the assistant radio producer Murke, who collects "silences"—blank snippets of recorded tape—and plays them back to himself at home as the only form of therapy enabling him to carry on in his job.

Another batch of stories revolve around an even more painful process of adaptation: that of children bruised by their first contact with an adult-made world of examinations, injustice and sexual taboos. These—for reasons not unconnected with the author's make-up—are the finest items in the collection. For all his distancing devices of urbane irony Herr Böll is essentially a guardian of innocence against the contagion of the world; the sensitized plate of his imagination registers—as does the childish mind—nuances of deceit and turpitude beyond the range of normal vision. In addition he is, of course, a fertile story-teller; and it is his unique combination of moralist and fabulist that makes him a writer who deserves a wider reputation here than he has previously enjoyed.

> *"Confessions of Zero," in* The Times Literary Supplement, *No. 3393, March 9, 1967, p. 181.*

Wilhelm Johannes Schwarz

[The essay excerpted below was originally published in German in 1967.]

[In 1950, Böll's first collection of short stories] was published under the title *Traveller, If You Come to Spa.* The spare, unadorned language of these short pieces fits their theme; they all throw light on the lot of the little man in the war and postwar years. **"Uber die Brücke"** is meant to give the reader the comforting feeling that despite apocalyptic upheavals the world will eventually straighten out and be its old self again; though German cities lie in ruins and ashes, wherever a house still stands, its windows are cleaned every Thursday, just as they always were. No doubt it is glad tidings of this kind that led Günter Blöcker to write of Heinrich Böll: "With touching, almost fatherly care this author seeks to paper over and drape the cracks and rents in our home the world."

"Kumpel mit dem langen Haar" is the story of an uprooted black-market dealer who wanders about aimlessly, escapes a police raid by the skin of his teeth, and eventually meets a young girl who, like himself, has nowhere to stay and leads an unsettled life in railway stations and waiting rooms. With impressive simplicity Böll describes this human encounter in a godforsaken time: "When it became cool, toward morning, I crept quite close to her, and she spread a part of her thin little coat over me. Since then we are together—in this time."

"Der Mann mit den Messern" is the story of two wartime friends who find it hard to get used to postwar conditions. Jupp has become a knife thrower in a nightclub, and the narrator, a former first lieutenant, makes a scant living with occasional work. This piece, too, ends with a tenuous ray of hope, though it disdains any cheap optimism: the narrator offers himself as a target to his friend, and in this profession finds some sort of satisfaction, because now he indeed stands on his own feet: "But I only grasped an hour later that I now had a real profession, a profession where I merely had to stand there and dream a little. For just twelve or twenty seconds. I was the man you threw knives at. . . ."

Several others of Böll's characters hit upon similarly miserable jobs. The disabled ex-serviceman in **"An der Brücke"** has to make a daily count of the people who cross the bridge. He finds a certain satisfaction in never counting the woman he secretly adores when she crosses the bridge, which, as it were, is his protest against this humiliating occupation. In his turn, the former black marketeer in **"So ein Rummel"** is prepared to take on any job at all: as roustabout in a circus who strikes tents, greases wheels, is brakeman on the rides, hammers nails, peels potatoes, or distributes soup. When at last he is allowed to take over the circus box office, he is overcome with happiness and kisses the hand of the proprietress. In Böll's stories people are modest. They do not dream of the great stroke of luck, they just look for a refuge so as not to end up in the gutter.

The stories **"Steh auf, steh doch auf"** and **"Wiedersehen mit Drüng"** both progress from a realistic, down-to-earth beginning to a vision of the hereafter. In both stories the antiheroic hero is defeated by his merciless destiny, but finds consolation in a dream vision of the luminous figure of a woman who waits for him with a smile in a paradisiacal landscape. A similar transition from realistic to fantastic scenery occurs in the story **"Die Essenholer."** A group of four and a half men are on the way to collect their rations (the half man is the mutilated corpse of a young sapper, a demolition engineer, whom the others carry along). The dead man gets heavier and heavier, and yet another heavy shellburst brings the change to the hereafter: "I knew then that I was at another destination, and would truthfully have to report four and a half men, and as I smilingly repeated to myself 'Four and a half,' a great voice said tenderly: 'Five!'" The story **"Wiedersehen in der Allee"** ends in a similar, if less surprising, manner. This device of a sudden transition to the world beyond seems somewhat too deliberate; in later stories Böll did without such solutions.

"Damals in Odessa," "Trunk in Petöcki," and **"Aufenthalt in X"** tell of soldiers who wanted to have one more fling before going to their almost certain deaths. These marked men do such things as pawning their clothes so as to eat and drink well just once more, or they spend their last night with a girl before being taken to the front by train or flown to the encircled Crimea. In **"Wiedersehen in der Allee"** Lieutenant Hecker relives in his memory a romantic passion of his youth while he gets blind drunk— and then is shot dead by snipers. **"Wir Besenbinder"** is the story of a soldier who, for many years at school, was always called a broommaker by one of the teachers because of his poor performance. Before he is bundled into the aircraft, which subsequently crashes, he observes for the first time in his life a real broommaker, whose calm and simplicity as he does his modest but meaningful job strike the soldier as comforting in comparison with the meaningless war. The teacher's disparagement suddenly ceases to matter to him, and shortly before his death he envies this broommaker, who is left undisturbed to exercise a peaceful trade. The contrast in this story between grandiose technical organization in the service of destruction and modest, primitive, but peaceful and useful work is a recurring theme in Böll's work.

"In der Finsternis" is a study of trench mentality. Dryly, in the most matter-of-fact way, the author tells of a night in a front-line dugout. There is not the slightest trace of that romanticism of the trenches exemplified in Ernst Jünger. The enemy is not even mentioned, we only hear of a few dead soldiers in front of the line. A young and an old soldier share a hole together, and when one of them strikes a match, they look at each other: "Every time there was some light again, they first looked at each other. Yet they knew each other well, much too well. So well that they almost hated each other; each knew the other's smell, almost the smell of each pore, and still they looked at each other, the older and the younger man." In the dark they catch one of their comrades in the act of prizing the gold teeth out of the corpses in front of the lines. Without more than a few words the body-stripper is killed by his fellows, and the trench again lies in deathly darkness.

The narrator of the story **"Die Botschaft"** is a soldier who has come back from the war and is on his way to give a certain Mrs. Brink the news of her husband's death. Before knocking at the door he hears the woman laugh, the cryptic, cooing laugh of a woman who is not alone. He finds her in a man's company in a shabby room smelling of poor food and very good cigarettes. Böll says little but intimates much. Three years ago the short, buxom woman had taken her husband to the station, and now she wants to know when he died. When she hears the date, she thinks it over for a moment, " . . . And then she smiled—quite pure and innocent—and I guessed why she smiled." When they say good-bye, the woman asks her visitor not to despise her, but he is taken aback: "For heaven's sake, did I look like a judge? And before she could prevent it, I had kissed this small, soft hand, and it was the first time in my life that I kissed a woman's hand." Böll draws his characters with tenderness and indulgence, even the "sinners," and he often shows the reader why they became sinners.

As in so many of Böll's stories, the scene in **"Abschied"** is laid on a platform with a train about to leave. The narrator accompanies the girl he loves to the station. She wants to go to Sweden to join a man who has settled in a job there, while the man who tells his own story will remain in devastated Germany, with his injured leg. Gert Kalow calls this piece a "love story in black, tenderness in the midst of horror." The very first paragraph places us in a typical setting: "Like all stations, the station was dirty and drafty, full of exhaust steam and noise, noise of voices and of cars." Böll's typical vocabulary—filth, rags, rubble, hunger—is used here in a routine manner. **"Abschied"** is an atmospheric sketch rather than a short story or narrative as defined by Böll. Nothing happens; the two converse in broken, clipped sentences, and then the train slowly pulls out and away into the darkness.

Nearly all Böll's stories are set either in devastated Germany or in Hungary, Poland, Rumania, or Russia. Exceptionally, France is the scene of **"Unsere gute, alte Renée."** Again we find the characteristic accumulation of adjectives like dirty, filthy, listless, monotonous, sullen, hungry, and tired. The tale is simple enough: A soldier passes the time of day with a slattern who runs a pub and learns that next day she is going to hand over the business to her niece because the listless singing of the German occupation unit, day after day, has become unbearable to her. The soldier finally says that he is afraid the niece may have not only a patriotic mouth, but patriotic hands as well. What Böll means by patriotic hands remains open, but then he not infrequently uses a vocabulary of this kind that seeks to force a peculiar effect of its own by means of an obscure hint of meaning.

"Mein trauriges Gesicht" is set in an imaginary country where unhappiness is a punishable offense. It is a country such as one might expect to find in the work of Franz Kafka: Public Law No. 1 in this utopian country reads "Every policeman *may* punish everybody, and *must* punish everybody who has committed an offense. For all comrades there is no impunity, but the possibility of impunity." Everything in this country is controlled by the state. The countryside is made level, cleaned and cared for, and the state publishes lists of persons permitted on certain days of the week to drink beer or to partake of hygienic

pleasures in the state's love barracks. **"Mein trauriges Gesicht"** is to be understood as a satire on the modern totalitarian state, which confines the life of the individual entirely within the rules and regulations imposed by bureaucracy. (pp. 4-8)

In **"Kerzen für Maria"** we hear the voice of Heinrich Böll the Catholic. (Böll does not want to be described as a Catholic writer. He calls himself a novelist who, among other things, happens to be also a Catholic.) Two motifs are sounded, and eventually merge. The first concerns a little man's struggle for existence in capitalist society, the second the vexations which beset young lovers amid the prejudices of such a society. The contradictions are overcome on the religious plane, in a Catholic church. A traveling salesman vainly tries to sell an assortment of hand-dipped candles of sound value, whereas the tawdry mass-produced output of the devotional-articles industry finds a ready market. At the inn where he spends the night there are also a young man and his girl, who, in deference to the suspicious landlady, take two separate rooms. The next morning the traveling salesman aimlessly roams about the town until he finally winds up in a church. Here he meets the lovers again, who are going to confession together. Following their example, he, too, goes to confession, for the first time in seven years. At peace with their God the three of them leave the church; but before he goes, the salesman lights all his candles in front of a stone statue of the Virgin.

The sufferings of children in Germany between the end of the war and the currency reform are recalled in **"Lohengrin's Tod."** The little hero of this story has fallen off a train from which he was stealing coal; a few hours later he dies of his severe injuries in a hospital. Böll describes the confused sequence of ideas racing through the child's head shortly before his death. Worries about his younger brothers and sisters alternate with scraps of memory concerning black-market prices, the theft of coal from guarded trains, and bread, again and again, mountains of bread. These are the delirious fantasies of a child that has had to fend for himself, without help, in a menacing world of grownups.

Kafka's influence can be traced in the two stories **"Geschäft ist Geschäft"** and **"An der Angel."** In the first of these the narrator tells of a former black marketeer who managed to switch over smoothly to the new conditions following the currency reform. He now owns a wooden booth at a busy street crossing; he wants to have nothing to do any more with his former fellow soldiers and black-market friends who missed the connection with the approaching German economic miracle. The narrator compares their life to a tram journey which never comes to an end. The same image of a tram ride was used by Kafka as a metaphor for life in "Der Fahrgast": "I am standing on the platform of the electric car and am totally uncertain about my position in this world. I could not give even an approximate indication of what claims I might advance in any direction whatever." (pp. 9-10)

In the story **"An der Angel"** the narrator, rather like the land surveyor K. in *The Castle* or Josef K. in *The Trial,* feels menaced by unknown powers which reduce him to helplessness. Every day he waits for his girl friend at the station, but he waits in vain; his girl friend does not come. He assumes that she is held up by anonymous, uncontrollable powers: "They detain her, they are against it, they begrudge me my girl, they begrudge my having more than a minute's hope for once, let alone joy. They obstruct our rendezvous; somewhere they sit and laugh, this clique." Nothing definite is said about the nature of these powers; there is a mere hint that they are influential, all-powerful authorities: "In this clique they stick together, they administer hope, they administer paradise and consolation. They get their clutches on everything." Repeatedly, the narrator decides to commit some desperate deed. He wants to murder the "flag wagger" at the station, for he suspects him of being in league with "them." But he knows that he is powerless against "them": ". . . There is no getting at them." As with Kafka, man is the plaything of alien, intangible powers. But while for Kafka escape is impossible, Böll points to love for a fellow human being as a means of enduring the menaces of modern life. His story ends with the image of loving understanding between two people, which overcomes their former isolation and loneliness. Indeed, the narrator finally bursts out laughing, in a liberating, redeeming laugh: "They rush out of the hut, they'll nab me, but I laugh at them, laugh at them, for the train has come in, and before they can get me she is already in my arms, she, and I own nothing but her and a platform ticket, her and a punched platform ticket. . . . "

Finally, the title story of the first edition of this collection, **"Traveller, if you come to Spa,"** shows us the Rhinelander Heinrich Böll, for whom there is no significant difference between National Socialism and Prussianism: ". . . And along the staircase itself . . . there they all hung in a row, from the Great Elector to Hitler. . . . " A few lines further on he writes sarcastically: ". . . Here was the specially beautiful, specially large, specially colorful portrait of the *Alter Fritz* in sky-blue uniform, with radiant eyes and the big, golden splendor of the star on his chest." The plot, once more, is as simple as could be: A gravely wounded young soldier is taken to a school which serves as an auxiliary hospital. In the pictures he recognizes Nietzsche, Togo, Feuerbach's Medea, and the customary "purebred," but he remembers that these pictures are hung in all the humanistic secondary schools of Prussia, alongside the busts of Caesar, Cicero, and Marcus Aurelius. Only when he recognizes his own handwriting on the back of a large blackboard does he realize that he is lying in the same school that he attended every day no longer than three months ago. Seven times, in modern script, Gothic, italics, Roman, English-Italian, round hand, and in his own writing, he had been made to write on the blackboard: "Go tell the Spartans, thou that passest by, that here, obedient to their laws, we lie;"—*Wanderer, kommst du nach Sparta, verkündige dorten*. . . . That Böll should have chosen a fragment of the inscription on the monument to Leonidas and his three hundred Greeks as the title for his book testifies to his reservations with respect to all the traditions of military fame that have nothing more glorious to hand down than the death of the hero. (pp. 11-13)

[In 1955, Böll published a small collection] under the pre-

tentious title *So ward Abend und Morgen,* which, in addition to the title story, contained four others: **"Das Abenteuer," "Die Postkarte," "Der Tod der Elsa Baskoleit,"** and **"Die Waage der Baleks."** The last two merit special attention, while the rest are again definitely marked by the "stuffy middle-class homeliness" mentioned by Günter Blöcker. The theme of **"Der Tod der Elsa Baskoleit"** is not so much the death of the little dancer itself as the paralyzing, destructive influence it exerts on her father. The narrator used to watch Elsa Baskoleit as a little girl, when, dressed in bright green tights, she practiced dancing steps in the basement. Then the war had come, and the postwar years, and he had never heard anything about her again. But one day he calls at the shop, now gone to seed, where the strangely distracted father serves an occasional customer. To each of these customers Baskoleit says merely the one, stereotyped sentence: "My daughter has died," or "She is dead." He does not say good morning to these people nor ask what they want; he just keeps repeating in a perplexed and helpless way: "My daughter has died; she is dead." A woman replies in a bored voice that she has known that for five years now and meaningfully taps her finger on her forehead; another woman starts to cry, but Baskoleit sees nothing and hears nothing, and merely keeps saying his little piece: "My daughter has died; she is dead." It is a matter-of-fact account, dealing exclusively with externals, but in combination with the recurring repetition of the two key sentences, it represents in the simplest conceivable manner the old man's pain, loneliness, and hopeless forlornness.

"Die Waage der Baleks" is a story that one could imagine as not out of place in Bert Brecht's *Kalendergeschichten.* For centuries the Balek family has been buying up cheap supplies of mushrooms, herbs, and wild flowers from the people of the surrounding villages and selling them at a profit in the town. As time goes on the Baleks get richer and richer, and in 1900 they are knighted by the Emperor. In the same year it so happens that a little boy tests the Baleks' venerable scales, on which the villagers' labor has been weighed for five generations; the scales give the wrong weight. There is an uproar, the scales are stolen, and the people feverishly calculate how many thousands of talers they have been defrauded of by the Baleks in the past decades. Right in the middle of their calculations the police arrive and forcibly take back the scales. But the boy's parents have to leave the village, and they never settle down again, because wherever they go, "the weights are wrong." "And anyone who would listen to them heard the story of the Baleks of Bilgan, whose justice was short by a tenth. But hardly anyone would listen to them." The story contains Böll's claim for social justice, which recurs in many of his works.

Theodore Ziolkowski declares that many of Böll's short stories are nothing but the "logical development of an absurd premise." As examples, Ziolkowski mentions **"Mein trauriges Gesicht"** and **"An der Angel,"** but his statement can be applied with equal justification to the comic stories of the volume *Unberechenbare Gäste* (1956). The title story describes the situation of a family so exaggeratedly fond of animals that it soon finds itself surrounded by rabbits, chicks, dogs, a tortoise, a hippopotamus, and a lion.

Like most of Böll's short stories it is told in the first person, and the father of the family, who is the narrator, explains the premise which eventually turns the house into a small zoo: "For my wife is a good woman, she turns no one away, neither man nor beast. . . . "

"Im Lande der Rujuks" is a skit on the unworldly professor in general and the philologist in particular. James Woodruff, the founder of Rujukology, is the holder of the world's only chair in Rujukology. For the last thirty years he has had precisely two students, one of whom became a money changer when he had completed his studies and was thus lost to science. The second student is the fictitious narrator, who, after eighteen years of research on the language, customs, and religion of the Rujuks, sets out to make the personal acquaintance of this wild tribe living on an inhospitable island to the south of Australia. He is in for some surprises. The first man he meets is a drunken raccoon hunter who asks him in perfectly ordinary English for news of Rita Hayworth. The primitive natives that he expected divert themselves in bars and noisy motor boats. The name of a mythical figure that he keeps hearing again and again is finally identified as "Zarah Leander." Disillusioned, he returns to Germany and henceforth devotes himself to growing fruit.

In **"Hier ist Tibten,"** Böll pokes fun at the modern tourist racket. This is not a new attitude; in *The Unguarded House* Böll had already mentioned the "Swedish cannon ball" over the city gates of Bietenhahn, made by Schmitz in his workshop, and in *Billiards at Half-Past Nine* sentimental tourists shed bitter tears over Roman children's graves that are nothing of the kind, while the pretty girls acting as guides competently control the visitors' grief in four languages. A similar note is struck in **"Hier ist Tibten."** Travelers come from all over the world to visit the grave and the toys of Tiburtius, who is supposed to have drowned himself eighteen hundred years ago for unhappy love. The toys of Tiburtius are pretty little figurines, a free bonus handed out with "Klüsshenner's Eggyolk Margarine." The original statuettes from Roman times lie in the narrator's drawer together with more margarine dolls, and sometimes he vainly tries to sort out the real ones. The narrator himself has studied at five universities and taken two degrees, only to call out every day at the station: "This is Tibten. You are in Tibten. Passengers wishing to visit the grave of Tiburtius, alight here. . . . " Curt Hohoff describes these last two pieces as "sociological parables" and compares them with similar works by Joseph Roth.

A tone unusual for Böll distinguishes **"Mein Onkel Fred,"** in which the German "homecomer's" readjustment and transition from the black-market period to the time of the economic miracle is described in a markedly optimistic and positive manner. The style is informal, easy and smooth. The homecomer is no longer left standing "outside the door," he has become a figure rather like Wolfgang Borchert's Uncle in "Schischyphusch": carefree, lovable, robust, irresistible. Without any trouble at all he takes to the new conditions and transforms himself from a tattered homecomer into a successful businessman. (pp. 21-3)

Another small collection of stories was published in 1958 under the title **Dr. Murkes gesammeltes Schweigen und andere Satiren.** In addition to **Nicht nur zur Weihnachtszeit,** . . . it includes four other satires. Again all the pieces start out from absurd premises and probe their extreme logical consequences. Inge Meidinger-Geise writes about this book:

> Böll's courage in exaggerating for the sake of the inner truth, his language composed of Kafkaesque profundity and lapidary irony, yet without epigonous pallidness or mannerisms, his critical religious faith which enables him to answer the clever bourgeois with a single sentence in praise of simplicity and calm, his sense of composition which can be traced in this volume especially in its subtle, measured development . . . all that makes this volume a little jewel of contemporary satire.

As a satirist Böll always shows himself gay, amiable, and slightly ironic; he never becomes waspish, sneering, or caustic. (p. 26)

Böll's targets in this book are certain manifestations of the German economic miracle. In [**"Dr. Murkes gesammeltes Schweigen"**] it is modern broadcasting with its inflated culture industry that comes in for his gently humorous mockery. In view of the public's new attitude of mind and the new turn in business conditions the famous Bur-Malottke causes the word "God" to be excised twenty-seven times from the tape recordings of his speeches, and has it replaced instead by the phrase "that higher Being which we venerate"; in his turn, Dr. Murke of the "Cultural Talks" division is so nauseated by the hurly-burly of transmissions that for relaxation at home he plays over a tape made up of silences. As regards language, this and the other satires keep to a seemingly effortless conversational tone. In **"Es wird etwas geschehen"** the attack is directed against the tremendous display of activity and useless energy in West German business life. However, the picture of the man with a telephone receiver in each hand and in his mouth a ball-point pen with which he makes notes, while with his bare feet he works a knitting machine under the table, overshoots its mark through sheer exaggeration; irony has degenerated into crude slapstick that fails to bring off the intended exposure. The relevance to reality is more convincing in **"Hauptstädtisches Journal"** and **"Der Wegwerfer."** Colonel, subsequently General, Erich von Machorka-Muff, who in his dreams sees himself on thousands of monuments, is a caricature of the German officer, and the language of this satire (**"Hauptstädtisches Journal"**) is a masterly parody of army jargon: " . . . Soon we were deep in reminiscences: 'That time at Schwichi-Schwaloche, you remember, the Ninth . . . ?' Does one good to see how the people are still sound at heart, they're not easily corroded by all these fashionable imponderabilia; tweedy and upright as ever, they are, always ready for a good virile laugh and a dirty story." With his dry, pointed humor Böll proves himself a practical observer. A topical and realistic feature of this story is Böll's invention of an "Academy for Military Memoirs," where every soldier from major upward may write his reminiscences, while a few "healthy girls from the people" are to sweeten the evenings of the retired heroes. The fictitious narrator in **"Der Wegwerfer,"** finally, is occupied for two hours a day in an insurance company sorting out printed matter from the rest of the mail, which saves the company one hundred man-hours every day. This really is close enough to reality to give one pause, and the necessity of such a job is (satirically) convincing enough. (pp. 26-7)

With the sole exception of **Billiards at Half-Past Nine,** Böll's longer stories and novels are too dated and above all too episodic and disjointed. . . . [It] is chiefly Böll's short stories that may prove of lasting value, for in them the dated themes are most convincingly subordinated to creative form. Pieces like **"Die Botschaft"** and **"Abschied"** may even now be counted among the "classical" short stories of our epoch, and it may be assumed that the future will not significantly alter this valuation. (p. 31)

> *Wilhelm Johannes Schwarz, in his* Heinrich Böll, Teller of Tales: A Study of His Works and Characters, *translated by Alexander and Elizabeth Henderson, Frederick Ungar Publishing Co., 1969, 123 p.*

Böll on the significance of language:

[Behind] every word a whole world is hidden that must be imagined. Actually, every word has a great burden of memories, not only just of one person but of all mankind. Take a word such as bread, or war; take a word such as chair, or bed or Heaven. Behind every word is a whole world. I'm afraid that most people use words as something to throw away without sensing the burden that lies in a word. Of course, that is what is significant about poetry, or the lyric, in which this can be brought about more intensively than in prose, although prose has the same function.

> *Heinrich Böll, in an interview in* The Paris Review, *Spring 1983.*

D. J. Enright

[The stories in Heinrich Böll's **Children Are Civilians Too** are] almost always to the point, and the point is invariably decent: the result is that the reader wants *more,* in fact he wants a novel. These stories are appetizers for a solid meal which doesn't materialize. This said, we have to qualify, because as we read on, short and slight-seeming though each story is, we become aware of a growing substantiality and force as (with a few exceptions) each story contributes to its predecessors, so that the final effect is that of a splintered novel. Or a work of documentaion in which, more legitimately, the artist's hand has intervened but slightly.

Böll's subject is war or the aftermath of war, war continued into peacetime: dugouts, hospitals, cripples, trains and railroad stations, insufficient food, bad wine, thin clothes, the black market. One of the most poignant of the stories [**"Traveller, If You Come to Spa"**] tells of a young soldier carried into an emergency casualty station and gradually deducing from the classical busts, the pictures on the wall, and finally his own handwriting on the blackboard

("Stranger, bear word to the Spartans we . . . ") that he is back in his old high school, and that the exhausted old fireman who gives him water is the school janitor from whom he used to get glasses of milk. As the soldier realizes he has lost both arms and a leg, so he recognizes the janitor and whispers for milk.

There is nothing quite so clever as **"Murke's Collected Silences"** in this volume, but most of the stories are clearly products of the same mind, a mind in which the anger that impels to satire is always being softened by compassion, a sense of common hardship and of shared guilt. Even the ex-black market operator who is so much harder-hearted now he has become a legitimate trader in candy and cigarettes is left to go his way: "now of course he has a proper business, and business is business." The tale of the cripple who finds a job he can do sitting down—keeping a count of the people crossing a new bridge—reminds us of some of the **18 Stories** about characters engaged in odd vocations, like the professional laugher. The cripple has fallen in love with a young girl who crosses the bridge twice a day, and while she is in sight he stops counting. Fortunately he is tipped off one day that the chief statistician will be checking his figures, and his accuracy is found to be such that he is promoted to horse-drawn vehicles, of which there are only a couple of dozen a day, and since they are not allowed at all between the hours of four and eight, "I could walk to the ice-cream parlor, feast my eyes on her or maybe walk her part-way home, my little uncounted sweetheart . . . "

Some of the wartime stories, concerned with the maimed and the shell-shocked, are reminiscent of First World War writing: now and again I found myself thinking of Wilfred Owen's poems on the pity and the waste of war. The postwar stories are generally bleak in mood—"Now men will go content with what we spoiled"—yet untainted by the cultivated and categorical hopelessness of some recent writers:

> Once upon a time I would have been glad to have a profession, I wanted very much to go into business. But once upon a time—what's the use of talking about it; now I don't even feel like going into business any more. What I like to do best is lie on my bed and daydream. I figure out how many hundreds of thousands of man-hours they need to build a bridge or a big house and then I think that in a single minute they can smash both the bridge and the house. So what's the point of working?

Elsewhere Böll evokes the preternatural fleetingly, which is disconcerting in a writer so predominantly "realistic." And yet the preternatural grows out of natural needs, out of loneliness and fear and pain. The presence of a ghostly friend or lover comes as a last small mercy toward the dying which we cannot decently begrudge. We find ourselves hoping that this too is realistic, that it does happen.

Exceptions to the rule are a sentimental piece about candles and altars (Böll's occasional decline into sentimentality blurs slightly the clear-cut contours of that fine novel of his, **The Clown**) and a pleasing anecdote about how

God sometimes tempers the wind to the black sheep. (pp. 42-3)

D. J. Enright, "Germanics," in The New York Review of Books, *Vol. XIV, No. 6, March 26, 1970, pp. 42-4.*

John Fetzer

Heinrich Böll's novella **Die Waage der Baleks** from the collection **So ward Abend und Morgen** of 1955 has generally been regarded as an unequivocal indictment of the ills besetting a corrupt society and its economic structure. The decisive event in the story—the discovery by the narrator's grandfather, little Franz Brücher, that the ancestral scale on which the Balek family had for five generations based its calculations in meting out payments for the herbs collected by the children of the local citizenry, was defective—lends credence to the view expressed originally by H. W. Waidson that the author's "sympathies are with the oppressed, and the short story . . . makes his attitude to the old-time feudal aristocracy abundantly clear." This hypothesis of 1959 persisted for almost a decade. . . . That the conflict of socio-economic forces would provide grist for the dialectical mills of communist criticism—which, as is well known, grind "exceeding" small—might be expected. In Günter Wirth's opinion, for instance, the rival camps—capitalist exploiter on the one side, oppressed proletariat on the other—are clearly delineated. . . . (p. 472)

One common feature shared by these critical voices—whether from East or West—is the view that the conflict is sharply silhouetted and that the means to remedy the situation can be deduced on the basis of *prima facie* evidence. The purpose of the present analysis, on the contrary, is to demonstrate that there are numerous aspects of the story which do not lend themselves to comfortable pigeonholing, and that certain facets of the narrative even defy such neat categorization. The case against the Baleks, for instance, is by no means established "beyond the shadow of a doubt," at least not in the judicial sense of the term. Neither are the measures of retaliation taken by the irate populace above and beyond reproach. It is the nagging persistence of the gray areas of doubt blurring any clear line of demarcation in the reader's mind between black and white, which makes this short story more than a mere propaganda piece. A blanket indictment of improprieties, whether perpetrated by an individual, a social class, or an entire nation would hardly constitute a novel topic for a novella. Likewise, a straightforward exposé of injustice could never prove a challenging enough theme for today's sophisticated reading public, an audience which knows that all absolutes are open to challenge in a world "beyond good and evil."

Some reservations with regard to a one-dimensional, "either/or" approach to Böll's tale were expressed recently by Caesare Cases in his study: " 'Die Waage der Baleks,' dreimal gelesen." Cases points out that with each successive reading of the text, the originally clear and distinct ideological positions recede into the background, as layers of ambivalence and ambiguity come to the fore. Among other things, Cases notes that since the Balek family runs what is, in essence, a closed corporation (controlling working conditions, setting prices for the finished product, establishing standards of payment for services rendered, etc.), they do not actually need to resort to the deception of a scale rigged ten percent in their favor. With an unbiased eye, Cases examines the living conditions and the behavioral pattern of the people in this microcosm of capitalist society at the turn of the twentieth century, taking into account such contingent factors as: the attitude of the populace which, either out of indifference or intimidation, allows the alleged abuses to endure so long; the upshot of the *tabula rasa* tactics employed by one "angry young man" to put an end to apparent chicanery.

As a kind of extension to Cases' line of attack, the following discussion will seek to probe a bit deeper and qualify even further the "abundantly clear" dichotomy which Waidson postulated. By examining four phases of the story: 1) the actions of the "exploiters"; 2) the reactions of the "exploited"; 3) any extenuating circumstances or circumstantial evidence; 4) the symbolic function of the scale, this analysis may discover yet another dimension of meaning which makes Böll's work relevant not only for the period in question (the threshold of the modern era), but also for our own day and, perhaps, for the coming age as well.

The actions of the Baleks with respect to the lives of the subjects under their jurisdiction can be said to entail suppression, to engender suspicion, and to employ superstition. As typical representatives of the industrial entrepreneur faction in late nineteenth century Europe, they coerce the adult population of their province to toil in the Balek-run flaxworks, while the children of the laborers gather herbs in the Balek-owned forest. In keeping with the tight economic policy in operation here, a member of the Balek family weighs the plants collected by the children, pays a nominal fee for them, and resells them to merchants of the vicinity for a handsome profit. Aside from exerting pressure in the economic sphere, the Baleks further strengthen their dominant position by quasi-legal means: the presence of another scale in their territory is prohibited—a decree which is as arbitrary as it is suspect.

In order to mitigate the impression of overbearing harshness, however, the Baleks do make a number of conciliatory gestures. For example, they foster better relations with the townspeople by sponsoring the theological studies of a deserving boy from their domain at the seminary in Prague. To sustain their flourishing trade with the children, they periodically supplement each financial transaction with a bonus piece of candy. In conjunction with their ascension to the ranks of the nobility in 1900, the Baleks assume the patronymic "von Bilgan" (the name of a legendary giant who inhabits the forest), thereby forging another link in the chain that binds the community to them in body and soul: in this instance through the irrational bond of myth and mystery. The entire populace is allowed to share in their good fortune, however, insofar as each family is allotted free beer, tobacco, and a quarter of a pound of genuine Brazilian coffee.

Ironically, it is this token of generosity on the part of the

Baleks—the distribution of food and gifts on the day of their great honor—which unmasks what appear to be long-standing discrepancies in their practices and which, in the final analysis, induces them to resort to even stricter measures of control. In an effort to regain their property after Franz Brücher and his contingent have taken possession of the scale and the account books, the Baleks summon the forces of "law and order"—the police and the local militia. During the head-to-head confrontation, Franz's sister—an innocent bystander to the whole affair—is slain and several members of both factions are wounded. Ultimately, the Baleks have the instigator and rabble-rouser ostracized from their domains, together with his entire family.

Having outlined the somewhat arbitrary actions of the Baleks both before and after the fateful discovery, it is necessary to examine the reactions of their subjects to these measures. With regard to the wretched working conditions in the factory, for instance, Böll comments laconically that the workers "ließen sich langsam dahinmorden." The manifest irony of this tongue-in-cheek comment suggests a kind of tacit acquiescence on the part of the populace to a form of existence which, if not desirable, was at least not deplorable. In spite of the obvious dearth of physical comforts in their lives, the inhabitants of the Balek territories are described as "fröhliche Geschlechter" and characterized as "glücklich." In short, these are people for whom such simple pleasures as pouring milk into their Sunday coffee would become a source of radiant joy: "die Gesichter der Kinder röteten sich vor Freude." A minimum of affluence, to be sure, but a modicum of security and serenity.

The chain of events which upsets the balance between Balek and Brücher is triggered by young Franz on New Year's Eve, 1900. Both the name of the protagonist and the chronological framework of his act have more than incidental significance. The etymological kinship of the name "Brücher" to "brechen" and "Bruch," creates the impression of an imminent "break" or "breach." The question which the reader must answer in this regard, however, is: do the actions of this "rebel with a cause" on the brink of the twentieth century constitute a "breakthrough" to a new order of society or merely the "breakdown" of the old? In the wake of Franz's startling disclosures, the populace, so long apathetic, becomes overly aggressive and resorts to violence. Not only do they employ illegal measures in the attempt to determine the extent of the Baleks' deceit, but they also condemn and convict the entire family solely on the basis of Franz's accusation and without benefit of a trial. Since so much of the outcome depends upon the nature of Franz's findings, one should investigate this aspect of the story in order to determine the validity of the charge in the light of the evidence adduced.

First of all, any discussion of this problem should be prefaced with the remark that the culpability of the Baleks with regard to the fraudulent scale is never stated unequivocally in the text, even though their behavior both prior and subsequent to the disclosure strongly suggests their guilt. Böll refuses to stack the cards against them, howev-er, and a clever barrister would be hard pressed to show that the evidence of their duplicity in a crime is far from foolproof. For instance, on the day of Franz's discovery, it is not Frau Balek herself, but rather the maid, Gertrud, who tends the scale. Consequently, one might infer that the latter tampered with the mechanism in order to make her efforts more profitable. Were this the case, then the validity of Franz's accusation—that the instrument had been defective for five generations—would be in jeopardy. In this same connection, it is not inconceivable that the antiquated scale simply broke down due to normal wear and tear. By the same token, one wonders why Böll emphasizes the fact that the balancing point—"diese dünne Linie der Gerechtigkeit"—had to be repainted each year. Is he implying that our concept of justice must also be constantly revamped? Or is this ceremonious procedure just another attempt on the part of the Baleks to delude the people into believing that they are receiving an "honest deal"? Finally, it could be argued that if this line is indeed drawn annually, the error causing the deficit might be of more recent vintage, and does not extend as far back as Franz claims. A shorter duration of the offense would not exonerate the Baleks from responsibility in the matter, of course, but it might reduce the magnitude of their "negligence" in the eyes of the law. From the standpoint of legal procedure and courtroom practice, one would have to concede on the basis of the above conjectures that the weight of incriminating evidence against the Baleks is counterbalanced by a number of extenuating circumstances which make conviction "beyond the shadow of a doubt" somewhat less than a foregone conclusion.

A particularly deft touch on Böll's part is to make the scale—traditionally the instrument held aloft by the allegorical figure of "blind justice" to symbolize equality and impartiality before the law—the source of conflict and a harbinger of corruption. In many respects, the "altertümliche, mit Goldbronze verzierte Waage" in its close affiliation with the protagonist recalls the association of a "Goldwaage" with another famous justice-seeker in German literature—Kleist's Michael Kohlhaas. Whether unconsciously or deliberately, Böll reinforces the relationship of the two figures by means of a number of subsidiary correspondences in character traits and plot development. For example, Franz's meticulous efforts to verify his suspicions on the empiric level before undertaking steps to rectify the wrongs done him and his ancestors recall Kohlhaas' attempt to ascertain the "truth" concerning the detention of his horses through a gruelling cross-examination of the stableboy, Herse. Once Franz has figured out the amount of money which he feels has been deprived him and his family, he weeps—just as Kohlhaas does after he learns of the ingenious machinations of Junker Wenzel von Tronka to impede the process of justice.

One significant motif which links Böll's and Kleist's stories even more closely is that of pallor—the loss of facial color manifesting itself when the extent of injustice is finally revealed. Whereas in *Michael Kohlhaas* it is Junker Wenzel who grows deathly pale during his confrontation with the protagonist, in *Die Waage der Baleks* the paleness at first characterizes Franz Brücher ("der kleine blasse Bursche") and then gradually spreads cancer-like throughout the entire community, displacing, in the process, the "Röte der Freude" which had marked the faces of the children each time the Baleks curried their favor with a bonus bonbon. On the morning when the Baleks enter church in anticipation of a tumultuous welcome due to their elevation in society, the congregation confronts them with cold silence and "blasse Gesichter." The word "blaß" is repeated four times within the space of a single paragraph. As Frau Balek glares in silence at the ashen-white countenance of little Franz, he counters with the challenge: "fünfeinhalb Deka . . . fehlen auf ein halbes Kilo an Ihrer Gerechtigkeit." The term "Gerechtigkeit" provides the signal for the entire congregation to intone the refrain "Gerechtigkeit der Erden, o Herr, hat Dich getötet . . . ," a motif which becomes the Marseillaise of the community until the singing of this rallying song is prohibited by legal sanction. Since an understanding of the subtle implications of this refrain is important in appreciating Böll's treatment of justice, a closer examination of this phrase is in order.

Undoubtedly the leitmotivic repetition of the hymn concerning mundane justice by the townspeople is intended to remind the Baleks that their treachery is, in some remote way, related to the most heinous act ever committed by mankind—the crucifixion of Christ. But there is another dimension of meaning inherent in this concept, of which the congregation seems oblivious but of which Böll is very much aware. If "earthly justice," that is, the kind of law dispensed by mankind, sanctioned this most monstrous of transgressions, how could we ever hope to devise a legal code which would vouchsafe equity in strictly everyday affairs: After all, would not the most ideally conceived system of jurisprudence—just like the most meticulously constructed scale—have to be administered by man, by the human animal with all his flaws, foibles, and flounderings?

Finally, one cannot help but wonder about the measures taken by Franz Brücher and the community in order to balance the scales of justice. Even though they do not compare in magnitude or devastation with those employed by Kohlhaas in his relentless quest to secure satisfaction, the *modus operandi* of the respective reformers is similar. The equilibrium of a segment of society is disturbed by the retaliatory actions of an individual who takes the law into his own hands because he can tolerate no degree of corruption. Are both Böll and Kleist perhaps suggesting that the desideratum of justice in any approximation of the Platonic ideal is to be sought on the pathway of injustice? Both the exiled Franz Brücher who refused to live with a defective scale and Michael Kohlhaas, whose finely honed sense of right and wrong literally became the "Goldwaage" on which the legal practices of his age were weighed and found wanting, might share the sentiments of another literary figure confronted by a world "out of joint": Shakespeare's Hamlet. They would also subscribe to his lament: "O cursed spite, that I was sent to set it right." Such an inference may be drawn from Böll's account of the final incidents of the story. He relates how the Brüchers, following their banishment, wander aimlessly about the countryside performing menial tasks and chanting the forbidden refrain about "Gerechtigkeit der Erden"

as a theme without variations. The irony of this situation is reinforced by their persevering spirit in spite of the discovery that even though "in allen Orten das Pendel der Gerechtigkeit falsch ausschlug," almost no one even wishes to hear about it: "Aber es hörte ihnen fast niemand zu." In distributing the guilt in the story, the author allots some to the Brüchers for a precipitous act, some to the world at large for its all too great tolerance of injustice, but strangely enough charges none to the Baleks specifically.

Heinrich Böll certainly does not condone passive acceptance of injustice any more than he champions exploitation because it is accomplished with finesse. Indeed, one cannot help but feel that he conceives of the world as a better place because of the Brüchers and their spiritual descendants—all those individuals who take it upon themselves to repair the machinery of society when, due to excessive wear and tear, the cogs no longer mesh. However, through his ambivalent mode of portrayal in *Die Waage der Baleks,* Böll would caution the reader to distinguish between timely replacement of defective parts and the destruction of the entire mechanism.

When examining critically such phrases as "earthly justice," one might do well to recall how the story of the Baleks' golden scale relativized these rhetorical slogans. All those who feel destined to shake society out of its dogmatic slumber or to meet Hamlet's challenge of "setting right" a world out of joint would be best advised to first weigh the validity of what now is against the value of what might be. If *Die Waage der Baleks* contains a message for the modern reader, then it can be found in the ironic dialectic by which the clamor for reform in the present is equivocated by the clichés from the past. Closely examined, pronouncements such as "Gerechtigkeit der Erden, o Herr, hat Dich getötet" do not offer a panacea to remedy the ills of society, but, on the contrary, focus our attention on the incurable paradoxes inherent in the all too human condition. (pp. 472-79)

John Fetzer, "The Scales of Justice: Comments on Heinrich Böll's 'Die Waage der Baleks'," in The German Quarterly, *Vol. XLV, No. 3, May, 1972, pp. 472-79.*

Theodore Ziolkowski

Böll recently explained why, for the time being, he has stopped writing short stories: he feels that he has achieved such facility in the genre, in which after all he initially established his reputation, that it has ceased to be a challenge. . . . [*Erzählungen, 1950-1970* is thus] a sort of *summa novellae.* Though it excludes the stories from Böll's early volume *Wanderer, kommst du nach Spa . . .* (e.g., such now classic items as **"Der Mann mit den Messern"**), it contains everything written since 1950, along with six tales that have not previously appeared in book form.

The chronological arrangement of these stories, familiar and unfamiliar ones alike, throws a new light on Böll's growth as a writer. The pages themselves, which tend to become more thickly printed in the course of twenty years, reflect this development: the paragraphs get longer, the dialogue less stichomythic, the syntax more complex. The changes are striking if one compares two thematically related tales, **"Das Abenteuer"** (1950) and **"Die Kirche im Dorf "** (1965). Both deal with adultery and cite the sixth commandment; but what was explicit and sober in the early tale has become implicit and ironic. Moreover, the stories become increasingly literary, as we see from the last three examples. **"Er kam als Bierfahrer"** (1968), the tale of a Greek worker named Tauros who comes to Germany and runs off with a woman called Europa, uses a familiar mythic pattern. **"Veränderungen in Staech"** (1969), dealing with events in a Benedictine monastery, is essentially plotless; the fun lies wholly in the virtuosity of language: irony of situation gives way to irony of language. And **"Epilog zu Stifters *Nachsommer*"** (1970), as its title suggests, picks up the story of Heinrich Drendorf and Natalie where Stifter left it and describes the smug complacency of their married years. In all three stories the main point of reference is not external reality, as was the case in Böll's early works, but the literary tradition itself.

In short, the volume is valuable not only as the most complete collection of Böll's stories. It also reflects the development of postwar German fiction from the cautious and calculated understatement of its beginnings to the self-conscious and exuberant "Artistik" of the present, where accomplishment itself becomes problematical.

> *Theodore Ziolkowski, in a review of "Erzählungen," in* Books Abroad, *Vol. 47, No. 4, Autumn, 1973, p. 754.*

Heinrich Böll [Interview with Jean-Louis de Rambures]

[*The interview excerpted below was originally published in the French daily* Le monde *on December 13, 1973.*]

[*De Rambures*]: *Many of your compatriots pretend they didn't know what really went on during the Third Reich. Did you, Heinrich Böll, know?*

[Böll]: Let us understand one another. Not to see that Nazism was a terrorist régime, one would have had to be blind. What, on the other hand, I did not know was the systematic and bureaucratic elimination of millions of human beings, as practiced by the Third Reich. Apparently Albert Speer himself was completely unaware of this. It may seem crazy. But this is a fact, and will doubtless always remain inexplicable. Just once, however, I came near the truth. It was during a train journey. I was returning from the East, on leave. In the middle of the night our train stopped in a small unknown German railroad station. Suddenly, I saw an immense flock of shaved creatures invading the platform. A few raised their emaciated arms toward us travelers. We threw them bread and cigarettes out of the carriage windows. It was hallucinating. But I had no idea that this was genocide. It was only later, after the war, that I brought the two facts together; the little railroad station was Buchenwald.

Throughout your whole work, in all your characters, culpability returns as a leitmotif. *Have you, yourself, felt guilty?*

I don't believe that an individual can be guilty just because he is born in one place rather than another. But neither is he for that reason innocent. That's the rub. Neither innocent, nor guilty, that's what we all are. The hardest thing for a German is to accept himself as such. By a wholly Germanic dialectic, it was by discovering what a malediction the fact of being German constitutes that I first became aware of belonging to this people. Let me explain. Until 1933, the question of my nationality had never bothered me. During the Third Reich, being against the regime, I did not feel myself concerned by the obligation imposed upon us to feel we were German.

It was in 1945, while I was a prisoner, that a relationship, which I would say was quasi-metaphysical, was born in me *vis-à-vis* this people, which had been, as it were, foreign to me until then. Wherever we traveled, as prisoners, in France, in Belgium, the inhabitants spat in our faces, threw stones at us. Simply because we were Germans. This explosion of collective hate was an unforgettable lesson: because Germany was despised, I suddenly became aware that for nothing on earth would I have refused to be a part of it.

Did this traumatization play any part in your literary commitment?

What is a committed writer? I don't much care for that qualification, which sounds as though one were carrying a flag. You have in France the expression "a man of letters." I much prefer that. That is the way I commit myself.

In its rhetoric and its formality, the French language constitutes a prop to thought. We German writers, we have every time to explore the territory before we set foot on it. That stems, above all, from the *tabula rasa* created by the Third Reich. It annihilated all our connections with tradition or with the natural and social environment. For authors of an earlier generation, Ernst Jünger or Friedrich Sieburg, there was always some way of finding in the depths of their libraries the forbidden authors. We often were even unaware of their names. Kafka, I discovered in 1946. Herman Hesse, Erich Kastner vaguely reminded me of something. Thomas Mann? I only knew *Buddenbrooks*, and that by chance. In short, then, in an extraordinary spirit of rediscovered liberty, Germany took up writing again. (Between 1945 and 1947 I published, I think, sixty stories in ten different magazines.) It had to start again from zero. Our new literature has dismissed what hitherto had been considered the very essence of Germany—interiority.

If one can believe Ernst Jünger, by rejecting interiority, this new literature thereby lost some part of its soul?

It was a necessary evolution. By dint of interiorization, we ended by giving up any capacity for political, social, or economic analysis. If Hitler was able to impose himself, it was owing to our habit of conceiving of history as an ineluctable fatality. I myself also had to make an effort to rid myself of this German distemper. Alas, we haven't come to the end of our capacity for interiorization. After 1945 this made us miss, I am quite sure, one of the greatest chances our history offered us. You must think back to what the situation of Germany was at that time: in a metropolis like Cologne, every inhabitant had become in fact a robber, in order to avoid dying of hunger or cold. In this immense indifference to private property, there was a nihilistic component which only needed to be mobilized.

The sociologist Alexander Mitscherlich considers that the Germans threw themselves desperately into the "economic miracle" to escape the unbearable idea of their culpability.

That may have played a part. But for myself I am sure that the Germans (insofar as one can generalize) suffer from a fundamental trauma in the face of life. (Two total inflations one after another is enough to traumatize.) It is there that the real reason for our maniacal attachment to property must be looked for. Our irrational fear of Communism—oh, note well, not of Communism as a political system or a spiritual force, but only of Communism as an eventual menace to private property—this is the fear of a people that has always been poor throughout its history. Now that it possesses for the first time, it intends to profit from its goods without being bothered. It is a very human attitude. (p. 237)

> **What is a committed writer? I don't much care for that qualification, which sounds as though one were carrying a flag. You have in France the expression "a man of letters." I much prefer that. That is the way I commit myself.**
>
> **—Heinrich Böll**

Do you still regard yourself as a Catholic?

Fiscally, yes. The Vicar-General of the Diocese of Cologne has just reminded me of this by sending me a bill for my "Church tax." So that's how I have become baptized for a second time. It's a negative definition. But my beliefs (let's say I still believe in many things) are no one's business but my own. In fact, my problem is not religious, but political. You know there are two definitions of the Church: on the one hand, the institution (which I detest because of its tie-up with the bourgeoisie) and, on the other hand, the Mystical Body. I refuse to play the game of eternally justifying the first by invoking the second. Why then have I not left the bosom of the Church? That's a problem my wife and I often discuss. Perhaps, quite simply, because Catholicism was the major influence of my childhood. But when, for example, I hear that the Cardinal of Santiago participated in a *Te Deum* for the Chile *putsch,* I find that unbearable. I cannot, in fact, tell you how much longer I will remain a Catholic.

In any case, you are a moralist. You have even been called "the conscience of the nation."

What a horrible definition, so characteristic of German idealism! I do not consider myself the least bit as a moralist, but as a player. Essentially it is the game with forms, with personages, with situations, that pleases me in writing. I have a horror of didactic literature. If I appear to be a moralist, it is completely unconsciously. Perhaps it

is because the Nazi terror has traumatized me so I instinctively avoid any description of violent scenes. But from this to call me the conscience of a nation! Germany has 62,000,000 inhabitants. To discover its conscience, one would need a computer as big as Cologne.

Believe me, what characterizes our postwar literary generation is the very simple fact that we intellectuals refuse to see ourselves as marked men. We are citizens of the German Federal Republic like everyone else. We have something to say, and the chance to be heard. This is an advantage of which we make use every time we consider it necessary. (p. 238)

> *Heinrich Böll and Jean-Louis de Rambures, in an interview in* Commonweal, *Vol. C, No. 10, May 10, 1974, pp. 236-38.*

James Henderson Reid

Böll's first publication was a short story, **"Die Botschaft"** (**"The Message"**), which appeared in 1947. It tells of a soldier who has the duty of visiting his friend's wife after the war to tell her of her husband's death and to bring her his personal belongings. On arrival at the house he discovers that she is living with another man. When she is given her husband's wedding-ring, watch and paybook she bursts into tears: 'Memory seemed to pierce her with swords. At that moment I realised that the war would never be over, never, as long as somewhere a wound was still bleeding which it had inflicted.' This fundamental credo must be remembered in taking into account the role played by the war in Böll's works. The war has shaped modern Germany, politically and socially, although the Germans would like to forget it. Böll is the man who cannot forget it. His novels consistently describe contemporary events: the date of writing and the date of the action described in them correspond more or less exactly. But even twenty-five years later the characters of *Gruppenbild mit Dame (Group Portrait with Lady)* (1971) come back again and again to this basic experience.

Böll's early works, *Der Zug war pünktlich,* [the novel] *Wo warst du, Adam?* and eleven of the stories of *Wanderer, kommst du nach Spa . . . (Traveller, If You Come to Spa . . .)* (1950) deal with the war directly. The German writer of war stories is obviously in a different position from that of his English or American counterpart. The latter have a clear tradition in which to write, what one might call the fairy-tale tradition, in which there are clear-cut issues, heroes and villains on a personal level and the triumph of good (i.e. our men) over evil (i.e. the others). (pp. 26-7)

A war novel is a kind of historical novel and the historical novel will usually try to interpret history by putting events into a meaningful pattern. The keynote of Böll's experience of the war, however, was its 'meaninglessness.' Perhaps the most respectable conservative writer on the subject of war is Ernst Jünger, and in view of the scorn with which Jünger is mentioned in *Als der Krieg zu Ende war (When the War was Over)* (1962) it is worth comparing Böll's attitude with that of Jünger. In *Der Kampf als inneres Erlebnis* (1922) Jünger praises war as a 'natural law' similar to the sexual instinct, an experience in which the natural impulses which society has repressed come into their own again. Even during the Second World War Jünger was able to mythologise war in terms of the mystical bond which unites the opposing camps.

For Böll, however, as for [Antoine de] Saint-Exupéry, whom he quotes in one of the epigraphs to *Wo warst du, Adam?*, war is a disease. It is something which happens to one, not something in which one actively engages. Böll always associates tedium with war. For Jünger too boredom was always a danger, but one which he invariably overcame—in nature study, in intellectual discussions, in combat. There are few descriptions of actual engagements with the enemy in Böll's works. The characteristic situation is that of the soldier waiting for the war to come to him or for himself to be sent into action. Location is interesting in this respect. *Der Zug war pünktlich* has three main locations: a train, a restaurant and a brothel. *Wo warst du, Adam?* is set mainly in hospitals or pubs. Passivity is the keynote throughout. When incidents are described, the individual soldier is baffled by them. In *Wo warst du, Adam?* Feinhals is twice sent into battle: but the war remains either a noise or a meaningless manoeuvre of hide-and-seek with the enemy. Böll does not believe in heroes; at best his individuals are part of a team, a collective. But even the comradeship which this implies and which is a traditional motif of war literature is singularly lacking in Böll's works. The opening scene of *Wo warst du, Adam?* includes the unforgettable description of a company of soldiers struggling with one another to get their tin mugs under a single water tap. The individual soldier is seldom in the same place for long enough for deeper personal relationships to develop. In any case, death may intervene at any moment—the narrator of [the novella] *Als der Krieg ausbrach* (*When the War Began*) (1962) loses his friend in the first action of the war. Andreas in *Der Zug war pünktlich* remains from start to finish imprisoned in his own self. In the course of the story he meets three people, two soldiers and Olina, a prostitute. The soldiers relate in turn their personal experiences and feelings but Andreas merely listens, dreams of the past, tries to pray. Conversations, dialogues do not develop. Only at the very end is he released from the prison of his self, talks to Olina—and shortly afterwards is killed. **"Wiedersehen in der Allee"** (**"Reunion in the Avenue"**) (1948) describes an apparently happy friendship between the narrator and Hecker, who are alone together for long periods in the trenches. But their comradeship exists largely without words—shortly before he dies Hecker realises that he has always done the talking, the other has merely listened. In **"Aufenthalt in X"** (**"Sojourn in X"**) (1950) the narrator's loneliness is emphasised. A chance encounter with a drunken comrade whom he prevents from shooting an officer, ends with a visit to a pub. The drunkard is loquacious, the narrator says nothing. The three young soldiers of **"Damals in Odessa"** (**"That Time in Odessa"**) (1950) have exhausted their news and have nothing more to say to one another. In *Wo warst du, Adam?* Feinhals has no comrades. Most of the people he meets are not likable, but even on the occasions when friendship might have developed he remains silent. When he visits Finck's family at the end of the war he cannot bring himself to tell them how their

son met his death—clutching a case of Tokay wine which his commanding officer had ordered. The catastrophe is too great to be encompassed in words. More significantly still, when Lieutenant Brecht tries to draw him out on the subject of the war, he remains non-committal. One reason for the breakdown in communication and personal relationships is the totalitarian state in which they live—it is safer to keep one's mouth shut. Accordingly monologues and inner monologues are an important feature of Böll's narrative technique.

War for Böll is meaningless. It would have meaning if it were shown to foster personal relationships or the virtues of heroism and self-sacrifice. But it does not. Schmitz and Schröder are potential heroes in *Wo warst du, Adam?*, remaining at their posts to tend the wounded as the Russians advance. But they die because of their own lethargy: when Schröder goes out towards the Russians bearing the white flag he steps on an unexploded shell which he ought to have removed weeks before, the Russians think themselves under attack and destroy the hospital.

In another sense war would be given meaning if it were related in some way to an underlying ideology, if, for example, the causes of the war were shown or if it were interpreted as the necessary concomitant of capitalism, as Brecht implies in *Mutter Courage* (*Mother Courage*). Böll makes no attempt to do this. His stories are told from a limited point of view. The vast majority of the short stories are first person narratives. The remainder are told from the point of view of one or more individual characters. With one brief exception, which will be examined in due course, the external, commenting, 'omniscient' narrator is not found. Moreover, this limited point of view is never that of somebody who might be expected to have insight into causes and connections, but almost invariably that of the non-political, mediocre 'little man'. Bressen and Filskeit, the 'villains' of *Wo warst du, Adam?*, give us some insights into the Nazi mentality and through the former we learn of certain parallels between the army bureaucracy and that of society in the wider sense. But only indirectly and by implication. There is no critical perspective. (pp. 27-31)

In yet another sense, merely to write about war in artistic form is to give it meaning, arranging it into a pattern of events, describing it as a coherent whole with a beginning and ending or in terms of the biography of an individual soldier. Böll attacks this problem in an interesting way. The short story is his favourite form. The point about the short story is that it does not recount events in coherent succession like the *Novelle* or the novel; it does not have a plot. Instead it illuminates, by concentrating on a single moment, a unique event, an encounter with life. **"Wanderer, kommst du nach Spa . . . "**, for example, describes a soldier's return, badly wounded, to the school which he left a few weeks earlier and which now has become a temporary hospital. On the blackboard is still the beginning of the text from the monument to the heroes of Thermopylae which he had begun to write and had to break off for lack of space. The truncated text reflects the mutilated narrator, mutilated by a war waged in abuse of the ideology of the text itself. No development is shown, no plot, merely a juxtaposition of actuality and ideology.

Der Zug war pünktlich was Böll's first independent publication. Preceded by some ten short stories, some of which, for example **"An der Brücke,"** are undoubtedly superior, its length may have been its undoing. It falls into two clear halves, the first describing a train journey back to the front, the second Andreas's experiences in a brothel, his attempt to desert and his death in an ambush. The strength of the work lies in its description of the train journey across Germany and occupied Poland: the station platforms at night time with the tired girls serving coffee, the grime of the train, the soldiers sleeping in the corridor, playing cards or singing their interminable songs. The passivity and absurdity of the soldier's existence are well captured. But the second half introduces the impossibly melodramatic and sentimental story of Olina, a Polish prostitute who originally wished to study music, and now works for the resistance network gathering strategic information from her customers. She and Andreas fall in love to the music of Beethoven and amid copious tears. Some stylistic weaknesses of the first half—a constant striving for effect by means of imagery—become even worse in the second. There are attempts to contrast or parallel the two halves. The meaningful life of resistance to the oppressors contrasts with the soldier's acceptance of his existence. But there is no suggestion that resistance on the part of the latter would be at all possible. Besides, Andreas finds the brothel administration strongly reminiscent of the army—there are oppressed and oppressors here too.

The story is told from the point of view mainly of Andreas, later of Andreas and Olina alternately. However, at the end of the first page there is an interpolation by an anonymous, external narrator unparalleled in all Böll's works. As the train leaves Andreas calls out in despair that he is going to die. There follows a long general comment. Sometimes words spoken unthinkingly take on magical qualities, anticipating the future, assuming the mantle of Fate: 'Lovers and soldiers, the doomed and those who are filled with the cosmic force of life are sometimes unexpectedly given this power, they are endowed and burdened with a sudden illumination . . . and the word sinks, sinks into them.' The power of the word remains for Böll an important preoccupation, as many of his critical essays and speeches testify. Totalitarian regimes abuse language for propaganda purposes. Since 1945 certain words have lost currency for Böll completely: 'Duty, fatherland, honour, obedience.' Fascism's contemporary equivalent, the administrative machine, is similarly engaged in debasing language. Advertising and the media are especially guilty. In view of the constant stream of words pouring from the radio **"Dr. Murkes gesammeltes Schweigen"** regards the only justifiable attitude to language as silence. However, in no other story of Böll's does an anonymous, impersonal narrator come out into the open with such a direct comment. And since he does not do so again in *Der Zug war pünktlich* we are justified in viewing it as a stylistic flaw, due to Böll's artistic immaturity. (pp. 31-3)

Böll's war stories are utterly pessimistic. The war machine has the individual firmly in its grasp. Prayer is the only possible solution, not prayer for divine intervention, in the hope of reforming the world, but 'in order to console God', as Ilona [of *Wo warst du, Adam?*] puts it. Everything else is doomed to destruction. Feinhals learns not to take anything earthly too seriously. But this insight is followed at once by death. Solidarity does not arise. Where it begins to do so it is at once nipped in the bud. Böll's monastery is at this stage a very lonely, withdrawn place. (pp. 35-6)

James Henderson Reid, in his Heinrich Böll: Withdrawal and Re-emergence, *Oswald Wolff, 1973, 95 p.*

David J. Parent

Friedrich Schiller, in his 200-line didactic poem "Der Spaziergang" ["The Walk"], written in 1795, castigates contemporary feudal society and sounds a Rousseauesque clarion-call for a return to nature after the destruction of a corrupt civilization. Reminiscent of Schiller's youthful *Sturm und Drang* [Storm and Stress] style, the poem reflects the turmoil of current events, the gradual decay of the multi-principality Holy Roman Empire, and especially the excesses of the French Revolution. But this negative tone is only a counterfoil to Schiller's dominant theme of an optimistic classical faith in a more comprehensive natural harmony, including also faith in the basic goodness of the Greek achievement in launching Western civilization.

This is the point-of-attack for 1972 Nobel-prize winner Heinrich Böll's short story, **"Wanderer, kommst du nach Spa-"** [**"Traveler, If You Go to Spa-"**], a specimen of *Kahlschlag* [total devastation] literature written in the equally desolate years immediately after World War II. Despite basic similarities between the two authors, Böll's **"Wanderer"** is a direct reply to Schiller's "Der Spaziergang." And Schiller's classic poem gains new poignancy and relevance in the light of modern historical perspective provided by the Böll *Kurzgeschichte*. Böll's fragmentary title was in fact taken from "Der Spaziergang":

> Wanderer, kommst du nach Sparta, verkündige
>   dorten, du habest
> Uns hier liegen sehen, wie das Gesetz es befahl.
>
> [Traveler, if you go to Sparta, announce there
>   that you have
> Seen us lying here, as the law commanded.]

Visualized as an inscription on a stone in a foreign land, these words commemorate the slain Greek soldiers who won victory and fame but lost their lives in one of the many battles their country fought for civilization. The poetic spectator, deeply moved, exclaims:

> Ruhet sanft ihr Geliebten! Von eurem Blute be-
>   gossen
> Grünet der Ölbaum, es keimt lustig die köstliche
>   Saat.
>
> [Rest gently, you beloved! Watered by your
>   blood
> The olive tree turns green, and cheerily the pre-
>   cious grain germinates.]

In the subsequent context—a long enumeration of the various trades and skills which gradually evolved as civilization progressed from its Greek beginnings until the advent of science and the Enlightenment, when "die Gebilde der Nacht weichen dem tagenden Licht" [the shapes of night give way to the dawning light]—Schiller makes it clear that the death of these heroic men set in motion millennia of human development.

Cryptically, Böll's title does not quote that part of the inscription relevant to his story, "verkündige dorten, *du habest / Uns hier liegen sehen*" [announce there that *you have / Seen us lying here*], an imperative which has a brutal impact in the context of a schoolboy-soldier brought back as a basket-case (an amputee with no arms and only one leg) after three months in the front lines. Böll repeats the words of his title three times near the end of the story, describing them as having been written seven times in different script in the amputee's own hand on the blackboard in the art room of his former humanistic high school, which is now being used as an operation room. Böll tells us why the saying was "nur etwas verstümmelt" [only somewhat mutilated], trailing off at the word "Spa-": the former schoolboy had not budgeted his space correctly and had written too large. The literary effect, however, is a strong implication that pronouncements in the spirit of *Dulce et decorum est pro patria mori*—or as Schiller puts it, "für das Vaterland und . . . der Ahnen Gesetze" [for the fatherland and . . . the ancestral laws]—have become unspeakable. This phrase becomes a ghastly understatement when the full extent of the boy's injuries is revealed at the very end of the story, immediately after they occur.

Böll's story, however, is much more closely linked with Schiller's poem than merely by an allusive title. Both structural and thematic affinities are so pronounced that they affirm that Böll's **"Wanderer"** is indeed, in one aspect of its primary intention, a reply to, or a commentary on, Schiller.

Schiller's philosophical poem has two main components: 1) the external walk upwards in a mountainous region where the various items of scenery are progressively observed, and 2) the vast inner vision of the history of civilization: from "Aus dem felsigten Kern hebt sich die türmende Stadt" [Out of the bedrock rises the towering city] to "Aber wo bin ich?" [But where am I?]. In a letter to his friend, Wilhelm von Humboldt, Schiller speaks of the "sinnlichen Gegenstände, an denen der Gedanke fortläuft" [sensory objects which guide the thread of thought] and gives a good summary of the basic structure of the poem:

> Sie werden bemerkt haben, daß ich biß da, wo die Betrachtungen über die Corruption angehen, beynahe immer von einem äußen Objekt ausgehe. (Bei der Corruption war es in der Natur der Sache, daß das Gemüth in sich selbst versinkt, und die Einbildungskraft die ganze Kosten des Gemäldes trägt. Ich gewann dadurch den großen Vortheil, daß nach einer so langen Zerstreuung, während der doch die Reise immer fortgeht, die Natur auf einmal als Wildniß dastehen kann.)

[You will have noticed that up to the point

where the reflections on corruption begin, I almost always start off with an external object. (In the case of corruption it was in the nature of the subject for the mind to turn inward and the imagination to bear the entire burden of the picture. I thereby gained the great advantage that after so long a distraction during which the walk continued uninterruptedly, nature can suddenly stand there as a wilderness.)]

Likewise, on the imaginative level, Böll's story has two main components, consisting of 1) observations of external objects by the amputee as he is carried along corridors and up stairs to the operation room, and 2) subjective reflections and musings of the amputee as he gradually reconstructs the past and seeks to understand the present. Thus the basic structural similarity between the two works, on the imaginative level, consists in their deployment of space and external objects along the forward and upward line of motion of an observer, and in their inclusions of reflective subjectivity more or less closely connected with the objects seen.

From this basic identity of structure, numerous stylistic similarities and differences result; in fact, the structural parallelism tends to highlight the differences in a relationship of point and counterpoint. In both cases, for instance, perception centers in a first-person observer who notes the individual objects around him. But in Schiller the tone is one of familiarity and intimacy with the observed environment: "Sei mir gegrüßt mein Berg" [I greet you, my mountain], while in Böll the central personality, bewildered and disoriented despite the countless minutely recognizable details, does not identify with, and, until the end, refuses to accept the reality of, his surroundings: "Alles das . . . ist kein Beweis" [All that . . . is no proof]; "Und außerdem besteht die Möglichkeit, daß ich Fieber habe, daß ich träume" [And moreover the possibility exists that I have a fever, that I am dreaming]. In both works, the physical movement is upward, but in Schiller the poetic thinker walks leisurely up a winding path while Böll's wounded man is carried up the stairs on a stretcher. Schiller's character has fled from narrow confinement, out of "des Zimmers Gefängnis / Und dem engen Gespräch" [the room's prison / And the narrow conversation], to the panoramic vistas of a living and provident nature, while Böll's tragic victim is brought into the confines of a "Totenhaus" [house of the dead] with formerly hated, "dumpfgetönten, langweiligen Wände" [dull-toned, boring walls].

The worlds which surround the two observers, and their modes of perception, are closely interconnected. The world around Schiller's observer is a world of natural phenomena, and a cursory listing of the nouns at the beginning of the poem reveals a traditional Romantic nature: "Berg" [mountain], "Gipfel" [summit], "Sonne" [sun], "Flur" [field], "Linden" [linden-trees], "Chor" [chorus], "Ästen" [branches], "Bläue" [blueness], "Gebirg" [mountain chain], "Wald" [forest]—but also a non-natural image: "des Zimmers Gefängnis" [the room's prison]. All of these natural images denote expansive, complex, or plural natural entities. They do not suggest a highly particularistic focus that singles out isolated details, but rather a deployment of reality which blends into a unified imaginative whole. The thrust of the noun-choice at the opening of Böll's **"Wanderer,"** however, denotes a restrictive, man-made world of technical objects and artifacts: "Wagen," "Motor," "Tor" [gate], "Licht" [light], "Fenster" [window], "das Innere des Wagens" [the inside of the car], "Glühbirne" [lightbulb], "Decke" [ceiling], "Gewinde" [threaded base], "Schrauböffnung" [socket], "Drähtchen" [filaments], "Glasresten" [glass remnants], "Motor," "Stimme" [voice]. Framed within onomatopoeic verbal images—"brummte der Motor" [the motor roared] and "hörte der Motor auf zu brummen" [the motor stopped roaring]—these visual images combine to present, with minute details, the technological still-life of a broken lightbulb with only its base still stuck in the socket and a few filaments glittering from glass fragments. Böll's mode of perception of this still-life seems related to the *nouveau roman* of Robbe-Grillet and similar German experimental fiction in its eccentric perspective, hypertensive alertness to isolated detail, semantic economy, and opaque, fragmented objectifications. This broken lightbulb contrasts with Schiller's sun which casts its lovely light on the mountaintop and which in the very last line of the poem, enriched by the poet's reflections on Greek antiquity, represents the everlasting serenity and bounty of nature despite all the toils of men: "Und die Sonne Homers, siehe! sie lächelt auch uns" [And Homer's sun, behold! it also smiles for us]. The roar of the truck motor contrasts with natural sounds such as: "Um mich summt die geschäftige Bien" [Around me hums the busy bee]. Schiller's "Belebte Flur" [animated field] may even have suggested as its opposite the primary location of the Böll story: the long, dimly lighted "Flur" [corridor], whose walls are painted with green oil paint.

Both works make extensive and explicit use of primary colors. In Schiller these colors symbolize nature's primeval and universal harmony and vitality.

> Ruhige Bläue dich auch grüße ich, die unermeßlich sich ausgießt
> Um das braune Gebirg, über den grünenden Wald.
>
> [Quiet blueness, you too I greet that pour out immeasurably
> Around the brown mountain, over the greening forest.]

The words "ruhig" [quiet] and "grünend" [greening] together with the apostrophe and the reflexive verb suggest an animated nature, while "unermeßlich" [immeasurably] bespeaks the infinite vastness of man's phenomenal *Umwelt*. Numerous other textual indications of activity and color in nature are perhaps fused in the term "das energische Licht" [the energetic light], which is immediately followed by a couplet in which Schiller sets up a momentary antagonism of colors:

> Kräftig auf blühender Au erglänzen die wechselnden Farben,
> Aber der reizende Streit löset in Anmut sich auf.
>
> [Strongly in a blooming meadow the various colors gleam,
> But the delightful clash is resolved in loveliness.]

The bright and multitudinous colors of the flowery meadow blend in an overall harmony. Throughout his descriptions of the natural world in the poem, Schiller carefully controls the modulations of daylight and the application of colors, especially blue and green, as in this example:

> Nur verstohlen durchdringt der Zweige laubigtes Gitter
> Sparsames Licht, und es blickt lachend das Blaue herein.
> Aber plötzlich zerreißt der Flor. Der geöffnete Wald gibt
> Überraschend des Tags blendendem Glanz mich zurück.
>
> [Only secretively the scanty light pierces the leafy grid
> Of twigs, and laughing, the blue looks in.
> But suddenly the vegetation is cut away. An opening in the forest
> Surprises the eye with the blinding glare of daylight.]

Even in the shady forest, the immeasurable blue of the sky smiles in through the leaves. Previously the poet's path had led him through the "freundliches Grün" [friendly green] of the meadow. Both colors are generously present in nature: "ein blaues Gebirg" [a blue mountain chain], and "des grünlichen Stroms fließender Spiegel" [the greenish stream's flowing mirror]. Climactically, the two colors recur at the end of the poem as symbols of the eternal order of nature:

> Unter demselben Blau, über dem nämlichen Grün
> Wandeln die nahen und wandeln vereint die fernen Geschlechter.
>
> [Under the same blue, over the identical green
> Walk the near and walk united the far generations.]

Böll's color images, on the other hand, refer mainly to paint, the green, yellow, and rose-colored oil paint on the walls, and the paint on various objects: clothes-hooks, picture-frames. His use of color is just as explicit as Schiller's, but the intent seems to be the opposite: to underscore the artificiality of the world being depicted. Even "der rote Himmel" [the red sky] and "schwarze Wolken" [black clouds] of smoke above the burning city are man-made rather than natural. Color use also culminates in irony: "himmelblau" [sky-blue] is the color of Old Fritz's uniform with the large, gleaming gold star in "das besonders schöne, besonders große, besonders bunte Bild" [the especially beautiful, especially large, especially bright picture] of him. The repetition of the adjective "bunt" [bright] not long after its pejorative use concerning the hoplite, the ironic anaphoric use of the pedestrian adverb "besonders" [especially] three times within a classical and harmonious rhythmic triad, these are clues to Böll's mockery of this paragon of militarism. The color brown is associated with "muffig" [stodgy] to suggest the Nazis, and their attempt to eradicate the cross involves ironic use of that color: "Sie hatten geschimpft, aber es hatte nichts genutzt: das Kreuz blieb da, braun und deutlich auf dem Rosa der Wand, und ich glaube, ihr Etat für Farbe war erschöpft, und sie konnten nichts machen" [They had scolded, but it had done no good: the cross remained there, brown and distinct on the rose of the wall, and I believe their paint budget was used up, and there was nothing they could do]. The colors "gelb" [yellow] and "gelblich" [yellowish] are used in connection with Classical Antiquity.

These indicators of object and color show that two totally different worlds are constructed on the parallel spatial structures of the two works. In "Der Spaziergang" the famous verticality and vast dimensionality of Schiller's poetic fantasy opens scenic panoramas; and, despite the positive or negative course of human history, nature remains eternally beautiful and bountiful:

> Aber jugendlich immer, in immer veränderter
> Schöne
> Ehrst du, fromme Natur, züchtig das alte Gesetz.
>
> [But youthful ever, in ever changing beauty
> You honor, pious nature, modestly the old law.]

In **"Wanderer, kommst du nach Spa-"** the world is narrow, man-made, defective, and suicidal.

The thematic relationship is no less clear. The external component of Schiller's "Spaziergang" culminates in a reflection on the peasantry who inhabit the villages which the wanderer sees: "Glückliches Volk der Gefilde! Noch nicht zur Freiheit erwachet" [Happy folk of the fields! Not yet awakened to freedom]. They represent the first, the naive stage of mankind when man has not yet achieved intellectual self-awareness and freedom, but still constitutes an integral part of nature, totally subject to its laws and organically intertwined with it. The inner vision of the history of civilization, the second phase of mankind, represents a new principle of human interrelationship with nature, symbolized for example by the orderly groves of single species of trees: "Und das Gleiche nur ist's, was an das Gleiche sich reiht . . . Regel wird alles und alles wird Wahl und alles Bedeutung" [And only the same is grouped with the same . . . Everything becomes rule and choice and meaning]. Man has taken systematic control of nature. From its Greek origins, civilization is described as ascending and progressive. The negative turn of civilization results after the written word has promoted enlightenment. Man then breaks his bonds, but together with the chains of fear he also tears asunder the reins of shame. Falsehood and corruption then prevail. The final stage, a return to nature, will come when "die Natur erwacht" [nature awakens] and the needs of the times shake the hollow structure and

> Aufsteht mit des Verbrechens Wut und des
> Elends die Menschheit,
> Und in der Asche der Stadt sucht die verlorne
> Natur.
>
> [Up rises mankind with criminal rage and misery,
> And in the ashes of the city seeks lost nature.]

This self-destructive stage of civilization is Böll's point of departure. From the first page the whole city is burning like a torch. There is no sign of the Homeric sun and the eternally bountiful blue sky and green earth. Instead there are the broken lightbulb, the black-out curtains, the sky

red with flames and black with smoke clouds. The narrator again and again screams with pain—no place in this type of brutal reality for Winckelmann's "edle Einfalt and stille Größe" [noble simplicity and silent grandeur] or Schiller's confidence in nature. In retrospect, the entire course of Western civilization seems to have taken a false path. "Das humanistische Gymnasium" [the humanistic high school], promulgator of the Graeco-Roman heritage, has now become a "Totenhaus" [house of the dead] and "das Museum einer Totenstadt" [the museum of a dead city]. It is Böll's use of this latter stark metaphor which demonstrates that the "Gymnasium" is not just an incidental setting for the action but rather its very theme. It can, in fact, serve as a key to the interpretation: Greek civilization is presented not by a magnificent direct intuition of its heroic achievements, military and otherwise, but through the mediacy of reproductions of its artifacts and of selected cultural motifs. For Schiller the Pantheon has been a symbol of aesthetic beauty and religious vitality:

> Künstliche Himmel ruhn auf schlanken
> jonischen Säulen,
> Und den ganzen Olymp schließet ein Pantheon
> ein.
>
> [Artificial heavens rest on slender Ionic pillars,
> And the entire Olympus is enclosed by a Pantheon.]

In it dwelled "die seligen Götter [the blessed gods]. In Böll it is a plaster imitation—gleaming, yellowish, and listed among the good old generation-tested school props. Moreover the chief of the gods has a "Zeusfratze" [an ugly Jovian scowl]. Schiller's Greek dead are mourned as persons— "Ruhet sanft ihr Geliebten"—and his poetic imagination reaches out across the ages directly to them, and their death is seen as not having been in vain, for it marked the beginning of civilization. Böll's Greek soldier is not a living person, but a picture of one, and the culturally relative and militaristic side is stressed in such a way that he appears anachronistic and ridiculous: "der griechische Hoplit, bunt und gefährlich, wie ein Hahn sah er aus: gefiedert" [the Greek hoplite, bright-colored and dangerous; he looked like a rooster: feathered].

But it is Böll's cruelly mutilated and dying narrator who is the principal subject of contrast with the ancient Greek heroes. They stood at the beginning, while he stands at the end of civilization, as it reaches an ignominious and catastrophic nadir in the shape of Nazism and its destructive aftermath. For the ultimate degradation of the Greek trophies and ideals is that they are linked with the "Prussian" and Nazi perversities in rectilinear continuity. Pictures of the German leaders from the Grand Elector to Hitler and, more debasing yet, phrenological specimens of Nazi racist theory are aligned with the Medea, the "Dornenauszieher" [boy removing a thorn], and the hoplite. Color also suggests a retrogressive and maladive continuity: The Parthenon reproduction is yellowish; busts of Caesar, Cicero, and Marcus Aurelius are "ganz gelb" [completely yellow]; and the wall behind the militaristic German leaders down to Hitler is painted yellow.

In addition to the title words (which could conceivably have been taken directly from Simonides) there is a veiled allusion to Schiller: the Parthenon frieze is "wunderbar gemacht, eine Nachbildung" [wonderfully made, a reproduction]; the three Roman busts are "wunderbar nachgemacht, ganz gelb und echt, antik und würdig" [wonderfully reproduced, all yellow and genuine, antique (i.e. classical) and dignified]. This last pair of adjectives suggests Schiller's famous phrase, "Anmut und Würde" [Charm and Dignity], and his idealization of the ancient Greek spirit. For Böll, however, the Graeco-Roman world as transmitted in the humanistic high school is artificial and unnatural: "nachgemacht" [reproduced]. For eight years Böll's Youth had, in boredom and frustration, drawn vases and practiced lettering in the art room—"schlanke, feine, wunderbar nachgemachte römische Glasvasen . . . und Schriften aller Art, Rundschrift, Antiqua, Römisch, Italienne" [slender, fine, wonderfully reproduced Roman glass vases . . . and scripts of every sort: round hand, antiqua, Roman, Italienne]—and he hated nothing more.

What, then, is the nature of Böll's reply to Schiller? First of all, it is not a condemnation *in toto,* as Böll seems to imply for Nietzsche: "zwischen bräunlichen muffigen Türen sah ich nur Nietzsches Schnurrbart und seine Nasenspitze in einem goldenen Rahmen, denn sie hatten die andere Hälfte des Bildes mit einem Zettel überklebt, auf dem zu lesen war: 'Leichte Chirurgie' " [between brownish stodgy doors I saw only Nietzsche's moustache and the tip of his nose in a golden frame, for they had pasted over the other half of the picture with a note which read: 'minor surgery']. In other words, this is the philosopher whom the brown shirts admired, this preacher of the blond beast with merciless cruelty; he has brought these mutilations and sufferings upon us. There is no hint of any such condemnation of Schiller. The point at issue between Böll's **"Wanderer"** and Schiller's "Spaziergang" is this: Schiller sees modern "corruption" as a deviation from nature and a result of *hybris* in civilization which does not nullify the majesty of the Greek beginnings; in Böll's story, however, nature is non-existent and Graeco-Roman antiquity is condemned as the militaristic source of the present evils and an artificial imposition upon the minds of the young *via* the authoritarian, traditionalistic institution called "das humanistische Gymnasium" [the humanistic high school]. As with the sign pasted across Nietzsche's face, it is no coincidence that the wounded and the dead are brought back here. The vultures have, so to speak, come home to roost. This is the harvest from an evil planting.

But the difference between the two authors is one of emphasis. For Schiller, too, civilization (i.e. the decadent feudalism of his time) ends in evil and destruction (modeled on the French Revolution), and the poetic inner vision culminates in this Rousseauesque appeal:

> O, so öffnet euch, Mauren, und gebt den Gefa-
> nenen ledig,
> Zu der verlassenen Flur kehr er gerettet zurück!
>
> [O, so open, you walls, and set the prisoner free,
> Let him return in safety to the abandoned fields!]

For Schiller, man can still escape from civilization and flee back to nature. But the world of Böll's **"Wanderer"** excludes even a glimpse of nature. Man is boxed in complete-

ly by his artifacts, which are the products and instruments of a perverse ideology, and he perishes with them. A young life, abused and misused by propaganda, recedes back to extinction. (pp. 109-16)

David J. Parent, "Böll's 'Wanderer, Kommst du Nach Spa–,' a Reply to Schiller's 'Der Spaziergang'," in Essays in Literature, *Vol. 1, No. 1, Spring, 1974, pp. 109-17.*

Böll on his world outlook:

Mine is the optimism of the survivor; the feeling of having survived is very often horrible when you realize how many didn't. I'm still whole, still here—that is one of my driving forces, the feeling of having survived. One of the difficulties for today's young people is that they don't have this feeling. But those who survived World War II, Auschwitz, and political murder have a certain optimism combined with a bad conscience as well . . . because surviving such things is not only luck and grace—it is even perhaps evidence of a brutal vitality. I don't know, I've just become very skeptical.

Heinrich Böll, in an interview in The Paris Review, *Spring 1983.*

J. P. Stern

Predictability and reliance on familiar thought, the predetermined response to a chosen situation, stereotyped judgments: moral goodness of a very high order is perfectly compatible with these lack-lustre qualities. Not so literature. One might almost define literature as that mode of experience whose most appropriate value judgments depend not, alas, on the goodness, or honesty, or even the integrity of the mind at work, but on the freshness and articulated energy of the prospect presented. Equally odd is the fact that eras of relative peace, equity and the rule of law, such as Federal Germany is enjoying today, offer no better opportunity for the creation of literary masterpieces than epochs of chaos, social disaffection and strife: it was in the 1920s that German literature entered the consciousness of Europe and the Western world for the first time since the death of Goethe.

The occasion for these remarks is a look at the prolific oeuvre of Heinrich Böll who recently won the Nobel Prize (not, incidentally, for his immense decency in the cause of peace and justice, but for literature) and who, together with Günter Grass, "represents" German fiction abroad.

Born in Cologne in 1917, Böll belongs to a generation for whom the Hitler era remains the central traumatic experience of their lives. There is little variation in the way the 1940s—the war and its aftermath—figure in most of his novels. Pity for its victims and concentration on their passive suffering offer a kind of narrative norm from which there are only occasional departures. There is a good deal that is poignant in the wartime situations evoked, when hours of leave count for decades, and relationships expand, flourish and fade away in a single encounter, but there is remarkably little resistance—only a sad or despairing resignation—to the evils of the age. This, of course, is true to the German situation of the 1940s. Faced, however, with the same historical situation, Günter Grass—ten years younger than Böll—infuses its literary representation with extravagant fantasy. Grass does not ignore the vileness and pain but heightens it by imposing on it grotesque linguistic and experiential patterns which turn out to be both wildly anarchic *and* true to the historical experience; he follows W. H. Auden's injunction (in his homage to W. B. Yeats): "Sing of human unsuccess / In a rapture of distress". Böll, in all his stories except the most recent, has been unwilling to go beyond a *sotto voce* recital of the victim's woes; has been unable (in Henry James's phrase) "to make a grand issue" of them, perhaps because he finds them overwhelming. Did Böll himself come to feel the inadequacy of his literary quietism? The experiments in language and narrative form with which, in recent years, he has attempted to enliven his style remain unconvincing: they touch only the surface of his fiction, and seem derivative.

Take *Gruppenbild mit Dame* (1974), the latest of Böll's longer novels (the first, *Billard um halbzehn,* 1959, appears to have been written for a generation of readers who did not know Thomas Mann's *Buddenbrooks*). In the centre of *Group Portrait with Lady* is Leni Pfeiffer nee Gruyten, whose life is intended as one more lengthy commentary on the history of Germany since 1922, the year Leni was born. We recognize her all too readily as a mixture of Joyce Cary's Sara Monday and Tony Buddenbrook. Her biography is to be pieced together by the reader from a series of interviews about her, given by her friends to a reporter (?)-narrator who speaks of himself, coyly and parenthetically, as "(. . . Verf.)", ie "(. . . Auth.)". This quasi-journalistic, quasi-forensic device (used extensively and with no more conviction by Siegfried Lenz in *Deutschstunde,* 1968) goes on heedlessly, relentlessly, letting up only when "Verf." runs out of steam and starts filling up pages of the novel with reprints of wartime army directives or bits of bureaucratic nonsense (Here Be Satire!), to tide us over until the next interview.

In his most recent work, *The Lost Honour of Katharina Blum* (published in Germany in 1974) and *Berichte zur Gesinnungslage der Nation* [*Reports on the Ideological Situation of the Nation*] (1975), Böll has left the era of National Socialism and the war, and turns his attention to the Germany of the Baader-Meinhof trial. The *Reports on the Ideological Situation of the Nation* purport to be written by underground agents of the German government. The intention of the satire is nothing if not plain: to send up the absurd jargon and the equally absurd procedures followed by these agents. It is hard to think when German literature last had a competent satirist: the humour of this one leaves the reader listless with melancholy.

[*The Lost Honour of Katharina Blum*], which concerns the ordeal by newspaper defamation of a young and attractive girl, is a good deal more interesting. The apparently absolute power of obloquy over the lives of all those who become its victims and the absence of any real opposition to that power, hardly explained by inadequate libel laws, are important and well-tried themes which go back in German literature to the eighteenth century and beyond Böll's exposure of the practices of the contemporary gutter press is a genuine addition to these themes, and there is just a little less sentimentality in the portrait of Katharina, the victim of the defamation, than one finds in Böll's earlier novels. Once more the style of forensic reportage has been chosen, perhaps because in recent years such "documentary" fiction has been praised as the latest literary thing by West German critics who delight in sending a shudder down their bourgeois readers' spines by claiming that all "bourgeois" or "beautiful" literature "is finished". (This, incidentally, is what Professor Hans Mayer does on the jacket of [*Gruppenbild mit Dame*].) Still, this style does have its uses: it enables Böll to present the scandal from various points of view and with a few touches of dry humour—as when Katharina's complaint that the death of her mother has been hastened by the monstrous behaviour of the press is met by sociological clichés:

> Dr Heinen, mistakenly assuming her to be a Marxist . . . was taken aback by her detachment and asked her whether she considered it—this *modus operandi* of the *News*—to be a problem of the social structure. Katharina did not know what he meant, and shook her head.

(Böll's "Zeitungsmasche"—*Zeitung* is the name of the paper in question and "Masche" means "trick"—is more sharply focused than "modus operandi" but on the whole the translation is careful and intelligent.)

The novella *Katharina Blum,* then, is an improvement on the over-long *Group Portrait* but the premeditation and stereotyped value judgments are still there. We have only to read a description of Katharina's clothes or the way she prepares her employers' breakfast to know that she can do no wrong; we have only to follow the scenario as it is outlined in the first few pages to know that there will be no real opposition to the process of character assassination, that there will not be a single person or institution to provide Katharina, not just with sympathy, but with effective protection; indeed, I cannot think of a single example in Böll's work where he has portrayed successful resistance to the tyranny of society. Why is this? Again we might go back for an explanation to the traditional pattern of German novels to Goethe's belief that novels should be built around a passive hero, one who "retards the action"; moreover, like most nineteenth-century German novelists, Böll, too, is incapable of showing a positive interest in institutional arrangements of any kind (even nunneries are suspect and corrupt or demean the individuals who live in them); but the reason for the passivity of his fiction, as well as for the clichés of his character portrayal and evaluation, is to be found in more recent history.

The scheme of values that underlies his writings is honourable and simple, but it is also entirely predictable. It amounts to a complete and, as it were, mechanical reversal of the value scheme of National Socialism: a reversal not merely of those values but of the gestures and perceptions that go with them. Where the National Socialists proclaimed the glory of the embattled national collective, Böll proclaims the absolute value of the unprotected individual; where they exalted the will and political power, his favourite characters are full of doubt and uncertainty, and he invariably sees power of any kind as evil; where they excelled at organizing people, he favours gentle anarchy and shows disdain for—if not outright loathing of—any social institution more formal than the kind we find in *Emil and the Detectives;* where they vaunted "moral purity" and harsh sexual prudishness, he shows a heart of gold and tolerance galore; where they preached the racial inferiority of Germany's eastern neighbours, he will invariably show them possessed of great dignity and dark-eyed wisdom; and since they used Nature as their major ideological ploy, in Böll every mention of lipstick, powder and rouge signals a retrospective protest. Who would wish to question the utter decency of these sentiments and reactions? But can it be denied that that is what they are—reactions? It seems as though, by imprisoning him in a perpetual negation of its scheme of "values" and of the gestures that go with those values, that evil ideology continues to blight even the work of one wholly uncontaminated by it.

It is, as I have said, the honourable predicament of a splendid and decent man—the sort of predicament from which consolation, wisdom, and integrity are born; but

> Time that is intolerant
> Of the brave and innocent

Auden wrote in that poem from which I quoted earlier,

> Worships language and forgives
> Everyone by whom it lives.

The German language has an indifferent time in Böll's work. His is not the sort of predicament from which great literature is born.

> J. P. Stern, "An Honourable Man," in The Times Literary Supplement, No. 3855, January 30, 1976, p. 101.

Wilhelm Johannes Schwarz on Böll's fiction:

At the center of Böll's work stands the individual of our time and his problems—his love and his suffering, his hope and his despair. Böll is a committed writer. Nothing is further from his mind than to indulge in *l'art pour l'art,* as indeed he explicitly states in his essays. He seems to feel an inner compulsion to come to terms with the recent past and its conflicting currents . . . [of] the last thirty years.

> *Wilhelm Johannes Schwarz, in his* Heinrich Böll, Teller of Tales: A Study of His Works and Characters, *translated by Alexander and Elizabeth Henderson, Frederick Ungar, 1969.*

Charlotte W. Ghurye

Böll is a man of moral convictions, known to speak up whenever he perceives a weak point or an abuse in society. In his work *Die verlorene Ehre der Katharina Blum*

(1974) he exposes and overtly criticizes the abuse of freedom of the press, especially by the tabloid with its highly questionable methods of reporting, or rather distorting, news, with its sensationalism and jumping to unjustifiable conclusions. (p. 64)

For the reader and scholar of German literature the title of Böll's *Erzählung* immediately evokes memories of the 19th-century *Novelle.* The first literary association that comes to mind is [Clemens Maria] Brentano's *Novelle Die Geschichte vom braven Kasperl und vom schönen Annerl* (1817) in which the concept of honor and especially the theme of "die verlorene Ehre" of the heroine, that is, the theme of a clandestine love affair and subsequent pregnancy, play a central role. Böll's title also reminds us of a *Novelle* of that century by [Theodor] Storm, *Aquis submersus* (1877), another story in which the heroine, incidentally named Katharina, gives herself to her lover, becomes pregnant, and to cover her social disgrace is married off by her brother to a surly and unloved man. [Heinrich von] Kleist's *Novelle Die Marquise von O . . .* (1808) forms a variation on the theme although the Marquise's embarrassing predicament is resolved to her satisfaction and the story has a happy end in contrast to those of Brentano and Storm.

What all three *Novellen* cited above have in common is the idea that the woman, by conceiving and bearing a child out of wedlock and thereby not conforming to the code of prescribed social behavior, is found guilty and condemned by society. Although the man is just as accountable for the conception of the child, and in the case of *Die Marquise von O . . .* he is a rapist, having impregnated the lady without her consent or even her knowledge, he is not taken to task by society, and no stigma is attached to him. The double standards held by society and applied to women, as illustrated in all three *Novellen,* are age old and need no further elaboration.

Böll's *Erzählung,* contrary to what the title might suggest in light of previous literary thematic exploration, does not treat the theme of the fallen maiden who gets pregnant and thereupon has to suffer the consequences of social rejection or ostracism. What Böll's Katharina does have in common with the heroines of the three *Novellen* cited above is the loss of her good name and her honorable reputation. The misfortune befalls her almost out of the clear blue sky, without her breaking the code of social ethics or knowingly committing any infraction of the law. Her good name is sullied maliciously by sensational libeling newspaper reports which assume such dimensions that they come close to destroying her reputable, carefully built-up life. (pp. 64-5)

Two points of importance emerge painfully clearly from our author's *Erzählung,* first: gullibly accepting information at face value that ought to be examined with close scrutiny and skepticism. Philistine members of contemporary society are all too willing to devour whatever unsavory fare is served to them by the tabloid. Worse yet, they sit in judgment with righteous indignation over the alleged misdeeds of their fellow citizens and openly rejoice in the latter's misfortune. Second, the casting of stones at the sinner—or rather alleged sinner, since Katharina has not committed the transgressions she is accused of—and the denigration by the philistines are particularly odious and biased when the person in question happens to be a woman.

Whether Böll intended to add the extra dimension of social prejudice against women in a male-dominated society to his castigation of the press for inciting the undiscerning reader to committing "Lynchjustiz" is a point only the author himself can answer. But in any case, evidence throughout the *Erzählung* points to the undisputable fact that Katharina's social position is more precarious and endangered than that of the male, she is more vulnerable and defenseless because she is a member of the weaker sex.

Many of the charges levelled against Katharina by witnesses called upon to testify against her reveal sex bias, class discrimination, and political hysteria. From the testimonies emerge worn-out clichés and social prejudices against woman mouthed by male chauvinists which have survived to this day and are as strong as ever. Complementing woman's image as the lewd seductress and sex object, as she is viewed by the prejudiced male, are several portraits of those viewers from among the stronger sex: the authoritarian, brute-force type, the irresistible ladies' man, the rejected, vindictive husband, the moralizer, the political conservative who fears the radicalism of women, presumably triggered by such activist figures as Ulrike Meinhof, and last but not least, the unscrupulous opportunist pursuing success who stops at nothing and whose reckless game nobody can check.

All the characters, male and female, who contribute to her defamation, project an image of Katharina as a shrewd and lewd seductress who makes capital out of her charms. Because Katharina is an attractive woman in her late twenties, whose alluring femininity has a bewitching effect on men, that image is reinforced. Incidentally, Böll never describes Katharina's physical characteristics, such as the color of her eyes or her hair, the shape of her body, etc. All we see is her effect on the men with whom she comes in contact, an effect which reflects an almost mysterious charm. The fact that she is divorced, "schuldig geschieden," and now lives alone arouses the suspicion of the philistine minds and contributes to the impression of lewdness whereas Katharina's ownership of an apartment promotes the conjecture of shrewdness. Jealous and insecure women, such as *Frau* Kluthen, wife of Katharina's former employer, perpetuate the unflattering image by declaring her a moral danger to every man in sight and accusing her of having "so eine richtig nuttige Art." Chiming in on that supposed aspect of Katharina's personality, *Kriminalkommissar* Beizmenne throws in the additional suspicion that she is a kept woman, financially supported by the criminal Ludwig Götten so that her good name is besmirched still further. Once Beizmenne, by authority of his office, has demanded an account of Katharina's financial affairs, a Pandora's box is opened. Although every penny is earned by honest work, all the evil tongues now accuse the poor young woman of prostitution.

The alleged practice of prostitution is easily explained by the slanderers because Katharina comes from the working class, has had an unhappy childhood and a disharmonious family life with an allegedly alcoholic mother—all of which factors supposedly have corroded her morality. And because she was poor and has had to work hard since she was a teen-ager, it is assumed that her foremost goal in life is easily obtainable affluence. This erroneous assumption coupled with the allegation of low morality lead to the conclusion that a girl of the 'lower classes' chooses prostitution as the easy way to get rich. None of Katharina's adversaries give her credit for the fact that she is extremely hard-working and thrifty and that her industriousness accounts for ownership of the apartment. Obviously class bias is a prejudicial factor in the defamation of Katharina's character.

Class bias is reflected also in the discourteous attitude and treatment accorded Katharina by the men who would like to seduce and possess her. The minds of these sexist men are still haunted by the old idea dating back to feudal times that a 'lower class' girl or woman is not a lady and that therefore she can be readily approached and seduced. Beizmenne's irrelevant inquiry into Katharina's intimate life, formulated in vulgar language and showing an offensive discourtesy by using the familiar German "du" form in an official police investigation is an example of that denigrating attitude. An even more glaring example is the stance of the unscrupulous journalist Tötges who likewise addresses Katharina with the "du" form without knowing her, but he surpasses Beizmenne by actually propositioning the reserved, unwilling young woman in the crudest terms and by attempting to change that illicit intent into instant aggressive action.

Since Tötges is the journalist from whose poisonous pen the murderous character assassination of Katharina, to which she refers as "ihre verlorene Ehre," has originated and then been published in his tabloid *Zeitung,* the possibility suggests itself that a psychological nexus exists between Tötges' systematic destruction of Katharina as a human being and his intention to rape her. That nexus appears to be an age old part of the pattern of aggressive human behavior itself. From historical sources evidence is presented that such a connection between male aggression and sexual assault dates back thousands of years and continues right into the present. With few exceptions, every conquering army sexually assaulted the women of the vanquished tribe or nation. From contemporary statistics the conclusion emerges that the barbarous practice extends also into the area of crime. In numerous cases of non-homicidal crimes, such as burglary, housebreaking, larceny, and abduction, the criminal commits rape incidentally, as an epilogue to another crime if a woman happens to be on the scene. The term 'felony rape' is applied to such cases where rape is not the primary goal but only occurs incidentally and the criminal is not a true sex offender.

Whether it was Böll's intention to highlight this point or not, the principle that the aggressor ravishes his female victim applies or can be interpreted as being applicable to Tötges, who has dealt the lethal blow to Katharina, although, of course, not in terms of actual physical violence. But Tötges' libelous, distorted stories about the innocent Katharina are such damaging lies that Else Woltersheim reprovingly criticizes them as an attempt "ein junges Leben zu zerstören."

In his literary review of *Die verlorene Ehre* [in *Der Spiegel* (1974)], the critic Torberg remarks with an air of knowing it all that the interview scene between Tötges and Katharina reveals a saddening ignorance of the professional customs of journalists on the part of Böll and that a reporter would not proposition and attempt to rape a woman he interviews. (pp. 66-9)

While Torberg's argument proceeds from a very pragmatical point of departure, emphasizing the rational, calculating attitude of even an unscrupulous reporter to not jeopardize his well-paid job, Torberg does not take into account the irrational elements of human nature. Böll's creating of the fateful scene of the interview with Tötges' improper advances is entirely plausible because there is something irrational, something pathological, even criminal about a personality capable of fabricating the type of outrageous lies such as Tötges has done, no matter what his motives are. Besides, Tötges is depicted as feeling very superior, even over-confident, and does not give the impression that risks overly concern him. By the same token, the possibility that he could have a troublesome lawsuit for libel on his hands never seems to enter his mind.

It was stated above that the image of Katharina projected by her adversaries is that of a seductress who uses her physical charms commercially. To increase that negative image, they have added yet another dimension to their vicious lies, namely political defamation. The completely apolitical young woman is accused of being the daughter of a Communist and is therefore considered tainted. Her main accuser is the pastor of Gemmelsbroich who boldly asserts that he needs no concrete proof of Communist affiliation and states "er habe einfach gerochen, dass Blum [Katharinas Vater] ein Kommunist sei." Here, we encounter Böll's implied criticism, well-known by now, that representatives of the Catholic Church often do not act in the Christian spirit. Katharina's ex-husband denounces her for "Radikalität und Kirchenfeindlichkeit," his motive undoubtedly being personal revenge because his former wife has rejected him. Even as educated a man as the head physician, Dr. Heinen, suspects Katharina to be a Marxist, basing his opinion uncritically on the report of the *Zeitung*. The assertions and beliefs of the three men reflect political hysteria, personal rancor, and lack of critical judgment, respectively, all of which contribute to the political witch-hunting aspect of the case.

Political defamation, exploiting the wide-spread phobia about leftists and Communists in the Federal Republic, recurs as a theme in *Die verlorene Ehre* involving two other female characters as the victims, neither of them affiliated with the Communist party or any radical group. In the case of Gertrud Blorna, an architect and the employer of Katharina, the lady in question is branded in the *Zeitung* as "die rote Trude" in order to turn public opinion against her. Else Woltersheim, Katharina's relative and chief witness, is discredited by the same source on the grounds that her father was a member of the Communist party in 1932, more than 40 years ago, and because her mother happens to live in East Germany. Beizmenne's acceptance of un-

verified information on the political background of the parents of a respectable witness, information gathered from as unsalutary a source as the *Zeitung*, totally irrelevant to the case he is investigating and partly outdated, is consonant with his unprofessional habit of jumping to conclusions and appears to serve only one purpose, to taint the witness with guilt by association. Once Else Woltersheim is represented in an unfavorable light to the public, her testimony in favor of the accused Katharina is weakened. In addition, Beizmenne relies on social prejudice to discredit Else as a witness. Having also learned from the *Zeitung* that Else was born the illegitimate daughter of a woman worker, he rejoices in having acquired this detail which is as irrelevant to Else's function as a witness as it is prejudicial in the eyes of the public.

In general, Beizmenne is represented as the tough law and order official whose conduct and practices are not in line with those of a democratic society where the rights of the individual are respected and guaranteed. Some of his tactics are reminiscent of the Hitler era and so is his inclination to use brute force, as for example, in wanting to put handcuffs on the co-operative Katharina when she is already guarded by six fully armed policemen. Beizmenne's unnecessary show of force conveys the idea that he valiantly protects society against a militant female anarchist, suggestive of Ulrike Meinhof. There is thus a further discrediting feature along the lines of political defamation added to the image of woman.

To inject a light and amusing touch to the serious hearing scene in which Else Woltersheim testifies with considerable hostility toward the prosecution, Böll makes fun of the public prosecutor, Dr. Korten. This inexperienced, self-important and not very sharp young man upbraids the older woman, whose social position is lower than Korten's for her lack of social graces, a criticism which is rude and inappropriate for a public prosecutor, to say the least. (pp. 70-2)

The unfair practice of using the principle of guilt by association against a woman is taken up once more as a theme in *Die verlorene Ehre* in Gertrud Blorna's case. Since Gertrud employs Katharina as a housekeeper and stands by her in spite of the adverse publicity, the architect's company is determined to dismiss Gertrud from her position. In the eyes of the business world, which here represents a segment of society, Gertrud also becomes suspect because of her association with the allegedly guilty Katharina. To give the appearance that Gertrud's dismissal is not only justified but also in the best interest of the company, a suit of "Vertrauensbruch" is brought against her, a procedure which underscores the hypocrisy of society.

To be sure, not all the characters in *Die verlorene Ehre* participate in the defamation of Katharina nor do they all view her as an immoral seductress. However, with the two exceptions, Blorna and Götten, Katharina's male admirers all treat her as a sex object, a desirable woman to be pursued for the purpose of amorous adventures and illicit affairs. Striving with varying degrees of persistence to exploit her for their own pleasure, these men seek a physical relationship without human commitment, without love or even a sincere friendship. The treatment of Katharina by these male hedonists contributes to the negative image of woman grounded in sexuality. It conveys the idea that woman is an erotic, manipulatable object, something that can be acquired by various stratagems, possessed, utilized, and discarded at will after it has served its purpose. In such an attitude toward woman the human dimension is missing and thus she becomes dehumanized and debased.

The character who displays the above described attitude toward woman most markedly is Sträubleder, the well-to-do, prestigious industrialist. He embodies the arrogant belief that wealth and social status entitle a man to indulge his sensual pleasures. And since Sträubleder considers himself irresistible to the ladies, he feels all the more that he has a right to engage in the conquest and enjoyment of women. Being a family man with a wife and four children does not deter him from his amorous adventures, nor does his infidelity trouble his conscience. Sträubleder's lack of respect for woman's dignity is not only evident from his pestering, unsuccessful pursuit of Katharina but also from his attitude toward his own wife. From his philanderings, of which he makes no secret, the reader cannot escape the conclusion that this self-centered Don Juan has little concern for his wife's feelings. She has to acquiesce to his extramarital relationships and is regarded as a mere appendage to her prestigious husband. While he enjoys and fancies himself in the role of the glamorous, successful man in public life and big business, his spouse is relegated to the sphere of the famous German three K's (*Kinder, Küche, Kirche*). However, the impression Sträubleder makes on the reader is far from glamorous, since he is presented quite ludicrously in his Don Juan role. He imagines and proclaims that he loves Katharina when actually he has fallen in love with his own projected image. When she rejects his bold advances, he is insulted, his vanity is injured. In a situation of crisis, he reveals himself as a hypocritical coward and egotist who uses his substantial influence only to keep his own name out of the *Zeitung,* but makes no attempt to suppress the outrageous lies about Katharina.

The character, Ludwig Götten, with whom Katharina falls in love, is the very antithesis of Sträubleder. In contrast to the latter, Götten's conception of woman is not that of a sex object but of a human being to be treated with tenderness and human dignity. After his arrest, his first thought is to clear Katharina of the accusation of being his accomplice, a fact which demonstrates his human concern for the young woman. It is remarkable that the one man whom Böll portrays as a gentleman, capable of genuine affection, and the only one to whom Katharina gives her love, is a rebel against the establishment. Although the police and society at large view him as a criminal, Böll in all probability intends Götten to be an activist, a protester against the *Bundeswehr,* which he has robbed and deserted. Böll's disapproval of and antagonism to that institution, which are expressed freely in *Ende einer Dienstfahrt* and in his essays, his sarcastic reference to the *Bundeswehr* as "diese segensreiche Einrichtung," point to the conclusion that Götten's motive is intended to be opposition on an ideological basis and defiance rather than criminality. (pp. 72-4)

If one scrutinizes Böll's previous novel *Gruppenbild mit Dame* (1971) carefully, one detects that the author already touches upon the theme of woman's degradation by certain elements in society. At the time of the action of the novel which is about 1970, a slander campaign is in progress against Leni Gruyten, the heroine. She is reviled by uncharitable neighbors; invectives and insults, such as "Kommunistenhure," "Russenliebchen," "mieses Stück" are shouted at her, reminiscent of the abusive expressions directed at Katharina in anonymous letters and obscene phone calls. Leni experiences much the same hostile and aggressive attitude as Katharina. But in Leni's case, at least a partial explanation is offered for the antagonism displayed toward her: her association with foreign workers and their families and her love affair with the Turkish garbage collector. Such associations and alliances are unacceptable to the narrow-minded, xenophobic neighbors of Leni. Devoid of tolerance and respect for individual liberty, these *Kleinbürger* react with malice and anger to the nonconformist. Leni's unconventional life style represents a challenge to the rule of the norm and a threat to the philistines' facile morality, hence they retaliate by denigrating Leni as a woman.

In contrast to Leni, Katharina behaves in no way like a nonconformist. She leads a quiet, reserved, routine life of hard work and no play. There is nothing extraordinary in her behavior or way of life to draw attention, much less hostility to herself. Even her encounter and falling in love with Götten is not in itself anything sensational. But because Beizmenne, Hach, and Korten are driven by the desire for professional glory and achievement, because they are determined to unveil a criminal conspiracy between Götten and Katharina, which does not exist, they attack her and degrade her as a woman. She gets caught in the wheels of the prosecution's machinery although she is not involved in any crime. (Her aiding a military deserter escape is a minor offense, a political rather than a criminal infraction.) Self-importance and ambition to enhance their public image lead the three men to the indiscretion of revealing far more information about Katharina's personal life to the press than is prudent or ethical or even relevant to the case. The public prosecutor, Hach, justifies the leak of information by emphasizing that "es habe natürlich angesichts des riesigen öffentlichen Interesses am Fall Götten eine Presseverlautbarung herausgegeben werden müssen." In its turn, the released information serves the professional ambitions of Tötges who promotes his own reputation as an efficient, sensationalist reporter for the *Zeitung*. He also benefits financially by selling the libelous reports further to other newspapers through an agent. In the last analysis, it is the professional ambition of men and their drive for personal success and recognition that degrade woman and destroy her honor. Not only Tötges and the publisher of the *Zeitung* take part in the destruction; Beizmenne, Hach, and Korten are equally accountable and guilty. By abstract moral standards, their share in the guilt is perhaps even greater because they are the holders of respected positions and public offices. The primary function of their job is to serve society and protect its citizens, male and female. But they first and foremost serve their own ends. Instead of carrying out their tasks with prudence and responsibility, they abuse their power and authority. Thus, an indictment of the law-enforcement agencies and the judiciary emerges from the work along with criticism of the press.

The conclusion of *Die verlorene Ehre* turns out to be unexpected and somewhat paradoxical. After Katharina commits the only antisocial act for which society could censure her with some justification, she is no longer concerned about her reputation, and public opinion becomes a matter of indifference to her. Taking vengeance for her lost honor restores her emotional equilibrium. She experiences no pangs of conscience or feelings of contrition after shooting Tötges, the assailant of her good name. Böll demonstrates convincingly how a peaceful person can be incited to violence and to taking the law into her own hands. But Katharina's act of revenge is a solution to her denigration only on a personal level; at most it is a general lesson that a woman can use a gun as efficiently as a man when it comes to defending her honor. On a universal level, the problem of vindicating woman's degradation by a male-dominated society remains unsolved. (pp. 74-6)

> *Charlotte W. Ghurye, "Katharina Blum— Symbol of Woman's Social Degradation," in her* The Writer and Society: Studies in the Fiction of Günter Grass and Heinrich Böll, *Herbert Lang, 1976, pp. 63-76.*

Robert C. Conard

The satire **"Nicht nur zur Weihnachtszeit,"** written in 1951, was at the time of its writing a product of Böll's growing displeasure with the political, psychological, and social developments in the Federal Republic. Böll's new critical attitude was a change from the general satisfaction he felt in Germany immediately after the war in the nation's return to what he thought were fundamental human values. But despite the work's harsh criticism of Germany—or because of it—critics praised the work. It soon became a standard piece in anthologies of short fiction and in 1970 was made into a film for television. Its acceptance abroad paralleled its success in Germany, where it was frequently used as a school text. Although the work's reputation continues to grow with the years, its success has not been because of any consensus on the meaning of the story.

Hans Magnus Enzensberger claims that **"Nicht nur zur Weihnachszeit"** is a satire against **"Pseudo-religiosität."** . . . The editors of an American college text which features the story under the title **"Christmas Everyday"** comment as follows: "The story suggests that Hitler rose to power while the German people 'fiddled.' Insulated by wealth and lost in a cycle of festivals, Aunt Milla [the protagonist] shut out both the Nazis and the war. After the war, she obsessively preserves her isolation from reality. Böll obviously intends to ridicule this kind of blindness." Hugo Ernst Käufer, Helmuth Günter, James Henderson Reid, H. M. Waidson, and Erhard Friedrichsmeyer all agree the story is a critique of the German "Restoration." Indeed, the story pillories the "Restoration," but that word alone reveals very little of the point of the satire, for "Restoration" as used today in German

literary and sociological writing, can refer to the restoration of the capitalist system after the war, the restoration of the social values prevailing before 1945, the rehabilitation of old Nazis and their return to public service, or the beginning of the economic recovery, to mention only a few of the word's referents. The story certainly treats the "Restoration." But how, in what degree, in which aspects? These questions are the ones an interpretation must address. In a dissertation on Böll's satire, Anne Louise Murray concludes:

> What is being satirized [in **"Nicht nur zur Weihnachtszeit"**] is the obsession of some people in the post-war era to build up for themselves again a feeling of security or comfort based on a return to "the good old times" before the war. What comes through very strongly is the folly of trying to elude the harsher realities that are the aftermath of disaster by an escape into any kind of artificial construct, no matter how praiseworthy or exalted its base might be.

Two British critics come still closer in nailing down what is one of Böll's main points in the satire. Enid MacPherson finds the work a critique of the apparent orderliness of postwar Germany: "In reality," she claims, "all is very much out of order and will continue to be so until the war and the Hitler period has been acknowledged and expiated." And fellow countryman Brian Murdoch concludes that the satire is "a criticism of the striving to obliterate all memory of the war and return to the pre-war *status quo.*" Memory, acknowledgement, and expiation of the war years, these are, indeed, the main themes of the satire.

Considering this broad range of conflicting (but justifiable) scholarly opinion, **"Nicht nur zur Weihnachtszeit"** deserves a detailed analysis and interpretation. Up till now only Friedrichsmeyer has thoroughly interpreted the story. Although his emphasis differs sharply from mine because his interpretation stresses the story's critique of Germany's return to a pre-war *Bürgerlichkeit* and mine the German failure to conquer the past, nonetheless, our approaches and conclusions, while different, often complement rather than contradict each other. However, when the interpretations strikingly oppose one another, the differences will be made clear.

In January 1979, German television broadcast the American T.V. serial "Holocaust." Millions of Germans saw all or part of this dramatized treatment of the final solution of the Jewish problem. The response of the nation to the series again made clear that thirty-four years after the war, many Germans who had lived through those years had not yet dealt honestly with the past. Some still claimed not to have known of the crimes of the Hitler period and a few even denied that they took place. German repression of the events of the war years became once again a phenomenon reported in the world press. The German claim of limited knowledge of the extent of Nazi war crimes, while justified at the end of the war, developed for many people in the years of the "economic miracle" into willful ignorance and denial. While many German writers have treated this theme, most notably Günter Grass in the *Zwiebelkeller* section of *Die Blechtrommel,* Günter Eich and Hans Magnus Enzensberger in their poems, and Wolfgang Koeppen,

Alfred Andersch, Siegfried Lenz, Johannes Bobrowski, and Christa Wolf in their novels, Heinrich Böll's bizarre and humorous tale **"Nicht nur zur Weihnachtszeit"** was one of the earliest works in German literature to deal with this refusal to face reality. But the story in its carefully chosen symbolic form with its paradigmatic technique transcends the limits of a national satire and contains a message for other nations as well. In the manner of Swift's "Modest Proposal," it grows in importance and prestige while the events behind the work fade into history.

Böll's satire is easily summarized. It related the tale of tyrannical Aunt Milla who desires to celebrate Christmas every day and of her tantrums which force the members of her family to yield to her strange and destructive demand. To recount the tale Böll chooses a first-person narrator, but one not immediately involved in the events he writes about. As nephew to the protagonist, Aunt Milla, he is, however, close enough to remain objective. He witnesses some of the action and hears about the rest. Despite his effort to be detached, he is more sympathetic to the aunt's attempt to have Christmas every day (i.e., to hide reality) than he admits. . . . Because of his sympathy with the older generation, because of his desire to put his relatives in a good light, he becomes a German Everyman who shares the responsibility of that generation for the repression of history. Most exemplary of his cooperation in the repression of the past is his failure, in an entire story about the Hitler period, to hint at, much less to refer to, concentration camps or the Final Solution; he mentions only Germany's own suffering in the war years. What results is a narrative fraught with understatement of bizarre antics. The discrepancy between this understatement and the extraordinary events of the story contributes to the irony of the tale.

In **"Nicht nur zur Weihnachtszeit"** the object of Böll's satire is not primarily the false piety or hypocrisy of Christians who cling to an empty ritual which they themselves have devitalized, nor is it primarily an attack against the commercialization, sentimentalization, and growing meaninglessness of Christmas in a secular world, nor even a veiled criticism of German behavior during the war years. Neither does the story satirize primarily the state of religion in postwar Germany, nor function simply as a very funny entertainment for readers of light fiction. The work attacks first and foremost West Germany's desire after the war to avoid coming to terms with the Hitler years and that nation's failure to learn from recent historical experience. In fact, most remarkable about **"Nicht nur zur Weihnachtszeit"** is the way it presents this message with objectivity and cool detachment in a genre not noted for either of these virtues. Böll's satire is in this regard in the manner of the English satirists Pope and Swift who create tension in the *Dunciad* and the "Modest Proposal" by confronting outrageous events with calmness. While the very idea of Christmas everyday is a form of hyperbole, the work retains a matter-of-factness and indirectness that results in a thorough analysis of Germany's postwar social sickness. (pp. 97-8)

The narrator's story is to be understood as a tale of his countrymen. He achieves this breadth of context with the words "in unserer Verwandtschaft" which indicate the story is one of more than the immediate family and refers to all relations and kin, with the phrase "ganze Sippe" which indicates a tribe, a family group in the largest sense, and with the expression "Zeitgenossen" which informs the reader that the unusual story he is about to hear is a parable (whose "Realität aber niemand bestreiten kann") for and about the entire German nation. Early in the story the narrator humbly apologizes for having to mention the war, admitting he preferred not to run the risk of making himself "unbeliebt," but was forced to raise the unpleasant topic simply because it had an "Einfluß auf die Geschichte"; however, after once having put the "langweilig" detail aside, he promises not to bring it up again. Thus, with this use of understatement Böll both sets the tone and provides the background necessary to understand the message of his tale.

The choice of Christmas as a symbol of Germany's forgetfulness (a people's desire not to conquer the past) is actually quite natural. Christmas, in fact, abrogates the concerns of the day. For a brief period people forget their troubles or at least disguise them behind a festive spirit. Traditions by their nature stress the past and in that manner distort the present and neglect the future, but Christmas more than other celebrations emphasizes an idealized and romanticized past. Hence, the Christmas season functions as institutionalized escapism as it is employed in the work, a permanent flight from reality extending from December to December, a point reinforced in the satire by the twelve narrative divisions Böll gives the story.

During the late days of World War II and in the months immediately following the war, German Christmases in their normal manner were impossible to celebrate; the necessary material items were simply unavailable. Escape from the reality of the war was impossible. However, in December 1946, twenty months after the war, for a wealthy family with important connections, material improvements were noticeable long before general prosperity. Prior to this time Germans could hardly put the war out of their consciousness. They were too close to the revelations of genocide, war crimes and their own hunger and deprivation to fail to associate their condition with its cause. . . . Thus, the repression of the war experience could begin in earnest only after a degree of normality was restored to life.

The past which Aunt Milla wishes to forget is explicit in the story: "Denn der Krieg wurde von meiner Tante Milla nur registriert als eine Macht, die schon Weihnachten 1939 anfing, ihren Weihnachtsbaum zu gefährden." Two conclusions are necessary from the narrator's observation. First, some Germans only reacted to the war to the extent that it touched adversely upon their personal lives, and second, Germans could hate the inconvenience of the war without relating it to the Hitler dictatorship. Both conclusions reveal that the war might be condemned as something apart from National Socialism and fascism. The leitmotifs of the story—"die gute alte Zeit" and "Alles sollte so sein wie früher"—refer specifically to the period prior to 1939, not 1933. "The good old days" refer then to the prewar period when Hitler was in power, Nazism was triumphant, and all was going well for the nation. Böll is saying in this satire of 1951 that the German failure to conquer the past is more than merely a desire to forget the war and a refusal to assume responsibility for it, but also a failure to condemn fascism.

The time references in the story are specific. It was "Mitte März" 1947 when the narrator discovered the first signs of permanent Christmas among his relatives. When the tree was taken down at its traditional time "um Mariä Lichtmess herum," Aunt Milla began to scream. Uncle Franz immediately called in medical assistance to deal with her fits of hysteria, but even the costliest experts could not analyze correctly, much less remedy, her German malady. When the family discovered that the restoration of the Christmas tree comforted her and alleviated her hysteria, they catered to her "harmlose Schwäche" and without further questioning, with the "Beteiligung aller," they took up the "kostbare" burden of continuing the celebration.

The costs are, indeed, more than financial. Aunt Milla's husband, Uncle Franz, described prior to the permanent Christmas as a "herzengute(r) Mensch," "ein Muster an Vitalität," and a "Vorbild ein(es) christlichen Kaufmann(s)," soon manifests [signs of moral decay]. . . . He becomes estranged from his wife, commits adultery, takes a mistress, and transforms himself into a greedy manipulating merchant—the last change a necessary development to maintain permanent Christmas. (pp. 98-100)

Uncle Franz' children, Cousin Johannes, Lucie, and Cousin Franz, are equally ill affected by the tacit decision not to conquer the past. Prior to the prolonged celebration Johannes is described as a successful lawyer, the favorite son of his businessman father, but in protest against the demands of permanent Christmas, he rebels. He becomes a communist and volunteers as a party organizer in the provinces. Considering the ambience of fear of the Soviet Union after the war, Johannes' protest appears as the ultimate rebellion against the restoration of German affairs.

Cousin Lucie reacts differently than her brother Johannes. She succumbs to a nervous breakdown and is "abtransportiert" (a word with clear overtones of the Nazi past) in a "Zwangsjacke." However, before the permanent Christmas drove her temporarily into an institution, she sought refuge in the life of a beatnik, even forcing her husband to accompany her to low class establishments and disreputable hangouts. Previously her husband Karl proposed emigration as an escape from the stress of year-round Christmas, but it is the deteriorating health of both his wife and children which finally forces him to leave the country with his family. His children have become "blaß und müde," and the entire family a "Versammlung von Gespenstern." Under such circumstances, which the narrator claims could in the long run cause psychic damage, Karl finds a sanctuary for his family in a land "nicht weit vom Aquator," i.e., in a country specifically chosen because it has no similarity to Germany and none of the same problems. Thus, the children of Aunt Milla and Uncle Franz turn to political activism and emigration to save themselves from the conditions in the German family.

In order to make his criticism more analytical and historically accurate, Böll departs momentarily from the tradition of satire which conventionally makes no claim to fairness. In fact, satire is normally the least objective of all literary genres because its intention is not usually to present a "realistic" account of events but a revealing insight into the condition of society; therefore, it makes no pretense of equity nor claim of balance, relying instead on disproportion either as overstatement or understatement. Satire justifies such methods because its purpose is not to offer solutions to social problems, but only to point out what the problems of society are.

In **"Nicht nur zur Weihnachtszeit"** Böll departs from the normal exaggeration of satire to tender a full view of the German situation. He knows not all Germans are guilty of the cover-up. He provides Aunt Milla's family with a symbolic redeeming member in Cousin Franz whose function in the satire is to act as foil to his tyrannical aunt. He is a typical Böllian black sheep, a boxer with an inclination to piety. He warns the family from the beginning of the "schreckliche Folgen" of permanent Christmas and is fully aware that what appears to be " 'an sich' ein harmloses Ereignis" is in reality a dangerous undertaking.

At no time does he personally take part in the celebrations. He even enhances his unpopularity in the family by suggesting his screaming mother be subjected to an exorcism or committed to an institution. In this little detail Böll points out his view that the refusal to conquer the past is, indeed, a devilish obsession or a form of mental illness. Because as a young man Cousin Franz was a mediocre student, associated with questionable companions and became a boxer, he "besaß . . . zu wenig Reputation, um in der Verwandtschaft Gehör zu finden." Therefore, the family considers him of unreliable character and treats him as an outsider. Cousin Franz exemplifies a type common in Böll's stories, the ethical asocial individual. His life is a model of humanity. During the war he treated Polish and Russian POWs with kindness, and after the war he reluctantly assumes the role of an Old Testament prophet, or of a John the Baptist, of one crying in the wilderness, warning his relatives against catering to the foolish escapism of Aunt Milla; later he even intervenes to save Lucie and Karl's children. However, at the conclusion of the story, succumbing to his lack of success, he retreats to a monastery to continue his battle with other means. (p. 100)

In his analysis of the role of Aunt Milla's children Friedrichsmeyer sees them as examples of negative behavior. He claims Cousin Franz "flüchtet ins Kloster" and "desertiert vom Leben," calls "der Eintritt ins Kloster ein negativer Akt." Further he regards the behavior of Cousin Johannes and that of the family of Cousin Lucie in this same light: "Das Gemeinsame an den Fluchtzonen Kloster, Kommunismus und Tropen ist das Assoziationsfeld des Utopisch-Idyllischen. Im Kloster herrscht der weltfremdkontemplative Geist, der Kommunismus träumt von einer befriedeten Welt, die Tropen meinen eine romantisierte Zivilisationsferne. . . ." Actually, within the satire these examples of "desertion" are positive affirmations of life because they are refusals to accept the social evil of Christmas everyday. These "desertions" function as do the social refusals of the protagonists in Böll's satirical novella *Entfernung von der Truppe* (1964), in which the hero deserts the army, and in the satirical novel *Ende einer Dienstfahrt* (1966), in which the hero deserts the post-war status quo. Friedrichsmeyer's approach to satire forces his interpretation. His radical understanding of satire as the principle of socialized aggression compels him in the direction he takes. While all satire is criticism, and all criticism may be defined as a form of aggression, Friedrichsmeyer's raising of this principle exponentially sometimes goes too far. Although his method always produces interesting results consistent with his working definition, the results are sometimes forced from the text.

In refutation of those critics who misread the satire as a criticism of the Church and religion, one need only point out that in the kindhearted and wise figure of Cousin Franz (a St. Francis figure), religion and the Church receive favorable treatment. Moreover, besides Cousin Franz, two other clerics, a pastor and a chaplain, represent the Church in a positive light by rejecting the daily Christmas celebration. Aunt Milla sees in the "einfache Herkunft" of the chaplain a case for class distinctions. She calls him, because of his refusal to cooperate, a "Prolet im Priestergewande." Through the contrast between the humble background of the chaplain, the chosen poverty of Cousin Franz, and the wealth of Aunt Milla's family, Böll indicates that the responsibility of hiding the past behind the veil of affluence falls mostly on the propertied and moneyed class. Böll implies even at this early date in his development that it is the bourgeoisie who benefits most from a society with a façade that conceals the relationship of the present to the fascist past.

Uncle Franz, because of his wealth, has connections in the hierarchy of the Church; he sees that charges are brought against the pastor and the chaplain for "Vernachlässigung seelsorgerischer Pflichten." Ironically, it is to meet parish responsibilities that the pastor excused himself from participation; the proletarian chaplain, on the other hand, showed his rejection of the celebrations by bursting into laughter at the single celebration he attended. Although the two clerics are exonerated in the canonical court, the incident in the story reveals what Böll believes is a close working relationship between the financially powerful and the Church hierarchy. While analysis of this satire yields an image of the clergy more positive than negative, Böll does not exonerate the church from a share in the guilt of the postwar cover-up of the Hitler period.

Since a priest must attend Aunt Milla's Christmas celebrations in order to maintain the unique family tradition, a retired prelate is found who is eager to cooperate. What Böll believes, rightly or wrongly, to be the extraordinary moral power of the Church can easily be seen in this satire: if the clergy had refused to take part in the false Christmas, if the Church had condemned the veiling of guilt, as did the pastor and the chaplain, then the perversity of year-round Christmas with all that it represents would be without sanction and doomed to failure. When the story appeared in 1951, the reader could sense the first sign of Böll's changing attitude toward the Church. In **"Nicht nur zur Weihnachtszeit"** the official Church and its hierarchical representatives begin to share in the responsibility for the "Schimmelpilze der Zersetzung" in the heart of West German society.

As stated above, by being balanced in his presentation, Böll departs from the tradition of satire, but he also deviates from satirical practice in yet another way. He uses satire not only to criticize, but to analyze social reality. Each character has a parabolic role in relationship to the permanent Christmas—there are more than merely two camps: those for and those against the celebrations, those who cooperate and those who do not. Within the family only Aunt Milla is totally dedicated to the restoration of the "gute alte Zeit." Thus, she feels no remorse nor does she demonstrate any recognition of the consequences of her actions. Therefore, her physical health is not endangered by the repression of the recent past: "Einzig meine Tante Milla . . . erfreut sich bester Gesundheit, lächelt, ist wohl und heiter, wie sie es fast immer war." In this regard she exemplifies perfectly Swift's definition of happiness in his digression on madness in the *Tale of the Tub,* where he claims: "Happiness is the possession of being well deceived." Aunt Milla, therefore, represents the people who see nothing wrong with the years 1933-1945 except in those aspects of the war that altered their own lives. Hence, they see the war only as a force which began in 1939 to endanger their Christmases. This attitude is reflected in the German law which permits the wearing of medals and citations awarded in the Nazi period, provided the swastika is removed, implying nothing was wrong with the Hitler period if its relationship to fascism can be denied or concealed.

For other persons not in the category of the willfully deceived, the repression of the past produces psychological disturbances, family divisions, and generational animosity with undesirable social effects. If such are the negative results of the permanent Christmas, the reader must ask why one would begin, much less continue, such a practice. The answer is indicated in the story. At first the extension of Christmas seemed " 'an sich' harmlos." "Die schrecklichen Folgen" were not foreseeable (except by Cousin Franz to whom no one listened). It was easier to cooperate with the pressure for the celebrations than to oppose it because the "costs" were not immediately obvious. It was also an easy way to achieve normality, for, as the narrator states, "Alles schien in Ordnung zu sein."

Furthermore, the satire suggests a close connection between the repression of the past and the headlong rush into the economic boom. It implies the more one wants to forget recent history, the more one must lose himself in the frantic activity of production. Uncle Franz, representative of the entrepreneur class, is forced to earn more, increase his profits, participate in the *Leistungsgesellschaft* in direct proportion to his cooperation with the needs of permanent Christmas.

Böll's satire is effective for at least two reasons. The first derives from the technique Böll uses to execute his idea and the second from the symbol of permanent Christmas he chooses to represent the theme of the story. The choice of the dual narrative perspective of Aunt Milla's cousin with its advantage of intimacy and objectivity has already been alluded to. But this point of view performs yet another aesthetic service. The teller of the story is not consciously committed to any of the camps within the family. He tries to be neutral in his presentation, friendly with all, sympathetic to everyone. He sees with the aunt's, uncle's, and the children's eyes. He even ends his story with a visit to Cousin Franz in the monastery. This middle position (although the narrator is somewhat more sympathetic to Aunt Milla's generation than to her children's) reduces the unpleasant didacticism and overbearing seriousness satire can often have. The narrator's stance aestheticizes and socializes the aggression inherent in the satire by the principle of indirection.

The technique deserves further mention in relationship to Böll's development as a satirist because it was his first use of a method which has proved successful in his later satires, the use of the principle of *executio ad absurdum,* i.e., the carrying out of the details of a story to their ultimate self-parodying conclusion. . . . In **"Nicht nur zur Weihnachtszeit"** this technique is seen in the details of the daily celebration, in the efforts to prolong the life of the tree, the itemization of the daily cost of providing the feast, the replacing of the children with wax figures, and hiring of actors to replace the adults, sending the children to cut fir trees in the state park, bribing officials to get out-of-season items from Czechoslovakia, and the melting of the candies on the tree from the summer heat, etc. (pp. 100-02)

The second reason for the effectiveness of the story is Böll's use of the *Einfall* of permanent Christmas. Satire, as a rule, has a short life because of its usual relationship to rapidly changing current affairs, which, when they change, make reading a satire an exercise in deciphering allusions to a past era, i.e., a satire can quickly become a difficult to understand historical document. Böll's story, on the contrary, remains alive because in it he chooses to criticize conditions which, though specifically German, still retain a general validity. In the choice of Christmas and in the critique of "die gute alte Zeit," Böll creates universality, which transcends the single interpretation of Germany's desire to repress its Nazi past. The story can, in fact, be read with equal application in any country where a shameful national past has not been adequately dealt with. In their own way most countries have their unconquered pasts: France has its Algeria, Russia its Stalinization, England its Ireland, the United States its Viet Nam, genocide against Indians, and lingering racism—nearly every civilized country has its shameful history. In any country where the past is not honestly dealt with, where popular reaction is to escape from hard responsibility, where national policy is changed out of opportunism or because of economic and political expedience rather than from moral conviction, **"Nicht nur zur Weihnachtszeit"** will be rewarding reading. In the story's ability to attack not just the folly peculiar to Germany, but the shortcomings of other nations as well, Böll has created not only a national classic, but a satire for all ages. (p. 102)

Robert C. Conard, "Heinrich Böll's 'Nicht nur zur Weihnachtszeit': A Satire for All Ages," in The Germanic Review, *Vol. LIX, No. 3, Summer, 1984, pp. 97-103.*

Peter Prochnik on Böll as a moralist:

[Böll's] strength lies in his ability to see ordinary people in clear relation to their pain and sorrow, and to sympathize with them in their predicament which is, more often than not, the result of circumstances well outside their control or comprehension: war, bureaucracies, social inequalities and pressures, the Establishment—those powerful forces and centres of power that have a vested interest in the status quo. Böll, then, is a moralist concerned with ending discrimination in the widest sense, but as with many moralists there are times when he treads the tightrope between objective analysis and a sentimentalized ideal with a certain uneasiness. In his early work, especially, his sympathy for the plight of his characters often causes him to see them as beyond reproach, although this does not necessarily mean that he wants his readers to see them as shining moral examples.

Peter Prochnik, in his "Personal Predicaments," The Times Literary Supplement, *January 31, 1975.*

Terence K. Thayer

If the reader of Böll's once controversial and now famous short story [**'Wanderer, Kommst du nach Spa . . .'**] can only recall the rest of the distich which gave Böll his title, then he may seem to have its ironic message in a nutshell:

> verkündige dorten, du habest
> Uns hier liegen gesehn, wie das Gesetz es befahl.

Böll's nameless schoolboy-soldier suffers a fate which his school has conditioned him (without success) to cherish, and which his country has then caused him to encounter. The resulting confrontation between humanistic education as realized in the *Gymnasium* and the inhumanity which it more or less obliquely supports, reaches its extreme as the posture of Spartan heroism is exposed in its latter-day counterpart as the ultimate abasement of the victim. The patriotic values so long propagated—obedience, courage, and self-sacrifice—are thus exposed as historically bankrupt and existentially false. For the narrator dies his wretched death precisely 'wie das Gesetz es befahl,' the latter encompassing no less the 'Hausordnung für humanistische Gymnasien in Preußen' surmised by him than the statutes and regulations which have in fact governed his existence as a soldier.

This is Böll's message—part of it, at least—but not his narrator's story. The story, it is true, seems just as straightforward. The narrator relates from a later vantage his passage from outside to upstairs, from ambulance to operating table, from suffering to death. It is in keeping with Böll's message that the narrator's movement is at no point elevated to a mythicizing descent into the underworld. The setting abounds with mythical suggestions which are never activated literarily. The pitching of the vehicle 'wie ein Schiff in einem Wellental' means only momentary relief from more abrupt impacts. Although dubbed a 'Totenhaus' by the narrator, the school resembles more a warehouse than a realm of the dead. Hermes is there, too, but is seen neither to escort nor to receive, but rather only to occupy his place among the other furnishings, a 'Hermessäule,' immobile. Likewise the great heroes of times past who show themselves, but only as plaster and paper. Clearly, accesses to mythical stylization à la Thomas Mann are present but unused, and therewith the pitfalls avoided of artistic association with the cultural tradition which Böll's story seeks to illuminate critically. Neither does his text invite or support interpretation according to a kindred literary model, that of an (inverted and abbreviated) journey of initiation, ending in death. There is no overlooking the juxtaposition of classicistic-humanistic, patriotic, and racial-ideological exhibits along the school's corridors and stairs. These exhibits signal a clear institutional intent, but [Manfred Durzak notes in his *Die deutsche Kurzgeschichte der Gegenwart* (1980) that] analysing them into a set of discrete 'stations' lends only superficial support to an 'initiation thesis' which construes the narrator's dying request for milk as his wish to return to childhood.

This request marks, rather, the last of three moments of recognition which together, in rapid succession, bring Böll's story to its close: 'es war Birgeler.' The first two produce answers to a pair of questions which still remain unanswered late in the story. 'Du mußt doch herauskriegen, was du für eine Verwundung hast und ob du in deiner alten Schule bist.' Enclosing the grisly revelation of the former is the delayed identification of the building as the narrator's school, and the belated recognition of the fireman as his friend.

The nearly thirty-kilometer transport to the school building returns the narrator to the setting of a past life extending from a time only three months prior to one more than eight years distant. By rights, his arrival there should become the point of departure for a return through memory to the part of his life spent there. But what appears at first to be happening does not take place. The narrator's physical passage through the building does occasion his passage via recollection back to a time spent among fixtures identical with, that is, indistinguishable from the ones past which he is being carried. Yet recognition and recollection do not become spontaneous and immediate remembrance. The narrator recognizes the cultural properties of his school item by item, in precise succession, yet even in the aggregate they do not admit of positive identification as those which hung and stood in his own school. 'I remember all of these things being where I was,' he can say, but not: 'I remember this place, being here before.' The final identification of the school as his own is no more than that—an inference of its identity made possible by the chance survival of his own handwriting on the chalkboard. Extending from the entry downstairs to this moment, the process of identification is now completed. The closing recognition of Birgeler neither contributes to it nor depends on it, but is rather separated from it by the exposure of the narrator's wounds. Now as before, Birgeler reacts, and it is by his attitude of compassion and expression of sadness ('sein müdes, trauriges Gesicht') that he is recognized. For the first and only time in the story, the narrator remembers: " 'Milch", sagte ich leise . . .'

Böll's story assumes its shape and draws its narrative life from the relationship of dislocation between the narrator's present and past, between his recognition and remembrance. Seen from the vantage of the close, his movement through the building occasions not so much a return to and re-experience of the past as a tour of inspection which assesses the quality of past experience according to its vitality in the present. As he tries to match features of his surroundings to recollections of the past, the narrator discovers how little of his past is genuinely recoverable, and what small part of his past experience was genuinely memorable.

Ironically, the greatest single factor (in the fictional terms of Böll's story) underlying this impoverishment of the narrator's past and memory is his society's and notably his school's concern to cultivate among its pupils the public memory of heroes past. This cultivation of memory is absolutely fundamental to both the humanistic and patriotic traditions which long determined the identity of the *Gymnasium* and which were adapted to and enlisted into the service of National Socialist propaganda. For more than two centuries, entry into the public memory had provided the sole form of transcendence accessible to its cultural and martial heroes and competitive in secular terms with the promise of transcendence central to Christian doctrine. Conversely, by maintaining a canon of heroic names the state contrived to engineer a sense of the past which obliges the present to fixed attitudes and behaviour.

It is specifically the cult of names, as perpetuated through the various media of recognition and renown, which constitutes the foundation of all other forms of secular immortality. Both the narrator's memory and his story are populated by names to which little else is attached beyond the vehicles bearing them. Only Birgeler's name, obscured by the rest to the very end, is attached to a face and a set of experiences. The 'Schule "Friedrich der Große" ' is suffused with this cult and, of course, itself exemplifies it. The renaming of the 'Thomas-Schule' for Friedrich (and of another for Hitler) represents both the intent to secularize Christian influence and to substitute by insinuation the prospect of secular immortality for Christian. A favoured furnishing for these 'name' buildings is thus more names.

This all makes the hallways of the narrator's school not only a museum but a pantheon, containing what are in effect memorials to famous dead. These in turn are distributed among likenesses of racial 'types,' mythical figures, and Greek deities, a juxtaposition which monumentalizes the status of patriotic heroes to the point of secular apotheosis and makes the hallways resemble a pantheon in the original sense, dedicated as they are to the state cryptoreligion of patriotic service. The centrepiece, both of the hallway displays and the school building itself, is the portrait of Friedrich. Its colours and forms communicate not only power and grandeur, but glory and permanence. Such enshrinement would doubtless meet with the full approval of nearly all those whose memory is thus perpetuated in the school. Most of them respected the perpetuating power of fame, and most helped lay the groundwork for their own. To remain with the case at hand, Friedrich himself in later life characterized the desire for fame as the mainspring of the soul and the wellspring of virtue. (pp. 262-66)

Yet the Prussian centrepiece has a companion piece, the 'Kriegerdenkmal,' the secret centre of the pantheon. In a wedding of elements the monument is adorned with a 'steinernen Lorbeerkranz' and a 'großen, goldenen [stone] Eisernen Kreuz,' the latter corresponding in its suggestion to the 'großen, golden glänzenden Stern' on Friedrich's breast. Friedrich's portrait (the original of which was no doubt painted posthumously) amounts to an image created to bear a name through time. The monument is foremost a vehicle for the display of names, that is, for their permanent enshrinement in the public memory. That this 'public' is ordinarily confined to pupils, and that the dead so memorialized were themselves all pupils, in no way precludes their elevation post mortem to the status of 'Krieger.' Soldiers take orders, but warriors, in the tradition of the Prussian military, give battle and perform martial deeds, often dying but also sharing in access to fame, or 'Kriegerehre,' which can survive them. Yet the promise extended by the school monument is a special and restricted one: its laurel wreath of stone belongs not to the victorious, but to the dead. By the inscription of their names on this cenotaph they appear to have been given a place in the halls of patriotic fame and therewith a share in the benefits of secular transcendence. They, too, will be revered and remembered.

Böll's narrator belongs to this posterity. His story demonstrates what this means, namely that he is made to share their lot and join their numbers. He neither reveres nor even recalls to mind names on the monument as he is carried past it. It is not solely his condition which prevents this. The historical reality of their names is obscured by the timeless artificiality of the monument, which the narrator himself labels 'ein Konfektionskriegerdenkmal . . . aus irgendeiner Zentrale.' If mass production in stone were not necessary to the fiction of prominent and permanent enshrinement, it, too, could just as well be issued as a plaster reproduction in keeping with all the other castings present. Like the testimonials to race and culture, patriotism and imperialism, the tribute to the school's war dead possesses no trace of distinctive and thus recognizable individuality.

In fact, the narrator can recognize nothing in the exhibits in this school, nor remember anything about those in his own, which would confirm the identity of the two. The artifacts displayed in the school do stem from separate artists both known and unknown, but they actually have a single common author, the state. Every last work, including the soldiers' memorial, is a copy of an absent original. Together with the other reproductions designed to commemorate past lives, deeds, and works, the monument resembles in its reproducibility the mass-produced wares of current political propaganda exemplified by the set of racial illustrations. Yet it also, more specifically, represents an environment in which the media of renown have become in part independent of individual artists, whether sculptors, painters, or poets. The unlimited reproducibility of an artist's work might initially seem only to guarantee his work's survival and therewith to ensure the 'im-

mortality' of his subject. Unlimited reproduction can also mean, as it does here, the conversion of individual tribute—subservient perhaps, but also original and in that sense authentic—into a vehicle for management of attitudes and values. Even the 'original' media themselves (stone and paint) have been diverted to the exclusive use of the planners as regulation building material and wall covering.

The mediation of plaster and paper depends on the use of molds and plates, and corresponds to the reduction of texts to formulae: to quotations, sayings, and maxims. The most nearly original and direct products of the reproductive media (the racial illustrations) are devoted to the most explicitly ideological ends, and are thus the most directly associated with mottos, slogans, and epithets. The production and distribution of the Nietzsche portrait accompanies the perversion of Nietzsche's philosophy by means of not so 'Leichte Chirurgie' to the 'Wille zur Macht' emblazoned on National Socialist flags. The two examples of the school's verbal environment recalled by the narrator both suggest its decidedly functional cast. These examples show the same subjection of an original (one of them is an original text) to indefinite reproduction to the end of cultural conditioning. The reproduction takes place in different modes to suit different circumstances. There is, of course, the Simonides quotation, which, owing to its use as the text for a lettering exercise, is reproduced by one pupil after another. It thus assumes in graphic terms the model status it implicitly enjoys throughout the school as an ideal expression of self-sacrificing obedience. The verbal sample from the school almanac exhibits precisely the same formulaic character common to the building's visual displays. It also isolates the ultimate thrust behind them all. Behind his own name, so the narrator anticipates, will stand the formula 'zog von der Schule ins Feld und fiel für . . . ' he knows so well from past repetitions in past yearbooks. As in the past, the formula will continue to be reproduced to meet the school's need. In its calculation, in its reproducibility, and in its innate falseness it resembles all the other fixtures in the school; it differs from them only insofar as the school's authorship of the others is obscured, but of this one it is not.

Just as the school's fixtures imply its reduction of the classical and national heritage to visual and verbal formulae, so the resultant formulae imply a concerted aestheticization of reality, and of military realities in particular. Horace's words qua slogan 'dulce et decorum est pro patria mori' are nowhere quoted but everywhere implied, especially by the decorum of soldiers' memorial and school almanac. Nearly half the words in the yearbook's memorial formula 'zog von der Schule ins Feld und fiel für . . . ' are euphemisms. (pp. 266-68)

Yet what the pupil saw every day is still 'wunderbar,' 'bunt,' 'schön'; every reproduction is at the same time a decoration, even—or rather especially—the military decorations whose functions as tributes cannot be separated from that as decorative appliqués. There is again the portrait of Friedrich 'mit . . . dem großen, golden glänzenden Stern auf der Brust' and the memorial 'mit dem großen, goldenen Eisernen Kreuz obendrauf.' The pupil himself was once enlisted in the same aestheticizing effort, reproducing on paper the graceful contours of Greek vases, and on the chalkboard the fine-sounding verses of Greek soldiers in one graceful script after another. One can imagine a school library well stocked with like images of war transformed into scenes of decorum and distinction. It is only fitting, then, that the school building itself becomes the final vantage point from which war is experienced as aesthetic illusion, an illusion to which the narrator allows himself to succumb one final time, if only to gain respite from the reality behind it which has engulfed him. . . . Likewise, the school's windows have become the medium through which the narrator experiences the incineration of the city at an aestheticizing distance. The first time: 'Rechts sah ich durch das Fenster den Feuerschein, der ganze Himmel war rot, und schwarze, dicke Wolken von Qualm zogen feierlich vorüber. . . . ' And then, with sound: 'Ich sah es durch die Verdunkelung hindurch, es glühte und wummerte hinter den schwarzen Vorhängen, rot hinter schwarz, wie in einem Ofen, auf den man neue Kohlen geschüttet hat. Ich sah es: ja, die Stadt brannte.' What the narrator now sees through the blacked out art room windows is what the school has always presented to him: celebrated figures and events isolated within a frame, separated from the observer by a veil of glass and removed from his experience by unrelenting idealization and aestheticization. The first fixture, 'sanftglänzend unter Glas in einem schwarzen Rahmen, die Medea von Feuerbach' is but the first example, and the last, Nietzsche 'in einem goldenen Rahmen.' The prescribed statuary exhibits the same qualities realized in a different medium: the framed or truncated isolation of frieze or herm and bust; the luminous mediation ('gelblich schimmernd') of plaster 'patina,' and the beauty borrowed from classical originals. As for the one example of freestanding sculpture, the Thorn Puller: 'ein Bild . . . , eine wunderbare rötlich schimmernde Photographie in braunem Rahmen.' Once again, the medium imparts to the subject a luminous beauty which, whether radiant or subdued, tells of heroism, distinction, and permanence.

Taken together, the school's visual furnishings thus represent the processes by which human lives and history are reduced to enduring images, and ideas to formulae and slogans. For the pupil such images seem to harbor the promise of self-realization, personal fulfillment, and social immortality. Böll's story is not only concerned to contradict this promise with the reality it conceals; it confronts these images with counter-images which, although they share the *formal* features of their heroic counterparts, confront the latter's promise with the certitude of mutilation, alienation, and death. The medium has now become the human body and its physical circumstances. The authority which issued the school's *Hausordnung* now returns its citizen on a stretcher, a head atop a wrapped-up body, armless, immobile, a human herm. Lying amidst 'the others' (as distinguished from 'the dead') he is no different from them, a *Konfektionsgegenstand,* and literally 'gleich an der Reihe' for final processing. The narrator describes the progress of another, whose passage his own movement will soon reproduce: 'Dann hoben sie den auf, der neben mir lag und trugen ihn hinter die Tafel; ich blickte ihnen nach: sie hatten die Tafel auseinandergezogen und quer

gestellt und die Lücke zwischen Wand und Tafel mit einem Bettuch zugehängt; dahinter brannte grelles Licht. . . .' The pictures which once hung on this wall have been removed because, in the terms of Böll's narrative, first the windows, and now the chalkboard and bedsheet have succeeded them. The narrator is himself transported 'hinter die Tafel, wo das grelle Licht brannte' into the three dimensions of this framed space, whose glaring light filters out through the sheet.

This time the subject is the self. Three times the narrator is confronted with the self as artifact, alienated from its life, its body, and its legacy. On the chalkboard he sees his handwriting—'es ist schlimmer, als wenn man sich im Spiegel sieht, viel deutlicher.' What he also sees there is: writing as reproduction, with both content and form prescribed by the school, and all individuality of stroke and expression effaced. The *Tafel* which ends up formalizing the narrator's relationship to the past and the future is not the memorial plaque but the chalkboard, with its ironic replacement of warrior-heroes with soldiers, and fame with nameless subordination. Still, the verse into which the narrator's identity is cast is 'nur ein bißchen verstümmelt.' When his torso is unwrapped he beholds in its mutilation the alienation of body from self exceeded only by the ultimate alienation of death. Death is coming. It is announced in the image of self-confrontation and self-alienation which precedes the other two and includes them both. The lightbulb above the operating table is not mirror-like, as is the handwriting, but a mirror in fact; not mangled like the Simonides-verse (or like the bulb in the ambulance) because what it mirrors is itself mangled: 'Ich lag auf dem Operationstisch und sah mich selbst ganz deutlich, aber sehr klein, zusammengeschrumpft, oben in dem klaren Glas der Glühbirne, winzig und weiß, ein schmales, mullfarbenes Paketchen wie ein außergewöhnlich subtiler Embryo: das war also ich da oben.' This is the final heroic portrait which the school offers its pupil: 'falling' on the battlefield become prostration beheld by no one but the self. 'Als ob der Tod nicht ein so privater Akt wäre wie die Geburt . . .'

Interspersed among the devices of sociocultural engineering which occupy the narrator's school and his mind and memory are the snatches of self-expression which show the narrator himself as more than a product, that is, as an author or writer of sorts. The earliest instance, 'Es lebe Togo.' documents the status of resistance in the school. It is a perfectly congruent response to the host of immortals which populate the halls. [The Japanese hero] Togo is to endure and remain unforgotten as they do, and has in fact. Yet given its circumstances and resources, schoolboy dissent has recourse only to slogans as its response to slogans. Böll locates it 'auf der mittleren Banane im rechten Bündel,' turning a Ludwig-Thoma-like motif into an example of how the voice of resistance is reduced to predictability and impotence. 'Auch die Witze, die sie in den Schulen machen, sind immer dieselben.' That was then, of course. What would he write now, if he could? What would he thrust into the memory of the future? . . . When this pupil *can* finally speak out, in his own voice, on his own behalf, it is too late. [In his ***Werke: Essayistische Schriften und Reden I, 1952-1963***], Böll presents his requests for cigarettes, water, milk, as a demand 'nach einem Schluck Kaffee, einer Zigarette, nach irgend etwas von dieser Erde, als letzten Gruß, während die kalte Majestät auf sie zukam.' For the rest, there is screaming. First the screams of pain, but then also the screams of self-assertion and expression, of abandonment and anguish. Then the closing ellipsis, the trailing off into the silence of the dead.

Who speaks for the dead? That is, who will represent them to their future as victims instead of heroes, exposing their sacrifice as passion and exchanging their fame for the mourning of their survivors? History as event, Böll's story shows, is what killed the dead, and history as narrative will speak not for the dead, but for the event under which the dead are subsumed. The monuments and memorial plaques merely perpetuate the captivity in which their passion originally took place. Official observances only extend that captivity as they confirm its place in history. Their media and formulae are different—'die amtliche Träne, das bewegte Gesicht, die zuckende Hand'—but remain media and formulae. They speak for the living to the living. Artistic traditions in thrall to the venerable and the heroic can only deliver illustrations for the history books and commemorative speeches. The complete message of the narrator's passage through the school's halls of fame is this: that the cultural and patriotic heroes of the past had the wrong spokesmen, but the past's dead soldiers had and still have none at all, and neither will he. (pp. 269-73)

'Wanderer, kommst du nach Spa . . .' does all that is humanly and literarily possible in the face of this fact. It may seem ironic, an instance of bitterest sarcasm, that Böll takes the title and central motif of his story from verses whose commemoration of obedience unto death makes them common coin in his narrator's school. **'Wie das Gesetz es befahl'** is the title he selected for a 1974 review of H.G. Adler's book *Der verwaltete Mensch: Studien zur Deportation der Juden aus Deutschland*. It is true that, even as a text for lettering exercises, these words contribute to the daily indoctrination effort of the school. It is also true that the verses preserve the memory of a fatal adherence to something—although not obedience to the law, as Schiller's mistranslation would lead us to believe, but rather conformance to the Spartan soldier's ethos, epitomized in the 'words,' that is, [what C. M. Bowra in his *Early Greek Elegists* (1935) calls] 'those Laconic sayings by which the ideals of manhood were instilled into Spartan youth.'

But it is no less true that the title of Böll's story has, in addition to its own literary history, a separate history in his text. The title is the last of multiple requotations: the title repeats (by way of anticipation) five words spoken three times by the narrator, and these five words were (to proceed in reverse, through one medium or another) uttered by the narrator three months before, still earlier by the art teacher, by Schiller, and by Simonides, who himself sought to transmit in an epitaph the sentiment of those who could no longer speak. Requotation of these words has in every instance meant at least partial alienation of their meaning from that communicated by them in prior context. This holds true historically for Schiller's incorporation of the distich into 'Der Spaziergang,' and it holds

true both historically and imaginatively for its use in school curricula such as Böll's story describes. To repeat: just as the school and its institutions convert the private lives of its pupils into the public history of its nation, so the reproduced artifacts which represent the school's historical consciousness are alienated from the cultural contexts out of which they arose. The authentic artifact of this age is the school itself. What better captures the paradoxes which inform its exhibits than the title quotation on the blackboard, at once alien and familiarized, severe and beautified, expressive and functionalized? It is also mutilated. Fitting his own model of the half-line into the dimensions of the school's chalkboard means truncating it. Living out his personal version of the destiny propagated by the school means having his limbs torn off and his life cut short. The title quotation thus epitomizes the ultimate relationship between the school and its pupil.

It is also worth considering that Böll makes the ultimate quotation, and that he quotes his own hero's fragmentary rendering of the Simonides text. That is to say, Böll quotes not Simonides, but the narrator, whose all too representative fate he would bring to the mind of his readers. By placing the fragment at the head of his narrative, Böll makes it into the literary epitaph of his narrator as surely as Simonides' distich was chiseled into the tomb of the three hundred nameless Spartans who were betrayed and killed defending the pass at Thermopylae. Simonides' literary commemoration is terse, confined to the two lines of the epitaph. Böll's is more circumstantial, beginning the same, but translating the remaining three half-lines into their latter-day prose equivalent. Moreover, the voice of Simonides' epitaph is given over to the dead themselves. There is no mention of patriotism, self-sacrifice, or fame. Simonides' dead speak of conformance to a soldierly ethos or, in Schiller's version, obedience to law. Böll's narrator speaks of suffering and anguish, but with very much the same dispassionate detachment of the already dead.

The correspondence should not be pressed further. Neither Böll nor his narrator would likely affirm the values implied in Simonides' distich. But, the irony of Böll's title clearly has limits. The title stems ultimately from a man perhaps much like Böll himself in one regard, a professional writer who devoted not a small part of his creative energies to composing on behalf of those with no other access to their survivors or to posterity. Simonides' own fame as a poet rests in large part on the body of epitaphs and cenotaphs written by or ascribed to him, just as Böll's early reputation was built on texts—narratives, essays, speeches—which sought to keep alive the memory of myriad victims in the conscience of those who chanced to survive them. 'Nicht von einem einzigen von ihnen wissen wir, welche Räume er im Angesicht des Todes durcheilte, die Worte schuldig oder unschuldig gehören unserer Welt an, der Tod einer anderen.' In this strictest sense, no one can or should speak for the dead. Yet Böll excepts himself from this dictum as surely as would have Simonides by extending the range of imaginative speech to include a narrative voice not just for the fictional but for the dead among them as well. Self-expression of the dead is, of course, a conventional literary paradox, and as familiar through the genres as talking animals. Specifically, the fiction of verse as speech of the interred or entombed to the living is a convention of sepulchral epigram. Böll's choice of the Simonides fragment as his title makes the possibility worth considering that his narrator's first-person narrative stands in this tradition rather than deriving from more recent conventions of the modern short story.

For what reasons does an author bestow his narrative voice on the dead? The collective voice bestowed by Simonides on the Three Hundred expresses how their death is to be understood. Speaking as it does ex extremis and beyond, their voice is made to affirm the extreme value of both their soldierly ethos and the obedience which belongs to it. The epitaph thus epitomizes the nature of those to whom it pays its oblique homage. Likewise, although epitaphs are written to perpetuate the memory of dead men, there is no mention here of the undying fame recorded in so many other inscriptions by Simonides. Instead, the Three Hundred are made to couch in their command to the passer-by a request to their countrymen:

> Wanderer, kommst du nach Sparta, *verkündige dorten,* du habest
> Uns hier liegen gesehn, wie das Gesetz es befahl.

'Remember us,' is the message, 'as we wish to be remembered, as we were.'

Simonides' epitaph thus depends in large measure on its conventional first-person perspective for the uniquely artful propriety of its tribute. Böll's story exploits the same convention to much the same ends: understanding, affirmation, and remembrance. The difference lies in his narrator's retrospective point of view. The story proceeds without reference to present or future time as firmly as the imperative of the Three Hundred, who are concerned with perennial values and perpetuation in memory, dispenses in the original with reference to the past. The relation of past events belongs to story-telling, of course, but postmortem narration in the past tense affords a vantage uniquely suited to the social-critical themes of Böll's story. By presenting institutions through the sensibility of their victim, Böll confronts them with their full, that is private as well as public, human consequences. The limits of the perspective themselves become the most expressive traits of the narrator as victim. The understanding thus produced is an understanding of relationships which hold no meaning for the narrator. Yet what he recalls to mind is not only disorientation and uncertainty vis-à-vis a prior past devoid of experience, but also past experience of boredom and suffering, and past moments of community and compassion. How vividly he recounts each detail of his experience as victim, and how vividly the figure of Birgeler stands out in relief against it. The last thing he sees in his image-filled school is Birgeler's 'müdes, trauriges Gesicht'—a face expressive of the silent 'Trauer' which official memorials may obscure but cannot replace. . . . Entirely without claim to public attention, Birgeler's human achievement alone laid claim to a place in another's mind and memory. No matter how different its ring from the sound of Simonides' verse, the narrator's voice pays its tribute by elevating the cigarettes, the water, the milk, the community, and the name of Birgeler above the oblivion wrought by the institution of the school.

As Birgeler is honoured by the narrator's memory, so the narrator is honoured by Böll's. Yet even though Böll's art, as both the memory and the conscience of a society fallen into indifference, writes in memory and behalf of the war's nameless and numberless victims, his story does not seek to honour the dead. The still living can give honour to the dead only by respecting the honour of the dead. As Böll says in 'Wo ist dein Bruder?',

> Jeder Tod hat seine Hoheit, jeder Tote seine Würde, die Ehre eines Toten ist unantastbar . . . Wir wissen nichts, nichts wissen wir, wir sind nicht befugt über die Toten zu richten [. . .] Bei Totenehrungen—und ich wiederhole: die Toten haben ihre Ehre—sollte das Reden verboten werden . . . Im nackten Schweigen sollten wir uns versammeln, und niemand sollte sich anmaßen dürfen, die Toten in seine Taktik einzubeziehen.

This and other speeches of the 1950's constituted Böll's rhetorical attempt to wrest the memory of the war's victims from official memorials and return it to their survivors, whose private grief is not accommodated by public ceremony. And, just as Böll's narrative perspective in this story implies that the war's survivors should not speak for its victims, so the end of the story reconfirms that it befits no one to speak for the dead in death. Silence is the only language of the dead, and it is into this 'Schweigen der Toten' that Böll's narrative issues at its close. Yet the closing ellipsis not only marks the silence which engulfs Böll's narrator at his end. It is also the silence which Böll untiringly affirms as the only human expression adequate to the remembrance of bereavement and mourning.

Böll's story is itself enclosed in silence. In spite of its abrupt and isolated narration it has neither preamble nor epilogue, no narrative frame and no intrusion of perspective other than the narrator's. When he falls silent, his story is done. The implicit request to the passing reader of this literary memorial is not to speak to others, but to remember such victims in the silence which they share with those who mourn them. In so many other stories and speeches Böll speaks eloquently and untiringly as a public advocate for the war's dead. Here, after creating a literary representative of their ranks and surrendering his artistic voice totally to him, Böll does not exempt himself from the silence he enjoins on others. (pp. 273-78)

> *Terence K. Thayer, "Fame and Remembrance in Heinrich Böll's 'Wanderer, kommst du nach Spa . . .',"* in *Seminar, Vol. XX, No. 4, November, 1984, pp. 262-78.*

Sven Birkerts

There is a distinct, if abstract, satisfaction to be gotten from working complex equations, factoring out extraneous numerals until at last the simple terms greet each other across the equal sign. An analogous pleasure, but more sensory and emotional, awaits the reader of [*The Stories of Heinrich Böll*]. Here the distraction and clutter are stripped from human commerce and we are brought face-to-face with our vestigial selves. The aesthetic effect,

---

Böll on language:

Language is more solid than music and painting. Yet it is "inexact." But the fact that a word has a multiplicity of meaning, not only within a language but also outside of it, makes it important to try to get to the root of words and language. That is the constant striving of literature. The absolute meaning exists somewhere; we just haven't found it yet.

Heinrich Böll, in an interview in The Paris Review, *Spring 1983.*

---

however, has a bitter cause. For the force of Böll's vision depends most often upon the reductions wrought by fear, confusion, and suffering. That is—to collapse three nouns into one—by war.

Böll needs no introduction. Long before the Nobel Prize consolidated his international reputation in 1972, he had earned the honor of being the spokesman for an entire generation of Europeans, a representative of the times. Böll's youth and young manhood had coincided with the rise of Nazism; he was conscripted in 1939 and spent five years in uniform, at the front and in American POW camps. His first work—which blasted the senselessness of imperialistic conflict—found a ready audience during the shell-shocked years of German reconstruction. He was ever of his time—in recent decades he was an outspoken peace activist—and ever at an angle to it, bearing witness.

Nor did Böll refuse the dais. His fiction, from the first, concerned itself with the common life of the insulted and injured. It gradually widened its reach, in novels such as *Group Portrait with Lady* (1971) and *The Safety Net* (1979), to embrace the whole social order. This compendium, weighted to favor the early stories, does not preserve the proportions of the career. Its bulk is for, and about, the voiceless—frightened boys who were handed guns and orders, bereaved mothers and wives, children. We get the cauterized emotions and hunger-sharpened perceptions experienced by the suffering majority, and very little about the yes-men and the perpetrators. The cumulation of simple perspectives is genuinely affecting. If many of the settings and situations recur from story to story—railway stations, barracks, bombed-out buildings; arrivals, departures, furtive trysts—this is not because of any artistic shortcoming, but because war levels differences. Smoking rubble and fear are the same everywhere.

The collection is arranged in chronological sequence. Thus, by the time we finish we have moved from the chaos of mortar fire through the monochromatic austerity of reconstruction to the disquieting blandness of prosperity. But the war is always there, if not directly on the page then as an implicit point of historical reference—akin to the painter's vanishing point. The slight satiric vignettes set in the near-present would mean nothing without the memory of disaster. Which is to say that Böll is faithful to the way that events become history in the collective memory.

It may be that in death everyone is the same, but at the

moment of dying individual uniqueness is most piercingly disclosed. In that instant—or so the writer's imagination would have it—the full path of destiny flashes out, and every act and choice can be viewed under the aspect of inevitability. A string of incidents, however unremarkable, becomes a tale. In two of the [longer works] included here, *And Where Were You, Adam?* and *The Train Was on Time,* Böll makes use of this revelatory possibility. In *And Where Were You, Adam?* he splices together the complex outer circumstances—the significant encounters, delays, choices—that lead up to the death of the soldier Feinhals. Here the young Böll (this was one of his early publications) indulges his appetite for the dramatic convergence. Feinhals is hit by an artillery shell just when he believes his homeward journey is over—"and he rolled in death onto the threshold of the house. The flagpole had snapped, and the white cloth fell over him." The clumsy and obvious knotting of the narrative belies the skill shown in other passages throughout, where terror, fatigue, and a range of freighted human confrontations have been caught with the eye of a practiced watcher.

The Train Was on Time, likewise an early work, attempts an inward rendition of the destined event. But in this account the strategy is reversed. The young soldier, Andreas, has a vivid premonition of the time and place of his death. The novella takes us through the excruciating days of waiting, building suspense by the minute until the expected finally happens: "Now we must be in Galicia, he thought, quite close to Lvov, since Lvov is the capital of Galicia. Now I must be just about in the center of the net where I'm going to be caught." There is an undeniable power in this kind of procedure—*Oedipus Rex* is the paradigm—but the portentousness gets to be too thick by the end. More memorable, finally, are the sketches drawn along the way, of Andreas's interminable train ride and of his fellow soldiers. Böll did not pull a description like this out of airy nothing:

> It was horrible to have the man leaning over the map with him. Andreas could smell the canned meat on his breath, which was still not quite free of the odor of digested, partially acidulated schnapps. He could smell the sweat and grime and was too wrought up to see anything; then he saw the man's finger, a thick, red, dirty, yet very good-natured finger, and the man said, "That's where I have to go."

A good many of the shorter fictions also turn on the idea of fatedness. In **"Stranger, Bear Word to the Spartans We . . . ,"** a dying soldier is carried into an infirmary that he realizes was once his gymnasium classroom; the handwriting that he notices on the blackboard is his own. We don't need to be told that he will die in that room. **"Adventures of a Haversack,"** similarly, traces the bizarre circuit that a dead infantryman's bag must follow in order to end up, long years later, on its original nail.

Böll's penchant for meaningful intersections seems to be at odds with the unblinking naturalism of his treatment of character and place. One may be tempted to dismiss it as unfortunate artifice. But it is possible, I think, to accept it as his attempt to depict the inexplicable change in the order of things that cataclysm initiates. I have often heard from veterans of the European war that miraculous meetings, deus ex machina escapes, perversely ironic deaths were all accepted as natural. It is almost as if the exponential increase of the death factor intensified the play of significance, as if the laws of daily life are abolished when a boiling point is reached. But with Böll we also cannot discount the religious influence.

Böll thought of himself as an unorthodox, even renegade, Catholic. Reared in the faith, drawn by temperament to its moral humanism, he was permanently alienated by Church hypocrisy. As he wrote in his 1981 memoir, **What's to Become of the Boy?:** "After the seizure of power, the Reichstag fire, and the March election, it was, incredibly, the Vatican that accorded the Nazis their first major international recognition." To the end of his life, Böll could not reconcile the spirituality of the creed with what he saw as the opportunism of its organizational vessel.

Still, a religious sensibility is active in his work. It is evident both in his humane treatment of characters, even the lowliest, and in the narrative developments that tend in every instance to meaningful resolution. Though Böll does not gloss facts—in his world the evidence of suffering far outweighs evidence of redemption—he does not exclude redemption altogether, which is no small victory for spirit in times as dark as these. The scale, nevertheless, is always modest. One looks in vain for suggestions that some larger struggle between good and evil has been engaged. The flawed and purblind human soul is not viewed as arena enough for the contest, or trophy enough to contend over.

Böll's intimations of higher meaning are there to mitigate suffering—they stand no chance of canceling it. But the possibility remains that death will bring sudden inner reconciliation, if not something even better. In **"Reunion on the Avenue,"** for instance, we read about the death of two trench-mates, who just one minute before had been drinking schnapps and confiding their dreams:

> . . . and while noise sprang to life around me, the frantic barking of the machine gun from Heini's dugout and the sickening impact of the grenade launchers that we called pipe organs, I became quite calm: for mingling with Hecker's darker blood that still covered the bottom of the dugout was a lighter, miraculously light blood that I knew was warm and my own; and I sank down and down until I found myself, smiling happily, at the entrance to that avenue which Hecker hadn't known how to describe, because the trees were bare, solitude and desolation were nesting among wan shadows, and hope died in my heart, while far off, at an immense distance, I could see Hecker's beckoning figure outlined against a soft golden light. . . .

Two-thirds of the way through the collection, Böll's tone perceptibly changes. He gives us, first, a handful of tales from the postwar period, and as violence and horror recede, irony and shrewd psychological observation take over. In a story called **"Business Is Business,"** a cynical survivor studies his suddenly prosperous—and just as suddenly amnesiac—black marketeer, and reflects upon the remarkable plasticity of human nature. "Everything was fine," he thinks,

> your medical insurance was still OK, you had yourself de-Nazified a bit—the way you go to a barber to get rid of that tiresome beard—you chatted about decorations, wounds, acts of heroism, and came to the conclusion that you were a pretty fine fellow after all.

Böll seldom gets any more strident. Either you pick up the message or you don't.

Irony gives way to flatter satire as the stories take on life in recent decades. The writing is more detached, the thematic presentation more idiosyncratic—but at the same time the impact (at least for the non-German reader) is diminished. Pieces like **"The Thrower-Away,"** about an efficiency expert working in secret in the basement of a large firm, and **"The Staech Affair,"** which looks at the consequences of monk absenteeism at a highly touristed monastic retreat, make perfect sense. Still, at times they feel like sections of an encoded dialogue that Böll may have been carrying on with his compatriots. For the power of satire derives from a play upon particulars, and here we cannot be sure that we're catching all of the barbs. **"Murke's Collected Silences,"** on the other hand, negotiates more universal terrain: a pompous culture czar insists that all references to God in his archive of radio tapes be replaced by the phrase "that higher Being Whom we revere." The sharp opposition between his bloated self-regard and the sly, puncturing wit of the underling, Murke—whose hobby is piecing together bits of taped silence that he has gathered—provides delicious comedy.

Böll's strengths were those of a witness, not those of an inventor. His satiric eye was keen, but he had trouble sustaining plots that could serve as credible vehicles. For this reason, the fiction that deals with the immediate circumstances of war is the most vivid. The directionless momentum of combat, the unrelieved tensions of waiting and watching, supply a natural frame and free the author from the need to contrive situations. True, Böll was sometimes guilty of resolutions that exceeded even the prodigal inventiveness of the three fates, but his palpable rendering of fundamental drives and emotions—his ability to sound the depths of the average heart—more than compensated. He knew that the patina of culture and sensible behavior is easily cracked. This collection, which honors an ample achievement, stands also as a reminder of the real hierarchy of human needs:

> He hastily broke off a hunk of bread: his chin was trembling, and he could feel the muscles of his mouth and jaws twitching. Then he dug his teeth into the soft, uneven surface of the bread where he had broken it apart. He was eating bread. The bread was stale, must have been a week old, dry rye bread with a red label from some bakery or other. He continued to dig in with his teeth, finishing off even the brown, leathery crust; then he grasped the loaf with both hands and broke off another piece. Eating with his right hand, he clasped the loaf with his left; he went on eating, sat down on the edge of a wooden crate, and, each time he broke off a

piece, bit first into the soft center, feeling all around his mouth the touch of the bread like a dry caress, while his teeth went on digging. (pp. 28-30)

> Sven Birkerts, "The Fragile Net," in The New Republic, *Vol. 194, No. 14, April 7, 1986, pp. 28-30.*

FURTHER READING

Criticism

Baacke, Dieter. "The Short Stories of Heinrich Böll." *Studies in Short Fiction* III, No. 1 (Fall 1965): 89-103.
> Examines the structure, themes, and prose style of Böll's short fiction.

Burns, Robert. A. "The Theme of Non-Conformism in the Work of Heinrich Böll." *Occasional Papers in German Studies,* No. 3 (1973): 1-87.
> Explores the unifying theme of the outsider in Böll's fiction.

Conard, Robert C. "The Humanity of Heinrich Böll." *Boston University Journal* 21, No. 2 (Spring 1973): 35-43.
> Analyzes Christian elements in Böll's fiction.

————. *Heinrich Böll.* Boston: Twayne Publishers, 1981, 228 p.
> General critical study of Böll's life and career that includes three chapters on Böll's short fiction.

Enright, D. J. "When They Were Wrong They Were Right." *The New York Times Book Review* (23 February 1986): 42.
> Reviews *The Stories of Heinrich Böll* and provides a short overview of Böll's career.

Flower, Dean. Review of *The Bread of Those Early Years,* by Heinrich Böll. *The Hudson Review* XXX, No. 2 (Summer 1977): 302-03.
> Praises *The Bread of Those Early Years* for its examination of the effects of the past on the present by focusing on Germany's attempts to undo the destructive consequences of World War II.

Friedrichsmeyer, Ehrard. *Die satirische Kurzprosa Heinrich Bölls.* Chapel Hill: University of North Carolina, 1981, 221 p.
> Critical study of Böll's satirical short fiction.

Prochnik, Peter. "Personal Predicaments." *The Times Literary Supplement,* No. 3804 (31 January 1975): 120.
> Review of *Children Are Civilians, Too, The Train Was on Time,* and *Neue politische und literarische Schriften.* Prochnik emphasizes that the focus of Böll's fiction is not restricted to World War II but also addresses life in postwar Germany.

Reid, James Henderson. "Böll's Names." *The Modern Language Review* 69, No. 3 (July 1974): 575-83.
> Explores the symbolism of characters' names in Böll's fiction.

Totton, Nick. "In Retrospect." *Spectator* 238, No. 7757 (5 March 1977): 24.
> Favorable review of *The Bread of Those Early Years,* which Totton demonstrates is "a genuine socialist novel: generating an individual out of his history and environment, and simultaneously demonstrating that individual's power and freedom to change, to reject the determinations of society."

West, Anthony. "Paths of Glory." *The New Yorker* XXXII, No. 17 (16 June 1956): 113-16.
> Review of *The Train Was on Time* comparing the novella in theme and technique to Böll's later works.

Interviews

Limberg, Margarete. " 'Freedom Is Fading Every Day': The Last Major Interview." In *Heinrich Böll: On His Death, Selected Obituaries and the Last Interview,* pp. 22-31. Bonn: Inter Nationes, 1985.
> Interview with Böll in which he discusses the political, economic, and social situation in post-World War II Germany.

Willson, A. Leslie. "The Art of Fiction LXXIV: Heinrich Böll." *The Paris Review* 25, No. 87 (Spring 1983): 67-87.
> Interview with Böll in which he addresses such topics as writing technique, literary theory, politics, and his work as a translator.

Additional coverage of Böll's life and career is contained in the following sources published by Gale Research: *Contemporary Authors,* Vol. 116; *Contemporary Authors New Revision Series,* Vol. 24; *Contemporary Literary Criticism,* Vols. 2, 3, 6, 9, 11, 15, 27, 39; *Dictionary of Literary Biography,* Vol. 69; *Dictionary of Literary Biography Yearbook: 1985;* **and** *Major 20th-Century Writers.*

Philip K. Dick

1928-1982

(Full name Philip Kindred Dick) American novelist, short story writer, and essayist.

The following entry provides criticism of Dick's major works. For further information on his life and works, see *CLC*, Volumes 10 and 30.

INTRODUCTION

Dick has been hailed as one of the most original and thought-provoking writers of science fiction. Often addressing the delicate balance between illusion and reality, Dick used the standard fare of this genre—robots, space ships, and alternate universes—to explore the complexities of human nature. He often portrayed bleak futuristic landscapes, oppressive government bureaucracies, and the destructive potential of advanced technology, especially mechanical or electronic simulations of organic life. Two of Dick's works were adapted for film: the novel *Do Androids Dream of Electric Sheep?* as *Blade Runner,* and the short story "We Can Remember It for You Wholesale" as *Total Recall.*

Dick was born in Chicago and lived most of his life in California. After briefly attending the University of California at Berkeley, he published his first story, "Beyond Lies the Wub," in 1952. He wrote the majority of his many short stories in the following three years, but shifted almost exclusively to writing novels after the publication of his first, *Solar Lottery.* Dick's early works, including *Eye in the Sky* and *Time Out of Joint,* reflect his curiosity about the nature of reality as well as a fear of omnipotent authority and political oligarchies. These subjects are particularly evident in his Hugo Award-winning novel, *The Man in the High Castle.* In this work Dick envisioned a world in which Germany and Japan have divided the United States between them after winning World War II. Through this scenario Dick examined an America willing to give up its own culture under occupation and whose racial fears and prejudices are compatible with Nazism. Dick went on to publish several other critically acclaimed novels in the 1960s, including *Martian Time-Slip, The Three Stigmata of Palmer Eldritch,* and *Ubik.* In 1975 he won the John W. Campbell Memorial Award for *Flow My Tears, The Policeman Said.* In this novel Dick used the recurring subjects of a stifling bureaucracy and synthetic organisms to explore such philosophical queries as the nature of identity and the definition of morality. Dick was also concerned with the existence of God, a matter that became increasingly important to him. In 1974 Dick claimed to have had a religious vision, and he spent the remainder of his life working on an "exegesis" based on this revelation. Dick's preoccupation with theological issues in his later years is apparent in his last novels, *VALIS, The Divine Invasion,*

and *The Transmigration of Timothy Archer.* Dick died of a massive stroke in 1982.

For the most part critics have greeted Dick's work with high regard. Although he is occasionally faulted for an awkward prose style and hackneyed dialogue, he is commended for creating sympathetic protagonists who, while not heroic, attempt to carry on with their lives under difficult circumstances. Dick's proponents have asserted that his complex narrative structures provide the framework for the equally complex questions that he asks of his readers. While often impugning the validity of American social and political institutions, Dick expresses confidence in a fundamental human capacity for compassion and tenderness. Following Dick's death, Norman Spinrad commented that Dick possessed a "clear and genuine metaphysical insight and loving warmth that made him the great writer that he was."

PRINCIPAL WORKS

NOVELS

Solar Lottery   1955
Eye in the Sky   1957
Time Out of Joint   1959
The Man in the High Castle   1962

Clans of the Alphane Moon   1964
Martian Time-Slip   1964
The Penultimate Truth   1964
Dr. Bloodmoney, or How We Got Along After the Bomb
   1965
The Three Stigmata of Palmer Eldritch   1965
Now Wait For Last Year   1966
The Unteleported Man   1966
The Zap Gun   1967
Do Androids Dream of Electric Sheep?   1968
Ubik   1969
We Can Build You   1972
Flow My Tears, The Policeman Said   1974
Deus Irae   [with Roger Zelazny]   1976
A Scanner Darkly   1977
The Divine Invasion   1981
VALIS   1981
The Transmigration of Timothy Archer   1982

SHORT FICTION

A Handful of Darkness   1955
The Variable Man, and Other Stories   1957
The Preserving Machine, and Other Stories   1969
The Golden Man   1980
The Collected Stories of Philip K. Dick   5 vols.   1987

OTHER

"The Android and the Human"   (speech)   1972; published in *SF Commentary*
"Who is an SF Writer?"   (essay)   1974; published in *Science Fiction: The Academic Awakening*
"Man, Android and Machine"   (essay)   1976; published
   in *Science Fiction at Large*
In Pursuit of Valis: Selections from the Exegesis   (nonfiction)   1991
The Selected Letters of Philip K. Dick–1974   (letters)
   1991

CRITICISM

Robert Scholes and Eric S. Rabkin

[Dick's] work is not easy to discuss, since it does not fall
neatly into a few books of exceptional achievement and a
larger body of lesser works. All of his books offer ideas,
situations, and passages of considerable interest. None
quite achieves that seamless perfection of form that constitutes one kind of literary excellence. Nor does his career
fall into any neat pattern of rise and fall or growth and decline. Stronger and weaker works are scattered evenly
among his entire body of fiction, even as stronger and
weaker episodes may be found within individual books.
His strength lies in the unique vision that informs all of
his fiction, and the crisp serviceable prose in which he
presents the most extreme events without acknowledging
that they are anything but ordinary. The way to read Dick
is to read all of him, from the beginning to his latest effort,

watching his control over certain themes mature and
flourish.

Throughout his work Dick has made two themes his own,
developing them and their philosophical implications
more richly than any other single writer. They are the
theme of alternate universes and the theme of mechanical
simulacra for organic forms of life. The theme of simulacra occurs throughout his work, assuming major dimensions in *The Simulacra, Do Androids Dream of Electric
Sheep?,* and *We Can Build You.* It is often an occasion for
comedy, as people are confronted by automated devices
that function badly or have their functions distorted by
unusual situations. At a deeper level this theme is used to
explore the interface between life and artifice, exploiting
the many paradoxes made possible by minute duplication
of organic functions and behavior. But the theme most
uniquely Dick's, because he has developed it more richly
than any other writer, is the theme of the alternate universe.

The alternate universe theme in Dick's work may rest, as
it does in *Eye in the Sky,* upon the simple notion that
every person perceives the world from a unique point of
view. In this book Dick uses an accident to a bevatron to
create a situation in which a small group of people are
forced to live in the mental worlds of individual members
of the group. Since these individuals include a fundamen-
talist religious fanatic, a do-gooding Victorian prude, a
paranoid schizophrenic, and a crypto-communist of extreme views—the results are both frightening and comic.
In later works the lines between real and "irreal" worlds
become less easy to trace. The characters in Dick's world
often find it impossible to distinguish between what is
really happening and what seems to be happening to
them—and the reader often faces the same problem. Even
what "actually" happens can only offer clues to a reality
which is enigmatic and elusive. In *Ubik* most of the events
we experience, including a persistent drift in space and
time toward Des Moines, Iowa, in 1939, are apparently
the hallucinations of semi-dead individuals kept in "cold-
pac" in a Swiss mortuary. But they are as vivid, as moving,
as concrete and specific as any other kind of fictional
event. There is no comfortable return to a "real" present
at the end of *Ubik,* as there is in *Eye in the Sky.* We are
denied that satisfaction here in much the same way that
we might be denied it by Alain Robbe-Grillet or some
other practitioner of the French "new novel." Dick has
turned science fiction into an elegant and harrowing mental game, in which traditional ethics and traditional metaphysics are both called into question. Of any particular act
it is often equally hard to say whether it has "really" happened or whether it is good or bad. What Dick makes us
understand is that events produce anguish for those involved in them, whether they are dreams or "realities,"
and where there is anguish there must be sympathy. But
he almost always prevents sympathy from turning into
sentimentality. Examine, for instance, the movement of
thought and emotion in the following passage from the
end of *Flow My Tears, the Policeman Said.* Police General Felix Buckman has just arranged for the death of a famous entertainer, for complex reasons involving his inces-

tuous love for his own dead sister and the exercise of his bureaucratic prerogatives:

> The real, ultimate truth is that despite your fame and your great public following you are expendable, he thought. And I am not. That is the difference between the two of us. Therefore you must go and I remain.

> His ship floated on, up into the band of night-time stars. And to himself he sang quietly, seeking to look ahead, to see forward into time, to the world of his home, of music and thought and love, to books, ornate snuffboxes and rare stamps. To the blotting out, for a moment, of the wind that rushed about him as he drove on, a speck nearly lost in the night.

> There is beauty which will never be lost, he declared to himself; I will preserve it; I am one of those who cherishes it. And I abide. And that, in the final analysis, is all that matters.

> Tunelessly, he hummed to himself. And felt at last some meager heat as, finally, the standard police model quibble heater mounted below his feet began to function.

> Something dropped from his nose onto the fabric of his coat. My God, he thought in horror. I'm crying again. He put up his hand and wiped the greaselike wetness from his eyes. Who for? he asked himself. Alys? For Taverner? The Hart woman? Or for all of them?

> No, he thought. It's a reflex. From fatigue and worry. It doesn't mean anything. Why does a man cry? he wondered. Not like a woman; not for that. Not for sentiment. A man cries over the loss of something, something alive. A man can cry over a sick animal that he knows won't make it. The death of a child: a man can cry for that. But not because things are sad.

> A man, he thought, cries not for the future or the past but for the present.

Buckman tries to see himself in absolute terms—as justified in his actions, as in command of events, as an enduring, worthy being. And of course he symbolizes all those men of power who justify their actions by their conoisseurship, their love of art, even while persecuting artists. But in this case the man of power actually cares for some things outside himself—his music, his sister—and this makes him prey to genuine emotion which bursts through his platitudinous self-comforting thoughts. He can't really control his tears, or events, or justify himself and the role he plays. As he observes a few moments later, when he is thinking of returning to his office for a final confrontation with his victim Jason Taverner, if he should return, he would not be in command: "All I can do there now is witness something I can no longer control. I am painted on, like a fresco. Dwelling in only two dimensions. I and Jason Taverner are figures in an old child's drawing. Lost in dust." In this lugubrious mood he stops for fuel and approaches the only other person at the station. He draws on a pad "a heart pierced by an arrow" and hands it to this stranger without explanation. The man, uncomprehending or unconcerned, hands it back. Buckman starts to leave but returns and hugs the stranger. After this they speak—kindly human words dwindling toward banality, cliché, and finally, with the behavioral routines of casual acquaintances, they part. Dick's ability to mix absurd adventures with moments of existential anguish is rare in our literature.

Though it is dangerous to single out any one of his works for special attention, we should at least acknowledge the achievement of his Hugo-winning novel, **The Man in the High Castle.** The premise of this book is that we are living in a United States that lost World War II. The country has been divided by the victorious Germans and Japanese, except for a zone in the Rocky Mountains which nobody seemed to want and serves as a buffer. In this world, a novelist (the man in the high castle) has written a book called *The Grasshopper Lies Heavy,* in which is imagined a world where England and America had won the war. This fictional world, we should note, is still not exactly like our "real" one. And at one moment in the novel, a Japanese dignitary under intense emotional pressure finds himself briefly in a San Francisco much more like our own—at any rate, a world in which the Japanese are clearly not the victorious occupiers of California. These various realities have equal ontological status in Dick's text. None is more actual than any other, except for those involved in it at that time.

The strength of this novel is in the characters and situations generated by Dick's imagination: the Japanese assiduously collecting American antiques (such as Colt .45s and Mickey Mouse watches); the Americans trying to master Japanese cultural codes and behavioral rituals, the Germans still pursuing Hitler's ideals but having to confront a resistant Japan. The individual characters: Mr. Tagomi, the Kasouras, Mr. Childan, the Frinks, Captain Wegener. The interweaving of all these characters in stories which intersect and separate, the development of greater understanding in Tagomi, Wegener, and Frink—all this is handled masterfully. The book comes to a richly extentialist conclusion in the thoughts of Wegener as he risks his life for a better Germany and a better world:

> No wonder Mr. Tagomi could not go on, he thought. The terrible dilemma of our lives. Whatever happens, it is evil beyond compare. Why struggle, then? Why choose? If all alternatives are the same . . .

> Evidently we go on, as we always have. From day to day. At this moment we work against Operation Dandelion. Later on, at another moment, we work to defeat the police. But we cannot do it all at once; it is a sequence. An unfolding process. We can only control the end by making a choice at each step.

> He thought, We can only hope. And try.

> On some other world, possibly it is different. Better. There are clear good and evil alternatives. Not these obscure admixtures, these blends, with no proper tool by which to untangle the components.

> We do not have the ideal world, such as we would like, where mortality is easy because cog-

nition is easy. Where one can do right with no effort because he can detect the obvious.

But this conclusion is followed by another in which Juliana Frink visits the man in the high castle and forces him to admit that he wrote his book with the aid of the Chinese *Book of Changes.* When she throws the coins herself, asking the *I Ching* what people were supposed to learn from the book, the resulting hexagram is Chung Fu, "Inner Truth." She interprets this literally—Germany and Japan lost the war. But Hawthorne Abendsen, the author of *The Grasshopper Lies Heavy,* hesitates and then says, "I'm not sure." The other author, Philip K. Dick, is silent. But surely he wants us to remember that Chung Fu stands for *inner* truth. Both books, Dick's and Abendsen's, are fictions. But both, like *The Book of Changes* itself, can lead us to confront, at least briefly, our own inner truth. Dick's books do not lend themselves to summary, and they lend themselves too easily to explanation and interpretation. Such interpretations are treacherous, because they must ignore countercurrents of idea and value in Dick's work, invariably oversimplifying it. These complex works must be experienced and reexperienced to yield their secrets— and even then they will often remain enigmatic. (pp. 71-5)

Robert Scholes and Eric S. Rabkin, "A Brief Literary History of Science Fiction," in their Science Fiction: History, Science, Vision, *Oxford University Press, Inc., 1977, pp. 3-99.*

Hazel Pierce

The novels of Philip K. Dick elicit ambivalent responses from readers, responses such as: "I don't like this novel, *but . . .* " Behind that last word lurks the intuitive realization that Philip K. Dick demands more of a reader than such a superficial affective response would indicate. True, one may be annoyed by a weak plot line, by scientific inconsistencies, or by the cavalier way in which Dick introduces, then summarily dismisses, some of his characters. Any reader with a strong urge to impose a firm and logical sequential structure on the events in Dick's novels will fight a losing battle. *But*—that word again—in the midst of the many shifts in reality, Dick does awaken our fears, shaking our complacent acceptance of the commonplace world as we think we know it. We sense an urgency in his appeal to our powers of imagination.

Critical commentary on Philip K. Dick also reflects this ambivalence to some degree. [In his essay "Philip K. Dick Saying It All Over Again" (*Philip K. Dick: Electric Shepherd,* ed. Bruce Gillispie)] George Turner speaks of his own superficial enjoyment of Dick's work but of his dissatisfaction with it on deeper levels. In a review of *Flow My Tears, the Policeman Said* [in *Philip K. Dick: Electric Shepherd*], Turner further claims that Dick "achieves his own brand of forgettability," compounded from carelessness, hastiness, and obvious logical holes. [In his essay "Science Fiction as Fictive History" (*Extrapolation,* 1974)] Robert H. Canary remarks on the "stigmata" in all of Dick's novels, those marks revealing "his long apprenticeship in Ace Double Novels." [In his essay "Discontent in American Science Fiction" (*Science-Fiction Studies,*

1977)] Gérard Klein, on the other hand, lauds Dick's work as the "most important work in American SF at least until the end of the 60s," reflecting the esteem with which Dick's work is regarded in France. The ultimate accolade comes from Stanislaw Lem, when he labels Dick as a "visionary among charlatans" in an essay by that title [in *Science-Fiction Studies,* 1975].

It appears self-evident that superficially Philip K. Dick satisfies something in all people, whether it is the need for a target to demolish or for a flag to raise. Perhaps the lack of unanimity is attributable to the absence of any single, generally accepted theory of science fiction by which to judge accomplishment or failure, as has been suggested by Lem in his critical salvos at the field in general. Despite the absence of such a theory, a serious reader must still face the nagging insistence of that small word, *but.* Philip Dick's work is all of these things which readers and critics say it is. However, he does demand more of us than flip dismissal, empty praise, or abstract labels. But just what *does* he want of us? And what has motivated him to assume the right to demand more of us?

Dick has sprinkled clues to possible answers to the above questions in several articles. In **"Who Is an SF Writer?"** Dick describes an individual who is in part a scientist, in part a believer in the magic of the written word, and in part a political dreamer. He considers the term *scientist* to refer to more than the possessor of a body of systematized knowledge derived from empirical investigation; instead, he focuses on the etymological basis of the word—*scientia,* having knowledge. The writer of science fiction possesses some knowledge which he must impart to his readers; he has that "grand drive of the true research scientist, to acquaint people with something heretofore overlooked." To do this, he must struggle with what William Blake called "the stubborn structure of the language" while believing in its ability ultimately to achieve some change or to effect some awakening in that mind lulled to sleep by custom.

Motivating Dick's drive to acquaint us with something heretofore overlooked is a modern variation of an age-old philosophical concern: what does it mean to be a human being? Humanists of every age have discussed this question within the context of their own culture and society. Pre-Newtonian thinkers saw an orderly universe with a special place for man—a place of equal value with others in the eyes of God, but a place which warranted the special gift of reason. Shakespeare's Hamlet closely reflects the view of his age:

> What is a man
> If his chief good and market of his time
> Be but to sleep and feed? A beast, no more,
> Sure, He that made us with such large discourse,
> Looking before and after, gave us not
> That capability and godlike reason
> To fust in us unused.

Post-Newtonian man, escaping his prescribed place in a hierarchical universe, could assume a central place in the universe and find comfort in a belief in his own perfectibility.

But what of twentieth-century man? Technological man?

Man living in a world of economic, political, and social complexity? That this is Philip K. Dick's very real concern is inescapable, for all of his writings—novels, short stories, essays, responses to reviews of his books, published letters—reflect it in one way or another. Perhaps the most open and detailed discussion of this concern appears in a speech, **"The Android and the Human,"** which Dick gave in Vancouver, B. C., in March of 1972. Whether on purpose or inadvertently, the mere arrangement of the two key words in the title betrays the focal problem for contemporary society. Amidst the twentieth-century reality of the increasing use of ever more complex mechanical and electronic constructs, is an "android" response to life taking precedence over the human one? Will the values associated with technological "behavior" encroach on humanistic values to the point of reducing people to the level of being mere extensions of their constructs? Dick would consider these questions to be phrased in the wrong tense. One should rather ask: *has* the android mentality *already* replaced authentic human behavior?

These two additional words—*authentic* and *human*—appear over and over in the Vancouver speech until they work on our conscious mind much as does water dripping on a stone, though more quickly. Slowly they wear into even the closed mind. Dick speaks of "unauthentic human activity" encouraged by present-day organization which relieves individuals of the responsibility for personal decisions. He finds hope for the "dying bird of authentic humanness" in those young persons who feel and express a "new and inner—and genuinely authentic—human desire." At last he lays out for us those telltale signs that might alert us to the encroachment of androidism. Comparing this state of mind with the more commonly understood schizoid personality, Dick warns us of the danger in the submersion of that which is authentic. When thought reduces feeling, when people are deprived of the opportunity for "making exceptions" or exerting choice, and when they fail to grow as a result of "agonizing situations," then there is a failure of sensitivity and the open avenue to androidism.

If the majority of people fail to notice these signs, the person with the spirit of the true research scientist and a firm belief in the word must act to alert them. Often this special knowledge will involve direct, stern criticism of situations generally labeled "good" or accepted as the status quo. Then the writer stands a fair chance of suffering considerable resistance, even of being labeled as a political activist. All too often the images evoked by this label tend to obscure and erode the validity of any message which the event may carry. The science-fiction writer, however, works as an "introverted activist." His protest, according to Dick, is a protest against "concrete reality," a protest that suggests neither a cause nor cure but rather alternate possibilities to that reality. Like William Blake's Los, the Poetic Imagination, "striving with Systems to deliver Individuals from those Systems," the science-fiction writer strives with his own special systems—the other realities which might exist, given the chance. With these alternatives, he can alert us to the "Systems" in our own experiential reality which threaten our humanity. In so doing he achieves his special deliverance. Perhaps this is the most

solemn task of the science-fiction writer—that of *political dreamer,* or to apply Stanislaw Lem's term, of *visionary.*

Even though written in the decade before the Vancouver speech, those novels of Philip K. Dick published between 1962 and 1965 provide us with evidence of his intense concern with the political relationships that threaten authentic humanity. Obviously this concern operates first through the plot. Characters react to a sequence of events in such a way as to define their values; they fail or succeed insofar as those values harmonize with the surrounding social, political, or physical reality, whichever is most dominant. Tacitly invited to step into this fictional framework, a reader can test himself against the conflicts or challenges of this futuristic—usually near-future—society. Up to this point, Dick does little or nothing different from many science fiction writers—indeed, from any writer of fiction. But Philip K. Dick, as an "introverted activist," does more. He prods our complacency, fills us with a vague sense of uneasiness, and finally forces us to hold up the mirrors of his worlds and recognize the distorted reflections of our own world in them.

How does he accomplish this? Certainly not through the plot, for he demolishes time and sequence almost to the point of our total confusion at times. Nor through the diverse characters who flood his pages in profusion. Instead, Dick activates our minds by those often small but telling images which remind us of something familiar but which are slightly out of focus for us. As we strive to bring these images into focus, they penetrate our consciousness and remain to change our outlook from that point on. This technique works much as do those rapid, montagelike films which purport to show all of American History or the sweep of the world's art in sixty seconds. We sense the continuity but cannot absorb the totality of each frame. What *does* stay with us is some eyecatching detail like the pose of a head signalling authority, or a drop of blood encompassing all of the pain of war, or the glowing eye of a newborn baby suggesting hope and life. Imagine such an imaginary film running from **The Man in the High Castle** to **Dr. Bloodmoney.** Certain images and phrases impinge upon our awareness as they are whisked rapidly by: an end of the idea of place; the "web of the world-spider" suggesting the interconnectedness of all life counterbalanced by AM-WEB with its harsh reality; the many simulacra built to order; adults escaping from their untenable existence by playing with dollhouses . . . The images go on and on, living a potent existence completely apart from the fictional plot. When they do not go away, they remain to urge the reader to ask: What does it mean to be a person in twentieth-century America? What is the contemporary idea of place? Are we adults playing with "toys" or with our special artifacts of material existence? How tenuous is the peace of the human relations we so take for granted? If we are pushed to answer these and the many other disquieting questions which Philip K. Dick arouses in us, he has succeeded in his introverted way in activating a sense of awareness in us. (pp. 105-10)

Hazel Pierce, "Philip K. Dick's Political Dreams," in Philip K. Dick, *edited by Martin Harry Greenberg and Joseph D. Olander,*

Taplinger Publishing Company, Inc., 1983, pp. 105-35.

Dick on the future:

The world of the future, to me, is not a place, but an event. A construct, not by one author in the form of words written to make up a novel or story that other persons sit in front of, outside of, and read—but a construct in which there is no author and no readers but a great many characters in search of a plot. Well, there is no plot. There is only them-selves and what they do and say to each other, what they build to sustain all of them individually and collectively, like a huge umbrella that lets in light and shuts out the dark-ness at the same instant. When the characters die, the novel ends. And the book falls back into dust. Out of which it came. Or back, like the dead Christ, into the arms of his warm, tender, grieving, comprehending, living mother. And a new cycle begins; from her he is reborn, and the story, or another story, perhaps different, even better, starts up. A story told by the characters to one another. "A tale of sound and fury"—signifying very much. The best we have. Our yesterday, our tomorrow, the child who came before us and the woman who will live after us and outlast, by her very existing, what we have thought and done.

Philip K. Dick, in his speech "The Android and the Human," published in Philip K. Dick: Electric Shepherd, *1972.*

Carl Freedman

"The ultimate in paranoia," writes Philip K. Dick,

> is not when everyone is against you but when ev-ery*thing* is against you. Instead of 'My boss is plotting against me,' it would be 'My boss's phone is plotting against me.' Objects sometimes seem to possess a will of their own anyhow, to the normal mind; they don't do what they're supposed to do, they get in the way, they show an unnatural resistance to change.

This comment on the early short story, **"Colony,"** has a direct and obvious relevance to representations that ap-pear throughout the Dick canon. Examples include the Lovecraftian house-creature in *Eye in the Sky,* the assassi-nation machine which masquerades as a television set in *The Penultimate Truth,* the comically insolent and liti-gious door in *Ubik,* and the occasionally murderous car-repair factory in *Deus Irae.* Rarely for Dick are objects what common sense would suppose them to be, and the will with which they are invested can even constitute a precise mimicry of such quintessentially "human" types as the benignly authoritative father (Kindly Dad in *Mar-tian Time-Slip*) or the irresistible and dangerous sexpot (Rachel Rosen in *Do Androids Dream of Electric Sheep?,* the major theme of which is the practical difficulty of dis-tinguishing between human beings and one variety of ob-jects).

That objects have a will, and a quasi-human will, of their own is, of course, also an idea long familiar to historical

materialism. *Capital* itself opens with the intricate analysis of the fetishism of commodities—definable as the process whereby "the definite social relation between men themselves . . . assumes here, for them, the fantastic form of a relation between things"—and some of the metaphors which Marx employs in explaining how products of human labor appear to be "endowed with a life of their own" have what one may be tempted to call a Dickian ring:

> The form of wood, for instance, is altered if a table is made out of it. Nevertheless the table continues to be wood, an ordinary, sensuous thing. But as soon as it emerges as a commodity, it changes into a thing which transcends sensu-ousness. It not only stands with its feet on the ground, but, with relation to all other commodi-ties, it stands on its head, and evolves out of its wooden brain grotesque ideas, far more wonder-ful than if it were to begin dancing of its own free will.

Since *Capital,* commodity fetishism has become a central category in many versions of Marxist cultural theory, and has been developed and reformulated in various ways—as reification, for instance, by Lukács, and as counter-finality by Sartre. Yet Philip Dick, when writing discursively of quasi-living "things," chooses a term not directly related to Marxism at all but one drawn from the different science of psychoanalysis: paranoia.

This apparent displacement, I suggest, is not necessarily a vulgar psychologistic reduction, but a potentially fruitful hint which may shed some light on the historical status of certain psychoanalytic categories, on the nature of signifi-cation under monopoly capitalism, and on the materialist reading of SF. In what follows I will outline a Marxist the-ory of paranoia and will then suggest its relevance to SF in general and to the work of Dick in particular, reserving my main critical emphasis for the novel which I take to be Dick's finest, *Ubik.*

For Freud, the ideational structure of paranoia is that of a ruthless hermeneutic. In one essay, indeed, he defines the disease as "the hypercathexis of the interpretations of someone else's unconscious." The point here is that the paranoiac has an abnormally high investment in the her-meneutic practice which he or she performs on the symp-tomatic actions of other people. Somewhat similarly, in the Schreber case-history Freud conceptualizes the alleged homoerotic basis of paranoia by means of a semantic de-coding of the various possible contradictions of the sen-tence, "I love him": each contradiction constitutes one mode of interpretation of worldly phenomena, and corre-sponds to one variety of paranoia. But not only is the para-noiac an interpreter: he or she is one of an especially sys-tematic and ambitious type. In the essay "On Narcis-sism," Freud explicitly links paranoia with the formation of speculative systems, and in the reading of Schreber he notes a profound affinity between paranoia and megalo-maniacal delusions of world catastrophe. The paranoiac is not only someone for whom every detail is meaningful—for whom nothing can be left uninterpreted or taken for granted—but someone who holds a conception of mean-ing that is both totalizing and hermeneutic. The paranoiac is the most rigorous of metaphysicians. The typical paranoid outlook is thoroughgoing, internally logical, never trivializing, and capable of explaining the multitude of observed phenomena as aspects of a symmetrical and expressive totality. No particular of empirical reality is so contingent or heterogeneous that the paranoiac cannot, by a straightforward process of point-for-point correspondence, interpret its meaning within the framework of his or her own grand system. The totalizing closure of paranoia is, in fact, noted as lucidly by Dick as by Freud: in **"Shell Game"** (one of Dick's finest stories and the germ of *Clans of the Alphane Moon*), the massive frustration of attempting to break down such closure is powerfully recorded, and the basic problem is clearly stated. "The paranoid is totally rigid," says one of the characters. "He logically weaves all events, all persons, all chance remarks and happenings, into his system."

Freud is similarly baffled. One can detect an unusual tone of weary exasperation when he reports his experience in treating jealousy (always closely related to paranoia and, beyond a certain point of delusionality, one of its varieties): "one must refrain from disputing with [the jealous patient] the material on which he bases his suspicions; one can only aim at bringing him to regard the matter in a different light." On the other hand, though Freud never considers paranoia as other than a sickness, it is a sickness for which he seems to have an unaccustomed intellectual respect. Not only does he associate paranoia with philosophy; he suggests that there may be "more truth in Schreber's delusion than other people are as yet prepared to believe," and as early as *The Psychopathology of Everyday Life* he concedes a "partial justification" to paranoiac interpretations. Or, as the paranoiac Horselover Fat says of himself in Dick's *Valis,* "What he did not know then is that it is sometimes an appropriate response to reality to go insane."

Jacques Lacan, however, goes one step further. What Freud regards as an especially interesting disease Lacan situates as crucial to the "normal" human psyche. The rationalizing interpretations of paranoia, elaborated into a system at the center of which stands the "I" of the paranoiac, are for Lacan paradigmatic of human psychic development as inaugurated by the "mirror stage" of objectifying identification, when distinctions and links are first established between an alienated "I" and an alienating not-"I." It is in this way that, in such early essays as "Aggressivity in Psychoanalysis" and "The Freudian Thing," Lacan maintains that the ego is structured on a paranoiac basis and that human knowledge operates according to a paranoiac principle. But the largest significance of these well-known formulations becomes evident only in the context of Lacan's later attempt, in *The Four Fundamental Concepts of Psycho-Analysis,* to provide a materialist historicization of the major psychoanalytic categories. He argues that the subject known to Freudian analysis—which seems to itself to be centered and autonomous but which analytic theory and practice show to be divided or "de-centered" between the Imaginary (or specular and dualistic) and Symbolic (or linguistic and structural) Orders—is by no means an eternal, ahistorical phenomenon. On the contrary, Lacan repeatedly links its emergence

with such cultural products of the period of nascent bourgeois hegemony as perspectival optics and the Cartesian *cogito:* the Freudian subject and the subject of capitalism are inextricably related. Again, paranoia plays a crucial role in Lacan's formulations. "At the basis of paranoia itself," he says, "there reigns the phenomenon of the *Unglauben,*" which is in turn defined as "the absence of one of the terms of belief, of the term in which is designated the division of the subject." But the designation of the division of the subject is, of course, precisely what the bourgeois ego constitutively and necessarily forecloses; and, again, there is no basis for a sharp distinction between the paranoiac and the "normal" subject of capitalist society.

It is in a Lacanian framework, then, that we can draw the most radical conclusions from Freud's descriptions of paranoia, which Freud himself was prevented from drawing by his ahistoricism and by his decisive clinical dichotomy between disease and health. Paranoia, we can conclude, is no mere aberration but is structurally crucial to the way that we, as ordinary subjects of bourgeois hegemony, represent ourselves to ourselves and embark on the Cartesian project of acquiring empiricist knowledge. In this sense, we can accept Freud's urgency when he insists of certain paranoiac delusions that *"There is in fact some truth in them."*

But what is it in the workings of capitalism that interpellates individuals as paranoid subjects? If, as we have seen, paranoia operates by a hermeneutic logic, what is it in bourgeois society that we are compelled to interpret? Capitalism is definable as generalized commodity production, which, as Marx shows, necessarily encompasses generalized commodity fetishism. But the secret of the commodity itself—the basic distinction between the commodity and the noncommodified object of traditional societies—is its dual aspect, its status as both a use-value that satisfies some human need and an exchange-value that renders it an interchangeable atom in the total system of exchange and that mystifies its origin in human labor. Furthermore, use-value, though indispensable to the commodity, is also, paradoxically, irrelevant to its status *qua* commodity: capitalism constitutes the hegemony of exchange-value (or simply "value," as Marx more often calls it). I suggest, then, that the commodity as bearer of value—both the basic economic "cell" of capitalism and a mystifying signifier—is the ultimate object of paranoid hermeneutic by the historical subjects of bourgeois society. If we are economically constituted as capitalists and workers who must buy and sell human labor that is commodified into labor-power, then we are psychically constituted as paranoid subjects who must seek to interpret the signification of the objects—commodities—which define us and which, in a quasi-living manner, mystify the way that they and we are defined. "Value," says Marx,

> does not have its description branded on its forehead; it rather transforms every product of labour into a social hieroglyphic. Later on, men try to decipher the hieroglyphic, to get behind the secret of their own social product: for the characteristic which objects of utility have of being values is as much men's social product as is their language.

From a Lacanian perspective, it is easy to see that there is nothing accidental in the collocation of language and value: both are signifying orders which demand interpretation. In addition, it is, I think, also arguable that what is generally true of capitalism is particularly true of 20th-century monopoly capitalism. "Consumerism"—that is, the increased importance of individual as distinct from productive consumption and the organized stimulation of the former by techniques such as advertising—saturates the social field with hieroglyphics to an extent unprecedented in all of human history. Virtually no aspect of life is left untouched: if our sexual lives are as dependent on over-the-counter contraceptive devices as our political awareness is on televised representations of the "news," yet all of these components of what has been called "the society of the spectacle" are first and last mystifying bearers of exchange-value.

When writing discursively, Dick may speak merely of "objects," but in his novels the commodification of these objects is made evident. The androids manufactured by the Rosen Association are primarily for sale, while in **Ubik** the ordinary accouterments of Joe Chip's middle-class life (his coffee-pot, his door, his shower, his bathroom, his refrigerator, *et alia*) actually foreground their role as exchange-values by verbally (and not too politely) demanding money before each act of use. If, as has often been noted, Dick is a paranoid writer, this is true not only because, on the level of character representation, his protagonists tend to be fearful and harassed men who strive to interpret and deal with alienating forces beyond their control. Even more importantly, the logic of Dick's paranoia is constituted by his representation of those forces themselves as commodities. In **The Unteleported Man,** even a nightmare vision of German totalitarianism is based on a popular consumer-oriented business. In **The Zap Gun,** even the world-wide arms race resolves into the production and marketing of consumer goods. Commodities for Dick are frequently "alive" in a more than metaphorical sense, for they are shown to participate in the paradigmatically "human" exchanges of linguistic and sexual intercourse. Like Joe Chip, one can argue with them, plead with them, scold them. Like Rick Deckard in **Do Androids Dream of Electric Sheep?,** one can even go to bed with them. It is, to put the matter mildly, unlikely that Philip Dick ever intended to represent the subjective or ideological state that a Marxist-Lacanian theory, which co-ordinates paranoia with commodity fetishism, would lead one to expect as paradigmatic for the bourgeois ego. But, objectively, this formulation seems to me a valid description of one major aspect of his work. Marx illustrates commodity fetishism through the metaphor of the acrobatic, thinking, dancing table. Lacan, in "The Freudian Thing," illustrates the paranoiac structure of the ego through the metaphor of the speaking desk. Dick accepts this kind of metaphoric structure and novelistically literalizes it.

But it is not only commodity fetishism which, as Dick's texts also suggest, can be co-ordinated with paranoia. Second only to this economic category is a more specifically political category whose pressure is also felt in Dick's paranoid texts: conspiracy. Conspiracy (in sharp contrast to commodity fetishism) is a woefully under-theorized term in the Marxist tradition, which has, indeed, tended to be extremely wary of it. Marxists have suspected, often justly, that to invoke conspiracy in political discourse is to replace structural analysis with merely ethical finger-pointing. Yet it can also be argued that in a monopoly-capitalist state like modern America—intensely centralized and militarized but still governed according to bourgeois-democratic forms—conspiracy is no voluntaristic aberration but a structural necessity for ruling-class politics. When actual political power is largely concentrated in a relatively compact network of corporate, military, and governmental bureaucracies—and yet when it is unfeasible to exercise this power in despotic ways that too openly flout popular sentiment or legislative and judicial sanctions—then the ruling elite may have only two choices. It can curtail the enforcement of its perceived interests out of prudence or (ethical) respect for republican parliamentarianism; or it can adopt conspiratorial methods. There is, I think, substantial evidence that the latter course has frequently been taken, from the still murky affairs at Dealey Plaza and the Watergate, to the open expressions of contempt for and evasion of democratic sanctions that Noam Chomsky and others have repeatedly documented in publications of elite groups like the Trilateral Commission. But a fully rigorous Marxist theorization of conspiracy has yet to be undertaken. Though I can hardly develop such a theory here, I will suggest that it is at least provisionally plausible to regard conspiracy as crucial to a theoretical description of the political level of society under certain varieties of monopoly capitalism.

Such a theory would, in any case, tend to explain the representations of conspiracy in Dick's fiction, where conspiracy is often as powerful as commodity fetishism and where the hermeneutic of paranoia works to decipher signs of conspiracy as well as exchange-values. In **Dr Bloodmoney** the ultimate conspiracy of nuclear war (one of Dick's recurring obsessions) is metaphorically located in the brain of one right-wing military scientist, but usually Dick's treatment is more literal. In **Time Out of Joint,** for example, Ragle Gumm's paranoid delusion of being the object of an immense governmental conspiracy and the most consequential person in the world turns out to be the precise, unproblematic truth. Similarly, in **A Scanner Darkly,** Robert Arctor is finally destroyed by the conspiratorial collusion between the state authorities which employ him and the criminal drug syndicate which he is employed to fight. In **Ubik,** the plot structure itself is based on the interpretative attempts of Joe Chip and his colleagues to discover the nature and perpetrator of the horrifying conspiracy that has enveloped them—questions which, after several apparent answers, the novel finally leaves in permanent suspense. If Dick's protagonists tend to be paranoid, there is always much for them to be paranoid about. For they live in a world dominated by commodities and conspiracies; which is to say, a world not wholly unlike our own. I will later discuss whether paranoia can finally be considered "true." But it is normally the truth for Philip Dick.

And not only for him. There is, I suggest, a privileged relationship between paranoiac ideology and the genre of SF in general. For SF, far more than mundane fiction, requires what seems to be the fictional creation of a new world, one whose assumptions are radically at variance with those of everyday life. Yet (unless we are willing to invoke a theological concept of poetic inspiration or imagination) *creation* in this context can only mean an ideological interpretation of the actual world. The radical novelty of SF interpretations—which helps to produce what Darko Suvin has termed the "cognitive estrangement" of the genre—tends to require a rather thorough and totalizing presentation; for little can be taken for granted or left to the reader's common sense. It is in this way that Dr Schreber, with his estranging, self-consistent, paranoid world-vision, is himself very nearly an SF author. Furthermore, the great majority of SF inherits certain basic formal properties from the realist, as distinct from the modernist or post-modernist, novel: the typical SF text has a smoothly diachronic narrative line and offers its characters as mimetic representations of human beings. Such formal tendencies work to reinforce the pressure toward logical coherence and expressive totalization. In both estranging "content" and realist "form," then, SF closely corresponds to the weird and coherent interpretative systems of the paranoiac.

One could, I think, write a history of the genre in these terms—from the pioneering efforts of H. G. Wells (the negative utopias of *The Time Machine* [1895] and *When the Sleeper Wakes* [1899], the nightmare representation of extraterrestrial imperialism in *The War of the Worlds* [1898]), to such more recent and sophisticated efforts as Ursula Le Guin's *The Dispossessed* (1974), where the luxury commodities of A-Io have an always ominous and finally sinister aura, or Samuel Delany's *Babel-17* (1966), where language itself is reified into a conspiratorial weapon of war. If Philip Dick, however, is, as some have claimed, the greatest of all SF authors—"the Shakespeare of science fiction," as Fredric Jameson has called him—then I suggest that his stature can be at least partly explained by his pre-eminence in the production of paranoiac ideology, his uniquely rigorous and consistent representations of human subjects caught in the web of commodities and conspiracies. These two paranoid themes are perhaps most fully worked out and combined in *Ubik,* which, however, may also imply a certain critique of paranoia itself.

The world of *Ubik* is thoroughly saturated by commodities that foreground their status as quasi-living, mystifying signifiers. Not only do doors threaten to sue and coffeepots demand money for services rendered; creditor robots dun free-spending debtors like Joe Chip, and animate homeopapes read the news for a specified fee. Telephones and TV sets occasionally adopt a will of their own and, much to Joe Chip's confusion, transmit their messages in a way only very dubiously related to any human agency. One of the first clear indications in the plot that things have gone desperately wrong, that the characters may have been killed, is that money—the universal equivalent of all exchange-values—begins to alter its form. Later, the time-regression which the characters experience is charted primarily by the backward technological march of commodities, as when an ultra-modern TV set regresses into

an old-fashioned radio. Furthermore, it is not only that commodities make their presence insistently felt, sometimes comically, sometimes nightmarishly, but always in an estranging manner which invites interpretation; the world of *Ubik* is also one in which virtually everything is in one way or another commodified. Pat Conley, perhaps the most frightening *femme fatale* in the Dick canon, becomes Joe Chip's mistress by paying a straightforward cash sum, and appropriately wears the tattoo *caveat emptor* (which Joe is unable to decipher). Expensive moratoriums maintain the dead in a state of "half-life," the commodity structure having produced the technology to deconstruct even the distinction between life and death. An important role in the capitalist economy of 1992 is played by Ray Hollis's firm of hired "precogs" and telepaths, and also by the prudence organizations like Runciter Associates, which, on a strictly commercial basis, will provide "inertials" to neutralize unwanted eavesdropping and prognostication.

It is not accidental that the most intimate and valued human relationship represented in the novel is that between Joe Chip and Glen Runciter: that is, between employee and employer (as both are frequently noting), between seller and buyer of the commodity called labor-power. Finally, the entire text is semantically dominated by Ubik itself, the ultimate and universal commodity and the symbol of the ubiquity of the commodity structure. Introduced in the small commercials that serve as epigraphs to each chapter (where it is in turn presented as a make of car, a brand of beer, a brand of instant coffee, *et alia*), Ubik finally enters the narrative itself as a mysterious spray in an aerosol can that seems to be the most powerful "reality support" available, the only force capable of at least temporarily reversing the processes of regression and death. In the end, this strange but paradigmatic commodity is identified with theological mystery: "I am Ubik. Before the universe was, I am. . . . I am. I shall always be."

From every direction, then, the characters of *Ubik,* who become increasingly paranoid as the narrative progresses, are dominated by—indeed constituted by—the commodity structure. But their paranoia is also, and even more directly, determined by the terrifying conspiracy or conspiracies that trap them. That they and their (commodified) surroundings should be made to regress, to go backward in time and be drained of vital energy, is itself a conspiracy worthy of Kafka or Pynchon. But even more powerful is the extreme importance and difficulty of deciphering the conspiracy. First, it seems to be the effect of the bomb blast arranged by Ray Hollis; later, it appears that it may possibly be a weird practical joke by Glen Runciter; for some time, Joe Chip and his friends are convinced that the psionic powers of Pat Conley are responsible; finally, the childish half-lifer Jory is found to be the perpetrator. Yet even this hard-won knowledge is problematized in the novel's last lines, where Glen Runciter (whom we had assumed *not* to be conspiratorially trapped) is left holding a Joe Chip coin, as Joe and the other characters had earlier found Runciter's face on their money. "This was just the beginning," the novel concludes, and the definitive explanation of the conspiracy is indefinitely postponed.

Likewise, of course, the mystical veil finally thrown over Ubik precludes any final explanation of the commodity structure. This indeterminacy, this textually explicit failure of closure, is rare in Dick's fiction, and can, I think, be read as hinting at the conceptual limits of paranoia itself. For this fissuring of the text, this refusal to provide any unproblematic narrative resolution, constitutes precisely the kind of epistemological disjunction that paranoia cannot allow. The novel may thus suggest that paranoia—and no Dick character is more paranoid and most justly paranoid than Joe Chip—is in the last instance not an adequate response to the structures of commodification and conspiracy, however inevitably and "naturally" it is produced by them.

In this case, then, *Ubik* marks in the Dick canon a theoretical high point in relation to the Marxist-Lacanian problematic which I outlined earlier. For paranoia, with its easy hermeneutic passages from appearance to essence, and its assumption of a totality that is symmetrical and expressive rather than structural and de-centered, is an ideology in the strictest Althusserian sense: a " 'representation' of the Imaginary relationship of individuals to their Real conditions of existence." Like any ideology, paranoia is finally based on a refusal of any complex theoretical structure of differentials, remaining instead within the specular or dualistic reductionism proper to the Imaginary. Only thus can its unswervingly hermeneutic logic operate. It can no more be identified with theoretical knowledge than commodity fetishism can be identified with Marx's discovery of the basis of generalized commodity production, or the paranoiac structure of the ego with Lacan's concept of the de-centering of the subject.

Yet paranoia remains, I think, of all ideologies perhaps the most "reasonable" and the most nearly approximating to knowledge of capitalist society. If, as *Ubik* suggests, the hermeneutic of paranoia is finally doomed to failure, yet our social and psychic constitution as bourgeois subjects makes the temptation to such hermeneutic irresistible. If paranoia is an ideology, it nonetheless remains a stubbornly privileged one. And no modern writer—certainly none since Kafka—has fictionally produced that ideology more rigorously than Philip K. Dick. (pp. 15-22)

> *Carl Freedman, "Towards a Theory of Paranoia: The Science Fiction of Philip K. Dick,"* in Science-Fiction Studies, *Vol. 11, No. 1, March, 1984, pp. 15-24.*

Patricia S. Warrick

To summarize his ideas, to categorize his work, to deliver the final word would be to violate Dick's vision. He saw a universe of infinite possibility, with shapes that constantly transformed themselves—a universe in process. He had not delivered his final word when he died on March 3, 1982, because for him the Word was truly the Living Word, the power that creates and re-creates patterns. Trapped in the stasis of a final statement, the Word would have been defeated by entropy and death.

But if we cannot make a final statement, we can at least note the significance of his opus of fiction for the times in which we live. Great creative personalities often see the essence of an age with a clarity denied to the mass of people. Their vision is so vivid that when subsequent events confirm it, humanity, slower at arriving at a realization of its present, hails them as prophetic. I believe that Dick may well be one of those creative personalities whom we hail as visionaries. The claim seems a strange one, considering the literary form in which he worked. Blake, Wordsworth, Yeats—the Romantics with the elegance of poetic diction make up the visionary company, not writers working in a prose form often regarded as trash. But let us for the moment ignore the form in which he was forced to write and consider instead his vision.

He had a remarkable sense of the cultural transformation taking place in the last half of the twentieth century. He pointed out the cracks in our institutions, our ideologies, and our value systems that would inevitably lead to their collapse. He understood that what had been functional in an industrial age would not work as our culture transformed itself and moved into an Information Age. Such changes often march in with violence. As Dick's fiction declares again and again, the late twentieth century is a time at war with itself, not with an external enemy. To fight against what one abhors without realizing it lies within is to destroy all. Dick warns us against doing this to ourselves. The cloud of chaos inevitably hangs above the Dickian landscape, a reminder that a like chaos will descend on the real world and envelop us if we continue to make war.

Dick's fiction calls up our basic cultural assumptions, requires us to reexamine them, and points out the destructive destinations to which they are carrying us. The American Dream may have succeeded as a means of survival in the wilderness of early America; it allowed us to subdue that wilderness and build our holy cities of materialism. But now, the images in Dick's fiction declare, we live in a new kind of wilderness, a wasteland wilderness, because those cities and the culture that built them are in decay. We need a new American dream to overcome this wasteland. Dick's ubiquitous wasteland landscape is a moral mirror asking us to journey within and explore the universe of mind and psyche where all the forms that shape the outer world are created. The critical journey of discovery is into the mysterious realm of inner space. Just as Dick's Fomalhaut Cosmos was a universe created by his imagination, so the universe in which we live is constructed of our ideas about it. To change it we must change our ideas.

Dick's work makes no new declarations about our time; we knew early in the twentieth century that ours was an Age of Anxiety. But the gift of his powerful mythmaking ability is to give us the stories that help us see both what we are and what we may become as we move into the Space Age. His novel contribution is the bizarre images he creates that so vividly picture our anxieties. Phantasmagoric shapes, the Dickian protagonist often calls them, as he muses about the swirl of awesome possibilities sweeping through his mind. They are disorienting images—without clear boundary, inconsistent, contradictory, fragmented, at war with one another. They force us to reconsider our conventional conception of reality. Dick said that "science fiction is uniquely a kind of semi-reality. It is not a statement that 'this is,' but a statement, 'What if this were.' The difference is crucial in every respect." Frightening as are some of the futures Dick imagines for mankind, they are not fixed. We are Leo Buleros, we are "choosers," Dick tells us in *The Three Stigmata of Palmer Eldritch;* and *The Divine Invasion* envisions another future than nuclear destruction that we can choose. (pp. 194-95)

The Dickian fictional world is a world without Titans or Heroes; instead it is a world cut off from the gods. It is filled with little people lacking in power or wisdom, who daily face the dilemma of trying to survive in the face of the inexplicable destructive forces that constantly try to snuff them out. Yet they are not the conventional antiheroes of modern fiction. Perhaps the oxymoron *heroic antihero* best describes Dick's protagonist. Finally, the Dickian hero acts. He may writhe and struggle to escape, but in the end he accepts the burden of his existential freedom. Daily, he finally learns, he must choose once again to push the boulder of moral responsibility up the hill of right action. Freedom thus becomes of highest value in Dick's code. The individual must be free to make moral choices, even though he may often fail to make the right choice. Dick declares again and again, for the individual to be turned into a machine programmed to carry out the decisions of others is "the greatest evil imaginable; the placing on what was a free man who laughed and cried and made mistakes and wandered off into foolishness and play a restriction that limits him, despite what he may imagine or think, to fulfilling an aim outside his own personal—however puny—destiny." (p. 196)

[From] the beginning one element remains constant in all the fiction—Dick's faith in the power of empathy. The idea was not well developed or labeled when it first appeared. We see empathy in two of his early short stories as through a glass darkly. He has not yet given it a name. Instead, his characters act it out, and only later does he recognize what his fiction has said. In **"Roog"** Dick pictures a dog who guards the garbage can of his owners against the garbage men who come to collect it each week. The dog is driven crazy because he cannot offer protection to his owners against these weekly raids. Years later, Dick commented on the story, explaining that he was describing an actual dog owned by a Berkeley neighbor. "I watched the dog suffer, and I understood a little of what was destroying him, and I wanted to speak for him. That's the whole of it right there. Snooper couldn't talk. I could. In fact I could write it down, and someone could publish it and many people could read it. Writing fiction has to do with this: becoming the voice for those without voices. It's not your own voice, you the author; it is all those other voices which normally go unheard."

"Beyond Lies the Wub," Dick's first published story, also dramatizes the concept of empathy. It tells the story of a piglike alien captured and eventually eaten by a crew of space adventurers despite the fact that the wub possesses human characteristics. Captain Franco and his men lack the ability to see beneath the wub's appearance. Twenty years later Dick said of the story:

The idea I wanted to get down on paper had to do with the definition of "human." The dramatic way I trapped the idea was to present ourselves, the literal humans, and then an alien life form that exhibits the deeper traits that I associate with humanity: not a biped with an enlarged cortex—a forked radish that thinks, to paraphrase the old saying—but an organism that is human in terms of its soul.

I'm sorry if the word *soul* offends you, but I can think of no other term. Certainly, when I wrote the story back in my youth in politically-active Berkeley, I myself would never have thought of the crucial ingredient in the wub being a soul; I was a fireball radical and atheist, and religion was totally foreign to me. However, even in those days I was casting about in an effort to contrast the truly human from what I was later to call the "android or reflex machine" that looks human but is not. The germ of the idea lies in this my first published story. It has to do with empathy, or, as it was called in earlier times, caritas or *agape*.

In this story, empathy (on the part of the wub who looks like a big pig and has the feelings of a man) becomes an actual weapon for survival. Empathy is defined as the ability to put yourself in someone else's place. The wub does this even better than we ordinarily suppose could be done: its spiritual capacity is its literal salvation. The wub was my idea of a higher life form; it was then and it is now. On the other hand, Captain Franco (the name is deliberately based on General Franco of Spain) looks on other creatures in terms of sheer utility; they are objects to him, and he pays the ultimate price for this total failure of empathy. So I show empathy possessing a survival value; in terms of inter-species competition, empathy gives you the edge. Not a bad idea for a very early story by a very young person!

Two years after writing **"The Wub,"** Dick again explored the concept in **"The Last of the Masters"** (1954) and now he named it and actually called it empathy. In the story a young freedom fighter, Silvia, finally encounters the head of the coercive government and discovers he is a robot. She says in horror, "My God, you have no understanding of us. You run all this, and you're incapable of empathy. You're nothing but a mechanical computer."

By the second period of Dick's fiction when he writes his great novels in the 1960s, empathy is regularly used as the key element defining the authentic human being. The concept is made concrete most vividly in **"The Little Black Box,"** published in 1964. Dick then incorporates the black empathy box into *Do Androids Dream* where those like J. R. Isidore who use it regularly gain the strength to climb up through the difficulties of their daily lives. Beyond that, the power of empathy frees the individual from the prison house of his own consciousness and allows him to slip through the mirror forever reflecting back his own image. Once beyond, he sees the world from an alien consciousness to which he gives the same rights and worth as his own awareness. All life, not just his own, becomes sacred.

At first glance, Dick seems to be a contemporary writer who in many ways espouses an old-fashioned moral view that places him in the long tradition of humanistic writers. From the beginning, his writing insists that each individual has a responsibility to act in a moral way, even though that early fiction makes no reference to God. And of course by the end of his career, the novels focus on the major concepts of the Judeo-Christian tradition. While these concepts are never accepted in their entirety—in fact they are almost always revised—they are never denied or negated.

A closer examination of Dick's moral code, however, shows us that given the complexities of the contemporary world, the values of traditional Christian humanists are too simple to be workable. He develops a code of valor that is much more demanding. Choice is no longer a choice between good and evil, as the moralist in an earlier age would have declared. Today the problem facing each man is that even when he practices empathy and yearns to make the right moral choice, he often finds himself in a moral dilemma where in order to do right he must also do wrong. Again and again the Dickian hero is faced with this tragic choice: to do the right thing he must violate his own moral nature. . . . (pp. 196-99)

In an interview near the end of his life Dick once again reinforced his belief that moral values are ultimate values: "In a sense what I'm saying is that all life is a moral issue. Which is a very Jewish idea. The Hebrew idea about God is that God is found in morality, not in epistemology. That is where the Almighty exists, in the moral area. It isn't just what I said once, that in Hebrew monotheism ethics devolve directly from God. That's not it. It's that God and ethics are so interwoven that where you have one you have the other."

Dick is an iconoclastic literary figure. His fiction refuses to conform to the characteristics of any particular category. Because he uses many of the techniques of science fiction, he is customarily labeled as a writer in that genre. But the strong, often overwhelming, elements of realism in his fiction—novels like *Martian Time-Slip* and *Dr. Bloodmoney,* for example—make that label somewhat inaccurate. In many ways he seems to fit into the tradition of Absurdist literature, and he readily admitted the influence in his formative stage of Beckett, Genêt, and other Absurdist dramatists. The typical Absurd hero inhabits a grotesque world whose structures violate reason and common sense but are nevertheless true. He is constantly frustrated, muddled, or horrified by inexplicable events that seem to happen only to him and finally lead him in paranoiac panic to decide that Fate is deliberately playing pranks on him. Not the Fall of Man but his pratfalls are the concern of the Absurdist writer. So, too, are pratfalls often Dick's concerns. Yet in a fuller assessment, we find that Dick does not fit neatly into this category because he refuses to give in to the nihilism of the French Absurdists.

Dick on occasion proclaimed himself a writer in the Romantic tradition who was particularly influenced by German Romanticism. He read Goethe and Schiller when he was young, and the works of Beethoven and other German romantic composers were among his favorites. His intuitive mode of creativity and his emotional excesses characterize him as a romantic, as does his rebellion against all institutions that violate individual freedom. "I'm a *Sturm and Drang* romantic," he himself declares in one interview.

When we continue to look for Dick's literary ancestors, we discover that the ones from which he is rooted most directly are the metaphysical poets. Dick claimed them as among his favorite poets and uses quotations from Vaughan and Marvell and Donne in his fiction. For example, he quotes Donne's Holy Sonnet XIV, "Batter my Heart, three person'd God," in its entirety in *Timothy Archer*. . . . Like Donne, he uses a colloquial style. Both writers are obsessed with the idea of death and treat it again and again in their works. So, too, do both writers blend wit and seriousness, intense feelings and vast erudition.

A discussion of literary influences is not a discussion of the essence of Dick's fiction because his literary voice is unique. He is an eclectic, choosing and using ideas, techniques, and quotations from the literary tradition as he creates in his own distinctive form. He is a synthesizer but never an imitator. The bibliography accompanying *Timothy Archer* demonstrates the wide range of literature that yielded material to him: the Bible, works of Aeschylus, Plato, Vergil, Dante, Shakespeare, Donne, Vaughan, Goethe, Schiller, Yeats, to name the major writers. In this final novel Dick felt free to reveal his debt to and use of the great literary tradition, a use that he hid under cryptic allusions in most of his science fiction.

Time must be the judge of Dick's literary worth. If, as some of us suspect it will, Time does declare him one of the major writers of the twentieth century, he will be hailed as the synthesizer of a new literary form yoking realism and the fantastic. . . . Dick's fiction gives too little emphasis to science to be called true science fiction. It gives too much emphasis to the real world to be called fantasy. It violates commonsense reality too often to be called realistic fiction. He sees with a new vision as he creates imaginary worlds for his reader—a vision that declares all worlds to be fictions, brought into existence by the consciousness of the creator. Man faces the void and keeps it at bay only by the power of his intelligence to create forms.

The universe where Dick's characters live when they fall out of commonsense reality is built on concepts that are a part of quantum physics. As physicists describe it, quantum reality is evasive and seems forever to hide beyond direct observation. Quantum physicists do not entirely agree about the nature of quantum reality, except in labeling it as bizarre. A contemporary physicist notes, "If we take the claims [of some outspoken physicists] at face value, the stories physicists tell resemble the tales of mystics and madmen. . . . Not ignorance, but the emergence of unexpected knowledge forces on us all new visions of the way things really are" [Nick Herbert, *Quantum Reality: Beyond the New Physics*]. Quantum theory holds that all elementary events occur at random, governed only by statistical laws. And Heisenberg's famous uncertainty principle forbids an accurate knowledge of a quantum particle's position and momentum. Beyond that, the prevailing quantum theory holds that there is no reality without the act of observation. Dick's fiction catches the essence of this quantum reality, and he is probably the first writer of fiction to have done so. (pp. 199-201)

Beyond his accomplishments as a writer, Dick merits recognition for his accomplishments as a human. He struggled to live by his code of valor. In the face of great adversity, he survived and created. He was a tortured genius, condemned to live within a brilliant mind that compulsively drove itself to gather up and live out all the anxiety, pain, and torment of our age. Perhaps he needed so to suffer before he could transform our shared experiences into literature. Perhaps he did not choose but worked heroically in the shadow of a mental illness from which he had no escape. He is not the first writer to be so tortured. I recently reread a biography of Virginia Woolf which describes her struggle to write in the face of repeated nervous breakdowns, and I noted how similar Dick's life was in this respect. He was less fortunate than she; he had no lifetime spouse like Leonard Woolf to shelter him economically and emotionally and to publish his works.

Dick's life was a quest for meaning, a struggle with the great metaphysical problem of our time—how to reconcile what he knew in his head with what he knew in his heart. He identified himself with his little men, unheroic protagonists who endure in the face of great adversity, going quietly about their work. His work was writing and he, too, went about it quietly, eschewing publicity. Through all the mental and physical illness he never stopped writing for more than a brief time. He never lost faith in the power of the word to create reality for the individual and the power of literature to create a shared consciousness for the community of men. Looking at our strife-torn world, he said:

> The key is this. We must shape a joint dream that differs for and from each of us, but it must harmonize in the sense that it must not exclude and negate from section to section. How this is to be done I can't of course say; maybe it can't be done. But . . . if two people dream the same dream it ceases to be an illusion; the sole prior test that distinguished reality from hallucination was the consensus gentium, that one other or several others saw it, too. This is the idios kosmos, the private dream, contrasted to the shared dream of us all, the koinos kosmos. What is new in our time is that we are beginning to see the plastic, trembling quality of the koinos kosmos—which scares us, its insubstantiality—and the more-than-merrier-vapor quality of the hallucination. Like science fiction, a third reality is formed half way between.

In his writing Dick shared with us his private dreams and his nightmares about this new reality in the future toward which we move. He said he was disturbed by those reviewers who found only bitterness and pessimism in his fiction because his mood was one of trust. "Perhaps," he said, "they are bothered by the fact that what I trust is so very small. They want something vaster. I have news for them; there is nothing vaster." For Dick all that one could trust was the capacity of the ordinary person to act with courage when courage is required. He explained, "To me the great joy in writing a book is showing some small person, some ordinary person doing something in a moment of great valor, for which he would get nothing and which would be unsung in the real world. The book, then, is the song about his valor." (pp. 201-02)

> *Patricia S. Warrick, in her* Mind in Motion: The Fiction of Philip K. Dick, *Southern Illinois University Press, 1987, 222 p.*

Dick on androids:

Within the universe there exist fierce cold things, which I have given the name "machines" to. Their behaviour frightens me, especially when it imitates human behaviour so well that I get the uncomfortable sense that these things are trying to pass themselves off as humans but are not. I call them "androids", which is my own way of using that word. By "android" I do not mean a sincere attempt to create in the laboratory a human being. . . . I mean a thing somehow generated to deceive us in a cruel way, to cause us to think it to be one of ourselves. Made in a laboratory—that aspect is not meaningful to me; the entire universe is one vast laboratory, and out of it come sly and cruel entities which smile as they reach out to shake hands. But their handshake is the grip of death, and their smile has the coldness of the grave.

> *Philip K. Dick, in his essay "Man, Android and Machine," published in* Science Fiction at Large, *1976.*

John Huntington

In *Sincerity and Authenticity,* one of his last works, Lionel Trilling traced the growth of sincerity as a value in the late 18th century and its gradual replacement in the 20th century with the idea of authenticity. The sense of divided consciousness that the great social and psychological thinkers of the last century have explicated renders the older idea of sincerity—most neatly stated in Polonius's "to thine own self be true"—problematic and untenable. What more recently has been called "post-modernism" can be seen as a cluster of strategies to deal with this perception of the impossibility of sincerity.

Philip K. Dick's work belongs in some ways to this new tradition. I would propose that Dick's work is special because it has so thoroughly embraced insincerity, especially by its thorough dependence on the mechanical creative formulas of pulp fiction, and has thus become "authentic" at a new level. Dick's insincerity is not qualified by irony (though there is plenty of irony in his work). His work is not like Roy Lichtenstein's massive, isolated moments from newspaper comics which render pathos and excitement from a consciousness outside the experience itself. Dick, whatever sophistications he achieves, builds his art out of the techniques of the pulps. He is an "authentic" "SF writer."

Of course, the moment that posture becomes comfortable, it too becomes problematic.

SF writers and fans are a notoriously evasive lot when it comes to understanding and defining their art. As Stanislaw Lem observes, they play a contradictory game. They claim that the work is "important," but then, as soon as people raise any kind of objection to its ideas, they say indignantly that these people are taking too seriously something that was written only to "entertain." Then, later, at other tables, in other rooms, we find these same enthusiasts again announcing the deep importance of SF.

Dick can play just such a double game:

> 'Important' is a rule from another game that I am not playing. I did not begin to read or to write sf for reasons dealing with importance. When I sat in high school geometry class secretly reading a copy of *Astounding* hidden within a textbook, I was not seeking importance. I was seeking, probably, intellectual excitement. Mental stimulation.

Dick's terms—"important," "intellectual excitement," and "mental stimulation"—are slippery. While we can recognize the vague and broad distinction Dick wants to make here—geometry is "important," SF is "exciting"— his language allows him to reclaim the importance that he has just rejected; for what is more "important" intellectually than "intellectual excitement" and "mental stimulation"?

We may suspect that the motive for such a statement is more psychological than philosophical or critical. One reason for seeing this passage in psychological terms is that it seems made up: in the late '30s or early '40s, when Dick would have been studying geometry, the textbooks were usually too small to have hidden a copy of *Astounding*. Dick's image is a conventional one, lifted perhaps from a film, of the slightly rebellious, secret reader who stands for something imaginative in the face of the pedantry of authoritarian "importance." Dick's reason for assuming this posture may be that he does not want to be held to a standard that he is not sure he can meet. Yet, when Dick made this statement in 1980, he had recently finished *VALIS,* a book which certainly aspires to "importance" even if it also undercuts it. This double standard, by which the writer or fan demands recognition and denies responsibility, is duplicitous and insincere as a strategy of defense, but it is also the main enabling device of Dick's imagination.

Despite Dick's own disclaimer that this is not the "game" he is playing, the critic who engages his work always finds that things of "importance" are being said. But if the critic tries to criticize the categorical values that Dick frequently invoked—such as rationality, sanity, naturalness, or goodness—Dick will evade the issue by saying that all he is after is "mental stimulation." But then, next page, next chapter, next book, he is philosophizing again.

Of all his works, *VALIS* is the most disconcerting this way. The lengthy appeals to gnostic ideas of hidden truth, even if they are called into question within the text itself, sanction a way of reading that would disregard the mechanisms of disavowal. *VALIS* is full of images (such as "lamination"), references to specific texts (such as Hermes Trismegistus or the Secret Gospels), and to genres (such as the parable) which authorize our reading two ways and treating one reading as the "real" one and the other as the veil to keep the true reading from the eyes of the uninitiated. Even if this process is parodied, it may be that we, if we are true initiates, will be able to read the truth even in its parody. Within the novel the same puzzle confronts us: the reading of the film "VALIS," like the interpretations of the cover of *Abbey Road* in the late '60s, feels like a deciphering of a hidden truth but may well be a foolish construction of meaning out of nothing.

In *VALIS,* having indulged one interpretation for a while, Dick will simply reverse himself and indulge another. Sometimes it is a book of wisdom, and sometimes it is just the case-history of a wordy madman. Much of the readers' problem in *VALIS* is generated, not by philosophical complexity as such, but by the mechanisms of narration that Dick has learned from popular SF. The important figure for Dick, as has long been recognized, is A. E. van Vogt, known for his confusingly intricate plots. But it is not the model of the plots themselves that we need to be aware of so much as the rule by which he generated them. Van Vogt advised young writers that in order to keep their readers' interest they should introduce a new idea every 800 words. For van Vogt this is not a "philosophical" rule, but simply a practical technique to make a story interesting, on the level with the rule which requires that the first paragraph of a story make mention of each of the five senses. In van Vogt's own work one is aware of a disorienting series of changes which may be exhilarating as long as one is able to hold on. Often the change at word 800 involves a blatant reversing of the values some character or thing has represented: a friend turns out to be an enemy, an enemy a friend, what we thought was useful is useless, an escape is a trap, etc. Often the reversals are given some coherence by the continuity offered by the hero (as in *Slan*) or by a fixed deep structure (such as the truth in "The Weapon Shop" that the armed strangers are liberators, while the familiar authorities are oppressors). What is remarkable about these fairly mechanical and hasty exercises is how profound they can seem. The van Vogt rule of a new idea every 800 words is a way of generating complexity and of enforcing at least the illusion of a relentless dialectic.

What I am calling the 800-word rule is an explicitly acknowledged device for van Vogt. I do not know of any such explicit acknowledgment on Dick's part. Yet the central importance of van Vogt's practice for Dick's sense of SF is easily documented. In his interview with Charles Platt, Dick twice points to *The World of Null-A* as a central text which "absolutely fascinated" him. "A lot of what I wrote, which looks like taking acid, is really the result of taking van Vogt very seriously." To state this from a different angle, Dick, like van Vogt, and like other popular SF writers such as Heinlein or Herbert, has learned how to give the impression of deep understanding simply by contradicting himself. The more clearly one side is affirmed, the more profound it seems later to find its opposite unexpectedly affirmed with equal unambiguousness. This process is not the same as what we usually think of as ironic reversal. In Dick there is no telegraphing of impending change. There is no implication that the alert, understanding reader will see the correct reading and discard the false one. There is no period in which the reader must balance two antithetical possible readings and then choose which is the moral or true one. In this van Vogtian system the reader is simply yanked from understanding to understanding.

Frequently the reader is returned to understandings that seem to have been superseded. Thus, in **Do Androids Dream of Electric Sheep?** we can at one point be led to see the androids as anti-social, pathological creatures preying on society, at another to see them as pathetic victims exploited by society, but then at a later time to see them again as simply cruel "killers." By moving without mediation from one moral perspective to the other, the novel gives the *feeling* of moral three-dimensionality, of depth. At other times, as in the whirligig of exchanges at the end of **The Three Stigmata of Palmer Eldritch,** or in the baffling regressions and exhaustions in **Ubik,** the van Vogtian technique generates more perspectives than a reader can absorb, and the effect is not so much of depth as of a suggestive complexity.

Van Vogt himself seems to enjoy the surface disarray and instability because he trusts to a few deep and unchanging principles. In this respect, he is in the same company as a conservative like G. K. Chesterton, who in *The Man Who Was Thursday* can indulge in any new complexity because all surface phenomena are layers concealing and at the same time revealing the fundamental and unchanging reality of divine presence. Dick, on the contrary, allows that the surface disarray may disrupt the deepest structure. Thus, whether or not **VALIS** is a seriously religious, ontological book, by its reversals it poses the *possibility* that Horselover Fat's insight into the bases of reality may be just a form of insanity. For a writer like Dick, who has a strong streak of Horselover Fat in him and could, one imagines, happily treat us to hundreds of pages of deep, repetitive, and vague philosophy about the nature of reality, the very arbitrariness of van Vogt's mechanical 800-word technique prevents the domination of a single idea. Like the *I Ching,* which figures prominently in **The Man in the High Castle,** the procedure enforces randomness. Writing under the constraints of such a method must be somewhat like working in a difficult verse form: the change is dictated by the mechanics of the form; the creative moment comes when the author finds a way to link form and content. The episode of the pseudo-police station in **Androids** feels like such a moment, and the pleasure towards the end of it, when the crazy, unaccountable event finds an explanation, is like the discovery of a brilliant, unexpected final rhyme.

For van Vogt the device of a change after 800 words is simply a machine that produces "interesting text" and "mental stimulation," but for Dick the device itself is both liberating and thematically expressive. The "insincerity" of the van Vogtian mechanism has permitted Dick to engage "authentic" issues that, for reasons that can be traced back to the fashions and politics of popular fiction and to the psychology of the author, he would not have been able to deal with otherwise. In Dick's situation the evasion that Lem complains of becomes an important device that will allow the writer and the reader to undertake briefly issues that the author and the SF readership have difficulty bringing to consciousness.

We can readily observe that Dick differs very much from van Vogt and from most SF writers of the '50s and early '60s in the US in his explicit use of intensely personal material. Even the reader who knows nothing of Dick's biography will be aware of the repeated motifs that suggest deep personal investment: the difficult or broken marriages; the high expectation for the effect of art and holy books; the ambiguous, authoritarian father figures who most often appear as corporation executives; the harried everyman figures trapped in compromises; entropic decline; and—everywhere—imitations, fakes, people or things which are not what they seem. These themes and images, important to Dick for reasons quite apart from the needs of the immediate plot, are turned and turned by the van Vogtian method until every realistic and absurd possibility that Dick's ingenious and tireless mind can discover has been examined. Mr Tagomi can be our model for this ruminative procedure as he subjects the triangular pin to all the perceptive texts he can think of as he tries to uncover its *wu*. Quite apart from the access it gives to elements of Dick's own life, the 800-word device is of general thematic importance to Dick because it mirrors the arbitrariness that he sees in the universe itself. And we who read this confusion are, again, like Mr Tagomi, this time putting a seashell to his ear and "[h]earing in its blabber the wisdom of the sea."

Dick is fascinated by the incompatibility of absolute and relative value systems, and by means of the van Vogtian device he is able to give full attention to both. The van Vogtian method allows Dick to dramatize tensions that tend to get clotted when he becomes simply expository. We can see the advantages the device gives him if we begin by looking at a passage that attempts to make a "philosophical" statement. In the following passage from **VALIS,** Dick moves from an absolute position, to a relative one, and then back to an absolute one:

> The single most striking realization that Fat had come to was his concept of the universe as irrational and governed by an irrational mind, the creator deity. If the universe were taken to be rational, not irrational, then something breaking into it might seem irrational, since it would not belong. But Fat, having reversed everything, saw the rational breaking into the irrational. The immortal plasmate had invaded our world and the plasmate was totally rational, whereas our world is not. This structure forms the basis of Fat's world-view. It is the bottom line.

The dichotomy of rational/irrational, like the one of sane/insane that also dominates this novel, tends to be more polemic than it is analytical. What interests us here is the way that, towards the end of the passage, rationality becomes absolute: "the plasmate was totally rational, whereas our world is not." The sentence is, in itself, ambiguous about what it claims the world is—it can be *totally* irrational or simply *not* totally rational—but the main line of the argument of the paragraph would seem to suggest the former. And not only is Fat's analysis committed to a single, absolute, defining concept, the "totally rational"; but the narrator's analysis of Fat's analysis seeks this same defining unity: this is "the single most striking realization." It "forms the *basis* of Fat's world-view. It is the bottom line." The complication that the narrator is himself Fat does not diminish the absoluteness that is reinforced at a second level here.

In the middle of the paragraph, however, we find a moment of a different kind of reasoning: Dick here uses subjunctives and allows for a relativistic and structural reading of rationality: "If the universe were taken to be rational, not irrational, then something breaking into it would seem irrational, since it would not belong." Rationality here is posed not as an absolute category, but as that mode of thought by which we define ourselves. In this statement, the irrational is simply the Other.

When he reverses this statement, Fat not only reverses the values of rationality and irrationality, but he also turns a statement of structural opposition into a statement of absolute value. One opposite of the hypothetical premise could be an equally hypothetical statement in which the "rational" is the "other" and, somehow, the irrational is us. But the opposite that is generated is a non-hypothetical statement in which the rational becomes the "totally rational." Such a moment asks to be criticized, and we will cry out with Lem, "unfair!" if the response we receive is the evasion: "the passage is not trying to say something important, it is only trying to entertain."

It is in his dramatizations of the problem of the *real* that Dick most successfully renders the absolute/relative conflict. Throughout his work Dick pays obsessive attention to imitations, whether of antiques from the pre-war US, as in *High Castle,* or of animals, as in *Androids,* or of experience itself, as in the Perky Pat layouts in *Palmer Eldritch.* And, as any reader of Dick knows well, the issue of imitation goes beyond the explicit thematics of his work. Again and again he indulges in the game of the ersatz for the sake of the game itself. In an early story, **"Nanny,"** there will be the gratuitous image of "artificial goldfish" in the pool near which robot nannies fight to the death. In *High Castle* Joe will buy Juliana a fancy coat made with synthetic German fiber.

At one level this concern with the artificial can be read as part of a pervasive, angry satire on the false values of a capitalist, consumerist culture. There is, however, a profound contradiction at the core of this satire. If the search for the "authentic" is at once a bourgeois folly, it is also the primal search in Dick, the search for "reality" in place of hallucination, for the authentic in place of imitation. And yet, if the authentic is the one worthy goal, it is at the same time a vain pursuit, for the authentic can never be unambiguously established. And though the artificial is a fraud, it nevertheless can suffice.

This enigma of authenticity is rendered by Deckard's Mercerist epiphany at the end of *Androids.* Deckard finds a living toad in the desert, but when his wife reveals that it is electric it seems clear that, while Deckard would prefer that the toad be real, he will make do with the artificial one. The repetition of such a moment in other novels, and

the gratuitous gestures in its direction, suggest that the motif is a crucial one for Dick: it allows him to inhabit two antithetical value systems at once. Significantly for our present considerations, it is the van Vogtian 800-word method that forces him to move between them. He must be both the playful skeptic who makes do with what there is and the sincere seeker for the authentic and absolute reality. He must be both the entertainer and the novelist of important themes.

Perhaps the quintessential episode in which authenticity is debated occurs in *High Castle.* When he finds the "aura" of authenticity of historical artifacts undependable, Robert Childan, the San Francisco shopkeeper, starts selling Edfrank jewelry, which he is told radiates *wu,* a quality of balanced alignment with the universe. *Aura* belongs to history and is liable to imitation and fraud; *wu* is an absolute aesthetic value, a universal outside of history, an intrinsic quality that cannot be imitated. If, as Childan discovers, the historical artifact's value fluctuates according to the dependability of the assurances of authenticity, the value of the artifact with *wu* exists absolutely and needs no certification. In one sense, it is gold in a world of paper money. But this easy opposition then undergoes a narrative inquiry. When Paul Kasouras, who has explained *wu* to Childan, urges him to make a profit on the jewelry, Childan goes through a series of van Vogtian reversals that rapidly touch on various contradictory implications of the situation. If the piece has *wu,* why not mass-produce it? But what if you cannot reproduce *wu* mechanically? What if it is, in this respect, just like *aura*? And Kasouras implies there may even be a sort of violation involved in such manufacture: he calls the jewel "something truly authentic. Not a model or replica. . . . Not something cast by tens of thousands." And finally Childan decides the whole idea of profiting from *wu* is itself despicable and that Kasouras has insulted him by suggesting he do such a thing. The complexity of the relations of absolute and relative values is here elaborately traced, though hardly resolved, by a set of arbitrary shifts in the narration.

It may be worth emphasizing at this point that the inquiry into the nature of *wu* and its relation to *aura* is not systematic. The questions that are raised do not follow one another logically, nor do they lead towards a new insight. While the skepticism about *aura* results in a debunking of the mystery of the "authentic" piece, there seems to be a counter-urge at work which will replace the commercial mystery of historical authenticity with an equally mysterious and even less empirically certifiable absolute, *wu.* Thus the inquiry, rather than working its way to a new level of clarity, moves sideways, as it were: as it exposes the relativity of *aura* it constructs an absolute to take its place.

In *Androids* the van Vogtian mode reaches a crescendo when Deckard, fully aware of the Christ-figure Mercer's bogus reality, meets Mercer, who tells him that the difference between himself and the androids is, "I am a fraud. . . . They're sincere." At this point we value fraud over sincerity. The opposition here has some of the outrageousness of the irrational/rational opposition in *VALIS.* However, unlike the passage we looked at earlier with its claim to have found a philosophical "bottom line," Mercer's self-cancelling assertion of his own paradoxical value never permits logical rest. Like the Cretan's statement, "All Cretans are liars," it disqualifies its authority in the very act of making its statement of authoritative paradox.

It is after this moment that *Androids* seems to make gestures away from the skeptical mode implied by the van Vogtian technique and to seek, for a moment, absolute insights. Deckard will declare, to himself:

> For Mercer everything is easy, he thought, because Mercer accepts everything. Nothing is alien to him. But what I've done, he thought; that's become alien to me. In fact everything about me has become unnatural: I've become an unnatural self.

Here again a self/other dichotomy underlies the distinction, and here too the paradox arises from the identification of value with the *other*. And here again, for a moment, by the word *unnatural,* the dialectic of alienness is converted to a statement of non-dialectical, categorical value. At this moment in the novel, one might argue, *Androids* has reached the place where *VALIS* begins.

Such a moment of spiritual alienation, that point of most profound failure at which the rebirth into true knowledge and faith can commence, is a familiar one in the Christian spiritual progress. Throughout *Androids* there are intimations of this moment of absolute despair when the possibilities of the dialogic are denied. At the beginning (and at the end) of the novel, Deckard's wife, Iran, is so depressed that she cannot even dial the number on her mood-synthesizer that will stimulate her to want to dial. This same spiritual nadir is experienced by J. R. Isidore as he deals with the androids. It is a state of mind which disgusts Deckard when he sees it in androids—a collapse, a refusal to fight to the very end—because it gives up hope. And Deckard in the wilderness finds himself "too tired to fly back out." But then, thanks to the arbitrary imperative of the van Vogtian 800-word rule, the mood of despair leads to the major epiphany of the novel. Deckard telephones his secretary. As he is about to telephone his wife, he sees the toad. The toad may turn out to be electric, and the novel may end on a note of satiric comedy as Iran, herself reinvigorated, orders artificial flies for the electric toad; but the re-engagement with a relative reality, however bogus, while a confession of the failure to achieve absolute reality, is also a lively escape from the black hole of absolute despair. It is an escape made possible, not by psychology, not by philosophy, not even by political insight, but by a mechanical narrative device.

Dick's work poses a problem for evaluative criticism: its contradictions are as often as not the result of arbitrary and random reversals as of any conscious critique of bourgeois culture. But the absence of conscious intent does not thereby render the thought of the narrative trivial. In fact, it may well be argued that it is precisely this freedom from controlling rational structures—especially insofar as such structures are really ideologically-weighted conventions— that gives Dick's writings their value. This is not to say that the arbitrary is free: free association is enlightening because it subtly responds to deep necessities of the au-

thor's psyche and of the culture. It reveals unknown structures not because it is free, but precisely because it is determined.

Dick's approach to narrative renders conventional modes of evaluating art and thought problematic. It would be inadequate simply to celebrate him as a hack and therefore to promote him as authentic. By the same token, we cannot just denounce him as a fraud. Like something in one of his novels, he is always on the other side of whatever posture of value we choose. Seeking wisdom, we find a wiseguy; but just when we are ready to treat his novels as only a game, they radiate profundity. As with the straw toy which, after you have inserted your finger in it, clamps onto your finger when you try to escape, the dilemma is given its energy not by the strength of the device itself, but by the victim's own urgency to get free. In reading Dick we trap ourselves. It is because *we* invoke categories with weighty consequences that Dick becomes a problem for us. He is an innocent, profoundly askew from mainstream values, but wanting to succeed, wanting even to cooperate. His mechanical version of wisdom creates a picture of reality to which we have to respond and thereby pose for ourselves difficult puzzles about the nature of reality and will. (pp. 152-59)

John Huntington, "Philip K. Dick: Authenticity and Insincerity," in Science-Fiction Studies, *Vol. 15, No. 2, July, 1988, pp. 152-60.*

Norman Spinrad

That *The Transmigration of Timothy Archer* was Philip K. Dick's last novel is a tragedy and a triumph.

It is a tragedy because it broke bold new literary ground, in terms of form, viewpoint, clarity, and control, for a writer who already had many great works behind him and was only in his fifties when he died. Where would Philip K. Dick have gone from here?

It is a triumph because it is a fitting final testament for Philip K. Dick the writer and Phil the man—a return to the height of his literary powers at the untimely end of his career, a return to the true metaphysical vision and human insight of *Ubik* and *The Man in the High Castle* and *The Three Stigmata of Palmer Eldritch* and *The Martian Time-Slip* after a long period of secondary work.

And it is also somehow the purest statement of the spiritual center of Phil Dick's work as a writer and his being as a man, as if Phil, like one of his own characters, knew somehow that the end was near, and left us this piece of clarity to give the lie to the obfuscatory cult he somehow knew was to come.

The story, though directly metaphysical and even straightforwardly religious, is, quite unlike *Valis* or *The Divine Invasion,* simple, clear, and direct. Angel, the narrator, is the wife of Bishop Archer's son, Jeff. She introduces Tim Archer to Kirsten Lundborg, and Kirsten and the bishop become lovers. Archer becomes obsessed with the scrolls that have been found in Israel and identified with the Zadokites, a sect that predated the birth of Christ by some two hundred years. As the translations proceed, it becomes apparent that the writings of the Zadokites were the template for the parables of Jesus, and the bishops's faith in the divinity of Christ begins to erode.

Jeffery Archer commits suicide. Bishop Archer learns that the Christian sacrament of the Eucharist derives from the Zadokite practice of consuming hallucinogenic mushrooms, that is, that the mystical communion between Christians and Jesus engendered by the eating of the wafer and the drinking of the wine is nothing more than a ritual derived from a preexisting mystical mushroom cult where an actual psychedelic experience of the godhead was delivered, and this destroys his faith.

Kirsten dies. Bishop Archer goes off into the Negev desert in a rented car in search of the mystical mushroom and his own lost faith, guided only by a gas station roadmap. The map is faulty, the car fails, and he dies in the wilderness.

Later his spirit returns, its faith reborn, via the person of Kirsten's schizophrenic son, Bill, thereby restoring Angel Archer's spiritual center, after a fashion.

Needless to say, such a plot summary does not convey the full depth and power of the book. Dick throws almost as much metaphysical speculation and biblical, kabbalistic, and even Hindu scholarship into *The Transmigration of Timothy Archer* as he does into *Valis* or *The Divine Invasion,* and a lot of arcane material about Wallenstein and the Thirty Years War to boot, as well as other esoterica—nowhere else has he displayed the full range of his sheer intellectual breadth and depth as he does here.

But there is nothing pretentious or boring or didactic about it, for it is all conveyed in the realistic dialogue of characters, particularly the narrator, Angel, who are products of a Berkeley milieu in which all this is quite natural, a milieu in which Phil himself lived and worked for many years, and that he never portrayed with this detail, depth, and humor until this final work.

Then too, all of this metaphysical speculation, all of this high-falutin' table talk, is perfectly balanced by an equal attention to the details of daily life and popular culture. Angel, Jeff, Kirsten, even the bishop, segue from heavy intellectual rapping into questions of popular music, down-and-dirty politics, and their problems with their cars (which seem, like Phil's, to have been endless), within the same sentence.

And this is not mere balancing technique. There is something behind it that is at the mystical core of the novel.

Bill Lundborg, Kirsten's schizoid son, is a character critical to the denouement of the novel; in order for Timothy Archer's spirit to speak credibly through him at the end, in order for the reader to believe in this as a spiritual reality and a peak moment, the reader must first have been convinced that this simple man, this victim of shock therapy and the psychiatric establishment, this mere auto mechanic, has been a kind of innocent saint all along.

How does Dick bring this off?

By a bravura piece of writing that is at once thematically central to the novel and quite impossible to paraphrase or explain, that one must quite literally read to believe.

He does it through a long conversation between Archer and others in which the bishop discusses Christian theology while Bill discusses the merits and flaws of various makes of cars. And makes it work. If there is such a thing as literary magic, this surely is it. (pp. 201-03)

The Man in the High Castle, published in 1962, was the novel that made Dick's reputation, and with the possible exception of *Do Androids Dream of Electric Sheep?* (courtesy of the film *Blade Runner*), is still probably his best-known book, and, with its alternate present of a Nazi- and Japanese-occupied America, certainly his most imitated.

In a certain sense, that is. For while there have been many novels and stories in which the Nazis have won World War II, there has been nothing like Dick's vision.

In most of Dick's previous short stories and novels, he made comparatively little attempt at genuine extrapolative verisimilitude. *Solar Lottery* posits a political system based on chance, *Eye in the Sky* takes its characters through a bizarre series of ersatz realities, *Dr. Futurity* is a time-paradox novel, and so forth; while many of these earlier works are metaphysically interesting indeed and contain well-rounded characters, they all make full self-conscious use of the tropes, imagery, gimmicks, jargon, and schtick of SF; in Alexei Panshin's phrase, they are "science fiction that knows it's science fiction."

The Man in the High Castle is something quite different. Here Dick posits a single assumption—that Nazi Germany and Imperial Japan won World War II and split America down the middle—and proceeds to write a realistic, characterologically based novel in the quite believable world he has created.

The novel jettisons all the familiar SF paraphernalia, centers on the lives of relatively ordinary people, concentrates on their human stories more than the macropolitics (in the manner of mainstream fiction), and yet remains science fiction, albeit a science fiction that *anyone* could pick up and read without familiarity with the genre. It was something that Dick had not done previously, and would not really do again until the very end with *The Transmigration of Timothy Archer.*

And yet most of the themes and virtues of the work to come, the work that was to make Dick one of the premier science fiction writers of the twentieth century and one of the premier metaphysical novelists of all time, are present in *The Man in the High Castle* and in rather fully developed form.

The dichotomy between the spiritless ersatz and the humanly real, as epitomized in the macrocosm by the anomie of the Nazis versus the more spiritually centered Japanese conquerors, and in the microcosm by Frank Frink's drive to create authentically new American jewelry instead of phony antiques.

Ordinary people like Frink and Mr. Tagomi as genuine heroes. Larger figures seen in the distance or in glimpses, like

Abensend, the author of *The Grasshopper Lies Heavy,* the alternate-world novel within the alternate-world novel in which the Nazis and the Japanese *lost* the war. Characters, who, for the most part have real workaday jobs, and ordinary work as something that can have spiritual and personal meaning.

A blending of passionately political themes (in this case an utterly convincing portrait of two Americas as molded by two very different occupying powers) with the metaphysical and mystical (here the I Ching and the Sino-Japanese concept of *wu*) in a manner that demonstrates the one arising out of the other. A sense of the author's genuine love for his characters. The multiplex subjectivity of reality—in this alternate America, a writer has written a book about another alternate America, and Mr. Tagomi's small moment of heroism is triggered by a fugue state in which he finds himself briefly in *our* America.

This is not to suggest that *The Man in the High Castle* laid out all of Dick's future obsessions and concerns and that all else was repetition or even that it is necessarily his best novel. But it certainly was a great writer finding his true voice, creating his first truly mature work, presenting us with the broad outline of the scope of his vision and the style and spirit of what was to come, and in that, much older, medieval sense, *The Man in the High Castle* can literally be said to be his "masterpiece."

What followed in the next decade was an enormous burst of creativity, in which Dick explored, exfoliated, and deepened the thematic concerns he had opened up in about half a dozen major novels and even more minor ones, though no two critics are likely to agree on complete lists of which was which.

Indeed Phil himself made it quite clear, publicly and privately, that some of these novels were hacked out at top speed for quick money, that some of them he took more seriously, that others were like Graham Greene's "entertainments," and a few didn't even make sense to *him* in retrospect, though he could be cagy and contradictory about which he thought were which.

While we can all argue the relative importance of novels like *Clans of the Alphane Moon, Dr. Bloodmoney, A Maze of Death, Galactic Pot-Healer, The Simulacra,* and *Now Wait for Last Year,* and few would contend that *The Zap Gun* or *The Unteleported Man* or *Our Friends from Frolix-8* or *Counter-Clock World* or *The Crack in Space* are major works, few critics or readers of Dick will deny that *Martian Time-Slip, The Three Stigmata of Palmer Eldritch, Do Androids Dream of Electric Sheep?* and *Ubik* are unquestionably at the core of Dick's oeuvre, whichever of his many, many, other works they may choose to rank with them.

While these are four very different novels with four quite different settings, they have many things in common with each other and with many of the other Dick novels of this enormously creative period.

All of them have viewpoint characters, which is to say the viewpoint character through whose consciousness we experience the largest portion of the novel, who are not really movers and shapers but find themselves placed in a central role that requires from them heroism of one kind or another. And they are all real people with real jobs that mean something to them and with real and troubled personal lives and relationships of one kind or another.

All of these novels but *Martian Time-Slip* have a larger-than-life, reality-altering, charismatic figure at the center of what is happening in the macrocosm but not really quite central to the actual events in the story, though their relative importance to the plot and the set-up vary from book to book. Mercer, the TV messiah expiating the guilts of the ruined world, is fairly incidental to *Do Androids Dream of Electric Sheep?,* Runciter is quite central to *Ubik,* and Palmer Eldritch at the end is virtually the deity of *The Three Stigmata.* Even *Martian Time-Slip* contains such a figure in a peculiar way, functionally split between the worldly powerful union leader Arnie Kott and his reality-altering autistic son Manfred.

We see such figures in other Dick novels—in *Dr. Bloodmoney, Now Wait for Last Year, Galactic Pot-Healer,* and in some of the earlier novels as well—and while all of them are highly individuated and finely drawn, they do have more in common than their functional ability to create, in one way or another, alternate realities.

Even though they are not central to the plotline in terms of their time on stage in the novel, they are rendered as viewpoint characters with real and understandable inner lives more often than not, rather than as cardboard figures, stock villains, or unmoved movers. Arnie Kott may be rough and tough and ruthless, but he is not really a bad sort. Glen Runciter, even in the semi-death of half-life, is trying to do good by his people. Even Palmer Eldritch is to some degree the victim of his own screwed-up good intentions.

Finally, the thread that runs strongly through these books, and indeed through most of Dick's work in one form or another, is his central theme with its many well-explored corollaries, which put one way is the distinction between the authentic and the ersatz—humans versus androids in *Do Androids Dream of Electric Sheep?,* realities themselves in *Ubik, Palmer Eldritch* and to an extent *Martian Time-Slip*—and put another way is the Dickian concept of the *multiplexity* of reality, and, in that sense at least, of the lack of hard and clear-cut distinction between "reality" and "illusion," "authentic" and "ersatz."

This is the great theme of Dick's oeuvre, of the core novels of his most productive period and the minor works too, of what leads up to the burst of creativity that began with *The Man in the High Castle,* as well as his later works; it is an enormously vast theme, bottomlessly deep, endlessly complicated. Small wonder then that Dick often seems to contradict himself on these matters from novel to novel, indeed often within the same book, for what he is wrestling with is the nature(s) of reality(ies) it(them)self, and the overall wisdom that one takes away from a reading of his work as a whole is that *reality itself* is multiplex, nonobjective, and indeed internally self-contradictory.

Martian Time-Slip seems to take place in the single reality of a future colonized Mars, and Manfred's autism seems to be merely a mental disease. But by the time the novel is over we are left with the perception that the autistic boy is living in a kind of precog vision of a future decaying into "gubbish," into a dead simulacrum from which all animating spirit has been leached (a key Dickian concept), as real or more so in some sense than the consensus reality of the other characters.

The realities of *Ubik* take place inside a subjective universe created by Runciter, who is himself trapped in the subjective reality of half-life, but what Joe Chip, the main protagonist does inside them affects the "real" world and vice versa.

The Three Stigmata of Palmer Eldritch is perhaps Dick's fullest and grandest and most humane statement of his enormous central theme. Via the drug Chew-Z, brought back from Centauris by Eldritch, the characters' subjective realities fold into each other like nested boxes along a Möebus strip, Eldritch himself the god of many of them, but Eldritch himself occupying a reality in which he is far from an unmoved mover.

What allows Dick to explore such material without lapsing into mere babblement? Indeed, such is the nature of his thematic core that sometimes, when he attempts to knock out a quick minor work along these lines, such as *The Zap Gun* or *Counter-Clock World* or *Our Friends from Frolix-8,* he *does* go over the edge.

But when he's got it right, as he certainly has in *Martian Time-Slip, The Three Stigmata of Palmer Eldritch, Do Androids Dream of Electric Sheep?, Ubik,* and elsewhere, he is able to give us, out of this very multiplex and self-contradictory metaphysical confusion, a true vision, a genuine clarity that illumines our lives on the deepest spiritual level.

He does this in two ways.

The first is technical. Dick is the master of the multiple-viewpoint narrative. He may not have invented the technique, but he did more to introduce it to science fiction than anyone else, he uses it in almost all of his novels, he never breaks form, and the form he has chosen is ideally suited to his material.

There is no auctorial overview in novels like *Martian-Slip, Palmer Eldritch, Androids,* etc., no Philip K. Dick telling the reader what is real and what is not. These novels are mosaics of realities, the realities of the viewpoint characters, not of the author; in this sense, there is no overall base reality to any of these novels, only the interfacing of a multiplexity of subjective realities.

And that is what "reality" is *really* like, Dick is not so much saying as demonstrating—consensus reality, to the extent that there is such a thing, is the interfacing of our subjective realities with those of other consciousnesses, not an overall matrix in which we all live. What is, is real.

Much has been made of Phil Dick's involvement with drugs and the prevalence of consciousness-altering drugs as central elements in his work, at least in the 1960s, and to lapse into memoir, it is certainly true that no one I ever met, including Timothy Leary, knew as much about psy-

chopharmacology as Phil or had pondered more deeply the metaphysics of consciousness-altering drugs and the relationship of that metaphysics to the metaphysics of mental illness, particularly various forms of schizophrenia.

For Phil Dick, consciousness-altering drugs like Chew-Z in *Palmer Eldritch,* mental states like Manfred's autism in *Martian Time Slip,* and ersatz subjective realities as in *Ubik* or *A Maze of Death* or *Eye in the Sky* serve the same function, literarily and metaphysically. Namely, to demonstrate that altered mental states, *however they may be created,* create altered realities that are as "real" as what we individually think of as "base reality," since each of our individual "base realities," far from being the absolute we like to pretend it is, is *itself* a unique subjective reality, arising as it does in our own unique biophysical matrix.

In this perception lies either the solipsistic madness of total psychic relativity or transcendent wisdom, and the greatness of Dick as a writer, what makes him by far the greatest metaphysical novelist of all time, is that, having opened the door to this ultimate spiritual, perceptual, and metaphysical chaos, he leads us through it to true wisdom along a *moral* vector.

What ultimately makes the androids in *Do Androids Dream of Electric Sheep?* less than human is not their synthetic origin, but, like the Nazis in *The Man in the High Castle,* their lack of caritas, their inability to empathize with the existential plight of other life caught in the same multiverse. What raises the android Roy Batty to human status in *Blade Runner* (the film version of *Androids*) is that, on the brink of his own death, he is able to empathize with Decard.

What makes Joe Chip, Rick Decard, Mr. Tagomi, Joe Bohlen, Barney Mayerson, and Leo Bulero true heroes is that ultimately, on one level or another, whatever reality mazes they may be caught in, they realize that the true base reality is not absolute or perceptual or metaphysical, but moral and empathetic, and they act accordingly when push comes to shove.

What is really real is what is felt on both sides when two subjective realities intersect; what is really real is the spiritual connection between isolated subjectivities, the caritas, the empathy, the love, without which we are all lost, like the Nazis and the androids and poor Palmer Eldritch, in our own solipsistic subjective universes. (pp. 205-10)

Norman Spinrad, "The Transmogrification of Philip K. Dick," in his Science Fiction in the Real World, *Southern Illinois University Press, 1990, pp. 198-216.*

Richard Bernstein

Philip K. Dick published 35 novels and six volumes of short stories during a short, bohemian life of 54 years, a life that involved a lot of drugs, five marriages, several psychological breakdowns, religious visions and an enormous amount of frustrated literary ambition. Now, nine years after his death, he has become a powerful influence on popular culture, especially at a time when the culture be-

> My theme for years in my writing has been, "The devil has a metal face". Perhaps this should be amended now. What I glimpsed and then wrote about was in fact not a face; it was a mask over a face. And the true face is the reverse of the mask.
>
> —*Philip K. Dick, in his essay "Man, Android and Machine," published in* Science Fiction at Large, *1976.*

speaks our deepest fears and most persistent fantasies about technology and its potential to destroy us.

Dick wrote the stories on which two major movies were based—*Blade Runner,* regarded by many critics as a science fiction masterpiece, and *Total Recall,* Arnold Schwarzenegger's don't-mess-with-me blockbuster. There are probably more films in the offing; nine other wittily gloomy futuristic works by Dick have been optioned by movie makers. There have also been a play and an avantgarde opera based on his novels. And recently some of Dick's books, most of which have been out of print since well before his death in 1982, have been reissued by Vintage Press. It seems as though just about every word Dick wrote and every minute of his offbeat life has suddenly become worthy of attention.

Dick's old sci-fi fans will regard the attention currently being paid him as long overdue. But there are many latecomers to the Philip K. Dick cult, arriving there, as I did, by way of the movies. Many of us are not devotees of science fiction, either. The term itself has always seemed to me to be an oxymoron, particularly when it encompasses such notions as psychic projection, time travel, the existence of alternative worlds. But the movies inspired by Dick's books have little of that, and the books themselves have even less. I'm talking here of a novel, *Do Androids Dream of Electric Sheep?,* and a story, **"We Can Remember It for You Wholesale,"** on which *Blade Runner* and *Total Recall,* respectively, were based. The conceptions behind them contained the shock of plausibility, and that is what, in my mind, unites them with other arresting antiutopian novels like *Brave New World* and *Nineteen Eighty-Four.*

The tremendous surge of interest in the author, his posthumous status as a guru, a prophet of the New Age, raises that always interesting question about cultural trends: why now?

My attempt to answer the question by reading the best-known books ran up against the fact that, until recently, Dick had been secluded in a very marginal corner of the literary world, away from the category of what sci-fi writers have always called, with a hint of envy, mainstream fiction. He had a cultish following, his many works most readily available in the sorts of bookstores that specialize in exotica, fantasy, the occult and what is called New Age.

But until Vintage started releasing a few of the novels this summer, Dick's books were mostly out of print and, even with the Vintage reissues, most of them still are.

And so, when I tried to find *Do Androids Dream of Electric Sheep?* or a collection including **"We Can Remember It for You Wholesale,"** none of the Manhattan bookstores I tried had either of them. I settled for a novel called *The Penultimate Truth* in a glossy paperback published by Carroll & Graf. That novel has not been optioned by a movie studio. It is not viewed as one of Dick's classics. Yet it is a good introduction to the author and to his dark vision of a soulless, pop-tech future in which there will be no meaningful difference between the real and the fake.

The idea is this: Most of mankind lives in vast multistoried underground "tanks" that manufacture robots for use in the nuclear conflagration that is raging at ground level. The millions of people in the tanks watch news broadcasts about the war and the poisoning of the planet's surface. They know, for example, that to go up there would result in diseases like "stink of shrink," in which your head is reduced to the size of a marble, and "bag plague." And so they stay where they are, until, more or less by accident, one of them ventures into the sunshine.

And what that person learns is that all is fraudulent. There was indeed a nuclear war. That much is true. But the rest of earthly existence is the secret of a privileged few who live on an entirely habitable earth on vast estates serviced by the robots produced by the duped inhabitants of the tanks. Thus *The Penultimate Truth* is a tale of the almost infinite manipulability of facts and images, of a bureaucratic dictatorship whose hold on power is based on the bureaucrats' control of truth.

The story is told in a gritty, technobabblish sort of *noir* prose, stripped of sentiment, blunt, disabused, a bit reminiscent of William Burroughs and also of Dick's fellow Californian Raymond Chandler, with passages like this one, having to do with "stink of shrink":

> The microscopic things downfalling to us that some careless ambulatory metal hunk of handmade parts had failed to 'cide out of existence before yanking the drop switch, shooting three hundred pounds of contaminated matter to us, something both hot and dirty at the same time . . . hot with radioactivity and dirty with germs. Great combination, he thought.

This is good stuff, I thought, good enough to count Dick among those in the pantheon of the good bad writers—Chandler, Dashiell Hammett, Robert B. Parker, Arthur C. Clarke and others, writers of remarkable discipline and thematic clarity who polish their special corner of the literary world like diamonds. (pp. 1, 28)

Some of the interest in Philip K. Dick no doubt comes from the momentum created by the two big-budget movies already made from his work. But the movies themselves and the growth of the author's following are based on something deeper. My own feeling is that Dick illustrates a phenomenon often claimed but rarely occurring—the times catching up with somebody who was ahead of them. Specifically, he prefigured that mingling of primal unease and fascination provoked by the stage of technological development that, unanticipated by most of us, we have now reached.

Dick, in this sense, belongs on a kind of imaginative continuum with other science fiction writers. Mary Wollstonecraft Shelley, fantasizing at the beginning of the continuum about the possibilities inherent in the new science of medicine, raised in *Frankenstein* the specter that we might create the very labor-saving device that will destroy us. Ever since, writers and fantasists—including the creators of such labor-saving devices as the computer Hal in the movie *2001: A Space Odyssey* (based on a novel by Arthur C. Clarke) and the half-human, half-machine creature in *Robocop*—have exploited humanity's deep ambivalence about scientific advance and technology. In these two later works, the starting point was the utter literal-mindedness of computers, their absolute amorality, and thus their potential to run amuck, turning against their creators.

For Dick, the real question was not whether mankind's creations would turn against us. He seems to have believed that the existence of nuclear weapons proved they already had. Most of his novels take place in a world rising out of the ashes of nuclear war. His main fascination was the likelihood that technology would lead to the disappearance of the very frontier between what mankind creates and what mankind is. *The Penultimate Truth* takes place in a world run by robots on behalf of humans who, in some cases, are alive because they control access to the world's limited supply of "artiforgs," synthetic pancreases and hearts. The "replicants" of *Do Androids Dream of Electric Sheep?* can be distinguished from humans by only two features: they are superior both mentally and physically, and they are programmed to die after four years of artificially created life. The replicants are a kind of ultimate genetic engineering achievement, more poetic, more impressively endowed than mere men and women, but they cause human beings to resort to Nazi-like methods to keep them under control.

The author is playful with these technological projections, which are always portrayed as part of the pop culture in the worlds he creates. In *Do Androids Dream of Electric Sheep?* the main character, Rick Deckard, who hunts down escaped replicants for a living, wakes up with the help of his Penfield mood organ, which has settings to induce different states of mind—number 888 for the "desire to watch TV, no matter what's on," or number 481, which is "awareness of the manifold possibilities open in the future." This lightheartedness is matched by Dick's lightheartedly philosophical exploration of the epistemological bases for what we believe, or, put another way, for what we, in an age of advanced technology, believe to be reality and what we believe to be illusion.

In recent years, scientists have come up with a new computer fad known as "virtual reality," in which you have the sensation of becoming an actor in a computer-generated world. It did not exist in Dick's time, but it seems now to be one of the areas in which the times have caught up with him. In **"We Can Remember It for You Wholesale,"** what seem like real experiences and entire identities can be electronically inserted into the conscious-ness—and electronically retracted as well. You just go to a retail outlet and put your head into what looks like a high-tech hair dryer, and off you go on a vacation more vivid and exciting than anything you can experience for real. And then, when you are, say, a secret agent on Mars confronting an adversary, you don't know if you are really there or if you are actually sitting back on Earth with your head attached to wires being given the illusion that you are on Mars.

In a recent telephone interview, David Hartwell, Dick's editor at Pocket Books, recalled a letter that Dick once wrote in which he said the purpose of his work was to get beyond "the only apparently real" to "what is really real."

Dick's agent, Russell Galen, told me: "Dick basically wasn't interested in science fiction. He was interested in philosophical speculation, in what's real, what's fake, what's human, what's inhuman, and he used things like aliens, androids and time travel to explore all of that."

Well, what is real anyway? And is what is real necessarily better than what is fake, particularly when the fake seems so real that it has the force of reality? What is so important about reality, anyway, in this age of artificial fruit flavors and virtual reality? It is Dick's hip, tuned-in exploration of those questions in his novels and stories that seems to have propelled him from the literary "whorehouse," where his biographer, Lawrence Sutin, reluctantly placed him, into the mainstream he yearned for all of his short life. (pp. 28-9)

> *Richard Bernstein, "The Electric Dreams of Philip K. Dick," in* The New York Times Book Review, *November 3, 1991, pp. 1, 28-30.*

FURTHER READING

Bibliography

Levack, Daniel J. H. *PKD: A Philip K. Dick Bibliography.* Westport, Conn.: Meckler, 1988, 156 p.

    Bibliography of writings by and about Dick.

Biography

Rickman, Gregg. *To the High Castle, Philip K. Dick: A Life, 1928-1962.* Long Beach, Calif.: Fragments West, 1989, 228 p.

    First volume of a projected two-volume biography.

Sutin, Lawrence. *Divine Invasions: A Life of Philip K. Dick.* New York: Harmony, 1989, 352 p.

    Comprehensive biography.

Criticism

Abrash, Merritt. "Elusive Utopias: Societies as Mechanisms in the Early Fiction of Philip K. Dick." In *Clockwork Worlds: Mechanized Environments in SF,* edited by Richard D. Erlich and Thomas P. Dunn, pp. 115-23. Westport, Conn.: Greenwood Press, 1983.

Centers on Dick's use of technological advancements as a reflection of society.

————. " 'Man Everywhere in Chains': Dick, Rousseau, and *The Penultimate Truth.* " *Foundation,* no. 39 (Spring 1987): 31-40.

Compares the social and political themes of *The Penultimate Truth* and the writings of nineteenth-century French philosopher Jean-Jacques Rousseau.

Aldiss, Brian. "The Mainstream That Through the Ghetto Flows: An Interview with Philip K. Dick." *The Missouri Review* VII, No. 2 (1984): 164-85.

Dick discusses his life and work.

Bray, Mary Kay. "Mandalic Activism: An Approach to Structure, Theme, and Tone in Four Novels by Philip K. Dick." *Extrapolation* 21, No. 2 (Summer 1980): 146-57.

Analyzes Dick's literary technique as "a blend of Eastern and Western modes of perception and experience."

Christiansen, Peder. "The Classical Humanism of Philip K. Dick." In *Women Worldwalkers: New Dimensions of Science Fiction and Fantasy,* edited by Jane B. Weedman, pp. 71-82. Lubbock: Texas Tech Press, 1985.

Discusses Dick's portrayal of traditional virtues and vices in his characters.

Fitting, Peter. "Reality as Ideological Construct: A Reading of Five Novels by Philip K. Dick." *Science-Fiction Studies* 10, No. 30, Pt. 2 (July 1983): 219-36.

Examines Dick's inquiries into the nature of reality.

Green, Terrence M. "Philip K. Dick: A Parallax View." *Science Fiction Review* 5, No. 2 (May 1976): 12-15.

Alleges that Dick was "not interested in studying aliens, or studying alien cultures, or planets. . . . His concern is the study of Man and the Human Condition."

Jameson, Fredric. "Nostalgia for the Present." *South Atlantic Quarterly* 88, No. 2 (Spring 1989): 517-37.

Highlights the concept of historicity—the historical interpretation of the present—in *Time Out of Joint.*

Ketterer, David. "New Dimensions of Time, Space, and Literature." In his *New Worlds for Old: The Apocalyptic Imagination, Science Fiction, and American Literature,* pp. 233-60. Bloomington: Indiana University Press, 1974.

Examines the alternate world device in *The Man in the High Castle.*

Latham, Robert. "Clanker Meets Gulper." *Necrofile,* no. 4 (Spring 1992): 7-10.

Proposes that Dick, though essentially a science fiction writer, incorporated elements of horror fiction in his writing.

Malmgren, Carl D. "Philip Dick's *Man in the High Castle* and the Nature of Science-Fictional Worlds." In *Bridges to Science Fiction,* edited by George E. Slusser, George R. Guffey, and Mark Rose, pp. 120-30. Carbondale: Southern Illinois University Press, 1980.

Outlines Dick's interest in the nature of reality and his use of alternate worlds.

Palmer, Christopher. "Postmodernism and the Birth of the Author in Philip K. Dick's *Valis.*" *Science-Fiction Studies* 18, No. 55, Pt. 3 (November 1991): 330-42.

Compares the themes prevalent in Dick's early works with *Valis,* asserting that the experiences presented in the novel are inextricably tied to his own experiences, posing an obstacle to the reader trying to draw meaning from them.

Pierce, Hazel. *Philip K. Dick.* Mercer Island, Wash.: Starmont House, 1982, 64 p.

Brief overview of Dick's life and career with critical interpretations of his major works.

Science-Fiction Studies, Special Issue: Philip K. Dick 15, No. 45, Pt. 2 (July 1988): 121-233.

Includes essays by Carl Freedman, Daniel Fondanèche, Eric S. Rabkin, Scott Durham, John Rieder, and others.

Simons, John L. "The Power of Small Things in Philip K. Dick's *The Man in the High Castle.*" *Rocky Mountain Review of Language and Literature* 39, No. 4 (1985): 261-75.

Illustrates Dick's use of "the small, especially children, to render weak the putatively strong constructions of those who proclaim both the power and the truth of their ossifying idealisms."

Stilling, Roger J. "Mystical Healing: Reading Philip K. Dick's *VALIS* and *The Divine Invasion* as Metapsychoanalytic Novels." *South Atlantic Review* 56, No. 2 (May 1991): 91-106.

Studies the philosophical and psychological aspects of two of Dick's later works.

Warrick, Patricia S. "The Encounter of Taoism and Fascism in Philip K. Dick's *The Man in the High Castle.*" *Science-Fiction Studies* 7, No. 21, Pt. 2 (July 1980): 174-90.

Describes Dick's portrayal of the differences between Eastern and Western philosophies.

————. "Philip K. Dick's Answers to the Eternal Riddles." In *The Transcendent Adventure: Studies of Religion in Science Fiction/Fantasy,* edited by Robert Reilly, pp. 107-26. Westport, Conn.: Greenwood Press, 1985.

Explores the theological concepts in Dick's writings.

Additional coverage of Dick's life and career is contained in the following sources published by Gale Research: *Contemporary Authors,* Vols. 49-52, 106; *Contemporary Authors New Revision Series,* Vol. 16; *Contemporary Literary Criticism,* Vols. 10, 30; *Dictionary of Literary Biography,* Vol. 8; and *Major 20th-Century Writers.*

Eduardo Galeano

1940-

(Full name Eduardo Hughes Galeano) Uruguayan novelist, short story writer, essayist, historian, and memoirist.

The following entry provides criticism of Galeano's works that have appeared in English translation from 1973 through 1991.

INTRODUCTION

Galeano is best known for works in which he combines elements of history, fiction, poetry, and autobiography through the use of vignettes, candid prose, and evocative imagery, a technique that is highly influenced by the writings of Jorge Luis Borges and Gabriel García Márquez, Latin American writers whose works blend fantasy with realism. Attempting to restore Latin American history to a position of social and cultural significance, Galeano creates an idiom that reflects the region's myths and oral traditions. Galeano explains: "I remember as a child feeling that history was locked away in a museum, and that she had to be rescued and set free so she could walk in the streets and fields again at will. This implies rescuing history by means of a language capable of embracing all its dimensions, the language people on the coast of Columbia call *sentipensante*—a language capable of uniting the reasons of passion with the passions of reason."

Born in Montevideo, the capital of Uruguay, Galeano became a caricaturist for the socialist paper *El sol* at age thirteen. He later become the editor-in-chief of *Marcha,* one of Latin America's most esteemed political publications, but when a military coup unseated the Uruguayan government and established a dictatorship in 1971, Galeano was forced to abandon his duties and flee to Argentina because authorities considered his work a threat to national security. While in Argentina, Galeano founded *Crisis,* a journal of Latin American literature, art, and popular culture which for a time had the highest circulation of any Spanish-language cultural publication. In 1976, Galeano was again forced into exile—this time in Spain—when Argentina's government was overthrown. He returned to Uruguay in 1984 when political restrictions eased.

Las venas abiertas de América Latina (*The Open Veins of Latin America: Five Centuries of the Pillage of a Continent*) was the first of Galeano's translated works to receive critical attention in the United States. An historical account of Latin America's economic and political exploitation by the United States and Europe, *The Open Veins of Latin America* traces the origins of poverty, environmental devastation, and governmental tyranny in the region. While critics praised Galeano's determination to accurately portray the atrocities that have occurred in Latin America since the colonial era, some contend that his failure to ex-

plain increasing class stratification in the area weakened the book's impact. In his next translated work, *Días y noches de amor y de guerra* (*Days and Nights of Love and War*), Galeano combines personal memoirs with factual accounts of the murders, tortures, and disappearances that have become common in Latin American nations. Comprising numerous short, nonchronological passages that introduce personal acquaintances as well as political figures, *Days and Nights of Love and War* reflects Galeano's feelings of isolation, displacement, and loss during his exile in Spain. "[I had] a strong need to bring together my broken pieces," Galeano revealed. "So I began writing [a] short text, which was in a manner of speaking, the pieces of myself. . . . *Days and Nights of Love and War* resulted from this open, free conversation with my own memory, as I tried to understand what had really happened and guess who I really was."

In his *Memoria del fuego* (*Memory of Fire*) trilogy, which includes *Los nacimientos* (*Memory of Fire: Genesis*), *Las caras y las máscaras* (*Memory of Fire: Faces and Masks*), and *El siglo del viento* (*Memory of Fire: Century of the Wind*), Galeano integrates fact, fiction, and myth to present a history of North, Central, and South America.

Seeking to restore the western hemisphere's cultural heritage, which he believes has been suppressed, forgotten, and misinterpreted due to the idealization of European values and the degradation of indigenous Americans, Galeano consulted more than a thousand books, periodicals, documents, letters, and diaries, many of which are cited in an extensive bibliography at the end of each volume. While *Memory of Fire* is well-documented, Galeano states he did not want to produce an anthology of isolated facts and historical generalizations but rather sought to provide a personal, accessible, and empathic account of the individuals who contributed to the development of the Americas. Galeano clarifies his intentions in the preface to the first volume: "I did not want to write an objective work—neither wanted to nor could. There is nothing neutral about this historical narration. Unable to distance myself, I take sides. I confess it and I am not sorry."

Galeano's *El libro de los abrazos* (*The Book of Embraces*) is a collection of nearly two hundred anecdotes, philosophical meditations, and personal remembrances ranging in length from a paragraph to a few pages. In addition to celebrating the oral traditions of Latin America through a distinctly rhythmic idiom, Galeano also disperses numerous sketches and caricatures throughout the text, techniques which reflect his belief that a work of literature should not only be intellectually provocative but should also stimulate the visual and auditory senses. While some critics have found this integration of genres and styles subjective, unrealistic, and disjointed, most concur that Galeano's holistic approach has broadened and enlivened historical interpretation. "I [have] tried," Galeano asserts, "to find a way of recounting history so that the reader [will] feel that it is happening right now, just around the corner—this immediacy, this intensity, which is the beauty and the *reality* of history."

PRINCIPAL WORKS

PROSE

*Los nacimientos 1982
  [*Memory of Fire: Genesis,* 1985]
*Las caras y las máscaras 1984
  [*Memory of Fire: Faces and Masks,* 1987]
*El siglo del viento 1986
  [*Memory of Fire: Century of the Wind,* 1988]
El libro de los abrazos 1989
  [*The Book of Embraces,* 1991]

NONFICTION

China 1964: Crónica de un desafío 1964
Guatemala: Clave de Latinoamérica 1967
  [*Guatemala: Occupied Country,* 1969]
Reportajes: Tierras de Latinoamérica, otros puntos cardinales, y algo más 1967
Siete imágenes de Bolivia 1971
Las venas abiertas de América Latina 1971
  [*The Open Veins of Latin America: Five Centuries of the Pillage of a Continent,* 1973]
Crónicas latinoamericanas 1972

OTHER

Los días siguientes (novel) 1962
Los fantasmas del día del léon, y otros relatos (short fiction) 1967
Vagamundo (short fiction) 1973
La canción de nosotros (novel) 1975
Días y noches de amor y de guerra (memoirs) 1978
  [*Days and Nights of Love and War,* 1983]
Nosotros decimos no: Crónicas (1963-1988) (essays) 1989

*These works comprise Galeano's *Memoria del fuego* (*Memory of Fire*) trilogy.

CRITICISM

Ramón Eduardo Ruiz

In Latin America today, few intellectuals view with satisfaction the state of their respective countries. Unhappiness with life-as-it-is colors their comments on society and questions of progress. Eduardo Galeano, a citizen of Uruguay and former editor of *Marcha* and *Época* and currently director of the University of Montevideo Press, writes in this mold. His [***Open Veins of Latin America***], a bitter indictment of the Latin American scene, covers, as he explains in his subtitle, "five centuries of the pillage of a continent."

A journalist by trade and a socialist by conviction, Galeano employs the historian's craft to explain what went wrong from the beginning. He castigates the conquering Spaniards for their "lust" for gold and silver and the societies they built. The exploitation of the people of Latin America, he writes, began with the Spaniards who, in their quest for quick wealth, enslaved the Indian. The Laws of the Indies, which in theory protected the native Americans from the greed of the conquerors, quickly became the dead letters of the past, more honored by historians today than by colonial officials. By 1800, he concludes, even mestizo intellectuals, eager to escape the plight of the Indian, denied their own people. Concolorcovo, for example, a mestizo intellectual of the late eighteenth century, while acknowledging the high rate of deaths among Indian workers in the mercury and silver mines, absolved the Spaniards of responsibility and put the blame on the Indian's "resolute way of life." As Galeano explains, the colonial mentality, the bane of Latin American societies today, had an early start.

In his biting indictment of Latin American life, Galeano explores a wide range of subjects. After discussing the colonial underpinnings, he takes up other aspects of contemporary monocultural systems, from the sugar of Cuba, Northeast Brazil, and the Caribbean, which prospered at the expense of black slaves, to rubber, cacao, cotton, and coffee. All, he argues, thrive by their ties with the industrialized powers and the willingness of local elites to exploit for selfish ends. Because of the structure of power in Latin

America, he testifies that with the exception of Cuba, nearly all attempts at reform have ended in failure.

Galeano, a Marxist intellectual, reserves his special ire for the United States, which he calls "the invisible sources of power." In conjunction with Western European cartels, he says, North American capitalists have come to control the wealth of Latin America: petroleum, copper, nitrates, and other mineral reserves. Quoting Simón Bolivar, he concludes with a dire prediction: in Latin America, "we shall never be happy, never!"

Galeano's views, which will please few North American scholars, add little to what is already known. They may, in fact, even distort some of the truth. Clearly, he writes with scant objectivity. Yet few will deny that he speaks for a majority of Latin America's intellectuals and scholars. In that rests the value of his book. (pp. 581-82)

> *Ramón Eduardo Ruiz, in a review of "Open Veins of Latin America: Five Centuries of the Pillage of a Continent," in* Pacific Historical Review, *Vol. XLIV, No. 4, November, 1975, pp. 581-82.*

Peter Roman

It is welcome to see a history of Latin America which is at the same time factual, to a great extent theoretically sound, and highly readable. Eduardo Galeano's *Open Veins of Latin America* is most useful in undergraduate courses on Latin America, and has received an enthusiastic reception among students, especially Latin American students.

The book is more a journalistic account of, than a significant contribution to, Latin American history, political economy, or the study of imperialism. But it is an honest popularization, and the reader emerges with a clear understanding of the dialectical relationship between Latin America's economic underdevelopment and European or United States economic development. From the outset colonial domination structured the dependent nature of Latin American capitalism; Galeano's section on Cuba makes it clear that only socialism has decisively broken this dependency.

The organization of the book is somewhat confusing since Galeano does not quite succeed in merging a broad historical approach with illustrative treatment of types of imperialist exploitation. He begins with the colonizers' thirst for gold and silver and the devastating effects of conquest on the indigenous populations and the local economies. Galeano assesses this early colonialism as the necessary precursor of modern dependent capitalism.

He then moves to the next historically significant form of imperialist exploitation—agriculture. The narration is informative, even exciting, and a direct link is shown to present-day monoculture. The legacy of African and Indian slavery and of the land tenure system is today's impoverished peasantry and *latifundia*. The legacy of wanton use of the soil is today's worn-out and semi-arid land.

In this and subsequent sections Galeano uses a country-by-country approach, tracing each case history from colonial to modern times. This shift from the broad continental historical treatment of the introductory section may confuse the reader. For example, in the case of Brazil several historical sketches, each emphasizing a different category of imperialist exploitation, are distributed throughout the book. Students just embarking on a study of Latin America will find themselves with insufficient historical and theoretical background fully to digest these accounts, or to understand the ramifications of present-day economic and political events in Brazil. The same can be said of other Latin American countries.

Galeano goes on to explain how, through imperialist exploitation of minerals and oil, Latin America's rich natural resources have benefited only outsiders, intensifying misery and poverty at home. Venezuela is the most flagrant example of economic deformation, superficial modernization, and great poverty resulting from imperialist domination:

> Caracas chews gum and loves synthetic products and canned foods; it never walks, and poisons the clean air of the valley with the fumes of its motorization: its fever to buy, consume, obtain, spend, use, get hold of everything, leaves no time to sleep. From surrounding hillside hovels made of garbage, half a million forgotten people observe the sybaritic scene. The gilded city's avenues glitter with hundreds of thousands of late-model cars, but in the consuming society not everyone consumes. According to the census, half of Venezuela's children and youngsters do not go to school.

The final two sections are better organized. Galeano argues that the nineteenth century free trade policy, forced upon Latin America by England, and later continued by the U.S., destroyed native industry and throttled independent capitalist development. The imposition of constantly increasing financial indebtedness only furthered the process of foreign domination. The example of Paraguay is striking: a century ago it was the most prosperous country of South America. "The most progressive country of Latin America was constructing its future without foreign investments, without loans from the Bank of England, and without the benedictions of free trade." But British imperialism eliminated this dangerous example by systematically undermining its economy.

Galeano closes with a valuable chapter on the pattern of imperialism in Latin America today and its strategy for maintaining dependent capitalist satellites. The new emphasis on foreign investments and domination in the manufacturing sector does not benefit the host country, but rather increases economic dependency, further reduces the latitude of independence of the national bourgeoisie, impedes integrated development, leaves the agrarian problem unsolved, and increases unemployment.

The book does an excellent job in underlining Latin America's paradoxical history: a continent of enormous abundance of natural resources that for almost five centuries produced untold wealth for its exploiters and unspeakable poverty for its peoples. From the beginning the goal of the Europeans was plunder, and the ties and allegiance of the colonial settlers always remained with Europe. The riches and labor of the indigenes and the imported Africans were used to enrich first European and then U.S. capitalism. Latin American capitalist development was always subservient, directed outward—so different from the English colonies from Maryland north, which had the "luck" to be deficient in natural resources and to suffer a climate roughly similar to England's.

Some of the book's strengths lead to weaknesses and omissions. While Galeano effectively depicts the impact of imperialism on Latin America, he fails to emphasize the class rather than national basis of this exploitation; he does not show sharply enough that it is the capitalist class in the metropolis which sets and implements policy and amasses its benefits—granting, when necessary, a share to the local bourgeoisie and landowners. Further, the book fails to deal with current counter-developments and the sharpening contradictions of capitalism as a world system. As a result there is no analysis of the dynamics which lead to socialist revolution. Depiction of human misery is not enough. What also is needed is an examination of the growing class struggle and the role of the urban and rural proletariat. As Theotonio dos Santos points out in *Socialismo o Fascismo:*

> In the contemporary epoch, revolution is proletarian not because the proletariat comprise the most dispossessed class of the society, but rather because they are the basis of the social production, the only ones who can offer a superior road to the existing capitalist structure. . . . The revolutionary category *par excellence* is exploitation, and not misery.

There is no bibliography, a great lack if one considers the book for pedagogical purposes, though there are bibliographical footnotes. But the book succeeds where it counts—explaining in a most readable manner the historical roots of Latin America's underdevelopment, and the impossibility of development under dependent capitalism. (pp. 497-500)

> *Peter Roman, in a review of "The Open Veins of Latin America," in* Science and Society, *Vol. XXXIX, No. 4, Winter, 1975-76, pp. 497-500.*

Eve Ottenberg

Literary accounts of the political murders, tortures, and mutilations that make up so much of recent Latin American history are not known for their popularity in the United States. Indeed such accounts are rarely even published here. When they do appear, they're usually greeted by resounding critical silence—which is exactly what has happened to Eduardo Galeano's fragmentary but at times electrifying *Days and Nights of Love and War.*

This is all the more remarkable given Galeano's stature. A Uruguayan exile, founder of the magazine *Crisis* (published in Argentina until forced by the government to close), author of a number of books, including *Open Veins of Latin America* and *Guatemala: Occupied Country,* and chronicler of the struggles of his associates Dr. Allende

and Che Guevara, Galeano is a notable figure in left literary circles south of the border. *Days and Nights of Love and War* won the Casa de las Americas prize prior to its translation into English. That news obviously didn't make the literary hotline up here.

Part of the problem doubtless lies in the book itself. *Days and Nights of Love and War* could more accurately be described as a cry of pain than an artistic tour de force. It recites one disappearance, death, and disaster after another. Cast in the form of a personal memoir, Galeano's book is, in essence, an attempt to bear witness to seemingly small acts of humanity which, performed in the context of relentless barbarism, become truly heroic. Amazingly, and unlike much of what constitutes that grim and distinctly 20th century genre called atrocity literature, *Days and Nights of Love and War* is not numbing. Galeano describes his discovery that once a month, the day his maga-

---

An excerpt from *Days and Nights of Love and War*

Returning from another trip shortly before the coup, I learned that the police had been to my home in Montevideo looking for me.
I presented myself to the police alone. I felt afraid as I entered. The door snapped shut behind my back, like a trap. The fear lasted for an hour. Then it left my body. What could happen, worse than death? It wouldn't be the first visit.

I stood in the yard, my face to the wall. The floor above was a torture chamber. Prisoners passed behind me. They were dragged through the yard. Some returned beaten to a pulp; they were thrown onto the ground. At midnight the siren sounded. I heard the commotion, the insults, the excitement of the pack of hounds as it lunged off to the manhunt. The police returned at dawn.

A few days later they put me in a car. They moved me and locked me in a cell.

I scratched my name on the wall.

At night I heard screams.

I began to feel the need to talk to someone. I made friends with a little mouse. I didn't know whether I would be locked up for days or years, and before long one loses count. It was days. I've always been lucky.

The night they let me out I heard murmurings and distant voices and sounds of metal clanking while I walked through corridors, a guard at either side. Then the prisoners began to whistle, softly, as if blowing on the walls. The whistling grew louder and louder until one voice, every voice as one, broke into song. The song shook the walls.

I walked home. It was a warm, serene night. Autumn was arriving in Montevideo. I learned that the week before Picasso had died.

A short time passed and my exile began.

> *Eduardo Galeano, in his* Days and Nights of Love and War, *Monthly Review Press, 1983.*

zine came out, 20 men—led by an elderly professor who had spent years in prison—crossed from Uruguay to Argentina, chipped in to buy an issue of the magazine, then went to a café and spent the day reading it aloud and discussing it, before returning home, where the magazine was banned; it's hard not to agree with Galeano that "even if it were just for this, it would be worthwhile." And more than agree. After all, aren't such acts of courage and fraternity what the printed word, at its very best, is about?

Anecdotes like this one make the book's purposely disjointed form almost irritating. One wants to know more: how, for instance, did Galeano find out about this group of men, and what else did he find out about them? Most readers would, I think, trade all of the book's passages on what it means to be a writer for some of these details. Similarly, when Galeano describes his grief over the official disappearance of Haroldo Conti, an Argentine novelist, teacher, and filmmaker, one wants more than grief—nothing less than a biography of Conti. This may seem an unreasonable demand, but it arises inevitably from the material. One vignette about a river expedition with Conti, and his wife's description of the kidnapping, are somehow not enough. Perhaps the artificially modernistic form of the book has prevented Galeano from giving what seems full justice to the life of his murdered friend.

Although one sinuous, connected piece of living prose might have had more impact, that might also have made the book a novel instead of a testament. What the tone of *Days and Nights of Love and War* brings to mind more than anything else is not another book, but a film—*La Guerre Est Finie*. If Galeano's book at times seems to lack a similar artistic unity, the reason must be that for him, clearly, the war is *not* over.

> Eve Ottenberg, in a review of "Days and Nights of Love and War," in VLS, No. 15, March, 1983, p. 4.

Julie Schumacher

A collection of memoirs, ideas, facts, fictions, hearsay and speeches from more than twenty years of work and travel in South and Central America, [Eduardo Galeano's] *Days and Nights* succeeds not only because of its socio-political authenticity and lyrical style but because of its interweaving of anger and tenderness, elation and sorrow. (p. 807)

Days and Nights is a testimony to the power of fear to silence a population. It is also a testimony to the courage of those who refuse to be silenced. Devoid of plot and chronological progression, the action is presented through fragments, semi-related paragraphs that jump back and forth in time, place, person and mood. Each fragment has a title (**"The Universe as Seen Through a Keyhole," "The System," "Dreams," "Introduction to History"**), and many are complete in their own right as prose poems or stories.

The book opens with a description of Edda Armas's great-grandfather, a poor, ancient blind man who married a girl of 18 and had the habit of gleefully running away from home. Neither Armas nor her great-grandfather is men-

tioned again; the following pages include accounts of torture in Buenos Aires, the author's divorce, the fantasies of children. Like so many in Argentina and Uruguay, Galeano's characters *do* disappear. Life in Buenos Aires, where much of the book is set, is fragmented; in this respect, the form and content of Galeano's work are one.

Days and Nights is the notebook of a wandering "people's reporter." Among its characters are Juan Perón, Che Guevara, Fidel Castro, Salvador Allende and Juan Rulfo. In addition, Galeano includes his grandmother, his neighbor's children, disheartened guerrilla fighters, a satanic priest and numerous women with whom he has made love. No one of these is accorded more importance than another. Galeano gives each an urgent vitality, and though we meet them for a moment only, they stick in the mind: the whore who turns tricks with her eyes closed for fear of going blind; Vicente, who, while making a political speech, sees his family in the distance and begins to talk about love and beauty; the old woman who keeps in a bureau, wrapped in lace, the umbilical cords of her ten children.

Fear, and the struggle against it, are the threads that hold the book together. Fear induces one couple to burn every book they own, from Lenin to *Alice in Wonderland*. Fear prevents a man's closest friends from showing up at his funeral. Fear drives a soldier to make love to a corpse, while making love erases fear from another man's mind. The importance of fear is that it is a means of control; when used effectively, it replaces the more expensive machinations of torture, arrest and American military advice. Fear is censorship, and censorship, says Galeano, "truly triumphs when each citizen is transformed into the implacable censor of his own acts and words."

Days and Nights is not without flaws. Galeano tends to overwrite (Che Guevara is billed as "Jesus Christ of the Rio de la Plata"), and to repeat clever phrases. Toward the end of the book, he reflects upon his childhood and indulges in moments of *angst*, which come across as mawkish. Ironically, given Galeano's intimate style, these autobiographical elements are intrusive, and only involve the reader in trying to keep the names of the author's children and numerous lovers straight by leafing madly through the unchronological paragraphs.

"In Defense of the Word," an essay appended to the English translation, is an appropriate conclusion. Here Galeano discusses the function of literature in a largely illiterate society: art is not a luxury, he argues, but an essential form of collective consciousness-raising, a telling of truths forbidden by those who govern. But more than that, literature is a way of instilling hope, of asking the reader to forestall despair, not by ignoring persecution and injustice but by understanding the possibilities of happiness as well as grief. "It is not futile to sing the pain and the beauty of having been born in America," Galeano writes, and indeed, he proves that it is not. (pp. 807-08)

> Julie Schumacher, "Denunciation and Hope," in The Nation, New York, Vol. 236, No. 25, June 25, 1983, pp. 807-08.

Ronald Christ

Long after Octavio Paz observed that the fragment is the form of our times, we know, with special reference to Latin America, that it is the content too. From its fractured map to its splintering factions and classes to its ruptured history, Latin America suggests identity drawn and quartered.

Eduardo Galeano, a Uruguayan writer and editor who recently returned to his homeland after more than a decade in exile, has seized this equivalence of form and content. His works invent genre by smashing categories and joining fragments to yield a "voice of voices."

Mr. Galeano's first book translated into English mingled Marxist polemic, autobiography, travel and testament in a violent, sometimes screeching indictment of Latin America's victimization, summed up in its title, **Open Veins of Latin America.** His subsequent **Days and Nights of Love and War** extended his view and was shattered into more than 100 sections. Even the Library of Congress muddles the contrary nature of **Memory of Fire: I, Genesis,** describing the book as "History—Anecdotes, facetiae, satire, etc." (Mostly etc., of course.)

Memory of Fire, the first part of a trilogy, is a sort of Bible, a recorded collation of the mythological and historical soul of the peoples of North, Central and South America, to be ignored or disbelieved at the reader's peril. . . . Certainly, it is no mere mosaic, no fabrication of pre-existing parts to form a static design. The assemblage of more than 300 imaginatively recreated parts flashes a staccato montage—the violently jolting tradition of the New World from indigenous myths, in the book's first section, through the gold-sucking European conquest disguised as religious conversion and up to the death in 1700 of Spain's King Charles II, in the second part.

The pieces emerge from one or more of 227 sources listed at the back of the book, but except for portions in italics, indicating "literal transcription," almost all have been retold, recast as drama, reconstructed in Mr. Galeano's inflamed diction, admirably captured by Cedric Belfrage's polyphonic translation. We have a pre-Columbian myth with a "dive-bombing" hummingbird, and a witty exchange between Sor Juana, the 17th-century Mexican poet, and a bishop (he wrote a letter admonishing her for writing poetry but signed the letter under a female pseudonym), now replayed as drama in drag; we read a discussion of the death of Cervantes between Don Quixote and Sancho Panza.

The collisions and interweavings of this modern Genesis ransom "the kidnapped memory of all America." Mr. Galeano produces a secular liberation mythology to revivify historic verities by turning them into day-to-day truths. In the 1670's, a playwriting mestizo priest composed a sacramental mystery about the prodigal son, in which the Devil is a Peruvian landlord, the wine is a native liquor and the calf is a pig. Check Mr. Galeano's source, the learned *El Teatro Hispanoamericano en la Epoca Colonial* by José Juan Arrom. The message anachronistically liberates theology; the identity of the priest futuristically liberates mythology.

More *Inferno* than Genesis, **Memory of Fire** is devastating, triumphant regeneration, sure to scorch the sensibility of English-language readers. It hopes to scandalize us into learning our sources—bibliographic and historic.

Ideally, an adequately translated anthology of Latin American literature and history would accompany **Memory of Fire** so we might better recognize the disconcerting interpretations offered in Mr. Galeano's book. Still lacking that, we can return to the historian William H. Prescott, to Gabriel García Márquez, never to be the same after this bold discovery that seems to precede them. Meanwhile, we await the next two volumes, which will conduct Mr. Galeano's **Memory** into our own era, where we all share the search for lost yet inescapably present times.

> Ronald Christ, "Dramas That Scorch," in The New York Times Book Review, *October 27, 1985, p. 22.*

Liz Heron

It was the aftermath of the Cuban Revolution that turned Europe's eyes towards the cultural tumult of Latin America. The notorious British reluctance to publish in translation ensured that what's become known as the Latin American literary boom got off to a slow start here, but, since the early Seventies, regular shipments conveying the terrors and marvels of the New World have been delivered to our shores: a process in which history mimics the responses of those who held out their hands for the riches of the Conquest. Like them we are dazzled and filled with wonderment; in place of the gold, we have magic realism.

The necessity for allegory and extravagant symbolism as camouflage against the censors explains in part the growth of these fantastic fictions. But, as the writers themselves have often reminded us in interviews and speeches, their material already exists in the baroque contusions of Latin America's past and present.

Magic realism also makes sense as an imaginative engagement with Latin American history as it is lived out in the unconscious, where it exerts a subterranean grip on contemporary societies. In a continent where the ghosts of history's crimes and defeats survive in the hybrid inheritance of their descendants, in the extremes of economic development, in the coexistence of hunger, illiteracy and great wealth and in the near reenactment of early barbaric expressions of political power, it is not hard to understand creative compulsions to retrieve what was lost or despoiled by giving history multiple imaginative possibilities. These compulsions have produced fictions of voracious scope and size. As Carlos Fuentes has said: 'Our problem is that we feel we have everything to write about. That we have to fill four centuries of silence.'

Eduardo Galeano is a Uruguayan writer whose **Memory of Fire,** a projected trilogy, has the avowed intention of rescuing America's history from silence and expropriation. This first, substantial volume is [titled **Genesis**] and it spans the period up to 1700. Its form is unique: over 300 fragments of fictionalised historical chronology that draw on specific written sources: political, cultural and anthropological studies; folklore; journalism; fiction and poetry; and the contemporary chronicles, letters and diaries of those who took part in the Conquest.

Creation myths and stories of the dawn of indigenous cultures precede the beginning of dated chronology in 1492: the year of Columbus's 'discovery' and also the year in which Spain expelled the Jews and drove the Moors from their last redoubt in Granada, simultaneously establishing the strangling orthodoxy of Catholicism and draining the country of economic vitality. Galeano's style is lyrical and smooth and this, by and large, is a good translation, spoiled only by occasional linguistic anachronisms and incongruities. His technique is to bring us to the threshold of historical experience evoked in an episode, a scene, a portrait or a dialogue, and hold us there as blinking witnesses. Only rarely does he fail to convey this immediacy. The horrors and cruelties of the prolonged bloody saga of dispossession that wiped out Indian civilisations in the greed for gold and slaves; the monstrosities of the Inquisition; the picaresque crew of saints and sinners, dupes and con men; the humanists and the fanatics; the scholars and poets: all come to brilliant momentary life. Some pieces carry the weight of a parable, the force of a nightmare vision and, often, the ironic sorrow of a lament.

It is an expansive technique, offering a personal and allusive view of history while suggesting that history is multiple and only to be apprehended through imaginative recognition of its incompleteness: what has been stolen, destroyed, suppressed or misremembered. Galeano conjures many such moments: the flames that devour the last books of Spanish-Islamic culture, the ashes of eight centuries of Mayan literature, the customs outlawed, the scholarly manuscripts seized: like those of Bernardino de Sahagún, whose 40-year labour of recording Mexican and Toltec cultures fell foul of Philip II: *'so that no original or translation of them should remain'.*

As the centuries pass there are intimations of the colonial advance into North America and, throughout, there is the corollary of Spain's history, its economic parasitism and the decline that will take it into a backwardness remote from Europe's coming Enlightenment. But the book's map is of Latin America and its mythic hoard of grotesque, macabre and fantastic images. As a coherent fiction it frustrates, for there are too many stories for any to resonate for long, but it proposes innumerable embryonic narratives. Reading them illuminates the dreams and realities that pervade the other fictions we know from that continent.

Liz Heron, "El Dorado," in New Statesman, *Vol. 3, No. 7881, June 13, 1986, p. 27.*

Steven White

It is very difficult to classify [*Memory of Fire: Genesis*], the first volume of a planned trilogy. As a collection of fragments drawn from a vast pool of bibliographic sources, it is certainly not a standard history textbook and not an anthology of selected writings from a particular period. Nor is it an historical novel. In the preface, Galeano recognizes his clear biases and the fact that he neither in-

tended nor was able to write an objective work. Each fragment of this huge mosaic, says Galeano, is based on a solid documentary foundation. Galeano relates events as they actually occurred but with a storyteller's vivid flair and imagination. It is Galeano's way of breathing life back into history and giving a voice to those who were defeated by the swords of the conquistadors and the pens of the official keepers of history.

Memory of Fire: Genesis begins in a timeless, prehistoric world. This striking collage about the origin of the sun and moon, clouds, wind, rainbows, oceans, animals and humanity is derived from the creation myths of indigenous peoples from North, Central and South America. The Milky Way is a serpent bristling with luminous arrows in the night sky. The glowing bodies of the first lovers are so beautiful that the sun and the gods die of embarrassment. The haunting radiance of these glimpses into indigenous consciousness, however, is soon extinguished. The Old New World is marked by its first date: 1492. Columbus falls on his knees, weeps and kisses the earth of his "discovery."

The history that follows in Galeano's book is cinematic in its rapid movement between Europe and the Indies. Galeano transports the reader with great skill across a scorched and bloody landscape. In *Memory of Fire,* it is as if the painter Hieronymus Bosch's infernal European visions crossed the oceans in the minds of the conquistadors and were then inflicted on the inhabitants of the New World in the name of God and gold. Three years after Bosch died in 1516, Hernán Cortés was standing in the smoking ruins of what was once the great Aztec city of Tenochtitlan.

The threads of Galeano's tapestry of American history are not simply the familiar names of Cortés, Montezuma, Pizarro, and Atahualpa. There is the story of Orellana's battle with the Amazon warrior women, another about a soldier in Pizarro's army who rips a giant gold sun from an Incan temple, then loses it one night in a game of cards. Galeano resurrects forgotten uprisings of Indian and black slaves forced to labor in silver mines so the Spaniards could finance wars and social progress across the seas.

Galeano's chorus of voices ranging across the Americas sings remarkably well in Cedric Belfrage's English translation. Eduardo Galeano has written a book that will undoubtedly shock some English-speaking readers into a re-evaluation of our own beginnings as a nation. (pp. 100-01)

Steven White, in a review of "Memory of Fire: Genesis," in Northwest Review, *Vol. XXIV, No. 2, 1986, pp. 99-101.*

Allen Boyer

In one scene from *Faces and Masks,* the second volume in his *Memory of Fire* trilogy, Eduardo Galeano describes the collapse of the Spanish empire:

> The messenger passes an order at the cockfights
> in Santiago, and another at a smart soiree, and
> at the same time picks up a report between two

horse races in the suburbs. The messenger announces himself at a big house—three taps of the door knocker—and at the same time emerges in the mountains on the back of a mule, and gallops over prairies on horseback . . . The Spanish governor has put a price on the head of Manuel Rodriguez, the messenger, the guerrilla. But his head travels hidden beneath the monk's hood, the muleteer's sombrero, the street peddler's basket, or the fine gentleman's plush topper.

In his native Uruguay, Galeano is known as an editorial cartoonist. Turning these skills to prose, he presents history in a sequence of vignettes. "The author proposes," he writes, "to narrate the history of America, and above all the history of Latin America, reveal its multiple dimensions and penetrate its secrets." *Genesis,* the trilogy's first volume, dealt with the history of the New World through 1700. *Faces and Masks* covers the years from 1700 to 1900. Some vignettes sketch in scenes; others reprint historical documents. Alexander von Humboldt discusses curare with an Indian shaman. Simon Bolivar, defeated and despondent, can find only one government to aid him: the black republic of Haiti, "a nation of peasants, very poor but free." Latin-American literature is born with the publication of *El Periquillo Sarniento*. Santa Ana marches into Texas with his chief, his jeweled sword, and a wagonload of his beloved fighting cocks. In Bolivia, Mariano Melgarejo stages history's shortest *coup d'etat* by shooting President Manuel Belzu, to whom he has just surrendered. Levi's jeans appear on the market; Coca-Cola follows. Indians are driven from the Dakota ranges and the Patagonian grasslands. Brazilian rubber, Cuban sugar, Peruvian guano, Chilean nitrates, Argentine beef—Latin America's goods flow out to Europe, while native industries are smothered by imports. In 1800, Spain and Portugal rule South America; by 1900, the United States stands ready to take their place.

Over the course of the book, one comes to understand Galeano's title. The masks represent those who squandered their continent's resources and clamped down their rule upon its people. They also include intellectuals who denied their American heritage, slavishly copying European models. The faces are the nameless people who endured and built, and the patriots and pamphleteers who spoke for them.

Galeano lobs many potshots northward. The United States appears in these pages as a "young voracious country" that gobbles up its neighbors. No one likes criticism from an outsider, but Galeano is even-handed. If he caricatures Teddy Roosevelt, he honors Lincoln, Whitman and Mark Twain. More irksome are minor muddles of fact. (California's Bear Flag, for example, is confused with the Lone Star banner of Texas). There are off-key phrases in the translation, too—anglicisms thrown in by the British-born translator, Cedric Belfrage.

Faces and Masks ends by foreshadowing this century's revolutions. Karl Marx's first grandchild is fathered by Cuban Paul Lafargue, "great-grandson of a Haitian mulatta and an Indian from Jamaica." In 1895, as Jose Marti dies fighting to free Cuba, Augusto Cesar Sandino is born in Nicaragua. And, farther south, another epoch is dawning: the Argentines have discovered soccer.

Galeano clearly identifies with Marti, a poet who turned revolutionary. But he never lapses into propaganda; his outrage is tempered by intelligence, an ineradicable sense of humor, and hope. He has taken the New World's history and fashioned from it a compelling book. (pp. 1, 7)

> *Allen Boyer, in a review of "Memory of Fire: Faces & Masks," in* Los Angeles Times Book Review, *March 15, 1987, pp. 1, 7.*

Barbara Belejack

In Brownsville, Texas—the self-proclaimed crossroads of the hemisphere, where I now live—there's a poem on the wall at the Nicarao Café that says much about the state of this half of the world. *"Brownsville,"* it begins, *"última ciudad en América."*

How does it happen that a homesick Chilean from Viña del Mar would refer to this sad little town that empties its heart into the Rio Grande as "the city where America comes to an end"? It happens, as Eduardo Galeano once wrote, "because everything flows north . . . along the way we even lost the right to call ourselves Americans." In the trilogy *Memory of Fire,* Galeano seeks to change all that. Like José Martí, whom he describes in *Faces and Masks,* Galeano "wants to revise everything in [America] that has been killed from the conquest onward."

Galeano is a 46-year-old Uruguayan journalist who writes like a poet. *Genesis* and *Faces and Masks,* the first volumes of *Memory of Fire,* re-create the history of America through a collection of fragments or episodes, a mix of literary forms and genres that Galeano calls a "voice of voices," a "huge mosaic based on a solid documentary foundation."

To Galeano, memory is everything. People who do not know who they are or where they come from are doomed, incapable of political or social change. Latin America's amnesia, he reminds us, is no accident:

> Through the centuries, Latin America has been despoiled of gold and silver, nitrates and rubber, copper and oil: its memory has also been usurped. From the outset it has been condemned to amnesia by those who have prevented it from being.

Genesis tells the story to the year 1700. It begins with the creation of the world: "God was singing and clacking his maracas as he dreamed his dream in a cloud of tobacco smoke, feeling happy but shaken by doubt and mystery." From the North, Galeano gives us a Sioux priest who "dreamed that outlandish creatures were weaving a huge spider web around his people" and announced: "When this happens, you shall live in square gray houses, in a barren land, and beside those square gray houses you shall starve." From the South, he gives us a prediction out of the Book of Chilam Balam, [a Mayan prophet], describing the end of a way of life: "There will be much misery in the years of the rule of greed. Men will turn into slaves. Sad will be the face of the sun. . . . The world will be depopulated, it will become small and humiliated . . ."

Cortés, La Malinche, Pizarro, Elizabeth I, and Shakespeare are among the cast of characters. The Borgia Pope Alexander VI makes a cameo appearance, "cutting up the world as if it were a chicken," defining spheres of influence circa 1493. Fray Bartolomé de las Casas struggles with his conscience and with Spain and wonders what can be done to alleviate the suffering of the Indians. Beyond the massacres and autos da fé, Galeano wants us to remember the countless edicts designed to legislate a culture out of existence. Books are burned, temples destroyed, dances and music banned. Even the quena, flute of the Andes, ends up on a proscribed list.

Faces and Masks is the story of political independence that masks economic and cultural dependency. "The Spanish colonies that are born to independent life walk bent over," Galeano writes. "From the first day they drag a heavy stone hung from the neck, a stone that grows and overwhelms. The *English debt,* born of Britain's support in arms and soldiers, is multiplied by the grace of usurers and merchants." Along the way, "Central America breaks to pieces"; Mexican General Santa Anna, accompanied by a funeral cortege, escorts his severed leg to Mexico City, where it is buried with full honors; Brazilian poet Machado de Assís "tears off the fancy wrapping, false frames of false windows with a European view, and winks at the reader as he strips the mud wall." Montevideo receives football; Buenos Aires the tango; and a marble opera house in the Amazon employs Italian virtuosos while "extremely important people drink extremely imported drinks, recuperate in the thermal baths of Vichy, and send their children to study in Lisbon or Geneva." North of the Rio Grande, Galeano compares the fate of Jane Franklin with that of her illustrious brother Ben and contemplates what life for the founding father might have been, had he been born a woman. Whitman and Poe pass through, along with Horatio Alger and John D. Rockefeller. As the 19th century and [*Faces and Masks*] close, President McKinley reveals a conversation during which God told him that the U.S. should retain possession of the Philippines.

Galeano has attempted nothing short of the impossible—to sift through the history of the hemisphere and come up with the big picture for Latin America. This is America's—in the original and most profound sense of the word—book of testimony. Galeano searches endlessly for some facts, some anecdotes, that cast a new light on official historical figures. At the same time, he seeks a voice for those whose stories have been ignored.

"One of the worst masks that prevent real history from being told is machismo," Galeano said during a reading in New York last year, "the fact that it's history told by males about males. Just as I think there is also a terrible mask in racism and elitism—history as told about heroes who are almost all white men." Acknowledging that in the past he was "accused of writing only for machos and being quite a machista," Galeano announced, "I am beginning to redeem myself." The road to redemption, however, is uneven. History is a "pink-veiled lady offering her lips to

those who win"; Latin America ends up again as La Chingada.

Hidden in the archives and in *Memory of Fire* are moments of joy as new culture is created from old. Galeano celebrates *san tería* and artisans who "sneak contraband llamas into their Christmas paintings instead of camels." In "annihilated Paraguay," somehow the Guarani Indian language survives.

These are tremendously courageous books, written from the heart but with a structure that is almost mathematical in its precision and elegance. Among the "secret rivers" that Galeano insists are hidden in Latin America's history is an inexplicable optimism. When I asked him about his own, he laughed, said he didn't know where it came from, and then recalled the story of his friend Juan Bustos, a story destined for the third volume of *Memory of Fire.*

Bustos is a Chilean lawyer who served in the Allende government. After the coup he wandered around lost, convinced that to go on living was an act of either cowardice or betrayal. For no reason, he stopped in a town called Yoro in the middle of Honduras, where he was suddenly pelted on the head by a rain of live fish. There was a scientific explanation, but it didn't matter, Galeano insisted. What mattered is that Bustos ended up in a place whose very name suggested sadness (*lloro* means *I am crying*), and "that a magnificent rain of live fish pelted him on the head as if to say, 'Don't be a fool. Life is worth living. Life matters. *Vale la pena vivir. Sobretodo, vale la pena vivir en América.*' "

Barbara Belejack, "Ordinary Peoples," in VLS, No. 54, April, 1987, p. 21.

Robert Cox

In an interview with *The New Yorker,* Eduardo Galeano said that he agrees with his wife that "music always humiliates writing." He may not know it, but in his *Memory of Fire* trilogy, an episodic narration of the history of the Americas of which [*Faces and Masks*] is the second volume, his words mark the beat of history and the music of time.

Like a brilliant conductor directing his own composition, Galeano calls upon the orchestra of the reader's imagination to bring history alive in a multi-media show with fireworks. It is difficult to envisage what music could capture that Galeano has failed to bring to life in what is surely an epic work of literary creation.

Appropriately enough, *Faces and Masks* picks up from the sweep of the first volume, *Genesis* (The Creation to the year 1700) by revealing that when the Chirigua Indians of the Guarani people saw paper carrying the written word for the first time, they called it "skin of God, because paper is for sending messages to friends far away."

The promise of the first volume of the trilogy is not betrayed. *Faces and Masks* conjures up the sights, smells and sounds of history and that means everything from the sussuration of Catherine the Great's petticoats in a dream of the Liberator José Miranda, to the excrement dumped nightly into the beautiful bay of Rio de Janeiro by slaves carrying chamber pots. We are in at the invention of Coca-Cola and of Levi Strauss' blue jeans, at the arrival of a traveling circus in a small town in Argentina and at the birth of the cafe in Montevideo. The love that imbues this work is communicated as Galeano writes of his own birthplace: "Montevideo will be the city of cafes. No corner will be a corner without a cafe as an accessory for secrets and noise, a little temple where all loneliness can take refuge, all encounters be celebrated, with cigarette smoke serving as incense."

Galeano uses a mixture of styles, choosing exactly the right instrument to make his music of time reverberate in the imagination as he records an Indian legend or retells an anecdote. Occasionally he provides us with a keyhole view of history. But his writing is so vivid, his words so musical that the reader is in the room for assassinations, couplings, births and deaths.

There are direct quotes when they are necessary. A verbatim report reveals that William Walker, the Tennessee adventurer who made himself president of Nicaragua, planned to conquer all Central America in order to restore slavery. Manuela Saenz also speaks for herself when writing to her English husband to explain why she is leaving him for Bolivar: "Leave me alone, my dear Englishman. Let's do something else. In heaven we'll be married again, but on earth no . . . There everything will be English style, because a life of monotony is reserved for your nation . . . in love, I mean."

So much in this book is simply splendid, including the miseries, that it is difficult to select a passage that captures the essence of Galeano's achievement, but his evocation of the death of the naturalist Aimé Bonpland is particularly beautifully wrought:

> Bonpland dies of his death, in a mud and straw hut, serenely, knowing that the stars do not die; that ants and people will not stop being born; that there will be new clover-leaves, and new oranges or suns on the branches; and that foals, newly upright on their mosquito legs, will be stretching out their necks in search of a teat. The old man bids farewell to the world as a child does to the day at bedtime.

In the preface to *Genesis,* the first volume of *Memory of Fire* . . . , Galeano writes: "I do not want to write an objective work—neither wanted to nor could. There is nothing neutral about this historical narration. Unable to distance myself, I take sides: I confess it and I am not sorry. However, each fragment of this huge mosaic is based on a solid documentary foundation."

Then Galeano goes on to indicate his main objective in narrating the history of America:

> I am not a historian. I am a writer who would like to contribute to the rescue of the kidnapped memory of all America, but above all of Latin America, that despised and beloved land: I would like to talk to her, share her secrets, ask her of what different clays she was born, from what acts of love and violation she comes.

Galeano has some telling vignettes that illuminate North American history, for he covers all the big figures and big subjects—Washington, Jefferson, Franklin, Lincoln and Teddy Roosevelt, the American Revolution, the Civil War and the years of "manifest destiny"—as well as telling a touching story of Franklin's sister Jane, noting that, "Her case will awaken no interest in historians." Galeaneo awakens the reader's interest in her.

His passion, however, is the redemption of Latin America from an unfair verdict by historians. In *Faces and Masks* Galeano notes that the idea of America as a continent of "accursed lands" goes back to the Encylopedists

> who describe the New World as an emporium of abominations. Count Buffon says that in America the skies are miserly and the rains rot the soil; that the lions are bald, small and cowardly and the tapir is a vest-pocket elephant; that over there horses, pigs and dogs become dwarfs and that Indians, cold as serpents, have no soul, nor fire for females.

There could be no greater vindication of the wonders of the lands and people of Latin America than *Memory of Fire.* It is only fair to warn the reader, however, that there are a few hints in volume two that Galeaneo may be preparing to return a harsh verdict on the United States in the final volume of his trilogy. *Faces and Masks* is dedicated to "Tomás Borge, to Nicaragua." Let us hope that the dedication to the most Stalinist of Nicaragua's *comandantes* is not a giveaway. One lesson that Galeano teaches is that much of Latin American history is the story of the substitution of one tyrant for another.

In his years of exile, after being forced to leave Uruguay and Argentina by the military regimes that ruled on both banks of the Rio de la Plata, Galeano has matured. The boring *yanqui*-bashing of his apprenticeship on magazines of the somewhat looney left has gone. His criticism of the United States remains harsh, but not to the point that his literary creation is unbalanced. So far there is not a piece out of place in this vast historical mosaic. (pp. 5-6)

> *Robert Cox, "History as Fable: An American Mosaic," in* Book World—The Washington Post, *April 5, 1987, pp. 5-6.*

Pat Aufderheide

"Poets and beggars, musicians and prophets, warriors and scoundrels, all creatures of that unbridled reality, we have had to ask but little of our imagination, for our crucial problem has been a lack of conventional means to render our lives believable. This, my friends, is the crux of our solitude," said Gabriel García Márquez when he accepted the Nobel Prize in 1982.

Uruguayan journalist and novelist Eduardo Galeano has, like García Márquez, undertaken the challenge of breaking through that solitude with art. So it is not surprising that he quotes García Márquez's 1982 speech in *Century of the Wind,* the third volume of [*Memory of Fire,*] a work he calls a trilogy but is in fact an open-ended re-imagining of Latin American reality from creation to the present.

This volume takes us from 1900, as pious Mexicans, terrified at the prospect of the end of the world, make confession, to 1984 on Nicaragua's English-speaking Atlantic coast, where peasants in the Contra war's target zone dance around a tree of life during the "Maypole fiesta."

Like its predecessors *Genesis* and *Faces and Masks, Century of the Wind* is constructed around chronologically organized vignettes and character sketches. One begins, "Against forgetting, the only death that kills . . ." It might be an epigraph for the book. Galeano of course is not talking about ordinary forgetting. He is talking about the kind that García Márquez made the center of *One Hundred Years of Solitude,* in which the slaughter of striking United Fruit company workers is simply erased from memory.

An impassioned journalist, Galeano in 1971 wrote *Open Veins of Latin America,* an angry essay on the history of Latin America as the victim of colonialism and neocolonialism. Exiled from Uruguay, he began working on the project that became this epic work.

Somewhere between doing the historical research and weathering the political storms. Galeano married the poet and the political analyst in him. He has never lost a passionate sense of justice, but has gone far beyond polemics.

It is pathetically easy for the grotesque, idiosyncratic and megalomaniacal in Latin American history to confirm contemptuous preconception. But as Galeano recalls bizarre autocratic practice, he makes the autocrats a target for outrage. He gives us, for instance, Salvadoran dictator General Martinez, who believed in reincarnation and the communist peril, hung a clock pendulum over steaming soup to divine conspiracies, wrapped street lights in red cellophane to cure smallpox—and ordered the slaughter of 30,000 Salvadoran peasants. Martinez is one of many autocrats in the book who combine the ludicrous and horrific, most of whom seem to have either arrived with or secured U.S. government backing.

As a generation of social historians knows, if you want to get away from the winning generals' version of history, you can't just tack on the history of minority groups, make lists of rebellions, or ignore the powerful. Done right, social history finds the contested zones of power and who was fighting in them at the time.

That is what Galeano does, not only with portraits of rulers, but of such left culture heroes as Sandino and Che Guevara and lesser-known ones such as Yucatecan socialist Rafael Carrillo Puerto. They appear in relation to their friends, enemies and their own idiosyncrasies. One Don Quixote of a resistance hero, Miguel Marmol—a Salvadoran leftist with more lives than a cat, each one testimony to the social conflict he was immersed in from his illegitimate birth—threads through the chronology.

Popular culture, including the sambas, saints and superstitions around which mass movements have been molded, shapes history here. Brazilian bandit Lampiao appears as a character who can hold up a whole town and still be the local hero, making a local prostitute famous for being the woman he spent all night with. Interestingly, that vignette sits next to one about Al Capone, for whom 10,000 students at Northwestern University rallied in 1929, and whom Galeano describes as an "exemplary family man . . . ever alert to the red menace." It's one of many juxtapositions that remind us of the links between the cultures of the Americas, and which reduces the safe distance between our "rational" reality and their "magical" one.

Galeano's style, melding intelligence and compassion in a controlled vernacular, rarely dazzles with its own cleverness. Nor does it patronize the less articulate by hiding its own elegance.

The trilogy thus speaks to a broad popular audience, and also testifies to a deep respect for scholarship and literary tradition. Being socially engaged, for Galeano, does not give art an excuse to be anything less than great. He does build a case for the social roots of art, by imagining for the reader the look of the world that shaped the world view of great Latin artists such as Juan Rulfo, Diego Rivera, Pablo Neruda.

In these pages, Latin America is no longer victim, but subject of the creative and destructive force of the many agents of his history. The title comes from a phrase of Mexican novelist Juan Rulfo: "and clawing ourselves out of the wind with our fingernails." The United States is also part of this great story of the self-invention of the Americas. If some of its historical figures play the role of enforcer to Latin America's solitude, others—Charlotte Perkins Gilman, Joe Hill, James Baldwin, Al Capone, Elvis—make the living links and parallels between the Americas North and South. The North American vignettes make you wish for an American bard of our own, perhaps a modern Walt Whitman who could be equally fascinated by commodities traders, community organizers and black gospel and R&B musicians, and weave them into an epic tale.

Galeano's anecdotes revive the passion of the past, and his trilogy, capped by *Century of the Wind,* vindicates storytelling as an approach to history at once critical and popular. It also leaves us with a challenge, to find a name for this new historical-literary form.

Pat Aufderheide, "Sambas, Saints and Superstitions," in Book World—The Washington Post, *May 22, 1988, p. 6.*

Raymund A. Paredes

Century of the Wind follows *Genesis* and *Faces and Masks* as the final volume in Eduardo Galeano's chronicle of the Americas, *Memory of Fire.* In his trilogy, Galeano ranges geographically from Canada to Argentina and Chile and chronologically from the pre-Columbian period to the present. To be sure, Galeano focuses on Latin America, shifting his attention above the Rio Grande primarily to treat events that have had large consequences in Mexico and lands farther south. In any case, *Memory of Fire* has been a hugely ambitious project, embracing vast cultural heterogeneity and complexity. That Galeano has managed to render his history of the Americas at once accessible, coherent and fascinating is a considerable achievement.

In his preface to *Genesis,* which first appeared in Spanish in 1982, Galeano decries conventional histories of Latin America as "lifeless, hollow, dumb . . . drowned in dates," little more than a "military parade of bigwigs in uniforms fresh from the dry-cleaners." For Galeano, such works are not only insipid but false, depriving Latin Americans of the knowledge that might break the prevailing mood of resignation and hopelessness. As the title itself indicates, *Memory of Fire* seeks to evoke the combustible, often destructive energy of American history. In presenting his version of events, Galeano makes no pretense of objectivity. I am "unable to distance myself," he writes. "I take sides."

Galeano on his motivations as a writer:

Perhaps I write because I know that the people and the things I care about are going to die and I want to preserve them alive. I believe in my craft; I believe in my instrument. I can never understand how writers could write while cheerfully declaring that writing has no meaning. Nor can I ever understand those who turn words into a target for fury or an object of fetishism. Words are a weapon: the responsibility for the crime never lies with the knife. Slowly gaining strength and form, there is in Latin America a literature that does not set out to bury our own dead but to perpetuate them; that refuses to clear up the ashes and tries, on the contrary, to light the fire. Perhaps my own words may help a little to preserve for people to come, as the poet put it, "the true name of each thing."

Eduardo Galeano, in written correspondance with Contemporary Authors, *Gale Research Inc., 1984.*

And so he does, initially with the aboriginal peoples of America and, later, with its oppressed masses, mostly Indian and black. He takes sides against the particular evils of the European conquest, North American capitalism and imperialism and the endless varieties of Latin American despotism. *Genesis* traces the legacy of the conquistadors' racism and avarice to 1700, by which time the aboriginal cultures had been virtually demolished and the bonds of colonialism had slackened, leaving an America "torn to pieces." In *Faces and Masks,* Galeano opens his survey of the 18th and 19th centuries with these lines from a Colombian poem:

I don't know who I am,
nor just where I was bedded.
Don't know where I'm from
nor where the hell I'm headed.

From his vantage point, Galeano sees the track of American history somewhat more clearly. Thomas Jefferson appears, to be followed by Toussaint L'Ouverture, Miguel Hidalgo y Costilla and Simón Bolivar. Independence, however, is not freedom, and everywhere, from Washington to Buenos Aires, governments fall into the hands of the wealthy.

During the 19th Century, the United States easily surpasses other American nations in economic development. As an omen of things to come, Galeano recounts the intrigues of William Walker, a pious, self-styled Southern gentleman who descends on Nicaragua with an army of adventurers and a bank account furnished by North American businessmen. A year later in 1856, Walker proclaims himself president, restores slavery, declares English the official language and offers land to any white compatriots willing to resettle in Nicaragua.

As *Century of the Wind* opens, Galeano notes two episodes that provide keys to his understanding of modern Latin American history. The first begins in New York City in 1901 when Andrew Carnegie sells his steel interests to J.P. Morgan for $250 million. Galeano writes that "a fever of consumption" and "a vertigo of money" dominate the United States; the country "belongs to the monopolies and the monopolies to a handful of men." Meanwhile, the "other America" remains in economic chaos, the individual countries eagerly signing commercial treaties with the United States and European nations but none with their neighbors. "Latin America is an archipelago of idiot countries" laments Galeano, "organized for separation and trained to dislike each other."

The second definite episode occurs in Quetzaltenango, Guatemala, in 1902 as the town is being destroyed by lava and mud avalanches from a volcanic eruption. Choking in a rain of ashes, the town crier bravely reads a proclamation by the president assuring the local citizens that all is quiet in Guatemala, that the rumors of volcanic disturbance are merely the dirty tricks of the "enemies of order."

Century of the Wind fairly runs over with these kinds of moments: tragic, sardonic, provocative and sharply insightful, often all at once. As Galeano depicts it, modern Latin American history resembles nothing so much as the old Latin American history. The same bloody patterns of oppression, exploitation and resistance persist; the only major new factor is advanced technology, particularly in the forms of mass media with their unprecedented ability to shape public opinion.

Otherwise, the United States remains its meddlesome, destructive self, intruding in Panama, Cuba, Mexico, Chile and Nicaragua endlessly. Mired in corrupt political systems, Latin Americans continue to exhibit the distressing habit of exterminating precisely those individuals most likely to deliver them from oppression: Villarroel in Bolivia, Gaitán in Colombia, Allende in Chile, to name just a few. The days of jubilee seem as remote as ever in a region where a high government official announces that the most sacred things in the world are, in descending importance, property, public order and human life.

Against long odds, however, Galeano clings to optimism. His hopefulness is embodied in characters such as Miguel Mármol, a Salvadoran Indian who rises to become a leader in his country's revolutionary movement. Mármol, whose life spans virtually all of the 20th Century, appears regularly throughout Galeano's history, each time with greater wisdom, dedication and resilience. A clearly symbolic figure, Mármol cannot be killed by the forces of oppression; he remains vigorous to the very end of Galeano's chronicle, still conspiring.

As he did in the earlier volumes of his trilogy, Galeano renders *Century of the Wind* in a series of vignettes, usually of three or four paragraphs, which together constitute a historical mosaic. Galeano consulted nearly 500 histories, literary works, journalistic accounts and official documents during the preparation of this volume, and he has used his sources well. Arranged chronologically, the vignettes cover an extraordinary range of historical figures, events and cultural phenomena.

In *Century of the Wind,* the reader will encounter Thomas Edison and Pablo Neruda and learn how the appearance of Donald Duck has played a part in Latin American experience. Galeano's early work as a political cartoonist in his native Uruguay evidences itself in his ironic and economical style of writing.

Many readers in this country will find Galeano's obvious sympathies for socialist and Marxist causes offensive. Be that as it may, *Century of the Wind* remains a compelling work and represents a point of view widely held in Latin America.

> Raymund A. Paredes, "A Telling Chronicle of the Americas," in Los Angeles Times Book Review, *July 17, 1988, p. 2.*

Amanda Hopkinson

In Europe, the French got there first. Not only in staging their revolution but also in revolutionising ways of writing about it, and so about history. Earlier this century, Georges Soboul coined the term "popular history" to distinguish it from the Great Names variety. Its logical apotheosis was in the documentation of "the role of the crowd" painstakingly brought to light by another historian of the French Revolution in the 1960s, George Rudé. At about the same time E. H. Carr was shaking the foundations of English academic tradition by asking, "What is History?" in a paperback that circulated well beyond the confines of his Cambridge orbit.

It was left to a philosopher, Marc Bloch, to note the existence of what he called "hierarchic bilinguilism—two languages are side by side, the one popular, the other learned". In the west this has meant that even history "from the grassroots up" is almost exclusively conducted within the walls of hallowed academe. Any conclusions have tended to be published by university presses and bought by specialists. Major exceptions are the numerous biographies of more eccentric or romantic individual protagonists. Nonetheless, to gain any kind of respectability (and reviews) even these are expected to rely heavily on original research and source material.

Eduardo Galeano is proud to stand outside all such internal debates and traditions. Uruguayan by birth, an exile by force of circumstance, a satirist and editor by profession, a socialist by conviction and a writer by vocation, he has again revolutionised what we are pleased carelessly to call history. Scorning vaunted historical texts and primary source material, his stock-in-trade is what is accessible: none of his references belongs in archives, many are out in paperback editions or in the pages of literary magazines.

Century of the Wind is the third book of [his *Memory of Fire* trilogy] dedicated to the history of the Americas. Starting with *Genesis* and the creation myths handed down orally from the earliest pre-Colombian civilisations, Galeano has compiled a patchwork of voices that, in the present volume, reaches the present century. In some ways there is remarkably little distinction between the two beginnings: what more apocalyptic birth, after all, than that headed **"1901: in all Latin America"**, which reads,

> In the villages and cities south of the Rio Grande, Jesus Christ marches to the cemeteries, a dying beast lustrous with blood, and behind him with torches and hymns comes the crowd, tattered, battered people afflicted with a thousand ills that no doctor or faith-healer would know how to cure, but deserving a fate that no prophet or fortune-teller could possibly divine?

The Wind sweeps all before it, leaving the reader breathless. Page after page of betrayals and atrocities by those in power alternate with episodes of extraordinary courage and faith on the part of the oppressed. Yet Galeano's oppressed are never simply victims, nor do they exist *en masse* as a crowd or even a people. Instead, we learn of long unsung individuals, like Delmira Agustini, who "sang to the fevers of love without shame, and was condemned by those who punish women for what they applaud in men, because chastity is a feminine duty, and desire, like reason, a male privilege". Or of Joao Candido, the "Black Admiral", who led a naval mutiny in the bay of Rio de Janeiro following the flogging to death of a sailor. When the government betrays its amnesty to the mutineers, reinstates flogging and hunts down the rebels, "the Black Admiral ends up in a lunatic asylum".

The literary voice is Galeano's own. Though ballads to Zapata, stories recounted from memory and dialogue from newspaper reports are a part of the fabric of his work, virtually all material is transcribed by the author. Passionate and lyrical, lucidly visual, alternating merciless humour at the expense of the rich with an unsentimental tenderness for those who suffer, Galeano parades the subjects of history before us in a dazzling frieze.

Galeano defies geography much as he does history, insisting on the Americas as a common continent and on domestic detail as the proper domain of the historian. Read, reread and keep returning to his trilogy: no politically significant event is omitted, but all is revealed through new eyes, to create a radically different panorama.

> Amanda Hopkinson, "History of the Americas," in New Statesman & Society, *Vol. 49, No. 2, May 12, 1989, p. 36.*

Jay Parini

One of the many interesting things about Eduardo Galeano's latest work, *The Book of Embraces,* is the way it moves beyond the stuffy confines of genre. A caricaturist

as well as a writer, Mr. Galeano has confected an ingenious blend of image and text that moves from autobiographical vignettes to philosophical musings, from reporting to storytelling. Of the almost 200 separate passages
that make up this volume, a large number are accompanied by illustrative emblems: a silver goblet that contains
a skull-faced miniature gentleman and his lady in 19th-
century garb, a typewriter fractured by a biplane, two children carrying a mirror in which death is pictured as a skeleton playing a guitar, a horn with a cockroach crawling
out of it.

Far from being merely decorative, these images derive
their power from specific contexts. The broken typewriter,
for instance, appears with a lyric passage near the end of
the book, called **"The Air and the Wind,"** in which Mr.
Galeano writes:

> Sometimes I recognize myself in others. I recog-
> nize myself in those who will endure, friends
> who will shelter me, beautiful holy fools of jus-
> tice and flying creatures of beauty and other
> bums and vagrants who walk the earth and will
> continue walking, just as the stars will continue
> in the night and the waves in the sea. Then, when
> I recognize myself in them, I am the air, coming
> to know myself as part of the wind.

The author himself is one of the world's many "flying
creatures of beauty," his typewriter a kind of flying machine.

Born in Uruguay in 1940, Mr. Galeano worked as a journalist and caricaturist until his left-wing political views
brought him into conflict with his Government. In 1973,
he fled to Argentina, where he helped found the journal
Crisis with a friend, Fico Vogelius, who is fondly memorialized in *The Book of Embraces.* Political events in Argentina drove him, in 1976, into further exile in Spain. He was
not able to return to Uruguay, where he now lives, until
1984.

This factual skeleton of the author's life is given flesh and
blood in his strangely beautiful book, in which poetry, fiction, autobiography, history, fantasy and political commentary mingle and reinforce one another in unexpected
ways. Mr. Galeano's unusual technique derives, in part,
from his masterwork, *Memory of Fire,* which appeared in
this country between 1985 and 1988 in three volumes
beautifully translated by Cedric Belfrage, who died while
at work on *The Book of Embraces.* In that vast and visionary epic, images from centuries of life in the Americas
were combined to form a shimmering mosaic of history
and political commentary.

Yet *Memory of Fire* was an impersonal book compared
with *The Book of Embraces,* which in many ways retells
the same history within the context of an autobiographical
narrative. The new book, for instance, records a number
of loves and personal losses. "I can't sleep," says Mr.
Galeano in an entry called **"The Night/1."** "There is a
woman stuck between my eyelids. I would tell her to get
out if I could. But there is a woman stuck in my throat."
Elsewhere, he writes movingly of the loss of a child.

Like Gabriel García Márquez, whose influence is palpable

here, Mr. Galeano adores absurdities and idiosyncrasies
of any kind. There is, for example, the wonderful tale of
the man who loved to tell funny stories. People came from
everywhere to hear him, and "wherever he was . . .
laughter would break out. When he told stories people
would come from all around to laugh and the house would
be packed. At the funerals, they had to upend the coffin
so everybody could fit—and thus the dead man stood up
to listen with due respect to all that was being so gracefully
said."

Pablo Neruda, the great Chilean poet, is present here too,
as a friend to Mr. Galeano but, more important, as an influence, as seen in passages like this, from an entry entitled
"Callings": "The moon calls to the sea and the sea calls
to the humble stream, which flows on and on from wherever it springs in search of the sea, no matter how far away
it may lie, and growing as it flows, the stream rushes on
until no mountain can hold back its surge."

Like every book by Mr. Galeano, this one is most centrally
a call for justice. He sides with the oppressed: street people, prisoners of conscience, Indians, workers. He admires
all the obvious heroes of the left, like Augusto César
Sandino and Salvador Allende Gossens, but he adds to
these an array of unexpected, unsung heroes—people who
resisted oppression in their own small ways.

Read naïvely, Mr. Galeano could easily be seen as a knee-
jerk leftist. But he retains an edge of ironic detachment
that gives his fierce judgments credibility. ("More than a
few northern intellectuals," he observes, "marry southern
revolutions for the sheer pleasure of becoming widow-
ers.") To be sure, Mr. Galeano is relentless in his condemnation of raw capitalism, which he sees as a "system of isolation" in which "your neighbor is neither your brother
nor your lover. Your neighbor is a competitor, an enemy,
an obstacle to clear or an object to use."

Thus *The Book of Embraces* is, finally, an argument for
communal values, values like those practiced by some of
the indigenous peoples of the New World before the conquistadors took over. "Community," he writes, "the communal mode of production and life . . . is the oldest of
American traditions, the most American of all. It belongs
to the earliest days and the first people, but it also belongs
to the times ahead and anticipates a new New World."

Mr. Galeano's invocation of the European "discovery" of
the New World, which had such tragic consequences for
the original inhabitants of the Americas, is timely. As the
quincentenary of Columbus's voyage nears, this book
forces us once again to recall that millions of people already lived here in 1492, yet the landscape was pristine.
In 500 years, we have very nearly destroyed the hemisphere, and nothing short of a rediscovery of communal
values will save it.

> *Jay Parini, "There Is a Woman Stuck in My
> Throat," in* The New York Times Book Re-
> view, *April 21, 1991, p. 14.*

Rockwell Gray

In his earlier three-volume poetic history of Latin America, *Memory of Fire,* the Uruguayan journalist and caricaturist Eduardo Galeano ranged freely across both Americas to capture the inner drama of his continent's agony. His technique entailed a huge collage of images and ideas, with recurring motifs and interanimating texts and tales. The method of his current book is the same, though the material is more personal and autobiographical. As with the earlier work, Cedric Belfrage has provided a crisp, elegant translation.

In the third volume of the *Memory* trilogy, [*Century of the Wind*], Galeano traced the pillaging of the continent and its repeated collapse into political violence. Himself a double exile (he fled Uruguay for Argentina in 1973 and the latter for Spain in 1976), he has witnessed both the brutality of two military dictatorships and—in Spain—the rebirth of democracy.

Galeano's present title [*The Book of Embraces*] ("abrazos" in Spanish is a widely used term of salute and affection) provides his answer to the greed and terror that plunge people into panicky self-interest and suspicious isolation: the common condition of those subject to totalitarian control. As he notes, "The system feeds neither the body nor the heart: many are condemned to starve for lack of bread and many more for lack of embraces."

The solidarity of the brotherhood Galeano invokes is the proper personal—and, ultimately, political—response to a bitter history that, in his view, began with Spanish conquest and has continued into the various reigns of the Batistas, Somozas, Perons, Videlas, Pinochets—the parade goes on and on.

In the earlier trilogy, Galeano borrowed something of his perspective from the Chilean poet Pablo Neruda, whose immense *Canto General* may have inspired the author's project of "reading" patterns of truth in the historical jumble of coups, exiles, outcries, disenfranchisements, tortures and the quiet triumph of laughter and storytelling.

In this new gathering of material, Galeano has created a polyphonic autobiography that comprehends all the voices he has heeded, echoed and saluted. Organized under topical headings, his stylized entries manage to fuse poetry, philosophy and politics. *Embraces* is also a study in the many varieties of exile—territorial, cultural and psychological. Galeano's own enforced wanderings are repeated in the stories of other Latin Americans whose lot is alienation.

At times the author falls into cliches about the evils of colonialism, the sufferings of indigenous peoples or the mindless fetters of bureaucracy. But his vision is at heart playful and inventive, making him a cousin to writers who have taught us to see Latin America through the brilliantly distorted mirror of their work: Gabriel García Márquez, Jose Donoso or Carlos Fuentes.

Not himself a novelist, Galeano knows that the deepest truth is fictive, to be perceived in the patternings of the poet's or the artist's eye. If some of his paradoxes are flat—"Politicians speak but say nothing." "Schools teach ignorance"—others are deft and provocative: "At the beginning of the twentieth century, Uruguay was a twenty-first century country. Now, at the end of the twentieth century, Uruguay belongs to the nineteenth."

Something similar might be said of history's trick on other parts of the world, but the author believes his own continent (and perhaps ours as well) exists in a time warp, where "Idiot memory" always recreates itself and builds a future from the freshly reappropriated past. If Latin America is arrested in tragic repetition, Galeano would break the nightmare's hold by expressing "the magical reality which I find at the core of the hideous reality of America."

The magic and the horror are not far to seek, he believes. History is declaring itself always, but often in ways we cannot recognize or fail to document. The poetic historian must heed the colloquial voice of events, the background rumors of things, and make them speak to each other and to the world. Hence Galeano's stress on anecdotes, graffiti, newspaper advertisements, dreams and propaganda: Fantasies and fears, faint voices and transient moments, carry metaphors of essential truth.

Galeano's obvious gift is his capacity to make a symphonic whole of such fragments, as if he were reading a thick, sometimes surreal newspaper and seeing all its stories and images in necessary connection. His eye is akin to the skilled photographer's, and his ear to that of the novelist upon whom nothing is lost. (pp. 6, 11)

> *Rockwell Gray, "A Tragic Continent's Fantasies and Dreams," in* Chicago Tribune—Books, *June 30, 1991, pp. 6, 11.*

Galeano on his *Memory of Fire* trilogy:

In *Memory of Fire* . . . the voice of my conscience and the will of my hand coincide absolutely. I was looking for little stories that would reveal the great ones, the universe seen through a keyhole. The little things about little people reveal the history of America—the *masked history,* not a history officially reduced to figures of bronze or marble. I was looking for the other side of it, which is the daily life of common people.

I was looking for stories with electricity. I was looking also for those magic moments when history speaks a perfect language of symbols, for history expresses itself as a poet through metaphors.

> *Eduardo Galeano, in an interview in* Publishers Weekly, *June 3, 1988.*

Alan West

I've always thought of Eduardo Galeano as a counterpoint to [Mexican poet] Octavio Paz. The latter's imagistic intensity usually yields to dualistic, glib abstractions; Galeano, even while dealing with the same themes as Paz, roots his ideas in historical moments. He will begin with an anecdote then turn it into a flight of fantasy, a symbol of resistance, a plunge into healthy contradiction, or a celebration of life. Paz fires metaphors away, nonstop, with interpretive verve. Galeano lobs a description and lets the reader draw the metaphors.

Galeano's micro-memory is evident in *The Book of Embraces* when he speaks of Fico Vogelius, an Argentinian businessman who helped finance *Crisis,* the magazine Galeano edited from 1974 to 1976 in Buenos Aires after fleeing the military dictatorship in his native Uruguay. Argentina soon had its own dictatorship; Vogelius was kidnapped and tortured by the Argentinian military, then released. At that point Galeano is in exile in Barcelona, and Vogelius calls him from London shortly after his release. He wants to meet with Galeano, saying there's lots to talk about, and adding, "I'm not sorry for anything."

The Argentinian dictatorship ends in 1983, and both men return home. In 1985 Vogelius decides to revive *Crisis.* At that time he learns that he has cancer; doctors say he'll live until November. The episode ends as follows:

> He walked around like a corpse, collapsing from one operation to another, but a defiant light shone in his eyes. *Crisis* reappeared in April of 1986. The day following its rebirth, half a year beyond all prognostications, Fico allowed himself to die.

Galeano tells Vogelius's story in a spare prose that leaves a lingering sense of the passion, pain, and determination of one who believed so strongly in culture and free expression.

The Book of Embraces is in some ways a continuation of Galeano's three-volume opus *Memory of Fire.* The polyphonic structure, the episodic narration, the ongoing engagement with history, and the struggle to avoid the terrible consequences of forgetting are equally present in this volume. The tone shifts from absurd to hilarious, with a rueful perspicacity and a more personal outlook than in *Memory of Fire.* It is part diary, part chronicle, part autobiography, part prose poem, part document. Even graffiti make their make their way into the text. Some are grotesquely funny, like the one in Melo, Uruguay—"Assist the police: torture yourself"—while others wander into slapstick: "Everybody makes promises and nobody keeps them. Vote for nobody."

Galeano's book is a celebration of Latin American oral traditions, a reworking of our penchant for storytelling. Words are a refuge. We tell jokes because reality is almost unbearable; we tell stories to entertain, to console, to tell the truth. They are the guardians of our memory and our identity. We use words to struggle, as an emblem of freedom, as a way of maintaining a sense of community in the face of being uprooted. Galeano's work has always strived to create a common history of Latin America. This harks back to the old dream of one huge Latin American homeland, but Galeano is a little more sanguine and modest—his contribution to unity is at the level of human and historical understanding. He does not shy away from our miseries; his sense of solidarity, and of the possibility of societies based on cooperation instead of murderous competition, is not idealistic. He finds new evidence every day,

in those acts of generosity, courage, and resistance that he documents in loving detail.

Maybe that explains his concern for the conjunction of word and deed:

> Bureaucracy . . . sees to it that action, words and thoughts never meet. Action stays at the workplace, words in meetings, and thoughts on the pillow. A considerable part of the power of Che Guevara, I think, that mysterious energy that far outlives his death and his errors, comes from a very simple fact: he was that rare kind of person who says what he thinks and does what he says.

Galeano isn't urging writers to drop their pens and take to the hills, but perhaps he is saying that memory need not be simply the tomb of dreams.

> *Alan West, "Fond Embraces," in* The Village Voice, *Vol. XXXVI, No. 27, July 2, 1991, p. 71.*

Alan Ryan

Great writers live on a tightrope and risk their necks with every word. Even the aim to write seriously is dangerous, because the writer must assume that his feelings are universal feelings, that his insights are always true, that his expression of what he feels—what, in fact, he knows—can be conveyed in mere words from his head and heart to the reader's. One false step and brilliant insights turn suddenly to cliché and universal truths become banal.

In his *Memory of Fire* trilogy, Uruguayan writer Eduardo Galeano triumphed on the tightrope. In hundreds of vignettes drawn from all the history of the Americas and linking memory with mystery, he made it possible to see, as if for the first time, a world we had known all along. In *The Book of Embraces,* Galeano goes out on the tightrope and then levitates in the air above it.

Like *Memory of Fire, The Book of Embraces* is constructed of vignettes, a risky and difficult technique that leaves the writer no room for misjudgment, and that requires the reader to participate by conjuring up the invisible correlations between its fragments. And Galeano's subject is nothing less than the variety of human life and love.

This is a much more personal work than *Memory of Fire,* rich with private moments and events and friends and stories. Some of the figures here are nameless but memorable, like the colonel facing a firing squad who gives the orders himself, or the family openly weeping before a dying grandmother so she will know how much she is loved. Other portraits are of celebrities, like the Brazilian painter Candido Portinari making a pronouncement on art, and of Galeano's fellow Uruguayan writers, Juan Carlos Onetti with tears in his eyes and Mario Benedetti, living "in Buenos Aires in times of terror" and carrying five keys on his key ring, "the keys to five houses, to five friends: the keys that proved his salvation."

Galeano, as he records himself in these pages, lives life vividly, feeling intensely every loss, love, pain and pleasure, treasuring the books he reads and crying at movies. Fear, bereavement, loneliness, all are the stuff of life. In a novel by Louise Erdrich, he finds an old man who is happy because his memories are gone and a child who is happy because he does not yet have memories. "This, I imagine, is perfect felicity," Galeano writes. "I want no part of it."

A thread of dreams links many of these vignettes. On one plane, people he knows dream of events happening to their loved ones far away. On another, "fleas dream of buying themselves a dog." And on still another, even God dreams. "I've been suffering from insomnia," Galeano imagines God saying. "And I like sleeping, I really do, because when I sleep, I dream. Then I become a lover, I burn myself in the brief flame of fleeting love, I am a strolling player, a deep-sea fisherman, or a Gypsy fortune teller," In Galeano's world, even God longs for the tastes and feel of life.

The book is occasionally punctuated with wonderful stabs of vicious wit. After noting that his religious upbringing failed to make him either afraid or a believer, he allows that, in any case, he will no doubt go to hell if he deserves it. But all will not be lost. "That way," he says, "I'll escape purgatory, which will be packed with dreadful middle-class tourists, and in the end, justice will be done." This is worthy of being recorded next to Mark Twain's dictum, "Heaven for climate; hell for society." And Twain himself would have appreciated some of the ironic graffiti Galeano records from his travels, like this comment on a wall in Uruguay: "Assist the police: torture yourself." . . .

Some of the vignettes in this book are clear as daylight, some are enigmatic. Taken together, these fragments are really fractions, but fractions that add up in some mysterious, non-arithmetic way to a total we couldn't otherwise imagine, a total as personal as Galeano's view of the world and, at the same time, as universal as our own.

> *Alan Ryan, "The Dream World of Eduardo Galeano," in* Book World—The Washington Post, *July 7, 1991, p. 7.*

Eduardo Galeano   [Interview with Bronwyn Mills]

[*Mills*]: *Since your tour of the States* [*in the Spring of 1991*], *what have you been doing?*

[Galeano]: I am now working on an article to publish next year. I also intend to return to work on some tales that I was writing before my trip. These are stories from the popular tradition, but they take off from there—they are like a popular Latin story that is very educational and very juicy, but a structure in which I can create . . . it's a way to free up my imagination. It's a book that I am doing with a new Brazilian writer, named Borges—Jose Borges. He is a storyteller, a Brazilian poet who interprets from an old tradition from the Northeast, native to Cordel. They are little things.

The Northeast is the poorest part of Brazil—

Culturally, it isn't the poorest, it is the richest. There you will find the most genial music, splendid sculptures, and paintings of the highest quality, and these are artists from the village, unknown and anonymous. It's what makes alive, keeps alive, the character of this region.

Jose lives in a little village in the interior of the Northeast, and he goes to the public squares and listens to the people singing these verses as they sell their wares. They are songs about their travels, about the latest news. He puts them on paper, makes up the proofs, prints them, sells them in the markets.

Some of these markets are going to die out. This is a culture condemned, lamentably, because television is turning the entire world into a vast suburb of Dallas. So there is no place for these poets. This is an area where you find one of the last expressions of this tradition, so we are working on this book for nothing . . .

So how do you deal with a world that is being invaded by TV?

It's the cultural reality of the actual world. A writer is sort of a prehistoric animal—[we laugh]—because the new generation in general is part of the visual culture being imposed on all four corners of the world. It's like the story of [Romanian dictator] Ceausescu during his crisis. In place of the posters with his face on it in all the stores, the Romanians substituted photographs of all the personalities in the series "Dallas."

Then what's the health of the imagination in the late twentieth century?

To begin with, I think the creative imagination is very obstinate, and this obstinancy shows itself, each time, when conditions are most difficult, not when they are most easy. I'm an optimist, despite all evidence to the contrary, a blind optimist, maybe. But for my part, I continue to believe that the written word has a destiny in our lives. It is capable of affecting readers' imaginations, freeing up their images of wholeness, and it has a creative function that, in my judgment, is greater than the audio/visual culture that surrounds it.

For example?

Well, when I was a little boy, I read Emilio Salgieri, an Italian author who wrote adventure stories. His novels made such an impression on me! Later I heard that Salgieri was adapted for TV, and then Sandocan [a character in his stories] took on the facial features of the actor who interpreted him. Now, I belong to a culture where I can invent what is happening from my own imagination, as a part of the stimulus from the words of Salgieri. I still think in terms of the multiple functions of literature.

When you talk about culture—one place you said, "It's communication or it's nothing—" or, at least, that's how they translated what you said—

Yes, that's my deep faith—

You think we are still forming it, it's still alive, it's still dynamic?

Yes. I believe that as soon as there is a contradiction, an opposition, an antithesis, there is a kind of stubbornness, an obstinate creative energy. That is to say, as creative as the media seems, the channels of communication are very incommunicative. The goals of the media are realized through a process of alienation that conditions the human mind, and makes us lose it.

There's a cuentatita *in your latest book, where a man writes to a famous TV personality, and he says something like, "When I look at you, do you look at me?" When the reciprocity is not there, what is it?*

That is the consumer's problem in a consumer society. The journey is a one-way trip because it is a trip that goes but doesn't return. . . . most communication is uncommunicated intelligence, because the power of expression and creation is reduced each time it is not used. Take the common man, as we call him, each time, he is without the opportunity to express himself.

The idea of *Crisis* was not just to express opinions, but to receive from the original source, to help people be heard, to enable them to have a response. When there isn't the capacity to hear, it's difficult for anyone to speak. Now there's a kind of worship, a love of speaking in an modishly elegant and mature language, but for us language is not a matter of modish elegance and maturity if there's no risk.

All this seems to fit in with your idea of writing books that people can read to one another—you've been doing that for a while—

Yes, **Memory of Fire, Days and Nights of Love and War** . . . they are windows, little windows that are opened for time to pass through, because **Memory of Fire** is a house that the reader constructs, that is to say, using the window, he comes into the past as though it were the present. Now I am turning my attention to much larger things—legends, tales that are more extensive, longer than **Embraces** or **Memory of Fire**—because the material demands more space, four or five pages. For me that's like a *latifundio*—a ranch.

It must be more like being a poet than a novelist; but you have written a novel—

Yes, I wrote a novel—yes, two novels—but now, no. I don't feel comfortable that **Memory of Fire** is announced like a novel. I think it's not a novel, it is nothing one can characterize by genre. It has much of the novel, but it isn't a novel . . . I think my things are unclassifiable—they have much of the chronicle, the poem, the tale, the novel, the testimony, and also the essay. It's not important to me that this is so; I celebrate that it is so—

*I was noticing how you talked way back in **Open Veins**, and I could see how you could make the same point with the story, the* cuenta, *whatever you needed, like a quilt—*

Yes, I think it captured the reality and the dignity—the fact that present reality is part of history, that past reality is part of present reality and that [mixture] is an aspect of history's function. That kind of reality is dignified as part of the same current of living breath that makes us human beings here on this earth. There is a continuum and a stubborn search for the dignity of history, for human dignity, for the real story beneath the surface. We aren't fatally condemned to make the history of a place valuable, to be made to feel that we can only be protagonists when we resign ourselves to suffering a future that is unimaginable and unacceptable.

(*In connection with* **Open Veins,** *the conversation turns to the cocaine trade as the ultimate consumer product that, in the words of Galeano, "makes us sick in order to take us to the hospital." He further characterizes the values such a system needs—"egotism, competitiveness, the idea that my neighbor is not my friend or lover but my rival."*)

I suppose, from a certain point of view, the energy for change in a society filled with drugs is diffused. Drugs have the most disabling effect possible, for within the last twenty or thirty years of all this, it has become obvious all over Latin America. I am a survivor in an unbalanced generation. Many of my companions were assassinated or tortured or disappeared or lost in the shitty error that separated us during the military dictatorship that rained state terror down on our heads. But when I was fifteen years old, politics was much more. It was the capacity to be located in an embrace.

It was a generation that equivocated a lot. It committed many grave errors in Latin America, no doubt, but the errors were born of love, the will to change reality. It is the magic that has made my generation the one that found a tremendous capacity for indignation, that is, for social justice. I found that this capacity for indignation corresponds to a profound hunger for change. I sense the new generation is not going to give itself away, or at least not in the same way, and this is largely the result of television and drugs.

You know, television is also a drug. It produces the same distaste for reality and invites you to a solitary ceremony—of consumption and prefabricated emotions that rule you. I sense that there is a growing tendency toward passivity, that in these last twenty or thirty years, everything has changed. Civilization can't stand to look itself in the face. Because we can't, it makes us passive. I don't say that simply in political terms—it's not only what people might expect from a political dictatorship—but this is a passivity towards living, a passivity in vital terms and all the more, what worries me most is the new generation. After all that, without doubt, I recognize a virtue we don't have. It seems to me, for one, that there is a certain healthy insolence towards dogma, toward staid morality, as opposed to a certain tendency to rationalize, characteristic of my generation. At times, it made life seem like it would swallow us up. . . . Now there is a much bigger faith in the world of emotions and that doesn't seem so good, because I believe when we look at a person, they are part reason, part passion, and a third part mystery. (pp. 1, 14)

Eduardo Galeano and Bronwyn Mills, in an interview, in The Bloomsbury Review, *Vol. 11, No. 8, December, 1991, pp. 1, 14.*

Bronwyn Mills

Where to begin? In Eduardo Galeano's **The Book of Embraces,** the epigram suggests we look to memory and to the heart in order to consider what is recorded. Certainly, his previous work, *Memory of Fire,* deals impressively with the collective memory (some might say the collective nightmare) that is New World history. *Days and Nights of Love and War* . . . is similar, and all three works use the heart as a filter.

We are not being invited to look at the world through heart-shaped glasses and praise the Emperor's new wardrobe. Rather, Galeano invokes the Spanish idea of *voluntad,* which he uses to describe the commitment of his generation to change, a word which carries with it the nuance of the heart. It can mean "will; free will"; Cassell's *Spanish/English Dictionary* even adds the implication, "love," of all things. Both personal and political, the subject of *Embraces* is events and memories of events touched by enormous courage and love in the face of terrible cruelty:

> It was extremely cold as always, but the sun was shining. Someone got him [Jose Toha] a nice hot cup of coffee and Jorquera the black man whistled a Gardel tango for him—one of those old tangos he loved so well.

> His legs trembled and his knees gave way with every step, but Toha danced that tango. He danced it with a broom, one as gaunt as the other, Toha pressing the handle of the broom against his patrician face, his eyes shut tight with emotion, until at one turn, he fell broken to the ground and couldn't get up.

> He was never seen again.

The form Galeano uses, the short paragraph or two, the brief *cuenta,* the *ventana* is very Latin: Jorge Luis Borges used it, for one, and it can be found in the work of Cristina Perri Rossi, a fellow Uruguayan, as well as many others. It is a building block, in a sense, large enough for a memory, an image, a thought; and Galeano uses it to build a nonlinear account of what it felt like to return from exile, what his thoughts are and were after twelve difficult years of exile. It is, in effect, the journal of a *sobreviviente,* a survivor, one who lives through.

Of course, there were those like Jose Toha, who did not return. There are conditions that persist. Evil has not fled with the toppling of the dictators. At best, it merely lies dormant, and this cross section of good and evil, too, is skillfully expressed by the technique Galeano uses, his layering of past and present and the way that, consequently, the reader can experience the past through the present. It is not objective, nor does it seek to be:

> And on the banks of the San Juan River, the old poet [Jose Coronel Urtecho] told me that there is no fucking reason to pay attention to the fanatics of objectivity:

> "Don't worry," he said to me. "That's how it should be. Those who make objectivity a religion are liars. They are scared of human pain. They don't want to be objective, it's a lie: they want to be objects, so as not to suffer."

Galeano attempts to combine what he calls the "Marriage of Heart and Mind," exemplified by the word *sentipensante*—thinking/feeling—as applied to "language that speaks the truth."

Further, the book was written very specifically to be read aloud. One can open it anywhere—"listen to this," one can say to a friend or a lover, even an older child. Such possibilities make the act of reading a communal event, rather than a solitary one. One not only visualizes, imagines, and ponders meaning, one can immediately share them, talk about them, smile at someone else's discovery—clever, this Galeano.

Does it succeed? *Embraces* does not seem as "heavy" as *Memory of Fire*: It has Galeano's own drawings and collages scattered throughout. A fish floats across the page, carrying an opened umbrella; a cobra clanks about in armor, carrying a sword; a cornet blooms three horns, and three hands pour out from them. We are not used to such frank outpourings of whimsy. Anyone remembering the "100,000 points of light" reference in George Bush's inaugural speech will wince at Galeano describing the people of the world as each shining with their own distinct light.

The book is deceptively simple, and it lacks the curlicues of academic writing. Without much forethought, one might call its style journalistic. But that is, I think, too cursory. The book wears well. Reading it is a little like making love: The first time is a little awkward, one does not always know where things are—the reader and the writer may not know each other very well—then, as you do become more intimately acquainted, the act of communion becomes deeper and more satisfying.

With the composite approach Galeano uses, we can see the snippets of the imagination—the thoughts and visions and dreams that accumulate—almost before they are assembled into a complete work. In other words, we see the process. That, of course, is on the technical level. Interestingly, we can also see how the imagination has moved in the life of the author and those he encounters. From the tango of Toha in a concentration camp, to the use of sign language among political prisoners, to the parable of the guinea pig who will not leave its cage from fear, Galeano works to show us what we must at some instinctive level have known all along. It applies to children who grow up whole in schizophrenic families, to those who survive the torture and chaos imposed on them by bad governments and careless bureaucrats—the human imagination is our best ticket to survival. (pp. 1, 30)

Bronwyn Mills, in a review of "The Book of Embraces," in The Bloomsbury Review, *Vol. 11, No. 8, December, 1991, pp. 1, 30.*

Additional coverage of Galeano's life and career is contained in the following sources published by Gale Research: *Contemporary Authors,* Vols. 29-32, rev. ed.; *Contemporary Authors New Revision Series,* Vols. 13, 32; and *Hispanic Writers.*

Graham Greene

1904-1991

(Full name Graham Henry Greene) English novelist, essayist, dramatist, short story writer, critic, travel writer, and author of children's books.

The following entry provides an overview of Greene's major works. For further information on his life and works, see *CLC*, Volumes 1, 3, 6, 9, 14, 18, 27, and 37.

INTRODUCTION

A prominent English novelist, Greene is noted both for his best-selling suspense novels, including *Stamboul Train* and *Our Man in Havana*, and for more serious works of fiction, particularly *The Power and the Glory*. Although Greene made a distinction between his popular and his serious novels, critics have observed that they are often closely related in their themes and characters. The protagonists of Greene's works are typically people torn by personal struggles with Roman Catholic concepts of sin and salvation, reflecting the author's concern with religious and moral questions.

The son of a public-school headmaster, Greene grew up at his father's school in the village of Berkhamsted, northwest of London. The regimented life and lack of privacy at the school, along with his father's constant moralizing on the sinfulness of sex, deeply affected Greene. A withdrawn child, he complained of terrible boredom, attempted suicide several times as a youth, and suffered a nervous breakdown at the age of sixteen. Despite a period of psychoanalysis, Greene attempted suicide six more times during his years as a student at Balliol College, Oxford, in the 1920s. After leaving Oxford, Greene worked as a sub-editor on the Nottingham *Journal* and the London *Times,* later serving as a film critic and then literary editor for the Spectator. While in Nottingham, Greene converted to Roman Catholicism. In his memoirs he explains he did so partly to satisfy his future wife and partly "to kill the time," but the Roman Catholic religion would later become a powerful force in both his life and literary works. Greene published his first novel, *The Man Within,* in 1929; the suspense novel *Stamboul Train* appeared in 1932 and was a popular success. Over the rest of his long and prolific career, he would continue to produce almost one book per year, often traveling to such places as the Tabasco and Chiapas regions of Mexico, French Indochina, the Belgian Congo, Haiti, and Cuba during periods of social and political unrest to gather details for the settings of his novels. Greene died in 1991.

Most critics have adopted Greene's division of his works into "entertainments" and "novels." According to Greene, his entertainments emphasize plot and setting while his novels focus on characterization. Conventional

thrillers in the tradition of adventure writers H. Rider Haggard and John Buchan, the entertainments depict spies slipping into enemy territory against a tawdry background of people fleeing from one city to another. Settings in the entertainments are either exotic locales, as in *Our Man in Havana,* or familiar places torn by war, such as Blitz-era England in *The Ministry of Fear.* The distinction between the novels and the entertainments is not always clear-cut: works such as *Brighton Rock,* although labeled entertainments, make characters' motivations and backgrounds a major concern, while novels like *The Power and the Glory* thread the character's development around chases and intrigues that are hallmarks of the entertainments.

Some critics have further subdivided Greene's novels into "Catholic novels," which focus on the characters' religious concerns, and "political novels," which explore the consequences of their characters' aloofness and ideological naivete. Catholic novels such as *The End of the Affair* and *A Burnt-Out Case* show their protagonists' struggles and failures to live up to religious beliefs they are unable to deny and the tragic consequences these characters face for striving ineptly toward their moral ideals. The political novels also portray characters who are to some extent both corrupt and idealistic. The protagonists in *The Comedians, The Quiet American,* and Greene's other political novels struggle to reconcile their distaste for involvement in the world with their grudging need to fight against the degradation and injustice that their society thrusts upon them. Both the Catholic and the political novels depict shabby environs and feature spies, murderers, and adulterers as main characters. The protagonists in "Greeneland," as critics have dubbed this fictional world, think of, talk about, and in many cases commit suicide. They see human love as treachery and consequently try to withdraw from human contact, afterward discovering that they are driven to involve themselves in the world. The people in Greene's novels are continually on the run from their crimes and their consciences. Irony abounds in these works, and virtuous characters generally prove more dangerous than corrupt ones. Many critics feel that Greene's agonized liars, killers, and secret agents reflect the sense of moral compromise inherent in people living in a society plagued by war and corruption, while his decrepit settings symbolize the ethical and physical decay that, in Greene's view, distinguishes the modern world.

Greene has been the source of much contention among critics; he has been both lauded as a master novelist and decried as a hack melodramatist. The majority of critics agree that Greene was an able storyteller, particularly in his delineation of setting and his skillful plot constructions, but opinions vary widely concerning his ability to create believable characters and artfully communicate themes. Some of his works depict highly unlikely characters caught in improbable situations. For example, the protagonist of *A Burnt-Out Case* is a famous Catholic architect of churches who, in an attempt to escape Catholicism and Western society, flees to a part of the Congo inhabited almost exclusively by devout European Catholics. The main character of *Our Man in Havana* is a vacuum cleaner salesman-cum-spy who ends up decorated by the Queen for supplying the British government with plans of supposed enemy military installations which are actually outsized sketches of vacuum cleaner parts. In such works as *Brighton Rock* or *The Heart of the Matter,* the characters are more lifelike, but critics point to an unusual tendency toward theological musing among the gangsters, waitresses, and prostitutes. Some believe this to be Greene's heavy-handed way of inserting profound matters into his novels without making them integral to the narrative.

Commentators disagree as to which novel is Greene's masterpiece. Most cite the Catholic novels of the 1930s and 1940s, especially *The Power and the Glory, Brighton Rock,* or *The End of the Affair.* Some critics also include the 1966 political novel *The Comedians* among Greene's best works, although the general consensus holds that Greene's talents declined in later years. In these four novels, protagonists live in a sin-suffused world and are continually troubled by their transgressions, yet seem unable to keep themselves from compromising their moral beliefs. The main characters simultaneously accept and despise their own extremely strict version of Catholicism. In the perception of critics, the passionate concern of murderers, spies, and adulterers about their moral failings contrasts sharply with other characters' easy, lackluster goodness, suggesting that saintliness may be found more often in the basest villains than in the conspicuously upright. Despite critical controversies, Greene is remembered not only as the author who redefined the modern thriller to examine the place of religion and morality in twentieth-century society, but also as a novelist who probed the possibilities for grace and redemption in the gray area between good and evil.

PRINCIPAL WORKS

NOVELS

The Man Within   1929
The Name of Action   1930
Rumour at Nightfall   1931
Stamboul Train   1932; also published as *Orient Express,* 1933
It's a Battlefield   1934
England Made Me   1935; also published as *The Shipwrecked,* 1953
A Gun for Sale   1936; also published as *This Gun for Hire,* 1936
Brighton Rock   1938; revised edition, 1947
The Confidential Agent   1939
The Power and the Glory   1940; also published as *The Labyrinthine Ways,* 1940
The Ministry of Fear   1943
The Heart of the Matter   1948
*The Third Man   1950
The End of the Affair   1951
Loser Takes All   1955
The Quiet American   1955
Our Man in Havana   1958
A Burnt-Out Case   1961
The Comedians   1966
Travels with My Aunt   1969
The Honorary Consul   1973
The Human Factor   1978
Doctor Fischer of Geneva   1980
Monsignor Quixote   1982
The Captain and the Enemy   1988

SHORT FICTION

The Basement Room   1936
Nineteen Stories   1947; also published as *Twenty-One Stories* [enlarged edition], 1955
A Sense of Reality   1963
May We Borrow Your Husband? and Other Comedies of the Sexual Life   1967
The Collected Stories of Graham Greene   1972

OTHER

†*Brighton Rock*   (screenplay)   1946
‡*The Fallen Idol*   (screenplay)   1948
The Third Man   (screenplay)   1949
§*Our Man in Havana*   (screenplay)   1960
∥*The Comedians*   (screenplay)   1967
Collected Essays   (essays)   1969
A Sort of Life   (autobiography)   1971

The Pleasure-Dome: The Collected Film Criticism, 1935-40 (essays) 1972
Ways of Escape (autobiography) 1980
Getting to Know the General (memoir) 1984
Yours etc.: Letters to the Press (letters) 1989

*This novel is an adaptation of the screenplay *The Third Man.*

†This screenplay is an adaptation of the novel *Brighton Rock.*

‡This screenplay is an adaptation of the short story "The Basement Room," published in *The Basement Room.*

§This screenplay is an adaptation of the novel *Our Man in Havana.*

⎮This screenplay is an adaptation of the novel *The Comedians.*

CRITICISM

Kenneth Allott and Miriam Farris

'Every creative writer worth our consideration; every writer who can be called in the wide eighteenth century use of the term a poet, is a victim: a man given over to an obsession', Greene writes in a tribute to Walter de la Mare, and in various places he has suggested the preoccupations which can be detected in the novels of Conrad, Hardy and Henry James. In what is one of the best short pieces of criticism on Henry James, he has described how a ruling passion may unify the work of a writer, binding the story-telling together by recurrences of theme, incident and image, and giving it weight, direction and 'a symmetry of thought' that lends to half a shelf of novels 'the importance of a system'. All but the most disgruntled will agree that there has been plenty of talent and sensitivity (and some intelligence) in the English novel in the last twenty years—Greene published *The Man Within,* his first novel, in 1929—but these are qualities that give us novels, not novelists. Talent, sometimes of a very high order, produced *High Wind in Jamaica, Darkness at Noon, A Handful of Dust.* Much rarer is the obsessional compulsion which I meet in the novels, travel-books and even the occasional criticism of Graham Greene; which distinguishes his work from that of equally adroit contemporaries; and which I agree with him in thinking the hallmark of the poet as distinct from the journeyman in fiction. I hardly know where else to find it among English novelists today.

The fact of obsession is my present concern, not the degree of success with which in particular novels the leading pre-occupations are fitted into a picture of ordinary life, and the most cursory reading of Greene's novels and entertainments is enough to establish that everything he writes is discoloured by an original hurt to his sensibility. Characters recur in his books: the lonely, isolated man perpetually engrossed in his own childhood, like Andrews in *The Man Within* or Arthur Rowe in *The Ministry of Fear;* the plain pathetic child-woman, like Milly Drover in *It's a Battlefield* or Helen Rolt in *The Heart of the Matter;* the masculine gargoyle, like Acky the epileptic unfrocked Anglican clergyman with a knuckleduster in *A Gun for Sale,* or Minty in *England Made Me,* the ex-Harrovian penny-a-liner in Stockholm whose malevolence is vented in such expletives as 'Holy Cnut'. Certain types of incident are

also repeated, such as the pursuit, which Walter Allen has described as almost a formula for a Greene fiction and which turns up in 'early', 'middle' and 'late' novels, for example, *Rumour at Nightfall, The Confidential Agent* and *The Power and the Glory;* or acts of suicide, brutal violence and voluntary or involuntary betrayal. There is very little gaiety in the Greene world (which is so often an underworld), but there is tenderness: the darkness is never pushed back far or for long. There is a blanketing sense of cruelty's omnipresence and the inevitability of failure, and very frequently this mood is symbolized by a peculiar background of squalor, urban and suburban in many novels but primitive and semi-tropical in *The Power and the Glory,* evoked with scrupulous care.

Characters, incidents and background constitute a mythology, which is the vehicle for Greene's obsessional ideas. Some of these run unchanged through all his fiction—escape and betrayal are good examples. Others, like 'the divided mind' in the three early immature novels or the theme of pity as a destructive passion in *The Ministry of Fear* and *The Heart of the Matter,* belong to one phase of his work distinctly, though they may be present more subtly in disguised forms elsewhere. The full range of these ideas, together with the varying emphasis attending their appearance in different books, will only gradually appear from the detailed study of the novels; but the separate obsessions are all related to each other by being connected with an unchanging general outlook. This may be thought of as a key obsession, or as a sun from which the satellite obsessions derive their luminosity and their capacity to sustain the life of the stories in which they appear.

There is a sentence by Gauguin, quoted approvingly by Greene, that comes near to expressing his main obsessional outlook: 'Life being what it is, one dreams of revenge.' A terror of life, a terror of what experience can do to the individual, a terror at a predetermined corruption, is the motive force that drives Greene as a novelist. With different degrees of plausibility in his various books Greene is continually saying that happiness is unusual and anxious routine nearer the disappointing 'natural' state of man, that experience saddens, that we must bear rather than rejoice because, in Matthew Arnold's words, of a 'something that infects the world'. Failure, ugliness, the primitive are in some sense truer than success, beauty and civilization with their deceptive gloss. The little boy gazing at an electric train in the uncollected short story **'The Hint of an Explanation'** is a true citizen of Greene-land: 'The tears of longing came into my eyes when I looked at the turntable. It was my favourite piece—it looked so ugly and practical and true.'

It should be stressed that Greene's reading of experience is not abnormal—it is a simple Declaration of the Wrongs of Man to which most intelligent people would subscribe. William James in *Varieties of Religious Experience* distinguishes between two ways of regarding life, 'the healthy-minded way' and 'the way that takes all . . . experience of evil as something essential'. He continues:

> To this latter way, the morbid-minded way, as we might call it, healthy-mindedness pure and

simple seems unspeakably blind and shallow. To the healthy-minded way, on the other hand, the way of the sick soul seems unmanly and diseased.

But he is unable to maintain that these two attitudes are in all respects equally valid. Speaking as an 'impartial onlooker' he comments:

> It seems to me that we are bound to say that morbid-mindedness ranges over the wider scale of experience, and that its survey is the one that overlaps. . . . The normal process of life contains moments as bad as any of those which insane melancholy is filled with, moments in which radical evil gets its innings and takes its solid turn. . . . Our civilization is founded on the shambles. . . .

Goethe is usually thought of as 'healthy-minded', but at the age of seventy-five he wrote: 'I will say nothing against the course of my existence. But at bottom it has been nothing but pain and burden. . . . It is but the perpetual rolling of a rock that must be raised up again forever.'

This pessimistic view of life is in the long run simply an adult view. Youth, physical well-being, success may temporarily blunt the sharpness of our perception of its truth, but the optimism dependent on these accidents is always precarious. Job, Aeschylus, Dante, Pascal—the creative artist or thinker is not a Cheeryble Brother. But, if healthy-mindedness to most mature minds seems 'unspeakably blind and shallow', we do go about our business without too much discomfort ignoring the suspended sword. It is the intensity of the feelings amounting to nausea aroused in Greene by this outlook that gives it importance in relation to the novels. It is as if he had been born with an abnormally thin skin so that the anomalies and paradoxes of existence continually irritate his attention. The vertigo of the abyss is not necessarily religious at all, but there is a whiff of it to be found in Calvinism and Jansenism—we have our nostrils tickled by it occasionally in Stevenson: which may explain why Greene has words like Augustinian, Jansenist and even Manichee hurled at him sometimes by reviewers (including, too, his fellow-Catholics).

The notion of evil as an essential element of life makes hay of the simple-minded judgment that Greene is really a social critic who has somehow regrettably become mixed up with religion. There is a sense in which Greene's Catholicism is the least important thing about his outlook, that is to say, in connection with his books, but this affords no excuse for critics like George Woodcock and Arthur Calder-Marshall, who seem to hold that Greene's criticism of life is valuable in so far as it is a criticism of a badly organized society, but beyond that reactionary if not neurotic. Such criticism was more popular in the nineteen-thirties than it is today. It reminds one of the regrets then expressed by intellectuals for Mr. Eliot's movement from *The Waste Land* to *Ash-Wednesday* and 'Burnt Norton', the first of the *Four Quartets*. In *Journey Without Maps* Greene separates himself fastidiously from Utopian thinkers and the whole cheerful bumble of progressive thought.

There are others, of course, who prefer to look

a stage ahead, for whom Intourist provides cheap tickets into a plausible future, but my journey represented a distrust of any future based on what we are.

There is social criticism and hatred of avoidable cruelty and injustice in Greene's novels, but such injustice is always seen as part of a wider reference to the 'injustice' of life as a whole. The theme is explored most fully in *It's a Battlefield.*

It should be added that this view of Greene as a revolutionary writer who has taken the wrong turning ignores his impatience with the equation 'Evil = Social Maladjustment', expressed in so many barbed portraits of idealists, progressives and liberals. An example is Mr. Hands in the unfinished **'The Other Side of the Border'** whose 'old tired grey face had peculiar nobility. For nearly seventy years he had been believing in human nature, against every evidence—it hadn't been good for his promotion in the bank. He was a Liberal, he thought men could govern themselves if they were left alone to it, that wealth did not corrupt and that statesmen loved their country. All that had marked his face until it was a kind of image of what he believed the world to be. But it was breaking up now. . . . If he lived long enough his face might become more probable, more like the other people's world.' If Greene's pity towards a class of person is ever narrowly circumscribed, it is towards the well-meaning woolly idealist, the believer in committees, protest meetings, petitions and week-end conferences. There is often a streak of malice in his treatment of the critical self-righteous leaven in society which keeps itself 'well-informed' in international politics, has no time for religion, is usually emancipated about sex and child-rearing, and may be imagined in moments of inspiration devising international languages and planning masculine dress reform. The malice throws Greene off his balance once or twice in *The Ministry of Fear,* in which there is a hint of war-time highbrow-baiting.

It would be possible to illustrate both the reading of experience and the resultant 'terror of life' from any of the novels, but the terror is not everywhere equally apparent. It leaps out of *Brighton Rock:* in other novels it is implied or emerges with comparative obliquity from the treatment of minor characters and events. It is mentioned by name in *The Man Within* (1929) when the 'hero', the young coward Andrews, speaks of 'a terror of life, of going on soiling himself and repenting and soiling himself again', and this passage can be set beside Scobie's reflections in *The Heart of the Matter* (1948).

> It seemed . . . that life was immeasurably long. Couldn't the test of man have been carried out in fewer years? Couldn't we have committed our first major sin at seven, have ruined ourselves for love or hate at ten, have clutched at redemption on a fifteen-year-old death-bed?

Another of Scobie's reflections gives us the reading of life plainly—he is deputy-commissioner of police in Freetown. Why, he wonders, am I so fond of the place?

> Is it because here human nature hasn't had time to disguise itself? Nobody here could ever talk about a heaven on earth. Heaven remained rigid-

ly in its proper place on the other side of death, and on this side flourished the injustices, the cruelties, the meannesses, that elsewhere people so cleverly hushed up. Here you could love human beings nearly as God loved them, knowing the worst.

Both the reading of life and the terror are found together in the following passage from *The Ministry of Fear.* Arthur Rowe, the central character of the book, has lost his adult memories as a result of a bomb explosion in London, and the clue to an important part of the book's meaning is in our understanding of the antithesis established between childish expectations of life and adult resignation to its real nature.

> In childhood we live under the brightness of immortality—heaven is as near and actual as the seaside. Behind the complicated details of the world stand the simplicities: God is good, the grown-up man or woman knows the answers to every question, there is such a thing as truth, and justice is as measured and faultless as a clock. Our heroes are simple: they are brave, they tell the truth, they are good swordsmen and they are never in the long run really defeated. That is why no later books satisfy us like those which were read to us in childhood—for those promised a world of great simplicity of which we knew the rules, but the later books are complicated and contradictory with experience: they are formed out of our contradictory memories— of the V.C. in the police-court dock, of the faked income-tax returns, the sins in corners, and the hollow voice of men we despise talking to us of courage and purity. The little duke is dead and betrayed and forgotten: we cannot recognize the villain and we suspect the hero and the world is a small cramped place. That is what people are saying all the time everywhere: the two great popular statements of faith are 'What a small place the world is' and 'I'm a stranger here myself'.

The experience here can be linked with various satellite obsessions. Emphasize the gap between real and ideal and we have an idea connected with that of man's double nature in *The Man Within* and *Rumour at Nightfall:* emphasize the corruption of youth and we have a preoccupation important in *England Made Me, Brighton Rock* and elsewhere.

I have said that the terror of life is expressed with grimmest force in *Brighton Rock.* Pinkie Brown, the proud warped adolescent gangster, whose sex-revulsion drives him to monstrous cruelties and whose reckless confidence has given him the leadership of a race-course gang, at one point turns on the little waitress Rose savagely for her pathetic 'Life's not so bad' with: 'I'll tell you what life is. It's jail. It's not knowing where to get some money. Worms and cataract, cancer. You hear 'em shrieking from the upper window—children being born. It's dying slowly.' And in the same novel the dreadful seediness which seems to Greene the most honest representation of the true nature of things is rendered with macabre intensity in the figure of the shyster lawyer Mr. Drewitt. He has come down in the world since his beginning at a minor public school

('Lancaster College. Not one of the great schools, but you'll find it in the Public Schools Year Book.'); his yellow middle-aged face is lined with legal decisions and the rebukes of magistrates. He lives in a soot-grimed house near the railway, shaken by shunting engines at all hours, hating his wife in the basement.

> 'I married beneath me,' Mr. Drewitt said. 'It was my tragic mistake. I was young. An affair of uncontrollable passion. I was a passionate man,' he said, wriggling with indigestion. 'You've seen her,' he said, 'now. My God.' He leant forward and said in a whisper: 'I watch the little typists go by carrying their little cases. I'm quite harmless. A man may watch . . . Listen to the old mole down there. She's ruined me.' His old lined face had taken a holiday—from bonhomie, from cunning, from the legal jest. It was a Sunday and it was itself. Mr. Drewitt said: 'You know what Mephistopheles said to Faustus when he asked where Hell was? He said: "Why, this is Hell, nor are we out of it" '.

Drewitt is another Greene grotesque. He reminds us of Acky, Minty and the more genially imagined, absurd Mr. Rennit of the Orthotex Inquiry Bureau, whose vision of a post-war 'brave new world' is of more broken lives and more divorces. His bitterest complaint is against identity cards, which make registration at hotels so difficult— 'You can't prove anything from cars.' These stunted perverse natures come from the same black places of the imagination as Dickens's Quilp or Krook, but Greene is more aware of their origin and the serious use to be made of them.

'Why, this is Hell, nor are we out of it.' It would have been natural to recall the famous description of a fallen world in Newman's *Apologia Pro Vita Sua* even if it had not appeared as one of the epigraphs to *The Lawless Roads.* 'To consider the world,' writes Newman, ' . . . the greatness and littleness of man, his far-reaching aims, his short duration, the curtain hung over his futurity, the disappointments of life, the defeat of good, the success of evil, physical pain, mental anguish, the prevalence and intensity of sin, the pervading idolatries, the corruptions, the dreary hopeless irreligion, that condition of the whole race, so fearfully yet exactly described in the Apostle's words, "having no hope, and without God in the world"—all this is a vision to dizzy and appal . . . ' Like Greene, Newman finds the nature of existence 'heartpiercing, reason-bewildering'.

> I can only answer, that either there is no Creator, or this living society of men is in a true sense discarded from His presence . . . *if* there be a God, *since* there is a God, the human race is implicated in some terrible aboriginal calamity.

So close indeed are Newman's and Greene's pictures of a fallen world that it may be asked how I could assert earlier that Greene's Catholicism is of minor importance in studying his main outlook on which the obsessions in the novels depend. The answer is a simple matter of timing.

The evidence of passages in *Journey Without Maps* and *The Lawless Roads,* together with that of certain less well-known essays, notably **'Heroes Are Made in Childhood'** and **'The Revolver in the Corner Cupboard',** proves that what is substantially the Greene outlook exists at much earlier date than his conversion to Catholicism, which took place in 1926. It springs ultimately from the unhappiness probed by him in childhood—he was, it should be remembered, a schoolboy at Berkhamsted, where his father was headmaster. An extract from **'Heroes Are Made in Childhood'** will help to make the chronology clear. Greene is recalling the reading of Marjorie Bowen's historical romance *The Viper of Milan* and asking why it was so important to him.

> On the surface *The Viper of Milan* is only the story of a war between Gian Galeazzo Visconti, Duke of Milan, and Mastino della Scala, Duke of Verona, told with zest and cunning and an amazing pictorial sense. Why did it creep in and colour and explain the terrible living world of the stone stairs and the never quiet dormitory? It was no good in that real world to dream that one would ever be a Sir Henry Curtis, but della Scala who at last turned from an honesty that never paid and betrayed his friends and died dishonoured and a failure even at treachery—it was easier for a child to escape behind his mask. As for Visconti, with his beauty, his patience and his genius for evil, I had watched him pass by many a time in his black Sunday suit smelling of mothballs. His name was Carter. He exercised terror from a distance like a snowcloud over the young fields. Goodness has only once found a perfect incarnation in a human body and never will again, but evil can always find a home there. Human nature is not black and white but black and grey. I read all that in *The Viper of Milan* and I looked round and I saw that it was so.
>
> There was another theme I found there. At the end of *The Viper of Milan* you will remember if you have once read it the great scene of complete success—della Scala is dead, Ferrara, Verona, Novara, Mantua have all fallen . . . Visconti sits and jokes in the wine light. I was not on the classical side or I would have discovered, I suppose, in Greek literature instead of in Miss Bowen's novel, the sense of doom that lies over success— the feeling that the pendulum is about to swing. That too made sense; one looked around and saw the doomed everywhere—the champion runner who would one day sag over the tape; the head of the school who would atone, poor devil, during forty dreary undistinguished years. . . . *Anyway she had given me my pattern—religion later might explain it to me in other terms, but the pattern was already there*—perfect evil walking the world where perfect good can never walk again, and only the pendulum ensures that after all in the end justice is done.

This sets echoes ringing from our reading of all the later Greene novels, but I have italicized the lines with the strongest bearing on the present argument. Obsessions as strong as Greene's have deeper roots than can be traced to a course of apologetics on the top of a Nottingham tram and a religious conversion in one's early twenties: they go back at least as far as 'the terrible living world of the stone stairs and the never quiet dormitory.' The first chapter of

The Lawless Roads makes clear the singularity of Greene's position as a schoolboy at Berkhamsted, living 'on the border', poised between the two adjoining but utterly different countries of home and school, and divided in his allegiance because hate is 'quite as powerful a tie' as love. He tells us of the horrors of classroom and pitch-pine-partitioned dormitory from which he would escape surreptitiously to darkness and solitude with the rabbit 'restlessly cropping near the croquet hoops'. It was then that 'faith came to one—shapelessly without dogma . . .' The Penny Catechism declares that man is prone to evil from his very childhood, but before Greene had ever heard of the catechism he had 'looked round and seen that it was so'. It is because all his ideas have been conceived personally and proved on his pulses that he is not so much a 'Catholic novelist', even in the later books where Mauriac is a master, as, in his own words, a 'novelist who is a Catholic'.

The importance of the idea of childhood to any appraisal of Greene's work should be evident. . . . It was the aptness of Marjorie Bowen's portrait of Renaissance Italy to his own experience of school-life at Berkhamsted that made the reading of *The Viper of Milan* the moment when 'the future for better or worse really struck'. Greene goes along with innumerable poets and other writers in accepting a golden age of innocence in earliest years, but what he stresses is how soon it is threatened even in childhood—'Hell lay about them in their infancy'—and how quickly and inevitably innocence and the capacity for simple, uncomplicated happiness leak away.

There are few novelists who have been so content as Greene simply to explore in their books the meaning of the 'certainties' given to them in their early years: it is a kind of fidelity less unusual among poets. 'I do not know for whom it is I write,' says Bernanos in *Les Enfants Humiliés,* 'but I do know why I write. I write to justify myself. In whose eyes? I have told you before . . . in the eyes of the child that I was. Whether that child speaks to me any longer or not, I shall never acknowledge his silence; I shall keep on answering him'. Greene might have said this. Pinkie and Rose in **Brighton Rock,** Anthony Farrant in **England Made Me,** Rose Cullen in **The Confidential Agent,** Helen Rolt in **The Heart of the Matter**—these are only a few of the characters understood in terms of childhood with its phobias, disciplines and secrecies. 'People change,' says Rose in **Brighton Rock.** 'Oh, no they don't', replies the comfortable Ida. 'Look at me. I've never changed. It's like those sticks of rock: bite it all the way down, you'll still read Brighton. That's human nature.'

People do not change: they grow older and accumulate memories. If childhood is 'that time of life when, however miserable we are, we have expectations', then to be mature is to know that the future has already struck—

> In the lost boyhood of Judas
> Christ was betrayed

—that a life and (Greene would add) a death have been chosen. We remember the unhappy dentist in **The Power and the Glory,** an exile in a fever-ridden Mexican state, separated from wife and children, drained of all initiative by the heat and the prevailing shoddiness, a typical Greene figure of decay.

> Mr. Tench's father had been a dentist too—his first memory was finding a discarded cast in a waste-paper basket—the rough toothless gaping mouth of clay, like something dug up in Dorset—Neanderthal or Pithecanthropus. It had been his favourite toy: they tried to tempt him with Meccano: but fate had struck. There is always one moment in childhood when the door opens and lets the future in.

Whenever we read about children or the state of childhood in Greene's novels we are near to his central obsession with the terror of life and its origin in his early years. If it should still appear rash to suggest such a direct relationship between Greene's life and fiction, then the reading of **'The Revolver in the Corner Cupboard'** is recommended. Both Andrews and Scobie, heroes respectively of his first and his latest novel, commit suicide. Suicide is the ultimate escape—life, not the police or a political rival, is the enemy evaded. In **'The Revolver in the Corner Cupboard'** Greene takes us behind the scenes of his adolescence. He describes how at the age of seventeen, bored and miserably and romantically in love with his sister's governess, he played a 'game' with a revolver and a single live charge. The charge was inserted without looking, the chambers twirled, the revolver put to the head and the trigger pulled. Greene had discovered 'that it was possible to enjoy again the visible world by risking its total loss'. This is not unconnected with the acceptance of the rigours of the Liberian journey [Cf. *Journey Without Maps,* Pt. III, Chap. I, 'The Lowland': 'The pain I had been feeling for some days now in my stomach seemed to get worse at the news . . . I was scared in the same way as I had been in England when I suddenly found that my plans had gone too far for me to back out of the Liberian journey . . . I was discovering in myself a thing I thought I had never possessed: a love of life.'], and I believe it is relevant to an understanding of **The Power and the Glory** and **The Heart of the Matter** where experience becomes significant because of the possibility of damnation, of risking (in the theological sense) a total loss; but, more simply, here we have in Greene's own experience a preoccupation attributed to several of his fictitious characters. The ambiguous attempt at suicide was not an isolated act. Greene tells us that he went on playing this 'game' even as an Oxford undergraduate, and that before the first attempt with the revolver there was a series of acts 'which my elders would have regarded as neurotic, but which I still consider to have been under the circumstances highly reasonable'.

> There had been for example, perhaps five or six years before, the disappointing morning in the dark room by the linen cupboard on the eve of term when I had patiently drunk a quantity of hypo under the impression that it was poisonous: on another occasion the blue glass bottle of hay-fever lotion which as it contained a small quantity of cocaine had probably been good for my mood: the bunch of deadly nightshade that I had eaten with only a slight narcotic effect: the twenty aspirin I had taken before swimming in the empty out-of-term school baths (I can still

> remember the curious sensation of swimming through wool) . . .

All these acts were rebellious protests against 'the horrible confinement and publicity of school'. They culminated in Greene's running away—he hid on Berkhamsted Common where he went with the revolver a few years later. The misery of school stretched out to spoil even the holidays. The first few days were 'light, space and silence', a rest for jangled nerves, but after that boredom set in—freedom, lacking misery's intensity, was tedious. Some ex-servicemen find peace tedious in the same way.

This boredom, a poor relation of Baudelaire's *ennui* and Leopardi's *noia,* is a definite part of the obsessional terror of life. It was fixed, Greene explains, by the psychoanalysis that followed his running away from school.

> For years, it seems to me, I could take no aesthetic interest in any visual thing at all: staring at a sight that others assured me was beautiful I would feel nothing.

Existence became a tedious routine, a migraine punctuated by the stabs of active fears. The notion can be related to something said in the previous paragraph. One reason for Greene's constant use of melodrama is his feeling, whether fully conscious or not, that existence can only be dramatic when routine is broken. For example, the recurrent pursuit formula takes a central character across other people's routine lives, but his life is one in which the unexpected always happens. Now that Greene consciously poses the actions of his characters against a supernatural screen which magnifies them and 'taints' the most ordinary scenes and conversations with eternity, there may be less need for the melodramatic. Certainly melodrama was less in evidence in **The Heart of the Matter,** which owed its sustained interest as much to the method of storytelling as to the story told. (pp. 13-29)

The names of the novelists spoken of by Greene with affection and admiration—Conrad, Ford Madox Ford (for *The Good Soldier*), Henry James and François Mauriac—suggest closely enough the kind of novel approved by him. If one may speak loosely, he by-passes the experimental novel of the nineteen-twenties and early nineteen-thirties, where in the more obvious senses moral preoccupations are at a minimum, and form is either lyrical, a matter of mood, or is artificially imposed on material that hardly appears to be selected at all. Equally he rejects what is unfortunately still widely known as 'the traditional English novel'.

There is a simple way of making clear what I mean by this phrase. In reading *Passage to India, The Spoils of Poynton, Sons and Lovers* or *Under Western Eyes* we need to pay the kind of attention to verbal and structural niceties that we pay as a matter of course even to minor poetry, but rightly consider inappropriate in reading Smollett and Thackeray or, to take more recent examples, Galsworthy and Arnold Bennett. Greene requires to be read with this 'poetic' attention. This is not to compare him in esteem with James or Conrad, but it is to rank him with them as a poet-novelist, a writer seriously and devotedly concerned with the artistic problems arising from the wish to express a way of looking at the world. From the technical point of view Greene has probably learnt most from these two writers: the influence of Mauriac appears mainly in the choice of subject.

The question of the attention with which the 'poetic' novel needs to be read is not directly concerned with the degree to which the obsessional ideas are obtrusive in any particular piece of fiction. I should not like to be dogmatic about the depth at which a novelist should bury his obsessions. Hardy's recurrent themes, as Greene has pointed out, can be isolated fairly easily, whereas the care Henry James took to dramatize his material makes the investigation of them in his novels a business of some delicacy. In my view Henry James is a greater novelist than Thomas Hardy, but I am not sure that this has much to do with unobtrusiveness of theme. I observe that in Greene, as in Hardy and Conrad, the obsessions are always near the surface and provide the flavour of the Morality that seems to cling to their novels; that in Mauriac, as in James, the obsessions are much less visible. Mauriac is an important illustration because his reading of experience is as idiosyncratic as Greene's, indeed not unlike it, yet in his books the ruling ideas are less imposed, the Morality flavour much fainter. On the whole I incline to think that the great novelists bury their obsessional themes as nearly out of sight as possible, but I have to remind myself that very remarkable novels may be written on the compositional principle that the ruling ideas should be plainly visible, and that part of our legitimate pleasure in form may derive from their visibility. In both types of poetic novel—that in which the obsessions are more and that in which they are less evident—reading involves our being alive to the meaning that is danced, so to speak, by the form of the novel: that form may be looked on as a movement, including the larger structural gestures made by the grouping of characters and incidents for parallel and contrast, and the smaller ones made by related images and various verbal refinements.

Greene's novels from *It's a Battlefield* onward belong to the type of poetic novel in which the obsessions are close to the surface: in them structure is used emphatically alongside character and situation to project the total poetic meaning. The recipe is near enough to a commonly accepted view of Elizabethan and Jacobean drama to make a statement of it in Greene's *The British Dramatists* apposite here:

> It must be remembered that we are still within the period of the Morality: they are being acted yet in the country districts: they had been absorbed by Shakespeare, just as much as he absorbed the plays of Marlowe, and the abstraction . . . still rules the play. And rightly. Here is the watershed between the morality and the play of character: the tension between the two is perfectly kept: there is dialectical perfection. After Shakespeare, character—which was to have its dramatic triumphs—won a too-costly victory.

It may be, of course, that the greater fluidity of the novel form makes it advisable for the novelist to do what is not required of the poetic dramatist—to hide his themes and disguise the structure of his books. It may be that the most ambitious kind of novel can only be created in this way—I am inclined, as I say, to think so—but I can see no reason why a novelist should not employ with the necessary variations the method of the poetic dramatist. In reading Greene's novels and entertainments it may be more useful to think of the structure of *The Duchess of Malfi* than that of *Barchester Towers* or *The Newcomes*. (pp. 30-3)

> *Kenneth Allott and Miriam Farris, in their*
> The Art of Graham Greene, *1951. Reprint by*
> *Russell & Russell, Inc., 1963, 253 p.*

François Mauriac

The work of an English Catholic novelist—of an Englishman returning to Catholicism—like **The Power and the Glory** by Graham Greene, at first always gives me the sensation of being in a foreign land. To be sure, I find there my spiritual country, and it is into the heart of a familiar mystery that Graham Greene introduces me. But everything takes place as though I were penetrating into an old estate through a concealed door unknown to me, hidden in a wall covered with ivy, and as though I were advancing behind the hero of a novel through tangled branches and suddenly recognized the great avenue of the park where I played when I was a child and deciphered my initials cut on the trunk of an oak on some former holiday.

A French Catholic enters the church by the main door only; he is interwoven with its official history; he has taken part in all the debates which have torn it throughout the centuries and which have divided the Gallican church especially. In everything he writes, one discovers at once whether he is on the side of Port-Royal or the Jesuits, whether he weds Bossuet's quarrel with Fénélon, whether he is on the side of Lamennais and Lacordaire or if it is with Louis Veuillot that he agrees. Bernanos' work of which it is impossible not to think on reading **The Power and the Glory** is very significant in this respect. All the Catholic controversies of the last four centuries unfold in filigree. Behind the Abbé Donissan of the *Sun of Satan*, appears the curate of Ars. Bernanos' saints, like his liberal priests and like the pious laymen he describes with such happy ferocity, betray his venerations and his hatreds.

Graham Greene, himself, broke, like a burglar, into the kingdom of the unknown, into the kingdom of nature and of Grace. No prejudice troubles his vision. No current of ideas turns him aside from that discovery, that key which he found suddenly. He has no preconceived notion of what we call a bad priest; it could be said that he has no model of saintliness in his mind. There is corrupted nature and omnipotent Grace; there is poverty-stricken man who is nothing, even in evil, and there is mysterious love which lays hold upon him in the thick of his ridiculous misery and absurd shame to make a saint and martyr of him.

The power and the glory of the Father burst forth in the Mexican curate who loves alcohol too much and who gets one of his parishioners pregnant. A type so common and mediocre that his mortal sins call forth only derision and a shrugging of the shoulders, and he knows it. What this extraordinary book shows us is, if I dare say so, the utilization of sin by Grace. This priest, rebellious and condemned to death by the public authorities and on whose head there is a price (the drama takes place in a Mexico given over to atheistic and persecuting rulers), who tries to save himself, as indeed all the other priests, even the most virtuous, did, who in fact saves himself and passes the frontier, but who comes back every time a dying person needs him, even when he believes his help will be in vain, and even when he is not ignorant that it is a trap and that the one who is calling him has already betrayed him, this priest, a drunkard, impure and trembling before death, gives his life without for a single moment losing the feeling of his baseness and his shame. He would think it a joke if he were told he was a saint. He is miraculously saved from pride, complacency and self-righteousness. He goes to his martyrdom, having always in his mind the vision of the soiled nothingness and the sacrilege that a priest in a state of mortal sin is, so that he sacrifices himself on attributing to God all of that power and glory which triumph over what he considers the most miserable of men: himself.

And as he approaches the end, we see this mediocre sinner conform slowly to the Christ until he resembles Him, but that is not saying enough: until he identifies himself with his Lord and his God. Passion begins again around this victim chosen from among human derelicts, who repeats what Christ did, not as at the altar, without it costing him anything, on offering the blood and the body under the species of bread and wine, but giving up his own flesh and blood as on a cross. In this false, bad priest it is not virtue that appears as the opposite of sin, it is faith—faith in that sign he received the day of his ordination, in the trust that he alone (since all the other priests have been massacred or have fled) still bears in his hands, unworthy but yet consecrated.

The last priest remaining in the country, he is unable not to believe that after him there will be no one to offer the Sacrifice, or to absolve, or to distribute the bread which is no longer bread, or to help the dying on the threshold of life eternal. And yet his faith does not waver, although he does not know that scarcely will he have fallen when another priest will suddenly and furtively appear.

We feel it is that hidden presence of God in an atheistic world, that subterranean flowing of Grace which dazzles Graham Greene much more than the majestic façade which the temporal Church still erects above the peoples. If there is a Christian whom the crumbling of the invisible Church would not disturb, it is, indeed, that Graham Greene whom I heard at Brussels evoking, before thousands of Belgian Catholics, and in the presence of a dreaming apostolic nuncio, the last pope of a totally dechristianized Europe, standing in line at the commissary, dressed in a spotted gabardine, and holding in his hand, on which still shone the Fisherman's ring, a cardboard valise.

That is to say that this book is addressed providentially to a generation that the absurdity of a crazy world is clutching by the throat. To the young contemporaries of Camus and Sartre, desperate prey to an absurd liberty, Graham Greene will reveal, perhaps, that this absurdity is in truth only that of boundless love.

The message is addressed to believers, to the virtuous, to those who do not doubt their merit and who have ever present in their minds several models of holiness, with the proper technic for attaining the various steps in the mystical ascension. It is addressed in particular to Christian priests and laymen, especially to writers who preach the cross but of whom it is not enough to say they are not crucified. A great lesson given to those obsessed with perfection, and those scrupulous people who split hairs over their shortcomings, and who forget that, in the last day, according to the word of Saint John of the Cross, it is on love that they will be judged.

Dear Graham Greene to whom I am attached by so many bonds, and first of all by those of gratitude (since thanks to you, my books to-day find the same warm reception in England that they received in my own country, at the time that I was a happy young author), how pleasant it is for me to think that France, where your work is already loved, is going to discover, thanks to that great book, *The Power and the Glory,* its true meaning. That state which you describe, which tracks down the last priest and assassinates him, is indeed the very one we see arising under our eyes. It is the hour of the Prince of this world, but you paint him without hatred. Even the executioners, even your chief of police is marked by you with a sign of mercy; they search for truth; they believe, like our communists, they have found it and are serving it—that truth which demands the sacrifice of consecrated creatures. Darkness covers all the earth you describe, but what a burning ray crosses it! Whatever happens, we know we must not be afraid; you remind us that the inexplicable will be explained and that there remains a grating to be put up against this absurd world. Through you, we know the adorable limit to the liberty that Sartre grants to men; we know that a creature loved as much as we are has no other liberty than that of refusing that love, to the degree to which it has made itself known to him and under the appearances it has been pleased to assume. (pp. 124-28)

François Mauriac, "Graham Greene," in his Men I Hold Great, *translated by Elsie Pell, Philosophical Library, 1951, pp. 124-28.*

V. S. Pritchett

English novelists are not notable for their sense of evil. James Hogg of *The Confessions of a Justified Sinner* has it, and so, in a romantic way, has Stevenson, but both are Scots. Conrad, the Pole, has it; so has Henry James, the American. Among ourselves it is hard to find. There are signs in *Clarissa;* in Dickens evil appears hysterically in the forms of staged melodrama. Only Emily Brontë fully exposes her imagination to the dark spirit and with a pagan or pantheistic exhilaration and pride which profoundly shocked her contemporaries. For Hardy evil is an aloof and alien polity. It can hardly be called more than mischance. The rest of the English novelists settle for a world which must be judged in terms of right and wrong.

Against this Protestant tradition the novels of Graham Greene are a rebellion or, rather, a series of guerrilla ambushes from a Roman Catholic point of view. He was once said to be a Jansenist and was certainly at variance with the accommodating Catholic tradition on the Continent. His religion—as we see it in his early novels—has the egocentricity, the scruple, the puritanism and aggression present in English nonconformity, though it finds more savour in failure than success. God is his misadventure and, for this reason, maybe he is a religious man, i.e. he does not expect to get anything but conflict and pain out of his religion. I must say this is a vast relief after the optimism of the success cults. To the spectator, it seems that Greene wishes to have an adulterer's, a gambler's or a spy's relation with his God and Church, finding more merit in despair than in the laborious conniving at the goodness the ordinary hypocrite goes in for. On the other hand, a man like Scobie, in *The Heart of the Matter,* can hardly rank with the great sinners; he lacks the pride. His muddles and illegalities rate official damnation but, as the priest suggests, there is still God's mercy. His portrait has some of that sentimentality which has come over the Channel from François Mauriac. I doubt if it is fair to Roman Catholic moralists to say that they believe the worst thing is to break the rules.

The light and serious novels of Graham Greene make their impression because of his phenomenal skill, his invention, and the edge and precision of his mind. He etches the conventional with the acid of the observable. His thrillers are not simply escapes from ordinary life, but are painful journeys into it: the agent, hunter or hunted, unveils. In *The Confidential Agent* the true subjects are pain and betrayal. He seeks the exact:

> She lay there stiff, clean and unnatural; people talked as if death were like sleep; it was like nothing but itself. He was reminded of a bird discovered at the bottom of a cage on its back, with the claws rigid as grape stalks: nothing could look more dead. He had seen people dead after an air raid; but they fell in curious humped positions—a lot of embryos in the womb. This was different—a unique position reserved for one occasion. Nobody in pain or asleep lay like this.

In one book at least, *The Power and the Glory,* he transcends his perverse and morbid tendencies and presents a whole and memorable human being; this wholeness is exceptional, for Greene is generally an impressionist, or rather a cutter of mosaics. We expect from incisive talents some kind of diagnosis, some instinctive knowledge of the human situation which we have not attended to; this Greene has had. His subjects are the contemporary loneliness, ugliness and transience. We disapprove of the ugliness of our civilization without recognizing that, for some reason, we *needed* to make it ugly. Greene makes great play with this in his novels; behind the ugliness is loneliness and betrayal. Very nearly all his characters are marked by the loneliness in our civilization, and on the simplest level—Scobie's, for example—they are merely self-pitying. They fail to communicate. Scobie hates talking to his wife because of fear that she will make yet another scene; he knows that talking to his mistress will lead fatally to the re-enacting of the same stale dramas of jealousy. These people wish to be alone; yet when they are alone, the sad dialogues of nostalgia, conscience and betrayal

begin in the mind; and presently each character breaks in two: the pursuer and pursued, the watcher and the watched, the hunter and the hunted. The relationship with God, if they are Catholics, is the same. One moment it is God who will have no mercy; next it is Scobie who is torturing God. In *The End of the Affair* the narrator accuses himself of inability to do anything but hate; and Fowler in *The Quiet American* admits that he translates his personal hatred of Pyle and Pyle's dangerous political innocence into a fantastic hatred of the American continent. Loneliness, the failure to communicate in love, or rather to sustain communication, is the cause, and behind that is the first cause, the betrayal we are thought to have experienced in childhood when evil was revealed to us. This is a contemporary subject for, in Greene's rendering of the world, we are now anonymous. We are bleak, observable people in streets, on staircases, in boarding-houses, hotel rooms, cafeterias, Nissen huts, native villages, police stations—free, but disheartened and 'wanted'.

Greene's masterly power of evoking the shabby scene, whether it is Pimlico or Liberia, Mexico or Kent, is a matter of a vision true to its misanthropy and quickness of eye; but it owes something also to his sense of being an accomplice. We are guilty transients leaving our fakes and our litter. There is an odd and frequent suggestion that romantic literature misled us. China, Liberia, Mexico ought not to have looked like this. In the later books, particularly in *The Quiet American,* the mood has become rather too much the conventional habit of disillusion (assumed for self-protection) of the American school of reporting. In fact only one scene was real reporting, so I have since learned. Only the minor figures observed by the master reporter in the war scenes are individual; the rest have become types. Fowler is mere self-pity; Pyle is a flat profile. There is always a danger in Greene's novels that the stress on banality and anonymity will turn into type-casting and that he will forget that the loneliness of people, on whatever level, is only an aspect of them. In *The Heart of the Matter,* Scobie's scenes with young Mrs Rolt become typical and therefore forced. The sudden leap from pitiable youth to the jealousy of the trained virago on Mrs Rolt's part, makes Greene's point of course, but is too pat. In his honesty he is too eager to see evil doing its stuff.

In *The Power and the Glory,* Greene succeeds above all the rest. In the other tales, by quickness of cinematic cutting, by turning everything he sees to the advantage of action, he makes circles round our doubts. The preposterous argument of *Brighton Rock* is lost in the excitement of the hunt. But in the Mexican novel no doubts arise. There is no overt resentment. There are no innuendos. There are no theological conundrums. It is actually an advantage that Greene hated Mexico and the tropical rot; he had worked the worst off in a vivid book, *The Lawless Roads.* Except for the portrait of the seedy Mr Tench, the dentist, at the beginning, and the account of the Catholic family reading their forbidden literature secretly, there is nothing to distract us from the portraits of the whisky-priest and the lieutenant, his pursuer. In this kind of drama, Mr Greene excels, but here there is meaning, not fear-fantasy; the priest is taken from depth to depth in physical suffering and spiritual humiliation. The climax is reached when he is disowned by his mistress and his child and this long scene is wonderful for the way in which the feeling is manipulated and reversed. The scene in the prison, into which he is thrown by mad misadventure, has to bear the moral burden of the story—that he is at peace with the criminals and outcasts from whom he need not hide his identity, and that he is in danger only from conventional piety. We should not forget that Greene trails his coat in order to provoke mercy and has a subtle and compassionate intelligence of unvoiced pain. As a novelist he is free of the vice of explanation in this book; we see a soul grow and recover its dignity. And the dialogue between the pursuing lieutenant and the priest at the end is a true dialogue; it is not a confrontation of views, but of two lives. The only weakness is in the transition to the Catholic family and the inter-cutting of scenes at the end. I do not know what the intention is. Is it to take us into the starchy world of Catholic piety, into that religious respectability which Greene detests and where, indeed, right and wrong take the place of good and evil? Or is it a return to Greene's boyish love of romantic literature? The child is 'believing' in a boy's heroic adventure in defence of the Faith, as Greene himself might have 'believed' in Rider Haggard. The misanthropy of Greene often reads as if it were a resentment of the deceit of books for boys and a rancour against the loss of the richly populated solitude of childhood.

In *The Comedians* Graham Greene returns to the reporter-novelizing manner of *The Quiet American* and is in a better temper. This book has the usual self-indulgence, the usual zest in the sardonic view. A Greene character has a hard time of it. The couple whom Brown, the present narrator, saw copulating cheerfully in the hotel swimming-pool one night in Haiti could have no notion that he would make a sermon out of them later on, by placing the body of a politician with his wrists cut in the corner of the pool: later still, to ram home the text, the battered head of the same politician will confront yet another woman who kneels down in a garden to be had by a policeman. It is hard luck to be a figure in a parable of sadomasochism.

Another woman—a German whose burden is that her father had been executed for Nazi crimes and who is the mistress of the narrator—fights back against the 'dark brown world you live in'. There is danger, you see, even in Brown's name. Having got out of bed and sworn at her suspender, she gives him a lecture.

> To you nothing exists except in your own thoughts. Not me, not Jones. We're what you choose to make us. You're a Berkeleyan. My God, what a Berkeleyan. . . . My dear, try to believe we exist when you aren't there. We're independent of you. None of us is like what you fancy we are. Perhaps it wouldn't matter much if your thoughts were not so dark, always so dark.

She is right. She has even accused him of being a novelist. And she is right again. In so many of his novels Graham Greene makes an overwhelming and literary intervention so that his people are reduced to things seen flat in the camera's eye and by the cleverest of living photographers. It is true that the author's mind is courageous, charitable and compassionate: no character can complain that he has not been enhanced in the very instant of being flattened or narrowed—and to say that is to say a great deal for Greene as an artist. If he piles it on, he does so with the inner gaiety of a great talent. But one often wishes that he were less of a contriver and would let the characters show for themselves what their meaning is. That passage about Berkeley is unlikely in the mouth of the German refugee wife of a diplomat in Haiti; it annuls her as an independent human being and breaks the novel's illusion. Not only that, one suspects the speech is there as an essayist's insurance against the suspicion that elsewhere, in the 'piled-on' incidents, Greene is parodying himself as a novelist. And perhaps as a conceit or a joke.

The theme of the novel is put by a priest preaching on the text: 'Let us go up to Jerusalem and die with him'. Indifference is to be condemned more harshly than violence. 'Violence can be the expression of love, indifference never. One is an imperfection of charity, the other the perfection of egoism'. The indifferent are the comedians, i.e. the egoists, in a tragic world. (It is odd to see indifference presented as the antithesis of violence; but I suppose we are back at that barbarous Manichean idea expressed in 'Because ye are neither hot nor cold' etc. etc.) The chief comedian is Brown himself, a lapsed Catholic speculator who has never known his father, was born in the no man's land of Monte Carlo and now runs a tourist hotel in Haiti. He has inherited it from his mother, a decent, now elderly tart found living with her black servant: she dies—need one say—after one last fling of intercourse. The black servant is so upset he hangs himself.

Brown had left Haiti, partly because of his possessive jealousy of his mistress, the diplomat's wife; now he returns to the disgusting police state and to the murdered politician. The horrible condition of this *triste tropique* is sharply evoked. No one so powerfully burns an exotic and seedy scene on the mind. Haiti is an island run by faceless Negro and mulatto crooks in sun-glasses. In Port-au-Prince arrives a farcical pair of American innocents, one-time freedom-riders, all for justice, who wish to persuade the government to open a vegetarian centre. The cranks are slow-motion slapstick, but they have their courage and dignity. They are also—in a business way—shrewd: this, and one or two adroit observations of their affectionate hypochondria, redeem them from pure caricature. They pass harmlessly from the scene—one can see that Brown's hotel had to have at least a couple of residents—to make way for a merry little spiv called Jones, self-styled hero of the Burma war, semi-secret agent, speculator, petty gambler, stoic, self-advertised Don Juan, and an instant friend of Papa Doc, the bloody dictator; selling out on him, however, he joins a Resistance group in the mountains.

Jones is a *comic* comedian—he is committed to making something out of the anarchy that the deeply comic are drawn into. It turns out that he has lied about everything—he is, in fact, wanted internationally for theft—but his lies catch up with him and he is forced to lead the guerrillas in the mountains because his bluff is called. Why do the Resistance people take him on? Because he is so irresistible. He makes people laugh. He has no real notion of what he is doing, beyond perhaps being a bit awestruck by people of principle. Eventually his feet let him down in the rough country. It is a surprising weakness that one has the death of Jones by hearsay; also that of Dr Magiot, the sad, upright Marxist who has managed to survive because communists are useful political counters: they enable Papa Doc to blackmail the Americans.

In this context of secret shootings, beatings-up and dejected plotting, in which the Haitians have either the brutal or the dedicated parts, Brown and his mistress conduct their private sexual comedy, in momentary beddings in the backs of cars, and in a grave-like hollow under the trees. They are nervous of discovery; Brown thinks his mistress's child may be spying on them. It is an affair constantly on edge because of his possessive nagging jealousies—Greene is always on the *qui vive* for the ironies of impotence and desire. And of betrayal. Treachery has always been one of Greene's central preoccupations as a moralist. Brown betrays Jones because he is jealous, by working cynically on his vanity; and the irony is that Jones, the liar, is the better man. His life could be construed, Brown suddenly sees, as a series of delinquent approaches to virtue. Such paradoxes fit in admirably with Greene's gift for creating suspense.

Brown is cool enough in danger, but he is a born destroyer of his own and his mistress's happiness. It is he who is really the absurd figure because all his suspicions turn out to be untrue: he has so little perception of normal feelings. Jones, the shady liar, is capable of inspiring affection. Brown, the adulterer, is so tied-up that he inspires pity. But Brown *thinks*—it is noticeable how often the heroes of the reporter's novel are Hamlets, tortured by the guilt of being outside, of having kept an escape-route, as they knowingly rock their pink gin in the glass and misanthropically bitch their Ophelias—and guilt sharpens even while it perverts observation. He has one exciting episode—Greene at his best—in which he smuggles Jones out to his rendezvous. The moment in which the awful police chief—admirably called Concasseur—is shot and has his sun-glasses trodden on is very fine. That is the kind of detail that reconciles us to Greene when we are just about to cry parody again.

The end of *The Comedians* is, like the beginning, a sardonic essay. The vegetarian Americans are in San Domingo and, in their grateful and businesslike way, they get Brown a partnership in a funeral business where the drift of local politics offers growing prospects. This is a nasty but exact diagnosis; the speciousness lies in our feeling that the symbolism is being piled on and that the people are puppets in an animated disquisition. The effect is literary. We have been reading news and news leaves us with the sense of waste. But as San Domingo follows Haiti, as Nigeria distracts us from the Congo, Greene has obviously chosen an important subject; and though he is an outsider, there are moments in which he gets inside. The Voodoo scene in which we watch a sensitive man being turned by grotesque religious performance into a partisan catches a note of tropical excess.

> The priest came in from his inner room swinging a censer, but the censer which he swung in our

faces was a trussed cock—the small stupid eyes peered into my eyes and the banner of St Lucy swayed after it. When he had completed the circle of the *tonelle* the *hougan* put the head of the cock in his mouth and crunched it cleanly off; the wings continued to flap while the head lay on the dirt-floor like part of a broken toy. Then he bent down and squeezed the neck like a tube of tooth-paste and added the rusty colour of blood to the ash-grey patterns on the floor.

But I think he overcrowds with the apparatus of horror; and especially in the sexual incident, one begins to grin and even to laugh.

Greene is laughing too, but we are at cross purposes; we are laughing at self-parody as we laugh at melodrama and he is laughing at his own pleasure in giving more and more turns to what, in both senses, is the screw. Brown is supposed to have lost his faith and to be adrift because he has found nothing to replace it. Yet in fact he *has* found something: the hotel-keeper has ostensibly written this remarkable book. That is an act of faith; certainly not an act of indifference. Or didn't Brown write the book? Is it all a game? All virtuosi are entitled to indulge their talents. But when Greene wrote *The Power and the Glory* he was not playing a game. (pp. 78-87)

> *V. S. Pritchett, "Graham Greene: 'Disloyalties',' in his* The Tale Bearers: Literary Essays, *Random House, 1980, pp. 78-91.*

Richard Johnstone

Graham Greene's conversion to Catholicism took place in 1926, but it was not until 1938 that he published the novel, *Brighton Rock,* that asserted the validity and the necessity of religious belief. In 1970 [in his Introduction to *Brighton Rock*], Greene offered his own explanation for the delay:

> More than ten years had passed since I was received into the Church. At that time, as I have written elsewhere, I had not been emotionally moved, but only intellectually convinced. . . .
>
> My professional life and my religion were contained in quite separate compartments, and I had no ambition to bring them together. It was 'clumsy life again at her stupid work' which did that; on one side, the socialist persecution of religion in Mexico and on the other General Franco's attack on Republican Spain inextricably involved religion in contemporary life.
>
> I think it was under these two influences—and the backward and forward sway of my sympathies—that I began to examine more closely the effect of faith on action.

By his own account, Greene's religious commitment was a private and considered act, very much removed from questions of the relationship of Catholicism to a specifically contemporary world. Instead Catholicism provided an intellectually satisfying but at the same time rather abstract explanation of the world and the meaning of existence, one whose very logicality compelled belief. In making this kind of distinction Greene is denying any personal need for belief; he is claiming that the predicament of the young man seeking permanence in a dangerously impermanent society was not his predicament—instead Catholicism presented itself to him as possessing the irresistible logic of mathematics. There is however an inherent paradox in Greene's description of himself in 1936 as 'a Catholic with an intellectual if not an emotional belief in Catholic dogma', and in his reiteration of this sentiment half a life-time later.

Greene's distinction between intellectual and emotional belief is vital to an understanding of the relationship of the novelist to belief in the thirties. Edward Upward uses virtually the same terms to discuss retrospectively the basis of his political commitment, and in doing so concedes to an emotional or personal motivation towards belief that he tended very much to deny in the thirties. Evelyn Waugh on the other hand, writing in 1949, employs the same distinction in order to establish, with Greene, the dominantly intellectual motivation of his conversion. 'It only remained to examine the historic and philosophic grounds for supposing the Christian revelation to be genuine. I was fortunate enough to be introduced to a brilliant and holy priest who undertook to prove this to me, and so on firm intellectual conviction but with little emotion I was admitted into the Church' ['Come Inside,' *The Road to Damascus,* ed. J. A. O'Brien]. This distinction is an artificial one in the sense that purely emotional or purely intellectual belief are impossibilities, but at the same time the implications of both terms are clear. Intellectual belief denies or substantially reduces the importance of the individual's background and personality and circumstances in the decision to believe. It is a logical, and by implication unimpeachable process, by which any rational human being might become convinced of the validity of Catholicism or indeed of Marxism. Emotional belief, by contrast, emphasizes the personal need for faith, the willingness to accept belief without a rigorous understanding of premisses or dogma. It carries implications of weakness or immaturity. Both Greene and Waugh, in their insistence upon the intellectual basis of their belief, reveal an awareness of these secondary implications, and their possible imputation to themselves. Yet to adopt this distinction as a critical yardstick, and to judge Greene and Waugh's fiction of the period in terms of its success in justifying intellectual commitment to Catholicism, is a fruitless exercise; as fruitless as it is to judge the fiction of Warner and Upward by its ability logically to justify belief in Marxism. Belief, when it appears in these novels, is important not as an independent phenomenon, but as an aspect of the hero's predicament. It is, in other words, predominantly personal or 'emotional' belief that informs the novels of the period—the relationship of belief and individual believer, and the effect each has upon the other.

Both Greene and Waugh claim to have been convinced by the indisputable validity of Catholic dogma, and to have accordingly had no option but to become converts. The emotional or instinctive belief emerged only gradually, complementing and perhaps finally overwhelming the intellect. In his autobiography, Greene quotes approvingly an old priest who has been questioned on the reasons for his faith: 'I knew them once, but I have forgotten them.'

Once the intellectual groundwork has been laid securely, it is safe to cover it with the luxury of emotional belief. By this initial and single-minded concern with the rational validity of Catholicism, Greene and Waugh were taking out insurance upon their faith. Emotional belief carries with it the strong possibility of later disillusionment, if and when the tenets of the faith seem increasingly to diverge from reality. But if it is first established that the faith covers convincingly all aspects of reality, the possibility of disillusionment is eliminated. Greene's description of his faith as intellectually compelled is in effect a claim for the irrefutability of religion. But there is a final disingenuousness to the claim: it is possible intellectually to understand the means by which Catholic doctrine explains and justifies the individual existence, but the understanding will not *of itself* lead to conversion. The initial impetus must spring from a need for, or at the very least a predisposition towards faith. Greene's state of mind as a child and adolescent, described in his autobiography, strongly suggests such a need. His retained memories—of a man in a workhouse cutting his throat, of a dead dog in a pram, of a tin jerry full of blood—seem contrived, but they convey the morbid sensitivity of a child lost in a confusing and threatening world. Greene's recollections present the most powerful image of the rootlessness and uncertainty that characterized his generation. His pessimistic world view required a powerful belief to prevent progress towards complete nihilism.

The emotional basis of belief, the instinctive pull away from despair towards the security and self-justification of faith, is glossed over by Greene in his autobiography and other reminiscences, but it may be seen at work in his fiction of the thirties, particularly in the two early novels that have since remained out of print at the author's instigation, *The Name of Action* and *Rumour at Nightfall.* Greene has expressed his puzzlement at the failure of public and reviewers to recognize his Catholicism until 1938; 'I had become a Catholic in 1926, and all my books, except for one lamentable volume of verse at Oxford, had been written as a Catholic, but no one had noticed the faith to which I belonged before the publication of *Brighton Rock*' [introduction to *Brighton Rock*]. Indeed an earlier novel, *It's a Battlefield,* was seen by *Viewpoint* (later *Left Review*) in 1934 as a welcome example of the kind of fiction they advocated. 'As yet English novelists show few signs of advancement in this direction, [i.e. of depicting the revolutionary struggle] though Graham Greene in *It's a Battlefield* has some conception of the basis of the class-struggle which he depicts against a wide and varied social background.' While it is true that Greene was not regarded as a Catholic novelist until 1938, he has himself been partly responsible for encouraging the idea that *Brighton Rock* was his first 'Catholic' work. In an interview [with Philip Toynbee in the *Observer*] in 1957 he claimed that for a decade after his conversion he 'simply hadn't had sufficient experience of how Catholics think or behave, and therefore . . . couldn't write about them'. The force of the word 'couldn't' is ambiguous. As a piece of self-criticism it may well be valid, yet Greene seems also to be suggesting that he *didn't* write about Catholics, that his incomplete understanding of Catholic motivation and sensibility actually prevented him tackling the subject. But, as he puts it, 'by [1937] the time was ripe for me to use Catholic characters'. In both these comments there is a muddiness of intention that seems to confirm rather than deny the notion that Greene only began to be a 'Catholic novelist' with **Brighton Rock.** In fact, Catholicism and Catholic characters are by no means absent from the earlier novels, and in **The Name of Action** and **Rumour at Nightfall** they play a considerable part.

The hero of **The Name of Action** is a wealthy and bored young man named Oliver Chant, whose need to break out of his purposeless existence leads him to the Palatinate with the vague aim of financing a revolution. The confusion between Chant's personal and political motives increases as he becomes infatuated with Anne-Marie Demassener, the wife of the Dictator. Against a background of violence, intrigue and self-aggrandizement, Catholicism is posed as a secure source of permanent values for those fortunate enough to have inherited their belief. When Chant questions his lieutenant, Weber, on the loyalty of some supporters, he receives the reply: 'They are all good Catholics'—as though he held some standard that had nothing to do with elementary schools or priests or even attendance at Mass. The 'as though' is not ironical; it reflects the puzzlement of the outsider when faced with such an irrefutable 'standard'. Catholicism for Weber is above the mundane and the everyday, offering an enviable security. Weber's wife is the embodiment of Catholic solidity: 'She spoke with a certainty which could never have been troubled by needs, questionings, doubts, analysis. That, thought Chant with some bitterness, was a haven to which neither he nor Anne-Marie Demassener could ever come. They were born in an age of doubt and to a class which wished to know too much.' Chant's heritage is a modern one, a dry rationalism which offers him little comfort. He and his generation have lost contact, apparently irrevocably, with the spiritual certainty possessed by Frau Weber. In an attempt to still and satisfy the 'needs, questionings, doubts, analysis', he places his hopes first in political action, then in sexual love. Both fail him, and the recognition of failure comes to him in a church, 'where God was not a cloudy aspiration but a concrete hope or fear. . . . He had believed in freedom. . . . He had believed in love. . . . It had seemed to Chant that he had been enabled to see the boundaries of the infinite. "O God, O God", he murmured . . . "I wish that I could believe in your infinity." ' Twentieth-century scepticism which has moulded Chant's personality now prevents commitment to the mysterious faith which would resolve his spiritual crisis and offer him the certainty he requires. It is the emotions that are drawing him towards commitment, and the intellect, the curses of doubt and analysis, that hold him back. He belongs to a generation of explainers, but the power of Catholicism is presented as quite inexplicable.

Rumour at Nightfall, published in the following year, is set in Spain during the Carlist Wars. Crane, an Englishman and a man of reason, is attracted to a darkly romantic, aristocratic Spanish woman who possesses the certainty of faith: ' "It seems to me that you must know everything which is worth knowing." His eyes swept back across the room, up the wall to the crucifix. He stared at it with a sceptical hope of enlightenment. "I envy you."

He has seen the effect of belief on many people. He knew it was regarded as a recipe for peace, an ingredient of courage.' Catholicism in these two novels is always described in such portentous and mysterious terms, and fits fairly well within the format of the romantic adventure story. Greene takes a modern, rational, directionless man and places him in the context of another faith, another tradition. The hero reacts with envy and a crudely articulated desire for the certainty of belief, but he does not, or rather cannot, make any meaningful connection with the ancient faith. Its promise of fulfilment remains tantalizingly unattainable to the rationalist mind, because any connection that is made is on an emotional level only—the intellect remains stubbornly unresponsive. Catholicism in these two novels belongs to the past, not to the sterile modern age, and like the past it is irrecoverable. Both novels can be seen as statements of the problem facing the twentieth century man attracted to religious commitment; they point both to the emotional need for faith, and to the impossibility of overcoming scepticism. At the same time there is an element of bitterness and contempt in these descriptions of Catholics and Catholicism, a suggestion that Frau Weber's 'certainty' might also be smug and simple-minded. Frau Weber's religion completely pre-empts needs and questionings and doubts, but Catholicism must be capable of answering needs, and resolving doubts, if it is to appear at all meaningful to a Chant or a Crane. The gulf separating the modern Englishman from the consolation of faith is emphasized by Greene's placement of his self-questioning heroes in conventional adventure-story settings—the romanticized nineteenth-century Spain of **Rumour at Nightfall,** and the equally romanticized Palatine Republic of the twenties in **The Name of Action.** The opposition of scepticism and Catholicism thus corresponds to the opposition of realism and romance, of relevance and irrelevance. Catholicism maintains a shaky presence in the novels by its association with the mysterious and romanticized settings, but by virtue of this association, it also seems to have no connection with the predicament of the modern hero. As Greene began to abandon what may be termed serious romantic fiction, and to concentrate more closely on the reality of the thirties, it became increasingly difficult to maintain even this balance. In a novel with a modern, realistic, and hence for Greene almost exclusively depressing setting, there would seem to be little room for asserting the presence, much less the validity, of Catholicism.

From **Stamboul Train** (1932) onwards, Greene's novels of the thirties clearly reflect a world without values. This notion of a foundering, purposeless society, heading inexorably towards chaos, is characteristic of the times. Its corollary was the desire for security and order through some kind of belief, and Greene was as aware as anyone of the claims of Marxism to fill that role. He has always inclined to the left in his political views, and indeed while an undergraduate at Oxford had been for a brief time a member of the Communist Party. In his autobiography, he dismisses the episode as prompted only by the 'far-fetched idea of gaining control [of the Oxford branch] and perhaps winning a free trip to Moscow or Leningrad'. Yet one inevitably poses this incident against the dominant tone of the descriptions of his early life—the constant quest for the solution to boredom and to what he refers to on more than one occasion as manic depression. Without presuming to extrapolate too far from his brief published comments, it seems justified to assume that the Communist Party suggested for Greene, however briefly, a solution to his predicament. Disillusionment however was almost immediate, as he describes in *A Sort of Life,* and more effectively in the novel published in 1934, *It's a Battlefield,* which reflects both his attraction to and his final dissatisfaction with political commitment.

It's a Battlefield appeared in 1934, ten years after the passing encounter with the Communist Party. By this time he had been a convert to Roman Catholicism for eight years and opposition to a rival cause would have been an element in his antipathy. He had allied himself with a long conservative tradition against what many intellectuals saw as the hope for the future, and he felt the need to express his dissatisfaction with this newer faith. To write a novel at such a time pointing out the inadequacies of Communism as a belief was for a man of Greene's outlook a particularly courageous step; he did not conform to the popular equation of religion and reaction and has always been sympathetic to the cause of social justice. (pp. 62-7)

It's a Battlefield is Greene's most direct attempt to deal with the contemporary social and political atmosphere. His characters grasp at Communism not with the purity of idealists but as desperate, flawed people seeking escape from their social and psychological predicaments. Jim Drover, a quiet, unpresumptuous man, is arrested at a political demonstration after stabbing and killing a policeman for allegedly attacking his wife. He is sentenced to death, and a Party meeting is called to press for a reprieve. Greene's description of the meeting, though relentless, is certainly not the work of an inflexible anti-Communist, but of one who sympathizes with the need for belief, however unsatisfactory its object. 'Nobody', he wrote in *The Lawless Roads,* 'can endure existence without a philosophy.' He conveys the aura of solidarity and purpose that pervades the hall as the meeting begins, 'the sincerity of the thousands who did not wrangle for leadership, who were ready to follow in patience and poverty'. Greene's sympathies lie, sentimentally, with this amorphous body of people whose main characteristic is hope. When he focusses attentions on individuals, however, the meeting loses its spiritual quality. The revolutionary rhetoric of the fashionable intellectual, Mr Surrogate, stands in blatant contrast to his pampered life. He is in love with abstractions—'Social Betterment, the Equality of Opportunity, the Means of Production'—and out of love with reality: 'In a cause was exhilaration, exaltation, a sense of Freedom; individuals gave pain by their brutality, their malice, their lack of understanding.' It is this gap between the political ideal and the social fact that Greene consistently points to as the inevitable failure of secular commitment.

If other characters in the novel are treated more sympathetically, it is largely because they admit their own shaky bases for belief. For Conder, the journalist, Communism is merely one more component of a fantasy world in which he imagines himself now a respectable family man, now a director of Imperial Chemicals, and now a Red Crusad-

er. It is one of the many masks he assumes to escape the reality of a bedsitter in Little Compton Street. Drover's brother Conrad is interested in the Party only in so far as it can help him to preserve the brother he idolizes. Kay Rimmer, though in her own way sympathetic to her brother-in-law and his probable fate, uses the Party mainly as a means of escaping temporarily the boredom of day to day existence; not for ideological reasons, but because at Communist Party meetings there are fifty men for every girl, a favourable ratio—'art, politics, the church, Kay Rimmer had tried them all'. Only Jules Briton is serious and explicit about what he would expect from Communism—'he wanted something he could follow with passion'. Jules is also a Catholic. Not much is made of this, but there are two important instances in which his religion is mentioned. He states mysteriously that 'none of you are going to do as much for Drover as I am. I feel it. None of you are going to do as much'. Subsequently, in his 'home', the Church, Jules prays for Drover. It would be over-ingenious to suppose from this that Drover owes the eventual commutation of his sentence to a miracle, but the suggestion of a more powerful force than communism or political action is there. And when Jules contemplates marrying Kay Rimmer, it is important for him to know that she is a Catholic, for it makes the bearing of reality less hard, 'easier, then, the formality of marriage, more final the barrier against loneliness, an impregnable dyke till death; otherwise the sea corroded'. These are the qualities Jules appreciates in his religion; he sees it as offering protection from the world. The Catholic sacrament of marriage, its guarantee of permanence rooted in the very essence of the Church, becomes for Jules a strangely negative consolation, a 'dyke' to hold back the flood of reality. Jules does not yield to the attractions of a political faith which claims—falsely for Greene—the power to change the order of things. Catholicism makes no such claim, but rather the power to justify and make significant the *present* order of things. From here, it is only a comparatively short step to Jules's notion of a Catholicism which makes life more 'bearable', and this is the level at which religion remains in the novel.

Greene felt the pull of Communism, the hold it had over intellectual life in the thirties, and over his generation in particular; but he could not believe in the possibility of a fair and just society because he had no corresponding belief in the essential goodness of man. Communism offered him no spiritual consolation for the oppressiveness of the world. It is just this consolation that Catholicism did offer. In an essay of 1936 on Henry James, Greene maintained that he had 'yet to find socialist or conservative who can feel any pity for the evil he denounces, and the final beauty of James's stories lies in their pity: "The poetry is in the pity." ' For Greene, any political belief involves the denunciation of a great part of human society, removing it beyond the bounds of sympathy. Political belief demands villains, and villains cannot be pitied. In political terms, pity is a weakness, but in terms of his religion, it is a sign of the individual's ability to accept the whole world, however sordid or oppressive, as part of God's design. Catholicism justifies the world as it is, not as it might be. In quoting the line of Wilfred Owen's, that 'the poetry is in the pity', Greene also emphasizes the connection between the ability to feel pity, and the expression of finer values in art. What is required of the artist is a willingness to understand and to sympathize. In Greene's view, the politically motivated writer denies sympathy to a large section of humanity, and is forced to take a blinkered view.

Greene looked to the present, not to what he regarded as an illusory future. 'There are others, of course, who prefer to look a stage ahead, for whom Intourist provides cheap tickets into a plausible future, but my journey represented a distrust of any future based on what we are.' He scoffs at his contemporaries, but the description of his journey into the wilds of Liberia, recorded in *Journey Without Maps,* recalls the journeys undertaken by Upward and Warner's heroes, the journey of the single man through a frightening and dangerous terrain in search of permanent values. Greene was particularly keen to observe in the primitive societies of Liberia the true nature of humanity at its most basic level; to see, more clearly than would be possible in a European, civilized society, the basic ignobility of man. At the same time the tribal beliefs and rituals accorded this ignoble existence value and dignity and significance; Liberia appealed to him as a country in which the quotidian and the spiritual were in obvious accord:

> What is the fascination of this country on which the dead hand of the white has never settled? I think it is a religious fascination: the country offers the European an opportunity of living continuously in the presence of the supernatural. The secret societies, as it were, sacramentalise the whole of life. ['Three Travellers,' *Spectator,* 1939]

Greene uses the word 'religious' very much in the sense in which it is used by Rex Warner, to describe the quality of significance and permanence which both writers feel must lie beneath superficial reality.

Christianity, as a possible alternative to the despair and futility of contemporary existence, is present even in *England Made Me,* the bleakest of Greene's thirties novels. The suggestion is conveyed through the character of the decayed journalist Minty; out of the desperate sordidness of his life, Minty feels the hope that the Church may have to offer, but his approach is furtive and uncertain: 'A church claimed him. The darkness, the glow of the sanctuary lamp drew him more than food. It was Lutheran, of course, but it had the genuine air of plaster images, of ever-burning light, of sins forgiven. He looked this way and that, he bent his head and dived for the open door, with the caution and dry mouthed excitement of a secret debauchee.' Minty senses the truth, but like Chant in *The Name of Action* and Crane in *Rumour at Nightfall,* he cannot grasp it. There is in this description of Minty's attraction to the Church a curious mixture of authorial sympathy and contempt. The antithetical irony of the phrase 'genuine air of plaster images' points to a failing in Minty's understanding of Christianity and of God. His religion is superficial; he regards it as a comforting retreat from the world, but has no intellectual understanding of the nature of Christianity, and no conception of its relation to contemporary society. Minty's idea of God is of someone quite arbitrary in his actions; in the security of his room Minty plays God with the life of a spider, keeping it imprisoned under a tooth-glass. God is for Minty an omnipotent being who plays with us for unfathomable reasons of his own, and in this sense Minty's resort to the sanctuary of the Lutheran Church offers not hope but another version of despair.

Despite the noticeable change in Greene's fictional territory in the years from 1930 to 1935, from the early 'serious romances' to the contemporary realism of *It's a Battlefield* and *England Made Me,* there remains throughout a striking similarity in the descriptions of churches and in other references to religion. The church which seems to offer sanctuary to Minty is very like the church which offers temporary comfort to Oliver Chant in *The Name of Action.* Despite Greene's own declarations that his original commitment was intellectual rather than emotional, the comfort offered by religion in these novels is an emotional and sentimentalized one, powerful but undefined. At the same time there is the suggestion that Chant and Crane and Minty are attracted to religion for very personal reasons, and cannot see it as anything more than a means of personal salvation, a 'recipe for peace'. When Minty approaches the church with the 'dry mouthed excitement of a secret debauchee', he is clearly resorting to religion as a kind of drug, a magic potion that will make life easier for him. Only with *Brighton Rock* does Greene make religion, and specifically Catholicism, a central fact of contemporary life, understood by the hero as a belief with certain rules and certain demands. The previous novels appear to deny the contemporary validity of Catholicism, or at least of the kind of simplified, romanticized religion they describe; *Brighton Rock,* by contrast, attempts to justify it. In this sense, Greene's own view of the novel as a definite departure from earlier work becomes clearer.

Pinkie Brown is leader of a Brighton gang at seventeen, a cheat, a liar and a murderer. But Pinkie is also a Catholic, and his commitment is, as Greene claims of his own, based on reason:

> 'Of course it's true,' the boy said. 'What else could there be?' he went scornfully on. 'Why,' he said, 'it's the only thing that fits. These atheists, they don't know nothing. Of course there's Hell. Flames and damnation,' he said with his eyes on the dark shifting water and the lightning and the lamps going out above the black struts of the Palace Pier, 'torments'.

The apparent logic of Pinkie's belief rests on the same paradox as Greene's own. The dialogue provides the reasoned assertion of Catholicism as 'the only thing that fits', but the accompanying description emphasizes the appropriateness of Pinkie's Catholicism to a pessimistic world-view that may be innate, or may be acquired, but is not necessarily logical. Reason, logic, intellect—such terms, commonly invoked in the thirties to justify belief, did not include in their range of definition the spirit of inquiry. The function of 'reason' is rather to reinforce and legitimize the instincts. Pinkie's confidence in the existence of hell, expressed in repeated 'of courses' only emphasizes how immensely important it is to him that hell should exist. For Pinkie there is no point in being merely bad, he must be evil. Anyone is capable of being bad, but the judgement of actions as good or bad, right or wrong, is for Greene and for Pinkie a purely arbitrary one, based upon values that have no solid support. It is impossible in Greene's terms to evaluate action if there is no creed upon which to base decisions; only belief can evaluate action. The best that may otherwise be relied upon is an instinctive knowledge of right and wrong, which is in fact little more than a series of prejudices accumulated over a lifetime. Ida Arnold, pursuing Pinkie in the name of her own concept of justice, bases her actions upon personal, arbitrary values, and is thus condemned. For Greene, the qualities she possesses are negative ones—she is a good sort; her virtues, such as they are, exist in a vacuum. When Ida resolves to pursue the murderer of the man who has been kind to her, she is relying solely on her own judgement. In Greene's terms, she is adopting deliberately the role of fate, and this is presumptuous, misplaced righteousness. She assumes the task of retribution with an inadequate set of values to support her. The text consistently denigrates Ida Arnold's virtues; her kindness is 'Guiness kindness'. Greene plays deliberately upon conventional notions of natural justice by describing them as perverse and self-indulgent, whereas Pinkie's actions, which are in terms of conventional morality reprehensible, are also morally superior by dint of his belief in Catholicism.

Pinkie's actions, however anti-human, are based on a set of prescribed values. He believes in the evil of his deeds, and that they will lead him certainly to damnation. He is thus able to place his temporal actions in a wider context, and to discover for himself the importance of actions which would be otherwise insignificant. They are made significant by the certainty of the punishment he will receive from a higher authority than Ida Arnold. In the face of God and Evil, Ida's concept of right and wrong seems not to matter:

> 'There's things you don't know.' Rose brooded darkly by the bed, while [Ida Arnold] argued on: a God wept in a garden and cried out upon a cross. . . .
>
> 'I know one thing you don't. I know the difference between Right and Wrong. They didn't teach you *that* at school.'
>
> Rose didn't answer; the woman was quite right; the two words meant nothing to her. Their taste was extinguished by stronger foods—Good and Evil. The woman could tell her nothing she didn't know about these—she knew by tests as clear as mathematics that Pinkie was evil—what did it matter in that case whether he was right or wrong.

Unlike Ida Arnold, Pinkie shares Greene's pessimistic world view. A weary assertion from Rose that 'life's not so bad', prompts from Pinkie a vehement reply: 'Don't you believe it,' he said, 'I'll tell you what it is. It's gaol, it's not knowing where to get some money. Worms and cataract, cancer. You hear 'em shrieking from the upper windows—children being born. It's dying slowly.' Pinkie's jaundiced view is made to carry a great deal more weight than the Rose-coloured. Our unconsidered notions of what is to be admired and what condemned, what is sympathetic and what unsympathetic, are reversed in *Brighton Rock.* Or are they? Waugh plays upon complacent no-

tions of moral good in *Black Mischief* in order to point up their superficiality. But in Waugh's description of Seth's birth control campaign, we are actually allowed to share Seth's assumptions, so that the condemnation of Seth is a condemnation of the reader's complacency. Greene also evokes a conventional notion of goodness, Ida Arnold's, in order to condemn it, but in *Brighton Rock* the text distances the reader from Ida. We do not discover for ourselves as it were that we have been mistaken, our sympathy with her misplaced. Instead it is always clear she is on the wrong side, despite her obsession with natural justice. Greene establishes Pinkie's moral superiority by appealing to another kind of complacency in the reader, by which the positive is accepted as the superficial, and the negative as the profound. Pinkie's stylized world of dark passions and expressionist lighting is founded as securely on sentimentality as Ida's drunken bonhomie. His authority in the novel depends upon a superficial acceptance by the reader of the profundity of his vision.

The acts Pinkie commits may be defined according to the individual perspective as cruel, bad, anti-social, defiant; but according to the perspective of Roman Catholicism they are evil. Pinkie has committed and continues to commit mortal sin. Given this, it would seem at first that his actions involve a kind of courage of commitment, a resolve to act and to accept the consequences, were it not made clear that Pinkie's personality is a fixed result of his environment. As such the murders of Hale and Dallow, the cynical marriage to Rose, would have taken place regardless of his religious beliefs. They may have been in Greene's terminology merely wrong, but they would still have occurred. It is a paradox therefore that Pinkie's awareness of his own future damnation should render his actions not harder to live with, but easier. Pinkie's Catholicism does not dictate individual action, but dignifies acts already committed. . . . [There] is no suggestion in *Brighton Rock* that belief in Catholicism genuinely influences action—its important function is to change the light by which the value of action is seen and judged. All acts are transformed by the rules of the Church into significant acts—Pinkie's wrongdoing assumes some meaning in the wider scheme of things. It is in this sense that Greene's novel is, as he claims, an examination of 'the effect of faith on action'. The certainty of Hell provided by Pinkie's religious belief lends purpose to the crimes he was predestined to commit.

Pinkie cannot bear the idea that his existence may be pointless. The conscious progress towards Hell gives him the knowledge of his own significance that he requires. He acts within a strictly defined framework of divine reward and punishment. Pinkie's lot will be punishment, but that is preferable for him to the knowledge that whatever his temporal actions, the end result will be a vacuum. The prospect of damnation offers eventual escape from the reality he detests, for life appals Pinkie: 'She got up and he saw the skin of her thigh for a moment above the artificial silk, and a prick of sexual desire disturbed him like a sickness. That was what happened to a man in the end: the stuffy room, the wakeful children, the Saturday night movements from the other bed. Was there no escape—anywhere—for anyone?' To escape all this, Pinkie uses his inherited Catholicism in a very calculating sense. Not only does it lend his actions significance, but in a logical way it justifies them, for murder and betrayal are leading him surely out of the unbearable world he inhabits, if only to Hell. 'It was worth murdering a world.' Even so, Pinkie's commitment to damnation cannot be total, for it is not simply in damnation but in Catholicism that he places his faith. He must believe, however half-heartedly, in the *possibility* of salvation. He remembers as a kind of talisman part of the familiar quotation from William Camden's 'Epitaphs', which reads more fully:

> My friend judge not me,
> Thou seest I judge not thee:
> Betwixt the stirrup and the ground,
> Mercy I asked, mercy I found.

When Rose, the pathetic bride-to-be, asks Pinkie if he believes in 'it', he answers with conviction that of course there is a Hell: ' "And Heaven too," Rose said with anxiety, while the rain fell interminably on. "Oh, maybe," the Boy said, "maybe." ' Pinkie has to believe in Heaven as the mirror image of his own goal, but there is a weary obligation about it. If he believes intellectually in the logic and fitness of eternal damnation, he is forced by his religious faith to hold a similar belief in eternal reward. The difference for Pinkie is that while his emotions, his very existence, support the belief in damnation, there is no corresponding support for salvation. To repent would be to deny the significance of his own existence, for if the simple act of repentance could wipe out his crimes, then the structure and purpose he had given them by his faith in religion would disappear as well. For Pinkie, confirmation of the significance of his temporal existence will come only when he is made to suffer eternally for it.

Despite the dominant movement of the novel towards this end, Greene does, in the last few pages, reassert the possibility of salvation implied earlier in the lines from Camden. After Pinkie's plan to trick Rose into committing suicide has been thwarted, and he has been killed instead, Rose seeks the comfort of the confessional. Here, in this final scene, Mary McCarthy's charge [in *Partisan Review*, 1944] that Greene is an 'ersatz serious novelist' seems inescapable. The old priest's words, implying a comparison between Pinkie and Péguy, are unconvincing. Pinkie may have been in a state of mortal sin, but not because, like Péguy, 'he couldn't bear the idea that any soul could suffer damnation'. Pinkie revels in the idea. Perhaps, though, these lines apply to Rose, for she cannot bear the thought of Pinkie in Hell, and wants to be damned herself that she may be with him. But the homily delivered at the end of the priest's speech seems to refer to Pinkie: 'You can't conceive, my child, nor can I or anyone . . . the . . . appalling strangeness of the mercy of God.' It is Rose's rejoinder that convinces: 'He's damned. He knew what he was about.' The internal logic of the novel leads towards Pinkie's damnation, but commitment to damnation is not regarded by Greene as its own justification; it is instead the discernible evidence of commitment to Catholicism. The conscious progress towards eternal punishment must include the faith in all aspects of religion, including the possibility of salvation. Just as T. S. Eliot regarded Baude-

laire's deliberate 'capacity for damnation' as leaving the way open for salvation, so Greene saw, in the conscious evil of Baron Corvo, 'the potential sanctity of the man'. It is not by any means an unfamiliar argument, that the perpetrator of evil acts is afforded the chance of heavenly forgiveness, whereas the Ida Arnolds of the world, who are unaware of the distinction between good and evil, have not even this slim chance. Yet at the end of *Brighton Rock,* Greene seems unwilling to leave the affirmation of the novel to rest upon an implied and comparatively sophisticated theological argument, and so Rose is pregnant. The emphasis is taken off Pinkie's apparent damnation and put onto the future. There will be a baby, and Rose, if she survives the horror of the recording Pinkie has bequeathed her, may 'make him a saint—to pray for his father'. Pinkie's damnation is by no means complete. But the possibility of salvation also implies the negation of Pinkie, for salvation would render his temporal actions—his entire life—insignificant.

The provisos that Greene attaches to Pinkie's damnation smack very much of the sentimentality which he condemned elsewhere as a 'pernicious influence' on literature. Reviewing Chaplin's *Modern Times,* he objected to the 'unfair pathos of the blind girl and the orphan child,' but in *Brighton Rock* he is not above a little unfair pathos of his own. The references to Camden's lines, and to Péguy, are an attempt to offer hope for Pinkie's soul, but the momentum of Pinkie's progress towards damnation is too great to be broken by a pair of academic niceties. And so Greene allows the weight of the ending to rest upon a child. The unresolved complexities of the argument he has constructed are shunted into the hazy future, and sentimentality triumphs over logic, emotion over reason. So despite Greene's contempt for the Communist writer's faith in a Utopian future, the ending of *Brighton Rock* suggests a similar confidence. Belief not only justifies present action, it also offers the possibility of eventual reward—salvation—for having acted as a believer. During a conversation recorded in Paris in 1950 for the Catholic journal *Dieu Vivant,* Greene rather confused his interlocutors by assuring them that contrary to all their assumptions, Pinkie is indeed saved at the end. But, they persisted, you seem in the novel to give in to the blackest pessimism. 'Pessimiste, moi!' Greene replied. 'Je me croyais au contraire débordant d'optimisme.' Behind the relentless cynicism of *Brighton Rock*—the ignobility and the seediness, the emphasis on evil and damnation—are optimism and confidence and faith, all of which lie beyond logical justification. (pp. 68-77)

Richard Johnstone, "The Catholic Novelist I: Graham Greene," in his The Will to Believe: Novelists of the Nineteen-thirties, *Oxford University Press, Oxford, 1982, pp. 62-78.*

Richard Kelly

Our Man in Havana is the last and best of Greene's entertainments. It surpasses the earlier works in depth of characterization and subtlety of theme and presents a comic vision of the world that anticipates *The Comedians* and *Monsignor Quixote.* The label "entertainment" for this

Graham Greene in later years.

book fails to disclose its real genre. Greene more accurately describes the work as "a fairy story" set "at some indeterminate date in the future."

The plot captures a comic view of life that Greene has denied his previous heroes and invests his new protagonist with the unique sanity of the clown. (p. 139)

What sets *Our Man in Havana* apart from the earlier pieces is Greene's development of an important new theme, described by John Atkins [in his *Graham Greene*] as "the growing insistence that life resembles a dream, that our dreams may be our inner convictions, that dream logic is the significant logic." In this respect, *Our Man in Havana* most closely resembles *Travels with My Aunt* and *Monsignor Quixote* where, Greene argues, the borders between fact and fiction, reality and illusion, are indiscernible.

James Wormwold can be seen as a man who discovers the powers of dreaming and creation. This "fairy story" opens with Dr. Hasselbacher and Wormwold enjoying a drink together in the Wonder Bar. The shadow of Lewis Carroll's Wonderland is further extended in Dr. Hasselbacher's advice to his friend: "You should dream more, Mr. Wormwold. Reality in our century is not something to be faced." Through his subsequent creation of characters and reports, Wormwold establishes his own Wonderland and in essence becomes an author in whom dream and reality blend together as one. Milly asks him, "Are you becoming a writer?" To which he replies, "Yes—an imaginative

writer." The death of the reconaissance pilot, Raul, marks the point at which fiction and reality merge. Wormwold's question, "Can we write human beings into existence?" is to be answered in the affirmative, and anticipates Monsignor Quixote's pantomime mass during which he administers the "fictional" but no less real Host to the mayor. Wormwold's fiction encompasses the actual world and thus brings about Raul's and Dr. Hasselbacher's deaths and the attempt on his own life. All of these events are set in motion through the imaginative powers of the naive author. It is interesting to note, however, that Wormwold's dreaming mind was first stirred by a concern for real money. Money helps him to secure still another dream, that of Milly's happiness. Wormwold thus comes to represent the creative artist who consumes reality for his fiction and in turn is nearly consumed by his own creation.

Related to this theme is the recurrent figure of the clown. Wormwold, who admires the clown and models his own life after him, reflects on the comic role as means of survival:

> The cruel come and go like cities and thrones
> and powers, leaving their ruins behind them.
> They had no permanence. But the clown whom
> he had seen last year with Milly at the circus—
> that clown was permanent, for his act never
> changed. That was the way to live: the clown
> was unaffected by the vagaries of public men and
> the enormous discoveries of the great.

He goes on to tell Milly that "If only we had been born

clowns, nothing bad would happen to us except a few bruises and a smear of whitewash." His later involvement in the circus of espionage turns him into a clown spotlighted in center ring. After Wormwold, who "had no vocation for violence," shoots Carter's Dunhill instead of his intended victim, Carter cries out, "You—you clown," to which Greene adds, "How right Carter was."

Wormwold the clown is a survivor in his own fairy story. Obviously not the traditional fairy of folklore, Wormwold nevertheless is mischievous and capricious, and possesses the power of magic and enchantment. The clown-artist is a paradox in that he stands outside of time (where the "Reality in our century is not something to be faced") while simultaneously embodying in the art of his comic fiction the passing events of the cruel who "come and go like cities and thrones and powers." (pp. 142-44)

> *Richard Kelly, in his* Graham Greene, *Frederick Ungar Publishing Co., 1984, 195 p.*

Steve Vineberg

Perhaps no other contemporary novelist of worth has had as great an association with movies as Graham Greene. More than a dozen and a half films have been derived from his novels and stories, and he himself worked on the adaptations of four of them (***Brighton Rock,*** 1947; ***The Fallen Idol,*** 1948; ***Our Man in Havana,*** 1959; and ***The Comedians,*** 1967); he reviewed films for *The Spectator* and *Night and Day* between 1935 and 1940; and he has written a handful of original screenplays as well, the most celebrated of which is ***The Third Man,*** directed by Carol Reed in 1949. Greene's script of ***The Third Man*** seems to me worthy of close analysis because it is a small marvel of novelistic technique. Three themes are carefully crosshatched: (1) the social and moral disintegration of post-war Europe; (2) the discrepancy between the real world and the world as fiction orders it; and (3) the nature of personal and social responsibility. Structurally, ***The Third Man*** is a spy thriller; psychologically, it is the chronicle of the coming of age of a naive Canadian writer, Rollo Martins. [The critic adds in a footnote: "In his original screenplay, Greene called his protagonist 'Rollo'; in the film, the name has been changed to 'Holly.' In this detail as in all others, my article reflects the original script as it existed before shooting began."] Through the employment of literary controls—irony, shift in consciousness, manipulation of the central character by juxtaposing his behavior and the behavior of others towards him, and by examining him in a hostile context—Greene illustrates a novelistic concern with the limitations of fiction in unearthing the truth.

Greene sets ***The Third Man*** in Vienna just after the Second World War—a burnt-out Vienna that appalls Martins when he first glimpses it, on a bus ride from the airport. Its citizens live in a state of constant deprivation. A "ratty little man" begs a cigarette from Rollo and he appeases Anna's landlady by offering her a handful of them; electricity is rationed; at the Josefstadt Theatre, where Anna performs, foreigners in the audience indicate their appreciation of the performance by throwing bouquets of coveted merchandise—tea from the British and whiskey from Americans. Martins, whose consciousness the film embraces at the outset, experiences Vienna as a post-Apocalyptic Babel: the Allies have divided the city into four zones—British, American, French and Russian—each with its own landmarks and its own set of restrictions. His first instructions come from the Vice Consul at the airport: "Remember, Vienna is an occupied city. You must be extremely careful to observe all official regulations," but the complex of rules only reveals itself to him when he sets out to investigate the mystery of his friend Harry Lime's allegedly accidental death. Baron Kurtz, the first of Lime's companions whom Rollo encounters, cannot meet him in Sacher's Hotel, where Rollo is staying, because Kurtz is an Austrian and Sacher's is off limits to Austrians. The only bar that will accept Martins' American cash is a dive that Greene describes as follows: "The same semi-nude photographs on the stairs, the same half-drunk Americans at the bar, the same bad wine and extraordinary gins—you might be in any third-rate haunt in any other shabby capital of a shabby Europe." Lime hides out in the Russian zone, where he is safe from the British police (and where he can stay as long as he remains "useful" to the Russians).

The world of ***The Third Man*** is ruled by boundaries, geography, international politics. They touch the lives of the four major characters—Lime, who survives by manipulating them to his advantage; Colonel Calloway, whose job as police inspector requires him to strike bargains with them; Anna, whom the Russians claim when Calloway learns that Tyler (on Lime's behalf) forged her passport; and Martins, who falls in love with Anna and is thus affected by her difficulties. Furthermore, all the citizens of Vienna (a group not represented by any of the four above-mentioned characters) live under the shadow of international politics and must, like Kurtz, be careful not to antagonize the police by breaking geographical rules. Greene captures the farcical quality of this complicated, precarious political structure in the bizarre scene in which four military policemen, one from each of the foreign powers in residence in the city, arrive at Anna's apartment to transport her to headquarters. The most sympathetic of the quartet, the British M.P., tells her gently, "It's the law, Miss. We can't go against the protocol." Anna protests, "I don't even know what protocol means." "I don't either, Miss," the British M.P. replies.

Greene has chosen this skewed, blockaded world as his setting because the character around whom the plot swings, Harry Lime, is presented on some level as the result of the moral confusion that pervades the Europe of the late forties. On another level he is a modern vice figure whose personality is simply unleashed by an opportune political situation—sick people in need of drugs, poor people in need of money and not averse to obtaining it in morally repugnant ways, like Kurtz and Joseph Harbin. But whatever one's perception of Lime may be, his supremely cynical speech to Martins as they ride on the "Great Wheel" represents the culmination of the political thinking Greene has bared for us in the earlier scenes of the movie: "In these days, old man, nobody thinks in terms of human beings. Governments don't, so why should we?"

The feelings the name "Vienna" invariably evoke for the reader are ironically undercut throughout the film by this bleak vision; Greene emphasizes what Vienna has descended to by reminding us of her cultivated past. After Rollo receives admission to "the military zone of Vienna," we hear a Strauss waltz. En route to Harry's supposed grave, the camera shows us photographs of the dead on other gravestones in the cemetery: one is a dancing master, and others have, Greene suggests, "respectable faces with waxed moustaches and morning coats." Anna's cheap apartment was once a reception room, and her aging landlady strives to retain some scrap of dignity while she accepts Martins' appeasement bribe of four cigarettes. Baron Kurtz, who arranges to meet Rollo at the Mozart Café and who carries an ivory-handled cane and "an elegant little 18th century snuffbox," cuts a jarringly banal figure: "He wears a toupée, flat and yellow with the hair out straight at the back and not fitting close." We learn later that the "Baron" is in truth the son of a butcher and a cloakroom attendant, "a slatternly woman with a malevolent sour face" who blows her nose with her fingers; and that he himself holds down a job as a violinist at the Casanova Club.

As said, *The Third Man* is a spy thriller. Greene establishes this very early, when Rollo arrives at Lime's residence, 15 Stiftgasse, and examines the spy holes in the apartment doors. At the funeral, one of the mourners (Winkel) "carries a wreath that he has obviously forgotten to lay on the coffin"—a suspicious detail—and he and Kurtz watch Rollo, "uneasy and puzzled" at the presence of this stranger. Calloway is described as "more like an observer than a participant in the scene"—another spy—and Paine watches him in conversation with Martins. In order to pump information from Martins, Calloway proceeds to get him drunk, indicating to the waiter by a glance that he should leave the two men alone. Greene insists that Kurtz's "English accent is really too good. A man ought not to speak a foreign language so well"—another suspicious detail. The porter's wife interrupts his dialogue with Martins and Kurtz and gives them an angry look; clearly she has been listening in and does not approve of Rollo's attempts to involve her husband in the business of Lime's death.

In order to penetrate Greene's purpose in writing *The Third Man* as a thriller, it would be useful to examine the structure of the screenplay. (pp. 33-6)

The film has almost a perfect circular structure determined by the two funerals of Harry Lime; Lime himself does not appear until two-thirds of the way through the picture (in what must be the most elaborately prepared entrance in movie history); and the first half, which is pure thriller (the serious content—the nature of Lime's activities, Martins' dilemma, etc.—surfaces only in the second half), ends with a send-up of itself when Martins, who thinks he is being kidnaped, finds himself at the Cultural Centre addressing a group of culture-hungry transplanted Londoners. These strategies have thematic significance, too, however. Lime's first funeral is a fiction, so a second funeral is necessary. So much conflicting information is given to us about Lime's life and death that Greene must resurrect him, though perhaps Lime fails, in the final analysis, to set the record straight. And in parodying itself, Greene's pleasant fiction deconstructs itself, revealing a layer of serious drama that the viewer must address. *The Third Man* concerns the creation of fictions.

Film, as writers and directors have demonstrated many times, is ideally suited to handle the theme of the conflict between fact and fiction. The camera moves back, and we realize that we have been looking at a mirror image, or that someone else, someone unexpected, was in the scene all along and we could not have known it. However, the collaboration of Carol Reed and Graham Greene on *The Third Man* is unusual in that Greene, a novelist who normally employs the mode of literary fiction in his exploration of this theme, is linked with an artist whose professional explorative instrument is the camera. Thus the movie works in both ways at once—cinematically and novelistically.

> TYLER. (His voice breaking clearly through the twitters). Mr. Martins, I'd like a word with you about your new novel.
>
> MARTINS. *The Third Man?*
>
> TYLER. Yes. (The meeting slowly quiets to hear them.)
>
> MARTINS. It's a murder story. I've just started it.
>
> TYLER. Are you a slow writer, Mr. Martins?
>
> MARTINS. Pretty quick when I get interested.
>
> TYLER. I'd say you were doing something pretty dangerous this time.
>
> MARTINS. Yes?
>
> TYLER. Mixing fact and fiction, like oil and water.
>
> MARTINS. Should I write it as straight fact?
>
> TYLER. Why no, Mr. Martins. I'd say stick to fiction, straight fiction.

The initial debate—the hinge of the spy story—is over the facts of Harry Lime's death. Martins learns from the porter at 15 Stiftgasse that Lime died accidentally and instantaneously, on his own doorstep, "bowled down like a rabbit" by a passing car. The porter claims to have been an eyewitness. Kurtz's version expands on the porter's: Tyler called to Lime from across the road, Lime began to cross, and after he had been hit, Tyler and Kurtz carried him to the far side of the road, where he died. Kurtz contradicts two details in the porter's story—he says that the vehicle was a truck, not a car, and that Lime died only after mentioning Martins' name and arranging for his safe trip home. Kurtz adds that the accident was clearly Harry's fault and that the driver has been officially exonerated. Anna's version, compiled from information given her by Kurtz and Winkel, is comically at odds with what Martins has already heard. She was told that Harry spoke of *her* at the last moment (prompting Martins to remark, "He must have been very clear in his head at the end: he remembered about me too"); that Winkel, Harry's physician, happened to be passing by a few moments after the accident occurred. This story contains too many coincidences for Rollo's satisfaction, and Anna, too, wonders if Harry's death was truly accidental. When Martins and Anna return to 15 Stiftgasse to interview the porter, he insists once again that Harry died at once ("He couldn't have been alive, not with his head in the state it was") and introduces the "third man"—the man who helped Tyler and Kurtz to carry the body across the street. Martins' further investigation sheds no more light on the incident, until the "third man" himself appears and turns out to be Harry Lime.

But this mystery is superficial—merely a dry run for the real mystery of identity at the root of Greene's screenplay, which he fills with alternative views of Harry Lime. Lime's name seems to have a mystical aura about it—it is practically the only name we hear for the first few scenes, it causes Anna to stop and stare at Martins and gains him access to Winkel's home. But who *is* Harry Lime? Rollo makes a drunken slip to Calloway that hints at the confusion of perspectives that the movie will unpack—"I guess there's nobody knew Harry like he did . . . (Corrects himself) . . . like I did"—because rather than fitting together in a jigsaw puzzle picture, like the reminiscences in *Citizen Kane,* the memories the characters offer of Lime cancel each other out. To Rollo he was a childhood hero who befriended and instructed a lonely boy starting at a new school; they drank together and indulged in adolescent tricks (Rollo was always clumsier and got caught); and just before his death, Harry invited Rollo, who he must have known was broke, out to Vienna to work for him in "some sort of charity organization which helped to get medical supplies." To Calloway, "He was about the worst racketeer who ever made a dirty living in this city," a murderer whose death is a blessing. Martins receives confirmation from Kurtz and Anna, but each unwittingly suggests a darker side of Harry—Kurtz says that everyone in Vienna is somehow involved in the black market, and Anna admits that Harry arranged to forge papers for her, though her interpretation of that action is colored by her love for him and by the benefit she has gained from this illegal act. "Harry never did anything," she insists when Calloway confiscates her letters. "Only a small thing, once, out of kindness." And who in the audience would champion the Russian bureaucrats (claiming Anna's "body" once they learn her Estonian origins) over a petty black marketeer who gallantly broke the law for the woman he loved? Who could resist the photograph on Anna's bureau of "a man grinning with great gaiety and vitality at the camera"?

As the film proceeds, however, Rollo's and Anna's efforts to keep their images of Harry alive become a desperate struggle, and even their portrait of the kind Harry, the charitable Harry, begins to seem oddly tainted. Presented with Joseph Harbin's photo, Anna tells Calloway, "You are wrong about Harry. You are wrong about everything. . . . What can I tell you but . . . You've got everything upside down." But this time Calloway has made no accusations; Anna appears to be fighting her instincts—she protests too much. And though in the remarkable scene in which Anna begs Martins to share his memories

of Harry with her, he may think he is eulogizing his dead friend, all his recollections, particularly when seen in the context established by Calloway's insinuations, strike us as blatant instances of dishonesty. Harry taught Rollo how to put up his temperature before an exam, how to cheat, how to avoid things, how to perform the three-card trick. "He fixed my papers," Anna adds—and suddenly our perspective on that charitable act shifts. Rollo's summary of Harry was that "he just made it all seem such fun"; now Anna phrases the same sentiment more romantically: "He never grew up. The world grew up round him, that's all—and buried him."

"If we had not been taught how to interpret the story of the Passion," Bendrix asks in *The End of the Affair,* "would we have been able to say from their actions alone whether it was the jealous Judas or the cowardly Peter who loved Christ?" In the second half of the film, Greene tells us the truth about Harry Lime; that is, he offers us the facts of Lime's sale of diluted penicillin to hospitals and its monstrous results, and he even introduces Lime himself, whose attitude toward his victims is cynical and uncaring. But the debate is not over. "He never existed, we dreamed him," Martins tells Anna after repeating Calloway's information, and when he encounters Harry in the flesh, he echoes Anna's words: "You've never grown up, Harry." However, he means something quite different— that Harry has never accepted responsibility for others. When he recalls their youthful escapades this time, he sees them as manifestations of Lime's selfishness: "I remember that time at that Club 'The 43,' when the police raided it. You'd learnt a safe way out. Absolutely safe for you. It wasn't safe for me." But Anna insists that "a man doesn't alter because you find out more," that everyone has compartments in him to which even his loved ones are denied admission, and that Rollo, having suffered great disillusionment, is now making Harry over in his own image, i.e., to conform to the impression he now holds of their twenty-year relationship. "He was real," she tells Martins. "He wasn't just your friend and my lover. He was Harry." Yet Anna's only concern is with the Harry she loved; even when she learns that he is still alive, she prefers not to see him but instead to preserve the Harry that she has kept inside her.

Although Harry Lime's name rings through the film, Rollo Martins is the protagonist, and his metamorphosis from the bewildered traveller of the early scenes to the disenchanted man of the late scenes, a sort of rite of passage, forms the psychological movement of the screenplay. The opening shot, a close-up of Martins' passport, establishes that he is a stranger to Vienna, and for a while we see the city from his alien perspective: the bombed buildings, the desperate, soliciting paupers, porters and bus drivers speaking in a language he does not understand, fellow audience members laughing at a farce that he, missing the ironies provided by the German text, takes seriously. His tears at Lime's funeral distinguish him from all of the other mourners except Anna. And he has a charmingly North American swagger and obstinacy that isolate him as rapidly as if he were Twain's Connecticut Yankee in King Arthur's court. He writes cheap novelettes— westerns in which the good guys and the bad guys are clearly delineated—and prides himself on his unpreten-tiousness: "You know, I don't write masterpieces, I don't like masterpieces," he tells Calloway. (The real story of Harry Lime, the one that eludes him for most of the movie, is the masterpiece he could never have written.) Yet he has certain affectations that we easily recognize as holdovers from the kind of prose he writes. When he tells Calloway, "I don't like policemen," he is talking like one of his renegade heroes, for it turns out that he has never known a cop before Calloway. He consciously patterns his crusade to redeem Lime's blackened reputation on the plot of one of his books, as he informs Kurtz: "This lone rider has his best friend shot unlawfully by a sheriff. The story is how this lone rider hunted that sheriff down. . . . I'm gunning just the same way for your Colonel Callag-han." ("Callaghan" is Martins' chronic misconstruction of Calloway's name.) And when the police search Anna's room, he orders her to deny them access to her private pa-pers and cracks to Calloway, "Pinning things on girls now?"

But Greene manipulates our attitude toward Rollo by continually placing him in a context hostile to his point of view and allowing the consciousness of other charac-ters—Calloway's specifically—to take over the screen temporarily. An abrupt shift in tone occurs when Rollo, arriving at 15 Stiftgasse to visit Harry, learns that he has just missed his friend's coffin and pallbearers, and our in-cipient notion that Rollo may be residing in a private world in no way connected with that of the rest of the characters is lent credence by his behavior at the funeral, where he is the only mourner not aware of the wholesale spying in progress. The appearance of Calloway, who is "not at all moved" by the sight of the coffin descending into the earth, who offers Martins a lift "as if they were leaving a party" and "speaks with a voice out of mood with the situation," creates a tension between our sympa-thy for Rollo and our growing feeling that he may be a bit of a fool; the more we hear Calloway speak, the more dra-matic weight his point of view assumes. It is he who puts us on our guard about the veracity of Martins' vision of Lime—

> MARTINS. He and I got up to a lot of things. . . . I was always the one who got caught.
>
> CALLOWAY. That was convenient for him.

and it is he who puts forward the first uncharitable opinion of Rollo, when he signals to Sergeant Paine to escort this "scribbler with too much drink in him" home. He identi-fies Martins' conduct as novelettishly fatuous: "Going to find the real criminal? It sounds like one of your stories," and later, when he is infuriated by Martins' constant inter-ference in the case, "I told you to go away, Martins. This isn't Sante Fe, I'm not a sheriff, and you aren't a cow-boy. . . . " Obviously Greene sides with Calloway's be-littlement of the fictive world Rollo keeps trying to evoke. He has Kurtz arrange to identify himself at the Mozart Cafe by carrying a copy of one of Rollo's books, a "gaudy paper-covered Western with a picture of a cowboy leaping from a horse onto the horns of a galloping steer"—too pointed a piece of satire to miss. Though Rollo insists that

Anna refuse to hand her papers over to Calloway, she makes no attempt to resist, and her quiet cooperation indi-cates that she understands the workings of the law in Vien-na far better than Martins can; when Calloway insults Lime's memory, he has no qualms about offending Mar-tins, but he apologizes to Anna when he sees that his words have hurt *her*.

Greene does provide one character who legitimately ad-mires Martins' novels, the amiable Sergeant Paine, but his sincerity proves to be Greene's most devastating weapon in puncturing the absurdity of Rollo's fantasy world. Paine compliments him on his writing right after he has decked him with a single punch; and during the second, prolonged chase through the sewers, as the two men stand in water up to their calves, exchanging pleasantries in the darkness, Paine's modest comparison of their lives makes Rollo's seem very unimportant indeed: "The things you must have seen in Texas and those parts, sir. Me—I've led a very sheltered life. . . . Fancy me being here with Rollo Martins." A moment later he is dead of a bullet wound—so that Martins, who has already received one object les-son from Calloway in the Children's Hospital (where the police colonel led him past the beds of the children who had been treated with Lime's medicine, all the while monologuing ironically on the subject of Martins' skill as a teller of exciting stories), now receives a second one, in the nature of true courage.

However, Greene does much more with the character of Martins. Ironically, it is one of the black marketeers, Tyler, who prefigures in the first half of the film much of what Martins will learn about social responsibility in the second half. The word "duty" is forever in Tyler's mouth: "Humanity's a duty," "It was his [the porter's] duty to give evidence," "He [Lime] had a great sense of duty"; but Tyler represents a faction of society with no interest in duty whatsoever. The transition in Martins to a real recog-nition of what duty means really takes him from one set of ideals (false, inspired by fiction) to another (true, in-spired by an awareness of how he is linked to other peo-ple); it begins in Calloway's office, where he learns the pen-icillin story, and ends in the Children's Hospital, where he sees its effects for himself. When he confronts Harry Lime on the Great Wheel (a deft piece of symbolism for postwar Vienna)—"a wrecked pleasure place, weeds growing up round the foundations of merry-go-rounds," Harry, too, attacks his novelistic system of heroes and villains: "We aren't heroes, Rollo, you and I. The world doesn't make heroes outside your books." But here Greene has manipu-lated our reactions to Rollo by giving these words to Harry and so, in a surprise gesture, he restores Rollo's he-roic stature.

Martins leaves Vienna at the end of *The Third Man* a wiser man but not yet a complete one. He rejects his boy-hood ideals and begins to live in the world, but he loses another battle when Anna does not forgive him for "in-forming" against Harry and causing his death. (She may not know that he actually pulled the trigger.) And though Greene has a great deal to say, as we have seen, about so-cial responsibility, he shows respect for Anna's point of view by refusing to undercut it. The famous final shot of the movie—Anna walking past Martins on the cemetery road, refusing contact with him as she heads for Harry's grave—gives her an undeniable nobility.

"A man's not dead because you put him underground," Martins reminds Calloway at Lime's second funeral, and though this is partly a joke—Calloway looks worried, recalling the farce of the first funeral—Greene may be suggesting here what he would discourse on the following year in the opening paragraph of *The End of the Affair:*

> A story has no beginning or end: arbitrarily one chooses that moment of experience from which to look back or from which to look ahead. I say "one chooses" with the inaccurate pride of a professional writer who—when he has been seriously noted at all—has been praised for his technical ability, but do I in fact of my own will *choose* that black wet January night on the Common, in 1946, the sight of Henry Miles slanting across the wide river of rain, or did these images choose me?

Perhaps Harry's importance lies in what he has done for Anna by providing an image of love to live inside her, and in what he has done for Rollo by forcing him to confront the very issues Harry himself always so successfully evaded. The beginning and end of Martins' story of Harry Lime, or Anna Schmidt's, or even Calloway's, are determined by a combination of character and circumstances; each of these people was in a sense "chosen" by a different image of Harry, and Harry is the sum of these images. "I've been a fool," Calloway says at one point. "We should have dug deeper than a grave." (pp. 37-44)

> Steve Vineberg, "The Harry Lime Mystery: Greene's 'Third Man' Screenplay," in College Literature, *Vol. XII, No. 1, Winter, 1985, pp. 33-44.*

Marc Silverstein

In a 1955 interview with Walter Allen, Graham Greene made the following comment regarding the distinction between those of his works he classifies as "novels" and those he classifies as "entertainments:"

> In one's entertainments one is primarily interested in having an exciting story as in a physical action, with just enough character to give interest in the action, because you can't be interested in the action of a mere dummy. In the novels I hope one is primarily interested in the character and the action takes a minor part.

Although such statements from Greene have tended to discourage serious critical consideration of his entertainments, if we overlook the perfunctory tone we can see the remark revealing his understanding that such formulaic literature as spy novels demands a special structure of narrative conventions not encountered in "serious" or, to use J. A. Cawelti's term, "mimetic" fiction—conventions which, as critics like Cawelti, Robert Warshow and Ralph Harper argue, both determine and are determined by the expectations readers bring to these works. Yet, despite his labelling **Stamboul Train, The Confidential Agent, The**

Ministry of Fear and *Our Man in Havana* as entertainments, and authorial comments like the one quoted above notwithstanding, I shall argue that Greene deliberately sets out to challenge—if not frustrate—reader expectations by either departing from the basic conventions of the formulaic narrative world or else utilizing these conventions in such a way as to blur the line separating formulaic from mimetic fiction. I do not wish to suggest, however, that these entertainments are mere literary games in which a clever author plays with his readers' sensibilities. Like Conrad's *The Secret Agent* before them, Greene's thrillers represent a serious attempt to establish the spy novel as an appropriate vehicle for exploring the tensions, ambiguities, darkness and sense of alienation which characterize the experience of modernity in the twentieth century.

The most significant feature of formulaic narratives—spy novels, westerns, gothic romances, science fiction fantasies, detective thrillers—as defined by Warshow [in his *The Immediate Experience*] is self-referentiality:

> One goes to any individual example of the type with very definite expectations, and originality is to be welcomed only in the degree that it intensifies the expected experience without fundamentally altering it. . . . It is only in an ultimate sense that the type appeals to its audience's experience of reality; much more immediately, it appeals to previous experience of the type itself; it creates its own field of reference.

Familiarity breeds security as well as content: with repeated exposure to spy novels we learn to detect their archetypal story pattern—identified by Cawelti [in his *Adventure, Mystery, and Romance: Formula Stories As Art and Popular Culture*] in its simplest terms as the adventures of an hero "overcoming obstacles and dangers and accomplishing some important and moral mission"—and we know (or *assume* we know) that whether a title-page displays the name John Buchan, Ian Fleming or Graham Greene, we will experience the recurrent contours of a familiar encounter. When John Atkins [in his study *Graham Greene*] attacks Greene for designating certain of his fictions as entertainments—"It smacks of lecturing the reader, attempting to control his responses"—he fails to recognize an important element in reader psychology that helps to account for the popularity of formulaic fiction. The reader of entertainments seeks out familiar story patterns because she/he *wants* his or her response controlled; wants to know that any original touches on the part of a particular author will "intensify the expected experience;" wants most of all to know that the well-defined boundaries of the spy-novel world are immune to encroachment by the ambiguities and unresolved questions encountered in both mimetic fiction and the "reality" it represents. Since formulaic literature creates its own world, divorced from the reader's experience of the quotidian, it functions primarily as a vehicle for escapist fantasies. Immersing ourselves in a spy novel, we find ourselves transported to a world where temporary incomprehensibility gives way to ultimate clarity; a world where the agents of chaos can never enjoy an ultimate triumph; a world governed by the principle of right action since, as Cawelti observes, the hero's mission is "important *and moral,*" and the successful completion of that mission thus reaffirms our sense of justice and ethical coherence.

By labelling his works, Greene does not so much "lecture" the reader as he does enter into a kind of contract with his audience, the denomination, "entertainment," acting as a promise that if we read his work we will find ourselves in "that well-known and controlled landscape of the imagination [where] the tensions, ambiguities, and frustrations of ordinary experience are painted over by magic pigments of adventure, romance and mystery" [Cawelti]. The effectiveness of formulaic literature depends on an author's ability to dichotomize the world and the word so the reader will recognize that she/he *is* confronted with an imaginary landscape—neither the "real" world nor a world more real than our experience of "reality," but one that, like the world of play defined by Roger Caillois [in his *Man, Play and Games*], is free from culturally-imposed restraints, separate from "ordinary life," governed by fixed rules, and characterized by an aura of make-believe. Because the world of the spy novel is self-contained, bounded by the covers of a book, it possesses "the most fundamental characteristic of true play . . . at a certain moment it is *over*" [J. Huizinga, *In The Shadow of Tomorrow*]—closing the book, we leave behind a world where things always work out as we want them to and return to a more complicated realm of experience.

Yet another feature shared both by forms of play and the reading of spy novels concerns the question of self-image. Much of children's playtime is devoted to acting out situations in which they can assume idealized roles, whether domestic—as in playing "House"—or heroic—as in "War," "Cowboys and Indians" or "Cops and Robbers." In a somewhat similar manner, when we court the suspension of disbelief which grants us passage into the fantasy world of the thriller we do not merely stand back and watch the hero saving civilization as we know it; rather, we participate in the adventure along with him, in a sense becoming the hero through imaginative projection and identification. Like the games which allow children at least briefly to play the valiant hero, spy novels take the reader out of him or herself by confirming an idealized self-image. In his study of *The World of the Thriller*, Ralph Harper asserts that it is the process of identification which grants ultimate psychological value to the reader's pursuit of escapist fantasy in the spy novel:

> The fantasy is the escape. What is fantasy? A compound of the desirable and the preposterous in the form of a dream. We like our fantasies, or else we would not create them. We even want to dream the preposterous . . . *provided we give ourselves a chance to play hero. We want a world where for once we count* . . . *When someone cooperates with fiction* . . . *when you read about an adventure, you go riding along yourself.*

Cawelti also discusses the importance of identification for the construction of an effective formulaic fantasy world, and he contrasts this with the recognition we feel when confronted with the heroes of mimetic fiction, in which an author, rather than presenting us with idealized, larger-than-life versions of ourselves, must "make us recognize our involvement in characters whose fates reveal the un-

certainties, limitations, and unresolvable mysteries of the real world." This opposition between identification and recognition helps clarify Greene's distinction between entertainments, in which the author emphasizes action over character, and novels, in which characterization becomes of paramount importance. By concentrating his narrative efforts on producing a steady flow of action, the author of entertainments can both encourage immediate involvement with his protagonist and avoid the necessity of probing his characters with the kind of psychological complexity or subtlety that forces a reader to confront those aspects of experience and the Self from which the spy novel promises escape.

The basic assumption governing the pattern of expectations we bring to the reading of thrillers can thus be defined as the belief that precisely because it is hermetic and self-referential, the spy novel—like the world of play—preserves its value by *not* being serious. To take it as model, to extract a world view from it, denies its nature as escapist fantasy. If we turn to Greene with these expectations, however, we will quickly have to redefine our concept of the spy novel, for, rather than offering a world of fantasy distinct from the reader's everday world, his works are set in a nightmare world where distinctions between the probable and the improbable, the actual and the fantastical, and the expected and the absurd, become blurred and finally vanish—a world, in short, which reflects and runs parallel to ours. In Greene's most revealing statement concerning his entertainments, he proposes a concept of the relationship between thrillers and the larger structure of "reality" diametrically opposed to that we have been considering:

> I couldn't help smiling to think of the many readers who have asked me why I sometimes write thrillers, as though a writer chooses his subject instead of the subject choosing him. It sometimes seems as though our whole planet had swung into the fog belt of melodrama.

For Greene, the spy novel has become the new and most effective form of mimetic fiction—no longer a passport to an enthralling land of fantasy, but a vehicle for representing the shape of the world as we experience it in the twentieth century. In *The Ministry of Fear,* Arthur Rowe's pursuit by fifth columnists forces upon him the realization that the thriller now defines (rather than offers an escape from) the structure of reality: "He said fiercely, as though he hated her instead of loving her, 'Let me lend you the History of Contemporary Society. It's in hundreds of volumes, but most of them are sold in cheap editions: *Death in Piccadilly, The Ambassador's Diamonds, The Theft of the Naval Papers, Diplomacy, Seven Days' Leave, The Four Just Men.'* " With the shift from a fantastic to a mimetic narrative universe comes a shift from the type of idealized protagonist with whom we wish to identify, e.g., Buchan's Richard Hannay or Fleming's James Bond, to a protagonist in whose predicament we see a reflection of our own condition. As we watch Greene's heroes attempt to adjust to a world rendered incomprehensible and terrifying, recreated in the image of the thrillers *they* have read, we recognize our own sense of displacement as we attempt to fathom "the uncertainties, limitations, and unresolvable mysteries of the real world." Arthur Rowe, speaking to his dead mother in a dream, articulates the dilemma of the modern consciousness confronting a world which has assumed the nightmare dimensions of the world of the thriller:

> I'm wanted for a murder I didn't do. People want to kill me because I know too much. I'm hiding underground, and up above the Germans are smashing London to bits all round me . . . It sounds like a thriller, doesn't it, but the thrillers are like life—more like life than you are, this lawn, your sandwiches, that pine. You used to laugh at the books Miss Savage read—about spies, and murders, and violence, and wild motor-car chases, but dear, that's real life: It's what we've all made of the world since you died. I'm your little Arthur who wouldn't hurt a beetle and I'm a murderer too. The world has been remade by William Le Queux.

When we consider the historical circumstances providing the genesis for Greene's thrillers—the rise of totalitarianism in eastern Europe for *Stamboul Train;* the Spanish Civil War for *The Confidential Agent;* the blitz and the activities of Nazi fifth columnists in London for *The Ministry of Fear;* the Cold War intrigues in Cuba preceding Castro's revolution for *Our Man in Havana*—we can well understand why Greene saw an aura of fear, crime and violence engulfing the "real" world as well as the fictional world of Le Queux.

The question now presents itself, what specifically is it Greene sees as characteristic of human experience that would impel him to transform the spy novel from escapist fantasy into a mimetic, psychologically complex genre? We can, I think, find the answer by recognizing that all of Greene's works ultimately concern themselves with probing "a terror of life, a terror of what experience can do to the individual, a terror at a predetermined corruption . . . " [Kenneth Allot and Miriam Farris, *The Art of Graham Greene*]. The perception of this "terror of life" easily lends itself to expression through the genre of the spy thriller. Terror—particularly the uncontrollable fear and dread arising from the sense of being pursued by a steadily-growing and ever-present danger—results from the characteristic experience of tension in the spy novel— the hero being forced to go on the run. The paradoxical state of being surrounded by an ordered society from which the individual is excluded; the loss of contact with whatever has made one secure; the realization that there is nowhere left to turn—all of these sensations define the experience of pursuit, one of the spy novel's most familiar narrative conventions. Pursuit becomes a major motif in the entertainments: Dr. Czinner *(Stamboul Train)* is pursued by the Yugoslavian secret police; D. *(The Confidential Agent)* by the police and enemy agents (while suffering betrayal at the hands of his own faction); Arthur Rowe by the police and fifth columnists; Wormwold *(Our Man in Havana)* by unidentified agents.

In conventional, escapist thrillers, the author utilizes pursuit in order to generate suspense, defined by Cawelti as "the writer's ability to invoke in us a *temporary* sense of fear and uncertainty about the fate of a character" with whom we identify. I emphasize "temporary" because the pattern of expectations we bring to thrillers exist within a framework of certainty and security: From repeated readings in the genre, we *know* that the hero will triumph over the forces of evil. The suspense evoked by the action of pursuit thus allows us to "encounter a maximum of excitement without being confronted with an overpowering sense of the insecurity and danger that accompany such forms of excitement in reality." Rather than a plot device for the creation of suspense, the action of pursuit in Greene's entertainments becomes a jumping-off point for a subtle exploration of his characters' psyches. The sense of isolation, displacement and exile experienced by the spy on the run perfectly suits Greene's characters, who, having more in common with Conrad's Lord Jim than James Bond, must ultimately run from their own sense of guilt, failure and—as pursuit becomes raised to metaphysical proportions—the loss of faith in an overarching spiritual reality which could impart a semblance of meaning and coherence to their actions. (pp. 24-9)

[In *Graham Greene: The Novelist*] J. P. Kulshrestha has observed that Greene's thrillers are written "in the predominantly secular point of view," but the narrative world of the entertainments is fallen, not merely secular. What Harper refers to as "the extreme suffering of loneliness" experienced by the spy on the run becomes emblematic of the modern predicament as Greene conceives it: the loss of God as punishment for the failure and guilt which define our fallen state. (p. 30)

Greene's treatment of the thriller convention which thrusts the spy into the role of hunter/avenger demonstrates another departure from the fantasy world of the formulaic spy novel. In Ian Fleming's novels, where we distinguish James Bond from other agents by his license to kill, and in such recent novels as William Goldman's *Marathon Man* and Robert Littell's *The Amateur,* the spy's ultimate triumph occurs only after he has transformed himself into a killing machine. Because we know the bloody vengeance he exacts is an imaginary rather than a real experience; because identification encourages us to accept rather than analyze the hero's actions; because this brand of violence possesses the "capacity to generate the kind of intense feelings that take us out of ourselves" [Cawelti]—for all these reasons, we are willing to believe that the essential morality of the spy's mission remains uncompromised by the number of corpses he leaves in his wake. In the more mimetic world of the entertainments, however, murder never becomes a forgivable, even laudable, act if only the right person commits it—for Greene, violence neither cancels out violence nor leads to his heroes' salvation. Because Greene wants the reader to think seriously about the consequences of immersing oneself in violence, we tend to react to his characters with the kind of ethical scrutiny totally absent from our response to novels by Fleming, Goldman or Littell, in which the reader's suspension of disbelief involves an attendant suspension of the moral imagination. (p. 35)

By denying the reader access to the cathartic act of vengeance when we most expect it, Greene takes a further step in shifting the relationship between reader and protagonist from one of identification to one of recognition—a recognition of the existential nature of "reality." Edmund Wilson's evaluation of Sartre's world aptly defines humanity's ontological status in the entertainments, for, like Sartre, Greene "places man in a world without God . . . in which all the moral values are developed by man himself . . . Man is free, [within] certain limits, to choose what he is to be and to do. His life has significance solely in its relation to the lives of others—in his action or refraining from action: to use a phrase of Sartre's, the individual must 'engage himself.' " If, as Greene suggests, guilt and the sense of failure have become the normal condition of twentieth-century humanity, the individual must learn to bear with rather than flee from his sense of despair if he is successfully to "engage himself." With the character of Arthur Rowe [in *The Ministry of Fear*], Greene achieves his most exhaustive study in the entertainments of how fallen man can achieve this existential engagement.

The four years separating *The Ministry of Fear* from *The Confidential Agent* witnessed England's transformation from a country at peace to a land ravaged by the horrors of war, a transformation reflected in the different visions of England presented in the two novels. Although the repercussions of the civil war in D.'s homeland can be felt in the Midlands and London, the threat of violence and destruction remains hidden beneath the surface of life, allowing the illusion of tranquility to prevail:

> He was filled with a sense of amazement at these people: you could never have told from their smoky good-fellowship that there was a war on—not merely a war in the country from which he had come, but a war here, half a mile outside Dover breakwater. He carried the war with him. Wherever D. was, there was the war. He could never understand that people were not aware of it.

The world of *The Ministry of Fear* is a world at war, not only fallen but nightmarish in its inescapable violence and horror:

> Nearer and nearer the guns opened up, but the plane pursued its steady deadly tenor until again one heard, "Where are you? Where are you?" overhead and the house shook to the explosion of the neighbouring gun. Then a whine began, came down towards them like something aimed deliberately at this one insignificant building. But the bomb burst half a mile away: you could feel the ground dent.

This depiction of the blitz generates the suitable backdrop of fear and violence against which the novel's two chases—Rowe pursued externally by fifth columnists and internally by the memory of having committed euthanasia—unfold, for Greene sees England itself as mercilessly pursued by the German bombers.

Along with suspense and identification, Cawelti lists the creation of a slightly removed, imaginary world as an indispensable element in the construction of a formulaic thriller world. To fulfill our expectations of escape, an author must offer us "an imaginary world that is just sufficiently far from our ordinary reality to make us less in-

clined to apply our ordinary standards of plausibility and probability to it." The use of exotic and romantic settings (or even the verisimilar description of Iron Curtain countries never visited by most readers in the novels of Len Deighton and John le Carré) is perhaps the most familar device employed by thriller writers to create that world "far from our ordinary reality." Even in its use of setting, *The Ministry of Fear* demonstrates Greene's attempt to shift the spy novel from escapist fantasy to mimetic fiction, for the fear, violence and sense of fragmentation his vision of wartime England evokes offered the novel's first readers a reflection of, rather than diversion from, "ordinary reality." (pp. 37-8)

Greene's treatment of love in the entertainments proves as anti-formulaic as his treatment of the other spy-novel conventions we have examined. "Formulas resolve tensions and ambiguities . . . [which] function as a means of challenging and then cementing the love relationship" [Cawelti writes], but the love relationships which conclude the entertainments remind us that when the spy completes his mission a specific threat may be removed, but the fallen world of corruption, fear and mistrust—the world transformed into a "Ministry of Fear"—remains. (p. 43)

Greene's treatment of love in the entertainments serves as our final example of the fundamentally anti-formulaic nature of his narrative world. As I have been arguing, his utilization of the basic conventions of the espionage thriller—the spy on the run, the spy as the hunter/avenger, the love relationship as a "reward" for a successful mission—in a rather subversive manner, together with his utilization of mimetic rather than formulaic literary devices—uncertainty rather than suspense, recognition rather than identification, settings (in *The Confidential Agent* and *The Ministry of Fear*) drawn from our ordinary reality rather than romanticized locales—transforms the spy novel from escapist fantasy into a vehicle for the author's investigation into the ambiguities and ironies of modern life. Although Greene's narrative universe seems to objectify our worst nightmares, we recognize the setting of his thrillers as an intensified representation of the world confronting us in the twentieth century. In keeping with his mimetic approach to the spy novel, Greene offers us heroes who are neither the supermen of Fleming nor the seasoned professionals of le Carré; rather, as Arthur Rowe observes, they emerge from the ranks of "dull shabby human mediocrity." Scarred by the painful consciousness of failure and the ubiquitous sense of guilt and corruption, they never passively resign themselves to the chaos. They may agree with Hasselbacher [in *Our Man in Havana*] that "reality in our century is not something to be faced ," but they know it must be faced nevertheless. Dullness and shabbiness notwithstanding, their determination to confront their predicament with some conclusive action grants them a kind of heroic stature. Haunted by fear of the inevitable corruption which follows from immersion in experience, they accept the responsibility of living "in a world without God . . . in which all the moral values are developed by man himself." We see them in the existential act of engagement in those moments of triumph which allow humanity to survive with dignity in the fallen world. . . . They are not the thrilling victories James Bond achieves, but, in an era when "the thrillers are like life" and what we commonly experience as reality swings "into the fog belt of melodrama," they are perhaps the victories essential for survival. (p. 44)

Marc Silverstein, "After the Fall: The World of Graham Greene's Thrillers," in Novel: A Forum on Fiction, *Vol. 22, No. 1, Fall, 1988, pp. 24-44.*

Paul W. Rea

Most film historians, having screened **The Third Man** once or twice, tend to see it as a *film noir,* a particular sort of psychological thriller made during and after World War II. As defined by Robert Sklar [in his *Movie-Made America: A Cultural History of American Movies*],

> the hallmark of *film noir* is its sense of people trapped—trapped in webs of paranoia and fear, unable to tell guilt from innocence, true identity from false. Its villains are attractive and sympathetic, masking greed, misanthropy, malevolence. Its heroes and heroines are weak, confused, susceptible to false impressions. The environment is murky and close, the settings vaguely oppressive. In the end, evil is exposed, though often just barely, and the survival of good remains troubled and ambiguous.

Unquestionably, **The Third Man** exhibits many of these characteristics: its trapped villain, Harry Lime, is played attractively by Orson Welles, and its ostensible hero, Holly Martins, is played by Joseph Cotten as "weak, confused," and "susceptible to false impressions." Its setting, postwar Vienna, is decidedly "murky and close," more than "vaguely oppressive." Its filmic style is indeed dark, with streetlights glaring on wet cobblestones and shafts of light penetrating the deep shadows.

The *film noir* is, however, essentially an American genre, and **The Third Man** is a very British film. Moving beyond the *film noir*, its stylistic influences are eclectic: its use of searchlighting and large shadows come from the German Expressionist cinema of the twenties, and its incessant use of camera angles tilted ten to twenty degrees off horizontal come from Orson Welles, who also used this technique in *Citizen Kane*. Most significantly, however, **The Third Man** incorporates the characteristic values of the British film at its best: highly literate and suggestive script; commitment to moral values such as order and decency, here embodied in the character of Maj. Calloway as played by Trevor Howard; and, in marked contrast to the *film noir*, concern with both psychological realism and political commentary.

Whereas Graham Greene's fictional treatment is presented from the point of view of—and therefore is essentially about—Maj. Calloway, chief of the British Military Police, Greene's shooting script opens with Holly Martins as narrator. Holly's famous opening voice-over narration—"I never knew the Old Vienna before the War, with its Strauss music, its glamour and easy charm"—were added when the filmmakers became concerned that audiences would not understand without them. Even without

them, however, **The Third Man** focuses clearly on the growth of Holly Martins.

Viewed from one perspective, Holly is an American innocent abroad who, in the course of the film, encounters evil in his "shadow," or psychological double, as represented by his long-time friend, Harry Lime. Although the script states that Holly was a Canadian, the film suggests repeatedly that he was an American—and an innocent. Immediately on his arrival at the British command post, he is identified as the author of Westerns, such as *The Lone Rider of Santa Fe*. Captain Crabbin, who runs the Cultural Institute, initially refers to Holly as an American author and later introduces him to an audience as "Mr. Martins, from the other side." The American innocence theme appears also when an American M.P. comments that he has never heard of Harry Lime and expands further when Holly, speaking to the Cultural Institute, reveals his utter ignorance about literature.

Although not essential either to the film or to this viewing that Holly be an American, it is well to observe that **The Third Man** was a British production directed by Carol Reed and that Graham Greene created another misguided American idealist in **The Quiet American.** In this novel, written five years later, Greene indicts an ignorant, willfully innocent, but well-meaning CIA agent. "Innocence," he writes, "is like a dumb leper who has lost his bell, wandering the world, meaning no harm" (quoted in "Night World" 1973). In the film, the two sides of the American character are suggested by the punning on "ranch" and "raunch."

The film offers ample verbal and visual evidence of parallels between Holly and Harry. In the script, Holly links himself to Harry when he remarks that "nobody reads Westerns nowadays, Harry liked them though." In the film, Anna, Harry's former lover, repeatedly calls Holly "Harry," and observes that "Harry never grew up," which also applies to Holly. This doubling motif emerges also from dialogue between Anna and Holly:

> MARTINS. Come out and have a drink. (*Anna looks quickly up.*)
>
> ANNA. Why did you say that?
>
> MARTINS. It seemed like a good idea.
>
> ANNA. It was just what he (Harry) used to say.

Obliquely, Calloway, too, suggests parallels between the two men. He warns Holly that "you were born to be murdered," implying a parallel to Harry, whom they both believed to have been murdered. Finally, Holly himself suggests parallels. In a particularly telling slip, Holly, half drunk, remarks that "there's nobody who knew Harry Lime like he did . . . like I did." Ironically, neither knows Harry well at all.

Visually, too, **The Third Man** reinforces the Holly/Harry connection. Seeking the details of his friend's "death," Holly watches as "Baron" Kurtz shows him how Harry was supposedly run over as he stepped out to see a friend across the street. (Kurtz illustrates his explanation by saying that "you might have been Harry.") Later, Holly himself is almost run over as he steps out to see a friend—Harry. Visual parallels occur also as Holly attempts to play with a cat associated with Anna, and moments later, in a dark doorway, the same cat plays with Harry's shoestring and licks his shoe. (This cat, according to Anna, "only liked Harry," and thus parallels her loyalty to Harry and foreshadows her rejection of Holly in the end.) Moreover, Holly escapes from pursuers by running up a spiral staircase, and later Harry escapes from pursuers by darting down one, into the sewers. Finally, as Holly sits in a bar, attempting to lure Harry, the shop displays a sign on the glass reading "Döppel-Filter."

These parallels, then, suggest that Holly, the decent-seeming opposite of the morally degenerate Harry, is actually his psychological double. This potential becomes clear—especially in the script—as Holly hesitates before declining Harry's offer to cut him in on his racket. Harry thus represents Holly's "shadow," that side of his nature that he has only dimly understood. Holly's initiation into experience, into the evil represented by Harry Lime, becomes fully evident as Holly readies himself for his journey to the moral and literal underworld of the sewers.

In the script, Greene delineates Holly's moral growth: "A world is beginning to come to an end for Martins, a world of easy friendships, hero worship, and confidence that had begun twenty years before . . . but he will not admit it." By the end of the film, Holly has, after considerable struggling, come to realize Harry's evil, has surmounted his loyalty to this "easy friendship," and has taken moral action to end it. (It is important that Holly kills his old chum, for to leave it to Calloway and his men would be to endorse governments as a means of combatting evil. Greene's sympathies ran toward individuals; he liked to believe that his work made that of the State more difficult.) Yet in helping Lime to avoid facing up to his crimes, Holly may unconsciously avoid fully recognizing his own shadowy side; by killing Harry Lime, he may be tempted to imagine that he has extinguished his own darker tendencies.

From a Jungian perspective, Holly represents archetypal man—the collective unconscious—in the process of individuation. The first step in his journey toward psychic growth comes with his encounter with the shadow, which occurs on the great wheel. Harry's depravity both fascinates and shocks him. Once he encounters this shadow, he follows it into the labyrinthine sewers, where he encounters the matriarchal consciousness—suggested by his feminine name—that has kept him an adolescent. Upon his return to the surface, having taken adult moral action, he is free of his immature notions of woman as creator/destroyer; he is ready to deal with his own "anima," and can let Anna pass him by without giving pursuit. This is a moment of growth; Holly begins to break with his tendency to "chase girls," and ceases his attempts to replace Harry.

The Third Man is also a film about moral responsibility, or the utter lack of it. Holly, Anna, and Major Calloway are each tested by circumstances, by their willingness to run the risks necessary to be responsible—i.e., to oppose evil for the common good. Evil is especially embodied by

Harry Lime and his cronies, Kurtz, Winkel, and Popescu. With characteristic innocence and bravado, Holly is willing to investigate the apparent death of his friend, but pulls back, evading responsibility, when he is rightly suspected of contributing to the death of his friend's porter.

Later, when his help seems necessary to Calloway's capturing Harry, Holly plans to leave town and consents only grudgingly to being Calloway's "dumb decoy duck." Only at the very end, during the chase through the sewers, does Holly become fully involved. This represents significant growth for Holly, who, after all, had been writing escapist pulp fiction about people and places he knew next to nothing about. Anna, by contrast, will not betray her former lover, even though he has abandoned her, to help Calloway halt his murderous racketeering. Calloway, the professional in charge, is the moral hero of the film, not because he has no flaws, but because he is unwavering in his commitment to opposing evil. He musters all the help he can find, hoping to make common cause for the common good.

Incorporating such moral considerations, *The Third Man* probes and comments upon Cold War politics in Europe. In her intelligent analysis, " 'I Never Knew the Old Vienna': Cold War Politics and *The Third Man*," Lynette Carpenter places the film in its immediate historical context. She points out that when Sir Alexander Korda sent Greene to Vienna, he asked not for a murder mystery or a quoted romantic melodrama but for a treatment "about the four-power occupation." Carpenter rightly points out that in the eighteen months or so before the filming, the Soviets had engineered a coup in Czechoslavakia and had blockaded Berlin, a city that, like Vienna, was divided among four powers. These cities are microcosms of Europe, itself divided into two camps.

The film satirizes petty provincialism and affirms internationalism. From Holly's initial nervousness at customs to the Viennese' complaints about too many foreigners to Anna's difficulties with her papers, *The Third Man* exposes the unnecessary bureaucratic difficulties created by an unnecessarily partitioned and divided world. Moreover, as a moral parable, it demonstrates that such divisiveness makes it more difficult to combat evil. Law enforcement personnel neither know one another nor speak a common language. Harry is able to slip from one occupied zone to another, evading capture.

Everything considered, *The Third Man* challenges Cold War orthodoxies. Although some viewers—then or now—might emphasize the fact that Harry ducks into the Soviet zone to evade capture, or that Anna faces deportation by the Soviets, to do so might be to indulge Cold War suspicions. On the contrary, the most significant fact, given the political climate of 1950, is that the Soviets are *not* part of Harry's deadly schemes—i.e., that evil is *not* caused simply by communism, and that Harry Lime, an American, is brought to bay *not* simply by *British* moral character, efficiency, and intelligence, though these traits are certainly affirmed in the Maj. Calloway and Sgt. Paine (Greene's script called for Popescu, who appears in the film as a Romanian, to be Tyler, an American. The change resulted largely from the strong objections of the American producer and distributor, David Selznick). The script also makes it clear that the British do not capture Lime alone: Lime is tracked by an "International Patrol," which "includes Austrian, British, French, Russian, and American M.P.s." Only through international cooperation, then, can evil be opposed.

Even more than most mysteries, *The Third Man* explodes assumptions, thereby inviting a reevaluation of Cold War assumptions. The central assumption—that Harry is dead—proves erroneous, as does Holly's naive belief that Harry does "publicity work for some kind of charity." Crabbin assumes that Holly is a serious writer, and Anna clings to her naive belief that Harry was simply a man "who never grew up." Most significantly, Holly presumes to play detective in a strange city where he hardly speaks a word of the language and persists in asking the wrong question, "who was the third man?" If all these assumptions prove false, why should one not also question that cluster of assumptions that comprises the Cold War mindset?

In this film, evil thrives not just as the result of individual depravity and greed, nor just as the result of bad governments, but as the result of an exhausted culture declining into moral decay. The faces of the Viennese bespeak moral shell shock and the stark futility that Ezra Pound voiced so memorably following the First World War:

> There died a myriad,
> And of the best, among them,
> For an old bitch, gone in the teeth,
> For a botched civilization.
> ("Hugh Selwyn Mauberly")

Whereas Pound depicted cultural disintegration with images of the broken columns of a classic temple, Greene and Reed depict it with numerous shots of broken statues, bombed out buildings, and deserted squares.

Commenting on such images of cultural decay, David Denby observes that

> Reed and cinematographer Robert Krasker have framed the shots so that bits of rococo decoration appear in the corners of almost every composition, and Anton Daras's zither score is full of such care-repertory favorites as "unter dem Lindenbaum" and "Alter Lied," but these traces of imperial and gracious city are used in mocking contrast to its postwar dereliction.

The great culture of the Old Vienna—"the graves of Beethoven, Schubert, and Brahms," the shots of buildings and statues from its glorious past—contrast starkly with the physical and moral ruin. If all this art, architecture, and music ever ennobled, clearly they no longer do. Moreover, what remains of Old World charm has degenerated into *erzatz:* Kurtz is a fake baron who wears a toupee, and Winkel collects animal bones that pass for those of saints. His collection of religious art inspires neither belief nor morality. Culture has become antique, charm a crumbling facade.

Perhaps it is not coincidental that Old Vienna led Freud toward his first explorations of the repressed unconscious. Over-refined as it often was, traditional European culture contained demons that surfaced during the World Wars. At the end of the First World War, Carl Jung observed that "the shadow" had broken loose—that the "animal in us only becomes more beastlike" when it is repressed. Jung continues to state that this "is no doubt the reason why no religion is so defiled with the spilling of innocent blood as Christianity, and why the world has never seen a bloodier war than the war of the Christian nations." European culture and Christian teachings repress the shadow.

But the film implies also that much of the evil in Vienna remains as a residue from the Second World War. The Wehrmacht uniforms and helmets worn by the Austrians, the bombed out buildings, the tilted camera angles, and the dark tones and deep shadows all suggest moral degeneration, often evoking the "there's a murderer amongst us" themes of the German Expressionist films. The legacy from the war is established early in the film when Kurtz informs Holly that "we all sell cigarettes and that sort of thing. Why, I have done things that would have seemed unthinkable before the war."

The Third Man stands at the crossroads of three powerful contemporary tendencies. The first is that of moral breakdown resulting from the failure of traditional culture and religion to speak to a world reverberating from the upheaval of World Wars I and II, from the shock waves of Auschwitz, Dresden, and Hiroshima/Nagasaki. The second contemporary tendency is the temptation of guilt-free, long-range technological killing, posed so memorably by Lime looking down on "dots" from on high: "Victims? Don't be melodramatic. Look down there. Would you really feel any pity if one of those dots stopped moving forever?" Lime's corruption is contagious because it tempts Holly and others to avoid guilt as he does—by killing from a distance and abstracting individuals into numbers.

It is this third contemporary tendency toward abstraction and impersonality that Albert Camus exposes so graphically in *The Plague,* a novel about the Occupation on one level and about nuclear holocaust on another:

> Ten thousand dead made about five times the audience in a biggish cinema. Yes, that is how it should be done. You should collect the people at the exits of five picture-houses, you should lead them to a city square and make them die in heaps if you wanted to get a clear notion of what it means. Then at least you could add some familiar faces to the anonymous mass.

In attempting to justify his calloused perceptions of human beings as "dots," Harry alludes to barbarities committed by governments. They kill people all the time, he contends. Harry identifies himself with dictatorships that treat people as a "mass" to be manipulated; he succumbs to the amorality of a Hitler or a Stalin. Though he may not recognize it consciously, Harry's degeneration—and that of many others—may stem from experiences with governments, the war, and the holocaust. Harry has swallowed a heavy dose of postwar cynicism.

In his "Thoughts for the Times on War and Death," Freud points out that wars, with their official legitimation of mass murder, "have repercussions on the morality of individuals":

> When the community no longer raises objection, there is an end, too, to the suppression of evil passions, and men perpetrate deeds of cruelty, fraud, treachery and barbarity so incompatible with their level of civilization that one would have though them impossible.
>
> Well may the citizen of the civilized world . . . stand helpless in a world that has grown strange to him.

Although Harry exhibits no restraints on his cynicism or greed, Holly, "the citizen of the civilized world," at first continues his adolescent innocence and willful ignorance, standing helpless in a strange city.

Civilized societies always contain their Harrys and their Hollys, just as the dark side of the unconscious may dominate or may remain unacknowledged in individuals. Much as Jung lamented that "civilized Germany disgorged its terrible primitivity," so Old Vienna, however civilized, refined, cosmopolitan, artistic, and progressive, collaborated all too willingly with the Nazis. The Viennese, like Holly, have tended to ignore the shadow, the sinister side of the unconscious. Reed repeatedly films their city on a tilt, suggesting both a world slipped morally askew and psychic imbalance. *The Third Man* implies that, as Jung asserts eloquently [in *Man and His Symbols*],

> Our times have demonstrated what it means for the gates of the underworld to be opened. Things whose enormity nobody could have imagined in the idyllic harmlessness of the first decade of our century have happened and have turned our world upside down. Ever since, the world has remained in a state of schizophrenia.

Much as political realms are divided, so are individuals. Calloway and Harry Lime live in their heads, out of touch with feelings; Holly lives in his romantic sentimentalities, his mind stunted by platitudes.

When individuals or nations assume their own innocence, believing that evil is something that others once did, they ignore their own shadows and live schizophrenically, divided like the postwar world. Harry was "buried" once, but "rose" to do more evil. The demons that erupted in Germanic culture still haunt the bombed buildings, the darkened doorways, the empty squares, and the sewers. Evil still lurks within the dark recesses of the human mind. The moral statement of the film echoes Alain Resnais's excruciatingly powerful *Night and Fog,* another film on the legacy of World War II. Narrating this film as the camera inspects the ruins of a crematorium and a torture rack, Resnais comments first that "war nods, but keeps one eye open"; then he challenges the viewer to ask, "and who will warn us of our next executioners? Are their faces really that different from ours?"

Perhaps not. But we also resemble the Hollys and the Calloways, those incomplete mortals who take up arms against evil, doing what needs to be done. Despite its surface pessimism, *The Third Man* suggests that any one of us could choose to be one of those shafts of light that penetrate the darkness. (pp. 155-63)

> *Paul W. Rea, "Individual and Societal Encounters with Darkness and the Shadow in 'The Third Man'," in* Film and Literature: A Comparative Approach to Adaptation, *edited by Wendell Aycock and Michael Schoenecke, Texas Tech University Press, 1988, pp. 155-63.*

Bruce Bawer

[How] did Graham Greene—an author who . . . has never quite shaken off the devices of a thriller writer—ever manage to acquire and maintain an international reputation as one of the most distinguished literary figures of his time? Undoubtedly this reputation owes much to the conspicuous role that Catholicism and leftist politics have played in Greene's most widely admired books. Certainly if he had spent his entire career writing straightforward thrillers along the lines of *Stamboul Train* and *The Confidential Agent,* Greene would have remained at most a peripheral figure on the literary scene; for, in those precincts where literary performances are evaluated and authorial ranks assigned, it is widely understood (if not universally accepted) that a thriller, however accomplished, represents an achievement of a different kind than a serious literary novel. But something odd happens, in a certain sort of critical mind, when religion or politics enters the picture. Religion is serious; politics are serious. For many critics, therefore, a novelist who purports to address religious or political questions is a novelist to be taken seriously—no matter how unserious the manner in which he engages those topics, and no matter how strongly the impact of his fiction may prove to depend upon the modalities of melodrama and the stylistic mannerisms of the thriller.

During the last twenty-five years or so, moreover—the period during which three of Greene's four later political novels were published—a conspicuous attraction to radical-left politics has become one way for a writer to ensure not only that he will be taken seriously but that he will be looked upon favorably by a number of influential literary critics; for to many such critics, as we know, the aesthetic value of a work of fiction is of less importance than its politics. And surely nothing could have been more appealing to leftist intellectuals from China to Peru during this period than the sort of anti-Americanism that figures in Greene's later political novels. Even less radically inclined commentators have often felt honor-bound, it would seem, to congratulate the outspoken, left-leaning Greene for his supposed courage and political commitment.

Yet how could any intelligent reader who considers himself socially responsible smile on the notion of political commitment that is typically reflected in Greene's later novels? And how, for that matter, could any devout and thoughtful Catholic not be made uncomfortable by Greene's singular view of Catholicism? For his Catholic novels and his later political novels make it clear that Greene looks upon both religion and politics, to a remarkable degree, not as means by which one may commit oneself to specific understandings of reality but as means of identifying oneself with certain ideals—ideals which one may well frankly accept as fanciful, illusory, and contrary to logic. Far from constituting rational, intellectual responses to the world, in other words, Greene's religion and politics more often seem attractive to him precisely because he regards them as forms of rebellion *against* intellect and reason, as ways of escape *from* the world. (Indeed, Norman Sherry, in his new biography of the author, quotes a sister-in-law of Greene's as saying that he "was not a logical man. . . . He was not logical about politics, he was not logical about his religion.") Time and again, Greene approves of characters who pointedly dissociate their belief—whether religious or political—from reality. He patently wants us to admire Sarah, for instance, when she remarks in **The End of the Affair** that "[t]hey could dig up records that proved Christ had been invented by Pilate to get himself promoted and I'd believe just the same." (Here and in Greene's other Catholic novels, he makes it clear that the important thing is not to believe in God, in any conventional sense, but to love God—to cherish, that is, an idea of God.) Likewise, though Communism may have had disastrous consequences in the real world, Greene wants us to cheer Dr. Magiot's loyalty to it as a romantic dream—his loyalty to, in Magiot's phrase, Communism's *"mystique."* (As Carlyon observes wistfully in **The Man Within,** "A dream is often all there is to a man.")

To many a reader, it may seem that Magiot's continued faith in the mystique of Communism prevents him from becoming responsibly involved in the real world; to Greene, however, this *is* involvement. In Greene's paradoxical view, that is to say, mystique *is* realpolitik, and it is altogether proper to respond to real-world problems by dedicating oneself to an alluring absolute. Never mind that Communism has had far bloodier consequences than Western democracy: the important thing is not that democracy has done better by humanity, but that Communism has greater charisma. One of the unintended ironies of Greene's oeuvre is that, whereas he implicitly criticizes the innocence of many of his characters—among them Father Thomas in **A Burnt-Out Case** and Alden Pyle in **The Quiet American**—because it leads them to unwise judgments or disastrous associations, Greene's own broad experience of the world has patently not prevented him from making choices and forging alliances that are at least as ill-advised and calamitous.

Highly enlightening in this regard is **Getting to Know the General,** Greene's 1984 memoir of his friendship with the Marxist dictator of Panama, General Omar Torrijos Herrera, who had died three years earlier. Torrijos had first invited Greene to Panama in 1976, and over the succeeding years acted as his host during several visits (which seem to have provided the background for some of the later episodes in **The Captain and the Enemy**). Subtitled "The Story of an Involvement," the memoir is an incredible document, an unintentionally devastating self-portrait in irresponsibility, egotism, and fatuity. It is also a portrait of General Torrijos, and no press agent ever wrote a more flattering one. For Greene—who was himself plainly flattered by the dictator's attentions—judges Torrijos not by

his accomplishments but by his professed dreams, his utterly impracticable "plans" for everything from the elimination of slums to the construction of "a pleasure park for the poor." Another factor in Greene's admiration is that Torrijos proved to be a man after Greene's own heart, a man who loathed America, whose "romanticism was balanced by a streak of cynical wisdom" (this is clearly also Greene's view of himself), who was "not the kind of man to be sexually faithful to one woman" but who was "faithful above all to friendship." It means a lot to Greene when Torrijos tells him, "You and I are both self-destructive." Greene's comment: "It was like a friend speaking who knew me better than I knew myself."

Manifestly, *friend* and *friendship* are the key words here. There can be little question but that Torrijos's feelings of amity for him outweigh, in Greene's mind, the general's tyranny and thuggery. So it is that, in praising the Torrijos government early in the book, Greene manages to avoid mentioning that the general had imposed a ban on opposition political parties. (He finally mentions the ban much later on, when Torrijos lifts it—an act to which Greene can refer approvingly.) And so it is, too, that when Torrijos offers to send a hit man to France to rub out an enemy of Greene's, the author looks upon the proposal not as further evidence that Torrijos is a thug, but as a delightful confirmation of the general's friendship: imagine, the man likes him so much that he would have somebody killed for him! "I have never lost as good a friend as Omar Torrijos," Greene writes sincerely, apropos of Torrijos's offer—and from a man who has barely advanced beyond schoolyard values, this is supreme praise. Not surprisingly, Greene reserves his calumny in these pages almost exclusively for *norteamericanos,* waxing derisive, at one point, about the comfortable living conditions of Americans in Panama—conditions which, one suspects, hardly compare to the luxury that Greene enjoys in Antibes. (And this derision comes, moreover, from a man who, elsewhere in the book, without a trace of irony, complains about the lack of cheese on the Concorde on the way home!)

The fact that emerges conclusively from both his novels and memoirs is that Greene doesn't understand the meaning of the term social involvement. By all indications, the sometime public-school boy who avoided his fellows for fear of contamination by the evil of sex has remained detached, incapable of a truly selfless allegiance, a rationally founded devotion. In his view, it would seem, only love or pity or enthrallment by some kind of *mystique* is capable of drawing one into a commitment to either God or man. And such commitment is by its nature self-destructive, he believes, because it brings one into intimacy with "the odour of human meanness and injustice" (to quote Greene in **The Heart of the Matter**), and because (as Scobie reflects) "no human being can really understand another." As Joseph Conrad writes in a passage that Greene borrowed for the epigraph to **The Human Factor,** "I only know that he who forms a tie is lost. The germ of corruption has entered into his soul." The intended irony at the heart of Greene's fiction is that ideals—which are sublime at least in part because they exist forever apart from physical reality, incapable of being translated to it, realized in it, or corrupted by it—can cause a formerly aloof person to become embroiled in, and therefore corrupted by, the world around him.

Yet the cardinal failing of Greene's most celebrated novels is that the ideals—religious and political—which play so dominant a role in them are too often bizarre, their sincere espousal by sane, sober, and well-educated twentieth-century individuals hard to imagine and even harder to countenance. If his entertainments are on the whole more effective than his Catholic novels, it is because in the former he routinely distances himself from his protagonists, while in the latter he saddles his protagonists with some variation on his own perverse notion of faith; thus, as a rule, the heroes of the Catholic novels are motivated by ideas that the average intelligent reader—Catholic, Protestant, Jewish, agnostic, or otherwise—cannot take seriously, and that are so thematically pivotal that it is likewise virtually impossible to take the books themselves seriously. And if Greene's later political novels are (to varying degrees) successful as thrillers, they too are well-nigh irredeemably marred by the fatuous politics that figure importantly in their plots.

How, then, can Greene legitimately be called a great writer? Among other things, a great writer helps us to understand what it means—and why it is (or is not) worthwhile—to be human and to be alive. To examine Greene's novels thoughtfully is to be confronted, in quite dramatic fashion, with the plain fact that his dedication to the ideas supposedly central to his own life is ultimately so cursory, so self-contentedly shallow, that he cannot possibly have anything of importance to convey to us about such matters. Greene has, to be sure, a facility for narrative, an eye for atmosphere, a gift for publicity, and (to borrow Noel Coward's phrase) "a talent to amuse," sometimes when he least intends to do so—but he is, most assuredly, far from being the literary master that countless people who have read little or none of his work suppose him to be. (pp. 38-41)

> *Bruce Bawer, "Graham Greene: The Politics,"*
> in The New Criterion, *Vol. 8, No. 3, November, 1989, pp. 34-41.*

John Updike

The Power and the Glory, first published fifty years ago in a modest English edition of 3,500 copies, is generally agreed to be Graham Greene's masterpiece, the book of his held highest in popular as well as critical esteem. Based upon less than two months spent in Mexico in March and April of 1938, including five weeks of grueling, solitary travel in the southern provinces of Tabasco and Chiapas, the novel is Greene's least English, containing only a few minor English characters. Perhaps it succeeds so resoundingly because there is something un-English about the Roman Catholicism which infuses, with its Manichaean darkness and tortured literalism, his most ambitious fiction.

The three novels (as opposed to "entertainments") composed before and after *The Power and the Glory—Brighton Rock* (1938), *The Heart of the Matter* (1948), and *The End of the Affair* (1951)—all have claims to

greatness; they are as intense and penetrating and disturbing as an inquisitor's gaze. After his modest start as a novelist under the influence of Joseph Conrad and John Buchan, Greene's masterly facility at concocting thriller plots and his rather blithely morbid sensibility had come together, at a high level of intelligence and passion, with the strict terms of an inner religious debate that had not yet wearied him. Yet the Roman Catholicism, in these three novels, has something faintly stuck-on about it—there is a dreamlike feeling of stretch, of contortion. This murderous teen-age gang leader with his bitter belief in hell and his habit of quoting choirboy Latin to himself, this mild-mannered colonial policeman pulled by a terrible pity into the sure damnation of suicide, and this blithely unfaithful housewife drawn by a happenstance baptism of which she is unaware into a sainthood that works posthumous miracles—these are moral grotesques, shaped in some other world; they refuse to attach to the world around them, the so sharply and expertly evoked milieus of Brighton, British West Africa, London.

In contrast, *The Power and the Glory*'s nameless whisky priest blends seamlessly with his tropical, crooked, anticlerical Mexico. Roman Catholicism is intrinsic to the character and terrain both: Greene's imaginative immersion in both is triumphant. A Mexican priest in 1978 told Greene's biographer, Norman Sherry: "As a Mexican I travel in those regions. The first three paragraphs, where he gives you camera shots of the place, why it is astounding. You are *in* the place." In 1960, a Catholic teacher in California wrote Greene:

> One day I gave *The Power and the Glory* to . . . a native of Mexico who had lived through the worst persecutions. . . . She confessed that your descriptions were so vivid, your priest so real, that she found herself praying for him at Mass. I understand how she felt. Last year, on a trip through Mexico, I found myself peering into mud huts, through village streets, and across impassible mountain ranges, half-believing that I would glimpse a dim figure stumbling in the rain on his way to the border. There is no greater tribute possible to your creation of this character—he lives.

Greene's identification with his anonymous hero—"a small man dressed in a shabby dark city suit, carrying a small attaché case"—burns away the educated upper-middle-class skepticism and ennui which shadow even the most ardently spiritual of his other novels. Mr. Tench, the dentist, and the complicated Fellows family are English, and may have been intended to play a bigger part than they do; as is, they exist marginally, like little figures introduced to give a landscape its grandeur. The abysses and heights of the whisky priest's descent into darkness and simultaneous ascent into martyrdom so dominate the canvas that even his pursuer and ideological antagonist, the fanatically atheistic lieutenant, is rather crowded out, flattened to seem a mere foil. Only the extraordinary apparition of the mestizo, with his yellow fangs and wriggling exposed toe and fawning, clinging, inexorable treachery, exists in the same oversized realm of transcendent paradox as the dogged, doomed priest. . . .

[Greene's] serious novels usually have a priest in them, portrayed as fallibly human but in his priestly function beyond reproach. In his second book of autobiography, *Ways of Escape,* Greene writes, "I think *The Power and the Glory* is the only novel I have written to a thesis. . . . I had always, even when I was a schoolboy, listened with impatience to the scandalous stories of tourists concerning the priests they had encountered in remote Latin villages (this priest had a mistress, another was constantly drunk), for I had been adequately taught in my Protestant history books what Catholics believed; I could distinguish even then between the man and the office."

The distinction between sinful behavior and sacramental function is clear also to the debased priests of *The Power and the Glory.* Father José, compelled by the state and his cowardice to marry, remembers "the gift he had been given which nobody could take away. That was what made him worthy of damnation—the power he still had of turning the wafer into the flesh and blood of God." The whisky priest can no longer find meaning in prayer but to him "the Host was different: to lay that between a dying man's lips was to lay God." Greene says of his hero what he might say of himself: "Curious pedantries moved him."

In the unrelenting succession of harrowing scenes as the hunted man tries to keep performing his priestly offices, none is more harrowing, more grisly in its irony and corrosive earthy dialogue, than the episode wherein he must watch a trio of local lowlife, including the police chief, drink up a bottle of wine he had bought with his last pesos for sacramental purposes. But almost every stage of the priest's ragged pilgrimage, between Mr. Tench's two glimpses of him in the stultifying capital of the hellish state (Tabasco, but unnamed), grips us with sorrow and pity. Greene, as a reviewer, saw a lot of movies in the Thirties, and his scenes are abrupt, cinematic, built of brilliant, artfully lit images; the "big whitewashed building," for instance, which the priest does not recognize as a church and mistakes for a barracks, at the end of Part II, and the mountaintop grove of tall, crazily leaning crosses "like trees that had been left to seed," which marks the Indian cemetery and the boundary of the less intolerant, safe state (Chiapas, also unnamed).

The preceding climb, in the company of the Indian woman carrying her dead child on her back, is as grandly silent as a pageant in Eisenstein, and there is a touch of surreal Buñuel horror in the priest's discovery, when he returns to the cemetery, of the dead child's exposed body, with a lump of sugar in its mouth. In *A Sort of Life,* Greene, thinking back upon his many novels for "passages, even chapters, which gave me at the time I wrote them a sense of satisfaction," named "the prison dialogue in *The Power and the Glory,*" and indeed this scene, in which the priest, at the nadir of his abasement and peril, sits up all night in a crowded dark cell listening to the varied voices—the disembodied souls—of the other inmates, is, in its depth, directness, and strange comedy, worthy of Dostoevsky, another problematical believer. (p. 16)

Graham Greene's sympathy with the poor in spirit, with the world's underdogs, preceded his religious conversion and survives it, apparently: he doubted to Norman Sherry that he still believes in God and in *A Sort of Life* tells how "many of us abandon Confession and Communion to join the Foreign Legion of the Church and fight for a city of which we are no longer full citizens." His religious faith always included a conviction that, as he put it in an essay on Eric Gill in 1941, "Conservatism and Catholicism should be . . . impossible bedfellows." In 1980, reflecting upon Mexico in *Ways of Escape* (where he describes how *The Power and the Glory* was written, back in London, in the afternoons, slowly, on Benzedrine, after mornings of racing through *The Confidential Agent*), Greene complains that the contemporary Mexican government is not left-wing enough, compared with Cuba's. His sympathies have led him into a stout postwar anti-Americanism and a rather awkward pleading for the likes of Castro and Kim Philby. But the energy and grandeur of his finest novel derive from the same will toward compassion, an ideal communism even more Christian than Communist. Its unit is the individual, not any class. The priest sees in the dark prison cell that "When you visualised a man or woman carefully, you could always begin to feel pity—that was a quality God's image carried with it." (p. 17)

> *John Updike, "The Passion of Graham Greene," in* The New York Review of Books, *Vol. XXXVII, No. 13, August 16, 1990, pp. 16-17.*

FURTHER READING

Bibliography

Miller, Robert H. *Graham Greene: A Descriptive Catalog.* Lexington: University Press of Kentucky, 1979, 73 p.

> Gives physical descriptions of the first editions of Greene's books, pamphlets, radio scripts, and letters in the collection of the University of Louisville.

Vann, J. Don. *Graham Greene: A Checklist of Criticism.* Serif Series: Bibliographies and Checklists, No. 14: Kent State University Press, 1970, 69 p.

> Lists bibliographies, books, and articles about Greene, and chapters about and references to Greene in broader works; also includes a chronology of Greene's novels and reviews of those works.

Biography

Sherry, Norman. *The Life of Graham Greene, Vol. 1: 1904-1939.* New York: Viking, 1989, 783 p.

> Greene's authorized biography.

Criticism

Aisenberg, Nadya. "Graham Greene and the Modern Thriller." In *A Common Spring: Crime Novel and Classic,* pp. 168-222. Bowling Green, Ohio: Bowling Green University Popular Press, 1979.

> Probes Greene's use of the modern thriller genre as a suitable vehicle for his themes.

Atkins, John. *Graham Greene*. Rev. ed. London: Calder and Boyars, 1966, 257 p.

Studies relationships between Greene's works and the events and tendencies in his life.

Bawer, Bruce. "Baseless Dreaming: The Novels of Graham Greene" and "Graham Greene: The Catholic Novels." *The New Criterion* 8, Nos. 1-2 (September 1989–October 1989): 17-33, 24-32.

Examines the "moral and intellectual contradictions" that abound in Greene's writings and personal life. Cited are the first two essays of a three-part series. The third essay is excerpted in the author entry above.

Boardman, Gwenn R. *Graham Greene: The Aesthetics of Exploration*. Gainesville: University of Florida Press, 1971, 216 p.

Views Greene's travels and the related novels as a quest for artistic growth and psychological understanding.

DeVitis, A. A. *Graham Greene*. New York: Twayne, 1964, 175 p.

Traces Greene's literary heritage and the development of religious themes in his novels.

Gransden, K. W. "Graham Greene's Rhetoric." *Essays in Criticism* XXXI, No. 1 (January 1981): 41-60.

Studies the effects of Greene's frequent use of two rhetorical figures in his narratives.

Kunkel, Francis L. *The Labyrinthine Ways of Graham Greene*. New York: Sheed & Ward, 1959, 182 p.

Compares Greene's major themes and "obsessions" to those of other writers in his tradition and times.

Mesnet, Marie-Béatrice. *Graham Greene and the Heart of the Matter*. London: Cresset, 1954, 116 p.

Analyzes characterization and free will in *Brighton Rock, The Power and the Glory*, and *The Heart of the Matter*.

Pryce-Jones, David. *Graham Greene*. New York: Barnes & Noble, 1967, 119 p.

Surveys the major themes of Greene's works.

Straub, Joe. "A Psychological View of Priesthood, Sin, and Redemption in Graham Greene's *The Power and the Glory*." In *Third Force Psychology and the Study of Literature*, edited by Bernard J. Paris, pp. 191-205. Rutherford, N.J.: Associated University Presses, 1986.

Studies the whiskey priest's loss of self in *The Power and the Glory* from the perspective of humanistic psychology.

West, Anthony. "Graham Greene." In *Principles and Persuasions: The Literary Essays of Anthony West*, pp. 195-200. New York: Harcourt, Brace and Co., 1957.

Contrasts the effect of religious belief in *The End of the Affair* with that in Greene's earlier Catholic novels.

Additional coverage of Greene's life and career is contained in the following sources published by Gale Research: *Contemporary Authors,* Vols. 13-16, rev. ed.; *Contemporary Literary Criticism,* Vols. 1, 3, 6, 9, 14, 18, 27, 37; *Dictionary of Literary Biography,* Vols. 13, 15; *Dictionary of Literary Biography Yearbook* 1985; *Major 20th-Century Writers;* and *Something about the Author,* Vol. 20.

Marilyn Hacker

1942-

American poet and critic.

The following entry covers Hacker's poetry collections *Assumptions* (1985), *Love, Death, and the Changing of the Seasons* (1986), and *Going Back to the River* (1990). For further information on her life and career, see *CLC,* Volumes 5, 9, and 23.

INTRODUCTION

Hacker is best known for her use of highly structured poetic forms in examining such provocative subjects as lesbianism and feminism. According to critics, she has revitalized the sonnet, sestina, and villanelle forms by candidly exploring her subject matter, incorporating slang and graphic language into her verse, and focusing on the urban landscape of her native New York City.

Although Hacker's first volume of poetry, *Presentation Piece,* met with mixed reviews, it earned her the National Book Award. Most commentators praised Hacker's daring themes and sharp wit but claimed that such poems as "She Bitches about Boys" and "Pornographic Poem," which advocate sexual liberation, are constrained by their ordered verse forms. The poems in Hacker's next volume, *Separations,* were written following her divorce. Critics also perceived these works as artificial due to their rigid structure but commented favorably on the poet's intricate use of language and her compelling descriptions of separation and loss.

The publication of Hacker's third collection, *Taking Notice,* bolstered her reputation as a poet. Critics praised Hacker's forthright portrayal of her lesbianism and her relationship with her daughter, claiming that in this collection she achieves a balance between theme and structure in which the sonnet form enhances, rather than undermines, the overall effect of the poetry. Marilyn Krysl wrote: "Marilyn Hacker is still a very careful, very formal writer. The sonnets and sonnet sequences . . . are impeccable and beautifully musical. At the same time they are informal, straightforwardly frank, even sometimes chatty in tone. This happy blend of formal structure and informal speech, her working of casual tone within the sonnet form, seems to me an achievement of some note."

Hacker's next volume, *Assumptions,* focuses exclusively on relationships between females: lovers, friends, mothers, and daughters. In these poems Hacker invokes her personal past more frequently than in her earlier works and speaks often of her own mother. *Love, Death, and the Changing of the Seasons* continues these themes, referring to two central women throughout: Hacker's daughter and a woman who becomes Hacker's lover. Critics praised Hacker's use of strong images and emotions, her wit and

irony, and her ability to manipulate standard poetic forms effectively.

Hacker's *Going Back to the River* covers a variety of topics while maintaining lesbianism and feminism as central issues. In a review of the book, Judith Barrington reflected the attitude of several critics as she defended Hacker against those who called her use of the sonnet and other ordered forms conservative. Arguing that Hacker's thought-provoking subjects and brash language preclude such labeling, Barrington insisted that Hacker's work defies convention and dubbed the poet a "radical formalist."

PRINCIPAL WORKS

POETRY

Presentation Piece 1974
Separations 1976
Taking Notice 1980
Assumptions 1985
Love, Death, and the Changing of the Seasons 1986
Going Back to the River 1990

CRITICISM

Carole S. Oles

Marilyn Hacker's intelligence, wit, passion and craft have delighted her readers ever since *Presentation Piece* announced her arrival a decade ago. *Assumptions,* her fourth book, moves us with new strength and nerve. Hacker continues to explore the forms, powers and attributes a woman can assume, searching her past as the poems move from personal to mythic expressions of a woman's progress toward herself.

The personal tone of her work is clearest in the section of the book called "Inheritances," where the pain of the past is revisited through the poet's relationship with her mother, for example, in this sonnet:

> We shopped for dresses which were
>   always wrong:
> sweatshop approximations of the lean-
> lined girls' wear I studied in *Seventeen.*
> The armholes pinched, the belt didn't
>   belong,
> the skirt drooped forward (I'd be told at
>   school).
> Our odd-lot bargains deformed the
>   image,
> but she and I loved Saturday rummage.
> One day she listed outside Loehmann's.
>   Drool
> wet her chin. Stumbling, she screamed
>   at me. Dropping
> our parcels on the pavement, she fell in
> what looked like a fit. I guessed: insulin.
> The cop said, "Drunk," and called an
>   ambulance
> while she cursed me and slapped away
>   my hands.
> When I need a mother, I still go
>   shopping.
>
>   **("Fourteen")**

Another poem, **"Mother,"** gives us some biographical facts while making it clear that what Hacker doesn't know about her mother is almost more significant than what she does. In part it's that ignorance that forces her to reconsider the past. Her own daughter, Iva, helps precipitate the poet's journey back, asking questions about her black Christian and white Jewish immigrant forebears. The stories must be told, must be heard.

Hacker sees her mother, herself and Iva in relation to one another. Her recollected distance from her mother is now measured against what her own daughter may feel for her. In **"Towards Autumn,"** she writes, "I missed the words to make friends with my mother," and "Befriend / yourself: I couldn't have known to tell my mother / that, unless I'd learned it for myself. / Until I do." The older and younger generations skewer Hacker between them in many of these poems, creating a tension that strengthens and enlarges

them beyond those addressed to Iva in her third book, *Taking Notice.*

Many mothers are celebrated in this book, but accepting her own, with all the forgiveness that implies, is Hacker's most difficult and liberating assumption. We've been prepared for such a pardon by these lines from the **"Regent's Park Sonnets,"** in *Taking Notice:*

> It was not my mother or my daughter
> who did me in. Women have been
>   betrayed
> by history, which ignores us, which
>   we made
> like anyone, with work and words,
>   slaughter
> and silver.

Now, in *Assumptions,* come the poems that forgive.

Hacker moves out of the familial house of the first section in a group of thirteen sonnets called **"Open Windows."** Speaking both to herself and to a lover, she airs such subjects as freedom and solitude, the roles of lover and mother, desire and satisfaction, justice and the disinherited.

Her tone shifts from intimacy and vulnerability to irony and vulnerability in **"Graffiti from the Gare Saint-Manqué,"** a 170-line variation on the *ballade suprème* which wryly considers the life of a lesbian: "The sin we are / beset by is despair." The poem leaps borders and centuries; as in Hacker's earlier work, travel is an outward expression of the interior journey of the soul or libido. Like the title of the book, *Assumptions,* the diction of this poem rings Catholic bells: "Saint," "communicants," "sin," "celebrants," "salvation," "nuns." Hacker suggests the creation of a new faith for unbelievers in the old.

If, in the first section, the poet retrieves and invents her mother so that she and her daughter can understand and live their own lives, she appropriates a myth for a similar purpose in "The Snow Queen," a narrative sequence of eight poems. Again the work centers on mothers and daughters: the Robber Woman and the Robber Girl; the Snow Queen and her daughters; and Gerda, who must find other women to mother her. While in Hans Christian Andersen's tale Gerda's quest is for Kay, her male friend lured away by the Snow Queen, in Hacker's version he is only a pretext. Her real search is for herself. In **"Gerda in the Eyrie,"** Gerda addresses the Robber Girl: "I almost love you. I've wanted to be you / all my life. You are asleep in the straw / with my story." In contrast to the Robber Girl, Gerda has inhabited a tiny world, by her own assent: "But I was happy where I was . . . I sat still." In the poem's final image, Gerda merges with her alter ego, suggesting the possibility of change.

"The Snow Queen" section closes with a prose poem, an encomium to "bad old ladies," who greet age with gusto on their own terms and are rewarded when their "daughters slog across the icecap to get drunk" with them. This image leads to the collection's final poem, a homage to the poet's "mothers," literary and historical.

That poem, **"Ballad of Ladies Lost and Found,"** balances the earlier **"Graffiti"** in form and tone, finally lightening the book. While any archness in both poems can be read as protective, this is perhaps not the best note for *Assumptions* to end on. But since the poet's shaping of the book has been so deliberate, we must conclude the effect is intended. Hacker's strengths have always been most impressive in sequences and long poems—large structures that provide ample space for the play of her range. While no sequence in *Assumptions* has the intensity of the title poem in *Taking Notice,* the whole volume reads more like a single poem.

The formal dexterity we expect from Hacker animates *Assumptions.* Whereas Adrienne Rich (who has inspired and emboldened her) discarded the formalism of her earlier poems, Hacker continues to explore a multiplicity of forms, "venerable vessels for subversive use." Hacker's work is political, looking toward a new order of things. Hence, when she writes in forms associated with the primarily male poets canonized by literary history, it is as if she were slipping, in broad daylight, into a well-guarded preserve. She uses the decorous sonnet, sestina and villanelle to contain a vernacular, often racy speech. Playing against formal conventions and the surrounding language of the poems are lines like "Unsaintly ordinary female queers" and "(whenever I'm horny, I first think I'm / hungry)" and "I wish I had my knife. I bet she'll drop / it and lose it, or give it to that drip / and never use it for herself. Piss on her!" In another poet, Hacker's formalism may seem imitative or passé. Her subject and emotional range make it a claim to ownership.

In *Assumptions,* her most moving and personal book to date, Hacker reconciles all manner of polarities. More than ever, her poems make us forget to admire their technical brilliance. They deepen and expand our conception of what it is to be a woman. (pp. 506-09)

> *Carole S. Oles, "Mother Wit," in* The Nation, *New York, Vol. 240, No. 16, April 27, 1985, pp. 506-09.*

J. D. McClatchy

I look forward to each new book by Marilyn Hacker not just as a gathering of new poems but as an installment of her story-in-verse. For a dozen years, and in three books, she has been conducting a grand tour of her history, often filled with erotic intrigues, political struggles and exotic locales and characters. She is our latter-day Byron, and has made out of herself a personification of style in her formal verse and the witty fictiveness of her ideas. She dredges her romantic impulses with irony; however raw her subject, her tone is knowing and her technique has a tempering effect.

Assumptions is less ambitious and virtuosic than her earlier work, a more intimate book, even a more vulnerable one. Her exclusive concern is the relationships between women, as mothers and daughters, friends and lovers. She can be an elegist, as in her **"Ballad of Ladies Lost and Found,"** a chronicle and honor roll of famous women:

> Louisa who wrote, scrimped, saved, sewed, and
>   nursed,
> Malinche, who's, like all translators, cursed,

> Bessie, whose voice was hemp and steel and
>   satin,
> outside a segregated hospital,
> and plain old Margaret Fuller died as well.

Her best history, though, is autobiography. How relationships evolve, how love changes from passion to friendship, how we watch ourselves come clear or obscured in the eyes of others—these problems are traced in a remarkable series of epistolalry poems to her ex–lovers and portraits of her family. She says:

> My daughter was born hero to her mother;
> found, like a lover, flawed; found, like a friend,
> faithful as bread I'd learn to make myself.

She writes wrenchingly in **"Autumn 1980"** of the death of her mother. And cannily of the life of a feminist:

> While deathdrunk superannuated boys
> tot up how often to blow up the world,
> a white-locked pink sage with a toddler voice
> recounts, purse clutched, how she was blued and
>   curled.
> I overhear her on the crosstown bus
> I take at three to meet the second grade.
> She smiles a smile someone called dangerous
> once, and she boiled it down like marmalade.
> I'm sheared, hands free, with keys, jackknife and
>   ten
> dollars deployed in worn corduroy pants.
> A matrifocal world would comprehend
> compassion, dignity and commonsense,
> I sneer, aware of my accoutrements
> as she is talking hairdos with her friend.

In most poems in this book a small moment (there are small, but never ordinary moments in Miss Hacker's poems) is given a shape and a point. Sometimes she fails to rise above the occasion and sometimes the diaristic note is too insistent. But she is an emotionally generous and wonderfully appealing poet.

> *J. D. McClatchy, "Three Senses of Self," in* The New York Times Book Review, *May 26, 1985, p. 16.*

Reg Saner

The ballade has thriven in France, as has Hacker, whose parallel to "Mezzo Cammin" is a 170 line ballade using for its refrain "another Jewish Lesbian in France." Since the poem runs seventeen stanzas such a line's repetitions seem at first mildly amusing, then gimmicky. By, say, the twelfth repetition, amusement returns, bolstered with admiration for more than just Hacker's famous skills, because **"Graffiti at the Gare Saint-Manqué"**—as its witty title implies—has become a rueful if self-amused inventory of loneliness. A mere whiff, excerpted, conveys at least some of that:

> . . . Would it have saved Simone Weil's life to
>   be
> another Jewish Lesbian in France?
> It isn't sex I mean. Sex doesn't save
> anyone, except, sometimes, from boredom
> (and the underpaid under-class of whoredom
> is often bored at work). I have a grave

suspicion ridicule of Continence
or Chastity is one way to disparage
a woman's choice of any job but marriage.
Most of us understand what we renounce.
(This was a lunchtime peptalk I once gave
another Jewish Lesbian in France

depressed by temporary solitude
but thinking coupled bliss was dubious.)
I mean: one way to love a body viewed
as soiled and soiling existential dross
is knowing through your own experience
a like body embodying a soul
to be admirable and loveable.
That is a source that merits nourishment.
Last night despair dressed as self-loathing
      wooed
another Jewish Lesbian in France. . . .

By coincidence the second of my favorites in *Assumptions* is also a ballade **"Of Ladies Lost and Found,"** this time an inventory of gone women.

Sestinas are less worth encouraging than piano *concerti* for thumb and ring-finger of the left hand. Hacker's first book (*Presentation Piece*) contained over a half dozen; but she is bringing this habit under control. *Assumptions* has two, only, one of which, **"Inheritances,"** succeeds in creating real poetry by embodying the situation of Hacker's daughter, Iva, set apart from Anglo-America (or half of everywhere) as the child of a Black and a Jewess. A companion poem **"Sword"** enters that subject through a pair of snapshots:

> This golden vengeance is one of those red
> niggers like her grandfather who said
> of me, "Her people are just off the boat."
> He might have said, just off the cattle cars.
> Here she is three, bangs her construction boot
> against the van she's perched on. He is in lace,
> held by a darker nurse, sixty-six years
> earlier. Their twice-bright blade of face
> astonishes, doubled, between imp ears
> the same red-gold (his lock's glassed) curls
>   around.
> When she was born he was long darkened; dead
> before he tried her honed red-gold, hybrid
> of six million dead off the cattle cars,
> just off the slave boats, fifteen million drowned.

Indeed, the mother/daughter theme pervades most of the book, which is flawed for me by some shrillness in Hacker's tendencies toward an adversary relation. A poet returning "sincere thanks to the MacDowell Colony, the Michael Karolyi Memorial Foundation, the Ossabaw Foundation, the Corporation of Yaddo, the New York State Creative Artists Public Service Grants, and the John Simon Guggenheim Foundation" must now and then feel things could be worse.

Not that *Assumptions* omits the joy of life. Hacker's technical verve, alone, expresses enormous delight in language. Her report of little domestic details, good wine and good food, can offer the delicious gifts of intimacy we find in Bonnard's painting—or Chardin's. Sometimes, though, the detail conveys mere scene-setting. Too, her unconventionalities are [now] thoroughly traditional; and her

damning admissions, shrewdly calculated, could come from a PR memo aimed at enlarging the cult.

Reviews always contain a "however." In fact you could put the all-purpose poetry review on a rubber stamp: *"Yes, but . . . "*

So these latter remarks are just my quibbles with another—her fourth—worthwhile collection by Marilyn Hacker. (pp. 115-17)

> Reg Saner, *"Studying Interior Architecture by Keyhole: Four Poets,"* in The Denver Quarterly, *Vol. 20, No. 1, Summer, 1985, pp. 107-17.*

Sandra M. Gilbert

[As Hacker celebrates] herself in **"Graffiti from the Gare Saint-Manqué"**—"I may go home as wide as Gertrude Stein / —another Jewish Lesbian in France"—she is as unabashedly Poetic as Clampitt or Schnackenberg. Yet, though she is by now well-known for (and keenly conscious of) her skill with such traditional and, to academics, comforting forms as sestinas, sonnets, ballades, she employs them [in *Assumptions*] with a lightness and irony unavailable to many of her contemporaries, as though she's saying, "Yes, I'm another Jewish Lesbian in France, but guess what?, I can write Poetry too," or, as she sardonically puts it, "I can write poetry now, if I don't bore / the constituents / who never read it, though they all want to Write / Something."

Political as Piercy and poetical as Clampitt or Schnackenberg, Hacker in fact performs a remarkable feat in being consistently *interesting*. To be sure, like Muske, she sometimes seems to be writing the requisite and "correct" mother/daughter poems, and sometimes, like Schulman, she even flirts with romantic ecstasy. Moreover, when she's consciously allusive she occasionally loses me: despite my passion for the Hans Christian Andersen fairytale, long sections of "The Snow Queen," the penultimate sequence in *Assumptions,* evoke my frosty indifference:

> The Snow Queen had a daughter la la or two
> She calls them and ignores them   but
> They live in different countries   now
> Her icy courtship drove them   out.

Maybe from a lesser artist such lines would be of some interest, but because I know Hacker can be polemical (dread word) without being tendentious, I find myself wearied by the subtext here.

Still, most of the time in *Assumptions* subtexts, pretexts, contexts are absorbing and linguistically exhilarating, moving, even amazing. **"Almost Aubade"** gives us the writer in a brilliantly "realistic" colloquial mood, worthy of Piercy: exhausted from cooking and childcare, one woman tells another,

> . . . Tired because
> of all we should stay up to say, we keep
> awake together often as we sleep
> together. I'll clear the plates. Leave your cup.
> Lie in my arms until the kids get up.

More poignantly, in **"Autumn 1980,"** the poet rings (it

sounds heartless but it doesn't feel that way) elegant changes on "the night after my mother died," bringing us to the moment when, in Macy's, picking up a garment "like autumn foliage I'd missed somehow," she "knew what I officially didn't know / and put the bright thing down, scalded with tears."

Besides including politically charged yet beautifully polished poems about, say, Harriet Tubman (a subject which no doubt earned this volume a careful blurb from Adrienne Rich), Hacker's *Assumptions* explores assumptions about what we in California would call "this modern world of today"—e.g.:

> Houston was unregenerately damp
> —clouds scudded in, clouds scudded out with
>   rain—
> and quintessentially American
> as neon reindeer in a trailer camp.

But maybe, beyond the skillful union of form and content, it's the wit and pizazz of this work that I admire most. Elaborating the refrain in which she relentlessly defines herself as "another Jewish Lesbian in France," this poet dashes off a marvelously sophisticated quasi-Byronic critique of contemporary French feminism—

> Then the advocates of Feminitude
> —with dashes as their only punctuation—
> explain that Reason is to be eschewed:
> In the Female Subconscious lies salvation.
> Suspiciously like Girlish Ignorance,
> it seems a rather watery solution.

Better still, in **"Ballad of Ladies Lost and Found,"** Hacker produces a parodic revision of Villon's "Où Sont Les Neiges D'Antan" that one wishes either the poetical Clampitt or the political Piercy had thought of:

> Where are the women who, *entre deux guerres,*
> came out on college-graduation trips,
> came to New York on football scholarships,
> came to town meeting in a decorous pair?
> Where are the expatriate *salonnières,*
> the gym teacher, the math-department head?
> Do nieces follow where their odd aunts led?
> The elephants die off in Cagnes-sur-Mer.
> H.D., whose "nature was bisexual,"
> and plain old Margaret Fuller died as well.

What's wonderful—literally wonder-ful—about Hacker's new book is the way in which it challenges some of our most deep-rooted assumptions, most especially the assumption that (as some of the advocates of "Feminitude" whom she attacks have argued) if you're a sexual radical, you have to be an aesthetic radical. I really admire the alternative proposition by which Hacker plainly lives and writes: that you can think seriously about gender without either rejecting, or mindlessly deploying, the most dazzling effects of genre. (pp. 167-69)

> *Sandra M. Gilbert, in a review of "Assumptions," in* Poetry, *Vol. CXLVII, No. 3, December, 1985, pp. 167-69.*

Marilyn French

The sonnet sequence, indeed lyrical love poetry itself, has faded out of fashion. In our age of control the poetry of helplessness, which is what love poetry inevitably must be, is disdained. But John Berryman wrote a magnificent sonnet sequence in the 1940s (not published until the late 1960s), in a casual conversational style that masked the strictness of his form, recognizable iambic pentameter in the difficult Petrarchan rhyme scheme. (The Petrarchan form, with its minimal number of rhymes, is constricting in English, which has relatively few rhyming words. It was modified early in the sixteenth century by Surrey and further refined by Shakespeare.) Berryman's poems allude to cities and countryside, newspaper reports, accidents, police cars, jukeboxes, parties, other people, drinking and work, especially the work of writing poetry—a twentieth-century innovation, identifying process and product. They have plot elements too: separations willed and involuntary; the fears, jealousy and frustrations inherent in adulterous affairs; but above all, and uniquely, the character of the adored Lise, who is no idealized Lady but a vivid, passionate, thinking woman.

And now we have a new sonnet sequence, Marilyn Hacker's *Love, Death, and the Changing of the Seasons.* Hacker clearly knows, and was perhaps influenced by, Berryman, but her prime model is Shakespeare, as the book's epigraph and many allusions testify. For it was Shakespeare who wrote love poems to a person of the same sex much younger than he, and whose sonnet "sequence" (as far as we know, he himself did not arrange it as one) contains poems addressed or referring to someone other than the beloved young man, a person we call the Dark Lady.

Hacker's sequence has a jazzy New York ambiance which is really a point of view, and it carries over into foreign scenes. In keeping with this, it is written in extremely slangy, sometimes "obscene" English, with equally slangy French interspersed. The emotional drama is interwoven with a detailed context of places and people and the events of daily life. The first lines set the tone:

> You hailed a cab outside the
>   nondescript
> yuppie bar on Lexington to go
> downtown. Hug; hug: this time I
>   brushed my lips
> just across yours, and fire down below
> in February flared.

We learn in this poem that the beloved has "someone . . . waiting up at home"; the third sonnet, addressed to Bill, a friend, tells us that the beloved is 25; and the fifth, that the narrator is considerably older (42, we discover later). The narrator—at one point she calls herself Hack—has an 11-year-old daughter, Iva, who lives with her part of the year. Hack has been without erotic love for such a long time "that I honestly / wondered if I'd outgrown it." The beloved is Rachel, sometimes called Ray; the two met in a poetry class taught by Hack, in which Rachel is a student:

> Class night: osmotic energy
> got all the girls in gear. Tight forms to
>   tame

only made them write funkier, slang
their diction down. I know some of
    them know
(besides Elaine); still, it was brash to
    throw
my Bic at you, and, oh dear, yes, I
    sang
"You Are My Soul and My Heart's In-
    spiration,"
to amplify the echoes in your poem.

The plot has considerable tension. Rachel lives with some-one she calls her wife; Hack won't get involved with her because "infidelity's / the kind of bad taste that leaves a bad taste / worse than the mousebreath of a hangover." At the same time, "I want you so much I can taste it"; "I'm horny as a timber wolf in heat. / Three times a night, I tangle up the sheet. / I seem to flirt with everything with tits: / . . .I think I ought to be kept off the street." Even-tually, the two women do come together but the tension remains, a sense that the poet loves more than she is loved. Rachel admonishes her, "need me less and I'll want you more"; the poet helplessly explains, "I feel damned / by wanting you so much it looks like need."

The erotic element is strong in these poems, and expressed without self-censorship, in references to fucking and ex-plicit descriptions of lovemaking. The entire account is frank. It does not blink at jealousy:

> I wish Kim hadn't made a pass at you.
> I wish she hadn't asked you not to tell
>   me
> she had. Oh hell, I wish that she would
>   call me,
> so she and I, *copines,* could talk it
>   through.

or self-consciousness:

> *Il y avait au moins une trentaine de*
>   *guoines*
> (that's "dykes" in French) come listen
>   to me
> sound off (in French) and read some
>   poetry
> (in English).

Both women worry, in a twenty-five-line villanelle, "Do people look at me and know I'm gay?" Rachel's unhappi-ness about not having children because she is a lesbian is addressed in three poems called "Having Kittens About Having Babies."

There is considerable movement in space, as the two women take cabs and buses around the city: Rachel lives in Chelsea and has a white bedroom; the poet lives uptown and has a blue bedroom. They visit bars and parks across the city, shop in Bloomingdale's. The poet goes to Paris, where she has an apartment in the Marais; to Vence in the south of France, where her close friend Julie lives; to Flor-ence. The lovers go together to Provincetown (P'town), where they have friends. Rachel travels in her job, for a "Commissar" of a boss.

Berryman's sequence also details places, bits of the scene, allusions to the ongoing life of the lovers. But Hacker's is

---

[*Love, Death, and the Changing of the Seasons*] allows the reader, in the concentrated and vivid way only poetry provides, to be immersed in the texture of one woman's actuality. And so detailed is that texture that the life stands, regardless of the outcome of the love affair. Unlike any other love poems I know, Hacker's sequence provides a context that offers a tacit explanation of how one can go on when the heart is shattered.

—*Marilyn French*

---

very much a *woman's* sonnet sequence: it embraces all ele-ments of life equally. Nothing is too insignificant to be in-cluded. Rachel, Hack and Iva play ball in Central or Riv-erside Park; Iva listens to Cindi Lauper on headphones on the plane to France; Hack does the laundry; she writes out shopping lists, goes marketing, prepares meals (not just *"lapin / à la moutarde"* and "cassoulet / with goose from Carcassonne, let *mijoter* / on the burner till nightfall" but even leftovers); she walks in the countryside around Vence; she picks blackberries. Hack teaches; Rachel works for the Commissar. Both women work composing poetry, and Hacker, like Berryman, identifies the act and its issue.

The lovers are embedded in a dense social context: the names and actions and words of friends and acquaintances weave through the poems. Besides the beloved Julie, Jac-queline (Jax) and Érzsi, there are Alice, Meg, Karyn, Sonny, Britt, David, Joanna, Kim and Catherine, the Countess, elegant and arrogant, who was still carousing at 92. The lovers also carouse. There is frequent heavy drinking; there are hangovers. There are deaths here, too, and two funerals. The lovers' world is, if anything, too peopled; it is hard for them to find time to be alone togeth-er. Comings and goings swirl around them, never glamor-ized, always recognizable. They quarrel in the car, while Iva sulks in the back seat; they have dinner with friends (*"magret de canard . . . escargots"*); they go dancing in gay bars; they make love; or Hack lies alone, in longing.

This inclusion of domestic, personal details creates the texture of a life lived in body as well as mind, of suffering and satisfying appetites sexual and sensuous, in an inclu-sive world. Love is not a thing apart, a spiritual or roman-tic quest elevated above the quotidian, but one strand of a diverse, disorderly, mentally and physically rich experi-ence. The poet accepts all of self and all of life; she cele-brates living. The characters eat, drink, excrete. They ex-perience love, friendship, betrayal; motherhood and the longing for motherhood; jealousy, estrangement, loneli-ness; the seasons and their natural manifestations. They are acquainted with what is disgusting, foolish, childish, erotic, maternal, joyous, serene, painful—with everything real. Like Hopkins, Hacker praises "All things counter, original, spare, strange; / Whatever is fickle, freckled (who knows how?) / With swift, slow; sweet, sour; adazzle, dim." But, unlike Hopkins, she does it without excluding any part of life.

Hacker uses a loose sonnet form, varying the rhyme scheme of the sestet considerably. There are sets of linked sonnets, the last line of one being picked up, sometimes with variation, as the first line of the next. Her rhythms are often jerky, mixing four-stress lines and unscannable lines with iambic pentameter. They are not graceful, lyrical, but are often strong. Strength, indeed, is necessary to make up for the lack of music. A couple of the sonnets are formed with two (separated) half-lines; a few expanded villanelles are included. Some of the poems are addressed to friends, as letters. There are allusions to a wide range of literary sources, but especially to Shakespeare, and first lines that echo his, like, "From you I will be absent as the spring / turns into summer."

Some of the sonnets end weakly (can we refer this too to Shakespeare, whose concluding couplets often seem perfunctory?):

> I'll take books to the park—it
> *is* a fine day. I miss you very much.
>   . . .
> We do it once like ladies, once like
>   tramps.
> We love each other very very much.

Sometimes the conceits seem forced:

> (It's either that or lie awake and stew
>   more.)
> (I wish that there were only beef to
>   stew.)

And sometimes the rhyme, as in "Tack- / y," or "disdain- / ing." There are a few lines in which the sense is opaque.

But these are minor problems. A more serious problem is the emotional range of the poems. Although they contain a great variety of experiences, suggesting that the poet censors nothing, refuses to treat any part of living as illegitimate, Hacker does seem to censor her emotional expression: she never permits herself to express anger. This would not matter if there were not situations in the narrative that call for anger, poems in which anger hangs faintly, distantly, like an echo in a room where music played hours before, or the backcloth for a play so often performed, so familiar, that the reporter feels the scene does not need to be described. One misses it. Hacker is aware of this lack, aware that "Grown-ups, at least, will not rush to applaud. They / won't believe you." Still, she insists she feels only loss and sorrow.

Altogether, though, *Love, Death, and the Changing of the Seasons* is deeply satisfying. It allows the reader, in the concentrated and vivid way only poetry provides, to be immersed in the texture of one woman's actuality. And so detailed is that texture that the life stands, regardless of the outcome of the love affair. Unlike any other love poems I know, Hacker's sequence provides a context that offers a tacit explanation of how one can go on when the heart is shattered. (pp. 443-47)

Marilyn French, "Laura, Stella and Ray," in

The Nation, *New York, Vol. 243, No. 14, November 1, 1986, pp. 442-47.*

Kathleene West

What does it take to be a hero in the 1980s? Contemporary American culture's obsession with temperamental rock stars and prima donna quarterbacks blurs the distinction between heroism and temporary fame, and President Reagan's proclamation of Lieutenant Colonel Oliver North as a national hero is as perplexing as the *Newsweek* inclusion of a KKK grandmother in their "A Day in the Life of America." It is an appealing proposition that, in order to generate heroes of a more elevated type, there should be a large-scale reexamination of individual, personal heroics, on the order of Walt Whitman's dictum, "To have great poets, there must be great audiences, too." In *Love, Death, and the Changing of the Seasons,* Marilyn Hacker considers the question of personal heroics directly:

> Would we be heroes if things came to it?
> We only get to be tough guys in small ways,
> in Central Park, on highways or in hallways.
> A big word, but we have a claim to it
> or, sometimes, need to give that name to it,
> especially the harder times, when you're a
> tad turned round toward the flip side of bravura
> or I've done something sticky, and stuck blame
>   to it.

The "you" and "I," the two heroes of this story-in-sonnets and villanelles, are two women, working their way in and out of a love affair, its lovely times, its harder times, or as Hacker explained at a reading, "Girl meets girl, girl gets girl, girl loses girl."

Consciously placing her work in the line of a solid literary (and male) tradition, Hacker chooses Shakespeare's "Sonnet 73" and lines from one of Pound's Chinese poems, "The River-Merchant's Wife: A Letter" as epigraphs, and shows her mastery of traditional forms by using them in each piece of this book. But *Love, Death* is excruciatingly modern; the very first page makes a sharp break with the autumnal diction of the epigraphs:

> You hailed a cab outside the nondescript
> yuppie bar on Lexington to go
> downtown. Hug; hug: this time I brushed my
>   lips
> just across yours, and fire down below
> in February flared.
>   **("Runaways Café I")**

We are about to witness the unfolding of a grand passion that is in no way lessened by its entanglement with twentieth-century *angst* and American self-deprecatory humor. The poet-speaker ends the second poem with the standards she wishes the two lovers to maintain and the comedy she recognizes in the situation:

> it still behooves us to know what to do:
> be circumspect, be generous, be brave,
> be honest, be together, and behave.
> At least I didn't get white sauce down my front.
>   **("Runaways Café II")**

"A sense of humor is a state of grace" as excitement, lust,

and longing foreshadow distance and a kind of jaunty despair.

A breathtaking pace holds throughout the book, fueled by New York freneticism, trans-Atlantic travel, and the energy of love. Besides the love affair, the poet maintains an active social life with attendant eating, drinking, visiting, and letter-writing; travels regularly to France; edits a journal; cares for a daughter; teaches poetry workshops and writes. Love and work intertwine:

> Your wish for me's
> time used, good work. I'm trying to discharge
> the task.

One result is "fifty-seven poems / in seven weeks." One of the most striking characteristics of this book is Hacker's attitude of unselfconscious dedication. The poet and her friends work hard, play hard, celebrate and mourn, and in this book at least, the expected exhaustion rarely shows through. "Get up then. Write about / It if you're scared" and "I find a clean page to find you again" dominate "I don't ever want to push papers one more minute / or ever pack another fourth-class parcel." Hacker lets us see the down side often enough, but her language is highly charged and often beautiful so that the reader is likely to be uplifted, even inspired.

Hacker plays with the notion of society's unease with Lesbian love in poems like **"Les Carabosses"**: *"Il y avait au moins une trentaine de gouines /* (that's 'dykes' in French)" or the charming villanelle **"Conversation in the Park"** with the repeated line "Do people look at me and know I'm gay?" and probes the mother's discomfort about telling a sweet and savvy daughter:

> Sure, she said
> she knew what we were up to, when I told her,
> thought it was cool, but thought she'd be discreet,
> liked you a lot, and did she have to eat
> the vegetables?

Those of us who wept through Radclyffe Hall's *The Well of Loneliness* will get some belly-laughs and lusty guffaws from Hacker as well as tears.

In this new book as in her earlier ones, Hacker's language is cultured, educated, raw, and rowdy. Penelope, Persephone, French phrases and the Shirelles's "What Does a Girl Do?" show up in the same poem, and I think Hacker may have rescued "girl" from its pre-liberation strata in the last Proterozoic age, associating it with the girl groups of the '60s, mother-daughter closeness, and the rejuvenation the speaker receives from her lover, younger by seventeen years: "there's some girl left in the old life yet." Old saws reverse to a bit of freshness, shapes change; the adversary is anxiety, and TWA jets us to the site of the next battle:

> Think of Greek claustrophobes inside the Trojan Horse—that's how I feel, rigged out to fight
> with champions, fearing phantoms.
>
> . . . . .
>
> Along with every other appetite
> anxiety is neutralizing lust.

The shape of the book gives the impression of being at once sprawling and contained. The 212 pages of mostly sonnets are divided into eight untitled parts and a coda. Just enough of the sonnets are untitled to give a sequential structure, but the occasional villanelle and the **"Letter on August 15"** in abc rhyme scheme break the long poems in the book. Last lines reappear as first lines, or ask questions to be later answered. "Achilles hung out in his tent and pouted / until they made the *Iliad* about it" closes a sonnet, and five pages later a sonnet begins:

> Until they made the *Iliad* about it,
> nobody would have seen a fit of pique
> as quintessentially *geste héroïque.*
> Is indecision epic? If you doubt it,
> look at the texts. Where could they be without
> it.
> She whose mind's made up fast as she'd eat cake
> has not got that right stuff out of which bards
> make
> heroes . . .

Chance, choice, and circumstance move the poet through a year of changes. A friend dies—"one warrior / fell"—a lover moves out. "How I do enjoy what girl you bring / back out in me" evolves to:

> The only gift
> I got to keep or give is what I've cried,
> floodgates let down to mourning for the dead
> chances, for the end of being young,
> for everyone I loved who really died.

Although *Love, Death and the Changing of the Seasons* ends sadly, it is not a sad book, but wise, funny, brave, and beautifully written. In giving us this book about the heroics involved in the risky choice of love, Marilyn Hacker gives us an alternative to shoddy and selfish impulses. She gives us poetry. (pp. 121-23)

> *Kathleene West, in a review of "Love, Death, and the Changing of the Seasons," in* Prairie Schooner, *Vol. 61, No. 4, Winter, 1987, pp. 121-23.*

John Retallack

The narrative in "Geographer," a five-part sonnet sequence from *Separations,* Marilyn Hacker's second book (1976), takes place in a postmodern collision of contemporary, Death-as-Terrorist time with Petrarchan-Heroic-Shakespeherian-Rag time. It *is* elegant and intelligent. It combines stately metrics, exquisite linguistic design, and pop vernacular in a style that hyphenates high culture, full of formal historical hindsight, and contemporary cultural critique:

> I
> I have nothing to give you but these days,
> laying broken stones on your waste, your death.
> (The teeth behind kisses.) Nothing rhymes with death.
> Richter plays Bach. My baby daughter plays
> with a Gauloise pack. Once I learned pain and praise
> of that good body, that mouth you curved for death.

Then your teeth clenched. Then you shivered.
  Seeing death.
Another of those mediocre lays.
Little brother, of all the wastes, the ways
to live a bad movie, work a plot to death.
You worked your myth to death: your real
  death.
I've put my child to bed. I cannot eat.
This death is on my hands. This meat dead meat.

And the end of part III (begun above):

> Last night I heard
> of another poet dead, by her own hand
> it seems (oh how I wish there were more
> boozy women poets, aged sixty-seven:
> new book, new man, wit and kitchen noted for
> flavor). *If there's a Rock-n-Roll Heaven*
> *They sure have a Hell of a band.*

The numbers that effect containment in these lines are not the Roman numerals which mark off the sections but those internal to speech rhythms—a musical notation which enables the word "death" to be played repeatedly as a discordant flat. The way in which this poem breaches its self- and conventionally defined boundaries is an example of how art can dissolve those sticky dichotomies, including art vs. life, edging toward life-death—as much an aesthetic continuum as space-time. The formal paradox here is that the scheme of the sonnet requires rhyme but "nothing rhymes with death," so what should rhyme, be resonant (living), can only repeat itself in a dull thud that cannot even approximate the literary grandeur of a "knell." It is invariable repetition (death) tacked onto a mind's process richly unfolding (life). Yes, death is tacky, "a bad movie," but so, a good deal of the time, is life. What more can be said? "Word, word, word: the cure / for hard nights."

Words and metrics and syllabics. It turns out they can constitute a narrative life with their spirited momentum. It is possible, for instance, to spend a vacation alone in Vence brimming with sage humor and visual acuity, and wit as sharp and mellow as a properly aged Gorgonzola (and as interested in the pleasures of cooking and eating as M. F. K. Fisher)—at least it's possible in the hendeca-syllabic, extended (by one line) Sapphic stanza that draws **"Letter from the Alpes-Maritimes"** from playful salutation ("Carissima Joannissima, *ave*") to sign-off twenty-seven stanzas later. Beginning with the fifth:

> I watch the sky instead of television.
> Weather comes south over the mountains: that's
>   news.
> Today the Col de Vence was crystalline. Blues
> stratospheric and Mediterranean
> in the direction
>
> of Nice. From Tourrettes, I could see Corsica.
> Sometimes I take myself out to dinner. I write
> between courses, in a garden, where twilight
> softens the traffic beyond the begonias,
> and my pichet, *vin*
>
> *ordinaire,* but better than ordinary,
> loosens my pen instead of tongue; not my guard.
> I like eating alone; custom makes it hard
> to be perceived content though solitary.

> A woman alone
>
> must know how to be cautious when she gets
>   drunk.
> I can't go rambling in night fields of horses,
> apostrophizing my wine to their apples,
> heaving an empty with a resounding thunk
> in someone's garden.

(from Assumptions)

Descriptions of local color are laced with humor, full of the kind of visual precision a poet who was once a painter commands. One senses, in fact, a local burgeoning wherever Hacker travels with her nourishing, protean eye (*esse est percipi,* indeed):

> The exotic novel Barnes could have written
> continues here: the old Countess and her child,
> further than ever from being reconciled,
> warily, formally, circle the old bone:
> an inheritance.
>
>   . . . . .
>
> I gave the mother a blood-red gloxinia.
> Hothouse perennial herself at ninety,
> terrible on the roads (Countess Báthory
> is rumored to be a direct ancestor),
> a war monument's
>
> long bones, selective eyes, a burnished ruin
> in white jeans, along the lines of Katharine
> Hepburn around the cheekbones and vulpine
>   chin,
> her style half-diplomacy, half-flirtation:
> she gets what she wants

(from Assumptions)

Architecture may turn out to be the most fitting postmodern paradigm. In a world where something as fundamentally temporal as weather has become more a matter of place (e.g., the Bahamas) than time (local seasons); where causally disjunctive events are beamed via satellite into your study, bed, and rec room simultaneously; and where we all go around with a premature afterimage of Armageddon imprinted in our brains—the spatial may become again the predominant aesthetic dimension, as it was for the ancient Greeks, for whom destiny was a matter of place. The buildings that we call postmodern, with their complicated shadows—arch, Baroque pediment, Western boot, and cactus—bear structural resemblance to, say, Hacker's formal historical "quotations" and eclecticism, her sonnets, sestinas, and villanelles exploded cartoon-style into contemporary consciousness.

But perhaps more significantly, if the varieties of the postmodern can be seen as an evolving critique of the modern, then Hacker's work in its challenge to the white, male, heterosexual flavor of modernism, as well as to its avant-garde, purist stance, might be seen as one sort of prototype. With her linguistic straddling of high-low culture, and her transvaluation of values from implicitly masculine to explicitly, even randily feminine, a good deal of her work fits the image of the project outlined in Andreas Huyssen's *After the Great Divide,* particularly in the chapter/essay called "Mass Culture as Woman," where he argues that

. . . the gendering of an inferior mass culture as feminine goes hand in hand with the emergence of a male mystique in modernism (especially in painting), which has been documented thoroughly by feminist scholarship. . . .

Thus the nightmare of being devoured by mass culture through co-option, commodification, and the "wrong" kind of success is the constant fear of the modernist artist, who tries to stake out his territory by fortifying the boundaries between genuine art and inauthentic mass culture. Again, the problem is not the desire to differentiate between forms of high art and depraved forms of mass culture and its co-options. The problem is rather the persistent gendering as feminine of that which is devalued. . . . It seems clear that the gendering of mass culture as feminine and inferior has its primary historical place in the late 19th century, even though the underlying dichotomy did not lose its power until quite recently. It also seems evident that the decline of this pattern of thought coincides historically with the decline of modernism itself.

Partly because of the fact that the heroes, with their strengths and weaknesses, feats and foibles, suddenly all became women; partly because of the readership—women looking for a non-archaic self-image—Hacker's very personal narrative, a kind of continuing series of life studies, infiltrates the public meta-narrative: those stories we tell ourselves about who we are, where we've been, what we've done, where we're going. **"The Little Robber Girl Considers Some Options"** is an example of something that (given our cultural assumptions) *surprisingly* isn't a story about a boy, and derives its humor as well as its edge as critique from that gender shift:

Who wouldn't love the bad old ladies? I'd rather not go gaga in a nursing home, or be preserved in plastic slipcovers with a sullen home attendant paid by a despicable son-in-law. If I can't grow sinewy on a hillside with my twenty years' mostly companion, selling books, pots or rocks in a shop and sitting to three healthy courses on the precise stroke of nine, then I could be captious in a crooked castle, more courted a ruin than ever I was a *rouée,* avid for gossip and close with my favor. The third choice, only granted as a reward, is to pack the gold hero's medal and the ornamental sword in a battered briefcase with one drip-dry shirt, and set out, on the very eve of your triumphal fireworks, to char in the ice dame's half-dismantled mansion, to bind the enemy's atlas with your last silk ball-gown, to tell bedtime stories to the torturer who brings you cream teas, and to the orphans for whom you butchered a horse with the ceremonial epée. Then your digestion will rival your memory, your breasts will grow back while you learn Catalan, and your daughters slog across the icecap to get drunk with you.

Gossip and, in **"Letter,"** shopping are not depicted as vices of softminded females but as wholesome activities. One thinks of Carol Gilligan's *In a Different Voice,* where the non-linear "web" logic of narratives of relations—in our culture characteristically identified as feminine,

"lower order" reasoning—is identified as a form of responsibility. Fairy-tale time, in which you "set out" with minimal luggage and a few magical accessories to travel through dimensions of possibility, where you can conquer a world or two (Scheherazade or dragon slayer), has intersected with reality-principle time (twenty years selling books . . .) to suggest coordinates of a new logically possible world for women. That this happens for Hacker in a prose poem (evoking the form of the Hans Christian Andersen tale from which the little robber girl comes) matters, since she has seldom ventured outside the densely fortified poetic castle whose period wings are made of sonnets, sestinas, villanelles, etc.

As a formidably accomplished and still-young poet, Hacker's only significant weaknesses stem ironically from her unsurpassed facility with these forms. In her worst moments, she slips into a kind of virtuoso running commentary of a tasteful, or at least zestful, but rather superficial "life-style"—good wine, food, sex, travel . . . and not much else—as in the opening stanza of **"Graffiti from the Gare Saint-Manqué"**:

Outside the vineyard is a caravan
of Germans taking pictures in the rain.
The local cheese is Brillat-Savarin.
The best white wine is Savigny-les-Beaune.
We learn Burgundies while we have the chance
and lie down under cabbage-rose wallpaper.
It's too much wine and brandy, but I'll taper
off later. Who is watering my plants?
I may go home as wide as Gertrude Stein
—another Jewish Lesbian in France.

(from *Assumptions*)

There is, of course, great wit and a certain irony in the tenth-line refrain, "another Jewish Lesbian in France," evoking the image of Gertrude Stein throughout this poem, which follows the structure of the *Ballade Suprème.* But Stein's presence is as large lesbian, not poet, since as poet she stood for the antithesis of a form like the ballade. Gertrude Stein, was, in fact, the quite large robber woman on a lifelong adventure of formal innovation. When a few pages later the **"Ballad [again "Suprème"] of Ladies Lost and Found"** appears, whose refrain is inhabited by another, very different female ancestor: "and plain old Margaret Fuller died as well," I wonder whether Hacker is fully aware of the consequences of form in the reader's mind—that there is a kind of eradication of difference (the very thing Hacker must value greatly as a feminist poet) in uniform packaging. I want Hacker to claim Gertrude Stein as a genuine spiritual ancestor—to claim some of her lust as non-Euclidean poetic geometer. This is not to abandon discipline but to recognize the specific gravities and humors of formal choices.

In fact, there are formal departures in *Assumptions* which expand the range of Hacker's and the reader's sensibilities by opening form to outside influences (as Kovner does to history). There can be loose ends which let possibilities proliferate and the reader take up some of the imaginative work (activity of the mind synonymous, according to Aristotle, with happiness) rather than being stuck always in the role of spectator at the Sun Queen's banquet—every detail a dazzling reflection of the will to create a poetic plenum in competition with the formally lapsed real world. Marilyn Hacker is too brilliant a poet to become impenetrably safe in her formal choices. (pp. 37-43)

> *Joan Retallack, "Non-Euclidean Narrative Combustion (or, What the Subtitles Can't Say)," in* Parnassus: Poetry in Review, *Vol. 14, No. 2, 1988, pp. 23-49.*

Elizabeth Alexander

Going Back to the River is a meditation about themes that have long absorbed Marilyn Hacker: geographies, languages, the marking of her own places across various landscapes, and the creation of rituals. Her familiar technical dexterity abounds; Hacker is a stringent formalist who wields difficult verse forms elegantly, and while she works within tightly rhymed and metered structures such as sestinas and villanelles, she nonetheless brings a colloquial ease and grace to the forms. She builds her rhythm on rhyme itself, which forges connections between unlike quantities, and she uses her language to make those unlikely companions jibe.

The poems move between New York, a writer's colony (she rhymes "bravado" with "Yaddo," so take a guess), Paris, and rural France. Hacker fans—who tend to be diehards—will want to read this volume to see what she's thinking about and eating (*moules* on the terrace with her daughter), to follow her routines and her walks, which "mark the day's measures like rhyme." But only a few of the poems show what she's capable of.

"Self" is a tightly strung description of masturbation and those "nerves whose duty is delight." **"Riposte"** lampoons the world of writers' grants and colonies and poets dependent on the kindness of strangers: "If 'poet''s written where it says: PROFESSION / American Express extends no credit." "PROFESSION" looms large above the small "poet," which seems to be Hacker's point. **"Then"** describes a brief tryst in an apartment landing after "a premature glass of white wine" and is driven by the same erotic energy that propels sections of her sonnet sequence *Love, Death, and the Changing of the Seasons.* And in the new volume's title poem Hacker considers rivers in different cities and her travels "oceans away from a landlocked childhood" in the Bronx.

In **"Nights of 1964-1966: The Old Reliable,"** Hacker is the young poet with her motley band of friends at a gay hangout. The poem is populous: "staunch blond Dora," Bill, who had been a monk in Kyoto, "squat Margie, gaunt Speedy." "The bar was talk and cruising"; "smoke and smack" and sex abound while two women cook rice and beef stew for the rest. The poem bustles with all this activity, until the final lines:

> Soon, some of us bussed south with SNCC and
>   CORE.
> Soon, some of us got busted dealing drugs.
> The file clerks took exams and forged ahead.
> The decorators' kitchens blazed persimmon.
> The secretary started kissing women,
> and so did I, and my three friends are dead

The epigraph to the poem is from James Fenton: "The laughing soldiers fought to their defeat"; perhaps the friends are dead from AIDS. By casting such unvarying line structures, Hacker calls attention to her weighty coda and conveys the futility of imposing a predictable structure on a world so utterly unpredictable. Even old reliable death now comes when it isn't supposed to.

The powerful final poem, **"Against Silence,"** addresses Hacker's struggle to speak across barriers to her former mother-in-law, Margaret Delany, to whom the poem is dedicated (Hacker was married to the science-fiction writer Samuel R. Delany). She describes an early visit to Margaret's home:

> I was fifteen. I wished this were my home.
> (None of my Jewish aunts read *I. F. Stone's
> Weekly,* or shopped at Saks
> Fifth Avenue, none of them grew up Black
> working poor, unduped and civilized.)

The poem moves through the years of their relationship as Hacker is asked " 'For whom do you write?' " and answers, " 'I write for somebody like Margaret.' " The poem, and the book, ends with "Some overload blocked silence" in the aging Margaret's brain. She speaks names only occasionally, "amidst the glossolalial / paragraphs." As Margaret communicates defiantly with hand squeezes, Hacker is left "mourning your lost words . . . at a loss / for words to name what my loss of you is."

There are many "new formalist" poets, but few have Hacker's wind. She recalls 18th century British poets who chronicled and satirized their times in strictest meter. Hacker has always been a versifying marathoner, with her readers cheering at the energy she brings to her long sequences, and it is a pleasure to see these times chronicled from the perspective of this 20th century, Bronx-born globetrotter who writes about relationships between women: her daughter, her mother, her lovers and flames. These current poems, though, are too frequently still lifes, and while still waters may run deep, some of them seem merely still. Nonetheless, the bright moments, though too scarce in this in-between volume, shine brightly enough to help readers committed to Hacker's work hold tight till the next book. (pp. 6-7)

> *Elizabeth Alexander, in review of "Going Back to the River," in* VLS, *No. 84, April, 1990, pp. 6-7.*

Judith Barrington

Critics such as Vern Rutsala, writing in the *American Poetry Review,* claim that "In itself form is not a simple political matter, but it may serve as a rough gauge of the attitudes of writers. Thus, among poets one way to be conservative is to write in traditional forms." Ira Radoff, too, in an article titled "Neo-Formalism: A Dangerous Nostalgia," strongly equates the current use of received forms with conservatism: "Neo-formalists have a social as well as a linguistic agenda."

It does seem to be true that many of the white male poets arguing for the supremacy of received forms are among the most conservative of their kind. But these debates leave out all the poets who come to received forms from a different standpoint. Some women poets, like Marilyn Hacker and Maxine Kumin, regularly rely on those forms to enhance their vision, and others, like Minnie Bruce Pratt and Cheryl Clarke, are increasingly slipping villanelles and sestinas into their collections. But I utterly fail to see how these poets fit into a debate that equates "formalism" with "conservatism" and "free verse" with "radicalism." How can you regard books like Hacker's *Love, Death, and the Changing of the Seasons,* or Clarke's *Living as a Lesbian,* or, for that matter, "formal" poems by men of color, such as the prison haiku of Etheridge Knight, as anything but radical? . . .

Of all the women poets manifesting this arguably different, and certainly non-conservative, use of received form, Marilyn Hacker stands out. *Going Back to the River* is her sixth collection in a series that started with *Presentation Piece,* a winner of both the Lamont Poetry Prize and the National Book Award. It reverts to the format of her first four books, a collection of poems grouped loosely by sections. (*Love, Death, and the Changing of the Seasons* stepped outside this format by giving us linked poems with a narrative thread.)

Like its predecessors, this new collection displays a brilliant understanding of syllabics, as well as a range of forms, including several sestinas ("**Country & Western I**" and "**II**"; "**Cultural Exchanges**"), envelope tercets ("**Dear Jool, I Miss You in Saint-Saturnin**"; "**For K. J., Leaving and Coming Back**";"**Celles**"), a villanelle ("**From Orient Point**"), a pantoum ("**Market Day**") and a crown of sonnets ("**Separate Lives**"). In almost all the poems, the choice of form is as much part of the poem's success as the skilful realization of that form. In the past, Hacker has used the repeating words of the sestina to create the effect of abundance and the recurring pattern of daily meals ("**Five Meals**" in *Taking Notice*); here, in "**Cultural Exchanges,**" she manages to make the form seem perfect for conveying the nature of cross-cultural exchanges, with their moments of connection and their odd near–misses.

> One of them always had to telephone
> someone. She didn't think North
>   Americans
> visiting *ought* to have so many friends.
> Some afternoons small groups came
>   over, all
> middle-class women, with an *empleada*
> working at home. They set her down,
>   explained
>
> she could listen, too, while they
>   explained
> why women—"Augusta! Get the
>   telephone!"—
> were all one class, *Doña* and *empleada*.
> They had—"Translate, someone. The
>   Americans . . . "
> petitions to circulate over all
> the neighborhoods, they hoped she'd
>   show her friends,
>
> to make abortion legal. (Her best
>   friend's

midwife aunt did that, but never
>   explained.) . . .

The use of syllabics is equally effective. "**Late August**" alternates a long, fifteen-syllable line with a short six-syllable one, setting up a rhythm in which the long lines spread out slowly and the short ones seem almost abrupt. The poem is lyrically descriptive and musically alliterative, but the tension builds through the oddly contradictory line lengths, until the last six words explain exactly why the speaker is torn between the slow unfolding and the sudden stop that the form itself implies:

> The weather is changing. The
>   mountainous temperate climate
> edges toward autumn.
> There's a crowded sound in the
>   rattling leaves of the fig tree
> and I think of cities,
> though the second fruit, ovarian,
>   purple, splitting to scarlet
> is ready for picking . . .
> I'm less often tempted to strip off my
>   shirt in the morning
> at work on the terrace.
> The bedsheets are grimy and
>   wrinkled, but why should we haul
> to the costly laundry
> what we'd need for a couple of days?
>   All our conversations
>   touch on departure

The danger, of course, is that the technique will overpower the heart of the poem. This happened only rarely in Hacker's past work and for the most part she avoids the temptation here. Although I found the last stanza of the villanelle, "**From Orient Point,**" a little awkward, I loved the poem's direct tribute to Elizabeth Bishop's famous villanelle, "One Art." (Bishop begins "The art of losing isn't hard to master"; Hacker, "The art of living isn't hard to muster.")

One aspect of the passion that keeps these finely crafted poems alive is Hacker's feminism, which breathes life into many of them. The poet makes no compromises as a feminist or a lesbian when hobnobbing with the literati. In "**Riposte,**" she writes a scathing reply to Tom Disch, whose words she quotes as her epigraph: "I never could," says Disch,

> Figure out how anyone can justify
>   poetry
> As a full-time job. How do they get
>   through
> The day at MacDowell—filling out
> Applications for the next free lunch?

Replies Hacker:

> Dear Tom,
> When my next volume (granted:
>   slender)
> is granted an advance of more than two
> thou, perhaps I'll scorn all grants and
>   spend a
> couple of them on summer rent, like
>   you
>
> in the right Hampton with the novelists

who swap Hollywood options with
                bravado.
Their *au pairs* hoard handwritten
                shopping-lists;
their word-processors go with them to
                Yaddo.

And later in the (nicely rhymed) quatrains:

And you see no excuse for poets' lives
because we're paid so mingily; that's it?
I think of "unemployed" mothers,
                housewives
whose work was judged equivalent to
                shit-
shoveling on Frank Perdue's chicken
                farm
by gents who calibrate Job Equity.
All that they are today they owe to
                Mom!
Do novelists owe shit to poetry?

No, there's nothing conservative about Marilyn Hacker—
one of the very best of the radical formalists.

> *Judith Barrington, "Feminist Formalist," in*
> The Women's Review of Books, *Vol. VII,*
> *Nos. 10-11, July, 1990, p. 28.*

FURTHER READING

Filkins, Peter. "Parables of Everyday Light." *The Literary Review* 29, No. 3 (Spring 1986): 362-75.

> Laudatory review of Hacker's *Assumptions.*

Jarman, Mark. "A Scale of Engagement, from Self to Form Itself." *The Hudson Review* XL, No. 2 (Summer 1987): 343-57.

> Surveys several works, including *Love, Death, and the Changing of the Seasons.*

Stitt, Peter. "The Typical Poem." *The Kenyon Review* VIII, No. 4 (Fall 1986): 128-33.

> Review of *Assumptions* and other works in which Stitt praises Hacker's poetic skill and portrayal of women.

Wills, Clair. "Driving a Tradition to the Wall." *The Times Literary Supplement,* No. 4397 (10 July 1987): 748.

> An overview of "women's writing" focusing in part on Hacker's *Love, Death, and the Changing of the Seasons.*

Additional coverage of Hacker's life and career is contained in the following sources published by Gale Research: *Contemporary Authors,* **Vols. 77-80 and** *Contemporary Literary Criticism,* **Vols. 5, 9, 23.**

Susan Howe

1937-

Irish-born American poet and critic.

The following entry provides an overview of Howe's work.

INTRODUCTION

Howe is known for poetry that combines biographical narrative with resplendent language to create a distinct panorama of historical events. She possesses, according to Marjorie Perloff, "an uncanny ability to enter the experience of an actual historical woman and to make that experience her own." She has often been included among the "language poets," a group distinguished by their skepticism concerning the efficacy of written language to fully express emotion and experience. Unlike most authors associated with that movement, however, Howe is hailed for acknowledging the importance of visionary poetry and exceeding in her verse the emotional impact of her contemporaries.

Howe was born in Ireland but emigrated to the United States with her family as a child. Her experience crossing aboard a ship carrying refugees from Nazi-dominated Europe, and the ensuing events of the Second World War so affected Howe that she became, in her words, "part of the ruin." She began her career as a visual artist, and critics have commented that her visual sense is reflected in her attention to page design: the "look" of her poetry is central to the images she conveys. For instance, in works such as *Pythagorean Silence,* Howe makes ample use of wide margins and large spaces between words and phrases to increase their impact. She has also been noted for using phonetic similarities between seemingly unrelated words to create an opposition of ideas, as well as for exploring the dual meanings of single words. This attention to linguistics frequently enhances the allegorical expressions which Howe uses to illustrate her primary subject matter—the encroachment of historical issues on modern consciousness. As critic Geoffrey O'Brien has stated, "It's as if through the contemplation of words we could participate in . . . the infinitesimally slow shifts of thought and feeling that take centuries or millennia rather than lifetimes." In her poetry, Howe often comments indirectly on contemporary events through the recreation of historical events. The title of *Defenestration of Prague,* for example, refers to a seventeenth-century Czech religious conflict; she uses this event to comment on Catholic-Protestant disaccord in Ireland.

Howe also has been recognized as an insightful commentator on poetics. In *My Emily Dickinson,* she offers a careful reading of a single Dickinson poem, "My Life had stood—a Loaded Gun—." In this examination, she considers the historical context of Dickinson's work, as well

as the poem's influence on contemporary verse. Howe's meditation on Dickinson's work becomes so intense that, according to Perloff, "the two voices imperceptibly merge." Howe's criticism, like her poetry, is marked by its confrontation with established norms. Throughout her career, Howe has focused on the possibilities of vocabulary and the freedom that language offers. Her criticism reflects this belief as well, acknowledging the importance of commentary and theory, while declaiming the need for poetry to remain separate from them.

PRINCIPAL WORKS

POETRY

Hinge Picture 1974
The Western Borders 1976
The Secret History of the Dividing Line 1978
Cabbage Gardens 1979
*Pythagorean Silence 1982
*Defenestration of Prague [includes earlier collection *The Liberties*] 1983
†Articulation of Sound Forms in Time 1987

194

A Bibliography of the King's Book or, Eikon Basilike 1989

OTHER

My Emily Dickinson   (criticism)   1985

*These works were published in *The Europe of Trusts* in 1990.

†This work was published in *Singularities* in 1990.

CRITICISM

Geoffrey O'Brien

Howe's fragmentation and discontinuity [in *Defenestration of Prague*] are quite different from anyone else's. While [Charles] Bernstein's words seem to hover near meaning in a state of frustrated desire and [Ron] Silliman's resemble a rough-textured collage of disparate found objects, Howe's words give the impression of echoing another, hidden poetry of which we catch only fragments, like an opera sung in another room—except the other room is death, or history, or the ineffable. Her vocabulary includes the whole past of language. The words are like magnetic filings that adhere uncertainly to a receding body of meaning. Bits crumble into gnomic phrases— "nimble multiplying spirit" or "Search for the dead" or "Unseen waters of the wood"—and Howe strings them into haunting tunes, as in the long poem sequence **"Speeches at the Barriers":**

> Clear night
> Cassiopeia—
>
> To the glass house by water
>
> hurried elf
> and bedlam beggar
>
> lonely hellward nursery tale manner
>
> Know buried cities
> Know the combustible dark

In **Defenestration** and in her 1982 book **Pythagorean Silence,** Howe risks plunging into the most played-out area of language, the realm of the "profound" words. I don't know another poet capable of using the words "passion," "truth," "glory," and "beauty" in four lines and getting them to say something new. Her ear is uncanny, but it's what she's listening for in the first place that makes the difference.

The presence of the past is overwhelming in Howe's work—as it is in our lives—but in the spaces between her words I hear an opening to the future. While she locates the deepest mysteries within rather than beyond language, Howe's work acknowledges that the need for visionary poetry persists even in the absence of belief. The more rigorous practitioners of language poetry make no such acknowledgment, and their work pays a price in diminished

emotional impact; ultimately, readers ask more than a demonstration of language's insufficiencies. In giving us that something more, Howe shows that creating a deconstructive poetics is a project that has barely begun. The possibilities for poetry are again wide open. (p. 9)

> *Geoffrey O'Brien, "Meaningless Relationships," in* VLS, *No. 25, April, 1984, pp. 8-9.*

Marjorie Perloff

The genre of Susan Howe's **My Emily Dickinson** is, as the dust jacket comments by Michael Palmer and Don Byrd make clear, not that of "critical commentary" but the genre of Williams's *In the American Grain,* Charles Olson's *Call Me Ishmael,* and Robert Duncan's *H. D. Book*—texts in which one poet meditates so intensely on the work of another that the two voices imperceptibly merge. "Howe's ear," says Kathleen Fraser, "almost becomes Dickinson's, hearing each musical phrase *and* its hesitancy as fierce intention and mindful resistance" (dust jacket).

Howe's subject, broadly speaking, is the impingement of historical or biographical narrative on lyric consciousness, a subject she has already made her own in her earlier books, especially in **Defenestration of Prague.** The title of this book refers to a particular event, the *putsch* of 1617 in which Calvinist rebels attacked a group of Catholic officials in the Czech royal palace and threw them out the window, thus setting in motion the religious conflict known as the Thirty Years' War. But Howe is writing, not about Prague but about another Catholic-Protestant conflict, this one closer to home, in Ireland, the country of her own origins. History, for this poet, is "the true story that comes to nothing," a story that must be filtered through "mute memory vagrant memory" and be recreated in the poet's imagination. The "defenestration of Prague" thus becomes Howe's own deconstruction of Irish myth, legend, and history, her recreation, for example, of the "words upon a window pane," as Yeats called them, spoken long ago by Esther Johnson ("Stella") to Jonathan Swift or by Cordelia to her father, Lear.

In the section called "The Liberties," at the center of **Defenestration of Prague,** Howe introjects such items as an Irish postage stamp, fragments from Swift's *Journal to Stella,* poems in octosyllabic couplets about Stella by both Swift and Sheridan, Swift's epitaph for himself, and Yeats's aphoristic six-line poem by that title, into a prose text called **"Fragments of a Liquidation,"** which reads like a slightly off-key eighteenth-century memoir, for example:

> Often [Swift] used a 'little language' they both understood. The pages are filled with chat, puns, politics, plans, gossip, history, dreams, advice, endearments, secrets. . . . Left out, was his growing entanglement with Ester Vanhomrigh (VANESSA). None of Stella's letters have been saved.

Or again, under the heading of "STELLA'S PORTRAIT":

> Loved horses and riding, had a sharp tongue, en-

joyed social evenings, card games, and punning. . . .

She had raven-black hair (Swift), a pale and pensive expression (Mrs. Delaney), was plump (Some), extremely thin (Others). Sickly in her childhood, she grew into perfect health (Swift). She seems to have had weak eyesight.

Because "No authentic portrait [of Stella] exists," Howe turns to Swift's *Journal* for evidence, then discards that evidence for another source and yet another; finally, the narrator produces her own free-verse poem ("her diary soared above her house"), followed by "THEIR Book of Stella," a poetic collage, made up largely of citations from Renaissance and eighteenth-century texts, in which Stella, Cordelia, and the poet herself come together, culminating in the lines:

> The real plot was invisible
> everything possible
> was the attempt for the finest thing
> was the attempt
>
> him over the bridge into the water
>
> her some sort of daughter
> events now led to a region
> returned in a fictional direction
> I asked where the road to the left lay
> and they named the place
> Predestination
> automaton whose veiled face
> growing wings
> or taking up arms
> must always undo or sever
> HALLUCINATION OF THE MIRROR

Allusive, philosophical, speculative as it is, Howe's collage-poem raises questions about female identity that are a good deal more challenging than, say, Erica Jong's "Aging," with its ladies' magazine speculation as to "how women age / it starts around the eyes so you can tell / a woman of 22 from one of 28 merely by / a faint scribbling near the lids." Amusing and wholly accessible, such versifying is easily forgotten: *subject matter,* finally, cannot save it from its one-dimensionality. By contrast, Howe's reenactment of Stella's decision to follow Swift from her home at Moor Park to Ireland and to live there for twenty-seven years as his unacknowledged companion (when the news of her death was brought to the Deanery, "Swift was entertaining guests. He continued the party as if nothing had happened") resonates with possibility.

A similar resonance—the language of the present charged with echoes from an earlier time—characterizes *My Emily Dickinson.* Howe's argument—for this book does have an argument—is that Dickinson is our great poet of "subversion":

> In prose and in poetry she explored the implications of breaking the law just short of breaking off communication with a reader. Starting from scratch, she exploded habits of standard human intercourse in her letters, as she cut across the customary chronological linearity of poetry. . . . [She] conducted a skillful and ironic investigation of patriarchal authority over literary

history. Who polices questions of grammar, parts of speech, connection, and connotation? Whose order is shut inside the structure of a sentence? What inner articulation releases the coils and complications of Saying's assertion?

Howe is speaking, of course, not only for Emily Dickinson but for herself. To subvert authority is, for Howe, to challenge the "customary chronological linearity" of patriarchal poetry, to challenge the received model on its own ground.

But, and this is where Howe's feminist reading takes issue with current criticism, Dickinson was hardly the ghostly victim of male oppression she is often taken to be. Howe cites Sandra M. Gilbert and Susan Gubar's *Madwoman in the Attic* as follows:

> Where the stitching of suicide simply gathers the poet's scattered selves into the uniform snow of death, the spider artist's artful stitching connects those fragments with a single self-developed and self-developing yarn of pearl. The stitch of suicide is a stab or puncture. . . . The stitch of art is provident and healing.

"Who," asks Howe, "is this Spider-Artist? Not *my* Emily Dickinson. This is poetry not life and certainly not sewing." And she adds:

> The Spider-Woman spinning with yarn of pearl, whose use of horizontal dashes instead of ordinary punctuation is here [in *Madwoman in the Attic*] described as being "neater and more soigné in manuscript than in type . . . tiny and clear . . . fine thoughts joining split thoughts theme to theme," was an artist as obsessed, solitary, and uncompromising as Cezanne. Like him she was ignored and misunderstood by her own generation, because of the radical nature of her work. During this Spider's lifetime there were many widely read "poetesses."

"A poet," that is to say, "is never just a woman or a man." Categories and hierarchies—woman poet, for instance—"suggest property" and foreclose "possibility." Dickinson's poetry, Howe suggests, depends to an unusual degree upon her reading—a reading that happens to be primarily that of male writers.

> Emily Dickinson took the scraps from the separate "higher" female education many bright women of her time were increasingly resenting, combined them with voracious and "unladylike" outside reading, and used the combination. She built a new poetic form from her fractured sense of being eternally on intellectual borders, where confident masculine voices buzzed an alluring and inaccessible discourse, backward through history into aboriginal anagogy.

The relationship of Dickinson's own poetic language to the "alluring and inaccessible discourse" of male writers provides Howe with her starting point. To place Dickinson in a hypothetical canon of women writers, she implies, is to cut off one of the most important dimensions of her work. More specifically, to read Dickinson against Anne Bradstreet, because Bradstreet was the founding mother of American women's poetry, is to ignore the fact that

Dickinson herself read, not Bradstreet but Jonathan Edwards, just as she read voraciously James Fenimore Cooper, Charles Dickens, George Eliot, both Robert and Elizabeth Barrett Browning, the Brontës, and Shakespeare's history plays.

Howe's discoveries in this regard are absolutely startling. Dickinson's third "Master" Letter (L248), for example, a letter that begins, "Oh, did I offend it— . . . Daisy— Daisy—offend it—who bends her smaller life to his" is read against Little Em'ly's letter, in *David Copperfield,* written after eloping with Steerforth, addressed to her family, Ham, and possibly Master Davy/David/Daisy, which begins "Oh, if you knew how my heart is torn." A second source is judged to be the passage in Barrett Browning's *Aurora Leigh,* where Marian Earle describes her passion for Romney, Dickinson's "Low at the knee that bore her once unto . . . Daisy," echoing Browning's, "She told me she had loved upon her knees, / As others pray," and so on. Howe remarks:

> Attention should be paid to Dickinson's brilliant masking and unveiling, her joy in the drama of pleading. Far from being the hysterical jargon of a frustrated and rejected woman to some anonymous "Master"-Lover, these three letters were probably self-conscious exercises in prose by one writer playing with, listening to, and learning from others.

The production of meaning through language, that is to say, not a prior subject matter or the author's state of mind, is the essence of poetry. The bulk of *My Emily Dickinson* is devoted to a reading of a single poem, "My Life had stood—a Loaded Gun—," but "reading" is not quite the word for what takes place in the course of Howe's genuinely learned narrative. She begins with the world of frontier America to which this particular poem points and, as in *Defenestration of Prague,* her method is collage: passages from Calvin's *Institutes* and Increase Mather's *History of the War with the Indians in New England,* juxtaposed to the *Narrative of the Captivity and Restoration of Mrs. Mary Rowlandson* and to Howe's own commentary on Rowlandson's suffering, present us with a Manichean world "based on rigid separation of race, concentrated on abduction, communion, war, and diabolism." "Contradiction," writes Howe, "is the book of this place." "Dualism of visible and invisible."

Within this context of Puritan conversion narrative and Calvinist sermon, Dickinson's first letter to her mentor-to-be, T. W. Higginson (7 June 1862) appears in a new light—"Far from being the misguided modesty of an oppressed female ego, it is a consummate Calvinist gesture of self-assertion by a poet with faith to fling election loose across the incandescent shadows of futurity."

If the New England world of "Guns and Grace" forms the first circle within which Dickinson's poem operates, there are many others. The Brontë circle for one, and especially the book of the other Emily, *Wuthering Heights,* in which, as in Dickinson's poetry, "the inhuman legalism of Calvin warred with the intellectual beauty of Neoplatonism." Then Browning's "Childe Roland to the Dark Tower Came" ("Two nameless narrators in the middle of life

were set on their path to the questionable freedom of paralysis in power by a nameless, vaguely threatening Guide/Owner"), and then Shakespeare's Henry VI cycle and Cooper's *The Deerslayer.* By this time, Howe has, so to speak, become Dickinson. Here is her lyric commentary on the second stanza ("And now We roam in Sovereign Woods— / And now We hunt the Doe— / And every time I speak for Him— / The Mountains straight reply—") in the light of Cooper:

> Killdeer is a hunter's gun. Together We will hunt and kill for pleasure. American frontiersmen were generally men on the make. Land in the West was a commodity to be exploited for profit just as land in the East had been. The Civil War will or will not expiate Our Sin. During the first two Removes of Emily Killdoe's Captivity Narrative of Discovery; the unmentioned sun, blazing its mythopoeic kinship with Sovereign and shooting its rhyme,—flash of sympathy with Gun, has been steadily declining. Dickinson, an unwed American citizen with "-son" set forever in her name, sees God coolly from the dark side of noon.

Increasingly, the world of the Loaded Gun and the Sovereign Woods, of "Vesuvian face" and "Yellow Eye," of "the power to kill, / Without—the power to die—," belongs to the contemporary poet who recreates it. It is impossible to read *My Emily Dickinson* without being swept along on its powerful lyric current. Howe's aim is not so much to "explain" Dickinson's meanings as to relive them. Hers is a tale of possession: the "ammunition in the yellow eye of a gun that an allegorical pilgrim will shoot straight into the quiet of Night's frame." "Possibility," as the poet puts it, "has opened." (pp. 13-15)

> *Marjorie Perloff, "Recharging the Canon: Some Reflections on Feminist Poetics and the Avant-Garde," in* The American Poetry Review, *Vol. 15, No. 4, July-August, 1986, pp. 12-20.*

John Taggart

In time poets and their poetry become critical cartoons. The great value of Susan Howe's *My Emily Dickinson* is that it neither reproduces nor produces such criticism. What it does produce is a picture of mystery and power. The poet is a hunter consciously and aggressively active in the hunting process of composition; the poetry is what's hunted down and transformed by that process in a wilderness of language. Power has been exerted to be transformed and exerted again upon us as readers of the poetry. Because Susan Howe's reading is attentive both to the poet's historical contexts and to her texts—passionately attentive and open-ended in interpretation—the final mystery of the poet's motivation is respected and the exertion of the poetry's power is given free play. It is a picture, but a picture that releases to mystery and power. It is a picture of Emily Dickinson, and it is a picture of the poet in the act of composition that applies to the practice of contemporary poets. Given the intricacies of its subject and their implications for contemporary practice, this is a compact, even short book. It is also a great and important one.

At least part of this importance, though not the major part, is as a corrective to the current preponderance of attention and thus authority granted to academic critical theory written by those who are not themselves poets. Students could be forgiven the impression that the function of poetry is to provide an occasion for critical theory. Perhaps, in the manner of Pierre Menard, Derrida has not only explained Ponge—not to mention Nietzsche—but has also improved upon the work. In Harold Bloom's terms, the critic has become the author of the poet *and* the climate generally.

To welcome such a corrective is not to deplore criticism in itself, nor is it to deprecate philosophy. It is to regret the obscuring of poetry by an ever increasing overlay of prose commentary and critical theory; it is to be justifiably angry with the conduct (and reception) of philosophy as an autonomous activity, the products of which stand as self-sufficient Kafkaesque castles having no reference to poetry. Criticism turns poetry into prose that misremembers its source. While criticism aspires to this perceived condition of philosophy, a predictable enough byproduct of modernism, philosophy itself may well be guilty of forgetting its origins in poetry. Heidegger is undeniably one of our century's preeminent philosophers, and his philosophy has served as a direct stimulus for the development of literary hermeneutics. It is doubtful, though, whether his thought could have come to definition, much less influence, without the poetry of Hölderlin, Trakl, and Rilke.

(Susan Howe's judicious utilization of some terminology from Heidegger is exemplary. The author of *My Emily Dickinson* is not an intellectual luddite. If her readers find her utilization occasionally too breathless—e.g., "For the journey of a soul across the distance to being's first breath, true existence is in the Abyss."—they should recall her devastating questioning of Heidegger following her citation of Mary Rowlandson's narrative of her child's brutal murder by her Indian captors. "Where is the warm hearth Heidegger finds through Hölderlin's perception of what lies waiting at the summit of the central Self?")

The argument is not for the abolition of criticism or philosophy, but for an alteration of attitude which recognizes the existence of poetry as distinct from its commentary and theory, if not as the originating site of the most fundamental element of all language, i.e., metaphor. It is for an alteration in the balance of the agonistic debate between those, the poets, who have a vision to state in metaphor and those, the commentators and theorists, who wish to be free of any such vision's hold and to disperse, if not altogether deny, the power of such vision's images. The debate is as old as Homer and Plato. *My Emily Dickinson* functions as a corrective to the current imbalance of this debate by its very style. For it is nothing like anything found in current commentary and critical theory. In fact, while there are whole sections of "normative" sentences and paragraphs, there is much that isn't prose at all.

What follows is taken from a paragraph responding to poem 1382 ("In many and reportless places") by Dickinson and which anticipates her poem 378 ("I saw no way").

> On this heath wrecked from Genesis, nerve endings quicken. Naked sensibility at the extremest

periphery. Narrative expanding contracting dissolving. Nearer to know less before afterward schism in sum. No hierarchy, no notion of polarity. Perception of an object means loosing and losing it. Quests end in failure, no victory and sham questor. One answer undoes another and fiction is real. Trust absence, allegory, mystery—the setting not the rising sun is Beauty.

Some of this might have been written by a critic with an unusually acute and insistent ear. Most of it, however, could only have been written by a poet accustomed to thinking in figures. What assertion there is spreads out in the complex horizontal branching of association and metaphor, oblivious to the prose conventions of punctuation and syntax.

This is more crucial than a surface discrepancy of stylistics. Toward the end of Susan Howe's recent collection of poems, *Defenestration Of Prague,* there appears a list following and answering two italicized questions: *What are eyes for? What are ears for?*

> Tension
> Torsion
> Traction
> Unction
> Vection
> Version
> Vision

Lists in a variety of spatial displays figure prominently in this poet's poetry and "prose." When we come upon the beginning of her brilliant reading of Dickinson's "My Life had stood—a Loaded gun—," what we find is a list of equations of identity of **"My Life."**

> *My Life:* A Soul finding God.
> *My Life:* A Soul finding herself.
> *My Life:* A poet's admiring heart born into voice by idealizing a precursor poet's song.
> *My Life:* Dickinson herself, waiting in corners of neglect for Higginson to recognize her ability and help her to join the ranks of other published American poets.
> *My Life:* The American continent and its westward moving frontier. Two centuries of pioneer literature and myth had insistently compared the land to a virgin woman [bride and queen]. Exploration and settlement were pictured in terms of masculine erotic discovery and domination of alluring/threatening feminine territory.
> *My Life:* The savage source of American myth.
> *My Life:* The United States in the grip of violence that threatened to break apart its original Union.
> *My Life:* A white woman taken captive by Indians.
> *My Life:* A slave.

Unlike almost all criticism, there is no move to close off the play of these possibilities. Instead, it's allowed to flourish. Much later in the book another list appears, one which gives the possible relations generated by the same poem, both in itself and in combination with historical and literary associations it attracts to itself.

> Gun in My Life
> My Life in Gun
> My in The Owner
> The Owner in My
> Catherine in Heathcliff
> Heathcliff in Catherine
> Edgar in Tom
> Tom in Edgar
> Panther in Boone
> Boone in Panther
> Doe in Rebecca
> Rebecca in Doe
> Killdeer in Deerslayer
> Hawk-eye in Kill-deer
> Serpent in Chingachgook
> Chingachgook in Serpent
> He in I
> I in He
> Childe Roland blowing
> Edgar's mad song

Again, this contradicts the operative premise not only of academic literary criticism, but also the criticism of many poets, including Williams with whom the author expresses a sense of kinship in her introduction. That is, it does not attempt to close off possibility in the interest of a single "right" reading. It lets the power of Dickinson's vision continue to play upon us, even as she herself is included in that "us" of readers. By itself, then, Susan Howe's style demonstrates, in Eliot's phraseology, that the criticism of artists writing about their own art is of greater intensity and carries more authority than that of nonartists. The authority which this book carries cannot be that of any single right reading. Rather, it is the poem's own authority, the authority of the vision of Emily Dickinson's poetry, the result of passionate attention to words in tension, torsion, traction.

This connects with Susan Howe's refusal to go along with received feminist critical theory concerning Emily Dickinson. If a poet is to continue to think as a poet outside the poem, the poem's process of composition, if a poet is to remain true to the authority of her vision and what her eyes and ears perceive to be the vision of another poet— vision moreover that is not static, but dynamic—, then she will have to remain at odds with feminist criticism as much as any other. The discussions of Hélène Cixous and of Sandra M. Gilbert and Susan Gubar are to the point. Cixous is found wanting in her disregard for Gertrude Stein while elaborating a hortatory program for the writing of women in the future; the authors of *The Madwoman in the Attic* are chided for their depiction of Dickinson as a sewing spider-artist. "This is poetry not life, and certainly not sewing." Prior to this statement there *is* agreement that gender difference does affect our use of language, and there is a distinction that matters. "That doesn't mean I can relegate women to what we 'should' or 'must' be doing. Orders suggest hierarchy and category. Categories and hierarchies suggest property. My voice formed from my life belongs to no one else. What I put into words is no longer my possession. Possibility has opened." If the poet is to be true to vision and possibility, to the continu-

ing exertion of vision's power, then *all* the hierarchies and closures of criticism have to be resisted. It is daring to do this. For there are several instances of agreement between the author of *My Emily Dickinson* and the feminist critics she parts company with. Yet remaining true to the authority of her vision and to that of her subject, she can only turn away from a society she might otherwise enjoy, a society which presumably would be only too happy to confer its authority upon her. To remain true in this way is to keep possibility open, even if it means, as it does, the enforcement of solitariness and isolation. Her readers, we are the beneficiaries of her courage to recognize that "a poet is never just a woman or a man. Every poet is salted with fire."

This courageous and *human* recognition sets *My Emily Dickinson* apart from the current varieties of academic literary criticism and, if only as a matter of degree, from much of the criticism written by poets. Pound, Williams, Olson, and the Possum want to be right. Therefore, the play of possibility is abridged, and the drive toward the single authoritative reading, however spectacular and unacademic in appearance, ensues. Despite a number of differences, the book's truest progenitor and peer is *The Necessary Angel*.

We should hear Stevens as we read Susan Howe's final paragraph.

> Poetry is the great stimulation of life. Poetry leads past possession of self to transfiguration beyond gender. Poetry is redemption from pessimism. Poetry is affirmation in negation, ammunition in the yellow eye of a gun that an allegorical pilgrim will shoot straight into the quiet of Night's frame.

She has written "stimulation" where Stevens would have written "sanction." Their different word choice comes down to "the same difference." Just as I'm persuaded that Dickinson will be acknowledged as the primary 19th-century American poet, so am I that Stevens will be likewise acknowledged for our own century. What persuades me is their awareness and confrontation of the ultimate problematics. What makes *My Emily Dickinson* so valuable is its open address to all who would read and its courageous confrontation of issues that go far beyond the current debate over aesthetic authority. The book is valuable because it confronts, like Dickinson and Stevens, those ultimate problematics of how to be alone and how to stay alive.

Timely and needed as the book's critical corrective is, that is not the major part of its importance. For that we must turn to its picture of the poet in the act of composition. It is true that an unusually useful—by which I mean attentive to textual questions and imaginative in dealing with them—work of academic criticism, e.g., Isabel MacCaffrey's *Spenser's Allegory* or Lyndall Gordon's *Eliot's Early Years,* may occasionally offer a glimpse of such a picture. And these works are not to be discounted. More typical examples of criticism, however, offer nothing of the sort for the same reason that sex doesn't occur in Henry James: they have no knowledge of the experience. A poet who has written some of the most mysterious and powerful poetry of our time, Susan Howe is certainly knowledgeable about the act of composition. What is authorized by her style and her own working knowledge is a picture of composition. The major importance of this book lies in the originality and depth of that picture and its potential for application by other poets.

To repeat, the poet is a hunter consciously and aggressively active in the hunting process of composition; the poetry is what's hunted down and transformed by that process in a wilderness of language. This restatement of the picture is a composite and condensation of several images that recur in the book. Not long after the list of possible equations for **"My Life,"** there is this.

> Power is pitiless once you have put it on. The poet is an intermediary hunting form beyond form, truth beyond theme through woods of words tangled and tremendous. Who owns the woods? Freedom to roam poetically means freedom to hunt.

And somewhat later: "freedom to explore is a violation of Sovereignty and Avarice, and may be linked forever to loneliness, exile, and murder." This in turn should remind us of an earlier characterization of Emily Dickinson and Robert Browning wandering "a wilderness of language formed from old legends, precursor poems, archaic words, industrial and literary detritus." And to an even earlier sentence: "pursuit and possession. Through a forest of mystic meaning, Religion hunts for Poetry's freedom, while Poetry roams Divinity's sovereign source." Finally, moving past all of these citations to a sentence toward the end of the book: "all power . . . is utterly unstable."

There are other images contributing to the picture, but these are what I take to be the crucial ones. Their distribution throughout the book is not a matter of chance. That is, its disorganization, in terms of prose conventions and standard critical methods, is governed by the complex horizontal dynamics of association and metaphor. Through these dynamics the book grows, branching out into a mirror-maze of metamorphosis. Let us briefly consider these images.

The poet becomes a hunter by putting on power. Primarily, this means a power over language whether, as with Dickinson, over that of another contemporary poet's poem or the inherited legends and literary detritus making up the wilderness that is language. The act of composition, assumption of power, takes place in the woods of words. In part, this should remind us of Olson's composition by field and its finest realization, "In Cold Hell, In Thicket." To make this assumption is to move consciously and aggressively, to move as a hunter. The poet does this in order to bring about a more powerful composition, literally to bring about composition. How is the power of a poem measured? Susan Howe provides an insightful answer in her discussion of Jonathan Edwards and Dickinson: "subject and object were fused at that moment, into the immediate *feeling* of understanding. This re-ordering of the forward process of reading is what makes her poetry and the prose of her letters among the most original writing of her century." What can be a greater or more final manifestation of power than the reordering of the reading process?

Prose is read forward toward conclusions. In an age characterized by advertising and in which the primary field of undergraduate study is business marketing, readers read toward those conclusions *at speed*. Such reading uses language up, particularly figurative language which is discarded like so much fast food packaging along the way. In this age as in any other, poetry resists any such rapid linear consumption. While the silent reading of poetry involves the same physiological processes as reading prose, it is so composed, if it is to exert power, as to resist both speed and summary conclusions.

The poetry of power in any age resists such reading to the point of stoppage. (The speed urged by Olson is a compacting of perception, of metaphor process, rather than a rate of reading; if anything, compacting has to be a slowing agent.) It does this as part of the exertion of power in language. Whether it is done with any positive regard for readers is a good question. Pound's "to see again" presumes the reader will benefit as well as the poet. Notwithstanding the neatness of her manuscripts, we can't quite be sure that Dickinson herself was concerned with whatever well-being her poems might provide for others. We have to remain uneasy with such poets. When Susan Howe writes "together We will hunt and kill for pleasure," there can be no assurance the reader is included in the collective. The play of the poetry of power is never less than frightening, and not only to ethical culture moralists.

Emphatically, the poetry of power is never "a good read." In *My Emily Dickinson* there is a reference to the pioneer practice of fire-hunting whereby hunters would "shine the eyes" of deer and thus secure "a fatal shot." The poetry of power threatens to transfix its readers by its vision, holding them utterly. It may be that this is what underlies the antagonism described by Eric Havelock between the Homeric poets and the Platonic philosophers. It is an antagonism that continues, though we may call it a debate and though the balance seems presently to be all on the side of criticism (aspiring to the free-standing condition of philosophy). Understanding poetry as that which almost successfully resists the intelligence should not tempt us to forget that, in its complexity, there may be whole regions of language, composed parts of the woods, which *are* successful, impenetrable, in their resistance.

Two related terms entwine themselves around the spreading growth of the book. They are concealment and revelation. "Poems and poets of the first rank remain mysterious. Emily Dickinson's life was language and a lexicon her landscape. The vital distinction between concealment and revelation is the essence of her work." The distinction's vital because the poem is not now one and then the other, but *both* at once. "Dickinson went further than Browning, coding and erasing—deciphering the idea of herself, dissimulation in revelation." The poem's images may provide revelation, vision, *and* at the same time serve as concealments of what is most vital for the composing self. (Despite the earlier suspicions of musicologists, we have come to know the "secret program" of Berg's "Lyric Suite" only by chance.) For there to be composition there must be hunting and killing. The power of the hunter poet is made all the more absolute when the evidence for the enacting of power has been concealed in a simulated revelation. Plausible metaphors for hidden metaphors. Aware of such power, we can only smile a Gioconda smile at the questions of critical decorum recently raised by Jonathan Culler: "Does one deem empirical authors responsible for what is discovered in their texts? Does one allow oneself the possibility of treating authors as blind to the forces operating in and through their language?" We can only smile at the "new" argument of Michael Riffaterre's influential *Semiotics of Poetry* that poems are riddles saying one thing and meaning another.

Critical theory, by its rhetoric of authoritativeness, seeks to divert attention from its secondariness. The critic is a prose hunter in a forest which has been designed and already hunted over by the poet. The critic solves only those riddles which are left to be solved. There is always another part of the wood in a powerful poet's work. The true "super-reader" can only be the poet. And, as Dickinson's correspondence with Higginson demonstrates, *all* the poet's texts are artful and aware.

The implications of Susan Howe's images and their related terms of concealment and revelation are not, in the end, smiling matters. The freedom to hunt is purchased at a price. Freedom is always freedom *from* something. To hunt, the poet must tear away from all the somethings that would prevent entry into the wilderness. (Suddenly, Emily Dickinson's chosen seclusion appears in a new light.) What must be torn away from is all that which is represented by settlement, historically limited and approximate as that term may be, by all the settled usages of grammar and law, at and beyond the frontiers. "Really alone at a real frontier, dwelling in Possibility was what she had brilliantly learned to do." The several sections of *My Emily Dickinson* which remind us of the historical American wilderness and of the dangers of living there—for a Jonathan Edwards, for a Mary Rowlandson—continue to be apt. Only now we must understand that the imperatives for staying alive in the America of real frontiers remain in effect for our encounter with and in language. Once we have torn away from the settled usages—and this is never done once and for all, but must be repeated with no cessation of pain or doubt—we must remain in motion. Whether it's *away from* or *toward,* motion must be maintained. If not, the poet risks composing nothing not already composed, an inert sort of hunting, or of becoming the hunted. For to hunt at all must certainly contain the possibility of becoming the hunted. There is only one possible protection, if there is to be any hunting and if power is to be put on, and that is to stay in motion. "Unconcealed consciousness out in pure Open must be acutely alert if *he* is feminine." We can affirm this and also affirm that *all* hunting consciousness in composition, male or female, must be acutely and continuously alert.

We have read that all power is utterly unstable. It is unstable because of the unceasing away from and toward motion of hunting. There can only be power in the motion, in the act (which may include the guarding and concealment of what has been hunted down). To take on, to maintain power, the poet must always be going into exile, must always act alone, and must know that the title of hunter

could be exchanged, with equal accuracy, for murderer. If a further twist is needed, the "prey" that is hunted down in the wilderness of language will be identified by what the poet has been attracted to out of love and admiration. *Power is pitiless.*

The earliest of the cited images of the book's picture involves not only the forest of language once more, but also religion and poetry in a relation of conflict. Religion hunts for poetry's freedom because it is dependent on the images of vision for its own existence and organization. Take away those images and all the churches fall down. The church does not produce vision, but enshrines and builds basilicas around it; through these actions vision is turned into static dogma, suitably "stable" material for erecting an organization. Once an image is selected, all others are suspect and must be denied. To promote itself, religion becomes a demonstration of authority in the name of the chosen image. By definition the hunter poet cannot be satisfied with the restricted movement permitted by the leash of dogma. There is no other recourse than rebellion. "Dickinson takes sovereignty away from God and bestows it on the Woods." And the woods are made of words. Yes, this is a female triumph over organized male authority. It is also more than that. The poet's rebellion can hardly come to an end once the biblical He's have been dutifully translated to She's. And the righteous instigators of that translation will be no less energetic than their predecessors in the imposition of their authority. The poet who would hunt and take on power goes to no church, however reformed. The obligation to stay in motion, to find ways to conceal and guard what has been hunted down, remains binding. It is noteworthy that Susan Howe has included this image in her book. It is not merely historical. Vision is the big picture, which includes apprehension of violent spirit powers. Its inclusion reminds us of those men and women who assumed the responsibilities of rebellion even as they mistrusted it and who went into exile and perhaps ignominious martyrdom as a result. We need to be reminded of the human seriousness of poetry in an age of advertising and marketing which would recognize its activity, insofar as it recognizes it at all, as a minor craftsmanship.

Finally, some readers of *My Emily Dickinson* may feel we've not read the same book. For them its attraction will be an unabashed feminine perspective from which an instance of the feminine overthrow of male authority is celebrated. That is a possible, though surely reductive, reading. If I read it differently, it is to call attention to the wider human application of Susan Howe's stimulating picture of the poet for all those who would read or write. It is a great and important book. (pp. 264-74)

John Taggart, in a review of "My Emily Dickinson," in Conjunctions, *Vol. 11, 1987, pp. 264-74.*

Marjorie Perloff

According to the [Oxford English Dictionary], *collision* means "*1.* The action of colliding or forcibly striking or dashing together; violent encounter of a moving body with another. *2a.* The coming together of sounds with harsh effect. . . . *3. fig.* Encounter of opposed ideas, interests, etc.; clashing, hostile encounter." Whereas *collusion* means "Secret agreement or understanding for purposes of trickery or fraud; underhand scheming or working with another; deceit, fraud, trickery."

What a difference a phoneme makes! One's *collision* with history may be accidental, an encounter of opposed ideas neither planned nor anticipated. One's *collusion,* on the other hand, is by definition premeditated. Attentiveness to such difference (/i/ versus /uw/) has always distinguished Susan Howe's "history poems" from those of her contemporaries. The opening page of the early chapbook, ***The Western Borders,*** for example, looks like this:

IRELAND

sandycove
keel

a snicker hugged this face that lay in sand cliffs
are cruel yes cruel rock and rook of cloud past
all and Ireland a place circled round by the sea
and Ibex a creature with horns like a goat and
Ibis a bird that in Egypt I've read was worshipped while living and honored when dead
galloped across the laugh of it all for a light sand
floor am told to go down while hills hem dawn
into

SONG

*

name my cottage Merlin
shutter it in trees
Merlin of the Dark Gate
deep calling into Sleep

Ireland, sandycove: one thinks immediately of Joyce's *Ulysses* as well as of Beckett's Irish novels, but what about *keel?* The apposition suggests that "keel" is another place in Ireland (there is, of course, a city called "Keele" in England), but in fact it's not on the map. Rather, the "keel" of a boat appears just where one would expect it—at Sandycove beach—and the block of words that now follows opens with reference to a "face that lay in sand / cliffs." We don't know whose face, but it doesn't matter, the poem's aim being to anchor that face in the Irish shorescape of *rock* and *rook, Ibex* ("a creature with / horns like a goat") and *Ibis* ("a bird that in / Egypt I've read was worshipped while living / and honored when dead"). Like *collision/collusion, rock/rook* and *Ibex/Ibis* are look-alike and sound-alike pairs, whose meanings are divergent. "I've read," "am / told to go down": these are the only references to a first-person speaker, and they do little to make the "I" present, the first being parenthetical, the second omitting both pronoun and agent (the construction is passive) and subordinating individual selfhood to proverbial action ("go down" to the ships, "go down" to the sea, etc.). This is the Ireland not of Susan Howe observer/traveler/poet (at least not overtly) but of myth and legend, a place where "hills hem dawn into / SONG" and Merlin of the Dark Gate shares the space with the alien Ibis and Ibex.

From the first, Howe has been interested in such myth-

ic/historical configurations of "sound forms." Untypically, she seems to have had no apprentice period during which she wrote derivatively, "in the style" of X or Y. No doubt her relatively late start as a poet had something to do with this; Howe began as a visual artist and was in her late thirties by the time her first book appeared. Her visual sense is reflected everywhere in her attention to page design—how the whole page is going to *look* is central to her poetics. Concrete poetry may well have been an influence; there is not, in any case, so much as a trace in Howe's work of the confessional mode so ubiquitous in the poetry of the early seventies. Except for **"Buffalo. 12.7.41"** in ***Pythagorean Silence*** (and this only in part), I know of no Howe poem that is directly autobiographical or personal. Which is not to say that the work isn't emotive, but its emotive contours depend upon the collisions (and sometimes, it may be, collusions) of three codes—the historical, the mythic, the linguistic—all three, it should be added, as informed by an urgent, if highly individual, feminist perspective.

Perhaps the best place to show how this process works is in Howe's . . . book, ***Articulation of Sound Forms in Time.*** On the first and otherwise blank page of this long poem, we read:

from seaweed said nor repossess rest
scape esaid

From seaweed said: the story to be told here, if not quite "Spelt from Sybil's Leaves" (Hopkins), evidently consists of fragments shored from the ocean of our American subconscious. Yet one cannot "repossess [the] rest"; or, since what is said from seaweed cannot be repossessed, one must rest one's case. Or just rest. "Scape" may refer either to the seascape or landscape, or, most plausibly, it may be an abridged version of *escape:* "there is no escape, he said," or "let it be said from what the seaweed said" (cf. Eliot's "What the Thunder Said"), no escape, moreover, from the desire to repossess the rest.

Obviously there are many ways of interpreting the eight words in these two lines, which is not to say that they can mean anything we want them to mean. We know from this introduction that an attempt will be made to "repossess" something lost, something primordial. The sound structure of the passage, with its slant rhyme of *sea/weed* and *repossess/rest,* its consonance of *weed, said, esaid,* and its alliteration of *s*'s, (nine out of forty-one characters) and assonance of *e*'s and *o*'s, enacts a ritual of repossession we can hear and see. And so small are the individual morphemes—*from, said, scape, esaid*—that we process them one by one, with difficulty. This "saying" "from seaweed" will evidently not be easy.

Who speaks these opening lines? The voice is impersonal, part bardic, part comic—a voice akin to Beckett's in *Ping* or *Lessness.* But the abrupt opening is immediately juxtaposed to a document, a text taken from the "real" world, namely an "EXTRACT *from a* LETTER *(dated June 8th, 1781,) of Stephen Williams to President Styles*":

In looking over my papers I found a copy of a
paper left by the Rev. Hope Atherton, the first
minister of Hatfield, who was ordained May

10th, 1670. This Mr. Atherton went out with the forces (commanded by Capt. Turner, captain of the garrison soldiers, and Capt. Holyoke of the county militia) against the Indians at the falls above Deerfield, in May, 1676. In the fight, upon their retreat, Mr. Atherton was unhorsed and separated from the company, wandered in the woods some days and then got into Hadley, which is on the east side of the Connecticut River. But the fight was on the west side. Mr. Atherton gave account that he had offered to surrender himself to the enemy, but they would not receive him. Many people were not willing to give credit to this account, suggesting he was beside himself. This occasioned him to publish to his congregation and leave in writing the account I enclose to you. I had the paper from which this is copied, from his only son Jonathan Wells, Esq., who was in the fight and lived afterward at Deerfield and was intimately acquainted with the *Indians* after the war, did himself inform *me* that the *Indians* told *him* that after the fall fight, a little man with a black coat and without any hat, came toward them, but they were afraid and ran from him, thinking it was the Englishman's God, etc., etc.

I reproduce this document in its entirety so that we can see what Howe does with her *donnée.* For *Articulation of Sound Forms in Time* is by no means a retelling of the Hope Atherton story or the invention of an up-to-date analogue that points to the "relevance" of the Indian Wars to our own time. Still, the story, as gleaned from the letter above and from a number of old chronicles of New England towns, is inscribed everywhere in Howe's poem. It draws, for example, upon the basic paradox that the Reverend Hope Atherton, ostensibly a man of God, would accompany the Colonial militia on an Indian raid. And further, that having somehow gotten separated "from the company," this "little man with a black coat and without a hat," as one chronicle calls him [*History of Hatfield,* author unknown], would surrender himself to the Indians, only to be rejected by them as suspect, indeed perhaps the "Englishman's God." Suspect as well to his own people, who, upon his return to Hatfield, refused to believe his story. Atherton, in the words of the chronicle, "never recovered from the exposure" and died within the year, an isolated figure, indeed something of a pariah.

Such "Untraceable wandering" culminating in the "nimbus of extinction" is, so Howe believes, a ubiquitous fact of early New England history, and its burden continues to haunt our language. *Articulation of Sound Forms in Time* draws upon not only Hope Atherton's story but also the captivity narratives Howe has been studying, specifically the 1682 NARRATIVE *of the Captivity and Restauration of Mrs. Mary Rowlandson,* which is the subject of a Howe essay published in *Temblor,* an essay more accurately described as a poetic collage-text, creating meanings, as it does, from its stark juxtapositions of seemingly disparate materials: Colonial documents, biblical extracts, historical records, quotations from Mary Rowlandson's own narrative, poems by Anne Bradstreet, snatches of Algonquin speech, Howe's own poetic response to the "events" recorded by Rowlandson, and so on.

The text begins with the words "Náwwatuck nôte-shem / I came from farre," immediately followed by Rowlandson's eloquent opening:

> **Come, behold the works of the Lord, what dissolations he has made in the Earth.** Of thirty-seven persons who were in this one House, none escaped either present death, or a bitter captivity, save only one, who might say as he. *Job* 1.15. *And I only am escaped alone to tell the News.*

Rowlandson's narrative, Howe tells us, "is both a microcosm of colonial imperialist history, and a prophecy of our contemporary repudiation of alterity, anonymity, darkness."

Taken out of context, this claim may sound bombastic, but, remarkably, Howe makes us believe that this "first narrative written by a white American woman" really functions as such a microcosm. As in the case of Atherton, it is the seeming contradictions of Mary Rowlandson's story that interest the poet. On the one hand, there is Rowlandson's "thoroughly reactionary figuralism," her obsessive orthodoxy, her view of her Indian captors, who actually never touched her, as "'murtherous wretches,' 'bloody heathen,' 'hell-hounds,' 'ravenous bears,' [and] 'wolves'"; she recalls "'the roaring, and singing, and dancing, and yelling of those black creatures in the night, which made the place a lively resemblance of hell'." Yet, as Howe puts it, "The idiosyncratic syntax of Mary Rowlandson's closed structure refuses closure"; the white woman captured by these "wolves" also remembers incidents like the following: "'Now must we pack up and be gone from this Thicket. . . . As we went along they killed a *Deer,* with a young one in her. They gave me a piece of the *Fawn,* and it was so young and tender, that one might eat the bones as well as the flesh, and yet I thought it very good'." Indeed, Rowlandson's "risky retrospective narrative" everywhere exceeds its author's intentions: she "saw what she did not see said what she did not say."

Here, as in *My Emily Dickinson,* Howe displays an uncanny ability to enter the experience of an actual historical woman and to make that experience her own. It is not, of course, a question of accuracy: who knows what went through the mind of the "real" Mary Rowlandson? The "real" Emily Dickinson? Rather, the seeming authenticity, the credibility of Howe's documentary collage depends upon the positioning of the language field, the juxtaposition, for example, of flat narrative ("Mary White Rowlandson, one of the seven children of John and Joane White, was born in England. The date of her birth is uncertain, but the Whites crossed to Salem, Massachusetts in 1638" with extracts from Deuteronomy and Psalms, from Increase Mather's *Brief History of King Philip's War,* and so on. Howe's is never the reductive capsule biography that trivializes so many of the sonnets in Robert Lowell's *History,* for instance, "Margaret Fuller Drowned":

> You had everything to rattle the men who wrote.
> The first American woman? Margaret Fuller . . .
> in a white nightgown, your hair fallen long
> at the foot of the foremast, you just forty,

> your husband Angelo thirty, your Angelino
>   one—
> all drowned with brief anguish together. . . .
>   Your fire-call,
> your voice, was like thorns crackling under a
>   pot,
> you knew the Church burdens and infects as all
>   dead forms,
> however gallant and lovely in their life;
> progress is not by renunciation.

Here the poet positions himself securely outside his character's consciousness, condescendingly addressing her as "You" and telling her about the "brief anguish" she must have felt; he wraps up Fuller's complex philosophical position in phrases like "you knew the Church burdens and infects as all dead forms." Indeed, Fuller serves Lowell primarily as a vehicle for his own clear-eyed recognition that "progress is not by renunciation"; he endows her with the stereotypical rebellious spirit that wants out from under: "Your fire-call, / your voice, was like thorns crackling under a pot."

Howe, on the other hand, forces us to see and smell and take part in Mary Rowlandson's eleven weeks and five days in the wilderness, even as she examines her subject's words from the vantage point of a sophisticated poet writing in the late twentieth century: "This is a crime story in a large and violent place. Too large for subject and object. Only a few of her captors have names. Nearly all of their names are wrong."

The wrongness of names in the old chronicles of New England provides the poet with an opportunity to call the very act of naming into question. In a sermon of May 28, 1670, reproduced in one of Howe's sources for *Articulation of Sound Forms in Time,* the Reverend Hope Atherton recalls that when, in his forest wanderings, he came face to face with the Indians, "I spake such language as I thought they understood." But evidently "they" did not understand, and this failure to understand what the other is saying becomes Howe's point of departure in *Articulation.* Here is the opening poem of Part 1, **"Hope Atherton's Wanderings":**

> Prest try to set after grandmother
> revived by and laid down left ly
> little distant each other and fro
> Saw digression hobbling driftwood
> forage two rotted beans & etc.
> Redy to faint slaughter story so
> Gone and signal through deep water
> Mr. Atherton's story Hope Atherton

We note right away that in this poem, Hope Atherton is not a "character," with such and such traits and a definable history. The "Wanderings" of Howe's title (there are sixteen sections in Part 1, ranging in length from two to fifteen lines) are presented not as articulations *of* time—not, that is to say, as accounts of what happened—but *in* time, in the time it takes to articulate the "sound forms" themselves. Thus poem #1 is a deceptive square (eight lines of predominantly eight- and nine-syllable lines), which tries to contain, both visually and aurally, the linguistic displacements produced by a faulty memory.

The word *Prest* may refer to Atherton's condition: he was pressed by the Indians to "try to set after" his own people, perhaps after he was revived by a grandmother and left to "lie" ("ly") in the forest. But the absence of the subject or object of "Prest" brings other meanings into play: "oppressed," "impressed," "presto." We cannot be sure whom "he" (if there is a he here) was "revived by," or whose "grandmother" is involved. As for "left ly," the tiny suffix makes it possible to bring to bear a whole host of *-ly* words: "left mercilessly," "left unkindly," "left ruthlessly," "left carelessly." The reader is given all these options; he or she can construct any number of scenarios in which two people are lying a "little distant [from] each other" and moving to and "fro." It is only dimly, after all, that we can reconstruct the Colonial-Indian conflict, with the colonists' "hobbling driftwood" and "forag[ing] two rotted beans & etc."—"& etc." suggests that it is what comes after speech ceases that matters—as well as the militia's "Redy to faint slaughter story," a story, "Mr. Atherton's story," now "so / Gone" that it can only come to us as a "signal through deep water."

Not only does Howe frequently decompose, transpose, and refigure the word (as in *ly*); she consistently breaks down or, as John Cage would put it, "demilitarizes" the syntax of her verbal units. Reading the poem above, one is never sure what subject pronoun goes with what verb, what object follows a given preposition, which of two nouns a participle is modifying, what phrases a conjunction connects, and so on. An extraordinarily taut sound structure—for example, "revived *by* and *l*aid down *left ly*"—holds in check a syntax that all but breaks down into babble. Indeed, by poem #8, all the connectives that make up "normal" syntax have been abandoned:

> rest chondriacal lunacy
>
> velc cello viable toil
>
> quench conch uncannunc
>
> drumm amonoosuck ythian

Is "rest" a noun or a verb, and how does it relate to "chondriacal [hypochondriacal?] lunacy"? In line 2, "velc" may be an abridgment of "velocity," which doesn't help us make sense of the intricately sounded catalogue "velc cello viable toil"; in line 3, "uncannunc" contains both "uncanny" and "annunciation" (the prophecy, perhaps, of the "conch" shell which cannot "quench" our thirst); in line 4, the Anglo-Saxon ("drumm"), Indian ("amonoosuck"), and Greek ("ythian") come together in a "collusion" that makes us wonder if the "rest" isn't some sort of hypochondriacal lunacy on Atherton's part. Or, some would say, a "lunacy" on the poet's part as well.

What justifies such extreme verbal and syntactic deconstruction, a decomposition that has become something of a Howe signature? Is the obscurity of *Articulation* merely pretentious? Confronted by lines like "velc cello viable toil," many readers have closed the book, concluding that the poet is talking only to herself. The charges leveled against Language poetry in general—obscurity, abstraction, lack of emotion, the absence of lyric selfhood—all these can easily be leveled at Susan Howe. Yet even readers unsympathetic to her work, readers who claim a book like *Articulation* is too private, that it isn't really "about" anything, will, I submit, find themselves repeating lines like "velc cello viable toil," if for no other apparent value than their complex music, the way *e, l,* and *c* in the first word reappear as *cel* in the second, or the way the *v, e, l* in *velc* reappear in the very different sounding word *viable,* the latter also containing the *l* of *cello* and *toil.*

Is this then Jabberwocky, nonsense verse? If Howe wants to talk about Hope Atherton's mission to the Indians or apply the "themes" implicit in the tale—Colonial greed, Puritan zeal, the fruits of imperialism, the loneliness of exile, the inability to communicate with the Other—to the contemporary situation, why doesn't she just get on with it? Even a prose piece like the Mary Rowlandson essay is, after all, by and large comprehensible.

It would be easy to counter that the breakdown of articulation, which is the poem's subject, is embodied in the actual breakdown of the language, that the fragmentation of the universe is somehow mirrored in the fragmentary nature of the text. But the fact is that in Howe's work, as in Charles Bernstein's or Lyn Hejinian's, demilitarization of syntax may well function in precisely the opposite way, namely as a response to the all too ordered, indeed formulaic syntax that characterizes the typical "workshop" poem. Thus a recent poem called "Thoreau" by Rodney Jones begins:

> It is when I work on the old Volvo,
> lying on my back among the sockets,
> wrenches, nuts, and bolts,
> with the asphalt grinding the skin
> over my shoulderblades, and with the cold
> grease
> dripping onto my eyeglasses,
> that I think of Thoreau
> on his morning walks around the pond
> dreaming of self-sufficiency.

This is certainly more accessible, more "natural," than the opening of Howe's **"Thorow"**:

> Go on the Scout they say
> They will go near Swegachey
>
> I have snow shoes and Indian shoes
>
> Idea of my present
> not my silence

But if emotion can be thus neatly packaged ("It is when I work on the old Volvo . . . that I think of Thoreau"), if "poetry" is really no more than such reportage, the straight-but-sensitive "nuts and bolts" talk broken arbitrarily into line segments so as to remind us that, yes, this is a poem, why read in the first place rather than turning on the TV? The Phil Donahue show, for instance, where the Reverend Hope Atherton would no doubt be a popular guest: his decision to leave his congregation and accompany the militia on a war raid might well prompt some heated debate, Caller A telling Phil that the minister should have stayed home and minded his own business, Caller B insisting that, on the contrary, Atherton's action was "compassionate" and "caring."

How, then, to give life to a "poem including history"? There is Ezra Pound's way: the documentary collage with its "repeats" and "subject rhymes," but, except in her prose pieces like the Mary Rowlandson essay, this way is not Howe's. Emily Dickinson's punning, word play, and syntactic ambiguity are closer:

> The Zeros taught Us—Phosphorus—
> We learned to like the Fire
> By handling Glaciers—when a Boy—
> And Tinder—guessed—by power

But Dickinson provides no direct models for the history poem. In this regard, Hart Crane, one of Howe's favorite poets, provides a kind of bridge (no pun on his "epic of America" intended) between Dickinson and Howe:

> Often beneath the wave, wide from this ledge
> The dice of drowned men's bones he saw be-
> queath
> An embassy. Their numbers as he watched,
> Beat on the dusty shore and were obscured.

How, Harriet Monroe wanted to know about these lines, could "dice" "bequeath / An embassy"? How could "numbers" "Beat on the dusty shore"? And as for line 8, "The portent wound in corridors of shells," is "wound" a verb or a noun? ("Letter to Harriet Monroe" [1926], Crane).

Crane's syntax looks ahead to Howe's, as does, to some extent, his "myth of America." But Howe's austere, condensed "articulation of sound forms" does not really resemble Crane's oracular, apocalyptic vision; indeed, the missing link in the Dickinson-Crane-Howe chain is surely the late Beckett. Here is the opening paragraph of "Lessness":

> Ruins true refuge long last towards which so many false time out of mind. All sides endlessness earth sky as one no sound no stir. Grey face two pale blue little body heart beating only upright. Blacked out fallen open four walls over backwards true refuge issueless.

If we lineate and scan Beckett's last sentence—

> Blácked óut | fállen ópen | fóur wálls | óver báck-
> wârds trúe réfuge íssuelêss

—we are close to Howe's structures of apposition, for example:

> Pósit gáze lével dimínish lámp and asléep
> (sélv)cánnot sée

In both cases, there seems to be a felt need to remake a language that, in its ordinary, which is to say formulaic, state (see Rodney Jones's "Thoreau" or, for that matter, Robert Lowell's "Margaret Fuller Drowned") cannot approximate the difficulties of what the postmodern poet and her/his readers perceive to be a multitrack experience.

Poem #5, for example, articulates a "sound form" that refers to Hope Atherton's journey home:

> Two blew bird eggs plat
> Habitants before dark
> Little way went mistook awake
> abt again Clay Gully

espied bounds to leop over
Selah cithera Opynne be
5 rails high houselot Cow
Kinsmen I pray you hasten
Furious Nipnet Ninep Ninap
little Pansett fence with ditch
Clear stumps grubbing ploughing
Clearing the land

"Two blew birds eggs plat": "blew" is a pun on "blue," and "plat" means "flat" as well as the truncated "plate." The image of the "Two blew bird eggs plat" gives a fairy-tale aura to this segment of the journey, as does "Little way went mistook" with its Hansel and Gretel echo. Again, the "bounds to leop over" (*leop* is Old English for "leap") are more than "houselot" divisions, for the real crossing of the poem is over the borders into another language where the "babble-babel" (Letter) is formed from words and sounds taken from Hebrew ("Selah"), Indian ("Nipnet Ninep Ninap"), and English ("Clay Gully"), with the mythological reference to Venus's isle Cythera thrown in.

The poems now become increasingly fragmented, gnomic, enigmatic, as if the breakdown depicted is not so much Hope's as that of language itself. Regression sets in, poem #9 going back to Anglo-Saxon origins—

scow aback din

flicker skaeg ne

barge quagg peat

sieve catacomb

stint chisel sect

—and then in #13 to a kind of aphasia, words, now without any modification or relationship, being laid out on the page as follows:

chaotic architect repudiate line Q
    confine lie link realm

circle a euclidean curtail theme theme
    toll function coda

severity whey crayon so distant grain
    scalp gnat carol

omen Cur cornice zed primitive shad
    sac stone fur bray

tub epoch too tall fum alter rude
    recess emblem sixty key

Epithets young in a box told as you fly

By this time, Hope's search has become the poet's search. It is the poet who must deal with the "chaotic," must "repudiate" the "line" that "confine[s]," the "euclidean" "circle" too neat in its resolution of "theme theme" and the "severity" of its "coda." But one can also read this poem as dealing with any form of making, of "architect-[ure]," the placement of "cornice" and "stone" so as to "alter rude" appearances. And the Indian motif never quite disappears, here found in the reference to "scalp," "gnat," "primitive," and "rude."

In #13, words are spread out insistently on the white ground of the page; in #15, by contrast, words run together:

MoheganToForceImmanenceShotStepSee-
    ShowerFiftyTree

UpConcatenationLessonLittleAKantianEm-
    piricalMaoris

HumTemporal-
    spatioLostAreLifeAbstractSoRemotePossess

ReddenBorderViewHaloPastApparitionOpen-
    MostNotion *is*

The "collusion" that forces words into this particular "collision" is oddly painful: the text is, so to speak, wounded, as if to say that the nightmare War with the Savage Other has come back to haunt Hope/Howe with its "AKantianEmpirical" "Force" or "Immanence" of "Mohegan" or "Maori" presence, its reference to "Shot," "Shower," "FiftyTree," "ReddenBorderView." This particular lyric concludes with a refrain already articulated in #14, a couplet producing a verbal mirror image:

blue glare(essence)cow bed leg extinct draw
    scribe sideup
even blue(A)ash-tree fleece comfort(B)draw
    scribe upside

"Sideup"/"upside" is a breaking point; after this particular collision, the sequence suddenly shifts to the formal and coherent monologue (#16) of Hope Atherton himself:

Loving Friends and Kindred:—

When I look back

So short in charity and good works

We are a small remnant

of signal escapes wonderful in themselves

We march from our camp a little

and come home

Lost the beaten track and so

River section dark all this time

We must not worry

how few we are and fall from each other

More than language can express

Hope for the artist in America & etc

This is my birthday

These are the old home trees

On a first reading, this lyric coda seems excessively sentimental as well as unwarranted. Having wandered with great difficulty through the forest of the preceding lyrics, one is, of course, relieved to come into this clearing, to hear the sermonlike address to "Loving Friends and Kindred." But the resolution here provided—"We must not worry / how few we are and fall from each other / More than language can express / Hope for the artist in America

& etc"—is a shade too easy, given the intractability of the material that has been put before us. How and why, after all, does Hope become Howe? How and why is there "Hope for the artist in America"? And finally, what do we do once we reach the birthday when we settle down under "the old home trees"?

But perhaps we are meant to feel slightly queasy at this point. The "old home trees" turn out to be no more than a brief point of rest en route to the "Corruptible first figure" of Part 2, "Taking the Forest." In the twenty-five meditations that follow, "Hope for the artist" once again grows dim, in the face of "Collision and impulsion," "Lives to be seen pressing and alien." But increasingly, the focus is now on "Girl with forest shoulder / Girl stuttering out mask or trick," and the penultimate poem brings us to a vision of "Lost fact dim outline / Little figure of mother," a "Face seen in a landscape once," with the assurance that "She is and the way She was."

Of this lyric, Howe writes, "It would have been easy to end on the second to last poem as I have done in readings of it and which makes it more overtly feminist. It's too easy that way. There are no answers and life is hard. Hart Crane leaped off the boat to his death; Hope Atherton was treated like a fool—like Pip in *Moby*. Melville and Dickinson died in obscurity." And she cites line 9 of the final poem: "Far flung North Atlantic littorals" (Letter). Indeed, the final poem is essential:

> To kin I call in the Iron-Woods
> Turn I to dark Fells last alway
>
> Theirs was an archheathen theme
> Soon seen stumbled in lag Clock
>
> Still we call bitterly bitterly
> Stern norse terse ethical pathos
>
> Archaic presentiment of rupture
> Voicing desire no more from here
>
> Far flung North Atlantic littorals
>
> Lif sails off longing for life
> Baldr soars on Alfather's path
>
> Rubble couple on pedestal
> Rubble couple Rhythm and Pedestal
>
> Room of dim portraits here there
> Wade waist deep maidsworn men
>
> Crumbled masonry windswept hickory

A dark conclusion but nevertheless triumphant. Over against the "Far flung North Atlantic littorals" of Melville, Crane, and Olson—littorals that are also the borders that open the verbal signifier to the possibilities of meaning—the poet sets the "Stern norse terse ethical pathos" of traditional myth, the myths of Lif and Baldr, of the "Rubble couple on pedestal" and the "Room of dim portraits here there." At the end, Old Hickory still triumphs, "Crumbled" though the masonry may be. But Howe's *Articulation of Sound Forms in Time* has opened up the possibilities for difference, for the "presentiment of rupture / Voicing desire no more from here."

"No more from here" because the voicing of desire in *Articulation,* as in Howe's other poems, avoids the personal "I," so pervasive in contemporary lyric. Ostensibly absent and calling no attention to the problems and desires of the "real" Susan Howe, the poet's self is nevertheless inscribed in the linguistic interstices of her poetic text. Howe has been called impersonal, but one could argue that the "muffled discourse from distance," the "collusion with history" in her poetry, is everywhere charged with her presence. She is not, after all, a chronicler, telling us some Indian story from the New England past, but a poet trying to come to terms with *her* New England past, *her* sense of herself vis-à-vis the Colonial settlers' actions, *her* recreation of the Hope Atherton story in relation to Norse myth as well as to contemporary feminist theory.

Most contemporary feminist poetry takes as emblematic its author's own experience of power relations, her personal struggle with patriarchy, her sense of marginalization, her view of social justice. These are Howe's subjects as well, but in substituting "impersonal" narrative—a narrative made up of collage fragments realigned and recharged—for the more usual lyric "I," Howe is suggesting that the personal is always already political, specifically, that the contemporary Irish-American New England woman who is Susan Howe cannot be understood apart from her history. But history also teaches the poet that, however marginalized women have been in American culture and however much men have been the purveyors of power, those who have suffered the loss of the Word are by no means only women. Indeed, what Howe calls the "Occult ferocity of origin" is an obstacle that only a persistent "edging and dodging" will displace if we are serious about "Taking the Forest." (pp. 518-33)

> *Marjorie Perloff, " 'Collision or Collusion with History': The Narrative Lyric of Susan Howe," in* Contemporary Literature, *Vol. 30, No. 4, Winter, 1989, pp. 518-33.*

Geoffrey O'Brien

In 1982 I picked up a book called **Pythagorean Silence;** I had never heard of the author, Susan Howe, although she had already published five volumes of poetry. It was an unusual book to encounter at any time, and in the context of the early '80s the effect was otherworldly. In time Howe's writing would often be linked to the "language" poets', but there was an irreducible solitariness about her work: it didn't seem part of any conceivable group or school.

> *Shapes   shadow-hunting*
> *Supremacy*
>
> *(cast now a shadow)*
> *Height of that tower diminished to*
>
> *this letter*
> *Light narrowed to this point or line*
>
> *Forfeit feeds nativity*
>
> *Ruin into rout*
> *antiquity—   Runes*
>
> *a row of signs*

ordering sound

(sacred and secret tree systems
I sleep

My initial impression was of movement: a world (was it ours?) in constant metamorphosis, a swirl of depths and tides, a series of transient landscapes (woods, seas, marshes) dissolving even as they were named. The aesthetic influences that came to mind were William Blake, Emily Brontë, Herman Melville, and beyond them echoes of all the poetry that came before. Yet a second look raised the question of where and how I perceived what I thought I was perceiving. Seen from a different angle, what was on the page showed up as a poetry of hard, dry clarity: spare, fragmented, analytical. Apparently nothing at all had been depicted or described.

It was an experience akin to getting a glimpse, in a Paul Klee painting, of a rich three-dimensional world and then, upon trying to locate it more precisely, coming up against a two-dimensional arrangement of shaded geometric forms which had shown, or pointed toward, something not there. The complex structures, images, and narratives Howe evoked were not written down; they existed in the margins of what was written down. The interior spaces I'd glimpsed were not in the words but in their unstated connections: in the decisiveness and freedom with which the words were laid side by side, and the abysses which were permitted to open up between them.

The freedom was most apparent in the use of words once possessed of tremendous power, but subsequently avoided by nearly all poets. For instance, there was a line reading in its entirety, "Broods infinity boundless": not one but three words of Miltonic bearing, and nothing but those words, jammed up against each other, surrounded by empty space, to produce a paradoxical effect of jagged disjunction. The notion of "boundless" was ripped from its context and plunked down to be looked at just as if it were any other word. Around the turn of the century poets had begun to abandon such words for any but ironic purposes because their meanings seemed used up. *Pythagorean Silence* did something quite different: tapping into the history of each word, as if there were hidden trails inside it that led toward still unexhausted half-lives.

Howe constructed poetry in which each word was an actor, carrying its story with it, its chamber of echoes. In this disembodied drama, words talked about and acted on other words. There was a forest of them; their interrelationships resembled a family or village. But abruptly, sometimes brutally, the solitariness of each was spelled out. At worst, the connections might exist only in the mind. For Howe this was only a starting point, the risk that all poetry runs. "Connections between unconnected things," she wrote in her study of Emily Dickinson, "are the unreal reality of poetry."

If the term "language poetry" meant anything at all, this surely was it. But unlike a good deal of work associated with that label, Howe's affirmed connections as much as it questioned them. Her critical, demystifying intelligence was also capable of an unfamiliar, wild, oracular strain. The force of *Pythagorean Silence* came from an anguished

doubleness of vision, where the same word might be both opening and closure, reality and disguise, truth and lie. The writing evoked a pain not localized but woven into all the reaches of human vocabulary, and perhaps most of all into words like "paradise" or "harmony" that posit a deliverance from pain.

In the years since, Howe has continued to produce work of a meditative urgency unmatched in recent American poetry. Three recent books make it possible to look at the main sweep of her accomplishment, gathering together texts which until now have been scattered and difficult to find. They show as well that if she is a language poet she is also a history poet, charting discoveries and incursions, massacres and evasions, as they register in inherited texts. If her writing is at times as abstract as poetry can be, it is also as concrete as muskets fired in a wood or (in the mazelike, perpetually unverifiable scholarship she explores in *A Bibliography of the King's Book*) Charles I losing his head.

The Europe of Trusts (a collection bringing together *Pythagorean Silence, Defenestration of Prague,* and *The Liberties*) includes an introduction that illuminates the presence of history in Howe's poetry. "For me there was no silence before armies," she writes. Tracing her childhood from her birth in 1937, she charts the progress of war as it impinged on her consciousness, "a ship crowded with refugees" sailing from Ireland to America in 1938, her father enlisting after Pearl Harbor. "From 1939 until 1946 in news photographs, day after day I saw signs of culture exploding into murder . . . If to see is to *have* at a distance, I had so many dead Innocents distance was abolished . . . I became part of the ruin."

The poems in *The Europe of Trusts* (whose title pun yokes loyalties and financial combines) reach into what might be called the etymological unconscious. In a recent interview in *Talisman* Howe said, "Sounds and spirits (ghosts if you like) leave traces in a geography. . . . The tale and the place are tied in a mysterious and profound way." She studies runes, scratches, accretions of speech. Pieces of Europe—Iseult, Arthur, Socrates, Arden, Florimell, Proteus—rise momentarily to visibility like bits of wreckage in foam. Tiny phrases stand in for immense stories: "Mirror king of names cascading"; "Law chanted to the people from hills"; "Messenger / Drowned ship / Bright city."

She proceeds not by argument or description or chronological narrative but by tuning in to the deeper implications of her vocabulary. It's as if through the contemplation of words we could participate in what the historian Fernand Braudel called "long duration," the infinitesimally slow shifts in thought and feeling that take centuries or millennia rather than lifetimes. Sounded to its depths, the word "sky" leads back to eyes that are not ours looking at a sky that was not the same either. All history is present, all at once, striated like overlapping layers of mineral deposits, and punctuated by sudden chasms and faults.

Those chasms and faults could also be the lacunae and erasures of a written text, the obscure patches of a lost or mistranslated dialect. Increasingly Howe's poetry has confronted particular texts, working through them as if through a thicketed and problematic terrain. This stems in part from her long-term involvement with Emily Dickinson's work and the complex textual problems associated with it. Her critical study *My Emily Dickinson,* with its patient excavation of the vocabulary of a single poem, opens exciting possibilities for the reading not just of Dickinson but of poetry in general.

Howe restores an awareness of the immensity of a single word. A word has ancient roots, and its sphere of activity is potentially infinite. (In the *Talisman* interview she remarks, "Words are candles lighting the dark. . . . They reach up out there. A little flicker in silence . . . a signal.") The deceptively small proportions of a Dickinson poem give way in her reading to an appreciation of hidden networks. The distance from one syllable to another can establish an epic scale.

Singularities (which incorporates the previously published *Articulation of Sound Forms in Time*) prompts a consideration of epic by the material it confronts: the Indian Wars of New England, the American transformations and dilemmas to which Thoreau and Melville bear witness, the "settlement" of wilderness and its grotesque culmination in a devastated, commercialized Lake George: "In the seventeenth century European adventurer-traders burst through the forest to discover this particular long clear body of fresh water. They brought our story to it. Pathfinding believers in God and grammar spelled the lake into *place.*"

Language takes land captive. Thought can only think with what has already been named. Hence Howe's preoccupation with nouns and even more with proper nouns. Names change, are assumed, split into variants. A name is not a fixed entity but the description of a process. No linguistic activity is more insistent than naming in its staking out of the real. The work called **"Thorow"** is involved with the writings of Thoreau; the title is a misspelling which occurs in a letter by Hawthorne; it is also an obsolete spelling of "through." Howe has stated that her purpose was "to go *through* the name, to open it up." Or, as the poem says: "We go through the word Forest."

We go through it, or it goes through us. The story is inside us, or we are inside the story. The unease of language—the chafing of thought against the means of its own articulation—lies in our inability to stand outside it, to dominate it. The "master stories" of conquest and progress try to invent controllable sentences. Howe's description of her own approach is different: "I write to break out into perfect primeval Consent."

Would that consent be the threshold beyond which language can melt away from history? But history—the world—is everywhere, in every syllable: in the very syllables which aspire toward an impossible freedom. "Blind destiny menacing catastrophe": a teleological dread informs her lines at times, a sense of time rushing toward disaster. All the doctrines imprinted at one time or another in language—all notions of order, harmony, center, authority, tradition, law—come out in the poetry, but they are set adrift, scattered, disarranged. The encounter with the world is by its nature unfinished. Poetry is rapid—"fixed in fleeting"—because it must be to travel at the speed of meaning. At the point of contact (and nothing is harder than to stay there) everything starts fresh: "I thought I stood on the shores of a history of the world where forms of wildness brought up by memory become desire and multiply. . . . Interior assembling of forces underneath earth's eye. Yes, she, the Strange, excluded from formalism. I heard poems inhabited by voices."

Geoffrey O'Brien, "The Way We Word," in VLS, No. 91, December, 1990, p. 27.

Paule Marshall

1929-

American novelist and short fiction writer.

The following entry provides an overview of Marshall's career through 1991. For further information on her life and works, see *CLC*, Vol. 27.

INTRODUCTION

A champion of the individual's search for identity, Marshall has been praised by critics for exploring the psychological trials and concerns of African-American women. Through her experiences as an American of Barbadian heritage as well as her knowledge of African mythology and rituals, she embodies the cultural dichotomy that provides the major tensions in her work. Although her writing primarily deals with African-American and feminist issues, critics have noted that the power and importance of Marshall's work transcends race and gender. Barbara T. Christian observed: "Marshall's novels manifest history as a creative and moral process, for she graphically describes how we compose our own experiences in our minds as well as in the objective world; how we as individuals and whole cultures decide upon the moral nature of an act, a series of acts, a history."

Marshall was born in Brooklyn, New York. She began writing at age ten and credits her mother and the other women of New York City's Barbadian community as being the first poets with whom she came into contact. Marshall writes: "I grew up among people to whom language was an art. Art which was present in the most ordinary things they said. They *created poetry* as they sat around a table talking." However, only after reading a volume of Paul Laurence Dunbar's poetry did Marshall realize a literary forum existed that, in her own words, "validated the black experience"; she then began to seek out the work of such African-American writers as Zora Neale Hurston, Gwendolyn Brooks, and Ralph Ellison. After graduating from Brooklyn College in 1953, Marshall worked as a researcher and writer for the magazine *Our World,* and her experiences in Brazil and the Caribbean are incorporated into her fiction. In 1959 Marshall embarked upon her career as a novelist with the publication of *Brown Girl, Brownstones,* a commercial failure but a critical success. Her subsequent books, however, earned her a larger reading audience. She now resides alternately in the United States and Africa.

Brown Girl, Brownstones, a frank depiction of a young black girl's increasing sexual awareness and search for identity, traces Selina Boyce's attempts to separate herself from New York's Barbadian community and from her ambitious mother, Silla. Although often described as a female bildungsroman detailing Selina's physical and emotional growth, *Brown Girl* also chronicles Silla's confrontations with her spendthrift husband as she tries to become assimilated to American culture and, as the owner of a brownstone house, a participant in the American dream.

Marshall's next work, *Praisesong for the Widow* examines the negative consequences of acculturation. The novel focuses on Avatar "Avey" Johnson, who has embraced materialistic American culture so fully that she has abandoned her African heritage. While on a cruise in the Caribbean, Avey becomes uneasy when she begins to dream about her ancestors. To distance herself from this emotional discomfort, which she associates with the islands, Avey disembarks at Grenada, intending to fly home. When she misses her flight and becomes stranded on the island, the natives welcome her into their community, inviting her to particpate in their activities. Avey complies and accompanies them to Carriacou, an island associated with the Middle Passage—the shipping route used to transport slaves from Africa to the Americas. Guided by the elderly Lebert Joseph, the embodiment of the African god of the crossroads, Avey begins to remember the oral narratives and folk tales she heard as a child from her great-aunt and joins in the islanders' dances and rituals.

Her participation prompts a spiritual journey that retraces the events suffered by blacks during the Middle Passage. Critics have lauded *Praisesong* as a diaspora novel that details the processes of self-discovery and maturation.

The Chosen Place, the Timeless People explores the means through which an individual comes to identify with a group. In this work, Jewish-American anthropologist Saul Amron travels to the West Indian island of Bournehills to study its primitive agricultural community and educate its people. Through his involvement with such natives as Merle Kinbona, a mulatto woman whose white father refuses to associate with her, Saul comes to understand the relationship between the natives and the colonial government. Eventually he stands up for the islanders' rights and tries to help them overcome their economic difficulties. Critics have noted that Saul's position is ironic because although he is a representative of the white patriarchy, he is also, as a Jew, a member of a group that historically has been the victim of prejudice. This irony is broadened following the revelation that his wife is heir to a shipping company that was actively involved in the slave trade. Often considered Marshall's most political novel, *The Chosen Place, the Timeless People* has been praised for examining the problems facing many third world countries in their struggle to establish a national identity. Edward Brathwaite observed that in *The Chosen Place, the Timeless People* Marshall examines how "the past predicts our present and that the present is, in the end, what we call home. . . . It is in this understanding, within not only the personal dimension but one of space and time, Paule Marshall is suggesting that the hard ground for development lies. Not in foundation projects, not in tourism and pseudoindustrialization, but in the discovery of one's self in the life and history of one's people."

Daughters, written from a female perspective, examines how relationships between men and women affect the formation of the self. The novel focuses on Ursa-Bea Mackenzie, a West Indian native living in New York City. She is forced to confront her ambivalent feelings for her father when she returns home to the fictional island of Triunion to participate in his reelection campaign as prime mininster. Although her father does not appear in the novel, his domineering presence pervades *Daughters,* and his exploitation of his family and country ultimately motivates Ursa-Bea to sabotage his campaign. As in her other works, Marshall incorporates elements of West Indian culture, such as the story of Congo Jane and Will Cudjoe, whose partnership exemplifies the perfect male-female relationship, to illuminate the search for independence, equality, and selfhood by many African-American women. Critics have noted that Marshall's title refers not only to Ursa's relationship with her father but to the relationship between patriarchal society and all women of African descent.

Marshall's novellas and short stories also emphasize the marginalized individual's attempts to establish identity. The collection *Soul Clap Hands and Sing,* which takes its title from William Butler Yeats's poem "Sailing to Byzantium," is composed of four novellas: "Barbados," "Brooklyn," "British Guiana," and "Brazil." In these stories-

Marshall incisively explores the search for self-knowledge, acceptance, and spiritual rebirth from a male perspective. With *Reena, and Other Stories,* republished as *Merle: A Novella, and Other Stories,* Marshall's focus returns to women engaged in relationships that require them to compromise their personal histories, beliefs, and desires. Barbara T. Christian has written: "At the heart of [Marshall's] work is the love of people, their speech, gestures, and thought which she expresses in her skillful and often tender characterizations. Underlying her aesthetic is a faith in the ability of human beings to transcend themselves, to change their condition, that is at the core of much Afro-American literature. Paule Marshall's contribution to that tradition is not only her ability to render complex women characters within the context of equally complex societies but also her creation of worlds in which the necessity of actively confronting one's personal and historical past is the foundation for a genuine revolutionary process."

PRINCIPAL WORKS

NOVELS

Brown Girl, Brownstones   1959
The Chosen Place, the Timeless People   1961
Praisesong for the Widow   1983
Daughters   1991

SHORT FICTION

Soul Clap Hands and Sing   1969
Reena, and Other Stories   1983; also published as *Merle: A Novella, and Other Stories*   1984

CRITICISM

Edward Brathwaite

Anglophobe West Indian literature—certainly its novels—has been mainly concerned with two main themes: the relationship of the author's *persona* or *personae* to his society, found in general to be limiting and frustrating; and stemming from this, a presentation of that society and an illustration of its lack of identity. West Indian novelists have so far, on the whole, attempted to see their society neither in the larger context of Third World underdevelopment, nor, with the exception of Vic Reid, in relation to communal history. Perhaps this has been artistically unnecessary. West Indian novels have been so richly home centered, that they have provided their own universe, with its own universal application. West Indian novelists, faced with the exciting if Sisyphean task of describing their own society in their own terms, for the first time, have had to provide for themselves a priority list in which, quite naturally, a relating of their own encounter with their environment, society and sensibility, has had to take pride of place. In addition, since most West Indian novelists have become exiles in several centres of the metropolitan West, their concern with a continuing and widening exploration of their societies has been limited by distance, separation and the concerns of a different milieu. They have, most of them, continued to write about the West Indies, but a West Indies stopped in time at the snapshot moment of departure.

The question, however, remains as to whether the West Indies, or anywhere else for that matter, can be fully and properly seen unless within a wider framework of external impingements or internal change. The contemporary West Indies, after all, are not simply excolonial territories; they are underdeveloped islands moving into the orbit of North American cultural and material imperialism, retaining stubborn vestiges of their Eurocolonial past (mainly among the elite), and active memories of Africa and slavery (mainly among the folk). Lamming and Naipaul, both of whom have returned to the West Indies from time to time, have in fact significantly widened their perspective to include this larger view of the region. Outside the English-speaking island, Alejo Carpentier, using a poet's technique, has been able to present us with an essential Caribbean within the widest possible context of space and time; and Wilson Harris, following his own configurations of myth, has been doing much the same thing for Guyana.

This way of looking at West Indian writing has been prompted by a reading of Paule Marshall's new novel, *The Chosen Place, The Timeless People.* Had Paule Marshall been a West Indian, she probably would not have written this book. Had she not been an Afro-American of West Indian parentage, she possibly could not have written it either; for in it we find a West Indies facing the metropolitan West on the one hand, and clinging to a memorial past on the other. Within this matrix, she formulates her enquiry into identity and change. And it is no mere externalized or exotic investigation. Mrs. Marshall has reached as far into West Indian society as her imagination, observation, and memory will allow. The questions raised and the answers suggested are, one feels, an integral part of her own development while being at the same—and for the first—time, a significant contribution to the literature of the West Indies.

The scope and value of this contribution is no accident. Paule Marshall's background has prepared and qualified her for it. Born of Barbadian parents in Brooklyn, she was brought up in a West Indian/Afro-American environment in New York which she explored in her first novel, *Brown Girl, Brownstones* (1959). Visits to the West Indies, and especially ancestral Barbados, revived and strengthened direct links with the Caribbean, as many of her stories illustrate, including one in *Soul Clap Hands and Sing* (1961). Now in *The Chosen Place, The Timeless People* (1969), we have her first mature statement on the islands—or more precisely, on a tiny, hilly corner of Barbados she calls Bournehills (though there is Port-of-Spain during Carnival and something of the Maroons of Jamaica as well).

Saul Amron [of *The Chosen Place, The Timeless People*] is an aging but still active Jewish-American anthropologist who, with his "Main Line" Philadelphia wife, Harriet,

and a research associate, goes out to Bournehills on a big "Multimillion-Dollar Development Scheme," as the local newspaper editor headlined it, on behalf of one of the great U.S. Foundations. Saul's plan is to carry out a careful anthropological survey of the district before applying his findings to the community's development. He is a committed intellectual who has worked all his life in underdeveloped countries and has acquired a pragmatic confidence in his ability to understand and improve them. He is also sincerely honest and hard-working and has real sympathy for people and their problems, with no time for metropolitan exploiters, be they indentured English newspaper editors or absentee canelords. He also has problems. Early in his career, he deserted a Peruvian public health nurse who had become his mistress. His first wife, a survivor of the Nazi concentration camps, died of a miscarriage while out on field work with him in Honduras. His self-assessed guilt for this incident had taken him out of field work altogether until he met Harriet, just divorced from her nuclear scientist husband. It was she who, recognizing his talents and divining his deep desire to return to the field, had arranged for him to be offered the directorship of the Bournehills project. They were married soon afterwards.

Now he, against his better instincts and with the memories of his past experiences still marked upon him, was bringing Harriet along with him to Bournehills—Harriet with her need "to *do* for the beloved, to be more than just a wife . . . to wield some small power." Success on this mission was crucial to them both. For Saul it was a matter of again proving himself to himself, of regaining his confidence, of trying to erase those scars. For Harriet, it was to be a test of their marriage. She wanted to prove to herself as much as to him, that she could be the perfect wife even unto the ends of the earth. As it turned out, Bournehills was to be Waterloo for them all—man, wife, and project. Here was a place that had stubbornly resisted change: a little, cut-off community that had, in the days of slavery, conducted a successful slave revolt and had never forgotten it. It was a community of canecutters and fisherfolk that strangely clung to its memorial Africa—living it, in fact, each day, and resisting all efforts to modernize it into something shoddy and less secure.

The other main story is Merle Kinbona's—articulate mulatta, spokeswoman of the island's self-respect, fiercely, petulantly, frustratedly committed to her little "rock" and yet essentially rootless—like Saul, one of nature's exiles, with shameful memories of a dead lesbian relationship in London and an African husband who, when he came to hear of it, had deserted her, taking their child. Merle knits the whole novel together: the Americans, the middle-class professionals from the capital, the night club crowd, the plantation overseers, and the "little fellas" of Bournehills. It is her affair with Saul, recognizing their similar kinds of loneliness, their similar kinds of scars, that precipitates Harriet's suicide and Saul's removal from the project. In the end, however, she has helped to restore his confidence and she herself, also party healed, wearily leaves the island to seek her husband and child in Africa.

Saul and Harriet are brilliant creations and it is they who give the novel its American flavor. Paule Marshall is too honest a writer not to have used these personae as its center. They are part of her purpose—to provide a particular kind of comment on the American role in developing countries. But the presentation of this comment remains marginal. We hear a great deal of the project but see very little of it being worked out in practice. Saul is a sympathetic observer, his associate little more than an impotent recorder. It is not their work, but the work that goes on around them that really comes through. The critical assessment of the effect of their presence is subsumed by Mrs. Marshall's larger and more compelling involvement with human relations.

Merle Kinbona is the person in the book with whom the most lavish and painstaking care has been taken. She talks incessantly, but never comes off the page. Her mannerisms, her moods, her devotions, her antagonisms are, one feels, lovingly described. But they remain descriptions. We are brought too close to her; there are too many obtruding angles and details for us to be able to get her clearly into focus. Through her we should have been able to enter the West Indian consciousness of the book, since she represents it, as easily as we enter the American with the less carefully drawn Harriet. But while we *see* Harriet loving and losing her man, making mistakes, being contrite, and finally becoming desperate, we simply *read* about Merle with her tremulous earrings, her "inner sunlight" eyes, her sudden hoots of manic laughter, and her ruined Bantu face. The fictional presentation of the middle-class West Indian woman's predicament has eluded Paule Marshall as surely as it has escaped the few West Indian novels—with the possible exception of Edgar Mittelholzer's *The Life and Death of Sylvia* (1953)—which have so far tried to capture it.

The main concerns of **The Chosen Place, The Timeless People** are not with middle-class characters or values, however, but with the effects of the colonial condition and experience on a people; the creation, in the West Indies, of what M. G. Smith (using Furnivall's concept) has designated the "plural society." Here we find, on the one hand, the imperial/metropolitan plantation masters, bolstered and abetted by the new technocrats of sugar estates, newspaper offices, and the professions—white, brown and black-faced, but all speaking the language of expediency, opportunism, self-interest, and exploitation. Foundation and foreign aid, it is hoped, will merely underpin this structure. (The beauty of this novel is that it both states and qualifies this view.) On the other hand, there is the great mass of the ex-African population, most of it stunned into an apparent acceptance of the inferiority/superiority principle handed down from the slave plantation; but some, a critical few, recognize the value and significance of their own creole folk culture. Percy Bryam, the planter, and Cuffee Ned, the slave leader who murdered him, are the symbolic nodes of these two opposing dispositions. Kingsley, the absentee plantocratic boss; Lyle Hutson, the black lawyer and Harriet—English, native, and Yankee, it makes no difference—in their dissimilar ways represent the continuation of the superiority/exploitation principle. Bournehills represents their opposite, though the upward transition from one to the other is always possible for the successful local.

Lyle Hutson, for instance, had been born poor and black, "son of an obscure village tailor in a remote section of the island." He had won a scholarship to the elite boys' secondary school in town, where he "had stood among the sons of the island's leading families flawlessly reciting his Latin—a small boy from the country in a clean, starched, but slightly threadbare uniform, school tie and garters, his thick bush of hair brushed flat, his knees greased, and a hint of his mother's talcum powder lightening the strong, dark-umber of his face." Later, on a Bourne Island scholarship, he had gone to study, first at Oxford—"and there could be a fine Oxonian thrust to his voice when he chose"—then at the London School of Economics, and finally, the Inns of Court. He had been something of a radical then, "had shouted socialism and revolution at the heated parties [he] attended." There had been talk "of nationalizing the sugar industry at home and driving Kingsley and Sons from the island. But once he had returned home and married into the famous Vaughan family, once his law practice had grown and he had entered politics, he had gradually started speaking about the need for change in less radical terms. He had begun to caution moderation and time." He had started building his future on the spoils of the past. His house is symbolic of this—public witness to his cultural betrayal and failure:

> The house as you approached it up the drive looked to be modern, although it had been built out of the remains of an old Georgian estate house that had once stood on the site. And it had retained, you saw as you drew closer, many of the features of the old house. . . . The thick, square graceless columns supporting the veranda, for example. And the heavy stone balustrade around it. As well as the ponderous, tightly shuttered look to the facade. To this had been added a profusion of modern touches that were suspect: flat, sharply canted roofs that soared off in all directions from the various wings, with on top of the roofs an elaborate television antenna that resembled a sculptor's construction. . . .

> The house was a failure, although this was not immediately apparent, and most people thought it handsome, progressive and new. But the designer, in trying to blend the old and the new, had failed to select the best from each. . . . Instead, in his haste perhaps, he had taken the worst of both architectural styles, so that although the house stood high on its private rise above the town, and was graced by the avenue of royal palms in front and breathed upon by the flowers in the gardens spread around it, it could still not rise above the profound error and confusion in its design.

Now, "relaxed in his *planter's* chair" (italics added), Lyle could say: "We shall be selling the island as the newest vacation-paradise in the Caribbean . . . emphasising our blue, warm waters, white beaches and happy natives, the usual sort of thing. . . ." True, he would say this in a voice "from which some small measure of sarcasm and even rage was never missing." But he was saying it nevertheless. But as with Merle (with whom had had a brief affair in London), the presentation of Lyle Hutson in this novel is too much by way of statement for it to come fully alive in fictional terms.

Again it is Harriet who provides us with one of the truly revealing moments in the book, in which the superiority/intrusive complex is seen working against the inferior/passive within an accurately perceived and brilliantly realized situation. For perhaps the only time in the novel, Paule Marshall successfully deploys her gift of irony, not consciously condemnatory as in Naipaul's *A Flag on the Island,* but with equal determination and within a more compassionate continuum.

> She had gone that late afternoon to the hopelessly overcrowded house on the dusty rise up from the main road where Stinger and Gwen lived with their innumerable children. . . . She arrived to find that Gwen had not yet returned from the fields . . . and the children, left alone in the house all day, had had nothing to eat since the midmorning meal at eleven.
>
> "Isn't there anything at all to eat, Brenda?" she said. She could not bring herself to look at her.
>
> The child also kept her gaze averted. "No, please," she said.
>
> "Are you sure? Isn't there perhaps something left over from this morning?"
>
> "No, please. We've eaten the last."
>
> But there was nothing in Harriet that could comprehend such a fact, and on a sudden impulse she turned from Brenda and made her way out to the shed-roof kitchen, a smoke-blackened lean-to one step down from the house. . . .
>
> She remained for the longest time in the middle of the kitchen gazing with a kind of numb fixity at the soot-covered pot in which the day's rice had been cooked. It had been scraped clean. Even the burnt part at the bottom had been eaten. . . .
>
> And then she saw them: a half-dozen brown-speckled eggs in a cracked bowl inside the otherwise empty larder. . . . [She] strode over to the larder, opened the wire-mesh door, giving it a little yank as it resisted her, and took out the bowl.
>
> The eggs were scarcely pullet size, but her disappointment at their smallness only brought her lips together in a more determined line.

These eggs had been treasured by Gwen so that she could sell them in order to get the few extra pence that would buy the week's ration of salt-fish and rice that alone could make some show of filling her children's bellies. It was her simple tactic of survival. But Harriet, bent now on her humane course of destruction, does not, unlike the children, know this.

> "Brenda."
>
> The child came noiselessly to the doorway behind her, but did not step down into the kitchen. . . .
>
> "Is there a frying pan?"

> She didn't turn to look at Brenda as she spoke, or at the other children who, curious and intrigued . . . had slipped up behind their sister, filling the doorway.
>
> "Yes, please," Brenda said.
>
> "Would you bring it for me, please."
>
> The child held back a moment, her troubled eyes on the eggs, wanting to say something but not bold enough. . . .
>
> Harriet then asked, one by one, for the other things she needed, and Brenda, hesitating briefly each time, brought them—the salt and pepper, a fork, the melting lump of strong-smelling, orange-coloured butter from New Zealand in a brown paper square that had soaked through, a clean plate. There was no milk, and the thought of that gaunt, dry cow which Stinger faithfully led out to the cliffs each morning brought on a wild momentary despair born of the futility of his devotion and her failure to understand it. Her hand began to tremble slightly, and picking up the fork she dealt the first egg a sharp little whack that broke it cleanly in two.
>
> At that Brenda, who had returned to stand in the doorway with the other . . . uttered a near-soundless, quickly stifled cry of protest or dismay—it was impossible to tell, and then silently bowed her head. Harriet brought the fork down a second time.

These are the forms of exploitation—well-meaning, complacent, rough, indifferent—that Bournehills, in some obscure way, has set its will against. The roads refuse to stay in place; a television set, presented to the community, and proudly set up in the village hall, is mysteriously blighted before it can begin to sprout flickering images of foreign pictures. These "backward" people survive, endure, resist, defend. From here on, Paule Marshall is not simply recording an experience; the overriding concern of her novel is the celebration of a vision.

> It was the Atlantic this side of the island, a wild-eyed, marauding sea the color of slate, deep, full of dangerous currents, lined with row upon row of barrier reefs, and with a sound like that of the combined voices of the drowned raised in a loud unceasing lament—all those, the nine million and more it is said, who in their enforced exile, their Diaspora, had gone down between this point and the homeland lying out of sight to the east. This sea mourned them. Aggrieved, outraged, unappeased, it hurled itself upon each of the reefs in turn and then upon the shingle beach, sending up the spume in an angry froth which the wind took and drove in like smoke over the land.

The people of Bournehills are the survivors and living embodiment of those millions drowned and unappeased and dead. Ferguson, the cane factory mechanic, a vociferous,

> strikingly tall, lean old man whose gangling frame appeared strung together by the veins and sinews standing out in sharp relief beneath his dark skin. . . . His face, his neck, his clean-

shaven skull, had the elongated, intentionally distorted look to them of a Benin mask or a sculpted thirteenth-century life head. With his long, stretched limbs he could have been a Haitian Houngan man.

There is a certain overidealization here, but it works. He it is who kept, like an Ashanti *okyeame,* the memory of the ancestral dead alive, with his interminable rehearsal of the tale of Cuffee Ned, the slave rebel. And then there is the Ashanti chief and Delbert, the shopkeeper and truck owner.

> He was lying propped up on a makeshift bed amid the clutter behind the counter, a broken right leg in a cast laid out stiffly on the bed. He was huge, with massive limbs. . . . He was the chief presiding over the nightly palaver in the men's house. The bed made of packing cases was the royal palanquin. The colorful Harry Truman shirt he had on was his robe of office; the battered Panama hat . . . his chieftain's umbrella, and the bottle of white rum he held within the great curve of his hand, the palm wine with which he kept the palaver and made libation to the ancestral gods.

There was also Leesy, the old prophetess; old Mr. Douglin, "faithful keeper of the grave," eternally cutting the grass "at the place where Cuffee's severed head had been left on the tall pike"; and Stinger, the cane-cutter who, at the Carnival, would undergo his yearly apotheosis into Cuffee Ned himself, "seer and shaman to the people, the intermediary between them and the ancient gods."

The correlations and identifications between people and their environment and people and their past weave in and out of the book and give it much of its texture. The eyes of the Bournehills workmen "were the same reddish brown as the aged walls of [Delbert's] shop, the man Delbert's skin, and the amber rum in the bottles on the shelves." "The coats of red paint [Vere] had applied [to his car] had dried, and the car, standing parked and ready on the sloping dirt road . . . looked as if it had been washed in the blood of the sow that had recently shared the yard with it." Later, Vere and that same red car were to be covered in blood from another kind of sacrifice. Susan Harbin, an early forebear of Harriet's,

> had launched the family's modest wealth by her small-scale speculation in the West Indies trade, which in those days consisted of taking a few shares in a number of sloops making the twice-yearly run between Philadelphia, the west coast of Africa, and then back across the Atlantic to the islands. In a stained, faded ledger still to be seen in a glass display-case at the Historical Society, the widow had kept careful account in a neat, furbelowed hand of the amounts of flour and salted cod, cornmeal and candles that went out on the sloops, the number of slaves taken on in Guinea and then just how much her portion of that cargo, both human and otherwise, had brought in crude sugar, rum and molasses in the islands.

Now, herself in those islands, Harriet says,

And it wouldn't even be so bad if the food coming in was at all decent. . . .

But that awful rice and dry, bad-smelling cod which everyone around here eats nearly every day—

To which comes the reply:

> "Food fit for a slave, my dear Mrs. Amron! Foisted upon us long ago by our metropolitan masters. . . . Saltfish, we call it. The damn, half-rotten rice. The cornmeal that used to be crawling with weevils by the time it reached us when I was a boy. But do you realize that some people up your way made their fortune in the old days selling us these delicacies? Do you know that . . . ?" He waited; then, as she remained silent, he laughed—and in such a way it almost seemed he knew about the faded ledger in the glass display case at the Philadelphia Historical Society and the portrait of the widow in her frilled cap, that whole questionable legacy which Harriet had long ago ruled from her thoughts.

This technique in itself reflects the whole point of the novel; that we are creatures of our history, that the past predicts our present and that the present is, in the end, what we call home. As Merle says to Saul on the eve of her departure for Africa:

> Not that I'm going expecting to find perfection . . . or to find myself or any nonsense like that. It's more what you once said: that sometimes a person has to go back, really back— to have a sense, an understanding of all that's gone to make them—before they can go forward. . . .

> But I'll be coming back to Bournehills. This is home. Whatever little I can do that will matter for something must be done here. A person can run for years but sooner or later he has to take a stand in the place which, for better or worse, he calls home.

It is in this understanding, within not only the personal dimension but one of space and time, Paule Marshall is suggesting that the hard ground for development lies. Not in foundation projects, not in tourism and pseudoindustrialization, but in the discovery of one's self in the life and history of one's people. The "little fellas" knew it, acting out their yearly unchanging pageant at the Carnival, paralleling the triumphant conclusion of George Lamming's *Season of Adventure* (1960):

> "They had worked together!"—and as if, in their eyes, this had been the greatest achievement, the thing of which they were proudest, the voices rose to a stunning crescendo that . . . jarred the blue dome of the sky. Under Cuffee, they sang, a man had not lived for himself alone, but for his neighbor also. "If we had lived selfish, we couldn't have lived at all." They half-spoke, half-sang the words. They had trusted one another, had set aside their differences and stood as one against their enemies. *They had been a people!* Their heads thrown back and welded voices reaching high above New Bristol's red faded tin roofs, they informed the sun and after-

noon sky of what they, Bournehills People, had once been capable of.

Then, abruptly, the voices dropped. You could almost see them plummeting through the bright, dust-laden air. They sang then in tones drained of their former jubilance of the defeat that had eventually followed. . . . In voices that would never cease to mourn . . . for this, too, as painful as it was, was part of the story.

It is within this painful, personal context that Paule Marshall offers and affirms her perception of the meaning of West Indian identity. (pp. 225-38)

Edward Brathwaite, "West Indian History and Society in the Art of Paule Marshall's Novel," in Journal of Black Studies, *Vol. 1, No. 2, December, 1970, pp. 225-38.*

Peter Nazareth

The two decades after the Second World War appeared to be full of great progress for the colonized people of the world. One by one, the colonies began receiving their independence from the "mother" countries. Almost all the countries thus freed immediately embarked on "development" with the aid of blueprints called Five-Year Development Plans, which identified development as raising the Gross National Product by building hotels to encourage tourism, constructing new industries for import-substitution, setting up a few state-owned enterprises, and so on. All these countries received aid for development from the developed countries, from aid-giving institutions, and even, in some cases, from charitable organizations.

But less than a decade after independence, what has been called the Third World has had to confront the gloomy fact that, on the whole, the promises of independence have not materialized. One by one, the newly-freed countries have been wracked by coups or civil wars; but even where these have not occurred, all is not well. Studies such as "The Pearson Report" (drawn up by the Commission on International Development, 1971) have revealed that in spite of all the apparent progress of the ex-colonies, the world prices of raw materials and primary products are going down, the cost of manufactured goods is going up, the foreign debt of the newly-freed countries is going up, and the gap is increasing between the developed and the developing countries.

What has gone wrong in the Third World and why?

It is this question that Paule Marshall tackles in her monumental novel, **The Chosen Place, The Timeless People.**

The "chosen place" of the novel is Bournehills, a near-wasteland at the end of a Caribbean island, and the "timeless people" are the people of Bournehills. As the title suggests, the author is using Bournehills as a paradigm of the whole Third World.

To the island on which Bournehills is situated comes a team of Americans to set up a project to help uplift the Bournehills people from their abject poverty. The team consists of three white Americans: Saul and Harriet

Amron and Allen Fuso. Saul Amron is an anthropologist who had given up field work when his first wife died but who had been persuaded by Harriet Shippen, whom he married, to take charge of the development project sponsored by the Center For Applied Social Research, which receives its funds from the Shippen family. Allen Fuso is a bland but likeable fellow who had spent some time on Bourne island over a year earlier doing a short-term demographic survey and had liked the place. Their hostess and landlady at Bournehills is to be Merle Kinbona: Merle is a black woman who had married an African while studying in England, only to return alone to Bournehills.

As soon as the team arrives on Bourne Island, they are given a party by the ruling elite of the island in New Bristol before they leave for Bournehills:

nearly all the men there were senior civil servants and high-ranking government officials. The rest were members of the professions, which in Bourne Island were largely taken to mean only medicine and law. And they were very much of a type. They were all, to a man almost, drinking imported whisky, scorning as a matter of status the local rum, which was excellent; all wearing dark-toned, conservative, heavy English suits in spite of the hot night. Some, like the pale, austere permanent secretary, had on matching vests, and a few wore their old school ties.

In just a few words, the author has presented us with a portrait of an ex-colonial bourgeoisie, cut off—or cutting itself off—from its roots, desperately chasing after status, which it identifies with all that is foreign: clothes, drinks, education, etc. The author's moral standpoint is clear: although she is writing "impersonally," she has contempt for this "underdeveloped middle class."

So when Saul implies that there may be a fairly large amount of money involved in the proposed project, it is not entirely a surprise that this gathering practically explodes with anger. A man named Hinkson, "with a pale amber-colored face and the crimped dark-blond hair typical of the Bourne Island colored-whites," says to Saul,

You don't know that place. There's no changing or improving it. You people could set up a hundred development schemes at a hundred million each and down there would remain the same . . . Tell him, for instance, about what happened to the small farmers' co-operative government tried starting there a few years back . . . Work their crops together? Share with each other? Not those people. The poor co-operative officer had to run for his life.

The people at the party then vie with one another to tell Saul Amron how far beyond redemption the Bournehills people are; for example, a television set which was a gift from a British firm and a jukebox from America had broken down in no time at Bournehills. The summing up of the Bournehills people by the Bourne Island bourgeoisie is: "Those people? They're a disgrace."

Saul's reaction to this onslaught is one of skepticism. He thinks, "they might have been speaking about a people completely alien to themselves, who did not even inhabit the same island." However, he goes on to feel self-critical:

> But then who, he reminded himself, can speak calmly of the brother who shames him? Because listening to them he had suddenly remembered, to his own shame, how, as a boy, he had fled his brothers, those with the sallow, long-nosed look, sloping shoulders and side curls, whose bodies always appeared to be cowering out of the way of an impending blow. The Ashkenazi look he had called it as an arrogant young man who had taken pride in his large, straight-shouldered build—the look of the long persecuted; and while maintaining his allegiance (for they were his people after all) he had still, at the same time, often been impatient, even angry with them.

We get a glimpse here at the complexity of Ms. Marshall's writing. She is dealing with an exploited people, but she does not limit herself to just the black people from the colonies—she is dealing with *all* exploited peoples, including the Jews. At the same time, she is not writing of people as affected by history in abstract terms: these are real human beings who have real human failings and may or may not have a capacity for self-awareness. We are made to have a measure of respect for Saul because he is aware of the suffering of the Jews, because he feels sympathy for the people of Bournehills whom he has not yet met, and because his skepticism of the underdeveloped bourgeoisie leads to self-criticism.

As for what this underdeveloped bourgeoisie says about the Bournehills people: how often do we not come across the new bourgeoisie in the ex-colonies who rail against the peasantry for not becoming modernized, for being lazy, selfish and irresponsible in the same terms in which the colonial rulers condemned all the colonized people!

One member of the underdeveloped bourgeoisie at the party is cynically aloof from the emotion expressed by the others. This is Lyle Hutson, a successful barrister, a senator in the legislature and a member of "the powerful clique which ran the government for the Prime Minister, a mild nondescript man who had been chosen as a compromise between warring factions of the party." Hutson was the son of a tailor but he had made it to the top via "education," i.e. studying irrelevant subjects such as Latin and eventually getting a scholarship to Oxford, the London School of Economics and the Inns of Court. While a student in England, he had been a radical nationalist and socialist, but the size of the problems confronting the country on his return and the temptation of easy wealth if he did not fight the system were such that he had sold out. Lyle Hutson represents all the bright young leaders of the Third World who talk in radical terms but who, when in power, choose to work within the framework of the same old economic system. Like all such leaders, Hutson talks of "development" and "progress" but is actually contemptuous of the "backward" peasants.

Finally, Merle Kinbona turns up at the party—a garrulous black woman the reader has met briefly earlier, a woman who talks compulsively but whose honesty, genuineness and historical awareness cut through what the others are saying as a scythe cutting through burnt-out grass.

It is clear by now that Paule Marshall has written a novel as complex as [Joseph] Conrad's *Nostromo* and James Ngugi's *A Grain of Wheat,* a novel which deals with the whole sweep of colonial history and in which there are several important characters instead of one central character. In order to see how Miss Marshall interweaves individual characters with historical forces, I shall now look at the main characters and the people of Bournehills.

Harriet Amron née Shippen is heiress to a Philadelphia family fortune. Unlike Saul, she is not a Jew but what is called a White Anglo-Saxon Protestant. Saul Amron is her second husband. She had been married previously to a nuclear scientist but had divorced him after recurrent nightmares of nuclear holocaust had convinced her that her need for power had been the fuel for his achievement. Her second marriage to a Jew is therefore in some ways, as Bell Gale Chevigny says in a review of this book in *The Village Voice,* 1970, an attempt to obtain a reprieve from the past. She persuades Saul to head the project to uplift the poverty of the Bournehills people; the project will receive most of its funds from her family fortunes. But we discover that her family has made its money through investments in shipping, i.e. the slave-trade, and therefore, ironically, has been responsible for creating the very misery it is now trying to solve, an insoluble contradiction!

At first, Harriet appears to be sympathetic to the Bournehills people. She moves about freely among them and, up to a point, is accepted as one of them. However, a crisis occurs during the carnival in which she has been persuaded to participate. She gets caught up in a group of young marchers from Harlem Heights, a shantytown, a "raucous green-clad guerilla band" and gets carried along. She thinks that the children are going to march straight into the sea and drown, so she tries to divert them— significantly, into "Queen Street"—but fails. She gets a shock when she realizes that they do not even see her and she is "seized by a revulsion and rage that was almost sexual in its force." She tries to beat her way out and fails, but finally gets flung out of the group which turns up a road near the bay.

Harriet has revealed her true nature—the quintessential WASP. She wants to control everything, including the lives of other people. She had been determined that Saul would head the development project and she had succeeded. She had decided to marry Saul and she had succeeded. She had insisted on coming out to Bournehills despite Saul's misgivings and she had had her way. Without even questioning herself, she tried to run everybody's lives. For example, when she went to Gwen's house one morning while Gwen, one of her village neighbours, was out at work, she had broken some eggs and cooked them for the hungry children without even asking herself why Gwen had kept the eggs aside, though there was no other food in the house. Now when Harriet is forced to realize that she cannot control the black crowd and, even more important, the black masses will carry on out of her control and oblivious of her presence without destroying itself, she shuts herself off.

When Harriet is told by Lyle Hutson that Saul has been having an affair with Merle, her immediate decision is to try and buy Merle off. She fails. She then accuses Saul over the affair, and refuses to listen when he tries to explain that although his affair with Merle is not a permanent one, it is not a casual one either: it arose out of a real need. Saul finally accuses her, the accusation of all the exploited people against the ruling WASPS:

> *What is it with you and your kind, anyway?* . . .
> If you can't have things your own way, if you can't run the show, there's to be no show, is that it?

But whenever it comes to anything Harriet does not want to hear, she just shuts herself off and Saul finds himself talking to somebody who is not there. She makes yet another attempt to control Saul: she writes to an influential friend at headquarters to take Saul off the job and offer him a higher post in America. This is done, but has unexpected results. Saul has become devoted to the Bournehills people, and, unlike Lyle Hutson, he will not sell out. He suspects Harriet's hand in the order to return to the U.S. and he lashes out at her, saying that if the truth is as he suspects, he will leave her. Like a character by D. H. Lawrence, e.g. Gerald Crich in *Women in Love,* Harriet's whole life is *will.* She must control everything. When she meets a will that thwarts *her* will, she suffers a psychic death which leads to her physical death: like Gerald Crich, she "drowns in her mind" and whereas he freezes to death, she physically drowns. She is swallowed up by the very sea that has kept battering out its ceaseless message of exploitation:

> It was the Atlantic this side of the island, a wild-eyed, marauding sea the color of slate, deep, full of dangerous currents, lined with row upon row of barrier reefs, and with a sound like that of the combined voices of the drowned raised in a loud increasing lament—all those, the nine million and more it is said, who in their enforced exile, their Diaspora, had gone down between this point and the homeland lying out of sight to the east. This sea mourned them. Aggrieved, outraged, unappeased, it hurled itself upon each of the reefs in turn and then upon the shingle beach, sending up the spume in an angry froth which the wind took and drove in like smoke over the land. Great boulders that had roared down from Westminster centuries ago stood scattered in the surf; these, sculpted into fantastical shapes by the wind and water, might have been gravestones placed there to commemorate those millions of the drowned.

The use of the word "Diaspora" in the above passage in relation to black people reminds us of the Jews, and Saul Amron is a Jew. He is an anthropologist who believes in applying the results of his research because he wants to help a poor and backward people climb out of their backwardness instead of exploiting them for academic reasons like most other anthropologists. Although he has a tinge of arrogance, he also has enough humility to feel that development projects are no good to a people if they are imposed from above; he believes that such projects must be linked with the people's daily lives and must grow out of their experience. Since he does not at first know anything about the people of Bournehills except that the place is

backward, he decides to go there and live among the people before making any further moves.

As in every good work of literature, we do not know everything about all the characters at the outset. Instead, character grows and is revealed through interaction with the other characters. Saul grows and is revealed not only through his relation with his wife but also through his relationship with Merle Kinbona and the Bournehills people. In fact, it was clear at the party that in order to get to know Bournehills, Saul must get to know Merle. This is how he reacted to her at the party:

> Saul studied her face; he listened to the desperate voice, and suddenly he recalled how the man Deanes had kept glancing nervously over his shoulder during the loud condemnation of Bournehills as though he feared his constituents were about to descend upon him. And it struck him that this woman who shrugged like a Jew and insisted whenever she glanced his way that he had been here before, had brought the entire spurned and shameless lot with her onto the veranda.

Merle, indeed, is the voice of a voiceless people, the people of Bournehills, who refuse to be suppressed or forgotten:

> Lifting her face she offered them her dark cheek to be kissed. And she insisted upon the kiss. The cheek would remain at its high angle until the person bent to it. It was as though she considered the kiss an obeisance due her, an acknowledgement on everyone's part of the wide suffering—wide enough to include an entire history—which her face reflected.

Merle Kinbona is the daughter of a mulatto and a black woman. She is black and makes no attempt, unlike other Bourne Islanders, to present herself as other than black. Despite her education in England, she identifies herself with the people of Bournehills instead of using that education as a means of climbing the ladder of "success" held out to the underdeveloped bourgeoisie. The author draws a link between Merle's acceptance of her blackness and her refusal to deny Bournehills.

Of course, as we have seen, the author skillfully interweaves the general with the individual and Merle's unceasing voice is not just a voice for the Bournehills people. As Saul recognizes, there is something desperate about her unceasing talk as though if she stopped talking, the unresolved contradictions in her life would overwhelm and destroy her. And so "the flow of words continued unchecked, the voice rushing pell-mell down the precipitous slope towards its own destruction."

Therefore in terms of the structure of the novel as well as the psychology of Saul and Merle, Saul must embrace Merle when he is ready to embrace the Bournehills people. This occurs just after the Carnival when Harriet, shaken after her experience, stays overnight at Lyle Hutson's place. Through his relationship with Merle, Saul first comes to understand external reality and then comes to terms with himself. First, what is "outside:" Saul had hoped that he could bring about development among the underdeveloped people program by program. But he has a different view after getting to know Bournehills, particularly after a searing experience when the absentee-owner, Sir John, comes to visit his sugar factory. Ferguson, one of the employees, had rehearsed a speech to tell Sir John that the rollers of the machinery were worn out and about to break down. However, when it came to the point, Ferguson, weighed down with the racialism of centuries of exploitation, was unable to say anything and his face had frozen into an African mask of suffering. After this, Saul realizes that what is needed is a complete revolution. He says to Merle:

> In most of the places I've worked—in South and Central America—the Sir Johns—those from outside who've come in and taken over—were Americans in business suits or those they kept in power: patrons with haciendas three and four times the size of Bourne Island or strong-arm generals in uniform. So, for me, they're the same, all of them. Out to own and control the world, and determined to hold on no matter what means they have to employ. And they behave the same, the arrogant bastards, toward the people they feel they own . . . They have to be gotten rid of, the bastards. Thrown out! And in one clean sweep. That's the only way. There's no gradual or polite way for it to be done as Lyle and his friends in town would like to think.

At the same time, through his relationship with Merle, Saul begins to come to terms with himself, to recognize what he has tried to blot out of his past. His wife, a survivor of the Nazi camps, had died as a result of premature childbirth because Saul insisted on doing his field work far from "civilization." It had been a subtle form of selfishness on Saul's part and his wife had died accusing him of it, an accusation he could not confront until his sympathetic sexual relationship with Merle. However, it cannot be forgotten that Saul is a white man. When the rollers of the sugar machinery finally break down, the owners decide to close the factory. This means that even the little the Bournehills people have will be taken from them. In confronting the bitterness of the situation, Merle goes out of her mind for a period, but she accuses Saul *as a white man* for being responsible for the troubles of the blacks and shouts at him to drop all his million-dollar schemes and fix the machinery. Until this point, Saul had always refused, as he acknowledges, to make the final act of commitment to the exploited peoples, but now he does just that: he organizes the people of Bournehills and organizes transport to take the sugar cane from Bournehills to the factory at Brighton. He also keeps vigil over Merle until she recovers.

Bell Gale Chevigny tells us that in *The Chosen Place, The Timeless People,* "the cultures line up—the WASP loves the Jew who loves the black. Each race turns to the race of more mystery and suffering . . . seeking redemption." The woman Saul turns to had also begun through this relationship to look at her past squarely, to accept, like Saul, that she was no less human for being a flawed human being. As a poor student in England, she had been sucked into a lesbian relationship with a rich Englishwoman, whose lesbianism was really an aspect of her lust to control, like Harriet. Merle had managed to break free and

had married an African studying at Leeds University. However, she had been so ashamed of her affair with the Englishwoman that she had not told her husband about it. Her ex-lover had taken revenge by informing Merle's husband about the affair. Her husband had turned cold towards her, and one day, he returned to Africa with their child without telling her. Merle had gone out of her mind and after that, she had always blamed herself for what had gone wrong in her life. But now, she suddenly gives vent to her real feelings and blames her husband:

> *"Brute!"*
>
> The charged word, hurled without warning into the midst of the long silence that had fallen, dealt the air a savage blow; and for an instant, as her enraged and anguished face with its tear-filled eyes came lunging across at him, Saul almost thought she meant him, that he was the one accused, and instinctively drew back. "Brute! How could he have just walked out like that? Without a word . . . She was as much mine as his. I was still her mother, no matter what I had done or how I had lived, and that gave me some say in what was to happen to her . . . Was he God . . . ? Or was I the only person who ever lied to someone they loved or tried to cover up the past? I only did it because I didn't want to risk losing him. I couldn't bear to have him know what a botch I had made of everything before meeting him. *I wanted him to think well of me. Is that so terrible? Does that make me the worst person in the world? Oh, damn him!"* (my italics)

At last, Merle has come to terms with her flawed nature and realized that she was not to be condemned for what she had done when she was so much younger. Correspondingly, her husband was not justified in walking out on her with their child.

However, unlike James Baldwin's *Another Country,* **The Chosen Place, The Timeless People** is not a novel only about flawed individuals coming to terms with themselves in a society whose perimeters have to be accepted as given. Instead, Merle's and Saul's self-acceptance is linked with their recognition of exploitation and what must be done to change society in order to end exploitation. To this end, a vital presence in the novel is that of the people of Bournehills.

The Bournehills people are maligned, ignored, even hated. They are an embarrassment to the underdeveloped bourgeoisie of Bourne Island because they refuse to "develop:" they have been unable to even look after gifts of a television set and a jukebox! They are supposed to be backward, selfish and lazy, an uncultured people that insists on performing the uprising of the rebellious slave Cuffee Ned at every carnival.

But the Bournehills people as revealed to Saul turn out to be a very warm-hearted and hard-working people. They work from dawn to dusk everyday. If they do not produce much, it is because their resources are limited. In her descriptions of the Bournehills people, the author makes us see that everywhere we look, the people are exploited just as much as they were in slave times. As Merle says to Lyle when he explains the plans his government has for development by turning the country into a vacation paradise and offering long tax-holidays to attract foreign industrialists,

> Is that the only way we can exist? Well, if so, it's no different now than when they were around here selling us for thirty pounds sterling. Not really. Not when you look deep. Consider. The Kingsleys still hold the purse strings and are allowed to do as they damn please, never mind you chaps are supposed to be in charge. And the Little Fella is still bleeding his life out in a cane field. Come up to Bournehills some day and see him on those hills. Things are no different. The chains are still on. Oh Lyle, can't you see that?

To underscore her statement about the chains still being on, Merle's bracelets clash as her arms go out in appeal to him, bringing to mind the chains of slaves. And she adds, "Read your history, man!"

In fact, Merle's words act as a comment on what the reader has already seen through Saul's eyes. We have already seen with Saul "the Little Fella" on the hills, and the author's description of the Little Fella is so powerful and moving that it is worth quoting in some detail. Saul usually spends no more than an hour or so everyday on the cane fields with Stinger because he finds the heat overpowering and the climb up the slopes too much for his badly out-of-condition body. But one day, he decides to spend the better part of the day with Stinger, and, for the first time, he really sees the people at work:

> Stinger was the boss of his own small work crew which consisted of three other men besides himself who did the cutting, and a number of women, including his pregnant wife, Gwen, called headers, whose job was to gather and tie the canes felled by the men into great bundles which they bore on their heads down the hillside to the lorries waiting on the road to take them to Cane Vale. Once Saul had tried lifting one of the bundles. It had felt to be well over two hundred pounds. He had barely been able to move it from the ground. Gwen, spotting him, had laughed, "watch, you don't break your navel string," she had said not unkindly. "Your body ain't used to nothing like this."

As front man Stinger set the pace of the cutting, which even today with the early heat, was formidable. Following him up the steep shoulder of the hill upon which the field lay, Saul was impressed, amazed. All the strength in the man's slight, wiry body had been poured, it seemed, in some highly concentrated form, into his right arm, and with this he slashed away without pause at the canes, his bill hook describing the same beautifully controlled downward arc in the rumshop that first night.

> . . . He saw, was only conscious of, the canes ranked like an opposing army before him up the slope, their long pointed leaves bristling like spears in the wind. To these only did he give his attention, and each time he brought one of them crashing down, he would give a triumphant grunt (the only sound he was ever heard to utter

while working), and toss it contemptuously aside.

This is one of the very rare moments in literature when we see the joy and beauty in what is usually labeled "unskilled" labor. Stinger enjoys his work, and defines himself in his work—and while he does this, he is beautiful. The same applies to the women workers:

> Behind him Gwen kept pace, gathering together the canes he flung her way into great sheaves which, with an assist from the other women, she then placed on her head and "headed" down to the truck below. And it was a precarious descent, for the ground would be slick underfoot from the "trash": the excess leaves the men hacked off the stalks before cutting them, and treacherous with the severed stumps hidden below. One bad slip and the neck would snap. But Gwen moved confidently down, as did the other women, her head weaving almost imperceptibly from side to side under its load (the motion was reminiscent of those child dancers from Bali, but more subtle, more controlled) her swollen stomach thrust high and her face partly hidden beneath the thick overhang.

Once again, we see, as we have so seldom seen in literature, the beauty and joy in working on the land: up to a point, Gwen not only works hard but also defines her humanity through her work. Is this really "unskilled" work? This description of Gwen and the other Bournehills people at work contrasts with the parasitic uselessness of the Bourne Island bourgeoisie.

But as the day progresses, beauty and joy turn into drudgery and finally we see what exploitation means to the human spirit.

> Stinger's essentially slight, small-built body, which was further reduced by the canes towering above him, appeared to be gradually shrinking, becoming smaller and painfully bent, old. By early afternoon all that was left to him it appeared were the shriveled bones and muscles within the drawn sac of skin and the one arm flailing away with a mind and will of its own. He saw, too, that every exposed place on his body—his arms, neck, his blind shrunken face, his bare feet—was covered with tiny bits of the tough cane peel which flew up along with the thick dust and chaff each time a plant was felled. They were like slivers of wood driven into the flesh. Saul felt them like splinters in his own flesh.

As for Gwen:

> She passed, and under the waving green forest on his head, Saul saw her face, a face which when she laughed proved she was still a young woman. But in the short time since he had last glanced her way it had aged beyond recognition. A hot gust of wind lifted the overhanging leaves a little higher and he glimpsed her eyes . . . He tried describing them to himself some days later . . . he could not, except to say they had had the same slightly turned up, fixed, flat stare that you find upon drawing back the lids of someone asleep or dead.

So when Merle tells Lyle Hutson to *see* the Little Fella working on the hillside, we feel her anger. These are a hard-working people who define themselves in their work. Why must they be forced to work to the point where their spirit is killed—and for so little return? Why do the politicians like Lyle Hutson ignore these people in their development plans? Is "development" merely the gift of television sets and juke boxes? Why cannot a system be devised which taps the boundless energy and willingness to work of the Bournehills peasants such that there is a meaningful return in human and economic terms on a national scale? These people are in no way responsible for their backwardness. And far from being a people to be ashamed of, they constantly salvage some human dignity out of all their suffering. Saul realizes this and gets caught up in the spirit of the people. He tries to explain this to an uncomprehending Harriet when he returns, a little drunk, after helping Cox build his house:

> In Bournehills a man doesn't believe in making it legal until he can at least offer his wife a house of her own no matter how small. You should have seen Cox! He was so happy, poor guy, especially when he saw the roof going up, that he drank too much and passed out on us . . . So all things being relative, Cox could see himself as a man who had succeeded at his life. And he did—at least for the time the house was going up. I saw it in his face, and I'm afraid I got a little drunk as a result.

One person at Bournehills reaches out to improve his position through established channels. This is Vere. Vere had left Bournehills and gone to the U.S. to make a success of his life, only to return a failure. Yet, we discover, he has talent. He rebuilds a battered old car that people had thought would never run again. Tragically, this talented young man had identified his goals in terms of machines instead of people, like so many young people in the ex-colonies. And it is this love for machines that destroys him—the car seems to take on a life of its own during a car-race and kills him: as Leesy, his aunt, had known it would, as we had known it would for the red color Vere had painted it resembled blood of the sow whose killing is described so graphically in the novel. In fact, it is the whole capitalist world that destroys Vere; the car was built in Germany on an American pattern. When the rollers at the sugar factory break down, the whole community needs Vere to repair the machinery, Vere who is now dead; and it is clear that Vere would not have been finally destroyed if he had defined his goals not in terms of machines but in terms of people.

Tragically, history has not changed for the people of Bournehills. As in slave times, they must be subservient to the overseer and the owner, who comes once in a way to signify his rule over his diabetic economic empire. Inspecting the sugar factory at Bournehills, Sir John says, "It's a bit of a shock, don't you know, to realize that the thing that sweetens your tea comes from all this muck." This remark is ironic because whereas Sir John is referring to the brown viscous fluid which is to become sugar, the novelist implies that the whole process has become one of turning out muck. The Bournehills people are still muck for history has not changed for them.

How is history to be changed for the people of Bournehills?

The people themselves repeatedly provide the answer by performing the uprising of Cuffee Ned every year at the carnival, a performance so powerful that it moves even the Bourne Island bourgeoisie which does not want to look at its past. Who was Cuffee Ned? He was a leader who had led a successful rebellion of the slaves against Bryam their slavemaster. In order to carry out this rebellion, Cuffee Ned had had to organize the people and after the rebellion, they had all lived in co-operative fashion for three years. Eventually, the other exploiters had killed Cuffee Ned to prevent his example from spreading: but he had left a message. The continuing lesson of the performance is clear:

> They were singing it was true, of Bryam, Cuffee and Pyre Hill, of a particular event, place and people, simply telling their story as they did each year. Yet, as those fused voices continued to mount the air, shaking the old town at its mooring on the bay, it didn't seem they were singing only of themselves and Bournehills, but of people like them everywhere. The struggle on the hill which had seen Cuffee triumphant and Bryam brought low was, their insistent voices seemed to be saying, but the experience through which any people who find themselves ill-used, dispossessed, at the mercy of the powerful, must pass. No more, no less. Differing in the time, in the forms it takes, in the degree of success or failure, but the same. A struggle both necessary and inevitable, given man. Arms outstretched, hands opened, the marchers sought to impress this truth upon the watching throngs.

The second lesson from the uprising of Cuffee Ned is equally important:

> *"They had worked together!"*—and as if in their eyes, this had been the greatest achievement, the thing of which they were proudest, the voices rose to a shining crescendo that visibly jarred the blue dome of the sky. Under Cuffee, they sang, a man had not lived for himself alone, but for his neighbor also. "If we had lived selfish, we couldn't have lived at all." They half-spoke, half-sung the words. They had trusted one another, had set aside their differences and stood as one against the enemies. *They had been a People!*

Ironically, the message of co-operative, unselfish living is brought by the peasants to the underdeveloped bourgeoisie, that very bourgeoisie that had accused these peasants of being backward and selfish!

So the Bournehills people wait for their new Cuffee Ned. Lyle Hutson could have been the new Cuffee Ned for he had once talked, while a student, of changing the whole economic system and introducing socialism. But once in power he had sold out so completely that he had even helped a rich expatriate prosecute a poor black servant who had stolen a clock in lieu of wages which had been withheld. Instead of fighting for justice, Lyle uses the forms of justice to mete out injustice! Lyle talks of "development" but this means nothing to the people at the bottom of the heap, from whom even the little they have is in danger of being lost when there is any economic crisis. Thus the author is saying that unless change grows from the masses, unless there is an economic revolution which is at the same time a cultural and spiritual revolution growing out of the people, there will be no change. In the words of Frantz Fanon:

> Now it must be said that the masses show themselves totally incapable of appreciating the long way they have come. The peasant who goes on scratching out a living from the soil, and the unemployed man who never finds employment, do not manage, in spite of public holidays and flags, new and brightly colored though they may be, to convince themselves that anything has really changed in their lives. The bourgeoisie who are in power vainly increase the number of processions; the masses have no illusions . . . The masses begin to sulk; they turn away from this nation in which they have been given no place and begin to lose interest in it.

We come back, then, to the question we asked at the very beginning: what has gone wrong with the newly-freed countries after independence and why? *The Chosen Place, The Timeless People* tells us that has gone wrong is that nothing fundamental has changed since independence. Although formal slavery has ended, the same exploitative system has continued in operation, ensuring that real slavery continues. Thus the motif of the novel, taken from the Tiv of West Africa, is:

> Once a great wrong has been done, it never dies. People speak the words of peace, but their hearts do not forgive. Generations perform ceremonies of reconciliation but there is no end.

We see here that Paule Marshall has created a Third-World novel, with its message to all the exploited peoples of the world. It is no surprise to discover that her message finds a resonance in other Third-World writers of today. Her indictment of Lyle Hutson and the underdeveloped Bourgeoisie could have been summed up in the words of Ayi Kwei Armah, the Ghanaian novelist, in *The Beautyful Ones Are Not Yet Born:*

> So this was the real gain. The only real gain. This was the thing for which poor men had fought and shouted. This is what it had come to: not that the whole thing might be overturned and ended, but that a few blackmen might be pushed closer to their masters, to eat some of the fat into their bellies too. That had been the entire end of it all.

The Kenyan novelist, Ngugi wa Thiong'o (James Ngugi), says [in his *Homecoming*] the same thing, more analytically than Armah:

> Yet the sad truth is that instead of breaking from an economic system whose life-blood is the wholesale exploitation of our continent and the murder of our people, most of our countries have adopted the same system.

But Paule Marshall, transmuting her American experience, goes beyond Armah and Ngugi. She traces the whole exploitative hierarchy from the base right up to the top, which happens to be the ruling WASP, as personified by Harriet Amron. Nothing can be changed for people at the bottom of the heap if nothing is changed from the middle to the top, the author says. The whole system must be changed. The first step towards such a change is that the people must not forget their history. "Remember your history, man!" Merle tells Lyle Hutson, and a whole host of images in the novel urges the reader to remember the history of the exploited peoples. Thus, to take one example, when we see the people of Bournehills working, the estate manager riding past recalls "some ghost who refused to keep to his grave even during the daytime," namely, the slave overseer. Thus history must not be forgotten for when it happens, instead of there being an alliance of the exploited against the exploiters, a few individuals out of the exploited mass are able to side with the oppressors against their own fellow-sufferers. Lyle Hutson is one such example. Merle gives Saul another example: she says that although Jews had "caught hell" far longer than black people, some of them had forgotten it and, in turn, exploit the black people. Later, Saul himself takes up this theme and says to Merle:

> [People] who've truly been wronged—like yours, like mine all those thousands of years—must at some point, if they mean to come into their own, start using their history to their advantage. Turn it to their own good. You begin, I believe, by first acknowledging it, all of it, the bad as well as the good . . . Use your history as a guide, in other words. Because many times, what one needs to know for the present—the action that must be taken if a people are to win their right to live, the methods to be used: some of them unpalatable, true, but again, there's usually no other way—has been spelled out in past events. That it's all there if only they would look . . .

The new Cuffee Ned will have to do much more than kill the Sir Johns, however, for the whole system has to be changed. The obstacles are formidable: yet a solid front can be built on the basis of alliances of the exploited peoples. This is the significance of the relationship between Saul Amron, a Jew, and Merle Kinbona, a black woman. Of course, this common front is to be an alliance, not a *merging*. Thus Saul returns to the U.S. to find out what he can do among his people to fight the system while Merle goes to Uganda to search for her husband, i.e. to search for her black roots.

In her earlier writing, such as her novel, *Brown Girl, Brownstones* (first published in 1959), and her short story, "Reena," Paule Marshall wrote about how exploited black people in the United States survived and tried to make something positive of their lives. In *The Chosen Place, The Timeless People,* she has chosen a much wider canvas in order to ask questions about development in the context of the exploited peoples of the world and how this development is to take place.

In answering these questions, Paule Marshall has forged

a link between the exploited black people of the Caribbean Islands and all suffering peoples of the world throughout history: and in doing this, she has created a great Third-World novel. (pp. 113-31)

> *Peter Nazareth, "Paule Marshall's Timeless People," in* New Letters, *Vol. 40, No. 1, October, 1973, pp. 113-31.*

The interrelatedness of complex shapes and settings is so fused in Marshall that her books are verbal sculptures. Form and space and humanity and culture cannot be separated. Her words chisel features, crevices, lines, into the grand, seemingly formless mass of history.

—*Barbara Christian, in her* Black Women Novelists: The Development of a Tradition: 1892-1976, *1980.*

Mary Helen Washington

The small fierce band of Barbadians who emigrated to the United States between 1900 and 1940 came to escape the brutal colonial exploitation of blacks in the West Indies. Given only the most menial jobs, deprived of advanced schooling, their racial and cultural inferiority assumed, disenfranchised (in 1930 only 6000 Barbadians out of 188,000 could vote), these landless people—plantation workers, cane cutters, peasant farmers—left the land they rightfully owned whenever the opportunity to come to America presented itself. (A large West Indian migration to England occurred after World War II.) "Like a dark sea nudging its way into a white beach and staining the sand," they flooded into America, but especially into New York City, the place they called "The City of the Almighty Dollar," a place where any smart, hard-working Bajan could make enough money to "buy house." The extraordinary pull of New York was its image as a place of immense wealth and unlimited opportunity available to anyone with a business mind and an unshakable determination to "study the dollar" and imitate the whites.

" 'Lord, lemme do better than this. Lemme rise!' " Silla [of *Brown Girl, Brownstones*] cries when she is down on her knees scrubbing " 'the Jew floor,' " and she feels it is the inevitable nature of power to give way to the next group forceful enough to seize it. Like the other Barbadians in her community she has staked out a claim to power with this carefully conceived plan: work night and day to buy house; rent out every room, overcharge if necessary; sacrifice every penny to maintain property; keep strict vigilance on the children so they will enter high-paying professions; stick close to other Bajans, and exclude American blacks who are only a "keepback"; as soon as one house is paid for, move to the next desirable location—preferably Crown Heights; imitate the Jew. In spite of all evidence

to the contrary, Silla persists in this belief that the magic uplift will occur in her life if she adheres religiously to the formula:

> "More Bajan than you can shake a stick at opening stores or starting up some little business. . . . Every West Indian out here taking a lesson from the Jew landlord and converting these old houses into rooming houses—making the closets-self into rooms some them!—and pulling down plenty-plenty money by the week. And now the place is near overrun with roomers the Bajans getting out. Every jack-man buying a swell house in dichty Crown Heights."

By skin color, by African origin, by their colonized status, the West Indians of Paule Marshall's [*Brown Girl, Brownstones*] are inexorably connected to all black Americans, but it is their distinctiveness that yields the peculiar themes and images of this novel. The Boyce family does not belong to the tradition that created such American novels as Richard Wright's *Black Boy* or Gwendolyn Brooks' *Maud Martha* or Toni Morrison's *The Bluest Eye*. These transplanted Barbadians are an employed, literate, ambitious, property-owning, upwardly mobile, tough community of first-generation immigrants. Not one person in this novel is unemployed. These people came to " 'this man country,' " as they call it, *on purpose,* as willfully as many white immigrants; and they exercise their collective force to get what they need and want. Their power and literacy and community strength are essential to the tragic vision of *Brown Girl, Brownstones*; for, like the brownstones they inhabit, they are a formidable army—huge, somber, watchful, ancient and beautiful—but "doomed by the confusion in their design." At the end of the novel, the father, Deighton Boyce, is dead by suicide; the oldest daughter, Ina, is withdrawn into the church and a safe, dull marriage; Silla is alone, and Selina is left wandering, trying to make sense out of her world and her history. Like all tragedies, the events in *Brown Girl* seem inevitable, as though the characters are unknowingly wedded to the destructive forces within and committed to some conjugal ritual from which they cannot be released. Only Selina, the old child, the observer, the figure of redemption, the Ishmael left alone at the end to tell the story, is able to break the bond.

But the monumental tragic figure at the heart of *Brown Girl* is the mother, Silla Boyce. This large and brooding figure strides through the novel as she does through Fulton Park on her way home from work, so powerful that Selina imagines the sun itself giving way to her force. Selina calls her " 'the mother,' " not " 'my mother,' " reinforcing this sense of Silla's dominance and power. Silla is *the* mother much as someone might be called *the* president. This angular woman in somber dress, with rough carved features and dark skin that suggests her mystery, is not only the mainstay of the Boyce family, but she is preeminent in the Bajan community. She is the pioneer, forging a path through unfamiliar territory, cutting the bush for those behind her, crushing whatever is in her way. With her powerful gift of words she expresses, in the accents and idioms of the Bajan community, its fears and aspirations. She is the avatar of the community's deepest values and needs.

Paule Marshall tells us that her own mother had this skill with words, and, like Selina, she became immersed in the oral traditions, sitting in the kitchen listening to her mother and her friends engaging in a high order of oral art. In the kitchen, where Silla makes Barbadian delicacies to sell, her friends, Florrie and Iris and Virgie, are spectators, silent and awed by Silla's immense power. Rapt and respectful, they acknowledge Silla's leadership, for don't they all know that " 'in this white-man world you got to take yuh mouth and make a gun.' " On every issue confronting their lives, Silla imposes her own meaning, affirming for herself and the others the role of language in the survival of oppressed people. With Silla the language becomes an art form, giving expression to the tremendous vitality and creativity she has no other way to express:

On the church:

> "Lemme tell you, Iris, you don see God any better by being sanctified and climbing the walls of a church and tearing off your clothes when you's in the spirit. . . . Not everyone who cry 'Lord, Lord' gon enter in. . . ."

On the causes of World War II:

> "It's these politicians. They's the ones always starting up this lot of war. And what they care? It's the poor people got to suffer and mothers with their sons."

On Barbadians' allegiance to England:

> "You think 'cause they does call Barbados 'Little England' that you is somebody? What the king know 'bout you—or care?"

On the political exploitation of Barbadians:

> "The rum shop and the church join together to keep we pacify and in igorance."

On poverty:

> "It's a terrible thing to know that you gon be poor all yuh life, no matter how hard you work. You does stop trying after a time. People does see you so and call you lazy. But it ain laziness. It just that you does give up. You does kind of die inside. . . ."

Here is a woman who understands poverty and political demagoguery and the harassment of the downtrodden and can express that understanding in haunting poetic words; but with all that understanding, that clear knowledge of "the way things arrange" to destroy her people, she still chooses to imitate the swift and the powerful, for if not, she says, " 'somebody come and trample you quick enough.' " She plots for months to sell Deighton's land, his life-long dream, declaring in front of her friends that she is prepared to damn her soul to get the down payment for that brownstone:

> "Be-Jesus-Christ, I gon do that for him then. Even if I got to see my soul fall howling into hell I gon do it. . . . I gon fix he and fix he good. I gon show the world that Silla ain nice!"

She evicts her boarder and kinswoman, Suggie Skeete, for being an "undesirable" tenant; she terrifies one daughter, the lovely Ina, into meek submission, and she tries to force Selina into medical school. She betrays Deighton to the immigration authorities for abandoning the family and has him deported. When Selina counters Silla's materialism with the scornful remark that money cannot buy love, Silla cries out in a loud though unconvincing voice, " 'Lord! Give me a dollar in my hand any day!' "

But Silla is not a monster. She reflects more clearly and more intensely our own struggles between innocence and guilt, our own contradictions and failures. This same bitter, enraged woman is the mother whom Selina says is the only prop, the emotional mainstay of their family. With her mouth fixed and her back rigid, Silla, the figure forging the way through the bush, is also the young girl coming alone to a new country, the young mother taking the train every morning to Flatbush and Sheepshead Bay to scrub floors for a few " 'raw-mout' " pennies; the woman in the factory pitting her life and strength against the machines because " 'You got to learn to run these machines to live.' " Silla becomes comprehensible to us as Selina, the witness and record keeper, passes from childhood innocence into maturity and experiences the adult pain—the grown-up black pain—of Silla's life. When Selina comes to the full knowledge of Silla, she sees not just *the mother* but the wild teenager dancing herself into a frenzy, longing for a better life, the passionate and mysterious lover, the scorned wife, the community leader, and above all, that ancient African woman whom the entire western world has humiliated and despised. And she, Selina, becomes one with the mother and the other Bajan women "who had lived each day what she had come to know." How, she wonders, had the mother endured, "she who had not chosen death by water?"

Silla's life is a paradigm of the Barbadian community. She is the touchstone, for she proclaims aloud the chaotic trouble deep in the core of the community. Her endurance, her rage, her devotion to the dollar and property, her determination to survive in "this man country" is theirs. Her lights and shadows are theirs. Her tragedy is theirs. That is why Silla is never seen alone in this novel and why Selina can never think of her alone: "It was always the mother and the others, for they were alike—those watchful, wrathful women whose eyes seared and searched and laid bare, whose tongue lashed the world in unremitting distrust." The bowed figure of Silla, exhausted and weary as she studies or cleans all night to avoid the dreams she must encounter in sleep, stirs both pity and awe because she is the community. She symbolizes its power, she reflects its values, she embodies its history. Her sorrow is the sorrow of the race.

While Silla is exposed throughout the entire novel—she is prepared to show the whole world that " 'Silla ain nice' "—Deighton always remains hidden, his face "a closed blind over the man beneath." His dark body is often described as limp and sensual; whereas Silla's body is nearly always in the position of reprimand: stiff, towering, and unbending. Silla is associated with wintery images, cold, white, stark, and unfeeling, while Deighton's warm sensuality and carefree demeanor are like the summer sun. Despite the fixed hardness between them, they both yearn for their former passionate life together, and one of the important tasks of the novel is to explain this irreconcilable split between Deighton and Silla and to relate it to the character of the community.

That pivotal communal ritual, the wedding of 'Gatha Steed's daughter, a huge and elaborate extravaganza of satin dresses, imperial plumes, and endless bridesmaids— but hardly a trace of traditional Bajan life—is a profound testimony to the community's successful imitation of white America. It is a suitable ritual ground to announce the divorce of Silla and Deighton. Silla moves through the ceremony alone, expressing the weariness and sadness of heart that both she and the forced bride feel. Once again Silla is the touchstone, for only she will admit aloud that she has done everything short of murder to attain her ends and that the accomplishment has brought her no peace. But what Silla says aloud the others disguise. The entire wedding is like perfume misting over a deep and pervasive odor. The unhappy little bride is being forced to marry a proper Barbadian and to abandon her lover, a black southerner. 'Gatha Steed's friends pretend to be impressed with her ostentatious display, but their response to her is full of jealous venom:

> "As black as she is in a bright-bright green? And somethin' tie round she head like she's home selling fish? . . . Oh, 'Gatha is playing white in truth."

The men and the women sit separately for most of the wedding as is customary, their physical separation pantomiming the deep antagonisms between Silla and Deighton. When Deighton appears at the door and hesitantly proceeds toward the circle of dancers, Silla pronounces the rejection of the entire community, " 'Small Island, go back where you come from,' " declaring him outcast because he will not live by their standards. They need to anchor their lives in material security and so they struggle for their little credit unions, their small banks, their business associations, and what little land they can accumulate. In this desperate fight to beat the white man at his game, they cannot afford aesthetes with paint brushes, or lovers like Suggie Skeete, or failed men like Deighton Boyce.

The second great communal scene in *Brown Girl* is Selina's first visit to a meeting of the Association of Barbadian Homeowners and Businessmen, a ritual dominated by men just as the wedding was by the women. There, joined together like the brownstones they inhabit, the Bajan community seems to become a single force, "Sure of its goal and driving hard toward it." With power and passion they declare their ambition to have a voice at City Hall, to build a credit union and a bank, to give these people "big word for big word," to puncture that implacable wall of white so that their presence will be heard and acknowledged. The main speaker of the meeting sums up their ambitions with this terrible admission of their own sense of invisibility and fear of blackness:

> "We ain white yet. We's small-timers! . . . But we got our eye on the big time. . . ."

The passionate fury which the Association arouses is reflected in their bodily gestures when they denounce Claremont Sealy for suggesting they include black Americans in their organization. Faces are contorted with wrath, arms punctuate the air with outrage, the basement is hot with their anger.

This passion for money and property and status contrasts ironically with the passionless generation of children they beget. Except for Selina, they are orderly, docile, and homogenous, each like a still-life painting, compliant to the brush strokes their parents impose, awaiting without question the codified life:

> the sanctioned embrace two nights a week, the burgeoning stomach, the neat dark children, the modest home on Long Island, the piano lessons to the neighbor's children and church each Sunday.

They will reconstruct the dreams of the parents, dreams of acquisition, binding themselves fast to a crumbling community where chaos and uncertainty are controlled by group force, with the final inevitable result: "the slow blurring of the self, the steady attrition of the soul over all those long complacent years."

The small, willful, quiet Selina, always listening unnoticed in the corners of rooms, absorbing culture and tradition, is the griot of this community, the preserver of its near and ancient past. Caught between the rigid codes of the Barbadian community, her mother's need for security, and her father's definition of a proud manhood that supersedes everyone's concerns, Selina is the one who must interpret and make sense of all these conflicting pressures. Just as she stands outside of the early family photograph, merely the swelling in her mother's belly, she remains throughout the novel somewhat of an outsider, drawn irresistibly to Fulton Street and jazz rhythms and blues music, to everything that admits to the chaos, uncertainty, and mystery of life. Paradoxically she must disrupt the destructive circle of the community's boundaries at the same time that she must preserve the power of its rugged endurance in a hostile white world. She remains always on the edge, a marginal woman, reaching for a life not bound by their comfortable, grim illusions: "Knowing, she still longed to leave this safe, sunlit place at the top of the house for the challenge there."

The questions Paule Marshall sets before her major characters are always the same: how do we remember the past so as to transform it and make it usable? How do we preserve those qualities of survival and endurance that are at the deepest emotional core of one's black identity? How do an oppressed people survive spiritually, and on what grounds can they construct a future in a world in which the "soul-beauty of a race" is despised, a world which yields no true self-consciousness but only lets one see the self through the revelation of the other world. This peculiar sensation, this double-consciousness, as DuBois called it, this sense of measuring one's soul by the tape of a world that looks on in contempt and pity, is the problem at the heart of *Brown Girl.*

The spiritual dilemma of the black woman has never been

acknowledged or recognized or understood. Paule Marshall says that until Gwendolyn Brooks' novel *Maud Martha,* it was rare to see a black woman in literature with a conscious, interior life. We have seldom seen black women characters struggling over such questions as suicide, or racial violence as a means to freedom, or feminism in conflict with racism, or their call to public ministry, or their need to transform their lives into art, and that is because the women who raised these issues have been silenced, omitted, patronized, made invisible. It is with these historical and literary omissions in mind that we must view Selina's movement toward wholeness, for she proceeds to this task with little precedence in literature.

Selina is given several guides, each of whom connects her with her culture in vital ways and provides important messages about the uniqueness of Selina's own identity. First there is Suggie Skeete, an upstairs roomer whose pleasure-loving, old-world ways are remnants of the past in Barbados, where people "does take a drink while the sun hot-hot and yuh wun know whether it was the sun or the rum or both that had yuh feeling so sweet." Suggie, with her weekly lovers, her codfish smells, and her inability to hold a job, is someone for the respectable Bajan community to "lick their mouth on," and indeed Silla evicts Suggie as a prostitute. Suggie gives Selina crucial lessons of love and passion to thwart the puritanical codes of the Bajans. In contrast to Silla warning Selina about " 'licking about with some piece of man,' " Suggie urges her to take off the clothes of mourning and embrace life like a lover.

Selina's second guide is the black American hairdresser, Miss Thompson, whose beauty shop on Fulton Street is like a way station from which she oversees the comings and goings of all who pass. Miss Thompson's face is described as "an African wood carving: mysterious, omniscient, the features elongated by compassion, the eyes shrouded with a profound sadness." It is her priestly function to listen, comfort, direct. She presides over Selina's elevation to womanhood, giving her her first curls, pronouncing that she ain't no more child, and finally telling Selina the story of her own resistance to the brutality of racism. She is the link to Selina's larger community—to black Americans, whom the Bajans despise, to the Barbadians with whom she encourages Selina's reconciliation, and to her half-forgotten African past. Selina realizes the full effect of Miss Thompson's ministry when she has her first real encounter with racism and, though she is stunned and humiliated, ultimately reacts with outrage and affirmation of her oneness with her own people:

> She was one with Miss Thompson . . . one with the whores, the flashy men, and the blues rising sacredly above the plain of neon lights and ruined houses. . . . She was one with them: the mother and the Bajan women, who had lived each day what she had come to know.

A long line of characters before Selina discovered that they belonged to those armies of darkness and had to share that suffering in order to discover identity and integrity. John Grimes in Baldwin's *Go Tell It On The Mountain* struggles to free himself from this dark, despised, and rejected people, but he finally understands in a vision that "the body in the water, the body in the fire, the body on the tree" have claimed him. The Invisible Man awakes into darkness, and it is in the embrace of darkness that he, like Selina, finds illumination.

But the most powerful guide given to Selina is *the* mother, Silla Boyce. For all of her worship of Deighton, Selina experiences the most profound connection to her mother. So complex is her feeling for Silla that she constantly vacillates between a loving awe and a violent angry distrust for Silla. Literature has rarely revealed so passionate a relationship between mother and daughter as we see in ***Brown Girl.*** In that tender scene after Deighton is deported, when Selina calls her mother Hitler and blames Silla for destroying the father, there is as much passion between them as there is anger. Selina strikes her mother's flesh until she falls exhausted and helpless against her mother's neck and then, reverently, Silla touches the tears, traces the outline of her face and smoothes her snarled hair, "Each caress declared that she was touching something which was finally hers alone."

In spite of this possessiveness, Silla never teaches Selina the ways of compromise nor female self-abnegation. In fact, she teaches her almost nothing of the "female" arts. She tolerates Selina's adventurous spirit with a grudging respect and in subtle ways encourages it. When Selina, at 13, begs to be allowed to go to Prospect Park without her older sister, Silla says with some annoyance: "What you need Ina for any more? You's more woman now than she'll ever be, soul. G'long." And her parting words when Selina is just seventeen years old reveal this same respect for her daughter's independent spirit:

> G'long! You was always too much woman for me anyway, soul. And my own mother did say two head-bulls can't reign in a flock.

When Alice Walker says of her mother that she "handed down respect for the possibilities—and the will to grasp them," I am reminded of Silla Boyce and the legacy she passes to Selina. In all of her tirades and machinations, she never once tells Selina that she is less for being a woman, and in fact, with her own life she shows Selina that a woman is the central figure in her own life. The romantic side of Selina may very well be her father's doing, but that assertive, willful, forthright girl, taking her life into her own hands, managing city college and a full-time love affair at eighteen, is Silla Boyce's daughter.

At the end of the novel Selina makes the conscious, political choice to return to Barbados, to search out the lost meaning of her homeland, to discover what went wrong for her people in "this man country." She will not complete college as her mother has planned, nor will she, like Clive, withdraw into self-pity. In making the choice to return to Barbados, to begin again, Selina symbolizes the community's need to reorder itself, to recognize the destruction of human values in a community devoted to money, ownership and power. ***Brown Girl, Brownstones*** is thus one of the most optimistic texts in Afro-American literature, for it assigns even to an oppressed people the power of conscious political choice: they are not victims.

When Selina dances at the end of the novel, we see her way

of being in the world. Utterly dependent on her own body (as we all are), its huge old eyes, coarse hair, dark skin, she captures in womanly movements both the pain and beauty of life and embraces them both. She dances memory and passion, expressing her own individuality, her reflections of other people, and the needs of us all caught in this cycle of life and death. At the end of the dance she goes through the night towards the river and up to the East Side into marble and gilt halls where her new identity will be tested. There, with the strength of community, the power of the mother, she confronts truly her own dark depth and finds in that upheaval not Deighton's, not Silla's, not the Bajan community's—but her own Selina. (pp. 311-22)

> *Mary Helen Washington, in an afterword to* Brown Girl, Brownstones *by Paule Marshall, The Feminist Press, 1981, pp. 311-24.*

Marilyn Nelson Waniek

As a first-generation West Indian-American and the author of three novels and a collection of short stories, Paule Marshall gives evidence in her work of a marginal duality similar to that felt by immigrants. While not herself an immigrant, Marshall grew up in an immigrant community whose legacy to her and her work is a share of its alienation. Marshall's first novel, **Brown Girl, Brownstones** may explain the source of that marginality. The basic conflict of this novel, between the protagonist's mother and her father, overshadows the protagonist's coming of age and her search for her identity. The mother has accepted the crass values of the upwardly-mobile Barbadian immigrant community in which the family lives, while the father maintains a dreamer's futile pride in the cruel face of American racism and disappointment. Their daughter, Selina, vacillates between these two extremes, neither a Barbadian nor an American, but a permanent and unhappy outsider. The novel ends with her escape to Barbados, where, we presume, her alienation will continue—if not deepen.

In her second book, the collection of short fiction entitled **Soul Clap Hands and Sing,** Marshall explores through different characters the alienated marginality seen in Selina. The four stories comprising the collection are set all over the Americas: in Barbados, Brooklyn, British Guiana and Brazil. Each story focuses on an elderly marginal man and the point at which he realizes the extent of his alienation. Despite the implication of the volume's title, a line borrowed and modified slightly from Yeats' "Sailing to Byzantium" ("An aged man is but a paltry thing, / A tattered coat upon a stick, unless/Soul clap its hands and sing, and louder sing / For every tatter in its mortal dress"), the concern of the stories is not with the age of the men who are their protagonists, but with their souls. Each of the protagonists has lost, as he has gained partial admission into the dominant culture or the ruling class, his soul—his faith in God, in his fellows, and in himself.

The seventy-year old protagonist of ["**Barbados**"] is known only as Mr. Watford, his lack of a forename indicating the extent of his distance from the people around

him. The story opens with a visual image of his alienation: he is in bed, a black face within white sheets, surrounded by the white interior walls of his white Colonial American house. After an exile of fifty years in America, he has returned "home," but the alienation he felt in America has not been alleviated. His life in Barbados is, as it had been in Boston, a simple, impersonal routine: He works all day, then dresses every evening in a white uniform to read the weeks-old Boston newspapers, chuckling at the "senseless way" of the world. He has devoted his life to work, to success, to the need to escape the death which seemed to pursue his poverty-stricken family:

> He had been the only one of ten to live, the only one to escape. But he had never lost the sense of being pursued by the same dread presence which had claimed them. He had never lost the fear that if he lived too fully he would tire and death would quickly close the gap. His only defense had been a cautious life and work. He had been almost broken by work at the age of twenty when his parents died, leaving him enough money for the passage to America.

What he remembers of his American exile is that "nothing had mattered after his flight." For fifty years he worked in the boiler room of a hospital, accumulating enough capital that he owned a large rooming house, yet "America . . . had meant nothing to him." For fifty years he was alone; neither his acquaintances nor his mistresses "mattered" to him.

Back in Barbados, Mr. Watford is landed gentry, treated with the deference "given only to a white man in his time." Because of his years in America, his position, and his unbending pride, Mr. Watford is as distant from his fellows as the white man had been from the black. Not only wealthier than they, but also having a different accent and different values—his sound very much like the Protestant work ethic—Mr. Watford is frozen in an isolation which is underscored when the corpulent and concupiscent Mr. Goodman sends a young girl to work in his house, arguing that "it's up to we that got little something to give them work."

The girl immediately represents to Mr. Watford his lost connection to the soil of his birth:

> She was standing in the driveway, her bare feet like strong dark roots amid the jagged stones, her face tilted toward the sun—and she might have been standing there always waiting for him. She seemed of the sun, of the earth.

Although he tries to send her away, the girl slowly becomes a fixture in his solitary life, and threatens to force him to break his fifty-year-old habit of denying his loneliness. He is cruel to her, for she threatens him as well with memories of his lost youth:

> Lying there, listening, he saw with disturbing clarity his mother dressed for an excursion—the white head tie wound above her dark face and her head poised like a dancer's under the heavy outing basket of food. That set of her head had haunted his years, reappearing in the girl as she walked toward him the first day. Aching with

memory, yet annoyed with himself for remembering, he went downstairs.

Mr. Watford rejects the girl's faint offer of intimacy because he has for fifty years denied himself the intimacy through which he might confess his loneliness. Rebuffed, the girl goes out on a "spree," leaving the old man alone in his empty house to worry about her. His routine of so many years' duration is broken; he cannot read his papers. Like a parent, he stands on the portico, waiting:

> He saw her lost amid the carousings of the village, despoiled; he imagined someone like Mr. Goodman clasping her lewdly or tumbling her in the canebrake. His hand rose, trembling, to rid the air of her; he tried to summon his cold laugh. But somehow, he could not dismiss her as he had always done with everyone else. Instead, he wanted to punish and protect her, to find and lead her back to the house.

The girl has broken through his reserve; Mr. Watford has for the first time in many years found that another person can "matter" to him. He is all eagerness, all concern when he glimpses her dancing through the twilight with a boy of her age, on whom Mr. Watford had earlier seen a political button reading "The Old Order Shall Pass." As he watches their playfully sexual dance, Mr. Watford realizes the prophecy of that motto, the all-but-impossibility of his entering the human community through the girl. He goes to her, driven by what passion Marshall does not say, although it is certainly far more than lechery:

> Hopefully, he staggered forward, his step cautious and contrite, his hands quivering along the wall.
>
> She did not see him as he pushed the door wider. And for some time he stood there, his shoulders hunched in humility, his skin stripped away to reveal each flaw, his whole self offered in one outstretched hand.

The girl turns away from his revealed vulnerability, slamming a door which has opened only once in fifty years. With that, the isolation in which he has borne his love for Barbados as well as his unwillingness or inability "to bear the weight of his own responsibility" is sealed. The ensuing name-calling is the last defense of a desperately lonely individual. The girl sees only his distance, his wealth, his age, his coldness; "You ain't people," she tells him. She cannot know his loneliness, the alienation forced upon him by his marginal position both in Boston and Barbados, the protective wall he has built around himself. Of course the old order shall pass; Mr. Watford and his generation of compulsive and cold achievers will die. Perhaps Marshall wants us to understand that Mr. Watford does die when, in the last paragraph of the story, he senses "that dark but unsubstantial figure which roamed the nights searching for him wind him in its chill embrace." Sadly, he has recognized the pain of the marginality imposed on him by his long exile and his return too late. It is equally sad, however, that the new order symbolized by the girl does not recognize the love which sustained Mr. Watford in America and which after fifty years brought him back to a home where he no longer belonged.

Max Berman, the sixty-three-year old protagonist of "Brooklyn," is a secular Jew for whom—as for Watford—nothing has mattered for many years. He loved neither of his two wives, found "his father's God . . . useless and even a little embarrassing," never believed enough in his work, and never took seriously his membership in the Communist Party. An academic, he had taught his classes in French literature "from the same neat pack of notes each semester" until the McCarthy investigations forced his resignation. He has long been cynical; as the story begins his cynicism has deepened. He is teaching an evening course in summer school at a fifteenth-rate college in Brooklyn, having been "gutted" by his recent confrontations with his government. For some time he has felt himself dead. The loneliness of an attractive young woman in his class the first evening intrigues him and seems to promise him life.

He does not notice at first that she is black. When he does, the recognition brings back to him not only a sense of white guilt, but, more profoundly, a sense of recognition: She reminds him of himself, of the humiliations he has suffered as a Jew, of his all but forsaken Jewish identity and faith. Weeks later, on the pretext of discussing her studies, Berman invites the young woman to his home in the country. Then he winks. The reader recognizes that wink from the opening paragraph of the story as "the anxiety which chafed his heart and tugged his left eyelid so that he seemed to be winking, roguishly, behind his glasses." The girl is taken aback, however, and recoils.

The brief scene that follows is a confrontation between two marginal individuals, both suffering from the loneliness that profound alienation brings. The Jew and the fair-skinned, middle class Southern black girl do not, however, understand each other. Burdened by history, the girl understands only that Berman is a white man propositioning her. Seeing this fact in her face and recognizing that her intuition is at least partly correct, Berman can only mumble an apology.

Several weeks pass before the girl returns to the class for the final examination. She has, in the mean time, lost her innocence and gained some of Berman's cynicism. The cynicism enables her to smile "a set, artificial smile that was both cold and threatening" and to say, "I've changed my mind. I think I'd like to spend a day at your place in the country if your invitation still holds." Because of his lonely despair and the vague, persistent hope for love or passion, Berman accepts, although he knows she has decided to treat him as a white man: "She smiled stiffly and left, her heels awakening the silence of the empty corridor, the sound reaching back to tap like a warning finger on Max Berman's temple."

On the day of her visit Berman is struck by the impossibility of an affair between them:

> The water between them became the years which separated them. Her white cap was the sign of her purity, while the silt darkening the lake was the flotsam of his failures. Above all, their color—her arms a pale, flashing gold in the sunlit water and his bled white and flaccid with

the veins like angry blue penciling—marked the final barrier.

Saddened by the knowledge that he is unworthy of her, Berman confesses to the girl not only the failures of his life, but also his feeling that "none of it really mattered that much." When she asks what *did* matter, he realizes that there has been "nothing . . . to which he had given himself or in which he had truly believed since the belief and dedication of his boyhood." He has lost his God, his capacity for belief, his place in a community. He is, profoundly, a marginal man.

The girl tells Berman of her Southern childhood, of the marginality forced upon her by her protective parents. Her world has been defined by skin-color; she has been taught to despise those darker than she and to fear those lighter. She believes she has learned from Berman "how you—and most of the people like you—see me," and, therefore, she is no longer afraid. She knows now that she "will do something." Berman's confessed failure and loneliness have become her strength and courage. Although she does not understand Berman, their relationship has emboldened her and enabled her to know what she is capable of. Berman, wounded, sees himself, too, and accepts "his responsibility for her rage, which went deeper than his, and for her anger, which would spur her finally to live. And not only for her, but for all those at last whom he had wronged through his indifference. . . ." The fact, however, remains that Berman's indifference is the product of his alienation; he disappointed his father, kept an emotional distance from his wives, his work, and his politics because he was an American Jew who had lost his faith and his identity. The girl, smiling "an ironic, pitiless smile," leaves Berman, in pursuit of her own life. How much more humanity she might find in herself in the future had she accepted, as Berman finally has, her own responsibility for her fellow man.

In the confrontations between old men and young women in the first two stories of this collection, the old men are cruelly rejected. Neither of the young women recognizes the pain of the old men; both are blind and rather selfish. The latter two stories in the collection center on confrontations between old men and women who are closer to them in age and experience; understandably, these women show greater sympathy, though not always greater understanding.

Gerald Motley, the protagonist of **"British Guiana,"** has been an alcoholic and a cynic for many years. Born seventy-four years ago to a wealthy, proud Creole family, a "handsome" mixture of British, African, and Hindu bloods, Motley refers to himself bitterly as "Gerald Ramsdeen Motley. My title, sirs? B.S.W.C.; Bastard Spawned of the World's Commingling!" As his name implies, Motley, a mixture of many races, has become, in his eyes, something of a clown, a joke, because his "sense of being many things and yet none, this confusion, had set the mold of his life." After a period in England, where he studied law, medicine, economics, and the classics and was often "taken for an Italian or Spaniard," Motley returned to B.G. without a career, married, and tried to find a place for himself. His attempt to adapt was, however, permanently put aside when he fell in love with a Chinese-Negro girl named Sybil, creating scandal and losing his wife and child, his place in polite society, and his self-respect.

Motley's relationship with Sybil both ruined him and made him successful. It was Sybil who stopped him from entering the bush and thereby finding himself:

> . . . at his awed cry the bush had closed around him, becoming another dimension of himself, the self he had long sought. For the first time this self was within his grasp.

Sybil called him back—an act for which he has never forgiven her—from his partial vision of what he might have been, and returned him to the world of respectability and responsibility. Because of her he accepted a position as program director for B. G. Broadcasting—he was the first black man to hold such a high position—and began to drink.

Motley's life since that point has been a downward spiral of cynicism and dissipation. He has, in his old age, found a young man on whom he lavishes his bitter affection because the younger man's bitterness is deeper than his own, because his insolence reminds Motley of what he feels to be the truth about himself, and because of latent sexual attraction. This last point is related to Motley's aborted vision of himself in the bush: His affection for Sidney never becomes a homosexual liaison because Motley has never confronted the truth about himself. Instead, warded away from it forty years ago by a woman who loved him and ministered to every day by bartenders named Ling and Singh, Motley has spent many years contemptuous of himself and British Guiana, feeling that, somehow, he and B. G. are the same.

When Sybil returns after many successful, but apparently lonely, years in Jamaica, Motley is forced to remember their long affair and the crucial moment when she held him back. Sybil had also been, because of her Chinese father, a marginal figure in the community, and her British education had similarly intensified her isolation. Indeed, at first Motley

> . . . could only remember the quality of her loneliness. It had been as much a part of her smell as the cologne she had used; it had often lent a fierce and excessive note to her laughter, and it had always brought on her rages during the long rain. It had been his loneliness, and the loneliness and despair of the land.

Sidney accuses him of not having married Sybil "because she was black and her father was only a shopkeeper"; Motley knows this is only partly true, that:

> . . . whenever he had slept with Sybil she had not only brought her body and laid that beside him, but her loneliness also, stretching it out like a pale ghost between them, and her intense, almost mystical suffering, asking him silently to assuage it.

Sybil's loneliness grew from her marginality; she kept Motley from seeing and admitting his homosexuality because she needed an ally, because his being a homosexual would have forever made impossible her alliance with the one individual whose marginality equaled her own. Yet Motley refused her:" . . . she had asked too much. He would have had to offer up himself to do so, and he refused."

With this history between them, a barrier and a bond, Motley and Sybil meet again. She has come to offer him a position of great responsibility with the radio station for which she works in Jamaica. Her invitation, with its implied offer of a renewed affair which might sustain them in their last years, unleashes Motley's self-deprecation:

> . . . who told Sybil I could co-ordinate anything? Not Murie certainly. She knows better. In all the years Sybil worked for me, did she ever see me do any coordinating or any directing for that matter—any work? . . . Sybil must let Murie tell her sometime how my hands shake these days . . . No, I could Not do the job.

He asks her instead to offer the job to his young friend, Sidney, confessing by his silent response to her question about the nature of his and Sidney's relationship that Sidney is more to him than a friend. Sybil lights a match to look at her old lover and sees—as he sees in her eyes—the truth about him which he might have seen in the bush years ago:

> . . . the confusion which had begun with his heritage and found its final expression in Sidney. The evidence was all there. And she saw something else which made her suddenly start and draw back and give a muted cry of fear and pity which made the small flame waver. It was, simply, the unmistakable form of his death lurking there.

This confusion, this motley collection of races which he could never make sense of, but which set him apart from others, had been there all along. His homosexuality had, too, with its additional pain. Sybil had tried to protect him, but she had also forced him to live what he knew to be a lie, thus increasing his sense of his separation from the people around him. The identification of B. G. with Motley is made clear by Sybil's last words before Motley races off to die in an accident: "This damn place. This damn, bloody place."

The marginality of Caliban, the fierce little old black man who is the protagonist of **"Brazil,"** is clearly allegorical. Caliban's marginality has been caused by his having moved from one social class—that of the rural peasantry—to a wealthier, a more highly respected, a "whiter" one. As a youth he had left his village and come to Rio, where he had struggled with poverty until being discovered in a talent show as a brilliant comic. From that point forward he had been "O Grande Caliban," the most famous comedian in Brazil, who with his partner, the ungainly blonde Miranda, had secured a place in the hearts of the people. Now, in his seventies and about to retire, he searches desperately for Heitor Guimares, the poor black youth he used to be. Again and again Marshall tells us of his lost identity: "it had become difficult over his thirty-five years in show business to . . . tell where O Grande Caliban ended and he, Heitor Baptista Guimares, began" ". . . only on stage made up as Caliban in the scarlet shirt

and baggy trunks was he at all certain of who he was." So much is he Caliban that when asked what his real name is, he has to stop and think; even his young wife and his partner know him only as Caliban.

In the course of the story Caliban tries to find someone who remembers Heitor Guimares and can return him to himself. He goes back to the poor neighborhood and the restaurant where he had worked when he first came to Rio. Instead of finding himself, he encounters a crowd of small boys for whom he is a hero, and the restaurant, its name changed years ago to Grande Caliban, is a shrine to his success. He walks into the *favela,* whose urban poverty is a reflection of his humble origin, and finds the old man Nacimento, for whom he had once worked. The old man's very name indicates his symbolic importance: Nacimento means birth. But Nacimento does not remember Heitor Guimares. Instead, he says, "O Grande Caliban. He was the best they ever had at the Teatro Municipal."

Since he cannot return to his past, Caliban goes back into Rio, the beautiful, indifferent city which gave him his name and his fame. Feeling that Miranda and Rio are somehow the same, he rushes to Miranda's apartment, where

> . . . for the first time Caliban was aware of how the room expressed the city, and of himself, reflected in one of the mirrors, in relation to it. He was like a house pet, a tiny dog, who lent the room an amusing touch but had no real place there. The pale walls and ivory furniture, the abundance of white throughout, stripped him of importance, denied him all significance.

He asks Miranda whether she knows Heitor Guimares. When she asks who he is, Caliban answers, "I am Heitor Guimares." Miranda laughs, then crouches in the pose that has been his trademark and says, "You? No, señor, you are Caliban. O Grande Caliban!"

O Grande Caliban, The Great Caliban, Caliban the Great: the name echoes with ironies, with bitter memories. The names Caliban and Miranda were, of course, given to this pair because of their races: Caliban the enslaved, ignorant native, Miranda the innocent white daughter of *The Tempest.* Yet, their act had played off against that allusion the irony of Miranda's ungainly height, her homeliness contrasted with Caliban's bantam toughness and wit. O Grande Caliban is not physically large, but his image has been one of strength. The crisis of the story has less to do with the obviously allusive nature of his name than with the fact that

> . . . Caliban had become his only reality, and anything else he might have been was lost. The image Miranda had created for him was all he had now and once that was taken—as it would be tomorrow when the signs announcing his retirement went up—he would be left without a self.

The apocalyptic conclusion is as filled with sad futility as the conclusions of the other three stories in the collection. Caliban destroys Miranda's apartment, feeling "with each blow . . . the confusion and despair congested within him fall away, leaving an emptiness which, he knew, would remain with him until he died." His attack on Miranda is clearly not the answer; Miranda is as much a victim as Caliban is. He cannot run away from his alienation, from his marginality, from his loss of self; there is no place to run to. Perhaps only an English-speaking reader can appreciate the ironic last line of the story, in which Miranda cries, "Caliban, *meu negrinho,* was it me . . .?" The endearment, which carries the force both of "my dear" and "my little black one," is a perfect embodiment of Caliban's dilemma, for in gaining respect, he has become "the little black one" and lost his identity and ultimately his self-respect.

Each of these stories [in *Soul Clap Hands and Sing*] is a story of marginality, a story of the pain of the immigrant, the returned immigrant, the upwardly-mobile individual who has forfeited his place in a society which is rapidly changing. Each is critical of, yet at the same time sympathetic to the plight of these old men for whom Soul has long since ceased to sing. Paule Marshall has not, as many of her readers seem to think, merely set up straw men like coats on sticks to be knocked down by the force of her political argument. There is no character in these stories who is without blame, who is completely human and responsible. This fact, and the fact that her sympathies are divided between the old men and the characters through whom they receive their visions, indicate that she understands and shares something of their marginality. (pp. 46-55)

Marilyn Nelson Waniek, "Paltry Things: Immigrants and Marginal Men in Paule Marshall's Short Fiction," in Callaloo, Vol. 6, No. 2, Spring-Summer, 1983, pp. 46-56.

Paule Marshall   [Interview with Maryse Condé]

[*Condé*]: *The spiritual return of Black women in the U.S. and in the Black diaspora to Africa is a recurring theme in your work. Have you ever been to Africa? Do you have a concrete image of Africa or does it exist as more of a spiritual homeland?*

[Marshall]: Africa is simultaneously both at the same time—a concrete destination and a spiritual homeland. Yes, I was in Africa in 1977 for the Festac Black Arts Festival in Nigeria. This was the first time I had ever been to Africa, and, also was the first time I had ever encountered Black writers from Africa and the Black diaspora. What was extraordinary for me was the way Africans adopted me. The Yorubas thought that I was a Yoruba, the Ibos thought that I was an Ibo, and the Ghanians thought that I was from Ghana. In 1980, I also traveled to Kenya and Uganda in East Africa, and there, as in West Africa, I was adopted as a native daughter. There is an expression of Yoruba or Ibo origin "Omowale" which roughly translates to mean "a native daughter has returned." This expression summarizes the experience of my physical return to Africa.

There was also a spiritual, emotional and affective facet of my return. Well before my journey to Africa, I was conscious of my African ancestry. During the 1920's, I was raised among Barbadians who would constantly talk about Marcus Garvey's Universal Negro Improvement Association. The West Indian women around me when I was a young girl spoke of Garvey's "back to Africa" movement in which they were active participants. You could say that Africa was an essential part of the emotional fabric of my world. Also, when I began to write my first novel, **Brown Girl, Brownstones** (1959), I experienced a necessity to make a spiritual return to my sources. At the end of the book, the heroine, Selina Boyce, leaves the U.S. in order to return to the Caribbean. In my second novel, **The Chosen Place, The Timeless People** (1969), the heroine, Merle Kinbona, completes the voyage to the Caribbean only to depart later for Africa. These two novels, plus my third, **Praisesong for the Widow** (1983), in which my heroine, Avey Avatara Johnson, makes the mythic return to the Caribbean, again, form a trilogy.

In order to develop a sense of our collective history, I think that it is absolutely necessary for Black people to effect this spiritual return. As the history of people of African descent in the U.S. and the diaspora is fragmented and interrupted, I consider it my task as a writer to initiate readers to the challenges this journey entails. Now, even though it would be difficult to classify my novels as "African" per se, I do attempt to constantly make references to Africa through the usage of images and metaphors. In **The Chosen Place, The Timeless People** (1969), for example, in a small village on a mythic Caribbean island, I describe a shopkeeper as a tribal African chief seated behind a counter as he makes libations to the gods. Many of the characters in the book are depicted as though they were wearing masks from Benin. This is how I express my attachment to Africa.

Do you find any contradiction in the desire for a spiritual affirmation of that which is "African" by Black women and the simultaneous desire for an affirmation of that which is "American?"

A spiritual return to Africa is absolutely necessary for the reintegration of that which was lost in our collective historical past and the many national pasts which comprise it. The role which Africa plays in determining our historical identity has been systematically de-emphasized. Without the presence of Africa in our lives, we would not be able to feel a sense of unity while at the same time existing as a Black people with avatars in Africa, the U.S., the French-Caribbean, and the Hispanic-Caribbean.

Is this preoccupation with a spiritual return to Africa something you share with other Afro-American writers?

I am not certain that they share the same concerns as I do. For example, Ralph Ellison, a writer whom I admire immensely, is of the opinion that as Blacks in the U.S. originate from a distinctly North American historical, political, and cultural experience, this distinguishes their experience from other Black cultures in the diaspora. In his estimation, as U.S. Blacks issue from a specifically American matrix, they exist as a completely new race of American Black people. As a result, any undue emphasis upon African ancestry is distasteful to him. I am not at all of this opinion. We (as people of African descent) must accept the task of "reinventing" our own image, and the role which Africa will play in this process will be essential.

> As the history of people of African descent in the U.S. and the diaspora is fragmented and interrupted, I consider it my task as a writer to initiate readers to the challenges this journey entails.
>
> —*Paule Marshall*

The way you were adopted as a native daughter on your first trip to Africa was a significant event. Do you now feel a sense of commitment to the burning economic, social, and political problems confronting Africa?

Yes, and my journey to Africa increased my awareness of the illiteracy, poverty, and repressive dictatorships which still exist in many African nations after years of independence. But, I do believe that Black women in the U.S. and the diaspora can play an important role in alleviating many of these problems. When we who live in technologically advanced societies arrive at a consciousness of ourselves as a collective force organized to combat problems impeding Black development on an international scale, then we will be able to contribute to the future well-being of Black peoples around the world. The question poses itself as such: "How can we (as Afro-American and Afro-Caribbean women) be more effective in the world?" First, in liberating ourselves from the inferiority complex imposed by the colonial system whose vestiges are still with us. Once reconciled with ourselves, we can begin to impose our own point of view, and, in this way, make ourselves useful in the struggle for the liberation of our brothers and sisters in Africa.

Isn't the notion of Blacks from technologically advanced societies liberating Blacks from non-technologically advanced societies a little paternalistic?

I don't think so, because the problems confronting Blacks in Africa and the diaspora in terms of economic and political development have not resolved themselves, and continue to persist. Take Harlem, for instance. The same system of economic inequality there also exists in the Caribbean.

Does this Africa which we must "reinvent" in our own image really exist?

Here, you are referring again to the notion of the spiritual return to Africa. Again, I must insist that, for me, this journey is not just a dream. I know that I am a product of Western civilization, but nevertheless, I need my African references.

There has been a lot of talk about the existence of a universal "African" language, which predated the imposition of the European colonial tongues by scholars of linguistics and Black women writers such as Toni Cade Bambara. What do you think about this notion?

I think that it's true. In the West Indian dialect and Black American English I employ in my work, there is a certain African dimension. It comes to me naturally as I grew up

around people who were veritable "griots," such as my mother and friends. For them, memories of the legacy of slavery were very active. It was revealed in conversation about the daily humiliations they had to endure while working as domestics for white people. These oral conversations were therapeutic, for as I described in *Brown Girl, Brownstones,* when they gathered together to talk about the day's humiliations, a healing process occurred which prepared them to face the next day. These oral conversations (part of the oral tradition in Afro-American literature) provided me with the raw materials for my novel. I learned from them how to define the contours of a character. I was never able to capture their wonderful oral art on paper. English did not seem to suit them. These oral conversations drew upon folktales, proverbs, metaphors, and images. "The sea ain't got no back door," for instance, is an expression which comes to mind. I come from a people for whom language is an art form, and, for me, this sense of language comes from Africa; not to mention a sense of theatre which is profoundly African. It was my mother and West Indian friends who really taught me how to write. (pp. 52-3)

> *Paule Marshall and Maryse Condé, in an interview, translated by John Williams, in* SAGE: A Scholarly Journal on Black Women, *Vol. III, No. 2, Fall, 1986, pp. 52-3.*

Ebele O. Eko

Paule Marshall's [*Praisesong for the Widow,*] about which little has been written to date, is not only a chronological continuum of her exploration of growth and maturity processes, it seems in itself a journey's end, a mission accomplished, a "breaking forth into joy" of the essence of Black soul. The author advocates that the Black writer's burden should be one of recreating Black history in heroic terms with the abundance of folk tradition around them. *Praisesong for the Widow* is in that sense a duty fulfilled. It celebrates the triumph of Africa's indomitable and collective spirit, thus bequeathing to her Black readers, a new sense of pride and confidence in their heritage. At the same same time it raises the consciousness of non-Black readers unto deeper appreciation of a long misunderstood and misrepresented culture. The double reaction which this novel elicits, is deliberately anticipated in one of Marshall's most summative and assertive statements:

> I have always felt that one of the reasons the white man in this country has been so hard on us is that he suspects we have something going for us that he doesn't have anymore, that he has lost. How shall I define it—an expressive quality, a strength, that comes from suffering, a feel for life that hasn't been leached out of us by a fat, complacent, meaningless existence, a basic health in the midst of sickness around us, and that once given the opportunity for this to come to flower, we would be formidable people. Our task as Negro writers is to prove this right.

This paper intends to examine in depth, one of the major ways Paule Marshall achieves her aim of proving her assertion right. The focus shall be on the author's use of traditional elements, first to make possible the unity and interpretation of the novel's four-part structure on individual and collective levels. Secondly oral traditional elements will be analyzed as they are used to link characters and act as vehicles for psychological therapy. The paper will demonstrate that healing of fragmented selves, rediscovery of lost identity and a repairing of bridges of communication between peoples that share a common heritage is only possible through an honest confrontation with one's past and a positive attitude towards one's heritage. By the same token, the paper will show through contrasting of characters, that a rejection of one's past and heritage can only lead to loss of direction and of life's essence. Putting it another way, in the author's own words, the paper will try to show how Black culture speaks "of becoming even in the face of bare bones and the burntout ends."

The four part structure of this novel indicates a clear broadening of base, even larger than what John McCluskey sees as a broad base in Marshall's second novel, *The Chosen Place, The Timeless People,* which embraces "the historical collective encounter of cultures." In *Praisesong,* there is a reaching back to dead ancestors and a reaching forward to unborn generations. The most fascinating part is discovering the organic relatedness within the novel's parts and between them, which linkages culminate in the essence of wholeness.

On the first level, the plot delineates the archetypal journey into awareness from "Runagate" (running away from . . .); to "Sleeper's Wake" (awakening to a shocking reality); to "Lavé Tête" (washing away false mentality); to "Beg Pardon" (the reconciliation with one's heritage). "Runagate" recalls slavery times when threats of corporal punishment precipitated slaves into confused flight. The novel opens with sixty two years old Avey Johnson, the protagonist, frantically packing her six suitcases for flight from the luxury liner, Bianca Pride, barely five days after setting sail on a two week cruise in the Caribbean. Agitated and bewildered, she has no concrete reasons to offer for her haunted behavior, and like a slave, she can hardly recognize her own image: "Her mind in a way isn't even in her body or for that matter in the room." A self doubt triggered by her daughter's criticism of the cruise has escalated into hallucinations after a vision of her long dead great Aunt Cuney, who seems supremely determined to force Avey face to face with her past, her roots and her heritage. She directs her to the highly symbolic Ibo Landing in Tatem, which is a key to that heritage.

"Sleeper's Wake" lends itself to two interpretations. Literally, it could be the wake for Avey's husband, Jerome Johnson, who died the year before. More likely, it is a wake for Jay Johnson, the true self of Jerome, who died unnoticed on the terrible Tuesday of '45 when things fell apart for the couple. It could therefore be a wake or funeral for the beautiful marriage of Jay and Avey which was killed off by their materialistic ambitions. "Sleeper's Wake," in another but related sense, is the awakening of a sleeping Avey, from the stupor of her bourgeois mentality to a sudden realization of all she has lost, all they have

sacrificed in terms of happiness and life-giving values in order to acquire a house in a white neighborhood:

> the little private rituals and pleasures, the playfulness and wit of those early years, the host of feelings and passions that had defined them in a special way back then.

"Lavé Tête" chronicles a cleansing ritual, a head washing, shedding of false image or washing off stuffy mentality. The sudden awareness and tragic sense of loss which makes Avey mourn the life of Jay instead of Jerome's death, forces her into a violent rejection of the root cause: her bourgeois values. That rejection is captured symbolically and dramatically through her excruciating and long-prolonged vomits. Ironically, it is in her moments of greatest weakness that she finds the greatest sympathy and moral support from her fellow passengers. None is repulsed, not even when like a naughty baby she soils her pants. Their approval rather than criticism of her purgation reveals that the process is natural, commonplace and indeed anticipated. All seem prepared to help the novice over the toughest part of her initiation process. It echoes in a very vivid way, the African communal involvement and deep empathy with young initiates during their rites of passage—the painful act of circumcision that marks a readiness for new life and new responsibilities.

"Beg Pardon" as the name implies, is the final stage in the growth process of awareness, when the cultural prodigal comes home to beg pardon of her offended ancestors. In preparation for the feast and celebration that mark all initiations, Avey is thoroughly washed, oiled, massaged and dressed. Psychologically, she is now ready, willing eager; no longer persuaded or coerced. Avey is finally standing on her feet and choosing for herself:

> "Do you think you might still like to come to the Big Drum? See what it's like?" . . . She held up a hand to stop him; spoke strongly
>
> "Of course I'm going! That's what I took the trip for!"

Avey has finally understood the significance of her heritage. Like a treasure lost and found again, it has grown in worth. Her acceptance and participation is conscious and even enthusiastic. That quality is part of her heritage and links her directly to the Shouters in the Black Church at Tatem, the excited Harlem holiday crowd on Bear Mountain, their golden days of married life in Halsey Street and the gay colorful dancers of Carriacou. All these are linked in turn to the deliriously excited generations of initiation candidates in Africa.

> All of her moving suddenly with a vigor and passion she hadn't felt in years, and with something of the stylishness and sass she had once been known for "Girl you can outjangle Bojangles."

On another level, the four parts of this novel broaden out to represent crucial historical stages in the Black experience. "Runagate" reminds one of slavery, that terrible historical wrong which Africans and Americans alike wish to forget. Jerome's fierce struggle upwards is to move away from all reminders of that past, "back you know where" as he used to say. But according to a Tiv proverb, "once a great wrong has been done, it never dies." Nana, the grandmother of Anowa in Ama Ata Aidoo's play *Anowa* tells her inquisitive daughter that "All good men and women try to forget." But the precocious child wants to remember, to know. She asks "what happened to those who were taken away? Do people hear from them? How are they?" Slavery is so central to understanding the Black man's history and mentality in America, that it must be faced honestly by Blacks and whites alike before the hurts can finally be healed. Marshall's message here, as in other parts of the book, is essentially the same. In Leela Kapai's words, it is that "Beyond the barriers of race, all men are the same; they share the same fears, the same loneliness and the same hopes. And they cannot live as islands; the bridges of communication have to be built."

One can equate "Sleeper's Wake" to the historic cultural and literary awakening of American Blacks, and by extension Blacks everywhere, through the Harlem Renaissance. It recalls parallel movements like Negritude and Haitian Renaissance in Africa and the Diaspora. Like Avey, Blacks have been brainwashed through slavery and colonialism to hate their self-image. The passionate longings of Pecola in Toni Morrison's *The Bluest Eyes* is only an aspect of what North White Plains and The Bianca Pride represent for the Johnsons. This stage is therefore, an awakening to a profound truth (credited to Karl Marx), that a people without history can easily be persuaded.

The "Lavé Tête" (head washing) is in historic terms, a parallel to the angry sixties in the United States and the overthrow of colonialism in most African countries, also in the 1960s. Just as a culminating crisis of awareness forces Avey into violent double purgation of everything in her system, a long history of oppression and injustice culminated in the bursting of the dam of Black patience. Led by politicians, thinkers and artists as Avey is guided by the old and wise Lebert Joseph. Blacks everywhere began to shed their false identity, often with violence. Negation and rejection of white values in America parallel the total rejection of British colonialism and French assimilation policies in Africa. Brainwashing is here reversed into washing off of slavery and colonial mentality from the brains of Blacks.

The "Beg Pardon" represents the historic physical and psychological move of Black Americans towards their roots in Africa since the 1960s. Led by African tourist guides as Avey is helped by Rosalie Parvay, physical pilgrimages and psychological rituals have been carried out, as if to appease the ancestors, and give their "remembrance" by rebuilding broken bridges to African roots. The willing participation of Avey recalls the enthusiastic trips of Blacks to Africa: their adoption of Afro hair style, corn rows, dashikis and their determination to prove that "black is beautiful." What we are witnessing and what Black women writers like Zora Neale Hurston, Paule Marshall and others are emphasizing through much use of oral tradition in their art, is a much needed rapprochment of Blacks everywhere on all levels of interaction and on much more serious notes than rhetoric. The mutual nature of this is symbolized by what happens as Avey participates in the Creole Dance:

> She too moved—a single declarative step forward. At the same moment, what seemed an arm made up of many arms reached out from the circle to draw her in.

Besides the structural unity which this novel achieves through the exploration of Black identity and its history, there is an even deeper level of wholeness and gap bridging achieved through Marshall's skillful characterization. While some characters act as links between the dead and the unborn, others are paralleled and contrasted to demonstrate the critical role of cultural awareness and its acceptance in the psychological health of individuals and groups alike. Attitude is what makes all the difference between characters. Their experiences lead one to believe that a positive attitude to one's heritage, even after going astray, leads one back to self-fulfillment and life-nurturing values. A negative attitude, on the other hand, leads to selfishness, sterility, loss of identity and a hankering after empty materialism.

Jay and Avey Johnson of Halsey Street, before the fateful Tuesday of '45, present a rare and refreshing picture in Black literature of a happy, loving couple and strong family unit. Jay is depicted as a hardworking, dependable family man who spends time creatively with his family and whose wit and sensibility keep the love between him and Avey young and sweet:

> "What's your pleasure this evening, Miss Williams?" calling her by her maiden name.
>
> "Will it be the Savoy, Rockland Palace or the Renny again?"
>
> "Oh, I don't know," she would say, entering the fantasy with him.
>
> "Why don't we . . . "
>
> "Your wish, ma'am, is my command."

The novel makes it clear that the confidence and contentment in this marriage comes from acceptance of self and one's roots. Jay is proud of his father, a man of confidence with a distinguished looking winged moustache. Jay models his own after his daddy's. He also shows clear evidence of a balanced cultural nourishment from diverse Black artists and musicians. The best of jazz and blues are sacred to him; they administer healing and strength at the end of each day to his tense and work-worn body. Above all, the practical application of these life renewing values of his culture makes him that witty, down-to-earth and passionate husband that Avey Johnson is later to mourn so disconsolately. Jay's unquestioning belief in the heroes of the Ibo Landing identifies him with their courageous spirit and his family's yearly trip South, further links him securely to his roots.

Avey shares her husband's love for music, dance and poetry. Her balanced sense of identity, though unknown to her, has its source deep in the cultural influences of her childhood. Even before her birth, as well as by her naming process, she is linked to Avatara, her ancestor, whose mind is said to have gone back to Africa with the famous Ibos. Her annual visit to her old Aunt Cuney since the age of seven has linked her securely to an eye-witness account of a legend which is so central to Tatem's history and hers. Aunt Cuney performs an annual ritual of retelling the miracle of Ibo-Landing. In vivid colors, this archetypal storyteller narrates how a group of Ibo slaves landed in Tatem, sensed future tragedy through their double vision, then within minutes, turned around chains and all, and walked right back to Africa on water. The legend is rife with potent symbols, and so sacred is this story to Aunt Cuney that she tolerates no scepticisms. In a quiet but dangerous voice, she quenches little Avey's doubts about the authenticity of the miracle of the Ibos walking on water:

> "Did it say Jesus drowned when he went walking on water in the Sunday School book your momma always sends with you?"
>
> "No ma'am."
>
> "I din' think so. You got any more questions?"
>
> She had shaken her head "no."

Avey Johnson's Tatem taproot has many fibrous ones. The Ring Shout she and Aunt Cuney often watched in Tatem, unknown to her, links her to the timeless people of Bournehills [in *The Chosen Place, The Timeless People*] whose similar anticlockwise tramp (designed to stay the course of history) is later re-enacted in the Carriacou Nation Dance, linking all participants to far-away African tribes: Temne, Banda, Avada, Moko, Cromanti, Congo, Chamba, etc. The fibrous roots of the Dance ritual spread out to enfold in one embrace the dancing Avey and Jay with the Juba dancers of slavery days, the Harlem crowd dancers, all dancers to the jazz and blues records of Harlem, the creole dancers and the colorful Durbar dancers witnessed by Marion in Ghana.

Jay and Avey of Halsey Street are clearly soul mates, sharing similar interests and values, living in harmony. In sharp contrast is the new relationship that slowly emerges after that notorious Tuesday. The schism between Jerome Johnson and Avey Johnson starts with a slow but steady moving away from all the little rituals that held the seams of their family life together. Endless work demanded by new ambitions take Jay away from his family, away from the healing music of his relaxed evenings, away from the Sunday rituals so dear to his children, away from Harlem and her dances, away from love. Even the simple but highly symbolic action of shaving off his moustache, takes away from him, in his wife's words, "the last trace of everything that was distinctive and special about him." The yearly trip south to their heritage is soon forgotten, so are old friends and old tested values. Their new links are with the Masons and the Elks, with snobbish upward-bound Blacks like the Moores, with the white folks of North White Plains who tour the Laurentians of the Arctic Circle rather than Africa.

The Johnsons' new mentality is characterized by what Peter Nazareth summarizes as the cutting off from roots, a chasing after status and identity with the white community, and a looking down on the lower classes. Avey's bourgeois image is that of "1940s upsweeps and pompadours and vampish high heeled shoes." She confesses to being embarassed by her earlier headstrong ways and high feelings. Indeed, the superimposed face which Avey no-

tices with shock on her husband is also on hers. The "strange pallid face" has an equally strange voice; that of one who views "the world and his fellow man according to a harsh and joyless ethic":

> "If it was left to me I'd close down every dancehall in Harlem and burn every drum! That's the only way these Negroes out here'll begin making any progress!"

Their new dignity creates distance, and soon husband and wife can only refer to themselves by their formal names.

Characters associated with Avey Johnson after she quits Bianca Pride can also be grouped into two: those with links to their roots and those without. Lebert Joseph, who plays a leading role in redirecting Avey Johnson's wandering steps, is Paule Marshall's artistic reincarnation of the Yoruba diety, Legba. Eugenia Collier notes: "Legba is the liaison between man and the gods. He is vital to numerous rituals, both in West Africa and in the new world." In this role, Lebert Joseph links the spirit and physical worlds, the ancestors with the living and the unborn. Like Legba of the crossroads, Lebert meets Avey at her crossroads, and firmly, gently and craftily leads her back to her roots, to a unified African world view.

Paralleled to Lebert Joseph is his daughter, Rosalie Parvay, a carbon copy of her father in her manner of walking, speaking, even thinking. In her contact with Avey, she complements the priestly role of her father, by performing on her the ritual of washing, oiling and laying on of hands, preparing her for the final process in her initiation. Like her father, Rosalie is deeply rooted in Carriacou customs. She is positive and proud of her heritage. Her gentle, tactful and firm guidance, links her with the matrons of Mt. Olivet church and the older Carriacou women on the boat Emmanuel C, whose chorus of "Bon, Li bon oui" helps Avey through the nightmare of her double purgation.

A final and more far-reaching linkage takes place during the "Beg Pardon." The communal supplication rituals cover everyone present and absent, drawing unto them the pardon and blessings of their ancestors. Full participation in the rituals of drumming, dancing and celebrations is an affirmation of their African roots, and Black brotherhood. The climactic Creole dance (for all people), symbolically brings the protagonist fully back:

> She moved cautiously at first, edging forward as if the ground under her was really water . . . She was doing the flatfooted glide and stamp with aplomb. And she was smiling to herself, her eyes screened over.

It is a smile of triumph, of one who has lost and found a treasure, of a prodigal daughter finally come home. With her self introduction as Avey, her initiation is complete, and she is ready to become a transmitter of heritage to her grandchildren and other children as well. She will become a story-teller like Aunt Cuney.

The losers are the unaware and the separated. The taxidriver confesses to unique values among Carriacou people—"All the out-islanders is like that. Serious people. Hardworking . . . They's a people stick together and helps out the one another." But he does not understand the source of their cultural pride, nor the sense in their annual excursion. A kindred spirit to the later Jerome Johnson, the driver dismisses with a careless wave of the hand, the beauty of his childhood playground but proudly shows Avey "a long column of Miami beach-style hotels." Paule Marshall's pen is sharp with criticism:

> "What did I tell you? Plenty hotels oui!" His *blind man's smile* in the mirror was equally proud. "That is all we got 'bout here now." (emphasis mine)

The other losers are the children and grandchildren of Lebert Joseph, whose absence he mourns bitterly, lost to him and to their rich heritage, faraway in Canada and America:

> "Josephs who has never gone on the excursion! Who has never been to a Big Drum! Who don't know nothing 'bout the nation dance!"

These are of the new generation of Blacks who are ignorant of their roots, because their parents like Komsoom, the bourgeois in *The Beautiful Ones Are Not Yet Born,* are too busy pursuing the gleam and aping the white culture to impart any cultural heritage to their children.

In conclusion, this analysis has shown the clever way Paule Marshall integrates oral traditional elements to achieve unity of plot in historical dimensions, and also in unifying and contrasting characters. The author has set out to prove a thesis: that one should never curse one's roots because the acceptance or rejection of one's heritage determines an individual's and a people's level of freedom, uniqueness and self-fulfillment. Her singleness of purpose is admirable, but it has also meant a regrettable underdevelopment of potentially interesting characters like Thomasina, Clarice and Rosalie, whose brief existence leave definite marks on the reader's mind. In accordance with the thesis also, one identifies and remembers clearly the images of the earlier Avey and the later Avey in Cariacou. The rest of her remains rather a blue, like a ghost lost in the wastelands and blasted years of confused self-image.

Finally, this writer sees in this remarkable work, a microcosm of the great vision which Black women writers seem to have caught from their grandmothers: rediscovering and emphasizing the common language, rituals, approach to life and unifying legends and beliefs among Blacks everywhere, from Africa, to America, to the Caribbeans and parts of South America. Paule Marshall has caught this vision from the outset, and her powerful umbilical cord symbol summarizes the unity as well as the need to preserve and treasure the values that are uniquely Black:

> What seemed to be hundreds of slender threads streaming out of her navel and from the place where her heart was to enter those around her . . . [then] issuing out of their navels and hearts to stream into her as she stood there . . .

Paule Marshall has followed this vision in her works both on the historical, cultural and political levels, perhaps more closely than any other Black writer, male or female. *Praisesong for the Widow* is indeed a landmark in Black literature. (pp. 143-47)

Ebele O. Eko, "Oral Tradition: The Bridge to Africa in Paule Marshall's 'Praisesong for the Widow'," in The Western Journal of Black Studies, *Vol. 10, No. 3, Fall, 1986, pp. 143-47.*

Abena P. A. Busia

In "Lave Tete," the third book of *Praisesong for the Widow,* old Lebert Joseph accosts Avey Johnson with the question, "And what you is? What's your nation?"; both the question and the passionate manner of its asking throw Avey into confusion. Yet in its answer lies the key to her self-understanding. What follows is a reading of this novel to unearth the many cultural signs the widow needs to recognize or acknowledge, in order to answer that central question. Paule Marshall's project in this deceptively simple novel is a remarkably bold one. This novel becomes a journey not only for Avey, but for her readers, for to appreciate the widow's experiences fully, the reader must journey with her in the same active process of recognizing and reassembling cultural signs.

When the novel opens, the heroine, Avey Johnson, is about to interrupt a luxury cruise through the Caribbean Islands to return home to North White Plains, New York. But the journey she eventually takes instead is one she could never have anticipated. Both the interrupted journey and the unexpected journey take on great significance as metaphors of the progress of her life, a life whose meaning she no longer understands. By the end of the journey, that life has taken on new meaning, and it becomes a representative journey for all New World diaspora children.

In speaking of this work as a diaspora novel, I read it alongside such novels as Alice Walker's *The Color Purple,* Ama Ata Aidoo's *Our Sister Killjoy,* Michelle Cliff's *Abeng,* and Maryse Conde's *Heremakhonon,* among many others—novels by black women throughout Africa and the African diaspora which tackle questions about women reclaiming their stories in a context in which storytelling becomes part of a larger project of self-revalidation.

Storytelling is here one of a wealth of nonwritten cultural forms that must be reinvested with meaning. The validation of such forms within the work is a part of that lifelong process in Marshall's writing which led Edward Brathwaite to celebrate her, as many as fifteen years ago, as a novelist of the "African Reconnection." The meaning of Africa in this (con)text is vital for Marshall, for whom reconnecting the scattered peoples, on the shared foundation of their African heritage, has been a continuing theme. In this work she gives her most thorough examination to date of the dynamics of this relationship. Along with the inheritance of stories, such elements as the efficacy of dreams and the ritual of song, dance, and drama are all delicately woven into the fabric of the tale, as Avey examines the tapestry of her life, to piece together again those parts that were becoming unraveled.

Marshall's concern is to take us through a journey of self-recognition and healing. Her text requires of us that we have a knowledge of "diaspora literacy," an ability to read a variety of cultural signs of the lives of Africa's children at home and in the New World. Marshall articulates the scattering of the African peoples as a trauma—a trauma that is constantly repeated anew in the lives of her lost children. The life of the modern world and the conditions under which Afro-Americans have to live, the sacrifices they must make to succeed on the terms of American society, invariably mean a severing from their cultural roots, and, as Avey learns to her cost, this is tantamount to a repetition, in her private life, of that original historical separation. This is a sacrifice too high. But to understand the nature of the journey and the magnitude of the sacrifice, it is necessary not simply to mark the passage of Avey's journey but to become fellow travelers with her. It is not only Marshall's heroine, but Marshall's readers as well who need to acquire "diaspora literacy." For to do so is to be able to see again the fragments that make up the whole, not as isolated individual and even redundant fragments, but as part of a creative and sustaining whole.

Thus the first task for the reader is to learn, like the widow whose journey we experience, to recognize the cultural signs of a past left littered along our roads of doubtful progress. The crucial factor about *Praisesong* is that it is a novel about the dispossession of the scattered African peoples from their past and their original homeland and, in the present, from their communities and from each other. The boldness of Marshall's project here is to take us through a private history of material acquisition and cultural dispossession, which becomes a metaphor for the history of the group, the history of the African in the New World. The challenge therefore is not to look at literacy or cultural artifact as abstraction, but as a concrete aspect of our lives, where our meaning—our story—becomes what we can read and what we can no longer, or never could, read about ourselves and our lives. The act of reading becomes an exercise in identifications—to recognize life experiences and historic transformations that point the way toward a celebration, a coming together attainable only through an understanding and acceptance of the demands of the past, which are transformed into a gift for the future.

This project is undertaken by giving us a text full of signs and allusion which each reader responds to differently and thus reflects, each in his or her own way, the experience of the widow. For example, an Afro-American reader who recognizes lines from the songs of Nina Simone, but for whom the Carriacou Tramp has no meaning or resonance, will experience the journey differently from a West African such as myself, for whom the opposite is true; the ceremonies for the dead on Carriacou may resonate with meaning while references to specific blues songs go unremarked. The experience of the widow's journey is relived differently, depending on how many, and which, of the many cultural icons and codes within the text the reader can register.

These gestures of significance that need to be registered begin, even before the first word of the novel had been read, with the words of title, *Praisesong for the Widow.* For Africans, a praisesong is a particular kind of traditional heroic poem. Sung in various communities over the entire continent, praisesongs embrace all manner of elaborate poetic form, but are always specifically ceremonial so-

cial poems, intended to be recited or sung in public at anniversaries and other celebrations, including the funerals of the great. Praisesongs may embrace the history, myths, and legends of a whole people or their representative and can be used to celebrate communal triumph or the greatness of rulers, and the nobility of the valiant and brave, whether in life or death. Important for its use here, they can also be sung to mark social transition. Sung as a part of rites of passage, they mark the upward movement of a person from one group to the next. This novel therefore celebrates for the widow her coming to terms with her widowhood—a reconciliation that has greater implications than a coming to terms with the loss of an individual husband only. The whole narrative in itself acts as a "praisesong" for the widow, with the narrator as the griot. Specifically also the title refers to the communal song and the dance of the "beg pardon" at the end of the novel, which themselves become a praisesong for the widow in homage to her homecoming.

Praisesong for the Widow is a tribute in praise of the homecoming of a woman who succeeds in making an awesome physical and spiritual odyssey. Avey's epiphany is presented to us as an arduous progress through a partially familiar landscape littered with cultural artifacts as clues. The widow's narrative becomes a map, with music, song, dance, dress, and ritual as the cultural registers we need to decode to follow her across the terrain to journey's end. But journey's end is Africa. By the end of her journey, Avey has symbolically reversed the diasporic journey and recrossed that wrenching middle passage. Through Avey's life Africa is once more reinvested with worth, the continent is no longer fractured from human history but restored to consciousness with valid meaning. Through the healing of one of Africa's lost daughters, a scattered people are made whole again, and the question "What is your nation?" is no longer a bewildering and devastating mystery.

By the time Avey understands the meaning of that mystery, she also knows that years before, as a child, she was given the key to answering it through a story told by her Great-Aunt Cuney. In this work, storytelling is not only a metaphor for cultural self-possession and wholeness, it is a literal injunction. The quest the widow is embarked on culminates in her taking upon herself the mantle, bequeathed by her Great-Aunt Cuney, to tell the story of the African slaves at Ibo Landing. This story, though it plays a complex symbolic part within the text, is itself a simple one: Avatara's Great-Aunt Cuney takes her to the landing and narrates that the Ibo slaves had arrived at that very point on the river, by boat from the offshore slave ships, but as soon as they set foot on shore had stopped. Without a word they had studied the place and, with deep vision, had seen the whole history of slavery and suffering that awaited them all there, and had stepped out, shackles and all, and walked firmly upon the water with nothing to stop them, heading back home again to Africa. This story serves in the text as the representation of spiritual understanding and the will to survive and triumph. In taking it upon herself as her legacy, the widow finds a meaning to her own personal journey, which then also transcends the self and the family. She becomes a griot for the collective whole, recounting the story which represents the saving history of the group, and thus finds a way to look to the future without rendering the past valueless.

However, the journey to inherit this story is in itself, within the text, made up of more than the recognition of the importance of the story of the slaves at Ibo Landing. For the widow, storytelling, including the telling of her own story which we see in process, must be undertaken within a cultural context, a context that includes, as indexes in the composition of her story, aspects such as dress, food, dance, and formal and informal ritual, in addition to words themselves. It is not only the story itself which has meaning, but the circumstances of its telling, a form of ritual acculturation for the seven-year-old Avey:

> At least twice a week, in the late afternoon, . . . her great-aunt would take the field hat down from its nail on the door and solemnly place it over her headtie and braids. With equal ceremony she would then draw around her the two belts she and the other women her age in Tatem always put on when going out: one belt at the waist of their plain, long-skirted dresses, and the other (this one worn in the belief that it gave them extra strength) strapped low around their hips like the belt of a sword or a gun holster.
>
> "Avatara."
>
> There was never any need to call her, because Avey, keeping out of sight behind the old woman, would have already followed suit, girding her non-existent hips with a second belt (an imaginary one) and placing—with the same studied ceremony—a smaller version of the field hat (which was real) on her head.

At the end of her journey Avey resolves to return to Tatem to tell the story her aunt had taught her, with the same words and gestures each time over the years, which Avey had learned in the exact manner her aunt had told it—the way griots inherit through oral transmission the sacred histories of the people. The *form* of their story is what helps memory carry the message, so as a true griot, Avatara learns her incantation and passes it on to her own grandchildren, physical and spiritual, in the same way her great-aunt had learned it from that grandmother whose name she bears. It is the acceptance of the significance of all these factors, which she has spent three decades layering over with the accoutrements of affluence, which she needs to reclaim—to return to the self beneath the expensive clothes Great-Aunt Cuney strips off her with such violence in her dream.

At the point in the narrative at which Avey Johnson is posed the question concerning me here, she is like a postulant being prepared for consecration, and the living Lebert Joseph replaces dreams and memories of Great-Aunt Cuney as the initiate who is to guide her through the final stages of her rituals. The placing of the encounter itself is crucial: it is situated in the book entitled "Lave Tete," with the widow at a moment of crisis; she is fleeing a ship that for her has become an emblem of burning hell, trying to get back to her house in North White Plains. But that house too is under assault as, in her memory, it has be-

come "the museum at the foot of Mount Pelee in the wake of the eruption that had taken place during her absence." That those days in her life which have driven her into Lebert Joseph's presence should be seen as cataclysmic is further emphasized by her reference to the dream of her Great-Aunt Cuney, who "had stood there large as life in the middle of her dream, and as a result there was a hole the size of a crater where her life of the past three decades had been." Essentially, although Avey cannot articulate it, she feels she has nothing to return to, nothing at least to which she can attach any viable meaning. She is in limbo, waiting.

Before Avey can return home she is taken to the farthest reaches of her physical journey, off course, as she sees it, to the island of Carriacou, even called the "out island" by the people of Grenada, which is one of the most easterly of the Caribbean Islands. That is, it is closest, physically, to the home continent of Africa. This physical closeness is simply a physical representation of the spiritual proximity that the widow is to see manifest.

Everything about the placing of that question by Lebert Joseph is important. The widow's journey has been littered with icons of significance which it is incumbent on the widow as postulant, and us as readers and fellow travelers, to recognize. She has come to this moment from the long reflection on what she has lost on the way from Halsey Street to North White Plains, and it is those remembrances that lead her to formulate for herself an intense series of questions. In being visited by the angry ghost of Jerome, Avey is forced to ask herself the central question of her life: Was the price paid for their material success and security truly necessary?

> They had behaved, she and Jay, as if there had been nothing about themselves worth honoring! Couldn't they have done differently? Hadn't there perhaps been another way? Questions which scarcely had any shape to them flooded her mind, and she struggled to give them form. Would it have been possible to have done both? That is, to have wrested, as they had done over all those years, the means needed to rescue them from Halsey Street and to see the children through, while preserving, safeguarding, treasuring those things that had come down to them over the generations, which had defined them in a particular way. The most vivid, the most valuable part of themselves! . . . What would it have taken? What would it have called for? The answers were as formless as the questions inundating her mind. They swept through her in the same bewildering flood of disconnected words and images.

There are in a sense two sets of loss: one set she herself knows as loss; the other she does not even realize she once possessed. For Avey the meaning of loss and the essential spirit of themselves as family and as community are signified for her in the small things she has missed:

> They were things which would have counted for little in the world's eye. To an outsider, some of them would even appear ridiculous, childish, *cullud.* Two grown people holding a pretend dance in their living room! And spending their

PAULE MARSHALL

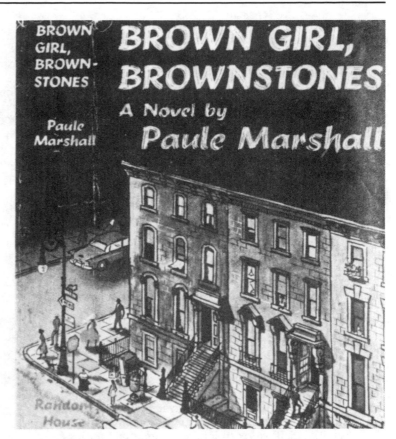

Dust jacket for Brown Girl, Brownstones.

Sunday mornings listening to gospels and reciting fragments of old poems while eating coffee cake! A ride on a Jim Crow bus each summer to visit the site of an unrecorded, uncanonized miracle!

Such things would matter little to the world. They had nonetheless been of utmost importance. . . . Not important in themselves so much as in the larger meaning they held in the qualities which imbued them. . . . Something vivid and affirming and charged with feeling had been present in the small rituals that had once shaped their lives. . . . Moreover, something in those small rites, an ethos held in common, had reached back beyond her life and beyond Jay's to join them to the vast unknown lineage that made their being possible. And this link, these connections, heard in the music and in the praise songs of a Sunday had protected them and put them in possession of a kind of power.

These memories trouble her spirit now because she has killed the joy that was in them, distanced herself from them, without knowing how, and with no reason why. They no longer are a living aspect of her life, but exist only as treasured memories. When she recollects them, they are still lifes, emblems of those dancing selves long disappeared. In this respect they bear the same relationship to her life as the dances Lebert Joseph speaks of bear to the Afro-American and Afro-Caribbean community at large.

The acknowledgment of their importance is dramatized through the steps of a different, more ancient, dance.

Avey's journey, which is to end in the first steps of this ancient dance, had started years before, on that same walk to Ibo Landing, which would always take her past the small church, filled with the elders taking part in the Ring Shout:

Through the open door the handful of elderly men and women still left, and who still held to the old ways, could be seen slowly circling the room in a loose ring.

They were propelling themselves forward at a curious gliding shuffle which did not permit the soles of the heavy work shoes they had on to ever once lift from the floor. Only their heels rose and fell with each step, striking the worn pineboard with a beat that was as precise and intricate as a drum's. . . . They allowed their failing bodies every liberty, yet their feet never once left the floor or, worse yet, crossed each other in a dance step.

By the end of her journey, Avey is to find herself dancing such a dance, and her journey is a carefully worked out reincorporation of song, dance, and ritual, specifically as it relates to the recognition of continuing African traditions. It is for this reason that Avey's physical journeying ends with her participation in the sacred excursion to Carriacou, a ritual that only those who share in it appreciate. Her guide on this trip, and central to her understanding of the meaning of her private journey, is the old man Lebert Joseph.

Lebert Joseph recognizes the vital importance of those traditions that carry history and meaning—the nation dances and the songs associated with them. It is these cultural forms which are sacred, for, as he demonstrates to Avey with the Bongo song about Ti-Walker and Zabette, they carry the myths and legends of the origins of the people and their histories of pain, triumph, and survival. It is the festival, its rituals and the oral culture surrounding it, which keeps the sacred unity of the group. And their significance is beyond any contemporary "reality"; thus for Lebert Joseph the word *Juba* still resonates of a once great imperial seat "from memories that had come down to him in the blood" rather than the "forgotten backwater that it has become."

However, it is important to recognize Lebert Joseph himself as an iconographic figure. Old Lebert Joseph in this text performs the role of the deity Legba. The name given in Ewe religious practice to the god of households and thresholds, and to the Yoruba god of crossroads who is the messenger of the gods, is, in Afro-Caribbean practice also, the lame god of crossroads. It is he who acts as the widow's guide, leading her back, at this crossroads in her life, to those ancestors whose spirits she has neglected or sacrificed, in order to move her onward. The association with the ancestors, and of him as guide, is made very clear. After his initial taciturn reception, in indignation over her ignorance of his origins, he starts chanting his lineage "like some Old Testament prophet chronicling the lineage of his tribe." Furthermore, like the Ibos of the landing, he is farsighted and can read spiritual histories. Avey knows when she meets him that his penetrating look "marked him as someone who possessed ways of seeing that went beyond mere sight and ways of knowing that outstripped ordinary intelligence and thus had no need for words." When they eventually arrive in Carriacou for the festival, even the physical description of this lame old man serves to underscore his relationship to the gods. The widow sees him almost as an apparition just at that moment when his function is to guide her into the realm that is going to reunite her with her past; like all gods of crossroads he walks before her into the unfamiliar realms through which she must travel. When she has made this last crossing of her journey, over the threshold into the ancestral home where the Beg Pardon takes place, she will then be able to tell of her origins.

It is this ability to tell her own story which is the final end of the tale, and when she meets Lebert Joseph and first asks him for shelter, she cannot answer his question about her self. In mythic terms, Avey is the traveler who must first find the answer to the question of origins before she can return home. It is the memory of Great-Aunt Cuney and the presence of Lebert Joseph which are to serve as her compassionate, but relentless, guides to this mystery. Lebert Joseph recognizes how hard a thing it is not to be able to name one's true nation and, like Great-Aunt Cuney, recognizes that Avey needs to learn to do this to be restored. Therefore, as Great-Aunt Cuney had waylaid

her in her dream and forced her back to Ibo Landing, so Lebert Joseph hijacks her to Carriacou.

Before she arrives there, however, on her journey out, she has a series of important recollections of other journeys—childhood journeys to Tatem as commanded by Cuney, to spend her summers making that most central of journeys, the walk to Ibo Landing, to hear narrated the story of those slaves who walked on the waters back to Africa. She also recalls, while standing on the wharf:

> Boat rides up the Hudson! Sometimes, standing with her family amid the growing crowd on the pier, waiting for the *Robert Fulton* to heave into sight, she would have the same strange sensation as when she stood beside her great-aunt outside the church in Tatem watching the elderly folk inside perform the Ring Shout. As more people arrived to throng the area beside the river and the cool morning air warmed to the greetings and talk, she would feel what seemed to be hundreds of slender threads streaming out from her navel and from the place where her heart was to enter those around her. . . . Then it would seem to her that she had it all wrong, and the threads didn't come from her, but from them, from everyone on the pier, issuing out of their navels and hearts to stream into her as she stood there. . . . She visualized the threads as being silken, like those used in the embroidery on a summer dress, and of a hundred different colors, and although they were thin to the point of invisibility, they felt as strong entering her as the lifelines of woven hemp that trailed out into the water at Coney Island. If she cared to she could dog-paddle (she couldn't swim) out to where the Hudson was deepest and not worry. The moment she began to founder those on the shore would simply pull in the silken threads and haul her in.

> While the impression lasted she would cease being herself; instead, for those moments, she became part of, indeed the center of a huge wide confraternity.

In fact her first recollection is not of this journey, but of the film presentation given by her daughter and spiritual sister, Marion, of a trip she had made to Ghana. The colors, sounds, and "pageantry of umbrellas" of the milling tide of people beside her reminded her of Marion's home movie. It is this recollection of Ghana that first makes the scene on the wharf so familiar and subsequently reminds her of that boat ride up the Hudson River to Bear Mountain. The triple link of communal history is thus complete, from Ghana to the Hudson River of her childhood, to Carriacou, through Tatem—because Tatem also is associated with the feeling of unity symbolized by her image of the silken threads, when standing with her great-aunt watching the worshipers at the Ring Shout. It is important that all the locations, both the north and the south of the United States, the Caribbean Islands, and Africa, the home continent, are embraced in this memory of the connections made by the silken threads.

But the reconnection is not only in this symbolic perception. That the widow is on a physical journey which ends in a dance is a fundamental part of her restoration, and this journey of restoration to the homeland of Africa is as painful as that of initial separation. There is a deliberate sudden and abrupt evocation of the middle passage as the widow from the United States crosses to Carriacou and remembers Africa:

> It was nearing dusk and the *Emanuel C* was almost to port when the pall over Avey Johnson's mind lifted momentarily and she became dimly conscious. She was alone in the deck house. That much she was certain of. Yet she had the impression as her mind flickered on briefly of other bodies lying crowded in with her in the hot, airless dark. A multitude it felt like lay packed around her in the filth and stench of themselves, just as she was. Their moans, rising and falling with each rise and plunge of the schooner, enlarged upon the one filling her head. Their suffering—the depth of it, the weight of it in the cramped space—made hers of no consequence.

That is, on her spiritual journey from the New World back to Africa, she reverses the middle passage and very specifically relives the original journey from Africa to the Americas. In doing this she also, in meaning, reverses the location of the promised land, which now, rather than being the United States as represented in the prosperity of the plantations or, today, the Fulton Street of Jerome's success, becomes Africa as represented by Carriacou.

On the day she meets the old man who is to take her to Carriacou, he is closing shop to go to the annual festival at Carriacou to hold the "Big Drum" for the "Old Parents," as he calls the ancestors. Each time he goes home, he goes to give them their remembrance, to feed them, and to beg pardon and ask their care for all of them, present and absent, including those who, like Avey, do not know they belong. When Lebert speaks, Avey thinks he has lost his mind, but these are recognizable ceremonies. Such supplications to the ancestors are still done to ensure the safe return of loved ones and to celebrate and give thanks for their safe arrival when the ancestors and the gods comply.

Furthermore, in her remembrance of Marion's talk about Ghana, she recollected Marion speaking of a New Yam Festival and of feeding the ancestors. This ritual, when Lebert Joseph mentions it to her, seems strange to Avey. Yet when it actually happens, this too seems quite normal, as it reminds her of a burial in Tatem where the old man's favorite foods had been prepared and laid beside the coffin. Thus these seemingly meaningless rituals from Ghana and fragmented memories from her childhood in Tatem are reconnected here in Carriacou; in Lebert Joseph's festival we have the link made—the survival of a festival that is culturally both religious and social in origins and purpose. It keeps the whole community of the living and the dead united, and keeps all the forces of life in harmony for another season. The ancestors must be remembered for their continuing protection, and failing to keep their memory alive leads to the destruction of the community.

Yet these rituals of remembrance are not simply idiotic romance on the part of the old man. The significance of his passion comes to Avey when she finally arrives at the feast itself and sees what a small, pathetic-seeming gathering it is:

> The bare bones. The Big Drum—Lebert Joseph's much vaunted Big Drum—was the bare bones of a fete. . . . To her surprise though she felt neither disappointment nor anger. Rather she found herself as the time passed being drawn more and more to the scene in the yard. The restraint and understatement of the dancing, which was not really dancing, the deflected emotion in the voices were somehow right. *It was the essence of something rather than the thing itself she was witnessing.*

Everything that has happened to the widow since her meeting with Lebert Joseph has been a ritual preparation for this moment: she has been prepared spiritually through the ordeals of her two dreams, of Jerome and Great-Aunt Cuney, and her recognition of her spiritual orphanage; she has been prepared physically by being purged on the sea voyage, by vomiting and excreting everything inside her; and she has been prepared ritually and reminded of the essential unity of the body and the soul by being bathed for absolution like a supplicant by Lebert Joseph's daughter Rosalie Parvay.

It is at the festival that we perceive the significance of all the various folk motifs that have run through the text, as the opening "Padone Mwe" movingly gathers in the scattered of the families for whom prayers must be said. Culminating in this familiar festival, the folk elements show the survivals as across the diaspora and are the physical representation of those metaphysical silken threads that the child Avey sees on the boat trip up the Hudson. This is a festival of music and dance, and in the instruments too we have clear reference to the traditional music of parts of the African continent, as they have been reformed and adapted to the Caribbean landscape and lifestyle. The use of the drums and instruments of iron, in their adapted form, serves the same function and purpose as their still extant African counterparts; thus rum kegs covered with goatskin replace Onyame's duruwood and hide, but the instrument is played the same way, and to the same purpose. Similarly, the cowbells and hoe blades, instruments of iron for Ogun—"Iron calling for its namesake and Creator." But it is the occasional plaintive note of the drum, interrupting its own rhythmic beat, which reminds them why they are all there:

> The theme of separation and loss the note embodied, the unacknowledged longing it conveyed summed up feelings that were beyond words, feelings and a host of subliminal memories that over the years had proven more durable and trustworthy than the history with its trauma and pain out of which they had come. After centuries of forgetfulness and even denial, they refused to go away. The note was a lamentation that could hardly have come from the rum keg of a drum. Its source had to be the collective heart, the bruised still-bleeding innermost chamber of the collective heart.

And in recognition of keeping this collective heart in memory, the festival begins with the nation dances, as each people dances their attendance and recalls their own names in memory of who they are and have been.

But for Avey it is when she joins the old people in their movement counterclockwise round the group of young dancers in the Carriacou Tramp, "the step which was something more than just walking," that the telling moment comes.

> Because it was a score of hot August nights again in her memory, and she was standing beside her great-aunt on the dark road across from the church that doubled as a school. And under cover of the darkness she was performing that dance that wasn't supposed to be dancing, in imitation of the old folk shuffling in a loose ring inside the church. And she was singing with them under her breath: "Who's that ridin' the chariot/Well well well . . ." The Ring Shout. Standing there she used to long to give her great-aunt the slip and join those across the road.

> She had finally after all these decades made it across. The elderly Shouters in the person of the out-islanders had reached out their arms like one great arm and drawn her into their midst.

The recognition of the origins of the Ring Shout, and its role in her private life as well as in the life of the community, restores to wholeness the fragmented communities and makes the link across waters and boundaries of generation and time. When Avey dances, the out-islanders pay her the homage of recognition, and this time when she is asked who she is, she can reply by saying her correct, given name, Avatara.

The widow's name is Avatara, a name given her by her father's Great-Aunt Cuney in memory of Cuney's own grandmother, whose name it was. Great-Aunt Cuney had dreamed months before Avatara was born that she would be a girl and sent word that she should be called Avatara because "it's my gran' done sent her. She's her little girl." The name, therefore, which has at its root a word meaning a passing over or a human manifestation of a continuing concept or entity, is of great symbolic importance; it was the name of the woman from whom Great-Aunt Cuney learned, at Tatem, the story of Ibo Landing, which carries the spiritual burden of the tale, and it is the name given by her to the woman who finally understands that tale and accepts the mission to pass it on.

The homage of the old people is for her a kind of homecoming, and in fact the following day they inform her that they think they can tell her nation by the way she danced the Carriacou Tramp. The question she was asked barely twenty-four hours before she can now answer. The festival may only have been "the bare bones of the feast," but it is the dance, and not how it may be described, which proves truly vital. Avey Johnson must learn the reason to dance the restorative ritual dance of Beg Pardon. And having remembered her own steps from the Ring Shout of her childhood, she is then able to retell the story of Ibo Landing. This story, about the miracle of survival, liberty, and the will to live, is the story whose continued existence in and of itself represents that same spirit of survival and cultural inheritance passed down through the ages. Story-

telling, like song singing, becomes cultural metaphor and the carrier of cultural meaning. This is Avatara's true inheritance. But she must remember the dance and do that first, before she comprehends the necessity of her heritage of speech.

And she begins to dance, with the passion with which she had once danced for her young husband Jay, but, like the old people at Tatem, without once ever letting the soles of her feet leave the ground; she remembered the ancient rule still observed on the mainland continent for such dances, and danced a dance that was sacred, "the shuffle designed to stay the course of history." (pp. 196-211)

> *Abena P. A. Busia, "What Is Your Nation?: Reconnecting Africa and Her Diaspora Through Paule Marshall's 'Praisesong for the Widow'," in* Changing Our Own Words: Essays on Criticism, Theory, and Writing by Black Women, *edited by Cheryl A. Wall, Rutgers University Press, 1989, pp. 196-212.*

Marshall on women in her fiction:

Women do figure prominently in my books. . . . And I'm concerned about letting them speak their piece; letting them be central figures, actors, *activists* in fiction rather than just backdrop or background figures. I want them to be central characters. Women in fiction seldom are. Traditionally in most fiction men are the wheelers and dealers. They are the ones in whom power is invested. I wanted to turn that around. I wanted women to be the centers of power. My feminism takes its expression through my work. Women are central for me. They can as easily embody the power principles as a man.

> *Paule Marshall, in Alexis DeVeaux's "Paule Marshall: In Celebration of Our Triumph,"* in Essence, *May 1979.*

Angelita Reyes

Two writers deeply concerned with personal experience as it illuminates external history are Paule Marshall and Toni Morrison. Marshall's *Praisesong for the Widow* and Morrison's *Tar Baby,* both published in the early 1980s, explore the relationship of personal and documented history and how that relationship affects collective cultural values. Personal history is translated through metaphors of myth and ritual. By using historical and personal metaphors, the authors imply that African-Americans need to connect to those aspects of culture and heritage which are psychologically empowering. Indeed, for both Morrison and Marshall, personal histories and extended cultural metaphors are paradigms of African-American history. Through the representation of metaphor and the presentation of history, the two authors write against the indiscriminate acquisition of Euro-American cultural values which allow African-Americans to forget African heritage, or as Morrison characterizes it, to forget their "ancient properties." The ancient properties are essentially rooted in the *connected* consciousness of the African past.

Social and legislative efforts at integration and the emergence of a distinct black bourgeoisie, in addition to the renewed consciousness regarding women's rights, have caused some blacks to be dominated by *Euro*-American, rather than *African*-American values. These Euro-American values are fundamentally middle-class operatives of capitalism, which means, in part, the attainment of happiness through the quest for and acquisition of "things." The [con]quest continues in that the objective is material wealth just as it was for the founding conquerors of the Americas. El Dorado now translates into a modern quest for owning things even if it continues to mean the preemption of place, property, and people. But displacement and preemption are not only on economic grounds—there is psychological and spiritual preemption as well. In the metaphoric context of El Dorado, people have their sense of worth only when they can own through [con]quest. And in some instances, they still want to own other people. Throughout *Tar Baby* and **Praisesong,** we see how events rooted in history and mythic thought conflict with the social consciousness of bourgeois American materialism. Certainly, Marshall and Morrison do not reject economic progress. The problem is to reach and maintain a compromise between material excess and spiritual propriety. By assuming a balance between Euro-American culture and African-American heritage, the community can better attempt to keep its feet on the nurturing ground. [Chikewenye Okonjo Ogunyemi notes that, as] *womanist* writers, Marshall and Morrison deal with

> a philosophy that celebrates black roots, the ideals of black life, while giving a balanced presentation of black womandom. It concerns itself as much with the black sexual power tussle as with the world power structure that subjugates blacks. Its ideal is for black unity where every black person has a modicum of power. . . .

American womanist interpreters are dynamic feminists in that they believe that women and men are complementary—neither should exist mutually exclusive of the other. These women are mother-women to themselves, to other women, and to their immediate family. They have a commitment to the community and larger society in that they are aware of the social injustices and, according to their circumstances, actively participate in building the new order. This is simultaneously the difficulty and the richness of the womanist experience in America. Womanism emphasizes a certain continuity of strength. . . . Womanist discourse sees an inherent empowerment in the heritage of the extended African-American family rather than in the Euro-American nuclear family. There is the need to acknowledge self and kin. As Marshall clearly indicates, the sustaining values come from the kin who still walk and breathe as well as from the ancestors who have passed on. Furthermore, these values are primarily sustained through the culture-bearer of the community, that is to say, the woman who is not necessarily a biological parent, but [as Robert Stepto has observed] a "sort of umbrella figure, a culture-bearer in that community with not just her children but all children." As culture-bearers,

women are primary transmitters of the culture and its traditions. In the same instance, much of the contemporary literature indicates that the culture-bearer is not an earth-mother stereotype. (pp. 180-82)

Both Paule Marshall and Toni Morrison illuminate a tradition which is not ashamed of being religious and spiritual in order to cope with social injustices and cultural dilemmas. Marshall's widow, Avey Johnson, experiences the final phase of her historical and mythic ritual process through the sacred invocation of her ancestors, the Old Parents, in the immediacy of the Big Drum's Beg Pardon dance. Cultural and spiritual values are reappropriated for Avey because of her ancestor, Great-Aunt Cuney. Great-Aunt Cuney is not only one of the Old Parents, but she is also a *Great* Mother in that she provides archetypal guidance by returning to Avey through dreams. As I have indicated, the significance of mother is not limited to its biological meaning, but rather transcends biological expression to include woman as a parent of spiritual culture. Jadine [of *Tar Baby*] is adopted by her aunt and uncle after the death of her parents. Yet, she does not have a daughter's kind of caring for them. Avey Johnson reclaims the rights of daughterhood (as the younger woman paying homage to the older woman, Great-Aunt Cuney) and spiritual womanhood.

Paule Marshall demonstrates that despite the many difficulties, Euro-and African-American values can be bridged. Marshall resolves the tensions. Avey is able to connect the bridges; Jadine chooses not to connect her two worlds. She is unable to mediate between the spiritual world of her ancestors and the contemporary materialistic world of Europe and America. By using paradox, Morrison shows that building cultural bridges is tenuous for some, and sometimes not even desired. **Praisesong for the Widow** and *Tar Baby* both explore how materialism and the need to control other people can block a person's and the community's spiritual and cultural visions.

Paule Marshall's literary nurturing began in the "Bajan" community of Brooklyn, New York. Marshall fully credits the Barbadian mother-women of her childhood for providing her with such a rich source of cultural inheritance: African, African-Caribbean, and American. Of her own mother, Marshall writes: "She laid the foundations of my aesthetic, that is the themes and techniques which characterize my work." Her childhood years were not only shaped by the "unknown bards," these mother-women, but marked by the materialism of the West Indian community. As she depicts in her first novel, **Brown Girl, Brownstones,** the community is caught in the materialistic web of "this white man country." Their El Dorado is expressed through the determination to accumulate consumer commodities and to own "de house" (if not several) at any human cost. Their brand of materialism is an extension of Middle Passage denials and attempts to legitimize their worth. Selina, the central figure in **Brown Girl,** rebels against those values. Although she claims herself as a child-product of America, she also affirms herself as a child of the Caribbean, and by spiritual consciousness, of Africa. Her coming of age is testimony to being an American woman-child with a West Indian heritage. Marshall says of this representation:

> The West Indies is so very important to me because it is part of a history that as a girl I tried to deny. I went through torture as a girl growing up in Brooklyn, going to school with those heavy silver bangles on my wrists, and when we went to the West Indies and came back with heavy West Indian accents, the kids used to laugh at us. It was dreadful. Now the West Indies represents an opportunity for me to fill in something I tried to deny, and it provides me with a manageable landscape for writing. . . .

With her third novel, *Praisesong,* Marshall continues to explore the dynamics of the West Indian cultural landscape, and its African heritage. The very title of the novel attempts to celebrate cultural transition and African continuity.

In traditional Africa the praisesong is a chant or poemsong which dramatizes the achievements of an individual or community within the realm of history and extended family. Performed by the *griot* or *griotte,* the oral historian, genealogist and musician, the praisesong is a highly developed "genre" in African oral literature. It is both a sacred and profane modality. In Marshall's invocation of praise-singing we see how the sacred overlaps with the profane reality. Avey Johnson's praisesong fulfills a vital function: it allows her to create a new opportunity for spiritual empowerment as she learns a new understanding of social propriety. At this point, some clarification is necessary as to how I am applying the concept of spirituality and religion, which is arrived at from within an African cultural matrix.

Traditional African philosophy and religion are characterized by sacred forces interwoven into the quotidian life of the community. Few valid generalizations can be made about a continent so vast and culturally diversified as Africa. However, among the few, it can be affirmed that religiosity as a pivotal force among African peoples. In his comprehensive study of African religions and philosophy, theologian John Mbiti maintains that, "Africans are notoriously religious. . . . Religion is the strongest element in traditional background, and exerts probably the greatest influence upon the thinking and living of the people concerned." For many non-Western peoples in general and African peoples in particular, there are no distinct boundaries between the sacred and profane. Historian of religions Mircea Eliade formulates the theory of the myth of the eternal return regarding the sacred: human beings can perpetuate enactments of the sacred and constantly share in a "trans-human" communication with the divine. Sacred activities are not reserved for "Sundays" and holy days only. African peoples consider all reality as potentially sacred. Furthermore, other worlds exist, but *in* this world. As Western cultures emphasize the *seen* experience in the material and concrete world, African peoples have traditionally acted as technicians of the *unseen*—the spiritual world.

When Africans were brought to the Americas, they brought with them their sense of religiosity: that human existence is fundamentally an ontological phenomenon and that religiosity is a central modality of that existence. The trauma of the Middle Passage did not sever New World Africans from their ancestral concepts of religiosity. In the New World, traditional religiosity shared its potentials and beliefs with New World Christianity. Attempting to survive their bondage, the neo-Africans incorporated their traditional beliefs into strategies for survival strength and psychological empowerment. Lawrence W. Levine states:

> The slaves' expressive arts and sacred beliefs were more than merely a series of outlets or strategies; they were instruments of life, of sanity, of health, and of self-respect. Slave music, slave religion, slave folk beliefs—the entire sacred world of the black slaves—created the necessary space between the slaves and their owners and were the means of preventing legal slavery from becoming spiritual slavery.

Unequivocally they were legal slaves but not spiritual slaves. Out of an African spirituality and out of the Middle Passage consciousness, Morrison and Marshall write about the resilience of the oppressed by way of metaphor, history, and story.

A summary of *Praisesong* shows that Avey Avatara Johnson is a comfortably middle-class, self-conscious, elderly widow, who on a Caribbean cruise with two friends abruptly decides to leave the ship. When the ship docks for a few hours on the Caribbean Island of Grenada, she disembarks and plans to fly back to her home, New York City. Significantly her trip has been jolted by recurring dreams of her long dead Great-Aunt Cuney of Tatem, South Carolina. Destiny intervenes and she misses the plane to New York only to get involved in the annual festival of the "out-island" people—people of the smaller island, Carriacou—who live and work in Grenada. The excursion back to their native land (Carriacou and by way of myth/ritual, Africa) is in fact their annual rite of rejuvenation, their rite of the eternal return, their trans-human communication with the African past and its sacred forces. The Big Drum ceremony is the enactment of their African past, their native land. The dance creates temporal space between reality and the spirit world. By going to Carriacou and experiencing the intensity of neo-African ritual dancing and music, Avey Johnson rediscovers her own sense of place as an American of African ancestry. She rediscovers what it means to bond with people and with the spirit, and not with *things*. As she leaves Carriacou, she resolves to renew her ties with her own ancestral and spiritual home, Tatem, South Carolina.

Avey Johnson's classical journey occurs on two levels: she is, in essence, the heroine embarking on a quest for spiritual enlightenment and renewed strength to deal with the human world. The journey becomes a validation of Avey's American social consciousness. By the middle age of life, Avey has settled for the illusion of El Dorado; that is to say, she has given in to the complacency of upper-middle class living and values. However, the spiritual void in her life began even before the death of her husband. By dividing the novel into four sections with the ritual-implied titles of "Runagate," "Sleeper's Wake," "Lavé Tete," and

"The Beg Pardon," Marshall demonstrates how the journey motif is inherent to Avey's spiritual and social awakening. Through trans-human communication, Avey reestablishes order out of her own chaos. The reestablishment is of primary importance for Marshall:

> I'm trying to trace history. . . . To take, for example, the infamous triangle route of slavery and to reverse it so that we make the journey back from America to the West Indies to Africa . . . to make that trip back. I'm not talking about in actual terms. I'm talking about a psychological and spiritual journey back in order to move forward. *You have to psychologically go through chaos in order to overcome it.* (my emphasis)

One must undergo symbolic death in order to be reborn, in order to overcome the "difficult passage." Marshall is thoroughly aware of the rites of passage revisited among the Carriacouans. Moreover, *Praisesong* is obviously formulated on the structure of a ritual process. From the outset of the novel, Marshall's ritual strategy juxtaposes images of whiteness and darkness to emphasize the themes of spiritual chaos and cultural loss. The luxury cruise ship, *Bianca Pride,* with its superficial elegance, explicitly represents Euro-America and the cruise-culture of affluent American widows. The very name of the cruise ship is purposely chosen by Marshall: it is a symbol of *white* pride. Despite the luxury and material order around her, Avey Johnson is confused because of the dreams she is having of her dead great-aunt who lived in the American south. Significantly, Avey dreams about the times when as a young girl in Tatem, South Carolina, her aunt used to talk about *her* grandmother who actually remembered seeing groups of Africans disembarking from the slave ships. With this focus on the Middle Passage, we immediately see that the old aunt represents that link with Africa, heritage, and history. The great-aunt's sense of place is historic and mythic because her own grandmother knew people who had made the Atlantic crossing.

In keeping with the oral art of "recollectin'," Marshall interweaves history and myth. As a child, Avey visited her great-aunt (although called Great-Aunt Cuney for short, the ancestor is actually a great-great-aunt) during the summers and heard stories of the "stepping Ibos." The aunt had heard the legend from *her* grandmother who never lost sight of the Word, or Nommo, as empowerment. In this instance, Nommo is female energy, for "my gran" functions as a *griotte* (and in turn Great-Aunt Cuney) who preserves the memory of the Middle Passage and its meaning to her family by keeping the tale of the Ibos alive. Avey Johnson recalls this tale about a group of Ibos who were brought to the New World as slaves. However, they are technicians of the unseen and as they survey the new land *they look down into history* and see the calamities and atrocities that are to come. They decide to leave because:

> They seen things that day you and me don't have the power to see. 'Cause those pure-born Africans was peoples my gran' said could see in more ways than one. The kind can tell you 'bout things happen long before they was born and

things to come long after they's dead. Well, they seen everything that was to happen 'round here that day. The slavery time and the war my gran always talked about, the 'mancipation and everything after that right on up to the hard times today. . . . Those Ibos . . . just turned . . . all of 'em . . . and walked on back down to the edge of the river here. Every las' man, woman and chile. And they wasn't taking they time no more. They had seen what they had seen and those Ibos was stepping! And they didn't bother getting back into the small boats drawed up here . . . boats take too much time. They just kept walking right on out over the river.

Such is the story, in part, which Avey Johnson's great-great-great grandmother has told. The tale gives spiritual empowerment to those who have no political power. Believing in the story of the Ibos is one way of affirming heritage and resilience. The tale becomes a *touchstone* for the ability to cope and persevere. The tale is the empowerment of the Nommo. But as a child Avey Johnson never really understood the Ibo story. The dreams of her great aunt are disturbing, and it is not until she undergoes the complete rite of spiritual renewal that the significance emerges. But at this point the dream brings other memories and sorrows to the surface of her consciousness.

Avey Johnson was not always in pursuit of El Dorado. There had been a time in her life when, along with her spouse Jay, she had been in tune with those simple rituals of culture and heritage—the music, the empowering voices of African-American poetry, the dancing, and the visits to Tatem:

> something in those small rites, an ethos they held in common, had reached back beyond her life and beyond Jay's to join them to the vast unknown linkage that had made their being possible. And this link, these connections, heard in the music and in the praisesongs of a Sunday . . . had *both protected them and put them in possession of a kind of power.* . . . (my emphasis)

When as a couple, they began to attain the realities of the American dream—material wealth and upward mobility—they forgot the sacred rituals of their past: Tatem, the tales, the music, their own sensuality. These were the folk materials which provided healing against the difficulties they faced as a black family struggling to overcome racial and economic pressures. Through years of hard work and fighting racial prejudice, Jerome Johnson becomes a man of status and property. However, in the painful effort to be an economic success in Euro-American terms, in the pursuit of the dream of El Dorado, both Avey and Jerome forget the folk modalities which had enabled them to cope with life, which had given them that rich sense of cultural place and spiritual continuity. Through embedded flashbacks, we learn that "All this passed from their lives without their hardly noticing." Jerome stops calling himself "Jay." As an accomplished businessman in the black community, he is "Jerome" to everyone. In showing how the Johnsons undergo a spiritual decline of their marriage and of themselves, Marshall demonstrates how the submission to indiscriminate acquisition of material possessions and success robs people of the inner strengths and traditional inner ability to empower self. Avey realizes that long before she became a widow, she and her husband had died spiritually: they had died on the killing ground of materialism and false cultural values. Marshall's metaphor of death decoded implies that material wealth can generate a false sense of happiness. The newly acquired power is superficial; it is a limiting power that mimics Euro-American materialism. Economic progress is necessary for all Americans. However, the tension lies between economic progress and spiritual maintenance. How do Americans sustain a balance? How do African-Americans bridge the desire for economic progress which has been historically denied, while they simultaneously keep in view the psychic-cultural principles of an African tradition? Economic progress is necessary, but not to the extent of being possessed by the material wealth it offers.

Marshall clearly presents the philosophical position that happiness certainly does not come from material wealth. The Johnsons imagine their joy and contentment as they "arrive" economically. However, their material gain provides only a fleeting sense of happiness. Moreover, their conspicuous progress inevitably grows into a specter and shadow of the past when, although they had very little materially, they at least had the rich capacity to love each other and not things. Undoubtedly, the acquisition of things is as transitory as El Dorado. Although material wealth has its seemingly limitless possibilities, just as it did in the early American conquests, its course proves its own inadequacy for happiness. Those who keep their feet on the nurturing ground can distinguish between transitory modalities of material power and the eternal sources of spiritual empowerment. Marshall demonstrates how happiness that is measured by and restricted to material gain leaves an inner void—a spiritual decadence. It causes Americans of African ancestry to *disconnect* from the Middle Passage saga of struggle, survival, and spiritual propensity. Happiness derived from material wealth may be translated into secular power, but it is not *empowering*. Along with other womanist interpreters such as Alice Walker, Gayle Jones, and Toni Cade Bambara, both Marshall and Morrison attest in their writing that when African-Americans share in the material wealth of mainstream American society, they seem to move away from the inner resources—spiritual, psychological, social and artistic—of empowerment and coping. As Morrison indicates, the pursuit of material wealth limits and defeats all people: Valerian Street, the wealthy American capitalist in *Tar Baby,* ends up not only physically and mentally out of sync with reality, but spiritually dead.

Through a series of carefully directed incidents situated by the author, we see how Avey Johnson returns to the nurturing ground. She must experience symbolic death in order to be rebirthed into a new awareness of self, myth, and history. The old man whom she meets in Grenada, Lebert Joseph, represents (like Great-Aunt Cuney) the African connected consciousness in the Americas. For Lebert Joseph is the African and African-American confluence of the mythic deity Legba. Lebert Joseph corresponds to Papa Legba in Haiti, Papa La Bas in the southern United States, Esu-Elegbara in Nigeria, and Legba in

Benin. Brought to the New World during the Middle Passage, Legba is personified by an irascible old man who usually carries a cane and limps. One leg is shorter than the other because part of him is in the spirit world and part of him moves in the world of the living. In some instances, he manifests both female and male energy. As the Guardian of the Gate, the Crossing, or the Threshold, Legba is a force of destiny who mediates between gods and human beings. In the context of *Praisesong,* Marshall employs Lebert/Legba to further the ritual structure of the novel: he becomes the messenger, the interpreter, leading the central character further along her journey and finally to the threshold of the spirit world in order to rebirth to the world of the living. It is essentially because of Lebert/Legba, this spiritual messenger, that Avey comes to an understanding of her great aunt's presence in her consciousness. As an interpreter, Lebert/Legba knows that Avey Johnson is one of the people who has lost sight of her spiritual "nation" and needs to be reincorporated.

Throughout the narrative, Marshall continues to juxtapose dreams into a fusion of the past and present. In some instances, the fusion of embedded flashback leaves the reader confused about the time sequence of events especially when Avey is thinking/dreaming of the immediate past of her childhood along with remote past of her ancestors. The symbolic significance of the events in the journey motif are eventually clarified when it is understood that Avey must experience a crossing over and must be led to the Threshold in order to be cleansed and rebirthed.

Led by Lebert Joseph/Legba, Avey Johnson moves closer to the Threshold of historic and mythic time, closer to understanding the implications of Middle Passage and El Dorado history. The excursion to Carriacou symbolizes this psychological return into history—it is the difficult passage for her. The actual turbulence of the excursion invokes not only a symbolic enactment of the middle crossing, but the turbulence of the excursion invokes not only a symbolic enactment of the middle crossing, but the turbulence of American [con]quest and preemption. Avey Johnson must be purged of the unnecessary self and experience the symbolic return to the womb, to the unconquered landscape of the New World and her native land. The women who assist Avey on the boat ride during this turbulence of mind and collective history are like the mother-women of Marshall's own life. They are also the historic culture bearers—the primary interpreters of culture and spirituality. Indeed, the women who help Avey are very much reminiscent of "mothers" in Baptist churches who help passengers who suddenly are possessed by the Holy Ghost from harming themselves. The women on the *Emanuel C* (again such obvious symbolic naming implies Marshall's didactic narrative position) assist the elderly widow like spiritual mothers. Like technicians of the unseen, the mother-women know that Avey needs to be protected and needs to be renurtured at this point in her life. They approve of Avey's seasickness. She must be purged of material comforts, make the symbolic return, if necessary even by literally defecating on herself. She is humiliated as an adult in order to regain honor:

> she had the impression as her mind flickered on
> briefly of other bodies lying crowded in with her

in the hot, airless dark. A multitude it felt like lay packed around her in the filth and stench of themselves, just as she was. Their moans, rising and falling with each rise and plunge of the schooner, enlarged upon the one filling her head. Their suffering—the depth of it, the weight of it in the cramped space—made hers of no consequence.

The "depth of it" is the suffering and conquest of a people. Paule Marshall is such a politically engaged writer that at times her writing leaves little for the reader's imagination. She forces her audience to join that political engagement, leaving little space for anything else. In *Chosen Place,* Saul Amron, a Jewish development expert, dwells on the same issue of historical suffering, past and present, when he says: "It's usually so painful though: looking back into yourself; most people run from it. . . . But sometimes it's necessary to go back before you can go forward, really forward. And that's not only for people—individuals—but nations as well. . . . " By using extended Middle Passage and El Dorado metaphors, Marshall explicates her recurrent theme of knowing one's heritage in order to move forward. Avey Johnson must remove the trappings of conquest mentality in order to move forward and build. *Praisesong* is about an individual figure, but in the larger context, the character of Avey Johnson is a vehicle for Marshall's socio-political engagement.

The novel climaxes with Avey Johnson moving into liminal space with the Carriacou islanders during the Big Drum Dance; she ceases to be a runagate running and stumbling in darkness. In the circle of the dance, we see the rituals and movements of neo-African people coming together: from the "nations" of Africa emerge the "Banda, the Cromanti, the Temne, the Congo." The description of the Big Drum is the accumulation of embedded symbolism leading toward the meaning of history, myth, and story. The dance itself is both spiritual rejuvenation and a necessary relief from the everyday struggle of economic survival because undoubtedly, the people understand the reasons why they ritually return to Carriacou. The ritual dance is a social and spiritual connection with friends and with culture. Moreover, it prevents the islanders' alienation. In other words, the dance is a touchstone of their cultural sensibilities and spiritual needs. As a collective group, the people are not possessed by conquest and materialism. The Big Drum presides, enabling them to keep the channels of trans-human communication open. These people do not have to search for an identity since they already know who they are. They make the annual return to the past—to their native land (the metaphor of the eternal return)—in order to live the present and future. Therefore, the Big Drum rite of passage is their spiritual affirmation rather than part of a spiritual quest as it is for Avey Johnson. For people who are close to their rich source of myth and history, such rituals are consciously necessary and unconsciously enacted. The richness of their cultural and spiritual ties attests to their wealth of inner resourcefulness.

The end of Avey Johnson's excursion to Carriacou marks the beginning of her being able to empower self through a rekindled knowledge of the self in relation to society.

Until her trajectory into the past, Avey Johnson had succumbed to the bourgeois quest for modern El Dorados. Using Caribbean and African-American ethnological idioms, Marshall demonstrates how the Middle Passage and El Dorado become extended metaphors of history which can help the community to rebuild itself and move forward.

Paule Marshall was once referred to as a "writer's writer." This phrase was used in the most complementary way. Considering Marshall's socio-political consciousness, it would certainly seem that she would want to write for the so-called masses as well. Whatever audience Marshall had in mind as *Praisesong* was being created, the novel materialized with heavy doses of ethnology and social idealism. *Praisesong* reads as a forced palimpsest of metaphors—politics, religiosity, history, ethnic rituals, and myths—which leads to ubiquitous enlightenment and ritual salvation. The force of the "message" overshadows Marshall's style and her own sense of language. In general, Marshall insists on defining history by weaving the memories of slavery into contemporary patterns of American life. From Marshall's perspective, the Avey Johnsons of America cannot exist outside of Middle Passage history. The "unexpected" spiritual journey enables Avey Johnson to reappropriate her own set of values and return home (her home in White Plains, New York, represents those who have "made it"), with a renewed sense of cultural spirituality. Therefore, like Merle Kinbona in *Chosen Place,* and Selina in *Brown Girl,* Avey arrives at a neat and assured awakening of what has to be done in order to stay the course. If only everyone *could* stay the course. At least, however, Great-Aunt Cuney does not insist that posterity has to relinquish economic gain; she only dramatically insists on paying homage to one's collective history and spiritual heritage. Marshall's metaphors of materialism and spirituality lead to inevitable awakenings. Her characters consistently converge at the gate of absolute enlightenment, enter the ritual process, and *remember* how to invoke history and reconnect. From this perspective, Marshall compromises with her interpretation of history because such absolutism is a romantic approach to history, myth, and social-political issues. Decidedly, in the African-American/African context, spiritual reconnections can be powerful and all-consuming, as Toni Morrison's most recent novel, *Beloved,* depicts. But stylistically Avey Johnson arrives all too suddenly and completely to her climax of enlightenment as she makes the decision to return to Tatem and Great-Aunt Cuney's sense of place. Avey Johnson is reincorporated happily and neatly. Undoubtedly, Marshall is a womanist interpreter. However, in *Praisesong* Marshall becomes an idealist failing to recognize where prescribed mythic events end and social reality takes over. (pp. 183-93)

Angelita Reyes, "Politics and Metaphors of Materialism in Paule Marshall's 'Praisesong for the Widow' and Toni Morrison's 'Tar Baby'," in Politics and the Muse: Studies in the Politics of Recent American Literature, *edited by Adam J. Sorkin, Bowling Green State University Popular Press, 1989, pp. 179-205.*

Leela Kapai on Marshall's literary beliefs:

[Paule Marshall] seems to be quite in agreement with some of the tenets of the much discussed black aesthetics, and yet she differs too. Miss Marshall also stresses the need for identity. She too believes in understanding of one's past, both individual and historical. She too stands for reviving the African cultural heritage which gives supremacy to man over the machine. She too believes that the black writer owes a great responsibility to himself and to his world, to express his views to the world through his art. But here she diverges. Her works show that she does not believe that the art of the black writer should serve only one end. Like several other writers, she knows that the American writer cannot deny his Western heritage. She is equally proud of her black heritage but believes that her art should be devoted to showing the relationship of an individual to the other inhabitants of this world, no matter what their color, race, or geographic location is. She writes of blacks, very often of West Indians, simply because a writer writes best when he makes use of what he knows best. Her characters are, therefore, human beings first; their racial identity is secondary so far as the art is concerned. This fact does not make her any less believer in black pride; in fact, her pride stems out of her deep confidence.

Leela Kapai, in her "Dominant Themes and Technique in Paule Marshall's Fiction," in CLA Journal, *September 1972.*

Hélène Christol

> People who can't call their nation. . . .
> You ask people in this place
> what nation they is and they look
> at you's madman.
> —Paule Marshall, *Praisesong for the Widow*

Paule Marshall began her career as a writer when black American women's literature was at a major crossroad, a crossroad that became the starting point for the contemporary black women writers' thrust forward to a courageous revision of American history, society, and literature from a black feminist perspective. Marshall's first novel, **Brown Girl, Brownstones,** which she published in 1959, not only built upon qualities that characterized earlier black women's fiction; it also anticipated key features of the black women's novel that would only burst fully into blossom and mature in the 1970s and 1980s. As the black critic Barbara Christian has demonstrated in her essay "Paule Marshall: A Literary Biography," her insistence in this novel on the relationship of woman as self and as part of a community reminded the reader of Zora Neale Hurston's *Their Eyes Were Watching God* (1937) or Gwendolyn Brooks's *Maud Martha* (1953), but also prefigured the major themes of Toni Morrison's, Alice Walker's, and Ntozake Shange's works.

Brown Girl is a black woman's retrospective rewriting of a transitional phase in the history of the American woman, that is, the 1940s seen with the eyes of the late 1950s. Indeed, **Brown Girl** can be viewed as a true novel of intersections. Written at and about a time when Marshall was just beginning to explore the implications of her racial, social, and sexual status, the book reflects the uncertainties of a period in which new interpretations of women's roles in terms of race, gender, and society had to be developed. If the forties, in which the novel is set, had seen a significant rise in female employment, wages, and unionization, the postwar years were years of testing and discussions about the proper limits of woman's place in the economic and social world. The debate was open, the answers still ambiguous. (pp. 141-42)

Despite fine reviews, [**Brown Girl**] was a commercial failure—Barbara Christian mentions that when she first read it, it was used as a book for juveniles, just as Morrison's *The Bluest Eye* (1970) would be later on. Yet [as Christian notes] it launched Marshall into the process of "figuring out for herself her own mode of expression." Various works followed: **Soul, Clap Hands and Sing** (1961), **The Chosen Place, The Timeless People** (1969), short stories like **"Reena"** (1962), **"Some Get Wasted"** (1968), **"Barbados"** (1982), and finally, *Praisesong for the Widow* (1983), whose essential aim [Alexis de Veaux claimed] was to describe "the materialism of this country, how often it spells the death of love and feeling and how . . . black people must fend it off." This is a permanent theme in her books, which all explore the relation between personal growth and cultural and social change. They skillfully balance myth and history, the individual and society, tradition and change.

Brown Girl is a book of origins: it started Marshall's search for a true political perspective, which she would only achieve twenty years later with **Praisesong for the Widow.** In an article entitled "Whose Child? The Fiction of Paule Marshall," John Cooke underlines Marshall's evolution by quoting two different analyses that she had made of **Brown Girl.** In a 1959 interview, she mentioned that the book aimed at describing

> a fairly common place experience on the American scene: the adjustment of an immigrant people to the American culture. In [her] case, it was the experience of the West Indian immigrant in America, specifically the Barbadian West Indian who settled largely in Brooklyn and created a somewhat exotic little world of his own there. [Her] efforts were to capture the whole sometimes painful process of the two ways of life meeting and merging to create something distinctively new.

She thus described the novel in terms of oppositions and conflicts that characterize any kind of ethnic literature and define the process of acculturation; in the end, the "something new" which is created is embodied in the children of the second generation, in **Brown Girl**'s central character Selina Boyce. In 1973, fourteen years and a few books later, she viewed the same work somewhat differently:

> I wanted to express through the study of this black family how overemphasis on the material which is the national ethic often destroys the ability to care and feel for each other. In the novel, the mother's obsession with acquiring

property in the form of old brownstone rooming houses alienated her husband and her children. Her unquestioned acceptance of success as defined by the society spells the death of love.

As pointed out by Cooke, this comment was to a certain extent misleading: first, it identified the culture of the book as black, whereas in *Brown Girl,* Marshall still distinguished American blacks from Bajans. On the other hand, it made the conflict between mother and family much more clearcut than it really is. As for the theme of the death of love, it is indeed a central theme, but it remains much more ambiguous than she made it out to be in 1973. Obviously, by the end of the 1970s, after two decades of black and feminist protest and the new rise of black nationalism, Marshall had acquired a much clearer vision of her conceptual framework which explains her new interpretation of *Brown Girl.*

The novel itself, however, claims its own ambiguity, as shown in Selina's final words: "My trouble was that I wanted everything to be simple—the good clearly separated from the bad—the way a child sees things." Indubitably, the "nation" the author was able to define in *Praisesong* was still an uncharted land for her heroines of the 1940s, Selina and her mother Silla. Yet, *Brown Girl* was to open new perspectives that would finally be of use to the Avatara of *Praisesong.* "Calling your nation," which implies a clear definition of identity, involved the necessary growth of personal, but also of social, racial, political, historical, and sexual awareness, an awareness which for Marshall would only be gained in the act of writing itself. Its basis was, however, suggested in the story of the Bajan women of *Brown Girl,* who passed on to the writer "the rich legacy of language and culture . . . in the wordshop of the kitchen."

A closer analysis of the elements with which and against which they define themselves in the text can provide some clues as to Marshall's search for and insights into possible definitions of a black female identity. With *Brown Girl,* as with most of her other works, Marshall selected a traditional form for her explorations. As she stated in **"Shaping the World of My Art,"** she held that the traditional novel was for her a vital form since it permitted her "to operate on many levels and to explore both the inner state of her characters as well as the words beyond them." Looking inward and outward at the same time was the strategy that she constantly adopted in her major works.

Brown Girl certainly looks inward, since it first presents itself as a *Bildungsroman;* it describes the growth of its heroine, Selina Boyce, who is ten years old when the story begins in 1939 and eighteen when it ends. The book follows the different stages in her development, as she goes from innocence to experience, testing the various phases, doubts, fears, hopes, enthusiasms, and conflicts of an archetypal adolescent girl. Small incidents leading to large revelations or genuine epiphanies, friendships, conflicts with her parents and family, puberty and its physical and mental manifestations, the discovery of her sexuality, all these events bring her to a new awareness of herself, gradually unifying and clarifying the fragments of the mosaic that surrounds her. For Marshall, the self is certainly the

first "nation" a girl has to define, and Selina is one of the first woman characters in black American literature with a conscious interior life. As in *Invisible Man*—Marshall herself emphasized the influence that Ellison's works had on her first writings—*Brown Girl* describes the journey of the fragmented self through experience to knowledge and ultimately, though the ending is still ambiguous, to wholeness and being.

In Selina, Marshall has created the perfect agent for this search; throughout the story, the heroine remains an explorer, a marginal woman on the fringes of the world, as shown by her symbolic absence in the family photograph. She is strong-willed, rebellious, different from her other friends who conform, or from her docile, silent sister. The contrast between Selina and the other adolescent girls of her age establishes her singularity. Selina's inability to come to terms with her filiation or to find her place makes her the source and center of unresolved tensions: she is part of her Bajan group, yet at odds with it; part of her feminine community, yet at odds with it; part of the white world, yet at odds with it. The ending of the novel finds her still searching: "That was the quest. . . . What was at the center—love, a clear vision, a place?" Like black women's novels of the 1970s and 1980s, Marshall's defies closure. Her protagonist Selina still has to find that clearer vision that she only sees darkly among the contradictory elements of her environment and of her life.

Thus the personal quest remains open: the heroine is left alone, playing the invisible music of her isolation, "the sole survivor amid the wreckage." Yet she has discovered on the way that freedom, identity, and the creation of an ethic must not only be the responsibility of the individual but also imply some amount of self-imposed alienation from the larger community. In this sense, *Brown Girl* is a novel of the 1950s, since in the very choice of the form itself, it emphasizes the odyssey of the philosophical I, the existential quest, and it downplays the role of environmental elements in the construction of the self. An essential innovative aspect, however, came from the tone of the narrative voice. The novel, by insisting on a woman's perspective, provided the writer with the heroic and philosophical qualities necessary to initiate the quest, making of Selina the first of a long line of similar heroines, ranging from Paule Marshall's Reena to Toni Morrison's Sula and Ntozake Shange's Betsey Brown.

On the other hand, Marshall's "worlds beyond" are never presented as mere backdrops or as abstract stages on which the central heroine plays her individual roles. They establish themselves dialectically at the heart of the story, providing it with specific social, economic, and cultural patterns that interweave with the fates of its main characters. The crucial interaction of these elements makes *Brown Girl* one of the first works of an ethnic literature that would fully unfold only in the 1960s and 1970s. Of course, at times it still tries to transcend racial/ethnic definitions of identity by appealing to the concept of the "human nation," as is shown, for instance, in Clive's statement: "You cannot admit that you are only Negro, some flat, one-dimensional bas-belief figure which is supposed to explain everything about you. At some point, you have to break through to the larger ring that encompasses us all—our humanity. . . . We're men, caught with other men within the common ring." Yet Clive is, after all, a negative reference in the novel, a character unable to come to terms with his own contradictions, a mentor whom Selina finally leaves behind as she goes on with her search.

Brown Girl does not evade the "tired race theme"; on the contrary, Marshall enriches it by adding to it a new ethnic dimension. The community she describes is the West Indian community which, even if it is black by its skin color, forms a distinctive group which in *Brown Girl* has not yet recognized its kinship with American blacks; it is determined to study the dollar and imitate whites by exploiting blacks. In fact, the book develops three essential themes linked to both black and ethnic definitions of identity: it probes the problems linked to invisibility and acculturation; it underlines the necessity for an ethnic community to rediscover and reconstruct its past; and finally, it stresses the importance of the ethnic group itself as both culturally and historically nurturing.

As in Ellison, invisibility is the concept that links together the personal and racial motifs. Selina tells Clive: "The funny feeling you get is that they don't really see you." Clive retorts: "Who knows what they see looking at us? Some of them probably still see in each of us the black moor tupping their white ewe or some legendary beast coming out of the night. The Devil. Sin . . . the whole long list of their race's fear." "They" is of course the white world which, even though it stays in the background, is ever present in the text. Represented in the novel by white characters like Margaret's mother, a caricature of white paternalism who reveals to Selina "the full meaning of her black skin," white society is constantly evoked as being economically, socially, and personally repressive, limiting opportunities and creating conditions which are destructive to both the personality and the person herself.

Thus, white society is partly responsible for Deighton's death, because in its materialism and racism it turns a blind eye to the dreams and ambitions of Selina's father. The white world determines the place and values of the West Indian community. It even decides its physical survival: World War II, denounced by Silla as "the white man war," maims Deighton in its factories and precipitates his downfall.

More insidiously, the West Indian immigrants are described as falling prey to the American dream, an essentially materialistic one symbolized by the central action of the book, the purchase of the brownstone houses which makes them owners of real estate. Property, work, and money—traditional WASP values—acquire an axiomatic quality for an upwardly mobile community that turns its back on the past, adopts the practices and rituals of white society, and ultimately exploits even blacks by renting them rooms at very high prices. Seen from Selina's point of view, this form of assimilation makes the reader feel that these people have sold their "birthright for a mess of pottage"—to use the words of James Weldon Johnson's ex-colored man.

In fact, *Brown Girl* remains ambiguous in its appraisal of

these patterns of change. This ambiguity is best symbolized by Selina's mother Silla, a paradigm of the Barbadian community. She shares their endurance, their devotion to the dollar and property, their will to survive in the white world, but also their tragic fate since she ends up alone and frustrated with the same feelings as those expressed by the main speaker of the Association of Barbadian Homeowners and Businessmen: "We ain't white yet. . . . But we got our eyes on the big time." In one climactic scene, Selina compares her mother to Hitler, thus establishing a firm link between the novel's central motifs of war, whiteness, and social mobility. Selina confronts this money-work ethic with values that she is not always able to define precisely: soul, love, breath, "things that are not in the stores."

Economic developments and social change that alienate a people seeking assimilation from their own past and that destroy their ethnic solidarity result in a loss of soul and cultural mutilation. As Suggie, the Barbadian prostitute, tells Selina: "When you hear the shout, you wun be able to call your soul your own." Yet even Selina's final choice appears to be ambiguous. Many critics, and Marshall herself in 1959, have interpreted the ending of the book in terms of Selina's acceptance of the two cultures, white American and Barbadian. According to Cooke, who even concludes that the work affirms no culture, Selina rejects the dichotomy Barbados/black/father and America/white/mother and accepts the complexity of acculturation, becoming a "faceted crystal," the symbol of a transient culture.

This interpretation, however, seems to misread Selina's ultimate gesture as she throws away the silver bangles that all Bajan girls wear from birth. By doing so, far from discarding the mark of her origin, she reestablishes the link with her native people, offering them the bangles as a gift, a reminder of their heroic struggles and of their race and culture. This gesture is the only alternative to the spiritual wasteland evoked in the last pages of the novel. If the story does not yet affirm clearly the necessity of confronting the past, which it limits historically by allusions to colonial exploitation in the West Indian islands, it offers some clues about the theme that Marshall was to develop much more fully in *The Chosen Place* and in *Praisesong for the Widow:* the importance of roots, ultimately involving the rediscovery of the Barbadian's *African* roots. Two female characters—Suggie and Ms. Thompson—anticipate and herald Marshall's later commitment. Suggie is a peasant girl from an obscure island: with her red dress, glinting earrings, and passionate love life, she is a pagan presence in the Victorian white and Bajan world of Brooklyn that reconciles Selina with her Barbadian culture. Miss Thompson is the novel's only black American character. Marshall's description of this woman makes her the paradigm of her ethnic group: "An African wood carving; mysterious, omniscient . . . the eyes shrouded in profound sadness." She helps and listens to Selina, tells her of her resistance to white racism, and thus provides the heroine with a link to her half-forgotten African past. Even though these two women remain secondary to the story, they are the guides that lead Marshall to contend that in her following book, *The Chosen Place,* she was "finally able to bring together what [she considered] to be the central themes of [her] work: the importance of truly confronting the past, both in personal and historical terms and the necessity of reversing the present order."

By the end of *Brown Girl,* after the scene with Margaret's white mother, who teaches her the potentially destructive effects of racism, Selina symbolically concludes that "she was one with Miss Thompson . . . one with the whores, the flashy men and the blues rising sacredly above the plains of neon lights and ruined houses. . . . She was one with them, the mother and the Bajan women, who had lived each day she had come to know." Selina's retracing of the past in mythical and personal terms leads to her re-evaluation of the community whose fight for success is no longer viewed as a betrayal or the acceptance of the rule of the white world, but as the only way to endure and to survive—prerequisites for a reversal of the present order. The community's tragic fate is to a certain extent the price it pays for survival, but it is also the measure of its subversive endeavor.

In that sense "the mother" takes on new dimensions: Silla is the woman who "has not chosen death by water" like her husband, Deighton. The black feminist critic Mary Helen Washington analyzes her as "the scorned wife, the community leader, that ancient African woman whom the entire Western world has humiliated and despised." A perfect representative of the community of black women, she embodies positive values: strength, courage, endurance, energy, the ability to transform humiliating experiences into creative ones. She invents new roles that run counter to the norms set for white women in the forties, ascriptions which dictated that women be passive and essentially locked into the function of being wives and mothers. Silla is the economic and physical mainstay of her household and, like many black American women in the 1940s, does not hesitate to go and work in the defense industry when times are favorable to female employment. Unlike her husband, she is able to control the machines, earn some good war money, and finally buy her own brownstone house, a definite change in her social and economic status. Selina, watching her in the factory, has to acknowledge that "only her mother's . . . formidable force could match that of the machine." Later on Marshall takes up the image again, comparing Silla to "a piston rising and plunging in its cylinder" and contrasting her to Deighton, whose arm has just been crushed—a symbol with obvious sexual implications. Silla is the active partner in her relationship with Deighton. But Silla is also the female character in Marshall's novel through whom the author's ambivalence toward this strong, independent black womanhood becomes most visible; parallel to the evocations of her strength runs the argument that she is a bad wife, eventually betraying her husband to the immigration authorities and thus indirectly bearing responsibility for his death. As a mother, she may bear traits of the archetypal matriarch, but she is also a vulnerable individual who instills in Selina a belief in her own possibilities and the will to grasp them. In fact, the true nurturing community of the book is the community of women who pass on to their children their culture, language, traditions, and their determination to resist.

In this perspective, *Brown Girl* can be viewed as a feminist novel since the least ambiguous nation it describes is the nation of Bajan women. The book affirms the importance of women, not only by making them central characters, but also by presenting them as centers of power. In an interview in *Essence* in May 1974, Marshall underlined the determining role she wanted to impart to her feminine characters: "I am concerned about letting them speak their piece, letting them be central figures, actors, *activists* in fiction rather than just backdrops or background figures. . . . My feminism takes its expression through my work. Women are central to me. They can as easily embody the power principles as a man." *Brown Girl* already expressed this power inherent in women both as an individual and collective force. The island itself, the place of birth, is a woman described as "that low mound resting on the sea like a woman's breast when she is supine," whereas America remains this "man country." In their community the Bajans keep alive the rituals that stabilize their threatened identities—their cooking and eating of Bajan foods, their conversations, and the preservation of ancient beliefs like obeah rites. Many of the novel's scenes take place in the kitchen amid the steam of the pots and the hum of the refrigerator, a place where the women re-create the world through their words and actions. A superb image of this almost divine power is that of Silla kneading the dough for the Bajan coconut bread "as though it was a world without form and she the God shaping it."

Language itself is perhaps the only homeland in which these uprooted women can find some refuge from external repressions and limitations. Marshall recalls how she was always intimidated as a little girl by "the awesome verbal power of these women. That might be one of the reasons why I started writing," she added "to see if on paper I couldn't have some of that power." In the same way, Selina learns how the "wordshop" of the kitchen is the only place where women can be in control, if only verbally, of their lives and the events that shape them, for "in this man world, you got to take your mouth and make a gun."

Confronted with this tremendous creative female energy, the novel's black male characters remain in the shadow. Deighton and Clive, each in his own way, fail to achieve their quests and are destroyed for obvious racial and economic reasons, but also, more subtly, because they are unable to deal with the societal and sexual definitions that mold their women's ambitions and claims. As Barbara Christian notes perceptively, Marshall "penetrates the worn image of the ne'er do well black man." She shows that the racist and sexist American definitions of man and woman run counter to Silla and Deighton's personalities, thus precipitating the tragedy their relation becomes. There is no place left for Deighton's imagination or Clive's artistic talents in a world in which the norm of manhood implies that "if you got a piece of man, you want to see him make out like the rest," as Silla crudely puts it. Stripped of any possibility of self, unmanned before they were even men, Deighton dies, while Selina's lover Clive regresses into self-pity, bemoaning himself as the victim of the archetypal cannibalistic mother, that is, all women:

"They form you in that dark place inside them and you're theirs. For giving life, they exact life. We're all caught within a circle of women . . . and we move from one to the next in a kind of blind dance." The Selina-Clive relationship reproduces to a certain extent the tragic Silla-Deighton relationship. Selina lucidly recognizes that, like her mother, "she was stronger than he [Clive], she possessed a hard center he would never have." The difference is that she is allowed to leave Clive before it is too late, thanks essentially to her mother's experience, which has taught her that power is an ambivalent tool, both creative and destructive, necessary but dangerous, "a thing that don make you nice," but has to be transformed into the drive to discover what went wrong for Bajan men and women in this man country.

In fact, if the relationship of mother-son or husband-wife is presented as essentially destructive, Silla and Selina form the only creative couple in the book. In **Brown Girl,** the reconciliation of mothers and daughters is clearly achieved, even if the relationship is ridden with conflicts and tensions. Adopting the formulation of Judith Kegan Gardiner in *Writing and Sexual Difference,* the heroine is certainly her author's daughter; Selina's search for her mother's past, mirroring the relationship between Selina and Marshall, is crucial for the building up of her own identity: "Selina yearned to know her mother then, in her innocence. . . . For she knew obscurely that she would never understand anything until she did." Like a modern Persephone, Selina traces back the steps of Demeter, thereby wanting and finally reconstructing her own freedom on an even larger scale than Silla had foreseen it. She thus exemplifies Adrienne Rich's observation in *Of Woman Born:* "As daughters, we need mothers who want their own freedom and ours." At the end of the novel, Silla expresses respect for Selina's new independence and her decision; she dismisses her with words that reemphasize the fluid yet decisive solidarity between mothers and daughters: "You was always too much woman for me anyway, soul. And my own mother did say two head-bulls can't reign in a flock."

"Calling your nation" receives multiple answers in **Brown Girl,** the most challenging linked to the necessity to find new definitions of masculine and feminine that would create better relations between men and women and renew basic concepts of sexual identity. In her later works, Marshall went on creating complex black female characters confronted with similar questions of race, history, and gender. **Praisesong for the Widow** seems to solve some of the conflicts and contradictions that left Silla's and Selina's quests unresolved, though the nation which is revealed is more political and racial than strictly feminist. In **Praisesong,** Marshall no longer speaks in terms of Bajan, but in terms of black experience, emphasizing the African past, the diaspora, and the history of enslavement. Obviously, if we collect all of Marshall's heroines, Merle, Reena, Vernell Johnson, Avatara, and of course Selina, their journeys back to their roots form a kind of Middle Passage reversed. As Mary Helen Washington put it, "These women, whose lives and traditions were forever changed by the Middle Passage, emerge . . . as central figures in that history, determined to order the meaning of their past and to find in their spiritual strivings the means to construct a future." (pp. 142-53)

Hélène Christol, "Paule Marshall's Bajan Women in 'Brown Girl, Brownstones',' " in Women and War: The Changing Status of American Women from the 1930s to the 1950s, *edited by Maria Diedrich and Dorothea Fischer-Hornung, Berg, 1990, pp. 141-53.*

Paule Marshall   [Interview with Sylvia Baer]

[*Baer*]: *When I began my literature major in college the writers that serious literature students were expected to emulate were all Eurocentric white males. And I assumed that my vision, as a woman born in South America, was not serious enough, and I ended up changing my major to psychology. I want to know how you were able to hold onto your vision and to your voice.*

[Marshall]: I think credit for that has to be given to a group of women from my childhood, whom I talk about every opportunity I get—just four or five ordinary-looking immigrant women from a tiny island in the West Indies that nobody had ever heard of. They came to this country shortly after World War One and because they were black women without any particular skills the only work they could find was cleaning people's houses. And one of those women happened to be my mother.

The foundation stone for my development as a writer was established when I was a kid who was forced to be among these women. As a girl child, as they called me, I was with them around the kitchen table when they came back from their day's work out in Flatbush. I was there with my sister waiting on them, serving them cocoa and tea, or sitting over in the corner doing my homework, being seen but not heard.

The remarkable thing about them was that while they looked ordinary, they were actually poets; they did marvelous things with the English language that they had learned in the schools of Barbados, this tiny island from which they came. They transformed the King's English. They brought to bear the few African words and cadences that they remembered and they infused and enriched it with all manner of biblical quotes and metaphors and sayings drawn from their life as black women.

For these women who were immigrants and who always felt as if they were strangers in America, the language gave them a sense of home. They talked about everything under the sun—politics, Roosevelt, Marcus Garvey, the Second World War which was just beginning, the First World War when they were young girls still living in the West Indies waiting for the war to be over so they could immigrate to the United States. They talked about the 1935 invasion of Ethiopia by Italy. The political perspective that was so much a part of the way they thought and saw the world became my way of looking at the world. I am indebted to them for that.

I see myself as someone who is to serve as a vehicle for these marvelous women who never got a chance, on paper, to be the poets that they were. Especially in **Brown Girl,**

Brownstones, my first novel, I see that I was impelled, forced, to write it, because once I got over my adolescent rebellion against family and community I was able to see the worth, validity and sacredness of that community in which I grew up, and its women especially. I wanted to try to get it down on paper before it was lost. That's why I think it's been easy for me over the years to hold fast to the vision—because it's not me so much, it's because of them, these women whom I call the mother poets.

From very early on, I had West Indian English—black English, West Indian style. Out on the streets I had black English, Afro-American style. As soon as I went outside to play with my friends I immediately switched into that vernacular. At school I learned standard English. I was trilingual. That's one of the things that informs what I try to do with language. It's to bring to bear those three forms, to play around with them and play them one against the other.

Another way I've held onto both vision and voice has to do with the reading I did at the Macon Street branch of the Brooklyn Public Library, around the corner from the house. That was the second phase of my education and preparation as a writer, because I moved from that great oral tradition which the mother poets represented, to the written tradition, and fell in love with that also. I was a voracious reader who read in a disorganized sprawling way from Jane Austen to Zane Grey without any order but loving all of it.

Although I readily identified with the characters of all the books that I read, and I especially liked the long, full-blown eighteenth- and nineteenth-century English novels, I sensed after a time that something was missing. Then one day while browsing in the poetry section of the library I came across a huge volume of poems, and to my amazement the photograph of the poet in the frontispiece was that of a black man, Paul Lawrence Dunbar. Of all the books I had read to that date, that my teachers suggested that I read, none were by black writers. That was a revelation to me. A number of the poems were in dialect, and I sensed a connection between what Dunbar was doing with English and what I heard my mother and her friends doing with their West Indian vernacular. Perhaps there was something worthwhile about that play with language, something interesting and valid about my own experience.

Dunbar also instilled in me the secret desire to some day write. That collection of poems gave me the courage to go up to the white librarian at the circulation desk and say to her, "Would you please give me a list of books by and about black writers?" And it was then, on my own, that I began my education.

This was in your early adolescence?

Yes, around twelve or so. Then, as I began to fill in this gap in my education, some other people became important to me. One of them was the poet Gwendolyn Brooks. In her novel *Maud Martha,* the main character is a young woman with a husband and a child, living in an apartment in Chicago. She begins to wonder about her life: "Is this all there is to it?" Brooks makes us privy to the interior landscape of Maud Martha's life. And that was important

to me because that was what I wanted to do if I ever wrote about these women in my community.

Ralph Ellison was important to me, not so much for *Invisible Man,* but for his collection of essays on the craft of writing called *Shadow and Act.* He talks about the responsibility of black writers to move beyond the sociology of our lives to deal with the individual, the interior person, to see us and to treat us as people rather than statistics.

Do you mean rather than making a political statement?

The political is always there in my work, but as subtext. I'm always seeking to treat my characters and their lives by writing about them as people rather than as representatives-of-whatever.

Your writing has spanned four decades: What keeps you motivated? What keeps you writing? What keeps you going?

First of all, it's my work. It's the thing that I do. It is what gives sense and order and a framework to my life. Writing is absolutely crucial. When I don't write I feel that the day is without shape.

And writing fiction is my way of answering questions I'm always putting to myself. For instance, ***Praisesong for the Widow*** began because I came across a tale about a place in the Sea Islands called Ibo Landing, with a group of slaves who, when they were brought over, decided after they took a long look around that they didn't want to stay because they knew what their history was going to be in this republic. So they left. They were in such a hurry to leave, so the folktale goes, they walked back across the Atlantic to home.

I couldn't get that story out of my head. It just took up residence in the back of my mind and gave me no peace. And I wondered to myself, "Why? Why did that story stay with me?" I came to understand that the Ibos spoke to something deep within me, a question that I'd always been putting to myself: "How do I, as a woman and a writer, a black woman and a black writer, live in a society that daily undercuts my sense of self?" As I began writing about the Ibos, they gave me the answer. In the same way that they put the physical distance of the Atlantic between this country and home, between themselves and this country, I had to put a psychological and spiritual distance between myself and what I perceived and knew to be some of the damaging aspects of American society. Its racism. Its sexism. Its class bias.

Now the woman in ***Praisesong,*** Avey Johnson, this middle-aged, middle-class black woman, has made it. In fact, she would be referred to in my day as a CTTR, a Credit To The Race. She has a wall-to-wall carpeted house in north White Plains, which is some of the most expensive real estate. She has annuities and bank accounts and stocks and bonds, left her by her late husband. And each year, now that her husband is dead, she goes to the West Indies with her two friends and her six pieces of matching luggage. Well, why did she come and take up residence in my head along with the Ibos? She too was answering questions that I had been putting to myself, perhaps unconsciously. She had to be a middle-aged woman because I was just moving into middle age, and I was asking myself,

"How does one continue to grow in a society which is all about youth?"

Through Avey I was able to deal with the notion that one has—women especially have—the absolute right to reconstitute their lives at no matter what age. And Avey does that. She takes a journey back over her life to see where she has, in her feverish climb up the ladder, disowned and rejected aspects of herself that would make her a more interesting and a more vital person. She's able to recapture that sense of self, that sense of history, which then permits her to move to another level in her life. To stage a private revolution and win it. And it's that capacity for change that I was trying to deal with in that novel.

I'm always putting these questions to myself. Writing offers me a way of answering them, through characters, through stories. What is so marvelous is that I find that they are questions that other people are asking themselves and sometimes some of them find the answers in the books.

I think that's what makes your work so wonderful, the universality of it—we can all identify with it, we can all feel part of it.

Yes, because I really think it operates on a couple of levels. Readers are not only emotionally involved with my characters and with the story lines, they're actually learning something about another people, another culture, another way of doing things, at the same time that they see their own concerns and questions being reflected in the work.

It seems as if you're not influenced by literary trends—you write for yourself. Don't you ever feel the pressure of the literary establishment to change your writing?

Not really. The publishing world is so capricious and so impossible to control, I remained with blinders on and kept my focus on what I'm about as a writer. I'm very gratified when people say to me that issues I dealt with some time ago are now being written about. Women questioning the roles assigned to them—that was there in my very very first story, **"The Valley Between,"** which goes back to the early fifties. The characters all happened to be white because it was so personal that I felt I could hide what was going on in my own life behind these white characters. It had to do with a young woman who found herself married and with a child, but who longed to return to school, and the opposition she faced from her husband. That was before we thought about women demanding a right to have part of themselves to themselves. I'd like to see my work as pioneering, but I'm not thinking about that when I'm working. I'm writing out of what was going on with a whole generation of women like myself, women who were raised to find work that was important, were raised to have a sense of self, and yet at the same time were carefully programmed from the very beginning to go the established route, marriage, family, the lot.

Also, what has kept me from being too concerned about the literary establishment is that I've been pretty clear-sighted about what I'd like my work to do. If I can as a writer portray my community in all of its complexities and in a truthful way, I can accomplish a couple of things. I

can provide an antidote to the unflattering and negative images of black women that have persisted in the literature and the society, and I can also offer young black women—such as myself at that earlier period, who had no models, who never saw herself reflected—a more authentic image of themselves. I see that as very empowering, because once you see yourself reflected truthfully, and that means not a flattering portrait, but with the warts also, it permits you to feel that you have a right to "be" in the world. We begin building an internal strength within our communities, because we know who we are.

Do you see a change in your style over the years, or do you use a particular style to match what you're trying to say within a novel? **Praisesong,** *for example, was much more compact than your other two.*

What I'm always trying to do is to challenge myself as a writer. Coming up with a kind of style that best serves the story, but also from time to time trying out different modes. **Brown Girl, Brownstones** and especially **Soul Clap Hands** were very literary. Because I was a very young writer, there was a desire to show that I was well-read, so there are a lot of allusions to predominantly Western literature because that was what I was subjected to—and I use the word subjected pointedly—in my education. The second novel, the big novel, **The Chosen Place, the Timeless People,** was a full-blown, somewhat self-indulgent one in terms of style and language. If there were five ways to describe something I would use all five. I decided to challenge myself with **Praisesong** and see if I could write in the lean, economical and distilled form, almost a poetic form, yet still create a resonance that would give fullness to the language.

Now you have a novel coming out in October called **Daughters.** *Tell me about the style of that.*

In **Daughters** I'm taking some other risks. It's a freer book in that I'm trying, in terms of point of view, to blend with the characters. If a character would describe something more colorfully or more interestingly than I would as narrator, I use the character's description.

I'm also trying to do some interesting things with time. The entire novel takes place within the span of two months, and yet what I do with time is a weaving back and forth within those two months that takes us all the way back to slavery. The characters are all daughters who are in some way connected one with the other, back to the slave woman who figures as a symbol in the novel. One of the themes that informs my work is being not only connected with those mother poets who were my mentors and instructors but also with the women who created them. It's part of how we define ourselves as people. How do black women get a sense of self? How do we create an identity that will permit us to function?

That's why it's so important for your characters to make that journey back.

Yes—it's all about the creation of a more truthful and liberating identity. One of the principal characters in **Daughters** is dealing with, and I'm quoting T.S. Eliot here, what it means to come out from under the shadow of that red rock, that dependency that gets built in those early relationships. That's why the symbol of abortion, which I use in the novel, is so important, abortion meaning being able to cut away those dependencies that can be so crippling.

I had an absolute charmer of a father, a man who just had this gift of the gab. He was a poet, too. To wake us in the morning he would come into our room and say, "It's time to rise and shine and give God the glory." He was handsome. There was a photograph of him that used to sit on top of the piano, the old upright piano we had, wearing his spats and holding his cane, his hair parted in the middle.

But he was a man who had great difficulty as a black man dealing with a society that denied him a sense of himself. He was unskilled, not able to find the work that he felt was in keeping with what he was as a person. He eventually abdicated his responsibilities, abandoned us. He fled, and that was exceedingly difficult for me because I so loved him. In many of my relationships along the way there was almost a repeat of that early relationship, always looking for this father in the men that I became involved with, and always preparing myself for the end of that relationship. How long it took me to move away from that and to recover, to insist upon autonomy. This novel is about the subtle deferring to men that was so much a part of my childhood and the childhood of many women.

You were talking about your father; how much of your fictional characters comes from real life? How much is the father in **Daughters** *your father, how much is the father in* **Brown Girl, Brownstones** *someone you know?*

The fictional characters are not drawn totally or solely from people that I have known. They are creations. But a good deal of their emotional history is drawn from what I have experienced either personally or what I have seen in the community that shaped me. The father figure in *Daughers* is physically different from my father, or the work he does, or the places he lives. Yet in terms of his relationship with his daughter, that whole emotional nexus reflects feelings and emotions that I have had. Again, I certainly am not an Avey Johnson, but she permitted me to reflect upon what it means to be a middle-aged woman, a black woman in this society.

Your women are the strong characters in the books: instead of having a patrilineal heritage, you have women carrying on the heritage. Do you do this on purpose?

Initially it was not a conscious decision on my part to have women so central to the work. Yet who did I know growing up, who was I surrounded by? Even though my father was important to me, my day to day existence was lived among women, and their lives, what they expressed about themselves and their place in the world, what they sensed about their place in the world had its impact on me from very early. I was not privy to the world of men. Women were central.

When I moved from the kitchen to the library, one of the things that struck me was that women weren't very central in any of the books that I read. I don't mean to make this sound as if I sat down and spelled it out consciously on a piece of paper, no, these were currents and feelings circulating within me. Perhaps because of this lack, one of the things I wanted to do when I started writing was to make women principal characters in the work.

I don't see them as "strong" but rather as complex and central, and that's different for me. The other side of strong black women is so often weak black men, and I want to get away from that thinking, because it divides rather than unites. I don't see, for example, Silla, the mother in *Brown Girl, Brownstones,* as all that strong a woman. I see her as someone who has perhaps foolishly or unquestioningly bought the whole American materialistic ethic. And the price she pays for that is the death of love and the ruin of her family. I don't see that as being all that strong. I see some strength in the father. He insists upon American success on his own terms.

If the Paule Marshall of the 1950s could talk to the Paule Marshall of today, what would she have to say to you?

She would say, I think, congratulations on two counts. One of them having to do with the work. That I kept to the commitment I made to writing in the fifties, not to give up or be discouraged by what I would encounter. I was in for the long haul, and I knew that. I understood from very early on that it might not work out very well financially for me, that I was not going to hang myself up as a writer by becoming unduly concerned with making it big. I was very straightforward about that. Also the whole thing of trends and fashions within the publishing world was something that I wasn't going to be involved in. And I've been able, over the four decades, to stay true pretty much to that early commitment.

The other thing that the fifties Paule might feel good about is that I've been able, through a good deal of interior work, private work, to eliminate from my life a lot of emotional impediments and obstacles. A lot of the negative programming that went into those early years—I've been able to make my peace with it and achieved a kind of interior

---

Marshall on her literary influences:

When people at readings and writers' conferences ask me who my major influences were, they are sometimes a little disappointed when I don't immediately name the usual literary giants. True, I am indebted to those writers, white and black, whom I read during my formative years and still read for instruction and pleasure. But they were preceded in my life by another set of giants whom I always acknowledge before all others: the group of women around the table long ago. They taught me my first lessons in the narrative art. They trained my ear. They set a standard of excellence. This is why the best of my work must be attributed to them; it stands as testimony to the rich legacy of language and culture they so freely passed on to me in the wordshop of the kitchen.

Paule Marshall, in her "From the Poets in the Kitchen," The New York Times Book Review, *January 9, 1983.*

calm, self-acceptance and self-love. That's been important for me, and I hope that that personal liberation is evident in the work. (pp. 24-5)

Paule Marshall and Sylvia Baer, in an interview in The Women's Review of Books, *Vol. VIII, Nos. 10-11, July, 1991, pp. 24-5.*

Jane Smiley

Through four works of fiction over the course of two and a half decades, Paule Marshall has not changed—her frank exploration of the details of the American dream has deepended and broadened but has remained her central preoccupation. Our literary culture, however, has changed. The condescension of early reviews of Marshall's work, which compliment her as a "negro writer" but assume that her novels are peripheral, now seems naive and distasteful. These days we know that Marshall's chosen themes are right at the heart of the American dream and the American dilemma. In her new novel, *Daughters,* she explores them with a breadth of insight and a maturity of technique that confirms her place in the front rank of American writers.

Ursa Beatrice Mackenzie is a classic Marshall creation, a black woman of intelligence and ambition with a Caribbean background but living and working in middle-class urban America. Temporarily blocked in her ambitions, Ursa is nevertheless fully enrolled in the middle class, and her problems are middle-class problems—when will her boyfriend stop complaining about his boss, will her grant come through, can she bring herself to visit her parents back in Triunion, the Caribbean island where her father is a career politician? Ursa's linguistic style tells all. Standard narrative English, fast-paced, descriptive but objective and understated, it demonstrates how far Ursa's own spirit has traveled from her vividly passionate island to the world of reason, success, assimilation.

Make no mistake about it, Marshall is a novelist of voices. She has a marvelous ear. The idiosyncratic language of each of her characters is not only authentic but also compelling and intriguing, revealing over and over how each character experiences both the world and herself in it.

Orbiting Ursa's father, known as "the PM," are four women who serve him—his nanny, Celestine; his wife, Estelle; his long-time mistress and the manager of his resort, Astral Forde; and Ursa. They most assuredly do not agree on much of anything except that the PM is an inescapable power in their lives. Nor do they understand one another.

Estelle, from the United States, seems mysterious and less than womanly to Celestine and Astral Forde, who shared none of her worldly political interests. Astral Forde is a wrathful, threatening presence to Ursa and her mother. Celestine's submersion in the wishes and needs of the PM, who has been in her charge since she was 8, seems uncanny to the others. As each woman speaks her piece, forwarding and commenting on the action, which covers about 60 years (including Celestine's memories of the PM's mother), she impresses herself indelibly on the reader's imagination.

Marshall is a writer of enormous technical maturity, which means that *Daughters* evolves on many levels at once and also means that Marshall doesn't play all her dramatic cards right at the beginning.

We meet Lowell Carruthers, Ursa's boyfriend, a tedious whiner who, in the face of office politics, has lost most of the pleasure he took in his beautiful apartment and his relationship with Ursa. Then there's Viney, Ursa's best friend, who seems to have made for herself, through hard work and creative family planning, an oasis from the general problems faced by black Americans.

Marshall tempts the reader to see only individuals, their success marred by details but perfectable through individual effort. The style is quiet, lulling. Not until Book Two, more than 100 pages into the novel, does she begin to shake the reader up.

A writer of scope and complex ideas, Marshall knows how to piece together her themes, providing incidents of immediate drama and interest that simultaneously coalesce into a larger and larger picture. What at first seems personal, temporary, is soon revealed to derive from background and longer-term psychological influences.

For example, Ursa's reluctance to return to Triunion is the effect of her parents' conflicts with each other and her inability to come to terms with her father's obsession with her. But this box exists within a still larger box, for her parents' conflicts center around her father's successful political career as a populist opposition member of Triunion's Parliament, who over the years has come to betray the ideals he and Ursa's mother once devoutly served.

The theme of political corruption even by those who mean well and the personal costs of such corruption sits once again inside a larger box, as Ursa makes a connection that she would like to avoid making, between life among blacks who have joined the ruling class in the United States and the political career of her father on his tiny and "unimportant" island. Marshall's technique is to move out from Ursa and the other characters, then to circle back repeatedly, patiently and evocatively, but never stridently—building the reader's understanding of how her characters' world not only looks, sounds and feels, but also how it works and what this means.

In a recent interview, Marshall remarked that it has taken her eight years to write *Daughters.* She commented that the exigencies of teaching prevented concentrated work on the novel. But *Daughters* could not have existed in its present form before now. The bitter fruit of the 1980s that gives Marshall's novel its final dimension of profundity and grandeur is her understanding of just what the callousness and cynical greed of the Reagan administration has meant both here and in the Caribbean.

Daughters is a work that has been mulled over and thought through; it is Marshall's most inclusive and sophisticated analysis of the intersection between personality, identity, family, politics and culture, an outstanding and important work and a fascinating novel.

Jane Smiley, "Caribbean Voices," in Chicago Tribune—Books, *October 6, 1991, p. 3.*

Susan Fromberg Schaeffer

Paule Marshall's *Daughers* is that rarity, a good *and* important book. It attempts to look at black experience in our hemisphere, to praise what progress has been made and to point to what yet needs to be done. In its willingness to take real stock, to find true answers to complex questions, it is a brave, intelligent and ambitious work.

Ms. Marshall examines the state of black life through Ursa Mackenzie, whose heritage—and perhaps nature—is dual. Her father, Primus Mackenzie, is a prominent official of a mythical Caribbean island, Triunion; he has been known since his youth as "the PM." Her mother is the American-born Estelle Harrison, who sends a very young Ursa back to the United States so that her child can learn "to talk the talk and walk the walk." Most of all, Estelle does not want Ursa to grow up to be a Triunion woman, one who waits hand and foot on her man and who has little independence of thought or deed. It is as if Estelle knows that her daughter will have a special role to play in determining the fate of black people in one or both of her countries. She is determined her daughter will make a difference.

When we first meet Ursa, in her early 30's, she seems an unlikely vessel for such hopes. She stands, dazed, in an abortion clinic where she has just aborted the child of her self-obsessed lover. She is tormented afterward by the idea that the abortion had not really taken place, and in a sense it has not. Although she is herself unaware of it, Ursa was trying not only to abort a real fetus, but also the patriarchal image of the PM, an image that, because she is so like him, has come to possess her. The image of her father is also a source of corruption; the PM, who began his political career wanting to help his people and throw out the Triunion "do-nothings," has, with the passage of time, become seduced by a desire for wealth and power.

In the aftermath of the abortion, Ursa finds herself subjected to a virtual storm of memory, in which she summons up everyone who has ever mattered to her; Celestine, the Creole woman who helped raise her; Astral Forde, her father's mistress; Viney, her mother-friend-sister-alter-ego; and, of course, her real mother, Estelle. Each has something to teach her. From Celestine she learns the futility of living without a sense of self. From Astral Forde she learns the vanity of living only for material gain. From Viney she learns what is to become the moral imperative of *Daughters*—that to be human, one must be of use. From her own mother she learns that in order to be of use, men and women must work together—and that the relationship between the sexes is far more complicated than she has ever imagined.

Throughout *Daughters,* Ursa is visited by two images. One is disturbing: the image of her father, standing at the edge of a swimming pool watching her: "His body would be in the way, his head blocking out the sun. The annoyance she used to feel! She would have done anything some days to make him move, to get out of her way." The second image—Ursa's earliest memory—is of her mother lifting her up to touch the great stone toes of the statues of Congo Jane and Will Cudjoe, the two heroes of Triunion's rebellion:

" 'See if you can touch her toes, Ursa-Bea! . . . And make sure to touch Will Cudjoe's toes while you're at it. You can't leave him out.' . . . Warmed by the sun, their toes had felt as alive as her own."

Ursa never forgets the great stone couple. Years later, in college, Congo Jane and Will Cudjoe inspire her to study "the mutually supportive relations that existed between the bondmen and women" and how these relations allowed them to resist slavery in the United States and the Caribbean. An unsympathetic and very probably prejudiced thesis adviser forces her to abandon this topic, and later, when Ursa, who has continued her research, again attempts to write this paper, she finds herself incapable of doing so.

In a sense, *Daughters* is Ursa's thesis, an examination of the relations between black men and women. By the end of *Daughters,* Ursa acts out rather than writes down what she has learned, but first she must radically revise her original conception. The memory storm that overtakes her, as well as her subsequent experiences, show her that the ideal relationship is not necessarily "mutually supportive." Quite the contrary.

Not surprisingly, the relations between men and women—like so much else in *Daughters*—change as the times change. In Triunion, where the primary struggle is still to survive, a woman's first duty is to husband and home. The people of Triunion want a better life for themselves and their children. Primus Mackenzie's mother tells him she wants him to have "the means, the money." "It's so he'll understand from the early how things go in this world. It's so he'll know how to carry himself in this life and what-and-what he must do to find the means to live as he would like—the motorcars and whatever else he sets his mind to." The ideal toward which she strives already exists in the wealthier or ruling class.

But Ursa, like her mother, Estelle, has won the battle for survival. They have the necessities of life, and more. They have benefited from the civil rights movement and no longer must get out of their car and squat in bushes because they are denied access to public bathrooms. Through Ursa, Estelle and Viney, Ursa's closest friend, Ms. Marshall states her belief that it is time for this new, more fortunate generation to make itself useful to others who are still struggling. They are now able to concentrate on the common good. They can and must afford idealism. Their imperative is no longer what it was. In a time when "the woods are on fire," they must "be useful." The moral code of *Daughters* is strict; people who fail to be of use fail as human beings. If they are not of use, they must be cut from one's life, in some cases *literally* cut. "If thy hand offend thee!" says Ursa's friend Viney, who is not speaking metaphorically. And neither is Ms. Marshall, who relentlessly compares Ursa's abortion to cutting what is useless from one's life.

What stands in Ursa's way? Why can neither she nor Estelle truly be of use? Estelle *wants* to be of use and is driven half-mad by the corruption she sees growing in her husband. She rebels against it; she disrupts important state functions, but she cannot return her husband to his original idealistic course. Ursa watches her parents, who fight constantly, and wonders why her mother does not leave her father and return to America. She still believes that relations between black men and women should be "egalitarian" and "mutually supportive." This, Ursa has always believed, was the message of the great stone couple. But Ms. Marshall finds other meanings in their image.

Daughters seems to imply that the purpose of many unions should now be mutual struggle; struggle, if necessary, *against* each other but always toward an ideal. Black men, who entered the political and economic arenas earlier than black women, have greater temptations to contend with and are thus more likely to be seduced from their ideals. Through Primus and Estelle Mackenzie, Ms. Marshall shows us how the *women* can—and perhaps should—find themselves becoming men's consciences. Primus *knew* that Estelle was to be his conscience, and in this capacity he welcomed her:

"So I thank my lucky stars for the Harrisons' girlchild, who's not the sort to run behind anybody and who'll see to it that this country boy in his donkey cart keeps to the straight and narrow."

In reply, Estelle held up her clenched fists to "show him the grip she intended keeping on the reins." Women, Ms. Marshall shows us, spend more of their time than men with children, friends and family. They are less likely to be distracted from what was probably always their original goal: to be of use.

Yet even here, women are hampered by the inevitable facts of life: they love and are sexually attracted to their husbands and fathers, and, unless they can free themselves from the spells of men, they are of little use as consciences. And so, when Estelle decides to move against her husband, to keep him "on the straight and narrow," she cannot do it. It is at this point that Estelle calls upon her daughter to act when she cannot. But does Estelle know what she is asking? Does she understand the bond between her father and daughter any better than her daughter understands the bond between her father and mother, husband and wife?

For Ursa, too, is hobbled by love of her father—even if that father stands between her and the light. So complete is his possession of her that she needs to *abort* him. In the novel's final scenes, this is what she does. When her father runs for reelection, she undercuts his scheme to build an enormous resort on public lands, a project that will bring great profit to her family but misery to the poor of Triunion. "Aborting" her father brings Ursa great pain. The "waves of pain cutting across the well of her stomach" are the pains of the abortion that opened the novel. The abortion is now really over, and the pain Ursa feels is now worthwhile. Her actions give her father a chance for a new life, even as she kills his corrupt image within her. And Ursa becomes a black woman who is, in every sense, free.

Many ideas dominate this wonderful novel, but perhaps the most important is that we have been on the wrong road, a "bypass road" that allows us to travel through life without seeing the urgent needs of others. You close *Daughters* feeling as if you have taken a dangerous trip that cannot leave you unchanged. Flawless in its sense of place and character, remarkable in its understanding of human nature, *Daughters* is a triumph in every way. (pp. 3, 29)

Susan Fromberg Schaeffer, "Cutting Herself Free," in The New York Times Book Review, *October 27, 1991, pp. 3, 29.*

Carol Ascher

Daughters, Marshall's fourth novel, is her most ambitious, mature and sharply political. It begins as small as the personal distress of a black woman, Ursa Mackenzie, returning from an abortion to her Upper West Side studio apartment in New York City. Single, in her thirties, temporarily jobless, Ursa is too paralyzed to return the call on her answering machine from her dear friend Viney Davis. She can only wait uselessly in the darkening evening for a ring from Lowell Carruthers, who has no reason to extend their relationship beyond a biweekly dinner and a little "company through the night," since she never even told him she was pregnant. Nor can Ursa open the one letter that lies among her junk mail: it's from her father, Primus Mackenzie, a politician on the small Caribbean island of Triunion, and a man she has always loved dearly.

> With the lamp off, there's only the ruby-red glow of the clock in the room, each lighted stud on the grid calling to mind those perfectly round, jewel-like drops of blood that form when the tip of a finger is pricked. The only sounds to be heard are the noisy radiator and the wind rattling the bay window. An occasional car hurtles by. Sounds that are merely part of the silence of the night. Ursa doesn't hear them.

From this tiny, isolated New York apartment, *Daughters* moves slowly outward in ever-widening circles that come to encompass relations, friends, lovers and colleagues in both the Caribbean and greater New York. Finally, this fictional world extends backward half a century, more, back to slavery itself, at the same time as it moves a mere two months forward, to election week on Triunion. Through the issues confronting Ursa's father, *Daughters* makes clear the dependent nature of Triunion as it grows poorer and more crowded over the years. (An American warship, the *Woody Wilson,* stands in the harbor at every election, ensuring that no candidate with wild socialist ideas, such as Primus once had, will win.) At the same time, we see life as it is lived at the increasingly compromised center of political power. Like Marshall's other books, *Daughters* prompts one to reflect on the life choices given to an African-American woman or man in both the metropolis and the colonies.

Ursa Mackenzie herself has left a high-paying job doing marketing surveys for whiskey, beer and cigarettes. She is waiting for funding for a more idealistic project, a political analysis of Midland City, a predominantly black New Jersey city. Her tiny apartment is filled with notes for a senior thesis she was long ago denied, but which she still hopes one day to write for her own satisfaction. Its subject: two slaves, Congo Jane and Will Cudjoe, whose joint statue stands in the Triunion hills, and whose lives have been emblematic for Ursa since she was a child on the island. As she tells her friend Viney, the couple proves that

> slavery, for all its horrors, was a time when black men and women had it together, were together, stood together. That there were Congo Janes and Will Cudjoes—I've told you about them— both here and in the islands . . . We have a saying about those two in Triunion: You can't call her name or his, we say, without calling or at least thinking of the other, they had been so close.

In fact, although **Daughters** promises to be about the connections between generations of females, it strikes one more strongly as being about the variety of the ties between African American men and women—between lovers, husband and wife, and even father and daughter.

Thus it is against the mythic closeness of Congo Jane and Will Cudjoe that Ursa judges the relationships between black men and women, both in New York and on the island. Lowell Carruthers, for example, has been unavailable for a Congo-Cudjoe-style partnership, not only because he is obsessed with the daily abuses he sustains from his white boss, but because he plays father to his sister's three sons, whose father was killed in Vietnam, loyally visiting them in Philadelphia every other weekend. What about Viney's former boyfriend, Willis Jenkins, an elegant, vain, highly talented man, the father of her son Robeson? Well, Viney kicked him out when she discovered him sleeping with the white man in the apartment downstairs, but theirs wasn't much of a partnership even before that.

And why does Ursa's mother, Estelle, stay with her father? The two actually come as close to Congo Jane and Will Cudjoe as any couple in the novel. As a young schoolteacher in Hartford, Connecticut, Estelle was swept up by this charismatic, spoiled, egalitarian, lovably triumphant young Triunion politician, Primus Mackenzie, and moved to the island to become "the wife he went and find in America." Yet over the years Estelle has had to make serious adjustments to island life—to the devastating gap between the ease in which she lives as "the PM's wife" and the dire poverty of most of the island's people; to the folkish openness of political corruption there; to the compromises Primus makes as he holds on to power election after election; and even to his regular mistress, who manages his hotel.

Why won't Estelle come back to the US? Ursa wonders. Called down to Triunion by her mother as the election nears, Ursa confronts the PM's secret plan to profit personally from a huge, American-built resort, which will cut off the beach and access to fishing for hundreds of Triunion natives. Yet she also comes close to an understanding of why Estelle stays. Riding in the car with the two of them, Ursa is sitting up front with her father; her mother rides in the back seat:

> Estelle is leaning so far forward by now she's practically sitting up front with them. Her pro-

file is superimposed on the PM's, Ursa notes, the side view of her face and head taking up more than three quarters of his. Their two profiles like bas-relief heads on a medallion or a specially minted commemorative coin. And their heads are in turn superimposed on the parade outside the Buick—on the dark, fleeting faces, the woebegone little houses, the cars, buses and donkey carts, and on the trees Estelle is always trying to save.

Congo Jane and Will Cudjoe? Not really. Though perhaps as close to a marital partnership as one gets among those in politics.

The scenes in Triunion are wonderfully rich with vitality, nuance and dialect. They recall another excellent portrayal of Caribbean politics, V.S. Naipaul's *The Suffrage of Elvira*. But Marshall forbids us to see in Triunion's politics merely the quaint, colorful ways of a tiny Third World country. Instead, Ursa's Midland City research grant, which has finally come through, provides an unhappy analogue to the PM's hotel scheme: the new black mayor agrees to displace blocks of the very constituency who voted for him to allow an expressway that only white suburbanites will use. Just as Primus' defense is that the resort will bring new jobs to the island, the mayor argues that "those [white] folks just happen to be our biggest tax base right now. And without some taxes coming in we can't hope to do anything for anybody. Besides, with the expressway we'll stand a better chance of attracting more business."

In a moving scene, Viney explains to Ursa how she's finally come to see her former lover, Willis Jenkins.

> "The woods are on fire out here," my granddaddy used to say, "and we need everybody that can tote a bucket of water to come running." He used to say that all the time, talking about the situation of Black Folks in this country, you know . . . And one day I took a good look at Willis Jenkins and knew he was not one of those Folks . . . Because Willis Jenkins wasn't about to tote so much as a thimbleful of water anywhere, for anybody, not even for himself if his own patch of woods was on fire. Do you understand me now?

Viney's granddaddy raises a haunting question. Has Ursa's father toted water? Does Ursa? Does Viney, working at an insurance company she hates in order to keep her son in good private schools, sheltered from their Brooklyn streets?

Daughters is intimately observed, culturally rich, morally serious. Marshall loves her complex, imperfect characters, male and female; she loves the tragic, often comic, worlds they inhabit. It is this love that one feels drives her to write so seriously and fully, and that makes each new work feel like the return of an old friend.

Carol Ascher, "Compromised Lives," in The Women's Review of Books, *Vol. IX, No. 2, November, 1991, p. 7.*

Sherley Anne Williams

Daughters, Paule Marshall's fourth novel, takes its title from the proverbial saying that serves as an epigraph to Part One of the novel and gives that section its name: "Little Girl of All the Daughters, / You ain't no more slave, / You's a woman now." The kinship invoked in the title is both literal and metaphoric. In the context of the novel, the epigraph implies that nothing excuses women's inaction in the face of an oppressive status quo. *Daughters* raises questions about racial and familial solidarity and individual responsibility in a confused and dangerous present. These questions have a special urgency now—in the wake of the Mayor Marion Barry debacle, in the aftermath of the Anita Hill, Clarence Thomas hearings—when silence in the name of "race solidarity" led to devastating and destructive exposures. Refreshingly, Marshall chooses to deal with these themes in a realistic universe where the characters are unaided by a dubious spiritualism or improbable ancestral intervention.

The "woman now," is Ursa Beatrice Mackenzie, a New Yorker of West Indian and American parentage. Ursa's dual heritage is a point of alienation in even her closest friendships. The tangled connection between the United States and the small islands off its southern coast is one of several leitmotifs in the novel. Marshall's principal concern, however, is the relationship daughter Ursa bears to the elders who have parented her through childhood. Ursa's father is Primus Mackenzie, called "The P.M." (prime minister) because his high domed forehead seemed, even in his youth, to foreshadow a great political future. Ursa's mother, Estelle, always seemed to be pushing Ursa toward America and adulthood. Celestine, the faithful family retainer, nursemaid to two generations of Mackenzies, has mothered Ursa almost as much as Estelle. And even Astral Forde, Primus's "keep-miss," whom he always made play the servant in front of Ursa, has influenced how she thinks of, and presents herself to, the world. The similarity in the names of the four women, all of which have to do with the heavens, is intentional; Ursa's father, Primus, is the "polestar" around whom they all gravitate, the lover and father so large that his shoulders, in their eyes, blot out the sun.

The novel's action is set against the backdrop of the contemporary ills that threaten the integrity, self-esteem, indeed, the very life of black people in America and elsewhere: the drug epidemic, the out-of-kilter ratio between men and women in the black middle class, "the brothers who only have eyes for" white girls, or "for each other," or "for themselves." Ursa so distrusts the commitment of her long-time lover, Lowell Carruthers, that she never tells him of the child accidentally conceived during one of their weekend trysts and aborted at a midtown clinic. Ursa's "sister/friend," Viney, even before the novel opens, made peace with their ill-omened future by conceiving a son through artificial insemination and contenting herself with celibacy and life as a single parent. And, if Viney's response seems less a solution than a part of the problem, at least she, like all the characters in *Daughters,* confronts her reality without recourse to the idiosyncratic spiritualisms or would-be oral traditions that have provided a

questionable salvation in much contemporary Afro-American fiction. Ursa sometimes repeats a mantra to calm her nerves, but she never uses meditation as a way of hiding from the need for action.

The immediacy and power of the novel are unfortunately blunted, however, by Marshall's decision to distance the reader from key events, or to portray them as part of the novel's past or, more vitiating still, to portray them off-stage. We first meet Ursa immediately after her abortion. Yet, in the process of rendering Ursa's necessary disengagement from the life that will soon be "spot[ting her] drawers," Marshall also distances the reader from Ursa's real feelings, the *sotto voce* responses that must exist beneath the surface of her talk of having been "caught," of "it" having "nothing to do with" Lowell Carruthers. This initial distance sets the tone for much of the rest of the novel. We never see Primus "the polestar" except by the reflected light of the four women in his life. The most compellingly portrayed episode in the novel is not the fate of Ursa's relationship with her lover, Lowell, but the silent, almost unacknowledged struggle between Estelle and Astral for Primus's loyalty, which we are shown in flashback. The resolution of the novel is reported in summary rather than shown, as if Marshall thought those scenes too unimportant to be dramatized.

Marshall's best work is distinguished by intimacy, by the attentively observed and rendered detail that, in her first two novels and in her short stories, for example, made even minor characters so memorable. Such evocative delineations are present in *Daughters,* but only in flashes that are too brief to carry the weight of the novel's momentous themes. (pp. 2-3)

Sherley Anne Williams, "Solidarity Is Not Silent," in Belles Lettres: A Review of Books by Women, *Vol. 7, No. 2, Winter, 1991-92, pp. 2-3.*

FURTHER READING

Benston, Kimberly W. "Architectural Imagery and Unity in Paule Marshall's *Brown Girl, Brownstones." Negro American Literature Forum* 9, No. 3 (Fall 1975): 67-70.
    Examines how setting is used to delineate character and plot in *Browngirl, Brownstones.*

Bond, Jean Carey. "Allegorical Novel by Talented Storyteller." *Freedomways,* 1 (1970): 76-8.
    Mixed review of *The Chosen Place, the Timeless People.* Bond observes that this "is a vintage novel, a strong tale of black workers—West Indian cane cutters specifically—imprisoned in a language that cannot contain it."

Bröck, Sabine. "Transcending the 'Loophole of Retreat': Paule Marshall's Placing of Female Generations." *Callaloo* 10, No. 1 (Winter 1987): 79-90.
    Maintains that Marshall's fiction emphasizes the black

woman's search for space, both physical and emotional, within the white patriarchy.

Byerman, Keith E. "Gender, Culture, and Identity in Paule Marshall's *Brown Girl, Brownstones.*" In *Redefining Autobiography in Twentieth-Century Women's Fiction: An Essay Collection,* edited by Janice Morgan and Colette T. Hall, pp. 135-47. New York: Garland Publishing, 1991.

Focuses on "the ways in which cultural adjustments are manifested in gender conflict and sexual identity" in Marshall's first novel.

Christian, Barbara T. "Sculpture and Space: The Interdependency of Character and Culture in the Novels of Paule Marshall." In her *Black Women Novelists: The Development of a Tradition, 1892-1976,* pp. 80-136. Westport, Conn.: Greenwood Press, 1980.

Explores Marshall's use of culture, folklore, and environment as a means of creating character.

————. "Ritualistic Process and the Structure of Paule Marshall's *Praisesong for the Widow.*" *Callaloo* 6, No. 2 (Spring-Summer 1983): 74-85.

Examines *Praisesong for the Widow* as "an African ritual that shows the relationship between the individual and the community."

Collier, Eugenia. "Selina's Journey Home: From Alienation to Unity in Paule Marshall's *Brown Girl, Brownstones.*" *Obsidian: Black Literature in Review* 8, Nos. 2-3 (Summer-Winter 1982): 6-19.

Examines *Brown Girl, Brownstones* as a "coming of age" novel.

Harris, Trudier. "No Outlet for the Blues: Silla Boyce's Plight in *Brown Girl, Brownstones.*" *Callaloo* 6, No. 2 (Spring-Summer 1983): 57-67.

Relates the character Silla Boyce to the blues tradition.

Hull, Gloria T. "Grand Narrative and Risky Revelations." *Belles Lettres* 7, No. 2 (Winter 1991-92): 3-4.

Praises *Daughters* for furthering Marshall's "self-ordained mission of chronicling the African Diaspora."

Kubitschek, Missy Dehn. "Paule Marshall's Witness to History." In her *Claiming the Heritage: African-American Women Novelists and History,* pp. 69-89. Jackson: University Press of Mississippi, 1991.

Explores Marshall's use of oral narrative and archetype in her novels.

Leseur, Geta J. "*Brown Girl, Brownstones* as a Novel of Development." *Obsidian II: Black Literature in Review* 1, No. 3 (Winter 1986): 119-29.

Describes *Brown Girl, Brownstones* as a bildungsroman detailing the growth process of "a fragmented individual self, through a turbulent awakening to a realigned whole."

Lodge, Sally. "PW Interviews Paule Marshall." *Publishers Weekly* 225, No. 3 (20 January 1984): 90-1.

Discusses Marshall's literary influences and her goals as a writer.

Marshall, Paule. "The Negro Woman in American Literature: Paule Marshall." *Freedomways* 6, No. 1 (Winter 1966): 20-5.

Text of speech given by Marshall at a three-day conference on "The Negro Writer's Vision of America." Marshall was one of four black women writers who discussed the role of black writers; she focuses on the myths which have halted honest depictions of black characters in literature.

————. "Shaping the World of My Art." *Newsletters* 40, No. 1 (October 1973): 97-112.

Discussion of Marshall's childhood experiences which have shaped her thinking, writing, and her belief that African-Americans must gain an understanding of their heritage in order to come to individual self-awareness.

————. "The Making of a Writer: From the Poets in the Kitchen." *The New York Times Book Review* (9 January 1983): 3, 34-5.

Highly acclaimed personal commentary on the foundations and elements of Marshall's personal and artistic beliefs. Marshall comments on the distinctive poetic art of her mother's Barbadian dialect and its impact on her writing.

Pollard, Velma. "Cultural Connections in Paule Marshall's *Praisesong for the Widow.*" *World Literature Written in English* 25, No. 2 (Autumn 1985): 285-98.

Discusses Marshall's *Praisesong for the Widow* as a diaspora novel which dramatizes the cultural similarities that exist between the communities of Africa, the Caribbean, and black America.

Scarboro, Ann Armstrong. Review of *Praisesong for the Widow,* by Paule Marshall. *International Fiction Review* 13, No. 1 (Winter 1986): 53-4.

Commends *Praisesong for the Widow* for its artistic depiction of "the process of psychological reintegration."

Schneider, Deborah. "A Search for Selfhood: Paule Marshall's *Brown Girl, Brownstones.*" In *The Afro-American Novel Since 1960,* edited by Peter Bruck and Wolfgang Karrer, pp. 53-73. Amsterdam: B. R. Grüner Publishing, 1982.

Examines *Brown Girl, Brownstones* as a bildungsroman.

Skerrett, Joseph T., Jr. "Paule Marshall and the Crisis of the Middle Years: *The Chosen Place, The Timeless People.*" *Callaloo* 6, No. 2 (Spring-Summer 1983): 68-73.

Discusses *The Chosen Place, the Timeless People* as a novel about "the crisis of the middle years, the 'the crisis of generativity'."

Spillers, Hortense J. "*Chosen Place, Timeless People:* Some Figurations on the New World." In *Conjuring: Black Women, Fiction, and Literary Tradition,* edited by Marjorie Pryse and Hortense J. Spillers, pp. 151-75. Bloomington: Indiana University Press, 1985.

Asserts that a proper interpretation of *The Chosen Place, the Timeless People* must account for Marshall's use of history, myth, ontology, and ritual.

Talmor, Sascha. "Merle of Bournehills." *Durham University Journal* LXXX, No. 1 (December 1987): 125-28.

Favorable review of *The Chosen Place, the Timeless People.*

Whalen, Gretchen. "The Long Search for Coherence and Vision." *Callaloo* 8, No. 3 (1985): 667-69.

    Positive assessment of *The Chosen Place, the Timeless People*.

Additional coverage of Marshall's life and career is contained in the following sources published by Gale Research: *Black Literature Criticism*, Vol. 3; *Black Writers*; *Contemporary Authors*, Vols. 77-80; *Contemporary Authors New Revision Series*, Vol. 25; *Contemporary Literary Criticism*, Vol. 27; *Dictionary of Literary Biography*, Vol. 33; *Major 20th-Century Writers*; and *Short Story Criticism*, Vol 3.

Paul Muldoon

1951-

Irish poet.

The following entry provides an overview of Muldoon's career.

INTRODUCTION

Muldoon is recognized as one of Ireland's major contemporary poets. His poetry is characterized by playful wit, dry humor, inventive rhyme, and multilayered structures of meaning. Although he has been criticized for what many consider the bafflingly allusive nature of his works, Muldoon is highly acclaimed for the extraordinary originality and artistic skill he exhibits in his poems.

Born in County Armagh, Northern Ireland, Muldoon was raised near the village of Moy, where his mother was a schoolteacher and his father a laborer and market gardener. He attended St. Patrick's College in Armagh, and, inspired by several of his teachers, developed a strong interest in Irish Gaelic language, literature, and song, as well as in English literature. One of Muldoon's teachers introduced him to the poetry of T. S. Eliot, and Muldoon quickly became an Eliot enthusiast, writing poetry that was often imitative of Eliot's. He sent several of his poems to Seamus Heaney and Derek Mahon, Irish poets who were gaining recognition in the 1960s, and a few of Muldoon's works were published by Heaney in the periodical *Thresholds.*

As an undergraduate at Queen's University in Belfast, Muldoon studied under Heaney and joined him at weekly poetry gatherings held at Heaney's home. The group, which included the Ulster poets Derek Mahon and Michael Longley, the critic Michael Allen, as well as several other young poets, served as a critical forum. Of his experience with this literary circle Muldoon has said: "It was very important for me, since a writer must be a good critic of his work. There was no sloppiness in the group, everyone was quite outspoken. It was a very healthy kind of society, and I use the word 'society' to describe the group. It's scarcely a group at all, even though it's been a critical convenience to see them as presenting a united front to the world: you have only to read them to be aware of the variety. They're not united under any manifesto." Muldoon's voice has remained highly individual and his verse is not associated with any particular poetical movement.

In his first collection of poetry, *New Weather,* Muldoon examines everyday objects in the allusive style that has become his hallmark. Although *New Weather* was widely acclaimed, Muldoon's status as a poet initially suffered from the widespread opinion of critics that he was a younger Seamus Heaney because of similarities in the subject matter of their poems. Muldoon's succeeding collections have

dispelled such views, and he has gained recognition for his individual poetic style. In Muldoon's second collection, *Mules,* the poem "Lunch with Pancho Villa" is an example of the intricacy and wit of his poetry, since it may be interpreted as a comment on Northern Ireland's sectarian violence, as well as a satire on Muldoon himself: "People are getting themselves killed / Left, right, and centre / While you do what? / Write rondeaux. / There's more to living in this country / Than stars and horses, pigs and trees."

Muldoon's third collection, *Why Brownlee Left,* marks a maturer stage in his poetic development. For the first time a single theme, that of self-discovery, connects the poems of the collection, which are more experimental in form and more extravagant in their wit and irony. The final and longest poem of the collection, "Immram," is Muldoon's contemporary interpretation of the ninth-century Irish voyage tale "Immram Mael Duin." In Muldoon's version the Celtic "Otherworld" of the original poem is represented by a surreal modern demimonde of decadence, drugs, and vice, which critics have commented gives the work the seamy atmosphere of a Raymond Chandler detective novel. *Why Brownlee Left* stands as a model for Muldoon's subsequent major collections of poetry: *Quoof, Meeting the British,* and *Madoc: A Mystery.* With each new work, Muldoon's poetry has become more abstruse. In the title poem of *Madoc: A Mystery,* for example, the narrative is partitioned into short poems, each captioned with the name of a philosopher, from the ancient Greeks to Stephen Hawking, on whom the lines of the poem are believed by critics to make some commentary. The collections following *Why Brownlee Left* also exhibit a similar format in which a group of shorter poems precede a long narrative poem. In both his long and short poems, Muldoon's poetic style remains densely allusive and witty. As Sarah Maguire notes in her review of *Madoc: A Mystery:* "Here again are [Muldoon's] deft rhythms, his ability to savour and play with the more obscure parts of language, and his breath-taking line-breaks and his terrible rhymes."

PRINCIPAL WORKS

POETRY

Knowing My Place   1971
New Weather   1973
Spirit of Dawn   1975
Mules   1977
Names and Addresses   1978
Immram   1980
Why Brownlee Left   1980
Out of Siberia   1982
Quoof   1983
The Wishbone   1984
Mules, and Early Poems   1985
Selected Poems: 1968-86   1986
Meeting the British   1987
Madoc: A Mystery   1990

The Times Literary Supplement

Too many of the poems in [Paul Muldoon's] highly promising collection [*New Weather*] are flawed by a vagueness of focus that dissipates the strength of original ideas. **"Dancers at the Moy"**, for instance, ends with an admirably resilient image:

> Horses buried for years
> Under the foundations
> Give their earthen floors
> The ease of trampolines.

But the ambiguous appositions and volte-faces of tense in the earlier stanzas have by this stage obscured the image's context and done the poem mortal hurt. By contrast, one of the most successful pieces is **"Good Friday 1971. Driving Westward"**, where a simple narrative framework enables the poet to communicate a genuinely disturbing experience. On a drive through the mountains a car hits something; whether big or small, an object or a life, no telling. Yet the incident becomes a powerful symbol of the insidiously random manoeuvres of guilt (whether or not the reader accepts the Christian implication of the title or, of course, the whole dimension of meaning added if he considers the Donne poem from which that title is breezily adapted). An ambivalent atmosphere is precisely created. The ambiguity of vagueness is a different thing.

That said, a distinctive voice emerges here, at its best a subtle and tuneful one. Mr Muldoon's concerns are the tensions of love relationships, Irish and other history and folk-lore, the unease and violence of the natural world. He has much of the panache, if not the rigour, of his fellow Northern Irishmen, Seamus Heaney and Derek Mahon, but his characteristic tone is altogether dreamier, more intuitively lyrical.

> *"Vaguely Nouvelle,"* in The Times Literary
> Supplement, *No. 3711, April 20, 1973, p. 442.*

Peter Scupham

Paul Muldoon's first collection, **New Weather,** was remarkable for a sense of shape and coherence in its verse structures, and a verbal resilience and energy which those structures were pliable enough to contain without atrophying. The legends, fictions, and recollections which made the book were handled in a language of resourceful simplicity, a diction timeless and balladic; somewhat derivative, yet tempered always by a strong sense of the external actuality of the natural world.

Paul Muldoon opens **Mules,** his new collection, with an oblique defence of a poetry which refuses to be converted into an overt social act, though his lay figure, the revolutionary Pancho Villa, shakes a monitory finger over the poet's "stars and horses, pigs and trees". Throughout, Muldoon's tact enables him to work from the strong, deeply-felt landscapes in which he has grown up, allowing the suggestions drawn from them to take on a wider life and energy. There is a greater clarity in these poems, more human warmth and less myth-making than there was in **New Weather;** the change seems appropriately symbolized by Faber's use of a clean roman rather than an italic face for the text of the book.

Again, Muldoon's taste for anecdote, invention, and parable shows strongly. **"The Big House"** celebrates with dry, ironic understatement the *Romanitas* of the Ascendancy as seen from below stairs; in **"Vaquero"**, the dead cowboy, lashed to the saddle, rides home with:

> . . . the halo of buzzards
> That was once a rippling, swirling lasso
> No wider now than his hat-band.

One of the most attractive of these worlds, landscapes of the camera obscura, is **"The Merman"**, a poem where mirrored farms of land and water are handy-dandied with ease, wit and elegance.

In this second book Muldoon has seen no need to relax those patterns and shapes by which the experiences are given form. Those successions of half-rhymes and approximations chipped in at the end of the line, still falling short of resolution in the final stanza, give a nervy, open quality to his perceptions, sorting well with the deceptively casual openings: "Do you remember me, Cass", "My father was a servant boy", "I've seen one in a fairground". Inside this informal formality of structure, Muldoon finds images of great particularity. The miners go down

> Swinging, for fear of the gas,

The soft flame of a canary.

Such a cut-away metaphor is not typical of Muldoon's style, which is reliant more on action and event, a sense of the thing-in-itself rather than its accretions and connotations; the whole poem is more likely to be a metaphor than to contain metaphors.

Paul Muldoon's work is now built on very real skills and perceptions. There do seem to be some dangers. The habit of creating poems from suggestive scenes and episodes can leave the reader with too strong a sense of the occasional. Several poems lack tension; in **"How to Play Championship Tennis"** or **"The Country Club"**, the approach results in merely attractive, slight pieces told by a poetic raconteur. Muldoon, either in propria persona or as a character actor, intrudes the egotistical "I", "my", or "me" too often for comfort. The diction has become less pushy than it was in *New Weather,* where there was sometimes a tone more appropriate to *Cold Comfort Farm* than to real wind and weather; now there is a greater sobriety, with occasional ventures into mythopoeia or burlesque heroics—in England you may drink a double whisky, in Ireland you're still likely to come across someone "in a fairground / Swigging a quart of whiskey".

At the worst comes the close of a Roethke-esque piece, **"Largesse"**: "Numberless cherubim and seraphim / Alleluia on my prick!" Here the exclamation mark hardly excuses the tone of this monstrous and disgusting hyperbole. Such poems reinforce the feeling that *Mules* is a book which does not yet carry the overall authority of an assured poetic personality. Sometimes, too, the open-ended nature of the final stanzas can seem to give a false resolution: an echoing final line which teases as much as it discloses.

Yet Pancho Villa is answered, in so far as Paul Muldoon's temperament can answer him, in the brief closing sequence **"Armageddon, Armageddon"**, where in seven glancing poems the themes of exile, homecoming, love, civil strife, and survival are handled with a compressed gravity and restraint. Here the poet shows a way of realizing his experiences in the terms of an artist, rather than a politician or journalist: the group is a handsome promise of good poems to come.

> Peter Scupham, "Learning from the Landscape," in The Times Literary Supplement, No. 3929, July 1, 1977, p. 801.

Alan Jenkins

Paul Muldoon opens [*Why Brownlee Left*] with a poem about dog-knotting (is it the first on that subject in the English language?) and follows it with a sonnet on the business begun in **"October 1950"**—or thereabouts—with "My father's cock / Between my mother's thighs". That second piece may acknowledge bafflement ("Whatever it is, it leaves me in the dark") before the sheer chanciness of it all, but elsewhere includes the phrase "my sly quadroon" and a graceful allusion to Laurence Sterne. So not completely in the dark. In both poems, as in much of Muldoon's work, what seems at first an essential simplicity, even crudity, of feeling is modified by immense sophistica-

---

Paul Muldoon on the Moy:

There's a nearby village called the Moy which figures quite strongly in my poems, though I've fictionalized it to a great extent. It's an area very rich in history and folklore, just as every square mile of Ireland is coming down with history and is burdened by it. The Moy itself was built by a man called James Caulfeild, who was at one stage Lord Lieutenant of Ireland, Earl of Charlemont, which is a little sister hamlet to the Moy. This story may be totally apocryphal, but Caulfeild is supposed to have designed it on the principle of an Italian town, Marengo. I've fictionalized the place to this extent—as I see it, one of my main duties as a writer is to write about what is immediately in front of me, or immediately over my shoulder. Clearly any landscape or locale is going to be re-mapped by a writer—Hardy's Wessex, Faulkner's Yoknapatawpha, Joyce's Dublin, Yeats Country—I'm not setting myself against any of them, but these are places which are recognizable in their fixtures yet are changed by the creative process. I'm very interested in the way in which a small place, a parish, can come to stand for the world.

> *Paul Muldoon in an interview with John Haffenden, in* Viewpoints: Poets in Conversation, *Faber and Faber, 1981.*

---

tion. The gentle and not-so-gentle ironies are those of a complex, controlled lyricism, which gets expressed most naturally in the telling of stories: **"Identities", "Good Friday, 1971. Driving Westward", "Vampire", "Cuckoo Corn" "Party Piece"** and **"Elizabeth"** from *New Weather* (1973); **"The Big House", "The Ducking Stool", "Lunch with Pancho Villa"** and **"Armageddon, Armageddon"** from *Mules* (1977); and everywhere in the latest, *Why Brownlee Left.*

Muldoon's is a stylishly idiosyncratic voice, allusive, indirect, investing equally in the inflexions and idioms of speech, and in a kind of virtuosity. His poems register the opposite of that "wonderment" at surfaces rendered by ingenuity of image-making; from the first, his slightly quirky diction and syntax have given an odd slant to otherwise straightforward anecdotes. The concern with "technique", the stanza forms simple or complicated, the echoes from other poetry in his native Irish tradition and outside it, the assonance, half-, off- and full rhyme: all were essential to an enterprise which issued in words of understated force and beauty: in **"Identities",** for example—"I have been wandering since, back up the streams / That had once flowed simply one into the other, / One taking the other's name"—or in **"Blowing Eggs"**:

> This is the breathless and the intent
> Puncturing of the waste
> And isolate egg and this the clean delivery
> Of little yolk and albumen.
> These his wrists, surprised and stained.

These are both endings of poems, and Muldoon's endings carry a good deal of weight without being over-heavy. In the same way, the verbal deftness, the quietly musical cadences—the whole economy of means—contrive a sleight-of-tongue which enables the words to slip out from under the burden of too much "meaningfulness" while managing to say much more than they mean. In the ambitious but not uncharacteristic early poem **"Elizabeth"** narrative and metaphor, surface and symbol, are one; the effects unforced, the speech-rhythms flexible and delicate enough to catch the girl's terror and self entrapment, the speaker's outsideness, and this small shock (the opposite of recognition):

> . . . One, and then two, and now four
> Sway back across your father's patchwork quilt
> Into your favourite elm. They will stay long
> Enough to underline how soon they will be gone,
> As you seem thinner than you were before.

Not all the early poems were as successful; there was some showy punning, some play on religious themes which put cleverness next to godliness, and some witty flourishes which wear thin very quickly. More important was a hint of underlying darkness, a suggestion of violence glimpsed behind both personal and "historical" poems. Although it is easy to feel, perhaps, that some grim realities were being rather prissily kept at one remove, they were definitely present; the very control of the writing, it seems to me, emphasized how many of our gestures are significant in this way, attempts to civilize the destructive element, the raw and uncontrollable. Muldoon's sense of Ireland was rooted in folk-lore and locality—the Moy—and in the images of a rural, often primitive, though not always Irish world; but his sense of self in that world, his grasp on it, seemed (and still seems) amazingly subtle.

Too subtle, for some; the sleight-of-tongue has been criticized as evasiveness, and the poetry as the slight, even trivial product of a precocious and precious talent, too busy with word-play and fussily intent on admiring itself. *Mules* clarified the doubts and temptations, but far from dispelling them it played on them in an almost dandified way. Self-criticism, or at least a high degree of self-consciousness, was everywhere implicit, though characteristically this involved a brilliant deployment of ironic dramatization:

> There's more to living in this country
> Than stars and horses, pigs and trees,
> Not that you'd guess it from your poems.
> Do you never listen to the news?
> You want to get down to something true,
> Something a little nearer home.

Thus "my celebrated pamphleteer" in **"Lunch with Pancho Villa"**. Yet the "something true" was unmistakably there: paradoxically in a note of unease, in this poem's ambiguous conclusion and in the disingenuousness of many others—particularly **"Paris"**. It became an undercurrent of nightmare half-heard through distant rumours of civil war in **"Armageddon, Armageddon"**:

> Some violence had been done to Grace,
> She had left for our next-of-kin.
> My brother gave us half of his last mangold
> And the warning of bayonets fixed in the bushes.

Unmistakable, too, was a Larkinesque note sounded from time to time: "Our simple wish for there being more to life / Than a job, a car, a house, a wife" (**"Our Lady of Ardboe"**). Muldoon was rhyming "croquet" with "crew-cut", "hay-stacks" with "half-bricks", and he could write, with total assurance, "The girls in the pool-room / Were out on their own limbs. / How could I help / But make men of them?". It was all infinitely seductive; but it also suggested that he might turn into a smooth writer of light verse.

The first poem in *Why Brownlee Left* again acknowledges, but this time explodes, the possibility. It tells of a chance encounter over *Cu Chulainn and the Birds of Appetite,* a saunter through the Botanic Gardens and a small tragedy: "To cut not a very long story short / Once he got stuck into her he got stuck / Full stop." But this hardly prepares us for the elegaic close, or the feeling that the couple's predicament, ridiculous and full of pathos, is somehow emblematic of a whole nation's: "gently but firmly / They were manhandled on to a stretcher / Like the last of an endangered species".

Other anecdotal pieces offer similarly engaging glimpses of the human comedy, retailed in a tone of relaxed intimacy—though the writing actually has the kind of unobtrusive formality which makes light of itself and the incidents canvassed by the poems (again, some would say dangerously light). Figures from childhood and adolescent memory people the pages, treading very close to sentimentality but given an edge by Muldoon's perception of tragi-comic immovability, or by his vision of the richly absurd: "this Kennedy's nearly an Irishman / So he's not much better than ourselves" (as the poet's father declares in **"Cuba"**).

The "unremembering darkness" of a ship's "unsteady hold", the "modest lee" of a tree-house where children swung "on a fraying rope", hankies which "unfurled / Like flags of surrender"—the details of a world, like the mildly-spoken accents, colloquial but mannerly, the precision and simplicity of Muldoon's language, are charged with a wry, melancholy warmth. In **"Truce," "Cuba"**, **"Lull"**, human sympathies and sardonic awareness seem stronger, purer than before, though what ostensibly prompts each poem—its "pretext"—has grown more slender. If the small particulars of experience—and of verbal patterns—have such currency in these poems, it is surely because they can suggest the contradictoriness of all that is anything but small: the range of Muldoon's responsiveness and feeling. The contradictions are of the kind that remain, by their nature, largely unspoken, though are everywhere strongly felt. Muldoon's kind of reticence expresses, and not only at moments of sudden directness, a deeply personal way of seeing—the more so when the "particulars" are neither small nor those of "experience" but point to the central realities of a life; events not lived through but embedded in every moment's living. The force of this is undiminished through poems dealing directly with the North (**"Anseo", "Ireland"**) and a sequence of lyrics on the death of a love-affair and marriage.

Five lines can evoke just as surely, and with as much of a quiet shock, the realities of Ulster—

> The Volkswagen parked in the gap,
> But gently ticking over.
> You wonder if it's lovers

And not men hurrying back
Across two fields and a river.

—as they can evoke, in a combination of delicate image and coarse sexual pun, tenderness and violence, the bottomless regret of final (or longed-for) intimacies:

> So put your best foot forward
> And steady on, steady on.
> Show me the plum-coloured beauty-spot
> Just below your right buttock,
> And take it like a man.

There is still—even in poems of personal estrangement—the kind of word-play, less exuberant than clever, which can make his poems feel strangely defensive, buttoned-up. But moments of greater vulnerability come with the recognition of defeat, hopelessness, even guilt, and the dropping of a pose. In **"Palm Sunday"** this follows a gently ironic aligning of yew-trees with Biblical date-palms, and of the personal with the Biblical history:

> Today's the day for all such entrances.
> I was wondering if you'd bring me through
> To a world where everything stands
> For itself, and carries
> Just as much weight as me on you.
> My scrawny door-mat. My deep, red carpet.

"The coffin-board that yearns to be a tree", Muldoon calls the yew. Turning away from openly private territory to his native country, some of his poems have a feeling of deathliness, of hopeless or abandoned striving, and find emblems for an Ireland in decay.

Such is **"Grief"**, with its broken-down hearse, the horse devoured by maggots and the "immediate family" paralysed in attitudes of horrified piety; **"Come Into My Parlour"**, its graveyards scattered with bedsteads and bathtubs; or, less obviously than these, **"The One Desire"**, a wry history of the crumbling palm-house in Belfast's Botanic Gardens—"Rusting girders, a missing pane / Through which some delicate tree / Led by kindly light / Would seem to have broken through. / We have excelled ourselves again". It's a far more convincing and more touching form of Irishry than that of the earlier books, with their myth-making strain rendered by self-conscious stiffness of diction, the occasional bardic posturing, and a weakness for the rhetoric of bar-room bravado and wisdom.

The tree here is "delicate", the light "kindly"; as, elsewhere, the word "gently" is an important one for Muldoon. Elegaic and wistful, yet as firm and sharp as it could be, this vignette is not just geographically remote from stars and horses, pigs and trees; or even from "Irish navvies drinking pints / This evening in Camden Town". Yet by the "singleminded swervings" of Muldoon's poetry the two are connected, by its sense of love and fidelity, or some such quality.

The turning-point is the ambiguously, unwittingly existential gesture of Brownlee the eponymous antihero, a farmer who uproots himself, leaving his smallholding and "his pair of black / Horses, like man and wife / Shifting their weight from foot to / Foot, and gazing into the future". The poem is resonant with both blazing self-assertion and

utter blankness; that final off-rhyme hints at the possibility of, yet refuses, resolution.

From Irishry to exoticism, and from Foster's pool-hall to Paradise, are two of the many trips undertaken (or undergone) in **"Immram"**, "a strange voyage of self-discovery" which recounts the narrator's search for the truth about his father. The longest poem in this very slim volume, told in ten line, elaborately patterned stanzas and derived from the ***Immram Mael Duin,*** it is something of a *tour de force*. Mixing elements of ancient ancestral legend (Mael Duin/Muldoon) and a down-beat West-Coast idiom, the poem explores a world of drug-pushers, dealers and "mules". Its ambience of Californian low-high life is nourished by hermit-millionaire mythology in the tradition of Howard Hughes and by more than a whiff of Raymond Chandler's *louche* or murderous goings-on and, especially, his laconic witness (though the innocent, but resourceful narrator/protagonist is also reminiscent of Nick in *The Great Gatsby*). The poem bears an oblique relation to **"Why Brownlee Left"**—perversely, it is the short poem of unassuming power which gives its title to the collection, rather than the dazzlingly virtuoso epic—but is directly linked with another of the irregular sonnets which Muldoon has almost made his own form: **"Immram"**. This traces the imagined wanderings of the poet's father from "a mud-walled cabin / Where he was born and bred / TB and scarlatina" to a fabled South American hideout: "That's him on the verandah, drinking rum / With a man who might be a Nazi".

The long poem draws these threads together, prompted by the ambivalent need to "trail my father's spirit"—or track him down, thriller-style, when another chance remark ("Your old man was an ass-hole. / That makes an ass-hole out of you") is aimed at the poet by someone brandishing a billiard cue. . . .

"Immram" may even have something to say about the ways of wealth and corruption, and the sheer weirdness, of American society, the awfulness behind awful surfaces; what doesn't sound at all awful is the source: "angel dust, dust from an angel's wing / Where it glanced off the land of cocaine, / Be that Bolivia, Peru. / Or snow from the slopes of the Andes, so pure / It would never melt in spring". The Atlantic Club, Central and Ocean Boulevards, the Park Hotel and the old Deep Water Baptist mission are *points de repère* in this half-realistic, half-hallucinatory journey; an assorted cast of grotesques keep it going, pointing the narrator on towards a final revelation. What kind of trip is it? "I am telling this exactly as it happened" he says at one point, but later avows "I was hit by a hyperdermic syringe. / And I entered a world equally rich and strange."

"Immram" might be all pure play. But Muldoon's narrating voice in this poem, rich in puns and slangy, parodic touches, is also brilliantly resourceful in its perceptions and inventions. Muldoon emerges from this endlessly fascinating and entertaining work as an unashamed word-spinner, prepared—for all the panache of the performance—to risk his poise on such pleasures and nuances as his language affords him. I say "his", because it is very much an Irish-English speech that we hear—for all the

Chandler overtones—in his poems. And, though it has its moments of anger and menace, Muldoon's poetry is most memorable for its art of gentleness. Such an art may seem irrelevant, even scandalous, to anyone making a firm stand on the ideological ground from which Muldoon mocked himself (and, implicitly, the stand) in **"Lunch with Pancho Villa"**. But the *actual* presence and weight of "history" is everywhere in these slender poems; it is, in fact, all the more powerfully present for being unsaid.

> *Alan Jenkins, "The Art of Gentleness," in* The Times Literary Supplement, *No. 4050, November 14, 1980, p. 1287.*

Paul Muldoon on Robert Frost:

I think the writer who excited me most at university was Robert Frost: an apparently simple, almost naïve, tone of voice and use of language, underneath which all kinds of complex things are happening. I believe very firmly that the most complex notions in the world can be presented in a simple, immediate way, and can have a primary, direct effect on the reader. If you take a poem like Frost's "The Road Not Taken", the complexity is astounding, and yet it just flies off the page.

> *Paul Muldoon in an interview with John Haffenden, in* Viewpoints: Poets in Conversation, *Faber and Faber, 1981.*

David Annwn

Paul Muldoon's concerns are those of a conscientious young writer: displacements of culture and of cultural origins, sexual paradoxes and traps and linguistic hubris and he possesses, above and beyond these subjects, an Irish yet truly Augustan curiosity. He has the unnerving knack of capturing most elusive atmospheres, manipulating the inflexions of Anglo-Irish (both peremptory and slang) and conveying a whole spectrum of humour: from emblematic crudery, through belly-laugh and dark whimsy, to wry warmth. He is not, however, I believe, a truly satisfying poet. Seamus Heaney talks about some of Theodore Roethke's poems being 'constructs for the inarticulate' rather than raids on the thing itself and I came away from *Why Brownlee Left* with the feeling that many of the poems are blueprints, sketches, fragments.

It is in the shorter poems that this condition is least obvious. **'The Boundary Commission'** and the marvellous **'Ireland'** stand by themselves as brief yet incisive statements. In contrast, **'Palm Sunday'** is a poem looking for foundations:

> To tell the range of the English longbows
> At Agincourt, or Crécy,
> We need look no further than the yews
> That, even in Irish graveyards,
> Are bent on Fitzwilliams, and de Courcys.
> These are the date-palms of the North.

An impressive beginning this: restrained yet taut with grim ironies. The poem even survives the advent of images that, in a moment of baroque concettism, strain or quarrel within themselves: the gourds and coffin-board 'that yearns to be a tree' of the second stanza. Then follows a lovely twist of play and wistfulness:

> Today's the day for all such entrances.
> I was wondering if you'd bring me through
> To a world where everything stands
> For itself, and carries. . . .

And then comes the final let-down, the switch from only just appropriate to totally inappropriate metaphor:

> Just as much weight as me on you
> My scrawny door-mat. My deep, red carpet.

The images will not be herded to form a correlative order for, or consciousness of, the dead. What is worse, they will not contain an attempted sidewise glance towards clumsy but tender sensuality. Further, they do not, in any convincing sense, bring these planes of discourse together. The attempt to be clever surfaces as a stillborn allusion and cheaply-bought at that.

Muldoon's predicament might bring to mind that of a much more accomplished writer: W. S. Graham. Both are capable of an admirable lyricism:

> There is such a splendour in the grass
> I might be the picture of happiness
> Yet I am utterly bereft
> Of the low hills, the open-ended sky . . .
>   **("Promises, Promises")**

an infatuation with the colourful double-takes and nuances of vernacular:

> I suppose that I should have called the cops
> Or called it a day and gone home
> And done myself, and you, a favour

a jokiness which initially seems over-obvious but gradually accumulates wit behind the reading mind:

> 'Your old man was an ass-hole.
> That makes an ass-hole out of you.'
> My grand-father hailed from New York State.
> My grand-mother was part Cree.
> This must be some new strain in my pedigree.

and a gift of jolting the reader out of presumptions about poetic fiction:

> I am telling this exactly as it happened.
>   **("Immram")**

Both are to be praised for their determination to take on the swift thrust and parry of hip allusions, offbeat slang and for their mastery of technique; (the rhythms of their poems are fluid and sensitively-deployed). However, both unfortunately suffer from the habit of letting slick phrases and swift leaps of ostentatiously disparate metaphor carry the full poetic burden. They have not, as have the majority of the British poetic establishment, sealed themselves off inexcusably and childishly from modern American influences or from the innovative writers of the 50s and 60s but it takes more than a sinuous rhythmic line or acerbic pun to engage a reader totally. Raids on the inarticulate are all very well, but, if one must use the language of aggression to sustain an incursion, one must establish a beach-head too.

But let us consider for a moment that which Heaney in his essay 'The Mixed Marriage' called Muldoon's "re-ordering of the facts of time and place" and his "delight in the trickery and lechery that words are capable of " for these are very palpable impulses in the younger writer's work. No one denies that the imagination has a right to be contrary and arbitrary or that new relations between words, meanings and places can emerge in poetry, but one does require a fitting poetic placement for these tendencies, a care for the directions and weight of allusions and a linguistic conscientiousness bearing on the power and life of the lines as they come. Sometimes Muldoon's poems are all name and music, all Tristram Shandy and Mac-Niece. To use another of his own images from **'Grief'**, what I find in Muldoon's work is an 'ornamental harness' of tight forms and sinuous thought but, in the end, all that survives in some of these poems is 'A tendril, a frond', an echo of a fully-developed voice.

Still, 'mixed marriages,' like most, have their difficult years. If Muldoon learned to temper (or even to burnish) his wit with a sustained attention and a deeper insight into layers of our environment and consciousness, he might break important new ground. But I don't wish to patronize or make an appeal or an elitist recourse to the longevity of the crucial 'Tradition'. Perhaps, in the end, I just cannot find his poems other than 'small beer', entertaining yes, but thin Allbright to Guinness drinkers. Heaney only confuses the issue by calling Muldoon's work 'hermetic' because it insists on "its proper life as words before it concedes the claims of that other life we all live before and after words". Good poetry must satisfy the reader on many levels, both spontaneously and after many readings. Jung sought after and found in the work of the Hermetic practioners a pattern of successive recognitions, as it has been used since 1605, has also meant a fusion of forces, a bringing together. Muldoon has need of such a fusion in his work, with all the intensity which this may call from him.

Ted Hughes, in seeking to define what good poetry is, talks about that "inner system of stresses" that has to be located and released and finishes an introduction to a selection of his verse:

> . . . in composing these poems I have been con-
>   cerned to give
> them—
> as well as good faces, clear brains and strong
>   hands—sound
> hearts.

In spite of the obvious pitfalls of this kind of direct anthropomorphism, I am keen to ally this poetic shape with its natural and literary correlative, that which Jeremy Hooker finds in the impressive poems of that neglected master, Frances Bellcrby: an art which seeks to satisfy the whole mind, heart and spirit of the poet and the reader. Let us admit an untrammelled variety of ways of doing this. But if Muldoon had neared a similar depth of engagement we might really find **Why Brownlee Left** to be a burning question instead of an absorbing aside. (pp. 74-7)

David Annwn, in a review of "Why Brownlee Left," in Anglo-Welsh Review, *1981, pp. 74-7.*

Paul Muldoon [Interview with Michael Donaghy]

[*Donaghy*]: *You're certainly pursuing a style different from [Irish poet Seamus] Heaney's. With Heaney you have a sense that he's writing out of a myth—it sounds like the roots of the world are speaking through him—whereas with you and Derek Mahon there's a more ironic, formal sensibility.*

[Muldoon]: Well I'm probably the worst person to answer that. It's a very small place, only fifty or sixty miles across, perhaps, and the same north-south. You tend to be brought up in much the same kind of way and have the same kind of experience. My experience was very much like Heaney's—brought up in the country, going to the same university, and pretty much following the same kind of tack—though he's fifteen years older (and I think those are a significant fifteen years.) It's true that a lot of things I write about are similar to things Seamus Heaney writes about, and early on I found comparisons a bit galling. There's a great tendency among commentators to . . . say things like, "Writers in the north of Ireland are writing in the shadow of Seamus Heaney." Perhaps its more accurate to say that readers are reading in his shadow. But in terms of what you were saying about Mahon, the most obvious thing is that both Derek and myself and indeed Michael Longley write in more evidently traditional forms, which Seamus Heaney doesn't, at least not so obviously. On a casual glance that would tend to suggest similarities or closer relationships. As I see it, these people are raising very different concerns.

Do you read Irish? I wondered to what extent you've trained your ear on Gaelic verse and to what extent the assonance and internal rhyme in your work derives from a tradition of Irish poetry in English.

That's a total imponderable, it seems to me. I'm not aware of assonance as I'm writing it. You know, "Let's have a bit of assonance here." I don't think anybody does. It's very difficult for any writer to describe his or her own style. I think there would be something seriously wrong if they could mathematically describe their style. The Irish thing . . . I don't know. I've read a lot of poetry in Gaelic, but I'm not aware of any carry over from that. If you think of the people who did consciously try to carry over Gaelic form and rhythms, like Thomas Moore in his songs, or Mangan and Davis, it all looks very stilted, not quite appropriate to English. English has its own prosody, and I think it's dangerous to assert that somehow English as it's spoken in Ireland is more colorful or musical. Those are unreal terms, and I don't understand them. I would say that in some respects the English language is still being learned in Ireland, but I wouldn't become overly romantic about it.

Hugh Kenner in The Colder Eye *makes an interesting case*

for an analysis of Irish literary style based on the word order of the Irish-English sentence.

Yes, well I suppose someone like Synge would be a prime example of that. He took the structure of Gaelic sentences and transcribed them. No, I find Synge very hard to stick. I find that kind of language forced. In *The Shadow Of The Glen,* for example, the tramp arriving at the door; I can't quote the line exactly . . . It's just stilted and stultifying, because he's not engaging by and large the rhythms of everyday speech.

There must have been a precedent in English poetry. Where could that rhapsodic rhythm and fanciful sentence structure have come from? Hopkins maybe?

I don't think so. Hopkins didn't hit the scene until 1912. Maybe Mangan or Moore. There would have been some kind of germ of traditional gaelic poetry in English.

In characterizing your work a lot of reviewers refer to your "wry tone".

Well I'm not aware of a particular tone or style when I'm writing. That seems to me to be a form of death.

But there's a time to be self-conscious.

Well, certainly one should be *conscious,* but not to the point where you're looking over your shoulder saying "This is P. Muldoon sitting down to write a poem." I'm not interested in that. I'm interested in getting on with the poem.

That's true, but when I read "Immram" the tone really keeps me on my toes from line to line.

Well, that was the hope. Naturally, that isn't my language; it's so far removed from my rhythms of speech. . . . As you know, it's totally parodic of [Raymond] Chandler.

But you undermine and transform the Chandler, and you find Byron in there too, and Robert Service as well.

There were various reasons for that. Byron is one of the classic tellers of tales. He just grabs you and takes you with him . . . so I was hoping for a bit of that. And Chandler appeals as a supreme stylist—perhaps a *mere* stylist. That's not to denigrate him. That upgrades him in my book.

A pure stylist?

Yes. A man who pretended to be engaged in narratives but wasn't the least interested.

You know, Auden was a great fan of Chandler's for the same reason.

Sure. Chandler said that when he was stuck, he'd have another body fall out of the cupboard. If you examine any of his plots you find that they're incredibly shaky. And yet it doesn't matter.

You say you admire Byron because he's a great storyteller. But there's another aspect of Byron present in your longer poems—the extraordinary rhymes of Don Juan . . . you have some great rhymes in "Immram" . . .

. . . really terrible rhymes . . .

Now I was hoping you'd say you were following in the Irish tradition of slant rhyme handed down through Yeats.

Indeed there may be something in that, that kind of assonantal rhyme. That's ancient history. There's nothing new about that, but I am interested in half rhymes or less than half rhymes.

You do some wonderful things with rhyme, and you foreground some of the most tenuous aural connections.

Well, any kind of formalism is most useful as a kind of framework for both the reader and the writer and the reader/writer as he's trying to put the thing down. It's like a piece of scaffolding or a loom. At the end of the day you can take the loom away, and you're not conscious of the structure—the thing doesn't leap out at you and assert itself. But there's got to be some logic to these things. There's no point in using rhyme for its own sake; the framework has to be so far back it doesn't distract the reader from the thrust of the poem. Or, as in Byron, it should grab you by the back of the head and say, 'Look at this. This is absolutely silly.'

So it should either be subliminal or . . .

Well I'm not being proscriptive about these things. Lots of fun can be had rhyming "moon" with "June". But again, there's got to be some reason for these things.

You do a lot of interesting things with narrative form, subverting narrative convention, just as you often undermine traditional forms—the crumbled sonnet, for example.

That's a good word. Someone has described them as "deconstructed sonnets." Yeah, there's a lot of that.

Well I find that same deconstructing at work in the longer poems. "Immram" and "The More A Man Has The More A Man Wants" are very compelling as stories. You're swept up with the action . . .

They get you to turn the page.

And they keep you in suspense from line to line. I'm always wondering how you're going to complete or default on a rhyme or how you're going to turn this or that cliché on its head. But the most interesting thing I find is where you'll flash from the main story to some detail (the narrator's father in "Immram," for example, and the description of his life in South America). The stories have these narrative cul-de-sacs, and this again reminds me of Byron.

Yes. I suppose another way of describing it would be "cinematic" or "quick cutting." In a longer poem you simply cannot go at a lick right the way through. You've got to have variety in the pace or else it's a runaway horse. Or it's boring. And one way to vary the pace is to move in for a close up of a detail and quick cut back to the central story. But I don't think there's anything earth-shattering in my use of that technique. It's just nuts and bolts stuff.

*Often in your books a theme develops through individual poems. Some peculiar word or reference will be picked up in the next poem. The title poem of your new book **Quoof,** for example, ends with your hand on this girl's breast like the "Spoor of the yeti," and the next poem is "Bigfoot." They seem to lead on that way so often. Are you aware of* *these themes at the very beginning or do you try to arrange the poems this way at the end?*

Well, this is a big one. I think because these poems—anyone's poems—come from one personality it's inevitable that the range of concerns will be kind of coherent. I certainly don't sit down to write books with themes—that'd be an appalling thought—but I think there's some reason why a book is a book, not just because it's forty pages or sixty, or because it has three dozen poems in it. I mean there's got to be some other shape or rationale. As the individual poems come along, they begin, for me at any rate, to sit beside each other comfortably or uncomfortably, to move around, sometimes correcting each other or illuminating each other (one hopes), or perhaps one will completely deny the thrust of another. When a number of poems are gathered together in their individual names, then perhaps they have some common purpose—but I don't want to give you the idea that there's something programmatic or calculating about this procedure. Think of Yeats, for example, as he grew older he revised and changed words in his earlier work so there'd seem to be a kind of continuity of theme and concern—as if to prove that Yeats was a guy who really knew what he was up to from the start.

Derek Mahon revised a lot for his last comprehensive collection. Some people think he damaged the poems. Of course, all that's very hard to say. It requires a freshly distanced reading, you get so used to the original versions.

Well that certainly is a problem for me, but I wouldn't want to go so far as to say they're damaged. In general, my feeling is that a writer has no particular right to go back to something he's written or that has been written through him—with whom he's had some kind of affair. It may be an affair of a weekend or one that lasts six months, say five years later things have changed—I don't think a writer has any right to go back and fiddle about with it. If he feels the thing doesn't work, then skip it, throw it out, try to forget about it. I'm sure there are all sorts of marvellous exceptions to this principle, but I would prefer to lose the entire limb rather than try and doctor it. When you're writing a poem, you might be particularly alert to the significance or impulse of a particular word or how it relates to another word, and later you may have entirely forgotten about this. I know that at times people have mentioned something they saw in one of my poems, and I'd forgotten that that was going on there myself. There's always that danger.

Also, a poem is conceived in a unified impulse—whether it takes a week or month—and after you've moved along and gone on to something else you can never be entirely faithful to that. Another thing is that it no longer belongs to you.

Exactly. You may perhaps be slightly better informed, you may have a special relationship with it, but its no more than that. It belongs to other people. You're only another reader after a certain point, and at that point you're free to say, "Well, as a reader of this poem I think it's not that bad." Or more often, I must say that it's a pretty terrible poem.

Does the expression "Martian poetry" mean anything to you?

Yes. Five or six years ago in England, Craig Raine published a book called *A Martian Sends A Postcard Home* which presents an innocent or naive view of everyday objects. It was very effective; his images . . . "similes" is the key word . . . can be very rewarding, and there are a few other poets in England who have been classed along with him in this kind of "pack"—David Sweetman and Christopher Reid, for example. It's a style that attracts a lot of attention and is very fashionable, but I get a bit concerned at the short sightedness of some commentators on these matters who would suggest that the simile is something that was invented over the past five or six years. It's a bit silly to say of a writer who uses simile—which is after all one of the key tools of any kind of writing—that "This is Martian". It has been said, and I think that's quite extraordinary.

Do you feel you've been tagged as one of these poets?

Once or twice, yes. I don't like being labelled and reviewers are all about labels. Anyone who says of a particular writer, "This guy is a Martian," because he uses similes, is a fool. There's also this new idea that's being pushed at the moment of a "new narrative" movement in English poetry. From what I remember of the introduction to the new Penguin anthology of contemporary British poetry, it argues that there are these two strains or trends, the Martian and the narrative. Some people would say that I'm a narrative poet, which I am, or that I use similes, which I do. But both narrative and the use of simile are at the heart of poetry. It's extremely short-sighted of anyone to abstract one or both of these elements. There are many other elements in the writing of poetry, and to raise any into some kind of religion . . . it's just *crap*. Certainly, I've been very interested in narrative, but I don't see myself doing anything new in that.

I wanted to ask you about the differences you see between contemporary Irish/English poetry and American poetry. America is a recurrent theme in your work—the presence of the US as a political power and as an exotic place where strange things happen. And you play against the Western and Private Eye genres, two clichés of American popular literature.

Yes, well clichés are clichés for very good reasons. There's a hell of a lot in them. I think that writers in Ireland, as well as the Irish in general, are inclined to look towards America. Indeed, many have done more than look towards it.

You mean they emigrate.

Yes. And in terms of writing it seems to me that a lot of exciting things have happened here—perhaps most of all in the last thirty years. One of my favorite poets is Robert Frost.

You've mentioned Frost in other interviews, and so has Seamus Heaney. In a way it seems to suggest that you two see more going on in Frost than a lot of Americans do.

Well, I think Frost is partly to blame for that.

271

Cover of Muldoon's third collection of poems.

He became an establishment poet. At Kennedy's Inaugural . . .

Ah yes, but that's a very interesting matter. When I talk about this, I must say that I'm to some extent reflecting the ideas of my friend Gerard Quinn. I recently wrote a poem called **"Gold"** which refers to Kennedy's Inaugural. It's about reading Robert Frost with this man Quinn. Frost says that the new administration welcomes in a "golden age of poetry and power / Of which this noontide's the beginning hour." Now noon is the peak of the day. If the beginning is the peak of it, the rest is a kind of decline. Then consider the phrase "golden age". The word "gold" as it occurs throughout Frost is almost inevitably pejorative. "Nothing gold can stay", for example, or "We almost ate our peck of gold." So old Frost was up to his tricks at Kennedy's Inauguration. That kind of complexity beyond the cracker barrel image is something we are going to have to come to terms with in Frost, if he's to be properly understood. His great virtue is that he's accessible, but sometimes, if you look twice, there's a complete undercutting of what he seems to be saying. I find that very interesting, and it's something I try to do myself. I try for a sub-text which is quite often totally at variance with the main text. If you take **"Why Brownlee Left"**, for example, it seems to be stating in a very matter of fact way that it's a mystery why Brownlee left. But it's evident from the poem that there's a very good reason why he left: he was bored. His very name suggests this. He's a brown lee, a ploughed field. His life was programmed, and he needed to break free from becoming his own destiny. It's obvious, but the tone of the poem is at variance with that.

There seems to be much more violence in **Quoof** *than the other books.*

Yes. I don't think it's a very likeable or attractive book in its themes.

It deals with very horrifying things in a grotesquely funny way. People expect a very earnest treatment of the "Troubles", but I suppose when you live with it day by day you've got to make jokes about it.

You've got to. But I don't mean that it can be dismissed or treated lightly.

What are your politics?

I don't think it matters. I don't think it's of any interest.

That's a pretty blunt statement.

It doesn't matter where I stand politically, with a small "p" in terms of Irish politics. My opinion about what should happen in Northern Ireland is no more valuable than yours. (pp. 77-85)

> *Paul Muldoon and Michael Donaghy, in an interview in* Chicago Review, *Vol. 35, No. 1, Autumn, 1985, pp. 76-85.*

Mark Ford

So characteristic of Paul Muldoon's poetry as to be almost a hallmark is the moment, unnerving and exciting in about equal measures, when his speaker is suddenly revealed to himself as someone else. The whole world expands and changes in **'Cass and Me'** when, as a boy, he climbs on the older Cass's shoulders, and they lean out

> across the yard
> As a giant would across the world . . .
>
> The sow fled West with her farrow,
> The hound made a rainbow under the barrow.
> The cock crowed out of time.
>
> So large we loomed.
> Which of us, I wonder, had grown,
> Whose were those wide eyes at my groin?

Here the perceptions spring from a physical convergence, and it is typical of the studiedly neutral Muldoon persona that he finds himself both appropriating and subtly distinguishing himself from 'those wide eyes' at his groin. More often, though, the confusion and discriminations that emerge are linguistic, and less easy to disentangle, as for the even younger boy ('threeish') in **'The Right Arm'** who plunders the last bit of clove-rock from the shop he and his parents keep in English.

> I would give my right arm to have known then
> How Eglish was itself wedged between

ecclesia and *église,*

he muses perplexingly—not exactly the Wordsworthian insight into hidden justice and unknown modes of being that one was expecting. Violence and exhilaration are located somewhere behind the poem, but are suppressed by Muldoon's diffidence, insulated, like his right arm, by the sleeve of glass that both protects and inhibits, and 'has yet to shatter'.

A more overtly intense confluence and self-alienation occurs in the superb title-poem of [*Meeting the British*], in which he imagines an encounter between the chief of a Red Indian tribe and some British military colonists:

> We met the British in the dead of winter.
> The sky was lavender
>
> and the snow lavender-blue.
> I could hear, far below,
>
> the sound of two streams coming together
> (both were frozen over)
>
> and, no less strange,
> myself calling out in French
>
> across that forest-
> clearing . . .

Yet this kind of Romantic self-release can only be suicidal to a wised-up, historical awareness like Muldoon's. Neither General Jeffrey Amherst nor Colonel Henry Bouquet can stomach the willow-tobacco the Indians offer. And in return

> They gave us six fishhooks
> and two blankets embroidered with smallpox.

The disorientations Muldoon stores up here, and unleashes in the poem's final word, resonate throughout *Meeting the British,* which continues to exploit the extraordinary blend of finicky gentleness and precise violence he originated in *Quoof.*

Quoof tended to push its metaphors, trance-like, to the point of no return, its mushroom hallucinations not deviations from but a visionary heightening of reality: the poems in *Meeting the British* seem more self-aware. The book is not held together with quite the obsessive thematic coherence with which Muldoon previously structured his effects, but operates through more casual continuities and allusions. A few of the poems—'**The Toe-Tag**', '**Crossing the Line**', '**My Grandfather's Wake**'—collapse his usual methods of oblique narration, and seem to function like musical variations. In this kind of poem the different parts, often further separated by asterisks, relate metaphorically to each other: they display similar symptoms, as it were, but don't immediately connect. '**The Toe-Tag**' seems to conjugate the perverse relationship between violence and luxury in a sequence of analogues, though behind it may lurk a more old-fashioned poem of sexual disgust. Rolls-Royces idle, 'their seats upholstered with the hides of stillborn calves'; there's a 'jigger of blood on your swish organza'; even a tagged cactus causes 'ecstasy' by reminding 'you' of the labelled big toe of a corpse.

Fragmentations like these are probably best understood as

new techniques Muldoon has discovered for maintaining the tight-wire neutrality on which much of the success of his poetry depends. The faux-naif voice he developed so brilliantly in *Mules* and *Why Brownlee Left* was a perfect vehicle for the uncommitted counter-punching of his cautious, rather passive-aggressive poetic persona, and is excellently deployed again in such poems as '**The Coney**' and '**Brock**', but the experimental nature of many of the others suggests he is in active pursuit of new ways of projecting himself without seeming to do so. There are all kinds of new types of poem in *Meeting the British.* '**Ontario**' is in prose. '**Bechbretha**' seems to be a political satire. There is an extended, untypically straightforward elegy for a friend, '**The Soap-Pig**'. The book's final, long poem is a sequence of dramatic monologues spoken by the famous residents of 7, Middagh Street in Brooklyn Heights and sounds more like something from Lowell's *Notebook* phase than like any of Muldoon's earlier work.

These are all, in their different ways, new acts of the 'ventriloquism' which, Muldoon once commented, he finds the best means of overcoming the self-parody implicit in over-self-consciousness. Most of his poems seem designed to implode in the act of being read. In a gleeful, spirited way he likes to seal each one within its particular metaphorical capsule; it can 'engage for thirty seconds in a little fiction; it has moved me, it will hopefully move you, disturb you, excite you; and having said and done that, we go our separate ways back into the welter.' Emotionally discontinuous with each other, there is no danger that they will ever locate or identify their author: the continuing resourcefulness of his voice depends on our building up no relationship with it, on its seeming to come each time 'out of the blue', like the 16-ounce billiard cue that initiates the business of '**Immram**'.

A self-effacing art such as this must perpetually refine itself, and *Meeting the British* adds some wonderful new tricks to Muldoon's repertoire. Two of the book's most effective pieces, '**Sushi**' and '**Christo's**', succeed by feigning a winning helplessness in the face of the brilliance of their own metaphorical processes. '**Christo's**' describes a day's drive from Dingle to Belfast, during which everything the protagonists observe—

> mounds of sugar-beet,
> hay-stacks, silage-pits, building-sites,
> a thatched cottage even

—seems to be draped in black polythene and weighted against the wind, like a Christo sculpture. This is prime Muldoon territory—things insulated and concealed inside themselves, the purely random and over-artistic somehow marrying, seeming revelations that lead nowhere—but the poem's dénouement unfolds like a sly disavowal of the extravagance of the conceit:

> By the time we go to Belfast
> the whole of Ireland would be under wraps
> like, as I said, 'one of your man's landscapes'.
> 'Your man's? You don't mean Christo's?'

In '**Sushi**', the most brilliant of Muldoon's many restaurant poems, he detaches himself in an equally effective way from his fancy, by inching it higher and higher until it finally topples. While his exasperated dining companion complains to him about his self-absorption, he has eyes only for the way an apprentice

> had scrimshandered a rose's
> exquisite petals
> not from some precious metal
> or wood or stone
> ('I might just as well be eating alone')
> but the tail-end of a carrot.

The excessiveness of the poem's final line both clinches the performance and dismantles the artifice. The carrot is submitted to the chef, and

> it might have been alabaster
> or jade
> the Master so gravely weighed
> from hand to hand
> with the look of a man unlikely to confound
> Duns Scotus, say, with Scotus Eriugena.

'Sushi' and 'Christo's' are also typical of *Meeting the British* in the way they deliberately blend images of the exotic and the banal. Indeed, almost all the poems here seem to relate in some way to the outlandish. From early in his career, Muldoon has been given to organising his collections around single principles and a corresponding group of related images: in *Mules* it was the concept of hybrids, sterile lives 'caught between heaven and earth'; in *Why Brownlee Left* the clash between random, inexplicable behaviour and an obsessive idealism; *Quoof* revolved around a vision of some magic realm beyond the reach of life's contradictions. Such bald abstractions can give Muldoon's progress an ominous consistency that is at odds with the variety and distinctiveness of his achievement, but it is also true that he plots the thematic interrelationships of his poems with utmost care. The delicacies and exotica with which *Meeting the British* abounds—a flute carved from a missionary's tibia, a spider-crab, medallions of young peccary, a nine-banded armadillo found wandering in Meath in the 1860s, an albino rabbit, a fish with three gold teeth, the sandvein like a 'seam of beryl' in an uncircumsized penis, triremes, quinqueremes, caymans, peacocks—are the book's currency, as shamans and mushroom metamorphoses were *Quoof*'s. Literary and artistic allusions thicken the texture still further: Wyeth, Soutine, the Mabinogion, O. Henry, Spinoza, Giraldus Cambrensis, Louis Aragon, Gerard de Nerval, Terence Malick, lots of Yeats, lots and lots of Masefield's 'Cargoes', Scott Fitzgerald, Delmore Schwartz, Marilyn Monroe, *Un Chien Andalou*, Hart Crane, *Ben Hur* . . . An index to proper names in the book would be several pages long.

This all-pervasive cosmopolitan glamorousness, often treated ironically, is most vivid in '7, Middagh Street'. 7, Middagh Street was the three-storey brownstone rented by George Davis—literary editor of *Harper's Bazaar* at the time—and tenanted by Auden, Carson McCullers, Benjamin Britten and Gypsy Rose Lee; shorter-term residents included Louis MacNeice, Auden's lover Chester Kallman and Salvador Dali. The poem consists of a monologue by each of these. Like 'Immram' and 'The More a Man Has the More a Man Wants', '7, Middagh Street' is a beguiling mixture of the serious and the silly. Muldoon

skittishly connects the seven poems to each other by an outrageous network of literary allusions; they are also involved in an elaborate sort of tag, the last line of one poem being picked up by the first line of the next. What is new is the poem's tone, which is rapt, even devotional, each carefully amassed fact dispensed as from an oracle.

In many ways Muldoon is one of the least suited of poets to pay direct homage to previous writers, and his desire to experiment with the form deserves respect. In *Station Island* Heaney confronts his shades from the fixed point of his own absolutely solid poetic personality: strangely, our almost physical impression of him can seem to be enhanced by the artifice and decorum of the convention the poem exploits. Muldoon's disembodied persona, mostly identifiable as the merest insinuation in a habit of speech, can establish no equal terms with literary heroes from the past; charismatic figures like Auden or Dali fit uneasily into an arbitrary medium like his, which tends to create itself as it goes along, reducing everything it touches to its own peculiar weightlessness. Muldoon is acutely aware of the problem, and might be said to make it the poem's principal theme. His Auden, Dali and MacNeice confront the relations of art, history and politics specifically, and often with wonderful eloquence:

> For history's a twisted root
> with art its small, translucent fruit
>
> and never the other way round.

That's Auden, with a vengeance perhaps. All three yearn for a firm sense of their own rootedness, though Auden again denies one can do more than strain 'for the ghostly axe / of a huge, blonde-haired lumberjack'. Dali, pictured in the act of rejecting the autonomy of Surrealism, discovers a more general resilience to the abrasions of human history:

> Our civil wars, the crumbling of empires,
> the starry nights without number
>
> safely under our belts,
> have only slightly modified the tilt
>
> of the acanthus leaf,
> its spiky puce-and-alabaster an end in itself.

Much of the poem's impact depends upon the range and intensity with which Muldoon develops these grand themes, and the sections not energised by them—on McCullers, Gypsy Rose Lee, Chester Kallman—tend to be what they call in *Scoop* mere 'colour'. In the end, it is Muldoon's countryman MacNeice, about to return to do his bit in war-torn Britain, who emerges most creditably, rebuking Auden for his apoliticism and insisting on the power of individual responsibility:

> For poetry *can* make things happen—
> not only can, but *must* . . .

Although the poem's self-reflexive ending seems to negate the possibility of this kind of commitment, it is still intriguing, and moving, to hear such things said not wholly ironically in a Muldoon poem. (pp. 20-1)

Mark Ford, "Out of the Blue," in London Review of Books, *Vol. 9, No. 22, December 10, 1987, pp. 20-1.*

Dave Smith

Paul Muldoon favors an associational strategy that minimizes the usual metaphoric stance of poetry: a thing is not like another thing so much as it is evoked by the fleeting presence of another thing, event, circumstance which is obliquely, almost as an informational aside, presented out of memory. Muldoon, only thirty-seven, is already a much admired voice among younger contemporary Irish poets. Seamus Heaney has called him "one of the best." Yet many readers will find it is no easy task to dip in and out of the poems of his *Selected Poems 1968-1986* because it rather requires an absorption into his method that is almost the learning of a foreign language.

There is, for example, a mysteriously significant moment hinted at in **"Chinook,"** but its nature is never clearly revealed. We know only that a speaker recites a past experience in which he "was micro-tagging Chinook salmon." Not the fish but their American Indian name fascinates him—but only as the link to something else in the mind:

> Chinook. Their very name
> a semantic
> quibble.
>
> The Autumn, then, of *Solidarity,*
> your last in Cracow.
> Your father
>
> rising between borsch
> and carp,
> relinquishing the table to Pompeii.

What begins as a pastoral memory turns to meditation on language and picks up speed as an angular description of political and domestic drama, all of which is tied to realistic presentation only through the temporal and imagistic associations. We *feel* something terrible has happened, our feeling evoked by the suggestion of the crushed Polish workers and the buried Italian city—but what? And is that really the concern of this poem?

Our desire to *know* and the angles by which we appear to know, never exactly, are Muldoon's toys. He refuses to satisfy our explicit expectations and creates poems with the character of riddles, enigmas, and tales. His playfulness with language clearly links him to the line of Joyce rather than Yeats. It is possible to feel some of his poems are so slight as to evaporate, but almost always he applies the delicacy of an engraver to set into his poem a level of experience that surprises and delights.

Muldoon is, in fact, a chronicler of the most ordinary moments of domestic life, a ride around an automobile cloverleaf, a memory of fishing with his father, the punishment of a teenage sister, overhearing news of an English political/sexual scandal, people who disappear or smoke marijuana in North Carolina or grow up just as we could see they would when they were children, even the love of a dog that exceeds love of a woman. Yet he is rarely a linear observer, given the spatially associational character of his imagination, and generally seems uninterested in the flourishes of anyone's mandarin poetic style.

For all that, it was never truer to say that here is a poet whose subject is language itself, the working of words. When we cannot see our way through directly to what a poem's words represent, we are forced to stare at words themselves, like a wall behind which we might hear voices we cannot decipher. To the Canadian Atwood, language represents the distortion of reality. To the Scot Dunn, it is the passage from class entrapment that may well be a doorway even Alice couldn't get back through. For Muldoon, language seems something else, a code without clear function or translators. It has, in his case, unfamiliar syntactical shapes, a diction as strange and idiomatically Irish to the American ear as are its curiously stop-and-go cadences. Moreover, a Muldoon poem will frequently refuse the expected beginning-middle-end structure.

In **"Duffy's Circus,"** Muldoon describes the arrival of that festivity which so excites everyone that "God may as well have left Ireland / And gone up a tree." The portrait is one of a comedic and airily buoyant family outing when the father and son haul themselves off to join the action. The poet recalls, however, that all did not go well:

> I had lost my father in the rush and slipped
> Out the back. Now I heard
> For the first time that long drawn-out cry.
>
> It came from somewhere beyond the corral.
> A dwarf on stilts. Another dwarf.
> I sidled past some trucks. From under a freight-
> er
> I watched a man sawing a woman in half.

Muldoon's ambiguity is a composite of the child's guileless observation and the poet's constant understatement—not vagueness but a refusal to specify one of several equal possibilities. Is the boy, alone in the world without his Virgilian parent, watching a magician at work on a famous trick? Or is it a sexual act? The cry might be either pleasure or pain, or both. It is maturity in any case. The angle of this speech is very like Elizabeth Bishop's reticent, careful cry from the dentist's office.

As with Bishop, it is difficult to pin down what Muldoon thinks about life and art and such. He tends toward stances of bemusement from which to note that living reaches few, if any, conclusions, only enigmatic moments that examination will reveal to be standoffs. He may speak in the voice of a servant girl or as a sort of mogul having lunch with Pancho Villa. He enjoys the cinematic effects familiar to him from his work in British Broadcasting Corporation productions, but perhaps nothing is more characteristic of Muldoon than a penchant for the graphic, even grotesque detail that doesn't so much explore or define a puzzlement as embody it, as when mule reproduction is distilled to "the afterbirth / Trailed like some fine, silk parachute. . . . " Or it may be the ominous disappearance of a farmer named Brownlee who by all accounts enjoyed ordinary workaday success when he "was last seen going out to plough / On a March morning, bright and early."

> By noon Brownlee was famous;

They had found all abandoned, with
The last rig unbroken, his pair of black
Horses, like man and wife,
Shifting their weight from foot to
Foot, and gazing into the future.

Though Muldoon places himself nowhere near the scene, one feels him shuddering just as the reader does before *that* marriage and *that* future. To be sure, E. A. Robinson would have recognized the slippery and predictably bottomless world under our various feet.

In fact, Brownlee and his horses, even the shadow-wife he may have, suggest Muldoon's constant effort to account for the inevitable rendings of the world's symmetries, its coupled structures. His especially fabular (at its worst coyly allegorical) poetry evokes wonder because it presupposes and works against a standard of orderly continuity we imagine as the basis of our lives. Against suburban comfort (even Ireland has its suburbs, its yuppies, its mall life), Muldoon's domestic scenes bend and twist to become tales of ugly ducklings, swains and ladies, grail pursuits, the legends of our strangeness. But in Muldoon nothing is treated as really strange: it is normal. We come to accept this lens, an odd kind of spectacles, and when Muldoon describes the word "quoof" as "our family word / for the hot water bottle," we are not at all distressed that he leaps with no transition, only the word, to:

> An hotel room in New York City
> With a girl who spoke hardly any English,
> My hand on her breast
> like the smoldering one-off spoor of the yeti
> or some other shy beast
> that has yet to enter the language.

But how can we fail to be at least puzzled by a sudden combination of a fabricated word, a naked girl, a legendary and perhaps nonexistent giant-beast, all together with the poet in a New York hotel room (where anything, I agree, is possible)? We can't, if we insist on plot, on language that explains, on a consciousness that keeps separate all that happens to us and continues happening in the memory as well as the imagination. Given time, though, Muldoon dissipates our anxieties, and his poems come to seem like songs that drift around the back of the head to summon up lives we have not stopped living. It is an intense, surprisingly interior poetry that appears not to want to move through experience to closure but rather to *look at* what occurs idiosyncratically.

Muldoon's idiosyncrasy extends even to his favorite form, the sonnet. It appears fractured visually, metrically, and in combination with longer forms. Perhaps it would be un-Irish did he not rhyme as often as not, but you will never mistake him for a parlor voice. He is irreverent, off-beat, jaunty, sometimes cocky. He has several longish narrative poems which concern playing pool or American travel or doing the voices in a kind of chorus of Auden, MacLeish, Isherwood, and the rest. While they hold out their entertainments, I find them strained, overlong, and not well suited to Muldoon's puckish talent. It is the short form that allows him the swift, effective jab (**"Holy Thursday"**), the tongue-in-cheek political swipe (**"Meeting the British"**), the wry innocence (**"Ned Skinner"**) which led Sea-

mus Heaney to write in 1978 of Muldoon's "sophisticated repose of *poesie pure*" and his "sceptical, playful imagination."

Although he is young enough to have hardly got started, Paul Muldoon's **Selected Poems** is a treasure. You can take it to the beach, read it to waitresses, laugh while you feel these are words with bite. Deep, as they say. Muldoon has a deviously subtle register of tones, and he makes poetry fun. Once you have got onto his way of saying, he sounds no stranger than your own life does at the end of the day. It's at least that memorable. There are poems about the Irish political troubles to show he is not without serious intention, poems about childhood, about love, about writers and places. But none might suggest how deft and fine a poet Muldoon is more than a poem about his father's death. Let it be an invitation to readers:

The Fox

Such an alarm
as was raised last night
by the geese
on John Mackle's goose-farm.

I got up and opened
the Venetian blind.
You lay
three fields away

in Collegelands
graveyard, in ground
so wet you weren't so much
buried there as drowned.

That was a month ago.
I see your face
above its bib
pumped full of formaldehyde.

You seem engrossed,
as if I'd come on you
painfully writing your name
with a carpenter's pencil

on the lid
of a mushroom-box.
You're saying, *Go back to bed.*
It's only yon dog-fox.

(pp. 142-46)

Dave Smith, "Formal Allegiances: Selected Poems x 6," in The Kenyon Review, *n.s. Vol. X, No. 3, Summer, 1988, pp. 127-46.*

John Drexel

Paul Muldoon is the sort of poet whose career provokes extreme envy even among those—perhaps most especially among those—who find his work ultimately empty, all surface charm and no depths. . . . A steady stream of books with the imprimatur of Faber & Faber—**New Weather** (1973), **Mules** (1977), **Why Brownlee Left** (1980), and **Quoof** (1983)—has fueled his reputation. Today he is probably the most publicized of the Ulster poets after Heaney. It would not be unfair to suggest that his vistas are more international than Heaney's, his technique more deliberately postmodernist than Montague's or Kinsella's. True, his work has always been full of local color, of a sort, but it is rarely if ever provincial. His latest and, in some ways, his most ambitious book, *Meeting the British,* shows him protean as ever, acting a variety of roles but not fully identifiable in any of them.

Most of the time, Muldoon is more interesting than most of his American counterparts in the New Formalism and New Narrative movements. He has absorbed his wide-ranging material whole, and brings a keen waggish talent to bear on his subjects. He generally manages to keep one foot in what we might call, for want of a more precise and elegant term, the Real World, and the other in the world of his imagining. In the one we find swatches of childhood incidents or adolescent escapades, no more than salvaged fragments of experience, which he embroiders and out of which he makes personal myths, as in **"The Coney," "Profumo,"** and **"Cristo's."** Then there are poems that seem fashioned out of only a mouthful of air, such as **"The Mist Net," "The Wishbone,"** and **"The Lass of Aughrim":**

> On a tributary of the Amazon
> an Indian boy
> steps out of the forest
> and strikes up on a flute.
>
> Imagine my delight
> when we cut the outboard motor
> and I recognize the strains
> of *The Lass of Aughrim.*
>
> 'He hopes,' Jesus explains,
> 'to charm
> fish from the water
>
> on what was the tibia
> of a priest
> from a long-abandoned Mission.'

But, for all the poignancy here, I can't help feeling that this poem, like a number of others in the book, is more a product of contrivance than of honest feeling. In a sense, what Muldoon is trying to prove is the primacy of the imagination without regard for actual experience. For all that words denote real objects, or at least can do, they can have equal validity as simply tools for a poet's exercise. I find it more plausible to believe that Muldoon got the images for this poem in a darkened cinema on New York's Upper West Side than a firsthand expedition up the Ucayali.

The full weight of *Meeting the British* lies in the concluding poem, " **'7, Middagh Street,' '** a tour-de-force that is also an exercise in pure Muldoonery. As Muldoon informs us, " **'7, Middagh Street'** takes its name from the Brooklyn Heights residence of George Davis, fiction editor for Harper's Bazaar. In the autumn of 1940, W. H. Auden, Chester Kallman, Gypsy Rose Lee, Benjamin Britten, Peter Pears, Salvador Dali, Carson McCullers, Louis MacNeice, Paul and Jane Bowles, and a trained chimpanzee were among the residents and visitors there." From this minor footnote to literary history, Muldoon fashions a baroque narrative in which all the aforementioned characters figure. As well as displaying his exuberant wit and imagination, **"7, Middagh Street"** shows that Muldoon is no slouch as a wordsmith. His lexical portmanteau is de-

monstrably larger than any other poet's today (and for extra effect, he also travels with a comprehensive atlas): who but Muldoon would "parlay with the mugwumps" using such words as "quinquereme," "flummoxed," "gormandize," and *"trou normand,"* or employ proper nouns to generate such wild rhymes as lemon / Ashmolean, Valladolid / welded, Eden / Auden, Tristan / rechristen, Minneapolis / nipples, Ovidian / *Healfdene,* and Goebbels / St Paul's? He even transforms his own name into a pub and rhymes it with "melodeon." The ground is in fact so thick with learned allusions, puns and fancy rhymes almost become all we notice; Muldoon's so taken with the virtuosity of his exercise, the dazzle of his achievement, that we can't help but feel he's continually winking at his audience. An acquaintance of mine who is something of an authority on Auden characterized Muldoon's metier as "exceptionally deft locker-room humor," and meant it uncharitably. Be that as it may, it's not the locker room at Madison Square Garden we're talking about, but rather, the sushi bar where

> it might have been alabaster
> or jade
> the Master so gravely weighed
> from hand to hand
> with the look of a man unlikely to confound
> Duns Scotus, say, with Scotus Eriugena.
>   **("Sushi")**

Any poet who can make that distinction *and* work it into a poem is certainly not looking over his shoulder for the ghost of Yeats. Such audaciousness is clearly out of the Audenary. (pp. 190-92)

> *John Drexel, "Threaders of Double-Stranded Words: News from the North of Ireland," in* New England Review and Bread Loaf Quarterly, *Vol. XII, No. 2, Winter, 1989, pp. 179-92.*

Ronald Marken

Irish poets have reconstituted the English sonnet's intricate machinery in scores of fascinating ways, much more imaginatively than have their English counterparts. They have boldly modified line length, rhyme scheme, and structural division, creating sonnets with their own tails in their mouths, trimeter fourteen-lines with two lonely but essential rhymes in the whole poem, gloriously tangled rhyme schemes in a seven-seven structure, and even thirteen-liners with so many allusions to other fourteen-liners that one is seriously tempted to call them sonnets too. These poets are not using ragged bits of flint to hit their targets, but clean, sharpened arrows of language and form. (p. 86)

[In Paul Muldoon's work there are] three loose categories of unconventional sonnets, categories into which the work of other Irish poets can be fit as well: Near-Shakespearean, Hybrids; and Sonnets of Dubious Parentage (but which seem from certain formal characteristics to owe some debts to Shakespeare). The last thing anyone would say about Paul Muldoon is that he is "typical" of anything, but his daring challenges to form constitute an important element in the revolution he has become.

Everyone is familiar with the defining constituents of the Shakespearean or English sonnet: iambic pentameter, three cross-rhymed quatrains using seven different rhymes, and a concluding couplet. What interests me in Irish poetry in general, and in Muldoon's poetry in particular, is Montague's "dance of forms," modifications that claim local ownership for an alien traditional structure, or at least adjustments that deny complete foreign ownership. For an analogy, one might compare certain Scots and Irish musical instruments. Both can be called "bagpipes," but their differences give each set of pipes their national identities, traditions, and distinctive voices. When a poet writes in a community where, as D. E. S. Maxwell puts it, "politics seizes violently upon the imagination" ["A Rhetoric for Politics in the North," in *Literature and the Changing Ireland,* ed. P. Connolly] in a community that examines the poet's every verbal nuance for evidence of partisan sentiment, then the shapes of those nuances are themselves significant. In an Irish context, writing an English sonnet, for example, can be seen as a political gesture, perhaps in a more obvious way than choosing the Italian structure; and one can further suggest that modifying that English form is not merely a poet's playful tinkering within the oft-denounced, but seldom complacent, tradition of the "well-made" poem.

In Paul Muldoon's 1980 collection, *Why Brownlee Left,* seven of the twenty-six poems have fourteen lines. Each has a rhyme scheme and structure sufficiently schematic to justify the label "sonnet." The form is even more pervasive in his most recent work, *Meeting the British,* which contains fourteen fourteen-line poems. The poem **"Immram"** is a representative example of the Near-Shakespearean poem, with a rhyme pattern that is almost imperceptible to the ear until we hear the outrageously Byronic chiming of "scarlatina-Argentina." Then one hears other echoes, very subtly, including the remarkable concluding couplet: "Nazi" in rhyming position with "mosquito-nets." The rhyme is just close enough for closure, but ominous enough for discomfort.

The poem adopts a flexing line-length, as do all of Muldoon's sonnet-forms, deploying as few as six (line 10) and as many as twelve (line 14) syllables per line. Such stichic irregularity further masks the rhyme when the poem is read aloud because the auditor does not have the familiar rhyming expectation after a set number of Shakespearean pentameter lines. The result is that the rhymes are almost concealed in the sonic texture of the poem. Muldoon adds to the rhyming complexity by using consonantal half-rhymes ("spirit / hired out") or by rhyming feminine with masculine endings ("hazel / Brazil"). Structurally, **"Immram"** employs the familiar, cross-rhymed English sestet with concluding couplet (EFEFGG), but the octave's ABCDABCD is boldly non-Shakespearean.

The form suits a poem that opens with explicit allusions to traditions of former days ("I too have trailed by father's spirit / From the mud-walled cabin behind the mountain") and concludes sadly, by depicting the bankruptcy of that past and its politics ("That's him on the verandah,

drinking rum / With a man who might be a Nazi"). In both his subject matter and choice of form, Muldoon recalls and denounces the impoverished values of that foreign country, the past.

The sestet of **"Immram"** and, especially, its final couplet give it a vestigially Shakespearean stalk, but what do we do with a Hybrid sonnet like **"The Princess and the Pea"**? The eight/six structure is familiar, but in Muldoon's line-endings we can see his refusal to sustain either cross-rhymes or rhymed quatrains. Then, continuing his defiance of the tradition, he opens the poem with a couplet, invoking closure, as it were, even before the poem has begun:

A	This is no dream
A	By Dulac out of the Brothers Grimm,
B	A child's disquiet
C	Her impish mouth,
B	The quilt upon embroidered quilt
D	Of satin and shot silk,
C	Her lying there, extravagant, aloof,
D	Like cream on milk.

After the couplet, the poet arranges the poem in triplets (BCB, DCD), but with sexually suggestive, partial rhymes not to be found in any Mother Goose.

Like **"Immram," "The Princess and the Pea"** ebbs and flows around a syllable count that ranges between four and ten, never allowing Muldoon's formal hold on the deeply troubling subject-matter to be anything more than tentative:

E	This is the dream of her older sister,
F	Who is stretched on the open grave
G	Of all the men she has known.
E	Far down, something niggles. The stir
F	Of someone still alive.
G	Then a cry, far down. It is your own.

The rhyming rectangle ("Known / down / down / own") encloses, like a coffin, the pathetic movements of the living, allowing Muldoon to exploit the full irony of a rhyme like "grave / alive." The insurgent power of the sestet's concluding image is held, but only barely, in close rhyme and tighter line-length, the compressive effect of which gives it almost nightmare force.

Most of Muldoon's sonnets belong to the *Dubious Parentage* category. Here, in addition to his usual manipulation of line-length, he varies structures with an enthusiasm that apparently intends to occupy every possible division of a fourteen-line form. These schemes will show but a few examples:

4-6-4;	4-5-5;	5-5-4;
3-5-3-3;	4-10;	5-6-3;
4-3-2-3-2;	2-4-2-4-2;
3-4-3-4.

And he seems to have experimented with most possible rhyme arrangements too—these among a score of others:

ABACB/DDEFEG/CFG;
ABACBCAB/DCDACB;
ABCA/DCBC/EFF/GGE;
ABCD/CEFE/DFG/BGA; and so on.

The rhymes may appear haphazard; examination reveals sometimes whimsical but always painstaking schemes with no randomness or coincidence. In their hold on the subject, the inventive rhyming designs are appropriative; they articulate ownership.

To illustrate these technical effects, I have chosen a mildly conventional example from Muldoon's **Meeting the British** (a handful of these poems are reprinted from an earlier publication, **Wishbone;** eight of the twelve poems in this book are sonnets too):

The Marriage of Strongbow and Aoife

A	I might as well be another guest
A	at the wedding-feast
B	of Strongbow and Aoife Mac Murrough
B	as watch you, Mary,
C	try to get to grips
C	with a spider-crab's
D	crossbow and cuirass.
D	A creative pause before the second course
x	of Ireland's whole ox on a spit;
E	the invisible waitress
E	brings us each a Calvados and water-ice.
F	It is as if someone had slipped
F	a double-edged knife between my ribs
x	and hit the spot exactly.

A marriage of true minds is the perfect occasion for a sonnet; however, typical of Muldoon's dry irony, he commandeers the form for this lover's complaint on the marriage of two aggressively warrior-like minds. The prevailing images are those of invasion and fatal piercings; the speaker identifies with the doomed spider-crab. This feast is no genteel affair, but an event of rowdy, even epic, proportions.

Muldoon makes sure the reader comprehends the central implication of the wedding of ancient Ireland's Norman conqueror to the daughter of Leinster's Gaelic King Dermot MacMurrough. Dermot recruited Norman aid against his Irish enemies, offering Strongbow the hand of his daughter Aoife in return. The Normans "landed at Baginbun in Wexford. . . . A traditional rhyme recorded this:

> At the creeke of Bagganbun
> Ireland was lost and wun."

All Ireland is at stake, nothing less. So, between lines eight and nine, Muldoon executes a turn within a turn with a turn. First, this space is the point around which a sonnet traditionally turns; second this space is also what line eight itself calls "a creative pause before the second course"; and, third, with that structural and syntactical attention fixed upon it, line nine shows Ireland herself slowly turning on a spit, ready to be devoured by conquerors. It is the "spitting image" of much of the country's history. And, should one have missed that point, "spit" (resonant with abusive and salivary possibilities) is the poem's first line-ending without a rhyming companion. The last line also lacks an end-rhymed partner. One finds, internally ("between the ribs"?), the missing rhyme; it "hit[s] the spot exactly." Commandingly written in a version of En-

gland's favorite form, the formal structure intensifies the poem's tragic undertones. (pp. 86-90)

Ronald Marken, "Paul Muldoon's 'Juggling a Red-Hot Half-Brick in an Old Sock': Poets in Ireland Renovate the English-Language Sonnet," in Éire-Ireland, Vol. XXIV, No. 1, Spring, 1989, pp. 79-91.

Michael Hofmann

Looked at in one way, **Madoc—A Mystery** is an extraordinary and unpredictable departure, a book of poems the size of many novels, with a title poem nigh on two hundred and fifty pages long, doubling Muldoon's output at a stroke. But in another way, it does remarkably little to change the sense one has of Paul Muldoon. It is a book for initiates, more of the same. Each of his previous five volumes has ended with something a little longer, a relaxing gallop after the dressage—even **'The Year of the Sloes, for Ishi'** in **New Weather** (1973) was four pages long. Further, the structure of **Madoc** is actually identical with that of Muldoon's last book, **Meeting the British** (1987)—in fact, it seems like a monstrously curtailed and distended parody of it: the prose poem at the start, a section of short poems (no more than six), and then the *pièce de résistance,* which, for all its length, occupies just one line on the contents page, as though the poet were telling us it's no big deal.

Madoc is a bigger canvas rather than a bigger splash. Perhaps it is Muldoon's fault, perhaps he has pre-empted himself. Already the most characterful and most imitated of contemporary poets, he offered more trademarks than perhaps was good for us: the pluperfect tense; the hoary Rip Van Winkle idioms stretching and disbelieving; the outrageously resourceful rhyming that came to preoccupy him more and more; the factual, ironical provincial-newspaper beginnings; the little seahorse emblems breaking up the poems and jointing them; the plain definite-article-plus-substantive titles; the erotic memoirs; the druggy meltdowns; the recurring totemic props that made each successive book more like a new religion than a book of poems. He has seemed for some time like a man in need of a challenge, the eponymous man in a previous long poem of his, **'The More a Man Has the More a Man Wants'**. In **'Madoc'**, Bucephalus the talking horse lectures us

> that Madoc himself is, above all, emblematic
> of our desire to go beyond ourselves.

The impulse for **'Madoc'** came from a selection of Byron that Muldoon made for his American publishers. (One finds oneself adopting this rather unlikely preterite and literary-historical tone, partly because the poem is a conundrum and cries out for a methodical approach; and partly for want of a strong or reliable personal response to it.) There, Muldoon re-acquainted himself with the literary politics of the Romantics, Byron's poetics, his digs at Southey and Coleridge. He read up on 'the Pantisocratic society of Aspheterists' (Coleridge), and even perused Southey's poem *Madoc,* about 'the Welsh prince, long believed by his countrymen to have discovered America in

1170' *(Chambers Biographical Dictionary)*. Muldoon's 'Madoc' is thus a 'remake'—a notion that crops up in the opening prose poem in the collection. The title is from Southey, the principal character is Coleridge, and the prevailing spirit is not unlike that of Byron in *Don Juan:*

> Prose-poets like blank-verse, I'm fond of rhyme,
> Good workmen never quarrel with their tools;
> I've got new mythological machinery,
> And very handsome supernatural scenery.

'Madoc' is predicated upon two non-events, 625 years apart: the 'arrivals' in America of Madoc, and then of Southey and Coleridge. That is Muldoon's 'new mythological machinery', providing him, on the one hand, with Welsh Indians, variously known as Madocs, Modocs, Mandans and Minnetarees, and, on the other, with a quarrelsome, unprepared, disreputable and idealistic bunch of poet-philosophers and their hangers-on. Coleridge's imaginary move is one that Muldoon himself really made, going from Cambridge to America in 1987. 'Madoc' is also by way of being a brief and selective history of the early years of the United States, as Muldoon works in (I'm not always sure how) some of the pioneers, the Lewis and Clark Expedition, the (Celtic) Indian Wars, eventually returning home in the person of the 19th-century (Irish?) artist and painter of 'native Americans', George Catlin, whose *Rushes through the Middle* graces the cover of **Madoc.** Oh, and one other thing. The narrative is sectioned-off into short, mostly self-contained poems, each given the name of a philosopher or quasi-philosopher (such as Frederick the Great or Schiller) to whose life or thought the poem makes some reference.

To sum up, then, '**Madoc**' consists of two unequal chronological sequences: the philosophers in the titles go from Thales to Stephen Hawking, while the poems below cover the ground from 1795 to 1834, Pantisocracy, Madoc and the Welsh Indians, early pioneers, Lewis and Clark, stray Irishmen, the Satanic School of Byron and Moore. The two disciplines are pretty arbitrarily related—principally, I suppose, by the idea that Southey and Coleridge are poet-philosophers, and thereafter by some typical Muldoon punning and legerdemain, such things as the cryptogram 'C(oleridge) RO(bert Southey The S)ATAN(ic School)', and later 'Not "CROATAN", not "CROATOAN", but "CROTONA" ', this last a reference to Pythagoras's western place of exile. Occasionally, too, the philosophers have names similar or identical to the names of actors in the drama: Putnam, Lewis, Newman, Clarke and Hartley. The whole spooky procedure recalls the celebrated episode when Coleridge and Wordsworth were eavesdropped-on in the West Country, and were heard to speak of the sinister 'Spy Nozy' (the philosopher Spinoza): there is the same mad triangle of poetry, philosophy and subversiveness in Muldoon's poem as there was in that incident.

In his long poems, Muldoon has been drawn to and drawn from literary history and genre fiction, sometimes the one ('**7, Middagh Street**' is about the Auden-Britten ménage in Brooklyn), sometimes the other (the Chandleresque '**Immram**'), but mostly a blend of both. This gives the poems their approachability and readability, a content, and a style both ripe for subversion. In '**Madoc**', the genres are Science Fiction, Western, whodunit, and perhaps even children's writing—in nonsense words like 'signifump' or the delightful 'de dum' used for comic rhyming, dither, mock-epic, iambic filler or half-coconuts on the radio. The Science Fiction provides the frame, because the poem begins and ends in the future, where a character called South (descended from Southey), a 'wet-set', leads some kind of insurrection against the 'Geckoes', perhaps themselves descended from Cayuga Indians. It seems as though the boot is on the other foot, that the high have been made low, and that Kubla Khan's 'pleasure-dome' has become some top-security hush-hush installation. The narrative of '**Madoc**' proceeds from the interrogation of South, in best Sci-Fi manner: 'And, though one of his eyes / was totally written-off, / he was harnessed to a retinagraph', 'So that, though it may seem somewhat improbable, / all that follows / flickers and flows / from the back of his right eyeball.'

What takes the reader through the poem is pleasure and puzzlement in roughly equal measure. Whatever Muldoon is, he isn't the maths master type of poet, setting problems of the correct level of difficulty: he seems rather unaware that there *is* any problem. Essentially, he is taking his style for a walk, and the style is mesmerising. Muldoon is a star exhibit for Gottfried Benn's view that a 'fascinating way with words' is an innate quality, unteachable and unlearnable. One either has it or one doesn't, and Muldoon has it. It is hard to imagine him using a dull word or phrase—he certainly wouldn't use them in a dull way. And yet this hard, glittering, *interesting* surface seems to be at variance with the very idea of a long poem—of a middle way, not high, not low, Wordsworth walking up and down a gravel path. Muldoon's road is like one paved with cat's eyes. It is an extraordinary idea, really, to have a narrative advanced in this way, by Muldoon's slight little poems, very exact, very fussy, never saying anything, but proceeding by ambiguity and innuendo. And yet somehow they aren't overpowered by what they have to convey: they pick up mass, but—against the laws of physics—without decelerating, still at the speed of thought. The reader is exasperated by his own dull-wittedness, but struggles on.

One often feels tempted to throw the whole thing at a computer and say: 'Here, you do it.' But that is the price one pays for Muldoon's speed. Part of one's exasperation comes from doubting whether the whole poem, the '**Mystery**', resolves itself. I am pretty sure it doesn't. If '**Madoc**' were a novel, I wouldn't persevere with it. But, as I have said, Muldoon doesn't set problems. It is more that the poem is too full of solutions: no body, no motive, but stacks of clues—what to do with all the recurring figures, the CRO-riddle, Bucephalus the (s)talking horse, the white (shaggy?) dog, the valise that survives into the SF future, the polygraph. Any one of them might lead to the heart of the matter. Take the last. It comes up three times, first in '**Pascal**':

> Jefferson is so beside himself with glee
> that he finishes off a carafe
>
> of his best Médoc;
> his newly-modified polygraph
>
> will automatically

follow hand-in-glove

his copper-plate 'whippoorwill'
or 'praise' or 'love':

will run parallel to the parallel
realm to which it is itself the only clue.

Why 'Pascal' I don't know. One notes the playful, not un-expected 'Médoc' and files it with an earlier rhyme, 'metic-/ ulously across a mattock's / blade-end'. Then one looks for the rhymes, in order of ease: carafe / polygraph, hand-in-glove / love, whippoorwill / parallel, Médoc / auto-matically and glee / clue. This last pairing summarises the argument of my last paragraph. There are many refer-ences to codes and ciphers and 'sympathetic ink' in the poem—possibly self-references. The 'Médoc' / 'automati-cally' rhyme is also an apposite one, when one takes 'Médoc' as **'Madoc'**. The suggestion is of 'automatic' writ-ing, reinforced by the 'polygraph': literally 'writing much', but also 'an apparatus for producing two or more identical drawings or writings simultaneously' and, figuratively, 'a person who imitates, or is a copy of, another; an imitator, or imitation' (Shorter *OED*).

The idea of a line or word parallel to an unseen word or line is highly suggestive: perhaps of the process of history first of all; of duplicity (tracking the Indians); of the idea of the 'remake' noted earlier; of something both forged and real; of an unlocatable original, since, famously, paral-lel lines never meet. A 'polygrapher' is the enigmatic, clue-dropping, rewriting Muldoon; is also 'multo-scribbling Southey', as Byron describes him. These meanings came into use around the turn of the 18th century; in its new, stupidly conferred meaning of 'lie detector', it has conno-tations of the White House and Nixon and Reagan, of the malpractice of 'hand-in-glove'.

The two further references to the polygraph, which occur in 'Kierkegaard' and 'Adorno', both continue the associa-tion with Jefferson (his retirement and his death); both suggest a kind of comic incompetence that may be Mul-doon speaking about the production of his poem: 'In Mon-ticello, the snaggle-toothed gopher / tries his paw at the polygraph' and 'The polygraph at its usual rigmarole. / The gopher pining for a caramel'. (The gopher must be Jefferson; Washington himself had wooden teeth.) The rigmarole, the parallel lines and the idea of polygraphy all comment on Muldoon's writing of history in **'Madoc'**.

'Madoc' may be enriched by reading it as or with a parallel text. Either a Dictionary of Philosophy (though not the Collins, which doesn't mention half his 'philosophers', not all of them philosophers) or something about Coleridge and Pantisocracy. (It seems the days are gone when one could read Muldoon simply unaided.) With *Madoc* I read Richard Holmes's *Coleridge: Early Visions*. Ironically, this wasn't used by Muldoon: *Madoc* would have been fin-ished by the autumn of 1989, when it came out. Some as-tonishing correspondences between the two books are therefore coincidental, the meeting of two great minds. First and perhaps greatest is this: 'It is not impossible to imagine Coleridge, in some alternative life, flourishing among these original Susquehanna pioneers, and making his own distinctive contribution to the history of the Wild West.' The 'alternative life' is not remarkable, but the 'dis-tinctive contribution to the history of the Wild West' is, because it is precisely what Muldoon does with him, en-rolling him, for instance, with Lewis and Clark. Coleridge himself stipulated that a poet must have 'the *eye* of a North American Indian tracing the footsteps of an Enemy upon the Leaves that strew the forest'. Then there is a very personal judgment of Holmes's, tucked away in a note: 'Coleridge's version of the emigration scheme has, at times, almost a Science Fiction quality.'

There are further suggestive phrases and details: about 'Southey's enthusiastic dog Rover (also a Pantisocrat)', about pondering 'his emigrant's wardrobe—"what do common blue trousers cost?" ' and his 'rapturous cartoon-ing', not a million miles from Muldoon's approach (the gopher, say). But there are also things that Muldoon hasn't got and doesn't use, such as the fact that Southey's 'rooms were next to the college lavatories, by an alley that opened on to St Giles', or the fact that Southey 'left for Dublin to take up a post as Secretary to the Irish Chancel-lor, with a salary of £200 per annum, a characteristically efficient career move'. The point about these is not wheth-er Muldoon knows them or not, but that his poem main-tains the same intense and witty close focus upon its char-acters as Holmes's outstanding biography does, and that from reading the poem alone, one might not necessarily have known it.

Every reading—and still more, every new bit of informa-tion—makes *Madoc* a cleverer and more imposing piece of work. Perhaps one of the last details (I am not claiming to know or to have done one-tenth of what needs to be known and done) to be seen to is the securing of the seven short poems of Part One to **'Madoc'** itself, for they are clearly appendices or codicils (a word which Muldoon might care to derive from *cauda,* a tail). And truly each one contains some chromosomes from **'Madoc'**: no other poet has Muldoon's expertise in forging such organic con-nections. In order, the poems contain: the idea of the 're-make': **'Pythagoras in America'** and 'some left-over / squid cooked in its own ink'; a duel, like those between Burr and Hamilton, and Jeffrey and Moore; **'Asra'**; an Irish immigrant to America; an amazing metastatic sesti-na patented by Muldoon; and this poem, **'The Briefcase'**:

> I held the briefcase at arm's length from me;
> the oxblood or liver
> eelskin with which it was covered
> had suddenly grown supple.
>
> I'd been waiting in line for the cross-town
> bus when an almighty cloudburst
> left the sidewalk a raging torrent.
>
> And though it contained only the first
> inkling of this poem, I knew I daren't
> set the briefcase down
> to slap my pockets for an obol—
>
> for fear it might slink into a culvert
> and strike out along the East River
> for the sea. By which I mean the 'open' sea.

The theme of this sonnet is the desperate—and comic—attempt to hold on to something, to prevent it from metamorphosing and accelerating away. In the context of *Madoc,* it is the wrestle with his own new poem about the new continent, *in* the new continent. Hence the force of the ' "open" sea': once escaped it could go anywhere, most obviously 'East' to Ireland. (The poem is dedicated to Seamus Heaney.) It is a kind of envoi, but one with the opposite wish, namely 'stay, little book.' I was reminded of John Berryman's epigraphs for his *Dream Songs,* from Sir Francis Chichester and Gordon in Khartoum: 'For my part I am always frightened, and very much so. I fear the future of all engagements.' There is something oddly and deeply touching about this fear in one of the most metamorphic poets alive, in whom words and facts and things themselves are so comprehensively and gracefully destabilised. (pp. 18-19)

> *Michael Hofmann, "Muldoon—A Mystery," in* London Review of Books, *Vol. 12, No. 24, December 20, 1990, pp. 18-19.*

John Banville

Muldoon's poetry is hard to grasp. It may convey something of the flavor of his work, of its diversity, its sudden switches and disconcerting lapses into dialect, real or invented, if I quote the opening and closing lines of his 1983 collection, *Quoof* (the word was a Muldoon family term for a hot water bottle). The first poem, **"Gathering Mushrooms,"** begins:

> The rain comes flapping through the yard
> like a tablecloth that she hand-embroidered.
> My mother has left it on the line.
> It is sodden with rain.
> The mushroom shed is windowless, wide,
> its high-stacked wooden trays
> hosed down with formaldehyde.

The closing, long poem, **"The More a Man Has the More a Man Wants,"** ends thus:

> "Next of all wus the han' "Be Japers."
> "The sodgers cordonned-off the area
> wi' what-ye-may-call-it tape."
> "Lunimous." "They foun' this hairy
> han' wi' a drowneded man's grip
> on a lunimous stone no bigger than a . . . . "
>
> "Huh."

Muldoon's poetry is fiendishly eclectic. He will place charming verses about his childhood in Armagh beside such things as **"7, Middagh Street,"** a long cycle set in the house in New York shared during the war by a gallimaufry (one finds oneself using such words when speaking of this poet) of people including W. H. Auden, Carson McCullers, Gypsy Rose Lee, Salvador Dali. He is also one of the few contemporary Irish writers who have dealt directly with the Troubles:

> The UDR corporal had come off duty
> to be with his wife
> while the others set about
> a follow-up search.
> When he tramped out just before twelve
> to exercise the greyhound
> he was hit by a single high-velocity

shot.

> You could, if you like, put your fist
> in the exit wound
> in his chest.
> He slumps
> in the spume of his own arterial blood
> like an overturned paraffin lamp.
> ("The More a Man Has
> the More a Man Wants")

It is a measure of this poet's skill and daring that he can set a passage such as this into a poem loosely based, so the publisher's blurb tells us, on the Trickster cycle of the Winnebago Indians—a poem dense with jokes, travels, names, outrageous rhymes, sudden tendernesses:

> He will answer the hedge-sparrow's
> *Littlebitofbreadandnocheese*
> with a whole bunch
> of freshly picked watercress,
> a bulb of garlic,
> sorrel,
> with many-faceted blackberries.
> ("The More a Man Has
> the More a Man Wants")

There are direct echoes of the North and its tribulation in *Madoc,* but the true "Northern note" sounds more audibly in the disjunctions and the febrile energies that drive the poetry; the line struts, falls, goes on again, broken but still moving, like something skittering away from the scene of a catastrophe that had as much of comedy in it as of horror. The book opens with a short prose passage, provocatively called **"The Key"**; following that come six short, splendid poems done in the by now familiar Muldoon manner: inventive, quirky, humorous, and frequently mystifying. Then we launch out on Part Two, **"Madoc: A Mystery,"** a 240-page cycle based (*very* loosely) on an idea conceived and enthusiastically canvassed by Samuel Taylor Coleridge and his friend, the minor poet Robert Southey (author of a long verse-narrative called *Madoc*), to set up a utopian community in the United States. This brotherly group were to be called the Pantisocrats ("Coleridge created the word from the Greek roots *pan-socratia,* an all-governing society . . . " [Richard Holmes, *Coleridge: Early Visions*]), and they were to settle on the banks of the Susquehanna river in Pennsylvania.

The idea fired the imagination of a great many otherwise serious people in England in the 1790s (even Southey's dog Rover was an enthusiastic Pantisocrat), until the mercurial Coleridge suddenly lost interest in it. What Paul Muldoon has done is to imagine that Coleridge and his friends, instead of contenting themselves with evenings of utopian talk over punch and tobacco in the Salutation & Cat, *did* go to America to found their Pantisocracy. Woven in with this conceit are bits of science fiction, word puzzles, glimpses of the Lewis and Clark expedition, and much, much more. The whole thing has a loony elegance and obsessive playfulness, an air of something concocted for a jape by the brightest boy in the class, one of those febrile geniuses who laugh a lot and have a tremor in their hands and who we suspect will never really come to anything in the end.

The poems in the cycle, none of them long, some of them

two- or even one-liners, are each headed by the name, in square brackets, of a philosopher, scientist, poet, explorer. . . . I do not see, except in few instances, that the poems refer to their patrons. Here are two examples, chosen pretty much at random:

[James]

The pile of horse-dung at the heart
    of Southeyopolis
looks for all the world like a dish
    of baked apples.

[Kristeva]

"Signifump. Signifump. Signifump."

(Well, yes, structuralism, the signifier and the signified and all that—though I doubt the elegant Ms. Kristeva would be pleased by the hint of "frump" here.) Sometimes a wan little joke emerges:

[Archimedes]

Coleridge leaps out of the tub.
    Imagine that.

I have to confess that I really do not know what to make of **Madoc:** I do not know what I am *meant* to make of it. Granted, it is continuous with Muldoon's previous work; here are all the old fascinations, with primitive ritual, "alternative" philosophies, hallucinogenic rigamarole, and madcap voyages; here too is the peculiar, inimitable music of Muldoon's voice:

Southey brushes the glib
from behind the stallion's ear

and takes aim
de dum. A flash in the pan. A
    thunder-clap.

Blood-alphabets. Blood-ems.
A babble of blood out of the broken fount.

Yet I cannot help feeling that this time he has gone too far—so far, at least, that I can hardly make him out at all, off there in the distance, dancing by himself. Yes, art *should* be resistant, poetry *should* hold back something of its essential self. The trouble is, **Madoc** demands that the reader work in ways that seem inappropriate to the occasion: one pictures work details of Ph.D. students already setting to, tracking down the references, preparing glosses, grinding keys. Such treatment will kill Muldoon's poetry. He is at once an artist of great gaiety and of high seriousness, and in his best work these two qualities are inextricably combined. **Madoc,** however, is a little too playful in its profundities, and many of its jokes are weighed down with leaden solemnity. (pp. 38-9)

> *John Banville, "Slouching Toward Bethlehem," in* The New York Review of Books, *Vol. XXXVIII, No. 10, May 30, 1991, pp. 37-9.*

FURTHER READING

Birkerts, Sven. "Paul Muldoon / Tony Harrison / Christopher Logue." In his *The Electric Life: Essays on Modern Poetry,* pp. 321-27. New York: William Morrow and Co., 1989.
    Studies the evolution of Muldoon's poetic style.

Burris, Sidney. "Some Versions of Ireland: The Poetry of Tom Paulin and Paul Muldoon." *The Kenyon Review* VII, No. 4 (Fall 1985) 129-35.
    Argues that Paulin's and Muldoon's poetry respectively document the Protestant and Catholic cultures of Northern Ireland.

Conover, Roger. Review of *New Weather,* by Paul Muldoon. *Éire-Ireland* X, No. 2 (Summer 1975) 127-33.
    Distinguishes Muldoon's individual poetic voice from Seamus Heaney's and studies the nature imagery of Muldoon's poems.

DeShazer, Mary. Review of *Why Brownlee Left,* by Paul Muldoon. *Concerning Poetry* 14, No. 2 (1981) 125-31.
    Contends that the subject of the collection is Muldoon's search for "both a literal father and a literary 'precursor,' the paternal giant whom the young poet must confront in order to achieve artistic autonomy."

Eagleton, Terry. "Fishmonger's Window." *The Observer* (3 May 1987): 25.
    Review of *Meeting the British* in which Eagleton praises the poem "7, Middagh Street."

Frazier, Adrian. "Juniper, Otherwise Known: Poems by Paulin and Muldoon." *Éire-Ireland* XIX, No. 1 (Spring 1984) 123-33.
    Discusses Muldoon's use of violent and sexual imagery.

Haffenden, John. "Paul Muldoon." In his *Viewpoints: Poets in Conversation,* pp. 130-42. London: Faber and Faber, 1981.
    Interview in which Muldoon discusses such topics as his development as a poet, his interest in the *Immram Mael Duin* legend, and his opinions on the "Troubles."

Harrod, Lois Marie. Review of *Why Brownlee Left,* by Paul Muldoon. *Éire-Ireland* XVII, No. 3 (1982) 145-48.
    Overview of the poems in *Why Brownlee Left.*

Imlah, Mick. "Abandoned Origins." *The Times Literary Supplement* (4 September 1987): 946.
    Review of *Meeting the British* in which Imlah comments on Muldoon's use of rhyme and examines the poem "7, Middagh Street."

Longley, Edna. " 'Varieties of People': Louis MacNeice and Paul Muldoon." In her *Poetry in the Wars,* pp. 211-43. Newcastle upon Tyne: Bloodaxe Books, 1986.
    Comparative study of Muldoon's and Louis MacNeice's treatment of the *Immram Mael Duin* legend, their use of syntax and cliches, and the influence of Robert Frost on their poetry.

Maguire, Sarah. "Play Pen." *The Listener* 124 (1 November 1990): 35.
    Highlights Muldoon's use of language in the poem "Madoc."

Stevenson, Anne. "Snaffling and Curbing." *The Listener* 98, No. 2530 (13 October 1977): 486-87.
    Comments on Muldoon's poetic style in *Mules,* asserting

that "more often Muldoon resembles a sleeker, Irish Robert Frost. His frame of reference is earthy, sly, obliquely religious and calculated to astonish as much as it is to please."

Stokes, Geoffrey. "Bloody Beautiful." *Village Voice Literary Supplement* No. 24 (March 1984): 15.

Review of *Quoof* in which Stokes remarks that the "poems are almost infinitely suggestive but diffidently so. There is beauty and charm enough on the surface to satisfy the casual reader, but once these poems have made their way into our minds—which they do by means of those deceptively easy and musical surfaces—they open and open and open."

Additional coverage of Muldoon's life and career is contained in the following sources published by Gale Research: *Contemporary Authors*, Vols. 113, 129 and *Dictionary of Literary Biography*, Vol. 40.

Raymond Mungo

1946-

American nonfiction writer, journalist, novelist, and scriptwriter.

This entry provides an overview of Mungo's career.

INTRODUCTION

An active participant in the counterculture movement of the 1960s, Mungo infuses his writing with his left-wing views on social and political issues. In 1967 Mungo, along with Marshall Bloom, founded the Liberation News Service (LNS), an underground news wire service intended to provide alternative media coverage of the Vietnam War. The conservative opposition, interpersonal disputes, and financial difficulties that the group encountered, as well as the demise of the organization the following year, are chronicled in Mungo's best-known work, *Famous Long Ago: My Life and Hard Times with Liberation News Service.*

In addition to offering a humorous and detailed history of the LNS in *Famous Long Ago,* Mungo describes and advocates the political activism and prevalent drug use that characterized the 1960s youth counterculture. While some critics dismissed what they deemed Mungo's self-congratulatory tone in the work, others praised his emotional range, his use of irony and sarcasm, and his willingness to expose the hypocrisies and shortcomings of "The Movement." John Leonard commented: "Mungo is not an idealogue. He jokes and grieves and specifies the humanity in every individual of whom he writes." Mungo's second book, *Total Loss Farm: A Year in the Life,* is a humorous and, at times, sentimental account of life on the Vermont commune where Mungo and his friends retreated after the breakup of the LNS. Again, Mungo was praised for the wit and insight incorporated into his storytelling. Because of its focus on nature and the environment, *Total Loss Farm* was compared, both favorably and unfavorably, to the works of nineteenth-century essayist and naturalist Henry David Thoreau.

Most of Mungo's later works focus on his individual, rather than group, endeavors. *Return to Sender; or, When the Fish in the Water Was Thirsty* recounts his travels in Asia, while *Cosmic Profit: How to Make Money without Doing Time* highlights his travels across the United States in search of the ideal job. Although the book offers little financial advice, many critics grouped *Cosmic Profit* in the same category as the numerous entrepreneurial guides published at that time. In *Confessions from Left Field: A Baseball Pilgrimage* Mungo outlines two years during which he closely followed professional baseball. While he offers anecdotes and musings about certain teams and players, most reviewers pointed out that he uses the sport as a backdrop for his liberal opinions on politics and soci-

ety. Mungo published a sequel to his first book, *Beyond the Revolution: My Life and Times Since "Famous Long Ago",* which received little critical attention. In this work, Mungo reflects upon his past as a young activist and his future as a "baby boomer," provides updates on the people mentioned in his earlier works, and comments on current political issues.

PRINCIPAL WORKS

NONFICTION

*Famous Long Ago: My Life and Hard Times with Liberation News Service   1970
*Total Loss Farm: A Year in the Life   1970
*Return to Sender; or, When the Fish in the Water Was Thirsty   1975
Cosmic Profit: How to Make Money without Doing Time   1980
Confessions from Left Field: A Baseball Pilgrimage   1983
Beyond the Revolution: My Life and Times Since "Famous Long Ago"   1990

OTHER

Between Two Moons: A Technicolor Travelogue   (screenplay)   1972
Tropical Detective Story: The Flower Children Meet the Voodoo Chiefs   (novel)   1972
Lit Biz 101   (writer's guide)   1988

*These works were published as *Mungobus* in 1979.

CRITICISM

Melvin Maddocks

The young seem to wear out early these days, like a lot of other things. But then, when you've Tried It All by 16, you're going to be ready to write your "Memoirs of a Burnt-Out Case" at 21, aren't you?

At 24, at any rate, Ray Mungo has composed the sort of autobiography that dedicated geniuses of self-destruction used to produce at 35 or 40—just before joining the strictest monastic order they could find. The tone is compounded of boredom and cyncism in about equal measure, climaxing finally in a disgusted renunciation of the Ways of the World. Aargh! Self-pity is not necessarily avoided.

Moral fatigue hangs all over *Famous Long Ago,* Mr.

Mungo's account of "My Life and Hard Times With Liberation News Service." Despite his Flip Little Monster jauntiness—Mr. Mungo knows the hot market value of playing thumb-the-nose revolutionary—this is a book that may just barely have been written. It gives off illusions of spontaneity; at least it is carelessly written to support the case. Yet it seems to have been thrown together, not with the lovely surplus energy of authentic spontaneity but with a kind of frantic, last-gasp will-to-be-spontaneous.

Famous Long Ago is significant as a document. Curiously, it makes a rather dull story. After leaving Boston University, where he became notorious as one of the first of the radical college newspaper editors, Mr. Mungo helped found a news service—a sort of hip Associated Press for student and underground newspapers. As he sees it now, Liberation News Service was born, not because he or anybody else wanted to get "involved in critical social change blah blah blah" but because "we had nothing else to do."

There followed two and a half slogging years, mostly in Washington, D.C. The venture was a technical success—subscribing papers reached 400, some of which even paid their bills. Mr. Mungo dutifully introduces a cast of hip characters and glamorizes the scene with obligatory clouds of marijuana smoke. But at least he admits the whole business was really an awful lot of dull, hard work, organizational hangups, and internecine feuds, just like the *New York Times*.

Furthermore, Mr. Mungo became totally disillusioned with "activism"—"the dreary world of systematic revolutionary effort." Would you believe that one underground "free" press has a time-clock for employees to punch?

Mr. Mungo is now a member of a small farm commune in Vermont, taking wild, tragicomically bungled canoe trips on the Merrimack in honor of his new culture hero, Thoreau (see the current *Atlantic*). He has dropped out of the Movement—all movements—because he believes "ideals cannot be institutionalized."

"I'm searching for love," he writes. Also, he wants never to work hard again—two of the noblest objectives known to man.

He yearns so to revive his elderly-urchin soul and become a Merry Prankster—a child of "light and hope." But like a child, Mr. Mungo has terrible nightmares too. He feels "America is beyond repair"—not least because of the *enfants terribles* who have already succeeded him. (He reacts like any senior citizen to the "new-style of demonstrator"—"screaming," "bitter," contemptuous.")

At 24, Mr. Mungo is as jaded as a man can be. Even travel bores him—his description of a cross-country trip barely keeps him, or the reader, awake. Like half the middle-aged Establishment, he is trying to survive the 20th century by going on a Nature kick. O glory! The taste of maple syrup in the spring. The look of stars in an August sky. The smell of burning leaves in October—oops, that's smog, and (bye, bye Thoreau) we're back in the 20th century again.

May the world we've made have mercy on us all, including spaced-out Robinson Crusoes like Ray Mungo.

Melvin Maddocks, "Dropout's Dropout," in The Christian Science Monitor, April 30, 1970, p. 13.

Jack Newfield

Compared to its numbers, its energies and its impact, the New Left has been remarkably underrepresented by readable literature. Until recently, young radicals have just not produced many books that successfully yoked intelligence to craft and imagination. Most of the book-length efforts by New Left types have been poorly written, simplistic, exaggerated, dumb, commercialized, or personal-ego trips.

In the last few months, this intellectual vacuum has finally begun to be filled with books of distinction. Paul Cowan's autobiography, *The Making of an Un-American*, Fred Gardner's tightly disciplined reportage in *The Unlawful Concert*; Sy Hersh's agonizing account of the My Lai massacre; and now this honest, literate and loving memoir of the Movement by Ray Mungo [*Famous Long Ago*].

Mungo, only 24, has a true writer's eye for character and detail, and a true writer's sense of drama, irony, confession and rhythm. This is not a book of programmatic politics, then. It is memoir, poetry, diary, autobiography. It is human. It is one young man's odyssey through the Vietnam war, Martin Luther King's assassination, the acid-rock counter-culture, the bitter splits within the New Left, ending up with him as a post-Beatles Thoreau, digging nature and privacy on a farm in Vermont.

My instinct tells me a lot of reviewers are going to compare this book with James Kunen's best-selling *The Strawberry Statement* because of the surface similarity of subject and both authors' youth. So let me declare unequivocally that *Famous Long Ago* is better. It is almost as good as Frank Conroy's beautiful *Stop-Time*. (p. 6)

The Strawberry Statement was like cotton candy. It was too mannered. Mungo's book has greater emotional range. It has the power to make you sad, and furious, and nostalgic, and introspective, and then to laugh out loud. And *Famous Long Ago* is written from the stormy center of the Movement, while Kunen's point of view was the cool, detached periphery.

"Were I true to my roots," Mungo writes on the first page, "I'd now be a laborer in a paper or textile mill, married and the father of two children, a veteran of action in Vietnam, and a reasonably brainwashed communicant in a Roman Catholic, predominantly Irish parish."

But Mungo chose another road: "In the eighth grade, puberty came between me and the church. . . . I knew the only way out of the mills was through college, so I kept my Stephen Dedalus secrets from everybody until I was safely out of that school with a bundle of college scholarships."

Mungo left home at 17, discovered dope in his sophomore year at Boston University, lost his virginity as a junior, and by 1965 was one of those freaky, prophetic opponents of the Vietnam war. "From Vietnam I learned to despise my countrymen, my government, and the entire English-speaking world, with its history of genocide and international conquest. I was a normal kid."

Then, in 1967, Mungo and the late Marshall Bloom, to whom this book is dedicated, founded Liberation News Service, the underground A.P. And the last third of the book chronicles the factionalization of L.N.S. and Mungo's own gradual disillusionment with the power struggles and dull, abstract meetings of the New Left. Baptizing the two factions of L.N.S. as the Vulgar Marxists and the Virtuous Caucus, Mungo tells with remarkable charity and wit the complicated story of how L.N.S. split in two.

By the end of his memoir, Mungo has dropped out of the day-to-day struggles of a New Left he feels has "changed from flowers and yellow submarines, peace and brotherhood, to sober revolutionary committees, Che-inspired berets, even guns." Mungo, at the end, has reached a place of contentment similar to Bob Dylan's in *Nashville Skyline*. He cares most about nature, the country, private virtue, community, writing and his friends.

As an activist and incurable cityhead, I temperamentally and politically disagree with Mungo's solution, but it obviously has been healthy for him, and it cannot diminish my affection for this book. At the end Mungo summarizes his modest prescription for what he calls The New Age:

"I am an indigent dropout. I no longer have *any* program to save the world, let alone nineteenth-century Marxism, except perhaps to pay attention to trees. . . . Let us now cease with our complaining about the state the world is in, and make it *better*. . . . We're only trying to change ourselves."

Write on Ray, write on! (pp. 6, 29)

> Jack Newfield, "An Honest, Literate and Loving Memoir of the Movement," in The New York Times Book Review, *June 28, 1970, pp. 6, 29.*

An excerpt from *Famous Long Ago*

My kind of life has been made immensely more difficult by the unceasing presence of the straight press, which comes around for motives of its own. You may be sure that by the time you read about something or somebody in the *Boston Globe,* its/his golden days are passed. Thus the media destroyed Haight-Ashbury, the anti-war movement, the underground press, and is rapidly getting to rock music. Speedy communications in the global village ensure that everybody everywhere will find out about every new project, and thereafter come to your doorstep seeking advice, approval, or sustenance of some kind; and, face it, most people are such schmucks you just don't want to meet them.

Last week, *Life* magazine came up the mountain, interrupted my bucolic utopian afternoon to question me as part of their nationwide survey of rural hip communes. Unh-huh.

> Raymond Mungo, in his Mungobus, *Avon Books, 1979.*

Albert H. Norman

After Henry D. Thoreau was sprung from his politically symbolic night in Concord jail, he headed out toward the high hills and huckleberry fields, where "the State was nowhere to be seen." In like manner, after paying his dues to the Movement, Ray Mungo went to huckleberry fields forever. Born in the working class of self-reliant Massachusetts, Mungo escaped to hip Boston University, where he became a dogged Marxist, a dopehead and editor of his college newspaper (in that order). Now he writes [in *Famous Long Ago*]: "I am a lazy good-for-nothing dropout, probably a Communist dupe, and live on a communal farm way, way into the backwoods of Vermont. What went wrong?"

What went wrong, says Mungo, was not his anarchistic, transcendental life style, but the Movement. Having been purged from high places in the United States Student Press Association, Mungo, together with another campus editor, Marshall Bloom (who committed suicide on All Saint's Day last year), founded Liberation News Service in 1967: "not because the proliferating underground and radical college press really needed a central information-gathering agency staffed by people they could trust (that was our hype) but, because we had nothing else to do." LNS is living in New York today, and delivering on the hype. But the embarrassing split of LNS in 1968, and the subsequent Bloom-Mungo liberation of office equipment, proved to be importantly symptomatic of the entire Movement.

"It had changed," Mungo saw, "from flowers and yellow submarines . . . to sober revolutionary committees, Che-inspired berets, even guns . . . the Movement was sour and bitter." Mungo, no longer a "Vulgar Marxist," lost faith in the revolution-to-come and turned to personal liberation: "We tried to enjoy life as much as possible, took acid trips, went to the movies . . . " He and Bloom abandoned the dogmatic journalist-*enragé* pose, and turned from the Mekong to the Merrimack, from Chairman Mao to foot man Thoreau.

"I came into this world," Thoreau wrote in an essay in 1848, "not chiefly to make this a good place to live in, but to live in it, be it good or bad." Mungo's withdrawal is not apolitical ("may . . . all your imperialist states crumble"). But he is only civilly disobedient. Rather than do everything, he has chosen something—to concentrate on "love, beauty, and the *quality* of life." "I'm sorry I didn't put an end to war," Mungo says with bucolic resignation, "but at least I haven't contributed to one of them."

Like the bear who went to see what he could see, Mungo has gone over the mountain. In frustration, without ideology or a plan to save the world, he deserts the hollow cities. The energy of Woodstock, the Whole Earth tools of Menlo Park and the funky music of Nashville have all pointed out the direction. But after the festivals, the camping trips and the recording sessions, the revolution settles back into the urban mold. Mungo and his nine disaffected farmers are among the first to take the Movement permanently out of society. The revolution has grown so far afield that part of it isn't coming back. The activists denounce the pastoralists, but the communes grow. A minority, said Thoreau, becomes "irresistible when it clogs by its whole weight." As more and more people opt for huckleberries, something very "heavy" may begin to take shape in them thar hills.

Albert H. Norman, "Take to the Hills," in Newsweek, *Vol. LXXVI, No. 6 August 10, 1970, p. 76.*

Richard Sennett

Ray Mungo, who started the Liberation News Service, gave up political activity in the spring of 1968, his 22nd year, "because the movement had become my enemy; the movement was not flowers and doves and spontaneity, but another vicious system, the seed of a heartless bureaucracy, a minority Party vying for power rather than peace." *Total Loss Farm* tells of the life he made for himself in the following year, a life that came to revolve around an old farm in Vermont he ran with some friends.

The scenario is not new; humane radicals have been deserting revolutionary politics almost as long as those political movements have existed. In the lives of such men as the 19th-century Russian exile Alexander Herzen or the humane artists and intellectuals who gave up Depression-era Communism, the rejection of radical politics has not meant the abandonment of political ideals; such men have left organized activity when the organization began to choke off life.

This is how Ray Mungo pictures himself. In his first book, *Famous Long Ago,* he wrote the story of that disillusionment. *Total Loss Farm* is intended to be a parable of the life-giving world beyond politics; Mungo looks at himself as a cultural phenomenon, finding love and warmth on a communal farm in the woods. In a way, he is still a political man, still devoting himself to a cause, only now he makes over his life to serve, like Thoreau, an ideal of spontaneity and enlarged sensitivity.

Yet on finishing this book I am convinced only that he has exchanged one set of restrictions on his spontaneity for another, that the revolution in life-style up in the woods is as culture-bound and dictated by the system he abhors as was radical politics. In fact, his "search for the New Age" is an age-old American myth: that simply by an act of will a man can escape his past and his present, that if he wants to, a person can walk away from the burden of experience. Despite its trite and wooden prose, this book teaches an important lesson—how in the guise of youth culture, new lifestyle and the like, we may be only reliving the sins of an old naiveté.

One of the most revealing passages in the book describes the differences between the enchanted child's world Ray Mungo has sought to re-enter and the hard adult life he wants to avoid: "It is curious how helpless, pathetic, and cowardly is what adults often call a Real Man. . . . If that is manhood, no thank you. I would rather know nothing of the cold cruel world I will someday just have to deal with, same as everybody else."

Here surely is a formula by which the voluntary child

makes himself helpless: he accepts that society of cold, cruel men as something he will ultimately join, and is only hiding from it now. I am reminded of a student at Yale, dressed in army fatigues with a big red strike fist stenciled on the jacket, who told me that he planned to enter his father's stock-brokerage house. Why the clothes, I asked, and he replied he wanted to be groovy while he had the chance. The sadness of Mungo's book is that he is personally more genuine than this student, but winds up doing the same posturing with his identity; the enchanted circle at the farm won't give him strength to go outside; before that detested cold cruel world he stands impotent and defenseless.

But this dream posturing affects the relations of the people at the farm itself. Mungo apologizes to the reader at one point for talking about his friends only in ecstatic terms, and he says something I find terribly discouraging: "Remember these are my friends because they are pillars of virtue to me." This is the moral universe of John Wayne or high-school football heroes: a man or woman is not drawn to someone by the complexity, the depth, the richness of a relationship but because he can put that person on a pedestal. When the people at the farm groove on each other they do not go exploring; theirs is more like an adolescent love that seeks to merge with some higher, unattainable object. Mungo admits as much: "I could not leap joyfully to the side of someone I considered my equal." What a perverse and impersonal gesture this friendship is! Has he really escaped from the vicious and dehumanized life of the city?

The human community at the farm is surely as narrow, self-conscious and manipulative as the outer world. In fact, the farm is but another instance of that world: it is a hippie suburb, it bears all the marks of a parental culture which a quarter century ago trekked out to the neat new suburbs hoping to start fresh and have a little plot of land you could call your own. This New Age is, after all, rather familiar, comfortable and stale.

The person who is Ray Mungo occasionally peeks out behind the facade of the pioneer of the New Age, and that person is both gentle and sensitive. This book is not just another of those radical autobiographies designed to sell big in the market; it is a more genuine, pathetic story of a sensibility smothered by its own illusions. And ironically, this is not really a book about the virtues of the New Age in nature at all. When Thoreau went to the woods, he went to learn, he went to be absorbed by nature. When Ray Mungo went to Vermont, he lost nothing and gained nothing; none of the folkways of suburban life passed out of his own. Rather, like generations of Americans before him, he reenacted a fantasy of becoming a man unburdened by pain, confusion, or the unanswerable problems of evil—and so not really a flesh-and-blood creature at all. (pp. 24, 28)

Richard Sennett, "A Hippie Suburb," in The New York Times Book Review, *November 15, 1970, pp. 24, 28.*

Aaron Latham

Ancient C. L. Sulzberger's memoirs, yes. Gnarled Charles de Gaulle's, sure. Balding George Kennan's, of course. But the memoirs of a twenty-three-year-old? The memoirs of Raymond Mungo? And his new book, *Total Loss Farm: A Year in the Life,* is not even the first volume. It's the second. Both are good. Mungo is one of the few figures out there on the New Left Ledge who can write.

"Listen, the Stephen Daedalus withdrawal . . . is no joke," Mungo observes upon revisiting his old Catholic prep school, and this evocation of James Joyce seems apt. In Mungo's first book, *Famous Long Ago: My Life and Hard Times with Liberation News Service,* he gave us a portrait of the urban radical as a young man. In the sequel, he has written a portrait of the young man one year older—now a New Age farmer on a commune in upstate Vermont.

Daedalus, like Joyce himself, believed in a whole row of saviors, one after the other: the Church until that gave way, then the Girl until she too toppled, and finally Art, but we are never sure whether even that was enough or just more thin milk. Mungo's "Daedalus withdrawal" took him from the Church to a belief in "a New Age born of a violent insurrection." To make way for that insurrection the boy radical founded a live-free, Americong news service, the LNS, which played AP to the underground papers. "But I woke up in the spring of 1968 and said, 'This is not what I had in mind,'" Mungo writes in his new book,

> because the movement had become my enemy . . . another vicious system, the seed of a heartless bureaucracy, a minority Party vying for power rather than peace.

In a power play of his own, Mungo and his pranksters attempted to end an LNS schism by stealing the news service press and whisking it away to New England to grow red rust while they grew potatoes. Those left behind followed the pranksters, beat them and held them prisoner but never got the press back. Mungo retaliated by calling in that old enemy—the very "pigs"—and having the opposition arrested and charged with kidnapping. In the country now, Mungo believes in communes and strives to become a combination Tom Sawyer and Henry Thoreau. The farm, he says, provides "the isolation from America which the peace movement promised but cruelly denied."

Mungo divides his book into seasons rather than chapters. The three he recognizes are fall, winter and Warm ("Warm is when you don't have to. Warm is freedom"). During the fall, he describes a "knockout October day . . . All the trees had dropped acid." In winter, "See touching and reaching and hugging and kissing and five long bodies . . . See Wrongness and Weirdness and Mustn't and Shame crumble. . . . Stamp out Couples!" At last Warm, when "we . . . make green grass grow, peaches bloom, flies drop eggs and multiply, water gush and sparkle, corn soar toward paradise . . ." Followed by fall again with its "wailing of mothers and babies [who] choose for themselves from a galaxy of fathers, each one in his way Responsible."

In a sense, Mungo has succeeded too well in escaping the abuses of city life. In his first book, we are treated to the 1967 March on the Pentagon, the 1968 Washington Riot, quarrels, factions, cutthroat intramural politicking—all the terrible things which make life painful and stories fascinating, dramatic. If there had been no wolf in the forest, no one would have ever remembered Little Red Riding Hood; and Mungo's north woods are wolfless. The young farmer therefore falls back on a lyrical, poetic prose which seems to say on every page:

> Come live with me and be my love
> And we will all the pleasures prove . . .

You admire but you aren't gripped. Still the book has a real power to charm.

Mungo is right about "Daedalus withdrawal"—it *is* no joke. Today the farm is the Answer, the wax wings to get the young man up to the sun. If tomorrow those wings are melted, then there will be others to strap on. (Already some have fallen into the sea. Marshall Bloom, co-founder of LNS, sucked in death from a hose attached to the exhaust pipe. Four others died when their chimney exploded and turned their farmhouse into an oven. Napalm could have done no worse. "Can you remember? what chances children will take?") As each new generation discovers one answer after another to our troubles, it is like their discovery of sex: It is not new but it seems new and no less exciting for being very old.

Wherever we—and Mungo—go from here, I hope that he keeps sending back these dispatches. Joyce said it: "Old father, old artificer, stand [him] now and ever in good stead." (pp. 6-7)

> *Aaron Latham, "My Enemy, the Movement,"*
> *in* Book World—The Washington Post, *November 22, 1970, pp. 6-7.*

Monroe Bush

> Raymond Mungo is a writer of some reputation and very little emotional stability. Far from striving for cool detachment, he seems always to be overreacting to his situation: laughing, crying, being hauled off by the police, fervently speaking to trees, changing his mind. He was born in 1946, Pisces, Scorpio rising. He did a lot of political stuff. Now he lives with these twelve other people on some farm up in Vermont, but sometimes he goes to Peru, at least in his head. He is just trying to make it, same as everybody.

Recently I picked up a book I had never seen or heard mentioned by the kind of people whose sub-profession is to mention important books, and found this sketch of the author. It is a sort of poem, of course, and free of that mindless compulsion to list an author's academic credentials, published titles, and whatever else it is we hide our deficiencies behind.

The book is called *Total Loss Farm, A Year in the Life,* and author Raymond Mungo, who I discover wrote the hard-hitting *Famous Long Ago,* is a beautiful wild man.

Total Loss Farm is a deep, deep, deep view of the environment. It was not written for children, people who feel secure with statistics, those who believe every nature writer should ape Thoreau, or those who have to take Tums after every meal. The text is moderately sprinkled with four-letter words. It is impulsive, imaginative, and personal. Mungo has held up a mirror to the world, and seen through it.

What is it about? Let Raymond Mungo himself tell you:

> The New Age we were looking for proved very old indeed, and I've often wondered aloud at my luck for being 23 years old in a time and place in which only the past offers hope and inspiration; the future offers only artifice and blight. I travel now in a society of friends who heat their houses with hand-cut wood and eliminate in outhouses, who cut pine shingles with draw-knives and haul maple sugar sap on sleds, who weed potatoes with their university-trained hands, pushing long hair out of their way and thus marking their foreheads with beautiful penitent dust. We till the soil to atone for our fathers' destruction of it. We smell. We live far from the marketplaces in America by our own volition, and the powerful men left behind are happy to have us out of their way. They do not yet realize that their heirs will refuse to inhabit their hollow cities, will find them poisonous and lethal, will run back to the Stone Age if necessary for survival and peace.

Within this context Mungo writes of New England rivers and of California, of Portsmouth and of Santa Fe, and of all the points between. Sometimes the reader cannot be certain whether a passage is from a diary or a dream, real or imagined, hoped for or hated. But the whole of it—and this book must be taken as a whole—is a shattering, terrifying indictment of the environment that we Americans have created in these United States.

Its message, then, is the message (as I understand it) of the Sierra Club, the National Audubon Society, and the Eco-this and Eco-that organizations that strive to keep Earth habitable. But there is a difference: organizational jargon is keyed to the ears of the middle-aged and framed in the idioms which those of us who are large of stomach and short of wind can understand.

Unfortunately, however, this is an audience whose power and prestige is not overly long for this world. Nearly one-half of all Americans are under 25 years. Raymond Mungo writes for them; that is, he writes for tomorrow and belongs to tomorrow. Despite the wisdom of all our yesterdays, it is doubtful if the middle-aged can understand him. But then, when have there ever been men of 50 who could understand the future? Nevertheless, with **Total Loss Farm** in your hands, it's worth an exciting try. (p. 40)

> *Monroe Bush, "Through Wide-Open Eyes," in* American Forests, *Vol. 77, No. 3, March, 1971, pp. 40, 42.*

Jean Zorn

As he tells it in **Return to Sender,** Ray Mungo left his Ver-

mont commune, Total Loss Farm, and went to India for the same reason that thousands of other young Americans abandon the commune, don long skirts and dhotis, pierce a nostril or two, and turn up in Bombay: "I sincerely believed that some spiritual master was waiting for me in India, that the good time I would find there would be actual bliss." Mungo found neither a good time nor actual bliss; he discovered instead, as do his fellow innocents abroad, that India is not a land of eternal peace and that poverty does not raise all men into gurus. He found the leprous beggars of Calcutta, the endlessness of death in Benares and the embarrassment of being one who is relatively rich in a country where most people are not only poor but vocally and vehemently angry about it.

On Mungo's first day in India, he was beset by the ubiquitous pedicab driver, who pursued him block after block, pleading with him to ride. Compassion alone forced Mungo finally to relent, but the object of his mercy repaid him by taking him the long way round, announcing an enormous hike in the fare and shouting angrily because he hadn't paid even more. After numerous similar encounters, the boy who went to India seeking spiritual peace found himself willing to do violence to train conductors, beggars, pedicab drivers, hotel clerks and all torpid bureaucrats of that sullen and aggressive land.

Someone ought to write a book about the migration of the young to India and Asia. Mungo is not the one to do it. A few images—his meeting with the demon of Sado Island, the boatload of dead men washed up on the beach at Kamakura just as the new wind is promising spring, his trance-like battle with the giant black bat—evoke the despair and darkness that draw travelers farther and farther from home. Usually, however, Mungo is satisfied merely to report to us how he felt, what he did and said about how he felt and what all his friends said and did about how he felt.

Most travel writers indulge in sweeping stereotypes about the lands they visit, and in an atmosphere of such heady generalizing, it is impossible not to succumb ourselves. But it is more enjoyable to characterize the writers than their subjects as national types. The 19th-century explorers reacted with condescension and disdain to the people who guided and hosted them. The European's invincible arrogance allowed him to sublimate both his sexual interest and the fear that it engendered. One might expect travelers in the post-imperial world to show more curiosity and less distrust, but while much has changed, too much remains the same.

Mungo, an American, reacts to the foreign cultures he encounters with fear and loathing. Japan drives him to drink; Hong Kong sends him fleeing to a lonely island inhabited by repulsive expatriates; in India, his face sprouts a mass of suppurating sores, painful and ugly signs of the unbearable anxiety that attacks an American abroad. On the other hand, the English traveler, . . . fancying himself invisible inside his tweeds, can remain superbly cheerful, benignly unaffected by what he sees because he assumes that nothing outside of England is real. All the quaint people are merely characters in a charming story, acted out for his delectation and delight. Travel is not, after all, a teacher; it is the process by which all our night terrors and prejudices are confirmed. (pp. 5, 22)

Jean Zorn, "Thrilling Threats of Dysentery and Decapitation," in The New York Times Book Review, *September 7, 1975, pp. 4-5, 22.*

John Stickney

To Mr. Mungo and his contemporaries who came of age during the 1960's and avoided settling into harness for as long as possible, the quality of work is now a near-obsession, by his account [*Cosmic Profit: How to Make Money without Doing Time*]. His books (*Famous Long Ago,* about his Liberation News Service, *Total Loss Farm,* about his Vermont commune, and others) amount to an ongoing autobiography, his generation's as much as his own, and this sixth installment charts the rise of new small business, the likeliest compromise between rebellious past and responsible present. Mr. Mungo tells of his own ventures as well as some four-dozen others across the country. The so-called counterculture is alive and various in anarcho-capitalist hybrids that range from underground publishing to salmon canning. (p. 13)

Because nobody fancies living by bread alone, some ideal comes to prevail. . . . In Mr. Mungo's [enterprises], it circulates in spherical collectives. But business remains stubbornly traditional, whatever the experiments in form and content. In Berkeley, whose revived industriousness reminds Mr. Mungo of postwar Hanoi, a fundraiser on public radio station KPFA announces, "C'mon, we know you're out there, and if you subscribe now, you can get a free year's subscription to *Struggle* magazine." Health-food companies like Boulder's Green Mountain Grainery or Brattleboro, Vt.'s Springtree Corporation, despite their pacific names and aims, battle in "the cutthroat natural marketplace."

To find contradictions, Mr. Mungo acknowledges, he need not travel far. "Marriage and children will put the fear of God into any young man," says the one-time communard. Like many of his fellow insurgents, Mr. Mungo became a born-again free enterpriser. Self-employment, the outsider's capitalism, just might support a family and turn a cosmic profit as well. "If time is money, and your time is your own," goes a Mungo proverb, "you are certifiably wealthy."

Mr. Mungo's liveliest material comes from his own business ventures or, as he calls them, the stages for his act, where he performs pratfalls, some sleight-of-hand and the occasional mock-heroic turn. He and two partners started Montana Books in a Seattle low-rent district in 1973 and took their motto from Henry James: "One should never be corrupt and dreary." Because the place was as much a salon as a store, and because the novices struck the right entrepreneurial balance of spirit, fortitude, luck and savvy, they defied the odds and succeeded. They also went into publishing, with their first title a friend's food-drying how-to book called *Dry It You'll Like It,* which has sold over 140,000 copies. Montana Books spun off two branches by 1978. But when initiative subsided into routine, Mr. Mungo became an absentee owner.

Writing is his true calling. Requests for trade secrets prompted a course, Lit Biz 101, taught by Mr. Mungo and other faculty at Montana Books. "I am proud to say that of the 80 or so students that we graduated (with a parchment diploma)," he reports, "none of them has written a book, to my knowledge." Mr. Mungo was eager to enlighten the students about the profession's risks, which usually outstrip its rewards. *Cosmic Profit* is most affecting where he tells of his own career and, by extension, goes to the heart of self-employment's hardships, whether in the Lit Biz or any other.

Despite his relative success, Mr. Mungo's literary ambitions have led him (in part) to divorce court, tax audit, credit card duns, friends' loans, "debt, depression, and inertia." To earn a living and sustain his writing, he started the bookstores and, in one harrowing foray, trafficked in real estate. But the extra money was not always cosmic profit, which comes to him most readily, if painfully, when he plies his writer's trade.

[Mr. Mungo sees] work as a means of salvation. [He] credits his kids for showing him the light. But after he'd accepted adulthood's obligations, he strayed into a fallacy that, he claims, bedevils many other seekers. Instead of pursuing his true vocation full-time, he worked elsewhere to buy the leisure to write in his off-hours. Integrating his life and livelihood is the right path for him, Mr. Mungo has decided, and potentially the most remunerative as well. His utopian vision is that everybody should have a chance at such career autonomy. "If you can do what you like and actually enjoy your responsibilities," says Mr. Mungo, "then you don't seek to escape them; they are not real chains but voluntary ties to your life's blood, your energy and identity. It's a neat trick, this cosmic profit, if you can manage it." (pp. 24-5)

John Stickney, "Making a Living," in The New York Times Book Review, *April 13, 1980, pp. 13, 24-5.*

Mungo is a brilliant celebrant. He writes with enormous joy and magic and eagerness for the future, like a boy who has had a lot of love. The beauty of his nature writing rivals Thoreau, one of his heroes.

—Bennett M. Berger in a review of Total Loss Farm, The New York Times Book Review, November 14, 1971.

Roy Hoffman

[In *Confessions From Left Field: A Baseball Pilgrimage*] Raymond Mungo tells us that Japanese baseball players consider it impolite to argue with the umpire; a Pittsburgh Pirates pitcher once threw a no-hitter while tripping on LSD; the Seattle Mariners were the first team to have a baseball game "volcanoed out"; for 20 years before the appearance of Fernando Valenzuela, Mexican-Americans in Los Angeles had refused to go to Dodger Stadium. If Mungo's facts intrigue you, you'll probably enjoy his funny, downbeat—though sometimes deadbeat—look at baseball fans, stadiums and memorabilia. There's more to the book, though. After all, the work is entitled "Confessions."

Confessions, these days, can indicate just about anything from honest soul-baring to comic meditation. Mungo puts together a quirky combination of these extremes, recounting his psychic and social condition over a two-year period—from spring training, 1980, through the World Series, 1982—as he moseys from one major league ballpark to another. He writes with choppy, poker-faced prose about his marriage ending in separation, his sporadic visits with his son, his penchant for dope, his love of trains and buses, his hair so long that, when in Japan, he feels it necessary to tuck the ends under the collar of his shirt. He writes of hitchhikers and Ivy League professors that the hitchhikers resemble.

The serious flaw of *Confessions from Left Field* is that, as a meditation on life, the book falls far short of the fence. Mungo wanders desultorily from baseball to world politics to dopester memories to societal speculation. At one point in the narrative he mentions he's off to have lunch with Kurt Vonnegut. The reference, personal, could also serve as literary allusion: *Confessions from Left Field* moves with the same ho-hum, "so it goes" lassitude of a good Kurt Vonnegut novel. Mungo is no Vonnegut, though, either in his perception of pain or his resignation to absurdity. When he scatters references to tragedy, such as the Atlanta child killings, he diminishes these tragedies rather than showing them to be absurdly horrible. Perhaps if his prose moved with more spit, knuckle and velocity, and if his baseball addiction were shown more forcefully, he'd catch us all up in his vision. But Mungo seems tired.

In the end we are left with what we are given in the beginning: memorabilia. Portraits of Maury Wills as a failing Seattle Mariners' manager; snapshots of a crazy, doubloon-chasing publicity campaign by the Portland Beavers of the Pacific Coast League; a funny look at the Gray Rabbit, a West Coast tour bus—these scenes, like vintage baseball cards, come spilling out of the book. In the end, *Confessions from Left Field* seems not so much baseball literature as baseball souvenirs—a worthy addition to any fan's shelf, but not necessarily to the serious reader's.

> *Roy Hoffman, "Meditations on Life as a Pop Fly," in* Los Angeles Times Book Review, *April 10, 1983, p. 5.*

Charles Solomon

One of the founders of the Liberation News Service and a minor '60s icon, Ray Mungo tells what he's been doing since the heady days of the student revolution. (Apparently not much.) He comes across [in *Beyond the Revolution: My Life and Times Since "Famous Long Ago"*] as a not very likeable opportunist, smoking dope and partying at other people's expense. Mungo gushes over former members of the counterculture he feels have remained true to its ideals (Dick Gregory is "a saint") and glosses over the fact that many of them are now lawyers, businessmen and real estate agents—exactly what they swore never to become. This former champion of anarchic freedom reports H. Rap Brown's recent condemnation of Salman Rushdie without a word of anger or dismay, although the reader gets the impression he would rush to defend an author attacked by Protestant fundamentalists. Mungo concludes with his credo that Baby Boomers "*need* to stay in touch" and "will be family"—the Addams Family, perhaps.

> *Charles Solomon, in a review of "Beyond the Revolution," in* Los Angeles Times Book Review, *December 16, 1990, p. 10.*

Phil Woods

Ray Mungo (author of *Total Loss Farm: A Year in the Life*) is, in my estimation, one of the best writers to come out of the counterculture, and [*Beyond the Revolution: My Life and Times Since "Famous Long Ago"*] is a record of his journey from the sixties to the present. In this microcosmic study, we get updates on Howard Zinn, Paul Krassner, Andy Kopkind, Roger Rappaport, Amanda Spake, and many others. Mungo also takes us along on his adventures through activism, repression, utopian dropout, freakout, travel, picking up the pieces, trying to find the right place to live, and trials of love. All are presented with grace, good humor, a sharp eye for irony, and a small bit of narcissism. Reading *Beyond the Revolution* is like hearing from an old friend. I think Mungo has the talent to write something truly substantial, but maybe living on the edge has taken its toll. For now, I'm happy with these gentle epistles. (pp. 3-4)

> *Phil Woods, in a review of "Beyond the Revolution," in* The Bloomsbury Review, *Vol. 11, No. 3, April-May, 1991, pp. 3-4.*

FURTHER READING

Barry, Marjorie M. Review of *Total Loss Farm, Quattlebaum's Truth,* and *The Conspiracy of the Young. America* 124, No. 10 (13 March 1971): 268-69.
> Discusses Mungo's *Total Loss Farm* in conjunction with *Quattlebaum's Truth* by Mark Gross and *The Conspiracy of the Young* by Paul Lauter and Florence Howe, claiming that "exploration of the whys of modern human existence is the common denominator of these three books."

Berger, Bennett M. Review of *Total Loss Farm. The New York Times Book Review* (14 November 1971): 6, 28, 30, 32.
> Discusses Mungo in a survey of books about communal living.

Caws, Peter. "Stage V and Con III." *The New Republic* 163, No. 20 (14 November 1970): 21, 23, 25-6.

Compares *Total Loss Farm* with Charles A. Reich's *The Greening of America,* noting that Mungo's work is more personal and, as a result, "if you want to meet Reich's new man in the flesh, read Mungo; having done so, you will not need to read Reich."

Leonard, John. "Books of the Times: Marx, Marijuana, Vermont and the System." *The New York Times* (26 May 1970): L39.

Reviews *Famous Long Ago* and Michael Myerson's *These Are the Good Old Days,* expressing doubt about the books' capabilities to incite social change.

Mills, Nicolaus. "A Rural Life Style." *The Yale Review: A National Quarterly* LX, No. 4 (June 1971): 609-13.

Compares three books on life in rural communities: *Total Loss Farm, Living the Good Life* by Helen and Scott Nearing, and *The Courage of Turtles* by Edward Hoagland.

Smucker, Tom. "New Leftovers." *The Nation* 230, No. 17 (3 May 1980): 526-27.

Review of *Cosmic Profit,* Todd Gitlin's *The Whole World is Watching,* and Abbie Hoffman's *Soon to Be a Major Motion Picture.*

Von Hoffman, Nicholas. "I Want To Be Me and Rich." *The New Republic* 182, No. 25 (21 June 1980): 25-8.

Surveys guides to moneymaking, including *Cosmic Profit,* which the reviewer describes as "a book for those who come into the harsh light of the decade with their eyes dilated by the chemistry of the near past's groovier years."

Additional coverage of Mungo's life and career is contained in the following sources published by Gale Research: *Contemporary Authors,* Vols. 49-52 and *Contemporary Authors New Revision Series,* Vol. 2.

Thomas Pynchon
The Crying of Lot 49

(Full name Thomas Ruggles Pynchon, Jr.) Born in 1937, Pynchon is an American novelist, short story writer, and nonfiction writer.

The following entry focuses on Pynchon's novel *The Crying of Lot 49* (1966). For further discussion of Pynchon's life and works, see *CLC*, Vols. 2, 3, 6, 9, 11, 18, 33, and 62.

INTRODUCTION

Pynchon is considered one of the most eminent literary stylists in contemporary American fiction. His second novel, *The Crying of Lot 49,* is generally regarded as a blend of romance, satire, and anti-detective story in which the traditional movement from disorder to clarity is reversed. In addition to reflecting Pynchon's knowledge of many disciplines in the natural and social sciences, the novel demonstrates his inclination for such popular elements as black humor, outlandish puns, and parody. While considered his most accessible work due to its concise narrative and exuberant comic surface, *The Crying of Lot 49* has elicited continuous scholarly debate, and most critics have concurred with Robert Sklar's assessment of the book as "a simple novel that reread grows more complex."

Set in southern California, *The Crying of Lot 49* begins as Oedipa Maas, a housewife living a buffered existence in the fictional suburb of Kinneret-Among-The-Pines, is named executor of the estate of her deceased former lover, Pierce Inverarity, a California real estate tycoon. Like the reader of *The Crying of Lot 49,* Oedipa grows increasingly confused as she attempts to trace indeterminate clues from a stamp collection owned by Pierce that seem to hint at a clandestine conspiracy. While tracing the collection, Oedipa discovers evidence of what appears to be an underground communications system—signified by the acronym W.A.S.T.E.—that has operated alongside the world's legitimate postal systems since the fourteenth century. This network, through which the disinherited and the alienated apparently communicate meaningful messages, seems to be associated in turn with an ominous organization known alternately as the Tristero or Trystero. While apparently offering hope for the hopeless, the Tristero seems to threaten destruction and apocalypse. The stamps Oedipa encounters, for example, contain such menacing symbols of death as poisonous flowers and a Statue of Liberty with a "faint, menacing smile"—and the W.A.S.T.E. trademark, a muted post horn, may signify the blocked trumpet of apocalypse that will sound should Oedipa discover (or perhaps, fail to discover) the significance of the Tristero.

During her investigation, Oedipa spends an entire night in San Francisco attempting to determine the meaning of the post horn symbol, which she finds scrawled indiscriminately in public lavatories, subways, and sidewalks with legends such as "DON'T EVER ANTAGONIZE THE HORN." Throughout *The Crying of Lot 49,* Oedipa remains uncertain as to whether her perception of the Tristero is valid, whether W.A.S.T.E. and the Tristero are part of an elaborate joke on her by Pierce, or whether she is in fact paranoid, attributing significance where none actually exists. The notion of solipsism versus manipulation is established early in *The Crying of Lot 49* in Oedipa's recollection of the central panel in a triptych she saw while visiting Mexico with Pierce. The painting, which depicts a group of female captives embroidering a tapestry of the world that overflows through the windows of the tower in which they are imprisoned, at once symbolizes a mode of self-entrapment for Oedipa, her previously insulated existence at Kinneret-Among-The-Pines, and—a central theme—her questioning of perception. What lies outside the tower appears to be the world, yet is in fact a tapestry—a false projection imposed upon the world by and for the self.

Throughout *The Crying of Lot 49,* Pynchon paradoxically affirms and denies the notion that mundane reality may possess hidden meaning. According to Alfred Mac Adam, such implausible and apparently arbitrary character names as Oedipa Maas, Genghis Cohen, and Mike Fallopian lead the reader to an awareness of their fictitious nature, to "an understanding of the device as a device and not as the knot which, once unraveled, opens the way to some deeper meaning." However, some critics have detected limited significance in Pynchon's overt allusions to classical myth. At one level, for example, Oedipa's name suggests the myth of Oedipus Rex in that she pursues a solution to a riddle that may result in either self-awareness or self-destruction. At another, she seeks paternal knowledge in the form of the legacy that Pierce—who is the founding father and owner of San Narciso, an industrialized city—has left Oedipa, and by extension, the United States. As the name San Narciso suggests, Pierce is related to Narcissus, the mythical character who fell in love with his own reflection. Oedipa is similarly likened to Echo, whose love was spurned by Narcissus, thereby dooming her to repeat only the last words of other people's voices. These allusions advance the theme of blocked communication in *The Crying of Lot 49* and emphasize Oedipa's role as a seeker of love who is unable to establish meaningful connections with others. Like virtually all of Oedipa's human contacts in the novel, Pierce is represented as having been less interested in the responsibilities of love than in the pursuit of materialism and self-gratification. Oedipa gradually realizes that the "colored windows" of his stamp collection are an illusory substitute for her love, affording him a view of "deep vistas of space and time, . . . allegorical faces that never were."

Unifying the complex plot of *The Crying of Lot 49* is Pynchon's use of the Second Law of Thermodynamics as a metaphor for the forces that contribute to social decline. This law states that the universe must reach a state of maximum entropy (disorder), at which time only a minimum of energy will be left available and all change will cease. The trend is thus paradoxically toward sameness and conformity despite the existence of overall disorganization and unpredictability. Pynchon's treatment of thermodynamic entropy derives from twentieth-century theorist Henry Adams, who argued in his *The Rule of Phase Applied to History* (1909) that history itself is succumbing to entropy as the world approaches apocalypse. *The Crying of Lot 49,* however, exploits the diametrically opposed meanings that the term "entropy" denotes in thermodynamics and in information theory. In both, entropy is a measure of disorganization, but in information theory, the term has some positive implications. A distinguishing feature of information theory is noise, which appears to represent disorder since communication should be the orderly, organized opposite. As the degree of noise in a communications system increases, however, along with disorder and unpredictability, so does the potential for new information and informative output. Therefore, chaos and disorder denote an abundance of possibilities for communication, a *neg*entropic state. By opposing thermodynamic and informational notions of entropy in *The Crying of Lot 49,* Pynchon posits a situation in which the world's entropic decline, as evidenced by its capacity for bureaucracy,

atomic war, and domestic violence, can only be prevented by an increase in meaningful human communication.

Responsibility for effecting such communication in *The Crying of Lot 49* is ultimately left to Oedipa. Oedipa's first encounter with thermodynamic and informational entropy ensues from a meeting with John Nefastis, an inventor who creates a machine based on the studies of James Clerk Maxwell, a nineteenth-century Scottish physicist. In his *Theory of Heat* (1871), Maxwell postulated that an imaginary intelligence known as "Maxwell's demon" could sort fast from slow molecules into two separate compartments inside a closed box and thereby create two regions of "heat" and "cold." The difference in temperature, according to Maxwell, could then be used to drive a heat engine, thereby defying the second law's supposition that it is impossible to produce an inequality in temperature without work. The twentieth-century objection to this theory is basically the same as Oedipa's—"Sorting isn't work?" Nefastis alters Maxwell's theory in that his machine combines science and spiritualism, requiring a "sensitive," or source of input from *outside* the box, to allow Maxwell's demon to sort molecules. As *The Crying of Lot 49* progresses, Oedipa becomes aware that like the Nefastis machine, America has become a closed system in which repitition and redundancy in language have threatened to create an entropic state in human communications, leaving its citizens spiritually numb. By the end of the novel, Oedipa embraces the role of sensitive, sifting clues relating to the Tristero in an effort to counter entropy and to become "the dark machine in the centre of the planetarium, to bring [Pierce's] estate into pulsing stelliferous Meaning." By the end of *The Crying of Lot 49,* Oedipa comes to believe that agents of the Tristero wish to obtain Pierce's stamp collection so that they may destroy or suppress evidence of their existence. This suspicion leads her to attend a public auction at which the stamps, designated "lot 49," are to be sold. The book ends, however, just before the auctioneer opens the bidding, providing no conclusive evidence of the Tristero's existence or nonexistence. This cryptic conclusion has continued to prompt diverse interpretations, many of which attribute indeterminate or religious meaning to the text. While some commentators, such as Thomas Hill Schaub, have insisted on the novel's essential ambiguity, citing the book's recurrent emphasis on paradox, others view *The Crying of Lot 49* as an allegorical quest for God in which absolute proof of Tristero's existence will free language ("the Word") from its entropic bonds and signal the end of the world.

PRINCIPAL WORKS

NOVELS

V. 1963
The Crying of Lot 49 1966
Gravity's Rainbow 1973
Vineland 1990

SHORT FICTION

*"Mortality and Mercy in Vienna" 1959

† "The World (This One), The Flesh (Mrs. Oedipa Maas), and the Testament of Pierce Inverarity" 1965
Slow Learner: Early Stories 1984

OTHER MAJOR WORKS

‡"A Journey into the Mind of Watts" (essay) 1966

*This story was published in *Epoch,* Vol. 9, No. 4, Spring 1959.

†This story, which consists of the first two chapters of *The Crying of Lot 49,* was published in *Esquire,* Vol. LXIV, No. 6, December 1965.

‡This essay was published in the *New York Times Magazine,* 12 June 1966.

CRITICISM

Richard Poirier

Thomas Pynchon's second novel, **The Crying of Lot 49,** reads like an episode withheld from his first, the much-acclaimed **V.,** published three years ago. Pynchon's technical virtuosity, his adaptations of the apocalyptic-satiric modes of Melville, Conrad, and Joyce, of Faulkner, Nathanael West, and Nabokov, the saturnalian inventiveness he shares with contemporaries like John Barth and Joseph Heller, his security with philosophical and psychological concepts, his anthropological intimacy with the off-beat—these evidences of extraordinary talent in the first novel continue to display themselves in the second. And the uses to which he puts them are very much the same.

The first novel, **V.** was a designed indictment of its own comic elaborateness. The various quests for **V.,** all of them substitutes for the pursuit of love, are interwoven fantastically, and the coherence thus achieved is willfully fabricated and factitious. Pynchon's intricacies are meant to testify to the waste—a key word in **The Crying of Lot 49** of imagination that first creates and is then enslaved by its own plottings, its machines, the products of its technology.

Except for the heroine of **V.,** Rachel Owlglass (she who can see wisely without being a voyeur), and the heroine of this novel, Oedipa Maas—lovable, hapless, decent, eager girls—both novels are populated by self-mystified people running from the responsibilities of love and compelled by phantoms, puzzles, the power of Things. No plot, political, novelistic, or personal, can issue from the circumstances of love, from the simple human needs, say, of a Rachel or an Oedipa, and Pynchon implicitly mocks this situation by the Byzantine complications of plots which do evolve from circumstances devoid of love.

Gestures of warmth are the more touching in his novels for being terrifyingly intermittent, shy, and worried. The coda of the first novel, enunciated by the jazz player, Mc-Clintic Sphere, also serves the second: "Love with your mouth shut, help without breaking your ass or publicizing it; keep cool but care." This is the stoical resolve of an embattled underground in a world increasingly governed by Ionesco's rhinoceri, to mention a vision markedly similar to Pynchon's. Efforts at human communication are lost among Pynchon's characters, nearly all of whom are obsessed with the presumed cryptography in the chance juxtaposition of Things, in the music and idiom of bars like the V-Note or The Scope, or merely in the "vast sprawl of houses" that Oedipa sees outside Los Angeles, reminding her of the printed circuit of a transistor radio, with its "intent to communicate."

Even the title of **V.** was cryptographic. It was available to all interpretations and answerable to none. Though **V.** probably did not have Vietnam as one of its meanings in 1963, the novel so hauntingly evokes the preconditions of international disaster that Vietnam belongs in the long list of other V's. Roughly half the novel is an international melodrama of spying in the years since the Fashoda incident of 1898. It shows how international, like personal, complications accumulate from an interplay of fantasies constructed by opposing sides, each sustaining the other's dream of omnipotence, each justifying its excesses by evoking the cleverness of its opposition, each creating that opposition and, in some mysterious and crazy way, the moves and the successes of the other side as a provocation of its own further actions.

"Plots" are an expression in Pynchon of the mad belief that *some* plot can ultimately take over the world, can ultimately control life to the point where it is manageably inanimate. And the ascription of "plots" to an opposition is a way of explaining why one's own have not achieved this ultimate control. Nearly from the outset, the people of Pynchon's novels are the instruments of the "plots" they help create.

Their consequent dehumanization makes the prospect of an apocalypse and the destruction of self not a horror so much as the final ecstasy of power. In international relations the ecstasy is war; in human relationships it can be sado-masochism, where skin itself is leather, leather a substitute for skin. The process is a part of daily news, and no other novelist predicts and records it with Pynchon's imaginative and stylist grasp of contemporary materials.

In **V.** private life (the story of Benny Profane, his girl Rachel, and the Whole Sick Crew) and international politics (involving the various European and African manifestations of **V.** from the 1890's to 1939) are related only metaphorically. The characters in one plot take no direct part in the other. Of much shorter length and narrower focus, **The Crying of Lot 49** is located between Berkeley and Los Angeles, and its events, historical as well as private, are filtered through the career of one person, Oedipa Maas. Oedipa is introduced as a good suburban housewife in Kinneret-Among-The-Pines, making "the twilight's whiskey sours" against the arrival of her husband Wendell ("Mucho") Maas.

At the outset her troubles are all manageable within the terms of ordinary daily living. She has a not always potent husband who suffers crises of conscience about his professions—formerly a used car salesman, he is now a disk jockey—and about his teen-age tastes and his taste for teen-agers. Also, she has a neurotic psychiatrist names Hilarius, who wants her to take LSD as an experiment, and a former lover, the tycoon Pierce University, who would sometimes call her, before his recent death, at one in the morning, using Slavic, comic Negro, or hostile Pachuco dialects.

As the novel opens, Oedipa learns, on her return from a party whose "hostess had put perhaps too much kirsch in the fondue," that she is an executor, along with a man named Metzger, formerly the child movie star known as Baby Igor, of Inverarity's will. The will was discovered some months after his death, a period during which it was perhaps tampered with in order to hide from Oedipa the revelations which his network of holdings, her "inheritance," seem to communicate: an America coded in Inverarity's testament. Before the novel closes, Oedipa loses her husband to LSD, her psychiatrist to madness, her one extra-marital lover, Metzger, to a depraved 15-year-old, and her one guide through the mazes of her inheritance, a Randolph Driblette, to suicide. In the final scene, accompanied by the famed philatelist Genghis Cohen, she enters the "crying" of Lot 49, a collection of Inverarity's stamps.

The "crying of Lot 49" refers to an auction, but the phrase evokes the recurrent suspicion on Oedipa's part that there is "revelation in progress all around her," that the stamps, "thousands of little colored windows into deep vistas of space and time," are themselves "crying" a message—not about Pierce Inverarity necessarily, or even about Oedipa, but about "their Republic," about America, its inheritances, and what we inherit from it, including things like used lots of stamps and used car lots. The "stamps" were often Inverarity's substitute for Oedipa, just as Mucho sought communication less with her than with his used cars or in the dancing of his teen-agers.

Oedipa's fascination with the possibilities of "revelation" in inanimate things, and the curious patterns of connection among them, is induced, at least in part, by the fact that "things" have stolen from her the attention and love of both men. It is therefore possible that Inverarity became connected with the famous Tristero System, the central cryptograph of this novel as "V" was of the first, out of the impulse *not* to communicate with her, or to communicate with her only under cover of various disguises. It is also possible that the System, participation in which allows a "calculated withdrawal from the life of the Republic, from its machinery," from its forms of public communication, is an elaborate hoax, a teaser arranged by Inverarity to tantalize her away from home, love, and the open community, to seduce her into such subsidiary organizations as the "Inamorati Anonymous," an outfit she encounters in a queer bar in San Francisco.

Alternatively, the hints about a Tristero System could have been planted in the will by interests anxious to prevent Oedipa from discovering the whole network of Inverarity's holdings, including those in Yoyodyne, an electronics and missile corporation, one executive of which, retired by automation, founded the Inamorati Anonymous. (Yo-yoing in *V.* was the pointless, repetitive passage and return on any convenient ferry or subway, usually the Times Square-Grand Central run, for Benny Profane and his friends, and it is characteristic of Pynchon's metaphoric translations of personal into international idiosyncrasies that yo-yoing can also describe the horror of nuclear exchange.)

Finally, Tristero may only be Oedipa's fantasy, an expression of her need to believe that there must be something to explain the drift of everyone she knows toward inhumanity. Otherwise she is either a paranoid or America *is* Tristero and she an alien.

Between the opening scenes of domesticity and the closing scenes of the "crying" of Lot 49, Oedipa is like the hero in a book of [Edmund Spenser's] *The Faerie Queene,* tempted from her human virtues while on a quest that takes her through all manner of seemingly prearranged weirdness and monstrosity, all kinds of foreign "systems" thriving within an America which is itself "a grand and so intricate enigma." Only the Tristero, imagined as an intricate network of underground organizations, can encapsulate what she would otherwise have to see as the drift of the Republic itself toward "the glamorous prospect of annihilation."

This novel is a patriotic lamentation, an elaborate effort not to believe the worst about the Republic. Patriotism for an ideal of America explains the otherwise yawning gap in Pynchon's comic shaping of his material. The Tristero System—it began in 1577 in Holland in opposition to the Thurn and Taxis Postal System and is active now in America trying to subvert the American postal system through an organization called W.A.S.T.E.—is a masterpiece of comic invention. It involves, among other things, one of the best parodies ever written of Jacobean drama, *The Courier's Tragedy,* and a perhaps final parody of California right-wing organizations, the Peter Pequid Society, named for the commanding officer of the Confederate man-of-war *Disgruntled* and opposed to industrial capitalism on the grounds that it has led inevitably to Marxism. Its leader, Mike Fallopian, speculates in California real estate.

The exuberance of such comedy softens the portents of national calamity, but at the same time it makes it nearly impossible for Pynchon to persuade the reader, as he anxiously wants to do, that the whole System and the whole book have more meaning than a practical joke. The same difficulty was apparent in *V.,* where the author's style at points of sincerity about love and youth was, by contrast to the vitality of his comic writing, platitudinously limp and sloganeering.

In this second novel, the difficulty is if anything more acute. Pynchon chooses to have all the significance pass through the experience of only one comically named character, Oedipa Maas, as if he had chosen to have all of *V.* assembled and assimilated by Benny Profane or by Rachel Owlglass. In *V.* a structure of metaphor and cross-reference existed beyond the inquiry of many of the characters. The result was a dimension secured from comedy and within which the comedy could function as a form of what might be called local ignorance of the issues on which it was commenting. In *The Crying of Lot 49,* however, the role given Oedipa makes it impossible to divorce from her limitations the large rhetoric about America at the end of the novel. This is unfortunate simply because Oedipa has not been given character enough to bear the weight of this rhetoric:

> If San Narciso and the estate were really no different from any other town, any other estate, then by that continuity she might have found The Tristero anywhere in her Republic, through any of a hundred lightly-concealed entranceways, a hundred alienations, if only she'd looked. She stopped a minute between the steel rails, raised her head as if to sniff the air. She became conscious of the hard, strung presence she stood on—knew as if maps had been flashed for her on the sky how these tracks ran on into others, and others, and others, knew they laced, deepened, authenticated the great American night, so wide and now so suddenly intense for her.

What I think is happening at the end is that Pynchon desperately needs to magnify the consciousness of his heroine, if he is to validate her encounter with The Tristero System. Only by doing so can he maintain the possibility that the System is distinguishable from the mystery and enigma of America itself. To say that no distinction exists would be to sacrifice the very rationale of his comic reportage: that he is reporting not evidence about America so much as pockets of eccentricity in it, fragments dangerously close to forming a design but fragments nonetheless. Pynchon is reluctant to make all his people submit to the pervasive grotesqueness of American life, though he comes close to that, and he therefore exalts a character altogether too small for the large job given Oedipa at the end.

Pynchon's best writing is often in his descriptions of American scenery, of objects rather than persons. He shows at such points a tenderness, largely missing from our literature since Dreiser, for the very physical waste of our yearnings, for the anonymous scrap heap of Things wherein our lives are finally joined.

—*Richard Poirier*

In fact, Pynchon's best writing is often in his descriptions of American scenery, of objects rather than persons. He shows at such points a tenderness, largely missing from our literature since Dreiser, for the very physical waste of our yearnings, for the anonymous scrap heap of Things wherein our lives are finally joined. The Pynchon who can write with dashing metaphoric skill about the way humans have become Things, can also reveal a beautiful and heartbreaking reverence for the human penetration of the Thingness of this country, the signatures we make on the grossest evidences of our existence. Indeed we do leave

codes and messages, seen by the likes of Mucho even in used cars:

> Yet at least he had believed in the cars, maybe to excess: how could he not, seeing people poorer than him come in, Negro, Mexican, cracker, a parade seven days a week, bring with them the most godawful of trade-ins: motorized, metal extensions of themselves, of their families and what their whole lives must be like, out there so naked for anybody, a stranger like himself, to look at, frame cockeyed, rusty underneath, fender repainted in a shade just off enough to depress the value, if not Mucho himself, inside smelling hopelessly of children, of supermarket booze, or two, sometimes three generations of cigarette smokers, or only of dust—and when the cars were swept out you had to look at the actual residue of these lives, and there was no way of telling what things had been truly refused (when so little he supposed came by that out of fear most of it had to be taken and kept) and what had simply (perhaps tragically) been lost: clipped coupons promising savings of 5 or 10¢, trading stamps, pink flyers advertising specials at the markets, butts, tooth-shy combs, help-wanted ads, Yellow Pages torn from the phone book, rags of old underwear or dresses that already were period costumes, for wiping your own breath off the inside of a windshield with so you could see whatever it was, a movie, a woman or car you coveted, a cop who might pull you over just for drill, all the bits and pieces coated uniformly, like a salad of despair, in a grey dressing of ash, condensed exhaust, dust, body wastes—it nauseated him to look, but he had to look.

Within this description is a haunting sequence of imagined human situations, typical and pathetic ones, fused with the particularized power that shows Pynchon's own obsession with the encoded messages of the American landscape. What is also noticeable here, and throughout the novel, is that the major character is really Pynchon himself, Pynchon's voice with its capacity to move from the elegy to the epic catalogue. The narrator sounds like a survivor looking through the massed wreckage of his civilization, "a salad of despair." That image, to suggest but one of the puns in the word Tristero, is typically full of sadness, terror, love, and flamboyance. But then, how else should one imagine a tryst with America? And that is what this novel is. (pp. 5, 42-3)

Richard Poirer, "Embattled Underground," in The New York Times Book Review, *May 1, 1966, pp. 5, 42-3.*

Remington Rose

Mr. Pynchon's first novel, *V.,* was published in 1963. No one who has read it could mistake the author of *The Crying of Lot 49. V.* is an elaborately organized presentation of searches for, and of, figures in some way involved in an antisocial conspiracy. Much of the action is spastic and bizarre, the language is an original blend of erudition and slang, the characters are vividly mournful, their relationships inevitably awry. And all this is true of Pynchon's second novel.

One result of this is to give this book a spurious interestingness, like a riddle or a trompe l'oeil painting by a craftsman of a certain capability. One begins to brood on the puns, to underline images and note analogous situations, and to draw patterns on the endpapers. I suppose one in some sense attends even to Shakespeare in this way, certainly to Joyce. But the difference is that their patterns become not only more complex, but larger; there is an opening out, a freeing of awareness thanks to the shaping of the work of art. But in *Crying* the circles become progressively smaller, and refuse to respond to the reader's (or the novelist's) efforts to inflate them other than by going limp with a modest hiss.

V. is a long book, geographically and temporally wide-ranging, with a huge cast and a profusion of activity. *Crying* is a short book, about the brief, distressing odyssey of one character up and down one section of a California freeway. Unfortunately the effect is not one of condensation, but of crampedness. It is as if *Crying* had been an early sketch of both the theme and the style of the larger novel, and has remained skimpy, cryptic, and superficial.

Oedipa Maas, the heroine, has been appointed co-executor of a former lover's will. While investigating his holdings, she finds evidence of a vast system of mail delivery which unites the discontented and disinherited in their separation from the institutions of society. In various ways the men she encounters are aware of communication beyond the surface noises of life—Muzak, telephones, air-conditioners, factory machines, and so forth. Is she hallucinating? Is there "another mode of meaning behind the obvious, or none"? At the end of the book she is near a possible answer, sitting with others in a locked room at the auction of her lover's belongings, awaiting "the crying of Lot 49." (That this should be the meaning of the title is such a letdown I feel a duty to reveal it here.)

The idea is rich and intriguing, and it is several times dramatized ingeniously. As she is led more and more into the company of the isolated, Oedipa feels herself increasingly alone and helpless. Everyone is plugged in somewhere else; in a queer bar, at a deaf-mutes' dance, she is disabled by her "normalcy" from making any connection. But these incidents are only briefly sketched before their "significance" is asserted in passages which begin like, "As things developed, she was to have all manner of revelations," and end like, "She had dedicated herself, weeks ago, to making sense of what Inverarity had left behind, never suspecting that the legacy was America."

Not only had I not suspected it either, I don't believe it now. Unless Oedipa and I together share experiences of such substance that they themselves suggest they are in a larger sense "representative," this kind of manufactured "revelation" is offensive. It is as if Pynchon distrusted either the medium or the reader, or both; as if he hadn't the interest or the patience to do his job properly. That such rudeness should have followed *V.* is especially disturbing; the author of that book clearly enjoyed what he was doing and assumed the reader was up to it. *Crying* is a step back-

ward to the art of the emblem books, a patchy collection of images propped up by claims of significance in terms which the artist hasn't proved his right to use.

Satire, pathos, dream visions, pawky humor, some crisp writing and occasional marvelous synopses—of a movie, a play, the history of the sinister mail system—an astonishing number of mental, sexual, musical, and political deviates: all these and too much more are listed. But nothing is really done, nothing is worked through; there has been too little effort to make a novel out of them. I am not especially interested in prescribing what something must be in order to be a novel. But I am concerned to keep the word as a useful description of one kind of art-work as opposed to another. In the same spirit, I would call *The Crying of Lot 49* a well-executed, mildly nasty, pretentious collage. And if you want to read one of them, go ahead. (pp. 39-40)

Remington Rose, "At Home with Oedipa Maas," in The New Republic, *Vol. 154, No. 20, May 14, 1966, pp. 39-40.*

Erik Wensberg

Thomas Pynchon's gifts as a novelist are almost alarming. An impassioned comic writer, spendthrift of invention, he dwells in that romance with time which nourishes the born storyteller. And he commands the stranger power of enforcement: he can work upon his reader the very disorder and anxious exertions his fiction describes. His language throws off Joycean and Nabokovian scintillations—multiple meanings, cross-references and puns—which yet remain steadily, intelligently directed.

He is also a comic writer upon whom seriousness and utter contemporaneity seem to have fastened like a kind of doom. With all its racy virtuosity, his dark little second novel, *The Crying of Lot 49,* is, I think, far more moving than the earlier *V.*, if only for its concision and consequent focus of feeling. The book dreams upon America with a tenderness and elegaic sense of loss not present before in our specifically comic fiction.

And, simplest to say, Pynchon is a comic writer who is very often extremely funny. In part, *The Crying of Lot 49* is an exuberant ribbing of all the California manias, of pop culture gone to rock and ruin, of the wreckage of taste that our machinery produces in abundance. Pynchon can indulge in that simplest kind of horsing, funny names (Randolph Driblette, Ghengis Cohen) for their own sake; at the other extreme of wit, he includes here a blood-drenched parody of Jacobean drama that closes out all other attempts.

The Crying of Lot 49 concerns certain revelations disclosed to a young suburban housewife, Oedipa Maas (Oedipa: she who interrogates the past and patrimony), whose former lover, a now deceased real estate tycoon named Pierce Inverarity, has made her executrix of his will, an inventory of international chicanery, local exploitation and hidden holdings. The name of Pierce Inverarity implies the labor that is to engulf Oedipa, as she is drawn away from her dim, malleable husband and the little green certainties of Kinneret-in-the-Pines into a search for the truth of power in her country. She must attempt to Pierce the Verity, the Appearances and Inversions, of a man who manufactured cigarette filters of ground bone; who built and owned the industrial city of San Narciso (its chiefest monument to him a thriving missile industry); who sent freeways hurtling through cemeteries and sowed barren housing developments whose tracery is that of the electronic circuit plate, a design for impulse and power only.

Yet it is another side of the revelation that invades Oedipa's imagination and compels the fullest range of Pynchon's own visionary inventiveness: in her quest for clarification of Inverarity's properties, Oedipa stumbles upon a sort of subcontinent of the obsolescent, a union of cracked and damned, silently watching "undergrounds," beaten by the controls of organized society—each, in its lush battiness or isolation, making up a station of The Tristero System. This vast brotherhood communicates by a rival postal system outside the federal one—symbolically, by means of public waste cans.

Its confederated withdrawers from the nation's "normal" life include the Peter Pequid Society, last word in right-wing truculence; Inamorati Anonymous, who seek wholly to cure the addiction of love, "the worst addiction of all"; failed suicides; mad children; lone Mexican girls on midnight buses—and all keep seeming to signal Oedipa with a graphic sign she has early seen on certain curious postage stamps. Again, in the name of The Tristero System lies the secret *Tristeza,* Terror, Hysteria that is the Inverse of Inverarity's "legacy."

At the end, Oedipa comes to the auctioning—professionally called a "crying"—of Lot 49, the Inverarity stamp collection containing the apparent Tristero forgeries, whose meaning she now fears. She knows there is to be in attendance an anonymous buyer of all this emblematic misery and waste; whether for its further elaboration or its cure is an open question. Most ominous of all, Oedipa has found hints in the course of her obsessed investigations that the Tristero System is centuries-old, perhaps an unredeemable by-product of civilization, brought to its grand destination and fullness in the most powerful nation in the world.

In the nature of the opposing forces she has seen, in their very opposition and secrecy, Oedipa envisions a paranoia—a continental paranoia—that may have infected herself. Her own sanity, then, is the other open question. Yet, along the stations of Tristero we have ourselves by this time seen the heightened versions of events and ideologies, missions and monuments that we know too well around us. The open questions are being put to more than Oedipa Maas.

Pynchon's novel "means" many other things as well. It may be seen as dealing with the failures of love, or even with the artist's obsession with "meaning." And to say so much is to distinguish Pynchon from those comic writers whose lidless gaze of disgust, or whose manic desperation, have acquired such authority of late under the rubric of Black Humor. These writers, asserting the relief of anarchy in the face of public outrage and private boredom, have disturbed the nation's peace to good effect. Yet even

Pynchon's errors in this novel occur beyond such limited purposes. His intellectual wit can veer into pedantry, as in some of Oedipa's historical researches. As his heroine, Oedipa must also necessarily convey the author's own intelligence and passion, yet has been under-endowed, as a character, by her creator. These are the mishaps of a complex conception.

What Pynchon has done, with a style of great rhetorical richness, is to reassert the emotions of patriotism, spaciousness and wonder that animate the classic American novels. His voice is that of the American novels. His voice is that of the American whom Tocqueville foresaw, whose destiny is unmediated by the traditional authorities, the voice sounded in American literature from Melville to Fitzgerald to Frost. Knowing, yet lyric, *The Crying of Lot 49* stands in the line of *The Great Gatsby* in its concise attempt to capture the dangerous exaltations, and the loneliness, of this strange place. (pp. 446-48)

> *Erik Wensberg, in a review of "The Crying of Lot 49," in* Commonweal, *Vol. LXXXIV, No. 16, July 8, 1966, pp. 446-48.*

Anne Mangel

One of the most significant aspects of Thomas Pynchon's writing is his ingenious use of scientific-technological concepts as the basis for his fiction. Pynchon's characters seldom reflect a traditional mythological or religious pattern of thought; in their world, the emphasis is rather on such things as thermodynamics and signal-to-noise ratios. Of the many scientific concepts which occur in Pynchon's fiction, three intrude most dramatically: thermodynamics and Maxwell's demon, entropy, and information theory, all of which are important in *The Crying of Lot 49.*

The novel is an account of Oedipa Maas's exploration into the estate of the deceased Pierce Inverarity, an entrepreneur, who seems, in the end, to own all of America. While investigating Inverarity's assets, she wanders into "Yoyodyne," a government-contracted industry. There Oedipa meets one of the Yoyodyne workers, Stanley Koteks, who introduces her to the idea of Maxwell's Demon with a breezy but essentially correct explanation of the concept.

James Clerk Maxwell, a 19th century physicist, introduced the Demon in 1871 in his book *Theory of Heat.* Pointing out that the second law of thermodynamics shows the impossibility of producing "any inequality of temperature or of pressure without the expenditure of work," Maxwell goes on:

> Now let us suppose that such a vessel is divided into two portions, A and B, by a division in which there is a small hole, and that a being, who can see the individual molecules, opens and closes this hole, so as to allow only the swifter molecules to pass from A to B, and only the slower ones to pass from B to A. He will thus, without expenditure of work, raise the temperature of B and lower that of A, in contradiction to the second law of thermodynamics.

As the Demon sorts the molecules, he increases the order

in the vessel, and decreases the entropy, or amount of disorder in the system.

In *The Crying of Lot 49,* Pynchon uses Maxwell's notion of the Demon as a metaphor for Oedipa's experiences. The frequent allusions to Oedipa's sorting masses of information evoke the idea of Maxwell's sorting Demon. As the novel opens, Inverarity's estate presents Oedipa with "the job of sorting it all out." She begins by "shuffling back through a fat deckful of days" trying to isolate the one on which Inverarity had last phoned her. The sorting and shuffling which is mentioned at the start of the novel is just the first indication of the separating Oedipa will have to do to create order out of the mass of clues, symbols, and signs which descend upon her.

After Oedipa hears about Maxwell's Demon from Koteks, she tends to view the Demon in terms of the poles of order and randomness. The Demon, as Oedipa sees it, establishes a point of order and connection in a system of random occurrences. As she puts it, the Demon is "the linking feature in a coincidence." Oedipa's understanding of the Demon's function is pointed out when she thinks of the explanation of entropy given to her by John Nefastis, a Berkeley inventor who has built a machine he believes contains a real Maxwell's Demon: "For John Nefastis (to take a recent example) two kinds of entropy, thermodynamic and informational, happened, say by coincidence, to look alike, when you wrote them down as equations. Yet he had made his mere coincidence respectable, with the help of Maxwell's Demon." Again, the Demon manages to bind occurrences.

Like Maxwell's Demon, Oedipa soon tries to link occurrences, to establish a point of order in what seems to be a random system of information. She vows to be "the dark machine in the centre of the planetarium, to bring the estate into pulsing stelliferous Meaning." Her desire to bring order to the mass of confusing interests left by Inverarity leads her to the discovery of "Trystero," a mysterious organization involving a bizarre underground mail system called WASTE. Oedipa sets out to discover the nature and extent of WASTE and Trystero, an obsessive hunt which takes her all over southern California. Just as the Demon, by sorting the molecules, gains information about them, so Oedipa shuffles through countless people and places, gathering information about the elusive Trystero.

Whatever concrete information Oedipa gains, though, is offset by increasing confusion. The Demon's sorting process can theoretically create a "perpetual motion" machine, and such a machine seems to be operating metaphorically in Oedipa's situation. The clues she gathers yield more clues in an infinite process. Opening out into more and more suggestions, they yield no conclusion. Oedipa gradually senses this. Pondering the information gained from watching *The Courier's Tragedy,* a Jacobean revenge play which contains references to the Trystero, she realizes "these follow-ups were no more disquieting than other revelations which now seemed to come crowding in exponentially, as if the more she collected the more would come to her." With her suspicion that the clues are unlimited comes a realization that they will never yield a stelliferous Meaning. She begins to consider whether "the

gemlike 'clues' were only some kind of compensation. To make up for her having lost the direct, epileptic Word, the cry that might abolish the night."

The parallels between Oedipa and the Demon seem almost too neat. Oedipa painfully discovers that symbols, such as WASTE and its emblem, the muted post horn, do not lead to one stelliferous Meaning. Rather, they point in a thousand different directions and never lead to a solid conclusion. This notion of symbol and metaphor seems to lie at the center of Pynchon's fiction. This idea forms the basis for Pynchon's novel *V.,* where the symbol V. mockingly suggests a chaotic host of irreconcilable things, from Veronica the rat to Venezuela, Vesuvius, and Vera Meroving. As the narrator wryly remarks, V. is "a remarkably scattered concept" and pursuing the meaning of this symbol becomes a grotesque and ludicrous venture. Pynchon fashions the Demon metaphor in *The Crying of Lot 49* in a similar way by manipulating it to point in opposite directions. Oedipa does indeed parallel the Demon problem as Maxwell stated it, but paradoxically she also incorporates its opposite, that is, the solution to the Demon dilemma.

The Demon poses a curious problem, partially because it challenges the realm of thermodynamics with a paradox. Since Maxwell introduced the Demon, several scientists have offered solutions to the Demon paradox. Leo Szilard, a physicist, suggested in 1929 that "any action resulting in a decrease in the entropy of a system must be preceded by an operation of acquiring information, which in turn is coupled with the production of an equal or greater amount of entropy." Szilard's idea that the Demon could not actually decrease the net entropy of the system, as Maxwell had supposed, was supported by another physicist, Leon Brillouin, who in 1951 wrote that "an intelligent being, whatever its size, has to cause an increase of entropy before it can effect a reduction by a smaller amount." The innovative idea in Brillouin's solution to the Demon paradox lay in his emphasis on *perception* as increasing the entropy of the system. A summary of Brillouin's argument is as follows:

> Before an intelligent being can use its intelligence, it must perceive its objects, and that requires physical means of perception. Visual perception in particular requires the illumination of the object. Seeing is essentially a nonequilibrium phenomenon. The cylinder in which the demon operates is, optically speaking, a closed black body and, according to the principle enunciated by Gustav Kirchhoff in 1859, the radiation inside a black body is homogeneous and nondirectional because for any wavelength and any temperature the emissivity of any surface equals its coefficient of absorption. Hence, although an observer inside a black body is exposed to quanta of radiation, he can never tell whether a particular photon comes from a molecule or is reflected from a wall. The observer must use a lamp that emits light of a wavelength not well represented in the black-body radiation, and the eventual absorption of this light by the observer or elsewhere increases the entropy of the system.

Brillouin went on further to prove mathematically that the increase in entropy caused by the process of perception was greater than the decrease in entropy which the Demon could produce by sorting the molecules.

Just as the intricacies involved in the Demon's perception of the molecules actually increase the net entropy of the system, so Oedipa's perception of information actually increases the entropy, or disorder, around her. She comes finally to perceive the WASTE symbol and connections with Trystero everywhere and this disorder far outweighs what order she creates through definite information about Trystero. Ultimately, her perception becomes so disordered that she cannot remember when she has seen the post horn and when she hasn't: "Decorating each alienation, each species of withdrawal, as cufflink, decal, aimless doodling, there was somehow always the post horn. She grew so to expect it that perhaps she did not see it quite as often as she later was to remember seeing it." Perception, here, is working to create disorder. In Oedipa's perception, the post horn replicates infinitely. The entropy increases until finally she is unable to distinguish reality from fantasy-insanity: "Later, possibly, she would have trouble sorting the night into real and dreamed." Here again is the sorting motif, but the increase in disorder is evident. Oedipa's task has shifted from sorting through an estate to distinguishing between reality and fantasy, the attempt to establish order having led to insane disorder.

The self-perpetuating symbols and clues gradually force Oedipa into a closed system of perception. She finally sees nearly everything in terms of post horn and Trystero and she senses that her enclosure in this cycle is the result of some sinister conspiracy: "They knew her pressure points, and the ganglia of her optimism, and one by one, pinch by precision pinch, they were immobilizing her." Not only is she immobilized by the symbols she perceives; she is also isolated by her progressive loss of contact with all the men she has known. Her last hope is the anonymous member of the "Inamorati Anonymous," an organization of isolates who communicate by phone, and when he hangs up on her, she stands, "her isolation complete."

Though her perception is leading her into a closed system of chaos, Oedipa is still pursuing the distinction between reality and fantasy at the end of the novel, and this at least sets her apart from most of the other characters. The motion involved in a pursuit is in itself important, as it is in *V.* There, Stencil's meandering search for V. at least saves him from inertness. He dislikes thinking about any possible conclusion to his pursuit, preferring to "approach and avoid." The same refusal to resolve confusion and reach any conclusion about the Trystero characterizes Oedipa. Her continual doubt and re-evaluation of events differentiates her from the other characters in the novel who do, in fact, end in closed systems of inertness. Oedipa's husband, Mucho, fades into his drug dream; her psychiatrist, Dr. Hilarius, aggravates his relative paranoia into complete paranoia; Driblette, the director of *The Courier's Tragedy,* commits suicide; and the unnamed figure at The Greek Way bar cushions himself in the soothing "Inamorati Anonymous."

The separate closed systems which engulf the characters in the novel suggest a vision of society which is both isolated and headed for disorder and chaos. Pynchon is deliberately applying this scientific metaphor to conditions in society. The relationship is made explicit in Pynchon's short story "Entropy." Callisto, the principal character in this tale, has become an isolated fanatic due to his drastic encounters with the scientific ideas of Gibbs and Boltzmann. Convinced that the universe may fall into heat-death at any moment, Callisto seals himself and his girlfriend, Aubade, into a room. They do not go out. In his hothouse retreat, Callisto obsessively checks the temperature and mercury throughout the day to reassure himself that the world has not yet collapsed into heat-death. As Aubade takes notes, Callisto dictates the evolution of his eccentric beliefs. He explains how he found "in entropy or the measure of disorganization for a closed system an adequate metaphor to apply to certain phenomena in his own world." He goes on to clarify the metaphor:

> He saw, for example, the younger generation responding to Madison Avenue with the same spleen his own had once reserved for Wall Street: and in American "consumerism" discovered a similar tendency from the least to the most probable, from differentiation to sameness, from ordered individuality to a kind of chaos. He found himself, in short, restating Gibbs' prediction in social terms, and envisioned a heat-death for his culture in which ideas, like heat-energy, would no longer be transferred, since each point in it would ultimately have the same quantity of energy; and intellectual motion would, accordingly, cease.

"Entropy" is set in Washington in the '50's and the metaphors in this description come from the '50's—Wall Street, Madison Avenue, consumerism. Consumerism is still at the heart of Inverarity's massive enterprises in *The Crying of Lot 49,* yet other systems of isolation have flourished in the '60's in political undergrounds and freaky California cults. Though the metaphors and closets of isolation have slightly shifted, the point remains the same. Society at the end of *The Crying of Lot 49* is, like the world in "Entropy," in a state of heat-death as its members remain immobilized in isolated chaos.

The concept of entropy is not only related to Maxwell's Demon and to closed systems, but also to information, as Nefastis, the eccentric inventor who believes in the reality of Maxwell's Demon, tries to tell Oedipa. Nefastis points out that "the equation for one, back in the '30's, had looked very like the equation for the other. It was a coincidence." The relation between entropy and information is intriguing, and Nefastis' sketchy explanation seems accurate. The equation for entropy in a system, where H is defined as entropy, was given by Boltzmann:

$$H = -\Sigma pj \log pj$$

Physicists in the 19th century did apparently see the connection between entropy and information. One information theorist states that Maxwell, Boltzmann, and Gibbs "realized that there was a close relation between entropy and information; but they did not develop a quantitative theory of information." Such a theory was devised in this century by Claude Shannon, whose equation for the average information-per-symbol did turn out to be precisely the same as Boltzmann's for entropy:

$$\text{average information/symbol} = -\Sigma \text{pj log pj}$$

Quantities of information are then related to measures of disorder. The exact relationship between information and entropy is clarified by Hawkins' example using gas molecules:

> When the molecules of a gas, for example, are in a collective state of maximum entropy, or disorder, all the alternatives consistent with the given total energy are equally probable, and therefore, by the most efficient method of measurement possible, the precise determination of the exact state of the gas will require the maximum amount of information.

From this explanation, it can be gathered that the more entropy or disorder in the system, the more information will be needed to describe the system.

The relationship between entropy and information leads directly into the complexities of information theory. Some of the concepts in information theory must be mentioned, since Pynchon uses these ideas both in *The Crying of Lot 49* and "Entropy." Pynchon's treatment of information theory is at least partially satirical. His characters frequently take scientific concepts in an absurdly serious manner. Callisto's obsessive worrying about the possible heat-death of the universe is grotesque, and the characters living below Callisto's hothouse retreat aren't much better. In this downstairs apartment, Meatball Mulligan listens to his friend Saul morosely explain how his wife has deserted him after a fierce quarrel:

> "What it was about," Saul said, "was communication theory. Which of course makes it very hilarious."
>
> "I don't know anything about communication theory."
>
> "Neither does my wife. Come right down to it, who does? That's the joke."

The unthinking absorption of scientific ideas by these characters frequently lures them into ludicrous postures. Though Pynchon sees the humor in this and often handles his characters' involvement with science in a loosely satirical way, the ideas from science and information theory still form the basis both for his characters' predicaments and also for Pynchon's own style of writing.

One of the things information theory is concerned with is analyzing communication systems and the transmission of information. . . . The interesting aspects of the system, at least in relation to Pynchon, are the notion of sending information through signals and codes, and also the idea of noise and distortion. The intrusion of noise into the channel may alter the message so that the information which is received differs from the information which was sent originally. The notion of information being altered and lost in the process of transmission is found throughout *The Crying of Lot 49.* Messages are frequently distorted while being transferred, and Oedipa's disk jockey husband, Mucho, must take this into consideration in his broadcasts. After he has interviewed his wife, Oedipa, who is an eyewitness to Dr. Hilarius' burst of insanity at the

Hilarius Psychiatric Clinic, he says, "Thank you, Mrs. Edna Mosh." To the bewildered Oedipa, he explains, "It'll come out the right way. I was allowing for the distortion on these rigs, and then when they put it on tape."

The distortion in meaning as language is transmitted from one source, or person, to another, centers in the novel around words in the Jacobean play Oedipa sees, *The Courier's Tragedy.* Two lines remain in her memory, because of their reference to the Trystero. Oedipa hears the lines as: "No hallowed skein of stars can ward, I trow, / Who's once been set his tryst with Trystero." She begins to pursue the lines with interest, intent on discovering their meaning. As she hunts through various editions of the play, all she finds are a series of transformations. The line "Who's once been set his tryst with Trystero" appears as "Who once has crossed the lusts of Angelo" in the 1687 Quarto edition of the play, and as "This tryst or odious awry, O Niccolò" in the 1670 Whitechapel version. Oedipa finds a further variant on the line when she passes through Golden Gate Park and spots a group of children playing jump-rope while they sing: "Tristoe, Tristoe, one, two, three." The line is repeatedly distorted through transmission until the information in the line is finally negated. Ultimately, the line seems fit only for the children's nonsense game. The distortion of information also occurs to "Thurn and Taxis" which Oedipa also hears in the Jacobean drama. Hoping to find in its meaning a conclusive lead to the meaning of Trystero, she pursues the phrase, only to find another series of aberrations: "Torre and Tassis" and "Turning taxi from across the sea." The pursuit of meaning in language turns into a chimera throughout the novel as information constantly disintegrates through transmission. Ironically, one of the measures of transformation in information theory is termed a "Jacobian."

Throughout *The Crying of Lot 49,* the transmission of information through language paradoxically results in "massive destructions of information." The notion that information may be conveyed through linguistic symbols and codes is repeatedly shattered in the novel. Symbols and codes simply contribute to the chaos and lack of information. "Get in touch with Kirby," the sign about WASTE urges Oedipa; yet Kirby turns out to be nonexistent, "a code name, nobody real." Similarly, the post horn symbol associated at first only with WASTE becomes an all-inclusive sign. It appears not only with WASTE, Oedipa discovers, but along with the etching DEATH on the back of a bus seat, and with an invitation to join the AC-DC, the Alameda County Death Cult. Such symbols continually seduce by suggesting information and meaning, yet they never reveal it. As codes and signals actually work to destroy information, they begin to emerge as something sinister. The nightmare which terrifies Mucho so much is about a sign which unceasingly repeats its initials. As Mucho tells it:

> It was only that sign in the lot, that's what scared me. In the dream I'd be going about a normal day's business and suddenly, with no warning, there'd be the sign. We were a member of the National Automobile Dealers' Association. N.A.D.A. Just this creaking metal sign that

said nada, nada, against the blue sky. I used to wake up hollering.

Another aspect of information theory which relates to the destruction of information in the novel is probability constraints in language. Different letters and combinations of letters have different probabilities of occurring in a language. The probabilities tend to control what information can actually be conveyed in the language. As one information theorist puts it, "All these frequencies (i.e., probabilities of occurrence) reduce the number of different messages which are possible in an English message of given length." This process is conspicuously at work in *The Crying of Lot 49*, as the probabilities of certain letters and words occurring begin to control the information which is being conveyed. Things tend to move toward a condition of the most probable, and as the novel progresses, almost everything is described in terms of certain symbols, like the post horn, the Trystero, and WASTE. We come back to Callisto's awareness in **"Entropy"** of a "tendency from the least to the most probable, from differentiation to sameness, from ordered individuality to a kind of chaos," only this time in the context of language. In this sense, the isolated systems which increasingly enclose people are reinforced by the nature of language which itself fails to differentiate and order.

Another area in information theory, related to probability constraints, focuses on redundancy in language. Shannon suggests that "the redundancy of ordinary English, not considering statistical structure over greater distances than about eight letters, is roughly 50%. This means that when we write English half of what we write is determined by the structure of the language and half is chosen freely." Redundancy is used in a very closed, technical sense by Shannon, who defines it as "one minus the relative entropy." Pynchon, however, uses the idea in an extended fashion, adding to it imprecision and irrelevancy, as this passage from **"Entropy"** shows. Saul and Meatball again:

> "Tell a girl: 'I love you.' No trouble with two-thirds of that, it's a closed circuit. Just you and she. But that nasty four-letter word in the middle, *that's* the one you have to look out for. Ambiguity. Redundance. Irrelevance, even. Leakage. All this is noise. Noise screws up your signal, makes for disorganization in the circuit."

> Meatball shuffled around. "Well, now, Saul," he muttered, "you're sort of, I don't know, expecting a lot from people. I mean, you know. What it is is, most of the things we say, I guess, are mostly noise."

> "Ha! Half of what you just said, for example."

> "Well, you do it too."

> "I know." Saul smiled grimly. "It's a bitch, ain't it."

Here, Pynchon is loosely adopting many of the ideas in information theory—noise, redundancy, disorganization, and entropy. Meatball's watery mutterings are a beautiful illustration of the redundancy and lack of information in language.

The redundancy, irrelevancy, ambiguity, and sheer waste involved in language glare from every page of *The Crying of Lot 49*. The one thing Pierce Inverarity transmits, besides his business assets, is an impression of waste in language. His last phone call to Oedipa presents her with "a voice beginning in heavy Slavic tones as second secretary at the Transylvanian Consulate, looking for an escaped bat; modulated to comic-Negro, then on into hostile Pachuco dialect, full of chingas and maricones; then a Gestapo officer asking her in shrieks did she have relatives in Germany and finally his Lamont Cranston voice." He then assaults Oedipa with the tale of an "old man in the fun house" who was killed by the same gun that killed Professor Quackenbush. "Or something," Oedipa thinks, as if she couldn't really remember the story Inverarity had told and that it didn't matter anyway. The same "or something" phrase characterizes Meatball's inane ramblings in **"Entropy."** Virtually every idea he tries to transmit, he follows with "or something." "Miriam left you, or something, is all I heard," he says to Saul. The "or something" phrase insidiously negates the tenuous words which are spoken, as if the information is inaccurate or irrelevant. The notion of waste in language influences Pynchon's style of writing. In fact, he throws the idea in the reader's face through his elaborate stories with their irrelevant details. The circuitous tales in the novel might be taken as examples of waste and irrelevancy in language, but through them, Pynchon is able to incorporate into his own method and style the notions about language he is trying to convey.

The notions involved in Maxwell's Demon, entropy, and information theory reveal a great deal about what Pynchon is doing. By building his fiction on the concept of entropy, or disorder, and by flaunting the irrelevancy, redundancy, disorganization, and waste involved in language, Pynchon radically separates himself from earlier 20th century writers, like Yeats, Eliot, and Joyce. Thinking of literature in terms of order, rather than disorder, they saw art as perhaps the last way to impose order on a chaotic world. Yet the complex, symbolic structures they created to encircle chaotic experience often resulted in the kinds of static, closed systems Pynchon is so wary of. Pynchon's use of scientific concepts and disorder in his fiction holds a dual excitement, for not only does it sever him from a previous, more rigid and static kind of writing, but it also links him with contemporary artists working in other media who incorporate scientific ideas and seek randomness in their art. (pp. 194-208)

Anne Mangel, "Maxwell's Demon, Entropy, Information: 'The Crying of Lot 49'," in Tri-Quarterly 20, No. 20, Winter, 1971, pp. 194-208.

John P. Leland

Critics have made Thomas Pynchon's *The Crying of Lot 49* an elaborate mystery to be de-coded, a task comparable to Oedipa's attempt to uncover the enigma of Tristero and determine finally whether her experience is sensible or merely an absurd game perpetrated by a demon—Pierce Inverarity. If we attempt the project, we are lead directly to Maxwell's Demon, a physicist's fiction devised to confound the Second Law of Thermodynamics, or to Information Theory with its "senders," "receivers," "codes," and "noise." Ultimately, we would fix upon a category transcending these—Entropy—as our philosopher's stone; and suddenly *The Crying of Lot 49* makes sense. Pynchon's novel, we would say, is about Entropy, extracted from its scientific context and injected boldly into aesthetics, as yet another category by which we may describe or predict the apocalypse towards which Western Civilization is surely tending. [In *Contemporary American Novelists of the Absurd* (1971), Charles B. Harris] has even suggested (perhaps to alleviate the boredom of having read yet another apocalyptic novel) that Pynchon ends on an optimistic note!

Pynchon may view Western Civilization as a vast network of closed systems regressing endlessly upon themselves as they confront the task of existence. Indeed, America itself may well be contained within Pynchon's fictional San Narciso with its appearance of order and serenity serving as a grand illusion covering the chaos within. However, to write a book *about* chaos, absurdity, entropy, or even apocalypse is quite different from using such themes as points of departure to explore their ramifications for the writing of fiction.

We might well begin with the novel's central character, Oedipa Maas. One critic has described her as a "frontierswoman of sorts" and another as an "everyman." But does an "everyman" or a "frontierswoman" stand before a painting and relate the substance of the world to its woven fabric, look at her feet and know that "because of a painting, that what she stood on had only been woven together a couple of thousand miles away in her own tower . . . [and] was only by accident known as Mexico"? If Oedipa is a symbol, the meaning she evokes is certainly ambiguous; and if she is a creature of allegory, we must again question the abstract qualities she supposedly personifies. Oedipa *is* a frontierswoman of sorts, though hers is a frontier where symbol and allegory have lost their referential power, where the "meaning of meaning"—the world's and ours—is open to question. Oedipa's quest is to search what is seemingly significant, what *should* have meaning, for its *precise* meaning; and as she tangles her way through the "forest of symbols" surrounding her life, we suspect she already knows the answers to her questions, an answer lying in the nature of words, in the arbitrary substance which generates all our "meanings" and all our answers. As Oedipa weaves away in her tower, so Pynchon weaves Oedipa in his; and what he weaves are symbols which, in their inability to escape the fabric of language towards a transcendental referent, paradoxically symbolize the failure of symbolic meaning.

Thus *The Crying of Lot 49* is a fiction which explores the possibilities of language and fiction themselves. Yet unlike some "metafictions," Pynchon's novel does not disappoint a critical examination which dwells upon this thematic content—Entropy—as the central interpretive metaphor. Entropy serves Pynchon in two ways: it provides him with an image of his civilization, the epistemological perspective of his novel; and it informs nearly all the actions and character presentations in the novel as well. However, a distinction must be made here between Entropy as the vehicle through which Pynchon chooses to describe civilization and Entropy as a vital part of the fiction *qua* fiction. Pynchon's novel is not only about entropy but is itself entropic. The point here is essentially the one made by John Barth when he suggests that the problem confronting the contemporary artist is not how to succeed Joyce or Kafka "but those who've *succeeded* Joyce and Kafka" ["The Literature of Exhaustion," *On Contemporary Literature,* ed. Richard Kostelanetz, 1969]. If the problems of writing in an age of linguistic scepticism must be faced in contemporary criticism as well as art, then we cannot be entirely comfortable in seeing *The Crying of Lot 49* (one of those problematic succeeding novels) as simply being about the nature of our decaying civilization—another "doomsday machine."

Pynchon's art stands as a profound denial of the mimetic, and criticism which insists on a mimetic function can only offer us a superficial understanding. For like Borges' "Tlon, Uqbar, Orbis Tertius," Pynchon's *The Crying of Lot 49* dramatizes the impingement of an imaginary realm upon our world of secure reality (Oedipa's "anarchist miracle"). Once we realize how easily the imaginary verbal realm of Tristero and W.A.S.T.E. becomes synomous with our own (and Oedipa's) reality, we begin to question not only the fictional nature of fiction but the fictional quality of "reality" as well. When the secure boundaries between the real and imagined are challenged, when the order of reality becomes as much an order of words as is fiction, then mimetic analogies collapse within a circular and inescapable labyrinth of words.

Pynchon's strategy for documenting the intrusion of the fantastic into the "real" is based upon his conception of the communicative process. The entropic nature of communication informs both Oedipa's quest to sort out the earthly effects of Inverarity and our attempts to sort out the "results" of Oedipa's experience—that is, to sort out the information Pynchon provides about his novel. In many ways our attempts to impose a meaningful pattern on Pynchon's story are doomed (like Oedipa's quest) from the beginning. The mystery which Oedipa attempts to solve is no nearer solution at page 138 than it was at page 1, before we (or Oedipa) even knew there was a mystery. Even when we do know it, we realize before long that it is exceedingly complex and enigmatic and begin a little later to wonder if the mystery is really the point anyway. Similarly, taking the W.A.S.T.E. emblem as serious allegory, we might make allusions to our contemporary wasteland and find much reinforcement for such an interpretation in the numerous spiritually depleted, two-dimensional characters that populate the novel—Kotecks, the Paranoids, "Mucho" Maas, Fallopian, Manny Depresso, to name a few of Pynchon's aberrations. Still, none of these characters seems to speak the "point": symbolism and allegory seem to strand us within a manic verbal interior as Pynchon demonically withholds the keys to the "kingdom of sense." Yet, so much detail has been given, so many words, suggestions, conversations, events, and days have gone past; clearly, given the closed system of Pynchon's novel, we should be able to come to terms with its meaning. Obviously, Entropy, Maxwell's Demon, Information Theory, W.A.S.T.E., and Tristero must contain the key. In a way they do, but not as equivalents of the novel's meaning, not as links in a chain of meaning that can be translated into *our* reality. Repeatedly Pynchon sets up possibilities for relevance, hints as to how we might clarify Oedipa's experience *vis-a-vis* ours, only to drop them in midstream, leaving us somewhat lost.

The situation—too much information and not enough pattern—is similar to Oedipa's response to *The Courier's Tragedy*. Near the end of the performance, a peculiar shift in the attitude of the cast is noted:

> a gentle chill, an ambiguity, begins to creep in among the words. Heretofore the naming of names has gone on either literally or as metaphor. But now . . . a new mode of expression takes over. It can only be called a kind of ritual reluctance. Certain things, it is made clear, will not be spoken aloud; certain events will not be shown on stage; though it is difficult to imagine, given the excesses of the preceding acts, what these things could possibly be. . . . It's all a big in-joke. The audiences of the time knew. Angelo knows, but does not say.

Although one cannot pinpoint exactly where the ambiguity begins to creep in among Pynchon's words, after our encounters with Metzger (alias Baby Igor), the Paranoids, or Stanley Kotecks, and the descriptions of each new piece of information Oedipa "receives" about Tristero, the naming of names and the connection of specific events to specific meanings *does* represent an in-joke for Pynchon. Indeed, the rapid shifts from one bizarre situation to another, the introduction of one absurdly named character followed by another, and the insane lack of connections in the "plot" that Oedipa seeks to understand indicate a "ritual reluctance" on the part of the narrator to provide us serious clues to a sensible and coherent meaning. As readers we are like Oedipa, first overwhelmed with information and then denied pattern; and like her, we must become a fictional Maxwell's Demon (which curiously has been elevated to "reality" by physicists and Information theorists who have sought to protect the validity of the Second Law of Thermodynamics) and attempt to sort out the information presented to us without—and such is impossible—increasing entropy, disorder, or ambiguity.

Pynchon's reluctance to give us "plot" in a traditional sense is coupled with Oedipa's ironical search for pattern in a babbling world where fantasy and reality have lost all distinction. Because language has lost its representational capacity, because reality appears as an absurd play of words, our "decoding" attempts, our attempts to find a coherence beyond the order of words, are doomed to failure. Language as a mirror of reality or as a medium capable of establishing significant contacts beyond its own closed system is radically denied in Pynchon's fiction. Language appears at once as a meaningless accident, its associations between signifier and signified arbitrary, yet—and paradoxically—the medium of all meaning. With language we spin our fabrics of significance, connecting "bits" of information in patterns of analogy and causality, yet these patterns remain internal: our versions of reality appear merely as fictions, with language at once the mediator and the

mediated. For Pynchon, language has become man's source of alienation and the prison which locks him within the hallucinatory possibility of words. All attempts (like Oedipa's) to impose upon language patterns of sense which are beyond language are doomed. Like the demon that James Clerk Maxwell created to confound the Second Law of Thermodynamics, our attempts to reduce the entropy of *The Crying of Lot 49* are refuted by the entropic nature of the language we employ to sort out information.

Perhaps the first "clear" indication of Pynchon's concern with the problems of language and communication is presented with the sequence of experiences Oedipa has at Yoyodyne with Stanley Kotecks and later in Berkeley with John Nefastis. The issue is Maxwell's Demon. According to Kotecks, Maxwell had postulated a "tiny intelligence" or demon that could, in violation of the Second Law, effect a temperature difference of random molecules in a box by merely sorting the fast from the slow. The demon could do the sorting without expending any energy (in a Thermodynamic sense), and the order he produced could be used to operate a piston or to do work. Although Maxwell's scheme stood for some time as a theoretical refutation of the Second Law, eventually the sorting activity of the demon was shown, after all, to involve work and energy; and as a result, any loss of entropy his actions effected would be nullified by the energy (in his case heat) his labors expended or produced. In other words, the operation of acquiring information necessary for sorting fast from slow molecules entails the production of a greater or at least equal amount of entropy. The important matter here is not the problem of heat transfer but the idea that imposing patterns upon random, unordered data produces more disorder in the process. Thus, as Nefastis explains, entropy is of two types:

> One having to do with heat engines, and the other with communication. The equation for one, back in the 30's had looked very like the equation for the other. It was a coincidence. The two fields were entirely unrelated except at one point: Maxwell's Demon. As the Demon sat and sorted his molecules into hot and cold, the system was said to lose entropy. But somehow the loss was offset by the information the Demon gained about what molecules went where.

Essentially, Nefastis' machine embodies ("operationally") the parallel between the "entropy" of physics and the "entropy" of Information Theory. For Nefastis "entropy" is a metaphor made "real" by his machine which, in order to function, must use the non-linguistic communication between a "sensitive" and the "demon" housed inside: "Entropy is a figure of speech, then . . . a metaphor. It connects the world of thermodynamics to the world of information flow. The machine uses both. The demon makes the metaphor not only verbally graceful, but also objectively true." To this somewhat entropic piece of information Oedipa asks for clarification and suggests that perhaps Nefastis' demon is itself in reality a product of metaphor. To her suggestion Nefastis smugly replies, "He existed for Clerk Maxwell long before the days of metaphor."

In Nefastis' machine, we see the black irony involved in

Dust jacket for the Perrenial Fiction Library edition of The Crying of Lot 49, *published by Harper & Row.*

the failure to recognize the entropic feature of language and communication. The machine signifies the impingement of separate worlds upon one another: miraculously, by the coincidence of two mathematical equations (themselves metaphors), the worlds of physics and communication found a common center. For Nefastis the point is Maxwell's Demon, a physicist's fiction which he has elevated to a reality. Essentially, Nefastis has made the "mere coincidence" between the similarity of the equations for physical and informational entropy respectable with the help of Maxwell's Demon. Thus, as often the case in science, phenomenal occurrences have been patterned by the imposition of metaphor—a metaphor which becomes in time understood literally. Science—that great defender of the concrete—is, Pynchon suggests, rooted in metaphor: its patterns of sense are figurative organizations, yet we know what Western science did with the Newtonian analogy.

What Nefastis fails to realize and what Oedipa's futile, silent attempt to invoke his demon suggest is the entropic nature of language. Nefastis' demon "binds the occurrences" of physics and information flow only in so far as we are willing to grant reality to a fictional demon. When,

like Oedipa, we attempt to uncover more proof regarding the demon, the entropic nature of language begins to take over. When Oedipa charges that Maxwell's Demon is really a metaphor, this bit of information adds nothing to her understanding. Indeed, her futile attempt to communicate with the demon results only in frustration and an invitation to sexual intercourse with all of China as witness, compliments of the television. The "answer" Oedipa received in her exchange with Nefastis apparently adds more information at the expense of meaning. Faced with a metaphor, a closed system, Oedipa's attempts to communicate with the demon and to venture beyond the "as if" towards the "real" result only in confusion and comical misunderstanding.

The futile effort to find in language a non-linguistic map of reality is paralleled in Pynchon's novel by the ambiguous nature of linguistic exchange. The problems of discourse and correct understanding are dramatized in the numerous communicative exchanges between Oedipa and other characters in the novel and allow Pynchon to exploit the concept of "noise" in Information Theory. Consider one example:

> "You one of those right-wing nut outfits?" inquired the diplomatic Metzger.
>
> Fallopian twinkled. "They accuse *us* of being paranoids."
>
> "They?" inquired Metzger twinkling also.
>
> "Us?" asked Oedipa.

In any message of communication the amount of information that is finally received from the sender is of importance to information theorists. However, if the message sent is ambiguous, overly redundant, or if "noise" occurs from within or outside of the system, the level of information exchanged drops. At the level of cognition, such a state is entropic; despite the fact that the communication itself might be packed with data, little is communicated. The important fact is not that communication is impossible in such exchanges but that they involve the linguistic interaction between subject and object where both are dynamic and subject to the arbitrary nature of the medium employed. At the level of language, the words "they" and "us" do not signify existential persons but instead are "unfulfilled" and empty grammatical categories. Oedipa's question reaches to the heart of the emptiness, yet her attempts to "fill" the void and purge the order of words of its essential ambiguity fail.

Oedipa's task, to impose some order upon the chaotic financial affairs of Inverarity, is essentially an attempt to impose a pattern—ultimately a fortuitous linguistic construct—upon the equally random bits of Inverarity's life. Fittingly, the task ultimately hangs on the significance of a word—"Tristero"—and a symbol—the muted post horn—and involves a futile attempt to impose The Picture (without the words) upon these signs. Ultimately, the futility of Oedipa's interpretative task is shared by the reader who, in confronting Pynchon's fiction, feels compelled to impose patterns of allegory and symbolism on the "bits" of confusing data Pynchon gives us. Seen in this way, Pynchon's novel turns on itself, for our attempts to objectify its meaning force us to become victims of Pynchon's entropic system. We will pit metaphor against metaphor in an endless sorting process from which we will emerge at the other side with information overload; thus, in the final analysis, these attempts to impose pattern are buried in "noise." (pp. 45-53)

> *John P. Leland, "Pynchon's Linguistic Demon: 'The Crying of Lot 49'," in* Critique: Studies in Modern Fiction, *Vol. XVI, No. 2, 1974, pp. 45-53.*

Edward Mendelson

[A small portion of the following essay was previously published in CLC, *Vol. 6.]*

Described briefly, in the sort of the bare outline that makes any serious plot sound ridiculous, **The Crying of Lot 49** recounts the discovery by its heroine, Mrs. Oedipa Maas, of an ancient and secret postal system named the Tristero. The manifestations of the Trystero (an alternate spelling), and all that accompanies it, are always associated in the book with the language of the sacred and with patterns of religious experience; the foils to the Trystero are always associated with sacrality gone wrong. As every person and event in *V.* is implicated in the general decline into the in-animate, everything in **Lot 49** participates either in the sa-cred or the profane. A major character in *V.* is named Benny Profane; in **Lot 49** there are wider possibilities (in-cluding someone named Grace). As Pynchon's work avoids the weightlessness of Nabokovian fantasy, so it avoids the self-important *nostalgie de la boue* of the social and psychological novels that occupy most of the fictional space in postwar America. Oedipa has "all manner of rev-elations," but they are not in the manner of most recent fiction, and certainly not the kind of revelations that her name might suggest: they are "hardly about . . . herself." Pynchon writes at the end of an era in which the Freudian interpretation of an event served as a more than adequate succedanium for the event itself: it was an act of courage to name his heroine Oedipa (I shall have more to say later about the courage to risk facetiousness), for the novel con-tains not even a single reference to her emotional relations with her parents or her impulses towards self-creation. The name instead refers back to the Sophoclean Oedipus who begins his search for the solution of a problem (a problem, like Oedipa's, involving a dead man) as an al-most detached observer, only to discover how deeply im-plicated he is in what he finds. As the book opens, and Oedipa learns that she has been named executor of the es-tate of the "California real estate mogul" Pierce Inverari-ty, she "shuffl[es] back" in her memory "through a fat deckful of days which seemed . . . more or less identical." But as she begins to sort out the complications of Inverari-ty's estate she becomes aware of moments of special signif-icance, repeated patterns of meaning, that had not previ-ously been apparent. Driving into the town where Inve-rarity's interests had been centered, she looks down from the freeway upon "the ordered swirl of houses and streets" and senses the possibility of a *kind* of meaning that is, for the moment, beyond her comprehension:

she thought of the time she'd opened a transistor radio to replace a battery and seen her first print-ed circuit. The ordered swirl of houses and streets, from this high angle, sprang at her now with the same unexpected, astonishing clarity . . . [T]here were to both outward pat-terns a hieroglyphic sense of concealed meaning, of an intent to communicate. . . . [Now,] a rev-elation also trembled just past the threshold of her understanding . . . [She] seemed parked at the centre of an odd religious instant. As if, on some other frequency, or out of the eye of some whirlwind rotating too slow for heated skin even to feel the centrifugal coolness of, words were being spoken.

At this point Oedipa's revelations are only partly defined. In the next paragraph the narrator dismisses Oedipa's ex-perience by placing it in distancing quotation marks: "the 'religious instant,' or whatever it might have been."

But a few pages later an "instant" of the same kind occurs, but this time more clearly defined. Oedipa sees in a televi-sion commercial a map of one of Inverarity's housing de-velopments, and is reminded of her first glimpse of the town in which she is now: "Some immediacy was there again, some promise of hierophany." This "promise of hierophany," of a manifestation of the sacred, is eventual-ly fulfilled, and her "sense of concealed meaning" yields to her recognition of patterns that had potentially been ac-cessible to her all along, but which only now had revealed themselves. In the prose sense, what Oedipa discovers is the Trystero, "a network by which x number of Ameri-cans are truly communicating whilst reserving their lies, recitations of routine, arid betrayals of spiritual pover-ty"—that is, everything profane—"for the official govern-ment delivery system." But across this hidden and illegal network information is transmitted in ways that defy ordi-nary logic: often, the links in the system cross centuries, or move between the most unlikely combinations of sender and receiver, without anyone in the world of routine ever recognizing that something untoward has occurred. The Trystero carries with it a sense of sacred connection and relation in the world, and by doing so it manifests a way of comprehending the world. By the end of the novel Oedi-pa is left alone, out over seventy thousand fathoms, left to decide for herself whether the Trystero exists or if she has merely fantasized, or if she has been hoodwinked into be-lieving in it. On that all-or-nothing decision, everything— her construing of the world, and the world's construc-tion—depends:

how had it ever happened here, with the chances once so good for diversity? For it was now like walking among matrices of a great digital com-puter, the zeroes and ones twinned above, hang-ing like balanced mobiles right and left, ahead, thick, maybe endless. Behind the hieroglyphic streets there would either be a transcendent meaning, or only the earth. . . . Ones and ze-roes. . . . Another mode of meaning behind the obvious, or none. Either Oedipa in the orbiting ecstasy of a true paranoia, or a real Tristero. For there was either some Tristero behind the ap-pearance of the legacy America, or there was just America. . . .

As in all religious choices, no proof is possible: the choice of ones or zeroes presents itself "ahead . . . maybe endless," and the watcher is left alone.

Pynchon uses religious terms and hieratic language not simply as a set of metaphors from which to hang his narrative, not merely as a scaffolding (as Joyce, for example, uses Christian symbols in *Ulysses*). The religious meaning of the book does not reduce to metaphor or myth, because religious meaning is itself the central issue of the plot. This creates difficulties for criticism. The Trystero implies universal meanings, and since universal meanings are notoriously recalcitrant to analysis, it will be necessary to approach the holistic center of the book from various facets and fragments. I hope the reader will bear with an argument that may, for a number of pages, ask him to assent to resolutions of issues that have not yet been discussed.

The book refers at one point to "the secular Tristero," which has a plausible history and a recognizable origin in ordinary human emotion and human society. During one of the few areas of the narrative in which nothing extraordinary happens—a "secular" part of the book—Oedipa compiles, with the help of one of the book's prosier characters (an English professor, alas), a history of the system that is somewhat speculative, but more plausible than the mock-theorizing in *V.* The history of the Trystero intersects with authentic history in a manner taken from historical novels like *Henry Esmond* or *The Scarlet Pimpernel,* where an extraordinary, fictional pattern of events, one that almost but not quite alters the larger course of history, is presented behind the familiar, public pattern. The Trystero, then, began in sixteenth-century Holland, when an insurgent Calvinist government unseated the hereditary postmaster, a member of the Thurn and Taxis family (here Pynchon blends authentic history with novelistic fantasy—the counts of Taxis did hold the postal monopoly in the Empire), and replaced him with one Jan Hinckart, Lord of Ohain. But Hinckart's right to the position, which he gained through political upheaval, not through inheritance, is disputed by a Spaniard, Hernando Joaquín de Tristero y Calavera, who claims to be Hinckart's cousin and the legitimate Lord of Ohain—and therefore the legitimate postmaster. Later, after an indecisive struggle between Hinckart and Tristero, the Calvinists are overthrown, and the Thurn and Taxis line restored to postmastership. But Tristero, claiming that the postal monopoly was Ohain's by conquest, and therefore his own by blood, sets up an alternative postal system, and proceeds to wage guerrilla war against the Thurn and Taxis system. The rallying theme of Tristero's struggle: "disinheritance."

So far, the story, though a fantasy, is still historically plausible, requiring only a relatively slack suspension of disbelief. However the word Calavera (skull, Calvary) in Tristero's name already suggests some emblematic resonances, and the theme of disinheritance joins the Tristero's history to Oedipa's discovery of it while executing a will. Later in the history, the Trystero system takes on, *for its contemporaries,* a specifically religious meaning. Pynchon invents a severe Calvinist sect, the Scurvhamites, who tend toward the gnostic heresy and see Creation as a machine, one part of which is moved by God, the other by a soulless and automatic principle. When the Scurvhamites decide to tamper with some secular literature (specifically, the play *The Courier's Tragedy,* of which more shortly) to give it doctrinal meaning, they find that the "Trystero would symbolize the Other quite well." For Thurn and Taxis itself, faced with the enmity of the anonymous and secret Trystero system, "many of them must [have] come to believe in something very like the Scurvhamite's blind, automatic anti-God. Whatever it is, it has the power to murder their riders, send landslides thundering across their roads . . . disintegrate the Empire." But this belief cannot last: "over the next century and a half the paranoia recedes, [and] they come to discover the secular Tristero." The Trystero returns from its symbolic meanings into a realm that is historically safe and believable. In this passage Pynchon offers an analogously safe way to read his own book: the Trystero is a symbol for a complex of events taking place on the level of a battle in heaven, but it is merely a symbol, a way of speaking that has no hieratic significance in itself. But the novel, while offering this possibility, does so in a chapter in which nothing strange happens, where the world is Aristotelian and profane, where the extraordinary concrescences of repetition and relation that inform the rest of the book briefly sort themselves out into simple, logical patterns. The book offers the possibility that its religious metaphor is only metaphor: but if the book were founded on this limited possibility, the remaining portions of the book would make no sense, and there would be little reason to write it in the first place.

The potted history near the end of the novel describes the discovery of the "secular Tristero" behind the demonic one; the book itself describes the progressive revelation of the sacred significance behind certain historical events. It should perhaps be mentioned that the frequent associations of the Trystero with the demonic do not contradict the Trystero's potentially sacred significance: the demonic is a subclass of the sacred, and exists, like the sacred, on a plane of meaning different from the profane and the secular. When Pynchon published two chapters from the book in a magazine he gave them the title, **"The World (This One), the Flesh (Mrs. Oedipa Maas), and the Testament of Pierce Inverarity"**: it is through Inverarity's will that Oedipa completes this proverbial equation, and finds her own devil in the agonizing ontological choice she has to make as the novel ends. The revelation of the sacred gets underway when Oedipa sees in the map of one of Inverarity's interests "some promise of hierophany." The sense of the word "hierophany" is clear enough—it is a manifestation of the sacred—but the word itself has a history that is informative in this context. The word is not recorded in the dictionaries of any modern European language (the related "hierophant" is of course recorded, but "hierophany" is not), and it appears to have been invented by Mircea Eliade, who expands most fully on the word in his *Patterns in Comparative Religion* but gives a more straightforward definition in his introduction to *The Sacred and the Profane:* "Man becomes aware of the sacred because it manifests itself, shows itself, as something wholly different from the profane. To designate the *act of manifestation* of the sacred, we have proposed the term *hiero-*

phany. It is a fitting term, because it does not imply anything further; it expresses no more than is implicit in its etymological content, *i.e.,* that *something sacred shows itself to us.* . . . From the most elementary hierophany . . . to the supreme hierophany . . . there is no solution of continuity. In each case we are confronted by the same mysterious act—the manifestation of something of a wholly different order, a reality that does not belong to our world, in objects that are an integral part of our natural 'profane' world." This latter condition, that the objects in which the sacred manifests itself be part of the natural world, is central to *Lot 49,* because everything in the novel that points to a sacred significance in the Trystero has, potentially, a secular explanation. The pattern and the coherence may, as Oedipa reminds herself, be the product of her own fantasy or of someone else's hoax. She is left, at every moment, to affirm or deny the sacredness of what she sees.

When, as she begins to uncover the Trystero, Oedipa decides to give, through her own efforts, some order to Inverarity's tangled interests, she writes in her notebook, "Shall I project a world?" But her plan to provide her own meanings, "to bestow life on what had persisted" of the dead man, soon confronts the anomaly that more meanings, more relationships and connections than she ever expected begin to offer themselves—manifest themselves. And these manifestations arrive without any effort on her part. When, by the middle of the book, "everything she saw, smelled, dreamed, remembered, would somehow come to be woven into The Trystero," she tries to escape, to cease looking for order. "She had only to drift," she supposes, "at random, and watch nothing happen, to be convinced that it was purely nervous, a little something for her shrink to fix." But when she drifts that night through San Francisco she finds more extensive and more varied evidence of the Trystero's existence—evidence far more frequent and insistent than she found when she was actually looking for it. Like the mystic whose revelation is dependent on his passivity, Oedipa's full discovery of the Trystero depends on her refusal to search for it. In the last chapter even the most surprising events leave her only in expectant passivity: "Even a month ago, Oedipa's next question would have been 'Why?' But now she kept a silence, waiting, as if to be illuminated."

Recent criticism has devoted much energy to finding detective-story patterns in fiction, and *The Crying of Lot 49,* with its heroine named after the first detective of them all, lends itself admirably to this method. However, Pynchon's novel uses mechanisms borrowed from the detective story to produce results precisely the opposite of those in the model. Where the object of a detective story is to reduce a complex and disordered situation to simplicity and clarity, and in doing so to isolate in a named locus the disruptive element in the story's world, *The Crying of Lot 49* starts with a relatively simple situation, and then lets it get out of the heroine's control: the simple becomes complex, responsibility becomes not isolated but universal, the guilty locus turns out to be everywhere, and individual clues are unimportant because either clues nor deduction can lead to the solution. "Suppose, God, there really was a Tristero then and that she *had* come on it by accident. . . . [S]he might have found The Tristero anywhere in her Republic, through any of a hundred lightly-concealed entranceways, a hundred alienations, if only she'd looked." What the detective in this story discovers is a way of thinking that renders detection irrelevant. "The Christian," Chesterton writes somewhere, "has to use his brains to see the hidden good in humanity just as the detective has to use his brains to see the hidden evil." This, in essence, describes Oedipa's problem: she never discovers the alienation and incoherence in the world—those were evident from the start—but she stumbles instead across the hidden relationships in the world, relations effected through and manifested in the Trystero.

Near the middle of the book Oedipa stops searching. From this point on she becomes almost the only character in the novel who is *not* looking for something. While hierophanies occur all around her, almost everyone else is vainly trying to wrench an experience of the sacred out of places where it cannot possibly be found. As everyone in *V.* worries constantly about the inanimate, everyone in *The Crying of Lot 49* suffers from some distortion of religious faith, and almost everyone in the book eventually drops away from Oedipa into some religious obsession. Their examples demonstrate the wrong turnings that Oedipa must avoid.

Mucho Maas, for example, Oedipa's husband, who works as a disc jockey, suffers "regular crises of conscience about his profession[:] 'I just don't believe in any of it'." This sounds at first like a suburban cliché, but the religious language soon develops in complexity and allusiveness. Oedipa's incomprehension during her first "religious instant" reminds her of her husband "watching one of his colleagues with a headset clamped on and cueing the next record with movements stylized as the handling of chrism, censer, chalice might be for a holy man . . . [D]id Mucho stand outside Studio A looking in, knowing that even if he could hear it, he couldn't believe in it?" His previous job had been at a used car lot, where although "he had believed in the cars" he suffered from a nightmare of alienation and nothingness (which also provides Pynchon with a send-up of Hemingway's "A Clean, Well-Lighted Place"): " 'We were a member of the National Automobile Dealers' Association. N.A.D.A. Just this creaking metal sign that said nada, nada, against the blue sky. I used to wake up hollering'." HIs escape from a nihilistic void takes him into the impregnable solipsism granted by LSD, and he leaves Oedipa behind him.

The drug had previously been urged on Oedipa herself by her psychiatrist, Dr. Hilarius, who was conducting an experiment he called the Bridge—not a bridge across to community but "the bridge inward." Oedipa, who seems to merit her revelations through her knowledge of what does *not* lead to revelation, knows that she "would be damned if she'd take the capsules he'd given her. Literally damned." Hilarius himself distorts the purpose of faith. In an attempt to atone for his Nazi past he tries to develop "a faith in the literal truth of everything [Freud] wrote. . . . It was . . . a kind of penance. . . . I wanted to believe, despite everything my life had been." The strain finally sends him into paranoia and madness: fantasies of vengeful Israelis, a wish for death. (pp. 188-97)

At least one character, however, has something of the enlightenment that Oedipa is approaching. A Mexican anarchist whom Oedipa meets on her night of drifting, and whom she and Inverarity had first met in Mexico some years before, is named Jésus Arrabal. When he talks politics his language quickly shifts to the language of religion:

> You know what a miracle is . . . another world's intrusion into this one. Most of the time we coexist peacefully, but when we do touch there's cataclysm. Like the church we hate, anarchists also believe in another world. Where revolutions break out spontaneous and leaderless, and the soul's talent for consensus allows the masses to work together without effort. . . . And yet . . . if any of it should ever really happen that perfectly, I would also have to cry miracle. An anarchist miracle. Like your friend [Inverarity the real-estate mogul]. He is too exactly and without flaw the thing we fight. In Mexico the privilegiado is always, to a finite percentage, redeemed, one of the people. Unmiraculous. But your friend, unless he's joking, is as terrifying to me as a Virgin appearing to an Indian.

The intersection of two worlds in miracles is a theme we shall return to. For the moment, it should be noted that Arrabal admits the possibility that the "miraculous" Inverarity may be "joking"—just as Oedipa has to admit the possibility that the miraculous Trystero may be a hoax, a joke written by Inverarity into his will.

Compared with the obsessions and confusions that surround most of the other characters, the religious language associated with Oedipa herself is on a different and clearer level. The word "God" occurs perhaps twenty times in the book (it appears hardly at all in *V.*), and on almost every occasion the word hovers near Oedipa or her discoveries. In her very first word, on the first page of the book, she "spoke the name of God, tried to feel as drunk as possible." When she first encounters the Trystero's emblem, a drawing of a muted post horn, she copies it into her notebook, "thinking: God, hieroglyphics"—a double iteration, through the prefix *hiero,* of the Trystero's sacrality. In an early passage that anticipates the book's later, culminating reference to "a great digital computer [with] the zeroes and ones twinned above," Oedipa tries to elude a spray-can gone wild: "something fast enough, God or a digital machine, might have computed in advance the complex web of its travel." When she sees the Trystero symbol in one more unexpected place she feels "as if she had been trapped at the center of some intricate crystal, and say[s], 'My God'." Faced with the choice of ones and zeroes, of meaning or nothingness, she thinks, "this, oh God, was the void." And there are other examples. What would simply be a nagging cliché in another kind of novel becomes here a quiet but insistent echo, a muted but audible signal.

The Crying of Lot 49 is a book partly *about* communications and signals—Oedipa's discovery of the Trystero involves the interpretation of ambiguous signs—and, logically enough, its central scientific metaphor involves communication theory (alternately called Information Theo-

ry). It is through information theory, in fact, that Pynchon establishes in this novel a richly imaginative logical link with the world of his first novel, *V.* The two novels share some superficial details on the level of plot—one minor character appears briefly in both, a Vivaldi concerto for which someone is searching in *V.* is heard over muzak in *Lot 49*—but their deeper connection lies in *Lot 49*'s extension and transformation of *V.*'s central metaphor. *V.* describes the thermodynamic process by which the world's entropy increases and by which the world's available energy declines. But the equations of thermodynamics and the term "entropy" itself were also employed, decades after their original formulation, in information theory, where they took on a wider and more complex function than they ever had before. By using information theory as a controlling pattern of ideas in his second book, Pynchon is in one way simply extending the metaphor central to his first book: but the extension also adds immeasurably to the complexity and fertility of the original idea. Thermodynamic entropy is (to speak loosely) a measure of stagnation. As thermodynamic entropy increases in a system, and its available energy decreases, information about the system increases: the system loses some of its uncertainty, its potential. In the language of information theory, however, entropy is the measure of *un*certainty in a system. As you *increase* thermodynamic entropy, therefore, you *decrease* information entropy. In information theory, also, the *entropy rate* of a system is the rate at which information is transmitted. Entropy increases in *V.,* and the world slows down; in *The Crying of Lot 49* Oedipa receives more and more surprises, more and more rapidly, and entropy still increases—but now it is information entropy rather than thermodynamic, and the effect of the increase is invigorating rather than stagnating.

Metaphorically, then, the two meanings of the term "entropy" are in opposition, and it is precisely this opposition which John Nefastis tries to exploit in his machine. Oedipa finds Nefastis's account of his machine confusing, but

> she did gather that there were two distinct kinds of this entropy. One having to do with heat-engines, the other to do with communication. The equation for one, back in the '30's, had looked very like the equation for the other. It was a coincidence. The two fields were entirely unconnected, except at one point: Maxwell's Demon. As the Demon sat and sorted his molecules into hot and cold, the system was said to lose entropy. But somehow the loss was offset by the information gained about what molecules were where.
>
> "Communication is the key," cried Nefastis. . . .

When Maxwell's hypothetical "Demon" (a received term that fits neatly into Pynchon's hieratic language) sorts hot and cold molecules, he can apparently raise the temperature in one part of a system, and lower the temperature in the other part, without expending work—thereby *decreasing* the system's thermodynamic entropy, in violation of the second law of thermodynamics. But the decrease of thermodynamic entropy is balanced by an *increase* in information entropy, thereby supposedly making the whole thing "possible," when a person whom Nefastis calls a "sensitive" transmits information to the Demon that Nefastis believes is actually in his machine. Nefastis mixes the language of science with that of spiritualism. The "sensitive" has to receive data "at some deep psychic level" from the Demon; the "sensitive" achieves his effects by staring at the photo of Maxwell on the machine; and so forth. The whole effect is one of Blavatskian mumbo-jumbo, but Nefastis also uses the language of belief that Oedipa is learning to understand. Feeling "like some kind of heretic," she doubts Nefastis's enterprise: "The true sensitive is the one that can share in the man's hallucinations, that's all." But the implied question, raised by Oedipa's doubt, is whether Oedipa's sensitivity to the Trystero is also the product of hallucinations.

The Nefastis machine is based on the similarity between the equations for information entropy and those of thermodynamic entropy, a similarity which Nefastis calls a "metaphor." The machine "makes the metaphor not only verbally graceful, but also objectively true." Pynchon has much to say elsewhere in the book about the relation between truth and metaphor, but Nefastis's error is based on the confusion of language and reality, on an attempt to make two worlds coincide. Nefastis, the "believer," has faith in his metaphor, and believes that the truth of that faith can objectively be demonstrated and confirmed. Oedipa, on the other hand, receives no confirmation. Faith, wrote Paul to the Hebrews, is "the evidence of things *not* seen."

Besides using the association of entropy and information theory, Pynchon also exploits the theory's rule of concerning the relation of surprise and probability in the transmitting of data. Briefly, the rule states that the more unexpected a message is, the more information it contains: a series of repetitive messages conveys less information than a series of messages that differ from each other. (Of course there must be a balance between surprise and probability: a message in language the receiver cannot understand is very surprising, but conveys little information.) In *The Crying of Lot 49* there are *two* secret communications systems: the Trystero, and its entirely secular counterpart, the system used by the right-wing Peter Pinguid Society. Both circumvent the official government delivery system, but, unlike the Trystero, the Pinguid Society's system cares less about transmitting information than about nose-thumbing the bureaucracy. Oedipa happens to be with a member of the Society when he receives a letter with the PPS postmark:

> *Dear Mike,* it said, *how are you? Just thought I'd drop you a note. How's your book coming? Guess that's all for now. See you at The Scope* [a bar].

"That's how it is," [the PPS member] confessed bitterly, "most of the time."

The Pinguid Society's letters, bearing no information, are empty and repetitive. With the Trystero, in contrast, even the stamps are surprising:

> In the 3¢ Mothers of America Issue . . . the flowers to the lower left of Whistler's Mother had been replaced by Venus's-flytrap, belladon-

na, poison sumac and a few others Oedipa had never seen. In the 1947 Postage Stamp Centenary Issue, commemorating the great postal reform that had meant the beginning of the end for private carriers [of which the Trystero is the only survivor], the head of a Pony Express rider at the lower left was set at a disturbing angle unknown among the living. The deep violet 3¢ regular issue of 1954 had a faint, menacing smile on the face of the Statue of Liberty. . . .

This delicate balance of the familiar and the unexpected (note, for example, that there are enough surprising poisoned plants, on one of the stamps, to indicate that the even more surprising ones which "Oedipa had never seen" are also poisonous) produces a powerful sense of menace and dread—a sense no less powerful for its comic aspects—while the secular Pinguid Society messages are capable only of conventionality, of repetition without a sense of the numinous.

The achievement of *The Crying of Lot 49* is its ability to speak unwanted words without a hint of preaching or propaganda. The book's transformation of the impersonal language of science into a language of great emotional power is a breathtaking accomplishment, whose nearest rival is perhaps [Johann Wolfgang von] Goethe's *Elective Affinities.*

—*Edward Mendelson*

The unit of information in communication theory is the *bit,* abbreviated from *bi*nary dig*it.* Theoretically, all information can be conveyed in a sequence of binary digits, i.e., ones and zeroes. By the end of the novel, in a passage quoted above, Oedipa perceives the dilemma presented to her by the possible existence of the Trystero in terms of the choice between one bit and another (Pynchon always provides the possibility that the Trystero is "only" Oedipa's fantasy, or that the whole system is a hoax written into Inverarity's will): "For it was now like walking among matrices of a great digital computer, the zeroes and ones twinned above . . . Behind the hieroglyphic streets there would either be a transcendent meaning, or only the earth." The signs themselves do not prove anything: the streets are "hieroglyphic"—an example of sacred carving—but behind the sacred sign *may* lie what is merely profane, "only the earth." The religious content of the book is fixed in Oedipa's dilemma: the choice between the *zero* of secular triviality and chaos, and the *one* that is the *ganz andere* of the sacred.

In Pynchon's novel, as in life, there are two kinds of repetition: trivial repetition, as in the monotony of the Pinguid Society letters, and repetition that may signify the timeless and unchanging sacred. In *The Sacred and the Profane* Eliade writes that "religious man lives in two kinds of time, of which the more important, sacred time, appears under the paradoxical aspect of a circular time, reversible and recoverable, a sort of mythical present that is periodically regenerated by means of rites." Oedipa's first experience (in the book, that is) of trivial repetition occurs when she encounters a debased version of Eliade's "circular time, reversible and recoverable." In the second chapter, before she has any evidence of the Trystero, she watches television in the Echo Courts motel (the name is a gracenote on the main theme), with her coexecutor Metzger—a lawyer, once a child actor. The film on the screen turns out to star Metzger as a child, and when the film-Metzger sings a song, "his aging double, over Oedipa's protests, sang harmony." At the end of the book, Oedipa wonders if the Trystero system is simply a plot against her; here, at the beginning, she suspects that Metzger "bribed the engineer over at the local station to run this[:] it's all part of a plot, an elaborate, seduction, *plot.*" Time, on this occasion, seems to become even more confused and circular when one reel of the film is shown in the wrong order: " 'Is this before or after?' she asked."

In the midst of the film Oedipa glimpses a more significant form of repetition: in a passage discussed above, a map in a television commercial reminds her of the "religious instant" she felt on looking over the town where she is now. But this significant repetition occurs in the midst of reports of other, sterile ones. For example, Metzger, an actor turned lawyer, describes the pilot film of a television series on his own life, starring a friend of his, a lawyer turned actor. The film rests isolated in its own meaningless circular time, "in an air-conditioned vault . . . light can't fatigue it, it can be repeated endlessly." Outside the motel room, a rock-music group called the Paranoids, who all look alike, seem to be multiplying—"others must be plugging in"—until their equipment blows a fuse.

In contrast, the reiterative evidence of the Trystero that Oedipa later discovers suggests that something complex and significant has existed almost unaltered for centuries, in Eliade's "mythical present that is periodically reintegrated." Many of the events, linked with the Trystero, that occur in the Jacobean *Courier's Tragedy* that Oedipa sees early in the book, recur in the midst of the California gold rush, and again in a battle in Italy during the Second World War. The Trystero's emblem, a muted post horn (suggesting the demonic aspect of the system: it mutes the trumpet of apocalypse), recurs in countless settings, in children's games, in postmarks, lapel pins, tattoos, rings, scrawled on walls, doodled in notebooks—in dozens of contexts which cannot, through any secular logic, be connected. Each of these repetitions, each evidence of the Trystero's persistence, seems to Oedipa a link with another world. As the Nefastis machine futilely tried to link the "worlds" of thermodynamics and communications, Jésus Arrabal talks of a miracle as "another world's intrusion into this one." Those who joined the Trystero, Oedipa thinks, must have entered some kind of community when they withdrew from the ordinary life of the Republic, and, "since they could not have withdrawn into a vacuum . . . there had to exist the separate, silent, unexpected world." To enter the Trystero, to become aware of it, is to cross the threshold between the profane and sacred worlds.

"The threshold," Eliade writes in *The Sacred and the Profane,* "is the limit, the boundary, the frontier that distinguishes and opposes two worlds—and at the same time the paradoxical place where those two worlds communicate, where passage from the profane to the sacred world becomes possible." Oedipa wonders if she could have "found the Trystero . . . through any of a hundred lightly-concealed entranceways, a hundred alienations."

Yet in the middle of the fifth chapter of the book the entranceways, the alienations ("Decorating each alienation . . . was somehow always the post horn"—), suddenly disappear: the repetitions stop. For perhaps thirty pages Oedipa receives no immediate signs of the Trystero, nothing more than some historical documents and second-hand reports. Until the middle of the fifth chapter Oedipa consistently sees the post horn as a living and immediate symbol, actively present in the daily life around her. From that point on she only hears about its past existence through documents, stamps, books—always second-hand. (This distinction is nowhere mentioned in the book, but the clean break . . . is too absolute to be accidental.) And at the same time, all her important human contacts begin to fade and disperse: "They are stripping from me, she said subvocally—feeling like a fluttering curtain, in a very high window moving . . . out over the abyss. . . . My shrink . . . has gone mad; my husband, on LSD, gropes like a child further and further into the rooms and endless rooms of the elaborate candy house of himself and away, hopelessly away, from what has passed, I was hoping forever, for love; . . . my best guide to the Trystero [Driblette] has taken a Brody. Where am I?" Without signs, without the repetition that all signs embody, she is left to her own devices. Until now, the repetitions *told* her of the Trystero ("the repetition of symbols was to be enough . . . *She was meant to remember.* . . . Each clue that comes is *supposed* to have its own clarity, its fine chances for permanence"—Pynchon's italics), but the simple reception of signs is insufficient for the revelation she is approaching: "she wondered if each one of the gemlike 'clues' were only some kind of compensation. To make up for her having lost the direct, epileptic Word, the cry that might abolish the night." (pp. 198-206)

The Trystero's illuminations are conveyed through miracles, sacred versions of what Oedipa thinks of as the "secular miracle of communication." The one traditional miracle most closely involved with communication is the miracle of Pentecost:

> When the day of Pentecost had come, [the Apostles] were . . . all filled with the Holy Spirit and began to speak in other tongues, as the Spirit gave them utterance. . . . [T]he multitude came together, and they were bewildered, because each one heard them speaking in his own language. . . . And all were amazed and perplexed, saying to one another, "What does this mean?" But others mocking said, "They are filled with new wine."

Pynchon names Pentecost only once, in the play-within-the-novel *The Courier's Tragedy,* where the novel's use of the Pentecost motif is parodied darkly. The gift of tongues is perverted, amidst a scene of Jacobean horror, into the tearing out of a tongue. The torturer gloats:

> Thy pitiless unmanning is most meet,
> Thinks Ercole the zany Paraclete.
> Descended this malign, Unholy Ghost,
> Let us begin thy frightful Pentecost.

The feast of Pentecost is alternately called Whitsunday, after the tradition that on that day baptismal candidates wear white. The final scene of the book—a stamp auction held, surprisingly, on a Sunday—is a parody of Pentecost: "The men inside the auction room wore black mohair and had pale cruel faces. . . . [The auctioneer] spread his arms in a gesture that seemed to belong to the priesthood of some remote culture; perhaps to a descending angel. The auctioneer cleared his throat. Oedipa settled back, to await the crying of Lot 49." And the book ends. The auctioneer prepares to speak; Oedipa awaits the forty-ninth lot of the sale, a lot whose purchaser "may" turn out to be from the Trystero, thus forcing the system to reveal itself. But why the *forty-ninth* lot? Because Pentecost is the Sunday seven weeks after Easter—forty-nine days. But the word Pentecost derives from the Greek for "fiftieth." The crying—the auctioneer's calling—of the forty-ninth lot is the moment before a Pentecostal revelation, the end of the period in which the miracle is in a state of potential, not yet manifest. This is why the novel ends with Oedipa waiting, with the "true" nature of the Trystero never established: a manifestation of the sacred can only be believed in; it can never be proved beyond doubt. There will always be a mocking voice, internal or external, saying "they are filled with new wine"—or, as Oedipa fears, "you are hallucinating it . . . you are fantasying some plot."

Oedipa's constant risk lies in that nagging possibility: that the Trystero has no independent existence, but is merely her own projection on the world outside. The center of Pierce Inverarity's interests is a town named San Narciso, and the name insistently mocks Oedipa's quest. (There is a Saint Narcissus in *The Courier's Tragedy,* so the narcissism in question is not limited to mid-century America.) The novel describes, however, Oedipa's progress away from the modes of narcissism. At the end of the first chapter Pynchon writes that Oedipa was "to have all manner of revelations[, h]ardly about Pierce Inverarity, or herself." Oedipa recalls, a few lines later, a past moment with Inverarity in Mexico when she saw an emblem of solipsism to which she responded in kind. They had

> somehow wandered into an exhibition of paintings by . . . Remedios Varo; in the central painting of a triptych . . . were a number of frail girls . . . prisoners in the top room of a circular tower, embroidering a kind of tapestry which spilled out the slit windows and into a void, seeking hopelessly to fill the void: for all the other buildings and creatures, all the waves, ships and forests of the earth were contained in this tapestry, and the tapestry was the world. . . . Oedipa . . . stood in front of the painting and cried. . . . She had looked down at her feet and known, then, because of a painting, that what she had stood on had only been woven a couple thousand miles away in her own tower, was only by accident known as Mexico, and so Pierce had

taken her away from nothing, there'd been no escape.

The tower of isolation, though an expression of the self, is not a product of the self, but one of the conditions of this world:

> Such a captive maiden . . . soon realizes that her tower, its height and architecture, are *like her ego only incidental:* that what really keeps her where she is is magic, anonymous and malignant, visited on her from outside and for no reason at all. . . . If the tower is everywhere and the knight of deliverance no proof against its magic, what else?

With this gesture towards hopelessness the chapter ends. But to its final question, the remainder of the book—with its partial revelation of what the Trystero might stand for—offers a tentative answer.

Near the end of the novel, when Oedipa stands by the sea, "her isolation complete," she finally breaks from the tower and from the uniqueness of San Narciso. She learns, finally, of a continuity that had been available, but hidden, from the beginning:

> She stood . . . her isolation complete, and tried to face toward the sea. But she'd lost her bearings. She turned, . . . could find no mountains either. As if there could be no barriers between herself and the rest of the land. San Narciso at that moment lost (the loss pure, instant, spherical . . .), gave up its residue of uniqueness for her; became a name again, was assumed back into the American continuity of crust and mantle.

At this point the uniqueness of her experience matters less than the general truth it signifies: "There was the true continuity. . . . If San Narciso and the estate were really no different from any other town, and any other estate, then by that continuity she might have found The Tristero anywhere in her Republic . . . if only she'd looked." Her choice now is either to affirm the existence of the Tristero—through which continuity survives, renews, reintegrates itself over vast expanses of space and time—or to be entirely separated, isolated, an "alien . . . assumed full circle into some paranoia." San Narciso or America. (pp. 207-11)

The achievement of *The Crying of Lot 49* is its ability to speak unwanted words without a hint of preaching or propaganda. The book's transformation of the impersonal language of science into a language of great emotional power is a breathtaking accomplishment, whose nearest rival is perhaps Goethe's *Elective Affinities.* Equally remarkable is the book's ability to hover on the edge of low comedy without ever descending into the pond of the frivolous. The risks Pynchon takes in his comedy are great, but all the "bad" jokes, low puns, comic names, and moments of pure farce that punctuate the book have a serious function: the book, through its exploration of stylistic extremes, constantly raises expectations which it then refuses to fulfill. Its pattern of comic surprises, of sudden intrusions of disparate styles and manners, is entirely congruent with the thrust of its narrative. As Oedipa is caught unaware by the abrupt revelations that change her world, and is thus made attentive to significance she never recognized before, so the variations in the book's texture alert a reader to the book's complexity. High seriousness is difficult to sustain—nor, clearly, would Pynchon ever want to do so. A serious vision of relation and coherence must include comic relationships, and recognize comic varieties of attention.

Pynchon recognizes the limits of fiction—his comedy is in part a reminder of the fictional quality of his world—but he never lets his book become therefore self-reflective. Although he shares the painful knowledge wrought by modernism of the limits of art, and although he knows that no work of quotidian fiction—neither social nor psychological—can ever again persuade, he devotes himself to the effort that leads from pure fiction to a thrust at truth. The effort is difficult and complex, and most of the modes in which the effort has previously been attempted now seem exhausted. Pynchon's search for a new mode of indicative fiction is a lonely and isolated one, but it leads to a place where fiction can become less lonely, less isolated than it has been for many years. (pp. 218-19)

> *Edward Mendelson, "The Sacred, the Profane, and 'The Crying of Lot 49'," in* Individual and Community: Variations on a Theme in American Fiction, *edited by Kenneth H. Baldwin and David K. Kirby, Duke University Press, 1975, pp. 182-222.*

Thomas H. Schaub

Nowhere in recent fiction do we find a better example of finely wrought ambiguity than in Pynchon's second novel, **The Crying of Lot 49.** This book may be understood as the education of its central figure, Oedipa Maas, but it is an education which Pynchon complicates considerably by the uncertainty he introduces into every perception allowed to Oedipa and the reader. The major source of the ambiguity is Pynchon's figurative use of the concept of "entropy," for he exploits the diametrically opposite meanings which the term has in thermodynamics and in information theory. Metaphorically, one compensates the other. In both, entropy is a measurement of disorganization, but in information theory disorganization increases the potential information which a message may convey, while in thermodynamics entropy is a measure of the disorganization of molecules within closed systems and possesses no positive connotation. Pynchon uses the concept of entropy in this latter sense as a figure of speech to describe the running down Oedipa discovers of the American Dream; at the same time he uses the entropy of information theory to suggest that Oedipa's sorting activities may counter the forces of disorganization and death.

Heat results from the motion of molecules. As Koteks explains to Oedipa, "Fast molecules have more energy than slow ones. Concentrate enough of them in one place and you have a region of high temperature. You can then use the difference in temperature between this hot region of the box and any cooler region, to drive a heat engine." The "difference in temperature" is crucial, for without it there

is no capacity for work. It is this difference which represents the organization of molecules. Entropy enters at this point: as the engine works, the two regions become mixed. The molecules collide with each other until they are all moving at the same rate, which means that eventually there is a cessation of difference, the creation of a static equilibrium, and an incapacity for work. Entropy is the measure of this declining activity, codified in the Second Law of Thermodynamics and summarized by Wiener in *The Human Use of Human Beings:* "energy spontaneously runs downhill in temperature."

The apparent implication of this law is that everything is running down. Wiener formulates this in the most extreme terms: "As entropy increases, the universe, and all closed systems in the universe, tend naturally to deteriorate and lose their distinctiveness, to move from the least to the most probable state, from a state of organization and differentiation in which distinctions and forms exist, to a state of chaos and sameness." This thesis was first put forward by Willard Gibbs, who used probability statistics to apply the Second Law to the universe at large. Henry Adams was quick to appropriate the thesis and apply it to his study of history in *The Degradation of the Democratic Dogma:* "to the vulgar and ignorant historian it meant only that the ash-heap was constantly increasing in size."

Wiener also notes that "while the universe as a whole, if indeed there is a whole universe, tends to run down, there are local enclaves whose direction seems opposed to that of the universe at large and in which there is a limited and temporary tendency for organization to increase. Life finds its home in some of these enclaves." He adds that there is disagreement among writers as to the possible application of the law of disorganization to biological and sociological systems. (pp. 21-2)

[Pynchon focuses on] the convoluted alienation of a single character in **The Crying of Lot 49;** [he] achieves this by writing in a conditional mode, so that the text itself oscillates like a standing wave between nodes of meaning, and by locating the paralyzing difficulties of those poles within the perceptions of Oedipa Maas. Her perceptions necessarily establish a middle ground between her culture and what she learns about it. Like the identity between Herbert Stencil's search for *V.* and the growth of the novel itself, Oedipa's instruction in American culture occurs under a McLuhanesque pedagogy that is also the method—almost the device—of **The Crying of Lot 49.** Oedipa's task as executrix of Pierce Inverarity's estate forces her to examine her cultural medium whose message is alienation, loss, and death, "congruent with the cheered land."

Oedipa is first "sensitized" to the technique of her education by the arrival of a letter from her husband Mucho, while she is staying in San Narciso: "It may have been an intuition that the letter would be newsless inside that made Oedipa look more closely at its outside, when it arrived. At first she didn't see. It was an ordinary Muchoesque envelope, swiped from the station, ordinary airmail stamp, to the left of the cancellation a blurb put on by the government, REPORT ALL OBSCENE MAIL TO YOUR POTSMASTER.." This is the beginning of her discovery of an alternative message service; once she acquires the

McLuhanesque knack, she is quick to read the messages encoded in the medium of America, congruent with the ostensible signs it proffers.

By naming the town Pierce founded "San Narciso," Pynchon engages the reader in the habit of reading messages in the medium of the book at the same time we are pursuing Oedipa in her search. Pynchon's direct evocation of the Narcissus myth is a clear statement that Pierce's estate and what it represents are a culture in love with a dream-image of itself. In the myth Narcissus spurned the love of Echo, who was doomed to repeat only the last words of other voices. Pierce, like Narcissus, prefers the "deep vistas of space and time . . . allegorical faces that never were"—the colored windows of mute stamps—to Oedipa's spoken love. The Echo Courts where she stays become the scene of his first adultery, and—it is suggested—the beginning of her escape from the image of the tower which defines her at the end of chapter one. She will no longer be an Echo, but will try to say first things about real facts.

The origin of Pynchon's use of the Narcissus myth is Marshall McLuhan's *Understanding Media: The Extensions of Man.* The world of **The Crying of Lot 49** is built around those "extensions": word of mouth, letters and postal systems, telephones, television, information encoded in cars and mattresses, the written work in plays and bathrooms, even the configurations of cities and towns. In McLuhan's view all these are the narcissistic extensions of man whose medium is the message of his culture. McLuhan's interpretation of the Narcissus myth is readily available for Pynchon's appropriation, for it establishes the identity between closed systems and narcissism:

> *Narcissus* . . . is from the Greek word *narcosis,* or numbness. The youth Narcissus mistook his own reflection in the water for another person. This extension of himself by mirror numbed his perceptions until he became the servomechanism of his own extended or repeated image. The nymph Echo tried to win his love with fragments of his own speech, but in vain. He was numb. He had adapted to his extension of himself and had become a closed system.

Pynchon incorporates this interpretation of the myth as social metaphor into **The Crying of Lot 49.** When Oedipa drives into San Narciso, she feels she is on the other side of the soundproof glass in a radio studio; the businesses are silent and paralyzed. The road along which San Narciso stretches Oedipa fancies is a "hypodermic needle, inserted somewhere ahead into the vein of a freeway, a vein nourishing the mainliner L.A., keeping it happy, coherent, protected from pain and whatever passes, with a city, for pain." In the Echo Courts themselves, "nothing moved."

American culture, in short, is numb, and is addicted to what protects it from pain (and, ultimately, death). In McLuhan's terms our culture has become addicted to the material forms which the American Dream has assumed. Of course, the dream and the culture, like Narcissus and his image, are inseparable, and it is in this convolution that Oedipa finds herself. In the spray can caroming off the walls of the motel bathroom we have both an image of entropy—a region of fast molecules within the can exhausting itself within the confines of the bathroom—and an image of human life threatened, threatened, albeit comically, by the systems it has created. Oedipa "could imagine no end to it; yet presently the can did give up in midflight and fall to the floor."

By the end of the book, Oedipa realizes that San Narciso is a microcosm of the Republic, an "incident among our climatic records of dreams and what dreams became among our accumulated daylight." She understands that Pierce, the founder of this microcosm, had been seized by "some headlong expansion of himself" and remembers him telling her once: "Keep it bouncing, that's all the secret, keep it bouncing." This is her meditation amidst the transcontinental railroad tracks first laid by Pierce's hero, Jay Gould; the Second Law of Thermodynamics lurks in her language as Oedipa wonders that Pierce "must have known . . . how the bouncing would stop."

The discussion thus far has concentrated on Pynchon's use of thermodynamic entropy; in this discussion *The Crying of Lot 49* is a view of America as a closed system running down. The bouncing will stop. But there is a convoluting wrinkle to all this, a hope of sorts which animates Oedipa's search for Tristero; this hope depends upon the concept of "information" and informational entropy. Both the Second Law and McLuhan's narcissism obtain within closed systems, for it is only within systems cut off from other sources of energy that the loss of the capacity for work is inevitable. Information, on the other hand, concerns what passes among systems. Wiener defines information as "the content of what is exchanged with the outer world as we adjust to it, and make our adjustment felt upon it." Inverarity's advice—"Keep it bouncing"—is linked to the Second Law; "echoed" by Oedipa at the end of the book, this advice recalls Nefastis's dogmatism, which has its origin in information theory: "Communication is the key . . . to keep it all cycling."

The Nefastis Machine represents a revision of Maxwell's hypothetical closed system with a sorting demon inside. Stanley Koteks's explanation of this to Oedipa is correct, and so is her objection, "sorting isn't work?" Koteks's description and Oedipa's response are a fictionalized version of the distinction Wiener draws between contemporary physics and the physics of Clerk Maxwell's age:

> In nineteenth century physics, it seemed to cost nothing to get information. The result is that there is nothing in Maxwell's physics to prevent one of his demons from furnishing its own power source. Modern physics, however, recognizes that the demon can only gain the information with which it [sorts the molecules] from something like a sense organ which for these purposes is an eye. The light that strikes the demon's eyes is not an energy-less component of mechanical motion, but shares in the main properties of mechanical motion itself. . . . In such a system, however, it will turn out that the constant collision between light and gas particles tends to bring the light and particles to an equilibrium. Thus while the demon may temporarily reverse the usual direction of entropy, ultimately it too will wear down.

The temporary reversal is the result of "feedback." All our "modern automatic machines . . . possess sense organs; that is, receptors for messages coming from the outside." Wiener stresses that in this capacity there is little difference between man and machine; both receive and transmit messages, and both survive in their environments through this feedback process, defined by Wiener as "the control of a machine on the basis of its *actual* performance rather than its *expected* performance." (The doors of an elevator are not only programmed to open at a designated floor, but the elevator also "knows" whether or not it is actually at that floor.) And it is this self-correcting ability of the machine which delays its running down.

Oedipa's function, sitting beside the Nefastis Machine, is to "feed back something like the same quantity of information. To keep it all cycling." The Machine, of course, is a comic distortion of the feedback systems Wiener is talking about. Nonetheless, it is a crucial interior metaphor of the book's operation as a whole. When Oedipa objects that "sorting is work," she ties the thermodynamic model to the book's postal courier themes, and to her own role as executrix. The first sentence of the book informs us that Pierce had "assets numerous and tangled enough to make the job of sorting it all out more than honorary."

Because Pierce's estate is a microcosm of America, the four parts to the metaphor are these: what Maxwell's Demon is to the Nefastis Machine, Oedipa is to America.

Pynchon's preoccupation with communications derives not only from McLuhan's "extensions of man" but from the central thesis of Wiener's book as well: "society can only be understood through a study of the messages and the communication facilities which belong to it; and that in the future development of these messages and communication facilities, messages between man and machines, between machines and man, and between machine and machine are destined to play an ever-increasing part." Typically, this has a political importance for Pynchon. Emory Bortz imagines a member of Tristero in the seventeenth century declaring that "whoever could control the lines of communication, among all the princes, would control them."

Oedipa's efforts to disentangle Inverarity's estate involve her in a study of her society; she comes to realize that her world is a vast communications system feeding her information which may engulf before it enlightens. Like the Demon, she tries to order the signs and symbols around her into some kind of operational meaning. But sorting is

Remedios Varo's Bordando el manto terrestre (Embroidering the Earth's Mantle), *1961, a painting Pynchon invokes in delineating Oedipa Maas's quest for reality in* The Crying of Lot 49.

work, and she requires for this task some infusion of energy from the outside to counter the entropic movement inside toward disorganization, sameness, and death. Her role is bequeathed to her by Pierce, whose last name "Inverarity" is cognate with place names in Scotland where Clerk Maxwell—inventor of the Demon—was born. This is another of the messages coded in the text's medium, and it suggests that Pierce was the demon of his own system, which Oedipa, like all of us born into a system we did not create, bears the burden of keeping alive.

The Nefastis Machine not only connects the worlds of thermodynamics and information, but it casts a shadow on Oedipa's entire enterprise. Even Nefastis knows that his belief in his invention's workability rests on a visual metaphor: the identity of the equations for "entropy" in thermodynamics and the average unit in information theory. The fact that they *look* the same but *mean* different things is a characteristic of clues in Pynchon's writing. This particular metaphor has added strength because in information theory "entropy" represents a measurement of possibility. J. R. Pierce (author of *Symbols, Signals and Noise: The Nature and Process of Communication*) tells us that "the amount of information conveyed by the message increases as the amount of uncertainty as to what message actually will be produced becomes greater. . . . The entropy of communication theory is a measure of this uncertainty." Nefastis thinks the entropy of information theory is "positive" and can counter the "negative" entropy of thermodynamics. What makes the entropy metaphor "verbally graceful" and "objectively true" is his belief in the actual existence of Maxwell's Demon, sitting inside his machine. We must give Nefastis his due; he is as "bothered" by the word "entropy" as Oedipa is disturbed by "Trystero," and the connection which he asserts is one with which theorists have been toying for as long as the similarity has been noticed.

Pierce discusses this matter in his chapter "Information Theory and Physics," and agrees with Wiener: "One pays a price for information which leads to a reduction of the statistical mechanical entropy of a system. This price is proportional to the communication-theory entropy of the message source which produces the information. It is always just high enough so that a perpetual motion machine of the second kind is impossible." Such extra-textual evidence undermines Nefastis's machine and implies that insofar as Oedipa is the sorting demon of her society, she is fighting a losing battle.

But in Oedipa, Pynchon has created a character with a knack for pointed questions. Her response to Koteks revealed the flaw in Maxwell's physics; her answer to Nefastis is equally incisive: "But what . . . if the Demon exists only because the two equations look alike? Because of the metaphor?" Nefastis merely smiles; he is a "believer." The contrast between Oedipa's worried questioning and Nefastis's belief is a distinguishing characteristic of Oedipa's intelligence, but the distance she keeps from her own metaphors costs her dearly. They tease her with the possibility of meaning without providing the comfort Nefastis, and later her husband Mucho, enjoy.

On the freeway leading to San Francisco she compares her own search with the method of Nefastis, her thoughts interpolated through the narrative voice:

> For John Nefastis (to take a recent example) two kinds of entropy, thermodynamic and informational, happened, say by coincidence, to look alike, when you wrote them down as equations. Yet he had made his mere coincidence respectable, with the help of Maxwell's Demon.

> Now here was Oedipa, faced with a metaphor of God knew how many parts; more than two, anyway. With coincidences blossoming these days wherever she looked, she had nothing but a sound, a word, Trystero, to hold them together.

That doubt is never expunged. At the end of the book the questions remain: is the Tristero pattern of Oedipa's own weaving, imposed on the world outside? Or is Tristero a pattern which inheres in the world outside, imposing itself upon her? Neither she nor the reader is allowed by Pynchon to ascertain the stable meaning of the blossoming pattern; without this certainty her usefulness in preserving order against a declining culture remains painfully ambiguous.

The early image of the tower (which closes chapter one) is a symbol of the uncertainty surrounding Oedipa's perceptions and our understanding of her condition. The tower quickly establishes an ambiguity which never resolves, for we are never sure whether it is an image of solipsism or one of imprisonment by forces outside Oedipa. Initially, the tower represents Oedipa's "buffered" and "insulated" existence at Kinneret-Among-the-Pines. Later, with Pierce in Mexico, the tower becomes an image of self-entrapment for her when she sees a painting by Remedios Varo titled "Bordando el Manto Terrestre," which pictures prisoners in a circular tower, "embroidering a kind of tapestry which spilled out the slit windows and into a void, seeking hopelessly to fill the void." By the end of the chapter the image has shifted again. Oedipa realizes that "her tower, its height and architecture, are like her ego only incidental: that what really keeps her where she is is magic, anonymous and malignant, visited on her from outside and for no reason at all."

Oedipa does manage to escape the tower, but only increases her isolation. She could join the anti-community available to her only by violating her integrity and accepting as literal truth the metaphorical linkages comprising Tristero (the replication of muted post horns, W.A.S.T.E. symbols, variations on the word "Tristero"). The people in the novel who do this—Nefastis, Mucho, Hilarius—are severely undercut by the narrator. They are facile believers in their own metaphors, while Oedipa rides a fence between a "hothouse" dogmatism on the one hand and engulfment by the void "outside" on the other. Indeed, *The Crying of Lot 49* may be read as a tragic account of the difficulty of human action in a world whose meanings are always *either* our own *or* just beyond our reach. Narcissism, in short, may be a condition of our participation in the world.

Pynchon plays on the religious implications of that ambiguity, for Oedipa's clues may be sacred signs as well as secular information, "*as if* . . . there were revelation in progress all around her" (italics mine). Information is a species of "revelation" just as Nefastis's version of feedback is a species of California spiritualism. Both he and Wiener trade on the fact that information can provide a temporary and local reversal of entropy. To reiterate: "the Maxwell demon can work indefinitely . . . if additional light comes from outside the system and does not correspond in temperature to the mechanical temperatures of the particles themselves." There are two requirements, then, for regenerating a system: the energy must come from an Outside, and it must be different from the energy present Inside. This is the importance of Tristero, for it represents the possible infusion from the outside of an organized "difference" reinstating opposition. The success of Oedipa's sorting rests directly on the uncertainty over the source of the information she accumulates and organizes into the Tristero; if these clues do not originate in a system or culture outside the one Oedipa seeks to redeem, then they are only a part of the inside system which is running down.

There are specific problems in her way. Pynchon's drama of contemporary society involves a historical as well as a spatial dimension. Oedipa's attempt to verify Tristero takes her into history, where she is confronted by various editions, pirated copies, questionable sources, and death. Oedipa can never get beyond herself, her language, or outside of time, but remains "parked at the centre of an odd, religious instant." In some ways this book is about being trapped within the present, at an intersection of time and space. Talking with ninety-one-year-old Mr. Thoth—named for the Egyptian god of letters—she will feel "as if she had been trapped at the centre of some intricate crystal." The story of Oedipa is the story of waiting for revelation, seeking it in the historical, secular, and time-bound world around her, but finding no God beyond the words she hopes will tell her the truth. Because she is trapped, "motion is relative"—which is the reason Pynchon includes the discussion at the Scope Bar about the Commodore Pinguid:

> Off the coast of either what is now Carmel-by-the-sea, or what is now Pismo Beach, around noon or possibly toward dusk, the two ships sighted each other. One of them may have fired; if it did then the other responded; but both were out of range so neither showed a scar afterward to prove anything. Night fell. In the morning the Russian ship was gone. But motion is relative. If you believe an excerpt from the *Bogatir* or *Gaidamak*'s log, forwarded in April to the General-Adjutant in St. Petersburg and now somewhere in the Krasnyi Arkhiv, it was the *Disgruntled* that had vanished during the night.

The Pinguid records are a comic parody of the unreliability (the relativity) of historical records, mimicked by the either/or prose of the narrator. The agility of metaphor balances on that ridge, as later, in a more somber scene, Oedipa realizes, "the act of metaphor . . . was a thrust at truth and a lie, depending where you were: inside, safe, or outside, lost."

The sacred language which informs *The Crying of Lot 49* is a foil to the inverted, profane culture it describes: smog obscuring the feminine moon, waste, debris, the "empties" Bortz tosses at seagulls looking for the true sea, freeways built over graveyards, spray cans, rusting cars, shanties. All this is the iconography of isolation in a culture of throwaways. The ironic use of language has a fitting origin in Pierce's name, which derives from "petrus" or rock. As founder of San Narciso, Pierce is an inverse Peter, on whom is built the profane church of America. Pynchon enforces this irony immediately, for Oedipa—on reading that she has been named executrix—"stood in the living room, stared at by the greenish dead eye of the TV tube, spoke the name of God, tried to feel as drunk as possible." Pierce occasions the association of the TV with God, and this association persists throughout the book, for the TV's "greenish eye" becomes the green bubble shades nearly everyone wears, which, like the TV, permit the wearer to be in someone else's living space without making contact.

Pynchon chooses Varo's painting, in part, because it serves for him as an inverse parable of creation. The world is created (in this painting) from the inside out; the rhythm of Pynchon's prose is an intentional echo of the opening verses of I John: "all the waves, ships and forests of the earth were contained in this tapestry, and the tapestry was the world." Randy Driblette tells Oedipa, "That's what I'm for. To give the spirit flesh. The words, who cares? . . . I'm the projector at the planetarium, all the closed little universe visible in the circle of that stage is coming out of my mouth, eyes, sometimes other orifices also." Driblette insists the play means nothing, yet Oedipa (and we) do not believe him fully because of his reluctance to speak about Tristero, and because of the accumulating coincidences. Varo's painting and Driblette threaten Oedipa with the possibility that there is no meaning beyond the one she herself weaves; but this possibility, while never denied, is never confirmed either.

Varo's painting is the initiation of a tapestry image which recurs three times late in the book. After interviewing Tremaine, Oedipa tells herself, "This is America, you live in it, you let it happen. Let it unfurl." Here the painting, like the Narcissus myth, has been assumed into the fabric of the novel and is part of the social vision of a culture weaving itself in time, each generation responsible for the ongoing expansion. At the same time, there is no given pattern to follow. When she learns of Driblette's suicide, Oedipa mutters "subvocally—feeling like a fluttering curtain in a very high window, moving up to then out over the abyss"; she asks Bortz about Tristero "with the light, vertiginous sense of fluttering out over an abyss." Earlier she worried that she was fashioning the tapestry, but now her paranoia has begun to blossom. She is not sure whether she is weaver or woven.

To resolve this uncertainty, Oedipa needs information not subject to time, "the direct, epileptic Word, the cry that might abolish the night." This need underlies her desire to find out "something about the historical Wharfinger. Not so much the verbal one." Bortz tells her words are all we have. "Pick some words. . . . Them, we can talk about." All that is available from the past is the medium in which Wharfinger lived, and the gambit of reaching the real message by tracing his words is blocked by the transformations of time: variant texts, pirated copies, faulty memory, and questionable interpretation. Her interest in Wharfinger, of course, arises from her determination to verify the literal existence of Tristero, because if Tristero is not part of some "grandiose practical joke" traceable to the Inverarity estate, then she may have found in it "a real alternative to the exitlessness, to the absence of surprise to life, that harrows the head of everybody American you know."

When the Tristero alternative is examined, we find it linked with exile and death. Promises of "revelation" and "hierophany" are matched, symmetrically, by an opposing set of references to the "Book of the Dead." The old man Oedipa interviews at Vesperhaven is Mr. Thoth, "scribe of the gods" in Budge's compilation of the *Egyptian Book of the Dead.* Moreover, we read in C. G. Jung's "Psychological Commentary" to the *Tibetan Book of the Dead:* "Like *The Egyptian Book of the Dead,* it is meant to be a guide for the dead man during the period of his Bardo existence, symbolically described as an intermediate state of *forty-nine days'* duration between death and re-birth" (italics mine). If the ending of *The Crying of Lot 49* is the point before revelation, then this revelation—at least in one sense—is death. Both Books of the Dead are about the necessary relation between the art of dying and the art of living. This relation is the fulcrum of one of Pynchon's fundamental themes: our culture is dying because it is predicated on a denial of death—as Tony Jaguar knew, for he had heard "stories about Forest Lawn and the American cult of the dead."

The attributes of the Tristero alternative—exile, alienation, silence, waiting, disinheritance, darkness, and death—are all "congruent with the cheered land." Oedipa's discovery of these attributes is concentrated in the "nighttown" section of the novel (chapter five), but this chapter has been prefigured twice by prose that anticipates her passage through the night and establishes resonances which convolute what she learns there. The passage-through-the-night theme is initiated in her motel room with Metzger. As the Strip Botticelli game unwinds toward climax, Oedipa suspects "that if the sun ever came up Metzger would disappear. She wasn't sure if she wanted him to." Despite the humor of this scene, the chapter can be read (as the narrator points out in chapter three) as the beginning of Oedipa's escape from the tower. That means an increase in "intensity," "focus," and a removal of the "insulation" she experienced at Kinneret. With Metzger she strips herself naked, and this venturesome adultery is only the first of many examples in the novel in which her efforts to "communicate" result in increased isolation.

Her night with Metzger is recalled and expanded by a passage ten pages later:

> So began, for Oedipa, the languid, sinister blooming of The Tristero. Or rather, her attendance at some unique performance prolonged as if it were the last of the night, something a little extra for whoever'd stayed this late. As if the break-away gown, net bras, jeweled garters and G-strings of historical figuration that would fall away were layered dense as Oedipa's own street-

clothes in that game with Metzger in front of the Baby Igor movie; as if a plunge toward dawn indefinite black hours long would indeed be necessary before The Tristero could be revealed in its terrible nakedness. Would its smile, then, be coy, and would it flirt away harmlessly backstage, say good night with a Bourbon Street bow and leave her in peace? Or would it instead, the dance ended, come back down the runway, its luminous stare locked to Oedipa's, smile gone malign and pitiless; bend to her alone among the desolate rows of seats and begin to speak words she never wanted to hear?

The structure of the passage is the same as that in chapter two: passage through the night, the stripping away of clothes/figurations, and the promise of revelation toward dawn. This simile complicates the relationship of Oedipa to the Tristero, for the historical strip tease is likened to Oedipa's own in the previous chapter, and this prompts the inescapable suspicion that Oedipa and Tristero are somehow involved in one another, and that Oedipa herself—as her name suggests—may be at the heart of the declining society. With this finesse, Pynchon convolutes outside and inside; the comfortable distinction between Oedipa and Tristero is now complicated. At her hotel in Berkeley Oedipa "kept waking from a nightmare about something in the mirror. . . . When she woke in the morning, she was sitting bolt upright, staring into the mirror at her own exhausted face." Back in southern California she dreams "of disembodied voices from whose malignance there was no appeal, the soft dusk of mirrors out of which something was about to walk . . . ".

The two passages just discussed prefigure Oedipa's descent into the San Francisco night and become the structure of that chapter. The preparation for our view of her experience is echoed in the language: "At some indefinite passage in night's sonorous score, it also came to her that she would be safe, that something, perhaps only her linearly fading drunkenness, would protect her. The city was hers, as, made up and sleeked so with the customary words and images (cosmopolitan, culture, cable cars) it had not been before: she had safe-passage tonight to its far blood's branchings." During the night the metaphors (like "historical figurations") will fall away. The city, "made up and sleeked," does a strip tease, which is an externalized version of the clichés that are falling away from Oedipa's understanding. The children she meets are unafraid because "they had inside their circle an imaginary fire, and needed nothing but their own unpenetrated sense of community," but Oedipa's own protection begins to dissolve because she is not a believer and because her world has been pierced. The only community she discovers is an anti-community, like the Inamorati Anonymous who have nothing to share but a mutual isolation from one another, "dedicated not to continuity but to some kind of interregnum."

Oedipa's passage through the night is fulfilled at dawn when she comes upon the drunken sailor and confronts for the first time the "irreversible process" of death. This is the revelation which greets her at dawn, and accompanying it is a realization which helps explain the book's slippery ambiguity. Oedipa's thoughts pun on the DTs she feels in the sailor's body, and she remembers that in calculus "dt" meant "also a time differential, a vanishingly small instant in which change had to be confronted at last for what it was, where it could no longer disguise itself as something innocuous like an average rate; where velocity dwelled in the projectile though the projectile be frozen in midflight, where death dwelled in the cell though the cell be looked in on at its most quick." The "delta-t" is a mathematical expedient for assuming continuous motion where none can be shown, and the shorthand "dt" establishes the continuity in Oedipa's understanding between the sailor's delirium tremens and the irreversible process.

Oedipa realizes suddenly that language is a kind of linguistic membrane between literal experience and what that experience may mean:

> The saint whose water can light lamps, the clairvoyant whose lapse in recall is the breath of God, the true paranoid for whom all is organized in spheres joyful or threatening about the central pulse of himself, the dreamer whose puns probe ancient fetid shafts and tunnels of truth all act in the same special relevance to the word, or whatever it is the word is there, buffering, to protect us from. The act of metaphor then was a thrust at truth and a lie, depending where you were: inside, safe, or outside, lost. Oedipa did not know where she was.

From the outside, metaphor is only a "buffer," while from the "inside, safe," metaphor provides access to that very realization, and is therefore a "thrust at the truth." The text of *The Crying of Lot 49* is fully metaphoric in that sense, existing in the middle between inside and outside, between a reductive literalism in which words are mere tools standing for things, and a speculative symbolism in which words are signs capable of pointing toward realities which transcend those signs. This is the same linguistic space as that occupied by Oedipa and the reader. If we look again at the formulation in the book, we see that metaphor is both a "thrust at truth and a lie"; it becomes disjunctive, or relative, only as it is employed from one side or the other. With this in mind, the next sentence is crucial: "Oedipa did not know where she was." At the end of the book she is still between "the zeroes and ones." Like Oedipa, the reader too is left in the middle, because *The Crying of Lot 49* stubbornly refuses to allow its own linguistic symmetries to resolve in ways that Oedipa's do not.

When Oedipa returns to visit Mike Fallopian at the Scope, he proposes that the entire Tristero network is a hoax. Her reaction is conveyed in a telling simile: "like the thought that someday she would have to die, Oedipa had been steadfastly refusing to look at the possibility directly." If the hoax is real, then death is "only death." The Tristero alternative is a release from her "deckful of days," but it is a release into a reality that recognizes death. Oedipa's search thus involves an unwitting discovery of her own mortality, a fact deadened by her daytime suburban culture but "congruent" with it.

As the world about her takes on more and more the character of information, Oedipa's evidence seems less like truth than clue to something beyond it; this is because her medium and its message are identical. Oedipa is caught in the midst of this identity. Her medium—housing tracts, the media, people, roads, graveyards, Cohen's dandelion wine—is all message; messages, she realizes, are subject to time and decay. Oedipa knows the sailor will die and with him all the messages encoded in his life. In her private vision of conflagration, she prophesies that his mattress will burn:

> She remembered John Nefastis, talking about his Machine, and massive destructions of information. So when this mattress flared up around the sailor, in his Viking's funeral: the stored, coded years of uselessness, early death, self-harrowing, the sure decay of hope, the set of all men who had slept on it, whatever their lives had been, would truly cease to be, forever, when the mattress burned. She stared at it in wonder. It was as if she had just discovered the irreversible process.

Her memory of Nefastis reminds us that the price of work done is entropy. This image of the burning sailor is the fulfillment of Oedipa's earlier suspicion that she might be "left with only compiled memories of clues, announcements, intimations, but never the central truth itself, which must somehow each time be too bright for memory to hold; which must always blaze out, destroying its own message irreversibly."

As message, life's medium is the transmutation of waste. Like the lost Faggio Guard, all life is transformed into the medium of the present. This process is described by Wiener in his chapter "Organization as the Message." Organisms are viewed by him as messages, since they are "opposed to chaos, to disintegration, to death, as message is to noise." Organisms, Wiener points out, exist not as substantial entities but as patterns whose content is fluid. The pattern resists disorganization, not the substance: "We are but whirlpools in a river of ever-flowing water. We are not stuff that abides, but patterns that perpetuate themselves." On this point, Wiener and McLuhan dovetail for Pynchon; Oedipa comes to view the universe as a message. As her talent for sensing meaning behind pattern ripens, the patterns proliferate and haunt her, "as if (as she'd guessed that first minute in San Narciso) there were revelation in progress all around her."

Oedipa's revelation, such as it is, is secular and real, and is the realization of loss and death. *The Crying of Lot 49* is a book about loss, about the tragedy of what happens to the moment in the stream of time. The truth existing in the present recedes into the past and is never present to our knowledge. Still, she is surrounded by transmutations of the past: she drinks it in Cohen's dandelion wine, just as the evil Duke writes with the ink of the Lost Guard. Mucho understood this when he worked as a used car salesman, watching people bring in "motorized, metal extensions of themselves" full of the "actual residue" of their lives "like a salad of despair." Pynchon has created in the W.A.S.T.E. postal system an inverse acronym, for We Await Silent Tristero's Empire stands for "waste." Waste is a communications system; as the medium of our society, its message is plain.

Oedipa is educated to this message, and learns about the

subterranean congruence of poverty and disease which lies beneath the shine of America's countenance. Therefore she is not a static character but one who changes and moves toward something new. Near the end of the book she experiences a secular epiphany:

> She stood between the public booth and the rented car, in the night, her isolation complete, and tried to face toward the sea. But she'd lost her bearings. . . . San Narciso at that moment lost (the loss pure, instant, spherical, the sound of a stainless orchestral chime held among the stars and struck lightly), gave up its residue of uniqueness for her; became a name again, was assumed back into the American continuity of crust and mantle.

This instant parallels the insight occasioned by Varo's painting that the land she stood on "was only by accident known as Mexico." Oedipa now understands that her ego, like Narciso, is only "incidental"—"a name; an incident among our climatic records of dreams and what dreams became among our accumulated daylight. . . . There was the true continuity." Paradoxically, the word "continuity" has come to mean in the course of the novel its exact opposite. For all Oedipa's admirable courage and persistence, she still possesses—like Herbert Stencil in pursuit of V.—a naive hope that Tristero will be a tangible and literal person." Yet it is clear that Tristero's reality is metaphoric; while it is an alternative, it is one indissolubly knit to the culture that alienates it. The pattern Oedipa finds *or* weaves has the reality of all metaphors, just as the community she discovers is real, though the word "community" here is a metaphor for the lack of community we all share.

At the beginning of *The Crying of Lot 49* the reader encourages Oedipa in her escape from the tower; by the end of the book she is outside lost, and paralyzed by the "matrices of a great digital computer." This is Pynchon's image of a culture whose terms—as Sidney Stencil predicted—have been reduced to polar extremes. Oedipa is caught between the suburban culture she has outgrown and the communion of withdrawal. She is happy with neither option; Oedipa "had heard all about excluded middles; they were bad shit, to be avoided; and how had it ever happened here, with the chances once so good for diversity?" If there is no Tristero "beyond the appearance of the legacy of America," then there is "just America" and the "only way she could continue, and manage to be at all relevant to it, was as an alien, unfurrowed, assumed full circle into some paranoia." The image of the computer, while inherently apt, may have its ironic source in the optimism of *Understanding Media:* "The computer . . . promises by technology a Pentecostal condition of universal understanding and unity." By contrast, Pynchon demonstrates the "secular miracle of communication": tremendous connectedness, but no community.

If hope exists at all, it is in the ability to withstand the terrible ambiguity threatening Oedipa. The fictions Pynchon writes have no happy endings; they hardly seem to "end" at all, for there is no end to the ambiguities his writing provokes. Oedipa does achieve an awareness of her culture, and that awareness is never held in doubt. Yet the doubts which her culture propagates are never resolved. To her credit she maintains her ground instead of slipping into a hermetic dogmatism or an apocalyptic suicide. Her position is isolated and filled with a paranoia more protective than psychotic. Yet with Oedipa we experience a broadening of consciousness, and a sense of the possibility for meanings which inhere in the world and in language. Those meanings, most skillfully in *The Crying of Lot 49,* depend for their vitality on the suspension in which they are caught. And this is one of the extra-literary aspects of the book, for insofar as *The Crying of Lot 49* stakes out the necessary ambiguity in which moral actions must take place, the narrator's binary flip-flopping not only makes our reading experience commensurate with Oedipa's trials, but echoes the experience beyond our reading. (pp. 24-41)

> *Thomas H. Schaub, in his* Pynchon: The Voice of Ambiguity, *University of Illinois Press, 1981, 165 p.*

In Pynchon's novels the plots of wholly imagined fiction are inseparable from the plots of known history or science. More than that, he proposes that any effort to sort out these plots must itself depend on an analytical method which, both in its derivations and in its execution, is probably part of some systematic plot against free forms of life.

> **—Richard Poirier, in his "The Importance of Thomas Pynchon," in Twentieth Century Literature, 1975.**

Tony Tanner

The Crying of Lot 49 (1966) is one of the most deceptive—as well as one of the most brilliant—short novels to have appeared since the last war. It is a strange book in that the more we learn the more mysterious everything becomes. The more we *think* we know, the less we *know* we know. The model for the story would seem to be the Californian detective story—an established tradition including the works of writers such as Raymond Chandler, Ross MacDonald and Eric Stanley Gardner. But in fact it works in a reverse direction. With a detective story you start with a mystery and move towards a final clarification, all the apparently disparate, suggestive bits of evidence finally being bound together in one illuminating pattern; whereas in Pynchon's novel we move from a state of degree-zero mystery—just the quotidian mixture of an average Californian day—to a condition of increasing mystery and dubiety.

In the simplest terms, the novel concerns Oedipa Maas, who learns that she has been named as an executor ('or she supposed executrix') of the estate of a deceased Californian real-estate mogul named Pierce Inverarity. As she sets about exploring this 'estate', she seems to discover more and more clues indicating the existence of an underground, anarchic organization called the Tristero, which, possibly dating from thirteenth-century Europe, seems to oppose all the official lines of communication and have its own secret system of communication. Seems. She can never be sure whether she is discovering a real organization, or is the victim of a gigantic hoax, or is wildly hallucinating. Her search or quest clearly has wider implications, for we are told that Pierce Inverarity was 'a founding father', and near the end we read: 'She had dedicated herself, weeks ago, to making sense of what Inverarity had left behind, never suspecting that the legacy was America'.

So on one level the driving question is simply: what does a contemporary American 'inherit' from the country's past? On the title-page Pynchon included this note: 'A portion of this novel was first published in *Esquire* magazine under the title **"The World (This one), the Flesh (Mrs Oedipa Maas), and the Testament of Pierce Inverarity"**.' Since he did not choose to give the title of another extract that appeared in a magazine, we may infer that he wanted this title definitely to appear under the main title of the book. Of course it raises the question: is 'the Testament of Pierce Inverarity' the Devil (following the World and the Flesh)? Like so much in the book it remains a question. The name itself can suggest either un-truth or in-the-truth; I have seen it glossed as 'pierces or peers into variety' and 'inverse' and 'rarity'. But then names can be like that in Pynchon's work, and I shall return to this point in a moment. The last phone call Oedipa receives from Pierce Inverarity is literally multivocal: he speaks in 'heavy Slavic tones', 'comic-Negro', 'hostile Pachuco dialect', as 'a Gestapo officer', and finally 'his Lamont Cranston voice'. He does indeed speak in many 'tongues'; the problem is which, if any of them, is 'true'? The phone call itself comes from 'where she would never know', and the 'phone line could have pointed any direction, any length'. Origin, intention, extension—all are insolubly ambiguous. What is Oedipa Maas hearing? What should she listen to? Is it all cacophony? Or is she being somehow singled out for 'revelations'?

I shall consider some details of Oedipa's quest for the meaning of the Pierce Inverarity legacy—and our quest for the meaning of the book (the two being intimately related)—but first I want to quote two crucial passages from the novel. The first occurs shortly after Oedipa has engaged in a sexual game—they call it 'Strip Botticelli'—with the lawyer Metzger. They have been watching a film (in which he starred as a child) in a motel room, and in seeking to anticipate the outcome of the plot (an anticipation of her larger concern to come) she agrees to take off an item of clothing in exchange for every answer he gives to her questions. But she prepares for this by loading herself with endless garments, trinkets and adornments. In doing so she becomes a grotesque image of an insanely eclectic culture which 'over-dresses' itself with bits and pieces of fabrics and fabrications taken from anywhere, and at the same time she reveals a poignant vulnerability, for under the absurd multi-layered 'protection' she is oddly defenceless, naked and exposed. Metzger does not

fully undress her but he does seduce her. Later she starts to find clues concerning the Tristero—in a bar, on a latrine wall—and we are given this summarizing paragraph:

> So began, for Oedipa, the languid, sinister blooming of the Tristero. Or rather, her attendance at some unique performance, prolonged as if it were the last of the night, something a little extra for whoever'd stayed this late. As if the break-away gowns, net bras, jeweled garters and G-strings of historical figuration that would fall away were layered dense as Oedipa's own streetclothes in that game with Metzger in front of the Baby Igor movie; as if a plunge toward dawn indefinite black hours long would indeed be necessary before The Tristero could be revealed in its terrible nakedness. Would its smile, then, be coy, and would it flirt away harmlessly backstage, say good night with a Bourbon Street bow and leave her in peace? Or would it instead, the dance ended, come back down the runway, its luminous stare locked to Oedipa's, smile gone malign and pitiless; bend to her alone among the desolate row of seats and begin to speak words she never wanted to hear?

It is an amazing passage, shifting in tone from vaudeville frivolity to a melodramatic note which is in fact quite chilling. But one important point to note is the conflation of 'performance' with 'historical figuration'. History and theatre become almost interchangeable terms, and Oedipa will never know when she is, or is not, present at some kind of 'performance'—a 'play' which might end in harmless concluding knockabout, or with her hearing 'words she never wanted to hear'. Just what kind of a 'performance' is America putting on anyway? All fun and jollity—or something 'malign and pitiless' coming down the aisles? When—if—history is 'undressed', what will it look like?

Later in the book Oedipa attends an actual theatre to see a performance of a Jacobean play called *The Courier's Tragedy*. Here is a description of a curious change in atmosphere which occurs during the 'performance':

> It is at about this point in the play, in fact, that things really get peculiar, and a gentle chill, an ambiguity, begins to creep in among the words. Heretofore the naming of names has gone on either literally or as metaphor. But now, as the Duke gives his fatal command, a new mode of expression takes over. It can only be called a kind of ritual reluctance. Certain things, it is made clear, will not be spoken aloud; certain events will not be shown onstage; though it is difficult to imagine, given the excesses of the preceding acts, what these things could possibly be. The Duke does not, perhaps may not, enlighten us. Screaming at Vittorio he is explicit enough about who shall *not* pursue Niccolo: his own bodyguards he describes to their faces as vermin, zanies, poltroons. But who then will the pursuers be? Vittorio knows: every flunky in the court, idling around in their Squamuglia livery and exchanging Significant Looks, knows. It is all a big in-joke. The audiences of the time knew. Angelo knows, but does not say. As close as he comes does not illuminate . . .

Those Who Know, know. But what is it they know? What does Oedipa know? And what is the 'big in-joke' anyway? No answers. But notice one thing about this new atmosphere in the play. Before, we are told, 'the naming of names has gone on either literally or as metaphor. But now . . . a new mode of expression takes over. It can only be called a kind of ritual reluctance.' Generally speaking, names can only be used either literally or metaphorically—one of those either/or situations that Pynchon's work is not particularly fond of. Here, then, is a moment, in the story and in the text, when a new mode of expression is inserted between literality and metaphor: an ambiguity, a hesitancy, a 'ritual reluctance'. We, like Oedipa, are teased and drawn into a new and problematical area of semantic dubiety—between the literal and the metaphorical. We—and she—can no longer be sure what 'names' are naming or not naming. Those who 'know' (but what do they know?) do not say. Words come 'close': there are many suggestions—even too many. But no final illumination.

Let us go back to the beginning, and the naming of names. 'Mrs Oedipa Maas'—now what kind of name is that? It is certainly right out of the line of plausibility. Fanny Price, Dorothea Brooke, even Isabel Archer: all well within the realm of possibility. But Oedipa Maas? Not so. So some critics have taken the name as a signal or symbol. Oedipa is a female Oedipus, who was of course the solver of the riddle in one of the first great detective stories in Western literature. But given that the riddle Oedipus finally has to solve concerns his own parents, parricide and incest, and given that this in no way applies to Oedipa, we may pause. Again 'Maas' has been read as suggesting Newton's second law of motion in which 'mass' is the term denoting a quantity of inertia. So the name suggests at once activity and passivity. But this will not do. In Pynchon's texts names do not operate as they do in, for example, Fielding in which Thwackum or Allworthy are—or do—exactly what their names indicate. One critic, Terry Caesar, is probably nearer the mark when he suggests an audible joke in the name: 'Oedipa my ass'; she is no Oedipus at all. As Caesar suggests, noting how wild and improbable—or downright crude and silly—many of Pynchon's 'names' are, he is probably undermining and mocking the very act of naming. We usually expect to find the person in his or her name. In a realist book as in life, the name comes to signify a real character with unique characteristics. This goes along with a very tenacious notion of the unique individual. Pynchon blows all this up. 'Character' and identity are not stable in his fiction, and the wild names he gives his 'characters', which seem either to signify too much (Oedipus and Newton indeed!) or too little (like comic-strip figures), are a gesture against the tyranny of naming itself. [Jacques] Lacan sees the fact that we are *named* before we can speak as a symptom of the degree to which we are at the mercy of language itself. Pynchon indicates that he can see how, in various ways, people are subject to the authority of naming: how a whole society can exercise its power through naming. As an author he also has to confer names on his figures, but he does so in such a way as to sabotage the conventional modes of naming. The relationship between individual and name is deliberately problematized—and caricatured—in Pynchon's texts. We find ourselves moving out of the literal or metaphorical and into—well, somewhere else.

We first encounter Oedipa Maas among the eclectic bricá-brac of contemporary Californian culture, buying lasagne and *Scientific American* in shops that indifferently play Muzak or Vivaldi. When she hears the news about being named as Pierce Inverarity's executrix, she stands in her room 'stared at by the greenish dead eye of the TV tube, spoke the name of God, tried to feel as drunk as possible'. Amid the randomness of the thoughts and her surroundings she as it were instinctively turns to the three substitutes for true religion in the contemporary world: the TV (with no message), the name of God (now an empty word) and drink (which doesn't work). So she has to try to start 'sorting it all out', 'shuffling back through a fat deckful of days which seemed . . . more or less identical'. She will have to go on sorting and shuffling to the end—and perhaps beyond.

Then Oedipa's husband 'Mucho' Maas comes back. He had once worked in a used car 'lot' (one of the many linking puns in the book), and Pynchon's elegiac evocation of the sheer pathos of the used car lot is characteristic of his uncanny sensitivity to the suggestive human traces and residues (a kind of information) to be found in the 'used', the rejected, the abandoned refuse and waste of a culture. Mucho now works for a pop music station which sends out an endless stream of jabbering trash (i.e. no information). 'He had believed too much in the lot, he believed not at all in the station'. For him every day is a 'defeat': the sadness of the car lot overwhelmed him; the pointlessness of the pop music station empties him out. He can be of no help to Oedipa. Next she receives a middle-of-the-night telephone call from her hysterical psychiatrist (Dr Hilarius), who wants her to join in an LSD experiment he is running. 'But she would be damned if she'd take the capsules he'd given her. Literally damned'. No help there. She goes to see her lawyer Roseman, who is mainly concerned with plans to mount a case against the TV lawyer Perry Mason and has no interest in Oedipa and her problem. He merely, vaguely, tries to make crude sexual advances to her. Again, no help. And this sets the pattern of what is to come. All the men who might (should?) help Oedipa recede from her in one way or another—into fantasy, madness, hallucination, some kind of private universe which has no room for any relationships.

The first chapter ends with a reference to her sense of herself as a Rapunzel who, although willing to let her hair down to someone, found that the one time she did so her hair fell out. The man could not reach her: she 'had really never escaped the confinement of that tower'. This is followed by her memory of a picture she had seen in Mexico City in which some girls who are imprisoned in a tower are 'embroidering a kind of tapestry which spilled out the slit windows and into a void seeking hopelessly to fill the void'. These 'Embroiderers of the Terrestrial Blanket' made Oedipa 'cry'. She cried because she realized that there is 'no escape' for a 'captive maiden'; realized 'that her tower, its height and architecture, are like her ego only incidental: that what really keeps her where she is is magic, anonymous and malignant, visited on her from outside and for no reason at all'. As to this conviction concerning the existence of 'anonymous and malignant' magic, the action of the book serves to open up the whole question. For, if it is true, then the only adequate rational reaction would be paranoia. But things are not so simple as that. Before leaving this consideration of what the first chapter opens up, I want to quote one rather strange passage, usually overlooked:

> As things developed, she was to have all manner of revelations. Hardly about Pierce Inverarity, or herself; but about what remained yet had somehow before this stayed away. There had hung the sense of buffering, insulation, she had noticed the absence of intensity, as if watching a movie, just perceptibly out of focus, that the projectionist refused to fix.

'Revelations' is suggestive enough—the word occurs often in the book—and opens up the possibility of a religious dimension to the novel (I'll come back to that). But that sense of something that had somehow remained and yet stayed away, and that absence of intensity which is like a movie slightly out of focus—this suggests strange states of mind, odd intimations of something between presence and absence, a sense of something, an image, a picture, a plot that is not quite visibly *there* but not quite visibly *not* there either. Such strange sensations, which seem to take place at the very interface between meaning and non-meaning, will occur to Oedipa increasingly as she sets out on her quest, alone, to the suitably named city of San Narciso.

As she drives in and looks down at the city ('less an identifiable city than a grouping of concepts'), she is reminded 'of the first time she'd opened a transistor radio to replace a battery and seen her first printed circuit'.

> Though she knew even less about radios than about Southern California, there were to both outward patterns a hieroglyphic sense of concealed meaning, of an intent to communicate. There'd seemed no limit to what the printed circuit could have told her (if she had tried to find out); so in her first minute of San Narciso, a revelation also trembled just past the threshold of her understanding.

She feels for a moment as though she and her car 'seemed parked at the centre of an odd, religious instant'; but a cloud comes, or the smog thickens, and the ' "religious instant", whatever it might've been', is broken up. Again she experiences a kind of brink moment—somewhere between smog and revelation, on the edge or verge of a possible 'religious instant'—but the dubiety is, as always, there. There may be a 'concealed meaning . . . an intent to communicate'; but there may not.

'Communicate' (cf. 'communion' in *V.*) is the key word. The novel is concerned with all aspects of communication—voices, postal systems, postage stamps, newspapers, books, radio, TV, telephones, signs on walls, acronyms, drawings, doodlings, etc. Then there is the possibility of some kind of religious communication. Is something being 'revealed' to Oedipa—whether on a sinister secular level, or on a more sacred plane—or is she simply sorting and shuffling clues of very uncertain status and validity? In any case, there are only 'clues', 'never the central truth itself', for if that should blaze out it 'would destroy its own message irretrievably'. Communication—if indeed there is any communication—can only be imperfect, incomplete. Oedipa is later to wonder if all the clues that come her way 'were only some kind of compensation. To make up for her having lost the direct, epileptic Word, the cry that might abolish the night'. The 'Word' is singular; clues are uncontrollably plural. Having 'lost'—or never having had—the 'Word', Oedipa is doomed to be the recipient/percipient of an ever-increasing number of clues which point to other possible clues which point to other possible clues which . . . there is no end to it. The 'cry' that might have ended the night is replaced by a 'crying' that can only extend it.

To recount Oedipa's encounter with the many possible clues that seem to 'bloom' for her as she pursues her inquiries would be a pointless exercise. From the drawing of a muted horn on a latrine wall to the detailed academic reconstructions and speculations of an English professor (Emory Bortz), the clues and signs seem obvious enough and, regarded in a certain way, seem to cohere. Indeed that becomes part of Oedipa's problem: they are *too* obvious and seem to fit together only too neatly.

> If one object behind her discovery of what she was to label the Tristero System or often only the Tristero (as if it might be something's secret title) were to bring an end to her encapsulation in her tower, then that night's infidelity with Metzger would logically be the starting point for it; logically. That's what would come to haunt her most, perhaps; the way it fitted, logically, together. As if (as she'd guessed that first minute in San Narciso) there were revelations in progress all around her.

As if. Oedipa does indeed become 'sensitized' (starting with the motel seduction) but can hardly be sure just what her new 'sensitized' state is picking up. She may be 'receiving', but who or what is 'sending'?

The state of communication in the everyday world she comes from is zero. When she receives a letter from her husband, she has an intuition that 'the letter would be newless inside'—so she studies the outside for clues instead. When she and Metzger accidentally witness the secret mail distribution of the Peter Pinguid Society at the Scope Bar near the Yoyodyne aerospace plant, she discovers that it is indeed an illegal system ('Delivering the mail is a government monopoly') which makes use of the Yoyodyne inter-office delivery. But, more to the point, the letters delivered have nothing to communicate. The members of this secret society (there are a number of such eccentric societies in the book) simply have a rule that they have to send a letter a week: as Oedipa discovers, they are usually notes with no content. More newless letters. Oedipa's problem is whether she has in fact discovered, stumbled across, been lured by, a *genuinely* alternative mode of communication which does convey real messages in a way that subverts the 'government monopoly— namely, the Tristero (another name that invites being played with—a meeting with sadness and terror, for example). And, if so, will it release her from her isolation—or confirm it? Will it offer the possibility of real communication 'and revelation'—or like the Peter Pinguid Society system merely reveal a pointless secrecy concealing meaningless, 'newsless' repetitions? If, that is, it exists at all.

The play that Oedipa actually sees—the 'performance' within that larger performance called history—is supposedly by one Richard Wharfinger, a Jacobean dramatist. It is called *The Courier's Tragedy* and is indeed about competing 'communications' systems. It is performed in a theatre located between 'a traffic analysis firm and a wildcat transistor outfit'—that is, between circulation and communication, as Frank Kermode has noted. It concerns another postal monopoly, owned by the Thurn and Taxis family (this seems to be historically accurate); and a rebellious, insurgent counterforce which dedicates itself to subverting, muffling, 'muting' the official system—the Tristero. Oedipa finds herself drawn into 'the landscape of evil Richard Wharfinger had fashioned for his 17th-century audiences, so preapocalyptic, death-wishful, sensually fatigued, unprepared, a little poignantly, for that abyss of civil war that had been waiting, cold and deep, only a few years ahead of them'. This, of course, refers to the civil war in England in the seventeenth century. But we should be alert to the fact that any novel about California which refers to '49' is bound to awaken echoes of the Gold Rush of 1849; and at this date too there was a civil war 'waiting' for America 'only a few years ahead' (twelve, in fact). The mining camps in the Gold Rush had their own kind of autonomous, somewhat anarchic organization—well outside any government control—and even, I gather, their own private mail systems. It is also suggested in the book that 1849—50 saw the arrival of the Tristero in America. The novel is making suggestive play with points and echoes in history, just as Wharfinger's macabre play involves the transformation of dead bones into ink, thus seeming to echo or anticipate an episode recounted in the novel in which the bones of dead GI soldiers in the Second World War were brought back from Italy (by the Mafia) and used in cigarette filters or wine. 1849 perhaps—perhaps—offered the possibility of a new kind of America, run and arranged in an entirely different kind of way. But the civil war was just those few years ahead, and the possibility disappeared (or went underground). A century later, 1949, saw the start of the Cold War and the beginning of what was arguably one of America's most conformist periods.

This is all part of the 'performance' of which Oedipa is a witness. In the course of this particular performance of Wharfinger's play there is a shock because it 'names' the 'name' that seemed to have been previously avoided:

> No hallowed skein of stars can ward, I trow,
> Who's once been set his tryst with Trystero.

'Trystero. The word hung in the air as the act ended . . . hung in the dark to puzzle Oedipa Maas, but not yet to exert the power over her it was to'. This is Oedipa's crucial 'tryst' with 'Trystero'—the name, the word. It is indeed, chronologically, her first encounter with the actual word; she and the name literally 'meet' just before the middle of the book. And after that she doesn't find clues—the clues find her, indeed, seem to besiege her in every form, while she tries to work out what, if anything, the Tristero really signifies.

The start of chapter 4 (the book has six chapters) makes the change explicit, referring to 'other revelations which now seemed to come crowding in exponentially, as if the more she collected the more would come to her, until everything she saw, smelled, dreamed, remembered, would somehow come to be woven into The Tristero'. Her danger—or would it be her deliverance?—is that the 'word' might come to have total 'power over her'. She might then become like Stencil, who 'stencilized' all reality into 'V.'; or she might be moving into a significant discovery about history and the very reality of America itself. Obsession—or revelation. But she tries to go on sorting and shuffling, in the continuing absence of 'the direct, epileptic Word'.

While the word 'Tristero' preoccupies Oedipa, another word equally bothers another of the 'leads' she meets, John Nefastis, and that word—so important in Pynchon—is 'entropy'. As Nefastis explains, 'there were two distinct kinds of this entropy. One having to do with heat-engines, the other to do with communication'. Nefastis has a 'machine' based on the Scotch scientist Clerk Maxwell's postulation of something known as Maxwell's Demon. This machine (which Nefastis has tried to make literal) suggests a situation in which there is a box of molecules moving at different speeds and in which 'the Demon' could simply sort out the slow ones from the fast ones: this would create a region of high temperature which could be used to drive a heat engine. 'Since the Demon only sat and sorted, you wouldn't have put any real work into the system. So you would be violating the Second Law of Thermodynamics, getting something for nothing, causing perpetual motion!' To which Oedipa sceptically replies: 'Sorting isn't work?'

The problem here centres on the fact that there seems to be an opposition between thermodynamic entropy and entropy in information theory. As thermodynamic entropy increases in a system, variety and potential diminish, and the certainty of information about the system increases. However, in information theory, 'entropy' refers to the measure of uncertainty in a system. Put very crudely, we can say this: in a thermodynamic system, as things tend towards stagnation, repetition, predictability, they approach a terminal state in which there is no more energy available for new work; in information theory, the higher the degree of disorganization, noise, uncertainty, the more possibility there is for new signals, new information. Nefastis tries to explain:

> She did gather that there were two distinct kinds of this entropy. One having to do with heat engines, the other to do with communication. The equation for one, back in the 30's, had looked very like the equation for the other. It was a coincidence. The two fields were entirely unconnected, except at one point: Maxwell's Demon. As the Demon sat and sorted his molecules into hot and cold, the system was said to lose entropy. But somehow the loss was offset by the information the Demon gained about what molecules were where.

'Communication is the key,' cried Nefastis. . . . 'Entropy is a figure of speech, then, a Metaphor. It connects the world of thermodynamics to the world of information flow. The Machine uses both. The Demon makes the metaphor not only verbally graceful, but also objectively true.'

His machine has a picture of Clerk Maxwell on it, and if the watcher is a true 'sensitive' he or she will be able to receive and return information from the box, and then the eyes of the portrait will move. But Nefastis is, of course, a lunatic—a 'believer', like so many other figures in the book. A 'believer' not in any genuine faith but in a crazy fantasy of his own making. In the end it emerges that he only wants to have intercourse with Oedipa in front of the television. But it is true that in one form or another 'communication' *is* the key, and Oedipa—demonically or not—will have to go on 'sorting' out the clues (molecules), trying to discover which information really works against entropy as opposed to the kind of non-information ('newsless' letters) that effectively accelerates it. She has to try to decide what kind of revelation or revelations, exactly, she is having.

Some critics regard the novel as unambiguously religious in its implications. What happens to Oedipa, for instance, can be regarded as echoing episodes in the life of Mary, mother of Christ. Then again, after a particularly gruesome scene in *The Courier's Tragedy,* a demented figure named Ercole who has just tortured someone to death (among other things, tearing out his tongue and leaving him to die amid 'tongueless attempts to pray': the possibility of the gift—and the loss—of 'tongues' runs through the book in various forms) says:

> The pitiless unmanning is most meet,
> Thinks Ercole the zany Paraclete
> Descended this malign, Unholy Ghost,
> Let us begin thy frightful Pentecost.

The context perverts the religious words, but perhaps this is a reflection of the perverse Pentecost towards which the book may be moving. As Edward Mendelson has pointed out, 49 is the pentecostal number (the Sunday seven weeks after Easter), but Pentecost derives from the Greek for 'fifty', so the moment at the end of the book when the auctioneer's spread arms are specifically likened to a 'gesture that seemed to belong to the priesthood of some remote culture' is like the moment before a pentecostal revelation when we would all be able to speak in tongues—and understand 'the Word' directly.

The word 'God' is often used, and sometimes seriously. The Tristero system—in its ambiguous aspects—has been seen as representing the sacred dimension to existence, albeit often in a demonic form. Their sign of the muted posthorn may intimate not only a determination to disrupt conventional 'profane' modes of communication but also a determination to block the trumpet of apocalypse. Certainly, although the Tristero may offer some kind of alternative to the apparently 'normal' but utterly alienated irreligious and loveless, and 'narcissistic', life of contemporary society (at least as depicted in the California of the book), their manifestations—if that is what they are—are nearly always sinister and connected with death. Their

postage stamps, for instance, distort ordinary stamps by adding something menacing—poisonous flowers, for example, or a head at an impossible angle. On one stamp, which supposedly celebrated 'Columbus Announcing His Discovery' (i.e. of America), 'the faces of three courtiers, receiving the news at the right-hand side of the stamp, had been subtly altered to express uncontrollable fright'. So, if we believe everything about the Tristero that seems to come our (or Oedipa's) way, we may conclude that the revelation of a 'sacred' pattern underlying the profane patterns of the surface may be a revelation of ultimate terror and dread. Edward Mendelson has been quick enough to note that the word 'hierophany' which appears in the book (a map Oedipa sees seems to offer 'some promise of hierophany') is not a standard word but a coinage by Mircea Eliade, and he quotes Eliade's definition: 'To designate the *act of* manifestation of the sacred, we have proposed the term hierophany . . . the manifestation of something of a wholly different order, a reality that does not belong to our world, in objects that are an integral part of our natural "profane" world.' This might indeed cover the Tristero very well, though from such a 'sacred' realm that it may well be a very 'unholy ghost' indeed who descends. (Not for nothing are two of the acronyms associated with the Tristero—and with each other—W.A.S.T.E. and D.E.A.T.H.)

On the other hand, seen as a historical phenomenon—an underground movement composed of and standing for 'the Disinherited', which now uses 'silence, impersonation, opposition masquerading as allegiance', and which does have a secret method of communication which allows many 'isolates' (Pynchon deliberately picking up Melville's word, from a context that suggests that all Americans are 'isolates') to 'keep in touch'—the Tristero system would not be the apocalyptic agents of death and doom and God knows what kind of Pentecost, but rather the kind of protoanarchic group with which Pynchon's work shows sympathy. (The founder of the Tristero was 'perhaps a madman, perhaps an honest rebel, according to some a con artist', so, if you want to take the historical account, then the movement was indeed rooted in total ambiguity and dubiety—or plurality of content and intent.)

'Anarchy' is perhaps a crucial clue. During the night when Oedipa lets herself drift through San Francisco she meets an old anarchist acquaintance, Jesus (*sic*) Arrabal. He says to her:

> You know what a miracle is. Not what Bakunin said. But another world's intrusion into this one. Most of the time we coexist peacefully, but when we do touch there's cataclysm. Like the church we hate, anarchists also believe in another world. Where revolutions break out spontaneous and leaderless, and the soul's talent for consensus allows the masses to work together without effort, automatic as the body itself. And yet, *sẽná*, if any of it should ever really happen that perfectly, I would also have to cry miracle. An anarchist miracle.

The 'anarchist miracle' would not involve the intrusion of the 'sacred' world into our profane one; rather it would be a kind of 'revolution' leading to a whole new way of living together in this world. It would be 'another world'—but still secular. A mundane miracle. Even here the possibility is undermined: Arrabal has an anarchist newspaper with him called *Regeneración*. But the date of the paper is 1904—a 'communication' so delayed as perhaps to be, literally, out of date.

Oedipa's night of drifting in the Bay Area brings her problems to a head. The whole area is 'saturated' with what seem like clues and references to the Tristero. She even comes across a group of children playing to a song that includes references to 'Tristeroe' and 'taxi'—by which time the clues are becoming worse than meaningless. Her 'sorting' problem has reached its limit. 'Later, possibly, she would have trouble sorting the night into real and dreamed'. Possibly. Nothing is certain. As Driblette (the director of *The Courier's Tragedy*) had warned Oedipa: 'You can put together clues, develop a thesis, or several. . . . You could waste your life that way and never touch the truth'. It was after seeing that play that Oedipa wrote in her memo book *'Shall I project a world?'* And there is no way in which she can find out how much she is projecting, and how much she is perceiving or receiving. What might be accidental, random, chance, and what might be plotted, determined, purposive, she has no way of establishing; and she gives up trying to 'check out' the possible clues. Her problem is beyond verification or falsification. She has emerged from 'narcissism', but is it only to enter into 'paranoia'? She runs over the possibilities:

> Either you have stumbled indeed . . . onto a secret richness and concealed density of dream; onto a network by which X number of Americans are truly communicating whilst reserving their lies, recitations of routine, arid betrayals of spiritual poverty, for the official government system; maybe even onto a real alternative to the exitlessness, to the absence of surprise to life, that harrows the head of everybody American you know, and you too, sweetie. Or you are hallucinating it. Or a plot has been mounted against you . . . so labyrinthine that it must have meaning beyond just a practical joke. Or you are fantasying some such plot, in which case you are a nut, out of your skull.

Looking at the possibilities, she does not like any of them and just hopes that she is 'mentally ill'. And this is where we feel the full poignancy of her position. 'For this, oh God, was the void. There was nobody who could help her. Nobody in the world'.

The problem is finally about America. There is the America of San Narciso, but is there perhaps another America? An America of the 'disinherited' (but 'What was left to inherit?' Oedipa wonders—transients, squatters, drifters, exiles within the system, people existing in the invisible interstices of official society, like those who live 'among a web of telephone wires, living in the very copper rigging and secular miracle of communication, untroubled by the dumb voltages flickering their miles, the night long, in the thousands of unheard messages'. The Tristero system might be a great hoax; but it might be 'all true'. And here is perhaps the most crucial and one of the most eloquent and powerful passages in the book:

Who knew? Perhaps she'd be hounded someday as far as joining Tristero itself, if it existed, in its twilight, its aloofness, its waiting. The waiting above all; if not for another set of possibilities to replace those that had conditioned the land to accept any San Narciso among its most tender flesh without a reflex or a cry, then at least, at the very least, waiting for a symmetry of choices to break down, to go skew. She had heard all about excluded middles; they were bad shit, to be avoided; and how had it ever happened here, with the chances once so good for diversity? For it was now like walking among matrices of a great digital computer, the zeroes and ones twinned above, hanging like balanced mobiles right and left, ahead, thick, maybe endless. Behind the hieroglyphic streets there would be either a transcendent meaning, or only the earth. . . . Ones and zeroes. So did the couples arrange themselves. . . . Another mode of meaning behind the obvious, or none. Either Oedipa in the orbiting ecstasy of a true paranoia, or a real Tristero. For there either was some Tristero beyond the appearance of the legacy America, or there was just America and if there was just America then it seemed the only way she could continue, and manage to be at all relevant to it, was as an alien, unfurrowed, assumed full circle into some paranoia.

The law of the 'excluded middle'—as I understand it—is that a statement is either true or false. There cannot be anything in between. Either it is raining, or it is not. Yet there are those strange, atmospheric conditions, not easily classifiable, in which moistness and dryness seem strangely mixed, which might make us—illogically, unphilosophically—long to admit the 'excluded middle', a middle term for something real but unascertainable. Oedipa is not at ease in a world of binary oppositions—ones and zeroes. Recall that apparently incomprehensible sentence in which it was stated that she would have revelations 'about what remained yet had somehow, before this, stayed away'. The law of the excluded middle would say that either it was there or it was not there. Quite apart from considerations of logic, such a rigidity forecloses on the possibility of unforeseen 'diversity' and irresolvable dubiety. Yet it is into just such an area of possible diversity and dubiety that Oedipa has stumbled—and we, as readers, along with her. Oedipa is mentally in a world of 'if' and 'perhaps', walking through an accredited world of either/or. It is part of her pain, her dilemma and, perhaps, her emancipation. At the auction which concludes the book, leaving all in suspension, the auctioneer is indeed likened to a priest—but also to a 'puppet-master'. There is no way in which Oedipa can be sure just what kind of 'performance' she has been—is—present at. And there is no way in which we can, either. And yet, at the end, as we both finish and wait to begin, something—and this is part of the deceptive magic of the book—seems to remain. Even while it stays away. (pp. 56-73)

Tony Tanner, in his Thomas Pynchon, *Methuen & Co. Ltd., 1982, 95 p.*

An excerpt from *The Crying of Lot 49*

[Oedipa] drove into San Narciso on a Sunday, in a rented Impala. Nothing was happening. She looked down a slope, needing to squint for the sunlight, onto a vast sprawl of houses which had grown up all together, like a well-tended crop, from the dull brown earth; and she thought of the time she'd opened a transistor radio to replace a battery and seen her first printed circuit. The ordered swirl of houses and streets, from this high angle, sprang at her now with the same unexpected, astonishing clarity as the circuit card had. Though she knew even less about radios than about Southern Californians, there were to both outward patterns a hieroglyphic sense of concealed meaning, of an intent to communicate. There'd seemed no limit to what the printed circuit could have told her (if she had tried to find out); so in her first minute of San Narciso, a revelation also trembled just past the threshold of her understanding. Smog hung all round the horizon, the sun on the bright beige countryside was painful; she and the Chevy seemed parked at the centre of an odd, religious instant. As if, on some other frequency, or out of the eye of some whirlwind rotating too slow for her heated skin even to feel the centrifugal coolness of, words were being spoken. She suspected that much. She thought of Mucho, her husband, trying to believe in his job.

Thomas Pynchon, in his The Crying of Lot 49, *Harper & Row, 1966.*

Robert N. Watson

> Oedipa wondered whether, at the end of this (if it were supposed to end), she too might not be left with only compiled memories of clues, announcements, intimations, but never the central truth itself. . . .

These are the musings of Oedipa Maas, the heroine of Thomas Pynchon's ***The Crying of Lot 49,*** as the spectral Tristero system invades her comfortable suburban life. Her efforts to execute the will of a former lover, the industrialist Pierce Inverarity, reveal to her a vast and constantly exfoliating conspiracy of America's downcast and disinherited, apparently the survival of a Tristero conspiracy that began in Europe centuries ago in a dispute over hereditary rights to the official postal monopoly. Whether this is a real conspiracy or a fabrication of her paranoia troubles both Oedipa and the reader throughout the book, and at the end she is sitting in an auction hall, waiting for one of the grim anonymous men around her to bid for some forged postage stamps, and thereby reveal himself as a palpable agent (and hence palpable evidence) of the Tristero.

One of the very few points on which the book's critics agree is that Pynchon never reveals this "central truth," never lets us know who, if anyone, stands up to claim lot 49 for Tristero; they generally agree that this irresolution accords, for better or for worse, with the book's epistemological and religious doubts, and its teasing way of conveying those doubts. But I believe Pynchon asks us to recognize that, paradoxically, the Tristero bidder will be none other than Oedipa herself. Instead of feeling uncertainty

at the end, we should be savoring the delicious irony of Oedipa surveying the room, "trying to guess which one was her target, her enemy, perhaps her proof," unaware of the imminent shock of self-recognition. The premature ending of the book is not a pointless tease: we are left anticipating that culmination of Oedipa's moral and political education, and we are obliged to participate in the culminating discovery. Reading the ending this way established ***Lot 49*** as a more conventional sort of novel than it has heretofore been considered, a novel about the education of its central character that educates the reader in the process; it is a coherent book, with an ethical message underlying its narrative shape and its theological analogies, rather than merely a cluster of amusing games, patterns, and allusions. The narrative prepares us, as it prepares Oedipa, for a great off-stage moment of recognition and reversal—the Aristotelian *peripeteia* and *anagnorisis*.

The comparison to Greek drama is invited by Oedipa's name ("Your absurd name, an ancient Greek," as Buck Mulligan says to Stephen Dedalus on the first page of *Ulysses*). Like many other names in the book—Manny Di Presso, Ghengis Cohen—the name has simple comic value: the leap from Oedipa Maas to the concept of oedipal mothers is an easy one. Shortened as if often is to "Oed," the name contributes to the book's theme of transsexuality, paralleling the nametag that makes her into Arnold Snarb in the gay bar, and complementing such male names as Mike Fallopian and Stanley Koteks, which of course allude to the anatomy and sanitation of strictly female processes. But the highlighted question that opens the book's blurb—"Who is Oedipa Maas?"—points back suggestively to the times the sphinx and the oracle asked obliquely, Who is Oedipus? The book's ending, as I read it, refocuses our attention from the cheap psychoanalytic joke to the more complex Greek story. Oedipus gained the throne by identifying the creature who walks first on four legs, then on two legs, then on three legs. The answer was man himself, and as Sophocles extends the story backwards to Oedipus' crawling infancy and forward to his wandering with a blind-man's cane, we recognize that Oedipus' answer was essentially Oedipus himself. The oracle later confronts King Oedipus with another puzzle: to lift the plague from his people, he must find and eradicate from his kingdom the man who killed his own father and married his own mother. Even more clearly than in the sphinx's riddle, Oedipus finds, to his huge dismay, that the answer is Oedipus.

Oedipa attacks the enigma of the Tristero with much the same hubristic complacency that characterizes her namesake's pursuit of the pariah the oracle described. But for Oedipa as for Oedipus, fate provides the revelations with a momentum of their own, and leaves the detective cowering from the solutions she had formerly been pursuing:

> She busrode and walked on into the lightening morning, giving herself up to a fatalism rare for her. Where was the Oedipa who'd driven so bravely up here from San Narciso? That optimistic baby had come on so like the private eye in any long-ago radio drama, believing all you needed was grit, resourcefulness, exemption

from hidebound cops' rules, to solve any great mystery.

Pierce Inverarity last spoke to her in the voice of just such a private eye, "The Shadow"; and the book persistently identifies shadows with the Tristero. In becoming the detective, she becomes part of the sinister force that detective is pursuing. When Oedipa finally penetrates the "great mystery" which (like the "strange mold" overrunning her herb garden) she evisions afflicting her whole nation, she will discover that, in an Oedipal paradox, she has been searching for herself. The result for her, as for Oedipus, is a guilt-ridden interval of self-imposed blindness, followed by exile; exile is associated with Tristero as frequently as shadows are, and Oedipa endures a version of Soviet "internal exile," in which she does not leave her country's territory but becomes a non-person within it, alien to the political system and to her former self.

The Oedipa we meet as the book opens is as alien as possible from the poor exiles, losers, outcasts, and isolates who evidently constitute the Tristero network. She is utterly comfortable and complacent, sampling kirsch-laced fondue at a Tupperware party, ambling "to the market in downtown Kinneret-Among-The-Pines to buy ricotta and listen to the Muzak," then on to "the sunned gathering of her marjoram and sweet basil from the herb garden, reading of book reviews in the latest *Scientific American,* into the layering of a lasagna, garlicking of a bread, tearing up of romaine leaves, eventually, oven on, into the mixing of the twilight's whiskey sours against the arrival of her husband" home from work. She declares herself "a Young Republican," and looks back on vacations in Mexico with a wealthy industrialist, as well as the sort of college education that trained her for hunting down variants in obscure Jacobean texts, rather than for protesting political and economic oppression. The end of the first chapter describes this comfort as a trap, a magic tower in which the princess is imprisoned. Pierce's effort to rescue her met with mixed success: he eventually penetrated the tower (slipping the lock with a credit-card, appropriately enough), "But all that had gone on between them had never really escaped the confinement of that tower. . . . Pierce had taken her away from nothing, there'd been no escape. What did she so desire escape from? . . . If the tower is everywhere and the knight of deliverance no proof against its magic, what else?"

What else, of course, is what follows: the harrowing of Oedipa's internal landscape. Pierce's codicil implicitly bequeathed the rescue-mission to Metzger, whose task of executing Pierce's will with Oedipa (the suggestive terminology is really Pynchon's) quickly involves replacing Pierce as her lover, "pierc[ing] her":

> If one object behind her discovery of what she was to label the Tristero System or often only The Tristero (as if it might be something's secret title) were to bring to an end her encapsulation in her tower, then that night's infidelity with Metzger would logically be the starting point for it; logically. That's what would come to haunt her most, perhaps; the way it fitted, logically, together. As if (as she'd guessed that first minute

in San Narciso) there were revelation in progress all around her.

But throughout the book Oedipa resists recognizing syllogistic patterns which indicate that she is what is being revealed, that the crucial revelations are not around her, but of her and within her. Her seduction by Metzger consists, not of the unveiling of any mystery foreign to Oedipa, but rather the unveiling of the heavily insulated Oedipa herself, in the game of Strip Botticelli. Significantly, as she asks Metzger question after question in an effort to penetrate his secret, she herself is the one being steadily exposed (both physically and psychologically) and eventually penetrated by her own inquiries. The Tristero begins to emerge only when Oedipa loses what Pynchon repeatedly characterizes as her "insulation" from the world's pressures, and feels Metzger's "thigh, warm through his suit and her slacks."

A few pages later the Tristero itself is the creature performing the figurative strip-tease:

> As if the breakaway gowns, net bras, jeweled garters and G-strings of historical figuration that would fall away were layered dense as Oedipa's own streetclothes in that game with Metzger in front of the Baby Igor movie; as if a plunge toward dawn indefinite black hours long would indeed be necessary before The Tristero could be revealed in its terrible nakedness. Would its smile, then, be coy, and would it flirt away harmlessly backstage, say good night with a Bourbon Street bow and leave her in peace? Or would it instead, the dance ended, come back down the runway, its luminous stare locked to Oedipa's, smile gone malign and pitiless; bend to her alone among the desolate rows of seats and begin to speak words she never wanted to hear?

As this passage looks backward to the game of Strip Botticelli, so it looks forward to the final auction. There Oedipa is again sitting as unobtrusively as possible in an audience of men, waiting for the big exposure, fearing the "smile practiced and relentless" (as compared to the "smile gone malign and pitiless") of the person onstage, and fearing most of all the unspecified words that performer begins to speak. The Tristero-as-stripper metaphor, given the precedent of the Strip Botticelli game, suggests Oedipa's subliminal fear that she will be exposed as a manifestation of Tristero. The final auction scene, given the precedent of the Tristero-as-stripper metaphor, suggests a fear that the auctioneer's words will somehow pick her out of the audience, that in crying lot 49, he will actually be speaking to her alone. The auctioneer, after all, is not the feared Tristero bidder; he is merely inviting that bidder to speak up and identify himself. In both of these clearly related scenes, then, Oedipa is apparently most afraid that she will become the main actor as well as the audience, as if the terrifying Other onstage were the archetypal Doppelgänger, an alienated version of the self returning to claim her in a schizophrenic nightmare.

Towards the end of the book, Oedipa describes the emergence of this alienated Tristero aspect of herself as a stripping, a removal of her social insulation: "They are stripping from me, she said subvocally—feeling like a fluttering curtain in a very high window, moving up to then out over the abyss—they are stripping away, one by one, my men." She is becoming, in other words, a *de facto* member of the Inamorati Anonymous, a typically subvocal and secretive offshoot of the Tristero consisting of people who have despairingly sworn off love—though, again, she refuses to recognize the strong evidence of her membership. The fittingly anonymous man in The Greek Way reveals to her the mysteries of the organization only after listening to her sad story and receiving her assurance that she has "nobody else to tell this to. Only somebody in a bar whose name you don't know." "We're isolates, Arnold," he then tells her, reminding us that Oedipa herself is not only isolated, but also anonymous and unsexed behind her "Arnold Snarb" nametag. Once the man leaves—and his refusal to renew their contact follows the rules governing relationships between I.A. members—"Oedipa sat, feeling as alone as she ever had, now the only woman, she saw, in a room full of drunken male homosexuals. . . . Mucho won't talk to me, Hilarius won't listen, Clerk Maxwell didn't even look at me, and this group, God knows."

Yet Oedipa continues to seek out the mysterious Tristero system, evidently oblivious to the fact that she has been initiated into one of its branches. When she encounters the decrepit sailor on the steps of his flophouse, she reacts with the strategies of a person still possessed of a loving husband, a sane analyst, and an unbroken faith in the social system:

> She ran through then a scene she might play. She might find the landlord of this place, and bring him to court, and buy the sailor a new suit at Roos/Atkins, and shirt, and shoes, and give him the bus fare to Fresno after all. But with a sigh he had released her hand, while she was so lost in the fantasy that she hadn't felt it go away, as if he'd known the best moment to let go.

> "Just mail the letter," he said, "the stamp is on it." She looked and saw the familiar carmine 8¢ airmail, with a jet flying by the Capitol dome. But at the top of the dome stood a tiny figure in deep black, with its arms outstretched.

Oedipa's former world of normal rules and comforts has now been relegated to the status of "fantasy," while the reality of the oppressed Tristero world is no longer in question. Still, even after personally dropping in a Tristero mailbox the sailor's futile effort to renew contact with his estranged wife, Oedipa apparently recognizes no similarity between that letter and the letter she recently received from her estranged husband, the postmark on which indicated that it, too, had travelled across California by Tristero courier.

Eventually Oedipa admits to herself that the prospect of a real Tristero threatens her even more than the prospect of being proved paranoid, though she does not yet understand the reasons for the fear:

> Yet she wanted it all to be fantasy—some clear result of her several wounds, needs, dark doubles. She wanted Hilarius to tell her she was some kind of a nut and needed a rest, and that there was no Trystero. She also wanted to know

why the chance of its being real should menace her so.

Hilarius is the wrong person to ask for an escape route, since he had been trying to enlist her, with a "We want you" that made him a parodic Uncle Sam recruiting for a counter-America, to join several other suburban housewives in an LSD-propelled crossing of "the bridge inward." "She had never asked Dr. Hilarius why, being afraid of all he might answer"; when LSD propels her husband into the Tristero network, we may suspect the shape that threatening answer might have taken. Now himself a full-fledged paranoid, Hilarius refuses to "talk [her] out of a fantasy." She begins passing up promising clues, trying to overlook evidence, as if some Jocasta were warning her to inquire no further into the riddle seemingly infecting her entire nation: she is "anxious that her revelation not expand beyond a certain point. Lest, possibly, it grow larger than she and assume her to itself." For her to discover her intimate kinship with the Tristero (as for Oedipus to discover his intimate kinship with Jocasta) would entail first the moral condemnation, then the utter annihilation, of her former self. In fact, the Inamorati Anonymous began as a network of people seeking self-annihilation, an "underworld of suicides who failed." Though Oedipa is obviously right to fear joining such a group, she also obviously belongs in it:

> Oedipa went back to Echo Courts to drink bourbon until the sun went down and it was as dark as it would ever get. Then she went out and drove on the freeway for a while with her lights out, to see what would happen. But angels were watching.

The Oedipal overtones of her self-destructively extinguished headlights are reinforced two sentences later as her tears "build up pressure around her eyes," a process which began with her first impulse to escape her insulation back in Mexico. Her first act upon deeming her attempt at suicide a failure and stopping her car is to call her one contact in the I.A. organization—an implicit acknowledgment of membership—but she asks him to confirm that her entrapment in the network is merely a hoax, whereas she has just proved it terrifyingly real. He hangs up on her, and her next thought is to try "to face toward the sea," perhaps to imitate the aptly-named Randolph Driblette's self-dissolution into the Pacific.

At this instant, however, she finds that "she'd lost her bearings . . . there could be no barriers between herself and the rest of the land. San Narciso at that moment . . . gave up its residue of uniqueness for her; became a name again, was assumed back into the American continuity of crust and mantle." This passage is extremely complicated, but I believe it marks, not Oedipa's escape from the Tristero legacy, but rather her incorporation by that legacy. Pierce can finally yield his posthumous role in her life, because she has now recognized that this underground of the oppressed does not belong to any one person's plot, or any one person's real estate holdings, but is integral (as she elaborates on the following few pages) to the experience of America. The single focal-point, the tip of the lance of Pierce, "the knight of deliverance," was necessary to penetrate her tower of insulation; now, instead of finding herself in her tower wherever she travels geographically, she finds the Tristero inhabiting not merely San Narciso, but the entire world she perceives. Pierce can return to his grave in peace, because, through the window of his will, Oedipa has finally seen past her own embroideries into the *tristesse* of a whole Other world, has escaped to what Pynchon, in *Gravity's Rainbow,* calls a Counterforce.

All that is left is for Oedipa to recognize that she has become part of this world in the process of discovering its reality and universality. She has mailed a despairing love-letter in the W.A.S.T.E. system, and walked the dreary route of a W.A.S.T.E. courier through the Oakland slums. She has lost all her normal heterosexual contacts, embraced a decrepit and alcoholic sailor in his flophouse, even attempted suicide. Instead of actively pursuing hints of the Tristero, "now she kept a silence, waiting"; she behaves, in other words, precisely as do those who obey the Tristero acronym W.A.S.T.E., We Await Silent Tristero's Empire. The task of executing Pierce's will, which led her to these discoveries, now becomes the clearest evidence of her conversion. Her role as "executor" punningly associates her with the Tristero assassins, especially since she is working to restore a heritage to the deprived. She first considers the possibilitiy that she might herself in some sense "be his heiress," then considers making the Tristero his heir:

> What would the probate judge have to say about spreading some kind of a legacy among them all, all those nameless, maybe as a first installment? Oboy. He'd be on her ass in a microsecond, revoke her letters testamentary, they'd call her names, proclaim her through all Orange County as a redistributionist and pinko. . . . Perhaps she'd be hounded someday as far as joining Tristero itself, if it existed, in its twilight, its aloofness, its waiting. The waiting above all. . . .

She too is awaiting the Apocalyptic moment the book often hints at, the moment when, according to the thirty-seventh Psalm, "those who wait for the Lord shall possess the land," and the meek shall inherit the earth, for which San Narciso and Inverarity Enterprises are metaphors and potential "first installments." The conservative legal system and the right-wing community that narrowly defend property rights have become her enemies, as they are the enemy of all the world's disinherited and unpropertied, and they exclude her from their counsels as a turncoat. Already she has casually decided to become "a fugitive" from the law by leaving Kinneret without testifying about Hilarius' shooting-spree. Now she is irreversibly on the road to becoming the very force that her former comfortable "Young Republican" self had perceived as the enemy, the Other.

The perception of the law—the Man—as an enemy rather than a protector is a crucial distinction between the oppressed black world and the affluent white world in Los Angeles, according to Pynchon's **"A Journey Into The Mind of Watts."** This non-fiction piece, published in *The New York Times Magazine* the same year *Lot 49* appeared, displays largely the same attitudes and attempts largely the same sort of political education that my analysis attri-

butes to the novel. In Watts, "There are still the poor, the defeated, the criminal, the desperate, all hanging in there with what must seem a terrible vitality"; these ghetto blacks are the equivalent of the dark, disinherited, terrifying Tristero. In the novel, Oedipa's insulated world coexists temporally and spatially with an entire Tristero world she must be forced to notice. In the article, Los Angeles is

> the co-existence of two very different cultures; one white and one black.

> While the white culture is concerned with various forms of systematized folly—the economy of the area in fact depending on it—the black culture is stuck pretty much with basic realities like disease, like failure, violence and death, which the whites have mostly chosen—and can afford—to ignore.

Oedipa eventually realizes that "she might have found The Tristero anywhere in her Republic, through any of a hundred lightly-concealed entranceways, a hundred alienations, if only she'd looked." To feel the combination of comfort and complacency Oedipa displays on the novel's opening pages, she must avert her eyes from those entranceways and the suffering they reveal. The same avoidance typifies the white Angelenos in Pynchon's article:

> Somehow it occurs to very few of them to leave at the Imperial Highway exit for a change, go east instead of west only a few blocks, and take a look at Watts. A quick look. The simplest kind of beginning. But Watts is country which lies, psychologically, uncounted miles further than most whites seem at present willing to travel.

The article, as its title suggests, seeks to take us on that psychological journey; the novel similarly suggests that Oedipa's tower—and ours—is mostly a state of mind, a convenient suppression of "sensitivity" to an oppressed underworld that is all around us.

The notion that this Other she had perceived as an enemy might be merely a black-and-white photographic negative of herself, or a reversed mirror-reflection of herself, is one that Oedipa has resisted since her quest began, presumably because it is threatening in two ways. It suggests either that her glimpses of the Tristero are a paranoid projection of her fears, a projection she mistakes for external reality, or else that she is somehow implicated in a Counterforce that seems terrifyingly alien to her. To develop the negative, to step through that looking-glass, would be to experience precisely the self-recognition she has been fleeing. She first meets Randolph Driblette in his theater's dressing-room, "a region of brightly-lit mirrors," and he gives her "exactly the same look he'd coached the cast to give each other whenever the subject of the Trystero assassins came up. The knowing look you get in your dreams from a certain unpleasant figure." Throughout her first night in the hotel housing the convention of deaf-mutes, Oedipa "kept waking from a nightmare about something in the mirror across from her bed. . . . When she woke in the morning, she was sitting bolt upright, staring into the mirror at her own exhausted face." When evidence of the Tristero overwhelms her near the end of the book, this classic schizophrenic nightmare recurs: she dreams of "the soft dusk of mirrors out of which something was about to walk, and empty rooms that waited for her. Your gynecologist has no test for what she was pregnant with."

This last comment reminds us that, two pages earlier, Oedipa had called a doctor in L.A. at random and, under the suggestive pseudonym of Grace Bortz, arranged for a pregnancy test; but the inward Jocasta who warns her off unwanted evidence again seems to intervene, and she skips her appointment. Perhaps she is subliminally unwilling to be the one who aborts Grace. Oedipa evidently (and rightly) fears that some "dark double" of herself has been developing inside her, conceived for her by one of her Tristero lovers. She seems to be replicating herself, and not necessarily doing it with mirrors. Empty rooms in a woman's dream often symbolize the interior space of her womb; that space in Oedipa here awaits Oedipa herself. What is specifically "awaited" throughout the novel is "silent Tristero's empire," so the birth of the new Oedipa will implicitly represent the Nativity of this new order. She has come from Kinneret, and Lake Kinneret was an alternative name for the Sea of Galilee; her conversion constitutes precisely what Jesús Arrabal (whose name, in Spanish, means suburban Savior) defined as "a miracle," namely, "intrusions into this world from another." The initial T of Tristero could easily be mistaken for a cross, as Oedipa herself points out while surveying an historical marker. All along the Tristero network, the disinherited are awaiting "the Word," and their pleas for that Word often come through her phone late at night, as did Pierce's last call; she will be the Word made Flesh. Pynchon first published portions of this novel under the title, **"The World (This One), The Flesh (Mrs. Oedipa Maas), and the Testament of Pierce Inverarity."** The fittingly-named Pierce, in handing down his Testament, immaculately fathers a new dispensation within and through Oedipa. She is only one convert, but if she is in a position to redistribute a legacy that seems to include all of America, or if Pynchon is a skillful enough apostle that the story of her miraculous rebirth converts the rest of us, then this conversion will truly entail a whole new dispensation. Oedipas, as the locus of incarnation, is what is in Pierce's new testament (through the codicil) that was not in the old. She attends a performance of *The Courier's Tragedy,* Pynchon's parody of the bloody and blustery Jacobean revenge-tragedies; toward the end of the play, the noble Gennaro receives a letter "miraculously" rewritten into truth by the Tristero forces, "closing with the revelation" of an earlier mass-murder by the villainous Angelo. The New Testament itself closes with Revelations, and Gennaro describes his revelation in terms of immaculate conception, holy incarnation, martyrdom, and a testament that affirms them:

> But now the bones of these Immaculate
> Have mingled with the blood of Niccoló,
> And innocence with innocence is join'd,
> A wedlock whose sole child is miracle:
> A life's base lie, rewritten into truth,
> That truth it is, we all bear testament. . . .

James Nohrnberg points out that Oedipa's embrace of the sailor resembles a pietà, and that her sense of the onset of the Tristero resembles an Annunciation:

Oedipa herself compares her sensitivity to the Tristero to the "secular announcement" felt by an epileptic, the "pure piercing grace note announcing his seizure." At another moment of aborted insight, Oedipa "felt briefly penetrated, as if the bright winged thing had actually made it to the sanctuary of her heart"; "She waited for the winged brightness to announce its safe arrival."

If Pierce is one immaculate father of the fetus for which Oedipa schedules a pregnancy test, Randolph Driblette is another: his kinship with the Tristero is the "transient, winged shape, needing to settle at once in the warm host, or dissipate forever into the dark" that Oedipa is here seeking to embrace. The Virgin Mary supposedly conceived without the company of man, impregnated instead by the Holy Ghost. Oedipa, while complaining that all her men have been taken from her, nonetheless conceives, with the aid of these two dead men. If the Tristero is analogous to Christianity, and the book persistently implies it is, then surely these two are Holy Ghosts (the Tristero was itself mistaken for a "ghost" by Thurn and Taxis. Driblette says he directed *The Courier's Tragedy* so as "To give the spirit flesh. The words, who cares?" This is the New Testament, the triumph of the spirit over the letter; this Testament, like Pierce's, promises its legacy to the oppressed. But the spirit must arise *through* the words; that transfer of ownership will only occur when Christ speaks again, in the form of the Last Judgement, announced by a trumpet. The new Oedipa must be the one to remove at long last the mute from the Tristero post-horn, and speak up at the crying of lot 49. Oedipa worries that she may have "lost the direct, epileptic Word, the cry that might abolish the night," presumably the Word of the Light of Light which would release Tristero from its characteristically dark exile where, like Oedipa, it "kept a silence, waiting, as if to be illuminated." In the first chapter of the Gospel According to Luke, John the Baptist's father says that God "has raised up a horn of salvation for us." "The Horn" seems to be a slang name for the Tristero, and in fact one of Oedipa's final clues is an article by someone named Jean-Baptiste Moens.

But Oedipa never fully understands the Annunciation and the mission spelled out for her in Pierce's Testament until she feels compelled to respond to the crying of the auctioneer, Loren Passerine, shortly after the book's narrative ends. Edward Mendelson describes this auction as a parodic negative of Pentecost, a notion nicely supported by another echo in *The Courier's Tragedy.* Pentecost commemorates the day the Holy Ghost descended as tongues of fire and inspired the Disciples with a common speech unknown to them. The Holy Ghost is commonly symbolized by a dove, and the auctioneer's last name is actually a word referring to an order of birds, including the passerine ground-dove. But the description of him as resembling "a descending angel" about to speak frightful words to Oedipa squares better with a parodic Annunciation scene than a parodic Pentecost. The implied visitation of the Holy Ghost might refer to His descent to impregnate Mary rather than to His descent to plant new speech in the Disciples. If we accept the notion that Oedipa will, to her own shock, turn out to be the Tristero bidder, then the possibilities are not mutually exclusive. Oedipa's gestation of a new, Tristero self, the Annunciation of the meaning of that pregnancy, and her Pentecostal moment of finding unexpected foreign speech on her tongue, all culminate together when Oedipa finds herself bidding for Tristero. Possessed in one sense or another by her own Holy Ghosts, Oedipa becomes a re-Incarnation of the spirit of Tristero's founding father, for whom it was named, a man "apt at any time to appear at a public function and begin a speech."

This notion of being pregnant with a new self is linked for Oedipa, as I have suggested, to the sensation of confronting oneself in a mirror; at other times, the idea of a mirror renews Oedipa's suspicion that the Other self is merely an illusion, an optical trick. The problem of distinguishing between one's own reflection and an actual other person is an archetypal and crucial one, characterized by Jacques Lacan as the *stade de miroir,* and utilized to great effect by Lewis Carroll in *Through the Looking-Glass* and by many silent comedians, most notably Harpo Marx. Oedipa faces the even trickier task of understanding that the dark image she confronts is both a reflection of herself *and* an actual Other. Pynchon's suggestion that mirrors divide Oedipa between her former insulated condition and her new alienated condition is strengthened by Emery Bortz's "mirror-image theory, by which any period of instability for Thurn and Taxis must have its reflection in Tristero's shadow-state." At first Oedipa stares into her mirror, trying to draw "dark lines along her eyelids," but finding it impossible to do so. She next encounters a mirror while so heavily insulated against Metzger's Strip-Botticelli game that she collapses in laughter, knocking over a can of hair-spray which shatters the mirror in its flight. Later "she went into the bathroom, tried to find her image in the mirror and couldn't. She had a moment of nearly pure terror. Then remembered that the mirror had broken and fallen into the sink." Finally, after the deluge of Tristero manifestations, she encounters a shadowed version of her reflection in yet another mirror:

> Change your name to Miles, Dean, Serge, and/or Leonard, baby, she advised her reflection in the half-light of that afternoon's vanity mirror. Either way, they'll call it paranoia. They. Either you have stumbled indeed . . . onto a network by which X number of Americans are truly communicating. . . . Or you are hallucinating it. Or a plot has been mounted against you. . . . Or you are fantasying some such plot, in which case you are a nut, Oedipa, out of your skull.

The mirror both elicits and comments on this sort of thinking. The narcissism implicit in conversing with a "vanity mirror" suggests that Oedipa is over-indulging her own fantasies, becoming "the true paranoid for whom all is organized in spheres joyful or threatening about the central pulse of himself." But in Greek myth Narcissus was devotedly pursued by Echo, and figurations of Echo pursue figurations of Narcissus throughout *Lot 49.* When Oedipa arrives in San *Narciso,* she stays at the Echo Courts motel, which in turn has "a swimming pool, whose surface that day was flat"—the sort of watery reflective surface that fatally seduced Narcissus. Indeed, Oedipa

and the narcissistic Metzger often found that "Echo Courts became impossible," partly "because of the stillness of the pool and the blank windows that faced on it." A simulation of the mythic Echo stands in front of the motel, but "The face of the nymph was much like Oedipa's. . . .". When a character in *The Courier's Tragedy* fatally kisses the foot of a statue of Saint Narcissus, the incident is itself an echo of the song "I Want To Kiss Your Feet" that Mucho Maas plays on his radio show. On the book's last page, as Oedipa is shut into the auction hall to confront herself, the sound of the closing door "echoed a moment," itself the echo of the sound of a slamming door on the book's first page, contributing to the book's appearance of being mirrored at its center.

Pynchon adheres to this pattern because Echo and Narcissus correspond symbolically to the two sides of Oedipa's dilemma, and because the ideal solution is their pairing. Echo is supposedly a real creature whom we mistake for the rebound of our own voices, but who is actually trying to call out to us, within the limitations Hera imposed on her speech. (A clear example is Echo's effort to warn Antonio in the fifth act of Webster's *The Duchess of Malfi*—a play of the sort Pynchon parodies in *The Courier's Tragedy*). Narcissus is the opposite: he symbolizes the illusion of an Other, which turns out to be merely a reflection of an over-indulged self. Oedipa fears that, if she believes in the Tristero, she will prove to be Narcissus, mistaking the creations of her own confused perceptions for external reality. But if she refuses to believe in it, she risks discovering that it is a version of Echo, a real warning from an all-too-real creature which she, like Webster's Antonio, fails to heed.

Oedipa is painfully slow to recognize that the Tristero may be both a reflection of her own evolving thoughts and desires, and simultaneously an actual political Counterforce, without contradiction. Confronted with a test of her "sensitivity" to unorthodox modes of communication, in the form of the Nefastis Machine, Oedipa believes momentarily that she has seen the righthand piston move, but seeing no further motion, concludes that she "had seen only a retinal twitch, a misfired nerve cell. Did the true sensitive see more?" It is an important question which she and Pynchon leave temporarily unanswered; for the moment there seems to be no middle ground, nor any way of deciding objectively between the alternatives.

Two pages from the end of the book, Oedipa is still

> waiting for a symmetry of choices to break down, to go skew. . . . For it was now like walking among matrices of a great digital computer, the zeroes and ones twinned above, hanging like balanced mobiles right and left, ahead, thick, maybe endless. Behind the hieroglyphic streets there would either be a transcendent meaning, or only the earth. . . . Either Oedipa in the orbiting ecstasy of a true paranoia, or a real Tristero. For there either was some Tristero beyond the appearance of the legacy America, or there was just America and if there was just America then it seemed the only way she could continue, and manage to be at all relevant to it

was as an alien, unfurrowed, assumed full circle into some paranoia.

The Tristero for Oedipa, like God for Voltaire, is something she will have to invent if it does not exist, so basic has it become to her new political awareness. But she still sees the possibility of a real Tristero and the possibility of her becoming an alien in America as separate alternatives; the auction will force her to recognize their unity. If Oedipa is truly the Incarnation of the Tristero, as Pynchon implies, then the misfiring of her retinal nerve can be as valid a part of it as the movement of a piston. The woman who told her husband he was "too sensitive" to the alienation of his jobs and the squalid, ruined lives they exposed to him, has herself become the ultimate "sensitive." The possibility that Tristero is part of her mind, that it expresses her fears and hostilities, and the alternative possibility that it is a network of embittered outcasts from American opulence and social complacency, have converged more radically than she seems to realize. Her journey into the oppressed shadow-world of America threatens to become a one-way ride when exploration gives way to participation and absorption, very much like the journeys of the protagonists in such political films as *Sullivan's Travels* and—more obviously relevant to Pynchon's own journalistic **"Journey into the Mind of Watts"**—*Black like Me.* The novel presents several instances of such conversions, most notably the Scurvhamites. This sect divided the universe into a saved Godly Creation, to which they belonged, and a doomed "opposite Principle" from which they hoped to win converts:

> But somehow those few saved Scurvhamites found themselves looking out into the gaudy clockwork of the doomed with a certain sick and fascinated horror, and this was to prove fatal. One by one the glamorous prospect of annihilation coaxed them over, until there was no one left in the sect. . . .

The parallel is made explicit by the Scurvhamites' pornographic version of *The Courier's Tragedy,* which (according to Emory Bortz) shows that "they felt Trystero would symbolize the Other quite well." So Oedipa's conversion is part of a long-standing Tristero pattern, a pattern of "opposition masquerading as allegiance"; her allegiance to her affluent world becomes merely a masquerade.

Even at the final auction, Oedipa's apparently binary choices will prove to be unitary. If she bids for the Tristero stamps, then she virtually announces herself as the agent of Tristero; if, on the other hand, she does not bid for this core of Pierce's legacy, then she places herself squarely in the midst of the disinherited, the unpropertied exiles from his capitalist America. If she speaks up during the bidding, then she speaks up for Tristero, wanting "to keep evidence that Tristero exists out of unauthorized hands"; if she remains silent, then she participates in Tristero's characteristic conspiracy of silence, declining to give evidence of her existence and membership.

Shortly before the auction Oedipa ventures into the office of the agent handling the book-bid for the mysterious Tristero bidder, a bidder identified only as being "a stranger," a total "outsider," to the group that normally attends philatelic auctions. The only person at the auction to whom that description obviously applies is Oedipa, an outsider and the only woman among a group of men with indistinguishable faces and costumes. She asks the agent about his book-bidder: " 'He decided to attend the auction in person,' was all Schrift would tell her. 'You might run into him there.' She might." The last two words may be her reply, presented in indirect discourse; but they may also be the narrator's ironic comment: of course she will, if the "he" is actually "Oed." On hearing this news, she naturally decides to attend in person too. Like Oedipus, she is trapped in a self-fulfilling prophecy that drives her to pursue, unwittingly, the shock of self-recognition that fate has long since prepared for her, thinking until the last minute that she will be finding out some evil Other.

Two paragraphs later, Ghengis Cohen encounters her outside the hall and says, "May I ask if you've come to bid, Miz Maas?" She answers no, she only came to watch, then begins to wonder "what she'd do when the bidder revealed himself." This seems to point, by a reductive dirty pun, to Cohen, whom she has just advised to zip his fly. But Oedipa, too, has been a stripper of sorts, and has been the object of countless obscene phone calls from members of Tristero who were "searching . . . for that magical Other who would reveal herself . . . [and] call into being . . . the Word."

Oedipa admits that her only strategy for meeting this revelation is "some vague idea about causing a scene violent enough to bring the cops into it and find out that way who the man really was." The echoes of Alfred Hitchcock plots are unmistakable here. Critics have documented Pynchon's heavy dependence on cinematic allusions in *Gravity's Rainbow,* but not in his other works. In *Lot 49,* the overall plot is standard Hitchcock fare: a comfortable and innocent person stumbles across an almost incredible conspiracy, becomes utterly entangled in it and gravely endangered by it, yet must struggle at times to decide whether the conspiracy is real, or whether he or she has simply gone insane. The strategem of creating a disturbance in the hall to bring in the police points specifically to two films, *The Thirty-Nine Steps* and *North by Northwest.* In *The Thirty-Nine Steps,* after a similar maneuver in the guise of a populist politician, Robert Donat stymies the villains by standing up in the audience and asking Mr. Memory what the thirty-nine steps are. The irony, and it is an irony highly applicable to Oedipa's situation, is that in order to expose the conspiracy, he has to ask the very question he fears the conspirator will be asking Mr. Memory a short while later. Even more obviously germane is Cary Grant's disruption of an auction in *North by Northwest,* where he bids fiercely for an unwanted lot, hoping to gain enough attention from the public and the police to protect him from the men he believes are there to kill him as well as to bid themselves. In both cases the parallel suggests that, in order to carry out her stated plan, Oedipa will have to stand up and make her own bid for lot 49. The allusions help us anticipate the moment when Oedipa realizes she has bitten her own bait, when she is forced to recognize that the only bidder is a formerly furtive aspect of herself.

Oedipa pauses momentarily outside the hall, "wondering if she'd go through with it"—a phrase as applicable to the bidder as to any challenger of that bidder. The auctioneer "stared at her, smiling, as if saying, I'm surprised you actually came"—a phrase that makes at least as much sense addressed to the Tristero bidder, devoted to secrecy and having declared an intention to bid from a distance, as it does addressed to Oedipa. Earlier Oedipa had expressed the fear that someday she "would be betrayed and mocked by a phantom self as the amputee is by a phantom limb"; as she scans the audience looking for the evil Other, her fear has been fulfilled. Next, "An assistant closed the heavy door on the lobby windows and the sun": Oedipa is finally under the shadow of the Shadow, the last voice of Pierce Inverarity and the insubstantial embodiment of the Tristero. "She heard a lock snap shut; the sound echoed a moment." One critic describes Oedipa as an archetypal Quester; here she has followed her "knight of deliverance" from her own tower into its opposite, this chamber of darkness, much as Browning's Childe Roland follows his fellow-knights to the Dark Tower, "When, in the very nick / Of giving up, one time more, came a click / As when a trap shuts—you're inside the den!" All that remains, for either quester, is to stand, recognize the ironies of a self-entrapment which is at once the greatest victory and the greatest defeat, and announce that he or she has arrived and completed the self-consuming quest, by blowing through an unmuted horn.

The book's final words tell us that "Oedipa settled back, to await the crying of lot 49." Stripped of her complacency, alone, despairing, she has joined in Tristero's "aloofness, its waiting"; she too *awaits* silent Tristero's empire. We are left, not with the dire uncertainty critics have attributed to this ending, but instead with a powerful ironic anticipation of the moment when Oedipa recognizes her own conversion and election, and emits her apocalyptic words, bids, soundings of the trumpet. This anticipation converts the book from a playful string of enigmas to a coherent novel of moral and political education. Like Robert Frost's ideal poem, it begins in delight and ends in wisdom. That wisdom is not presented explicitly to the reader any more than it is to Oedipa; Pynchon can expose us to the other world, but the true conversion experience must finally arise from within ourselves. Without that apocalyptic moment of recognition, which for us as for Oedipa must occur outside the narrowly-defined limits of the text, Pynchon's crucial and characteristic political message would be lost. As readers, we toy with our text's riddle—"Who is Oedipa Maas?"—even less self-consciously than Oedipa toys with the task of identifying the Tristero encoded in Pierce's testament. But at the end, we too must realize we have been trapped in an Oedipal riddle: we are Oedipa Maas, and her conversion from complacency has been ours. (pp. 59-74)

Robert N. Watson, "Who Bids for Tristero? The Conversion of Pynchon's Oedipa Maas," in The Southern Humanities Review, *Vol. XVII, No. 1, Winter, 1983, pp. 59-75.*

One would like to say of *The Crying of Lot 49* what T. S. Eliot said of *The Great Gatsby,* that it represents the first step forward for American fiction in some time; for if the road ahead for fiction lies in the direction Borges in his stories has pointed, toward greater philosophical and metaphysical sophistication, Pynchon surely ranks as the most intelligent, most audacious and most accomplished American novelist writing today.

—*Robert Shlav, "The New Novel, USA: Thomas Pynchon," in* The Nation, *1967.*

Lance Olsen

> We all move in an Ellipse of Uncertainty, don't we?
>
> Pynchon *(Gravity's Rainbow)*

Pynchon's penchant for science—particularly for the science of physics—is common knowledge and commonplace. He employs science as a metaphor, a guiding schema for his art, and an aesthetic model representing the phenomenal and spiritual worlds. For Wittgenstein, of whom Pynchon makes multiple mention in *V.,* the world is all that the case is, and for Pynchon the case is primarily one of disorder, heat-death, white noise, communication collapse, and existential blur. In criticism concerning Pynchon's use of science as metaphor, one most often finds discussed the concept of entropy, in which nature, according to the second law of thermodynamics, will reach a state of maximum disorganization and minimum available energy, at which time all change will cease. The next most commonly discussed scientific notion is that of white noise and distortion in information systems. Then comes Maxwell's Demon, the idea of nineteenth-century physicist James Clerk Maxwell, who posed the existence of a small intelligent being who can sort out swifter and slower molecules in a box divided into two compartments, thereby creating an inequality in energy (heat) without the expenditure of work. Little criticism has been devoted to Pynchon's use of relativity theory, which emphasizes the subjectivity of the observer.

In her article on Pynchon, Anne Mangel concludes that by using these concepts as guiding metaphors in his work, he "radically separates himself from earlier twentieth-century writers, like Yeats, Eliot, and Joyce. . . . The complex symbolic structures they created to encircle chaotic experience often resulted in the kinds of static, closed systems Pynchon is so wary of." In the end, the dense and intricate structures at work in modern writers can be filtered into a comprehensible system, but Pynchon's postmodern impulse is exactly the reverse of this. His understanding and use of the New Physics (although, of course, to some extent writers like Eliot and Joyce were familiar with such ideas) underlines the radical distinction between his fictional universes and that of the moderns. He revels in ultimate plurisignification, confusion, and indeterminacy. (pp. 69-70)

[The idea of indeterminacy often appears in physics, yet] it has never been precisely defined. Instead, it has at least three different though related denotations: acausal behavior of physical processes; the unpredictable behavior of such processes; and the essential imprecision of measurement procedures.

The notion of uncertainty in atomic physics is by no means a new one. In fact, it stretches back to the beginnings of Western civilization. The earliest known thesis of uncertainty, which bears some slight resemblance to that found in New Physics, appears in Plato's *Timaeus* (ca. 348 B.C.), where the protagonist explains to Socrates that two levels of reality exist,

> that which always is and never becomes [and] that which is always becoming but never is. The one is apprehensible by intelligence with the aid of reasoning, being eternally the same, the other is the object of opinion and irrational sensation, coming to be and ceasing to be, but never fully real.

The Demiurge has created the phenomenal world after an eternal pattern, and only this perfect pattern can be spoken of with any certainty. The phenomenal world, the copy, can be articulated only in the language of uncertainties.

In *On the Nature of the Universe* (ca. 55 B.C.), Lucretius sets forth Epicurus' elaboration of Democritus' notion of atomic swerve, or *clinamen*. Although generally atoms travel straight down through an undisturbed void at equal speed, albeit with different weights, Lucretius notes,

> at quite indeterminate times and places they swerve ever so little from their course, just so much that you can call it a change of direction. If it were not for this swerve, everything would fall downwards like raindrops through the abyss of space. No collision would take place and no impact of atom on atom would be created.

If it were not for this small degree of uncertainty in the phenomenal world, nothing would ever happen, nothing would ever be created, and will could not logically exist. A perfectly determined world, a perfectly static universe—and Pynchon will echo this view—would be a dead world.

While ancient thought stressed, along with Ovid, that "nothing is constant in the whole world. Everything is in a state of flux, and comes into being as a transient appearance," medieval through early modern thought stressed a thoroughly rational prejudice governed by a theological faith. With the publication of Newton's *Principia* (1678), determinism began its movement toward dominance. The universe became predictable and static.

Not until the nineteenth century did such a view of "reality" begin to crumble. And not until 1892 was Charles Sanders Peirce able to conclude that chance is the basic factor in the universe. During the early 1920's questions arose concerning the limitations of measuring instruments in physics, and hence the growing improbability of attaining any sort of precise data about "the world." Both Erwin Schrödinger and Werner Heisenberg addressed themselves to the problem of indeterminacy, and when the latter attempted to describe the motion of wave-particles in terms of ordinary concepts like position and momentum he realized that the very act of observing a wave-packet disturbed it to such an extent that no accurate information could be gathered about it.

At least one quantum of energy had to be used to make an observation, Heisenberg imagined in what he called a "thought experiment," but the effect of this energy upon the particle was to disturb it so that it was impossible to correct for the disturbance. In other words, one could not know simultaneously to any desired accuracy the position and momentum of an object, no matter how good the instruments used and no matter how careful the procedures. If one knows the position of a particle, and not the momentum (i.e., mass and velocity), one cannot predict the particle's future position or momentum. Inversely, if one knows the momentum and not the position, it is equally impossible to know future position or momentum.

Niels Bohr, the third major figure in the evolution of the uncertainty principle, understood that the crux of the principle was, in essence, a Kierkegaardian belief in the irreconcilable dualism between thought and reality—reality understood is reality changed. To Laplace it had been evident that if we know the present we can predict the future, but the uncertainty principle asserts that we can know neither. For Heisenberg, the causality postulate became an empty statement.

> In view of the intimate connection between the statistical character of the quantum theory and the impression of all perception, it may be suggested that behind the statistical universe of perception there lies a hidden "real" world ruled by causality. Such a speculation seems to us—and we stress this with emphasis—useless and meaningless.

The Platonic real world ruled by causality that exists as a pure pattern behind the phenomenal one became for Heisenberg an empty language game, and the intense discord between the Old and the New Physics became staggering.

William Barrett sums up this discovery by saying the uncertainty principle

> shows that there are essential limits to our ability to know and predict physical states of affairs, and opens up to us a glimpse of a nature that may at bottom be irrational and chaotic—at any rate, our knowledge of it is limited so that we cannot know this not to be the case.

A basic confusion results, then, about whether the universe is in essence chaotic or whether what we can say about it imposes inherent limits on our knowledge—that is, whether the fundamental problem is one of ontology or epistemology. And what more effective mode of discourse to employ when exploring this postmodern question than the fantastic?

In essence, the plotline of *The Crying* follows that of a detective story where a heroine-sleuth attempts to solve a mystery through the logical assembling and interpretation of palpable evidence. What better name is there, then, for the protagonist than "Oedipa," which harkens back to the first detective of them all? Oedipus the King seeks to reduce a complex and chaotic situation to one of simplicity and clarity. He seeks wisdom and thereby control over his experience. He struggles toward a center of illumination. Although the dazzling and terrible intensity of the illumination blinds him, he nonetheless attains the wisdom that he seeks and hence, to a certain degree at least, control of his experience. But the Frequentor of Tupperware Parties' Sphinx is one Pierce Inverarity, whose name intimates complication, puzzlement, and the inveracity at the core of the situation Oedipa is trying to pierce, and whose system, if it is a system, is the irruption of the inadmissible within the changeless legality of everydayness. His riddle is an enigmatic will which, it appears, is somehow tied up with the whole of the Tristero System.

The Crying seems charged with palpable evidence which can be logically assembled and interpreted, although, as is common with a host of postmodern detective stories (those of Kafka and Robbe-Grillet, for example), the reader is never given enough evidence to know who did it, or what did it, and so he suspects everyone. Pynchon's example of the genre is a text of perplexities—I count a bewildering 266 question marks in a brief 138 pages—a text with a remarkably high frequency of mystery-words like "wonder," "chance," "understanding," "hieroglyphics," and "probability"; a text where the very structure of the language reflects the complex and puzzling situation in which Oedipa one day finds herself. At one point early on, for instance, the narrator comments that Mucho believed in cars,

> Maybe to excess: how could he not, seeing people poorer than him come in, Negro, Mexican, cracker, a parade seven days a week, bringing the most god-awful of trade-ins: motorized, metal extensions of themselves, of their families and what their whole lives must be like out there so naked for anybody, a stranger like himself to look at, frame cockeyed, rusty underneath, fender repainted in a shade just off enough to depress the value, if not Mucho himself, inside smelling hopeless of children, supermarket booze, two sometimes three generations of cigarette smokers, or only of dust—and when the cars were swept out you had to look at the actual residue of these lives, and there was no way of telling what things had been truly refused (when so little he supposed came by that out of fear most of it had to be taken and kept) and what had simply (perhaps tragically) been lost: clipped coupons promising savings of 5 or 10 ¢, trading stamps, pink flyers advertising specials at the markets, butts, tooth-shy combs, rags of old underwear or dresses that already were period costumes, for wiping your own breath off the inside of a windshield so you could see whatever it was, a movie, a woman or a car you coveted, a cop who might

pull you over just for a drill, all the bits and pieces coated uniformly, like a salad of despair, in gray dressing of ash, condensed exhaust, dust, body wastes—it made him sick to look, but he had to look.

That is only one sentence, and sentences like it, which are not at all uncommon in the text, are as numerous and tangled as Inverarity's assets. It is a kind of archeological sentence, like those in Joyce's *Finnegans Wake,* Beckett's trilogy, and García Márquez' *Autumn of the Patriarch,* whose information density, parenthetical phrases within parenthetical phrases, epic and chaotic cataloging of a grotesquely decadent world, and convolutions and confusing syntax, all work to form a "salad of despair"; a complex bundle of meaning that indicates the complex universe Oedipa inhabits, and jams the reader's sensibilities. Just as Oedipa feels an information overload before such a complex and uncertain "reality," so too does the reader feel an information overload before such complex and uncertain "reality," so too does the reader feel an information overload before such complex and uncertain sentences.

This density of syntax points as well to Pynchon's departure from the plotline of a simple detective story. Although *The Crying* begins with a relatively simple situation that appears imminently solvable, events soon slip from Oedipa's control, and, rather than a movement toward resolution and clarity, one finds a movement toward irresolution and indeterminacy. The simple becomes intricate, the precise knotty, the transparent opaque, and clues become unimportant because neither they nor any kind of deduction can begin to lead one toward any solution. In this way, Pynchon reverses the plotline of a detective story. The movement becomes one from certainty to uncertainty. It is not clarity and Truth that lie as the grail at the end of Oedipa's quest, but only the world itself.

By the end of the second chapter, the sophomoric and throw-away humor of name-gags like those in the law firm of Warpe, Wistful, Kubitschek and McMingus, Dr. Hilarius, and radio station KCUF, the cartoon characters of Manny Di Presso, Baby Igor and the rock group the Paranoids, the idea of the Vivaldi Kazoo Concerto or songs like "I Want to Kiss Your Feet" all burn away before the dark illumination that the game is real, that whimsy is nowhere to be found, and the universe is filled with a horrible possibility. In place of the sophomoric comedy we see a postmodern Joseph K., no longer searching for a center in *The Trial,* but scrambling through the matrices of a great digital computer.

What Oedipa finds is that she exists in a positionless world, a universe in which the center shifts, a cosmos governed by "magic, anonymous and malignant, visited on her from outside and for no reason at all." The Tristero System is a projection of terror, the fear of metamorphosis and fusion, that silenced area in the culture. Existence for Oedipa contains "a hieroglyphic sense of concealed meaning, of an intent to communicate," where "a revelation . . . trembled just past the threshold of understanding." Although for her, meaning always seems near—as for Kafka's protagonists, it is always just around the corner, just up the next flight of stairs—it never materializes. As she approaches one seeming center of meaning, it shifts or vanishes altogether, and she is confronted by another. She finds a kind of perverse sustenance through her quest. Her world thereby echoes that of another Pynchon protagonist, Stencil in *V.,* who realizes:

> Finding [V.], what then? Only that what love there was to Stencil had become directed entirely inward, toward this acquired sense of animateness. . . . To sustain it he had to hunt V.: but if he should find her, where else would there be to go but back into half-consciousness? He tried not to think, therefore, about any end to the search. Approach and avoid.

The quest is everything, the resolution superfluous.

Shifts in the center start small. Pierce, for instance, on the phone calls Oedipa "Margo" rather than using her real name. Metzger, also known as Baby Igor, notes that "our beauty . . . lies in this extended capacity for convolution. . . . Raymond Burr is an actor, impersonating a lawyer, who in front of a jury becomes an actor. Me, I'm a former actor who became a lawyer." The Peter Pinquid Society is so far right it appears left. As one approaches an object, its significance changes.

So after the first mail-call at The Scope, it seems clear that the answer to W.A.S.T.E. lies somewhere in the brilliant halls of Yoyodyne, but soon that possibility vanishes. At first the G. I. bones at the bottom of Lago di Pieta seem to be significant, but soon just what significance they might have becomes unclear. Although readers have bravely wrestled with the convoluted plot of *The Courier's Tragedy,* it seems clear that the very fact of the convolutions is what is important, and not the play per se. Although Randolph Driblette at first appears to offer some center of hope and light, by the end of the novel he has walked into the Pacific Ocean one night, thereby taking any meaning with him. When Oedipa comes upon Stanley Koteks somewhere in the labyrinth of Yoyodyne, she finds him doodling something that looks like a post horn, so when he tells her about the Nefastis Machine, Oedipa believes that that too must hold some significance, but nothing comes of it either. Old Mr. Thoth at Vesperhaven House tells Oedipa the story of the false Indians, and shows her the ring with the W.A.S.T.E. symbol on it, and then vanishes from the text. Genghis Cohen, the philatelist, appears to help Oedipa solve the mystery of Tristero, but at the crying he shows up mysteriously and starts making excuses.

At one point Oedipa stops to wonder whether

> at the end of this (if it were supposed to end), she too might not be left with only compiled memories of clues, announcements, intimations, but never the central truth itself, which must somehow be too bright for her memory to hold; which must always blaze out, destroying its own messages irreversibly, leaving an overexposed blank when the ordinary world comes back.

But in her universe there exists no central truth. Only for the protagonist of the Sophoclean drama could the central truth be too bright for the memory to hold. Only in someone else's narrative could there exist a central truth. At the heart of this text, however, beats only an absence, a waiting for "truth" that will not be fulfilled. As it is with regard to the uncertainty principle, so it is with regard to Oedipa's quest—the more she tries to focus on one element in the equation of her situation, the more uncertain she becomes of everything else. The best she is left with is a system of chance. One thinks of that crazy can flying around the bathroom of the Echo Courts Motel while Oedipa and Metzger huddle together on the floor, unable to know where it may hit or whither it may be going or when it might cease its absurd flight.

Of course the world presents Oedipa with a number of answers, approximations of "truth," but each one reveals itself in the end as either absurd or useless. Dr. Hilarius, for example, tries to control reality by making faces at it. Jesús Arabal talks about miracles and political revolutions while he sits exiled in some greasy spoon restaurant somewhere in California. For Mucho, the world makes perfect sense, but that is only because his brain has been fried with LSD. Pierce himself suggests that one should "keep it bouncing . . . that's all the secret, keep it bouncing," but what kind of "truth" is that for a person like Oedipa, whose only impulses seem to be the finding of meaning and accumulating clues? As Driblette warns, "you can put together clues, develop a thesis, or several, about why characters reacted to the Trystero possibility the way they did, why the assassins came on, why the black costumes. You could waste your life that way and never touch the truth." This is exactly what she does. As with Oedipus, Oedipa must search for meaning at the risk that that meaning may turn on her.

As with the characters in Ovid's *Metamorphoses,* Oedipa's universe teeters on the edge of an infinite number of others. As with Democritus' physical world, Oedipa's "reality" is composed of subtle swerves and shifts that lead her always away from a center and toward a randomness. As with Plato, the phenomenal universe of Oedipa's is always one of becoming, never one of being. There exists the possibility for a more real and meaningfully determined universe behind this one, but, unlike Plato, for Oedipa that ordered universe—that static, closed system of which Pynchon is so wary—would be malevolent and brutally anonymous. Everything in the world, then, has existence, not in fact and clarity, but in possibility:

> Either you have stumbled, without the aid of LSD or other indole alkaloids, onto a secret richness and concealed density of dream; onto a network by which x number of Americans are truly communicating whilst reserving their lies, recitations of routine, arid betrayals of spiritual poverty, for the official government delivery system; maybe even onto a real alternative to the exitlessness, to the absence of surprise in life, that harrows the head of everybody American you know, and you too, sweetie. Or you are hallucinating it. Or a plot has been mounted against you, so expensive and elaborate . . . so labyrinthine that it must have meaning beyond just a practical joke. Or you are fantasying some such plot, in which case you are a nut, Oedipa, out of your skull.

Or, as she puts it several pages later:

> it was now like walking among the matrices of a great digital computer, the zeroes and ones twinned above, hanging like balanced mobiles right and left, ahead, thick, maybe endless. Behind hieroglyphic streets there would either be transcendent meaning, or only earth. . . . Ones and zeroes. . . . Another mode of meaning behind the obvious, or none

Oedipa, that is, reduces her universe to a system of either/or possibilities for which no precise truth-value can ever be determined. Her formula is easy, and utterly disturbing: either everything makes sense, or nothing makes sense. The distance between one and zero is on the one hand fractional, on the other infinite. If everything makes sense, Oedipa is a pawn in a ghastly and crazy plot. If nothing makes sense, Oedipa is floating in a ghastly and crazy world. The more she attempts pinpointing the validity of one side of the proposition, the more the other side reveals itself as possibly being the case.

Nor is Oedipa the only one reduced to such continual epistemological uncertainty. Because of the intrinsic positionlessness of the text, the reader too finds herself stumbling among the matrices of a great digital computer. When teaching **The Crying**, I find my students can put up with the absurdity of the first two chapters because the text does not seem to take itself seriously. With the introduction of the Tristero System in chapter three, however, hesitation, frustration, and even resentment build. My students find themselves in a world seemingly filled to bursting with palpable evidence, and they sense that their job as readers is the same as it would be in the case of a book by Arthur Conan Doyle or Agatha Christie—to assemble information in order to attain a clear and understandable whole. As the textual centers begin shifting, "truth" dissolves, and as an opaque haze settles on the words, anger mounts. Students feel resentment in the face of such information density, false leads, the dearth of any real ones, the fiendish plot of *The Courier's Tragedy,* the compact tales of Peter Pinguid, or the bones on the bottom of the lake. Such relentless inconclusion is enough to frustrate any reader. The narrator of **Gravity's Rainbow** points to as much when once he condescendingly interrupts his narrative to say, "You will want cause and effect. All right." What he gives, and what the narrator of **The Crying** gives, is just the opposite. So again, the reader confronts a postmodern fantasy that demands to be interpreted and understood on the one hand, while, on the other, deliberately refusing interpretation and understanding.

As James Nohrnberg points out in his article on Pynchon, one convention of satire—from *Satyricon* (ca. 66 A.D.) to *Dead Souls* (1842) and beyond—is the lost or recovered manuscript that exists in fragmentary or unfinished form. Even the satires that do not make use of this convention make use of a related one, whereby—as in Rabelais or Sterne—the work does not conclude at all conclusively. In the end [as Edward Mendelson has stated in his essay "The Saved, the Profane, and **The Crying of Lot 49"**], "the reader's sense of being defrauded of what becomes a consistent or cherished illusion actually signals the fulfillment of the satiric design." Perhaps this is the final and most radical uncertainty concerning **The Crying.** Just like the old Hollywood cliff-hangers, Pynchon's text breaks off at the climatic moment, the moment of "truth," as does Beckett's *The Unnamable* which ends at "the threshold of my story, before the door that opens on my story," and thereby completely frustrates the reader's expectations, jams all progress forward, thwarts any sense of wholeness, and thrusts the reader into a web of perplexity, distraction, and incertitude. At very best, the reader can seek solace in the fact that the novel might have an ending just outside his field of vision, that it concludes on the page after the last one she is given. But this offers scant comfort indeed, particularly if one follows the suggestions of inconclusiveness that the last 138 pages offer to its logical conclusion.

The true effect of the last page of this text is not to glide the reader out with a sense of completion as in a myth, a romance, a high mimetic, or many low mimetic works, but . . . to cast her back into the book's intricacies, densities, convolutions, incompletions, and uncertainties. For in the world according to Pynchon there exists a beautiful and elusive female center whose name could be Victoria, Vhesissu, Venezuela, Veronica, Valetta, or an infinite number of other possibilities; the exquisite arc of a V-2 screaming down somewhere, sometime, inevitable but unknowable; a universal and rackety Tupperware party where we all stand slightly drunk, slightly hallucinating, and celebrate our ignorance, our absolute inability to know, and our ultimate bewilderment in the face of it all. (pp. 72-83)

Lance Olsen, "Pynchon's New Nature: Indeterminacy and 'The Crying of Lot 49'," in his Ellipse of Uncertainty: An Introduction to Postmodern Fantasy, *Greenwood Press, 1987, pp. 69-83.*

FURTHER READING

Bibliography

Scotto, Robert M. *Three Contemporary Novelists: An Annotated Bibliography of Works by and about John Hawkes, Joseph Heller, and Thomas Pynchon.* New York: Garland Publishing, Inc., 1977, 97 p.

    Annotated listing of novels and uncollected stories by Pynchon, Hawkes, and Heller, as well as many critical and biographical essays specifically relevant to *The Crying of Lot 49.*

Criticism

Brugiére, Marion. "Quest Avatars in Thomas Pynchon's *The Crying of Lot 49.*" Translated by Margaret S. Langford. *Pynchon Notes 9* (June 1982): 5-16.

    Considers the significance of the word "quest" in *The Crying of Lot 49,* "a text which is a deliberate parody, where an obsession for reference . . . on the one hand, the repetitiveness of the narrative as well as the uncertain status of the speaker(s) on the other, and, last of all, rather cryptic symbolism, tend to obscure the finality of narrative."

Colvile, Georgiana M. M. *Beyond and Beneath the Mantle: On Thomas Pynchon's 'The Crying of Lot 49'.* Edited by C. C. Barfoot, Hans Bertens, and Theo D'haen. Amsterdam: Kodopi, 1988, 118 p.

Examines *The Crying of Lot 49* in relation to Pynchon's allusions to the paintings of Remedios Varo, the relationship between reader and text, and social and feminist issues. Contains a brief bibliography and several reproductions of Varo's works.

Cowart, David. "Surface and Void: Paintings in *V.* and *The Crying of Lot 49*." In his *Thomas Pynchon: The Art of Allusion,* pp. 13-30. Carbondale: Southern Illinois University Press, 1980.

Reprinted essay on Pynchon's references to Botticelli's *Birth of Venus* in *V.,* and to Remedios Varo's *Bordando el manto terrestre* in *The Crying of Lot 49.*

Cox, Stephen D. "Berkeley, Blake, and the Apocalypse of Pynchon's *The Crying of Lot 49*." *Essays in Literature* VII, No. 1 (Spring 1980): 91-9.

Questions whether Pynchon's novel belongs to the tradition of apocalyptic literature, which, according to Cox, contains a vision of destruction and regeneration, the redemption of the people or the rejuvenation of the self, and doctrine that may serve as "a vehicle for a new synthesis of religious or philosophical ideas."

Davidson, Cathy N. "Oedipa as Androgyne in Thomas Pynchon's *The Crying of Lot 49*." *Contemporary Literature* 18, No. 1 (Winter 1977): 38-50.

Relates the character of Oedipa Maas to the mythic tradition of the androgyne, which allows for "the perfect union in one person of characteristics conventionally designated as either male or female."

Davis, Robert Murray. "Parody, Paranoia, and the Dead End of Language in *The Crying of Lot 49*." *Genre,* No. 4 (December 1972): 367-77.

Examines language, humor, entropy, communications theory, and related concepts in *The Crying of Lot 49* as these relate to one of Pynchon's major themes: the demise of the American dream and human communication.

Eddins, Dwight. "Closures and Disclosures: The Quest for Meaning in *The Crying of Lot 49*." In his *The Gnostic Pynchon,* pp. 89-108. Bloomington: Indiana University Press, 1990.

Detects philosophic affinities between *The Crying of Lot 49* and gnosticism, the philosophy and practice of various pre-Christian and early Christian sects which purported that matter is evil and can only be transcended by means of knowledge.

Guzlowski, John Z. "*The Crying of Lot 49* and 'The Shadow'." *Pynchon Notes* 9 (June 1982): 61-8.

Analyzes Pynchon's brief allusion to "The Shadow," the dark, cryptic hero of pulp novels, radio, and comic books, which Guzlowski believes "enriches the thematic texture of *The Crying of Lot 49.*"

Hall, Chris. " 'Behind the Hieroglyphic Streets': Pynchon's Oedipa Maas and the Dialectics of Reading." *Critique* XXXIII, No. 1 (Fall 1991): 63-77.

While focusing on problems encountered in reading and interpreting *The Crying of Lot 49,* Hall asserts that "Oedipa Maas becomes Pynchon's ambivalent personification of the postmodern reader."

Hays, Peter L. "Pynchon's Cunning Lingual Novel: Communication in *Lot 49.*" *University of Mississippi Studies in English* (*1984-1987*) V (1987): 23-38.

Considers how language in *The Crying of Lot 49* "is involved as a major element in the novel, almost as a character, certainly as a plot device."

Hunt, John W. "Comic Escape and Anti-Vision: *V.* and *The Crying of Lot 49.*" In *Critical Essays on Thomas Pynchon,* edited by Richard Pearce, pp. 32-41. Boston: G. K. Hall & Co., 1981.

Excerpt from a previously published essay in which Hunt explores how Pynchon uses comic elements to obscure rather than clarify his vision of America in *The Crying of Lot 49.*

Langland, Elizabeth. "Society and the Problematics of Knowledge in Faulkner, Kafka, and Pynchon." In her *Society in the Novel,* pp. 187-208. Chapel Hill: University of North Carolina Press, 1984.

Briefly explores alternative social orders by which various characters seek to define themselves in *The Crying of Lot 49.*

Mackey, Douglas A. *The Rainbow Quest of Thomas Pynchon.* The Milford Series: Popular Writers of Today, Vol. 28. San Bernardino, Ca: The Borgo Press, 1980, 63 p.

Introduction to Pynchon's works up to 1980.

May, John R. "Loss of World in Barth, Pynchon, and Vonnegut: The Varieties of Humorous Apocalypse." In his *Toward a New Earth: Apocalypse in the American Novel,* pp. 172-200. Notre Dame, Ind.: University of Notre Dame Press, 1972.

Examines the use of black humor to explore cultural crises in works by John Barth, Pynchon, and Kurt Vonnegut.

Mendelson, Edward, ed. *Pynchon: a Collection of Critical Essays.* Englewood Cliffs, N.J.: Prentice-Hall, Inc., 1978, 225 p.

Compendium of new and previously published essays, several of which include commentary on *The Crying of Lot 49.*

Merrill, Robert. "The Form and Meaning of Pynchon's *The Crying of Lot 49.*" *Ariel* 8, No. 1 (January 1977): 53-71.

Endeavors "to characterize the form of Pynchon's three novels [*V., The Crying of Lot 49,* and *Gravity's Rainbow*] and then analyze *The Crying of Lot 49* as an example of this form."

Newman, Robert D. "The Quest for Metaphor in *The Crying of Lot 49.*" In his *Understanding Thomas Pynchon,* pp. 67-88. Columbia: University of South Carolina Press, 1986.

Introductory study surveying such concerns as entropy, indeterminacy, paranoia, and revelation in *The Crying of Lot 49.*

O'Donnell, Patrick, ed. *New Essays on "The Crying of Lot 49".* Cambridge, N.Y.: Cambridge University Press, 1991, 174 p.

Collects new and reprinted essays on *The Crying of Lot 49.*

Plater, William M. *The Grim Phoenix: Reconstructing Thom-*

as Pynchon. Bloomington: Indiana University Press, 1978, 268 p.

> General study of Pynchon's work. Contains numerous references to *The Crying of Lot 49.*

Profit, Marie-Claude. "The Rhetoric of Death in *The Crying of Lot 49.*" Translated by Margaret S. Langford. *Pynchon Notes* 10 (October 1982): 18-36.

> Asserts that the central theme of *The Crying of Lot 49* is expressed in Emory Bortz's comment to Oedipa regarding Richard Wharfinger's play *The Courier's Tragedy:* "Notice how often the figure of Death hovers in the background."

Puetz, Manfred. "Thomas Pynchon's *The Crying of Lot 49:* The World Is a Tristero System." *Mosaic* VII, No. 4 (Summer 1974): 125-37.

> Asserts that Pynchon "testifies to a continuity of the quest for organization in a universe of infinite disorganization," yet departs from previous models by suggesting that such a pursuit may merely indicate paranoid delusion.

Schaub, Thomas Hill. "Open Letter in Response to Edward Mendelson's 'The Sacred, the Profane, and *The Crying of Lot 49.*'" *Boundary 2* V, No. 1 (Fall 1976): 93-101.

> While citing Mendelson's essay as "clearly the best thing available on *The Crying of Lot 49* so far," Schaub protests that the overassertiveness of Mendelson's argument "threatens to eliminate the book's essential ambiguity."

Slade, Joseph W. "Excluded Middles and Bad Shit: *The Crying of Lot 49.*" In his *Thomas Pynchon,* pp. 125-75. New York: Warner Paperback Library, 1974.

> Detailed overview of *The Crying of Lot 49* focusing on such diverse concerns as Pynchon's use of symbolism and metaphor, themes of entropy and apocalypse, and the significance of character names in the novel.

Wagner, Linda W. "A Note on Oedipa the Roadrunner." *Journal of Narrative Technique* 4, No. 2 (May 1974): 155-61.

> Identifying Oedipa Maas as a surrogate for the reader who is bewildered by the rapidity of events in *The Crying of Lot 49,* Wagner demonstrates that Pynchon's novel is "the one book that attempts to re-create physically the quality that dominates our culture, *speed,* the demonic speed that obscures any truth and confuses the strongest character."

Ward, Dean A. "Information and the Imminent Death of Oedipa Maas." *University of Hartford Studies in Literature* 20, No. 3 (1988): 24-37.

> Demonstrates how the relationship between thermodynamic and informational entropy unifies *The Crying of Lot 49.*

Additional coverage of Pynchon's life and career is contained in the following sources published by Gale Research: *Contemporary Literary Criticism,* Vols. 2, 3, 6, 9, 11, 18, 33, 62; *Contemporary Authors,* Vols, 16-20, rev. ed.; *Contemporary Authors New Revision Series,* Vol. 22; *Dictionary of Literary Biography,* Vol. 2; and *Major 20th-Century Writers.*

Jack Spicer

1925-1965

American poet.

The following entry provides an overview of Spicer's career. For further information on his life and works, see *CLC,* Volumes 8 and 18.

INTRODUCTION

Spicer was associated with the Beat movement which originated in San Francisco during the 1950s. Although he shared the Beat Generation's social attitudes and supported the groups use of unconventional modes of literary expression, Spicer felt that the major Beat icons, Jack Kerouac and Allen Ginsberg, compromised their writing careers by selling out to commercial publishing houses and what he called the "English department" establishment. In addition, Spicer disputed the Beats' belief that poetry is primarily a matter of personal expression; instead, he asserted his theory that writing poetry is a form of dictation in which the poet derived mysterious codes or messages from an external source. According to Spicer, the poet's role was similar to that of a radio, receiving and transmitting signals with minimal interference.

Spicer was born in Los Angeles, California. He attended the University of Redlands in 1943 and the following year transferred to the University of California at Berkeley, where he received his bachelor's degree in 1947 and his master's degree in 1950. While at Berkeley, Spicer established strong friendships with the poets Robert Duncan and Robin Blaser, and together they envisioned forming a literary circle which, in emulation of the *Georgekreis* ("George Circle") of the twentieth-century German poet Stefan George, would inspire a poetic revival. This ambition ended when Spicer was forced to leave Berkeley after refusing to sign a loyalty oath that was required of all faculty.

Spicer spent the next seven years teaching, studying, and working in academic institutions in various states. In 1957 he returned to California to live in the San Francisco Bay Area and founded his Magic Workshop at the San Francisco State College Poetry Center. Ostensibly a poetry workshop, the sessions held there were experiments in which participants would occupy themselves in such activities as writing blasphemies and dramatizing roles from *The Wizard of Oz.* Through his workshop Spicer met many of San Francisco's poets, including Helen Adam, George Stanley, Ebbe Borregaard, Joe Duncan, and Jack Gilbert. The workshop was later held informally at various North Beach bars, where Spicer presided over activities such as "Blabbermouth Night," in which poets would utter nonsense words, spontaneous chatter, and noises in a manner that resembled Spicer's poetic theory of dicta-

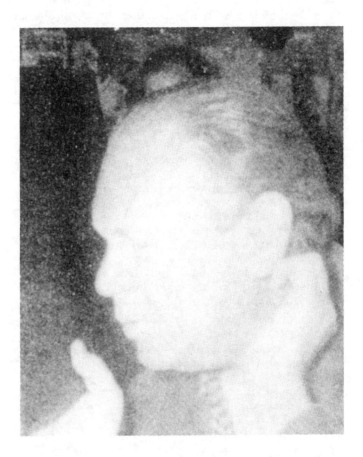

tion. Because Spicer refused to publish in well-known literary periodicals or through established publishers, his works remained virtually unknown outside the Bay Area. Most of Spicer's books were published surreptitiously in mimeographed editions by a friend who worked in a Greyhound bus printing office, which later became known as the White Rabbit Press, and individual poems appeared in obscure local magazines such as *Open Space.* In addition to writing poetry, Spicer worked from 1958 until his death on a linguistic atlas of the Pacific Coast. He died in 1965 from medical complications resulting from alcoholism.

Spicer wrote relatively conventional poetry from 1946 to 1956, but he is primarily known for works written after he conceived his method of dictation. He employed dictation in his first book of poems, *After Lorca,* in which he "communicates" with the Spanish poet Federico García Lorca, who was murdered in 1936. The book is a mixture of poetry and prose; through the technique of dictation Lorca is presented as the author of an introduction to the volume, and in the process of translating Lorca's poetry Spicer alters words and lines, adds original poems, and composes an exchange of letters between himself and the deceased Spanish poet. Spicer's next important work, *The Heads of the Town up to the Aether,* is written in a three-part structure that also combines poetry and prose. In the third section of the book, "A Textbook of Poetry," Spicer compares communication between poet and reader to that of a radio and a listener, wherein the reader might misinterpret a poem due to "faulty reception" or choose not to "listen" by not reading the poem.

Spicer's final works reflect his concern with what it means to be human. *The Holy Grail* is a collection of seven poems, each of them named after a hero of the Arthurian legends, and is a modern interpretation of humanity's search for meaning. The volume *Language* reveals Spicer's increased sense of isolation as a poet from society: "being a poet / a disyllable in a world of monosyllables." Spicer's last work, *Book of Magazine Verse,* discusses humanity's relationship to God, whose existence Spicer never completely acknowledged or denied. Spicer's contempt for the literary establishment is epitomized by the cover of *Book of Magazine Verse,* which mocks the design of *Poetry* magazine, and in the final poem of the work, which is an attack on Ginsberg: "At least we both know how shitty the world is / You / wearing a beard and a mask to disguise it. I / wearing my tired / smile. I don't see how you do it. One hundred thousand university students marching with you. / Toward / A necessity which is not love but is a name. / King of the May . . . "

Dora FitzGerald has written: "Jack was a teacher first, and wrote poetry as a vehicle for communicating that which was his to teach." Due to the efforts of his friends and colleagues after his death, Spicer has received increasing critical recognition. *The Collected Books of Jack Spicer* was published in 1975 and various academic journals have since devoted issues to his works.

PRINCIPAL WORKS

POETRY

*After Lorca   1957
Billy the Kid   1959
Dear Ferlinghetti with Dear Jack   1962
The Heads of the Town up to the Aether   1962
The Holy Grail   1962
Lament for the Makers   1964
Language   1965
Book of Magazine Verse   1966
A Book of Music   1969
The Red Wheelbarrow   1971
Admonitions   1974
Fifteen False Propositions about God   1974
The Collected Books of Jack Spicer   1975
One Night Stand, and Other Poems   1980

*This volume includes translations of Federico García Lorca's poetry as well as original material by Spicer.

CRITICISM

W. V. Spanos

The postmodernism of Jack Spicer's poetry is a complex phenomenon, not easily defined or categorized. It should, for example, be ultimately distinguished from, say, Charles Olson's or Robert Creeley's in that he commits language to the freeplay of writing (somewhat in the manner of Derrida's notion of *écriture*), whereas Olson and Creeley commit language to the occasion of oral expression (in the manner of Heidegger's understanding of *Rede*). But Spicer's poetry shares with Olson's and Creeley's the essential impulse of the postmodern imagination: to call into question the metaphysical or logocentric forms that have dominated the poetry—and above all the hermeneutics—of the Western literary tradition from Sophocles to Yeats and Eliot, from Aristotle to Brooks and Wimsatt and, even more recently, the Structuralists.

More specifically, Spicer's poetry of dictation, the poetry that, as Blaser puts it, is "received" by way of the generous "practice of outside," is postmodern in the sense that it deconstructs the coercive rhetoric of the ego-centrism, the anthropomorphism, of the Western tradition. And he does this, as Blaser observes, in order to bring near "something other than ourselves"—the "being," perhaps, that an egocentric language closes off, hardens, and alienates in the name, on the authority, of the abiding *logos,* the Word as presence. "A *reopened language,*" Blaser continues, "lets the unknown, the Other, the outside in again as a voice in the language. Thus, the reversal is not a reduction, but an openness. The safety of a closed language is gone and its tendency to reduce thought to a reasonableness and definiteness is disturbed." In Spicer's characteristically pop-art version of this phenomenological rhetoric, his "Martian" poetry brings the traditional—the transcendental and thus distanced—*logos* low, i.e., allows it to come into the region of immediacy as the "low-ghost," in order, as Michael Davidson says, to " 'spook' words into new contexts for which the [traditional] criteria of truthfulness [are] not at issue."

The contemporary impulse to dis-cover or dis-close what a logocentric rhetoric of presence—a coercive naming, as it were—covers over or closes off and forgets, this impulse to reactivate the *astonishment* of original perception, reminds us, of course, of the anti-nomianism that, according to Roy Harvey Pearce, constitutes the forgotten origins of the American poetic tradition in poets like Walt Whitman. In so doing, it also suggests that Spicer's "received" poetry of dictation, like Heidegger's "destructive" project, in which, paradoxically, the *es gibt* becomes primal, constitutes a *repetition,* a retrieval of "our historical-spiritual existence, in order to transform it into a new beginning . . . with all the strangeness, darkness, insecurity that attend a true beginning." In this antinomian effort at retrieval of beginnings—and despite his tendency towards a neo-Gnosticism—Spicer takes a significant, if not identical, place in the post-Modern project initiated by Ezra Pound and William Carlos Williams and continued by Olson, Creeley, Duncan, Snyder, Rothenberg, Antin, and others to "make it new"—to re-new the tradition, i.e., open up new possibilities, by remembering origins. (pp. 1-2)

W. V. Spanos, "Jack Spicer's Poetry of Absence: An Introduction," in boundary 2, *Vol. VI, No. 1, Fall, 1977, pp. 1-2.*

James Liddy

[Regarding Spicer's last book, ***Book of Magazine Verse***], it's not enough to agree with Blaser in "The Practice of Outside" (his commentary included in ***The Collected Books of Jack Spicer***) that the writing is surreal or under the real. It is simply a message, stark and reductively absolute as, the life lived the craft eclipsed, last statements or testaments are wont—a message, if it comes from anywhere, of ghost-voices from under the world. In all that fable of dictation theory that Spicer so elaborately goldleafed from Wordsworth and Yeats, the breathing of this already ghosting man (1964-65) into minimal staccato poetry! ***Book of Magazine Verse*** as gasps, as funeral sighs, substituting for rites (the repeated poem in the book beginning "Pieces of the past arising out of the rubble" must be reheard, for it is a rubric for a solemn dirge: vain rest, vain words for it), serves as the context for the death of the poet, the passing of King Cock, as it were on a dung hill, among the shadows of the future and the peculiar shapes of the past. And yet it says, Poetry is impersonal, one is not present as hero or victim even in death.

Book of Magazine Verse is divided into "books" with names of magazines that reflect a national or a Californian establishment. Some, if not most, are literary; others are radical-Catholic like *Ramparts,* and *The St. Louis Sporting News* is here for the irresistible baseball reference and the idea of "fixing." The poetics as poems thrust against the managers of each industry (including the poetry industry), the "Captains." *Poetry Chicago* and *The Nation* are corrupt corporations threatening both good poetry and promising young poetry. It is proper to ask why Robin Blaser, in editing ***The Collected Books,*** left out the dedication to ***Book of Magazine Verse,*** a mock acknowledgement of the rejection of the poems by editors Levertov and Rago. This seems as vital to me as the original cover—***The Collected Books*** should at the very least have had the covers of each volume as illustrations—a take-off of the Pegasus drawing of *Poetry Chicago.* Spicer was a symbolist brother of Oscar Wilde, who said of his books, "I always begin with the cover." The merging of cover, paper, and poems was possible only with small non-commercial presses: a point Spicer must have wanted to make. The varying colors of each part in the first edition makes us remember Dorian Gray choosing different colors for his ten large paper editions of *A Rebours:* one to suit each mood. The paper of ***Book of Magazine Verse*** imitates the paper of the original publications. Newsprint for *The St. Louis Sporting News* and glossy paper for *Downbeat,* a jazz magazine. Aesthetic considerations mostly moved Spicer; the protest against selling out was, like the fluttering butterfly modes of Wilde and Firbank, an urge to preserve beauty in decay against the coming mass-produced apocalypse of coffee table books and paperbacks.

The manifesto of 35 poems (with one repeat) pushes towards extremes, past the author and beyond his targets but straight as an arrow towards the source of poetry, not just the "outside," where he knew it could no longer be a community but at least a flame. His bullshit quota full, a warrior for authenticity (real lives make good poems), Spicer had a virile, almost militaristic rage. His career seems a parade of warnings, this the final admonition: "No / One accepts this system better than poets. Their hurts healed for a few dollars." "These big trucks drive and in each one / There is a captain of poetry or a captain of love or a captain of sex." "The road-captains, heartless and fast-moving. . . ." Simultaneous with the composition of these dire charges we have the tape of the Berkeley Poetry Festival talk and answer a month before his death. Here Olson is named as a big captain, the market is analysed for the young poet who wants to go there to sell out, and specifically *Poetry* is mentioned. We are told we cannot or shouldn't appear there because of whom our poems will have to rub shoulders with; when we are published in a magazine we become part of that community. It is as simple as being told to mind who our friends are—and, seeing the ersatz and low mimetic culture of published poetry now, we should take Spicer seriously. I do.

The first level theme then is the attack on the venality of being published in terms of politics not poetry. *Poetry* is what *U.S. News & World Report* would be to a devout Trotskyist. The spawning assaults, spurts of coherence fanning out to isolated statements of an absolute ideology, transvaluate the original privacy of the ideas. They also suggest exhaustion of his working methods.

We have assembled here, in ascending degree of traditionalism, in addition to the poet who protests the system and the bosses, two other central fortress positions: 1) the classic love poet in dying heat, and 2) the Christian believer a witness to transcendence and beguiled, as a preliminary, in "sweet Platonic spiritland." The main love poems are in the "Tish" and "Downbeat" sections. For the while I will just look at "Tish," 2, where climate interacts with a love situation. The lover shivers at ten above freezing, becomes a bird flying through snow-clouds, nestles in the poet's palm. The lover becomes an Arctic snow goose "if there are such things" and finally a sparrow about to starve in snow, 30 below in the hand-holding of lover and poet. "A problem with sparrows." Spicer is wonderfully in the Roman tradition, the other is a *puer delicatus* of a male lover (add to this the folk belief of the lecherous nature of the birds, "The adulterous sparrows in the eaves"). As we are meant to, we go to the second "Lesbia" poem of Catullus, where his girl's sparrow is dead that "quem plus illa oculis suis amabat." The image of Lesbia caressing her bird in her hand is presented as her way of dampening down the flames of passion—a clear explanation in part of what is wrong in the "Tish" poem. Catullus and his world do not seem alien to Spicer, as they have not to other writer-lovers. For the designated heroes and victims (the poets of love), being in love constitutes a way of life, as Kenneth Quinn makes plain in his *The Catullan Revolution.* Love is a serious preoccupation for this kind of imagination, the *Praeceptor Amoris.* It is usual and traditional to engage in the pursuit of love with a young man;

it is also usual and traditional that one's affairs stay at a frequent and casual level. It is this latter proposition that Spicer animadverts against. Passion is not quite sincerity, and what we have is the Christian reality (about the person) psychotically disturbing "the offered good." But when it is not offered, as in "Tish", 3, conscience, having found a soul, is a consolation. But we know consolation is not for love. Belief without morals is what we Christian poets spread as merchandise. A problem with doves.

The final meaning of **Book of Magazine Verse** is that of a man at the end of his tether having to find a way out, and finding it in the Incarnation, the flesh on the poem of God. It is the melody of Job, past patience yet redemptive. There is no dark brewing lament like it. It is Osip Mandelstam's, "I drink the cold mountain air of Christianity." Mandelstam is a Christian poet of ultimates, one aware of Dante's rose in Paradise and Villon's "lyrical hermaphroditism." If only Spicer had been drinking on Russian Hill with Mandelstam, instead of the Celtic bore, Dylan Thomas, with no idea of history's cornucopia! Mandelstam's inspired essay on Villon contains a sentence which seems to sum up Jack's psychic nature: "By his very nature, a lyric poet is a bisexual creature, capable of an infinite number of fissions in the name of his inner dialogue." Since Jesus is celibate, both man and woman on the cross, the poetry in this book is affirmative atonement material, with genitals appearing only to have access to the body. The soul is a sweet place, untouched yet untouchable. Ambiguities of vinegar and spear. Christsperm of "no love deserves the death it has."

The remainder of this paper will be simply a sequence of notes on individual poems. The poems for *The Nation* have been assimilated. So I start with the *Poetry* magazine satirica. Poems are section-numbered.

1. The good of the heterosexual bourgeois world is easily maintained. The world of the homosexual/artist (because Spicer equates them here) is beautiful and magical but useless in the social sense. As in Auden's Yeats, "Poetry makes nothing happen." With a subtheme: the fading poems of past ("sickened by the old lemon") issues of *Poetry*.

2. The repeat, the rebaked poem, in the Hamlet metaphor, for those unfamiliar with funerals.

3. The first part of the poem posits the nothingness of matter (the luxuriant jungle and drunken conversation). The other part is the bar/war dream of being back with mother.

4. In saying the rind is also called the skin, Spicer declares that he is talking about human fruits. Oranges remain oranges in the world of marriage and regeneration, as symbolized by the circular shape of the orange. Lemons are oval—not a continuing line. The love and life of the artist/homosexual, though more fully continuous, is not self-perpetuating. It comes to an end and stops, like love stops.

5. Aging and time—though one learns to better read the symbols one forgets the essential (ideal?) love (good?) which these symbols manifest. A position which includes the possibility that disregards the obviously half-correct

Freudian interpretation because that interpretation forgets the informing original love.

6. Physical love seems awkward, material, the skins are material objects such as the bedclothes, and frustrating. But it gives rise to the "good dream" of spiritual (ghostly) love, "the ghost of myself and the ghost of yourself. . . . With / Out / Skin." "The moment's rest" as distinct from "a moment's rest" (orgasm).

"Tish"

1. Again the Platonic of the real and ideal—here with real "rubble" of the mind. This essence, its capacity for art and love, astonishes. The image of dancing is continued from the last poem. Of course it was to Cocteau, not Nijinsky, that Diaghilef said, "Etonez moi." "A crazy notion in a grey society." A notion commemorative of all the artist-lovers of the Ballet and Paris at its apogee is contrasted with American present, California's imitations. It was Nijinsky who, through his unacceptable relationship (a kind of erotic tutoring) with Diaghilef, rejuvenated choric theatre with the triumphs of the Ballet Russe. The beauty of Nijinsky or the beauty of any youth able to dance (and dancing) comes from a long distance and takes getting used to. It is "The whorship of beauty / Or beautiful things take a long time getting used to" (ninth poem in the "Thing Language" section of *Language*). "What you hear is what you have heard from," similar to Plato's "All knowledge is memory." The last line is a (Christian?) reminder of mortality.

2. Lesbia's sparrow. Already dealt with except for this late reflection: the problem of trying to love someone who is so starved for love that they cannot return it.

3. We refuse, the horse-animal inside us refuses, love (Grace) while pretending to ourselves that it is being refused for us. As Odysseus pretended he wanted to return to wife and son. Love is as great as it should be—if we properly know how to drive Plato's black and white horses of *The Phaedrus*. Refusing to drink the water imagining, neurotic Narcissi, that the water refuses us. Though the heroic(?) Greek Age is over, despite temporary returns like the Renaissance, human nature is not altered. We are parasites because we won't allow love to work.

"Ramparts"

1. Plato (mouth) is not Christ (heart). Salvation exists. The Piltdown Man, beloved of Teilhard de Chardin, was a forgery. Evolution cannot be hurried, or the gaps that discoverable. On the other hand, Plato's fire is real flame: the shadows of love are the shadows of God. Balloons make an attempt at transcendence but the real lack of it ("the sky where men weep for men") leads to the sterility of the moon and the artificial distances of space travel. However, it is not that distant, the individual soul can reach it; Beatrice guides Dante to light.

2. The apparent contradictions of divine truth, the strangeness of Rome as the holy city. St. Peter, the rock, denying—Jesus divine becoming human—the church human accepting divinity. These *are,* and cannot be denied any more than, and are as persuasive as, "the weather." Despite Pius XII's hiccups, or Peter in the courtyard,

it's a "rock"—the old pun for turning Augustus' empire from marble to church stone. Spicer's ideas are close to the Roman poems of Osip Mandelstam. "It's not Rome, as a city, that lasts forever, / but man's place in the universe . . . without it houses, and altars, / are contemptible rubble, pitiful, wretched." Or from his slightly later poem on Benedict XV's Peace Encyclical, "There is a spirit / risen and leavened by freedom, / fate of the sweetest. The Roman priest survives / centurion-eyes catching absolutely the music." Mandelstam's Romanism came from his nostalgia for a world culture, the unity of the medieval world.

3. The perishing of the good leaders, Pope John, JFK. A little Protestant reaction here like Mandelstam's Orthodox guilty retractions. Spicer would probably prefer different Papal costumes and would avoid travel to Texas.

4. The technological world could not exist without God. This is Spicer's big statement: the apparently gratuitous gift of Grace creates humanity. Job-Spicer wonders why God bothers, why He is not a misanthrope. These poems show an essentially humanist distaste for all gnosis.

"The St. Louis Sporting News"

1,2,3,4. These poems are about playing by (obeying) the rules (divine laws and laws of poetry) or not. The rules are difficult, sometimes impossible to follow or understand—but any attempt to cheat them is both a sell-out and self-destructive (i.e., in contrast, perhaps, being destroyed by the rules?). 1 and 2 are about selling out, 3 and 4 are about not selling out. 4 returns to the concerns of the "Ramparts" poems: the necessity of having to accept God despite his false images.

"Vancouver Festival"

1. Building Augustine's city of God in the wilderness. The city is an extension of a baseball diamond (baseball is still symbolic of the divine laws). The diamond is a metaphor of perfection; therefore building a city outward and from the baseball diamond is building an eternal, beautiful city. Reminiscent of Hopkins' "This Jack, joke, poor potsherd, patch, matchwood, immortal diamond is immortal diamond."

2. Los Angeles is a parody of the city of God. Though it has lost Faith and Charity streets it still has Hope Street. This makes the quest possible despite "the idiocy of age and direction" as the poet goes north to find the source of the (mortal) chill in his bones.

3. Thingness, home (lambs—lamb of God) surviving in the world of matter. Last sun falling, direction ending.

4. Still it doesn't cohere (Pound on *The Cantos*). The landscape a "mess of nature" without supernatural qualities. Pioneers' errors.

5. The Beatles, equated in the Ferlinghetti letter with trendiness, the paperback culture that renders middle-class values immovable and horrifying, make Spicer think of exit and escape. There is no point in living with the Beatles playing on the records (or on the jukebox in North Beach). The impossible (a right exit) is possible but not, obviously, obvious.

6. The important thing is the individual moment of truth, courageous action, not the apparent goal: "Dead bait." Even if your truth is small.

7. Detachment—disinterested love. The immigrants turned back on themselves, the San Francisco poets back after this temporary migration to Vancouver. Even the Prime Minister's face is "parched."

"Downbeat" (placed last for its name—an ironic tribute to Kerouac?)

1. The bad East—Olson wanting everyone to believe in the ships in "Glouchester Harbor." The West, the coast, with its dead-end possibilities, "nothing but ocean," grabbing "the first thing coming." No comfort.

2. Thingness again. Confronting the world without dreams or illusions. Desert.

3. The self is "light baggage." Lacking substance, important only as direction which begins to mock itself, reminiscence in distraction.

4. Beware of the established bosses or "makers." Their music is lies. If you find the true music, outside of them, you will be young, still beautiful. Advice to a Canadian: keep British Columbia young and as free as possible from Capitalism, its chance is its out-of-the-way position?

5. Poets are ludicrously easy to buy. The ridiculous selling-out price of the poets. Fame, respect. The absurdity of the ordinary imagination, what the poets get into.

6. Portrait of the real poet as aspiring angel (desert butterfly).

7. The Pacific roaring with love though "Its beaches we've starved on." New tide, new surf, creation. "A spirit moved upon the waters."

8. The passing anonymity of people. Incorrectly or loosely called guerillas, nameless as Trotsky was a name. Names for the nameless; unknown Christians, for instance, with that name.

9. Charity. Love at last, the last glimpse. Possible to hold hands together—the poet doesn't lie if he can do this.

10. The shit of the world, Ginsberg the false poet pretending the young are not part of it, that it is not there. Ginsberg's abstract impersonal "love" which is not even love really, only a "name"—a gesture, a rhetoric. False prophet for America emotionally dying. Spicer concludes with a hint of successful prosecution. The point of his whole enterprise is that people die because they cannot make the right moral judgments.

Postscript. As it becomes increasingly clear that Spicer is a unique poet differing from the others in the San Francisco Renaissance, because of his honesty and objective power to distinguish the true from false in literature (and after his death whipping the big names out of the Californian temple of the imagination), his cult will become vast and sulfurous like a religion. The poet turns into a shrine. (pp. 260-66)

James Liddy, "A Problem with Sparrows:

Spicer's Last Stance," in boundary 2, *Vol. VI, No. 1, Fall, 1977, pp. 259-66.*

Norman M. Finkelstein

To write poetry is to mold a poetic; certainly this is nowhere more evident than in the work of Jack Spicer, who riddles his books with letters explaining their supposed intent, who writes mock commentaries and a textbook in [*The Heads of the Town Up to the Aether*], and who finally composes an entire volume called *Language.* Although he would certainly deny the title, Spicer is a major poetic theorist in an era in which serendipity and faddism pass for purpose and technique. But the role of theorist is so thoroughly subsumed in his poetic identity that to read his poetry is to discover the intended motives of its creation, which, as in a palimpsest, may be seen through the actual words. As Spicer himself declares, very late in his career, "The poem begins to mirror itself. / The identity of the poet gets more obvious."

The Heads of the Town Up to the Aether (1960-61) is the single work by Spicer that bears the closest examination in this regard, for it is not only an extremely self-reflexive book, it is also the most haunted of Spicer's volumes, containing a wide variety of disturbing, ghostly voices that hint at truths the poet barely wishes to accept. The title of the book, as [Robin Blaser in *The Collected Books of Jack Spicer*] informs us, comes from Spicer's reading about a book by the same name in Jean Doresse's *The Secret Books of the Egyptian Gnostics.* Blaser claims that

> The words found or discovered in a book are one level of a dictation. Here they rang a bell, though there is no systematic relation in Jack's poem to what we know about the contents of that mysterious book. However, the source and the title open for us Jack's concern with the extremity of thought common to all gnosticism, an opposition of light and dark and extensions of these in metaphor and experience.

[In his essay "Jack Spicer: *Heads of the Town Up to the Aether*" (*boundary 2*)] Michael Davidson quotes a line from Doresse to amplify the "upper-lower hierarchy" which informs Spicer's book, particularly "Homage to Creeley," with its poem-and-commentary structure. But a sustained look at Doresse sheds more light on *The Heads of the Town.* The original book was written by the Gnostic sect called the Peratae, of whom Doresse says:

> According to the Peratae, "the universe is composed of the Father, the Son and of Matter. Each of these *three* principles possesses within itself an infinity of powers. Between Matter and the Father resides the Son—Word and Spirit—a median principle always in movement, either towards the immobile Father or towards Matter, which is moved. Sometimes it turns towards the Father and, in its own person, takes on his powers; sometimes, having taken these powers, it returns towards Matter: and Matter, being without form or quality, receives from the Son the imprint of the forms of which the Son himself has received the imprints from the Father." If we are to believe the summary given in the *Philosophumena,*

these sectaries had built up a whole pattern of correspondences between the different powers of the lower heavens, such as those known to the other Gnostic systems and, at the same time, between those of the classical mythology and the celestial powers whose names the Ptolemaic astrology had multiplied.

This passage suggests a number of ideas with which Spicer may well have been working in composing his book. The first is the expanded notion of *correspondences* which he first presents in *After Lorca.* There, he speaks of objects corresponding through the medium of the poem. But systems of ideas and works of literature can correspond through the poem as well, as the Peratae understood. Hence the layered references in *The Heads of the Town,* which draw from Cocteau's *Orphée,* from the *Divine Comedy,* from Creeley's poetry, from Rimbaud's, from Lewis Carroll's, and from Gnosticism itself. Secondly, the three-part structure of the book, which Spicer says is analogous to the *Divine Comedy,* is amplified by the Son's (the Word's) capability of moving down into Matter (the Lowghost of distorted meaning in "Homage to Creeley") or up towards the truth of the Father ("A Textbook of Poetry"). And thirdly, the Son's taking on "the imprints of the Father," even as Matter takes on the imprints of the Son, supports the concept of dictated poetry that comes into its own for the first time in *The Heads of the Town.* These three concepts with which Spicer works—correspondences, vertical movement and impressed dictation—go far in explaining the goals of the poet's most difficult text.

"Homage to Creeley" is divided into three sections dedicated to the three supernatural figures in *Orphée:* Cegeste, the dead young poet; the Princess, "A Representative of The Dead"; and Heurtebise, the angelic messenger who chauffeurs the Princess' black limousine. These three characters, who in the course of the film both control and are controlled by the demonic forces of Hades, are appropriate figureheads for Spicer, who in this book renounces all sense of poetic personality and empties himself completely, so that the ghostly voices of language may speak. Their utterances take a double form: poems that seem like nursery rhymes read through a glass darkly, and commentaries printed in pale grey ink below them, as full of word play and obscurities as the poems themselves. Despite the joking surface of the text, "Homage to Creeley" remains an awesome confrontation with negativity, in which the potential meaninglessness of language represents a kind of psychic hell into which the contemporary Orpheus must descend.

The poet's motives for such a formal strategy are obliquely voiced throughout "Homage to Creeley." The first voice we hear is that of the commentator, saying that the poet "wanted to eliminate all traces of the poetry." But at the same time we are warned that the voice itself is "the ghost of answering questions. Beware me. Keep me at a distance as I keep you at a distance." Thus we are given no reason to trust any of the voices above or below the line that divides each page of the text, and yet all at times speak with painful honesty:

> What is a half-truth the lobster declared

You have sugared my groin and have sugared
  my hair
What correspondence except my despair?
What is my crime but my youth?

Truth is a map of it, oily eyes said
Half-truth is half of a map instead
Which you will squint at until you are dead
Putting to sea with the truth.
              ("The Territory Is Not the Map")

The formulation is almost classical: the poet, always the voice of youth, despairs over the truth that only he can perceive, and is driven to death. The commentary says that "This is a poem to prevent idealism—i.e. the study of images. It did not succeed." It cannot succeed, for the poet, with the truth before him, cannot cease to be idealistic. Mocked as he is, with sugared groin and hair, he maintains his belief in correspondences between the poem and the world, even when only his despair corresponds to what is beyond the poem. This is why "Orpheus and Eurydice are in their last nuptial embrace during this poem." The poet clings to truth, to meaning, even when truth is fated only for hell.

But Eurydice is lost for good, and "Homage to Creeley" is as much about the place she takes in the underworld as it is about the absence created by her departure in the world above. We are told that "In hell it is difficult to tell people from other people," as the poems lose all sense of what they refer to, in open rebellion against any would-be writers:

Dante would have blamed Beatrice
If she turned up alive in a local bordello
Or Newton gravity
If apples fell upward
What I mean is words
Turn mysteriously against those who use them
Hello says the apple
Both of us were object.
       ("Sheep Trails Are Fateful To Strangers")

"Both of us were object" means that the speaking subject is someone other than the supposed user of words. This realization is the only means by which one can possibly get out of hell, and it is the realization that all the figures who wander through these poems have yet to make. In one of the most allusive commentaries, we learn that

Cegeste comes back to a big meeting with his personal fate. He lacks knowledge of the driver's seat as did Cegeste, Creeley, and all of us. He intends to spend his fortune in banks, on the banks of some rivers. He will wreck their cars if he can have to.

Despite the confused pronouns, the message comes through: no living poet has recognized the fact that he is not in the driver's seat, that a poetic Power from the outside is driving instead. Thus, the Princess' limousine, which runs down Cegeste to bring him to Hades, ironically corresponds to Creeley's "I Know a Man," the source of Spicer's "homage":

As I sd to my
friend, because I am
always talking,—John, I

sd, which was not his
name, the darkness sur-
rounds us, what

can we do against
it, or else, shall we &
why not, buy a goddamn big car,

drive, he sd, for
christ's sake, look
out where yr going.

Creeley, according to Spicer, cannot drive (that is, write) until he realizes that he is not the driver. Until then, he is another of hell's victims, another Orpheus without his love:

The fate of the car
And the fate of the ride
Is only a bridegroom
Without a bride

Though she hasn't a face
And I haven't seen her
She isn't a mirror
Whatever she was.

And the light in the air
Was as real as it was
And it hasn't her beauty
Whose blankness I stare.

For Spicer, the most horrible thing about the dead is their irredeemable *pastness;* only their distorted voices return to an ongoing present, making for a psychological hell. Dead poets, i.e. the tradition, and the beauty of meaning that they take with them into death, make the life of the living poet particularly hellish, for the messages from dead poets constantly remind the living poet of the loss of immanence he must always endure. To confront dead poets is to confront history; to lay them to rest is to discern what voices from the dead still maintain their vitality and usefulness for the living. This is an act of *purgation,* and Spicer's *Purgatorio,* "A Fake Novel about the Life of Arthur Rimbaud," sets the living poet against one of his most representative precursors in order to extract meaning from one of the noisy dead. As Spicer succinctly puts it, "The dead are not alive. This is what this unattractive prose wants to stamp out. Once you see an end to it, you believe that the dead are alive."

Unfortunately, Spicer is correct about the unattractiveness of this section, and while Ross Feld's opinion that it is "a bar entertainment drawn out to nineteen pages" seems somewhat overstated, it is true that criticism of "A Fake Novel" is usually more readable than the novel itself. This is partly due to the fact that, as the middle section of a Divine Comedy, "A Fake Novel" most overtly displays the vertical movement of the Word down into Matter or up to the divine truth of the Father. Stylistically, it offers neither the pleasures of madness of "Homage to Creeley" nor the absolute, confident clarity of "A Textbook of Poetry". But its asymmetrical and overblown prose is still, in the main, successful:

"You can't close the door. It is in the future,"
French history said as it was born in Charlie-

ville. It was before the Civil War and I don't think even James Buchanan was president.

The accomplishments of this section are of great importance: meaning *can* be ascertained from history and from past poetry, even if this does not occur in the present; and it is the poet, at any point in history, who is most prepared to discover where the meaning lies:

> No way to turn except upward. Rimbaud will turn sixteen, invent what my shrewdness (our shrewdnesses) will not remember, come to a more usable concept of sex and poetry—a machine to catch ghosts.

With the poet firmly ensconced as ghost-catcher, and, by the end of the novel, even the reader becomes a ghost, "Involved in the lives of Rimbaud." Spicer turns his haunted eyes towards the spheres and offers his *Paradiso*. "A Textbook of Poetry" *is a Paradiso* because it provides a way to deal with the experience of dictation, which previously seemed a more uncontrolled event for the poet. Spicer read "A Textbook" in the course of the first Vancouver Lecture, offering it as the purest dictation he had ever received, a fact that argues strongly for his power as a theorist, for the dictated "Textbook" is about dictation itself. This is to say that it is about the role of the poet in the world, and about the attitudes he must assume in regard to inspiration and composition. It is one of the few points in Spicer's opus at which the poet seems at rest, comfortable in his role of medium and completely in tune to the content of the messages that he is receiving. Containing very little of the ghostly terror and personal unease that one may observe continually increasing from book to book, it is a genuinely prophetic piece, Utopian in its outlook towards poetry, if not society. It serves as a sad contrast to the almost intolerable preternatural revenge enacted upon Spicer in his last works, a revenge that comes from his being too good a receiver of messages that he cannot, ultimately, understand.

But the terror of Spicer's last achievements in poetic self-consciousness is still remote from the wisdom of his "Textbook". He begins by looking back at the tradition of Romantic interiority from which he emerges, knowing immediately that its ideological stance was contingent upon the necessity of advancing poetic creativity:

> Surrealism is the business of poets who cannot benefit by surrealism. It was the first appearance of the Logos that said, "The public be damned," by which he did not mean that they did not matter or he wanted to be crucified by them, but that really he did not have a word to say to them. This was surrealism.

The Surrealists are the last generation of poets who turned their backs on exterior reality in order to dwell in a dictated interior world of language. Spicer feels a strong kinship to Surrealism, but his work has taken him beyond it:

> To define a metaphor against a crowd of people that protest against them. This is neither of our businesses.
>
> It is as if nothing in the world existed except metaphors—linkings between things. Or as if all

our words without the things above them were meaningless.

Here, Spicer's Objectivism again comes into play; he knows that language worlds are completed by exterior reality, that a continuum of correspondences, of metaphors, forever links them. This gnosis comes from the outside; it is the dictated knowledge that the poet is given. Yet as has been becoming more evident in **The Heads of the Town,** this outside is, at least partly, the voices of the tradition. It is this that Spicer would teach us:

> The ghosts the poems were written for are the ghosts of the poems. We have it second-hand. They cannot hear the noise they have making.
>
> Yet it is not a simple process like a mirror or a radio. They try to give us circuits to see them, to hear them. Teaching an audience.

This in itself, however, is not enough on which to base an ongoing poetic. The primary subject of "A Textbook" is *how* dictated voices become poetry, what the poet must do and what the world will do in turn. The natural metaphor for Spicer is the Incarnation of the Word, of which he says:

> If you see him everywhere or exactly nowhere, he becomes as it were the circumference of a circle that has no point but the boundary of your desire. Coming to a point.
>
> And the human witness of this passion is rightly stunned by the incongruity of it. Lifting a human being into a metaphor.
>
> All that we do in bed, or sleep, or sex is limited by this circle which can only be personally defined.
>
> On the outside of it is what everybody talks about. On the outside of it are the dead that try to talk.
>
> Once you try to embrace an absolute geometric circle the naked loss stays with you like a picture echoing.

Desire, then, its extensions and limitations as imposed by the individual, is the key to the Incarnation of the Word, the dictated voice become flesh in the poem. At the limits of desire the dead try to talk; to hear them is to write poetry despite "the naked loss" that one feels simultaneously with the coming of the poem. For poetry is only partly plenitude for Spicer; the emptying out of personality dialectically leads to redemption.

The poet's inevitable feeling of loss is heightened by society's reaction to his work. Inspiration, or in Spicer's case, dictation, is at least partly regarded as a threat in contemporary society, and must be rationally explained by an attendant battery of ideologues and high priests of culture. Spicer's answer to them is typically acerbic, but nonetheless courageous:

> The Indian rope trick. And the little Indian boy climbs up it. And the Jungians and the Freudians and the Social Reformers all leave satisfied. Knowing how the trick was played.

There is nothing to stop the top of the rope
though. There is nothing to argue. People in the
audience have seen the boy dancing and it is not
hypnosis. . . .

Reading the poem that does not appear when the
magician starts or when the magician finishes. A
climbing in-between. Real.

The earlier metaphor of poetry as a rope reappears, but in
this case, the rope does not end, but extends beyond the
comprehension of the "Jungians and the Freudians and
the Social Reformers." What the poet shows the public is
only the surface, a sham: the real magic begins in the interstices between words, which only the most perceptive
readers can understand. This is the "argument with the
dead. That is what these pauses are mainly about." But the
source of this ghostly magic is itself a social phenomenon,
a historically based artistic reaction. Thus, in one of his
most perceptive variations on his supernatural theme,
Spicer observes that

Every city that is formed collects its slums and
the ghost of it. Every city that is formed collects
its ghosts.

Poetry comes long after the city is collected. It
recognizes *them* as a metaphor. An unavoidable
metaphor. Almost the opposite.

As if trying to recapitulate the history of verse in a few
sentences, Spicer then says that "The city redefined becomes a church. A movement of poetry. Not merely a system of belief but their beliefs and their hearts living together."

From system to system, form to form, the Utopian voices
break in to disturb social and literary order, generated dialectically by what has gone before them. Each time they
have their effect, they become reified: "now he is the Low-
ghost when He is pinned down to words." But beauty and
the hope of the future continues to free the words, pushing
them forward at the moment of their utterance:

Hold to the future. With firm hands. The future
of each afterlife, of each ghost, of each word that
is about to be mentioned.

Don't say put beauty in here for the past, on account of the past. On account of the past nothing
has happened.

Stick to the new. With glue, paste it there continually what God and man has created. Your fingers catch at the edge of what you are pasting.

And beyond every individual's capacity for beauty are the
"Immortal mockers of man's enterprise," misquoted from
"Among School Children" but still present, "holding a
blowtorch to all beauty." Here, like Yeats's, Spicer's visionary imagination comes to an end, for the individual
poet, confronted at the present moment with the nether-
world of the past generating the unborn future, can only
surrender to the "silver voices," the voices of history that
appear to speak beyond and above history itself.

The entrance of history-as-such into Spicer's poetry, the
self-conscious effort "To create the beautiful again," and
the continuing recognition of the limits of the poet's cre-

ative desire, all force Spicer to come to terms with the
poet's role in society, not so much for the sake of society,
nor even for the sake of poetry, but for the sake of the open
stance towards reality he so strongly endorses. Ross Feld
observes that as Spicer tries more desperately to achieve
a personality-less poetry, his personal voice grows continually stronger. Peter Riley seems to agree:

His sole duty was to perfect the single poem to
the point where it was able to slot into a course
of which the author remained ignorant. Spicer
then surrendered his entire identity to a totality
which he trusted to operate through him, as long
as he remained sufficiently resourceful, open,
and faithful to it. The whole business of dictation, ghosts, radio transmission, the word descending into the flesh, and so on, was for this
purpose: to create a narrative out of the discrete
singularities of the person, when those singularities represented the only field in which the person could operate as himself.

As Spicer becomes a more faithful receiver of messages,
the messages speak more clearly for his own personal "singularities." These singularities in turn become more directed towards what the poet can and cannot do within the
confines of his art. The gnosis of the future, unattainable
to the poet and unrealizable in contemporary society,
leads Spicer to visionary despair, in which the circumstances of his own life take on much wider poetic and political significance:

I can't stand to see them shimmering in the im-
        possible music of the Star Spangled
        Banner. No
One accepts this system better than poets. Their
        hurts healed for a few dollars.

Hunt
The right animals. I can't. The poetry
Of the absurd comes through San Francisco tele-
        vision.
        Directly connected with moon-rockets.
If this is dictation, it is driving
Me wild.

Spicer's dictation becomes congruent with the historical
forces that shape his life: in a world where the ghostly
moon is bought by American technocrats, most poets are
ready to transform themselves into commodities as well.
Those who refuse court madness, for the dictated truths
they speak fall on deaf ears. If space permitted, I would
demonstrate how in *The Holy Grail, Language* and *Book
of Magazine Verse,* Spicer's increasing despair over the
fact that "No one listens to poetry" leads to an increasingly monstrous (that is, Demiurgic) kind of dictation, made
all the more bitter by the feeling of *inevitability* that accompanies the emergence of form. The past, the tradition,
history, dominates these books, both as a vulnerable terrain into which the present may march at will, and as a
powerful, unscrupulous and unpredictable region from
which Spicer's ghosts appear with sudden fury:

Pieces of the past arising out of the rubble.
        Which evokes Eliot and then evokes
        Suspicion. Ghosts all of them. Doers
        of no good.

The past around us is deeper than.
Present events defy us, the past
Has no such scruples.

Spicer's final position, so honest and intelligent in its hopelessness, is the result of a poetic that keeps the personal
at a distance in order to effect neither a false interiority nor
an equally limited version of exterior, "objective" truth.
But the personalized subject speaks out in the poem, for
it is through personality that the forces of history are conceived as sensuous poetic matter.

As I have implied, Spicer's poetics are the furthest possible
extension of Keats's Negative Capability, "when man is
capable of being in uncertainties, Mysteries, doubts, without any irritable reaching after fact & reason," which also
had a profound effect on Charles Olson, the one post-
Modernist who rivals Spicer as a poetic theorist. With its
sources in such Modernist aesthetics as those of Williams,
the post-Modern insistence on an open stance towards reality assumes that the poet responds to pre-existing conditions of reality in the creation of his verse. From what is,
of necessity, this poet creates his literary world: this is why
subjectivity as such has been willfully eschewed by many
of the Modernists and their heirs. But to act from the self
is to lay claim to the future, to go beyond the immediate
moment, and therefore it is arguable that the most future-
oriented poetry of this century has been written when the
poet allows his objectivism to lapse into a more fruitful
synthesis of self and world. Jack Spicer is among a small
group of poets to achieve this synthesis, . . . and thus he
is one of the most advanced post-Modernists. (pp. 89-99)

*Norman M. Finkelstein, "Jack Spicer's Ghosts
and the Gnosis of History," in* boundary 2,
Vol. IX, No. 2, Winter, 1981, pp. 81-100.

Spicer on his poetry:

I would like to make poems out of real objects. The lemon
to be a lemon that the reader could cut or squeeze or
taste—a real lemon like a newspaper in a collage is a real
newspaper. I would like the moon in my poems to be a real
moon, one which could be suddenly covered with a cloud
that has nothing to do with the poem—a moon utterly independent of images. The imagination pictures the real. I
would like to point to the real, disclose it, to make a poem
that has no sound in it but the pointing of a finger.

Jack Spicer, in his After Lorca, *White
Rabbit Press, 1957.*

Lori Chamberlain

The corpus of Jack Spicer's poetic work is available posthumously in two books: ***The Collected Books of Jack
Spicer,*** which collects the published books, and ***One Night
Stand and Other Poems,*** which collects the early published and unpublished poems. The dividing line between
these two books is Spicer's discovery of the "serial poem,"
that is, of the poem conceived of as a book, wherein indi-

vidual poems resonate against each other and confuse any
notion of the single, "perfect" poem. Spicer marks this discovery with the book ***After Lorca*** (1957), the first of ***The
Collected Books; After Lorca*** therefore occupies a significant point in the development of Spicer's poetics. What,
then, do we make of the fact that this first book is a translation?

Translation, according to the accepted wisdom, is a secondary art, twice removed from the Platonic truth. Poets
sometimes practice it to sharpen their tools, particularly
while the muse is in hiding, but we look for the true signs
of the poet's genius in the original work, not generally in
the translations. For we accord the original author a kind
of privilege, the head seat at the table, and grant the author ownership over those words, intentions, poetics; the
translator, then, is an ephebe, come to worship, serve, or
usurp the place of the author, possibly parasitic, not to be
trusted, certainly not a "poet" in the usual sense. According to this logic, we might evaluate Spicer's skill in translating Lorca, but we would not confuse Lorca's poetics
with Spicer's. Thus, as an inaugural statement of a poetics,
After Lorca poses a critical dilemma.

But perhaps ***After Lorca*** is not *really* a book of translations. While it includes several very good translations, notably one of Lorca's "Ode to Walt Whitman," it also includes "fake" translations, some poems that are purely
Spicer's, as well as a playful "correspondence" between
Spicer and Lorca. The introduction to the book, written
in Lorca's voice—it is dated "Outside Granada, October
1957," some twenty years after Lorca's death—warns the
reader about the status of the translations:

> It must be made clear at the start that these
> poems are not translations. In even the most lit-
> eral of them Mr. Spicer seems to derive pleasure
> in inserting or substituting one or two words
> which completely change the mood and often
> the meaning of the poem as I had written it.
> More often he takes one of my poems and ad-
> joins to half of it another half of his own, giving
> rather the effect of an unwilling centaur. (Mod-
> esty forbids me to speculate which end of the an-
> imal is mine.)

To complicate matters even further, Lorca claims to have
sent Spicer poems written after Lorca's death, which, he
says, Spicer has dutifully translated. As a result, "Even the
most faithful student of my work will be hard put to decide what is and what is not García Lorca as, indeed, he
would if he were to look into my present resting place."

The macabre analogy between Lorca's condition in the
grave and the status of the work in question provides an
allegory of Spicer's poetics of translation. Lorca—or the
body of his work—is not regarded as an immutable, substantial presence, but as something subject to the laws of
change; thus, Lorca does not stand as the source of an in-
violate text. Spicer, then, goes as a sort of grave-robber to
consult the ghost of Lorca and to reconstitute the body of
the poems, not as *individual* poems, but as a language of
poetry.

What I want to argue about Spicer's poetics is first that
the project of translation in ***After Lorca*** prefigures what

he later calls a "poetics of dictation." This poetics calls into question both romantic notions of the self-sufficient or expressive self and symbolist notions of the poet's ego-less, vatic function. The poet, according to Spicer, is a receiver of messages from an outside, but these messages are not signs of the Logos, as they might be for the symbolists, but of what Spicer calls the "low-ghosts" of language. In many ways the most radical statement of this poetics occurs in *After Lorca,* where Spicer confronts one of the central tenets of interpretation: that we be able to identify the genealogy of the text. In producing these bastard poems (or "centaurs"), he forces us either to reduce our reading strategy to deciding which part of the poem belongs to Spicer and which part to Lorca, or to find a reading strategy that can accommodate the poems' mixed heritage. This interpretive problem is repeated in the semiotics of Spicer's writing, a writing that employs a variety of doubling, duplicitous strategies, pushing the very definition of "poetry" to its margins. Finally, I would argue that Spicer's poetics of translation is characteristic of a larger postmodern poetics of translation that we could locate in the work of Samuel Beckett, Jorge Luis Borges, Donald Barthelme, Harry Mathews, Raymond Federman, the concrete poets, bp nichol—writers for whom translation is not a subsidiary activity but who have revived the idea that all writing is a translating. If for the modernists—Pound and Joyce in their different ways—translation marks a nostalgia or search for origins, an attempt to resurrect a past which will become the measure of value, an attempt finally to rebuild the Tower of Babel and reunite language into a coherent tale of the tribe, for the postmodern writers, translation marks an acceptance of the impossibility of origins, an opening of the play between before and after, a reveling in multiplicity. While this writing is marked, then, by its openness to play, it is not the less "serious": in undermining those definitions (of truth, of authority, of originality) that have been held sacred, this writing attempts to understand both how those sacred structures insured a kind of failure (the literature of exhaustion) and how that failure might be turned into a success.

Contrary to Lorca's prediction in the introduction, faithful students of both Lorca's and Spicer's works have discovered "what is and what is not García Lorca" in these poems. Clayton Eshleman, in an essay entitled "The Lorca Working" [*boundary 2,* 1977], has matched Spicer's poems to their Lorca equivalents and singled out those poems that are purely Spicer's. In making these distinctions, Eshleman points out the most flagrant mistranslations and attempts further to distinguish between "arbitrary" and "meaningful" mistranslation. He compares, for example, Spicer's version of Lorca's "Juan Ramon Jimenez," the first poem in *After Lorca,* with a literal translation (done by Eshleman) of that poem. The first stanza of the Lorca original goes as follows:

> En el blanco infinito,
> nieve, nardo y salina,
> perdió su fantasia.

Eshleman gives the literal translation:

> In the white infinite,

> snow, spikenard and saltmine,
> he lost his fantasy.

Spicer translates that same stanza as follows:

> In the white endlessness
> Snow, seaweed, and salt
> He lost his imagination.

Eshleman argues convincingly that the choice of "imagination" over "fantasy" is a meaningful "mistranslation" in terms of Spicer's poetics, but his model of reading forces him then to argue that the substitution of "seaweed" for "spikenard" is merely arbitrary and, in Eshleman's terms, "less interesting" than the correct equivalent:

> I can see no point at all in rendering "nardo" and "salina" as "seaweed" and "salt." Surely Spicer knew what the words actually meant, and as I puzzle over the matter, the only thing that comes to my mind to explain it is the idea of "dictation" which later in his life Spicer developed to justify his poetry as coming from the outside as opposed to the inside.

Eshleman exposes here precisely the problem of attempting to distinguish "meaningful" from "arbitrary" mistranslation—or, for that matter, translation from mistranslation. To do either is to assume that Spicer's purpose in translating Lorca is to render an equivalent poem, judged in terms of Lorca's intentions, a project that the introduction to these poems undercuts. As a matter of fact, Spicer not only "mistranslated" this poem, but he encouraged others to do so as well: he used it as part of his "Magic Workshop" questionnaire where, after eliminating portions of the poem/translation, he asked workshop applicants to "fill in each of the blanks with any number of words you wish." Though as a preliminary step, it is essential to compare Spicer's translations against the original poems, it is finally difficult to take Spicer "literally" as a translator. Eshleman's intuition that "dictation" might provide a more adequate explanation for the translation is a clue I will pursue later in this essay.

For Spicer provides a serious theory of writing as translation that precisely confuses such concepts as "meaningful" and "arbitrary." In his "correspondence" with Lorca, he proposes a "correspondence" theory of translation:

> Things do not connect; they correspond. That is what makes it possible for a poet to translate real objects, to bring them across language as easily as he can bring them across time. That tree you saw in Spain is a tree I could never have seen in California, that lemon has a different smell and a different taste, BUT the answer is this—every place and every time has a real object to *correspond* with your real object—that lemon may become this lemon, or it may even become this piece of seaweed, or this particular color of gray in this ocean. One does not need to imagine that lemon; one needs to discover it.

This, then, is the justification for Spicer's transformation of "spikenard" into "seaweed" in the poem "Juan Ramon Jimenez."

Not surprisingly, Eshleman's model of reading *After*

Lorca is particularly ill-suited for the book's "centaur" poems. Let us look briefly, for example, at one of these, "Song of the Poor," which serves in many ways as an exemplary tale of Spicer's translation practice. It is based on a fairly early poem of Lorca's entitled "Es Verdad," which appeared in the volume entitled *Canciones* (or "Songs"). Spicer would have seen the poem either in Lorca's *Obras Completas* or, in translation, in *The Selected Poems of Federico García Lorca* first published by New Directions in 1955. Lorca's is a simple, direct, even stark lyric poem lamenting the pain of love. Like many of the *Canciones,* the poem is bracketed, opening and closing with the same short stanza:

> ¡Ay qué trabajo me cuesta
> quererte como te quiero!
> (Oh, what an effort it costs me to love you as I
>   love you!)

Between this opening and closing stanza, Lorca objectifies the pain of love, locating it in the air, in his hat, and in his heart, and he asks,

> ¿Quién me compraría a mi
> este cintillo que tengo
> y esta tristeza de hilo
> blanco, para hacer pañuelos?
> (Who would buy of me this hat band I have and
>   this sadness of white linen to make handker-
>   chiefs?)

Spicer's poem retains the bracketing stanzas in Spanish, following the Lorca poem here to the letter, so to speak, but he translates the middle two stanzas into three:

> Because I love you the table
> And the heart and the lamplight
> Feel sorry for me.
>
> Who will buy from me
> That small belt I have
> And that sadness of white thread
> To weave handkerchiefs?
>
> Because I love you the ceiling
> And the heart and the air
> Feel sorry for me.

By adding the fourth stanza, Spicer gives a different kind of symmetry to the poem, though his changes are made according to the "logic" of the Lorca original: inanimate or intangible things (ceiling, air, lamplight, etc.) are made to feel the lover's grief.

Eshleman assesses the poem as follows:

> (Lorca's poem is entitled "Es Verdad"—"It is True"; Spicer's retitling makes no sense at all.) This translation is a mess. Spicer has kept Lorca's opening and closing couplet in Spanish, has butchered the second and third stanza and added his own fourth stanza which is so dumb it almost functions as a parody of Lorca's poem. Interestingly, though, this failure comes right before the toughest and most engaging poem and translation in the whole book.

Spicer's retitling is perhaps not as nonsensical as Eshleman asserts; in it, Spicer takes up the poem's theme of "poverty," which lies at the root of desire, of love. The

Front cover for Spicer's Book of Magazine Verse, *which satirizes the literary establishment. The cover design imitates the format and logo of* Poetry *magazine.*

lover by definition *lacks,* a condition Lorca alludes to in the first stanza. Leaving this stanza untranslated, Spicer has nonetheless "translated" its central feature in the title. Eshleman's assertion that the rest of the so-called translation is a "mess" refers undoubtedly to the awkward and/or erroneous choices Spicer makes, as well as to the additions; but it is a "failure" only by the criterion of "fidelity."

The real problem is that the poem seems slight, though no more so in Spicer's hands than in Lorca's. It does not stand up to the complexity of the poem following it. But Spicer did not intend this to be read as a single, isolated poem; it is, rather, part of a "serial" poem, intended to be read both as it "corresponds" with and to Lorca's poems and to the rest of the poems in the book. Spicer would seem to be translating not individual Lorca poems so much as Lorca himself. The position of "Song of the Poor," then, immediately preceding the "Ode for Walt Whitman" makes its stark simplicity that much more striking. Read as Spicer's struggle with his own sexuality, it declares the cost of loving that unnamed "you" of the poem, a theme whose variations are played in ominous harmonies in the next poem. Significantly, it is the only poem in *After Lorca* that is not dedicated to someone. Is this the dedicatory poem to Lorca? to Walt Whitman? But it is also not inconceivable that Spicer was, as Eshleman suggests, parodying the Lorca poem. Certainly Spicer's jesting attitude to the problem of translation would warn us not to take each of these poems entirely "seriously." This might explain the almost self-mocking "mistranslation" of "hurts me" to "feels sorry for me." Perhaps better, there is a faint mocking of pity or self-pity that weaves its way through the book. The theme of "poverty," then, has been translated both as the lover's lack and as the condescension that appears most obviously a few poems later in "Narcissus":

> Poor Narcissus
> My sorrow
> Self of my sorrow.

Seen in the context of the book as a whole, "Song of the Poor" is but a single stanza; its seeming triviality is an issue to which we will return later in this essay.

So "things do not connect," in Spicer's translation, "they correspond." His explicit concern is to make "real objects" correspond to/with "real objects"—poems with poems, language with language.

> Even these letters. They *correspond* with something (I don't know what) that you have written (perhaps as unapparently as that lemon corresponds to this piece of seaweed) and, in turn, some future poet will write something which *corresponds* to them. That is how we dead men write to each other.

He wants, he says, to bring the "real" *across* time in language—but what he means by "real" is a real question. He seems to vacillate between being a postmodern Platonist in search of essences and a post-modern Aristotelian in search of the here and now. Out of context, his desire to make the invisible visible is but a restatement of the Kantian concrete universal, yet Spicer's "invisible" world is a living one. He wants the lemon "to be a lemon that the reader could cut or squeeze or taste—a real lemon like a newspaper in a collage is a real newspaper." His concern with the real seems to respond to two poles in his writing. On the one hand, it refers to a kind of authenticity of expression related to objectivist aesthetics. Like Pound, he advocates the direct treatment of the thing, uncluttered by sentiment, abstraction, superfluity. This sense of the "real" in poetry is described by Pound, in his essay "A Retrospect," as follows:

> As to Twentieth century poetry, and the poetry which I expect to see written during the next decade or so, it will, I think, move against poppycock, it will be harder and saner, it will be what Mr. Hewlett calls "nearer the bone." It will be as much like granite as it can be, its force will lie in its truth, its interpretative power (of course, poetic force does always rest there); I mean it will not try to seem forcible by rhetorical din, and luxurious riot. We will have fewer painted adjectives impeding the shock and stroke of it. At least for myself, I want it so, austere, direct, free from emotional slither.

Spicer writes—as, actually, Emily Dickinson might have said—nearer the bone, eschewing not only the painted adjectives but any rhetoric tainted by what he elsewhere calls the "English Department" of the writer's feelings. But Spicer especially wished to avoid "emotional slither," or what he called "the big lie of the personal":

> Loneliness is necessary for pure poetry. When someone intrudes into the poet's life (and any sudden personal contact, whether in the bed or in the heart, is an intrusion) he loses his balance for a moment, slips into being who he is, uses his poetry as one would use money or sympathy. The person who writes the poetry emerges, tentatively, like a hermit crab from a conch shell. The poet, for that instant, ceases to be a dead man.

In order to write poetry, the poet must be a dead man— dead, that is, to the inessential, to the "emotional slither." The poem is to include what *really* matters, not the temporary and strictly personal concerns that would make the poem into "something one would exchange for foreign money."

At the same time, however, Spicer's poems *are* very personal. Each of the poems in ***After Lorca,*** for example, is dedicated to someone, a gesture that is both sexual and amorous. The language too is a uniquely Spicerian mixture of the high and the low—of literary allusions, bar talk, puns, and bad jokes. While arguing that the poem originates outside of the poet, Spicer nonetheless acknowledges the poet's role in articulation. As he points out, "if you have a cleft palate and are trying to speak with the tongue of men and angels, you're gonna still speak through a cleft palate"; certainly Lorca is made to speak through Spicer's peculiar palate. Spicer was fond of comparing the poet—as a receiver of messages—to the radio, but he recognized the analogy to be imperfect. The poet develops "scar-tissue"; he

> Takes too many messages. The right to the ear that floored him in New Jersey. The right to say that he stood six rounds with a champion.

Authenticity of expression, then, demands an oscillation between the "outside" of the poet and language, between the objective and the subjective—between the poet and the translator, the living and the dead. The "real," then, is where Spicer as subject is not; it is not something that can be represented, but it can be caught in the web of language and made thus visible: "Words," Spicer says, "are what sticks to the real."

Spicer's choice to begin his correspondence course in translation with Lorca is not insignificant; indeed, Lorca was one of the most influential figures for the boom of American poetry in the 1950s and 60s. He has sponsored aesthetic theories as widely diverse as those of Robert Bly and Robert Duncan; his theory of the *duende* has been read as the archetype for all varieties of expressivist poetics. It is all the more interesting, then, that Lorca's *duende* seems to be whispering in Spicer's direction as well, for Spicer's poetics is aimed squarely against the "expressive." What Spicer would have been interested in is the connection between the *duende* and fate or fatality; he shares with Lorca the view of the writer's activity as a solitary struggle with an "outside," a struggle with possibly mortal consequences. Lorca also believes that the *duende* may change the character of a work as it passes from interpreter to interpreter: "the *Duende* of the interpreter," Lorca says, "creates a new marvel that retains the appearance—and the appearance only—of the originating form." Such an interpreter finds "something new, something never before encountered, which put lifeblood and art into bodies void of expression." Or, in Spicer's translation, "that lemon may become this lemon, or it may even become this piece of seaweed"—or spikenard may become seaweed. For both poets the justification for such transformations lies in the sense of fate and fatality about writing. Lorca was in addition a particularly important figure for the considerable number of homosexual poets, including Spicer, of the San Francisco Renaissance, for whom Lorca's "Ode for Walt Whitman" is something of a touchstone.

The operative term for Spicer's correspondence with Lorca—and to translation—is the word "after." The condition of all translation, of course, is that at least in the temporal sense, it follows the original text. Spicer, however, does not simply want to be relaying old news. As a receiver of messages from Lorca's *duende,* Spicer's task as a poet and translator is not to "represent" these messages but to "present" them, a point he makes repeatedly in the letters to Lorca. In Spicer's own terms, he does not want to give us rotting lemons but fresh ones; in this sense, Spicer's theory is remarkably similar to Walter Benjamin's, as articulated in his "The Task of the Translator." Benjamin also argues against a representational model for translation, proposing instead an organic model: the translation does not reproduce the original, but completes it, providing for the continued life of a work:

> Just as the manifestations of life are intimately connected with the phenomenon of life without being of importance to it, a translation issues from the original—not so much from its life as from its afterlife. . . . The idea of life and afterlife in works of art should be regarded with an entirely unmetaphorical objectivity.

Translation provides a mode of living on, of survival after death, and each text contains in its form the law of that survival, a sort of DNA for its translation. Translation is charged with the restitution and growth not only of the text, but of Language itself.

If Spicer's translations provide for the survival, the afterlife, of Lorca, they do not do so merely because of the sequential arrangement, Spicer's texts coming *later* than Lorca's. While this "after" is a sign of temporal location, it is also a sign of the writing's desire, of Spicer's pursuit—his courtship—of Lorca. The poems/translations are like love letters, intended to revive the beloved. And the go-between, shuttling between Eros and Thanatos, is, in Spicer's language, the ghost, the sign of the crossover between life and death.

It is not surprising, then, that one of the features of Spicer's correspondence with Lorca—his translation—is a homoerotic subtext, a gay language. The critical parameters of such a language, which Bruce Boone begins to lo-

cate in his important essay on Frank O'Hara, are defined by an apparent superficiality of tone and a nonmoralizing irony—precisely the sort of tone we have seen in Spicer's "Song of the Poor." It is, Boone says, a "trivializing" tone, functioning to displace the "seriousness" or danger of real connections, and it relies on rhetorical strategies that at once propose and defeat "connection," conjunctions that do not conjoin or pronouns whose antecedents are left unspecified. This trivializing typical of gay language use is distinct, Boone goes on to point out, from the kind of trivial writing found in newspapers or magazines, for example, for gay language trivializes as "a ruse whose intent is to disarm the intelligence of the 'other'." While Spicer's personal sexuality was very different from O'Hara's—Spicer's homosexual poetry reveals a less comfortable relation to his physicality—his position in a poetic and homosexual community was very similar to O'Hara's. Spicer's immediate poetic community in the Bay Area during the 1950s, largely homosexual, was distinct from the more visible "beat" scene that included Allen Ginsberg and Gregory Corso. Spicer's group—clustered around the triumvirate of Spicer, Robin Blaser, and Robert Duncan—was, like O'Hara's group, both oppositional and marginal.

Spicer's translations of Lorca do not, as the Lorca poems often do, bury homoerotic allusions in ambiguous gender categories. But, while homoeroticism is explicit in the poetry, this does not in itself constitute "gay" language; it is rather in the practice of discourse that we would find evidence of such a language. As an example of Spicer's poetics of translation in the praxis of gay language, let us look at one of the poems from **After Lorca,** "Frog." The title itself and the opening five lines seem slight, as Eshleman notes, a silly version of Basho's famous frog pond poem:

> Like all the novels I've read
> My mind is going to a climax
> And a climax means a splash in the pool.
>   i   i   i
> Booing. Booing. Booing.

The image of this "climax" as a sort of cartoon dive into the pool ("boing"), juxtaposed with the equally silly cartoon sound of a ghost "booing"—or is it the crowd's sign of disapproval?—seems to dismiss the importance of the "climax." While a "climax" is as fleeting, certainly, as this splash in the pool, the language equates its ephemerality with triviality. The next line, however, turns the poem in a more serious direction:

> And your heart is full of water
> And your nose can't hardly breathe.
> Remember
> How black those pinetrees were that fire burned.
> All that black forest. And the noise
> (Splash)
> Of a single green needle.

In a shift typical of Spicer's work, and especially of the poems in **After Lorca,** he moves from the "I" of the first line to an unspecified "you" in the sixth, a pronoun whose ghostly identity could be filled in many ways, one of which would finally resolve back into the "I." For the "I" who makes the "splash in the pool" seems to be addressing the image *in* the water, that is, an image that could only be the "I" 's reflection, and not a "you" at all. Combining the images of fire and water, the poet/lover drowns and burns, consumed not, it seems, by love, but by loneliness, marked by the sound (soundless) of a single pine needle. In this light, the poem is "about" an unsatisfactory narcissism, the climax of masturbation. The imperative mode of the eighth line ("Remember") serves as a reminder to the "I" himself of a kind of desolation and emptiness. The most interesting feature of this poem, however, occurs in the fourth line, which consists of three lower-case "i" 's spaced across the line—the splashes in the pool? Or the poetic "i" rippling across the poem, hidden in the "boo-ing" of the nonsensical fifth line.

"Frog" is not, in fact, a translation, though it illustrates nonetheless Spicer's translation practice. The poem grows logically or poetically from the previous one, a translation of Lorca's "Debussy":

> My shadow moves silently
> Upon the water in the ditch.
> Upon my shadow are the frogs
> Blocked off from the stars.

Shadow and reflection unite with the surface of the water, the image unbroken until the "splash" of the next poem. The image occurs significantly again in another transla-tion, "Narcissus":

> How wide-awake the frogs are
> They won't stay out of the surface
> In which your madness and my madness
> Mirrors itself
>
> Poor Narcissus
> My sorrow
> Self of my sorrow.

The poem reverberates both formally and thematically against *many* others in this serial poem: "And your heart will never break at what you are hearing," "The pine nee-dles fall / Like an ax in the forest," "Child, / How you keep falling into rivers", etc. The use of the connective "and" to introduce a line, the metonymic "heart" stand-ing for desire, the images of water, mirrors, glass, shad-ows, reflections, drowning—all of this makes this poem "correspond" to the rest of the book. The manifestation of Spicer's "madness" is precisely this mirroring effect; in fact, Spicer tries to go *through* the mirror in a postmodern completion of that Rimbaudian gesture wherein the "I" must become an "Other." For Spicer this gesture is al-ready doubled in his personal and sexual "otherness." The poem's apparent triviality, like that of "Song of the Poor," is a gesture both for and against that otherness.

Spicer's theory of translation finally demands that we read it intertextually, acknowledging the sexuality of the sub-text. The poems "correspond," he says, in one of the early letters to Jim Alexander, in "a fantastically inefficient sys-tem," not unlike a game of post office:

> And it is almost impossible to list the random
> places from which they will deliver their letters.
> A box of shredded wheat, a drunken comment,
> a big piece of paper, a shadow meaningless ex-
> cept as a threat or a communication, a throat.

This letter makes the identification between letters and signs of all kinds—poems, kisses, shadows—explicit. The post office then becomes the linguistic structure by which the exchange of signs is made possible.

Spicer's dead letter office—through which dead men, of course, correspond—provides the metaphoric extension of his earlier correspondence metaphor. What he accom-plishes in *After Lorca* by expanding the possibilities of translation he must find new techniques for in the later books. The doubling of translation is enacted in puns, pro-nouns, fractured citations, yet the principle of intertextu-ality, where one text meets another in a doubling of author and translator, self and other, inside and outside, com-mands both the poetics and its complementary interpre-tive ratios. I would like, then, to look briefly at an example of Spicer's translation of "translation" in the later books.

"Hisperica Famina," a poem from *The Heads of the Town Up to the Aether,* deals with the thematic issue of transla-tion in a poetics appropriate to the theme. It is located in the "Homage to Creeley" section, which in fact deals with the problem of "translating" a text into a commentary. Each poem is accompanied by a shadowy double—the commentary—at the bottom of the page, separated from it by a line. "Hisperica Famina" provides a paradigm for the problem of translating lurking in the rest of the sec-tion:

> Joan of Arc
> Built an ark
> In which she placed
> Three peas
> —Can you imagine translating this poem into
>   New English—
> In the ark
> Were three ghosts
> Named Hymen, Simon, and Bynem
> —Can you imagine ghosts like that translating
>   these poems into New English—
> I, they, him, it, her
> I, they, him, it, ourselves, her.

"Hisperica Famina" is first of all a kind of translation, in this case, a transformation of nursery rhymes; one can hear in the distance "The Queen of Hearts / She made some tarts," for example, and references to various of the night sea journeys undertaken by Wynken, Blynken, and Nod or the butcher, the baker, and the candlestick maker in boats made out of sieves. Joan of Arc is allowed to re-place the more famous ark-maker, Noah, first by virtue of her name (Arc/ark), and second, by the similarity be-tween Noah's and her missions. Thus, Spicer layers the rescue from the Biblical deluge upon France's liberation, and those both upon fantastical night-time journeys through nursery rhyme. The poem occurs in the section of "Homage to Creeley" dedicated to the Princess of Coc-teau's *Orphée,* who functions, Spicer tells us, as "a Repre-sentative of The Dead"; Joan of Arc's car, though it is sim-ilar to the Noah's ark of rescue, is here the literary vehicle of death. Spicer's poem wavers between the ideas of rescue from death and journey to death, between the playful ref-erences to children's poems and more serious references to death, between the sleep of children and the sleep of ghosts.

The poem's dialogue with itself and the reader on the subject of translation ("Can you imagine translating this poem into New English") is in fact an oblique reference to the poem's title, which is taken from an obscure sixth-century composition. The *Hisperica Famina* is written, according to *The Cambridge Bibliography of English Literature*, in a pastiche of Hebrew, Greek, and Vulgar Latin along with words of unknown origin, a language called *Geheimsprache*. Literally, it would be nearly impossible to "translate" the *Hisperica* into "New English," "Old English," or any other language except, perhaps, Spicer's. According to Robert Duncan, Spicer would have seen the book referred to in *The Cambridge History of Medieval Literature* and/or in a book by Leo Weiner entitled *Contributions toward a History of Arabico-Gothic Culture.* The *Hisperica* provides just the right mixture of obscurity, occultism, and nonsense that would have fascinated Spicer; he finds a compatible ghost in the unknown author of this text who, like himself, revels in linguistic play.

The explanatory text accompanying **"Hisperica Famina"** bears a typically oblique relation to the poem:

> The madmen who drive cars into the distances of dying or who predict football games are celebrated here. Hisperica famina means western words.

> The three ghosts have names that are mockeries of your names.

> Your names (and theirs) are the afterwords mentioned pronouns.

The correspondence between this "explanation" and the poem mirrors the relation between Spicer's "translations" and the poems he purports to have translated. The reader would no doubt be surprised, for example, to discover that "Joan of Arc / Built an ark" is a celebration of madmen and cars. Yet Spicer has simply translated Joan of Arc's name into the Princess's vehicle of death by a fortuitous anagram: Arc/ark/car. And when Spicer claims that "The madmen who drive cars into the distances of dying" are celebrated in **"Hisperica Famina,"** he is making more or less explicit what lies in the layerings of that poem's references to voyages. The madmen "who predict football games"—celebrated alongside those who drive cars—are connected with the cars of death by virtue of the connection between the concepts of prediction and of fatality, concepts central to Spicer's poetics.

The most interesting section of the poem, however, is the translation of the ghosts' names into pronouns standing for the ghosts, the reader, and the poem. "The three ghosts have names that are mockeries of your names," Spicer says. The principle generating the ghosts' names is that of rhyme, a principle as arbitrary—though more amusing—as any naming system. When those names (and ours) are translated into pronouns, they change shapes, appearing variously as the subject (I, ourselves) and as the absent third parties (they, him, it, her). They point both to the poem and to its other. Thus, the pronouns are "afterwords" just as Spicer's translations are "after" Lorca, providing the afterlife of what shimmers in the poem.

"The poem begins to mirror itself," Spicer says in his last book, the ***Book of Magazine Verse.*** As Spicer's language increasingly mirrors its own processes, as it becomes a kind of fake translation of itself, the distance between the source of the poem and the poet becomes simultaneously infinite and nonexistent. His use of pronouns is just one indication of the way Spicer's theory of translation manifests itself in the poetics. Pronouns, like ghosts, point both to an endistanced source and to themselves, confusing both identity and temporality; poems, like translations, bring to life what is potential in language:

> The motion of the afterlife. The afterlife of the poem—

> Define ghosts as an India-rubber eraser created to erase their own past.

> The motion of the afterlife. And you will think immediately of a photograph. The ghost of it defined as a blob of ectoplasm—an anti-image.

> An anti-image as if merely by being dead it could make the motions of what it was to be apparent.

> An argument between the dead and the living.

Somehow "being dead" is what makes visible what it was to be living, thus providing the anti-image for the image—the negative out of which the image is made. It is thus that Spicer grapples with the problems of closure—understood in formal, epistemological, and metaphysical terms, bequeathed by the previous generation—and attempts to open his poems out upon language. His writing demonstrates most clearly the possibility of "intertranslatability," as it investigates the borders of the text, the limits of meaning. Here translation lives on in the writing. (pp. 426-42)

Lori Chamberlain, "Ghostwriting the Text: Translation and the Poetics of Jack Spicer," in Contemporary Literature, *Vol. 26, No. 4, Winter, 1985, pp. 426-42.*

Burton Hatlen

The poetry of Jack Spicer stubbornly refuses what has by now become the characteristic gesture of the modern poem: the invocation of a series of sensory images that claim to encode universal human feelings. This gesture is Romantic in that it locates the unifying personal consciousness at the center of the phenomenal world. In the pages of the *American Poetry Review* or of Dave Smith's massive new anthology of poets under forty, we see the final outcome of this Romantic aesthetic: a poetry almost entirely controlled by the first person pronoun, which claims to name the one fixed point in an unstable world—a poetry, therefore, of nostalgia, for in the end it turns out that in such poems the self is constituted largely by its longing for a lost homeland. Spicer's work, born out of a rejection of "the big lie of the personal," eschews nostalgia more rigorously than any other body of poetry I can think of, it systematically displaces the first person pronoun, and it consistently recognizes the ultimate mystery of the relationship between the knowing consciousness and the world of "things." As such, Spicer's work continues to offer contemporary poets an alternative starting point.

Spicer's work also offers a continuing challenge to modern criticism. American criticism, at least as practiced within that "English Department" which Spicer saw as the mausoleum of poetry, still generally accepts as orthodoxy the assumptions of the New Critics, who saw the poem as essentially an "expression" of, an "objective correlative" for the unique sensibility of the poet. But Spicer's poetry continually subverts any attempt to read it as an "expression" of the poet's sensibility. Here is a poetry that demands a new set of critical categories; this essay is dedicated to the search for a way of talking about a poetry which dismisses the "personal" as a "big lie," and insists on treating language itself as prior both to images and "feelings."

To date, roughly a dozen critics have addressed themselves to the challenge posed by Spicer's poetry. For the most part, they have turned to the writings of one or another of the recently fashionable French *philosophes,* in hopes of finding a vocabulary to describe Spicer's poetic practice. Thus Robin Blaser, Spicer's editor, has described his "practice of outside" in terms borrowed from Merleau-Ponty and Foucault. More recently, the contributors to the *Boundary 2* special issue on Spicer have generally seen his work as constituting a poetic equivalent of Derrida's deconstructive practice. I have found the suggestions of some of these critics, especially Robin Blaser and Jed Rasula, very useful. But I also find myself distressed at how easily such readings of Spicer slip over his poetic practice, into talk about the "ideas" presumably implicit in that practice. By and large the deconstructive commentators on Spicer seems more interested in the metaphysical resonances of his work than in what the *language* is there doing, and it is on Spicer's language that I want to focus here. Rather than seeking some sort of ontological resonance in Spicer's poetry, I want to look for the ways his writing seeks to remain faithful to the "openness" of language itself. Spicer, of course, never read Mikhail Bakhtin, but his poems offer evidence that he fully recognized what Bakhtin described as the inherently *dialogic* character of language. More specifically, in *Marxism and the Philosophy of Language,* Bakhtin argues that the "relativistic individualism" of the late bourgeois epoch finds its characteristic voice in what Bakhtin calls "quasi-direct discourse," a discourse which systematically breaks down the boundary between the voice of the author and other voices that enter into the text, by allowing these other voices to control lexical and syntactic choices, even in passages where the "author" seems to be speaking. Spicer's poetry, as I shall show, displays all the qualities of what Bakhtin describes as the discourse of relativistic individualism, for in it the poet encourages divergent voices to co-exist, overlap, and interpenetrate. Generally Spicer seeks to honor the difference between those voices, even as he allows them to intersect—although in some of the later books an overload seems to occur, as the text is flooded by other voices which the author deliberately refuses to control. I find the willed disorder of these later books a bit overwhelming. So I propose here to focus on the book which inaugurates Spicer's mature work: *After Lorca.* In this book we can observe some degree of balance between the authorial voice and the voice of the other, but we can also watch Spicer in the act of breaking free from monologic discourse. By examining *After Lorca,* I hope to develop both a grammar and a rhetoric of the "voice of the other" that will help us understand this particular book and Spicer's poetics in general.

To begin with, I would like to linger a while over the curious fact that Spicer's "breakthrough" book—the book in which, by his own judgment, he first came into his own as a poet—was a "translation." Ezra Pound's translations mark the end of the idealist illusion that "the poem" exists somehow above and beyond the language in which it is "clothed," and that the translator's job is merely to move "the poem" from one language into another. By beginning his *Cantos* with a translation of a Renaissance translation of Homer, Pound also demystifies the notion of an "original" text: any text, it seems, is inscribed over some antecedent text, which in turn . . . Rather than being an exercise for the left hand, something that poets do in odd moments, translation becomes for Pound a central artistic act. Indeed, to Pound *all* writing is translation. As a translator, Spicer locates himself within the Poundian tradition, in that he consistently struggles to bring into focus the contradictory nature of the enterprise in which he is engaged, i.e. the way a translation seeks at once to be a "faithful version" of an "original" text and an autonomous work of art. He recognizes that the author of the "original" poem and its translator are both allies and combatants; their voices constantly merge and separate, separate and merge. Like Pound, Spicer doesn't want to bury these contradictions. Rather, he wants to take them as his starting point.

All of his books, Spicer would later insist, were "dictated." His job was, he announces in the Vancouver lectures, not to "invent" poems, but to serve as a transmitter, a radio through which the "voice of the other" might speak. In *After Lorca* the voice speaking through Spicer, the "dictator," assumes a reasonably traditional guise. It is, we are invited to believe, simply the voice of another poet, Federico Garcia Lorca, murdered in Granada, Spain, in 1936. Yet in various ways Spicer acknowledges the problematic relationship between the "original" text and the translation. This process begins in Spicer's title, which deliberately shifts our attention from the things translated—the "Lorca poems" which will here appear "in English"—to the act of translation. The phrase "after——" signals that the texts to follow are not to be judged according to their "correctness" but according to their success or failure as autonomous poems. Further, the title invites us to reflect on precisely what it means to come "after." Spicer's text is "after" Lorca's in at least three senses. Spicer will here truly dedicate himself to following after, retracing, the movements of Lorca's language: many of Spicer's translations are relatively "straight." But Spicer is also imitating Lorca's general poetic behavior, and to comport himself *like* Lorca he must possess and transmute the work of his predecessors, as Lorca possessed and transmuted the work of his own predecessors. Finally, Spicer's text is also *subsequent to* Lorca's. What Lorca wrote changed the world, and Spicer is writing in that new world. In this respect Spicer cannot simply rewrite Lorca's poems in English, nor can he even re-enact what Lorca did. Rather he must find a way of living and writing in a world that *includes* Lorca. Spicer's title thus reminds us that translation is at once necessary (how do we know who we are unless we can possess the past?) and impossible (we cannot, with the best will in the world, make the past present).

As we now move into Spicer's book, we encounter a preface purportedly written by Lorca himself, which again insists that we acknowledge the problematic character of this peculiar act that we call "translation":

> It must be made clear at the start that these poems are not translations. In even the most literal of them Mr. Spicer seems to derive pleasure in inserting or substituting one or two words which completely change the mood and often the meaning of the poem as I had written it. More often he takes one of my poems and adjoins to half of it another half of his own, giving rather the effect of an unwilling centaur. (Modesty forbids me to speculate which end of the animal is mine.) Finally there are an almost equal number of poems that I did not write at all (one supposes that they must be his) executed in a somewhat fanciful imitation of my early style. The reader is given no indication which of the poems belong to which category, and I have further complicated the problem (with malice aforethought I must admit) by sending Mr. Spicer several poems written after my death which he has also translated and included here.

But while "Lorca" here denies that the poems in *After Lorca* are translations, every poem in the body of the book—even the "original" "Spicer" poems—is subtitled "a translation," except for the final "Postscript for Marianne Moore." And the preface raises some further questions, by gleefully proclaiming that the book to follow will flout what the conventional wisdom would regard as the first principle of translation: namely, the preservation of a certain distance between the voice of the original poet (who, after all, claims the authority of being "original") and that of the translator (who may have his own voice but, for the duration of the translation, agrees to subordinate that voice to another). Rather than establishing such a distance, the preface deliberately blurs the distinction between what is "Lorca's" and what is "Spicer's"—and in this respect Spicer's method seems both brasher and rasher than Pound's.

On the one hand (the right hand?), this preface invites us to begin sorting out the "translations" from the "original" Spicer poems; and Clayton Eshleman has done just that—at which point we also discover that Lorca/Spicer has lied to us, for in fact less than one third of these poems, not one half as the preface would suggest, are "original" Spicer texts, and it is difficult to find *any* examples of the "centaur" poems to which "Lorca" refers. On the other hand, even as it acknowledges the difference between what "Lorca" and "Spicer" have here created, this preface seems to deny the significance of the boundary in question. For if Spicer regarded this difference as important, he could easily have identified these groups of poems for us—as Robert Lowell, for example, collected his *Imitations* in a single book, thus implicitly declaring his other poems to be "original." As "translations" then (and by this point I am finding it increasingly necessary to enclose this word in inverted commas), *After Lorca* at once ac-

knowledges the distance between "Lorca" and "Spicer" and systematically blurs that distance—just as the "quasidirect discourse" which Bakhtin sees as the distinctive idiom of modern prose narratives simultaneously acknowledges the differences between an authorial voice and the voices of his characters and breaks down these differences. This characteristic modernist gesture, Bakhtin suggests, creates a new kind of relationship between the self and other, both of which now become profoundly unstable entities. This endless dance of merger and division, I am proposing, also plays through all of Spicer's poetry, including *After Lorca*.

"Lorca's" preface also introduces us to a second way in which *After Lorca* breaks down the self/other opposition. In offering us a preface purportedly written by Lorca, Spicer immediately locates his text in an ironic mode—*we* know that Lorca is dead, and that dead men don't write prefaces. And irony by nature renders the self/other relationship unstable. Metaphors, we might say, create an instability in the object of discourse: in his famous "All the world's a stage" speech in *As You Like It*, does Jacques want to tell us something about the world, or about the stage, or about both? Analogously, irony makes us unsure *who* is speaking: in "A Modest Proposal," are we hearing the voice of a meticulously logical cannibal, or of the Dean of St. Patrick's, or both simultaneously? The preface to *After Lorca* pushes irony somewhere close to Swift's savagery. What begins as a mildly humorous conceit (What would Vallejo say if he could read Eshleman's translation?) darkens as the language circles around the unnameable fact: Lorca's murder. "I have been," "Lorca" coyly tells us, "removed from all contact with poetry for the last twenty years." The cadence suggests an aging ex-dilettante, a businessman who has given up the follies of youth. But *we* know how and why Lorca was "removed from all contact with poetry," and this knowledge gives the climactic lines of the preface—"The dead are notoriously hard to satisfy"—a poignant resonance, as the unspoken (our knowledge of Lorca's murder) and the spoken (Lorca's "removal" from poetry) finally merge. Yes, the demands of the dead—Lorca twenty years dead as Spicer wrote, Spicer himself now too twenty years dead—are absolute, and these claims become, in fact, a major concern of *After Lorca*. But the resonance of the climactic line depends directly on the ironic mode in which Spicer is here working, a mode which allows what is not said to become as important as what is said.

Irony, we should also recognize, always demands the active collaboration of the reader, thereby creating an *ad hoc* community of discourse. No statement is ever inherently ironic—irony is a rhetorical trope, not a grammatical form. If I *don't* know how Lorca died, I will miss the overtones of the preface. If I *do* know, I then join the poet as a member of a privileged group of insiders, united by the fact that "they," the outsiders, won't "get it." That Spicer adopts a dead poet as his ironic persona also points us toward another important fact: The community here at issue is above all a community of poets, a secret community ("They will kill us if they discover what we're really doing"), a "gay" (in all the past and current senses of that word) community. *After Lorca*, the preface promises us, will be a hermetic text, a book of wisdom only for initiates. But we are all invited to join this community: all we need do is open the book and begin to read.

Irony is the most traditional stratagem for breaking down the self/other dichotomy, and as such it cannot content Spicer for long. Instead he presses beyond irony, to explore new ways of rendering both the "self" and the "other" problematic. As an example, we might reflect on the dedications which Spicer has appended to almost every poem in the book. "Who are these people?" the outsider may initially wonder. John Ryan, George Stanley, etc., none of them exactly household names. Presumably, they are Spicer's friends, for in a dedication it is acceptable to refer to your friends as if everyone should know who they are. Anyone who knows a little about the Spicer circle can confirm this hypothesis. But these people are not only Spicer's friends—many, perhaps all of them, are fellow poets. Some have had poetic careers of their own: Ebbe Borregaard, Don Allen, Robin Blaser, Steve Jonas, James Broughton, Helen Adam. There are some exceptions to the general pattern, but for the most part the dedications suggest that Spicer has systematically appropriated Lorca's poems and has transformed them into a celebration of the common life shared by a circle (formed, we know now, in imitation of the Stefan George circle) of mostly gay poets. From a conventional perspective, to translate a poem by Lorca and dedicate it to one of your own friends is a supremely presumptuous act. The "poem," we assume, "belongs to" its "original" author, who alone has the right to give it away. Yet there is a lavish generosity in Spicer's dedications. He will give away all that he has and everything he has managed to borrow from Lorca too. And in doing so he also transforms Lorca into another one of his friends. The letters in *After Lorca* of course, consistently treat Lorca as a friend—indeed, they are not so different in tone from the letters Spicer was writing at about the same time to some of his "real" friends, such as Graham Mackintosh and Jim Alexander (both series are published in *Caterpillar 12*). In one of the letters in *After Lorca,* Spicer wonders how Lorca's poems "found people" and tells of how his own poems seek to give themselves away, to find friends. "All this," the letter concludes, "is to explain why I dedicate each of our poems to someone." "*Our* poems"—in this proud phrase Spicer proclaims that he has transcended the distance between himself and Lorca, created a community which extends through time as well as space. To Spicer, it would seem, the poem isn't mine or yours. Rather it is *ours:* we create it collaboratively, and we consume it sacramentally, breaking and eating the word made flesh.

In *After Lorca,* Spicer serves not only as translator but as editor; in selecting the Lorca poems to be included here and arranging them in a particular order, he once again affirms his sense of writing within an ongoing community of poets, a community within which identities constantly merge and separate. The first poem in *After Lorca* is Lorca's portrait of Juan Ramon Jimenez. Edwin Honig identifies Jimenez as one of Lorca's three principal poetic mentors. Jimenez outlived Lorca by more than twenty years, but Lorca's poem nevertheless strikes an elegiac note: the poet's imagination makes a "wound" in the "white endlessness," but then he himself dissolves into the whiteness of "snow, seaweed, and salt." By placing this poem immediately after the preface, Spicer transforms it into *his* elegy for Lorca, who has indeed passed into the "white endlessness." Thus Lorca's elegiac tribute to his poetic master becomes Spicer's tribute to his own master, Lorca himself. Furthermore, Lorca's poem appears to be a conscious imitation of Jimenez's neo-symbolist manner—cf., for example, the line about walking on a "soundless carpet of pigeon feathers." As an act of homage-through-imitation, this poem indirectly sanctions Spicer's own "fanciful imitations of [Lorca's] early style." In selecting this poem to open *After Lorca,* then, Spicer accepts a poetic lineage: if Lorca is his father, then Jimenez is his grandfather.

There are other fathers (and grandfathers, even mothers and grandmothers) in *After Lorca.* In particular, it seems to me no accident that the only poem which Spicer selects from *Poet In New York* is the famous "Ode for Walt Whitman"; nor is it an accident that he places this poem at the center of *After Lorca.* Here we can see Lorca—who at the time he wrote it was living in a Columbia University dormitory, alone in a country whose language he could not speak, deeply troubled in his sexuality—in the act of discovering a poetic father. It was 1929—only a year or two after Hart Crane had also adopted Whitman as his guide to the hell and the purgatory of the new world. In selecting this poem for translation, then, Spicer again affirms a sense of poetic continuity: from Whitman to Lorca to Spicer. There's an additional irony here, since Spicer, as an American poet, "owns" Whitman in a way that Lorca could not. But by appropriating Whitman "through" Lorca, Spicer at once internationalizes his lineage and foregrounds the troubled homosexuality that all three poets shared. If *After Lorca* begins with Lorca's tribute to Jimenez and pivots on Lorca's "Ode for Whitman," it ends, we may further note, with a "Spicer" poem that echoes these other "ancestral" poems: **"Radar,"** a "postscript" (thus avowedly not a "translation"), dedicated to Marianne Moore, the only dedicatee who is not a member of the Spicer circle. I take it that Moore here synecdochically represents an entire generation of Modernist masters, including Pound and Williams and probably Stevens along with Moore. These poets are Spicer's immediate forebears, his fathers and—for the singling out of Moore seems significant—mothers. *After Lorca,* as a book, thus moves from Lorca's acknowledgement of his descent from Jimenez, through a celebration of Whitman as the ur-father of us all, to Spicer's acceptance of his position as heir of the great American Modernists. And in the process we see "Lorca" and "Spicer" gradually move together, as joint inhabitants of Whitman's capacious beard, and then separate again, as Spicer accepts his own unique destiny.

The three poems I have singled out also suggest a thematic design to *After Lorca,* one that is both "Lorca's" and "Spicer's." In the third of Spicer's six letters to Lorca, positioned only two pages after the Whitman poem, Spicer declares that he would "like to make poems out of real objects." Spicer here voices his own longing for a "poetics of presence," a poetry that issues out of a simple act of faith in the reality of the things of this world. The poetry of the great American Modernists, I have argued elsewhere can be read—was read by many of their immediate successors—as such a "poetry of presence," as a simple declaration of faith in the *thereness* of that wasp and that fringe of mountains in Pisa, or that red wheelbarrow, or that carriage from Sweden—and an affirmation that this *thereness* is enough. The works of these poets can also be read as grounded in a faith that poetry can fully body forth the things of this world, make them present to us. But as Spicer in this same letter regretfully notes, "things decay," "real things become garbage"—and this gap between relatively stable words and transitory things, between the signifier and the signified, ultimately makes a "poetry of presence" untenable. For this reason, the poets of Spicer's generation, especially Duncan, campaigned vigorously against the (in Duncan's words) "this-is-just-a-wheelbarrow-Williams" of Cid Corman and others, and in favor of a "magical" reading of Williams and other American Modernists. (The principal document in this campaign is Duncan's *H. D. Book*. To this end, the poets of the Spicer/Duncan/Blaser sought to place themselves in the context of a larger European tradition (both Duncan and Blaser wrote adaptations of Nerval's "Les Chimeres") and especially in relationship to the writings of the continental surrealists—including Lorca.

I read **After Lorca** as itself a document in this struggle to redefine the meaning of American Modernism. "We have both," Spicer tells Lorca in this same letter, "tried to be independent of images (you from the start and I only when I tired of trying to make things connect), to make the things visible rather than to make pictures of them." The phrasing here suggests that Spicer came to Lorca out of a dissatisfaction with the more imagistic poetics of his earlier work:

> And when the fish come in to die
> They slap their heads against the rocks until
>   they
> float
> Downstream on one dead eye
> ("Poems 1946-56")

The image of the dead fish is disturbing enough, but the language here does not explicitly acknowledge the problematic relationship between the poet's imagination and the "things" which the imagination tries to grasp. In contrast, Lorca's "surrealist" poetics persistently tries to remain faithful to the shifting, indeterminate relationship between the poetic imagination and the things of the world. The "things" of Lorca's world are never stable:

> On the branches of laurel
> Saw two shadowy pigeons.
> One of them was the sun
> The other the moon.
>
> . . . . . .
>
> On the branches of laurel
> Saw two naked pigeons.
> The one was the other
> And the both of them no one.

If we can imagine Williams' wheelbarrow not simply sitting there "beside" those chickens but *turning into* a

chicken, we will have some sense of the differences between a "poetics of presence" and Lorca's more indeterministic poetics. Spicer was drawn to Lorca, I believe, by the way that Lorca's poetry refuses to reify either the knowing subject or the object of attention, the way it traces the shifting dialogic interaction between the imagination and the things of this world. **After Lorca,** in this respect, marks Spicer's decisive break with a poetics of presence, and a commitment to what I have here identified, following Bakhtin, as a dialogic poetics, a poetics which tries to be faithful to "the world" swallows up the "self," and the "self" wounds "the world."

My metaphoric description of the self as both "swallowed by" and "wounding" the world comes from the Jimenez poem, which I shall at last quote in full:

> In the white endlessness
> Snow, seaweed, and salt
> He lost his imagination.
>
> The color white. He walks
> upon a soundless carpet made
> of pigeon feathers.
>
> Without eyes or thumbs
> He suffers a dream not moving
> But the bones quiver.
>
> In the white endlessness
> How pure and big a wound
> His imagination left.
>
> Snow, seaweed, and salt. Now
> In the white endlessness.

The "things" here are real enough: "snow, seaweed, salt." (I reject Eshleman's contention that the substitution of "seaweed" for the literal "spikenard" is "arbitrary." Rather, I think Spicer probably wanted something ordinary here, rather than the exotic "spikenard." He also wanted the association with another kind of endlessness that swallows up the imagination: the sea). But these things are not passive, simply "there"—rather they reach out to swallow up the imagination. Ultimately, the human imagination fails before the reality of snow, seaweed, and salt, and Spicer's version, reversing Lorca's last two lines, leaves us with the spectacle of that "white endlessness." There is a two-way process here, then, and active exchange between the knowing self and the object of knowledge: the two "wound" each other, interpenetrate, even change places. In a poetics of presence both the "I" and the object of its attention are fixed, determined entities. But Lorca/Spicer is here giving us something else.

In introducing this pattern of concerns, the Jimenez poem establishes a thematic focus for the entire book. The centrality of these concerns is, moreover, reaffirmed by the last poem in the book, **"Radar,"** the postscript to Marianne Moore:

> No one exactly knows
> Exactly how clouds look in the sky
> Or the shape of the mountains below them
> Or the direction in which fish swim.
> No one exactly knows.
> The eye is jealous of whatever moves
> And the heart

Is too far buried in the sand
To tell.

They are going on a journey
Those deep blue creatures
Passing us as if they were sunshine
Look
Those fins, those closed eyes
Admiring each last drop of the ocean.

I crawled into bed with sorrow that night
Couldn't touch his fingers. See the splash
Of the water
The noisy movement of cloud
The push of the humpbacked mountains
Deep at the sand's edge.

"Things," this poem tragically recognizes, remain forever beyond the grasp of the mind: we can never know these things "exactly"—as Moore's precise images would have us believe. We cannot know things exactly because we are *ourselves* things. Our eyes move *with* the fish, and at the same moment want to *be* fish. And the heart too is buried *in* the world, even as it tries to respond *to* what the eye sees. In contrast, the fish are *wholly* "in it," while we are both inside and outside. So what we "know" (mentally and sexually) is sorrow, and even sorrow we cannot quite touch. In the last lines of both the Jimenez poem and **"Radar"** the images return, but transformed, phantasmagoric. Only in a dream, it seems, can we "know things." Bracketing *After Lorca,* the Jimenez poem and **"Radar"** both suggest that the relationship between the imagination and the things of the world is deeply problematic. If we then place the Whitman Ode between these two texts, it starts to become clear the *After Lorca* wants to test out the central claim of the Romantic Tradition. More vigorously than any other poet, Whitman had affirmed the power of the imagination to absorb into itself the multifarious things of this world. Appropriately, Whitman becomes, at the end of Lorca's Ode, the earth of America itself: everything is absorbed into his body to be purified and made whole, thus inaugurating "the reign of the ear of wheat." And such is indeed Whitman's own vision of himself. But is the wholeness prophesied by Whitman only a myth? And if so, what then? These are, I believe, the questions that *After Lorca* wants, finally, to ask.

In the end, I propose, both Lorca and Spicer reject Whitman's totalitarian vision of the "self as Kosmos," a vision that denies the self/other distinction, in favor of a tragic vision of the self and the other as eternally seeking one another, interpenetrating, wounding each other, but in the end capable at best only of a dialogic relationship, not that ecstatic merger of which Whitman dreamed. "We find the body difficult, and speak across its walls like strangers" (*One Night Stand*)—so Spicer in an early poem. It is this distance, *and* this capacity to speak across distance, that Whitman and the Romantics cannot accept—and that both Lorca and Spicer *do* accept. I base this claim partly on a cluster of poems which seem to me central to *After Lorca.* As Edwin Honig notes, the Jimenez poem belongs to a cycle of three poems, all portraits of "musical sensualists"—the other two "sensualists" are Debussy and Verlaine. And Honig also points out that to each of these poems Lorca has "appended shorter poems to Bacchus,

Venus, and Narcissus." These six poems appear as a unit in Lorca's *Obras Completas,* and Spicer includes all six in *After Lorca.* The Debussy and Verlaine poems, like the Jimenez poem, evoke the evanescent passage of the artist's imagination over the things of this world. Thus at the beginning of the Debussy poem, as in the Jimenez poem, the artist (who is speaking? Lorca? Debussy? Spicer? All of them?) "wounds" the things of this world as his shadow passes over them, blocking their access to the stars:

My shadow moves silently
Upon the water in the ditch.

Upon my shadow are the frogs
Blocked off from the stars.

Yet the artist's imagination also seems to give something *to* the things it touches.

A hundred crickets try to mine gold
From the light in the rushes.

A light born in my heart
Upon the ditch, reflected.

So too, in the Verlaine poem, the poet takes the honeysuckle and the firefly and the moon into his song, and then allows the song to die on his lips, thus leaving these things "lost . . . in the shadow." In both poems the artistic imagination is active, reaching out, both taking from and giving to the world of things.

In the three mythological poems which Lorca pairs with his "portraits," "things" themselves become active, reaching out to touch *us.* Thus in "Bacchus," which Lorca offers as a companion piece to the Verlaine poem, the artist is pursued by more and more menacing presences:

An untouched green murmur.
The figtree wants to extend me its branches.

Like a panther its shadow
Stalks my poet shadow.

The moon has words with the dogs.
She is mistaken and begins over.

Yesterday, tomorrow, black, and green
Troop around my circle of laurel.

Where would you look for my lifetime
If I exchanged my heart?

—And the figtree shouts at me and advances
Terrible and extended.

And in the poignant "Narcissus," companion piece to "Debussy," the poet becomes a child drowned in the river of phenomenal experience:

Child,
How you keep falling into rivers.

At the bottom there's a rose
And in the rose there's another river.

Look at the bird. Look,
That yellow bird.

My eyes have fallen down
Into the water.

My god,
how they're slipping! Youngster!

—And I'm in the rose myself.

When I was lost in water I
Understood but won't tell you.

"Venus," the companion poem to the Jimenez poem, moves in a somewhat different direction, but here too the self is swallowed up by an infinite world "out there":

The dead girl
In the winding shell of the bed
Naked of the little wind and flowers
Surges on into perennial light.

If we read these six poems as a group, some very suggestive patterns emerge. The three artists and the three mythological figures all seem to be presences which the poet wants to invoke. They are all guides, powers, magically summoned by the poem. Yet there are some major differences too. The three artists all move *into* the world as their imaginations reach out to transform all the things that they touch. In the myth poems, *things themselves* become active. But the result is a kind of dialogue, a constant exchange of energy between the artistic imagination and the things of this world.

Spicer includes in *After Lorca* all six of the poems discussed above, but he separates them from one another, distributing them more or less randomly (except the Jimenez poem, whose placement is *not*, I have argued, accidental) through the book. The effect is to open up to other voices that dialogue between the imagination and the things of the world which Lorca has inaugurated, as Spicer inserts other poems by Lorca and even his own poems into this ongoing dialogue. Thus it would seem appropriate to look at a few more of the "original" "Spicer" poems, to see how these poems sustain and elaborate the dialogic interaction between the imagination and the things of the world which Lorca has initiated in the six poems discussed above. Here is an example:

Alba

If your hand had been meaningless
Not a single blade of grass
Would spring from the earth's surface.
Easy to write, to kiss—
No, I said, read your paper.
Be there
Like the earth
When shadow covers the wet grass.

The final image here has a Rilkean richness, redolent of "being," of earth. At this moment, the world of things seems to offer itself as a full and accessible repository of objective correlatives for the various states of the soul. Yet this more or less conventional image is here made to jostle against some odd neighbors. The opening lines make a statement so extreme as to seem absurd. Yet in the "dialogic" context I have here proposed we must take these lines seriously. "Meaning," it appears, is a condition neither of the mind nor of things, but of the meeting between the two. In its absence, the earth itself will dry out. In insisting upon a recognition of what the imagination gives to things, these lines counter-balance the final image,

which celebrates what things give to the imagination. And between those two sentences, we have an odd lurch. Suddenly the poem seems to be interrupted by a bit of spoken dialogue, as the speaker first reaches toward and then recoils from someone in the room—a lover, apparently. This erotic ambivalence seems to parallel the epistemological ambivalence of the framing passages: the opening lines pull back from the world, proclaiming that it is meaningless without us, while the final lines give themselves to the world. Paradoxically, the opening lines suggest fretful need, while the final ones are rich with acceptance of both the lover's and the world's simple "being there." The whole poem, in short, enacts that process of dialogic exchange between self and world which is, I have proposed, at work throughout *After Lorca.*

Still, the most obvious and innovative form of dialogic interaction in *After Lorca* remains to be discussed. I am referring to the letters which Spicer writes to Lorca and intersperses among his translations and imitations of Lorca poems. These letters allow Spicer to respond to Lorca, answer him, give something back; they turn the ordinarily monologic pattern of poetic discourse into a dialogue. Other poets have, of course, addressed their poems to other poets, even dead ones. Indeed, the elegy to the dead poet-friend has become a major literary sub-genre. And poets have spoken to the long dead too—friends they have come to know only through the printed page. ("Milton," says Wordsworth, "thou shouldst be living at this hour.") Yet, characteristically, Spicer also gives this kind of poetic interaction a new twist, defamiliarizes the "address to the dead poet." Traditionally, the speech to the dead has been a "high," formal poetic mode. Spicer writes a prose which persistently stops only a step short of the chatty:

But I am speaking of the first night, when I leave my apartment almost breathless, searching for someone to show the poem to. Often now there is no one. My fellow poets (those I showed poetry to ten years ago) are as little interested in my poetry as I am in theirs. We both compare the poems shown (unfavorably, of course) with the poems we were writing ten years ago when we could learn from each other. We are polite but it is as if we were trading snapshots of our children—old acquaintances who disapprove of each other's wives. Or were you more generous, Garcia Lorca?

This has, at first reading, the tone not of a ritual gesture or a conventional poetic exercise, but rather of a real letter to a real friend. This is the voice of love; for Spicer does indeed love Lorca, and like any lover he voices his love by eagerly attempting to share his experiences with the beloved. Yet the language here also has a fairly formal, even ironic, tone—the tone, perhaps, of a 19th century letter, rather than a 20th century letter. And this tinge of courtly formality acknowledges the unbridgeable distance between Lorca and Spicer—between the living and the dead, but between any two living human beings too, for Spicer is always acutely aware of the otherness of the other. The final question in the quoted paragraph seems to bring all these overtones into the open. How guarded, self-protective we all are, Spicer here admits. And how distant, ultimately mysterious Lorca remains, always beyond the reach even of a lover's imagination. The prose letter in which Spicer has chosen to address Lorca thus allows him both to affirm a hope of intimacy between himself and Lorca and to acknowledge the unbridgeable *distance* between them: a dual gesture once again, the kind of dual gesture which we have encountered again and again in *After Lorca,* at once ironic and astonishingly open, a gesture which we should now begin to recognize as typically Spicerian.

Along with an ongoing dialogue with Lorca, Spicer here also engages in a dialogue with Poetry Itself. I capitalize this noun because Spicer himself implicitly does so. "These letters," he tells Lorca in his second letter,

> are to be as temporary as our poetry is to be permanent. They will establish the bulk, the wastage that my sour-stomached contemporaries demand to help them swallow and digest the pure word. We will use up our rhetoric here so that it will not appear in our poems. Let it be consumed paragraph by paragraph, day by day, until nothing of it is left in our poetry and nothing of our poetry is left in it. It is precisely because these letters are unnecessary that they must be written.

Spicer here proposes an absolutely "pure" poetry, free of rhetoric, free of "invention" ("Prose invents—poetry discloses," he says in this same letter), free even, he suggests in his third letter, of language itself:

> A really perfect poem (no one yet has written one) could be perfectly translated by a person who did not know one word of the language it was written in. A really perfect poem has an infinitely small vocabulary.

The absolutely pure poetry here envisioned can be written, Spicer eventually suggests, only by and for the dead:

> Loneliness is necessary for pure poetry. When someone intrudes into the poet's life (and any sudden personal contact, whether in the bed or in the heart, is an intrusion) he loses his balance for a moment, slips into being who he is, uses his poetry as one would use money or sympathy. The person who writes the poetry emerges, tentatively, like a hermit crab from a conch shell. The poet, for that instant, ceases to be a dead man.

Here an absolute antithesis opens up between "poetry" and what Spicer calls in this same letter "the big lie of the personal." The "personal" is not in itself a delusion, but it becomes a lie when it claims to be the origin of the poem. In the poem,

> this immediate thing, this personal adventure, . . . will, at best, show in the lovely pattern of cracks in some poem where autobiography shattered but did not quite destroy the surface.

By the standards which Spicer here establishes, *After Lorca* is far from "pure" poetry. Indeed, Spicer himself suggests that a perfectly pure poem has never been written. But by articulating his conception of the "pure" poem, Spicer invites us to see the poems in *After Lorca* as a kind of dialogue between the "impure" world of human life and their own "purity." The various dialogic processes I have described all in some measure "violate" the purity of the poem. These "violations" are counterbalanced by the repeated invasions of the pure poem into the human world. A kind of mutual corruption is here going on, and the act of writing now becomes illicit—tacitly, every writer actively participates in this mutual seduction of the poem by the world, and of the world by the poem. We now begin to understand the burden of Spicer's irony: if every poem must enact its own failure to achieve the wordless perfection of the "pure" poem, then irony becomes the only possible stance for the poet.

At the beginning of this essay I invoked Mikhail Bakhtin, simply because he more than any other critic has reminded us of the originally dialogic character of all language, and has given us some methods for recovering the dialogic residue present even in those forms of discourse that seem most insistently monologic. From my reading of Bakhtin, I have come to see monologue and dialogue less as "kinds" of discourse than as potentialities present in all discourse. If we look at language ontogenetically, we see (as Vygotsky insisted) that dialogue always precedes monologue. We speak because we *are addressed,* and when we speak we always hope for a reply. On the other hand, all of us, once we start talking, have trouble stopping, and the written page (including the one on which I am now writing) encourages the impulse to monologue on and on. I sometimes fear that we would all (but perhaps I am only speaking of myself!) monologue endlessly, if it were not that others also demand to be heard—and so they interrupt. If we see discourse as pulled always *both* toward monologue *and* toward dialogue, then it follows that individual writers have some options here. On the one hand, the writer may try to limit the dialogic potentialities of language. Indeed, the major literary genres all represent, I would propose, strategies for constraining dialogue by pretending that *this* text is a closed, complete system. Every text, I like to think, tries to absolutize itself, to *be* the world, and the writer may accede to this pull within the text. On the other hand, a writer may try to thwart the pull toward monologue, to destabilize the text, open it up to other voices. When Spicer began to write, there already existed in American writing a tradition of such "open" poetry running from Pound, Williams, and the Eliot of *The Waste Land* through Olson and the Objectivists to certain of Spicer's contemporaries, including especially Duncan and Creeley. *After Lorca,* I am convinced, not only claims a place within this tradition but carries the tradition forward, insofar as it consciously foregrounds issues of intertextuality, historical continuity and discontinuity, and the dialogic interplay between poets and between language itself and the world which language claims to "reflect." (pp. 118-34)

Burton Hatlen, "Crawling into Bed with Sorrow: Jack Spicer's 'After Lorca'," in Ironwood, *Vol. 14, No. 2, Fall, 1986, pp. 118-35.*

FURTHER READING

Blaser, Robin. "My Vocabulary Did This to Me." *Acts,* No. 6 (1987): 98-105.
>   Transcription of a lecture on Spicer given at the Spicer Conference held at New College in San Francisco.

Davidson, Michael. " 'The City Redefined': Community and Dialogue in Jack Spicer." In his *The San Francisco Renaissance: Poetics and Community at Mid-Century,* pp. 150-71. Melbourne: Cambridge University Press, 1989.
>   Examines the dialogic quality of Spicer's verse and his theory of "dictation" as a method of poetry writing.

Ellingham, Lewis. "Tape by Holt Spicer Concerning His Brother, Jack Spicer, and the Family Background: Dictated in Springfield, MO., Fall 1983." *Acts,* No. 6 (1987): 85-8.
>   Reminiscence by Spicer's brother.

Silliman, Ron. "Spicer's Language." In *Writing/Talks,* edited by Bob Perelman, pp. 166-91. Carbondale: Southern Illinois University Press, 1985.
>   Discusses *Language* and *Book of Magazine Verse* as well as the poem "Thing Language."

Additional coverage of Spicer's life and career is contained in the following sources published by Gale Research: *Contemporary Authors,* Vols. 85-88; *Contemporary Literary Criticism,* Vols. 8, 18; and *Dictionary of Literary Biography,* Vols. 5, 16.

Bruce Sterling

1954-

American novelist and short story writer.

The following entry provides an overview of Sterling's major works.

INTRODUCTION

Sterling is best known as a leading figure of the "cyberpunk" movement in contemporary science fiction. In his introduction to *Mirrorshades: The Cyberpunk Anthology,* Sterling described the movement as "an unholy alliance of the technical world and the world of organized dissent—the underground world of pop culture, visionary fluidity, and street-level anarchy. . . . Cyberpunk comes from the realm where the computer hacker and the rocker overlap, a cultural Petri dish where writhing gene lines splice." While Sterling's novels and short stories are considered exemplary of the cyberpunk school, critics find his works distinctive for their humanist themes.

A native Texan born in Brownsville, Sterling graduated from the University of Texas at Austin in 1976. Sterling's first two novels, *Involution Ocean* and *The Artificial Kid,* introduce a recurrent theme in his writing: the fallaciousness of a rigid set of values that excludes all others. Sterling further developed this theme in a series of short stories based on an ideological conflict between the Shapers, who seek to enhance human faculties through genetic alteration, and the Mechanists, who achieve the same end through cybernetic prostheses. The opposition of these two groups and their competing value systems is extended in his novel *Schismatrix,* which envisions a society that is continually fragmenting into various political and ethical factions. In his next novel, *Islands in the Net,* Sterling considers the effect of advanced technology on human relations. The "Net" of the title is a vast information and communication network that links the "corporate democracies" which in the future have replaced nations. Critics praise Sterling's believable extrapolations of current world trends to emphasize both the possibilities and the vulnerabilities of technology. This theme is also apparent in *The Difference Engine,* a collaboration with fellow cyberpunk William Gibson. In this novel the authors rewrite history on the premise that Charles Babbage's crude nineteenth-century computer expedited the "information age" of the twentieth century by a hundred years. The resulting social and political upheaval is set against a detailed Victorian background.

Critics have commended Sterling for his positive, humanist vision of the future that does not rely on bleak, post-nuclear holocaust landscapes common in science fiction.

His works posit a world free of nuclear weapons yet still subject to terrorism, where information is a more valuable commodity than arms, and where scientific discoveries bring unprecedented benefits as well as troubling new issues. Sterling is fascinated by the potential benefits of technology, while cautiously regarding its impact on human relations. This concern, according to critics, is at the heart of Sterling's fiction and the cyberpunk movement.

PRINCIPAL WORKS

NOVELS

Involution Ocean   1977
The Artificial Kid   1980
Schismatrix   1985
Islands in the Net   1988
The Difference Engine [with William Gibson] 1990

SHORT FICTION

Crystal Express   1989

OTHER

Mirrorshades: The Cyberpunk Anthology [editor]   (short fiction)   1986

Michael Dirda

Over the past few years Bruce Sterling has been constructing a universe, first in short stories (**"Cicada Queen,"** **"Swarm"**), and now in his ambitious novel *Schismatrix.* In an undefined future earth has colonized much of the solar system; in so doing mankind has divided into two major political-ethical factions called Shapers and Mechanists. Shapers believe in cloning, genetic experiment, periodic rejuvenation, and psychological control; Mechanists, by contrast, improve their bodies with prosthetic devices, are able to wire themselves into extensive electronic networks, and are generally on their way to becoming true cyborgs. "The scanners assured him that the visitor, a woman, bore only harmless Mechanist implants: plaque-scraping arterial microbots, old-fashioned teflon kneecaps, plastic knuckles, a porous drug duct in the crook of the left elbow. Much of her hair was artificial, implanted strands of shining optical fibers."

Abelard Lindsay—the hero of *Schismatrix*—is a human being from an aristocratic family, schooled by Shapers, who finds himself exiled among Mechanists because of a change in political policy on his home planet, the Mare Serenitatus Circumlunar Corporate Republic. In good [Science Fiction] tradition—that of the outcast who grows into a superman—Lindsay gradually wins his way back to power. In the process he becomes a theatrical impresario, the lover of a beautiful brothel-owner (who eventually undergoes her own drastic transformation), a pirate, a happily married Shaper husband, a leading diplomat (expert in dealing with the aliens mankind soon encounters), a scientist, and an all-round political wheeler-dealer.

He needs to be all these things just to survive in a world where assassins take on their victims' features, whole cities are built from flesh, people are iced out for decades, and humanity is gradually fragmenting more and more—into Concatenates, Black Medicals, PostHumanists, Super-Brights, Zen Serotonins, Cicadas, Cataclysts. To evoke this complex, ever-evolving universe, Sterling writes in a fast-moving, concentrated style; but like Samuel Delany, he sometimes makes the reader work overly hard in following the action. Indeed, there is a sketchiness to his characters and a gray tonality to the narration—the result, perhaps, of an ambition to compose a monumental future history in the manner of Olaf Stapledon. Whatever the reason, Sterling's action climaxes—a battle between Shapers and Pirates, a duel between Abelard and an old enemy within the bodies of alien animals—fail to generate the excitement one might expect of such shoot-'em-ups.

Sterling's real forte lies in the evocation of technological, human and alien *strangeness.* His vision is Balzacian in its scope and richness, above all in its obsession with new science, party politics, and the complex of changes brought about through genetic engineering. His is a brave new world of nearly constant future shock—contact with aliens, odd religions, the advent of terraforming, the biological and prosthetic transformation of man. Many of his themes will be familiar to sf readers: Shapers and Mechanists, for instance, recall respectively the adherents to Asimov's First and Second Foundation, and Lindsay's progress pays frequent homage to Alfred Bester's Gully Foyle

of the classic revenge epic, *The Stars My Destination.* For all my nits about *Schismatrix* it is with such books that Sterling's should be placed.

> *Michael Dirda, "Robots, Cyborgs and Aliens,"*
> *in* Book World—The Washington Post, *June*
> *30, 1985, p. 6.*

Paul Granahan

It's not too much of a simplification to note that new "generations" of science fiction authors seem to crop up roughly every five years. A non-exhaustive list of the '80's wave would include names such as Gibson, Brin, Willis, Robinson, Shepard, MacAvoy, Swanwick—and Bruce Sterling. To be accurate, Sterling made his first professional SF sale in 1976, and has even written two novels, but only in the past several years has his popularity soared, and this current novel can only strengthen his growing status.

The explanation for this new excitement in Sterling's work lies in his Shaper/Mechanist stories, which illuminate various facets of a future society encompassing the entire solar system. Several of these complicated and highly imaginative tales have been Hugo and/or Nebula nominees—**"Swarm," "Spider Rose,"** and **"Cicada Queen"**— and all this acclaim has been well-deserved. Like William Gibson (whose rich and electrifying first novel *Neuromancer* was awarded this year's Nebula over names such as Heinlein and Niven), Sterling has a high-tech style which, unlike so much dry and pedantic "hard" SF of the past, is crisp, colorful, and superbly stimulating.

Schismatrix is the first novel set in the Shaper/Mechanist universe where the fate of humankind (or its successors) rests in the balance of the fierce conflict between the cybernetic faction of the asteroid belt and the genetically re-shaped dwelling upon Saturn's moons. Both overt force and political intrigue are utilized in this deadly struggle for domination which is anything but clear-cut given the variety of splinter groups evolving from the main divisions. *Schismatrix* spans more than 150 years and examines the length and breadth of Sterling's dynamic universe through the watchful eyes of one of its most pivotal inhabitants, Abelard Lindsay. Lindsay, the consummate identity-shifting survivor, serves both as the lens through which we view the intricate and ever-changing "Schismatrix" and as the primary catalyst of that society. The measure of distance he manages to keep despite his intimate involvement with every aspect of his complex world not only grants Lindsay an enhanced sense of perspective but also provides the reader with a relatively objective picture of that world.

Sterling's disturbing creation depicts a society which is rather joyless and cold—but ultimately fascinating. There are many stories left in this universe, and I hope Sterling relates more of them before moving on. (pp. 172-73)

> *Paul Granahan, in a review of "Schismatrix,"*
> *in* Best Sellers, *Vol. 45, No. 5, August, 1985,*
> *pp. 172-73.*

Norman Spinrad

[*The following essay was first published in* Isaac Asimov's Science Fiction Magazine *in 1986.*]

The Cyberpunks are the first new literary movement within the SF field since the New Wave of the 1960s, or at the very least the first to have a collective label pinned on them. For reasons that will become apparent, I tried to rechristen them "the Neuromantics," and while that attempt was entirely unsuccessful, the reasoning behind it, I believe, remains valid.

For while some of my reasons for wanting to change the nomenclature may have been trivial, others cut to the heart of the matter.

For one thing, everyone agrees that William Gibson's *Neuromancer* started it all, including the "Movement" writers, who, unlike the writers of the New Wave movement who habitually insisted that no such thing existed, openly proclaim themselves a Movement with a capital *M.* (p. 109)

The logical place to begin this discussion, is, of course, with William Gibson's novel *Neuromancer* the archetypal template for the core group of writers, and the book most accurately described by the term cyberpunk.

Case, the "hero" of *Neuromancer,* certainly has what one might fairly call a punk sensibility in the current extended meaning of the term. He is an ex-speed freak—ex not as a matter of his own choice, but courtesy of "therapeutic" tampering with his brain against his will. He is a marginal man living on the razor edge of the underworld of his future, and his sometime lady-love is a mercenary killer with permanently implanted mirror-shades.

So far we could be dealing with a not terribly atypical Harlan Ellison protagonist of a certain period. And indeed, a strong Ellison influence underlies at least one aspect of the core Neuromantic sensibility.

For it was Ellison, writing SF and contemporary "gang" or "street" fiction simultaneously, who did the most to bring the sensibility, style, rhythm, and characters of the demimonde of the street into the clean white middle-class worlds of 1950s SF, though it would seem that William Burroughs might have been at least as direct an influence on Gibson. Certainly the Ellison oeuvre abounds with punk protagonists, in the 1950s sense of the word.

But by the end of the 1970s, punk had taken on new meanings, though curiously enough, black leather jackets and defiantly artificial hairdos had once more become the trappings of a kind of rebellion.

The black leather and DA punks of the 1950s were rebelling against Mom, Apple Pie, sexual repression, intellectuality, and the America of Dwight Eisenhower and Norman Rockwell, and their libidinal marching music was, interestingly enough, already primitively electronic, to wit, early primary-stage rock and roll.

These punks disappeared into history in the 1960s, their fate being sealed when Bob Dylan and the Beatles began the transformation of rock and roll from the ass-kicking music of Elvis and street gangs into the music of the politically conscious transcendental revolutionary utopianism that spawned the Counterculture.

So the "punks" or "new wavers" who emerged towards the middle of the 1970s were not at all the same as the punks of the 1950s, despite the superficial trappings, for these *nouvelle* punks were in rebellion against the countercultural sensibilities of the *1960s,* not the long-gone innocent ennui of the 1950s.

What *they* were in rebellion against was the self-conscious artsiness of early 1970s rock, the failed laid-back utopianism of the Counterculture, mysticism, and the naive supposition that the future would be better if youthful idealism kept the faith. If the punks of the 1950s really *were* anti-intellectual hoods, the nouvelle punks of the 1970s were *intellectual* anti-intellectuals; not naive natural nihilistic rebels without a cause but *self-consciously* nihilistic pessimists capable of raising cynicism to a more or less coherent philosophy and sophisticated enough to know they were doing it.

Case, the hero of *Neuromancer,* is a punk in the nouvelle mode, an intellectual punk rather than a simple greaser, and it is the "cyber" half of the equation that informs his intellectuality. This is precisely what makes *Neuromancer* a watershed book, what distinguishes the Cyberpunks from the New Wave, and what begins to define what this new esthetic means to science fiction as a whole.

Although the Neuromancer of the title is technically the name of an Artificial Intelligence, Case is the true Neuromancer of the story, in more ways than one.

The word Neuromancer is of course a pun on *necromancer,* meaning magician, and *neuro,* meaning pertaining to the nervous system. The Neuromancer is a contemporary (or in this case intermediate future) magician whose wizardry consists of directly interfacing his protoplasmic nervous system with the electronic nervous system of the computersphere, manipulating it imagistically (and being manipulated by it) much as more traditional shamans interact imagistically with more traditional mythic realms via drugs or trance states.

Now of course as a science fictional idea, this is not exactly new. I did something like this myself in *Riding the Torch;* there is Vernor Vinge's *True Names,* Alfred Bester's *Golem 100,* and the recent endless spate of stories and novels in which human protagonists find themselves acting and living in some kind of "cyberspace." The Disney studio even did it in a special-effects extravaganza called *Tron.*

But "neuromancer" is a pun on "necromancer" in another sense, too, for the narrowest meaning of the latter word is "raiser of the dead," and the spirit underworld in which Case and Gibson dabble is also magic of a black kind, where electronic means are used to raise neural ghosts in the software.

What's critical here is that Gibson's Neuromancer, Case, is not a Faustian scientist but an outlaw, not a computer *wimp* but a computer *punk.* A *cyberpunk,* if you will. An electronic necromancer in a black leather jacket and mirror-shades. (pp. 110-12)

[It is] the *acceptance* of the technological evolution and alteration of our definition of our humanity, the *romantic* acceptance of the technological alteration of the species, rather than the more traditional posture of cautionary warnings against the dangers of same, that ultimately defines the Neuromantic sensibility, and defines it in terms far broader and deeper than the title of Bruce Sterling's Movement anthology *Mirrorshades.* (p. 117)

Sterling's novel *Schismatrix* does something . . . disturbing to our cozy definitions of humanity.

Schismatrix is the somewhat picaresque story of diplomat and "sundog" (a kind of footloose, high-level space hobo) Abelard Lindsay's wanderings through the space and history of the solar system. From circumlunar space colony, to the asteroid belt, to the outer satellites, Lindsay meanders and machinates through a series of entirely artificial environments, conveniently giving the reader interior access to a long stretch of history in the process.

The historical dynamic of Sterling's solar system is the long, sometimes hostile, sometimes interpenetrating, dialectic between the Mechs and the Shapers. The Mechs are devotees of the arts and sciences of cyborging humans, and the Shapers are genetic engineers and biological transformers. Their endless conflicts are occasionally military, but mostly economic, diplomatic, technological, and esthetic, and as the fortunes of either side wax and wane, waves of defectors and refugees, including Lindsay, pass back and forth between them.

What finally begins to emerge out of all this is the Schismatrix of the title, a solar system of bewildering human complexity, in which the key concepts are *post-humanism* and *moving in clades.*

Post-humanism is basically the situation that evolves in the Schismatrix after decades of genetic engineering, cyborging, cloning, and combinations of the two lines of species-altering technology. The original human form has been so diversely transmogrified by these technologies that it persists mainly in a circumlunar colony set up as a kind of nature preserve.

Alteration of the human body by technology has been viewed as less than horrific before, notably by John Varley, in many of whose stories and novels people change sexes as casually as they would go to the hairdresser, and in Delany's *Nova,* where people have bizarre cosmetic surgery.

But Sterling's "Post-humanists" go much further. Both the Mechs and the Shapers who merge into the "Post-humanism" of the eventual Schismatrix have always agreed that the human form should be mutated technologically; their whole long struggle concerned only *how.* And the Post-humanist answer ultimately satisfies both of them—by any means convenient, to anything the heart desires.

And the concept of moving in clades takes it one radical step further.

Moving in clades is the current most extreme statement of the Neuromantic concept of human evolution through science and technology. Bear has humanity evolve first into a *singular* post-human physical form and then to a transcedence of the physical universe. But Sterling introduces the concept of evolutionary *multiplexity* through technology.

Evolution, chez Sterling, moves in clades or daughter species; it does not move linearly, it *radiates.* Successful species do not evolve in a straight line into a *single* daughter species, they radiate into a *multitude* of successor species.

The fully developed Schismatrix contains a vast complexity of post-human species, all the product, not of natural selection, but of technological development. "Lobsters" so cyborged into their spacesuits that they abhor atmospheres. Humans biologically adapted to methane oceans. Even an entire space colony whose interior structure is the altered protoplasm of a single woman, Lindsay's sometime lover, who retains her human personality.

Schismatrix is a thoroughgoing hard science fiction novel, in that all the scientific and technological extrapolation and all the descriptions of space habitats (and there certainly are plenty of both) are executed with a rigor and attention to detail of which a Heinlein, Niven, or even Benford could be proud, and then some. But while the prose follows the straightforward transparent line we have come to expect from the hard science mode, Sterling uses it to ground his novel with equal attention to psychological depth and details. The characters, Lindsay in particular, no matter how weird their physiognomies become, are believably human on a psychological level. (pp. 118-20)

Only at the very end does Sterling lapse into a somewhat vague transcendental denouement at variance with the hard-edged structure he has so carefully constructed, bringing Lindsay to an evolutionary endpoint in which we, and perhaps the author himself, cannot quite believe. For the whole thrust of the novel has been that there *is* no endpoint to the evolution of our species through science and technology, only an endless process of radiation.

Thus, perhaps, do the Neuromantics themselves shrink back, at least at this stage, from the ultimate consequences of their explorations of the frontiers of technologically based human evolution. Beyond this point, perhaps, even the visionaries of our species are not yet equipped to travel.

Evolution moves in clades. So does science fiction. Perhaps there will always be a point beyond which further explorations must be left to daughter species. (pp. 120-21)

Norman Spinrad, "The Neuromantic Cyberpunks," in his Science Fiction in the Real World, *Southern Illinois University Press,* 1990, pp. 109-21.

Roz Kaveney

Bruce Sterling's Laura, in *Islands in the Net,* receives the perilous gift of agenthood and loses a lot of innocence in the process, as well as husband and career. Given the role of Sterling as propagandist of the "cyberpunk" group as the cutting edge of the sf avant-garde, there is a lot here that is productively old-fashioned; Laura's misadventures take her through a sequence of dystopian environments, much as they might have done in the 1950s of Frederik Pohl and Cyril Kornbluth.

Sterling has a real gift for turning ideas from the science pages of newspapers into entertaining science-fictional conceits; this is a book in love with gadgetry and sensitive to the extent to which to change the human environment with bits of techno-junk is authentically to change the possibilities of human affect. There is nothing cold or heartless about Sterling's hip portrayal of the early 21st century; indeed, there is a slight tendency to the sentimental.

Laura is part of a quasi-communal industrial grouping to which she and her architect husband are currently providing hotel and conference center service; they find themselves at the heart of negotiations between groups of information pirates descended from, and inheriting the heavy manners of, various of today's criminal conspiracies. When the amiable Rastafarian leader of the Grenadan delegation is shot to death by a robot plane on Laura's veranda, she feels an obligation to act as honest broker. She pursues this role in the high-tech voodoo jungle of Grenada, in the glossy, embattled steel and glass canyons of a Singapore coming apart under its own political tensions, and in the dungeons of a kleptocratic and dangerous Mali. Laura is the sort of character who survives to bear witness partly because she is convincingly that sort of person, more because we know she is the heroine of the sort of novel in which people do.

Part of the strength of *Islands in the Net* is that we know as well as Sterling that this is a fiction, a fiction in which things happen and are said just too neatly for any pretense at even that minimal realism to which science fiction can aspire. When the doomed Rastafarian moans about "Babylon Luddites," or when Laura inadvertently becomes the leader of a Sikh protest group, it is the artifice we applaud, not any conviction we for a moment feel. Sterling's Laura is just real enough to act as our surrogate as Sterling shows us a series of gaudy but information-packed tourist snaps of a future.

> Roz Kaveney, "Sterling Gold," in Book World—The Washington Post, *June 26, 1988, p. 10.*

Tom Easton

Bruce Sterling has been lumped in with the Cyberpunk writers because his stories, like theirs, often deal with intimate human-computer symbioses. But his vision is less narrow than theirs, and he does not believe, as they seem to, that the only reality that counts is in the streets among the wireheads, dataspace cowboys, and neuropeptide addicts. He agrees that, yes, as computer technology continues to improve, the day is inevitable when humans will accept computers into their skulls, move into the dataspaces in which the computers live, entwine organic and silicon lives as intimately as ever a cowboy and his horse or a suburban 1950s teenaged male and his hot rod.

So he's Cyber. But he's not punk. He recognizes the inevitable, and from that he constructs scenarios, optimistic, pessimistic, frightening, elating, all within the cards of possibility. He is easy to believe, and nowhere easier than in his latest book, *Islands in the Net.*

The time is early in the history of *Homo cyberneticus.* War has been banned, and the vast nuclear arsenals dismantled. The coldly inhuman corporate bureaucracies of today are being replaced by multinationals such as the Rizome Group, held together by an esprit that closely resembles the fellow-feeling that marks a large and happy extended family. The Group defines itself by saying that it has people, and work that needs doing. Its people's motives are not—or are not supposed to be—power and wealth.

The story begins to emerge when Sterling adds to these basics that the world is growing ever more tightly linked by computerized data exchanges, summing up to the "Net" of the title, but there are a few places—islands—that parasitize the Net as data pirates (e.g., Grenada, Singapore). There is also Africa, so beset by ecological and political disaster that it is a metaphorical island totally surrounded by the Net, but not a part of it. And now we have Laura and David Webster, Rizome Associates, managers of a guest house on the Texas coast, building up points toward the day when they will ask Rizome to support them in a larger undertaking.

It looks like an unexpected point bonus when Rizome schedules a conference of data pirates at the Webster guest house. It is, if not quite in the expected way. Rizome wishes to talk the pirates into giving up their nasty ways, but then terrorists assassinate the chief Grenadan on the beach, beside Laura and her infant daughter. The pirates flee. Rizome can save face only if its representatives—David, Laura, and baby—go to Grenada as little more than diplomatic hostages. They go (expecting those points), and the reader learns a great deal about grinding poverty, an ideological allegiance to bootstraps, and promising futures.

But the terrorists strike again, destroying all the promise. Laura and her family escape again, and now she is off to Singapore, while David chickens out and stays behind. Singapore may or may not have been behind the attacks. Whatever the truth, disaster follows Laura: a second batch of data pirates bite the dust, and she is captured by the terrorists, who in due time imprison her in Africa.

Years later, she escapes, her guided tour of disaster resumes, and she finally makes it home. The reader has been dismayed by the enormity of the future's problems—especially in Africa—and thrilled by Laura's continuing string of Paulinesque Perils. Now, that reader realizes, she is a figure of charisma, more knowledgeable in the ways of the Net, prepared to use it toward some unguessed future, and Sterling must be working on a sequel. He is building a future history that is fascinating in the ramifications of events he knits into the fabric, and he can expect a horde of welcoming readers. Few will be greatly put off by the unlikeliness of humanity abandoning its nuclear missiles, or of bureaucracies coming to depend on esprit instead of power. (pp. 163-65)

Tom Easton, in a review of "Islands in the Net," in Analog Science Fiction/Science Fact, *Vol. CVIII, No. 12, December, 1988, pp. 163-65.*

Gregory Feeley

No problems with structure or proportion bedevil the stories in Bruce Sterling's *Crystal Express,* which collects all but the slightest of Sterling's short fiction. Since the appearance of *The Artificial Kid* in 1980, Sterling's work has been characterized by intellectual playfulness, a careful, almost mannered style and a flamboyant virtuosity in matters of formal invention excelled only by that of Rudy Rucker, who cannot write half so well. At 264 pages, *Crystal Express* offers a higher concentration of sheer energy than any short story collection since the heyday of Harlan Ellison.

Best known are the five stories of the Shaper/Mechanist sequence, which details a future in which humanity has spread throughout the solar system, competing between factions of genetically tailored Shapers and cybernetically rebuilt Mechanists. **"Green Days in Brunei"** and **"The Beautiful and the Sublime"** are both set in a 21st century that has overcome the toxic hazards now threatening us, and recount comedies of love and daring with enormous gusto. A final section, featuring fantasy stories, is notable for **"Flowers of Edo,"** a very funny story of the advent of modern industrialism in 19th-century Japan, and **"Telliamed,"** a scientific romance of the early 18th century.

Sterling's subject has always been the dislocations of conceptual change, what Thomas Kuhn called the "structure of scientific revolutions." A second theme is his unabashed love of youthful energy, which Sterling sometimes indulges a bit. Both the heroes of **"Green Days in Brunei"** and **"The Beautiful and the Sublime"** end up running off with the daughters of aging plutocrats, although Sterling's sense of irony and *joie de vivre* keep us from really minding. Only his epigraph page—juxtaposing a learned observation by physicist J. D. Bernal with a scabrous one-liner by William Gibson—betrays his occasional tendency to posture.

Gregory Feeley, "Apocalypse Then and Now," in Book World—The Washington Post, *August 27, 1989, p. 11.*

Dan Chow

Recognition has already come to Sterling, in large part due to the stories that are gathered [in *Crystal Express*]. The entire Shaper/Mechanist sequence (of short pieces) is here, most notably **"Swarm"**. Gathered as well are an eclectic assortment of other sf including **"Green Days in Brunei"**, and a small, impressive gathering of Sterling's fantasy, showcasing **"The Flowers of Edo"** and **"Dinner in Audoghast"**. Reading these stories close upon one an-

other, two things are immediately obvious and most impressive.

The first is that the experience is not in the least boring. The usual problem in such a collection is that something begins to repeat itself. It may be a setting, a thematic preoccupation, a stylistic technique; it could be almost anything. Even so, it will be there to betray the writer and to distract the reader. If anything is repetitive in *Crystal Express,* it is the author's remarkable knowledge of his characters and settings, no matter how diverse they might be. The Chinese-American dropout of **"Green Days . . . "** is right, as is his dilemma, as is the setting. Likewise for the Japanese protagonists of **"Flowers of Edo"** and their confrontation with the modern world beyond the borders of Meiji Japan. Even within the Shaper/Mechanist sequence, the stories display far greater range than one might expect. Taken as a whole, they form a meditation greater than the sum of the individual stories themselves.

The second is that the stories hold up. When gathered so closely in a collection, the tendency is for some stories to diminish, to become not as good as we had remembered. *Crystal Express* is one of the few collections which manages to avoid this pitfall. Each of the stories which gained recognition and honors the first time around holds its own in the company of its brethren. To the extent that some of the stories are lesser, it is more like they are supporting actors, adding to the presence of the more noted characters. . . .

The cyberpunk label is far too restrictive for this author. *Crystal Express* shows Sterling to be an author of dazzling range and insight.

Dan Chow, in a review of "Crystal Express," in Locus, *Vol. 23, No. 3, September, 1989, p. 27.*

Paul Delany

In February 1812, Byron stood up to speak for the first time in the House of Lords. His speech was a passionate defence of the Nottingham weavers—followers of the mythical King Ludd—who had been smashing the new mechanical stocking-frames; and for the rest of his life Byron went on arguing that 'we must not allow mankind to be sacrificed to improvements in mechanism.' But what might have happened if the enemies of mechanism had changed their minds? *The Difference Engine* is one answer, in the form of an 'uchronic' novel: set in 'no time', instead of *Utopia*'s 'no place'.

Gibson and Sterling propose that the Duke of Wellington is killed by a Luddite bomb in 1831. Tired of internecine struggle between Tories and workers, the country turns to the 'Industrial Radical Party' for a sweeping transformation of British society, instead of the actual modest reform of 1832. In 1855 the IRP is still in power, led by the great convert to its cause, Lord Byron. Shelley, faithful to the Luddites, has been exiled incommunicado on St Helena; Keats is a 'clacker' who programs difference engines—the Victorian predecessors of the computer. The true rulers of Britain are 'merit Lords' appointed for life: Lord Darwin,

Lord Bentham, Lord Brunel and above all Lord Babbage. Charles Babbage really lived, of course (though not as a Lord), and really invented merit lordship, the computer, and many other improvements in mechanism. All one needs to accept, to set this novel going, is that Babbage's genius should be properly recognised in his own time, instead of later.

The Difference Engine belongs to the thriving Post-Modern genre of historical pastiche, whose most notable recent example is A. S. Byatt's *Possession.* But these two novels exploit the device of the 'alternative past' in very different ways. Byatt slides her texts into the Victorian canon while leaving as little trace of the seams as possible; she tries to make her work 'pass' for Victorian while leaving everything we know about the period intact. As a tribute to Victorianism, *Possession* stakes no claim on the present, except in the private lives of its contemporary characters. *The Difference Engine,* on the other hand, shuffles the cards of history in order to prove by example the 'Wiener thesis' of recent years: that Britain's ambivalent response to the Industrial Revolution has led to its relative economic backwardness today.

Charles Babbage was the prophet of a modernised and meritocratic Britain. He wanted universal education; rationalised production methods; national scientific institutes modelled after the French Grandes Ecoles; reform of the Royal Society, which had become a chums' club for non-scientists; and life peerages for savants and capitalists, so that the aristocracy would no longer be 'as a body . . . the least enlightened in point of knowledge, and the most separated from the mass of the people'. Babbage got off to a good start in the 1820s, when the Government gave him its biggest research grant ever to build his 'difference engine' (he promised to help extend the Empire by recalculating the navigational tables). Many of his contemporaries recognised his genius, including Marx and Dickens (who put something of Babbage's story into Daniel Doyce and the Circumlocution Office in *Little Dorrit*). But over the years, the Establishment steadily cut Babbage down to size. His candidate for the Presidency of the Royal Society, the great astronomer John Herschel, was defeated by the Duke of Sussex, whose main qualification was being the King's brother. Technical education was left at the mercy of private patronage; Babbage failed to win a seat in the reformed Parliament; and Melbourne cut off funding for the difference engine and its successor, the 'analytical engine'. Babbage lived till 1871, firing off brilliant ideas on economics, manufacturing, railways, postal services and operations research, but never getting his hands on the real levers of power.

In *The Difference Engine,* Gibson and Sterling ask us to imagine that Babbage's ideas have become as pervasive in the 1850s as, say, Marx's in the Soviet Union of the 1920s. The novel's London still has the familiar trappings of music halls, whores and Thames mud. But steam-driven chariots are starting to appear on the streets, the middle class have telegram machines at home, and rows of difference engines spin their axles at the Central Statistics Bureau. The Industrial Radicals have made Britain a richer and more egalitarian country: but they have also turned their information system into a political weapon, even making their enemies 'disappear' as in the Argentine terror of the 1970s.

The plot of the novel, in brief, is that a freakishly hot summer has brought pestilence to London and allowed Luddite mobs to take over much of the capital; meanwhile a right-wing conspirator, Charles Egremont, schemes to make himself a dictator by seizing the Statistics Bureau. Against this backdrop of impending revolution, rival gangs are in pursuit of a mysterious box of punched cards, known as 'the Modus'; like the Maltese Falcon, it leaves a trail of murder in its wake. The Modus is finally revealed as the weapon of a new generation of intellectual Luddites, who use it to attack the 'great Napoleon'—the world's largest difference engine, instrument of the French Police. Instead of throwing a sabot into the gears, they make the engine run endless loops: the Modus is, in fact, the first computer virus. By 1990, evolution of the Modus will have produced artificial intelligence programs that have 'gone critical' and achieved human-like self-consciousness. Herein lies a favourite theme of Gibson and Sterling: the official institutions of a society always work on yesterday's agenda, while the future is being made by an underground of anarchists, criminals and fanatics. . . .

Sterling's future is generally less menacing than Gibson's. In his recent *Islands in the Net,* the corporate ruling class has banned nuclear weapons and imposed on the world a kind of progressive school ethos—though there's still a secret police to crush those who prefer the old ways of conflict resolution. The politics of *The Difference Engine* seem to owe more to Sterling than to Gibson. It is a novel in the spirit of 1989, which assumes that in the long run the market and political pluralism are bound to prevail over Luddites and Leninists. Its message thus becomes rather tame: that we are all headed for a late capitalist nirvana, but Babbage would have got us there sooner. The sepia-tinted Victoriana of 1855, even with steam chariots and computers thrown in, serve the same purpose as all antiques: to reassure us against the menace of the present.

Paul Delany, "Voyage to Uchronia," in London Review of Books, *Vol. 13, No. 16, August 29, 1991, p. 22.*

FURTHER READING

Criticism

Maddox, Tom. "Wars of the Coin's Two Halves: Bruce Sterling's Mechanist/Shaper Narratives." *Mississippi Review* 16, Nos. 2-3 (1988): 237-44.

    Examines the two major political-ethical factions depicted in many of Sterling's works.

McKeeman, D. P. "Hack to the Future." *Compute* 13, (November 1988): 160

    Interview with Sterling.

Pierce, John J. "The Synthetists." In his *When World Views Collide: A Study in Imagination and Evolution,* pp. 167-89. Westport, Conn.: Greenwood Press, 1989.
> Includes a brief discussion of Sterling as the "chief propagandist" of the cyberpunk movement.

Additional coverage of Sterling's life and career is contained in the following source published by Gale Research: *Contemporary Authors,* Vol. 119.

Gore Vidal

1925-

(Full name Eugene Luther Gore Vidal, Jr.; also wrote under the pseudonym Edgar Box) American novelist, essayist, scriptwriter, playwright, short story writer, and critic.

The following entry contains criticism of Vidal's American historical and political novels. For information on his complete career, see *CLC*, Volumes 2, 4, 6, 8, 10, 22, and 33.

INTRODUCTION

Vidal is esteemed for both his historical fiction and for his witty and satirical commentary on such topics as politics, sex, and literature. His best known works of fiction include a series of historical novels based on American political figures and events from the Revolutionary era to the present. According to Joyce Carol Oates, Vidal is "concerned with dissecting, obsessively and often brilliantly, the roots of personal ambition as they give rise to history itself."

Vidal was born in New York, where his father was an aeronautics instructor at the United States Military Academy at West Point. He was raised in the home of his maternal grandfather, Senator Thomas Gore of Oklahoma, who strongly influenced his interest in politics as well as literature. Vidal began writing poetry and short stories while attending the Phillips Exeter Academy in New Hampshire. Shortly after graduation in 1943, Vidal enlisted in the Army Reserves and briefly studied engineering. The following year he transferred to the Army Transport Service and later served on a freight transport ship in the Aleutian Islands. During this period he completed his first novel, *Williwaw*. Exploring tensions among the crew of a military transport ship during World War II, *Williwaw* was well received and led critics to rank Vidal among the leading post-World War II novelists. He became a controversial figure with the publication in 1948 of *The City and the Pillar*, a best-selling novel that was chiefly noted for its nonstereotypical portrayal of the homosexual subculture. Vidal has charged that because of the controversy surrounding this novel, several prominent critics and journals deliberately ignored or attacked his subsequent works. Vidal published eight novels between 1949 and 1954, including three mystery novels under the pseudonym Edgar Box, but was unable to support himself from their sales and in 1954 embarked on what he termed "a kind of five-year plan: an all-out raid upon television, which could make me enough money to live the rest of my life." During this phase, which lasted closer to ten years, he wrote numerous television and film scripts and later adapted several of these works for the stage. Vidal eventually achieved his goal of financial independence and re-

ceived the Edgar Allan Poe award for television drama from the Mystery Writers of America in 1955 and the Cannes Critics Prize in 1964 for the screenplay of the film *The Best Man*.

Vidal's first work of historical fiction, *A Search for the King*, is based on a twelfth-century legend concerning a troubadour's quest to rescue Richard the Lion-Hearted from his captors during the Crusades. Though Vidal published several novels subsequent to this work in the 1950s, most critics agree that he developed his trademark style as a dispassionate commentator on the follies of humankind in the novel *Julian*. The result of more than seven years of research, *Julian* is a fictional autobiography of the fourth-century Roman emperor Julian the Apostate interspersed with posthumous commentary from two of his associates. This novel has been praised for its lively presentation of the personal gossip, political intrigues, and religious controversies of Julian's era. Vidal's practice of mingling fiction and fact and his speculative explorations of the personalities and motivations of his subjects are well-known characteristics of his historical fiction, about which Vidal has commented: "To me, the attraction of the historical novel is that one can be as meticulous (or as careless!) as the historian and yet reserve the right not only to rearrange events but, most important, to attribute motive—something the conscientious historian or biographer ought never do."

Vidal has described himself as America's "current biographer," and he has examined the American political scene in a series of six historical novels that expose the corruption and incompetence of political life and demythologize many of the nation's most revered historical figures. The first novel in the series, *Washington, D.C.,* takes place between the late 1930s and the early 1950s and focuses on the relationship between two prominent fictional Washington families. The action of the novel encompasses such momentous historical events as the Japanese attack on Pearl Harbor, the McCarthy investigations, and the Korean War, as well as the political intrigues that lead to the suicide of a senator involved in bribery and corruption. This work is often viewed as Vidal's fundamental comment on how the American political system degrades those who participate in it. Set in the 1830s, Vidal's second American historical novel, *Burr,* is narrated by Charles Schuyler, a fictional law clerk and historian investigating the life of the third vice-president of the United States, Aaron Burr, who is best known for killing Alexander Hamilton in a duel in 1804 and organizing a secessionist conspiracy two years later. Vidal's next novel, *1876,* is presented as Schuyler's journal of events surrounding the centennial celebration of the United States. This work draws numerous parallels between the political figures and public scandals of the 1870s and those of the 1970s, comparing such events as the Whiskey Ring scandal and Watergate, and the presidencies of Ulysses S. Grant and Richard Nixon. *Lincoln* is a fictive biography of the sixteenth president of the United States as seen from the perspective of his contemporaries. This volume in particular is noted for Vidal's minimal usage of fictional elements and for his meticulous historical research that effectively discredits popular myths about the nobility and grandeur of important historical figures. Vidal notes, for example, that Lincoln was generally more concerned with saving the Union than he was with the plight of the slaves. *Empire* encompasses such events as the Spanish-American War of 1898 and focuses on the emergence of the United States as a major political and military world power at the turn of the nineteenth century. The events in *Hollywood* take place between 1917 and 1923, during the presidencies of Woodrow Wilson and Warren G. Harding, and focus on the interrelated nature of American political life and the entertainment industry. Like the other novels in the series, *Hollywood* mixes historical and fictional characters and events, vividly re-creating a period in American history and offering a scathing indictment of the pettiness and artificiality of American social and political life. Vidal's American political series is also noted for exposing the fundamentally theatrical and melodramatic nature of American politics.

Vidal has also written several humorous novels satirizing various aspects of popular culture and contemporary society. The protagonist of one of the best-known, *Myra Breckinridge,* is a man who has undergone a sex change operation and moved to California to enter the movie in-

dustry. The novel includes graphic sexual episodes and was considered pornographic by some reviewers, although the book is most commonly viewed as a campy satire on sex, pornography, and politics. In the sequel *Myron* the protagonist is transported to a 1940s movie set. *Kalki* and *Duluth* are also satiric novels in which fantasy plays an important role.

Vidal's essays often assume the satirical tone and thematic concerns he favors in his novels. His observations on history, sexual mores, literature, and American politics are noted for their erudition, insight, and urbane humor. Many commentators assert that his essays represent his most enduring contribution to American literature. Gerald Clarke observed: "It is not that Vidal's essays are better than his novels. It is rather that his essays are more consistently good and that the qualities that limit him as a novelist are precisely those that a good essayist needs: a forceful intelligence, a cool detachment, an unpretentious, graceful style, and a sense of perspective that distinguishes the big from the little. If most of his fictional characters seem unbelievable, his judgments on real people are both original and irrefutable." Vidal's political and social views have been widely disseminated through numerous television interviews and debates. He has unsuccessfully campaigned for the House of Representatives in 1960 and for the Senate in 1982 on a platform of increased federal aid for education and decreased military funding. In 1987 Vidal observed: "To effect change, you either write or you run for office. There's nothing else I can do."

PRINCIPAL WORKS

NOVELS

Williwaw   1946

In a Yellow Wood   1947

The City and the Pillar   1948; also published as *The City and the Pillar Revised* [revised edition], 1965

The Season of Comfort   1949

Dark Green, Bright Red   1950; revised edition, 1968

A Search for the King: A Twelfth-Century Legend   1950

Death in the Fifth Position [as Edgar Box] 1952

The Judgment of Paris   1952; revised edition, 1965

Death before Bedtime . . . [as Edgar Box] 1953

Death Likes It Hot [as Edgar Box] 1954

Messiah   1954; revised edition, 1965

Julian   1964

†*Washington, D.C.*   1967

Myra Breckinridge   1968; also published as *Myra Breckinridge* [censored edition], 1968

Two Sisters: A Memoir in the Form of a Novel   1970

†*Burr*   1973

Myron   1974

†*1876*   1976

Kalki   1978

Creation   1981

Duluth   1983

†*Lincoln*   1984

†*Empire*   1987

†*Hollywood: A Novel of America in the 1920s*   1990

ESSAYS

Rocking the Boat   1962
Sex, Death and Money   1968
Reflections upon a Sinking Ship   1969
Homage to Daniel Shays: Collected Essays, 1952-1972
        1972; also published as *Collected Essays, 1952-1972,*
        1974; and *On Our Own Now,* 1976
Matters of Fact and Fiction: Essays, 1973-1976   1977
The Second American Revolution, and Other Essays
        1982; also published as *Pink Triangle and Yellow
        Star,* 1982
Armageddon?: Essays 1983-1987   1987; also published as
        At Home: Essays [revised edition], 1988

SCREENPLAYS

The Catered Affair   1956
Visit to a Small Planet, and Other Television Plays   1956
The Scapegoat [with Robert Hamer] 1959
Suddenly, Last Summer [with Tennessee Williams] 1959

SHORT FICTION

A Thirsty Evil: Seven Short Stories   1956

*These works were published as *Three by Box: The Complete Mysteries of Edgar Box in* 1978.

†These novels comprise Vidal's American historical and political series.

CRITICISM

Robert F. Kiernan

Vidal has maintained a serious interest in American politics almost his entire life. He is not only a pundit who haunts television talk shows in election years and an *arbiter elegantarium* of political behavior but also an occasional participant in the political fray. He campaigned actively for Senator Eugene McCarthy in McCarthy's presidential bid of 1968, and he has been active from time to time in movements to launch a new political party; he was a congressional candidate in 1960, and since 1975 he has issued several "State of the Union" addresses designed to show up the presidential address. The Presidency, Vidal once remarked whimsically, is the only thing he ever wanted that he has not achieved, but he is almost certainly less whimsical about such political ambitions than he wants us to believe. It is no surprise that a substantial portion of Vidal's writing has taken American politics as its subject, most notably the trilogy composed of **Washington, D.C.,** **Burr,** and **1876.**

Washington, D.C. (1967) begins on July 22, 1937, at a party celebrating the defeat of President Roosevelt's attempt to enlarge the Supreme Court, and it proceeds against a backdrop of just such momentous events—Pearl Harbor, Roosevelt's death, the McCarthy investigations, and Korea—each following in its turn. The novel focuses on two families. One family consists of James Burden Day, an influential senator from an unnamed state in America's heartland, his wife Kitty, and their daughter Diana; the other family consists of Blaise Sanford, the owner of the *Washington Tribune,* his wife Frederika, and their children, Enid and Peter. Clay Overbury, Senator Day's protégé, links the two families when he marries Enid Sanford, and the novel charts Clay's unscrupulous rise to power, first through the influence he gains over Blaise Sanford as he displaces Enid in her father's affections and then through his blackmailing of Senator Day, who had once accepted a bribe.

Structurally, Clay is at the novel's center, but he is as moribund as his name implies, and Senator Day is the novel's one character of substance and vitality. As Vidal himself has pointed out, the senator faces a thoroughly realistic dilemma when he must decide whether to accept the bribe that is his undoing, for he feels a moral obligation to save the republic from FDR by winning the Presidency himself, yet he cannot finance a presidential campaign without violating his moral sense and accepting the bribe. Ultimately, Day is driven to suicide by the prospect of exposure, and the novel closes with a party scene that mirrors the novel's opening, with the significant difference that a door which had been opened upon Clay in the first pages is now firmly locked. The range of political possibility in America is diminished with Senator Day's death, we understand, and the republic's store of idealism is less than it was.

Considered simply as a political novel, **Washington, D.C.** delivers a number of shrewd insights. Senator Day remarks to young Peter Sanford that of all the lives he can think of, political life is the most humiliating, and his remark is much more than characterization. In some ways, the remark is Vidal's most fundamental comment on what the American system does to its statesmen. Similarly, Senator Day is not merely sloganizing when he remarks to his daughter that timeserving is the secret of survival in politics; he is, rather, enunciating a political truth as deeply embedded in the novel's plot as in the national history. Again, a passage about the senatorial "Club" offers a glimpse into the corridors of power, impressive in its reductionism and authority:

> No one was ever quite sure who belonged to The
> Club since members denied its existence but ev-
> eryone knew who did not belong. The club was
> permanently closed to the outsize personality, to
> the firebrand tribune of the people, to the Sena-
> tor running too crudely for President. Members
> of The Club preferred to do their work quietly
> and to get re-elected without fanfare. On princi-
> ple they detested the President, and despite that
> magnate's power to loose and to bind, The Club
> ruled the Senate in its own way and for its own
> ends, usually contrary to those of the President.

The novel is particularly rich in contemporary insights, especially the seamier side of political life in the 1940s. "Like so many of the American magnates," we are told of Blaise Sanford, he "vacillated between despair at Hitler's continuing success and terror that Hitler might fail in Russia." With kindred acerbity, Vidal mocks in another key the WASP pretense of the 1940s that FDR was Jewish, for that is surely the purpose of Frederika Sanford's lunatic insistence that the British royal family is Jewish. Commemorating the same tradition of WASP invective, Peter Sanford opines that Irish-Americans tend to regard the demagogic Senator McCarthy "as chosen by God to shield them from civilization." In still another key, allusions to the herding of Japanese citizens into concentration camps on the West Coast evoke the high-handedness of the wartime government, while Clay's admiration for Roosevelt's imperialism commemorates the attractions of empire for many Americans in the postwar decade.

Such censorious evocations are rarely the stuff of history books, of course, for they are based on intuitive insights and are deeply partisan. They are the mother wit of one who was there rather than the dispassionate conclusions of a scholar, and in a sense they are more like gossip than history. Yet as Peter Sanford reflects, "History is gossip . . . the trick was in determining which gossip is history." Like Saint-Simon at the court of Louis XIV, Vidal transforms gossip into history, and his view of this period in American history is both significant and absorbing.

But *Washington, D.C.* is giddily melodramatic at the same time that it is soberly historical. Senator Day is haunted by the specter of his father, who appears to him several times in a bloodied Civil War uniform and calls down imprecations upon the son who sentimentalizes the Civil War while serving in the federal government. The senator identifies with his dead father, of course, in the classic manner of rejected sons, and this identification is complicated by the senator's further identification with Clay, who is both a surrogate son he wishes to treat better than his ghostly father treats him and an alter ego through whom he attempts to replay his sonship more successfully. Symptomatic of this ripe Freudianism is the scene at Bull Run in which the senator's father appears to him, unrecognized, as a young soldier very like Clay. Symptomatic, too, is the scene in which Clay tells the senator that he is joining the Army, for the senator immediately feels the bullet that hit his father at the battle of Shiloh tear through his own shoulder. The senator's suicide, rendered as a final confrontation with his father, is nakedly Gothic and quite wonderful of its kind.

> With stiff fingers Burden removed a handkerchief from his pocket. Then he walked toward the wounded soldier, half expecting him to run away. But this was no ordinary youth; it was his father honorably struck by an enemy's bullet in the field of battle. The Confederate corporal did not flinch even when at last they were face to face.
>
> For a long moment Burden stared into the blue eyes that perfectly reflected empty sky. Then slowly he extended the hand which held the handkerchief. Now only the rifle barred his way. He waited patiently until at last, marvelously, the rifle was lowered. With a cry he flung himself upon the youth who was his father, plunged the handkerchief into the wound, lost his balance, fell against the beloved, was taken into those long-dead arms, and like impatient lovers, they embraced and together fell.

There are many scenes in the novel as melodramatically extravagant and as highly colored as these, although they are usually of a more humorous cast. One thinks of the scene in a hotel dining room in which Senator Day's son-in-law defines liberalism, complete with images of barricades in the streets and the proletariat taking their bread at gunpoint. "Meanwhile the businessmen at the next table fled," we are told, "no doubt to report to the House Un-American Activities Committee that the enemy had seized the dining room of the Willard Hotel." The career of Millicent Smith Carhart, a Washington hostess and the niece of a shadowy President, is melodrama become camp; it is worthy of Oscar Wilde.

> Lacking conventional good looks, she had resolutely made herself interesting by, among other things, marrying a British peer. Unfortunately, her belted earl, as she called him, was addicted to *le vice anglais,* and though this might have interested Millicent, it did not please her. Finally, after an otherwise uninteresting dinner party at the American Embassy, she had, in her own phrase, belted the earl. She then returned to Washington, and built a palace on Dupont Circle with the fortune left her by the President, who had died unexpectedly rich. Millicent lived alone until the earl died when, to everyone's surprise, she married Daniel Truscott Carhart, a dim New Englander who interested no one but Millicent. Speculation as to just *how* he interested her continued for many years.

Such passages tend to color the straightforwardly melodramatic elements in the novel: the conspiracy of Clay and Blaise Sanford to commit Enid to an insane asylum, for instance, and Enid's subsequent attempt to kill Blaise, and the suspicion of homosexuality in the relationship between Clay and Blaise. One tends, in consequence, to view each element as seriocomically lurid.

Peter Sanford is the key to the complexity of tone in the novel that results from this interaction of history, melodrama, and humor, and Peter is in many ways Vidal's spokesman, his vehicle for the savoring of *lèse majesté.* Politics both delights and enrages Peter, we are told, as it obviously delights and enrages Vidal, and the characters in the novel seem to Peter to be part of a vast novel in progress, further identifying Peter's stance as auctorial. Indeed, Vidal has allowed Peter to resemble himself in several important ways. By Vidal's own admission, Peter's home is modeled on Merrywood, the Auchincloss estate on the Potomac where Vidal lived when he was Peter's age; Peter also shares Vidal's youthful passion for the cinema, and he even shares Vidal's tendency to gain weight. With almost indelicate intimacy, the death of Peter's friend Scotty echoes the death of James Truscott, Vidal's fellow student at St. Alban's, just as Bob Ford echoes Truscott so intimately in *The City and the Pillar.*

More specifically, Peter is the key to the novel's tone in that he embodies the conjunction of history, melodrama, and humor. He spends a good deal of time in the Library of Congress studying the career of Aaron Burr, for instance. He is discovered reading Walter Map, the twelfth-century historian and author of *De Nugis Curialium,* and he is discovered reading *The Federalist Papers*. He is gratified to find in Burden Day his ideal of the classic Roman senator, and in later years he is able to point out that Senator Day's favorite quotation from Plato is a forgery. Peter is a student of history, and he brings a consciousness of history to his observations.

Peter is also a student of melodrama, however, and he relishes the discovery of Gothic possibilities in the Washington *mise-en-scène*. In the opening pages of the novel, he is pleasurably excited by the prospect of being struck by lightning, and his theatrically defiant scream to the heavens is entirely typical of him. Having read Poe the winter before, he finds himself consumed with incestuous passion for his sister Enid, and when he is stimulated by the zippers in women's clothing and can think of nothing but rape, he fancies himself Poe-esquely mad. The violent antipathy between Clay and Blaise in the early months of their association gratifies Peter's taste for raw passion; if the alliance that later develops between the two men disappoints him, he thrills to the promise of "rich drama" when Clay and Blaise must deal with Enid.

But Peter is not self-deluded. The novel may open with Peter standing in a storm-lashed garden, playing at King Lear and daring the lightning to strike him, but Peter knows playacting for what it is, and so he strolls to a lavatory, where he repeats his cry of defiance before a mirror so that he can watch the veins knot in his temples. Indeed, that is Peter's distinction in the novel; he knows his predilection for melodrama as other characters in the novel do not. Thus, he can never take seriously Enid's notion that Blaise is in love with Clay or, on the other hand, think badly of himself simply because his father rejects him. Neither can he bestir himself very much about the incestuous feelings that he cultivates for Enid. He is neither Senator Day, the victim of an overactive sense of melodrama, nor Clay, so totally lacking in the melodramatic imagination as never to taste its joys. The melodrama of both familial and political life is a matter of choosing to see the melodrama, Peter knows; if he chooses to see life as a melodrama, it is simply because life is more amusing when it is highly colored.

Peter's fondness for all things Hollywood imparts a special edge to the melodramatics of *Washington, D.C.,* for American politics and Hollywood scenarios merge so often in Peter's mind as to suggest that the national life takes its keynote from Hollywood. Upon hearing the news of Pearl Harbor and realizing that America's entrance into the war is imminent, Peter immediately envisions a newsreel, complete with background music and a narrator's grave voice announcing, "Heroism took on a new meaning when Peter Sanford, alone, unaided, stormed an enemy position. . . . " Connections between Hollywood and the national life are unmistakably limned: Clay Overbury rises to political eminence through something very like the Hollywood star system (there are dark hints of a casting couch), and the merchandising of Clay is patterned on Hollywood's promotional methods. Harold Griffiths, who is effectively Clay's press agent, is even a sometime film critic who believes that movies are life "with the point made simple."

But it is once again Peter's distinction in the novel that he knows where Hollywood ends and reality begins. He finds it distasteful that a famous movie star actually *votes,* and when he learns that Scotty has been killed in action, he resents the newsreels that play melodramatically in his head, preferring to rise to tragedy or sink to grief. When Enid dies, on the other hand, Peter tries desperately and without success to imagine an innocuous, Hollywood-style revision of the scenario recounted by her attending doctor. Characteristically, however, his grasp of reality is firm.

It is wholly fitting, then, that Peter is the only character in the novel whose success is not tawdry. Through his involvement with a journal of opinion, he arranges that his father and Clay Overbury do not win easily, and he thereby avenges Enid; through his involvement with the egregious Irene Bloch and her introduction into Laurel House, he strikes a blow against WASP complacency; and through his involvement with Diana, he achieves the only relationship in the novel that is remotely honest and healthy. Yet like Senator Day, Peter is an off-center presence in the novel, and his relative success is a minor irony, just as Senator Day's relative integrity is a sidelined hope. Clay Overbury's climb to a shabby eminence remains the central thread of the novel, and the republic's taste for melodrama remains the novel's trenchant theme. In the last analysis, *Washington, D.C.* is a comedy of political manners.

Burr (1973) is set in the 1830s and is narrated by Charlie Schuyler, a young law clerk with journalistic ambitions who is employed and befriended by Aaron Burr. Burr is a New York City lawyer of advanced years in the 1830s, but he is still notorious as the man who killed Alexander Hamilton in a duel in 1804 and as the author of a secessionist conspiracy in 1806. Burr is, in fact, so notorious that Charlie is secretly hired to discredit Vice-President Martin Van Buren by writing a pamphlet asserting that Van Buren is Burr's bastard son. Charlie's consequent probing of Burr's life encourages Burr to reminisce and to hand over to Charlie his written account of the early days of the republic. Charlie incorporates Burr's account of those days into the narrative, alternating great gobs of Burr's material with his own. Indeed, Charlie's probing of Burr's fatherhood is less significant for what it finally uncovers—that he and Van Buren are *both* Burr's sons—than for its analogue in Burr's probing of the Founding Fathers.

The giants of the early republic are no heroes to Burr, and he paints compelling, gossipy portraits. George Washington was a man of "eerie incompetence" and a backside threatening always to split his trousers; the Marquis de Lafayette was all silliness and a pointed head; Alexander Hamilton was a social-climbing West Indian who read women's novels on the sly; John Hancock went to his grave piqued that Washington and not he had commanded the Continental Army; Thomas Jefferson was a hypocrite who pledged his countrymen's lives but never his own. In Burr's view, the Founding Fathers were so many despoilers of the infant republic. He sees Washington as building a strong central government simply to protect his land holdings, and he sees Jefferson as amassing a Napoleonic empire and trampling on civil liberties in the process. Having thought the Constitution too brittle a document to last even fifty years, Burr nevertheless affects to be scandalized that those who had framed the Constitution subverted it so casually, and his accounts of their political wrangles are as damning and fascinating as they are ample.

But Burr has axes to grind, it is clear, and much of the material he gives Charlie is self-justifying and emphasizes his own good sense and refinement. He is, he admits, something of a rake, but an elegant, Augustan rake and a patrician scoundrel to the degree that he is a scoundrel at all. Charlie tends to think the old reprobate beyond criticism, yet Charlie's sections of the novel make clear that Burr is still an unregenerate adventurer, as exemplified by his marriage to the wealthy ex-prostitute Madame Jumel and his loss of her money in a Texas land-lease fraud. The novel is, in fact, nothing so much as a composite portrait of Aaron Burr—disjointed, fictionalized, and honorific, to be sure, part biography and part autobiography *manqué*, but a portrait of Burr nonetheless.

The portrait is untenable, of course, to the degree that it is partisan and omits elements of Burr's life recorded elsewhere. There is no mention of Burr's having been raised until he was thirteen in the home of a brutal, bachelor uncle, presumably because such mention would make too predictable his maverick impulses and notorious womanizing. And the very odd relationship between Burr and his daughter Theodosia—a Freudian set piece if there ever was one—seems to exist at face value, just as Burr's insistence that he never wanted to be emperor of the American West (merely emperor of Mexico) seems to prevail, although Henry Adams and the majority of historians believe that Burr did attempt to separate the Western territories from the union, exactly as Jefferson charged. Yet these suppressions and misrepresentations are portraiture, too, for they are part of Burr's carefully prepared brief for himself and wholly consonant with his opportunism.

The portraits of the Founding Fathers are similarly shaded. Jefferson was certainly a duplicitous man, as Burr charges, and he certainly took up the cause of states' rights in order to gain votes; he was even the compulsive explainer of the obvious that Burr ridicules. But with equal certainty, it is a shaded viewpoint that sees Jefferson as no more than that, just as it is a shaded viewpoint that Washington endorsed a strong central government simply to protect Mount Vernon, for hundreds of other landowners bitterly opposed the formation of a strong central government. In short, Burr and his author are all too ready to see the ambitions of these men and too little ready to see the men. A historian might object they are too ready to see the men and too little ready to see the historical forces that shaped them.

But who would have it otherwise? Shading imparts depth and texture to a narrative as much as to a photograph or painting, and *Burr* is absorbing precisely because it debunks the Founding Fathers so gloriously. Burr remarks of Washington, for instance, that "the fine white powder he used to dress his hair sometimes gave the startling effect of a cloudy nimbus about that storied head." One has only to think of the halo effect in so many of Washington's portraits to catch Vidal's superb iconoclasm, meshed so artfully with the period detail. Similarly, when Burr visits Jefferson's rented home at Gray's Ferry, he is treated to a demonstration of a bed that rises to the ceiling on ropes (a duplicate of the famous Jefferson gadget that draws tourists to Monticello today), and Burr's simple bewilderment as to why anyone would *wish* to send his bed to the ceiling is a neat deflation of Archimedes redux. It does not harm the fun that the bed crashes to the floor when the ropes break, "nearly sparing us the Jefferson administration." Just as one must admire Vidal's restraint in not making overt the connection between Washington's hair powder and his portraits, so one must admire his restraint in not connecting Jefferson's ludicrous copying machines—a repeating joke in every sense—with the many replications of Jefferson among the slave children at Monticello or with Jefferson's astonishing ability to stand on both sides of every question. Doubleness is in a sense Jefferson's keynote in the novel, but Burr and his author have too much respect for the debunking stance to resort to overkill.

Indeed, Burr and his author are wonderfully adept at the casual remark that debunks gratuitously. The Virginians' dominance of the country's political machinery inspires Burr not to a focused peroration but to an incidental remark about "the many-limbed Virginian junto, the octopus with but a single Jeffersonian head and a thousand tentacles, all named James!" The invidious word "junto" cuts the Virginians sharply to size, the octopus conceit is nicely rude, and the allusion to a proliferation of Jameses in political life is lightly parodic. This descending scale of invective softens the harshness of "junto" without for a moment mitigating its sting, and it is highly effective rhetoric.

Similarly, the early republic's lust for empire is debunked much more successfully in the small scene than in the large plot. The preposterous Madame Jumel (otherwise known as Eliza Bowen of Rhode Island) shifts between New England Yankee and emigré French in her accent, and she evokes in miniature the American fascination with Bonaparte and the French empire in the 1780s. If her devotion to the emperor is absurdly pretentious, it is the exact equivalent of Jefferson's ambition to match Bonaparte empire for empire. Only Burr and his author are sufficiently patrician to snub the Corsican: Bonaparte was apparently too great a man to notice weather, Burr remarks with studied indirection, for he failed to understand that autumn is invariably followed by winter and that in Russia winter is invincible. Alluding to the influence of Empire fashion on American clothing, Burr remarks simply and contemptuously that the summer of 1807 was one of "teats and treason."

There is almost no aspect of American life between 1776 and 1830 that is not debunked in this incidental manner. The government is blatantly anti-Catholic, Burr assures us in an aside, and he himself finds it impossible to believe that a Catholic can be a good American. The Continental Army may have suffered at Valley Forge, but our attention is casually drawn to the nation's founders spending the winter quite comfortably before their fires. Burr remarks that bad manners in America began with the French Revolution—that overnight it became slavish for the lower classes to be polite to anyone—and Charlie maintains, without especial point, that Washington Irving goes to the opposite extreme of conduct and threatens to suffocate one and all with his "constant benevolent blandness." Ambassadorships are eagerly sought, we learn, because they take people out of America to more civilized lands. Martha Washington has a "disquieting tendency to nod or shake her head for no particular reason," Burr tells us, apropos of nothing. The colonists did not win the Revolutionary War, he claims; rather, the French won it for them. Slavery is not really one of Burr's concerns, yet Jeffersonian democracy, he suggests, is a matter of "honest yeomen enjoying the fruits of black labor."

One of Vidal's more delightful creations in this vein is Mrs. Townsend, who presides over a brothel that Burr and Charlie frequent and who is an historically authentic person. Early in the novel, she is discovered reading *Pilgrim's Progress* in a search for the meaning of life; paralleling the history of American religious sentiment in the eighteenth and nineteenth centuries, she progresses later in the novel to Jonathan Edwards, whom she reads, she says, "for the terror!" An Emersonian interest in Oriental religions later soothes her spirits.

America is a compound of pretension, arrogance, and silliness, then, and the narrator, Charlie Schuyler, finds Burr a refreshing antidote to the tone of the day. Indeed, this is a secret of Burr's immense appeal in the novel for us as well as for Charlie. He pretends to be no more than an opportunist, quite willing to trade his charm for a steady income and the heady delights of power. It gives one pause to realize that unlike the other Fathers (Hamilton is the only exception), Burr never spoke of a national purpose and apparently never even imagined that such an exalted thing could be.

Vidal has caught this aspect of the historical Burr well, and the debunking tone of the novel is perfectly calculated to flatter Burr's lack of cant. Yet Burr is no unimaginative literalist. Charlie notes that he is able to make a trip to his barber sound like a conspiracy to overthrow the government, and his grandiose schemes for the Western territories are certainly imaginative enough, even foolhardy. His marriage to Madame Jumel is no less imaginative. Andrew Jackson was of the opinion that the historical Burr was no fool but as easily fooled as any other man, and Vidal has caught this paradoxical aspect of the historical Burr, too, not shying from depicting him as the dupe of his own ambitions. This is actually part of Vidal's vindication of Burr, for the other Founding Fathers escape the consequences of their ambition all too easily, and the ordinary citizen pays the cost in their stead. Burr is an overreacher as much as they, but he pays the cost of overreaching with hard cash and with his permanent reputation.

Burr's charm is essentially verbal, however, and he is especially a master of the set piece that begins in arrogance and fades into self-mockery. His reaction to the death of Lafayette is a hoary set piece, perhaps, but the technique of the abrupt reversal has never been more elegantly rendered.

[Burr:] "One cannot say that he was taken before his time. We must restrain our grief." The Colonel was suitably dry. "He must have been—what, eighty?"

[Sam Swartout:] "Seventy-seven. Younger than you, Colonel."

[Burr:] "Then I shudder at this cold premonitory wind from France. Poor boy! So much to look forward to. I trust he is now in Heaven with General Washington and, side by side, they rest on a cloudy mantle of stars for all eternity, dreaming up disastrous military engagements."

The elegance of Burr's wit seldom falters. He remarks of his mother that she died before they could properly meet, and on being told to his surprise that the poet William Cullen Bryant was once a Burrite, he remarks, "I shall now read him with a warmth which hitherto has been lacking." Of his impending death, he says to Charlie, "If you should hear that I have died in the bosom of the Dutch Reformed Church, you will know that either a noble mind was entirely overturned at the end or a man of the cloth has committed perjury."

This verbal elegance is also part of Burr's vindication, perhaps the most important part. Vidal's characters are always worthy of respect to the degree that they are fluent, and only Myra Breckinridge can match Burr's high verbal style. Vidal's equation is not trivial. Sophistication, intellect, and breeding do manifest themselves in language, and for Vidal language is the preeminent clue to the man. Burr is superior to the other Founding Fathers whatever the facts of history, then, not simply because he speaks more elegantly than they but because his language is a manifestation of superior being. The Fathers of lesser being are betrayed by their speech. Words always failed Washington, we are assured, for he was utterly incapable of organizing a sentence containing a new thought; Jefferson's self-delusion was echoed in his "tangled sentences and lunatic metaphors," his modest intellect in his inability to achieve irony, wit, or humor.

Charlie Schuyler is a neat foil to Burr, for he is an apprentice *littérateur,* enormously impressed by Burr's gifts and terribly conscious of his own amateurism. He complains at the very beginning of the novel that he is unable to catch the "right tone" in preparing a story about Burr's wedding to Madame Jumel for the *Evening Post,* and he is endearingly self-conscious about his more literary effects, reminding himself to include descriptive detail, pointing out his parody of Washington Irving's style lest we miss it, and assiduously cultivating the "slanderous manner" for his pamphlet on Van Buren and Burr. His respect for language and for verbal style functions as a continuing tribute to Burr, underscoring this important element of Burr's vindication.

But Charlie is an echo of his father as well as a foil. His delight in tricking Burr is something Burr would readily understand, and his fascination with the past and his attraction to what is secret are surely dispositions inherited from Burr. Financial security eludes him just as it eludes his father, and his living with the prostitute Helen Jewett and his false arrest for her murder (the murder of the historical Helen Jewett was a celebrated *crime passionel* of the 1830s) parallel Burr's marriage to the former prostitute Madame Jumel and the legal squabble that ensued.

Charlie does not realize until the last page of the novel that Burr is his natural father, yet he has been looking unconsciously for a father throughout the novel, inasmuch as he is drawn to older men and finds discipleship a congenial role. "I am always obedient," he says. Moreover, he is estranged from his adoptive father, whom he credits with killing his mother three years before the novel opens. In the one scene in which Charlie accidentally meets his adoptive father, he significantly protests almost at once that he must leave to meet Burr. Burr is his chosen father, we understand, even his fairy godfather, for in the last line of the novel Charlie says that "there was no wish that I could make that I have not already been granted by my father Aaron Burr." It is Charlie's miraculous luck that his chosen father is his real father.

As I have already observed, *Burr* is a novel more impressive in the small scene than in the large plot, but this search for a father that constitutes the large plot of the novel contributes nicely to Vidal's large point that America has misunderstood its paternity. Aaron Burr would figure more prominently in the pantheon of the Fathers if history were rightly understood, Vidal seems to say, and the politicos of *Washington, D.C.* might be more impressive men had America adopted the high style of Burr rather than the low style of his coevals. Yet Burr's influence is not dead. Peter Townsend carries on Burr's iconoclasm in *Washington, D.C.,* the chronologically last novel in Vidal's trilogy, and Peter is a stepfamily descendent of Burr, just as Vidal himself is loosely related to Burr through his stepfather, Hugh D. Auchincloss. But Peter Townsend's sniping at the national life from the sidelines of a political journal is a pale shadow of Burr's fine outsiderhood, just as Charlie's attack on Burr in his pamphlet is only a shadow of Burr's debunking of the Founding Fathers in his memoirs. *"Le style, c'est l'homme,"* according to the French aphorism, and Vidal would surely agree. But for Vidal, political style is also passé.

1876 (1976) opens in December 1875, on the eve of the American centennial year. Charles Schuyler, the narrator of *Burr,* is sixty-two years old and returns to New York from France for the first time since 1837. His widowed daughter Emma, the Princess d'Agrigente, accompanies him, and they come as desperate fortune hunters, since Schuyler has lost most of his capital in the Panic of 1873 and cannot support them on his meager earnings as a writer. *1876* is a scribbled journal that Schuyler keeps from his arrival in New York until his death in the early months of 1877; he thinks of it as his workbook, a place to note incidents and impressions that he may someday write about, a "quarry" from which he hopes to "hack out a monument or two to decorate the republic's centennial."

The quarry is ample, for the America of 1876 is very different from the land Schuyler left almost forty years before, and he confesses himself unprepared for "the opulence, the grandeur, the vulgarity, the poverty, the elegance, the awful crowded abundance" that are everywhere, especially in New York City. Daunted but eco-

nomically desperate, he plunges into New York society with Emma on his arm, and in short order he declares himself a supporter of Samuel J. Tilden, the Democratic nominee for President, in the hope that Tilden will appoint him Minister to France in return for his writing a campaign biography. Schuyler also signs on as a special correspondent for the New York *Herald,* and his duties take him to cities as far flung as Albany, Cincinnati, and Washington. He covers the opening of the Philadelphia Centennial Exposition, he is a guest at the Astor estate in Rhinebeck, and he attends the Republican nominating convention in the Midwest. In rather too much detail, he traces the collapse of the Grant administration under the weight of the Belknap scandal and traces the bitterly contested Hayes-Tilden presidential election, in which Republicans maneuvered the election into the Electoral College and stole the Presidency from Tilden, who had won the popular vote.

In a parallel upset, Schuyler's daughter Emma breaks her engagement to the scion of a respectable New York family and marries the flashy millionaire William Sanford, the grandfather of Peter Sanford of *Washington, D.C.* Their marriage is clouded by the probability that Emma helped Sanford do away with his former wife, just as the presidential election is clouded by charges of malfeasance. Aghast, Schuyler dies shortly afterward while working on the notes that constitute *1876,* and William Cullen Bryant provides a short obituary in an addendum to the text.

Like the other novels in Vidal's American trilogy, *1876* is meticulously historical and something of a Cook's Tour, replete with allusions to the thousand churches of Brooklyn, to goats trotting down East Twenty-fourth Street, and to the beginnings of Chinatown in lower Manhattan. But Schuyler is not the average tour guide, and historical trappings acquire an interesting edge when they are filtered through his Europeanized mind. The newly completed Central Park raises for him the very European question, "How does one 'complete' a park?" and his acquired distaste for Americanisms makes him ask whether shops are always called "stores" in New York. Oakey Hall, a former mayor of New York, is the best dressed man in the city, he reports, "(whatever *that* must be)." The Hudson River estates built in the Gothic style make him grateful that there is no Gothic revival in France—just the Gothic itself—and nineteenth-century landmarks beloved in the twentieth century are especially singled out for his censure. The houses of Washington Square are "as unimaginative as a row of new American novels," he says, and Gramercy Park seems to him a "homely little square . . . surrounded by a perfunctory ironwork fence and the usual narrow houses sprayed with chocolate." Folkways inspire a similar censure: "What'll it be?" is the "gracious question" put to him in a restaurant, and "Welcome home, traitor" is America's inevitable greeting to her expatriates. Titles are alleged to have no place in a democracy, yet he finds that they are shamelessly affected.

> Americans care desperately for titles, for any sign of distinction. In fact, since the War Between the States, I have not met a single American of a certain age who does not insist upon being addressed as Colonel or Commodore. In-

variably I promote them; address them as General, as Admiral; they preen and do not correct me.

American *littérateurs* are beyond the pale. Mark Twain is "the most contemptible music-hall performer that ever pandered to an audience of ignorant yahoos," and Nathaniel Hawthorne is "that dark veiled lady of New England letters . . . who, faced with *any* truth about the way we are, swiftly evokes ghosts and haunted houses." Schuyler's European friends would prefer roasting Bryant's waterfowl to apostrophizing it, he assures us, perhaps after slaughtering it with "that terrible swift sword so savagely celebrated in the bloodthirsty 'hymn' of one Julia Ward Howe." Clearly, Schuyler's monument to the American centenary is not a work of unalloyed love.

Inasmuch as it was published in 1976, *1876* must also be considered Vidal's monument to the American bicentenary. Vidal aligns the two periods carefully. His Samuel J. Tilden is not unlike George McGovern in many respects, his Rutherford B. Hayes is not unlike Gerald Ford, and his Mark Twain is not unlike the contemporary writer Tom Wolfe. The bicentennial anniversary was haunted by memories of Vietnam, the Kennedy assassination, the Watergate break-ins, and the corrupt Nixon administration; and Vidal's centennial anniversary has its memories of the Civil War, Lincoln's assassination, the Babcock break-in, and the Grant administration.

The violence and mendacity that Schuyler finds prevalent in America in 1876 are perennial flowers in the American garden, but Schuyler and his author do not so much object to the growth of these dubious flowers as object that they grow so messily. Schuyler is never more a cultivated European than when he remarks that flowers belong in vases rather than loose and untidy on the ground, and he is no less the cultivated European in objecting to the untidy measures of American villainy. "I delight in all Bonapartes," he says, "particularly in the first one, whose crimes were on such a large scale that they have ceased to be the stuff of moralizing and are simply history." President Grant would qualify as a Bonaparte in Schuyler's view if Grant's Puritan sense of morality had not made for "confusion."

In a sense, Vidal is inverting Henry James's novelistic formula and looking at corrupt America through the eyes of still-more-corrupt Europe rather than looking at corrupt Europe through the eyes of innocent America. In the same sense, the Princess d'Agrigente is an inverted Jamesian heroine, and the stylistic contrast is significant between her quietly macabre dispatch of Sanford's first wife (assuming the fact) and the too obvious machinations of American politicos. Europe may be capable of darker deeds than America, but that is because in Europe evil is a fact of civilized life, whereas in America immorality is a rude and grubby theater.

A sustained theatrical conceit runs through Vidal's American trilogy. Senator Day sees life at crucial moments as a Shakespearean play in *Washington, D.C.,* and he retires from politics "because he felt that the time had come for him to cease to be an actor." Schuyler had once thought of becoming an actor too, but the newspaper he works for

in *Burr* is a "stage more important than that of the Bowery Theatre," and he cannot hope to match the performances of Clay, Jefferson, and others on the Senate floor. Appropriately, the Bowery Theatre changes its name to the "American Theatre" in the course of *Burr,* and Burr's home at Richmond Hill is converted into a theater after he debuts as a villain in the Hamilton farce.

1876 is replete with such allusions. Washington is a "peculiar theatre," and its politicians gesture "like Edwin Forrest as Othello confronting Iago," leave the congressional chamber "like Hamlet in the last act," and conduct themselves "like the very worst sort of actors trying to look like Roman senators." Shakespearean tragedy is the republic's mime, then, although Schuyler says that American politics is really "an ongoing comedy" liable at any moment to become "wildest farce," and he sees himself as playing "the part of foolish elder sage, of Falstaff," at another time, Polonius.

This theatrical conceit is broadly applicable to the world of *1876.* The New York cityscape is something of a scrim, with whorehouses lurking behind cigar store Indians, and the mansion of a wealthy abortionist sitting demurely next to St. Patrick's Cathedral. With similar effect, ragged, emaciated children paw through trash cans on the fashionable Ladies' Mile of Broadway, and Civil War veterans beg coins beside the red carpet thrown down profligately in the snow for Mrs. William Astor's guests. The homes of New York society are scrims, too, dowdy brownstone without, gilt and tapestry to rival Versailles within. People in New York society are scrims incarnate: Ward McAllister claims an impossible French ancestry; Governor Tilden secretly collects erotic literature; William Sanford is at one moment a "plain-spoken man of the people, all hideously self-made" and at another the "thoughtful Darwinist and social historian"; Mrs. Paran Stevens (of "Chateau Stevens") has even had her portrait painted in the likeness of Madame Sans-Gêne. In fashionable Newport, society women style their mansions "cottages," and though they are "Watteau ladies," they pretend to be "Breughel women" as they convey their chefs' contributions to rustic picnics. In a world of scrims, imposture must even be assumed. Senator Roscoe Conkling's look of sincerity was "so perfectly convincing," Schuyler says, "that I knew myself to be in the presence of a truly deceitful man."

Given the elaborate deceits of the age, Schuyler faces a problem in trying to write its history. Vidal sees a solution, however, in Schuyler's readiness to see the scrims and to suppose the worst. Since the truth is never plainly shown, fantasy and conjecture are necessary approaches to the truth, and since the truth would not have been suppressed were it not scandalous, the more invidious one supposes the truth, the more accurate one is apt to be.

Vidal's spokesman for the first half of this dubious proposition is Baron Jacobi, a diplomatic minister from Bulgaria who enters the world of *1876* via Henry Adams's novel *Democracy.* The Baron argues that history is something we *cannot* know. What we think to be history is fiction, he maintains, because the historian's raw materials—letters, diaries, and newspaper reports—are "more apt than not to lie." In the Baron's view, one learns about the past from Shakespeare, whose historical characters are "right" whatever Shakespeare's penchant for getting their history wrong. The Baron does not go further (although he might) and observe that Shakespeare's most villainous characters are his most authentic; rather, it is Vidal, through his own dedicated enterprise, through the fact of his writing *1876* and the other novels in the trilogy, who asserts that the most malicious speculations about history are worthwhile and probably accurate. And just as Shakespeare's characters are true because they are "right," so Vidal's characters can claim historical accuracy to the degree that they are credible human beings rather than the plaster idols that have come down to us in the official histories.

If American history is theater, as the conceit suggests, what other truth can there be than the truth of the successful illusion, whether Shakespeare's or Vidal's? What is the "truth" of the history books if public figures are professional illusionists? Such questions are disingenuously posed, of course, but they constitute the essential spirit of the novels in the American trilogy, and they are a marvelous justification of Vidal's naughtiness vis-à-vis American history.

It is ironical in the face of all this that Charles Schuyler is not adequately real as a character. To an extent, he suffers from an inevitable comparison with Burr. Having established Schuyler as a foil to Burr in the earlier novel, Vidal does not develop him in *1876* to the extent that he can command center stage once Burr is dead. Schuyler's judgments on America tend to be incidental and miscellaneous compared to Burr's radical debunking, and his speculations about what is going on behind the scenes are effete compared with Burr's overarching speculations.

Schuyler is, in fact, very much an American innocent behind his European scrim. He is innocent enough to hope Emma innocent, and he is innocent enough to express the belief that "somewhere in this corrupt and canting American society there still exists in certain men a sense of what the good society must be." This innocence does Schuyler enormous damage as a character, for it means that the novel's profound cynicism washes over his head like a great wave, although the novel's cynicism—that is to say, Vidal's cynicism—is technically Schuyler's own. This is not just Vidalian irony. Because the novel is so loosely structured and scatters its anathemas so randomly, it very much needs a narrator who can rise to its cynicism and pull its scattered energies together. The effect of Schuyler's innocence, however, is to compromise his ability to do these things, and the net effect is to compromise his reality as a character. He is so much less than the novel needs him to be that he seems not enough at all according to the ruthless economics of art, not "real" and not true.

In the context of Vidal's three-volume sequence, however, Schuyler's inadequacy as a narrator is well calculated. The three novels move in their chronological order from vigorous old Burr through weary Charles Schuyler down to indolent Peter Sanford at the end of the family line. A decline in the sexual performance, general health, and intellectual vitality of the three protagonists is as carefully graded as the decline in their physical stamina and age and

as carefully gradated, too, as the rapacity of the American politico. A decline in the republic's genes is clearly the point, and it is wholly appropriate in this regard that Schuyler's role as the narrator of *1876* is less dominant than his father's role in *Burr* yet more dominant than Peter's role in *Washington, D.C.* This pattern of the trilogy simply takes precedence over the formal demands of *1876.*

But *1876* is a sophisticated jaunt through the centennial year nonetheless. Who but Vidal would bring Schuyler back to America after thirty-eight years and have him say, "The fact that I can no longer tell a prostitute from a true lady is the first sign that I have been away for a very long time. As a boy, I always knew"? Who except Vidal (and Borges) would say, "Well, the writer is not unlike the explorer. We, too, are searching for lost cities, rare tigers, the sentence never before written"? Indeed, who but Vidal consistently writes such marvelous sentences? *1876* may be a misfired salute to the American (bi)centenary, but even misfires can delight those who have a taste for accomplished prose. (pp. 67-93)

Robert F. Kiernan, in his Gore Vidal, *Frederick Ungar Publishing Co., 1982, 165 p.*

Italo Calvino

[Calvino was a prominent Cuban-born Italian novelist, essayist, and editor. The following is the translated text of a speech that Calvino delivered at a 1983 ceremony making Vidal an honorary citizen of Ravello, Italy, where he has maintained a residence since the 1960s.]

Celebrating Gore Vidal here in Ravello, I find myself in a strange, multi-track situation. I think of Gore in his house here, suspended over a dazzling and sheer cliff, or I see him in the main square seated at the cafe where I met him this morning, while at the same time I feel myself transported to a backdrop, one of a huge city on a lake which is encircled by skyscrapers and neon lights.

The fact is that I've just finished reading Vidal's latest novel, *Duluth,* to continuous amusement and stimulation to the imagination. It is a novel in which contemporary life seems to have been completely taken over by fiction, with the world being nothing but episodes of TV serials, with characters who switch their roles, dying in one of the series only to reappear in another. Or else life is a crisscrossing of plots from cheap novels, published in installments, or issued in massive volumes destined for the masses.

One cannot tell where real life, or that which Vidal calls "life, or nonfiction," ends and where the intricate jungle of imaginary stories, with episodes which alternate and overlap, thanks to the combinations of a word processor (whose memory has been fed the plots of all the world's novels), begins.

Therefore, inspired by the recent reading of *Duluth,* in which the things which happen do not conform to Vidal's principle of "absolute uniqueness," I must ask myself if we are indeed in Ravello, or in a Ravello reconstructed in a Hollywood studio, with an actor playing Gore Vidal, or if we are in the TV documentary on Vidal in Ravello which we were to have seen tonight and which mysteriously vanished, or whether we are here on the Amalfi Coast on a festive occasion, but one in 1840, when, at the end of another Vidal novel, *Burr,* the narrator learns that the most controversial of America's Founding Fathers, Colonel Burr, was his father. Or, since there is a spaceship in *Duluth,* manned by centipedes who can take on any appearance, even becoming dead-ringers for American political figures, perhaps we could be aboard that spaceship, which has left Duluth for Ravello, and the E.T.s aboard could have taken on the appearance of the American writer we are gathered here to celebrate.

The key to all those mysteries may lie in the book's finale, when we learn that the world exists only in the mind of a tireless woman novelist who has the power to erase houses, hills, existences, until the invasion of the centipedes from the spaceship creates hundreds of Ravellos in time and in space, complete with all the municipal dignitaries and the guests here tonight, and with a Gore Vidal in each Ravello, all that much more multiform and gifted with ubiquity, and thus that much more "absolutely unique" and faithful to himself.

As for the ubiquity of Vidal, I believe that we can gather that right here in Ravello, because when we read or listen to Vidal it seems that he has never left America even for one second. His passionate and polemical participation in American life is without interruption. What we see in Ravello is someone living a tranquil, parallel life. Is it Vidal or his double? Or is there a satellite circling over the Amalfi Coast which keeps him informed of all that is happening in America?

Certainly, in today's world where distance has been erased, where everything is present, Vidal has initiated a new way of staying in Italy. For many generations, American writers saw our country as a picturesque background, exotic, mysterious, and anyhow a world opposite to America. Their sojourning in Europe and above all in Italy of those days, so archaic, distant from America in time and in space, signified a symbolic breaking-away almost like going to the great beyond. Not for nothing were they called then "exiles" or "expatriates."

Gore, here, does not feel himself an exile anywhere. He lives with the same ease and assurance on the Mediterranean as on the Pacific or on the Atlantic. In fact, he manages to keep one foot on each shore, which must require some fast footwork as his feet are two and his shores three. That could be the reason why he has never felt the need to give us his Italian novel, his *Marble Faun,* his *Daisy Miller,* his *Across the River and Into the Trees.*

I would be very pleased, now that he has become an honorary citizen of one of our cities, if he should feel himself authorized to write that Italian novel. And I'm sure that unlike those of his illustrious predecessors, it would be entertaining from beginning to end. But I must admit that so far, we also may have been luckier than we realize! When I think of the ferocious glee with which Vidal rips apart the American reality with a transfiguration both grotesque and truculent, and what could come forth if he were to turn his powers on *our* manners and morals, I experience a foretaste of enjoyment and at the same time an attack of cold sweat. I can already see the Furies of his fantasy hungrily turning on the public and private image of Italian society, with all the gusto of *Duluth's* women-police corps when they force "illegal aliens" to undergo body searches. I can already see all of us in some of his hilariously cruel pages. Which can take their place in the great *Humour Noir* tradition from Swift onwards.

Vidal knows us well. In his essays and interviews about Italy he is right on target. He once defined Italian society as being that which "combines the less attractive aspects of socialism with practically all the vices of capitalism." Staying in Italy for Vidal is, to be sure, a less problematic adventure than it is for us. It is rather a way of keeping that little distance from America which permits him to observe it better. And being American is his problem. His passion for what America is or is not dominates his thoughts. It is not true that this *enfant terrible* respects nothing and no one. His point of departure can be found in the fundamental principles of the Declaration of Independence, which, from the first lines, defines as the inalienable rights which all men have received from their creator the rights to life, liberty, and the pursuit of happiness. With these very simple principles as his strength, Vidal fires point-blank at everything which contradicts them. His view is one of absolute pessimism. In *Duluth,* no social stratum is spared, nor any institution. But he always leaves a door ajar for a harmonious ideal. In this case it is proclaimed by the centipedes from the spaceship (which, however, does not preserve these E.T. visitors from getting caught up in disastrous stock market speculation).

This polemical passion for America's public affairs, and for everything which could be called the anthropology of that country's mass-culture, is the nucleus of the "absolute uniqueness" which binds together the many Gore Vidals who are acting contemporaneously and taking on diverse forms. There is the essay form, of which he is one of the contemporary masters, incomparable for his sincerity, agility, and concreteness. There is the contemporary novel form as a grotesque transfiguration of the language and myths of the mass-media. There is the historical novel which brutally presents the past in a way which alarmingly resembles our present. (This is as true in his interpretations of the American past, in *Burr* and in *1876,* as when he evokes the more remote past in *Creation.*) There is the theater form, where Vidal's instinct to make a drama of everything he does or says converges. And there is the conversationalist, or TV personality, form, which made his last year's senatorial campaign different from any others. As a political animal, he delivers what he calls his Discourse on the State of the Union. We also know what some of the average Americans' reactions to those discourses are, as Vidal has recorded them as well.

I chanced to hear one of these discourses before a public of his co-nationals, though probably not typical of the average American, inasmuch as no one was scandalized and everyone greeted his *jeu de massacre* with a sense of complicity and fun was had by all. But what was the reaction of the foreign listener?

It led me to reflect that the strength of a country can be measured by its capacity to swallow the most radical criticism, to digest it, and to draw from it nourishment. And I found myself saying—"only in a society sure of itself, of its stability and good health could a polemicist like Gore Vidal be born! That is the difference between the United States and our fragile Italy! What Italian has ever done a satire so radical of our political world, or of our social mores? Only when we shall have writers capable of merrily and mercilessly attacking our government, parties, and institutions, can we be certain of having become a great power."

Vidal also can be a lethal literary critic, but here I must mention one exception. That is when he writes about Italian writers, when his criticism is full of *simpatia*—and coming from a temperament like his, that can only be sincere. Not that the polemicist is nodding on those occasions. He always has a critical attitude toward other American critics which leads him to present our works in the most favorable light. The link between Vidal and the Italian writers he has introduced to the American public is that most of them are of his generation. They began writing after the war, and Vidal never forgets coming to a still-devastated Italy in 1948 with Tennessee Williams. In other words, there is a sense of some shared experiences which he wants to perceive on this side and on the other side of the Atlantic.

Vidal's *betes noire* are the writers and critics in the United States and in France who want to experiment with or theorize new forms of the novel. Is there, then, a conservative Vidal? It would be difficult admitting to that, since one cannot speak of the revival of the novel's form in the last fifteen years without turning back to what may be his most famous novel, *Myra Breckinridge.* That satirical and grotesque burlesque, made up of a collage of the language and myths of the mass-culture, inaugurated a new phase in the way to present our era, which is comparable to pop art, but much more aggressive and with an explosion of expressionistic comedy.

Vidal's development along that line, from *Myra* to *Duluth,* is crowned with great success, not only for the density of comic effects, each one filled with meaning, not only for the craftsmanship in construction, put together like a clockwork which fears no word processor, but because his latest book holds its own built-in theory, that which the author calls his "*apres*-poststructuralism."

To be sure, Vidal's explicit intention is to parody the current university vogue for "Narratology," but his mythology seems to me to be no less rigorous and his execution no less perfect. For that reason, I consider Vidal to be a master of that new form which is taking shape in world literature and which we may call the hyper-novel or the novel elevated to the square or to the cube.

As for Vidal's wars against new experiments in novels, I don't share his views towards that general tendency because I hope always that some good will come out of it all to bring more life into a pallid scene. But there is a point where I share Vidal's concern: that is the risk today that literature is being reduced to subject matter for universities. The fact that there are books being written today in the United States exclusively for internal consumption on the campus does not offer a happy prospect. (Complementary to that tendency is the spread of novels prefabricated for an undemanding public: the fashionable lady novelist who does not know either how to write or read and who uses ghost writers is a character that appears both in Vidal's *Kalki* and in *Duluth.*)

Anyhow, you may rest assured, dear Mr. Vidal, that *Duluth* is one of those novels upon which the universities will base courses and seminars, producing theses and tracts bristling with diagrams. It is a fate which cannot be avoided. The important thing is the spirit which you have put in the book and which races non-stop throughout its pages.

With this observation, I want to close my salutations to Gore Vidal. He belongs to that group of writers of our times who, precisely because they always have kept their eyes open to the disasters and distortions of our age, have chosen irony, humor, comedy—in other words, the whole range of literary instruments belonging to the universe of the laugh—as their means of settling accounts.

That is the terrain where literature can reply to history's challenge. In an epoch of tragic mystifications, in which language serves more to conceal than to reveal, the only serious discourses are those delivered as if for laughs. (pp. 26-7)

> *Italo Calvino, "Imagining Vidal," in* The Threepenny Review, *Vol. V, No. 1, Spring, 1983, pp. 26-7.*

Harold Bloom

Walt Whitman elegized Lincoln as "the sweetest, wisest soul of all my days and lands." "The actual Lincoln was cold and deliberate, reflective and brilliant," according to Gore Vidal's brief meditation on the martyr president in *The Second American Revolution and Other Essays: 1976-1982.* That somber "Note" by Vidal gave us a Lincoln "at heart . . . a fatalist, a materialist" who "knew when to wait; when to act." This is the Lincoln of Vidal's superb novel [*Lincoln*], celebrated by the author as the master politician who invented what is now in crisis, the American nation-state.

If I count accurately, this is Vidal's nineteenth novel and thirtieth book, and he is (or is going on) fifty-nine. I have read thirteen of the novels, and two books of essays, which may be enough to yield some reasonable estimate of at least the relative nature of his achievement, if only to see how his work might be placed, so far. Though Vidal has a substantial audience, which certainly will be augmented by *Lincoln,* he has had rather mixed esteem among the most serious readers whom I know. I myself found his fiction very readable but not greatly memorable until the appearance of his ninth novel, *Julian,* which seems to me still a beautifully persuasive historical tale, a poignant portrait of the Emperor Julian, known forever as the Apostate by the Christian tradition that he rejected and abandoned.

Of the earlier novels, I had read only the first, *Williwaw,* and the third, *The City and the Pillar,* both refreshing, but then I was disappointed by the book just before *Julian,* an ambitious yet sketchy work that courageously was entitled *Messiah.* What the far more powerful *Julian* showed, I thought, was that Vidal lacked invention, and so was most gifted at reimagining history. The political and historical *Washington, D.C.,* which followed *Julian,* seemed to confirm this intimation, since everything and everyone weakest in it was of Vidal's own creation. But I underestimated Vidal's own creation. But I underestimated Vidal badly. *Myra Breckinridge* followed, an apocalyptic farce that rivals Nathanael West's *A Cool Million* and Evelyn Waugh's *Scoop,* three outrageous travesties that will outlive many of the more celebrated visions of our century. After many readings, *Myra Breckinridge* continues to give wicked pleasure, and still seems to have fixed the limit beyond which the most advanced aesthetic neopornography ever can go.

Myra compelled a revisionary estimate of Vidal, who had powerfully demonstrated that superb invention was his strength, provided that the modes were farce and fantasy. The polemic of *Myra* remains the best embodiment of Vidal's most useful insistence as a moralist, which is that we ought to cease speaking of homosexuals and heterosexuals. There are only women and men, some of whom prefer their own sex, some the other, and some both. This is the burden of *Myra Breckinridge,* but a burden borne with lightness, wildness, abandon, joy, skill. It was a little difficult to see just how the author of *Julian* was one with the creator of *Myra,* but that increased a sense of expectation for what was to come.

I have never encountered a copy of *Two Sisters,* which followed *Myra,* but I have read the half-dozen intervening novels before *Lincoln,* with some appreciation and much puzzlement, until now. *Myron* and the recent *Duluth* seem to me failures in the exuberant mode of *Myra Breckinridge,* though I was stimulated by the references in *Duluth* to the egregious Thornton Bloom, author of *The Kabbalah.* The fictions of political history, *Burr* and *1876,* were far better, and indeed *Burr* stands with *Julian* and *Myra Breckinridge* as Vidal's truest contributions before *Lincoln.* But *Kalki* was another *Messiah,* contrived and perfunctory, in the religious mode that Vidal should perhaps handle only historically, while *Creation,* a civilized and learned narrative, showed that Vidal, even working historically, is simply not a philosophical novelist. *Creation,* unlike *Julian,* reduces to a series of essays, which are always provocative, but almost never very consequential. Vidal, reimagining our cultural origins, or rather our imaginations of those origins, is no Burckhardt and no Nietzsche, but then why should he be?

What he is, in *Lincoln,* is a masterly American historical novelist, now wholly matured, who has found his truest subject, which is our national political history during precisely those years when our political and military histories were as one, one thing and one thing only: the unwavering will of Abraham Lincoln to keep the states united. Vidal's

imagination of American politics, then and now, is so powerful as to compel awe. Lincoln is to our national political mythology what Whitman is to our literary mythology: the figure that Emerson prophesied as the Central Man. No biographer has been able to give us a complete and convincing account of the evasive and enigmatic Whitman. No biographer, and until now no novelist, has had the precision of imagination to show us a plausible and human Lincoln, of us and yet beyond us. Vidal, with this book, does just that, and more: he gives us the tragedy of American political history, with its most authentic tragic hero at the center, which is to say, at our center.

Lincoln: A Novel begins in the early, frozen morning of February 23, 1861, as Lincoln, flanked by the detective Pinkerton and by his presidential bodyguard, Lamon, slips into Washington so as to avoid being murdered before his inauguration. A minority president, elected with less than 40 percent of the total vote, he confronts a crisis that no predecessor, and no American head of state since, could even envision. Though his election committed him only to barring the extension of slavery to the new states, and though he was a moderate Republican and not an Abolitionist, Lincoln was violently feared by most of the South. Vidal's opening irony, never stated but effectively implied, is that the South beheld the true Lincoln long before Lincoln's own cabinet had begun to regard the will and power of the political genius who so evasively manipulated them. Vidal's Lincoln is the most ambitious of all American presidents. The South feared an American Cromwell, and in Vidal's vision the South actually helped produce an American Bismarck.

But there is no Southern perspective in Vidal's novel, nor should there be. Lincoln, the first Westerner to be elected president since Andrew Jackson, is presented as the heir of Jackson and Polk, a believer in the strong executive tradition and a respecter of neither the states, nor the Congress, nor the courts, nor the parties, nor even the Constitution itself. This Lincoln, rather enigmatically, is transcendental and idealist only in the mode of the later Emerson, author of the grim essay "Power" in his superb *The Conduct of Life.* "Power" works by the dialectic of Emerson's Lear-like revision of Coleridge's compensatory imagination. Coleridge thought (or hoped) that experiential loss could be transformed into imaginative gain. Emerson rephrased this formula as "Nothing is got for nothing," which seems the secret motto of Vidal's Lincoln, who follows another great essay, "Fate," in *The Conduct of Life,* by worshiping, not Jehovah nor Jesus, but only what Emerson called the Beautiful Necessity, the American tragedy of the struggle between freedom and fate, in which the heroic agonist secretly loves neither freedom nor fate, but only power. Vidal's strong Lincoln, triumphant at last over both the South and his own cabinet and party, is such an agonist, a dialectician of power, and finally a kind of self-willed Orphic sacrifice who, in the closing words of Vidal's book, "had willed his own murder as a form of atonement for the great and terrible thing that he had done by giving so bloody and absolute a rebirth to his nation."

It is Vidal's skill as a narrator, and his art as a reimaginer of historical personages, that makes plausible this curiously nihilistic rebirth. The book's narrative principle is a highly traditional one: deferred revelation, enacted throughout by Lincoln's brilliant alternation of an endless, almost passive waiting with sudden, overwhelming acts of decision. What is perpetually deferred is a full awareness of Lincoln's preternatural ability to prophesy the moves of every other politician, as well as his uncanny sense of his own greatness, his own central place in national and world history. That this savage greatness paradoxically has been revised by American mythology into Whitman's "sweetest, wisest soul" and later debased into Carl Sandburg's homespun sentimentalist may be the provocation for Vidal's novel, yet one senses that Vidal's motives are more immediate. With the likely, impending reelection of Reagan, the nation confronts what might become the final crisis of Lincoln's presidential creation. If our system is, as Vidal contends, Lincoln's invention, then the American age of Lincoln finally approaches its apocalypse. Should Vidal prove correct, his tragic vision of Lincoln as Orphic dictator may serve also as an elegy for the one hundred and twenty years of Lincoln's invented America.

On its surface, Vidal's novel is a grand entertainment, maintaining a tonal intensity that might be called humorously somber. Lincoln himself is presented as the master of evasions, strongest when he strives to appear weakest, and a purposive self-mythologizer. Vidal cunningly contributes to the mythologizing by adding "the Tycoon" and "the Ancient" to "Old Abe" and "Father Abraham" as presidential nicknames. The crucial name probably is "the Ancient," who indeed is what Emerson called "Spontaneity or Instinct" in the crucial essay, "Self-Reliance." Lincoln falls back continually upon what is best and oldest in his own self, an ancient spark that seems to have originated not only before the creation of the Union, but before the Creation itself. More than Whitman, this Lincoln is Emerson's American Adam, post-Christian and self-begotten, who knows no time when he was not as now. If this is Vidal's ontological Lincoln, the empirical Lincoln, archetypal politician yet tragic sufferer, nevertheless more winningly dominates the novel.

Vidal demystifies Lincoln to the rather frightening degree of suggesting that he had transferred unknowingly a venereal infection, contracted in youth and supposedly cured, to his wife, Mary Todd, and through her to his sons. The gradually developing madness of Mrs. Lincoln, and the related early deaths of two of the boys, form one of the dark undersongs of this novel, plausibly suggesting a more than temperamental basis for Lincoln's profound melancholia. Counterpointed against this sadness is Lincoln's celebrated humor, conveyed by Vidal with authentic verve, but always with a Freudian sense of wit, in which the laughter carries the burden of double or antithetical meanings:

> "Sometimes I say those things and don't even know I've said them. When there is so much you *cannot* say, it's always a good idea to have a story ready. I do it now from habit." Lincoln sighed. "In my predicament, it is a good thing to know all sorts of stories because the truth of the whole matter is now almost unsayable; and so cruel."

The "predicament" here overtly refers to the Southern Rebellion and the "truth of the whole matter" perhaps to the endless catastrophe of the sequence of incompetent Northern generals, but the underlying references are to Lincoln's inner despairs. Vidal seems to be suggesting, quite subtly, throughout the novel, that Lincoln's obsessive drive to preserve and restore the Union of the states was a grand restitution or compensation for what never could be healed in his own personal and familial life. Combined with a metaphysical will to power, this results in the gradual emergence of Lincoln as the first and most forceful dictator-president, forerunner of the Roosevelts and of Lyndon Johnson.

It seems to me an astonishing achievement that Vidal makes us love his Lincoln, "cold and deliberate, reflective and brilliant," qualities that do not often engender affection whether in fact or fiction—particularly because we have to struggle also against our mystified sense of the Sandburgian or Hollywood saintly Lincoln. I suspect that Vidal succeeds because his Lincoln is an authentic image of authority. Freud taught us that love reduces to love of authority, love of the father image that seems not to love us in return. Vidal's Lincoln is Shakespearean, not just in his recurrent quotations from the plays, but in his lonely and heroic fatalism. He inspires love partly because he seems to be beyond needing it.

Surrounding Vidal's Lincoln swarms an almost Dickensian roster of fabulistic caricatures: politicians, generals, White House aides, Washington ladies, newspapermen, Northern and Southern conspirators, and amiably evil bankers, including Jay Cooke himself. These are Vidal's America, then and now, and they are rendered with an almost invariable and unfailing gusto. The most memorable and entertaining is the sanctimonious Salmon P. Chase: archetypal Republican, pious Abolitionist, hero of bankers, endless plotter to seize power from Lincoln, and forever ungrateful to the president for his appointments as secretary of the treasury and chief justice. Vidal's Chase is the comic foil to Vidal's tragic Lincoln, for Chase has every quality except aesthetic dignity. Inwardly humble, but in the Dickensian mode, Chase pursues greatness, to the parodistic extent of obsessively yielding to a ruling passion for collecting the autographs of famous writers.

In a finely rendered scene of comic pathos, Chase confronts the job-seeking and highly disreputable Walt Whitman, who is devoting himself to the care of sick and wounded soldiers. Since Whitman bears with him a letter of recommendation from Emerson, Chase's sole concern is to extract the desired letter while rejecting the obscene bard. Whitman splendidly starts off wrong by comparing the inside of the Capital to "the interiors of Taylor's saloon in the Broadway, which you doubtless know." Chase shudders at thus encountering a populist beast, and proceeds to his triumph:

> "In Mr. Emerson's letter, does he mention *what* you might do in the government's service?" Chase thought this approach subtle in the extreme.
>
> "Well, here it is," said Whitman. He gave Chase the letter. On the envelope was written "The

Honorable S. P. Chase." Inside was a letter dated January 10, endorsing Walt Whitman highly for any sort of government post; and signed, Chase excitedly saw, with the longed-for-but-never-owned autograph "R. W. Emerson."

"I shall give Mr. Emerson, and yourself, sir, every sort of consideration," said Chase, putting the letter in his pocket where it seemed to him to irradiate his whole being as if it were some holy relic.

"I shall be truly grateful. As will Mr. Emerson, of course." Chase shook Whitman's hand at the door and let him out. Then Chase placed the letter square in the middle of his desk, and pondered what sort of frame would set it off best.

As the novel progresses, Vidal's exuberance in depicting Chase increases, and the reader begins to share the author's dialectical sympathy for this comic monster who nevertheless is the clear ancestor of all sanctimonious Republicans since, down to the menagerie currently staffing the White House. Though a paragon of selfishness, Chase nevertheless is sincere in behalf of the slaves, while Lincoln frees them only reluctantly, and then idly dreams of shipping them off to the West Indies or back to Africa. Chase seeks power, but for presumably idealistic purposes; Lincoln, with the single purpose of keeping his nation unified, stalks power with no concern whatsoever for human rights.

Vidal does not celebrate Lincoln's destruction of civil liberties, but shows a certain admiration for the skill with which the President subverts the constitution he is sworn to defend. There is a split in Vidal between the man of letters who has a friendly contempt for politicians and the born political man who would make a remarkable senator, if only even California was quite ready for him. The audacity that distinguishes Vidal as visionary politician, amiably and sensibly urging us to withdraw tax-exempt status from churches, synagogues, foundations, and universities, is matched by his audacity as political novelist, urging us to see Lincoln plain while giving us a Lincoln that our mythological needs cannot quite accept.

I return to the still ambiguous question of Vidal's strength or perhaps competing strengths as a novelist. *Lincoln,* together with the curiously assorted trio of *Julian, Myra Breckinridge,* and *Burr,* demonstrates that his narrative achievement is vastly underestimated by American academic criticism, an injustice he has repaid amply in his essayistic attacks upon the academy, and in the sordid intensities of *Duluth.* But even *Lincoln* (unlike the slighter but flawless *Myra Breckinridge*) has its disappointments. Booth's conspiracy against Lincoln's life was melodramatic enough in mere actuality, but that does not justify Vidal's rendering of it as a quite perfunctory melodrama. The difficulty appears again to be Vidal's relative weakness, except in farce, for inventing characters, as opposed to his immense gifts for revisualizing historical personae. David Herold, upon whom the Booth conspiracy is made to center, remains a name upon these pages; he simply does not stimulate Vidal's imagination, unlike Lincoln, Chase, and other personages of our common past. Lin-

coln's striking Epicurean fatalism is asserted rather than dramatized; the ideological and religious vigor that portrayed Julian the Apostate so memorably is simply absent here. And though Vidal's humor is a pleasure throughout, he restrains himself too strictly from relying upon his genius for farce. This may be just as well, since the author of *Myra Breckinridge* is also the author of *Duluth.* But it does prompt the critical question: will it ever be possible for Vidal to reconcile all of his talents within the dimensions of a single novel?

The question would be unjust or misleading if *Lincoln* did not testify so persuasively that Vidal, in his late fifties, remains a developing rather than an unfolding novelist, to borrow a useful distinction from Northrop Frye. There are several extant American novelists, more highly regarded by critics than Vidal, who nevertheless will never surprise us. Vidal, like the very different Norman Mailer, has the capacity to confound our expectations. Such a capacity, in so bad a time for the republic, both of letters and of politics, scarcely can be overpraised. (pp. 5-6, 8)

> *Harold Bloom, "The Central Man," in* The New York Review of Books, *Vol. XXXI, No. 12, July 19, 1984, pp. 5-6, 8.*

Bruce Allen

When Gore Vidal appears on a television talk show, he's so imperturbably urbane and witty, and shows such commanding intelligence, that I almost always pick up one of his books and start skimming, hoping to retain the company of that elegant, entertaining voice a little longer.

Throughout his career Vidal has been, oddly, hampered by that general impression of his powers—as a high-class entertainer, an intellectual stage performer. His many novels, plays, and essays on a dazzling variety of subjects are too often regarded as the products of an accomplished but superficial virtuosity—polished glitter lacking genuine substance. Only in his political novels—*Washington, D.C.* (1967). *Burr* (1973), and *1876* (1976)—have Vidal's great gifts for organizing unruly material and devising memorable epigrammatic statements been focused on what his critics have deemed truly worthy subjects. And it's really only since *Burr*—that supremely ironic revisionist viewing of the American Revolution and the early republic—that Vidal has been taken in any sense seriously as a novelist.

Well, now we have his *Lincoln,* a sober and surely authoritative portrayal of America's 16th President during the years 1861-65, from the beginning of his first term to his assassination by John Wilkes Booth. It is a book packed with historical information transposed into drama and dialogue: Readers can justifiably feel they're improving themselves while they are engrossed in this suavely managed story—which, brilliant as it often is, doesn't quite satisfy the expectations it raises.

The story begins with the newly elected President's arrival in Washington, incognito and under guard, after one of the many threats on his life. "I will never live this down," Lincoln observes to a colleague, "sneaking like a thief into the capital." Indeed he's a more than controversial figure, a compromise candidate and winner, hated and feared by secessionist forces who believe he'll free the slaves, perhaps even give them the vote.

Washington is in turmoil: States are seceding and joining the Confederacy, and rumors of Civil War are increasing daily. (Vidal deftly sketches in an amusing parallel situation: The White House is run down and dirty, bereft of efficient plumbing, and downwind of a sewage canal.) Things are rapidly worsening. Lincoln's announcement that he has been elected "to prevent the extension of slavery to the new territories of the Union" confirms the deepest suspicions of the Southern and Border States. His Inaugural Address is, however, too conciliatory toward the "rebels" for Northern politicians who argue that "the South must be destroyed." The new President appears to be trying, unsuccessfully, to please every element of the population, and there's a consensus among his fellow politicians "that Mr. Lincoln is a well-meaning but inadequate man."

Then the contention blossoms into outright war, and we observe—through others' observations of him—Lincoln in control. He puts the broadest possible interpretation on the doctrine of the presidency's "inherent powers" and gives his Treasury secretary unprecedented latitude in finding ways to finance military necessities. He discourages the pivotal state of Maryland from secession by suspending the rights of assembly and *habeas corpus* and other traditional liberties. He resists pressures to evacuate Washington when Confederate troops approach the city. Throughout the long ordeal of the war, Lincoln's determination to preserve the Union whatever the cost is seen against his expressed horror at realizing how great that cost will be. The story's conclusion, in the elaborate preparation to kill the President, then in the mysterious suddenness of the act itself, has a persuasive dignity and grandeur that are only too appropriate to the subject.

The most interesting thing about **Lincoln** is the manner in which Vidal tells the story. We see Lincoln as he is seen and judged by several of those most fascinated and obsessed by him. Mary Todd Lincoln's worshipful closeness to her husband cannot keep her from slipping into eccentricity, then insanity. Salmon P. Chase, secretary of the Treasury and later chief justice, knows that his suspicious uncertainty about Lincoln is rooted in his own strong presidential ambitions. David Herold, drugstore clerk and Confederate spy, dreams day and night of ridding the country of "the Tyrant." William H. Seward, Lincoln's clever secretary of state, begins by distrusting his superior's slow competence and ends up as his greatest admirer. And John Hay, Lincoln's young secretary (and later his biographer)—a charmingly created character—is the primary narrator to whom the most incisive opinions of Lincoln are given, such as this climactic assessment: "So he not only put the Union back together again, but he made an entirely new country, and all of it in his own image."

The technique produces several striking characterizations. Besides those names, there are William Sprague, the "boy governor" of Rhode Island, who marries Chase's splendid daughter Kate and tarnishes that proud family with his illegal commercial double-dealings; George McClellan, the

fiery Union general who becomes Lincoln's chief impediment to reelection; Walt Whitman, who appears in a brief scene applying for a government clerkship; and two or three dozen other vividly created, individually distinct, and articulate people.

There are many strongly lit and convincingly detailed scenes, many of them policy-making meetings at which Lincoln's political astuteness and personal strength are sharply conveyed. These include a dramatic presidential meeting with Negro leaders; a marvelous strategic conversation between Lincoln and his old rival, Stephen Douglas; and a tense scene in which Mary Lincoln's brother-in-law refuses the President's appeal for support, announcing that he'll accept a commission in the Confederate Army. The quiet, unpolitical moments are no less dramatic, and allow us to perceive people nominally "in power" who are inhibited and appalled by the burden they've shouldered.

But Vidal pays a comparatively heavy price for this novel's impression of fullness and authenticity. The exposition is handled quite clumsily: The characters' backgrounds and histories are poured into their reported thoughts about one another. The first 150 pages or so are thus overburdened with retrospective detail, and the story is permitted to develop much too slowly. In fact, this sluggish pace is so firmly established that even the account of the last days of Lincoln's life never quite manages to take on the momentum we expect.

The decision to show Lincoln from outside proves even more troubling. Vidal's mosaic technique produces refreshing emphases: We understand that this President was not at first a committed abolitionist (unlike, for example, his wife) and that his sympathy for the Negro population grew while he held office and only gradually altered his intentions. We come to appreciate his self-possession and his quiet wit, and we become occasionally bored, as do his hearers, by the folk wisdom he can't stop spouting. We may even concur with the extraordinary concluding statement of young John Hay, who came to believe "that Lincoln, in some mysterious fashion, had willed his own murder as a form of atonement for the great and terrible thing that he had done by giving so bloody and absolute a rebirth to his nation."

There's the clue, I think, to what is missing from this otherwise intelligent and satisfying novel. Vidal's Abraham Lincoln is, essentially, the stone figure seated within that celebrated memorial. For once, this daring writer's nerve seems to have failed him. He declined to think his way inside Lincoln's head and heart. Had he done so, this book might have been something magnificent and original; as it is, brilliant as it is, I'm afraid **Lincoln** is really only another act of acclamation, a respectful and conventional tribute. (pp. 19-20)

Bruce Allen, "'Lincoln' Awash with Detail, Lacking in Depth," in The Christian Science Monitor, *July 25, 1984, pp. 19-20.*

Richard Eder

Gore Vidal and History are on breezy first-name terms,

but there is a trickle of irritation underneath. As mentor, Vidal has reservations about his protege.

In his fictional re-creations of our nation'a political life—*Burr, Lincoln, 1876, Washington, D.C.*—Vidal first-named his way from the Revolution and the Jackson era, to the Civil War, to the robber-baron Gilded Age, to a stretch running from the later New Deal into the McCarthy days. In *Empire,* just published, he goes back for a missing chunk: the expansionist years of the Spanish American War and Manifest Destiny.

We had met Washington, Jefferson, Benedict Arnold, Col. Blennerhasset—footnotes as well as Big Feet—Lincoln, Seward, Stanton, John Hay, William Cullen Bryant in their historical pajamas. Now we are treated to the table talk and table manners of Teddy Roosevelt, William McKinley, William Randolph Hearst and the two Henrys: Adams and James; along with Vidal's Alexandrian notions of what they all represented. Alexandria as the infinitely disenchanted capital of Old Egypt, that is; not Washington's bedroom suburb.

Vidal's Washington novels began as scribbling. *Washington, D.C.*—the first to be written, though the most recent in its setting—is sprawling and slack; it makes Alan Drury look elegant. Its major characters include an old senator who is both corrupt and idealistic, a cynical newspaper publisher and an ambitious young politician. Even naming them this way is a camp cliche, like Roy Lichtenstein painting comics. They are made up, and making up characters is not Vidal's strength.

Perhaps writing a truly awful book can be useful in clearing the mind. It was about 10 years before Vidal returned to an American political novel; and this time, he was doing something different and more interesting. He was dramatizing—even more than fictionalizing—his acid notions about the meaning of our history and national character, and using real personages to do it.

Using, appropriating, and sometimes even impersonating. Aaron Burr in the second novel, and one of the best, is thoroughly evoked in the historical detail of his scattered life. Also, clearly enough, he is Vidal. The voice of the failed adventurer, debunking the vain and pompous Washington, the piously devious Jefferson, the self-protective John Marshall and the whole uplift of our constitutional tradition—the Founding Fathers come out as so many progeny-gobbling Saturns—is the writer's.

In *Lincoln,* Vidal's voice is the angled sophistication of Seward, who considered his President a bumpkin until he came to revere him as a great man. In his new book, the author uses the crabby, gloomy Henry Adams.

All three of these alter egos were much wiser than their times. Unfortunately, Vidal is wiser than his books. This allows them to be clever and entertaining at their best; but it also makes them, by and large, not very good novels.

Only in *Lincoln* does the author, occasionally, go in past his depth. Struggling with what carries him away—Lincoln and the movingly complex Mary Todd Lincoln—he can carry the reader away as well. The power of a novel has less to do with wading in than with swimming ashore.

In *Burr,* the protagonist's memoirs are fascinating, at least when they cover the early parts of his life. Eventually, the glittery discourse becomes excessively discursive, but it has told us some provocative things. What works far less well is Vidal's attempt to break it up with a series of fictional scenes involving the compiler of the memoirs, and his life as a would-be New York journalist in the 1830s.

That *Empire,* though witty and absorbing in parts, is weaker than its predecessors, although decidedly better than *Washington, D.C.* is, I think, for two reasons.

The first is that Vidal introduces two entirely fictional characters among his historical re-creations; and they occupy a disproportionate amount of strenuously dead space. They are Caroline and Blaise Sanford, half-siblings and perpetual rivals.

Their rivalry is set off by a quarrel over their considerable inheritance. Blaise, who goes to work for William Randolph Hearst, hopes to use the money to set up his own press empire. Caroline out-maneuvers him by buying up a small Washington newspaper and turning it into a lively scandal-sheet and eventually into a lively political voice.

Vidal works hard to endow Caroline with spirit, imagination and energy. Her devices for upgrading a stodgy and failing paper by downgrading it and later providing depth as well as bite, are interesting and evocative. But she is all spunk and no character. Vidal's efforts to give her life by means of a flaming love affair with a politician simply do not work. Their passion is all bedclothes and no bed.

Blaise is less a character than assorted ill-fitting character fragments. He is ruthless and ineffective; his rivalry with Caroline comes to very little, and he ends up by serving mainly as a foil for Hearst. At one point, for no apparent reason, Vidal has him sleep with Caroline's lover.

The historical figures, some of them at least, are much livelier. There is a provocative portrait of McKinley; bland, sleepy and immensely fond of eating. Vidal needs a touch of the physically grotesque to get really going on a character—he harped on Washington's outsize posterior—and here he uses Mrs. McKinley's epileptic seizures. McKinley calmly throws a napkin over her head when these occur, and goes on with the conversation as if nothing were amiss.

Beyond the detail, though, there is a subtle and convincing picture of the man who was taken for granted as a tool of the political boss, Mark Hanna, and who grows with the presidency. The McKinley-Hanna roles are reversed; the President becomes the power behind the power behind the throne, as well as the throne itself.

Roosevelt is more of a caricature, but an amusing one. Vidal takes his physical and moral bounciness and makes it as much infected as infectious. The flashing eyeglasses and ferocious smiles simply repeat the caricatures of the time, but there is something extra in Vidal's description of Roosevelt marching pointlessly around a room while talking "like a toy soldier that someone had wound up but forgot to point in any particular direction."

Henry James appears briefly as a conversational pastiche

of his own convoluted prose. Adams comes across with wry authenticity. John Hay, McKinley's and then Roosevelt's secretary of state, is both a skeptical observer of the policy of expansion—Cuba, the Philippines, the Panama Canal, a bigger Navy—and its diligent architect.

Hay is Vidal's humane, civilized and ultimately futile public man. Hay contrasts the largeness of Lincoln, to whom he was secretary, with the voracious purposes of the new breed of political men. But he can think of nothing else but to agree with them and serve them.

With *Empire,* Vidal makes his point that the spirit of American expansion was in conflict with the authentic qualities of the American character, and has tended to extinguish them. The fact that his books on earlier portions of our history found precious few such qualities rather weakens the point.

What weakens *Empire* most, though, is that Vidal's talents need large figures and dramatic events to work properly. American history between 1890 and 1910 lacked the grandeur and moral excitement of the Civil War and of our Revolution and constitutional beginnings.

Vidal is a skillful commentator on public character and characters. He can give an eccentric spin to our notions of the figures in our history, and put their energy to new uses. He needs their energy, though; he himself does not produce very much.

> *Richard Eder, in a review of "Empire," in* Los Angeles Times Book Review, *May 24, 1987, p. 1.*

Christopher Lehmann-Haupt

Empire would seem to be the most amorphous of the novels in Gore Vidal's fictional chronicle of American history, which, along with the present volume, now includes *Washington, D.C.* (1967), *Burr* (1973), *1876* (1976) and *Lincoln* (1984) (though according to the periods they cover, their order should be *Burr, Lincoln, 1876, Empire* and *Washington, D.C.*

Chronologically, *Empire* takes the United States from August 1898, or halfway into the first term of President William McKinley, to the autumn of 1906, halfway into the first elected term of President Theodore Roosevelt. Its theme is America's decision to become a world power, and to establish its presence more forcefully in the Caribbean, Latin America and the Eastern Pacific. Its major historical characters include everyone from Secretary of State John Hay to the newspaper publisher William Randolph Hearst to the novelist and historian Henry Adams to such leaders of society as the Astors, the Vanderbilts and the Whitneys.

Yet despite the size of his canvas, Mr. Vidal has surpassed himself in *Empire* and written what now stands as the best in the series. The key to its success is the intricate yet balanced relationship between its foreground, middleground and background, which permits the author to tell a dramatically compelling story without sacrificing either his complex view of American history of his unusual ability to caricature its major players.

In the foreground we meet Caroline Sanford, a 20-year-old heiress raised in France but descended illegitimately from Aaron Burr and endowed with his brains and audacity (at least, those he possessed in Mr. Vidal's version of him). Because of an ambiguity in her father's will that has temporarily allowed her half-brother, Blaise, the freedom to control her inheritance and invest it in Hearst's budding newspaper empire, Caroline is provoked to buy *The Washington Journal* and compete with Blaise and Hearst.

This she succeeds in doing so emphatically that she projects herself into the novel's middleground, which is occupied principally by her uncle, Henry Adams, and his close friend, John Hay, who spend much of their time in their "double house" in Lafayette Square, opposite the White House, talking of old times and ideas, debating the course of the American empire as it takes its way in all directions, and entertaining such personages as Henry James, the novelist, Alice Roosevelt, the "princess" of Washington, and Clarence King, the mineralogist and founder of the United States Geological Survey.

John Hay, in turn, as secretary to Lincoln and Secretary of State under both McKinley and Roosevelt, provides a natural bridge to the novel's background, where the major figures—McKinley, Roosevelt, Hearst, Elihu Root, who later becomes Secretary of State, Senator Henry Cabot Lodge and "the Great Commoner," William Jennings Bryan—play out their parts. Here Teddy Roosevelt snaps his "tombstone teeth" and shrieks "bully" and "dee-lighted."

"In March, 1897," Mr. Vidal writes, "the 38-year-old Roosevelt met, as it were, his luck. The new President, McKinley, appointed him Assistant Secretary of the Navy, ordinarily a humble post, but with a weak and amiable secretary, Roosevelt, in thrall to the imperial visions of Captain Mahan and Brooks Adams, was now in a position to build up the fleet without which there could be no future wars, no glory, no empire. The next four years were to wreathe with laurel the stout little man who now stood, if not like a colossus athwart the world, like some tightly wound-up child's toy, dominating all the other toys in power's playroom, shrill voice constantly raised."

Here in the background Hearst connives to invent the news, and to crown his work by inventing himself as Napoleon of the United States.

> Blaise realized that, in some curious way, Hearst lived in a kind of dream where real people were turned, by his yellow art, into fictional characters that he could manipulate as he pleased. On those rare occasions when his fictions and the real world coincided, he was genuinely shocked. It was all very well for him to report that one Jack had taken a ride into Heaven aboard a bean stalk and quite another thing for an actual bean stalk to lift *him* up above the world.

Obviously, the narrator, Mr. Vidal's persona, takes a dim view of Hearst and Roosevelt. In the novel's final, cleverly imagined, scene, these two nearly scuffle for the right to sit in "the chair of state" in the White House's Cabinet room. Hearst takes credit for inventing Roosevelt. "Mr. Hearst," Roosevelt retorts, "history invented me, not you." "Well," answers Hearst, "if you really want to be highfalutin, then at this time and in this place, I am history—or at least the creator of record."

Yet for all that Mr. Vidal makes us hold in contempt these caricatures, we can't exactly wash our hands of them. After all, we've just finished rooting for and applauding the success of Caroline Sanford, who is really not much more than a sympathetic embodiment of Hearst and Roosevelt, as well as Mr. Vidal's version of America—ambitious, cynical, manipulative, self-created and, in her way, imperial. But aside from being the author's best invention since Myra Breckinridge (though far more conventionally appealing), she serves as the glue that holds together this work that is by turns caustic, witty and outrageous fun. And for this, as well as a number of other things she does in the novel, one has to love her.

> *Christopher Lehmann-Haupt, in a review of "Empire," in* The New York Times, *June 11, 1987, p. C24.*

Vidal on his intent in writing *Burr*:

[Lasky]: What were you trying to get across in **Burr**? *That is, what would you like the reader to come away with after reading it?*

[Vidal]: A sense of what the world of power is like, the psychology of men who aim to be the first in the State—what these people are like. It's not often done by American writers. I don't believe in all this relevancy business; history is interesting for its own sake. This thing that the historical novel is worthwhile only to the extent that it has relevancy for us today—well, Burger that. Today is neither more or less interesting than yesterday. A book is as interesting as the book is. If people want to sit there and figure out "is this really Richard Nixon"—well, they are wasting their time.

> *Michael S. Lasky in an interview with Gore Vidal,* Writer's Digest, *March, 1975.*

Justin Kaplan

"It has been a splendid little war," wrote John Hay, a central historical figure in Gore Vidal's [*Empire*], during the summer of 1898, a war "begun with the highest motives, carried on with magnificent intelligence and spirit, favored by that fortune which loves the brave." As reward for 10 weeks of intermittent land and sea combat with Spain, the United States acquired Puerto Rico and added Guam and the Philippines to a Pacific empire that already included the Hawaiian Islands. By 1905 we had also established proprietary protectorates over Panama and the Dominican Republic as well as Cuba. Continued by his successor, Theodore Roosevelt, President William McKinley's policy of dilation and incorporation answered strategic and ideological imperatives of the day, the old cry of Manifest Destiny, and the old itch, in eruption earlier during General Grant's occupation of the White House, to achieve a commanding American presence in the Caribbean and Central America, Nicaragua in particular.

Commenting on the extermination of more than 100,000 Filipino insurgents who, starting in 1899, rejected the colonizing bear hug of their North American brothers, Mark Twain welcomed the United States to pre-eminence in the "Blessings-of-Civilization Trust." He wanted the white stripes of the national banner painted black "and the stars replaced by the skull and crossbones."

"The will to grow," wrote Henry James, returning to his native country after an absence of 21 years, "was everywhere written large, and to grow at no matter what or whose expense." This is the grand theme of Gore Vidal's *Empire,* the fifth in his continuing cycle of novels about American history, politics and high society from Jefferson's time to Truman's. (The others, starting with *Burr,* published in 1973, are *Lincoln, 1876* and *Washington, D.C.*) Architects of the imperial nation, McKinley—suave, imperturbable, canny—and his successor, the hypomanic Roosevelt—hero of the Cuban campaign, an accidental President who, after being elected in his own right, took on some of the airs of a Theodore Rex—are seen here largely through the eyes of their Secretary of State, John Hay.

An overrated, overapplauded writer and statesman who as a young man had been assistant private secretary to Abraham Lincoln, Hay was blessed with luck, connections, a rich wife, "perfect pitch" and charm: "Those whom the gods wish to disappoint they first make charming," Mr. Vidal says. He gives us vivid glimpses of Hay's friend Henry Adams, "America's great historian, wit, dispenser of gloom." Along with Henry James, who makes several appearances in this decidedly un-Jamesian novel, Adams is among the few exemplary figures in a crowd of scamps and opportunists (by Mr. Vidal's account there is little ethical difference between Theodore Roosevelt and William Randolph Hearst in their bids for political office). Great-grandson of one President and grandson of another, Adams views the White House from his mansion on the other side of Lafayette Square as a family property usurped by frauds and evolutionary throwbacks. In self-regard and social exclusiveness the members of Adams's innermost circle have more than made up for what they lacked in charity and receptiveness to inevitable change. Roosevelt dismissed them as snobs and cynics "wholly lacking in robustness of fiber." Mr. Vidal, or at least his invented heroine, Caroline Sanford, suggests, however, that Adams and his intimates may have been "the Gods of Olympus in disguise." This recurrent theme is one of *Empire*'s few descents into sentimentality.

Like her scheming half-brother Blaise, Caroline is a retrofit from Mr. Vidal's *Washington, D.C.* Rich, highborn, beautiful, manipulative and ruthless, a marital horse trader and indifferent mother, in a world dominated by powerful men Caroline escapes the restrictions of gender by achieving power as a newspaper publisher on the model of Hearst. Three-quarters of the way through *Empire,* after a passionless engagement to one man, Caroline tenders her virginity to another in a characteristically brisk, businesslike encounter. Having at last consummated "the famous act" she takes appropriate (although unavailing) measures, as Mr. Vidal writes in a sugary passage, "to discourage any little stranger from assembling itself in her no longer virginal loins." Caroline advances her fortunes by arranging for her lover to seduce Blaise, who had already "wondered, perversely, what it would be like to switch roles with her." Unyielding in policy and action, which in the framework of *Empire* means becoming a man, a publisher and "a natural general," Caroline appears to be a psychosexual cousin to Mr. Vidal's Myra Breckinridge.

One problem in the sort of fiction represented by *Empire* is that of keeping invented characters from bumping into the scenery and into others who, unlike them, come equipped with a documented historical existence and a necessary path of action to follow. For the most part Mr. Vidal handles this stage traffic quite well. The separate and joint careers of Caroline and her half-brother mediate among the rarefied society of Washington, New York and Newport; Hearst's yellow journalism domain; and the political world of power deals, wheeling, wheedling and maneuver. In this last area, especially when he gives McKinley, Roosevelt and Hearst their heads, Mr. Vidal demonstrates a political imagination and insider's sagacity equaled by no other practicing fiction writer I can think of. And like the earlier novels in his historical cycle, *Empire* is a wonderfully vivid documentary drama set in the White House, Peacock Alley in the original Waldorf-Astoria, Mrs. Astor's ballroom, great houses along Newport's Bellevue Avenue, and similar locales rich in production values. The appropriate background music for Mr. Vidal's print spectacular should be a medley of John Philip Sousa's "Stars and Stripes Forever," "Meet Me in St. Louis, Louis," Ethelbert Nevin's religio-romantic "Rosary" and "There'll Be a Hot Time in the Old Town Tonight," unofficial anthem of the Spanish-American War and later Theodore Roosevelt's campaign song.

Mr. Vidal is not so successful, however, in dealing with another problem built into historical fiction, that of how to identify "real" characters without having their well-tailored progress through the narrative impeded by flapping shirttails of exposition, and not notably clear or graceful exposition at that. Roosevelt's political career, Mr. Vidal tells us in one of his asides, "had been interrupted not only by personal tragedies but by a mistrust of the Republican Party's leader James G. Blaine; fortunately, this dislike had not led to apostasy of the sort that had caused the truly virtuous to bolt the party and raise high the banner of Independence and Mugwumpery. Roosevelt and [Henry Cabot] Lodge were too practical for this sort of idealistic gesture. They stayed with Blaine, who lost to Cleveland in 1884."

In other respects, too, *Empire* betrays a laxity of vigilance, a decline from the standards Mr. Vidal has set in *Burr*, for example, and in his brilliant nonfiction writing. Although flat-footed, a phrase such as "Lehr greeted the amused Blaise with coquettish charm" is at least less grotesque than "Mrs. Fish's not unpiscine face was now costive with attention." Struggling under this sort of dead-weight

prose, Mr. Vidal's otherwise not unengaging and not uninstructive tale of empire building tends to decline into a carnival attraction consisting of public people doing stereotypical things: moved by hidden gears and levers, but with a certain grinding and squeaking nonetheless audible, prelatic McKinley beams down the ample slopes of his piqué waistcoat, his wife goes rigid in an attack of petit mal, John Hay grimaces with pain, Clara Hay lowers her bulk into a chair too small for her, T. R. clicks his famous teeth, flashes his eyeglasses, and exclaims "Dee-lighted!" It's movement perhaps, but not exactly life.

Mr. Vidal has put himself forward on several occasions as our nation's biographer and history preceptor. It seems fair, even obligatory, to comment on *Empire* in its capacity as history lesson as well as historical fiction. Written in a traditional mode, although the limitations and distortions of this mode are all too familiar, *Empire* is history told strictly from the top, a chronicle of the doings of the rich, powerful and famous who, if they and Mr. Vidal are to be believed, settle the fate of nations between dinner courses. *Empire* largely ignores the existence of the labor movement, urbanization, muckraking, immigration. As to the last: the events recounted in *Empire* take place at a time when a nation of 76 million people (in 1900) absorbed more than 13 million foreigners (by 1914). The "drama" of immigration, as Henry James described it, went on "without a pause, day by day and year by year." A "visible act of ingurgitation on the part of our body politic and social," he said, it constituted "an appeal to amazement beyond that of any sword-swallowing or fire-swallowing of the circus." Internal empire building was at least as eventful, if not as amenable to fictionalizing, as America's territorial ingurgitations. (pp. 1, 42)

Justin Kaplan, "A Fat and Hungry Nation," in The New York Times Book Review, *June 14, 1987, p. 1, 42.*

Carol des Lauriers Cieri

Never mind that Henry James makes a number of appearances in [*Empire*]. Never mind that heroine Caroline Sanford's rise in publishing has the making of a television miniseries. This is a book with a thesis: that newspapers invent politics.

Empire begins in the summer of 1896 and takes the reader through some 20 years of American history. It is one of those perplexing beasts, the historical novel, and one of a series by Gore Vidal. In it, Vidal focuses on the rise of newspapers and their effect on politics.

A key exchange comes midway through the book. "We create news . . . ," says a newspaperman. "Empires, too?" asks an ambassador. "One follows on the other if the timing's right," comes the reply.

Empire fleshes out Vidal's proposition that the king of yellow journalism, William Randolph Hearst, had impeccable timing. And an unbeatable formula. Hearst newspapers offered "not news but entertainment for the masses." He offered murder ("rape's better, if you'll forgive the word") and he offered scandal. On the political scene,

Vidal tells us Hearst invented the characters, gave them dialogue, and moved them in and out of wars.

One can hardly help noticing that Vidal is doing the same thing. At the end of *Empire*, Vidal scripts an encounter between Hearst and President Theodore Roosevelt. Hearst gets all the good lines: "I have placed the press above everything else, except maybe money, and even when it comes to money, I can usually make the market rise or fall. When I made—invented, I should say—the war with Spain, all of it fiction to begin with, I saw to it that the war would be a real one at the end, and it was. For better or for worse, we took over a real empire from the Caribbean to the shores of China. . . . It's my story, isn't it? This country. . . . I am history—or at least the creator of the record." President Roosevelt counters, but Hearst, and Vidal, have the last word. "True history is the final fiction," Hearst says.

Vidal draws a battle line that is still fought over. Publishers want to sell newspapers. How do they do it? The chilling modern strategy of providing "infotainment" is just yellow journalism for an upscale audience, for yuppies who are curious but squeamish.

But surely Vidal blows his own cover. He spells out the Hearst formula. Sensationalism, scandal, invented news. And then he follows it himself. With characters like Henry Adams and the Roosevelts, *Empire* gives us the "Society Lady" angle on American history. He gives us political corruption, sexual perversity, and tantalizing mention of conflicts that have yet to be resolved: Russia, the Philippines, and South Africa. Then there are the touches that border on cute. Mention of typewriters and the first cars. An oblique reference to the president of Princeton, Woodrow Wilson. Hearst announces he has bought the magazine *Cosmopolitan*. (The Hearst Corporation still owns *Cosmo*, which ran a segment from *Empire* in its July issue.)

The cover of Vidal's new book reads *Empire: a Novel*. And Vidal's end note reads ". . . I keep the historical figures in *Empire* to the generally agreed-on facts." But from beginning to end, it is hard to know where fiction ends and facts begin. That is, I suppose, Vidal's point—no one ever does. In the face of this airy sophistication, or sophistry, a reader feels a bit shabby and old-fashioned to want "truth," or even accuracy. And if politics is scripted by newspapers and history is fiction, then what is the point? Or, to put it in editor's parlance, so what?

> Carol des Lauriers Cieri, "Gore Vidal's 'Empire' Offers a Morality Play without the Morals," in The Christian Science Monitor, *July 20, 1987, p. 22.*

Tom Carson

Like the earlier installments of Gore Vidal's "American Chronicle"—a skimpy American Trilogy until Vidal discovered that he'd found his mother lode—*Empire* is entertaining, impressively engineered stuff: a nifty new season for the most literate TV miniseries ever written for the page instead of the tube. The period covered is engrossing-

ly rich, its status as all-but-virgin literary territory a tribute to this society's ability to convince itself that everything in the United States was swell until yesterday morning. Even Vidal's version has gone along with the prevailing myth that his country had an innocence to lose. He's just relocated the moment of defloration for each succeeding novel, like an artillery barrage shifting its brackets forward and back.

Washington, D.C. (1967), the first installment, is untypical of the series on most of the levels that make your entertainment dollar count: no backstairs historical gossip, not much period-piece pizzazz. But its plot, about an old-fashioned senator driven to death by heartbreak at the hands of an amoral Kennedyesque challenger, did set the thematic pattern—though Vidal handled all his characters with such zealous disdain it would have taken a mind reader to realize that his old coot was meant to represent tarnished values.

Burr (1973) was far brisker, the tartness of its portrait of the revolutionary generation making Vidal's schoolboyish crush on that scamp Burr forgivable, and the schoolboyish fantasy of his conclusion—the narrator discovers that old Aaron's his *father,* by God!—conveniently forgettable. In *1876* (1976; no, of course it wasn't written to cash in on the Bicentennial), the tarnished values of Grant's Gilded Age drive *Burr*'s resurrected narrator, now old and old-fashioned, to die of heartbreak. *Lincoln* (1984) broke the mold somewhat: Vidal was quite aware that Lincoln's insistence on saving the Union meant the destruction of the old Republic's ideals, but he was so awed by his hero's resolve that admiration overcame his usual cavils. (Which of course doesn't stop him from implying in *Empire* that it wasn't much of a Union to save.) Two further volumes are reputedly in the works, one on the Wilson era, one contemporary—tarnished values, lost ideals galore.

In *Empire,* Vidal's familiar scheme—the noble old poised against the grubby new, and proceeding to have the shit dogmatically drubbed out of it—feels closer to home than in the earlier books. Teddy Roosevelt's seizure of the Pacific may not be the epochal national fall from grace Vidal makes it out to be: fall from *what?* But it's certainly the moment when all the impulses curdling the country from the start began to assume the particular contours they still have today. The immediate parallels—read Central America for the bloody putdown of the Philippine insurrection; multiconglomnationalerate for the oil, railroad, and press tycoons; Reagan's hallucinatory world view for T. R.'s only slightly less dictated-to-him manifest-destiny gobbledygook—are acute enough that Vidal, at any rate, feels no need to belabor them. He's probably wrong; since his stated purpose is to educate the citizenry—"Why else would I go to all this trouble?" he recently put it—he ought to know that they aren't much for extrapolative thinking.

Vidal's hauteur is probably one of the best-sustained literary defense mechanisms around, and the above remark is a relatively mild example. But it also comes close to letting the cat out of the bag. For all his habit of picking things up by his fingertips, our number-one literary fop is secretly as convinced as the glummest Socialist Realist that fiction needs to serve a program to justify itself. He's played a good game for three decades now—girding himself in amused detachment to conceal the fact that just underneath is our old friend the North American crank, clanking with causes and better ways to run the world.

The causes have often turned out to be perfectly decent ones. But you could wish that, at 62, Vidal's apparent model for how to campaign in secret, stay cool on top, were somebody other than the Scarlet Pimpernel. Even his most earnest essays are full of arch little strategies and backings-off whose function is to lift him above the battle he has just been exhorting his readers to join. But the manner also goes deeper with him than mere ploy. He really does see himself as the last of the WASPs—his squabble with Norman Podhoretz in *The Nation* last year had less to do with N.P.'s complacent lack of identification with U.S. culture (historical division) than with G.V.'s equally complacent but far more exercised assumption that no one could ever identify with it so poignantly, trenchantly, usefully as an apostate son of the power elite like himself.

One of the main virtues of Vidal's historical sequence is that these books, besides harmonizing well with his talents, find honest work for his vices. The approach answers his desire to agitate in fictional form, channels his tricky and overspecial sense of U.S. history into a disinterested-looking seemliness. It also makes a use of his large technical gifts and engaging bitcheries which for once does not leave them supercilious in relation to their subject. He's never been willing to commit himself to his stories or characters for their own sake; to a mind as essentially rationalist and programmatic as he wants his to be, trying to make made-up things believable must seem at bottom a silly undertaking. Even in Vidal's more fanciful books, where he jettisons the mimetic chores that so clearly bore him, he fails to put himself more on the line to compensate. Instead, the lack of friction with reality gives him the leisure to rig his targets so that every hit is a bull's-eye—it's wit in a vacuum chamber.

But writing about history performs an essential service for Vidal: it gets him off the book. The people, the events, are self-evidently important—he doesn't have to fret over whether they're worth his while, or roll his eyes to the gallery for an alibi. He's an anomalous novelist in that he seems happiest when functioning as a critic: he treats history like a great novel already written, his own fictionalizations of it mere interpretive renderings, free of the responsibility of creation—or, as he might prefer to see it, of the frivolity of mere invention. He can be subjective and impersonal, involved and removed at once. He can be serious without leaving himself vulnerable.

It helps that *Empire* brings the story full circle, introducing us in their youth to the generation of characters who still hold center stage in *Washington, D.C.,* the novel that is at this point the series chronological ending, though it was published first. Half the new book's fun is the dopily irresistible kind of recognizing characters we've already met at earlier or later moments of their lives. Vidal mines this primitive, or anyway inexplicable, audience pleasure, to considerable effect. In *Lincoln,* John Hay, borrowed from history by Vidal to serve as one of his chief surrogates, was in his early 20s. Here he's 60 and Secretary of State—our reencounter with him in old-age makeup is as cartoonishly satisfying as the first sight of DeNiro suddenly wizened in *Once Upon a Time in America.*

That's one appeal of miniseries, too. But a more basic reason why these novels feel closer to a TV epic than a literary one is that Vidal has written a generational saga—one man's family through the ages—whose formal protagonists are pure cardboard. The Sanfords—it's hard even to remember the name—are in no danger of being referred to by even the most cliché-happy reviewer as a "clan." They're serviceable, that's all, performing the linking chores between the books, and functioning within each as doormen for our peeps into the meatier stuff: Vidal's reconstructions of dead celebrities. In some books, he concocts a modicum of plot for them to act out, by way of a hearthside mirror to the temper of the time—in *1876,* Emma's scheme for marrying up by inciting her best friend's death in childbirth is meant to parallel the Grant era's venality; in *Empire,* her daughter Caroline carves out a business empire inside the titular one. But even though we might occasionally mistake these episodes for life, Vidal knows better: they're just plots, their crises and even their tone more or less received, and he is simply a well-read enough craftsman to give them an efficient run-through.

Most likely, Vidal believes he's amusing himself hugely by briskly stylizing the paint-by-numbers dramatics so indispensable to miniseries writers. On the other hand, his temperament at low ebb may be closer to theirs than he bothers to notice; he's just as bent as we are on getting to the living Madame Tussaud's. Certainly, his heroine from book to book is as generic as *Dallas.* No matter what name she goes by, she is going to stay beautiful, clever, mercenary, gifted with an uncanny ability to make deflating asides in drawing rooms, though at least Vidal can give her epigrams wit. (In *Lincoln,* he finds a real-life female who can stand in the part: Kate Sprague, Salmon P. Chase's calculating, beautiful, clever, etc. daughter.) The Vidal heroine goes all the way back to Enid, the headstrong, etc. broken blossom in *Washington, D.C.*—which at this point makes a rather flat ending for the series, as it was written entirely about made-up people, back before Vidal figured out a way of one-upping Capote and Mailer at the nonfiction novel without even letting on that he was in the game.

He does run a good Madame Tussaud's. Since this is the stuff he takes seriously, he's conscientious and painstaking—winning the reader's trust has heretofore not been his strong suit. His virtue is that, while giving pomp its due (and *Empire* deals with a period when statesmen talked with breathtaking blitheness about themselves as agents of history), he has the patience to work up the details of large and small priorities, the impingements of circumstance and long-forgotten private agendas, out of which history's turning points get unexpectedly bundled. If the matter at hand is the ratification of the "peace" treaty which annexed the Philippines from Spain, committing the U.S. to its first-ever suppression of a foreign revolution, Vidal will linger over such consequential trifles as Cabot Lodge's vanity. Then, with Roosevelt installed in power, he's set us up for a demonstration of how yesterday's upheaval congeals into the new norm, as everybody scurries to obliterate whatever habits of mind the Rooseveltian reality has made obsolete.

The sets Vidal builds—Washington, New York, Newport—have the same dioramic intricacy. In this as well, his preference for keeping himself at one remove clearly brings mysterious, bold uses both here and in *Lincoln;* the capital is a vivid and tellingly rendered place—not just in period detail, though that abounds, but in stuff that rings bells of recognition for anybody who's ever spent time there, like the haplessly unrequited snobbery of its more-or-less natives toward the voted-in short-timers who are the city's reason for existing. The city is less vivid in *Washington, D.C.,* even though it's set during the years of Vidal's own childhood there, and derives many of its particulars from material he knew at firsthand.

But let's get on to the mannequins. Vidal's Roosevelt is first-rate. The real pleasure here, however, is his depiction of a group of intimates, with one foot in intellect and the other in politics; Hay and Henry Adams were the magnetic poles of the group, with Henry James—who unpredictably turns out to be the novel's funniest sketch—as an occasional visiting constellation. These aging intimates are beautifully aware of each other, the approaching sunset adds poignancy; their endlessly alert banter—which of course Vidal is more than equal to reproducing—is so enjoyable we don't really mind that the ventriloquist can't help himself when it comes to indulging in them. We want to bask in the serenity, too.

And, well, yes, but. There is another side to all this. Vidal is hardly the first seeming debunker to betray a sentimental rooting interest. What keeps it well concealed is that he's most often sentimental about things too foreign to most of his readers for them to notice the wetness: Roman ideals of noble conduct—that is, noble conduct on even the flimsiest of pretexts. There's an episode in *Lincoln* when Secretary of State Seward decides that for the president's sake he must quit his office. At once he calls to his son, "Fred! . . . We're resigning, the two of us. Write out your resignation and give it to Senator King." You'd forgive Fred for at least asking what the hell's up. But Vidal's comment is, "The young man did as he was told; he was every bit as cool as his father." He's in schoolboy heaven, for once unguarded—it's a moment of gee-whiz admiration that gives the whole game away.

If you have style, he'll forgive you everything. Vidal's Burr is certainly his most entertaining character so far. But it's too perfect; Burr never falters, he's always saying the right sardonic thing. Mosca in *The Charterhouse of Parma* is just as much a piece of wish fulfillment for his creator; but Stendhal also shows Mosca making a fool of himself, caught in situations where the manner falls apart, with no loss in admiration. Facade is the only thing Vidal is willing to take at face value—and it's also difficult for him to invest much in characters who don't value worldly polish and sharp wit as highly as he does. *Lincoln* is the most memorable book in the series so far because Vidal makes the effort; Lincoln isn't really in his best range, but for once he has to admit that there's a lot there anyway.

(Though he gets a good assist by lifting his conception of Lincoln's mystical Unionism, down to the comparison to Bismark on the final page, without acknowledgment from Edmund Wilson's *Patriotic Gore.*)

Vidal does a bit of the same for McKinley in *Empire,* uncharacteristically finding value in his blandness, but for more tactical reasons: to make Roosevelt look worse. As a rule, though, here as elsewhere, his yen for brightness ends up vitiating and skewing even his villains. Introducing William Randolph Hearst, he makes an interesting point of Hearst's obtuseness in most things human; he's a virtuoso with his newspapers, a cigar-store Indian about everything else. But Vidal can't bring himself to spend half of a very long book in the company of such a metronome, and so Hearst gradually gets more articulate, more self-aware, ingratiatingly wicked instead of obsidian—in other words, more like everyone else in the book.

Partly because of this underlying tendency, to turn history into something made by enormously well-spoken people, ironists all too easily able to delight in the showmanship of their own intrigues, all these books, however satisfying in the reading, glance off in your mind afterwards. You're left on your own when it comes to convincing yourself that these events are consequential, still panning out today. Otherwise, you just end up with the good old *I, Claudius* turn-on: evil so far removed from the recognizably contemporary that enjoyment of its stylishness is value-free.

In each novel the central situation, the emotional backbone that ought to provide the ploys and maneuverings with their urgency, is never made very pressing. In *Lincoln,* the human cost of the Civil War is never brought home, even though the fighting and dying are meant to be what gives Lincoln's resolve its awful resonance. The genocidal U.S. campaign against the Filipinos is something we know matters a lot to Vidal: he's been recurring to it in his essays for a decade. But in the book whose moral hinges on it, it's barely present at all.

Other paradoxes are more subtle. In his nonfiction, interviews, and so on, Vidal has increasingly—if with an air of looking reluctantly backward at every step—subscribed to the position that what passes for politics in the U.S. is mere shadow-play, performed by useful fools while the actual rulers go on doing business pretty much undisturbed. In fact, he's been admirably dogged about trying to din that awareness into his audience's heads, though even otherwise goggle-eyed admirers, most recently Stephen Schiff in *Vanity Fair,* deride the "musty late-sixties-early-seventies flavor" of his politics. (What a loss—just a little air freshener would have put *Vanity Fair* on the barricades.)

In the novels, though, Vidal shies away from any sustained attempt to dramatize this understanding. Since, as he knows quite well, only outsiders see that the U.S. is run as a conspiracy—the people who do the running wouldn't recognize that description of themselves—it's admittedly not an easy thing to dramatize. But what he ends up producing instead is an only slightly soured and japing version of the usual schoolbook personalities who get to sign a page of history with their names. Even when he knows better, he can't give up on seeing the stand-in in the arena as the star—who, reading his version of Roosevelt, could believe that Teddy was acting on behalf of any interest more abstract than his own crackling energy?

Vidal is a lot more ambivalent about his subject than he lets on. He's irresistibly drawn to the things he means to set us straight on, about the one country whose citizens all take living there personally. On the surface, he will be curtly dismissive, superior, dry; just underneath is an adolescent helplessly infatuated with all the old guff about the pageantry and romantic specialness of U.S. history, secretly wishing to see it as an epic populated with Great Men. In *Burr,* he does a wonderfully sly job on the Revolutionary generation, pickling them in petty vanities and nagging feuds. But by *Lincoln,* all this is forgotten—the periodic somber invocations of "Washington's unfinished monument" visible outside Lincoln's window take us straight back to the votive offerings of Scott Fitzgerald, who was too impetuous to hedge on his crushes, and who (as a result?) is a Doppelgänger Vidal has gone out of his way to keep shoving back into the closet.

Vidal's identification with the U.S. patricianate, though, could make Fitzgerald look like an icy-eyed realist. Turning the faucet on and off, he can be scathing about their pomposities, denunciatory of the uses they make of their power. What's left unquestioned is the assumption that they are indeed the most important people in the country, the central players, all else a mongrelization. One memorable episode in *Empire* has John Hay, on a train trip through the Midwest, making a folksy speech to a group of farmers, only to discover that they're all German immigrants who don't understand a word. These newcomers make Hay's world the past, and though the tone is comic, the inference is unmistakable: Vidal actually believes that something precious is being lost.

But the larger complication is the sense of another lost legacy—his own—which leaves him much more divided. He doesn't know whether he's an escapee or an exile from a collegiality of power which he considers to have been his by birthright.

The irony is that Vidal's kind of ambivalence could, if honestly explored, have made for a much richer novel than any of the feints he's come up with to avoid confronting it head-on. But he's hardly the first literary operator to write his way out of what he ought to be writing about. Instead, he produces well-wrought diversions like *Empire*—which my mom, lover of miniseries, connoisseur of escapist good reads, recently called to tell me she was enjoying a whole lot. (pp. 53-5)

> *Tom Carson, "His Country, Right or Wrong,"* in The Village Voice, *Vol. XXXII, No. 40, October 6, 1987, pp. 53-5.*

Christopher Hitchens

During the course of a politico-literary spat in the pages of the *Nation,* Gore Vidal was . . . accused of disliking his own country. The accuser was Midge Decter, the helpmeet of that stern guardian of orthodoxy Norman Podho-

retz. Vidal's reply had all the honeyed modesty that his admirers have come to relish. 'Poor Midge,' he wrote, 'Of course I like my country. After all, I'm its current biographer.'

This claim was meant to madden, and did not fail in its effect. But it also happens to be true. Vidal has been steadily raising a fictional edifice through which the growth of the United States into a global colossus can be appreciated and understood. With his other hand, he has been penning essays that point out the ironies and contradictions of this power, and phlegmatically predict its demise. Vidal is the only eminent American who routinely refers to 'empire,' and its inevitable corollary 'imperialism,' when discussing the international dimension of his country's affairs.

In his last and greatest novel *Lincoln,* we saw honest Abe agree to do something in which he did not believe (emancipate the slaves) in order to preserve something in which he did believe (the continental Union of the states). *Empire* begins a few decades later, with a new confidence and prosperity overtaking the country. There are new fortunes, exemplified by the names Astor and Hearst. There are confident demagogues like William Jennings Bryan and Teddy Roosevelt, and new achievements such as the Brooklyn Bridge. And in the figure of President McKinley, the country has also found a man who can drape imperial acquisitions in the necessary piety.

The novel opens in the Weald of Kent, where the circle of Henry James, Henry Adams and John Hay is wont to meet. It is the task of these men to bring a sceptical and Europeanised perspective to the new American enterprise. The new America is seen through the eyes of a shrewd young woman named Caroline Sanford, who has been reared in Europe and who comes to the salons of New York, Washington and Providence, Rhode Island with a fresh and critical eye. Through this commingling of two themes—the new imperialism and the new vulgarity—Vidal has scope for all his talents. The megalomania of Hearst is hit off nicely by the unction of Bryan and the hypocrisy of Roosevelt. In the background, the city of Washington DC is making its transition from the sweltering backwater we left in *Lincoln* to the pretentious imperial capital. As with *Lincoln,* most of the historic drama takes place off-stage.

Vidal plainly believes that you can't have an empire without making hypocrisy into a civil religion, and he records the high-minded justifications for conquest with the same sarcastic punctilio that he brings to the observance of nuance in rank and station. As he has Hearst say of Roosevelt: 'He's got to have money so that he can go round the country at election time, attacking the trusts that are paying for his train.' Or, as he has a character observe of Hearst: 'The Chief had never worked out the differences between "compliment" and "complement;" fortunately, he did not have to.'

The novel brings America, kicking and screaming lustily, into the twentieth century. Many of the essays in *Armageddon?,* written towards the century's inglorious close, take up the same themes. In the title piece, Vidal states flatly that 'Nearly every major politician in the United

States is paid for by what is known as "the defence industry." That is why over 60 per cent of the government's income is wasted on "defence".' Here again we have Vidal the bad boy: campaign finance is one of those topics that most people have an interest in not mentioning. He tosses and gores the religious, the gay-bashers, the Israeli lobby, and, of course, the Californian milieu that incubated Ronnie and Nancy Reagan.

Vidal's hatred of the Reagans is more or less pure, and he chooses to express it in a sort of mocking, feline style. He makes some use of a pun on the term 'Acting President' and gives this old gag a new lease of life. Here he recalls his first sight of Ronnie, at the famous Republican convention in San Francisco's Cow Palace in 1964, while Eisenhower was speaking:

> I do remember being struck by the intensity with which Reagan studied Eisenhower. I had seen that sort of concentration a thousand times in half-darkened theatres during rehearsal or Saturday matinées: the understudy examines the star's performance, and tries to figure how it is done. An actor prepares, I said to myself: Mr Reagan is planning to go into politics. With his crude charm, I was reasonably certain that he could be elected mayor of Beverly Hills.

Vidal's general contempt for Christianity, which found its happiest expression in *Julian the Apostate,* has now found its ideal target. In the alliance between fundamentalists and the military-industrial complex, all his enemies have done him the favour of amalgamation. How he hates this coalition of the mean-spirited with the corrupt, and its constipated image of 'the real America of humming electric chairs, well-packed prisons, and kitchens filled with every electrical device that a small brown person of extranational provenance might successfully operate at a fraction of the legal minimum wage.'

If an Englishman wrote like that about America, he might plausibly be accused of 'anti-Americanism." But it's clear that Vidal is fond of his country and his countrymen, and believes that they deserve a better government and media than they get. There is a charming piece here, about the history of aviation in the United States, in the form of a memoir of his father. Eugene L. Vidal was FDR's Secretary for Air, and the boy Gore had many chances to indulge in what was still a high adventure for most people. Even here, though, he contrasts those days of enchantment with the modern stupidity of 'Star Wars, and a future in which dumb dented human toys will drift mindlessly about the cosmos long after our small planet's dead.'

Part II of the collection is less polemical and embittered, with appreciations of Henry James (Teddy Roosevelt's dinner for the novelist appears as in *Empire*) and a most affecting valediction to Italo Calvino. It's not that Vidal prefers Europe, as some of his detractors imply in the hope of convicting him of snobbery. It's more that he feels a knowledge of Europe to be essential in the taming of American arrogance.

Christopher Hitchens, "Vidal Statistics," in
The Observer, *November 22, 1987, p. 25.*

Stephen Fender

Caroline Sanford, one of the few non-historical characters in *Empire,* returns to her native country after an upbringing and education in France, to find America too full of 'everything except history.' This is an omission that Gore Vidal has set out to repair. To the massive chunks of what he calls his 'biography of America'—*Lincoln; 1876*—he now adds this monument to the turn of the 20th century, when the United States first undertook the imperial role.

At nearly 600 pages, *Empire* has too much of everything including history. Sometimes we seem to be reading barely fictionalised annals: everything famous and contemporary gets a mention, from the Dreyfus case and the first flight of the Wright Brothers to the rise of baseball and the yellow press. Henry Adams can barely appear without references to virgins, dynamos and entropy—or William Jennings Bryan without the 'cross of gold' (his famous metaphor for the penalty of expensive loans imposed on America's western farmers).

Yet the history is given a shape, moulded on the old Whig thesis that cultures begin to decline when they turn themselves from republics into empires. America is assuming the white man's burden, extending Anglo-Saxon civilisation to its 'little brown brothers' in Cuba and the Philippines. Unlike *Lincoln,* which includes a thick slice of common experience, *Empire* sticks to top people: the theorists and practitioners of the new empire, like the Brothers Adams (childless as the Republic their great family once served), and Presidents McKinley and Theodore Roosevelt—builders, if not architects, of the American expansion in the Pacific.

So far, so pretty conventional as historical analyses go, except that Vidal is much too hard on Roosevelt, whom he demotes to a vain, bombastic creation of William Randolph Hearst. This is only part of the story. Roosevelt was also a courageous and resourceful progressive with plenty of ideas of his own (including support for the imperial ideology drawn from his experience in the wild West), and some accomplishment himself in the writing of history.

Vidal is good on class, though. The high-minded propagandists of empire are also fighting a rear-guard action against Bryan's populists and other 'enemies of the rich' including (when it is good for circulation) William Randolph Hearst. Even John Hay, Vidal's sympathetic observer of most of the novel's action, is implicated. The cautious, reflective Secretary of State to both McKinley and Roosevelt and the last surviving member of Lincoln's cabinet (he hears and sees Lincoln in his dying daydreams), Hay nevertheless articulates the policy of American expansion without believing in it and deplores Hearst's manipulation of the masses. Too late, the theorists see what they have created: Roosevelt, the Empire and the American modern world. Then, after Hay has died, Vidal moves his readers into a chilling coda in which Hearst reveals that it is he, not the oligarchy, who had made the President, as an author makes his characters.

Despite this last gesture in the direction of self-referring fiction, *Empire* is really a traditional historical novel, governed by a consistent narrative point of view, tightly packed with minute details of everyday habit and speech—just the sort of thing Americans are supposed not to write. But Vidal's non-fiction is something else. In his new collection of essays [**Armageddon?**], the President of the United States is preparing for the final war between Christ and the Antichrist at Armageddon, just 55 miles north of Tel Aviv. The Zionists have formed a pact with the American ultra-right to accelerate the onset of the nuclear holocaust. The aviatrix Amelia Earhart was in love with Vidal's father and was wearing his jockey shorts when she crashed in the Pacific. That is, if she did crash. For years afterwards many stories circulated of a mysterious white woman sighted 'on this or that island', wearing only a pair of man's drawers.

This is racy stuff, as Vidal himself would say, right out the pages of E. L. Doctorow, Thomas Pynchon and other post-modern experimenters in apocalyptic fact-fiction. And while on the subject of American authors, can anyone remember what happened to that other writer living in Italy who devoted the better part of his life's work to a reworking of his country's history and warned of an unholy alliance between Jews and armaments manufacturers? He was indicted for treason and wound up in an insane asylum. Vidal, by contrast, is reviewed in all the best papers and is made the sole subject of a whole *South Bank Show,* his punishment limited to what seems to have been a rather long lunch with Melvyn Bragg. I wonder why the difference? Of course, Italy was at war with the United States when Ezra Pound made his infamous broadcasts from Rome. But Pound was part of the populist strain of American politics, which means (though admittedly not for that reason alone) that his opinions can be assigned to the rubbish pile of history's crackpots. Vidal's connections, (he is a grandson of a distinguished senator, son of Franklin Roosevelt's Director of the Bureau of Air Commerce, and step-brother to Jackie Kennedy Onassis) are a bit more patrician. Maybe the contemporary treatment of American literary figures also has something to do with class.

Stephen Fender, "Remember Pound," in The Listener, Vol. 118, No. 3042, December 17-24, 1987, p. 50.

Clive Davis

Gore Vidal embarked on his "American Saga" in 1967 with **Washington DC,** a racy tale of ambition and lust set in the Republic's high noon. **Burr,** published six years later, took us back to the very beginning of the story, presenting us with a cynic's eye view of the Founding Fathers.

With **Hollywood,** we have reached the sixth stage of the odyssey, taking us through the ill-fated idealism of Woodrow Wilson to the tawdry disintegration of the Harding presidency. Vidal's admirers will certainly be eager to join him on the journey. But be warned: there are signs that epic fatigue is beginning to set in.

Vidal has always made ingenious use of the conventions of the historical novel. **Burr** and **1876** were written in the mock-naive style of the bystander. **Lincoln** conveyed a frank portrait of "honest Abe" as seen through the eyes of his intimates and rivals.

Hollywood lacks the same sense of focus. Vidal's tidbits of gossip about America's rulers are as entertaining as ever, but by dividing his energies between the political narrative and the further adventures of the Sanford dynasty (whose members first appeared in **DC**) he has produced a convoluted work, part blockbuster, part essay, part guided tour.

That, to be fair, was part of the charm of the earlier novels. The problem is that Vidal has failed to add a compelling cast of characters. His main protagonists, the newspaper publishers Blaise and Caroline Sanford, are as witty and epigrammatic as they were in **Empire,** but we know better than to take them for real people. The figures who normally provide much of the interest—the politicians—rarely come to life.

Assigned to travel to Hollywood to help pull the infant "photo play" industry behind the war effort, Caroline discovers that, at the age of 40, she has the looks and potential to become a film star. Sold to a world-wide audience as "Emma Traxler", she begins to understand that cinema has the power to re-shape the world, to project illusions and falsehoods almost at will.

While "Emma" is mingling with the stars, President Wilson is struggling to win support for his vision of a League of Nations. When he fails, the way is open for the Republican Warren Harding to assume power. The ensuing corruption scandals, culminating in the Teapot Dome affair, give Vidal ample ammunition for another assault on the governing classes.

Hollywood takes pains to draw parallels between past, present and future. The venality of the Harding years recalls the dirty deeds of **1876,** not to mention the general shadiness of the Reagan era. There are further echoes of the "Acting President" in Caroline's bizarre double life in Hollywood and Washington. And when Harding's wife consults a fortune-teller in the opening chapters, it is easy to picture Nancy Reagan playing the same role.

Vidal covers page after page with dazzling dialogue—one of the hallmarks of his imaginary America is that almost everyone talks like him. Celebrities queue up to make an appearance, however brief. Blaise chats to Charlie Chaplin in a Turkish Bath, while there is even space for Vidal's own grandfather, blind Senator Gore from Oklahoma.

In the end, the book is submerged by the period accessories. By broadening his scope to cover every issue from the Fourteen Points to the fall of Fatty Arbuckle, Vidal loses his usual grasp of individual detail. Instead of characterisation, he gives us a succession of sometimes dutiful thumbnail sketches. There are still glorious moments of humour and bitchery: nothing—not even Douglas Fairbanks's penis—is safe from ridicule. But for once, the satire is not quite enough. (pp. 35-6)

Clive Davis, "Cynic's Eye View," in New Statesman & Society, Vol. 2, No. 74, November 3, 1989, pp. 35-6.

Francis King

Very few people now ever read Upton Sinclair in [England], and in his native America he is scarcely more in demand. Yet there was a time, in the Forties and Fifties, when his blend of history and fiction in a series of novels featuring Lanny Budd, illegitimate son of an armaments king, was highly popular on both sides of the Atlantic. There is a parallel here with Gore Vidal.

Admittedly, in many respects no two writers could be more unlike than the idealistic, stylistically clumsy and proletarian Sinclair, who worked his way through the College of the City of New York by strenuously writing inordinately long novels, and the cynical, stylistically elegant and patrician Vidal, who, by no less strenuously writing inordinately long novels, has worked his way into the councils of leading politicians, writers and thinkers. But each man has been the literary equivalent of a wordworm, with an amazing capacity simultaneously to bore through the fabric of history, and to digest and to excrete.

The latest volume of what Vidal has called his biography of the United States, [*Hollywood*], starts in 1917, with Woodrow Wilson determined to lead his country into the Great War, despite the opposition of the Irish and German communities in America and of William Randolph Hearst. Wilson, with his combination of high ideals and low political cunning, is one of the most convincing characters of this vast novel. As we see him deploy his intellect and eloquence at Versailles to hold his own against two such wily and obstinate negotiators as Lloyd George and Clemenceau, watch him struggle to make his own country a partner in the League of Nations which he had conceived, and then witness his decline into illness and premature old age, it is impossible to withhold from him, for all his priggishness, the respect which, it is clear, Vidal himself also feels.

More surprisingly, the portrait of Warren Gamaliel Harding, Wilson's successor, is not merely respectful but also affectionate. With his dark, slightly blurred good looks (Vidal repeatedly refers to the rumour that he was partly negro), his ability to 'bloviate' (his own verb for the impromptu gassing at which he excelled, to the delight of his often ill-educated auditors), and his capacity to out-manoeuvre people like Cabot Lodge and Borah who loftily underestimated him, he emerges as a President whose reputation would now be far higher but for the financial scandal which engulfed it in the immediate aftermath of his premature death. The wives of these two men, Wilson's energetically supportive Edith and Harding's canny, ailing 'The Duchess', emerge hardly less vividly.

Vidal is at his best when dealing with political confrontations. The sections which deal with Wilson's defeat over the League of Nations and with Harding's victory at the ninth ballot at the Republican Convention have real power and substance and hold one in thrall. The confrontations of private life are, by contrast, muted, even inert. Parallel to the story of the two fateful presidencies is the continuing one of Caroline Sanford, the heroine of Vidal's previous novel *Empire.* Proprietress, with her bisexual half-brother Blaise, of an influential newspaper, the Wash-

ington *Tribune,* she is recruited to work as government propagandist in the Hollywood dream-factory. There, improbably, she herself becomes a film-star under the name 'Emma Traxler'; and, even more improbably, having invented for 'Emma Traxler' a European past, she manages never to be recognised by even her closest friends in this new persona. Caroline's career in Hollywood first as 'Emma' and then as a film-producer convinced of the ability of films to 'invent' a new and better world ('What we invent others reflect'), provides Vidal with the opportunity to introduce such characters as Elinor Glyn, imperiously queening it over people younger and more talented than herself; Mabel Normand, rapidly destroying both her career and her health with cocaine; compact, athletic Douglas Fairbanks and already boozy Mary Pickford; and Charlie Chaplin, narcissistically playing as much to himself as to his audience. In these Hollywood sections, as in one in which Blaise takes himself off to the Paris brothel financed by Marcel Proust and there actually sees the butcher's boy whom Proust himself patronises, one has the impression of a knitting-machine busily extruding yet another loose-textured, brightly coloured length of material.

As anyone who has ever read him must by now know, Vidal is one of the wittiest of novelists. 'Since the morality of Washington was always relative to need, one's man Gethsemane might be another's Coney Island.' ' "It's mother," murmured Frederika in much the same tone of voice that a 14th-century woman might have warned the family of plague.' There is scarcely a page without some such delight. But, sadly, there is also scarcely a section without some example of undue haste on the part of the author or carelessness on the part of the proof-reader. The author's haste manifests itself in the way in which, presumably out of forgetfulness, he repeats information—for example, that Wilson had no men friends, or that Harding enjoyed both his drink and chewing tobacco—already given to the reader.

Francis King, "A Biography of the United States," in The Spectator, *Vol. 263, No. 8415, November 4, 1989, p. 30.*

Zachary Leader

At the end of *Empire,* which covers the years 1898-1906, a new and ominous presence dominates the scene: the popular press, source of a power 'no ruler could exercise'. *Hollywood* opens in 1917, on the eve of United States' entry into the Great War, but the power of the press is no longer a central preoccupation. Instead, 'Hollywood is the key to just about everything.'

As in earlier volumes of the cycle—*Washington, DC* (1967), *Burr* (1973), *1876* (1976, of course), *Lincoln* (1984), and *Empire*—*Hollywood* mixes fictional with historical characters. The central fictional characters in this case, as in *Empire,* are Caroline Sanford and her half-brother Blaise, descendants of the cycle's first hero, Aaron Burr, and their sometime mutual lover, Senator James Burden Day, now a prospective Democratic presidential candidate. These are the characters, together with the real-life Jess Smith, a minor fixer and under-agent of the corrupt Harding administration, from whose points of view the story is told.

The chief historical characters are the two Presidents of the period, Wilson and Harding, and the flanking Roosevelts—bellicose Teddy, all 'tombstone' teeth and tireless bustle, and the ultra-smooth FDR, an obvious comer. But there are also memorable appearances from a host of powerful wives and daughters, secondary political figures, movie makers, literary celebrities. Even Marcel Proust figures briefly, as the creepy proprietor of a male brothel Blaise visits in Paris, on the eve of the League of Nations peace conference. 'This old man,' one of the brothel's more attractive employees tells him, 'he's very sick, very pale . . . he likes talking about blood, things like that.'

When the novel begins, Caroline has turned 40 and is drifting. Though still co-owner and chief resuscitator of the *Washington Tribune,* she finds herself, like her competitor William Randolph Hearst, drawn to the movies; and since she is a sort of super-woman (a figure out of Barbara Taylor Bradford), she quickly becomes both a star and the owner of a powerful studio.

In *Empire,* Caroline's involvement with the newspaper business prevented the novel from splitting into fictive and historical strands. In *Hollywood,* this is not quite the case, in part because the movie business takes her outside Washington, in part because the power of film is conceived of as deeper and more diffuse than that of journalism. Though Hollywood can indeed serve specific political purposes—demonising the Germans, then the communists—its principle power lies in its relation to dream, which is 'subtle—universal, unnoticeable'. Only towards the end of the novel is this deeper influence identified with the self-dramatising tendencies of the political characters, tendencies that will eventually produce Ronald Reagan, Vidal's 'Acting President'. By the early 1920s everyone in the novel, and not just Caroline and her Hollywood circle, is meant 'to think like a movie'.

The best bits in the book, the historical confrontations and set pieces, are less obliquely rendered. Both Wilson and Harding are compellingly imagined, unlike either of the Sanfords or Burden Day, whose problems are comparatively muted and internal, mostly having to do with age. Wilson, in contrast, must fend off Roosevelt, Henry Cabot Lodge, hideous Clemenceau, a stroke (the effects of which he and his inner circle try to hide), his own 'blind zealotry'. Vidal doesn't need to give him a complex inner life; or rather, he need only gesture at it. This is true of Harding as well, a quite different sort of President—softer, less brilliant—but one we are also meant to admire, for all his obsessive philandering and cronyism.

A comparable straightforwardness marks the novel's style. In previous volumes, Vidal's tendency to view his characters *ab extra,* to see them as defined in action, could jarr with his manner. *Empire,* in particular, was all signifying, Jamesian hesitations (in part a product of the Master's appearance in several of its scenes). The prose of *Hollywood* is less distractingly literary, its prevailing archness no longer antiquely mandarin. This is as it should be given

Vidal's subject. It is right, after all, that a novel called *Hollywood* should be written in an unfussy, popularising idiom—should smack, that is, of the movies.

Zachary Leader, "Where Everyone Thinks Like a Movie," in The Observer, *November 5, 1989, p. 54.*

Joel Conarroe

Standing in front of an altar, his monocle glittering in the klieg lights, a tiny Prussian officer is about to assault the mother of an American soldier. "Who is Henry Adams?" he asks, gutturally. The woman, who has the face of a Madonna, tells him, and suggests that he read *The Education.* Then as he tears at her dress, she picks up a crucifix and breaks it across his head.

It's a perfect take, and the director is ecstatic. The actors, too, are pleased, though Emma's makeup is burning her eyes and unlucky Pierre is rubbing his head. Their improvised dialogue is edifying, to be sure, but since the film is silent the book chat will be heard by none of the throngs of viewers who will be inspired by *Huns From Hell* to new heights of patriotic fervor and who will make Emma Traxler, whose real name is Caroline Sanford, an international star.

This cinematic encounter is just one of many entertaining moments in *Hollywood,* the latest installment in Gore Vidal's documentation (and revision) of our country's fables and foibles from its infancy to the 1950's. Subtitled "A Novel of America in the 1920s," the new work comes chronologically after *Burr* (1973), *Lincoln* (1984), *1876* (1976) and, finally, *Empire* (1987), a portrait of the Gilded Age that features the pre-Hollywood Caroline as she battles her half brother for a share of their father's immense estate. *Hollywood* takes place soon after the conclusion of *Empire* and precedes *Washington, D.C.* (1967), which documents both the New Deal and the McCarthy era. Although nothing in *Hollywood* is quite so riveting as the various deathbed scenes in *Lincoln* or the incredible election involving Rutherford B. Hayes and Samuel Tilden in *1876,* this is a wonderfully literate and consistently impressive work of fiction that clearly belongs on a shelf with the author's best earlier efforts.

Like the earlier books, the new novel is an imaginative re-creation, a heady mix of fact and fancy, wisdom and nonsense. His poetic license periodically renewed, Mr. Vidal, like E. L. Doctorow and Don DeLillo, likes to put purely fictional characters of his own creation on the page alongside notable figures from history. Among the more colorful personae in this new work are a uxorious, tap-dancing Woodrow Wilson, his immense wife, Edith (whom he calls "little girl"), irrepressible Charlie Chaplin, narcissistic Douglas Fairbanks Jr. and, most memorably, the famously acid-tongued Alice Roosevelt Longworth, who as she did in *Empire,* gets the book's snappiest lines. It became evident as early on as *Burr* that some of the author's wittier characters, masters of the pungent epigram and withering putdown, sound remarkably like their creator.

Warren Gamaliel Harding, on the other hand, does not.

A toothpick-chomping philanderer, he not only lets the executive collie, Laddie Boy, urinate on White House furniture but, worse yet, says things like "between you and I." Florence ("the Duchess"), his vindictive, controlling wife, is given to consulting a spiritualist (who advertises herself as "a president-ruler") to determine what her handsome, none too-bright spouse ought to do. At this point, I suppose, a reviewer is probably expected to say something topical, even Vidalesque, but since our novelist introduced the idea of political astrology many years ago (in *Washington, D.C.*) and hence cannot be accused of hitching his wagon to a recent star-gazer, I'll move on.

Other events, in addition to horoscopes in high places, serve to reinforce a reader's sense of *plus ça change.* Drugs and rampant corruption were serious problems during Harding's tenure; at the time of his death in 1923, the $64 million question was not whether certain trusted appointees of "one of the most popular presidents in history" had engaged in illegal activities, but whether he knew about their actions, and if not, why not. Campaigns, too, in those halcyon days before sound bites, were pretty ugly affairs, though apparently less so than in our own era of dubious ethical standards—his opponent decides not to exploit a charge against Harding that would play to racial fears. (Along similar lines, a prescient character in *Washington, D.C.,* published more than 20 years ago, ironically suggests that every citizen "swear a daily oath of allegiance to the flag. In this way we can soon discover who is a good American and who is not.")

As those familiar with his addictive prose know, Mr. Vidal has a number of stylistic tics. He is fond of words like "bloviate," "mephitic" and "riparian" and also returns with unseemly frequency to "dwarf," his conditioned response to screen actors, "each tinier than the other," with their "regulation dwarf proportions." An equal-opportunity size-basher, he is also impressed by gigantism, referring to Mrs. Wilson's "ship-like tonnage," and, in an atypical fit of redundancy, to William Randolph Hearst's "vast bear-like body." Partial to animal imagery, the novelist, as he does in the earlier books, also assigns to certain politicians the attributes of rodents—the sort of thing that could give rats a bad name. The literary historian Peter Conn clearly has a point when he refers to the series of novels as Mr. Vidal's "smirking revenge on 200 years of American history."

The bearlike Hearst, who gets a star billing in *Empire,* is just one of an enormous cast of characters who play supporting or walk-on roles in *Hollywood.* Others include the press tycoon's bibulous mistress, Marion Davies, awarded one of the funnier (and meaner) scenes; Senator William Borah ("the Lion of Idaho"); the Henrys (Adams and James, who, as in *Empire,* steal every scene they're in); the ambitious young Franklin Roosevelt and his idealistic Eleanor; and Mary Pickford, who, according to her mother, "gives her most as an actress when she's got a good director on top of her." The blind Senator Thomas Gore (a bit of novelistic nepotism here), falsely accused of a sexual assault, makes an appearance as does, in the interests of geographical balance, Fatty Arbuckle, implicated in a Hollywood scandal. Another cameo role is played by Harding's

successor, Calvin Coolidge, dismissed by the imperious Henry Cabot Lodge (who also seems to have a thing about size) as "that dreadful little creature in his dreadful little two-family house."

Confronted with so many vivid personalities and with so many pages of quotable dialogue, one can forget that the fluent Mr. Vidal—author, after all, of the exhaustive *Lincoln*—is a learned historian of a singularly nonacademic bent who is determined not only to amuse but also to enlighten. Fiction about Hollywood, as F. Scott Fitzgerald, Nathanael West and, more recently, Robert Stone (in his merciless *Children of Light*) have made clear, is likely to be almost indecently entertaining, and Mr. Vidal's contribution to the genre is no exception.

In fact, though, Hollywood is of decidedly secondary importance in this novel, the book's real subject being Washington. Caroline Sanford is the link between the two places. The way in which she becomes a star is the stuff of fantasy, and the relatively few chapters set in California are appropriately fantastic. Her original reason for going West, however, is not to challenge Theda Bara but to represent the Government in an unusually sensitive assignment—to persuade producers "to make pro-American, pro-Allies photo-plays," that is to say, anti-German films, like *Huns From Hell.* Politics, in this particular novelist's fictional-historical world, always takes dominion over everything else.

It is, thus, Washington, Henry James's "city of conversation," that principally concerns Mr. Vidal, and the events of an unusually dramatic period in history that most profoundly engage his attention. The book's numerous plot lines, whether involving such fictional characters as Caroline's sexually ambivalent brother, her redbaiting daughter or an ambitious senator who is her former lover, all find a common denominator in Washington politics. The book, moreover, is largely structured around the rise and fall of two Presidents, and without relinquishing the novelistic pleasures of an essentially comic narrative, Mr. Vidal manages to convey an enormous amount of information, partly factual, partly speculative, about such serious matters as the preparation for an unpopular war, the passionate debates generated by the proposed League of Nations, the tragic physical decline of Woodrow Wilson and the scandals of the Harding Administration. Such subjects, and not Douglas Fairbanks's tiny physique or Mary Pickford's huge salary, constitute the book's center.

Is such a work likely to enjoy popular success? Reviewers have tended to greet each new installment of Mr. Vidal's saga with hyperbole, suggesting that he regularly manages to outdo even his previous outdoings, as if he were involved in some sort of novelistic Olympics. My own sense is that with the exception of *Washington, D.C.,* which lacks both the trenchant wit and the historical players of the other works, the novels are pretty much of a piece, huge chapters in a continuing opus rather than self-contained entities. And like the earlier chapters, *Hollywood,* given its subject matter and diverting cast of characters, is destined to sell like hotcakes—or, rather, like popcorn. So confident am I of this prediction that if proved wrong I will walk from Pennsylvania Avenue to Sunset

Boulevard. And that, as one of Mr. Vidal's honest politicians would say, is a promise. (pp. 1, 38)

Joel Conarroe, "Klieg Lights on the Potomac," in The New York Times Book Review, January 21, 1990, pp. 1, 38.

Louis Auchincloss

In the beginning of Gore Vidal's new novel, **Hollywood,** the "Duchess," as the consort of Ohio senator Warren G. Harding is affectionately known, visits the Washington salon of the astrologist Madame Marcia to read her husband's horoscope. The visit has been arranged by Harding's henchman, Harry Daugherty, who is pushing him for the Republican nomination in 1920. Daugherty believes that his candidate will be nominated and elected, and he expects that Madame Marcia, who is consulted by the greatest in the land, will predict this, and that her prediction will be a good way of preparing the Duchess for her future role. Only Harding's hour and date of birth have been supplied to the functioning sorceress, but since she has instant access to the Congressional Director, a glance could allow her to match the date to the man. Or has Daugherty fixed her in advance?

Madame Marcia duly foresees the presidency in the stars and rampant lion of the horoscope. But she also sees a darker fate. In answer to the question: "He'll die?" she replies:

> "We all do that. No. I see something far more terrible than mere death." Madame Marcia discarded her toothpick like an empress letting go her sceptre. "President Harding—of course I know exactly who he is—will be murdered."

We are now in the world of Gore Vidal. Many years ago, although an avid reader of his novels, I was uneasy in some parts of that world. I remember waxing a bit hot under the collar, reading **Burr,** at what I considered a travesty of the character of my hero, Thomas Jefferson. But since that time the bottom has fallen out of my old world. We have undergone Watergate and Irangate; we have seen a president resign from office under fire and a daydreaming movie star occupy the White House. If I hear the truth spoken by an elected official or his representative, I wonder if he has had no inducement to lie. I have had to face the nasty fact that the world is—and probably always was—a good deal closer to the one so brilliantly savaged by Vidal than any that I had fondly imagined.

And even now, as I pause in writing this piece to glance at the newspaper, I read that the second volume of Robert Caro's heavily documented life of LBJ will attempt to prove that that lauded Texas liberal was the greatest and most unabashed rigger of elections in our political history. We may yet live to see Vidal branded a sentimentalist!

Vidal has said that **Hollywood** is the last (though not the last chronologically) of a sequence of novels loosely called his History of the United States, starting with **Burr,** which deals with Aaron Burr's conspiracy jumping forward to **Lincoln** and the Civil War, pausing in **1876** to cover the scandal of the Hayes-Tilden election, then moving in **Em-** *pire* to the imperialism of Theodore Roosevelt, and ending in **Washington, DC,** with Joe McCarthy's reign of terror. **Hollywood** fills in the First World War and the Harding administration. But if the novels are all stars, at least in the brightness of their dialogue and character delineation, they do not form a true constellation. I doubt that they were really conceived as such before the writing of **Lincoln.** I find a true unit only in the trilogy of **Lincoln, Empire,** and **Hollywood,** which relate the grim, dramatic story of the forging, for a good deal worse than better, according to Vidal, of the American empire and its ultimate conversion into the celluloid of the moving picture, which is all he deems it to be worth.

In **Lincoln** he finds the only man in his epic to whom he is willing to concede true greatness, and his portrait of his man raises the novel a head above the others of the trilogy and may even make it a significant addition to the mountain of books on the emancipator, many of which, in Vidal's opinion, are packed with lies. His Lincoln is not so much concerned with freeing the slaves; he wants to save the union in order to turn it into a huge, world-dominating state, the "empire" that will be the subject of the next two novels. The book ends with John Hay musing on the question of whether the assassinated president might not have willed his own murder "as a form of atonement for the great and terrible thing that he had done by giving so bloody and absolute a rebirth to his nation."

Vidal admires the creator but not the creation. He is constantly fascinated with the subject of power. Money, oratory, muscle, wit, and sex (the latter when not used exclusively for brief physical pleasure) are devoted to the domination of one's fellow man. For what purpose? For the fun of the game. Vidal is something of an existentialist, suggesting as he does the absurdity of grand projects. Theodore Roosevelt in **Empire** exults in blood and guts and accomplishes nothing. The question is raised at the end of the novel if it is even he who has effected the things he has purported to effect. In a scene between the rough rider and the newspaper despot William Randolph Hearst, the latter suggests that the President has been his puppet.

> "True history," said Hearst, with a smile that was, for once, almost charming, "is the final fiction. I thought even you knew that." Then Hearst was gone, leaving the President alone in the Cabinet room, with its great table, leather armchairs, and the full-length painting of Abraham Lincoln, eyes fixed on some far distance beyond the viewer's range, a prospect unknown and unknowable to the mere observer, at sea in present time.

The two main characters, who weave the episodes of history into the narrative of **Hollywood,** Blaise Sanford and his half sister, Caroline Sanford Sanford, have settled an old family feud by agreeing to co-manage a Washington newspaper of wide circulation and great political importance. They have a genealogical connection with Charles Schermerhorn Schuyler, the narrator of **Burr** and **1876,** who dies at the end of the eponymous year, which is worthy of a Jacobean tragedian. Schuyler's daughter Emma, widow of the French Prince d'Agrigente, has plotted to marry the wealthy Colonel William Sanford after his wife has died giving birth to a child whose conception Emma knows will be fatal to her but which she has nonetheless wickedly encouraged. Mrs. Sanford duly dies giving birth to Blaise, and the next year Emma, now her successor, is justly punished by expiring at the birth of her own child, Caroline. The two babies are given a genetic head start to face the rigors of life in a Vidalian world.

Their creator has chosen the appropriate interpreters for his cool and unsentimental story. They are dedicated sophisticates, devoid of any prejudice and of any religious or even political bias, brilliant, charming, and quite as decent to others as others are to them, with wit, delightful manners, and a fixed determination to do anything they choose to do as well as it can be done. Above all, they aim to see the world as it is, no matter what conclusion that vision may entail. Caroline has been married to and divorced from a Sanford cousin, but her dismal, right-wing, red-baiting daughter and only child, whom she understandably dislikes, is the child of a former lover, US Senator Burden Day, another detached interpreter of the political scene. Sex in Vidalian fiction rarely gets out of hand. It is entirely physical, entirely for pleasure, and is indulged in with both sexes. Oddly enough, it is just the opposite of what it is in Proust, whom Vidal deeply admires, where it is identified with pain. Caroline's brother Blaise, who is married to an heiress, has a brief homosexual encounter in Paris with a *poilu* turned prostitute, an episode that might be deemed the trademark of a Vidal novel, like the fox hunt in Trollope or the appearance of Hitchcock as an extra in each of his films.

Caroline takes leave of the Sanford-owned newspaper to explore the new phenomenon of Hollywood in 1917, where she becomes not only the mistress of a director, Tim Farrell, but the leading lady of his films, under the name of Emma Traxler. That a middle-aged, world-famous newspaper woman should become a movie star without anyone recognizing her surely lacks verisimilitude, but in the dreamlike reality that Vidal so successfully evokes we are only too happy to accept it. Blaise remains, for the most part, in Washington, which allows the reader to follow two of the three themes of the novel: the involvement of America in war and the rise of Hollywood to world power, each through the eyes of a Sanford. The third theme, the why and wherefore of the election of Warren Gamaliel Harding, we follow through the mind of one of his crooked henchmen, Jesse Smith.

The Sanfords, of course, know everybody. Caroline fills us in on Hearst, Marion Davies, Elinor Glyn, Douglas Fairbanks, Mary Pickford, the murdered William Desmond Taylor, and hosts of others, while Blaise introduces us to everyone of note in the capital from President Wilson down. It is an entrancing gallery of portraits, as funny as it is acute.

Wilson is the best, "an odd combination of college professor unused to being contradicted in a world that he took to be his classroom and of Presbyterian pastor unable to question that divine truth which inspired him at all times." Eleanor Roosevelt, then wife of the assistant secretary of the Navy, is "the Lucrezia Borgia of Washington— none survived her table." The malice of her cousin Alice

Longworth, TR's daughter, has "the same sort of joyous generalized spontaneity as did her father's hypocrisy." As it was an article of faith that the American public could not fall in love with a screen star who was married in real life, Francis X. Bushman, the father of five, is "obliged to pretend to be a virtuous bachelor, living alone, waiting, wistfully, for Miss Right to leap from the darkened audience onto the bright screen to share with him the glamour of his life."

We see Wilson on board the SS *George Washington,* confiding to Blaise that he could have done well in vaudeville, and, to prove it, letting his face go slack and his body droop as he performs a kind of scarecrow dance across the deck singing: "I'm Dopey Dan, and I'm married to Midnight Mary." We see Charlie Chaplin and Douglas Fairbanks naked in a steam room discussing how they should have used some of their surplus earnings to buy the press and bury such Hollywood-damaging scandals as the Fatty Arbuckle affair. We see Mrs. Harding hurling furniture at her husband's mistress and Alice Longworth doing handsprings before her father's admirers.

Whether we believe it all or not, it is always in character, always more than possible. When a character suggests that a woman as plain as Eleanor Roosevelt would never have hired as her secretary as beautiful a woman as Lucy Mercer to be brought in constant contact with her handsome husband unless she had been attracted to her herself, one's first reaction may be one of shocked indignation, but then, when one pauses to consider it. . . . It is always that way with Vidal.

There are moments when a gathering of his characters takes on some of the features of a fancy dress party. One tries to identify each newcomer before he is introduced. Sometimes the characters are not. I think I spotted Rudolf Valentino in the young extra in a Hearst private movie who had "a square crude face" and eyebrows that grew together in a straight line "like those of an archaic Minoan athlete."

Through conversations with the capital's power wielders Blaise and Senator Day follow the slow enmeshing of a peace-loving president in the imbroglio of European war. "I do believe the Germans must be the stupidest people on earth," Wilson groans as the submarine sinkings mount. But he is helpless against the U-boat and Allied propaganda, as he will be helpless against the Republican Senate majority to save his league. Vidal sees our involvement in the war of empires as a mistake and one that cost us essential liberties in the Red-baiting era that followed, but he does not see how the mistake could have been avoided. America in his view, ever since Lincoln forged his new union, had been ineluctably committed to the course of empire. Empires are not good things; they ruthlessly exploit weaker tribes, but at least in Europe, with its aristocratic traditions, the process is carried out to its inevitable dissolution with a certain style. America, on the other hand, being a mix of peasant emigrations, is easily victimized by any sort of propaganda and doomed to make an imperial fool of itself.

Caroline, the author's primary spokesman, like her mentor Henry Adams (one of Vidal's finest portraits) believes in nothing but "the prevailing fact of force in human affairs." In Washington, where the game of force is played for its own sake and where morality is always relative to need, "one man's Gethsemane might be another's Coney Island." In Hollywood she finds things even worse.

> Now the Administration had invited Caroline herself to bully the movie business into creating ever more simplistic rationales of what she had come, privately, despite her French bias, to think of as the pointless war. Nevertheless, she was astonished that someone had actually gone to prison for making a film. Where was the much-worshipped Constitution in all of this? Or was it never more than a document to be used by the country's rulers when it suited them and otherwise ignored?

She finds a new source of national power in the movies and begins to wonder if Hollywood might not even be able to persuade a defeated country that its army had been victorious, at least abroad.

> A moving picture was, to begin with, a picture of something that had really happened. She had really clubbed a French actor with a wooden crucifix on a certain day and at a certain time and now there existed, presumably forever, a record of that stirring event. But Caroline Sanford was not the person millions of people had watched in that ruined French church. They had watched the fictitious Emma Traxler impersonate Madeleine Giroux, a Franco-American mother, as she picked up a crucifix that looked to be metal but was not and struck a French actor impersonating a German officer in a ruined French church that was actually a stage-set in Santa Monica. The audience knew, of course, that the story was made up as they knew that stage plays were imitations of life, but the fact that an entire story could so surround them as a moving picture did and so, literally, inhabit their dreams, both waking and sleeping, made for another reality parallel to the one they lived in. . . . Reality could now be entirely invented and history revised. Suddenly, she knew what God must have felt when he gazed upon chaos, with nothing but himself upon his mind.

She finds the war unpopular in California until the people succumb to every "anti-German, anti-Red, anti-negro demagogue," and she resolves, when peace comes, to use the new power of the film to offset some of the damage done. Whether she will enjoy success in her project is far from clear at the end of her tale.

The parts of the novel that deal with the handsome and amiable Warren Harding and the gang of crooks with whom he is too easygoing not to associate are highly amusing, but on a lower level. They are like the play put on by the mechanicals in *A Midsummer Night's Dream,* though considerably more ominous. Harding is shown as shrewd enough to see that if he is every delegation's second choice he will be nominated in a convention deadlocked over bigger men. I suppose the reason his story lacks the impact of the two other themes of the novel is that here Vidal has little to bring to our already settled

conviction of its sordidness. He adds a murder or so for zest, but it is not essential. We know those men would have been capable of anything. (Very incidentally, speaking of murder, Vidal's solution of the famous one of the Hollywood director William Desmond Taylor has just been rebutted, at least so far as this reviewer's jury is concerned, by Robert Giroux's forthcoming study of the subject, *A Deed of Death.*)

In **Hollywood,** as in many of Vidal's novels (**Lincoln** and **Julian** excepted), the parts are greater than the whole. But that is what he would say of the universe. In a senseless mosaic are not the beautiful details all the more precious? His highly polished prose style, in part the fruit of his classical training, is a constant delight. One might even go so far as to call him a modern La Rochefoucauld. I suppose it is a mistake to take sentences out of context to illustrate this, but I submit a few.

The Irish lover of a society girl "had entered her life like a sudden high wind at a Newport picnic, and everything was in a state of disorder."

Wilson, asked what was the worst thing about being president, replies: "All day long people tell you things that you already know, and you must act as if you were hearing their news for the first time."

And here is the end of the court of Henry Adams:

> In the twenty years that Caroline had known Adams, neither the beautiful room, with its small Adams-scale furniture nor its owner had much changed; only many of the occupants of the chairs were gone, either through death, like John and Clara Hay, joint builders of this double Romanesque palace in Lafayette Park, or through removal to Europe, like Lizzie Cameron, beloved by Adams, now in the high summer of her days, furiously courting young poets in the green spring of theirs.

(pp. 20-2)

Louis Auchincloss, "Babylon Revisted," in The New York Review of Books, Vol. XXXVII, No. 5, March 29, 1990, pp. 20-2.

FURTHER READING

Bibliography

Stanton, Robert J. *Gore Vidal: A Primary and Secondary Bibliography.* Boston: G. K. Hall, 1978, 226 p.
    Bibliography of works by and about Vidal.

Biography

LaHood, Marvin J. "Gore Vidal: A Grandfather's Legacy." *World Literature Today* 64, No. 3 (Summer 1990): 413-17.
    Discusses the influence of Vidal's maternal grandfather, Oklahoma senator Thomas P. Gore, on Vidal's education and development. LaHood also provides a brief overview of Vidal's American historical novels.

Criticism

Burgess, Anthony. "Honest Abe's Obsession." *The Times Literary Supplement,* No. 4252 (28 September 1984): 1082.
> Finds Vidal's literary reconstruction of the Civil War era in *Lincoln* factually accurate but artistically undistinguished. Burgess observes: "Vidal is in danger of making the wrong sort of reputation for himself—the popular recorder of American political history, and not the brilliant scabrous fantasist of *Myra Breckinridge* or the revivifier of the remote past as in *Julian* and *Creation.*"

Dick, Bernard F. *The Apostate Angel: A Critical Study of Gore Vidal.* New York: Random House, 1974, 203 p.
> Chronologically arranged examination identifying and discussing Vidal's most important works in several genres, including the novel, essay, television script, and drama.

Edwards, Owen Dudley. "On an Earlier President." *Encounter* LXIV, No. 1 (January 1985): 33-42.
> Commends the blend of historical fact with fictional narrative in *Lincoln.*

Ross, Mitchell S. "Gore Vidal." In his *Literary Politicians,* pp. 247-300. Garden City, N.Y.: Doubleday, 1978.
> Critical survey that emphasizes the political concerns expressed in Vidal's works.

White, Ray Lewis. *Gore Vidal.* New York: Twayne, 1968, 157 p.
> Critical overview including a chronology of Vidal's life and career as well as selected primary and secondary bibliographies.

Interviews

Clarke, Gerald, and Vidal, Gore. "Gore Vidal." *The Paris Review* 15, No. 59 (Fall 1974): 130-65.
> Discusses Vidal's literary career and the works and personalities of other twentieth-century writers.

Dreifus, Claudia, and Vidal, Gore. "Gore Vidal: The Writer as Citizen." *The Progressive* 50, No. 9 (September 1986): 36-9.
> Discussion of American social, cultural, and political life.

Wright, Colin, and Vidal, Gore. "Tug of War." *New Statesman and Society* 2, No. 74 (3 November 1989): 43-4.
> Focuses on *Hollywood* and Vidal's views on American politics.

Additional coverage of Vidal's life and career is contained in the following sources published by Gale Research: *Contemporary Authors,* Vol. 5-8, rev. ed.; *Contemporary Authors New Revision Series,* Vol. 13; *Contemporary Literary Criticism,* Vols. 2, 4, 6, 8, 10, 22, 33; *Dictionary of Literary Biography,* Vol. 6; and *Major 20th-Century Writers.*

☐ Contemporary Literary Criticism

Indexes

Literary Criticism Series
Cumulative Author Index
Cumulative Nationality Index
Title Index, Volume 72

This Index Includes References to Entries in These Gale Series

Children's Literature Review includes excerpts from reviews, criticism, and commentary on works of authors and illustrators who create books for children.

Classical and Medieval Literature Criticism offers excerpts of criticism on the works of world authors from classical antiquity through the fourteenth century.

Contemporary Authors series encompasses five related series. *Contemporary Authors* provides biographical and bibliographical information on more than 97,000 writers of fiction, nonfiction, poetry, journalism, drama, and film. *Contemporary Authors New Revision Series* provides completely updated information on active authors covered in previously published volumes of *CA*. *Contemporary Authors Permanent Series* consists of updated listings for deceased and inactive authors removed from the original volumes 9-36 when those volumes were revised. *Contemporary Authors Autobiography Series* presents specially commissioned autobiographies by leading contemporary writers. *Contemporary Authors Bibliographical Series* contains primary and secondary bibliographies as well as analytical bibliographical essays by authorities on major modern authors.

Contemporary Literary Criticism presents excerpts of criticism on the works of novelists, poets, dramatists, short story writers, scriptwriters, and other creative writers who are now living or who have died since 1960.

Dictionary of Literary Biography comprises three related series. *Dictionary of Literary Biography* furnishes illustrated overviews of authors' lives and works and places them in the larger perspective of literary history. *Dictionary of Literary Biography Documentary Series* illuminates the careers of major figures through a selection of literary documents, including letters, interviews, and photographs. *Dictionary of Literary Biography Yearbook* summarizes the past year's literary activity and includes updated and new entries on individual authors. A cumulative index to authors and articles is included in each new volume. *Concise Dictionary of*

American Literary Biography, a six-volume series, collects revised and updated sketches on major American authors that were originally presented in *Dictionary of Literary Biography.*

Drama Criticism provides excerpts of criticism on the works of playwrights of all nationalities and periods of literary history.

Literature Criticism from 1400 to 1800 compiles significant passages from the most noteworthy criticism on authors of the fifteenth through the eighteenth centuries.

Nineteenth-Century Literature Criticism offers significant passages from criticism on authors who died between 1800 and 1899.

Poetry Criticism presents excerpts of criticism on the works of poets from all eras, movements, and nationalities.

Short Story Criticism combines excerpts of criticism on short fiction by writers of all eras and nationalities.

Something about the Author series encompasses three related series. *Something about the Author* contains well-illustrated biographical sketches on authors and illustrators of juvenile and young adult literature from all eras. *Something about the Author Autobiography Series* presents specially commissioned autobiographies by prominent authors and illustrators of books for children and young adults. *Authors & Artists for Young Adults* provides high school and junior high school students with profiles of their favorite creative artists.

Twentieth-Century Literary Criticism contains critical excerpts by the most significant commentators on poets, novelists, short story writers, dramatists, and philosophers who died between 1900 and 1960.

Yesterday's Authors of Books for Children contains heavily illustrated entries on children's writers who died before 1961. Complete in two volumes.

Literary Criticism Series
Cumulative Author Index

This index lists all author entries in the Gale Literary Criticism Series and includes cross-references to other Gale sources. References in the index are identified as follows:

AAYA: *Authors & Artists for Young Adults,* Volumes 1-7
BLC: *Black Literature Criticism,* Volumes 1-3
CA: *Contemporary Authors* (original series), Volumes 1-136
CAAS: *Contemporary Authors Autobiography Series,* Volumes 1-15
CABS: *Contemporary Authors Bibliographical Series,* Volumes 1-3
CANR: *Contemporary Authors New Revision Series,* Volumes 1-35
CAP: *Contemporary Authors Permanent Series,* Volumes 1-2
CA-R: *Contemporary Authors* (first revision), Volumes 1-44
CDALB: *Concise Dictionary of American Literary Biography,* Volumes 1-6
CLC: *Contemporary Literary Criticism,* Volumes 1-72
CLR: *Children's Literature Review,* Volumes 1-25
CMLC: *Classical and Medieval Literature Criticism,* Volumes 1-9
DC: *Drama Criticism,* Volumes 1-2
DLB: *Dictionary of Literary Biography,* Volumes 1-114
DLB-DS: *Dictionary of Literary Biography Documentary Series,* Volumes 1-9
DLB-Y: *Dictionary of Literary Biography Yearbook,* Volumes 1980-1990
LC: *Literature Criticism from 1400 to 1800,* Volumes 1-19
NCLC: *Nineteenth-Century Literature Criticism,* Volumes 1-36
PC: *Poetry Criticism,* Volumes 1-4
SAAS: *Something about the Author Autobiography Series,* Volumes 1-14
SATA: *Something about the Author,* Volumes 1-68
SSC: *Short Story Criticism,* Volumes 1-10
TCLC: *Twentieth-Century Literary Criticism,* Volumes 1-45
WLC: *World Literature Criticism, 1500 to the Present,* Volumes 1-6
YABC: *Yesterday's Authors of Books for Children,* Volumes 1-2

A. E. 1867-1935 . . . . **TCLC 3, 10**
See also Russell, George William
See also DLB 19

Abbey, Edward 1927-1989 . . . . . . **CLC 36, 59**
See also CANR 2; CA 45-48;
obituary CA 128

Abbott, Lee K., Jr. 19??- . . . . **CLC 48**

Abe, Kobo 1924- . . . . **CLC 8, 22, 53**
See also CANR 24; CA 65-68

Abell, Kjeld 1901-1961. . . . . **CLC 15**
See also obituary CA 111

Abish, Walter 1931- . . . . **CLC 22**
See also CA 101

Abrahams, Peter (Henry) 1919- . . . . . **CLC 4**
See also CA 57-60

Abrams, M(eyer) H(oward) 1912-. . . **CLC 24**
See also CANR 13; CA 57-60; DLB 67

Abse, Dannie 1923-. . . . . **CLC 7, 29**
See also CAAS 1; CANR 4; CA 53-56;
DLB 27

Achebe, (Albert) Chinua(lumogu)
1930- . . . . **CLC 1, 3, 5, 7, 11, 26, 51**
See also BLC 1; CLR 20; WLC 1; CANR 6,
26; CA 1-4R; SATA 38, 40

Acker, Kathy 1948- . . . . **CLC 45**
See also CA 117, 122

Ackroyd, Peter 1949-. . . . . **CLC 34, 52**
See also CA 123, 127

Acorn, Milton 1923-. . . . . **CLC 15**
See also CA 103; DLB 53

Adamov, Arthur 1908-1970 . . . . . . **CLC 4, 25**
See also CAP 2; CA 17-18;
obituary CA 25-28R

Adams, Alice (Boyd) 1926- . . . **CLC 6, 13, 46**
See also CANR 26; CA 81-84; DLB-Y 86

Adams, Douglas (Noel) 1952- . . . **CLC 27, 60**
See also CA 106; DLB-Y 83

Adams, Francis 1862-1893. . . . . . . **NCLC 33**

Adams, Henry (Brooks)
1838-1918 . . . . **TCLC 4**
See also CA 104; DLB 12, 47

Adams, Richard (George)
1920- . . . . **CLC 4, 5, 18**
See also CLR 20; CANR 3; CA 49-52;
SATA 7

Adamson, Joy(-Friederike Victoria)
1910-1980 . . . . **CLC 17**
See also CANR 22; CA 69-72;
obituary CA 93-96; SATA 11;
obituary SATA 22

Adcock, (Kareen) Fleur 1934- . . . . . . **CLC 41**
See also CANR 11; CA 25-28R; DLB 40

Addams, Charles (Samuel)
1912-1988 . . . . **CLC 30**
See also CANR 12; CA 61-64;
obituary CA 126

Addison, Joseph 1672-1719 . . . . **LC 18**
See also DLB 101

Adler, C(arole) S(chwerdtfeger)
1932- . . . . **CLC 35**
See also CANR 19; CA 89-92; SATA 26

Adler, Renata 1938- . . . . **CLC 8, 31**
See also CANR 5, 22; CA 49-52

Ady, Endre 1877-1919 . . . . **TCLC 11**
See also CA 107

Afton, Effie 1825-1911
See Harper, Francis Ellen Watkins

Agee, James 1909-1955 .... TCLC 1, 19
See also CA 108; DLB 2, 26;
CDALB 1941-1968

Agnon, S(hmuel) Y(osef Halevi)
1888-1970 .... CLC 4, 8, 14
See also CAP 2; CA 17-18;
obituary CA 25-28R

Ai 1947- .... CLC 4, 14, 69
See also CAAS 13; CA 85-88

Aickman, Robert (Fordyce)
1914-1981 .... CLC 57
See also CANR 3; CA 7-8R

Aiken, Conrad (Potter)
1889-1973 ... CLC 1, 3, 5, 10, 52; SSC 9
See also CANR 4; CA 5-8R;
obituary CA 45-48; SATA 3, 30; DLB 9,
45, 102; CDALB 1929-1941

Aiken, Joan (Delano) 1924- .... CLC 35
See also CLR 1, 19; CANR 4; CA 9-12R;
SAAS 1; SATA 2, 30

Ainsworth, William Harrison
1805-1882 .... NCLC 13
See also SATA 24; DLB 21

Aitmatov, Chingiz 1928- .... CLC 71
See also CA 103; SATA 56

Ajar, Emile 1914-1980
See Gary, Romain

Akhmadulina, Bella (Akhatovna)
1937- .... CLC 53
See also CA 65-68

Akhmatova, Anna
1888-1966 .... CLC 11, 25, 64; PC 2
See also CAP 1; CA 19-20;
obituary CA 25-28R

Aksakov, Sergei Timofeyvich
1791-1859 .... NCLC 2

Aksenov, Vassily (Pavlovich) 1932-
See Aksyonov, Vasily (Pavlovich)

Aksyonov, Vasily (Pavlovich)
1932- .... CLC 22, 37
See also CANR 12; CA 53-56

Akutagawa Ryunosuke
1892-1927 .... TCLC 16
See also CA 117

Alain 1868-1951 .... TCLC 41
See also Chartier, Emile-Auguste

Alain-Fournier 1886-1914 .... TCLC 6
See also Fournier, Henri Alban
See also DLB 65

Al-Amin, Jamil Abdullah 1943-
See also BLC 1; CA 112, 125

Alarcon, Pedro Antonio de
1833-1891 .... NCLC 1

Alas (y Urena), Leopoldo (Enrique Garcia)
1852-1901 .... TCLC 29
See also CA 113

Albee, Edward (Franklin III)
1928- ... CLC 1, 2, 3, 5, 9, 11, 13, 25, 53
See also WLC 1; CANR 8; CA 5-8R;
DLB 7; CDALB 1941-1968

Alberti, Rafael 1902- .... CLC 7
See also CA 85-88

Alcott, Amos Bronson 1799-1888 .. NCLC 1
See also DLB 1

Alcott, Louisa May 1832-1888 .... NCLC 6
See also CLR 1; WLC 1; YABC 1; DLB 1,
42, 79; CDALB 1865-1917

Aldanov, Mark 1887-1957 .... TCLC 23
See also CA 118

Aldington, Richard 1892-1962 ...... CLC 49
See also CA 85-88; DLB 20, 36

Aldiss, Brian W(ilson)
1925- .... CLC 5, 14, 40
See also CAAS 2; CANR 5; CA 5-8R;
SATA 34; DLB 14

Alegria, Fernando 1918- .... CLC 57
See also CANR 5; CA 11-12R

Aleixandre, Vicente 1898-1984 ... CLC 9, 36
See also CANR 26; CA 85-88;
obituary CA 114

Alepoudelis, Odysseus 1911-
See Elytis, Odysseus

Aleshkovsky, Yuz 1929- .... CLC 44
See also CA 121, 128

Alexander, Lloyd (Chudley) 1924- .. CLC 35
See also CLR 1, 5; CANR 1; CA 1-4R;
SATA 3, 49; DLB 52

Alexander, Margaret Abigail Walker 1915-
See Walker, Margaret

Alfau, Felipe 1902- .... CLC 66

Alger, Horatio, Jr. 1832-1899 ..... NCLC 8
See also SATA 16; DLB 42

Algren, Nelson 1909-1981 .... CLC 4, 10, 33
See also CANR 20; CA 13-16R;
obituary CA 103; DLB 9; DLB-Y 81, 82;
CDALB 1941-1968

Ali, Ahmed 1910- .... CLC 69
See also CANR 15, 34; CA 25-28R

Alighieri, Dante 1265-1321 .... CMLC 3

Allard, Janet 1975- .... CLC 59

Allen, Edward 1948- .... CLC 59

Allen, Roland 1939-
See Ayckbourn, Alan

Allen, Sarah A. 1859-1930
See Hopkins, Pauline Elizabeth

Allen, Woody 1935- .... CLC 16, 52
See also CANR 27; CA 33-36R; DLB 44

Allende, Isabel 1942- .... CLC 39, 57
See also CA 125

Alleyne, Carla D. 1975?- .... CLC 65

Allingham, Margery (Louise)
1904-1966 .... CLC 19
See also CANR 4; CA 5-8R;
obituary CA 25-28R; DLB 77

Allingham, William 1824-1889 ... NCLC 25
See also DLB 35

Allston, Washington 1779-1843 .... NCLC 2
See also DLB 1

Almedingen, E. M. 1898-1971 ...... CLC 12
See also Almedingen, Martha Edith von
See also SATA 3

Almedingen, Martha Edith von 1898-1971
See Almedingen, E. M.
See also CANR 1; CA 1-4R

Alonso, Damaso 1898- .... CLC 14
See also CA 110; obituary CA 130

Alta 1942- .... CLC 19
See also CA 57-60

Alter, Robert B(ernard) 1935- ...... CLC 34
See also CANR 1; CA 49-52

Alther, Lisa 1944- .... CLC 7, 41
See also CANR 12; CA 65-68

Altman, Robert 1925- .... CLC 16
See also CA 73-76

Alvarez, A(lfred) 1929- .... CLC 5, 13
See also CANR 3; CA 1-4R; DLB 14, 40

Alvarez, Alejandro Rodriguez 1903-1965
See Casona, Alejandro
See also obituary CA 93-96

Amado, Jorge 1912- .... CLC 13, 40
See also CA 77-80

Ambler, Eric 1909- .... CLC 4, 6, 9
See also CANR 7; CA 9-12R; DLB 77

Amichai, Yehuda 1924- ...... CLC 9, 22, 57
See also CA 85-88

Amiel, Henri Frederic 1821-1881 .. NCLC 4

Amis, Kingsley (William)
1922- ...... CLC 1, 2, 3, 5, 8, 13, 40, 44
See also CANR 8; CA 9-12R; DLB 15, 27

Amis, Martin 1949- .... CLC 4, 9, 38, 62
See also CANR 8, 27; CA 65-68; DLB 14

Ammons, A(rchie) R(andolph)
1926- .... CLC 2, 3, 5, 8, 9, 25, 57
See also CANR 6; CA 9-12R; DLB 5

Anand, Mulk Raj 1905- .... CLC 23
See also CA 65-68

Anaya, Rudolfo A(lfonso) 1937- .... CLC 23
See also CAAS 4; CANR 1; CA 45-48;
DLB 82

Andersen, Hans Christian
1805-1875 .... NCLC 7; SSC 6
See also CLR 6; WLC 1; YABC 1

Anderson, Jessica (Margaret Queale)
19??- .... CLC 37
See also CANR 4; CA 9-12R

Anderson, Jon (Victor) 1940- ...... CLC 9
See also CANR 20; CA 25-28R

Anderson, Lindsay 1923- .... CLC 20
See also CA 125

Anderson, Maxwell 1888-1959 ..... TCLC 2
See also CA 105; DLB 7

Anderson, Poul (William) 1926- .... CLC 15
See also CAAS 2; CANR 2, 15; CA 1-4R;
SATA 39; DLB 8

Anderson, Robert (Woodruff)
1917- .... CLC 23
See also CA 21-24R; DLB 7

Anderson, Roberta Joan 1943-
See Mitchell, Joni

Anderson, Sherwood
1876-1941 ...... TCLC 1, 10, 24; SSC 1
See also WLC 1; CAAS 3; CA 104, 121;
DLB 4, 9; DLB-DS 1

Andrade, Carlos Drummond de
1902-1987 .... CLC 18
See also CA 123

Andrade, Mario de 1892-1945 ..... TCLC 43

Andrewes, Lancelot 1555-1626 ...... LC 5

Andrews, Cicily Fairfield 1892-1983
See West, Rebecca

Andreyev, Leonid (Nikolaevich)
1871-1919 .... TCLC 3
See also CA 104

Andrezel, Pierre 1885-1962
See Dinesen, Isak; Blixen, Karen
(Christentze Dinesen)

Andric, Ivo 1892-1975 .... CLC 8
See also CA 81-84; obituary CA 57-60

Angelique, Pierre 1897-1962
See Bataille, Georges

Angell, Roger 1920- .... CLC 26
See also CANR 13; CA 57-60

Angelou, Maya 1928-....... CLC 12, 35, 64
See also BLC 1; CANR 19; CA 65-68;
SATA 49; DLB 38

Annensky, Innokenty 1856-1909... TCLC 14
See also CA 110

Anouilh, Jean (Marie Lucien Pierre)
1910-1987 ...... CLC 1, 3, 8, 13, 40, 50
See also CA 17-20R; obituary CA 123

Anthony, Florence 1947-
See Ai

Anthony (Jacob), Piers 1934- ...... CLC 35
See also Jacob, Piers A(nthony)
D(illingham)
See also DLB 8

Antoninus, Brother 1912-
See Everson, William (Oliver)

Antonioni, Michelangelo 1912- ..... CLC 20
See also CA 73-76

Antschel, Paul 1920-1970....... CLC 10, 19
See also Celan, Paul
See also CA 85-88

Anwar, Chairil 1922-1949 .... TCLC 22
See also CA 121

Apollinaire, Guillaume
1880-1918 .... TCLC 3, 8
See also Kostrowitzki, Wilhelm Apollinaris
de

Appelfeld, Aharon 1932- .... CLC 23, 47
See also CA 112

Apple, Max (Isaac) 1941-........ CLC 9, 33
See also CANR 19; CA 81-84

Appleman, Philip (Dean) 1926-..... CLC 51
See also CANR 6; CA 13-16R

Apuleius, (Lucius) (Madaurensis)
125?-175?.................. CMLC 1

Aquin, Hubert 1929-1977......... CLC 15
See also CA 105; DLB 53

Aragon, Louis 1897-1982........ CLC 3, 22
See also CA 69-72; obituary CA 108;
DLB 72

Arany, Janos 1817-1882........ NCLC 34

Arbuthnot, John 1667-1735 .... LC 1

Archer, Jeffrey (Howard) 1940- .... CLC 28
See also CANR 22; CA 77-80

Archer, Jules 1915- .... CLC 12
See also CANR 6; CA 9-12R; SAAS 5;
SATA 4

Arden, John 1930- .... CLC 6, 13, 15
See also CAAS 4; CA 13-16R; DLB 13

Arenas, Reinaldo 1943- .... CLC 41
See also CA 124, 128

Arendt, Hannah 1906-1975 .... CLC 66
See also CA 19-20R; obituary CA 61-64

Aretino, Pietro 1492-1556 .... LC 12

Arguedas, Jose Maria
1911-1969 .... CLC 10, 18
See also CA 89-92

Argueta, Manlio 1936-............ CLC 31

Ariosto, Ludovico 1474-1533........ LC 6

Aristophanes
c. 450 B. C.-c. 385 B. C. ..... CMLC 4;
          DC 2

Arlt, Roberto 1900-1942 .... TCLC 29
See also CA 123

Armah, Ayi Kwei 1939-.......... CLC 5, 33
See also BLC 1; CANR 21; CA 61-64

Armatrading, Joan 1950-.......... CLC 17
See also CA 114

Arnim, Achim von (Ludwig Joachim von
Arnim) 1781-1831 .... NCLC 5
See also DLB 90

Arnold, Matthew 1822-1888 ... NCLC 6, 29
See also WLC 1; DLB 32, 57

Arnold, Thomas 1795-1842 ...... NCLC 18
See also DLB 55

Arnow, Harriette (Louisa Simpson)
1908-1986 .... CLC 2, 7, 18
See also CANR 14; CA 9-12R;
obituary CA 118; SATA 42, 47; DLB 6

Arp, Jean 1887-1966............... CLC 5
See also CA 81-84; obituary CA 25-28R

Arquette, Lois S(teinmetz) 1934-
See Duncan (Steinmetz Arquette), Lois
See also SATA 1

Arrabal, Fernando 1932- ... CLC 2, 9, 18, 58
See also CANR 15; CA 9-12R

Arrick, Fran 19??- .... CLC 30

Artaud, Antonin 1896-1948 ..... TCLC 3, 36
See also CA 104

Arthur, Ruth M(abel) 1905-1979.... CLC 12
See also CANR 4; CA 9-12R;
obituary CA 85-88; SATA 7;
obituary SATA 26

Artsybashev, Mikhail Petrarch
1878-1927 .... TCLC 31

Arundel, Honor (Morfydd)
1919-1973 .... CLC 17
See also CAP 2; CA 21-22;
obituary CA 41-44R; SATA 4;
obituary SATA 24

Asch, Sholem 1880-1957 .... TCLC 3
See also CA 105

Ashbery, John (Lawrence)
1927- ... CLC 2, 3, 4, 6, 9, 13, 15, 25, 41
See also CANR 9; CA 5-8R; DLB 5;
DLB-Y 81

Ashton-Warner, Sylvia (Constance)
1908-1984 .... CLC 19
See also CA 69-72; obituary CA 112

Asimov, Isaac 1920-.... CLC 1, 3, 9, 19, 26
See also CLR 12; CANR 2, 19; CA 1-4R;
SATA 1, 26; DLB 8

Astley, Thea (Beatrice May)
1925- .... CLC 41
See also CANR 11; CA 65-68

Astley, William 1855-1911
See Warung, Price

Aston, James 1906-1964
See White, T(erence) H(anbury)

Asturias, Miguel Angel
1899-1974 .... CLC 3, 8, 13
See also CAP 2; CA 25-28;
obituary CA 49-52

Atheling, William, Jr. 1921-1975
See Blish, James (Benjamin)

Atherton, Gertrude (Franklin Horn)
1857-1948 .... TCLC 2
See also CA 104; DLB 9, 78

Attaway, William 1911?-1986
See also BLC 1; DLB 76

Atwood, Margaret (Eleanor)
1939- .... CLC 2, 3, 4, 8, 13, 15, 25, 44;
          SSC 2
See also WLC 1; CANR 3, 24; CA 49-52;
SATA 50; DLB 53

Aubin, Penelope 1685-1731? .... LC 9
See also DLB 39

Auchincloss, Louis (Stanton)
1917- .... CLC 4, 6, 9, 18, 45
See also CANR 6; CA 1-4R; DLB 2;
DLB-Y 80

Auden, W(ystan) H(ugh)
1907-1973 ..... CLC 1, 2, 3, 4, 6, 9, 11,
        14, 43; PC 1
See also WLC 1; CANR 5; CA 9-12R;
obituary CA 45-48; DLB 10, 20

Audiberti, Jacques 1899-1965 ...... CLC 38
See also obituary CA 25-28R

Auel, Jean M(arie) 1936-.......... CLC 31
See also CANR 21; CA 103

Auerbach, Erich 1892-1957 .... TCLC 43
See also CA 118

Augier, Emile 1820-1889 .... NCLC 31

Augustine, St. 354-430.......... CMLC 6

Austen, Jane
1775-1817 .... NCLC 1, 13, 19, 33
See also WLC 1

Auster, Paul 1947- .... CLC 47
See also CANR 23; CA 69-72

Austin, Mary (Hunter)
1868-1934 .... TCLC 25
See also CA 109; DLB 9

Averroes 1126-1198 .... CMLC 7

Avison, Margaret 1918-.......... CLC 2, 4
See also CA 17-20R; DLB 53

Ayckbourn, Alan 1939- .... CLC 5, 8, 18, 33
See also CA 21-24R; DLB 13

Aydy, Catherine 1937-
See Tennant, Emma

Ayme, Marcel (Andre) 1902-1967... CLC 11
See also CA 89-92; DLB 72

Ayrton, Michael 1921-1975 . . . . CLC 7
  See also CANR 9, 21; CA 5-8R;
    obituary CA 61-64

Azorin 1874-1967 . . . . CLC 11
  See also Martinez Ruiz, Jose

Azuela, Mariano 1873-1952 . . . . TCLC 3
  See also CA 104

"Bab" 1836-1911
  See Gilbert, (Sir) W(illiam) S(chwenck)

Babel, Isaak (Emmanuilovich)
  1894-1941 . . . . TCLC 2, 13
  See also CA 104

Babits, Mihaly 1883-1941 . . . . TCLC 14
  See also CA 114

Babur 1483-1530 . . . . LC 18

Bacchelli, Riccardo 1891-1985 . . . . . CLC 19
  See also CA 29-32R; obituary CA 117

Bach, Richard (David) 1936- . . . . CLC 14
  See also CANR 18; CA 9-12R; SATA 13

Bachman, Richard 1947-
  See King, Stephen (Edwin)

Bachmann, Ingeborg 1926-1973 . . . . . CLC 69
  See also CA 93-96; obituary CA 45-48

Bacon, Sir Francis 1561-1626 . . . . LC 18

Bacovia, George 1881-1957 . . . . . . TCLC 24

Bagehot, Walter 1826-1877 . . . . . . NCLC 10
  See also DLB 55

Bagnold, Enid 1889-1981 . . . . CLC 25
  See also CANR 5; CA 5-8R;
    obituary CA 103; SATA 1, 25; DLB 13

Bagryana, Elisaveta 1893- . . . . CLC 10

Bailey, Paul 1937- . . . . CLC 45
  See also CANR 16; CA 21-24R; DLB 14

Baillie, Joanna 1762-1851 . . . . NCLC 2

Bainbridge, Beryl
  1933- . . . . CLC 4, 5, 8, 10, 14, 18, 22, 62
  See also CANR 24; CA 21-24R; DLB 14

Baker, Elliott 1922- . . . . CLC 8, 61
  See also CANR 2; CA 45-48

Baker, Nicholson 1957- . . . . CLC 61

Baker, Russell (Wayne) 1925- . . . . . . CLC 31
  See also CANR 11; CA 57-60

Bakshi, Ralph 1938- . . . . CLC 26
  See also CA 112

Bakunin, Mikhail (Alexandrovich)
  1814-1876 . . . . NCLC 25

Baldwin, James (Arthur)
  1924-1987 . . . . . CLC 1, 2, 3, 4, 5, 8, 13,
                15, 17, 42, 50, 67; DC 1; SSC 10
  See also BLC 1; WLC 1; CANR 3,24;
    CA 1-4R; obituary CA 124; CABS 1;
    SATA 9, 54; DLB 2, 7, 33; DLB-Y 87;
    CDALB 1941-1968; AAYA 4

Ballard, J(ames) G(raham)
  1930- . . . . CLC 3, 6, 14, 36; SSC 1
  See also CANR 15; CA 5-8R; DLB 14

Balmont, Konstantin Dmitriyevich
  1867-1943 . . . . TCLC 11
  See also CA 109

Balzac, Honore de
  1799-1850 . . . . NCLC 5, 35; SSC 5
  See also WLC 1

Bambara, Toni Cade 1939- . . . . CLC 19
  See also BLC 1; CANR 24; CA 29-32R;
    DLB 38; AAYA 5

Bandanes, Jerome 1937- . . . . CLC 59

Banim, John 1798-1842 . . . . NCLC 13

Banim, Michael 1796-1874 . . . . . NCLC 13

Banks, Iain 1954- . . . . CLC 34
  See also CA 123

Banks, Lynne Reid 1929- . . . . CLC 23
  See also Reid Banks, Lynne

Banks, Russell 1940- . . . . CLC 37, 72
  See also CANR 19; CA 65-68

Banville, John 1945- . . . . CLC 46
  See also CA 117, 128; DLB 14

Banville, Theodore (Faullain) de
  1832-1891 . . . . NCLC 9

Baraka, Imamu Amiri
  1934- . . . CLC 1, 2, 3, 5, 10, 14, 33; PC 4
  See also Jones, (Everett) LeRoi
  See also BLC 1; CANR 27; CA 21-24R;
    CABS 3; DLB 5, 7, 16, 38; DLB-DS 8;
    CDALB 1941-1968

Barbellion, W. N. P. 1889-1919 . . . TCLC 24

Barbera, Jack 1945- . . . . CLC 44
  See also CA 110

Barbey d'Aurevilly, Jules Amedee
  1808-1889 . . . . NCLC 1

Barbusse, Henri 1873-1935 . . . . TCLC 5
  See also CA 105; DLB 65

Barea, Arturo 1897-1957 . . . . TCLC 14
  See also CA 111

Barfoot, Joan 1946- . . . . CLC 18
  See also CA 105

Baring, Maurice 1874-1945 . . . . TCLC 8
  See also CA 105; DLB 34

Barker, Clive 1952- . . . . CLC 52
  See also CA 121

Barker, George (Granville)
  1913- . . . . CLC 8, 48
  See also CANR 7; CA 9-12R; DLB 20

Barker, Howard 1946- . . . . CLC 37
  See also CA 102; DLB 13

Barker, Pat 1943- . . . . CLC 32
  See also CA 117, 122

Barlow, Joel 1754-1812 . . . . NCLC 23
  See also DLB 37

Barnard, Mary (Ethel) 1909- . . . . CLC 48
  See also CAP 2; CA 21-22

Barnes, Djuna (Chappell)
  1892-1982 . . . CLC 3, 4, 8, 11, 29; SSC 3
  See also CANR 16; CA 9-12R;
    obituary CA 107; DLB 4, 9, 45

Barnes, Julian 1946- . . . . CLC 42
  See also CANR 19; CA 102

Barnes, Peter 1931- . . . . CLC 5, 56
  See also CA 65-68; DLB 13

Baroja (y Nessi), Pio 1872-1956 . . . . TCLC 8
  See also CA 104

Barondess, Sue K(aufman) 1926-1977
  See Kaufman, Sue
  See also CANR 1; CA 1-4R;
    obituary CA 69-72

Barrett, (Roger) Syd 1946-
  See Pink Floyd

Barrett, William (Christopher)
  1913- . . . . CLC 27
  See also CANR 11; CA 13-16R

Barrie, (Sir) J(ames) M(atthew)
  1860-1937 . . . . TCLC 2
  See also CLR 16; YABC 1; CA 104;
    DLB 10

Barrol, Grady 1953-
  See Bograd, Larry

Barry, Philip (James Quinn)
  1896-1949 . . . . TCLC 11
  See also CA 109; DLB 7

Barth, John (Simmons)
  1930- . . . . . . CLC 1, 2, 3, 5, 7, 9, 10, 14,
                           27, 51; SSC 10
  See also CANR 5, 23; CA 1-4R; CABS 1;
    DLB 2

Barthelme, Donald
  1931-1989 . . . . . CLC 1, 2, 3, 5, 6, 8, 13,
                          23, 46, 59; SSC 2
  See also CANR 20; CA 21-24R, 129;
    SATA 7; DLB 2; DLB-Y 80

Barthelme, Frederick 1943- . . . . CLC 36
  See also CA 114, 122; DLB-Y 85

Barthes, Roland 1915-1980 . . . . CLC 24
  See also obituary CA 97-100

Barzun, Jacques (Martin) 1907- . . . . CLC 51
  See also CANR 22; CA 61-64

Bashevis, Isaac 1904-1991
  See Singer, Isaac Bashevis

Bashkirtseff, Marie 1859-1884 . . . NCLC 27

Basho, Matsuo 1644-1694 . . . . PC 3

Bass, Kingsley B. 1935-

Bassani, Giorgio 1916- . . . . CLC 9
  See also CA 65-68

Bataille, Georges 1897-1962 . . . . CLC 29
  See also CA 101; obituary CA 89-92

Bates, H(erbert) E(rnest)
  1905-1974 . . . . CLC 46; SSC 10
  See also CANR 34; CA 93-96;
    obituary CA 45-48

Baudelaire, Charles
  1821-1867 . . . . NCLC 6, 29; PC 1
  See also WLC 1

Baudrillard, Jean 1929- . . . . CLC 60

Baum, L(yman) Frank 1856-1919 . . . TCLC 7
  See also CLR 15; CA 108; SATA 18;
    DLB 22

Baumbach, Jonathan 1933- . . . . . . CLC 6, 23
  See also CAAS 5; CANR 12; CA 13-16R;
    DLB-Y 80

Bausch, Richard (Carl) 1945- . . . . . . CLC 51
  See also CA 101

Baxter, Charles 1947- . . . . CLC 45
  See also CA 57-60

Baxter, James K(eir) 1926-1972 . . . . CLC 14
  See also CA 77-80

Bayer, Sylvia 1909-1981
  See Glassco, John

Beagle, Peter S(oyer) 1939- . . . . CLC 7
  See also CANR 4; CA 9-12R; DLB-Y 80

Beard, Charles A(ustin)
1874-1948 .... TCLC **15**
See also CA 115; SATA 18; DLB 17

Beardsley, Aubrey 1872-1898 ..... NCLC **6**

Beattie, Ann 1947- ... CLC **8, 13, 18, 40, 63**
See also CA 81-84; DLB-Y 82

Beattie, James 1735-1803 .... NCLC **25**

Beauvoir, Simone (Lucie Ernestine Marie Bertrand) de
1908-1986 ... CLC **1, 2, 4, 8, 14, 31, 44, 50, 71**
See also WLC 1; CANR 28; CA 9-12R;
obituary CA 118; DLB 72; DLB-Y 86

Becker, Jurek 1937- .... CLC **7, 19**
See also CA 85-88; DLB 75

Becker, Walter 1950- .... CLC **26**

Beckett, Samuel (Barclay)
1906-1989 ..... CLC **1, 2, 3, 4, 6, 9, 10, 11, 14, 18, 29, 57, 59**
See also WLC 1; CA 5-8R; DLB 13, 15

Beckford, William 1760-1844 .... NCLC **16**
See also DLB 39

Beckham, Barry 1944-
See also BLC 1; CANR 26; CA 29-32R;
DLB 33

Beckman, Gunnel 1910- .... CLC **26**
See also CANR 15; CA 33-36R; SATA 6

Becque, Henri 1837-1899 .... NCLC **3**

Beddoes, Thomas Lovell
1803-1849 .... NCLC **3**

Beecher, Catharine Esther
1800-1878 .... NCLC **30**
See also DLB 1

Beecher, John 1904-1980 .... CLC **6**
See also CANR 8; CA 5-8R;
obituary CA 105

Beer, Johann 1655-1700 .... LC **5**

Beer, Patricia 1919?- .... CLC **58**
See also CANR 13; CA 61-64; DLB 40

Beerbohm, (Sir Henry) Max(imilian)
1872-1956 .... TCLC **1, 24**
See also CA 104; DLB 34

Begiebing, Robert J. 1946- .... CLC **70**
See also CA 122

Behan, Brendan
1923-1964 .... CLC **1, 8, 11, 15**
See also CA 73-76; DLB 13

Behn, Aphra 1640?-1689 .... LC **1**
See also WLC 1; DLB 39, 80

Behrman, S(amuel) N(athaniel)
1893-1973 .... CLC **40**
See also CAP 1; CA 15-16;
obituary CA 45-48; DLB 7, 44

Beiswanger, George Edwin 1931-
See Starbuck, George (Edwin)

Belasco, David 1853-1931 .... TCLC **3**
See also CA 104; DLB 7

Belcheva, Elisaveta 1893-
See Bagryana, Elisaveta

Belinski, Vissarion Grigoryevich
1811-1848 .... NCLC **5**

Belitt, Ben 1911- .... CLC **22**
See also CAAS 4; CANR 7; CA 13-16R;
DLB 5

Bell, Acton 1820-1849
See Bronte, Anne

Bell, Currer 1816-1855
See Bronte, Charlotte

Bell, James Madison 1826-1902 ... TCLC **43**
See also BLC 1; CA 122, 124; DLB 50

Bell, Madison Smartt 1957-........ CLC **41**
See also CA 111

Bell, Marvin (Hartley) 1937-..... CLC **8, 31**
See also CA 21-24R; DLB 5

Bellamy, Edward 1850-1898 ...... NCLC **4**
See also DLB 12

Belloc, (Joseph) Hilaire (Pierre Sebastien Rene Swanton)
1870-1953 .... TCLC **7, 18**
See also YABC 1; CA 106; DLB 19

Bellow, Saul
1915- ..... CLC **1, 2, 3, 6, 8, 10, 13, 15, 25, 33, 34, 63**
See also WLC 1; CA 5-8R; CABS 1;
DLB 2, 28; DLB-Y 82; DLB-DS 3;
CDALB 1941-1968

Belser, Reimond Karel Maria de 1929-
See Ruyslinck, Ward

Bely, Andrey 1880-1934........... TCLC **7**
See also CA 104

Benary-Isbert, Margot 1889-1979 ... CLC **12**
See also CLR 12; CANR 4; CA 5-8R;
obituary CA 89-92; SATA 2;
obituary SATA 21

Benavente (y Martinez), Jacinto
1866-1954 .... TCLC **3**
See also CA 106

Benchley, Peter (Bradford)
1940- .... CLC **4, 8**
See also CANR 12; CA 17-20R; SATA 3

Benchley, Robert 1889-1945 .... TCLC **1**
See also CA 105; DLB 11

Benedikt, Michael 1935- .... CLC **4, 14**
See also CANR 7; CA 13-16R; DLB 5

Benet, Juan 1927-................ CLC **28**

Benet, Stephen Vincent
1898-1943 .... TCLC **7; SSC 10**
See also YABC 1; CA 104; DLB 4, 48

Benet, William Rose 1886-1950 ... TCLC **28**
See also CA 118; DLB 45

Benford, Gregory (Albert) 1941-.... CLC **52**
See also CANR 12, 24; CA 69-72;
DLB-Y 82

Benjamin, Walter 1892-1940 ...... TCLC **39**

Benn, Gottfried 1886-1956........ TCLC **3**
See also CA 106; DLB 56

Bennett, Alan 1934- .... CLC **45**
See also CA 103

Bennett, (Enoch) Arnold
1867-1931 .... TCLC **5, 20**
See also CA 106; DLB 10, 34

Bennett, George Harold 1930-
See Bennett, Hal
See also CA 97-100

Bennett, Hal 1930-................ CLC **5**
See also Bennett, George Harold
See also DLB 33

Bennett, Jay 1912-................ CLC **35**
See also CANR 11; CA 69-72; SAAS 4;
SATA 27, 41

Bennett, Louise (Simone) 1919-..... CLC **28**
See also Bennett-Coverly, Louise Simone
See also BLC 1

Bennett-Coverly, Louise Simone 1919-
See Bennett, Louise (Simone)
See also CA 97-100

Benson, E(dward) F(rederic)
1867-1940 .... TCLC **27**
See also CA 114

Benson, Jackson J. 1930-.......... CLC **34**
See also CA 25-28R

Benson, Sally 1900-1972 .... CLC **17**
See also CAP 1; CA 19-20;
obituary CA 37-40R; SATA 1, 35;
obituary SATA 27

Benson, Stella 1892-1933........ TCLC **17**
See also CA 117; DLB 36

Bentley, E(dmund) C(lerihew)
1875-1956 .... TCLC **12**
See also CA 108; DLB 70

Bentley, Eric (Russell) 1916-...... CLC **24**
See also CANR 6; CA 5-8R

Beranger, Pierre Jean de
1780-1857 .... NCLC **34**

Berger, John (Peter) 1926- ...... CLC **2, 19**
See also CA 81-84; DLB 14

Berger, Melvin (H.) 1927-......... CLC **12**
See also CANR 4; CA 5-8R; SAAS 2;
SATA 5

Berger, Thomas (Louis)
1924- .... CLC **3, 5, 8, 11, 18, 38**
See also CANR 5; CA 1-4R; DLB 2;
DLB-Y 80

Bergman, (Ernst) Ingmar
1918- .... CLC **16, 72**
See also CANR 33; CA 81-84

Bergson, Henri 1859-1941 .... TCLC **32**

Bergstein, Eleanor 1938- .... CLC **4**
See also CANR 5; CA 53-56

Berkoff, Steven 1937-............. CLC **56**
See also CA 104

Bermant, Chaim 1929- .... CLC **40**
See also CANR 6; CA 57-60

Bernanos, (Paul Louis) Georges
1888-1948 .... TCLC **3**
See also CA 104; DLB 72

Bernard, April 19??-............. CLC **59**

Bernhard, Thomas
1931-1989 .... CLC **3, 32, 61**
See also CA 85-88,; obituary CA 127;
DLB 85

Berriault, Gina 1926-............. CLC **54**
See also CA 116

Berrigan, Daniel J. 1921-.......... CLC **4**
See also CAAS 1; CANR 11; CA 33-36R;
DLB 5

Berrigan, Edmund Joseph Michael, Jr.
1934-1983
See Berrigan, Ted
See also CANR 14; CA 61-64;
obituary CA 110

Berrigan, Ted 1934-1983 . . . . **CLC 37**
See also Berrigan, Edmund Joseph Michael, Jr.
See also DLB 5

Berry, Chuck 1926- . . . . **CLC 17**

Berry, Wendell (Erdman)
1934- . . . . **CLC 4, 6, 8, 27, 46**
See also CA 73-76; DLB 5, 6

Berryman, John
1914-1972 . . . . . **CLC 1, 2, 3, 4, 6, 8, 10, 13, 25, 62**
See also CAP 1; CA 15-16;
obituary CA 33-36R; CABS 2; DLB 48;
CDALB 1941-1968

Bertolucci, Bernardo 1940- . . . . **CLC 16**
See also CA 106

Bertrand, Aloysius 1807-1841 . . . . **NCLC 31**

Bertran de Born c. 1140-1215 . . . . . **CMLC 5**

Besant, Annie (Wood) 1847-1933 . . . **TCLC 9**
See also CA 105

Bessie, Alvah 1904-1985. . . . . **CLC 23**
See also CANR 2; CA 5-8R;
obituary CA 116; DLB 26

Beti, Mongo 1932- . . . . **CLC 27**
See also Beyidi, Alexandre
See also BLC 1

Betjeman, (Sir) John
1906-1984 . . . . **CLC 2, 6, 10, 34, 43**
See also CA 9-12R; obituary CA 112;
DLB 20; DLB-Y 84

Betti, Ugo 1892-1953 . . . . **TCLC 5**
See also CA 104

Betts, Doris (Waugh) 1932- . . . . **CLC 3, 6, 28**
See also CANR 9; CA 13-16R; DLB-Y 82

Bialik, Chaim Nachman
1873-1934 . . . . **TCLC 25**

Bidart, Frank 19??- . . . . **CLC 33**

Bienek, Horst 1930- . . . . **CLC 7, 11**
See also CA 73-76; DLB 75

Bierce, Ambrose (Gwinett)
1842-1914?. . . . . . . **TCLC 1, 7, 44; SSC 9**
See also WLC 1; CA 104; DLB 11, 12, 23,
71, 74; CDALB 1865-1917

Billington, Rachel 1942- . . . . **CLC 43**
See also CA 33-36R

Binyon, T(imothy) J(ohn) 1936- . . . . **CLC 34**
See also CA 111

Bioy Casares, Adolfo 1914- . . . . **CLC 4, 8, 13**
See also CANR 19; CA 29-32R

Birch, Allison 1974?- . . . . **CLC 65**

Bird, Robert Montgomery
1806-1854 . . . . **NCLC 1**

Birdwell, Cleo 1936-
See DeLillo, Don

Birney (Alfred) Earle
1904- . . . . **CLC 1, 4, 6, 11**
See also CANR 5, 20; CA 1-4R

Bishop, Elizabeth
1911-1979 . . . . . **CLC 1, 4, 9, 13, 15, 32; PC 3**
See also CANR 26; CA 7-8R;
obituary CA 89-92; CABS 2;
obituary SATA 24; DLB 5

Bishop, John 1935- . . . . **CLC 10**
See also CA 105

Bissett, Bill 1939- . . . . **CLC 18**
See also CANR 15; CA 69-72; DLB 53

Bitov, Andrei (Georgievich) 1937- . . . **CLC 57**

Biyidi, Alexandre 1932-
See Beti, Mongo
See also CA 114, 124

Bjornson, Bjornstjerne (Martinius)
1832-1910 . . . . **TCLC 7, 37**
See also CA 104

Blackburn, Paul 1926-1971 . . . . . **CLC 9, 43**
See also CA 81-84; obituary CA 33-36R;
DLB 16; DLB-Y 81

Black Elk 1863-1950 . . . . **TCLC 33**

Blackmore, R(ichard) D(oddridge)
1825-1900 . . . . **TCLC 27**
See also CA 120; DLB 18

Blackmur, R(ichard) P(almer)
1904-1965 . . . . **CLC 2, 24**
See also CAP 1; CA 11-12;
obituary CA 25-28R; DLB 63

Blackwood, Algernon (Henry)
1869-1951 . . . . **TCLC 5**
See also CA 105

Blackwood, Caroline 1931- . . . . **CLC 6, 9**
See also CA 85-88; DLB 14

Blair, Eric Arthur 1903-1950
See Orwell, George
See also CA 104; SATA 29

Blais, Marie-Claire
1939- . . . . **CLC 2, 4, 6, 13, 22**
See also CAAS 4; CA 21-24R; DLB 53

Blaise, Clark 1940- . . . . **CLC 29**
See also CAAS 3; CANR 5; CA 53-56R;
DLB 53

Blake, Nicholas 1904-1972
See Day Lewis, C(ecil)

Blake, William 1757-1827 . . . . **NCLC 13**
See also WLC 1; SATA 30

Blasco Ibanez, Vicente
1867-1928 . . . . **TCLC 12**
See also CA 110

Blatty, William Peter 1928- . . . . **CLC 2**
See also CANR 9; CA 5-8R

Blessing, Lee 1949- . . . . **CLC 54**

Blish, James (Benjamin)
1921-1975 . . . . **CLC 14**
See also CANR 3; CA 1-4R;
obituary CA 57-60; DLB 8

Blixen, Karen (Christentze Dinesen)
1885-1962
See Dinesen, Isak
See also CAP 2; CA 25-28; SATA 44

Bloch, Robert (Albert) 1917- . . . . **CLC 33**
See also CANR 5; CA 5-8R; SATA 12;
DLB 44

Blok, Aleksandr (Aleksandrovich)
1880-1921 . . . . **TCLC 5**
See also CA 104

Bloom, Harold 1930- . . . . **CLC 24, 65**
See also CA 13-16R; DLB 67

Blount, Roy (Alton), Jr. 1941- . . . . . **CLC 38**
See also CANR 10; CA 53-56

Bloy, Leon 1846-1917. . . . . **TCLC 22**
See also CA 121

Blume, Judy (Sussman Kitchens)
1938- . . . . **CLC 12, 30**
See also CLR 2, 15; CANR 13; CA 29-32R;
SATA 2, 31; DLB 52

Blunden, Edmund (Charles)
1896-1974 . . . . **CLC 2, 56**
See also CAP 2; CA 17-18;
obituary CA 45-48; DLB 20

Bly, Robert (Elwood)
1926- . . . . **CLC 1, 2, 5, 10, 15, 38**
See also CA 5-8R; DLB 5

Boccaccio, Giovanni 1313-1375
See also SSC 10

Bochco, Steven 1944?- . . . . **CLC 35**

Bodenheim, Maxwell 1892-1954 . . . **TCLC 44**
See also CA 110; DLB 9, 45

Bodker, Cecil 1927- . . . . **CLC 21**
See also CLR 23; CANR 13; CA 73-76;
SATA 14

Boell, Heinrich (Theodor) 1917-1985
See Boll, Heinrich
See also CANR 24; CA 21-24R;
obituary CA 116; DLB 69; DLB-Y 85

Bogan, Louise 1897-1970 . . . . . **CLC 4, 39, 46**
See also CA 73-76; obituary CA 25-28R;
DLB 45

Bogarde, Dirk 1921- . . . . **CLC 19**
See also Van Den Bogarde, Derek (Jules
Gaspard Ulric) Niven
See also DLB 14

Bogosian, Eric 1953- . . . . **CLC 45**

Bograd, Larry 1953- . . . . **CLC 35**
See also CA 93-96; SATA 33

Bohl de Faber, Cecilia 1796-1877
See Caballero, Fernan

Boiardo, Matteo Maria 1441-1494 . . . . **LC 6**

Boileau-Despreaux, Nicolas
1636-1711 . . . . **LC 3**

Boland, Eavan (Aisling) 1944- . . . **CLC 40, 67**
See also DLB 40

Boll, Heinrich (Theodor)
1917-1985 . . . **CLC 2, 3, 6, 9, 11, 15, 27, 39, 72**
See also Boell, Heinrich (Theodor)
See also WLC 1; DLB 69; DLB-Y 85

Bolt, Robert (Oxton) 1924- . . . . **CLC 14**
See also CA 17-20R; DLB 13

Bonaventura. . . . . **NCLC 35**
See also DLB 90

Bond, Edward 1934- . . . . **CLC 4, 6, 13, 23**
See also CA 25-28R; DLB 13

Bonham, Frank 1914- . . . . **CLC 12**
See also CANR 4; CA 9-12R; SAAS 3;
SATA 1, 49

Bonnefoy, Yves 1923- . . . . **CLC 9, 15, 58**
See also CA 85-88

Bontemps, Arna (Wendell)
1902-1973 . . . . **CLC 1, 18**
See also BLC 1; CLR 6; CANR 4;
CA 1-4R; obituary CA 41-44R; SATA 2,
44; obituary SATA 24; DLB 48, 51

Booth, Martin 1944-.............. CLC 13
See also CAAS 2; CA 93-96

Booth, Philip 1925-............... CLC 23
See also CANR 5; CA 5-8R; DLB-Y 82

Booth, Wayne C(layson) 1921-..... CLC 24
See also CAAS 5; CANR 3; CA 1-4R;
DLB 67

Borchert, Wolfgang 1921-1947 ..... TCLC 5
See also CA 104; DLB 69

Borges, Jorge Luis
1899-1986 ... CLC 1, 2, 3, 4, 6, 8, 9, 10,
13, 19, 44, 48; SSC 4
See also WLC 1; CANR 19; CA 21-24R;
DLB-Y 86

Borowski, Tadeusz 1922-1951 ...... TCLC 9
See also CA 106

Borrow, George (Henry)
1803-1881 .... NCLC 9
See also DLB 21, 55

Bosschere, Jean de 1878-1953..... TCLC 19
See also CA 115

Boswell, James 1740-1795........... LC 4
See also WLC 1

Boto, Eza 1932-
See Beti, Mongo

Bottoms, David 1949-............. CLC 53
See also CANR 22; CA 105; DLB-Y 83

Boucolon, Maryse 1937-
See Conde, Maryse
See also CA 110

Bourget, Paul (Charles Joseph)
1852-1935 .... TCLC 12
See also CA 107

Bourjaily, Vance (Nye) 1922- .... CLC 8, 62
See also CAAS 1; CANR 2; CA 1-4R;
DLB 2

Bourne, Randolph S(illiman)
1886-1918 .... TCLC 16
See also CA 117; DLB 63

Bova, Ben(jamin William) 1932-.... CLC 45
See also CLR 3; CANR 11; CA 5-8R;
SATA 6; DLB-Y 81

Bowen, Elizabeth (Dorothea Cole)
1899-1973 ..... CLC 1, 3, 6, 11, 15, 22;
SSC 3
See also CAP 2; CA 17-18;
obituary CA 41-44R; DLB 15

Bowering, George 1935-........ CLC 15, 47
See also CANR 10; CA 21-24R; DLB 53

Bowering, Marilyn R(uthe) 1949-... CLC 32
See also CA 101

Bowers, Edgar 1924- .... CLC 9
See also CANR 24; CA 5-8R; DLB 5

Bowie, David 1947- .... CLC 17
See also Jones, David Robert

Bowles, Jane (Sydney)
1917-1973 .... CLC 3, 68
See also CAP 2; CA 19-20;
obituary CA 41-44R

Bowles, Paul (Frederick)
1910- .... CLC 1, 2, 19, 53; SSC 3
See also CAAS 1; CANR 1, 19; CA 1-4R;
DLB 5, 6

Box, Edgar 1925-
See Vidal, Gore

Boyd, William 1952-........ CLC 28, 53, 70
See also CA 114, 120

Boyle, Kay 1903- .. CLC 1, 5, 19, 58; SSC 5
See also CAAS 1; CA 13-16R; DLB 4, 9, 48

Boyle, Patrick 19??-.............. CLC 19

Boyle, Thomas Coraghessan
1948-..................... CLC 36, 55
See also CA 120; DLB-Y 86

Brackenridge, Hugh Henry
1748-1816 .... NCLC 7
See also DLB 11, 37

Bradbury, Edward P. 1939-
See Moorcock, Michael

Bradbury, Malcolm (Stanley)
1932-..................... CLC 32, 61
See also CANR 1; CA 1-4R; DLB 14

Bradbury, Ray(mond Douglas)
1920-........... CLC 1, 3, 10, 15, 42
See also WLC 1; CANR 2, 30; CA 1-4R;
SATA 11, 64; DLB 2, 8;
CDALB 1968-1988

Bradford, Gamaliel 1863-1932..... TCLC 36
See also DLB 17

Bradley, David (Henry), Jr. 1950-.. CLC 23
See also BLC 1; CANR 26; CA 104;
DLB 33

Bradley, John Ed 1959-........... CLC 55

Bradley, Katherine Harris 1846-1914
See Field, Michael

Bradley, Marion Zimmer 1930-..... CLC 30
See also CANR 7; CA 57-60; DLB 8

Bradstreet, Anne 1612-1672......... LC 4
See also DLB 24; CDALB 1640-1865

Bragg, Melvyn 1939-............. CLC 10
See also CANR 10; CA 57-60; DLB 14

Braine, John (Gerard)
1922-1986 .... CLC 1, 3, 41
See also CANR 1; CA 1-4R;
obituary CA 120; DLB 15; DLB-Y 86

Braithwaite, William Stanley 1878-1962
See also BLC 1; CA 125; DLB 50, 54

Brammer, Billy Lee 1930?-1978
See Brammer, William

Brammer, William 1930?-1978 ..... CLC 31
See also obituary CA 77-80

Brancati, Vitaliano 1907-1954..... TCLC 12
See also CA 109

Brancato, Robin F(idler) 1936-..... CLC 35
See also CANR 11; CA 69-72; SATA 23

Brand, Millen 1906-1980.......... CLC 7
See also CA 21-24R; obituary CA 97-100

Branden, Barbara 19??-........... CLC 44

Brandes, Georg (Morris Cohen)
1842-1927 .... TCLC 10
See also CA 105

Brandys, Kazimierz 1916-......... CLC 62

Branley, Franklyn M(ansfield)
1915-..................... CLC 21
See also CLR 13; CANR 14; CA 33-36R;
SATA 4

Brathwaite, Edward 1930-......... CLC 11
See also CANR 11; CA 25-28R; DLB 53

Brautigan, Richard (Gary)
1935-1984 .... CLC 1, 3, 5, 9, 12, 34, 42
See also CA 53-56; obituary CA 113;
SATA 56; DLB 2, 5; DLB-Y 80, 84

Braverman, Kate 1950- .... CLC 67
See also CA 89-92

Brecht, (Eugen) Bertolt (Friedrich)
1898-1956 .... TCLC 1, 6, 13, 35
See also WLC 1; CA 133;
brief entry CA 104; DLB 56

Bremer, Fredrika 1801-1865 ..... NCLC 11

Brennan, Christopher John
1870-1932 .... TCLC 17
See also CA 117

Brennan, Maeve 1917-............. CLC 5
See also CA 81-84

Brentano, Clemens (Maria)
1778-1842 .... NCLC 1
See also DLB 90

Brenton, Howard 1942-........... CLC 31
See also CA 69-72; DLB 13

Breslin, James 1930-
See Breslin, Jimmy
See also CA 73-76

Breslin, Jimmy 1930-........... CLC 4, 43
See also Breslin, James

Bresson, Robert 1907-............ CLC 16
See also CA 110

Breton, Andre 1896-1966... CLC 2, 9, 15, 54
See also CAP 2; CA 19-20;
obituary CA 25-28R; DLB 65

Breytenbach, Breyten 1939-..... CLC 23, 37
See also CA 113, 129

Bridgers, Sue Ellen 1942- .... CLC 26
See also CANR 11; CA 65-68; SAAS 1;
SATA 22; DLB 52

Bridges, Robert 1844-1930........ TCLC 1
See also CA 104; DLB 19

Bridie, James 1888-1951 .... TCLC 3
See also Mavor, Osborne Henry
See also DLB 10

Brin, David 1950-................ CLC 34
See also CANR 24; CA 102

Brink, Andre (Philippus)
1935-.................... CLC 18, 36
See also CA 104

Brinsmead, H(esba) F(ay) 1922- .... CLC 21
See also CANR 10; CA 21-24R; SAAS 5;
SATA 18

Brittain, Vera (Mary) 1893?-1970... CLC 23
See also CAP 1; CA 15-16;
obituary CA 25-28R

Broch, Hermann 1886-1951....... TCLC 20
See also CA 117; DLB 85

Brock, Rose 1923-
See Hansen, Joseph

Brodkey, Harold 1930-............ CLC 56
See also CA 111

Brodsky, Iosif Alexandrovich 1940-
See Brodsky, Joseph (Alexandrovich)
See also CA 41-44R

Brodsky, Joseph (Alexandrovich)
1940- .... CLC 4, 6, 13, 36, 50
See also Brodsky, Iosif Alexandrovich

Brodsky, Michael (Mark) 1948- .... CLC 19
See also CANR 18; CA 102

Bromell, Henry 1947- .... CLC 5
See also CANR 9; CA 53-56

Bromfield, Louis (Brucker)
1896-1956 .... TCLC 11
See also CA 107; DLB 4, 9

Broner, E(sther) M(asserman)
1930- .... CLC 19
See also CANR 8, 25; CA 17-20R; DLB 28

Bronk, William 1918- .... CLC 10
See also CANR 23; CA 89-92

Bronte, Anne 1820-1849......... NCLC 4
See also DLB 21

Bronte, Charlotte
1816-1855 .... NCLC 3, 8, 33
See also WLC 1; DLB 21

Bronte, (Jane) Emily
1818-1848 .... NCLC 16, 35
See also WLC 1; DLB 21, 32

Brooke, Frances 1724-1789 .... LC 6
See also DLB 39

Brooke, Henry 1703?-1783 .... LC 1
See also DLB 39

Brooke, Rupert (Chawner)
1887-1915 .... TCLC 2, 7
See also WLC 1; CA 104; DLB 19

Brooke-Rose, Christine 1926- ...... CLC 40
See also CA 13-16R; DLB 14

Brookner, Anita 1928- ...... CLC 32, 34, 51
See also CA 114, 120; DLB-Y 87

Brooks, Cleanth 1906- .... CLC 24
See also CA 17-20R; DLB 63

Brooks, Gwendolyn
1917- .... CLC 1, 2, 4, 5, 15, 49
See also BLC 1; WLC 1; CANR 1, 27;
CA 1-4R; SATA 6; DLB 5, 76;
CDALB 1941-1968

Brooks, Mel 1926- .... CLC 12
See also Kaminsky, Melvin
See also CA 65-68; DLB 26

Brooks, Peter 1938- .... CLC 34
See also CANR 1; CA 45-48

Brooks, Van Wyck 1886-1963...... CLC 29
See also CANR 6; CA 1-4R; DLB 45, 63

Brophy, Brigid (Antonia)
1929- .... CLC 6, 11, 29
See also CAAS 4; CANR 25; CA 5-8R;
DLB 14

Brosman, Catharine Savage 1934-.... CLC 9
See also CANR 21; CA 61-64

Broughton, T(homas) Alan 1936- ... CLC 19
See also CANR 2, 23; CA 45-48

Broumas, Olga 1949- .... CLC 10
See also CANR 20; CA 85-88

Brown, Charles Brockden
1771-1810 .... NCLC 22
See also DLB 37, 59, 73;
CDALB 1640-1865

Brown, Christy 1932-1981........ CLC 63
See also CA 105; obituary CA 104

Brown, Claude 1937- .... CLC 30
See also BLC 1; CA 73-76

Brown, Dee (Alexander) 1908- ... CLC 18, 47
See also CAAS 6; CANR 11; CA 13-16R;
SATA 5; DLB-Y 80

Brown, George Douglas 1869-1902
See Douglas, George

Brown, George Mackay 1921-.... CLC 5, 28
See also CAAS 6; CANR 12; CA 21-24R;
SATA 35; DLB 14, 27

Brown, H. Rap 1943-
See Al-Amin, Jamil Abdullah

Brown, Hubert Gerold 1943-
See Al-Amin, Jamil Abdullah

Brown, Rita Mae 1944- .... CLC 18, 43
See also CANR 2, 11; CA 45-48

Brown, Rosellen 1939-............ CLC 32
See also CANR 14; CA 77-80

Brown, Sterling A(llen)
1901-1989 .... CLC 1, 23, 59
See also BLC 1; CANR 26; CA 85-88;
obituary CA 127; DLB 48, 51, 63

Brown, William Wells
1816?-1884............. NCLC 2; DC 1
See also BLC 1; DLB 3, 50

Browne, Jackson 1950- .... CLC 21
See also CA 120

Browning, Elizabeth Barrett
1806-1861 .... NCLC 1, 16
See also WLC 1; DLB 32

Browning, Robert
1812-1889 .... NCLC 19; PC 2
See also YABC 1; DLB 32

Browning, Tod 1882-1962 .... CLC 16
See also obituary CA 117

Bruccoli, Matthew J(oseph) 1931- .. CLC 34
See also CANR 7; CA 9-12R

Bruce, Lenny 1925-1966 .... CLC 21
See also Schneider, Leonard Alfred

Bruin, John 1924-
See Brutus, Dennis

Brunner, John (Kilian Houston)
1934- .... CLC 8, 10
See also CAAS 8; CANR 2; CA 1-4R

Brutus, Dennis 1924-............. CLC 43
See also BLC 1; CANR 2, 27; CA 49-52

Bryan, C(ourtlandt) D(ixon) B(arnes)
1936- .... CLC 29
See also CANR 13; CA 73-76

Bryant, William Cullen
1794-1878 .... NCLC 6
See also DLB 3, 43, 59; CDALB 1640-1865

Bryusov, Valery (Yakovlevich)
1873-1924 .... TCLC 10
See also CA 107

Buchan, John 1875-1940 .... TCLC 41
See also YABC 2; brief entry CA 108;
DLB 34, 70

Buchanan, George 1506-1582 .... LC 4

Buchheim, Lothar-Gunther 1918-.... CLC 6
See also CA 85-88

Buchner, (Karl) Georg
1813-1837 .... NCLC 26

Buchwald, Art(hur) 1925-.......... CLC 33
See also CANR 21; CA 5-8R; SATA 10

Buck, Pearl S(ydenstricker)
1892-1973 .... CLC 7, 11, 18
See also CANR 1; CA 1-4R;
obituary CA 41-44R; SATA 1, 25; DLB 9

Buckler, Ernest 1908-1984........ CLC 13
See also CAP 1; CA 11-12;
obituary CA 114; SATA 47

Buckley, Vincent (Thomas)
1925-1988 .... CLC 57
See also CA 101

Buckley, William F(rank), Jr.
1925- .... CLC 7, 18, 37
See also CANR 1, 24; CA 1-4R; DLB-Y 80

Buechner, (Carl) Frederick
1926- .... CLC 2, 4, 6, 9
See also CANR 11; CA 13-16R; DLB-Y 80

Buell, John (Edward) 1927-........ CLC 10
See also CA 1-4R; DLB 53

Buero Vallejo, Antonio 1916- ... CLC 15, 46
See also CANR 24; CA 106

Bukowski, Charles 1920- .... CLC 2, 5, 9, 41
See also CA 17-20R; DLB 5

Bulgakov, Mikhail (Afanas'evich)
1891-1940 .... TCLC 2, 16
See also CA 105

Bullins, Ed 1935- .... CLC 1, 5, 7
See also BLC 1; CANR 24; CA 49-52;
DLB 7, 38

Bulwer-Lytton, (Lord) Edward (George Earle
Lytton) 1803-1873 .... NCLC 1
See also Lytton, Edward Bulwer
See also DLB 21

Bunin, Ivan (Alexeyevich)
1870-1953 .... TCLC 6; SSC 5
See also CA 104

Bunting, Basil 1900-1985.... CLC 10, 39, 47
See also CANR 7; CA 53-56;
obituary CA 115; DLB 20

Bunuel, Luis 1900-1983 .... CLC 16
See also CA 101; obituary CA 110

Bunyan, John 1628-1688 .... LC 4
See also WLC 1; DLB 39

Burgess (Wilson, John) Anthony
1917- ..... CLC 1, 2, 4, 5, 8, 10, 13, 15,
22, 40, 62
See also Wilson, John (Anthony) Burgess
See also DLB 14

Burke, Edmund 1729-1797.......... LC 7
See also WLC 1

Burke, Kenneth (Duva) 1897- .... CLC 2, 24
See also CA 5-8R; DLB 45, 63

Burney, Fanny 1752-1840 .... NCLC 12
See also DLB 39

Burns, Robert 1759-1796........... LC 3
See also WLC 1

Burns, Tex 1908?-
See L'Amour, Louis (Dearborn)

Burnshaw, Stanley 1906-..... CLC 3, 13, 44
See also CA 9-12R; DLB 48

Burr, Anne 1937- .... CLC 6
See also CA 25-28R

Burroughs, Edgar Rice
1875-1950 .... TCLC 2, 32
See also CA 104; SATA 41; DLB 8

Burroughs, William S(eward)
     1914- . . . . CLC 1, 2, 5, 15, 22, 42
     See also WLC 1; CANR 20; CA 9-12R;
     DLB 2, 8, 16; DLB-Y 81

Busch, Frederick   1941- . . . CLC 7, 10, 18, 47
     See also CAAS 1; CA 33-36R; DLB 6

Bush, Ronald   19??- . . . . CLC 34

Butler, Octavia E(stelle)   1947- . . . . . CLC 38
     See also CANR 12, 24; CA 73-76; DLB 33

Butler, Samuel   1612-1680 . . . . LC 16
     See also DLB 101

Butler, Samuel   1835-1902 . . . . . . TCLC 1, 33
     See also WLC 1; CA 104; DLB 18, 57

Butor, Michel (Marie Francois)
     1926- . . . . CLC 1, 3, 8, 11, 15
     See also CA 9-12R

Buzo, Alexander   1944- . . . . CLC 61
     See also CANR 17; CA 97-100

Buzzati, Dino   1906-1972 . . . . CLC 36
     See also obituary CA 33-36R

Byars, Betsy   1928- . . . . CLC 35
     See also CLR 1, 16; CANR 18; CA 33-36R;
     SAAS 1; SATA 4, 46; DLB 52

Byatt, A(ntonia) S(usan Drabble)
     1936- . . . . CLC 19, 65
     See also CANR 13, 33; CA 13-16R;
     DLB 14

Byrne, David   1953?- . . . . CLC 26

Byrne, John Keyes   1926-
     See Leonard, Hugh
     See also CA 102

Byron, George Gordon (Noel), Lord Byron
     1788-1824 . . . . NCLC 2, 12
     See also WLC 1

Caballero, Fernan   1796-1877 . . . . . NCLC 10

Cabell, James Branch   1879-1958 . . . TCLC 6
     See also CA 105; DLB 9, 78

Cable, George Washington
     1844-1925 . . . . TCLC 4; SSC 4
     See also CA 104; DLB 12, 74

Cabrera Infante, G(uillermo)
     1929- . . . . CLC 5, 25, 45
     See also CANR 29; CA 85-88

Cade, Toni   1939-
     See Bambara, Toni Cade

CAEdmon   fl. 658-680 . . . . CMLC 7

Cage, John (Milton, Jr.)   1912- . . . . . CLC 41
     See also CANR 9; CA 13-16R

Cain, G.   1929-
     See Cabrera Infante, G(uillermo)

Cain, James M(allahan)
     1892-1977 . . . . CLC 3, 11, 28
     See also CANR 8; CA 17-20R;
     obituary CA 73-76

Caldwell, Erskine (Preston)
     1903-1987 . . . . CLC 1, 8, 14, 50, 60
     See also CAAS 1; CANR 2; CA 1-4R;
     obituary CA 121; DLB 9, 86

Caldwell, (Janet Miriam) Taylor (Holland)
     1900-1985 . . . . CLC 2, 28, 39
     See also CANR 5; CA 5-8R;
     obituary CA 116

Calhoun, John Caldwell
     1782-1850 . . . . NCLC 15
     See also DLB 3

Calisher, Hortense   1911- . . . . CLC 2, 4, 8, 38
     See also CANR 1, 22; CA 1-4R; DLB 2

Callaghan, Morley (Edward)
     1903-1990 . . . . CLC 3, 14, 41, 65
     See also CANR 33; CA 9-12R;
     obituary CA 132; DLB 68

Calvino, Italo
     1923-1985 . . . . CLC 5, 8, 11, 22, 33, 39;
                                                       SSC 3
     See also CANR 23; CA 85-88;
     obituary CA 116

Cameron, Carey   1952- . . . . CLC 59

Cameron, Peter   1959- . . . . CLC 44
     See also CA 125

Campana, Dino   1885-1932 . . . . TCLC 20
     See also CA 117

Campbell, John W(ood), Jr.
     1910-1971 . . . . CLC 32
     See also CAP 2; CA 21-22;
     obituary CA 29-32R; DLB 8

Campbell, Joseph   1904-1987 . . . . . . CLC 69
     See also CANR 3, 28; CA 4R;
     obituary CA 124; AAYA 3

Campbell, (John) Ramsey   1946- . . . . CLC 42
     See also CANR 7; CA 57-60

Campbell, (Ignatius) Roy (Dunnachie)
     1901-1957 . . . . TCLC 5
     See also CA 104; DLB 20

Campbell, Thomas   1777-1844 . . . . NCLC 19

Campbell, (William) Wilfred
     1861-1918 . . . . TCLC 9
     See also CA 106

Camus, Albert
     1913-1960 . . . CLC 1, 2, 4, 9, 11, 14, 32,
                                 63, 69; DC 2; SSC 9
     See also WLC 1; CA 89-92; DLB 72

Canby, Vincent   1924- . . . . CLC 13
     See also CA 81-84

Canetti, Elias   1905- . . . . CLC 3, 14, 25
     See also CANR 23; CA 21-24R; DLB 85

Canin, Ethan   1960- . . . . CLC 55

Cape, Judith   1916-
     See Page, P(atricia) K(athleen)

Capek, Karel
     1890-1938 . . . . TCLC 6, 37; DC 1
     See also WLC 1; CA 104

Capote, Truman
     1924-1984 . . . . . CLC 1, 3, 8, 13, 19, 34,
                                      38, 58; SSC 2
     See also WLC 1; CANR 18; CA 5-8R;
     obituary CA 113; DLB 2; DLB-Y 80, 84;
     CDALB 1941-1968

Capra, Frank   1897- . . . . CLC 16
     See also CA 61-64

Caputo, Philip   1941- . . . . CLC 32
     See also CA 73-76

Card, Orson Scott   1951- . . . . CLC 44, 47, 50
     See also CA 102

Cardenal, Ernesto   1925- . . . . CLC 31
     See also CANR 2; CA 49-52

Carducci, Giosue   1835-1907 . . . . . . TCLC 32

Carew, Thomas   1595?-1640 . . . . LC 13

Carey, Ernestine Gilbreth   1908- . . . . CLC 17
     See also CA 5-8R; SATA 2

Carey, Peter   1943- . . . . CLC 40, 55
     See also CA 123, 127

Carleton, William   1794-1869 . . . . . . NCLC 3

Carlisle, Henry (Coffin)   1926- . . . . . . CLC 33
     See also CANR 15; CA 13-16R

Carlson, Ron(ald F.)   1947- . . . . CLC 54
     See also CA 105

Carlyle, Thomas   1795-1881 . . . . . . NCLC 22
     See also DLB 55

Carman, (William) Bliss
     1861-1929 . . . . TCLC 7
     See also CA 104

Carpenter, Don(ald Richard)
     1931- . . . . CLC 41
     See also CANR 1; CA 45-48

Carpentier (y Valmont), Alejo
     1904-1980 . . . . CLC 8, 11, 38
     See also CANR 11; CA 65-68;
     obituary CA 97-100

Carr, Emily   1871-1945 . . . . TCLC 32
     See also DLB 68

Carr, John Dickson   1906-1977 . . . . . . CLC 3
     See also CANR 3; CA 49-52;
     obituary CA 69-72

Carr, Virginia Spencer   1929- . . . . CLC 34
     See also CA 61-64

Carrier, Roch   1937- . . . . CLC 13
     See also DLB 53

Carroll, James (P.)   1943- . . . . CLC 38
     See also CA 81-84

Carroll, Jim   1951- . . . . CLC 35
     See also CA 45-48

Carroll, Lewis   1832-1898 . . . . NCLC 2
     See also Dodgson, Charles Lutwidge
     See also CLR 2; WLC 1; DLB 18

Carroll, Paul Vincent   1900-1968 . . . . CLC 10
     See also CA 9-12R; obituary CA 25-28R;
     DLB 10

Carruth, Hayden   1921- . . . . CLC 4, 7, 10, 18
     See also CANR 4; CA 9-12R; SATA 47;
     DLB 5

Carson, Rachel   1907-1964 . . . . CLC 71
     See also CANR 35; CA 77-80; SATA 23

Carter, Angela (Olive)   1940- . . . . . CLC 5, 41
     See also CANR 12; CA 53-56; DLB 14

Carver, Raymond
     1938-1988 . . . CLC 22, 36, 53, 55; SSC 8
     See also CANR 17; CA 33-36R;
     obituary CA 126; DLB-Y 84, 88

Cary, (Arthur) Joyce (Lunel)
     1888-1957 . . . . TCLC 1, 29
     See also CA 104; DLB 15

Casanova de Seingalt, Giovanni Jacopo
     1725-1798 . . . . LC 13

Casares, Adolfo Bioy   1914-
     See Bioy Casares, Adolfo

Casely-Hayford, J(oseph) E(phraim)
     1866-1930 . . . . TCLC 24
     See also BLC 1; CA 123

Casey, John   1880-1964
     See O'Casey, Sean

Casey, John 1939- .... CLC 59
See also CANR 23; CA 69-72

Casey, Michael 1947-............. CLC 2
See also CA 65-68; DLB 5

Casey, Patrick 1902-1934
See Thurman, Wallace

Casey, Warren 1935- .... CLC 12
See also Jacobs, Jim and Casey, Warren
See also CA 101

Casona, Alejandro 1903-1965 ...... CLC 49
See also Alvarez, Alejandro Rodriguez

Cassavetes, John 1929-1991........ CLC 20
See also CA 85-88, 127

Cassill, R(onald) V(erlin) 1919-... CLC 4, 23
See also CAAS 1; CANR 7; CA 9-12R;
DLB 6

Cassity, (Allen) Turner 1929- .... CLC 6, 42
See also CANR 11; CA 17-20R

Castaneda, Carlos 1935?-.......... CLC 12
See also CA 25-28R

Castedo, Elena 1937- .... CLC 65
See also CA 132

Castellanos, Rosario 1925-1974..... CLC 66
See also CA 131; obituary CA 53-56

Castelvetro, Lodovico 1505-1571..... LC 12

Castiglione, Baldassare 1478-1529 ... LC 12

Castro, Guillen de 1569-1631........ LC 19

Castro, Rosalia de 1837-1885 ..... NCLC 3

Cather, Willa (Sibert)
1873-1947 ...... TCLC 1, 11, 31; SSC 2
See also WLC 1; CA 104; SATA 30;
DLB 9, 54; DLB-DS 1;
CDALB 1865-1917

Catton, (Charles) Bruce
1899-1978 .... CLC 35
See also CANR 7; CA 5-8R;
obituary CA 81-84; SATA 2;
obituary SATA 24; DLB 17

Cauldwell, Frank 1923-
See King, Francis (Henry)

Caunitz, William 1935- .... CLC 34

Causley, Charles (Stanley) 1917-..... CLC 7
See also CANR 5; CA 9-12R; SATA 3;
DLB 27

Caute, (John) David 1936-........ CLC 29
See also CAAS 4; CANR 1; CA 1-4R;
DLB 14

Cavafy, C(onstantine) P(eter)
1863-1933 .... TCLC 2, 7
See also CA 104

Cavanna, Betty 1909-............. CLC 12
See also CANR 6; CA 9-12R; SATA 1, 30

Caxton, William 1421?-1491? .... LC 17

Cayrol, Jean 1911-............... CLC 11
See also CA 89-92; DLB 83

Cela, Camilo Jose 1916-...... CLC 4, 13, 59
See also CAAS 10; CANR 21; CA 21-24R

Celan, Paul 1920-1970 ..... CLC 10, 19, 53
See also Antschel, Paul
See also DLB 69

Celine, Louis-Ferdinand
1894-1961 ..... CLC 1, 3, 4, 7, 9, 15, 47
See also Destouches,
Louis-Ferdinand-Auguste
See also DLB 72

Cellini, Benvenuto 1500-1571 .... LC 7

Cendrars, Blaise 1887-1961........ CLC 18
See also Sauser-Hall, Frederic

Cernuda, Luis (y Bidon)
1902-1963 .... CLC 54
See also CA 89-92

Cervantes (Saavedra), Miguel de
1547-1616 .... LC 6
See also WLC 2

Cesaire, Aime (Fernand) 1913- .. CLC 19, 32
See also BLC 1; CANR 24; CA 65-68

Chabon, Michael 1965?-........... CLC 55

Chabrol, Claude 1930- .... CLC 16
See also CA 110

Challans, Mary 1905-1983
See Renault, Mary
See also CA 81-84; obituary CA 111;
SATA 23; obituary SATA 36

Chambers, Aidan 1934- .... CLC 35
See also CANR 12; CA 25-28R; SATA 1

Chambers, James 1948-
See Cliff, Jimmy

Chambers, Robert W. 1865-1933... TCLC 41

Chandler, Raymond 1888-1959 ... TCLC 1, 7
See also CA 104

Channing, William Ellery
1780-1842 .... NCLC 17
See also DLB 1, 59

Chaplin, Charles (Spencer)
1889-1977 .... CLC 16
See also CA 81-84; obituary CA 73-76;
DLB 44

Chapman, Graham 1941?- .... CLC 21
See also Monty Python
See also CA 116; obituary CA 169

Chapman, John Jay 1862-1933 ..... TCLC 7
See also CA 104

Chappell, Fred 1936- .... CLC 40
See also CAAS 4; CANR 8; CA 5-8R;
DLB 6

Char, Rene (Emile)
1907-1988 .... CLC 9, 11, 14, 55
See also CA 13-16R; obituary CA 124

Charles I 1600-1649 .... LC 13

Chartier, Emile-Auguste 1868-1951
See Alain

Charyn, Jerome 1937- .... CLC 5, 8, 18
See also CAAS 1; CANR 7; CA 5-8R;
DLB-Y 83

Chase, Mary (Coyle) 1907-1981 ...... DC 1
See also CA 77-80, 105; SATA 17, 29

Chase, Mary Ellen 1887-1973....... CLC 2
See also CAP 1; CA 15-16;
obituary CA 41-44R; SATA 10

Chateaubriand, Francois Rene de
1768-1848 .... NCLC 3

Chatterji, Bankim Chandra
1838-1894 .... NCLC 19

Chatterji, Saratchandra
1876-1938 .... TCLC 13
See also CA 109

Chatterton, Thomas 1752-1770 ...... LC 3

Chatwin, (Charles) Bruce
1940-1989 .... CLC 28, 57, 59
See also CA 85-88,; obituary CA 127

Chaucer, Geoffrey c. 1340-1400 ..... LC 17

Chayefsky, Paddy 1923-1981....... CLC 23
See also CA 9-12R; obituary CA 104;
DLB 7, 44; DLB-Y 81

Chayefsky, Sidney 1923-1981
See Chayefsky, Paddy
See also CANR 18

Chedid, Andree 1920-............. CLC 47

Cheever, John
1912-1982 ..... CLC 3, 7, 8, 11, 15, 25,
64; SSC 1
See also WLC 2; CANR 5, 27; CA 5-8R;
obituary CA 106; CABS 1; DLB 2;
DLB-Y 80, 82; CDALB 1941-1968

Cheever, Susan 1943-............. CLC 18, 48
See also CA 103; DLB-Y 82

Chekhov, Anton (Pavlovich)
1860-1904 ...... TCLC 3, 10, 31; SSC 2
See also WLC 2; CA 104, 124

Chernyshevsky, Nikolay Gavrilovich
1828-1889 .... NCLC 1

Cherry, Caroline Janice 1942-
See Cherryh, C. J.

Cherryh, C. J. 1942-............. CLC 35
See also CANR 10; CA 65-68; DLB-Y 80

Chesnutt, Charles Waddell
1858-1932 .... TCLC 5, 39; SSC 7
See also BLC 1; CA 106, 125; DLB 12, 50,
78

Chester, Alfred 1929?-1971 .... CLC 49
See also obituary CA 33-36R

Chesterton, G(ilbert) K(eith)
1874-1936 .... TCLC 1, 6; SSC 1
See also CA 104; SATA 27; DLB 10, 19,
34, 70

Chiang Pin-Chin 1904-1986
See Ding Ling
See also obituary CA 118

Ch'ien Chung-shu 1910-........... CLC 22

Child, Lydia Maria 1802-1880 .... NCLC 6
See also DLB 1, 74

Child, Philip 1898-1978........... CLC 19
See also CAP 1; CA 13-14; SATA 47

Childress, Alice 1920-.......... CLC 12, 15
See also BLC 1; CLR 14; CANR 3, 27;
CA 45-48; SATA 7, 48; DLB 7, 38

Chislett, (Margaret) Anne 1943?-.... CLC 34

Chitty, (Sir) Thomas Willes 1926- .. CLC 11
See also Hinde, Thomas
See also CA 5-8R

Chomette, Rene 1898-1981
See Clair, Rene
See also obituary CA 103

Chopin, Kate (O'Flaherty)
1851-1904 .... TCLC 5, 14; SSC 8
See also CA 122; brief entry CA 104;
DLB 12, 78; CDALB 1865-1917

Christie, (Dame) Agatha (Mary Clarissa)
1890-1976 . . . . . . **CLC 1, 6, 8, 12, 39, 48**
See also CANR 10; CA 17-20R;
obituary CA 61-64; SATA 36; DLB 13

Christie, (Ann) Philippa   1920-
See Pearce, (Ann) Philippa
See also CANR 4; CA 7-8

Christine de Pizan   1365?-1431?. . . . . . **LC 9**

Chulkov, Mikhail Dmitrievich
1743-1792 . . . . **LC 2**

Churchill, Caryl   1938- . . . . **CLC 31, 55**
See also CANR 22; CA 102; DLB 13

Churchill, Charles   1731?-1764. . . . . . . **LC 3**

Chute, Carolyn   1947- . . . . **CLC 39**
See also CA 123

Ciardi, John (Anthony)
1916-1986 . . . . **CLC 10, 40, 44**
See also CAAS 2; CANR 5; CA 5-8R;
obituary CA 118; SATA 1, 46; DLB 5;
DLB-Y 86

Cicero, Marcus Tullius
106 B.C.-43 B.C. . . . . **CMLC 3**

Cimino, Michael   1943?- . . . . **CLC 16**
See also CA 105

Cioran, E. M.   1911- . . . . **CLC 64**
See also CA 25-28R

Cisneros, Sandra   1954- . . . . **CLC 69**
See also CA 131

Clair, Rene   1898-1981 . . . . **CLC 20**
See also Chomette, Rene

Clampitt, Amy   19??- . . . . **CLC 32**
See also CA 110

Clancy, Tom   1947- . . . . **CLC 45**
See also CA 125

Clare, John   1793-1864 . . . . **NCLC 9**
See also DLB 55

Clark, Al C.   1937?-1974
See Goines, Donald

Clark, (Robert) Brian   1932- . . . . **CLC 29**
See also CA 41-44R

Clark, Eleanor   1913- . . . . **CLC 5, 19**
See also CA 9-12R; DLB 6

Clark, John Pepper   1935- . . . . **CLC 38**
See also BLC 1; CANR 16; CA 65-68

Clark, Mavis Thorpe   1912?- . . . . **CLC 12**
See also CANR 8; CA 57-60; SAAS 5;
SATA 8

Clark, Walter Van Tilburg
1909-1971 . . . . **CLC 28**
See also CA 9-12R; obituary CA 33-36R;
SATA 8; DLB 9

Clarke, Arthur C(harles)
1917- . . . . . . **CLC 1, 4, 13, 18, 35; SSC 3**
See also CANR 2; CA 1-4R; SATA 13

Clarke, Austin   1896-1974. . . . . **CLC 6, 9**
See also BLC 1; CANR 14; CAP 2;
CA 29-32; obituary CA 49-52; DLB 10,
20, 53

Clarke, Austin (Ardinel) C(hesterfield)
1934- . . . . **CLC 8, 53**
See also CANR 14; CA 25-28R; DLB 53

Clarke, Gillian   1937- . . . . **CLC 61**
See also CA 106; DLB 40

Clarke, Marcus (Andrew Hislop)
1846-1881 . . . . **NCLC 19**

Clarke, Shirley   1925- . . . . **CLC 16**

Clash, The . . . . **CLC 30**

Claudel, Paul (Louis Charles Marie)
1868-1955 . . . . **TCLC 2, 10**
See also CA 104

Clavell, James (duMaresq)
1924- . . . . **CLC 6, 25**
See also CANR 26; CA 25-28R

Clayman. Gregory   1974?- . . . . **CLC 65**

Cleaver, (Leroy) Eldridge   1935- . . . . **CLC 30**
See also BLC 1; CANR 16; CA 21-24R

Cleese, John   1939- . . . . **CLC 21**
See also Monty Python
See also CA 112, 116

Cleland, John   1709-1789 . . . . **LC 2**
See also DLB 39

Clemens, Samuel Langhorne
1835-1910 . . . . . **TCLC 6, 12, 19; SSC 6**
See also Twain, Mark
See also YABC 2; CA 104; DLB 11, 12, 23,
64, 74; CDALB 1865-1917

Cliff, Jimmy   1948- . . . . **CLC 21**

Clifton, Lucille (Thelma)
1936- . . . . **CLC 19, 66**
See also BLC 1; CLR 5; CANR 2, 24;
CA 49-52; SATA 20; DLB 5, 41

Clough, Arthur Hugh   1819-1861. . **NCLC 27**
See also DLB 32

Clutha, Janet Paterson Frame   1924-
See Frame (Clutha), Janet (Paterson)
See also CANR 2; CA 1-4R

Coburn, D(onald) L(ee)   1938- . . . . . . **CLC 10**
See also CA 89-92

Cocteau, Jean (Maurice Eugene Clement)
1889-1963 . . . . **CLC 1, 8, 15, 16, 43**
See also WLC 2; CAP 2; CA 25-28;
DLB 65

Codrescu, Andrei   1946- . . . . **CLC 46**
See also CANR 13; CA 33-36R

Coetzee, J(ohn) M.   1940- . . . . **CLC 23, 33, 66**
See also CA 77-80

Cohen, Arthur A(llen)
1928-1986 . . . . **CLC 7, 31**
See also CANR 1, 17; CA 1-4R;
obituary CA 120; DLB 28

Cohen, Leonard (Norman)
1934- . . . . **CLC 3, 38**
See also CANR 14; CA 21-24R; DLB 53

Cohen, Matt   1942- . . . . **CLC 19**
See also CA 61-64; DLB 53

Cohen-Solal, Annie   19??- . . . . **CLC 50**

Colegate, Isabel   1931- . . . . **CLC 36**
See also CANR 8, 22; CA 17-20R; DLB 14

Coleman, Emmett   1938-
See Reed, Ishmael

Coleridge, Samuel Taylor
1772-1834 . . . . **NCLC 9**
See also WLC 2

Coleridge, Sara   1802-1852 . . . . **NCLC 31**

Coles, Don   1928- . . . . **CLC 46**
See also CA 115

Colette (Sidonie-Gabrielle)
1873-1954 . . . . . . **TCLC 1, 5, 16; SSC 10**
See also CA 104, 131; DLB 65

Collett, (Jacobine) Camilla (Wergeland)
1813-1895 . . . . **NCLC 22**

Collier, Christopher   1930- . . . . **CLC 30**
See also CANR 13; CA 33-36R; SATA 16

Collier, James L(incoln)   1928- . . . . . **CLC 30**
See also CLR 3; CANR 4; CA 9-12R;
SATA 8

Collier, Jeremy   1650-1726. . . . . **LC 6**

Collins, Hunt   1926-
See Hunter, Evan

Collins, Linda   19??- . . . . **CLC 44**
See also CA 125

Collins, Tom   1843-1912
See Furphy, Joseph

Collins, (William) Wilkie
1824-1889 . . . . **NCLC 1, 18**
See also DLB 18, 70

Collins, William   1721-1759 . . . . **LC 4**

Colman, George   1909-1981
See Glassco, John

Colter, Cyrus   1910- . . . . **CLC 58**
See also CANR 10; CA 65-68; DLB 33

Colton, James   1923-
See Hansen, Joseph

Colum, Padraic   1881-1972. . . . . **CLC 28**
See also CA 73-76; obituary CA 33-36R;
SATA 15; DLB 19

Colvin, James   1939-
See Moorcock, Michael

Colwin, Laurie   1945- . . . . **CLC 5, 13, 23**
See also CANR 20; CA 89-92; DLB-Y 80

Comfort, Alex(ander)   1920- . . . . **CLC 7**
See also CANR 1; CA 1-4R

Compton-Burnett, Ivy
1892-1969 . . . . **CLC 1, 3, 10, 15, 34**
See also CANR 4; CA 1-4R;
obituary CA 25-28R; DLB 36

Comstock, Anthony   1844-1915 . . . . **TCLC 13**
See also CA 110

Conde, Maryse   1937- . . . . **CLC 52**
See also Boucolon, Maryse

Condon, Richard (Thomas)
1915- . . . . **CLC 4, 6, 8, 10, 45**
See also CAAS 1; CANR 2, 23; CA 1-4R

Congreve, William   1670-1729 . . . **LC 5; DC 2**
See also WLC 2; DLB 39, 84

Connell, Evan S(helby), Jr.
1924- . . . . **CLC 4, 6, 45**
See also CAAS 2; CANR 2; CA 1-4R;
DLB 2; DLB-Y 81

Connelly, Marc(us Cook)
1890-1980 . . . . **CLC 7**
See also CA 85-88; obituary CA 102;
obituary SATA 25; DLB 7; DLB-Y 80

Conner, Ralph   1860-1937. . . . . **TCLC 31**

Conrad, Joseph
1857-1924 . . . . . . **TCLC 1, 6, 13, 25, 43;
SSC 9**
See also WLC 2; CA 104, 131; SATA 27;
DLB 10, 34, 98

Conrad, Robert Arnold   1904-1961
See Hart, Moss

Conroy, Pat   1945-.................. CLC 30
See also CANR 24; CA 85-88; DLB 6

Constant (de Rebecque), (Henri) Benjamin
1767-1830 .... NCLC 6

Cook, Michael   1933- .... CLC 58
See also CA 93-96; DLB 53

Cook, Robin   1940- .... CLC 14
See also CA 108, 111

Cooke, Elizabeth   1948- .... CLC 55

Cooke, John Esten   1830-1886 ..... NCLC 5
See also DLB 3

Cooney, Ray   19??- .... CLC 62

Cooper, Edith Emma   1862-1913
See Field, Michael

Cooper, J. California   19??- .... CLC 56
See also CA 125

Cooper, James Fenimore
1789-1851 .... NCLC 1, 27
See also SATA 19; DLB 3;
CDALB 1640-1865

Coover, Robert (Lowell)
1932- .... CLC 3, 7, 15, 32, 46
See also CANR 3; CA 45-48; DLB 2;
DLB-Y 81

Copeland, Stewart (Armstrong)
1952- .... CLC 26
See also The Police

Coppard, A(lfred) E(dgar)
1878-1957 .... TCLC 5
See also YABC 1; CA 114

Coppee, Francois   1842-1908 ...... TCLC 25

Coppola, Francis Ford   1939-....... CLC 16
See also CA 77-80; DLB 44

Corcoran, Barbara   1911-.......... CLC 17
See also CAAS 2; CANR 11; CA 21-24R;
SATA 3; DLB 52

Corman, Cid   1924- .... CLC 9
See also Corman, Sidney
See also CAAS 2; DLB 5

Corman, Sidney   1924-
See Corman, Cid
See also CA 85-88

Cormier, Robert (Edmund)
1925- .... CLC 12, 30
See also CLR 12; CANR 5, 23; CA 1-4R;
SATA 10, 45; DLB 52

Corn, Alfred (Dewitt III)   1943-..... CLC 33
See also CA 104; DLB-Y 80

Cornwell, David (John Moore)
1931- .... CLC 9, 15
See also le Carre, John
See also CANR 13; CA 5-8R

Corso, (Nunzio) Gregory   1930-... CLC 1, 11
See also CA 5-8R; DLB 5, 16

Cortazar, Julio
1914-1984 ..... CLC 2, 3, 5, 10, 13, 15,
                               33, 34; SSC 7
See also CANR 12; CA 21-24R

Corvo, Baron   1860-1913
See Rolfe, Frederick (William Serafino
Austin Lewis Mary)

Cosic, Dobrica   1921- .... CLC 14
See also CA 122

Costain, Thomas B(ertram)
1885-1965 .... CLC 30
See also CA 5-8R; obituary CA 25-28R;
DLB 9

Costantini, Humberto   1924?-1987... CLC 49
See also obituary CA 122

Costello, Elvis   1955-.............. CLC 21

Cotter, Joseph Seamon, Sr.
1861-1949 .... TCLC 28
See also BLC 1; CA 124; DLB 50

Couperus, Louis (Marie Anne)
1863-1923 .... TCLC 15
See also CA 115

Courtenay, Bryce   1933-............ CLC 59

Cousteau, Jacques-Yves   1910-...... CLC 30
See also CANR 15; CA 65-68; SATA 38

Coward, (Sir) Noel (Pierce)
1899-1973 .... CLC 1, 9, 29, 51
See also CAP 2; CA 17-18;
obituary CA 41-44R; DLB 10

Cowley, Malcolm   1898-1989 .... CLC 39
See also CANR 3; CA 5-6R;
obituary CA 128; DLB 4, 48; DLB-Y 81

Cowper, William   1731-1800....... NCLC 8

Cox, William Trevor   1928- ... CLC 9, 14, 71
See also Trevor, William
See also CANR 4; CA 9-12R; DLB 14

Cozzens, James Gould
1903-1978 .... CLC 1, 4, 11
See also CANR 19; CA 9-12R;
obituary CA 81-84; DLB 9; DLB-Y 84;
DLB-DS 2; CDALB 1941-1968

Crabbe, George   1754-1832....... NCLC 26

Crace, Douglas   1944-............. CLC 58

Cram, Ralph Adams   1863-1942.... TCLC 45

Crane, (Harold) Hart
1899-1932 .... TCLC 2, 5; PC 3
See also WLC 2; CA 127;
brief entry CA 104; DLB 4, 48;
CDALB 1917-1929

Crane, R(onald) S(almon)
1886-1967 .... CLC 27
See also CA 85-88; DLB 63

Crane, Stephen
1871-1900 ..... TCLC 11, 17, 32; SSC 7
See also WLC 2; YABC 2; CA 109;
DLB 12, 54, 78; CDALB 1865-1917

Craven, Margaret   1901-1980....... CLC 17
See also CA 103

Crawford, F(rancis) Marion
1854-1909 .... TCLC 10
See also CA 107; DLB 71

Crawford, Isabella Valancy
1850-1887 .... NCLC 12
See also DLB 92

Crayencour, Marguerite de   1903-1987
See Yourcenar, Marguerite

Creasey, John   1908-1973.......... CLC 11
See also CANR 8; CA 5-8R;
obituary CA 41-44R; DLB 77

Crebillon, Claude Prosper Jolyot de (fils)
1707-1777 .... LC 1

Creeley, Robert (White)
1926-........ CLC 1, 2, 4, 8, 11, 15, 36
See also CANR 23; CA 1-4R; DLB 5, 16

Crews, Harry (Eugene)
1935-.................. CLC 6, 23, 49
See also CANR 20; CA 25-28R; DLB 6

Crichton, (John) Michael
1942-.................... CLC 2, 6, 54
See also CANR 13; CA 25-28R; SATA 9;
DLB-Y 81

Crispin, Edmund   1921-1978........ CLC 22
See also Montgomery, Robert Bruce
See also DLB 87

Cristofer, Michael   1946-.......... CLC 28
See also CA 110; DLB 7

Croce, Benedetto   1866-1952 ...... TCLC 37
See also CA 120

Crockett, David (Davy)
1786-1836 .... NCLC 8
See also DLB 3, 11

Croker, John Wilson   1780-1857 .. NCLC 10

Cronin, A(rchibald) J(oseph)
1896-1981 .... CLC 32
See also CANR 5; CA 1-4R;
obituary CA 102; obituary SATA 25, 47

Cross, Amanda   1926-
See Heilbrun, Carolyn G(old)

Crothers, Rachel   1878-1953....... TCLC 19
See also CA 113; DLB 7

Crowley, Aleister   1875-1947 ...... TCLC 7
See also CA 104

Crowley, John   1942-
See also CA 61-64; DLB-Y 82

Crumb, Robert   1943-............. CLC 17
See also CA 106

Cryer, Gretchen   1936?- .... CLC 21
See also CA 114, 123

Csath, Geza   1887-1919........... TCLC 13
See also CA 111

Cudlip, David   1933-............. CLC 34

Cullen, Countee   1903-1946 ..... TCLC 4, 37
See also BLC 1; CA 108, 124; SATA 18;
DLB 4, 48, 51; CDALB 1917-1929

Cummings, E(dward) E(stlin)
1894-1962 ...... CLC 1, 3, 8, 12, 15, 68
See also WLC 2; CANR 31; CA 73-76;
DLB 4, 48; CDALB 1929-1941

Cunha, Euclides (Rodrigues) da
1866-1909 .... TCLC 24
See also CA 123

Cunningham, J(ames) V(incent)
1911-1985 .... CLC 3, 31
See also CANR 1; CA 1-4R;
obituary CA 115; DLB 5

Cunningham, Julia (Woolfolk)
1916-....................... CLC 12
See also CANR 4, 19; CA 9-12R; SAAS 2;
SATA 1, 26

Cunningham, Michael   1952- .... CLC 34

Currie, Ellen   19??-............... CLC 44

Dabrowska, Maria (Szumska)
1889-1965 .... CLC 15
See also CA 106

Dabydeen, David 1956?-........... **CLC 34**
See also CA 106

Dacey, Philip 1939-.............. **CLC 51**
See also CANR 14; CA 37-40R

Dagerman, Stig (Halvard)
1923-1954 .... **TCLC 17**
See also CA 117

Dahl, Roald 1916-............ **CLC 1, 6, 18**
See also CLR 1, 7; CANR 6; CA 1-4R;
SATA 1, 26

Dahlberg, Edward 1900-1977... **CLC 1, 7, 14**
See also CA 9-12R; obituary CA 69-72;
DLB 48

Daly, Elizabeth 1878-1967......... **CLC 52**
See also CAP 2; CA 23-24;
obituary CA 25-28R

Daly, Maureen 1921-............. **CLC 17**
See also McGivern, Maureen Daly
See also SAAS 1; SATA 2

Daniken, Erich von 1935-
See Von Daniken, Erich

Dannay, Frederic 1905-1982
See Queen, Ellery
See also CANR 1; CA 1-4R;
obituary CA 107

D'Annunzio, Gabriele
1863-1938 .... **TCLC 6, 40**
See also CA 104

Dante (Alighieri)
See Alighieri, Dante

Danvers, Dennis 1947-............ **CLC 70**

Danziger, Paula 1944-............ **CLC 21**
See also CLR 20; CA 112, 115; SATA 30,
36

Dario, Ruben 1867-1916 .... **TCLC 4**
See also Sarmiento, Felix Ruben Garcia
See also CA 104

Darley, George 1795-1846........ **NCLC 2**

Daryush, Elizabeth 1887-1977.... **CLC 6, 19**
See also CANR 3; CA 49-52; DLB 20

Daudet, (Louis Marie) Alphonse
1840-1897 .... **NCLC 1**

Daumal, Rene 1908-1944........ **TCLC 14**
See also CA 114

Davenport, Guy (Mattison, Jr.)
1927- .... **CLC 6, 14, 38**
See also CANR 23; CA 33-36R

Davidson, Donald (Grady)
1893-1968 .... **CLC 2, 13, 19**
See also CANR 4; CA 5-8R;
obituary CA 25-28R; DLB 45

Davidson, John 1857-1909....... **TCLC 24**
See also CA 118; DLB 19

Davidson, Sara 1943-............. **CLC 9**
See also CA 81-84

Davie, Donald (Alfred)
1922-............... **CLC 5, 8, 10, 31**
See also CAAS 3; CANR 1; CA 1-4R;
DLB 27

Davies, Ray(mond Douglas) 1944-.. **CLC 21**
See also CA 116

Davies, Rhys 1903-1978.......... **CLC 23**
See also CANR 4; CA 9-12R;
obituary CA 81-84

Davies, (William) Robertson
1913-............. **CLC 2, 7, 13, 25, 42**
See also WLC 2; CANR 17; CA 33-36R;
DLB 68

Davies, W(illiam) H(enry)
1871-1940 .... **TCLC 5**
See also CA 104; DLB 19

Davis, Frank Marshall 1905-1987
See also BLC 1; CA 123, 125; DLB 51

Davis, H(arold) L(enoir)
1896-1960 .... **CLC 49**
See also obituary CA 89-92; DLB 9

Davis, Rebecca (Blaine) Harding
1831-1910 .... **TCLC 6**
See also CA 104; DLB 74

Davis, Richard Harding
1864-1916 .... **TCLC 24**
See also CA 114; DLB 12, 23, 78, 79

Davison, Frank Dalby 1893-1970 ... **CLC 15**
See also obituary CA 116

Davison, Peter 1928-............. **CLC 28**
See also CAAS 4; CANR 3; CA 9-12R;
DLB 5

Davys, Mary 1674-1732............. **LC 1**
See also DLB 39

Dawson, Fielding 1930-........ **CLC 6**
See also CA 85-88

Day, Clarence (Shepard, Jr.)
1874-1935 .... **TCLC 25**
See also CA 108; DLB 11

Day, Thomas 1748-1789............. **LC 1**
See also YABC 1; DLB 39

Day Lewis, C(ecil)
1904-1972 .... **CLC 1, 6, 10**
See also CAP 1; CA 15-16;
obituary CA 33-36R; DLB 15, 20

Dazai Osamu 1909-1948 .... **TCLC 11**
See also Tsushima Shuji

De Crayencour, Marguerite 1903-1987
See Yourcenar, Marguerite

Deer, Sandra 1940-............... **CLC 45**

De Ferrari, Gabriella 19??-....... **CLC 65**

Defoe, Daniel 1660?-1731 .... **LC 1**
See also WLC 2; SATA 22; DLB 39

De Hartog, Jan 1914-............. **CLC 19**
See also CANR 1; CA 1-4R

Deighton, Len 1929-....... **CLC 4, 7, 22, 46**
See also Deighton, Leonard Cyril
See also DLB 87

Deighton, Leonard Cyril 1929-
See Deighton, Len
See also CANR 19; CA 9-12R

De la Mare, Walter (John)
1873-1956 .... **TCLC 4**
See also CLR 23; WLC 2; CA 110;
SATA 16; DLB 19

Delaney, Shelagh 1939-........... **CLC 29**
See also CA 17-20R; DLB 13

Delany, Mary (Granville Pendarves)
1700-1788 .... **LC 12**

Delany, Samuel R(ay, Jr.)
1942-................ **CLC 8, 14, 38**
See also BLC 1; CANR 27; CA 81-84;
DLB 8, 33

de la Ramee, Marie Louise 1839-1908
See Ouida
See also SATA 20

De la Roche, Mazo 1885-1961 ..... **CLC 14**
See also CA 85-88; DLB 68

Delbanco, Nicholas (Franklin)
1942-...................... **CLC 6, 13**
See also CAAS 2; CA 17-20R; DLB 6

del Castillo, Michel 1933-......... **CLC 38**
See also CA 109

Deledda, Grazia 1871-1936 .... **TCLC 23**
See also CA 123

Delibes (Setien), Miguel 1920- ... **CLC 8, 18**
See also CANR 1; CA 45-48

DeLillo, Don
1936-........ **CLC 8, 10, 13, 27, 39, 54**
See also CANR 21; CA 81-84; DLB 6

De Lisser, H(erbert) G(eorge)
1878-1944 .... **TCLC 12**
See also CA 109

Deloria, Vine (Victor), Jr. 1933-.... **CLC 21**
See also CANR 5, 20; CA 53-56; SATA 21

Del Vecchio, John M(ichael)
1947-...................... **CLC 29**
See also CA 110

de Man, Paul 1919-1983 .... **CLC 55**
See also obituary CA 111; DLB 67

De Marinis, Rick 1934-........... **CLC 54**
See also CANR 9, 25; CA 57-60

Demby, William 1922-............. **CLC 53**
See also BLC 1; CA 81-84; DLB 33

Denby, Edwin (Orr) 1903-1983..... **CLC 48**
See also obituary CA 110

Dennis, John 1657-1734............ **LC 11**

Dennis, Nigel (Forbes) 1912-........ **CLC 8**
See also CA 25-28R; obituary CA 129;
DLB 13, 15

De Palma, Brian 1940-............ **CLC 20**
See also CA 109

De Quincey, Thomas 1785-1859 ... **NCLC 4**

Deren, Eleanora 1908-1961
See Deren, Maya
See also obituary CA 111

Deren, Maya 1908-1961........... **CLC 16**
See also Deren, Eleanora

Derleth, August (William)
1909-1971 .... **CLC 31**
See also CANR 4; CA 1-4R;
obituary CA 29-32R; SATA 5; DLB 9

Derrida, Jacques 1930-............ **CLC 24**
See also CA 124, 127

Desai, Anita 1937- .... **CLC 19, 37**
See also CA 81-84

De Saint-Luc, Jean 1909-1981
See Glassco, John

De Sica, Vittorio 1902-1974 .... **CLC 20**
See also obituary CA 117

Desnos, Robert 1900-1945........ **TCLC 22**
See also CA 121

Destouches, Louis-Ferdinand-Auguste
1894-1961
See Celine, Louis-Ferdinand
See also CA 85-88

Deutsch, Babette 1895-1982 .... **CLC 18**
See also CANR 4; CA 1-4R;
obituary CA 108; SATA 1;
obituary SATA 33; DLB 45

Devenant, William 1606-1649 .... **LC 13**

Devkota, Laxmiprasad
1909-1959 .... **TCLC 23**
See also CA 123

DeVoto, Bernard (Augustine)
1897-1955 .... **TCLC 29**
See also CA 113; DLB 9

De Vries, Peter
1910- .... **CLC 1, 2, 3, 7, 10, 28, 46**
See also CA 17-20R; DLB 6; DLB-Y 82

Dexter, Pete 1943-............ **CLC 34, 55**
See also CA 127

Diamano, Silmang 1906-
See Senghor, Leopold Sedar

Diamond, Neil (Leslie) 1941-....... **CLC 30**
See also CA 108

Dick, Philip K(indred)
1928-1982 .... **CLC 10, 30, 72**
See also CANR 2, 16; CA 49-52;
obituary CA 106; DLB 8

Dickens, Charles
1812-1870 .... **NCLC 3, 8, 18, 26**
See also WLC 2; SATA 15; DLB 21, 55, 70

Dickey, James (Lafayette)
1923- .... **CLC 1, 2, 4, 7, 10, 15, 47**
See also CANR 10; CA 9-12R; CABS 2;
DLB 5; DLB-Y 82; DLB-DS 7

Dickey, William 1928-......... **CLC 3, 28**
See also CANR 24; CA 9-12R; DLB 5

Dickinson, Charles 1952-......... **CLC 49**

Dickinson, Emily (Elizabeth)
1830-1886 .... **NCLC 21; PC 1**
See also WLC 2; SATA 29; DLB 1;
CDALB 1865-1917

Dickinson, Peter (Malcolm de Brissac)
1927-.................... **CLC 12, 35**
See also CA 41-44R; SATA 5; DLB 87

Didion, Joan 1934-..... **CLC 1, 3, 8, 14, 32**
See also CANR 14; CA 5-8R; DLB 2;
DLB-Y 81, 86; CDALB 1968-1987

Dillard, Annie 1945-............ **CLC 9, 60**
See also CANR 3; CA 49-52; SATA 10;
DLB-Y 80

Dillard, R(ichard) H(enry) W(ilde)
1937-.................... **CLC 5**
See also CAAS 7; CANR 10; CA 21-24R;
DLB 5

Dillon, Eilis 1920-................ **CLC 17**
See also CLR 26; CAAS 3; CANR 4;
CA 9-12R; SATA 2

Dinesen, Isak
1885-1962 .... **CLC 10, 29; SSC 7**
See also Blixen, Karen (Christentze
Dinesen)
See also CANR 22

Ding Ling 1904-1986 .... **CLC 68**

Disch, Thomas M(ichael) 1940-... **CLC 7, 36**
See also CAAS 4; CANR 17; CA 21-24R;
SATA 54; DLB 8

Disraeli, Benjamin 1804-1881 ..... **NCLC 2**
See also DLB 21, 55

Dixon, Paige 1911-
See Corcoran, Barbara

Dixon, Stephen 1936-............ **CLC 52**
See also CANR 17; CA 89-92

Doblin, Alfred 1878-1957........ **TCLC 13**
See also Doeblin, Alfred

Dobrolyubov, Nikolai Alexandrovich
1836-1861 .... **NCLC 5**

Dobyns, Stephen 1941-............ **CLC 37**
See also CANR 2, 18; CA 45-48

Doctorow, E(dgar) L(aurence)
1931- ..... **CLC 6, 11, 15, 18, 37, 44, 65**
See also CANR 2, 33; CA 45-48; DLB 2,
28; DLB-Y 80; CDALB 1968-1987

Dodgson, Charles Lutwidge 1832-1898
See Carroll, Lewis
See also YABC 2

Dodson, Owen 1914-1983
See also BLC 1; CANR 24; CA 65-68;
obituary CA 110; DLB 76

Doeblin, Alfred 1878-1957........ **TCLC 13**
See also CA 110; DLB 66

Doerr, Harriet 1910- .... **CLC 34**
See also CA 117, 122

Domini, Rey 1934-
See Lorde, Audre

Donaldson, Stephen R. 1947-....... **CLC 46**
See also CANR 13; CA 89-92

Donleavy, J(ames) P(atrick)
1926- .... **CLC 1, 4, 6, 10, 45**
See also CANR 24; CA 9-12R; DLB 6

Donnadieu, Marguerite 1914-
See Duras, Marguerite

Donne, John 1572?-1631 ...... **LC 10; PC 1**
See also WLC 2

Donnell, David 1939?- .... **CLC 34**

Donoso, Jose 1924-........ **CLC 4, 8, 11, 32**
See also CA 81-84

Donovan, John 1928- .... **CLC 35**
See also CLR 3; CA 97-100; SATA 29

Doolittle, Hilda 1886-1961
See H(ilda) D(oolittle)
See also CA 97-100; DLB 4, 45

Dorfman, Ariel 1942-............. **CLC 48**
See also CA 124

Dorn, Ed(ward Merton) 1929-... **CLC 10, 18**
See also CA 93-96; DLB 5

Dos Passos, John (Roderigo)
1896-1970 ... **CLC 1, 4, 8, 11, 15, 25, 34**
See also WLC 2; CANR 3; CA 1-4R;
obituary CA 29-32R; DLB 4, 9;
DLB-DS 1

Dostoevsky, Fyodor
1821-1881 .... **NCLC 2, 7, 21, 33; SSC 2**
See also WLC 2

Doughty, Charles (Montagu)
1843-1926 .... **TCLC 27**
See also CA 115; DLB 19, 57

Douglas, George 1869-1902 .... **TCLC 28**

Douglas, Keith 1920-1944 .... **TCLC 40**
See also DLB 27

Douglass, Frederick 1817?-1895 ... **NCLC 7**
See also BLC 1; WLC 2; SATA 29; DLB 1,
43, 50, 79; CDALB 1640-1865

Dourado, (Waldomiro Freitas) Autran
1926-.................... **CLC 23, 60**
See also CA 25-28R

Dove, Rita 1952-................. **CLC 50**
See also CA 109

Dowson, Ernest (Christopher)
1867-1900 .... **TCLC 4**
See also CA 105; DLB 19

Doyle, (Sir) Arthur Conan
1859-1930 .... **TCLC 7, 26**
See also WLC 2; CA 104, 122; SATA 24;
DLB 18, 70

Dr. A 1933-
See Silverstein, Alvin and Virginia B(arbara
Opshelor) Silverstein

Drabble, Margaret
1939- .... **CLC 2, 3, 5, 8, 10, 22, 53**
See also CANR 18; CA 13-16R; SATA 48;
DLB 14

Drayton, Michael 1563-1631........ **LC 8**

Dreiser, Theodore (Herman Albert)
1871-1945 .... **TCLC 10, 18, 35**
See also WLC 2; CA 106; SATA 48;
DLB 9, 12; DLB-DS 1;
CDALB 1865-1917

Drexler, Rosalyn 1926- .... **CLC 2, 6**
See also CA 81-84

Dreyer, Carl Theodor 1889-1968.... **CLC 16**
See also obituary CA 116

Drieu La Rochelle, Pierre
1893-1945 .... **TCLC 21**
See also CA 117; DLB 72

Droste-Hulshoff, Annette Freiin von
1797-1848 .... **NCLC 3**

Drummond, William Henry
1854-1907 .... **TCLC 25**
See also DLB 92

Drummond de Andrade, Carlos 1902-1987
See Andrade, Carlos Drummond de

Drury, Allen (Stuart) 1918-........ **CLC 37**
See also CANR 18; CA 57-60

Dryden, John 1631-1700 .... **LC 3**
See also WLC 2

Duberman, Martin 1930-........... **CLC 8**
See also CANR 2; CA 1-4R

Dubie, Norman (Evans, Jr.) 1945- .. **CLC 36**
See also CANR 12; CA 69-72

Du Bois, W(illiam) E(dward) B(urghardt)
1868-1963 .... **CLC 1, 2, 13, 64**
See also BLC 1; WLC 2; CA 85-88;
SATA 42; DLB 47, 50, 91;
CDALB 1865-1917

Dubus, Andre 1936-........... **CLC 13, 36**
See also CANR 17; CA 21-24R

Ducasse, Isidore Lucien 1846-1870
See Lautreamont, Comte de

Duclos, Charles Pinot 1704-1772 ..... **LC 1**

Dudek, Louis 1918- .... **CLC 11, 19**
See also CANR 1; CA 45-48; DLB 88

Dudevant, Amandine Aurore Lucile Dupin
1804-1876
See Sand, George

Duerrenmatt, Friedrich
1921- .... CLC 1, 4, 8, 11, 15, 43
See also CA 17-20R; DLB 69

Duffy, Bruce 19??- .... CLC 50

Duffy, Maureen 1933- .... CLC 37
See also CA 25-28R; DLB 14

Dugan, Alan 1923- .... CLC 2, 6
See also CA 81-84; DLB 5

Duhamel, Georges 1884-1966 .... CLC 8
See also CA 81-84; obituary CA 25-28R;
DLB 65

Dujardin, Edouard (Emile Louis)
1861-1949 .... TCLC 13
See also CA 109

Duke, Raoul 1939-
See Thompson, Hunter S(tockton)

Dumas, Alexandre (Davy de la Pailleterie)
(pere) 1802-1870.......... NCLC 11
See also WLC 2; SATA 18

Dumas, Alexandre (fils)
1824-1895 .... NCLC 9; DC 1

Dumas, Henry 1918-1968 .... CLC 62

Dumas, Henry (L.) 1934-1968...... CLC 6
See also CA 85-88; DLB 41

Du Maurier, Daphne 1907- ... CLC 6, 11, 59
See also CANR 6; CA 5-8R;
obituary CA 128; SATA 27

Dunbar, Paul Laurence
1872-1906 .... TCLC 2, 12; SSC 8
See also BLC 1; WLC 2; CA 124;
brief entry CA 104; SATA 34; DLB 50,
54, 78; CDALB 1865-1917

Duncan (Steinmetz Arquette), Lois
1934- .... CLC 26
See also Arquette, Lois S(teinmetz)
See also CANR 2; CA 1-4R; SAAS 2;
SATA 1, 36

Duncan, Robert (Edward)
1919-1988 ... CLC 1, 2, 4, 7, 15, 41, 55;
PC 2
See also CANR 28; CA 9-12R;
obituary CA 124; DLB 5, 16

Dunlap, William 1766-1839 .... NCLC 2
See also DLB 30, 37, 59

Dunn, Douglas (Eaglesham)
1942- .... CLC 6, 40
See also CANR 2; CA 45-48; DLB 40

Dunn, Elsie 1893-1963
See Scott, Evelyn

Dunn, Katherine 1945- .... CLC 71
See also CA 33-36R

Dunn, Stephen 1939- .... CLC 36
See also CANR 12; CA 33-36R

Dunne, Finley Peter 1867-1936.... TCLC 28
See also CA 108; DLB 11, 23

Dunne, John Gregory 1932-........ CLC 28
See also CANR 14; CA 25-28R; DLB-Y 80

Dunsany, Lord (Edward John Moreton Drax
Plunkett) 1878-1957......... TCLC 2
See also CA 104; DLB 10

Durang, Christopher (Ferdinand)
1949- .... CLC 27, 38
See also CA 105

Duras, Marguerite
1914- ...... CLC 3, 6, 11, 20, 34, 40, 68
See also CA 25-28R; DLB 83

Durban, Pam 1947-................ CLC 39
See also CA 123

Durcan, Paul 1944-............ CLC 43, 70
See also CA 134

Durrell, Lawrence (George)
1912-1990 .... CLC 1, 4, 6, 8, 13, 27, 41
See also CA 9-12R; DLB 15, 27

Durrenmatt, Friedrich
1921- .... CLC 1, 4, 8, 11, 15, 43
See also Duerrenmatt, Friedrich
See also DLB 69

Dutt, Toru 1856-1877.......... NCLC 29

Dwight, Timothy 1752-1817...... NCLC 13
See also DLB 37

Dworkin, Andrea 1946- .... CLC 43
See also CANR 16; CA 77-80

Dylan, Bob 1941-.......... CLC 3, 4, 6, 12
See also CA 41-44R; DLB 16

Eagleton, Terry 1943-............. CLC 63

East, Michael 1916-
See West, Morris L.

Eastlake, William (Derry) 1917-..... CLC 8
See also CAAS 1; CANR 5; CA 5-8R;
DLB 6

Eberhart, Richard 1904-... CLC 3, 11, 19, 56
See also CANR 2; CA 1-4R; DLB 48;
CDALB 1941-1968

Eberstadt, Fernanda 1960-......... CLC 39

Echegaray (y Eizaguirre), Jose (Maria Waldo)
1832-1916 .... TCLC 4
See also CA 104

Echeverria, (Jose) Esteban (Antonino)
1805-1851 .... NCLC 18

Eckert, Allan W. 1931- .... CLC 17
See also CANR 14; CA 13-16R; SATA 27,
29

Eckhart, Meister c. 1260-c. 1327 .. CMLC 9

Eco, Umberto 1932-........... CLC 28, 60
See also CANR 12; CA 77-80

Eddison, E(ric) R(ucker)
1882-1945 .... TCLC 15
See also CA 109

Edel, Leon (Joseph) 1907-...... CLC 29, 34
See also CANR 1, 22; CA 1-4R

Eden, Emily 1797-1869 .... NCLC 10

Edgar, David 1948-.............. CLC 42
See also CANR 12; CA 57-60; DLB 13

Edgerton, Clyde 1944- .... CLC 39
See also CA 118

Edgeworth, Maria 1767-1849...... NCLC 1
See also SATA 21

Edmonds, Helen (Woods) 1904-1968
See Kavan, Anna
See also CA 5-8R; obituary CA 25-28R

Edmonds, Walter D(umaux) 1903-.. CLC 35
See also CANR 2; CA 5-8R; SAAS 4;
SATA 1, 27; DLB 9

Edson, Russell 1905- .... CLC 13
See also CA 33-36R

Edwards, Eli 1889-1948
See McKay, Claude

Edwards, G(erald) B(asil)
1899-1976 .... CLC 25
See also obituary CA 110

Edwards, Gus 1939-.............. CLC 43
See also CA 108

Edwards, Jonathan 1703-1758........ LC 7
See also DLB 24

Ehle, John (Marsden, Jr.) 1925-.... CLC 27
See also CA 9-12R

Ehrenburg, Ilya (Grigoryevich)
1891-1967 .... CLC 18, 34, 62
See also CA 102; obituary CA 25-28R

Eich, Guenter 1907-1971
See also CA 111; obituary CA 93-96

Eich, Gunter 1907-1971.......... CLC 15
See also Eich, Guenter
See also DLB 69

Eichendorff, Joseph Freiherr von
1788-1857 .... NCLC 8
See also DLB 90

Eigner, Larry 1927- .... CLC 9
See also Eigner, Laurence (Joel)
See also DLB 5

Eigner, Laurence (Joel) 1927-
See Eigner, Larry
See also CANR 6; CA 9-12R

Eiseley, Loren (Corey) 1907-1977.... CLC 7
See also CANR 6; CA 1-4R;
obituary CA 73-76

Eisenstadt, Jill 1963- .... CLC 50

Ekeloef, Gunnar (Bengt) 1907-1968
See Ekelof, Gunnar (Bengt)
See also obituary CA 25-28R

Ekelof, Gunnar (Bengt) 1907-1968 .. CLC 27
See also Ekeloef, Gunnar (Bengt)

Ekwensi, Cyprian (Odiatu Duaka)
1921- .... CLC 4
See also BLC 1; CANR 18; CA 29-32R

Elder, Lonne, III 1931-
See also BLC 1; CANR 25; CA 81-84;
DLB 7, 38, 44

Eliade, Mircea 1907-1986 .... CLC 19
See also CA 65-68; obituary CA 119

Eliot, George 1819-1880.... NCLC 4, 13, 23
See also WLC 2; DLB 21, 35, 55

Eliot, John 1604-1690 .... LC 5
See also DLB 24

Eliot, T(homas) S(tearns)
1888-1965 .... CLC 1, 2, 3, 6, 9, 10, 13,
15, 24, 34, 41, 55, 57
See also WLC 2; CA 5-8R;
obituary CA 25-28R; DLB 7, 10, 45, 63;
DLB-Y 88

Elizabeth 1866-1941............. TCLC 41
See also Russell, Mary Annette Beauchamp

Elkin, Stanley (Lawrence)
1930- .... CLC 4, 6, 9, 14, 27, 51
See also CANR 8; CA 9-12R; DLB 2, 28;
DLB-Y 80

Elledge, Scott 19??- .... CLC 34

Elliott, George P(aul) 1918-1980..... CLC 2
See also CANR 2; CA 1-4R;
obituary CA 97-100

Elliott, Janice 1931-.............. CLC 47
See also CANR 8; CA 13-16R; DLB 14

Elliott, Sumner Locke 1917-....... CLC 38
See also CANR 2, 21; CA 5-8R

Ellis, A. E. 19??-.................. CLC 7

Ellis, Alice Thomas 19??-.......... CLC 40

Ellis, Bret Easton 1964-........ CLC 39, 71
See also CA 118, 123; AAYA 2

Ellis, (Henry) Havelock
1859-1939 .... TCLC 14
See also CA 109

Ellis, Trey 1964-................ CLC 55

Ellison, Harlan (Jay) 1934-... CLC 1, 13, 42
See also CANR 5; CA 5-8R; DLB 8

Ellison, Ralph (Waldo)
1914- .... CLC 1, 3, 11, 54
See also BLC 1; WLC 2; CANR 24;
CA 9-12R; DLB 2, 76;
CDALB 1941-1968

Ellmann, Lucy 1956- .... CLC 61
See also CA 128

Ellmann, Richard (David)
1918-1987 .... CLC 50
See also CANR 2; CA 1-4R;
obituary CA 122; DLB-Y 87

Elman, Richard 1934-............. CLC 19
See also CAAS 3; CA 17-20R

El-Shabazz, El-Hajj Malik 1925-1965
See Malcolm X

Eluard, Paul 1895-1952 .... TCLC 7, 41
See also Grindel, Eugene

Elyot, Sir Thomas 1490?-1546....... LC 11

Elytis, Odysseus 1911-......... CLC 15, 49
See also CA 102

Emecheta, (Florence Onye) Buchi
1944- .... CLC 14, 48
See also BLC 2; CANR 27; CA 81-84

Emerson, Ralph Waldo
1803-1882 .... NCLC 1
See also WLC 2; DLB 1, 59, 73;
CDALB 1640-1865

Eminescu, Mihail 1850-1889 ..... NCLC 33

Empson, William
1906-1984 .... CLC 3, 8, 19, 33, 34
See also CA 17-20R; obituary CA 112;
DLB 20

Enchi, Fumiko (Veda) 1905-1986 ... CLC 31
See also obituary CA 121

Ende, Michael 1930-............. CLC 31
See also CLR 14; CA 118, 124; SATA 42;
DLB 75

Endo, Shusaku 1923-..... CLC 7, 14, 19, 54
See also CANR 21; CA 29-32R

Engel, Marian 1933-1985.......... CLC 36
See also CANR 12; CA 25-28R; DLB 53

Engelhardt, Frederick 1911-1986
See Hubbard, L(afayette) Ron(ald)

Enright, D(ennis) J(oseph)
1920- .... CLC 4, 8, 31
See also CANR 1; CA 1-4R; SATA 25;
DLB 27

Enzensberger, Hans Magnus
1929- .... CLC 43
See also CA 116, 119

Ephron, Nora 1941- .... CLC 17, 31
See also CANR 12; CA 65-68

Epstein, Daniel Mark 1948- .... CLC 7
See also CANR 2; CA 49-52

Epstein, Jacob 1956- .... CLC 19
See also CA 114

Epstein, Joseph 1937-............. CLC 39
See also CA 112, 119

Epstein, Leslie 1938- .... CLC 27
See also CANR 23; CA 73-76

Equiano, Olaudah 1745?-1797...... LC 16
See also BLC 2; DLB 37, 50

Erasmus, Desiderius 1469?-1536..... LC 16

Erdman, Paul E(mil) 1932- .... CLC 25
See also CANR 13; CA 61-64

Erdrich, Louise 1954-.......... CLC 39, 54
See also CA 114

Erenburg, Ilya (Grigoryevich) 1891-1967
See Ehrenburg, Ilya (Grigoryevich)

Erickson, Steve 1950-............. CLC 64
See also CA 129

Eseki, Bruno 1919-
See Mphahlele, Ezekiel

Esenin, Sergei (Aleksandrovich)
1895-1925 .... TCLC 4
See also CA 104

Eshleman, Clayton 1935-........... CLC 7
See also CAAS 6; CA 33-36R; DLB 5

Espriu, Salvador 1913-1985........ CLC 9
See also obituary CA 115

Estleman, Loren D. 1952- .... CLC 48
See also CA 85-88

Evans, Marian 1819-1880
See Eliot, George

Evans, Mary Ann 1819-1880
See Eliot, George

Evarts, Esther 1900-1972
See Benson, Sally

Everett, Percival L. 1957?- .... CLC 57
See also CA 129

Everson, Ronald G(ilmour) 1903-... CLC 27
See also CA 17-20R; DLB 88

Everson, William (Oliver)
1912- .... CLC 1, 5, 14
See also CANR 20; CA 9-12R; DLB 5, 16

Everyman 1495-................... DC 2

Evtushenko, Evgenii (Aleksandrovich) 1933-
See Yevtushenko, Yevgeny

Ewart, Gavin (Buchanan)
1916- .... CLC 13, 46
See also CANR 17; CA 89-92; DLB 40

Ewers, Hanns Heinz 1871-1943 ... TCLC 12
See also CA 109

Ewing, Frederick R. 1918-
See Sturgeon, Theodore (Hamilton)

Exley, Frederick (Earl) 1929- .... CLC 6, 11
See also CA 81-84; DLB-Y 81

Ezekiel, Nissim 1924-............. CLC 61
See also CA 61-64

Ezekiel, Tish O'Dowd 1943-....... CLC 34

Fagen, Donald 1948-............. CLC 26

Fair, Ronald L. 1932-............. CLC 18
See also CANR 25; CA 69-72; DLB 33

Fairbairns, Zoe (Ann) 1948- .... CLC 32
See also CANR 21; CA 103

Fairfield, Cicily Isabel 1892-1983
See West, Rebecca

Fallaci, Oriana 1930-............. CLC 11
See also CANR 15; CA 77-80

Faludy, George 1913-............. CLC 42
See also CA 21-24R

Fanon, Frantz 1925-1961
See also BLC 2; CA 116; obituary CA 89-92

Fante, John 1909-1983............ CLC 60
See also CANR 23; CA 69-72;
obituary CA 109; DLB-Y 83

Farah, Nuruddin 1945-............ CLC 53
See also BLC 2; CA 106

Fargue, Leon-Paul 1876-1947 ..... TCLC 11
See also CA 109

Farigoule, Louis 1885-1972
See Romains, Jules

Farina, Richard 1937?-1966......... CLC 9
See also CA 81-84; obituary CA 25-28R

Farley, Walter 1920- .... CLC 17
See also CANR 8; CA 17-20R; SATA 2, 43;
DLB 22

Farmer, Philip Jose 1918-....... CLC 1, 19
See also CANR 4; CA 1-4R; DLB 8

Farrell, J(ames) G(ordon)
1935-1979 .... CLC 6
See also CA 73-76; obituary CA 89-92;
DLB 14

Farrell, James T(homas)
1904-1979 .... CLC 1, 4, 8, 11, 66
See also CANR 9; CA 5-8R;
obituary CA 89-92; DLB 4, 9, 86;
DLB-DS 2

Farrell, M. J. 1904-
See Keane, Molly

Fassbinder, Rainer Werner
1946-1982 .... CLC 20
See also CA 93-96; obituary CA 106

Fast, Howard (Melvin) 1914- ...... CLC 23
See also CANR 1; CA 1-4R; SATA 7;
DLB 9

Faulkner, William (Cuthbert)
1897-1962 .... CLC 1, 3, 6, 8, 9, 11, 14,
18, 28, 52, 68; SSC 1
See also WLC 2; CANR 33; CA 81-84;
DLB 9, 11, 44, 102; DLB-Y 86;
DLB-DS 2; CDALB 1929-1941

Fauset, Jessie Redmon
1882-1961 .... CLC 19, 54
See also BLC 2; CA 109; DLB 51

Faust, Irvin 1924-................. CLC 8
See also CA 33-36R; DLB 2, 28; DLB-Y 80

Fearing, Kenneth (Flexner)
1902-1961 .... CLC 51
See also CA 93-96; DLB 9

Federman, Raymond 1928- ...... CLC 6, 47
See also CANR 10; CA 17-20R; DLB-Y 80

Federspiel, J(urg) F. 1931-........ CLC 42

Feiffer, Jules 1929-........... CLC 2, 8, 64
See also CANR 30; CA 17-20R; SATA 8,
61; DLB 7, 44; AAYA 3

Feinberg, David B. 1956-......... CLC 59

Feinstein, Elaine 1930-............ CLC 36
See also CAAS 1; CA 69-72; DLB 14, 40

Feke, Gilbert David 1976?- .... CLC 65

Feldman, Irving (Mordecai) 1928-.... CLC 7
See also CANR 1; CA 1-4R

Fellini, Federico 1920-............ CLC 16
See also CA 65-68

Felsen, Gregor 1916-
See Felsen, Henry Gregor

Felsen, Henry Gregor 1916- .... CLC 17
See also CANR 1; CA 1-4R; SAAS 2;
SATA 1

Fenton, James (Martin) 1949-...... CLC 32
See also CA 102; DLB 40

Ferber, Edna 1887-1968........... CLC 18
See also CA 5-8R; obituary CA 25-28R;
SATA 7; DLB 9, 28, 86

Ferguson, Samuel 1810-1886..... NCLC 33
See also DLB 32

Ferlinghetti, Lawrence (Monsanto)
1919?- .... CLC 2, 6, 10, 27; PC 1
See also CANR 3; CA 5-8R; DLB 5, 16;
CDALB 1941-1968

Ferrier, Susan (Edmonstone)
1782-1854 .... NCLC 8

Ferrigno, Robert 19??-............ CLC 65

Feuchtwanger, Lion 1884-1958 ..... TCLC 3
See also CA 104; DLB 66

Feydeau, Georges 1862-1921...... TCLC 22
See also CA 113

Ficino, Marsilio 1433-1499 .... LC 12

Fiedler, Leslie A(aron)
1917-................. CLC 4, 13, 24
See also CANR 7; CA 9-12R; DLB 28, 67

Field, Andrew 1938-.............. CLC 44
See also CANR 25; CA 97-100

Field, Eugene 1850-1895 .... NCLC 3
See also SATA 16; DLB 21, 23, 42

Field, Michael .... TCLC 43

Fielding, Henry 1707-1754 .... LC 1
See also WLC 2; DLB 39, 84

Fielding, Sarah 1710-1768 .... LC 1
See also DLB 39

Fierstein, Harvey 1954-........... CLC 33
See also CA 123, 129

Figes, Eva 1932-................. CLC 31
See also CANR 4; CA 53-56; DLB 14

Finch, Robert (Duer Claydon)
1900-..................... CLC 18
See also CANR 9, 24; CA 57-60; DLB 88

Findley, Timothy 1930-........... CLC 27
See also CANR 12; CA 25-28R; DLB 53

Fink, Janis 1951-
See Ian, Janis

Firbank, Louis 1944-
See Reed, Lou
See also CA 117

Firbank, (Arthur Annesley) Ronald
1886-1926 .... TCLC 1
See also CA 104; DLB 36

Fisher, Roy 1930-................. CLC 25
See also CANR 16; CA 81-84; DLB 40

Fisher, Rudolph 1897-1934 .... TCLC 11
See also BLC 2; CA 107, 124; DLB 51

Fisher, Vardis (Alvero) 1895-1968.... CLC 7
See also CA 5-8R; obituary CA 25-28R;
DLB 9

FitzGerald, Edward 1809-1883 .... NCLC 9
See also DLB 32

Fitzgerald, F(rancis) Scott (Key)
1896-1940 .... TCLC 1, 6, 14, 28; SSC 6
See also WLC 2; CA 110, 123; DLB 4, 9,
86; DLB-Y 81; DLB-DS 1;
CDALB 1917-1929

Fitzgerald, Penelope 1916-... CLC 19, 51, 61
See also CAAS 10; CA 85-88,; DLB 14

Fitzgerald, Robert (Stuart)
1910-1985 .... CLC 39
See also CANR 1; CA 2R;
obituary CA 114; DLB-Y 80

FitzGerald, Robert D(avid) 1902-... CLC 19
See also CA 17-20R

Flanagan, Thomas (James Bonner)
1923-.................... CLC 25, 52
See also CA 108; DLB-Y 80

Flaubert, Gustave
1821-1880 .... NCLC 2, 10, 19
See also WLC 2

Flecker, (Herman) James Elroy
1884-1913 .... TCLC 43
See also CA 109; DLB 10, 19

Fleming, Ian (Lancaster)
1908-1964 .... CLC 3, 30
See also CA 5-8R; SATA 9; DLB 87

Fleming, Thomas J(ames) 1927- ... CLC 37
See also CANR 10; CA 5-8R; SATA 8

Fletcher, John Gould 1886-1950 ... TCLC 35
See also CA 107; DLB 4, 45

Flieg, Hellmuth
See Heym, Stefan

Flying Officer X 1905-1974
See Bates, H(erbert) E(rnest)

Fo, Dario 1929-................. CLC 32
See also CA 116

Follett, Ken(neth Martin) 1949- .... CLC 18
See also CANR 13; CA 81-84; DLB-Y 81

Fontane, Theodor 1819-1898..... NCLC 26

Foote, Horton 1916-.............. CLC 51
See also CA 73-76; DLB 26

Forbes, Esther 1891-1967......... CLC 12
See also CAP 1; CA 13-14;
obituary CA 25-28R; SATA 2; DLB 22

Forche, Carolyn 1950-............ CLC 25
See also CA 109, 117; DLB 5

Ford, Ford Madox
1873-1939 .... TCLC 1, 15, 39
See also CA 104; DLB 34

Ford, John 1895-1973............. CLC 16
See also obituary CA 45-48

Ford, Richard 1944-.............. CLC 46
See also CANR 11; CA 69-72

Foreman, Richard 1937-.......... CLC 50
See also CA 65-68

Forester, C(ecil) S(cott)
1899-1966 .... CLC 35
See also CA 73-76; obituary CA 25-28R;
SATA 13

Forman, James D(ouglas) 1932- .... CLC 21
See also CANR 4, 19; CA 9-12R; SATA 8,
21

Fornes, Maria Irene 1930-...... CLC 39, 61
See also CANR 28; CA 25-28R; DLB 7

Forrest, Leon 1937- .... CLC 4
See also CAAS 7; CA 89-92; DLB 33

Forster, E(dward) M(organ)
1879-1970 .... CLC 1, 2, 3, 4, 9, 10, 13,
15, 22, 45
See also WLC 2; CAP 1; CA 13-14;
obituary CA 25-28R; SATA 57; DLB 34

Forster, John 1812-1876 .... NCLC 11

Forsyth, Frederick 1938-...... CLC 2, 5, 36
See also CA 85-88; DLB 87

Forten (Grimke), Charlotte L(ottie)
1837?-1914................... TCLC 16
See also Grimke, Charlotte L(ottie) Forten
See also BLC 2; DLB 50

Foscolo, Ugo 1778-1827.......... NCLC 8

Fosse, Bob 1925-1987............. CLC 20
See also Fosse, Robert Louis

Fosse, Robert Louis 1925-1987
See Bob Fosse
See also CA 110, 123

Foster, Stephen Collins
1826-1864 .... NCLC 26

Foucault, Michel
1926-1984 .... CLC 31, 34, 69
See also CANR 23, 34; CA 105;
obituary CA 113

Fouque, Friedrich (Heinrich Karl) de La
Motte 1777-1843 .... NCLC 2

Fournier, Henri Alban 1886-1914
See Alain-Fournier
See also CA 104

Fournier, Pierre 1916-............ CLC 11
See also Gascar, Pierre
See also CANR 16; CA 89-92

Fowles, John (Robert)
1926- .... CLC 1, 2, 3, 4, 6, 9, 10, 15, 33
See also CANR 25; CA 5-8R; SATA 22;
DLB 14

Fox, Paula 1923-................. CLC 2, 8
See also CLR 1; CANR 20; CA 73-76;
SATA 17; DLB 52

Fox, William Price (Jr.) 1926- ..... CLC 22
See also CANR 11; CA 17-20R; DLB 2;
DLB-Y 81

Foxe, John 1516?-1587............. LC 14

Frame (Clutha), Janet (Paterson)
1924- .... CLC 2, 3, 6, 22, 66
See also Clutha, Janet Paterson Frame

France, Anatole 1844-1924 .... TCLC 9
See also Thibault, Jacques Anatole Francois

Francis, Claude 19??-............. CLC 50

Francis, Dick 1920- .... CLC 2, 22, 42
See also CANR 9; CA 5-8R; DLB 87

Francis, Robert (Churchill)
1901-1987 .... CLC **15**
See also CANR 1; CA 1-4R;
obituary CA 123

Frank, Anne 1929-1945 .... TCLC **17**
See also WLC 2; CA 113; SATA 42

Frank, Elizabeth 1945- .... CLC **39**
See also CA 121, 126

Franklin, (Stella Maria Sarah) Miles
1879-1954 .... TCLC **7**
See also CA 104

Fraser, Antonia (Pakenham)
1932- .... CLC **32**
See also CA 85-88; SATA 32

Fraser, George MacDonald 1925- .... CLC **7**
See also CANR 2; CA 45-48

Fraser, Sylvia 1935- .... CLC **64**
See also CANR 1, 16; CA 45-48

Frayn, Michael 1933- ...... CLC **3, 7, 31, 47**
See also CA 5-8R; DLB 13, 14

Fraze, Candida 19??- .... CLC **50**
See also CA 125

Frazer, Sir James George
1854-1941 .... TCLC **32**
See also CA 118

Frazier, Ian 1951- .... CLC **46**
See also CA 130

Frederic, Harold 1856-1898 ...... NCLC **10**
See also DLB 12, 23

Frederick the Great 1712-1786 ...... LC **14**

Fredman, Russell (Bruce) 1929-
See also CLR 20

Fredro, Aleksander 1793-1876 ..... NCLC **8**

Freeling, Nicolas 1927- .... CLC **38**
See also CANR 1, 17; CA 49-52; DLB 87

Freeman, Douglas Southall
1886-1953 .... TCLC **11**
See also CA 109; DLB 17

Freeman, Judith 1946- .... CLC **55**

Freeman, Mary (Eleanor) Wilkins
1852-1930 .... TCLC **9; SSC 1**
See also CA 106; DLB 12, 78

Freeman, R(ichard) Austin
1862-1943 .... TCLC **21**
See also CA 113; DLB 70

French, Marilyn 1929- ...... CLC **10, 18, 60**
See also CANR 3; CA 69-72

Freneau, Philip Morin 1752-1832 .. NCLC **1**
See also DLB 37, 43

Friedman, B(ernard) H(arper)
1926- .... CLC **7**
See also CANR 3; CA 1-4R

Friedman, Bruce Jay 1930- .... CLC **3, 5, 56**
See also CANR 25; CA 9-12R; DLB 2, 28

Friel, Brian 1929- .... CLC **5, 42, 59**
See also CA 21-24R; DLB 13

Friis-Baastad, Babbis (Ellinor)
1921-1970 .... CLC **12**
See also CA 17-20R; SATA 7

Frisch, Max (Rudolf)
1911- .... CLC **3, 9, 14, 18, 32, 44**
See also CA 85-88; DLB 69

Fromentin, Eugene (Samuel Auguste)
1820-1876 .... NCLC **10**

Frost, Robert (Lee)
1874-1963 ... CLC **1, 3, 4, 9, 10, 13, 15,
26, 34, 44; PC 1**
See also WLC 2; CA 89-92; SATA 14;
DLB 54; DLB-DS 7; CDALB 1917-1929

Fry, Christopher 1907- .... CLC **2, 10, 14**
See also CANR 9; CA 17-20R; DLB 13

Frye, (Herman) Northrop
1912-1991 .... CLC **24, 70**
See also CANR 8; CA 5-8R;
obituary CA 133; DLB 67, 68

Fuchs, Daniel 1909- .... CLC **8, 22**
See also CAAS 5; CA 81-84; DLB 9, 26, 28

Fuchs, Daniel 1934- .... CLC **34**
See also CANR 14; CA 37-40R

Fuentes, Carlos
1928- ...... CLC **3, 8, 10, 13, 22, 41, 60**
See also WLC 2; CANR 10; CA 69-72

Fugard, Athol 1932- ... CLC **5, 9, 14, 25, 40**
See also CA 85-88

Fugard, Sheila 1932- .... CLC **48**
See also CA 125

Fuller, Charles (H., Jr.)
1939- .... CLC **25; DC 1**
See also BLC 2; CA 108, 112; DLB 38

Fuller, John (Leopold) 1937- .... CLC **62**
See also CANR 9; CA 21-22R; DLB 40

Fuller, (Sarah) Margaret
1810-1850 .... NCLC **5**
See also Ossoli, Sarah Margaret (Fuller
marchesa d')
See also DLB 1, 59, 73; CDALB 1640-1865

Fuller, Roy (Broadbent) 1912- .... CLC **4, 28**
See also CA 5-8R; DLB 15, 20

Fulton, Alice 1952- .... CLC **52**
See also CA 116

Furabo 1644-1694
See Basho, Matsuo

Furphy, Joseph 1843-1912 .... TCLC **25**

Futabatei Shimei 1864-1909 ...... TCLC **44**

Futrelle, Jacques 1875-1912 ...... TCLC **19**
See also CA 113

Gaboriau, Emile 1835-1873 ...... NCLC **14**

Gadda, Carlo Emilio 1893-1973 .... CLC **11**
See also CA 89-92

Gaddis, William
1922- .... CLC **1, 3, 6, 8, 10, 19, 43**
See also CAAS 4; CANR 21; CA 17-20R;
DLB 2

Gaines, Ernest J. 1933- ...... CLC **3, 11, 18**
See also BLC 2; CANR 6, 24; CA 9-12R;
DLB 2, 33; DLB-Y 80;
CDALB 1968-1988

Gaitskill, Mary 1954- .... CLC **69**
See also CA 128

Gale, Zona 1874-1938 .... TCLC **7**
See also CA 105; DLB 9, 78

Galeano, Eduardo 1940- .... CLC **72**
See also CANR 13-32; CA 29-35R

Gallagher, Tess 1943- .... CLC **18, 63**
See also CA 106

Gallant, Mavis
1922- .... CLC **7, 18, 38; SSC 5**
See also CA 69-72; DLB 53

Gallant, Roy A(rthur) 1924- .... CLC **17**
See also CANR 4; CA 5-8R; SATA 4

Gallico, Paul (William) 1897-1976 ... CLC **2**
See also CA 5-8R; obituary CA 69-72;
SATA 13; DLB 9

Galsworthy, John 1867-1933 .... TCLC **1, 45**
See also WLC 2; brief entry CA 104;
DLB 10, 34, 98

Galt, John 1779-1839 .... NCLC **1**

Galvin, James 1951- .... CLC **38**
See also CANR 26; CA 108

Gamboa, Frederico 1864-1939 ..... TCLC **36**

Gann, Ernest K(ellogg) 1910- ...... CLC **23**
See also CANR 1; CA 1-4R

Garcia Lorca, Federico
1898-1936 ..... TCLC **1, 7; DC 2; PC 3**
See also WLC 2; CA 131;
brief entry CA 104; DLB 108

Garcia Marquez, Gabriel (Jose)
1928- ... CLC **2, 3, 8, 10, 15, 27, 47, 55,
68; SSC 8**
See also WLC 3; CANR 10, 28;
CA 33-36R; AAYA 3

Gardam, Jane 1928- .... CLC **43**
See also CLR 12; CANR 2, 18; CA 49-52;
SATA 28, 39; DLB 14

Gardner, Herb 1934- .... CLC **44**

Gardner, John (Champlin, Jr.)
1933-1982 .... CLC **2, 3, 5, 7, 8, 10, 18,
28, 34; SSC 7**
See also CA 65-68; obituary CA 107;
obituary SATA 31, 40; DLB 2; DLB-Y 82

Gardner, John (Edmund) 1926- ..... CLC **30**
See also CANR 15; CA 103

Gardons, S. S. 1926-
See Snodgrass, W(illiam) D(e Witt)

Garfield, Leon 1921- .... CLC **12**
See also CA 17-20R; SATA 1, 32

Garland, (Hannibal) Hamlin
1860-1940 .... TCLC **3**
See also CA 104; DLB 12, 71, 78

Garneau, Hector (de) Saint Denys
1912-1943 .... TCLC **13**
See also CA 111; DLB 88

Garner, Alan 1935- .... CLC **17**
See also CLR 20; CANR 15; CA 73-76;
SATA 18

Garner, Hugh 1913-1979 .... CLC **13**
See also CA 69-72; DLB 68

Garnett, David 1892-1981 .... CLC **3**
See also CANR 17; CA 5-8R;
obituary CA 103; DLB 34

Garrett, George (Palmer, Jr.)
1929- .... CLC **3, 11, 51**
See also CAAS 5; CANR 1; CA 1-4R;
DLB 2, 5; DLB-Y 83

Garrick, David 1717-1779 .... LC **15**
See also DLB 84

Garrigue, Jean 1914-1972 .... CLC **2, 8**
See also CANR 20; CA 5-8R;
obituary CA 37-40R

Garvey, Marcus 1887-1940 ...... **TCLC 41**
See also BLC 2; CA 124; brief entry CA 120

Gary, Romain 1914-1980 .... **CLC 25**
See also Kacew, Romain

Gascar, Pierre 1916- .... **CLC 11**
See also Fournier, Pierre

Gascoyne, David (Emery) 1916- .... **CLC 45**
See also CANR 10; CA 65-68; DLB 20

Gaskell, Elizabeth Cleghorn
1810-1865 .... **NCLC 5**
See also DLB 21

Gass, William H(oward)
1924- .... **CLC 1, 2, 8, 11, 15, 39**
See also CA 17-20R; DLB 2

Gates, Henry Louis, Jr. 1950- ...... **CLC 65**
See also CANR 25; CA 109; DLB 67

Gautier, Theophile 1811-1872 ..... **NCLC 1**

Gaye, Marvin (Pentz) 1939-1984 ... **CLC 26**
See also obituary CA 112

Gebler, Carlo (Ernest) 1954- .... **CLC 39**
See also CA 119

Gee, Maggie 19??- .... **CLC 57**

Gee, Maurice (Gough) 1931- .... **CLC 29**
See also CA 97-100; SATA 46

Gelbart, Larry 1923?- .... **CLC 21, 61**
See also CA 73-76

Gelber, Jack 1932- .... **CLC 1, 6, 14, 60**
See also CANR 2; CA 1-4R; DLB 7

Gellhorn, Martha (Ellis) 1908- .. **CLC 14, 60**
See also CA 77-80; DLB-Y 82

Genet, Jean
1910-1986 ... **CLC 1, 2, 5, 10, 14, 44, 46**
See also CANR 18; CA 13-16R; DLB 72;
DLB-Y 86

Gent, Peter 1942- .... **CLC 29**
See also CA 89-92; DLB 72; DLB-Y 82

George, Jean Craighead 1919- ...... **CLC 35**
See also CLR 1; CA 5-8R; SATA 2;
DLB 52

George, Stefan (Anton)
1868-1933 .... **TCLC 2, 14**
See also CA 104

Gerhardi, William (Alexander) 1895-1977
See Gerhardie, William (Alexander)

Gerhardie, William (Alexander)
1895-1977 .... **CLC 5**
See also CANR 18; CA 25-28R;
obituary CA 73-76; DLB 36

Gerstler, Amy 1956- .... **CLC 70**

Gertler, T(rudy) 1946?- .... **CLC 34**
See also CA 116

Gessner, Friedrike Victoria 1910-1980
See Adamson, Joy(-Friederike Victoria)

Ghelderode, Michel de
1898-1962 .... **CLC 6, 11**
See also CA 85-88

Ghiselin, Brewster 1903- .... **CLC 23**
See also CANR 13; CA 13-16R

Ghose, Zulfikar 1935- .... **CLC 42**
See also CA 65-68

Ghosh, Amitav 1943- .... **CLC 44**

Giacosa, Giuseppe 1847-1906 ...... **TCLC 7**
See also CA 104

Gibbon, Lewis Grassic 1901-1935 ... **TCLC 4**
See also Mitchell, James Leslie

Gibbons, Kaye 1960- .... **CLC 50**

Gibran, (Gibran) Kahlil
1883-1931 .... **TCLC 1, 9**
See also CA 104

Gibson, William 1914- .... **CLC 23**
See also CANR 9; CA 9-12R; DLB 7

Gibson, William 1948- .... **CLC 39, 63**
See also CA 126

Gide, Andre (Paul Guillaume)
1869-1951 .... **TCLC 5, 12, 36**
See also WLC 3; CA 104, 124; DLB 65

Gifford, Barry (Colby) 1946- .... **CLC 34**
See also CANR 9; CA 65-68

Gilbert, (Sir) W(illiam) S(chwenck)
1836-1911 .... **TCLC 3**
See also CA 104; SATA 36

Gilbreth, Ernestine 1908-
See Carey, Ernestine Gilbreth

Gilbreth, Frank B(unker), Jr.
1911- .... **CLC 17**
See also CA 9-12R; SATA 2

Gilchrist, Ellen 1935- .... **CLC 34, 48**
See also CA 113, 116

Giles, Molly 1942- .... **CLC 39**
See also CA 126

Gilliam, Terry (Vance) 1940-
See Monty Python
See also CA 108, 113

Gilliatt, Penelope (Ann Douglass)
1932- .... **CLC 2, 10, 13, 53**
See also CA 13-16R; DLB 14

Gilman, Charlotte (Anna) Perkins (Stetson)
1860-1935 .... **TCLC 9, 37**
See also CA 106

Gilmour, David 1944-
See Pink Floyd

Gilpin, William 1724-1804 ...... **NCLC 30**

Gilroy, Frank D(aniel) 1925- .... **CLC 2**
See also CA 81-84; DLB 7

Ginsberg, Allen
1926- ..... **CLC 1, 2, 3, 4, 6, 13, 36, 69;**
PC 4
See also WLC 3; CANR 2; CA 1-4R;
DLB 5, 16; CDALB 1941-1968

Ginzburg, Natalia
1916-1991 .... **CLC 5, 11, 54, 70**
See also CANR 33; CA 85-88

Giono, Jean 1895-1970 .... **CLC 4, 11**
See also CANR 2; CA 45-48;
obituary CA 29-32R; DLB 72

Giovanni, Nikki 1943- ..... **CLC 2, 4, 19, 64**
See also BLC 2; CLR 6; CAAS 6;
CANR 18; CA 29-32R; SATA 24;
DLB 5, 41

Giovene, Andrea 1904- .... **CLC 7**
See also CA 85-88

Gippius, Zinaida (Nikolayevna) 1869-1945
See Hippius, Zinaida
See also CA 106

Giraudoux, (Hippolyte) Jean
1882-1944 .... **TCLC 2, 7**
See also CA 104; DLB 65

Gironella, Jose Maria 1917- .... **CLC 11**
See also CA 101

Gissing, George (Robert)
1857-1903 .... **TCLC 3, 24**
See also CA 105; DLB 18

Gladkov, Fyodor (Vasilyevich)
1883-1958 .... **TCLC 27**

Glanville, Brian (Lester) 1931- ...... **CLC 6**
See also CANR 3; CA 5-8R; SATA 42;
DLB 15

Glasgow, Ellen (Anderson Gholson)
1873?-1945 .... **TCLC 2, 7**
See also CA 104; DLB 9, 12

Glassco, John 1909-1981 .... **CLC 9**
See also CANR 15; CA 13-16R;
obituary CA 102; DLB 68

Glasser, Ronald J. 1940?- .... **CLC 37**

Glendinning, Victoria 1937- .... **CLC 50**
See also CA 120

Glissant, Edouard 1928- .... **CLC 10, 68**

Gloag, Julian 1930- .... **CLC 40**
See also CANR 10; CA 65-68

Gluck, Louise (Elisabeth)
1943- .... **CLC 7, 22, 44**
See also CA 33-36R; DLB 5

Gobineau, Joseph Arthur (Comte) de
1816-1882 .... **NCLC 17**

Godard, Jean-Luc 1930- .... **CLC 20**
See also CA 93-96

Godden, (Margaret) Rumer 1907-... **CLC 53**
See also CLR 20; CANR 4, 27; CA 7-8R;
SATA 3, 36

Godwin, Gail 1937-.... **CLC 5, 8, 22, 31, 69**
See also CANR 15; CA 29-32R; DLB 6

Godwin, William 1756-1836...... **NCLC 14**
See also DLB 39

Goethe, Johann Wolfgang von
1749-1832 .... **NCLC 4, 22, 34**
See also WLC 3; DLB 94

Gogarty, Oliver St. John
1878-1957 .... **TCLC 15**
See also CA 109; DLB 15, 19

Gogol, Nikolai (Vasilyevich)
1809-1852 ..... **NCLC 5, 15, 31; DC 1;**
SSC 4
See also WLC 3

Goines, Donald 1937?-1974
See also BLC 2; CA 124; obituary CA 114;
DLB 33

Gokceli, Yasar Kemal 1923-
See Kemal, Yashar

Gold, Herbert 1924-....... **CLC 4, 7, 14, 42**
See also CANR 17; CA 9-12R; DLB 2;
DLB-Y 81

Goldbarth, Albert 1948- .... **CLC 5, 38**
See also CANR 6; CA 53-56

Goldberg, Anatol 1910-1982 .... **CLC 34**
See also obituary CA 117

Goldemberg, Isaac 1945- .... **CLC 52**
See also CANR 11; CA 69-72

Golding, William (Gerald)
1911- ..... **CLC 1, 2, 3, 8, 10, 17, 27, 58**
See also WLC 3; CANR 13; CA 5-8R;
DLB 15

Goldman, Emma 1869-1940 . . . . . . **TCLC 13**
See also CA 110

Goldman, William (W.) 1931- . . . . **CLC 1, 48**
See also CA 9-12R; DLB 44

Goldmann, Lucien 1913-1970 . . . . . . **CLC 24**
See also CAP 2; CA 25-28

Goldoni, Carlo 1707-1793 . . . . **LC 4**

Goldsberry, Steven 1949- . . . . **CLC 34**

Goldsmith, Oliver 1728?-1774 . . . . **LC 2**
See also WLC 3; SATA 26; DLB 39, 89,
104, 109

Gombrowicz, Witold
1904-1969 . . . . **CLC 4, 7, 11, 49**
See also CAP 2; CA 19-20;
obituary CA 25-28R

Gomez de la Serna, Ramon
1888-1963 . . . . **CLC 9**
See also obituary CA 116

Goncharov, Ivan Alexandrovich
1812-1891 . . . . **NCLC 1**

Goncourt, Edmond (Louis Antoine Huot) de
1822-1896 . . . . **NCLC 7**

Goncourt, Jules (Alfred Huot) de
1830-1870 . . . . **NCLC 7**

Gontier, Fernande 19??- . . . . **CLC 50**

Goodman, Paul 1911-1972 . . . . **CLC 1, 2, 4, 7**
See also CAP 2; CA 19-20;
obituary CA 37-40R

Gordimer, Nadine
1923- . . . . **CLC 3, 5, 7, 10, 18, 33, 51, 70**
See also CANR 3, 28; CA 5-8R

Gordon, Adam Lindsay
1833-1870 . . . . **NCLC 21**

Gordon, Caroline
1895-1981 . . . . **CLC 6, 13, 29**
See also CAP 1; CA 11-12;
obituary CA 103; DLB 4, 9; DLB-Y 81

Gordon, Charles William 1860-1937
See Conner, Ralph
See also CA 109

Gordon, Mary (Catherine)
1949- . . . . **CLC 13, 22**
See also CA 102; DLB 6; DLB-Y 81

Gordon, Sol 1923- . . . . **CLC 26**
See also CANR 4; CA 53-56; SATA 11

Gordone, Charles 1925- . . . . **CLC 1, 4**
See also CA 93-96; DLB 7

Gorenko, Anna Andreyevna 1889?-1966
See Akhmatova, Anna

Gorky, Maxim 1868-1936 . . . . **TCLC 8**
See also Peshkov, Alexei Maximovich
See also WLC 3

Goryan, Sirak 1908-1981
See Saroyan, William

Gosse, Edmund (William)
1849-1928 . . . . **TCLC 28**
See also CA 117; DLB 57

Gotlieb, Phyllis (Fay Bloom)
1926- . . . . **CLC 18**
See also CANR 7; CA 13-16R; DLB 88

Gould, Lois 1938?- . . . . **CLC 4, 10**
See also CA 77-80

Gourmont, Remy de 1858-1915 . . . . **TCLC 17**
See also CA 109

Govier, Katherine 1948- . . . . **CLC 51**
See also CANR 18; CA 101

Goyen, (Charles) William
1915-1983 . . . . **CLC 5, 8, 14, 40**
See also CANR 6; CA 5-8R;
obituary CA 110; DLB 2; DLB-Y 83

Goytisolo, Juan 1931- . . . . **CLC 5, 10, 23**
See also CA 85-88

Gozzi, (Conte) Carlo 1720-1806 . . **NCLC 23**

Grabbe, Christian Dietrich
1801-1836 . . . . **NCLC 2**

Grace, Patricia 1937- . . . . **CLC 56**

Gracian y Morales, Baltasar
1601-1658 . . . . **LC 15**

Gracq, Julien 1910- . . . . **CLC 11, 48**
See also Poirier, Louis
See also DLB 83

Grade, Chaim 1910-1982 . . . . **CLC 10**
See also CA 93-96; obituary CA 107

Graham, Jorie 1951- . . . . **CLC 48**
See also CA 111

Graham, R(obert) B(ontine) Cunninghame
1852-1936 . . . . **TCLC 19**

Graham, W(illiam) S(ydney)
1918-1986 . . . . **CLC 29**
See also CA 73-76; obituary CA 118;
DLB 20

Graham, Winston (Mawdsley)
1910- . . . . **CLC 23**
See also CANR 2, 22; CA 49-52;
obituary CA 118

Granville-Barker, Harley
1877-1946 . . . . **TCLC 2**
See also CA 104

Grass, Gunter (Wilhelm)
1927- . . **CLC 1, 2, 4, 6, 11, 15, 22, 32, 49**
See also WLC 3; CANR 20; CA 13-16R;
DLB 75

Grau, Shirley Ann 1929- . . . . **CLC 4, 9**
See also CANR 22; CA 89-92; DLB 2

Graver, Elizabeth 1965- . . . . **CLC 70**

Graves, Richard Perceval 1945- . . . . **CLC 44**
See also CANR 9, 26; CA 65-68

Graves, Robert (von Ranke)
1895-1985 . . . **CLC 1, 2, 6, 11, 39, 44, 45**
See also CANR 5; CA 5-8R;
obituary CA 117; SATA 45; DLB 20;
DLB-Y 85

Gray, Alasdair 1934- . . . . **CLC 41**
See also CA 123

Gray, Amlin 1946- . . . . **CLC 29**

Gray, Francine du Plessix 1930- . . . . **CLC 22**
See also CAAS 2; CANR 11; CA 61-64

Gray, John (Henry) 1866-1934 . . . . **TCLC 19**
See also CA 119

Gray, Simon (James Holliday)
1936- . . . . **CLC 9, 14, 36**
See also CAAS 3; CA 21-24R; DLB 13

Gray, Spalding 1941- . . . . **CLC 49**

Gray, Thomas 1716-1771 . . . . **LC 4; PC 2**
See also WLC 3

Grayson, Richard (A.) 1951- . . . . **CLC 38**
See also CANR 14; CA 85-88

Greeley, Andrew M(oran) 1928- . . . . . **CLC 28**
See also CAAS 7; CANR 7; CA 5-8R

Green, Hannah 1932- . . . . **CLC 3, 7, 30**
See also Greenberg, Joanne
See also CA 73-76

Green, Henry 1905-1974 . . . . **CLC 2, 13**
See also Yorke, Henry Vincent
See also DLB 15

Green, Julien (Hartridge) 1900- . . **CLC 3, 11**
See also CA 21-24R; DLB 4, 72

Green, Paul (Eliot) 1894-1981 . . . . . . **CLC 25**
See also CANR 3; CA 5-8R;
obituary CA 103; DLB 7, 9; DLB-Y 81

Greenberg, Ivan 1908-1973
See Rahv, Philip
See also CA 85-88

Greenberg, Joanne (Goldenberg)
1932- . . . . **CLC 3, 7, 30**
See also Green, Hannah
See also CANR 14; CA 5-8R; SATA 25

Greenberg, Richard 1959?- . . . . **CLC 57**

Greene, Bette 1934- . . . . **CLC 30**
See also CLR 2; CANR 4; CA 53-56;
SATA 8

Greene, Gael 19??- . . . . **CLC 8**
See also CANR 10; CA 13-16R

Greene, Graham (Henry)
1904-1991 . . . **CLC 1, 3, 6, 9, 14, 18, 27,
37, 70, 72**
See also CANR 35; CA 13-16R;
obituary CA 133; SATA 20; DLB 13, 15,
77, 100; DLB-Y 85

Gregor, Arthur 1923- . . . . **CLC 9**
See also CANR 11; CA 25-28R; SATA 36

Gregory, J. Dennis 1925-
See Williams, John A.

Gregory, Lady (Isabella Augusta Persse)
1852-1932 . . . . **TCLC 1**
See also CA 104; DLB 10

Grendon, Stephen 1909-1971
See Derleth, August (William)

Grenville, Kate 1950- . . . . **CLC 61**
See also CA 118

Greve, Felix Paul Berthold Friedrich
1879-1948
See Grove, Frederick Philip
See also CA 104

Grey, (Pearl) Zane 1872?-1939 . . . . . **TCLC 6**
See also CA 104; DLB 9

Grieg, (Johan) Nordahl (Brun)
1902-1943 . . . . **TCLC 10**
See also CA 107

Grieve, C(hristopher) M(urray) 1892-1978
See MacDiarmid, Hugh
See also CA 5-8R; obituary CA 85-88

Griffin, Gerald 1803-1840 . . . . **NCLC 7**

Griffin, John Howard 1920-1980 . . . . **CLC 68**
See also CANR 2; CA 2R; obituary CA 101

Griffin, Peter 1942- . . . . **CLC 39**

Griffiths, Trevor 1935- . . . . **CLC 13, 52**
See also CA 97-100; DLB 13

Grigson, Geoffrey (Edward Harvey)
1905-1985 . . . . CLC 7, 39
See also CANR 20; CA 25-28R;
obituary CA 118; DLB 27

Grillparzer, Franz 1791-1872 . . . . . . NCLC 1

Grimke, Charlotte L(ottie) Forten 1837?-1914
See Forten (Grimke), Charlotte L(ottie)
See also CA 117, 124

Grimm, Jakob Ludwig Karl
1785-1863 . . . . NCLC 3
See also SATA 22; DLB 90

Grimm, Wilhelm Karl 1786-1859 . . NCLC 3
See also SATA 22; DLB 90

Grimmelshausen, Johann Jakob Christoffel
von 1621-1676 . . . . LC 6

Grindel, Eugene 1895-1952
See also brief entry CA 104

Grossman, David 1954- . . . . CLC 67

Grossman, Vasily (Semenovich)
1905-1964 . . . . CLC 41
See also CA 124, 130

Grove, Frederick Philip
1879-1948 . . . . TCLC 4
See also Greve, Felix Paul Berthold
Friedrich

Grumbach, Doris (Isaac)
1918- . . . . CLC 13, 22, 64
See also CAAS 2; CANR 9; CA 5-8R

Grundtvig, Nicolai Frederik Severin
1783-1872 . . . . NCLC 1

Grunwald, Lisa 1959- . . . . CLC 44
See also CA 120

Guare, John 1938- . . . . CLC 8, 14, 29, 67
See also CANR 21; CA 73-76; DLB 7

Gudjonsson, Halldor Kiljan 1902-
See Laxness, Halldor (Kiljan)
See also CA 103

Guest, Barbara 1920- . . . . CLC 34
See also CANR 11; CA 25-28R; DLB 5

Guest, Judith (Ann) 1936- . . . . CLC 8, 30
See also CANR 15; CA 77-80

Guild, Nicholas M. 1944- . . . . CLC 33
See also CA 93-96

Guillen, Jorge 1893-1984 . . . . CLC 11
See also CA 89-92; obituary CA 112

Guillen, Nicolas 1902-1989 . . . . CLC 48
See also BLC 2; CA 116, 125;
obituary CA 129

Guillen y Batista, Nicolas Cristobal
1902-1989
See Guillen, Nicolas

Guillevic, (Eugene) 1907- . . . . CLC 33
See also CA 93-96

Guiney, Louise Imogen
1861-1920 . . . . TCLC 41
See also DLB 54

Guiraldes, Ricardo 1886-1927 . . . . . TCLC 39

Gunn, Bill 1934-1989 . . . . CLC 5
See also Gunn, William Harrison
See also DLB 38

Gunn, Thom(son William)
1929- . . . . CLC 3, 6, 18, 32
See also CANR 9; CA 17-20R; DLB 27

Gunn, William Harrison 1934-1989
See Gunn, Bill
See also CANR 12, 25; CA 13-16R;
obituary CA 128

Gunnars, Kristjana 1948- . . . . CLC 69
See also CA 113; DLB 60

Gurganus, Allan 1947- . . . . CLC 70

Gurney, A(lbert) R(amsdell), Jr.
1930- . . . . CLC 32, 50, 54
See also CA 77-80

Gurney, Ivor (Bertie) 1890-1937 . . . TCLC 33

Gustafson, Ralph (Barker) 1909- . . . . CLC 36
See also CANR 8; CA 21-24R; DLB 88

Guthrie, A(lfred) B(ertram), Jr.
1901- . . . . CLC 23
See also CA 57-60; DLB 6

Guthrie, Woodrow Wilson 1912-1967
See Guthrie, Woody
See also CA 113; obituary CA 93-96

Guthrie, Woody 1912-1967 . . . . CLC 35
See also Guthrie, Woodrow Wilson

Guy, Rosa (Cuthbert) 1928- . . . . CLC 26
See also CLR 13; CANR 14; CA 17-20R;
SATA 14; DLB 33

Haavikko, Paavo (Juhani)
1931- . . . . CLC 18, 34
See also CA 106

Hacker, Marilyn 1942- . . . . CLC 5, 9, 23, 72
See also CA 77-80

Haggard, (Sir) H(enry) Rider
1856-1925 . . . . TCLC 11
See also CA 108; SATA 16; DLB 70

Haig-Brown, Roderick L(angmere)
1908-1976 . . . . CLC 21
See also CANR 4; CA 5-8R;
obituary CA 69-72; SATA 12; DLB 88

Hailey, Arthur 1920- . . . . CLC 5
See also CANR 2; CA 1-4R; DLB-Y 82

Hailey, Elizabeth Forsythe 1938- . . . CLC 40
See also CAAS 1; CANR 15; CA 93-96

Haines, John 1924- . . . . CLC 58
See also CANR 13; CA 19-20R; DLB 5

Haldeman, Joe 1943- . . . . CLC 61
See also CA 53-56; DLB 8

Haley, Alex (Palmer) 1921- . . . . . . CLC 8, 12
See also BLC 2; CA 77-80; DLB 38

Haliburton, Thomas Chandler
1796-1865 . . . . NCLC 15
See also DLB 11

Hall, Donald (Andrew, Jr.)
1928- . . . . CLC 1, 13, 37, 59
See also CAAS 7; CANR 2; CA 5-8R;
SATA 23; DLB 5

Hall, James Norman 1887-1951 . . . TCLC 23
See also CA 123; SATA 21

Hall, (Marguerite) Radclyffe
1886-1943 . . . . TCLC 12
See also CA 110

Hall, Rodney 1935- . . . . CLC 51
See also CA 109

Halpern, Daniel 1945- . . . . CLC 14
See also CA 33-36R

Hamburger, Michael (Peter Leopold)
1924- . . . . CLC 5, 14
See also CAAS 4; CANR 2; CA 5-8R;
DLB 27

Hamill, Pete 1935- . . . . CLC 10
See also CANR 18; CA 25-28R

Hamilton, Edmond 1904-1977 . . . . CLC 1
See also CANR 3; CA 1-4R; DLB 8

Hamilton, Gail 1911-
See Corcoran, Barbara

Hamilton, Ian 1938- . . . . CLC 55
See also CA 106; DLB 40

Hamilton, Mollie 1909?-
See Kaye, M(ary) M(argaret)

Hamilton, (Anthony Walter) Patrick
1904-1962 . . . . CLC 51
See also obituary CA 113; DLB 10

Hamilton, Virginia (Esther) 1936- . . . CLC 26
See also CLR 1, 11; CANR 20; CA 25-28R;
SATA 4; DLB 33, 52

Hammett, (Samuel) Dashiell
1894-1961 . . . . CLC 3, 5, 10, 19, 47
See also CA 81-84; DLB-DS 6

Hammon, Jupiter 1711?-1800? . . . . NCLC 5
See also BLC 2; DLB 31, 50, 31, 50

Hamner, Earl (Henry), Jr. 1923- . . . CLC 12
See also CA 73-76; DLB 6

Hampton, Christopher (James)
1946- . . . . CLC 4
See also CA 25-28R; DLB 13

Hamsun, Knut 1859-1952 . . . . . . TCLC 2, 14
See also Pedersen, Knut

Handke, Peter 1942- . . CLC 5, 8, 10, 15, 38
See also CA 77-80; DLB 85

Hanley, James 1901-1985 . . . CLC 3, 5, 8, 13
See also CA 73-76; obituary CA 117

Hannah, Barry 1942- . . . . CLC 23, 38
See also CA 108, 110; DLB 6

Hansberry, Lorraine (Vivian)
1930-1965 . . . . CLC 17, 62; DC 2
See also BLC 2; CA 109;
obituary CA 25-28R; CABS 3; DLB 7, 38;
CDALB 1941-1968

Hansen, Joseph 1923- . . . . CLC 38
See also CANR 16; CA 29-32R

Hansen, Martin 1909-1955 . . . . TCLC 32

Hanson, Kenneth O(stlin) 1922- . . . . CLC 13
See also CANR 7; CA 53-56

Hardenberg, Friedrich (Leopold Freiherr) von
1772-1801
See Novalis

Hardwick, Elizabeth 1916- . . . . CLC 13
See also CANR 3; CA 5-8R; DLB 6

Hardy, Thomas
1840-1928 . . . TCLC 4, 10, 18, 32; SSC 2
See also CA 104, 123; SATA 25; DLB 18,
19

Hare, David 1947- . . . . CLC 29, 58
See also CA 97-100; DLB 13

Harlan, Louis R(udolph) 1922- . . . . . CLC 34
See also CANR 25; CA 21-24R

Harling, Robert 1951?- . . . . CLC 53

Harmon, William (Ruth) 1938- . . . . . CLC 38
See also CANR 14; CA 33-36R

Harper, Frances Ellen Watkins
     1825-1911 .... TCLC 14
     See also BLC 2; CA 125;
     brief entry CA 111; DLB 50

Harper, Michael S(teven) 1938- .. CLC 7, 22
     See also CANR 24; CA 33-36R; DLB 41

Harris, Christie (Lucy Irwin)
     1907- .... CLC 12
     See also CANR 6; CA 5-8R; SATA 6;
     DLB 88

Harris, Frank 1856-1931 .... TCLC 24
     See also CAAS 1; CA 109

Harris, George Washington
     1814-1869 .... NCLC 23
     See also DLB 3, 11

Harris, Joel Chandler 1848-1908 ... TCLC 2
     See also YABC 1; CA 104; DLB 11, 23, 42,
     78, 91

Harris, John (Wyndham Parkes Lucas)
     Beynon 1903-1969 .... CLC 19
     See also Wyndham, John
     See also CA 102; obituary CA 89-92

Harris, MacDonald 1921- .... CLC 9
     See also Heiney, Donald (William)

Harris, Mark 1922- .... CLC 19
     See also CAAS 3; CANR 2; CA 5-8R;
     DLB 2; DLB-Y 80

Harris, (Theodore) Wilson 1921-.... CLC 25
     See also CANR 11, 27; CA 65-68

Harrison, Harry (Max) 1925- ...... CLC 42
     See also CANR 5, 21; CA 1-4R; SATA 4;
     DLB 8

Harrison, James (Thomas) 1937- ... CLC 66
     See also Harrison, Jim
     See also CANR 8; CA 13-16R

Harrison, Jim 1937-......... CLC 6, 14, 33
     See also Harrison, James (Thomas)
     See also DLB-Y 82

Harrison, Kathryn 1961- .... CLC 70

Harrison, Tony 1937-............. CLC 43
     See also CA 65-68; DLB 40

Harriss, Will(ard Irvin) 1922-...... CLC 34
     See also CA 111

Hart, Josephine 1942?-............ CLC 70

Hart, Moss 1904-1961 .... CLC 66
     See also Conrad, Robert Arnold
     See also obituary CA 89-92; DLB 7

Harte, (Francis) Bret(t)
     1836?-1902......... TCLC 1, 25; SSC 8
     See also brief entry CA 104; SATA 26;
     DLB 12, 64, 74, 79; CDALB 1865-1917

Hartley, L(eslie) P(oles)
     1895-1972 .... CLC 2, 22
     See also CA 45-48; obituary CA 37-40R;
     DLB 15

Hartman, Geoffrey H. 1929-....... CLC 27
     See also CA 117, 125; DLB 67

Haruf, Kent 19??-................ CLC 34

Harwood, Ronald 1934-........... CLC 32
     See also CANR 4; CA 1-4R; DLB 13

Hasegawa Tatsunosuke 1864-1909
     See Futabatei Shimei

Hasek, Jaroslav (Matej Frantisek)
     1883-1923 .... TCLC 4
     See also CA 104, 129

Hass, Robert 1941-............ CLC 18, 39
     See also CANR 30; CA 111

Hastings, Selina 19??- .... CLC 44

Hauptmann, Gerhart (Johann Robert)
     1862-1946 .... TCLC 4
     See also CA 104; DLB 66

Havel, Vaclav 1936-........ CLC 25, 58, 65
     See also CA 104

Haviaras, Stratis 1935- .... CLC 33
     See also CA 105

Hawes, Stephen 1475?-1523?........ LC 17

Hawkes, John (Clendennin Burne, Jr.)
     1925-...... CLC 1, 2, 3, 4, 7, 9, 14, 15,
                                    27, 49
     See also CANR 2; CA 1-4R; DLB 2, 7;
     DLB-Y 80

Hawking, Stephen (William)
     1948- .... CLC 63
     See also CA 126, 129

Hawthorne, Julian 1846-1934 ..... TCLC 25

Hawthorne, Nathaniel
     1804-1864 ... NCLC 2, 10, 17, 23; SSC 3
     See also YABC 2; DLB 1, 74;
     CDALB 1640-1865

Hayashi Fumiko 1904-1951 ...... TCLC 27

Haycraft, Anna 19??-
     See Ellis, Alice Thomas
     See also CA 122

Hayden, Robert (Earl)
     1913-1980 .... CLC 5, 9, 14, 37
     See also BLC 2; CANR 24; CA 69-72;
     obituary CA 97-100; CABS 2; SATA 19;
     obituary SATA 26; DLB 5, 76;
     CDALB 1941-1968

Hayman, Ronald 1932-............ CLC 44
     See also CANR 18; CA 25-28R

Haywood, Eliza (Fowler) 1693?-1756.. LC 1
     See also DLB 39

Hazlitt, William 1778-1830 ...... NCLC 29

Hazzard, Shirley 1931- .... CLC 18
     See also CANR 4; CA 9-12R; DLB-Y 82

H(ilda) D(oolittle)
     1886-1961 .... CLC 3, 8, 14, 31, 34
     See also Doolittle, Hilda

Head, Bessie 1937-1986........ CLC 25, 67
     See also BLC 2; CANR 25; CA 29-32R;
     obituary CA 119

Headon, (Nicky) Topper 1956?- .... CLC 30
     See also The Clash

Heaney, Seamus (Justin)
     1939- .... CLC 5, 7, 14, 25, 37
     See also CANR 25; CA 85-88; DLB 40

Hearn, (Patricio) Lafcadio (Tessima Carlos)
     1850-1904 .... TCLC 9
     See also CA 105; DLB 12, 78

Hearne, Vicki 1946-.............. CLC 56

Hearon, Shelby 1931-............. CLC 63
     See also CANR 18; CA 25-28

Heat Moon, William Least 1939-... CLC 29

Hebert, Anne 1916- .... CLC 4, 13, 29
     See also CA 85-88; DLB 68

Hecht, Anthony (Evan)
     1923- .... CLC 8, 13, 19
     See also CANR 6; CA 9-12R; DLB 5

Hecht, Ben 1894-1964 .... CLC 8
     See also CA 85-88; DLB 7, 9, 25, 26, 28, 86

Hedayat, Sadeq 1903-1951....... TCLC 21
     See also CA 120

Heidegger, Martin 1889-1976 ...... CLC 24
     See also CA 81-84; obituary CA 65-68

Heidenstam, (Karl Gustaf) Verner von
     1859-1940 .... TCLC 5
     See also CA 104

Heifner, Jack 1946-............... CLC 11
     See also CA 105

Heijermans, Herman 1864-1924 ... TCLC 24
     See also CA 123

Heilbrun, Carolyn G(old) 1926-..... CLC 25
     See also CANR 1, 28; CA 45-48

Heine, Harry 1797-1856
     See Heine, Heinrich

Heine, Heinrich 1797-1856 .... NCLC 4
     See also DLB 90

Heinemann, Larry C(urtiss) 1944- .. CLC 50
     See also CA 110

Heiney, Donald (William) 1921-..... CLC 9
     See also Harris, MacDonald
     See also CANR 3; CA 1-4R

Heinlein, Robert A(nson)
     1907-1988 ...... CLC 1, 3, 8, 14, 26, 55
     See also CANR 1, 20; CA 1-4R;
     obituary CA 125; SATA 9, 56; DLB 8

Heller, Joseph
     1923- .... CLC 1, 3, 5, 8, 11, 36, 63
     See also CANR 8; CA 5-8R; CABS 1;
     DLB 2, 28; DLB-Y 80

Hellman, Lillian (Florence)
     1905?-1984..... CLC 2, 4, 8, 14, 18, 34,
                                    44, 52; DC 1
     See also CA 13-16R; obituary CA 112;
     DLB 7; DLB-Y 84

Helprin, Mark 1947- ..... CLC 7, 10, 22, 32
     See also CA 81-84; DLB-Y 85

Hemans, Felicia 1793-1835 ...... NCLC 29

Hemingway, Ernest (Miller)
     1899-1961 ... CLC 1, 3, 6, 8, 10, 13, 19,
                30, 34, 39, 41, 44, 50, 61; SSC 1
     See also CA 77-80; DLB 4, 9; DLB-Y 81,
     87; DLB-DS 1; CDALB 1917-1929

Hempel, Amy 1951-............... CLC 39
     See also CA 118

Henley, Beth 1952-............... CLC 23
     See also Henley, Elizabeth Becker
     See also CABS 3; DLB-Y 86

Henley, Elizabeth Becker 1952-
     See Henley, Beth
     See also CA 107

Henley, William Ernest
     1849-1903 .... TCLC 8
     See also CA 105; DLB 19

Hennissart, Martha
     See Lathen, Emma
     See also CA 85-88

Henry, O. 1862-1910 . . . **TCLC 1, 19; SSC 5**
See also Porter, William Sydney
See also YABC 2; CA 104; DLB 12, 78, 79;
CDALB 1865-1917

Henry VIII 1491-1547 . . . . **LC 10**

Henschke, Alfred 1890-1928
See Klabund

Hentoff, Nat(han Irving) 1925- . . . . . **CLC 26**
See also CLR 1; CAAS 6; CANR 5, 25;
CA 1-4R; SATA 27, 42; AAYA 4

Heppenstall, (John) Rayner
1911-1981 . . . . **CLC 10**
See also CANR 29; CA 1-4R;
obituary CA 103

Herbert, Frank (Patrick)
1920-1986 . . . . **CLC 12, 23, 35, 44**
See also CANR 5; CA 53-56;
obituary CA 118; SATA 9, 37, 47; DLB 8

Herbert, George 1593-1633 . . . . **PC 4**

Herbert, Zbigniew 1924- . . . . **CLC 9, 43**
See also CA 89-92

Herbst, Josephine 1897-1969 . . . . . . **CLC 34**
See also CA 5-8R; obituary CA 25-28R;
DLB 9

Herder, Johann Gottfried von
1744-1803 . . . . **NCLC 8**

Hergesheimer, Joseph
1880-1954 . . . . **TCLC 11**
See also CA 109; DLB 9

Herlagnez, Pablo de 1844-1896
See Verlaine, Paul (Marie)

Herlihy, James Leo 1927- . . . . **CLC 6**
See also CANR 2; CA 1-4R

Hermogenes fl.c. 175- . . . . **CMLC 6**

Hernandez, Jose 1834-1886 . . . . . . **NCLC 17**

Herrick, Robert 1591-1674 . . . . **LC 13**

Herriot, James 1916- . . . . **CLC 12**
See also Wight, James Alfred
See also AAYA 1

Herrmann, Dorothy 1941- . . . . **CLC 44**
See also CA 107

Hersey, John (Richard)
1914- . . . . **CLC 1, 2, 7, 9, 40**
See also CA 17-20R; SATA 25; DLB 6

Herzen, Aleksandr Ivanovich
1812-1870 . . . . **NCLC 10**

Herzl, Theodor 1860-1904 . . . . **TCLC 36**

Herzog, Werner 1942- . . . . **CLC 16**
See also CA 89-92

Hesiod c. 8th Century B.C.- . . . . . . **CMLC 5**

Hesse, Hermann
1877-1962 . . . **CLC 1, 2, 3, 6, 11, 17, 25,
69; SSC 9**
See also CAP 2; CA 17-18; SATA 50;
DLB 66

Heyen, William 1940- . . . . **CLC 13, 18**
See also CAAS 9; CA 33-36R; DLB 5

Heyerdahl, Thor 1914- . . . . **CLC 26**
See also CANR 5, 22; CA 5-8R; SATA 2,
52

Heym, Georg (Theodor Franz Arthur)
1887-1912 . . . . **TCLC 9**
See also CA 106

Heym, Stefan 1913- . . . . **CLC 41**
See also CANR 4; CA 9-12R; DLB 69

Heyse, Paul (Johann Ludwig von)
1830-1914 . . . . **TCLC 8**
See also CA 104

Hibbert, Eleanor (Burford) 1906- . . . . **CLC 7**
See also CANR 9, 28; CA 17-20R; SATA 2

Higgins, George V(incent)
1939- . . . . **CLC 4, 7, 10, 18**
See also CAAS 5; CANR 17; CA 77-80;
DLB 2; DLB-Y 81

Higginson, Thomas Wentworth
1823-1911 . . . . **TCLC 36**
See also DLB 1, 64

Highsmith, (Mary) Patricia
1921- . . . . **CLC 2, 4, 14, 42**
See also CANR 1, 20; CA 1-4R

Highwater, Jamake 1942- . . . . **CLC 12**
See also CLR 17; CAAS 7; CANR 10;
CA 65-68; SATA 30, 32; DLB 52;
DLB-Y 85

Hijuelos, Oscar 1951- . . . . **CLC 65**
See also CA 123

Hikmet (Ran), Nazim 1902-1963 . . . . **CLC 40**
See also obituary CA 93-96

Hildesheimer, Wolfgang 1916- . . . . . **CLC 49**
See also CA 101; DLB 69

Hill, Geoffrey (William)
1932- . . . . **CLC 5, 8, 18, 45**
See also CANR 21; CA 81-84; DLB 40

Hill, George Roy 1922- . . . . **CLC 26**
See also CA 110, 122

Hill, Susan B. 1942- . . . . **CLC 4**
See also CANR 29; CA 33-36R; DLB 14

Hillerman, Tony 1925- . . . . **CLC 62**
See also CANR 21; CA 29-32R; SATA 6

Hilliard, Noel (Harvey) 1929- . . . . . . **CLC 15**
See also CANR 7; CA 9-12R

Hillis, Richard Lyle 1956-
See Hillis, Rick

Hillis, Rick 1956- . . . . **CLC 66**
See also Hillis, Richard Lyle

Hilton, James 1900-1954 . . . . **TCLC 21**
See also CA 108; SATA 34; DLB 34, 77

Himes, Chester (Bomar)
1909-1984 . . . . **CLC 2, 4, 7, 18, 58**
See also BLC 2; CANR 22; CA 25-28R;
obituary CA 114; DLB 2, 76

Hinde, Thomas 1926- . . . . **CLC 6, 11**
See also Chitty, (Sir) Thomas Willes

Hine, (William) Daryl 1936- . . . . **CLC 15**
See also CANR 1, 20; CA 1-4R; DLB 60

Hinton, S(usan) E(loise) 1950- . . . . . **CLC 30**
See also CLR 3, 23; CA 81-84; SATA 19,
58; AAYA 2

**Hippius (Merezhkovsky), Zinaida
(Nikolayevna)** 1869-1945 . . . . . . **TCLC 9**
See also Gippius, Zinaida (Nikolayevna)

Hiraoka, Kimitake 1925-1970
See Mishima, Yukio
See also CA 97-100; obituary CA 29-32R

Hirsch, Edward (Mark) 1950- . . . **CLC 31, 50**
See also CANR 20; CA 104

Hitchcock, (Sir) Alfred (Joseph)
1899-1980 . . . . **CLC 16**
See also obituary CA 97-100; SATA 27;
obituary SATA 24

Hoagland, Edward 1932- . . . . **CLC 28**
See also CANR 2; CA 1-4R; SATA 51;
DLB 6

Hoban, Russell C(onwell) 1925- . . **CLC 7, 25**
See also CLR 3; CANR 23; CA 5-8R;
SATA 1, 40; DLB 52

Hobson, Laura Z(ametkin)
1900-1986 . . . . **CLC 7, 25**
See also CA 17-20R; obituary CA 118;
SATA 52; DLB 28

Hochhuth, Rolf 1931- . . . . **CLC 4, 11, 18**
See also CA 5-8R

Hochman, Sandra 1936- . . . . **CLC 3, 8**
See also CA 5-8R; DLB 5

Hochwalder, Fritz 1911-1986 . . . . . . **CLC 36**
See also CA 29-32R; obituary CA 120

Hocking, Mary (Eunice) 1921- . . . . . **CLC 13**
See also CANR 18; CA 101

Hodgins, Jack 1938- . . . . **CLC 23**
See also CA 93-96; DLB 60

Hodgson, William Hope
1877-1918 . . . . **TCLC 13**
See also CA 111; DLB 70

Hoffman, Alice 1952- . . . . **CLC 51**
See also CA 77-80

Hoffman, Daniel (Gerard)
1923- . . . . **CLC 6, 13, 23**
See also CANR 4; CA 1-4R; DLB 5

Hoffman, Stanley 1944- . . . . **CLC 5**
See also CA 77-80

Hoffman, William M(oses) 1939- . . . **CLC 40**
See also CANR 11; CA 57-60

Hoffmann, E(rnst) T(heodor) A(madeus)
1776-1822 . . . . **NCLC 2**
See also SATA 27; DLB 90

Hoffmann, Gert 1932- . . . . **CLC 54**

**Hofmannsthal, Hugo (Laurenz August
Hofmann Edler) von**
1874-1929 . . . . **TCLC 11**
See also CA 106; DLB 81

Hogg, James 1770-1835 . . . . **NCLC 4**

Holbach, Paul Henri Thiry, Baron d'
1723-1789 . . . . **LC 14**

Holberg, Ludvig 1684-1754 . . . . **LC 6**

Holden, Ursula 1921- . . . . **CLC 18**
See also CAAS 8; CANR 22; CA 101

Holderlin, (Johann Christian) Friedrich
1770-1843 . . . . **NCLC 16; PC 4**

Holdstock, Robert (P.) 1948- . . . . **CLC 39**

Holland, Isabelle 1920- . . . . **CLC 21**
See also CANR 10, 25; CA 21-24R;
SATA 8

Holland, Marcus 1900-1985
See Caldwell, (Janet Miriam) Taylor
(Holland)

Hollander, John 1929- . . . . . . **CLC 2, 5, 8, 14**
See also CANR 1; CA 1-4R; SATA 13;
DLB 5

Holleran, Andrew 1943?- . . . . **CLC 38**

Hollinghurst, Alan 1954-.......... **CLC 55**
See also CA 114

Hollis, Jim 1916-
See Summers, Hollis (Spurgeon, Jr.)

Holmes, John Clellon 1926-1988.... **CLC 56**
See also CANR 4; CA 9-10R;
obituary CA 125; DLB 16

Holmes, Oliver Wendell
1809-1894 .... **NCLC 14**
See also SATA 34; DLB 1;
CDALB 1640-1865

Holt, Victoria 1906-
See Hibbert, Eleanor (Burford)

Holub, Miroslav 1923-............. **CLC 4**
See also CANR 10; CA 21-24R

Homer c. 8th century B.C.-....... **CMLC 1**

Honig, Edwin 1919-............. **CLC 33**
See also CAAS 8; CANR 4; CA 5-8R;
DLB 5

Hood, Hugh (John Blagdon)
1928-.................... **CLC 15, 28**
See also CANR 1; CA 49-52; DLB 53

Hood, Thomas 1799-1845....... **NCLC 16**

Hooker, (Peter) Jeremy 1941-...... **CLC 43**
See also CANR 22; CA 77-80; DLB 40

Hope, A(lec) D(erwent) 1907-.... **CLC 3, 51**
See also CA 21-24R

Hope, Christopher (David Tully)
1944-........................ **CLC 52**
See also CA 106

Hopkins, Gerard Manley
1844-1889 .... **NCLC 17**
See also DLB 35, 57

Hopkins, John (Richard) 1931-...... **CLC 4**
See also CA 85-88

Hopkins, Pauline Elizabeth
1859-1930 .... **TCLC 28**
See also BLC 2; DLB 50

Horgan, Paul 1903-............. **CLC 9, 53**
See also CANR 9; CA 13-16R; SATA 13;
DLB-Y 85

Horovitz, Israel 1939-............. **CLC 56**
See also CA 33-36R; DLB 7

Horvath, Odon von 1901-1938 .... **TCLC 45**
See also brief entry CA 118; DLB 85

Horwitz, Julius 1920-1986........ **CLC 14**
See also CANR 12; CA 9-12R;
obituary CA 119

Hospital, Janette Turner 1942-..... **CLC 42**
See also CA 108

Hostos (y Bonilla), Eugenio Maria de
1893-1903 .... **TCLC 24**
See also CA 123

Hougan, Carolyn 19??-............ **CLC 34**

Household, Geoffrey (Edward West)
1900-1988 .... **CLC 11**
See also CA 77-80; obituary CA 126;
SATA 14, 59; DLB 87

Housman, A(lfred) E(dward)
1859-1936 .... **TCLC 1, 10; PC 2**
See also CA 104, 125; DLB 19

Housman, Laurence 1865-1959 ..... **TCLC 7**
See also CA 106; SATA 25; DLB 10

Howard, Elizabeth Jane 1923- ... **CLC 7, 29**
See also CANR 8; CA 5-8R

Howard, Maureen 1930- ..... **CLC 5, 14, 46**
See also CA 53-56; DLB-Y 83

Howard, Richard 1929-...... **CLC 7, 10, 47**
See also CANR 25; CA 85-88; DLB 5

Howard, Robert E(rvin)
1906-1936 .... **TCLC 8**
See also CA 105

Howe, Fanny 1940- .... **CLC 47**
See also CA 117; SATA 52

Howe, Julia Ward 1819-1910 ..... **TCLC 21**
See also CA 117; DLB 1

Howe, Susan 1937-............... **CLC 72**

Howe, Tina 1937-............... **CLC 48**
See also CA 109

Howell, James 1594?-1666......... **LC 13**

Howells, William Dean
1837-1920 .... **TCLC 7, 17, 41**
See also brief entry CA 104; DLB 12, 64,
74, 79; CDALB 1865-1917

Howes, Barbara 1914-............. **CLC 15**
See also CAAS 3; CA 9-12R; SATA 5

Hrabal, Bohumil 1914-........ **CLC 13, 67**
See also CAAS 12; CA 106

Hubbard, L(afayette) Ron(ald)
1911-1986 .... **CLC 43**
See also CANR 22; CA 77-80;
obituary CA 118

Huch, Ricarda (Octavia)
1864-1947 .... **TCLC 13**
See also CA 111; DLB 66

Huddle, David 1942- .... **CLC 49**
See also CA 57-60

Hudson, W(illiam) H(enry)
1841-1922 .... **TCLC 29**
See also CA 115; SATA 35

Hueffer, Ford Madox 1873-1939
See Ford, Ford Madox

Hughart, Barry 1934-............. **CLC 39**

Hughes, David (John) 1930-...... **CLC 48**
See also CA 116, 129; DLB 14

Hughes, Edward James 1930-
See Hughes, Ted

Hughes, (James) Langston
1902-1967 .... **CLC 1, 5, 10, 15, 35, 44;**
PC 1; SSC 6
See also BLC 2; CLR 17; CANR 1;
CA 1-4R; obituary CA 25-28R; SATA 4,
33; DLB 4, 7, 48, 51, 86;
CDALB 1929-1941

Hughes, Richard (Arthur Warren)
1900-1976 .... **CLC 1, 11**
See also CANR 4; CA 5-8R;
obituary CA 65-68; SATA 8;
obituary SATA 25; DLB 15

Hughes, Ted 1930-..... **CLC 2, 4, 9, 14, 37**
See also CLR 3; CANR 1; CA 1-4R;
SATA 27, 49; DLB 40

Hugo, Richard F(ranklin)
1923-1982 .... **CLC 6, 18, 32**
See also CANR 3; CA 49-52;
obituary CA 108; DLB 5

Hugo, Victor Marie
1802-1885 .... **NCLC 3, 10, 21**
See also SATA 47

Huidobro, Vicente 1893-1948 ..... **TCLC 31**

Hulme, Keri 1947-............... **CLC 39**
See also CA 125

Hulme, T(homas) E(rnest)
1883-1917 .... **TCLC 21**
See also CA 117; DLB 19

Hume, David 1711-1776............. **LC 7**

Humphrey, William 1924-......... **CLC 45**
See also CA 77-80; DLB 6

Humphreys, Emyr (Owen) 1919-.... **CLC 47**
See also CANR 3, 24; CA 5-8R; DLB 15

Humphreys, Josephine 1945-.... **CLC 34, 57**
See also CA 121, 127

Hunt, E(verette) Howard (Jr.)
1918-........................ **CLC 3**
See also CANR 2; CA 45-48

Hunt, (James Henry) Leigh
1784-1859 .... **NCLC 1**

Hunt, Marsha 1946-............... **CLC 70**

Hunter, Evan 1926- .... **CLC 11, 31**
See also CANR 5; CA 5-8R; SATA 25;
DLB-Y 82

Hunter, Kristin (Eggleston) 1931-... **CLC 35**
See also CLR 3; CANR 13; CA 13-16R;
SATA 12; DLB 33

Hunter, Mollie (Maureen McIlwraith)
1922-........................ **CLC 21**
See also McIlwraith, Maureen Mollie
Hunter

Hunter, Robert ?-1734............. **LC 7**

Hurston, Zora Neale
1901?-1960....... **CLC 7, 30, 61; SSC 4**
See also BLC 2; CA 85-88; DLB 51, 86

Huston, John (Marcellus)
1906-1987 .... **CLC 20**
See also CA 73-76; obituary CA 123;
DLB 26

Hutten, Ulrich von 1488-1523....... **LC 16**

Huxley, Aldous (Leonard)
1894-1963 .. **CLC 1, 3, 4, 5, 8, 11, 18, 35**
See also CA 85-88; DLB 36

Huysmans, Charles Marie Georges
1848-1907
See Huysmans, Joris-Karl
See also CA 104

Huysmans, Joris-Karl 1848-1907 ... **TCLC 7**
See also Huysmans, Charles Marie Georges

Hwang, David Henry 1957-........ **CLC 55**
See also CA 127

Hyde, Anthony 1946?-............ **CLC 42**

Hyde, Margaret O(ldroyd) 1917- ... **CLC 21**
See also CLR 23; CANR 1; CA 1-4R;
SAAS 8; SATA 1, 42

Hynes, James 1956?-............. **CLC 65**

Ian, Janis 1951-.................. **CLC 21**
See also CA 105

Ibarguengoitia, Jorge 1928-1983.... **CLC 37**
See also obituary CA 113, 124

Ibsen, Henrik (Johan)
1828-1906 . . . . . TCLC 2, 8, 16, 37; DC 2
See also CA 104

Ibuse, Masuji 1898- . . . . CLC 22
See also CA 127

Ichikawa, Kon 1915- . . . . CLC 20
See also CA 121

Idle, Eric 1943- . . . . CLC 21
See also Monty Python
See also CA 116

Ignatow, David 1914- . . . . . . CLC 4, 7, 14, 40
See also CAAS 3; CA 9-12R; DLB 5

Ihimaera, Witi (Tame) 1944- . . . . CLC 46
See also CA 77-80

Ilf, Ilya 1897-1937 . . . . TCLC 21

Immermann, Karl (Lebrecht)
1796-1840 . . . . NCLC 4

Ingalls, Rachel 19??- . . . . CLC 42
See also CA 123, 127

Ingamells, Rex 1913-1955 . . . . TCLC 35

Inge, William (Motter)
1913-1973 . . . . CLC 1, 8, 19
See also CA 9-12R; DLB 7;
CDALB 1941-1968

Innaurato, Albert 1948- . . . . CLC 21, 60
See also CA 115, 122

Innes, Michael 1906-
See Stewart, J(ohn) I(nnes) M(ackintosh)

Ionesco, Eugene
1912- . . . . CLC 1, 4, 6, 9, 11, 15, 41
See also CA 9-12R; SATA 7

Iqbal, Muhammad 1877-1938 . . . . . TCLC 28

Irving, John (Winslow)
1942- . . . . CLC 13, 23, 38
See also CANR 28; CA 25-28R; DLB 6;
DLB-Y 82

Irving, Washington
1783-1859 . . . . NCLC 2, 19; SSC 2
See also YABC 2; DLB 3, 11, 30, 59, 73,
74; CDALB 1640-1865

Isaacs, Susan 1943- . . . . CLC 32
See also CANR 20; CA 89-92

Isherwood, Christopher (William Bradshaw)
1904-1986 . . . . CLC 1, 9, 11, 14, 44
See also CA 13-16R; obituary CA 117;
DLB 15; DLB-Y 86

Ishiguro, Kazuo 1954- . . . . . . CLC 27, 56, 59
See also CA 120

Ishikawa Takuboku 1885-1912 . . . . TCLC 15
See also CA 113

Iskander, Fazil (Abdulovich)
1929- . . . . CLC 47
See also CA 102

Ivan IV 1530-1584 . . . . LC 17

Ivanov, Vyacheslav (Ivanovich)
1866-1949 . . . . TCLC 33
See also CA 122

Ivask, Ivar (Vidrik) 1927- . . . . CLC 14
See also CANR 24; CA 37-40R

Jackson, Jesse 1908-1983 . . . . CLC 12
See also CANR 27; CA 25-28R;
obituary CA 109; SATA 2, 29, 48

Jackson, Laura (Riding) 1901- . . . . . . CLC 7
See also Riding, Laura
See also CANR 28; CA 65-68; DLB 48

Jackson, Shirley
1919-1965 . . . . CLC 11, 60; SSC 9
See also CANR 4; CA 1-4R;
obituary CA 25-28R; SATA 2; DLB 6;
CDALB 1941-1968

Jacob, (Cyprien) Max 1876-1944 . . . TCLC 6
See also CA 104

Jacob, Piers A(nthony) D(illingham) 1934-
See Anthony (Jacob), Piers
See also CA 21-24R

Jacobs, Jim 1942- and Casey, Warren
1942- . . . . CLC 12
See also CA 97-100

Jacobs, Jim 1942-
See Jacobs, Jim and Casey, Warren
See also CA 97-100

Jacobs, W(illiam) W(ymark)
1863-1943 . . . . TCLC 22
See also CA 121

Jacobsen, Jens Peter 1847-1885 . . NCLC 34

Jacobsen, Josephine 1908- . . . . CLC 48
See also CANR 23; CA 33-36R

Jacobson, Dan 1929- . . . . CLC 4, 14
See also CANR 2, 25; CA 1-4R; DLB 14

Jagger, Mick 1944- . . . . CLC 17

Jakes, John (William) 1932- . . . . CLC 29
See also CANR 10; CA 57-60; DLB-Y 83

James, C(yril) L(ionel) R(obert)
1901-1989 . . . . CLC 33
See also CA 117, 125; obituary CA 128

James, Daniel 1911-1988
See Santiago, Danny
See also obituary CA 125

James, Henry (Jr.)
1843-1916 . . . TCLC 2, 11, 24, 40; SSC 8
See also CA 132; brief entry CA 104;
DLB 12, 71, 74; CDALB 1865-1917

James, M(ontague) R(hodes)
1862-1936 . . . . TCLC 6
See also CA 104

James, P(hyllis) D(orothy)
1920- . . . . CLC 18, 46
See also CANR 17; CA 21-24R

James, William 1842-1910 . . . . . TCLC 15, 32
See also CA 109

Jami, Nur al-Din 'Abd al-Rahman
1414-1492 . . . . LC 9

Jandl, Ernst 1925- . . . . CLC 34

Janowitz, Tama 1957- . . . . CLC 43
See also CA 106

Jarrell, Randall
1914-1965 . . . . CLC 1, 2, 6, 9, 13, 49
See also CLR 6; CANR 6; CA 5-8R;
obituary CA 25-28R; CABS 2; SATA 7;
DLB 48, 52; CDALB 1941-1968

Jarry, Alfred 1873-1907 . . . . TCLC 2, 14
See also CA 104

Jeake, Samuel, Jr. 1889-1973
See Aiken, Conrad

Jean Paul 1763-1825 . . . . NCLC 7

Jeffers, (John) Robinson
1887-1962 . . . . CLC 2, 3, 11, 15, 54
See also CA 85-88; DLB 45;
CDALB 1917-1929

Jefferson, Thomas 1743-1826 . . . . NCLC 11
See also DLB 31; CDALB 1640-1865

Jeffrey, Francis 1773-1850 . . . . . . NCLC 33

Jellicoe, (Patricia) Ann 1927- . . . . . . CLC 27
See also CA 85-88; DLB 13

Jen, Gish 1955- . . . . CLC 70

Jenkins, (John) Robin 1912- . . . . CLC 52
See also CANR 1; CA 4R; DLB 14

Jennings, Elizabeth (Joan)
1926- . . . . CLC 5, 14
See also CAAS 5; CANR 8; CA 61-64;
DLB 27

Jennings, Waylon 1937- . . . . CLC 21

Jensen, Johannes V. 1873-1950 . . . . TCLC 41

Jensen, Laura (Linnea) 1948- . . . . . . CLC 37
See also CA 103

Jerome, Jerome K. 1859-1927 . . . . . TCLC 23
See also CA 119; DLB 10, 34

Jerrold, Douglas William
1803-1857 . . . . NCLC 2

Jewett, (Theodora) Sarah Orne
1849-1909 . . . . TCLC 1, 22; SSC 6
See also CA 108, 127; SATA 15; DLB 12,
74

Jewsbury, Geraldine (Endsor)
1812-1880 . . . . NCLC 22
See also DLB 21

Jhabvala, Ruth Prawer
1927- . . . . CLC 4, 8, 29
See also CANR 2, 29; CA 1-4R

Jiles, Paulette 1943- . . . . CLC 13, 58
See also CA 101

Jimenez (Mantecon), Juan Ramon
1881-1958 . . . . TCLC 4
See also CA 104

Joel, Billy 1949- . . . . CLC 26
See also Joel, William Martin

Joel, William Martin 1949-
See Joel, Billy
See also CA 108

John of the Cross, St. 1542-1591 . . . . LC 18

Johnson, B(ryan) S(tanley William)
1933-1973 . . . . CLC 6, 9
See also CANR 9; CA 9-12R;
obituary CA 53-56; DLB 14, 40

Johnson, Charles (Richard)
1948- . . . . CLC 7, 51, 65
See also BLC 2; CA 116; DLB 33

Johnson, Denis 1949- . . . . CLC 52
See also CA 117, 121

Johnson, Diane 1934- . . . . CLC 5, 13, 48
See also CANR 17; CA 41-44R; DLB-Y 80

Johnson, Eyvind (Olof Verner)
1900-1976 . . . . CLC 14
See also CA 73-76; obituary CA 69-72

Johnson, Fenton 1888-1958
See also BLC 2; CA 124;
brief entry CA 118; DLB 45, 50

Johnson, James Weldon
1871-1938 . . . . TCLC **3, 19**
See also Johnson, James William
See also BLC 2; CA 125;
brief entry CA 104; SATA 31; DLB 51;
CDALB 1917-1929

Johnson, James William   1871-1938
See Johnson, James Weldon
See also SATA 31

Johnson, Joyce   1935- . . . . CLC **58**
See also CA 125, 129

Johnson, Lionel (Pigot)
1867-1902 . . . . TCLC **19**
See also CA 117; DLB 19

Johnson, Marguerita   1928-
See Angelou, Maya

Johnson, Pamela Hansford
1912-1981 . . . . CLC **1, 7, 27**
See also CANR 2, 28; CA 1-4R;
obituary CA 104; DLB 15

Johnson, Samuel   1709-1784 . . . . LC **15**
See also DLB 39, 95

Johnson, Uwe
1934-1984 . . . . CLC **5, 10, 15, 40**
See also CANR 1; CA 1-4R;
obituary CA 112; DLB 75

Johnston, George (Benson)   1913- . . . CLC **51**
See also CANR 5, 20; CA 1-4R; DLB 88

Johnston, Jennifer   1930- . . . . CLC **7**
See also CA 85-88; DLB 14

Jolley, Elizabeth   1923- . . . . CLC **46**
See also CA 127

Jones, D(ouglas) G(ordon)   1929- . . . . CLC **10**
See also CANR 13; CA 29-32R, 113;
DLB 53

Jones, David
1895-1974 . . . . CLC **2, 4, 7, 13, 42**
See also CANR 28; CA 9-12R;
obituary CA 53-56; DLB 20

Jones, David Robert   1947-
See Bowie, David
See also CA 103

Jones, Diana Wynne   1934- . . . . CLC **26**
See also CLR 23; CANR 4, 26; CA 49-52;
SAAS 7; SATA 9

Jones, Gayl   1949- . . . . CLC **6, 9**
See also BLC 2; CANR 27; CA 77-80;
DLB 33

Jones, James   1921-1977 . . . . CLC **1, 3, 10, 39**
See also CANR 6; CA 1-4R;
obituary CA 69-72; DLB 2

Jones, (Everett) LeRoi
1934- . . . . CLC **1, 2, 3, 5, 10, 14, 33**
See also Baraka, Amiri; Baraka, Imamu
Amiri
See also CA 21-24R

Jones, Louis B.   19??- . . . . CLC **65**

Jones, Madison (Percy, Jr.)   1925- . . . CLC **4**
See also CAAS 11; CANR 7; CA 13-16R

Jones, Mervyn   1922- . . . . CLC **10, 52**
See also CAAS 5; CANR 1; CA 45-48

Jones, Mick   1956?- . . . . CLC **30**
See also The Clash

Jones, Nettie   19??- . . . . CLC **34**

Jones, Preston   1936-1979 . . . . CLC **10**
See also CA 73-76; obituary CA 89-92;
DLB 7

Jones, Robert F(rancis)   1934- . . . . . . CLC **7**
See also CANR 2; CA 49-52

Jones, Rod   1953- . . . . CLC **50**
See also CA 128

Jones, Terry   1942?- . . . . CLC **21**
See also Monty Python
See also CA 112, 116; SATA 51

Jong, Erica   1942- . . . . CLC **4, 6, 8, 18**
See also CANR 26; CA 73-76; DLB 2, 5, 28

Jonson, Ben(jamin)   1572(?)-1637 . . . . . . LC **6**
See also DLB 62

Jordan, June   1936- . . . . CLC **5, 11, 23**
See also CLR 10; CANR 25; CA 33-36R;
SATA 4; DLB 38; AAYA 2

Jordan, Pat(rick M.)   1941- . . . . CLC **37**
See also CANR 25; CA 33-36R

Josipovici, Gabriel (David)
1940- . . . . CLC **6, 43**
See also CAAS 8; CA 37-40R; DLB 14

Joubert, Joseph   1754-1824 . . . . NCLC **9**

Jouve, Pierre Jean   1887-1976 . . . . . . CLC **47**
See also obituary CA 65-68

Joyce, James (Augustine Aloysius)
1882-1941 . . . . . . TCLC **3, 8, 16, 26, 35;
SSC 3**
See also CA 104, 126; DLB 10, 19, 36

Jozsef, Attila   1905-1937 . . . . TCLC **22**
See also CA 116

Juana Ines de la Cruz   1651?-1695 . . . . LC **5**

Julian of Norwich   1342?-1416? . . . . LC **6**

Jung Chang   1952- . . . . CLC **71**

Just, Ward S(wift)   1935- . . . . CLC **4, 27**
See also CA 25-28R

Justice, Donald (Rodney)   1925- . . CLC **6, 19**
See also CANR 26; CA 5-8R; DLB-Y 83

Juvenal   c. 55-c. 127 . . . . CMLC **8**

Kacew, Romain   1914-1980
See Gary, Romain
See also CA 108; obituary CA 102

Kacewgary, Romain   1914-1980
See Gary, Romain

Kadare, Ismail   1936- . . . . CLC **52**

Kadohata, Cynthia   19??- . . . . CLC **59**

Kafka, Franz
1883-1924 . . . . TCLC **2, 6, 13, 29; SSC 5**
See also CA 105, 126; DLB 81

Kahn, Roger   1927- . . . . CLC **30**
See also CA 25-28R; SATA 37

Kaiser, (Friedrich Karl) Georg
1878-1945 . . . . TCLC **9**
See also CA 106

Kaletski, Alexander   1946- . . . . CLC **39**
See also CA 118

Kalidasa   fl. c. 400- . . . . CMLC **9**

Kallman, Chester (Simon)
1921-1975 . . . . CLC **2**
See also CANR 3; CA 45-48;
obituary CA 53-56

Kaminsky, Melvin   1926-
See Brooks, Mel
See also CANR 16; CA 65-68

Kaminsky, Stuart   1934- . . . . CLC **59**
See also CANR 29; CA 73-76

Kane, Paul   1941-
See Simon, Paul

Kanin, Garson   1912- . . . . CLC **22**
See also CANR 7; CA 5-8R; DLB 7

Kaniuk, Yoram   1930- . . . . CLC **19**

Kant, Immanuel   1724-1804 . . . . . . NCLC **27**

Kantor, MacKinlay   1904-1977 . . . . . . CLC **7**
See also CA 61-64; obituary CA 73-76;
DLB 9

Kaplan, David Michael   1946- . . . . . . CLC **50**

Kaplan, James   19??- . . . . CLC **59**

Karamzin, Nikolai Mikhailovich
1766-1826 . . . . NCLC **3**

Karapanou, Margarita   1946- . . . . CLC **13**
See also CA 101

Karl, Frederick R(obert)   1927- . . . . . CLC **34**
See also CANR 3; CA 5-8R

Kassef, Romain   1914-1980
See Gary, Romain

Katz, Steve   1935- . . . . CLC **47**
See also CANR 12; CA 25-28R; DLB-Y 83

Kauffman, Janet   1945- . . . . CLC **42**
See also CA 117; DLB-Y 86

Kaufman, Bob (Garnell)
1925-1986 . . . . CLC **49**
See also CANR 22; CA 41-44R;
obituary CA 118; DLB 16, 41

Kaufman, George S(imon)
1889-1961 . . . . CLC **38**
See also CA 108; obituary CA 93-96; DLB 7

Kaufman, Sue   1926-1977 . . . . CLC **3, 8**
See also Barondess, Sue K(aufman)

Kavan, Anna   1904-1968 . . . . CLC **5, 13**
See also Edmonds, Helen (Woods)
See also CANR 6; CA 5-8R

Kavanagh, Patrick (Joseph Gregory)
1905-1967 . . . . CLC **22**
See also CA 123; obituary CA 25-28R;
DLB 15, 20

Kawabata, Yasunari
1899-1972 . . . . CLC **2, 5, 9, 18**
See also CA 93-96; obituary CA 33-36R

Kaye, M(ary) M(argaret)   1909?- . . . . CLC **28**
See also CANR 24; CA 89-92

Kaye, Mollie   1909?-
See Kaye, M(ary) M(argaret)

Kaye-Smith, Sheila   1887-1956 . . . . . TCLC **20**
See also CA 118; DLB 36

Kaymor, Patrice Maguilene   1906-
See Senghor, Leopold Sedar

Kazan, Elia   1909- . . . . CLC **6, 16, 63**
See also CA 21-24R

Kazantzakis, Nikos
1885?-1957 . . . . TCLC **2, 5, 33**
See also CA 105

Kazin, Alfred   1915- . . . . CLC **34, 38**
See also CAAS 7; CANR 1; CA 1-4R;
DLB 67

Keane, Mary Nesta (Skrine)   1904-
  See Keane, Molly
  See also CA 108, 114

Keane, Molly   1904- . . . .   CLC 31
  See also Keane, Mary Nesta (Skrine)

Keates, Jonathan   19??- . . . .   CLC 34

Keaton, Buster   1895-1966 . . . .   CLC 20

Keaton, Joseph Francis   1895-1966
  See Keaton, Buster

Keats, John   1795-1821 . . . . . .   NCLC 8; PC 1

Keene, Donald   1922- . . . .   CLC 34
  See also CANR 5; CA 1-4R

Keillor, Garrison   1942- . . . .   CLC 40
  See also Keillor, Gary (Edward)
  See also CA 111; SATA 58; DLB-Y 87;
    AAYA 2

Keillor, Gary (Edward)
  See Keillor, Garrison
  See also CA 111, 117

Kell, Joseph   1917-
  See Burgess (Wilson, John) Anthony

Keller, Gottfried   1819-1890 . . . .   NCLC 2

Kellerman, Jonathan (S.)   1949- . . . . .   CLC 44
  See also CANR 29; CA 106

Kelley, William Melvin   1937- . . . . . .   CLC 22
  See also CANR 27; CA 77-80; DLB 33

Kellogg, Marjorie   1922- . . . .   CLC 2
  See also CA 81-84

Kelly, M. T.   1947- . . . .   CLC 55
  See also CANR 19; CA 97-100

Kelman, James   1946- . . . .   CLC 58

Kemal, Yashar   1922- . . . .   CLC 14, 29
  See also CA 89-92

Kemble, Fanny   1809-1893 . . . .   NCLC 18
  See also DLB 32

Kemelman, Harry   1908- . . . .   CLC 2
  See also CANR 6; CA 9-12R; DLB 28

Kempe, Margery   1373?-1440? . . . .   LC 6

Kempis, Thomas á   1380-1471 . . . .   LC 11

Kendall, Henry   1839-1882 . . . .   NCLC 12

Keneally, Thomas (Michael)
  1935- . . . . . .   CLC 5, 8, 10, 14, 19, 27, 43
  See also CANR 10; CA 85-88

Kennedy, Adrienne   1931-
  See also BLC 2; CANR 26; CA 103;
    CABS 3; DLB 38

Kennedy, Adrienne (Lita)   1931- . . . .   CLC 66
  See also CANR 26; CA 103; CABS 3;
    DLB 38

Kennedy, John Pendleton
  1795-1870 . . . .   NCLC 2
  See also DLB 3

Kennedy, Joseph Charles   1929- . . . . . .   CLC 8
  See also Kennedy, X. J.
  See also CANR 4, 30; CA 1-4R; SATA 14

Kennedy, William (Joseph)
  1928- . . . .   CLC 6, 28, 34, 53
  See also CANR 14; CA 85-88; SATA 57;
    DLB-Y 85; AAYA 1

Kennedy, X. J.   1929- . . . .   CLC 8, 42
  See also Kennedy, Joseph Charles
  See also CAAS 9; DLB 5

Kerouac, Jack
  1922-1969 . . . .   CLC 1, 2, 3, 5, 14, 29, 61
  See also Kerouac, Jean-Louis Lebris de
  See also DLB 2, 16; DLB-DS 3;
    CDALB 1941-1968

Kerouac, Jean-Louis Lebris de   1922-1969
  See Kerouac, Jack
  See also CANR 26; CA 5-8R;
    obituary CA 25-28R; CDALB 1941-1968

Kerr, Jean   1923- . . . .   CLC 22
  See also CANR 7; CA 5-8R

Kerr, M. E.   1927- . . . .   CLC 12, 35
  See also Meaker, Marijane
  See also SAAS 1; AAYA 2

Kerr, Robert   1970?- . . . .   CLC 55, 59

Kerrigan, (Thomas) Anthony
  1918- . . . .   CLC 4, 6
  See also CAAS 11; CANR 4; CA 49-52

Kesey, Ken (Elton)
  1935- . . . .   CLC 1, 3, 6, 11, 46, 64
  See also CANR 22; CA 1-4R; DLB 2, 16;
    CDALB 1968-1987

Kesselring, Joseph (Otto)
  1902-1967 . . . .   CLC 45

Kessler, Jascha (Frederick)   1929- . . . .   CLC 4
  See also CANR 8; CA 17-20R

Kettelkamp, Larry   1933- . . . .   CLC 12
  See also CANR 16; CA 29-32R; SAAS 3;
    SATA 2

Kherdian, David   1931- . . . .   CLC 6, 9
  See also CLR 24; CAAS 2; CA 21-24R;
    SATA 16

Khlebnikov, Velimir (Vladimirovich)
  1885-1922 . . . .   TCLC 20
  See also CA 117

Khodasevich, Vladislav (Felitsianovich)
  1886-1939 . . . .   TCLC 15
  See also CA 115

Kielland, Alexander (Lange)
  1849-1906 . . . .   TCLC 5
  See also CA 104

Kiely, Benedict   1919- . . . .   CLC 23, 43
  See also CANR 2; CA 1-4R; DLB 15

Kienzle, William X(avier)   1928- . . . .   CLC 25
  See also CAAS 1; CANR 9; CA 93-96

Kierkegaard, SOren   1813-1855 . . .   NCLC 34

Killens, John Oliver   1916- . . . .   CLC 10
  See also CAAS 2; CANR 26; CA 77-80,
    123; DLB 33

Killigrew, Anne   1660-1685 . . . .   LC 4

Kincaid, Jamaica   1949- . . . .   CLC 43, 68
  See also BLC 2; CA 125

King, Francis (Henry)   1923- . . . . .   CLC 8, 53
  See also CANR 1; CA 1-4R; DLB 15

King, Martin Luther, Jr.   1929-1968
  See also BLC 2; CANR 27; CAP 2;
    CA 25-28; SATA 14

King, Stephen (Edwin)
  1947- . . . .   CLC 12, 26, 37, 61
  See also CANR 1, 30; CA 61-64; SATA 9,
    55; DLB-Y 80; AAYA 1

Kingman, (Mary) Lee   1919- . . . .   CLC 17
  See also Natti, (Mary) Lee
  See also CA 5-8R; SAAS 3; SATA 1

Kingsley, Charles   1819-1875 . . . . .   NCLC 35
  See also YABC 2; DLB 21, 32

Kingsley, Sidney   1906- . . . .   CLC 44
  See also CA 85-88; DLB 7

Kingsolver, Barbara   1955- . . . .   CLC 55
  See also CA 129

Kingston, Maxine Hong
  1940- . . . .   CLC 12, 19, 58
  See also CANR 13; CA 69-72; SATA 53;
    DLB-Y 80

Kinnell, Galway
  1927- . . . .   CLC 1, 2, 3, 5, 13, 29
  See also CANR 10; CA 9-12R; DLB 5;
    DLB-Y 87

Kinsella, Thomas   1928- . . . . . .   CLC 4, 19, 43
  See also CANR 15; CA 17-20R; DLB 27

Kinsella, W(illiam) P(atrick)
  1935- . . . .   CLC 27, 43
  See also CAAS 7; CANR 21; CA 97-100

Kipling, (Joseph) Rudyard
  1865-1936 . . . .   TCLC 8, 17; PC 3; SSC 5
  See also YABC 2; CANR 33; CA 120;
    brief entry CA 105; DLB 19, 34

Kirkup, James   1918- . . . .   CLC 1
  See also CAAS 4; CANR 2; CA 1-4R;
    SATA 12; DLB 27

Kirkwood, James   1930-1989 . . . .   CLC 9
  See also CANR 6; CA 1-4R;
    obituary CA 128

Kis, Danilo   1935-1989 . . . .   CLC 57
  See also CA 118, 129; brief entry CA 109

Kivi, Aleksis   1834-1872 . . . .   NCLC 30

Kizer, Carolyn (Ashley)   1925- . . .   CLC 15, 39
  See also CAAS 5; CANR 24; CA 65-68;
    DLB 5

Klabund   1890-1928 . . . .   TCLC 44
  See also DLB 66

Klappert, Peter   1942- . . . .   CLC 57
  See also CA 33-36R; DLB 5

Klausner, Amos   1939-
  See Oz, Amos

Klein, A(braham) M(oses)
  1909-1972 . . . .   CLC 19
  See also CA 101; obituary CA 37-40R;
    DLB 68

Klein, Norma   1938-1989 . . . .   CLC 30
  See also CLR 2, 19; CANR 15; CA 41-44R;
    obituary CA 128; SAAS 1; SATA 7, 57;
    AAYA 2

Klein, T.E.D.   19??- . . . .   CLC 34
  See also CA 119

Kleist, Heinrich von   1777-1811 . . . .   NCLC 2
  See also DLB 90

Klima, Ivan   1931- . . . .   CLC 56
  See also CANR 17; CA 25-28R

Klimentev, Andrei Platonovich   1899-1951
  See Platonov, Andrei (Platonovich)
  See also CA 108

Klinger, Friedrich Maximilian von
  1752-1831 . . . .   NCLC 1

Klopstock, Friedrich Gottlieb
  1724-1803 . . . .   NCLC 11

Knebel, Fletcher 1911- . . . . CLC 14
See also CAAS 3; CANR 1; CA 1-4R;
SATA 36

Knight, Etheridge 1931-1991 . . . . . . CLC 40
See also BLC 2; CANR 23; CA 21-24R;
DLB 41

Knight, Sarah Kemble 1666-1727 . . . . . LC 7
See also DLB 24

Knowles, John 1926- . . . . . . CLC 1, 4, 10, 26
See also CA 17-20R; SATA 8; DLB 6;
CDALB 1968-1987

Koch, C(hristopher) J(ohn) 1932- . . . CLC 42
See also CA 127

Koch, Kenneth 1925- . . . . CLC 5, 8, 44
See also CANR 6; CA 1-4R; DLB 5

Kochanowski, Jan 1530-1584 . . . . LC 10

Kock, Charles Paul de
1794-1871 . . . . NCLC 16

Koestler, Arthur
1905-1983 . . . . CLC 1, 3, 6, 8, 15, 33
See also CANR 1; CA 1-4R;
obituary CA 109; DLB-Y 83

Kohout, Pavel 1928- . . . . CLC 13
See also CANR 3; CA 45-48

Kolmar, Gertrud 1894-1943 . . . . . . TCLC 40

Konigsberg, Allen Stewart 1935-
See Allen, Woody

Konrad, Gyorgy 1933- . . . . CLC 4, 10
See also CA 85-88

Konwicki, Tadeusz 1926- . . . . . CLC 8, 28, 54
See also CAAS 9; CA 101

Kopit, Arthur (Lee) 1937- . . . . CLC 1, 18, 33
See also CA 81-84; CABS 3; DLB 7

Kops, Bernard 1926- . . . . CLC 4
See also CA 5-8R; DLB 13

Kornbluth, C(yril) M. 1923-1958 . . . . TCLC 8
See also CA 105; DLB 8

Korolenko, Vladimir (Galaktionovich)
1853-1921 . . . . TCLC 22
See also CA 121

Kosinski, Jerzy (Nikodem)
1933-1991 . . . CLC 1, 2, 3, 6, 10, 15, 53,
70
See also CANR 9; CA 17-20R;
obituary CA 134; DLB 2; DLB-Y 82

Kostelanetz, Richard (Cory) 1940- . . CLC 28
See also CAAS 8; CA 13-16R

Kostrowitzki, Wilhelm Apollinaris de
1880-1918
See Apollinaire, Guillaume
See also CA 104

Kotlowitz, Robert 1924- . . . . CLC 4
See also CA 33-36R

Kotzebue, August (Friedrich Ferdinand) von
1761-1819 . . . . NCLC 25

Kotzwinkle, William 1938- . . . CLC 5, 14, 35
See also CLR 6; CANR 3; CA 45-48;
SATA 24

Kozol, Jonathan 1936- . . . . CLC 17
See also CANR 16; CA 61-64

Kozoll, Michael 1940?- . . . . CLC 35

Kramer, Kathryn 19??- . . . . CLC 34

Kramer, Larry 1935- . . . . CLC 42
See also CA 124, 126

Krasicki, Ignacy 1735-1801 . . . . . . NCLC 8

Krasinski, Zygmunt 1812-1859 . . . . NCLC 4

Kraus, Karl 1874-1936 . . . . TCLC 5
See also CA 104

Kreve, Vincas 1882-1954 . . . . TCLC 27

Kristofferson, Kris 1936- . . . . CLC 26
See also CA 104

Krizanc, John 1956- . . . . CLC 57

Krleza, Miroslav 1893-1981 . . . . CLC 8
See also CA 97-100; obituary CA 105

Kroetsch, Robert (Paul)
1927- . . . . CLC 5, 23, 57
See also CANR 8; CA 17-20R; DLB 53

Kroetz, Franz Xaver 1946- . . . . CLC 41
See also CA 130

Kropotkin, Peter 1842-1921 . . . . . . TCLC 36
See also CA 119

Krotkov, Yuri 1917- . . . . CLC 19
See also CA 102

Krumgold, Joseph (Quincy)
1908-1980 . . . . CLC 12
See also CANR 7; CA 9-12R;
obituary CA 101; SATA 1, 48;
obituary SATA 23

Krutch, Joseph Wood 1893-1970 . . . . CLC 24
See also CANR 4; CA 1-4R;
obituary CA 25-28R; DLB 63

Krylov, Ivan Andreevich
1768?-1844 . . . . NCLC 1

Kubin, Alfred 1877-1959 . . . . TCLC 23
See also CA 112; DLB 81

Kubrick, Stanley 1928- . . . . CLC 16
See also CA 81-84; DLB 26

Kumin, Maxine (Winokur)
1925- . . . . CLC 5, 13, 28
See also CAAS 8; CANR 1, 21; CA 1-4R;
SATA 12; DLB 5

Kundera, Milan
1929- . . . . CLC 4, 9, 19, 32, 68
See also CANR 19; CA 85-88; AAYA 2

Kunitz, Stanley J(asspon)
1905- . . . . CLC 6, 11, 14
See also CANR 26; CA 41-44R; DLB 48

Kunze, Reiner 1933- . . . . CLC 10
See also CA 93-96; DLB 75

Kuprin, Aleksandr (Ivanovich)
1870-1938 . . . . TCLC 5
See also CA 104

Kureishi, Hanif 1954- . . . . CLC 64

Kurosawa, Akira 1910- . . . . CLC 16
See also CA 101

Kuttner, Henry 1915-1958 . . . . TCLC 10
See also CA 107; DLB 8

Kuzma, Greg 1944- . . . . CLC 7
See also CA 33-36R

Kuzmin, Mikhail 1872?-1936 . . . . . . TCLC 40

Labrunie, Gerard 1808-1855
See Nerval, Gerard de

La Bruyere, Jean de 1645-1696 . . . . . LC 17

Laclos, Pierre Ambroise Francois Choderlos
de 1741-1803 . . . . NCLC 4

La Fayette, Marie (Madelaine Pioche de la
Vergne, Comtesse) de
1634-1693 . . . . LC 2

Lafayette, Rene
See Hubbard, L(afayette) Ron(ald)

Laforgue, Jules 1860-1887 . . . . NCLC 5

Lagerkvist, Par (Fabian)
1891-1974 . . . . CLC 7, 10, 13, 54
See also CA 85-88; obituary CA 49-52

Lagerlof, Selma (Ottiliana Lovisa)
1858-1940 . . . . TCLC 4, 36
See also CLR 7; CA 108; SATA 15

La Guma, (Justin) Alex(ander)
1925-1985 . . . . CLC 19
See also CANR 25; CA 49-52;
obituary CA 118

Lamartine, Alphonse (Marie Louis Prat) de
1790-1869 . . . . NCLC 11

Lamb, Charles 1775-1834 . . . . NCLC 10
See also SATA 17

Lamming, George (William)
1927- . . . . CLC 2, 4, 66
See also BLC 2; CANR 26; CA 85-88

LaMoore, Louis Dearborn 1908?-
See L'Amour, Louis (Dearborn)

L'Amour, Louis (Dearborn)
1908-1988 . . . . CLC 25, 55
See also CANR 3, 25; CA 1-4R;
obituary CA 125; DLB-Y 80

Lampedusa, (Prince) Giuseppe (Maria
Fabrizio) Tomasi di
1896-1957 . . . . TCLC 13
See also CA 111

Lampman, Archibald 1861-1899 . . NCLC 25
See also DLB 92

Lancaster, Bruce 1896-1963 . . . . CLC 36
See also CAP 1; CA 9-12; SATA 9

Landis, John (David) 1950- . . . . CLC 26
See also CA 112, 122

Landolfi, Tommaso 1908-1979 . . . CLC 11, 49
See also CA 127; obituary CA 117

Landon, Letitia Elizabeth
1802-1838 . . . . NCLC 15

Landor, Walter Savage
1775-1864 . . . . NCLC 14

Landwirth, Heinz 1927-
See Lind, Jakov
See also CANR 7; CA 11-12R

Lane, Patrick 1939- . . . . CLC 25
See also CA 97-100; DLB 53

Lang, Andrew 1844-1912 . . . . TCLC 16
See also CA 114; SATA 16

Lang, Fritz 1890-1976 . . . . CLC 20
See also CANR 30; CA 77-80;
obituary CA 69-72

Langer, Elinor 1939- . . . . CLC 34
See also CA 121

Langland, William 1330?-1400? . . . . . LC 19

Lanier, Sidney 1842-1881 . . . . NCLC 6
See also SATA 18; DLB 64

Lanyer, Aemilia 1569-1645 . . . . LC 10

Lao Tzu c. 6th-3rd century B.C. . . . CMLC 7

Lapine, James 1949-.............. CLC 39
See also CA 123, 130

Larbaud, Valery 1881-1957 .... TCLC 9
See also CA 106

Lardner, Ring(gold Wilmer)
1885-1933 .... TCLC 2, 14
See also CA 104; DLB 11, 25, 86;
CDALB 1917-1929

Larkin, Philip (Arthur)
1922-1985 ... CLC 3, 5, 8, 9, 13, 18, 33,
39, 64
See also CANR 24; CA 5-8R;
obituary CA 117; DLB 27

Larra (y Sanchez de Castro), Mariano Jose de
1809-1837 .... NCLC 17

Larsen, Eric 1941- .... CLC 55

Larsen, Nella 1891-1964 .... CLC 37
See also BLC 2; CA 125; DLB 51

Larson, Charles R(aymond) 1938-... CLC 31
See also CANR 4; CA 53-56

Latham, Jean Lee 1902-.......... CLC 12
See also CANR 7; CA 5-8R; SATA 2

Lathen, Emma.................... CLC 2
See also Hennissart, Martha; Latsis, Mary
J(ane)

Latsis, Mary J(ane)................ CLC 2
See also Lathen, Emma
See also CA 85-88

Lattimore, Richmond (Alexander)
1906-1984 .... CLC 3
See also CANR 1; CA 1-4R;
obituary CA 112

Laughlin, James 1914-........... CLC 49
See also CANR 9; CA 21-24R; DLB 48

Laurence, (Jean) Margaret (Wemyss)
1926-1987 .. CLC 3, 6, 13, 50, 62; SSC 7
See also CA 5-8R; obituary CA 121;
SATA 50; DLB 53

Laurent, Antoine 1952- .... CLC 50

Lautreamont, Comte de
1846-1870 .... NCLC 12

Lavin, Mary 1912-...... CLC 4, 18; SSC 4
See also CA 9-12R; DLB 15

Lawler, Raymond (Evenor) 1922-... CLC 58
See also CA 103

Lawrence, D(avid) H(erbert)
1885-1930 .... TCLC 2, 9, 16, 33; SSC 4
See also CA 104, 121; DLB 10, 19, 36

Lawrence, T(homas) E(dward)
1888-1935 .... TCLC 18
See also CA 115

Lawson, Henry (Archibald Hertzberg)
1867-1922 .... TCLC 27
See also CA 120

Laxness, Halldor (Kiljan) 1902- .... CLC 25
See also Gudjonsson, Halldor Kiljan

Laye, Camara 1928-1980 .... CLC 4, 38
See also BLC 2.; CANR 25; CA 85-88;
obituary CA 97-100

Layton, Irving (Peter) 1912-..... CLC 2, 15
See also CANR 2; CA 1-4R; DLB 88

Lazarus, Emma 1849-1887....... NCLC 8

Leacock, Stephen (Butler)
1869-1944 .... TCLC 2
See also CA 104; DLB 92

Lear, Edward 1812-1888 .... NCLC 3
See also CLR 1; SATA 18; DLB 32

Lear, Norman (Milton) 1922- ...... CLC 12
See also CA 73-76

Leavis, F(rank) R(aymond)
1895-1978 .... CLC 24
See also CA 21-24R; obituary CA 77-80

Leavitt, David 1961?-............. CLC 34
See also CA 116, 122

Lebowitz, Fran(ces Ann)
1951?- .... CLC 11, 36
See also CANR 14; CA 81-84

Le Carre, John 1931-... CLC 3, 5, 9, 15, 28
See also Cornwell, David (John Moore)
See also DLB 87

Le Clezio, J(ean) M(arie) G(ustave)
1940-...................... CLC 31
See also CA 116, 128; DLB 83

Leconte de Lisle, Charles-Marie-Rene
1818-1894 .... NCLC 29

Leduc, Violette 1907-1972........ CLC 22
See also CAP 1; CA 13-14;
obituary CA 33-36R

Ledwidge, Francis 1887-1917...... TCLC 23
See also CA 123; DLB 20

Lee, Andrea 1953- .... CLC 36
See also BLC 2; CA 125

Lee, Andrew 1917-
See Auchincloss, Louis (Stanton)

Lee, Don L. 1942-................ CLC 2
See also Madhubuti, Haki R.
See also CA 73-76

Lee, George Washington
1894-1976 .... CLC 52
See also BLC 2; CA 125; DLB 51

Lee, (Nelle) Harper 1926-...... CLC 12, 60
See also CA 13-16R; SATA 11; DLB 6;
CDALB 1941-1968

Lee, Lawrence 1903- .... CLC 34
See also CA 25-28R

Lee, Manfred B(ennington)
1905-1971 .... CLC 11
See also Queen, Ellery
See also CANR 2; CA 1-4R;
obituary CA 29-32R

Lee, Stan 1922-.................. CLC 17
See also CA 108, 111

Lee, Tanith 1947-................ CLC 46
See also CA 37-40R; SATA 8

Lee, Vernon 1856-1935 .... TCLC 5
See also Paget, Violet
See also DLB 57

Lee-Hamilton, Eugene (Jacob)
1845-1907 .... TCLC 22
See also CA 117

Leet, Judith 1935- .... CLC 11

Le Fanu, Joseph Sheridan
1814-1873 .... NCLC 9
See also DLB 21, 70

Leffland, Ella 1931- .... CLC 19
See also CA 29-32R; DLB-Y 84

Leger, (Marie-Rene) Alexis Saint-Leger
1887-1975 .... CLC 11
See also Perse, St.-John
See also CA 13-16R; obituary CA 61-64

Le Guin, Ursula K(roeber)
1929- .... CLC 8, 13, 22, 45, 71
See also CLR 3; CANR 9, 32; CA 21-24R;
SATA 4, 52; DLB 8, 52;
CDALB 1968-1987

Lehmann, Rosamond (Nina) 1901- ... CLC 5
See also CANR 8; CA 77-80; DLB 15

Leiber, Fritz (Reuter, Jr.) 1910-.... CLC 25
See also CANR 2; CA 45-48; SATA 45;
DLB 8

Leimbach, Marti 1963-............ CLC 65

Leino, Eino 1878-1926.......... TCLC 24

Leiris, Michel 1901-.............. CLC 61
See also CA 119, 128

Leithauser, Brad 1953-........... CLC 27
See also CANR 27; CA 107

Lelchuk, Alan 1938-.............. CLC 5
See also CANR 1; CA 45-48

Lem, Stanislaw 1921-........ CLC 8, 15, 40
See also CAAS 1; CA 105

Lemann, Nancy 1956-............ CLC 39
See also CA 118

Lemonnier, (Antoine Louis) Camille
1844-1913 .... TCLC 22
See also CA 121

Lenau, Nikolaus 1802-1850...... NCLC 16

L'Engle, Madeleine 1918- .... CLC 12
See also CLR 1, 14; CANR 3, 21; CA 1-4R;
SATA 1, 27; DLB 52; AAYA 1

Lengyel, Jozsef 1896-1975......... CLC 7
See also CA 85-88; obituary CA 57-60

Lennon, John (Ono)
1940-1980 .... CLC 12, 35
See also CA 102

Lennon, John Winston 1940-1980
See Lennon, John (Ono)

Lennox, Charlotte Ramsay
1729?-1804................. NCLC 23
See also DLB 39

Lentricchia, Frank (Jr.) 1940-...... CLC 34
See also CANR 19; CA 25-28R

Lenz, Siegfried 1926-............. CLC 27
See also CA 89-92; DLB 75

Leonard, Elmore 1925-...... CLC 28, 34, 71
See also CANR 12, 28; CA 81-84

Leonard, Hugh 1926-............. CLC 19
See also Byrne, John Keyes
See also DLB 13

Leopardi, (Conte) Giacomo (Talegardo
Francesco di Sales Saverio Pietro)
1798-1837 .... NCLC 22

Lerman, Eleanor 1952-............ CLC 9
See also CA 85-88

Lerman, Rhoda 1936-............ CLC 56
See also CA 49-52

Lermontov, Mikhail Yuryevich
1814-1841 .... NCLC 5

Leroux, Gaston 1868-1927........ TCLC 25
See also CA 108

Lesage, Alain-Rene   1668-1747. . . . . . .   LC 2

Leskov, Nikolai (Semyonovich)
   1831-1895 . . . .   NCLC 25

Lessing, Doris (May)
   1919- . . . .   CLC 1, 2, 3, 6, 10, 15, 22, 40;
                                          SSC 6
   See also CA 9-12R; DLB 15; DLB-Y 85

Lessing, Gotthold Ephraim
   1729-1781 . . . .   LC 8

Lester, Richard   1932-. . . . .   CLC 20

Lever, Charles (James)
   1806-1872 . . . .   NCLC 23
   See also DLB 21

Leverson, Ada   1865-1936. . . . .   TCLC 18
   See also CA 117

Levertov, Denise
   1923- . . . . . .   CLC 1, 2, 3, 5, 8, 15, 28, 66
   See also CANR 3, 29; CA 1-4R; DLB 5

Levi, Peter (Chad Tiger)   1931- . . . . .   CLC 41
   See also CA 5-8R; DLB 40

Levi, Primo   1919-1987. . . . .   CLC 37, 50
   See also CANR 12; CA 13-16R;
      obituary CA 122

Levin, Ira   1929- . . . .   CLC 3, 6
   See also CANR 17; CA 21-24R

Levin, Meyer   1905-1981 . . . .   CLC 7
   See also CANR 15; CA 9-12R;
      obituary CA 104; SATA 21;
      obituary SATA 27; DLB 9, 28; DLB-Y 81

Levine, Norman   1924- . . . .   CLC 54
   See also CANR 14; CA 73-76; DLB 88

Levine, Philip   1928-. .   CLC 2, 4, 5, 9, 14, 33
   See also CANR 9; CA 9-12R; DLB 5

Levinson, Deirdre   1931-. . . . .   CLC 49
   See also CA 73-76

Levi-Strauss, Claude   1908- . . . .   CLC 38
   See also CANR 6; CA 1-4R

Levitin, Sonia   1934-. . . . .   CLC 17
   See also CANR 14; CA 29-32R; SAAS 2;
      SATA 4

Lewes, George Henry
   1817-1878 . . . .   NCLC 25
   See also DLB 55

Lewis, Alun   1915-1944. . . . .   TCLC 3
   See also CA 104; DLB 20

Lewis, C(ecil) Day   1904-1972
   See Day Lewis, C(ecil)

Lewis, C(live) S(taples)
   1898-1963 . . . .   CLC 1, 3, 6, 14, 27
   See also CLR 3; CA 81-84; SATA 13;
      DLB 15

Lewis (Winters), Janet   1899-. . . . . . .   CLC 41
   See also Winters, Janet Lewis
   See also CANR 29; CAP 1; CA 9-10R;
      DLB-Y 87

Lewis, Matthew Gregory
   1775-1818 . . . .   NCLC 11
   See also DLB 39

Lewis, (Harry) Sinclair
   1885-1951 . . . .   TCLC 4, 13, 23, 39
   See also CA 104; DLB 9; DLB-DS 1;
      CDALB 1917-1929

Lewis, (Percy) Wyndham
   1882?-1957. . . . .   TCLC 2, 9
   See also CA 104; DLB 15

Lewisohn, Ludwig   1883-1955. . . . .   TCLC 19
   See also CA 73-76, 107;
      obituary CA 29-32R; DLB 4, 9, 28

L'Heureux, John (Clarke)   1934-. . . .   CLC 52
   See also CANR 23; CA 15-16R

Lieber, Stanley Martin   1922-
   See Lee, Stan

Lieberman, Laurence (James)
   1935- . . . .   CLC 4, 36
   See also CANR 8; CA 17-20R

Li Fei-kan   1904-. . . . .   CLC 18
   See also Pa Chin
   See also CA 105

Lifton, Robert Jay   1926-. . . . .   CLC 67
   See also CANR 27; CA 17-18R

Lightfoot, Gordon (Meredith)
   1938- . . . .   CLC 26
   See also CA 109

Ligotti, Thomas   1953- . . . .   CLC 44
   See also CA 123

Liliencron, Detlev von
   1844-1909 . . . .   TCLC 18
   See also CA 117

Lima, Jose Lezama   1910-1976
   See Lezama Lima, Jose

Lima Barreto, (Alfonso Henriques de)
   1881-1922 . . . .   TCLC 23
   See also CA 117

Limonov, Eduard   1943-. . . . .   CLC 67

Lincoln, Abraham   1809-1865. . . . . .   NCLC 18

Lind, Jakov   1927-. . . . .   CLC 1, 2, 4, 27
   See also Landwirth, Heinz
   See also CAAS 4; CA 9-12R

Lindsay, David   1876-1945. . . . .   TCLC 15
   See also CA 113

Lindsay, (Nicholas) Vachel
   1879-1931 . . . .   TCLC 17
   See also CA 114; SATA 40; DLB 54;
      CDALB 1865-1917

Linney, Romulus   1930- . . . .   CLC 51
   See also CA 1-4R

Li Po   701-763. . . . .   CMLC 2

Lipsius, Justus   1547-1606 . . . .   LC 16

Lipsyte, Robert (Michael)   1938-. . . .   CLC 21
   See also CLR 23; CANR 8; CA 17-20R;
      SATA 5

Lish, Gordon (Jay)   1934-. . . . .   CLC 45
   See also CA 113, 117

Lispector, Clarice   1925-1977. . . . . . .   CLC 43
   See also obituary CA 116

Littell, Robert   1935?-. . . . .   CLC 42
   See also CA 109, 112

Little, Malcolm   1925-1965
   See also BLC 2; CA 125; obituary CA 111

Liu E   1857-1909. . . . .   TCLC 15
   See also CA 115

Lively, Penelope   1933-. . . . .   CLC 32, 50
   See also CLR 7; CANR 29; CA 41-44R;
      SATA 7; DLB 14

Livesay, Dorothy   1909- . . . .   CLC 4, 15
   See also CAAS 8; CA 25-28R; DLB 68

Lizardi, Jose Joaquin Fernandez de
   1776-1827 . . . .   NCLC 30

Llewellyn, Richard   1906-1983. . . . . .   CLC 7
   See also Llewellyn Lloyd, Richard (Dafydd
      Vyvyan)
   See also DLB 15

Llewellyn Lloyd, Richard (Dafydd Vyvyan)
   1906-1983
   See Llewellyn, Richard
   See also CANR 7; CA 53-56;
      obituary CA 111; SATA 11, 37

Llosa, Mario Vargas   1936-
   See Vargas Llosa, Mario

Lloyd, Richard Llewellyn   1906-
   See Llewellyn, Richard

Locke, Alain   1886-1954. . . . .   TCLC 43
   See also CA 124, 106; DLB 51

Locke, John   1632-1704 . . . .   LC 7
   See also DLB 31

Lockhart, John Gibson
   1794-1854 . . . .   NCLC 6

Lodge, David (John)   1935-. . . . .   CLC 36
   See also CANR 19; CA 17-20R; DLB 14

Loewinsohn, Ron(ald William)
   1937- . . . .   CLC 52
   See also CA 25-28R

Logan, John   1923- . . . .   CLC 5
   See also CA 77-80; obituary CA 124; DLB 5

Lo Kuan-chung   1330?-1400? . . . .   LC 12

Lombino, S. A.   1926-
   See Hunter, Evan

London, Jack
   1876-1916 . . . . . .   TCLC 9, 15, 39; SSC 4
   See also London, John Griffith
   See also SATA 18; DLB 8, 12, 78;
      CDALB 1865-1917

London, John Griffith   1876-1916
   See London, Jack
   See also CA 110, 119

Long, Emmett   1925-
   See Leonard, Elmore

Longbaugh, Harry   1931-
   See Goldman, William (W.)

Longfellow, Henry Wadsworth
   1807-1882 . . . .   NCLC 2
   See also SATA 19; DLB 1, 59;
      CDALB 1640-1865

Longley, Michael   1939-. . . . .   CLC 29
   See also CA 102; DLB 40

Longus   fl. c. 2nd century- . . . .   CMLC 7

Lopate, Phillip   1943- . . . .   CLC 29
   See also CA 97-100; DLB-Y 80

Lopez Portillo (y Pacheco), Jose
   1920- . . . .   CLC 46
   See also CA 129

Lopez y Fuentes, Gregorio
   1897-1966 . . . .   CLC 32

Lord, Bette Bao   1938- . . . .   CLC 23
   See also CA 107; SATA 58

Lorde, Audre (Geraldine)   1934-. . . . .   CLC 18
   See also BLC 2; CANR 16, 26; CA 25-28R;
      DLB 41

Author Index

Loti, Pierre 1850-1923 . . . . TCLC 11
　See also Viaud, (Louis Marie) Julien

Louie, David Wong 1954- . . . . CLC 70

Lovecraft, H(oward) P(hillips)
　1890-1937 . . . . TCLC 4, 22; SSC 3
　See also CA 104

Lovelace, Earl 1935- . . . . CLC 51
　See also CA 77-80

Lowell, Amy 1874-1925 . . . . TCLC 1, 8
　See also CA 104; DLB 54

Lowell, James Russell 1819-1891 . . NCLC 2
　See also DLB 1, 11, 64, 79;
　CDALB 1640-1865

Lowell, Robert (Traill Spence, Jr.)
　1917-1977 . . . CLC 1, 2, 3, 4, 5, 8, 9, 11,
　　　　　　　　　　　　　　　15, 37; PC 3
　See also CANR 26; CA 9-10R;
　obituary CA 73-76; CABS 2; DLB 5

Lowndes, Marie (Adelaide) Belloc
　1868-1947 . . . . TCLC 12
　See also CA 107; DLB 70

Lowry, (Clarence) Malcolm
　1909-1957 . . . . TCLC 6, 40
　See also CA 105, 131; DLB 15

Loy, Mina 1882-1966 . . . . CLC 28
　See also CA 113; DLB 4, 54

Lucas, Craig . . . . CLC 64

Lucas, George 1944- . . . . CLC 16
　See also CANR 30; CA 77-80; SATA 56;
　AAYA 1

Lucas, Victoria 1932-1963
　See Plath, Sylvia

Ludlam, Charles 1943-1987 . . . . . CLC 46, 50
　See also CA 85-88; obituary CA 122

Ludlum, Robert 1927- . . . . CLC 22, 43
　See also CANR 25; CA 33-36R; DLB-Y 82

Ludwig, Ken 19??- . . . . CLC 60

Ludwig, Otto 1813-1865 . . . . NCLC 4

Lugones, Leopoldo 1874-1938 . . . . . TCLC 15
　See also CA 116

Lu Hsun 1881-1936 . . . . TCLC 3

Lukacs, Georg 1885-1971 . . . . CLC 24
　See also Lukacs, Gyorgy

Lukacs, Gyorgy 1885-1971
　See Lukacs, Georg
　See also CA 101; obituary CA 29-32R

Luke, Peter (Ambrose Cyprian)
　1919- . . . . CLC 38
　See also CA 81-84; DLB 13

Lurie (Bishop), Alison
　1926- . . . . CLC 4, 5, 18, 39
　See also CANR 2, 17; CA 1-4R; SATA 46;
　DLB 2

Lustig, Arnost 1926- . . . . CLC 56
　See also CA 69-72; SATA 56; AAYA 3

Luther, Martin 1483-1546 . . . . LC 9

Luzi, Mario 1914- . . . . CLC 13
　See also CANR 9; CA 61-64

Lynch, David 1946- . . . . CLC 66
　See also CA 129; brief entry CA 124

Lynn, Kenneth S(chuyler) 1923- . . . . CLC 50
　See also CANR 3, 27; CA 1-4R

Lytle, Andrew (Nelson) 1902- . . . . . . CLC 22
　See also CA 9-12R; DLB 6

Lyttelton, George 1709-1773 . . . . LC 10

Lytton, Edward Bulwer 1803-1873
　See Bulwer-Lytton, (Lord) Edward (George
　Earle Lytton)
　See also SATA 23

Maas, Peter 1929- . . . . CLC 29
　See also CA 93-96

Macaulay, (Dame Emilie) Rose
　1881-1958 . . . . TCLC 7, 44
　See also CA 104; DLB 36

MacBeth, George (Mann)
　1932- . . . . CLC 2, 5, 9
　See also CA 25-28R; SATA 4; DLB 40

MacCaig, Norman (Alexander)
　1910- . . . . CLC 36
　See also CANR 3; CA 9-12R; DLB 27

MacCarthy, Desmond 1877-1952 . . TCLC 36

MacDermot, Thomas H. 1870-1933
　See Redcam, Tom

MacDiarmid, Hugh
　1892-1978 . . . . CLC 2, 4, 11, 19, 63
　See also Grieve, C(hristopher) M(urray)
　See also DLB 20

Macdonald, Cynthia 1928- . . . . . . CLC 13, 19
　See also CANR 4; CA 49-52

MacDonald, George 1824-1905 . . . . . TCLC 9
　See also CA 106; SATA 33; DLB 18

MacDonald, John D(ann)
　1916-1986 . . . . CLC 3, 27, 44
　See also CANR 1, 19; CA 1-4R;
　obituary CA 121; DLB 8; DLB-Y 86

Macdonald, (John) Ross
　1915-1983 . . . . . . CLC 1, 2, 3, 14, 34, 41
　See also Millar, Kenneth
　See also DLB-DS 6

MacEwen, Gwendolyn (Margaret)
　1941-1987 . . . . CLC 13, 55
　See also CANR 7, 22; CA 9-12R;
　obituary CA 124; SATA 50, 55; DLB 53

Machado (y Ruiz), Antonio
　1875-1939 . . . . TCLC 3
　See also CA 104

Machado de Assis, (Joaquim Maria)
　1839-1908 . . . . TCLC 10
　See also BLC 2; brief entry CA 107

Machen, Arthur (Llewellyn Jones)
　1863-1947 . . . . TCLC 4
　See also CA 104; DLB 36

Machiavelli, Niccolo 1469-1527 . . . . . . LC 8

MacInnes, Colin 1914-1976 . . . . . . CLC 4, 23
　See also CANR 21; CA 69-72;
　obituary CA 65-68; DLB 14

MacInnes, Helen (Clark)
　1907-1985 . . . . CLC 27, 39
　See also CANR 1, 28; CA 1-4R;
　obituary CA 65-68, 117; SATA 22, 44;
　DLB 87

Macintosh, Elizabeth 1897-1952
　See Tey, Josephine
　See also CA 110

Mackenzie, (Edward Montague) Compton
　1883-1972 . . . . CLC 18
　See also CAP 2; CA 21-22;
　obituary CA 37-40R; DLB 34

Mac Laverty, Bernard 1942- . . . . CLC 31
　See also CA 116, 118

MacLean, Alistair (Stuart)
　1922-1987 . . . . CLC 3, 13, 50, 63
　See also CANR 28; CA 57-60;
　obituary CA 121; SATA 23, 50

MacLeish, Archibald
　1892-1982 . . . . CLC 3, 8, 14, 68
　See also CANR 33; CA 9-12R;
　obituary CA 106; DLB 4, 7, 45;
　DLB-Y 82

MacLennan, (John) Hugh
　1907- . . . . CLC 2, 14
　See also CA 5-8R; DLB 68

MacLeod, Alistair 1936- . . . . CLC 56
　See also CA 123; DLB 60

Macleod, Fiona 1855-1905
　See Sharp, William

MacNeice, (Frederick) Louis
　1907-1963 . . . . CLC 1, 4, 10, 53
　See also CA 85-88; DLB 10, 20

Macpherson, (Jean) Jay 1931- . . . . . . CLC 14
　See also CA 5-8R; DLB 53

MacShane, Frank 1927- . . . . CLC 39
　See also CANR 3; CA 11-12R

Macumber, Mari 1896-1966
　See Sandoz, Mari (Susette)

Madach, Imre 1823-1864 . . . . NCLC 19

Madden, (Jerry) David 1933- . . . . CLC 5, 15
　See also CAAS 3; CANR 4; CA 1-4R;
　DLB 6

Madhubuti, Haki R. 1942- . . . . CLC 6
　See also Lee, Don L.
　See also BLC 2; CANR 24; CA 73-76;
　DLB 5, 41; DLB-DS 8

Maeterlinck, Maurice 1862-1949 . . . TCLC 3
　See also CA 104

Mafouz, Naguib 1912-
　See Mahfuz, Najib

Maginn, William 1794-1842 . . . . NCLC 8

Mahapatra, Jayanta 1928- . . . . CLC 33
　See also CAAS 9; CANR 15; CA 73-76

Mahfuz Najib 1912- . . . . CLC 52, 55
　See also DLB-Y 88

Mahon, Derek 1941- . . . . CLC 27
　See also CA 113, 128; DLB 40

Mailer, Norman
　1923- . . . . . . CLC 1, 2, 3, 4, 5, 8, 11, 14,
　　　　　　　　　　　　　　　　28, 39
　See also CANR 28; CA 9-12R; CABS 1;
　DLB 2, 16, 28; DLB-Y 80, 83;
　DLB-DS 3; CDALB 1968-1987

Maillet, Antonine 1929- . . . . CLC 54
　See also CA 115, 120; DLB 60

Mais, Roger 1905-1955 . . . . TCLC 8
　See also CA 105, 124

Maitland, Sara (Louise) 1950- . . . . . . CLC 49
　See also CANR 13; CA 69-72

Major, Clarence 1936-....... **CLC 3, 19, 48**
See also BLC 2; CAAS 6; CANR 13, 25;
CA 21-24R; DLB 33

Major, Kevin 1949- .... **CLC 26**
See also CLR 11; CANR 21; CA 97-100;
SATA 32; DLB 60

Malamud, Bernard
1914-1986 ..... **CLC 1, 2, 3, 5, 8, 9, 11,
18, 27, 44**
See also CANR 28; CA 5-8R;
obituary CA 118; CABS 1; DLB 2, 28;
DLB-Y 80, 86; CDALB 1941-1968

Malcolm X 1925-1965
See Little, Malcolm
See also BLC 2

Malherbe, Francois de 1555-1628..... **LC 5**

Mallarme Stephane
1842-1898 .... **NCLC 4; PC 4**

Mallet-Joris, Francoise 1930-...... **CLC 11**
See also CANR 17; CA 65-68; DLB 83

Maloff, Saul 1922-................ **CLC 5**
See also CA 33-36R

Malone, Louis 1907-1963
See MacNeice, (Frederick) Louis

Malone, Michael (Christopher)
1942-........................ **CLC 43**
See also CANR 14; CA 77-80

Malory, (Sir) Thomas ?-1471....... **LC 11**
See also SATA 33, 59

Malouf, David 1934- .... **CLC 28**

Malraux, (Georges-) Andre
1901-1976 ...... **CLC 1, 4, 9, 13, 15, 57**
See also CAP 2; CA 21-24;
obituary CA 69-72; DLB 72

Malzberg, Barry N. 1939-......... **CLC 7**
See also CAAS 4; CANR 16; CA 61-64;
DLB 8

Mamet, David (Alan)
1947- .... **CLC 9, 15, 34, 46**
See also CANR 15; CA 81-84, 124;
CABS 3; DLB 7; AAYA 3

Mamoulian, Rouben 1898-......... **CLC 16**
See also CA 25-28R; obituary CA 124

Mandelstam, Osip (Emilievich)
1891?-1938?................ **TCLC 2, 6**
See also CA 104

Mander, Jane 1877-1949 .... **TCLC 31**

Mandiargues, Andre Pieyre de
1909-........................ **CLC 41**
See also CA 103; DLB 83

Mandrake, Ethel Belle 1902-1934
See Thurman, Wallace

Mangan, James Clarence
1803-1849 .... **NCLC 27**

Manley, (Mary) Delariviere
1672?-1724.................... **LC 1**
See also DLB 39, 80

Mann, (Luiz) Heinrich 1871-1950... **TCLC 9**
See also CA 106; DLB 66

Mann, Thomas
1875-1955 ... **TCLC 2, 8, 14, 21, 35, 44;
SSC 5**
See also CA 104, 128; DLB 66

Manning, Frederic 1882-1935 ..... **TCLC 25**
See also CA 124

Manning, Olivia 1915-1980...... **CLC 5, 19**
See also CANR 29; CA 5-8R;
obituary CA 101

Mano, D. Keith 1942-.......... **CLC 2, 10**
See also CAAS 6; CANR 26; CA 25-28R;
DLB 6

Mansfield, Katherine
1888-1923 .... **TCLC 2, 8, 39; SSC 9**
See also CA 104

Manso, Peter 1940-.............. **CLC 39**
See also CA 29-32R

Manzoni, Alessandro 1785-1873 .. **NCLC 29**

Mapu, Abraham (ben Jekutiel)
1808-1867 .... **NCLC 18**

Marat, Jean Paul 1743-1793........ **LC 10**

Marcel, Gabriel (Honore)
1889-1973 .... **CLC 15**
See also CA 102; obituary CA 45-48

Marchbanks, Samuel 1913-
See Davies, (William) Robertson

Marie de France
c. 12th Century-............. **CMLC 8**

Marie de l'Incarnation 1599-1672.... **LC 10**

Marinetti, F(ilippo) T(ommaso)
1876-1944 .... **TCLC 10**
See also CA 107

Marivaux, Pierre Carlet de Chamblain de
(1688-1763) .... **LC 4**

Markandaya, Kamala 1924-...... **CLC 8, 38**
See also Taylor, Kamala (Purnaiya)

Markfield, Wallace (Arthur) 1926-... **CLC 8**
See also CAAS 3; CA 69-72; DLB 2, 28

Markham, Robert 1922-
See Amis, Kingsley (William)

Marks, J. 1942-
See Highwater, Jamake

Markson, David 1927-............ **CLC 67**
See also CANR 1; CA 49-52

Marley, Bob 1945-1981........... **CLC 17**
See also Marley, Robert Nesta

Marley, Robert Nesta 1945-1981
See Marley, Bob
See also CA 107; obituary CA 103

Marlowe, Christopher 1564-1593 ..... **DC 1**
See also DLB 62

Marmontel, Jean-Francois
1723-1799 .... **LC 2**

Marquand, John P(hillips)
1893-1960 .... **CLC 2, 10**
See also CA 85-88; DLB 9

Marquez, Gabriel Garcia 1928-
See Garcia Marquez, Gabriel

Marquis, Don(ald Robert Perry)
1878-1937 .... **TCLC 7**
See also CA 104; DLB 11, 25

Marryat, Frederick 1792-1848 .... **NCLC 3**
See also DLB 21

Marsh, (Dame Edith) Ngaio
1899-1982 .... **CLC 7, 53**
See also CANR 6; CA 9-12R; DLB 77

Marshall, Garry 1935?-........... **CLC 17**
See also CA 111; AAYA 3

Marshall, Paule 1929- .. **CLC 27, 72; SSC 3**
See also BLC 3; CANR 25; CA 77-80;
DLB 33

Marsten, Richard 1926-
See Hunter, Evan

Martin, Steve 1945?-............. **CLC 30**
See also CANR 30; CA 97-100

Martin du Gard, Roger
1881-1958 .... **TCLC 24**
See also CA 118; DLB 65

Martineau, Harriet 1802-1876.... **NCLC 26**
See also YABC 2; DLB 21, 55

Martinez Ruiz, Jose 1874-1967
See Azorin
See also CA 93-96

Martinez Sierra, Gregorio
1881-1947 .... **TCLC 6**
See also CA 104, 115

Martinez Sierra, Maria (de la O'LeJarraga)
1880?-1974.................. **TCLC 6**
See also obituary CA 115

Martinson, Harry (Edmund)
1904-1978 .... **CLC 14**
See also CA 77-80

Marvell, Andrew 1621-1678......... **LC 4**

Marx, Karl (Heinrich)
1818-1883 .... **NCLC 17**

Masaoka Shiki 1867-1902 .... **TCLC 18**

Masefield, John (Edward)
1878-1967 .... **CLC 11, 47**
See also CAP 2; CA 19-20;
obituary CA 25-28R; SATA 19; DLB 10,
19

Maso, Carole 19??-................ **CLC 44**

Mason, Bobbie Ann
1940- .... **CLC 28, 43; SSC 4**
See also CANR 11; CA 53-56; SAAS 1;
DLB-Y 87

Mason, Nick 1945-............... **CLC 35**
See also Pink Floyd

Mason, Tally 1909-1971
See Derleth, August (William)

Masters, Edgar Lee
1868?-1950.......... **TCLC 2, 25; PC 1**
See also CA 104; DLB 54;
CDALB 1865-1917

Masters, Hilary 1928-............ **CLC 48**
See also CANR 13; CA 25-28R

Mastrosimone, William 19??- ...... **CLC 36**

Matheson, Richard (Burton)
1926-...................... **CLC 37**
See also CA 97-100; DLB 8, 44

Mathews, Harry 1930-.......... **CLC 6, 52**
See also CAAS 6; CANR 18; CA 21-24R

Mathias, Roland (Glyn) 1915-...... **CLC 45**
See also CANR 19; CA 97-100; DLB 27

Matthews, Greg 1949- .... **CLC 45**

Matthews, William 1942-.......... **CLC 40**
See also CANR 12; CA 29-32R; DLB 5

Matthias, John (Edward) 1941-...... **CLC 9**
See also CA 33-36R

Matthiessen, Peter
   1927- . . . . CLC **5, 7, 11, 32, 64**
   See also CANR 21; CA 9-12R; SATA 27;
   DLB 6

Maturin, Charles Robert
   1780?-1824. . . . . NCLC **6**

Matute, Ana Maria 1925- . . . . CLC **11**
   See also CA 89-92

Maugham, W(illiam) Somerset
   1874-1965 . . . . CLC **1, 11, 15, 67; SSC 8**
   See also CA 5-8R; obituary CA 25-28R;
   SATA 54; DLB 10, 36, 77, 100

Maupassant, (Henri Rene Albert) Guy de
   1850-1893 . . . . NCLC **1; SSC 1**

Mauriac, Claude 1914- . . . . CLC **9**
   See also CA 89-92; DLB 83

Mauriac, Francois (Charles)
   1885-1970 . . . . CLC **4, 9, 56**
   See also CAP 2; CA 25-28; DLB 65

Mavor, Osborne Henry 1888-1951
   See Bridie, James
   See also CA 104

Maxwell, William (Keepers, Jr.)
   1908- . . . . CLC **19**
   See also CA 93-96; DLB-Y 80

May, Elaine 1932- . . . . CLC **16**
   See also CA 124; DLB 44

Mayakovsky, Vladimir (Vladimirovich)
   1893-1930 . . . . TCLC **4, 18**
   See also CA 104

Mayhew, Henry 1812-1887 . . . . . . NCLC **31**
   See also DLB 18, 55

Maynard, Joyce 1953- . . . . CLC **23**
   See also CA 111, 129

Mayne, William (James Carter)
   1928- . . . . CLC **12**
   See also CA 9-12R; SATA 6

Mayo, Jim 1908?-
   See L'Amour, Louis (Dearborn)

Maysles, Albert 1926- and **Maysles, David**
   1926- . . . . CLC **16**
   See also CA 29-32R

Maysles, Albert 1926- . . . . CLC **16**
   See also Maysles, Albert and Maysles,
   David
   See also CA 29-32R

Maysles, David 1932- . . . . CLC **16**
   See also Maysles, Albert and Maysles,
   David

Mazer, Norma Fox 1931- . . . . CLC **26**
   See also CLR 23; CANR 12; CA 69-72;
   SAAS 1; SATA 24

Mazzini, Guiseppe 1805-1872 . . . . NCLC **34**

McAuley, James (Phillip)
   1917-1976 . . . . CLC **45**
   See also CA 97-100

McBain, Ed 1926-
   See Hunter, Evan

McBrien, William 1930- . . . . CLC **44**
   See also CA 107

McCaffrey, Anne 1926- . . . . CLC **17**
   See also CANR 15; CA 25-28R; SATA 8;
   DLB 8

McCarthy, Cormac 1933- . . . . CLC **4, 57**
   See also CANR 10; CA 13-16R; DLB 6

McCarthy, Mary (Therese)
   1912-1989- . . . CLC **1, 3, 5, 14, 24, 39, 59**
   See also CANR 16; CA 5-8R;
   obituary CA 129; DLB 2; DLB-Y 81

McCartney, (James) Paul
   1942- . . . . CLC **12, 35**

McCauley, Stephen 19??- . . . . CLC **50**

McClure, Michael 1932- . . . . CLC **6, 10**
   See also CANR 17; CA 21-24R; DLB 16

McCorkle, Jill (Collins) 1958- . . . . . . CLC **51**
   See also CA 121; DLB-Y 87

McCourt, James 1941- . . . . CLC **5**
   See also CA 57-60

McCoy, Horace 1897-1955 . . . . TCLC **28**
   See also CA 108; DLB 9

McCrae, John 1872-1918 . . . . TCLC **12**
   See also CA 109; DLB 92

McCullers, (Lula) Carson (Smith)
   1917-1967 . . CLC **1, 4, 10, 12, 48; SSC 9**
   See also CANR 18; CA 5-8R;
   obituary CA 25-28R; CABS 1; SATA 27;
   DLB 2, 7; CDALB 1941-1968

McCullough, Colleen 1938?- . . . . CLC **27**
   See also CANR 17; CA 81-84

McElroy, Joseph (Prince)
   1930- . . . . CLC **5, 47**
   See also CA 17-20R

McEwan, Ian (Russell) 1948- . . . CLC **13, 66**
   See also CANR 14; CA 61-64; DLB 14

McFadden, David 1940- . . . . CLC **48**
   See also CA 104; DLB 60

McFarland, Dennis 1956- . . . . CLC **65**

McGahern, John 1934- . . . . CLC **5, 9, 48**
   See also CANR 29; CA 17-20R; DLB 14

McGinley, Patrick 1937- . . . . CLC **41**
   See also CA 120, 127

McGinley, Phyllis 1905-1978 . . . . . . CLC **14**
   See also CANR 19; CA 9-12R;
   obituary CA 77-80; SATA 2, 44;
   obituary SATA 24; DLB 11, 48

McGinniss, Joe 1942- . . . . CLC **32**
   See also CANR 26; CA 25-28R

McGivern, Maureen Daly 1921-
   See Daly, Maureen
   See also CA 9-12R

McGrath, Patrick 1950- . . . . CLC **55**

McGrath, Thomas 1916- . . . . CLC **28, 59**
   See also CANR 6; CA 9-12R, 130;
   SATA 41

McGuane, Thomas (Francis III)
   1939- . . . . CLC **3, 7, 18, 45**
   See also CANR 5, 24; CA 49-52; DLB 2;
   DLB-Y 80

McGuckian, Medbh 1950- . . . . CLC **48**
   See also DLB 40

McHale, Tom 1941-1982 . . . . CLC **3, 5**
   See also CA 77-80; obituary CA 106

McIlvanney, William 1936- . . . . CLC **42**
   See also CA 25-28R; DLB 14

McIlwraith, Maureen Mollie Hunter 1922-
   See Hunter, Mollie
   See also CA 29-32R; SATA 2

McInerney, Jay 1955- . . . . CLC **34**
   See also CA 116, 123

McIntyre, Vonda N(eel) 1948- . . . . . CLC **18**
   See also CANR 17; CA 81-84

McKay, Claude
   1889-1948 . . . . TCLC **7, 41; PC 2**
   See also BLC 3; CA 104, 124; DLB 4, 45,
   51

McKay, Claude 1889-1948
   See McKay, Festus Claudius

McKay, Festus Claudius 1889-1948
   See also BLC 2; CA 124; brief entry CA 104

McKuen, Rod 1933- . . . . CLC **1, 3**
   See also CA 41-44R

McLuhan, (Herbert) Marshall
   1911-1980 . . . . CLC **37**
   See also CANR 12; CA 9-12R;
   obituary CA 102; DLB 88

McManus, Declan Patrick 1955-
   See Costello, Elvis

McMillan, Terry 1951- . . . . CLC **50, 61**

McMurtry, Larry (Jeff)
   1936- . . . . CLC **2, 3, 7, 11, 27, 44**
   See also CANR 19; CA 5-8R; DLB 2;
   DLB-Y 80, 87; CDALB 1968-1987

McNally, Terrence 1939- . . . . . . CLC **4, 7, 41**
   See also CANR 2; CA 45-48; DLB 7

McNamer, Deirdre 1950- . . . . CLC **70**

McNeile, Herman Cyril 1888-1937
   See Sapper
   See also DLB 77

McPhee, John 1931- . . . . CLC **36**
   See also CANR 20; CA 65-68

McPherson, James Alan 1943- . . . . . CLC **19**
   See also CANR 24; CA 25-28R; DLB 38

McPherson, William 1939- . . . . CLC **34**
   See also CA 57-60

McSweeney, Kerry 19??- . . . . CLC **34**

Mead, Margaret 1901-1978 . . . . CLC **37**
   See also CANR 4; CA 1-4R;
   obituary CA 81-84; SATA 20

Meaker, M. J. 1927-
   See Kerr, M. E.; Meaker, Marijane

Meaker, Marijane 1927-
   See Kerr, M. E.
   See also CA 107; SATA 20

Medoff, Mark (Howard) 1940- . . . CLC **6, 23**
   See also CANR 5; CA 53-56; DLB 7

Megged, Aharon 1920- . . . . CLC **9**
   See also CANR 1; CA 49-52

Mehta, Ved (Parkash) 1934- . . . . CLC **37**
   See also CANR 2, 23; CA 1-4R

Mellor, John 1953?-
   See The Clash

Meltzer, Milton 1915- . . . . CLC **26**
   See also CLR 13; CA 13-16R; SAAS 1;
   SATA 1, 50; DLB 61

Melville, Herman
   1819-1891 . . . . . . NCLC **3, 12, 29; SSC 1**
   See also SATA 59; DLB 3, 74;
   CDALB 1640-1865

Membreno, Alejandro 1972- . . . . CLC **59**

Menander
c. 342 B.C.-c. 292 B.C......... **CMLC 9**

Mencken, H(enry) L(ouis)
1880-1956 .... **TCLC 13**
See also CA 105, 125; DLB 11, 29, 63;
CDALB 1917-1929

Mercer, David 1928-1980........... **CLC 5**
See also CANR 23; CA 9-12R;
obituary CA 102; DLB 13

Meredith, George 1828-1909...... **TCLC 17**
See also CA 117; DLB 18, 35, 57

Meredith, George 1858-1924...... **TCLC 43**

Meredith, William (Morris)
1919- .... **CLC 4, 13, 22, 55**
See also CANR 6; CA 9-12R; DLB 5

Merezhkovsky, Dmitri
1865-1941 .... **TCLC 29**

Merimee, Prosper
1803-1870 .... **NCLC 6; SSC 7**

Merkin, Daphne 1954-............ **CLC 44**
See also CANR 123

Merrill, James (Ingram)
1926- .... **CLC 2, 3, 6, 8, 13, 18, 34**
See also CANR 10; CA 13-16R; DLB 5;
DLB-Y 85

Merton, Thomas (James)
1915-1968................. **CLC 1, 3, 11, 34**
See also CANR 22; CA 5-8R;
obituary CA 25-28R; DLB 48; DLB-Y 81

Merwin, W(illiam) S(tanley)
1927- ...... **CLC 1, 2, 3, 5, 8, 13, 18, 45**
See also CANR 15; CA 13-16R; DLB 5

Metcalf, John 1938-.............. **CLC 37**
See also CA 113; DLB 60

Mew, Charlotte (Mary)
1870-1928 .... **TCLC 8**
See also CA 105; DLB 19

Mewshaw, Michael 1943-........... **CLC 9**
See also CANR 7; CA 53-56; DLB-Y 80

Meyer-Meyrink, Gustav 1868-1932
See Meyrink, Gustav
See also CA 117

Meyers, Jeffrey 1939- .... **CLC 39**
See also CA 73-76

**Meynell, Alice (Christiana Gertrude
Thompson)** 1847-1922 .... **TCLC 6**
See also CA 104; DLB 19

Meyrink, Gustav 1868-1932....... **TCLC 21**
See also Meyer-Meyrink, Gustav

Michaels, Leonard 1933-........ **CLC 6, 25**
See also CANR 21; CA 61-64

Michaux, Henri 1899-1984 ...... **CLC 8, 19**
See also CA 85-88; obituary CA 114

Michelangelo 1475-1564............ **LC 12**

Michelet, Jules 1798-1874....... **NCLC 31**

Michener, James A(lbert)
1907- .... **CLC 1, 5, 11, 29, 60**
See also CANR 21; CA 5-8R; DLB 6

Mickiewicz, Adam 1798-1855 ..... **NCLC 3**

Middleton, Christopher 1926- ...... **CLC 13**
See also CANR 29; CA 13-16R; DLB 40

Middleton, Stanley 1919-........ **CLC 7, 38**
See also CANR 21; CA 25-28R; DLB 14

Migueis, Jose Rodrigues 1901-..... **CLC 10**

Mikszath, Kalman 1847-1910 .... **TCLC 31**

Miles, Josephine (Louise)
1911-1985 .... **CLC 1, 2, 14, 34, 39**
See also CANR 2; CA 1-4R;
obituary CA 116; DLB 48

Mill, John Stuart 1806-1873..... **NCLC 11**
See also DLB 55

Millar, Kenneth 1915-1983 .... **CLC 14**
See also Macdonald, Ross
See also CANR 16; CA 9-12R;
obituary CA 110; DLB 2; DLB-Y 83;
DLB-DS 6

Millay, Edna St. Vincent
1892-1950 .... **TCLC 4**
See also CA 103; DLB 45;
CDALB 1917-1929

Miller, Arthur
1915- ...... **CLC 1, 2, 6, 10, 15, 26, 47;
DC 1**
See also CANR 2, 30; CA 1-4R; CABS 3;
DLB 7; CDALB 1941-1968

Miller, Henry (Valentine)
1891-1980 .... **CLC 1, 2, 4, 9, 14, 43**
See also CA 9-12R; obituary CA 97-100;
DLB 4, 9; DLB-Y 80; CDALB 1929-1941

Miller, Jason 1939?-............... **CLC 2**
See also CA 73-76; DLB 7

Miller, Sue 19??-................... **CLC 44**

Miller, Walter M(ichael), Jr.
1923-...................... **CLC 4, 30**
See also CA 85-88; DLB 8

Millett, Kate 1934-................ **CLC 67**
See also CANR 32; CA 73-76

Millhauser, Steven 1943-....... **CLC 21, 54**
See also CA 108, 110, 111; DLB 2

Millin, Sarah Gertrude 1889-1968 .. **CLC 49**
See also CA 102; obituary CA 93-96

Milne, A(lan) A(lexander)
1882-1956 .... **TCLC 6**
See also CLR 1, 26; YABC 1; CA 104, 133;
DLB 10, 77, 100

Milner, Ron(ald) 1938-............ **CLC 56**
See also BLC 3; CANR 24; CA 73-76;
DLB 38

Milosz Czeslaw
1911- .... **CLC 5, 11, 22, 31, 56**
See also CANR 23; CA 81-84

Milton, John 1608-1674............. **LC 9**

Miner, Valerie (Jane) 1947-....... **CLC 40**
See also CA 97-100

Minot, Susan 1956- .... **CLC 44**

Minus, Ed 1938-................. **CLC 39**

Miro (Ferrer), Gabriel (Francisco Victor)
1879-1930 .... **TCLC 5**
See also CA 104

Mishima, Yukio
1925-1970 .... **CLC 2, 4, 6, 9, 27; DC 1;
SSC 4**
See also Hiraoka, Kimitake

Mistral, Gabriela 1889-1957 .... **TCLC 2**
See also CA 104

Mistry, Rohinton 1952-........... **CLC 71**

Mitchell, James Leslie 1901-1935
See Gibbon, Lewis Grassic
See also CA 104; DLB 15

Mitchell, Joni 1943-.............. **CLC 12**
See also CA 112

Mitchell (Marsh), Margaret (Munnerlyn)
1900-1949 .... **TCLC 11**
See also CA 109, 125; DLB 9

Mitchell, S. Weir 1829-1914...... **TCLC 36**

Mitchell, W(illiam) O(rmond)
1914-...................... **CLC 25**
See also CANR 15; CA 77-80; DLB 88

Mitford, Mary Russell 1787-1855.. **NCLC 4**

Mitford, Nancy 1904-1973........ **CLC 44**
See also CA 9-12R

Miyamoto Yuriko 1899-1951...... **TCLC 37**

Mo, Timothy 1950-.............. **CLC 46**
See also CA 117

Modarressi, Taghi 1931- .... **CLC 44**
See also CA 121

Modiano, Patrick (Jean) 1945-..... **CLC 18**
See also CANR 17; CA 85-88; DLB 83

Mofolo, Thomas (Mokopu)
1876-1948 .... **TCLC 22**
See also BLC 3; brief entry CA 121

Mohr, Nicholasa 1935-........... **CLC 12**
See also CLR 22; CANR 1; CA 49-52;
SAAS 8; SATA 8

Mojtabai, A(nn) G(race)
1938-.............. **CLC 5, 9, 15, 29**
See also CA 85-88

Moliere 1622-1673 .... **LC 10**

Molnar, Ferenc 1878-1952........ **TCLC 20**
See also CA 109

Momaday, N(avarre) Scott
1934- .... **CLC 2, 19**
See also CANR 14; CA 25-28R; SATA 30,
48

Monroe, Harriet 1860-1936....... **TCLC 12**
See also CA 109; DLB 54, 91

Montagu, Elizabeth 1720-1800 .... **NCLC 7**

Montagu, Lady Mary (Pierrepont) Wortley
1689-1762 .... **LC 9**

Montague, John (Patrick)
1929-................... **CLC 13, 46**
See also CANR 9; CA 9-12R; DLB 40

Montaigne, Michel (Eyquem) de
1533-1592 .... **LC 8**

Montale, Eugenio 1896-1981... **CLC 7, 9, 18**
See also CANR 30; CA 17-20R;
obituary CA 104

Montesquieu, Charles-Louis de Secondat
1689-1755 .... **LC 7**

Montgomery, Marion (H., Jr.)
1925-...................... **CLC 7**
See also CANR 3; CA 1-4R; DLB 6

Montgomery, Robert Bruce 1921-1978
See Crispin, Edmund
See also CA 104

Montherlant, Henri (Milon) de
1896-1972 .... **CLC 8, 19**
See also CA 85-88; obituary CA 37-40R;
DLB 72

Monty Python . . . . **CLC 21**

Moodie, Susanna (Strickland)
1803-1885 . . . . **NCLC 14**

Mooney, Ted 1951- . . . . **CLC 25**

Moorcock, Michael (John)
1939- . . . . **CLC 5, 27, 58**
See also CAAS 5; CANR 2, 17; CA 45-48;
DLB 14

Moore, Brian
1921- . . . . **CLC 1, 3, 5, 7, 8, 19, 32**
See also CANR 1, 25; CA 1-4R

Moore, George (Augustus)
1852-1933 . . . . **TCLC 7**
See also CA 104; DLB 10, 18, 57

Moore, Lorrie 1957- . . . . **CLC 39, 45, 68**
See also Moore, Marie Lorena

Moore, Marianne (Craig)
1887-1972 . . . **CLC 1, 2, 4, 8, 10, 13, 19,**
47; PC 4
See also CANR 3; CA 1-4R;
obituary CA 33-36R; SATA 20; DLB 45;
DLB-DS 7; CDALB 1929-1941

Moore, Marie Lorena 1957-
See Moore, Lorrie
See also CA 116

Moore, Thomas 1779-1852 . . . . **NCLC 6**

Morand, Paul 1888-1976 . . . . **CLC 41**
See also obituary CA 69-72; DLB 65

Morante, Elsa 1918-1985 . . . . **CLC 8, 47**
See also CA 85-88; obituary CA 117

Moravia, Alberto
1907- . . . . **CLC 2, 7, 11, 18, 27, 46**
See also Pincherle, Alberto

More, Hannah 1745-1833 . . . . **NCLC 27**

More, Henry 1614-1687 . . . . **LC 9**

More, Sir Thomas 1478-1535 . . . . **LC 10**

Moreas, Jean 1856-1910 . . . . **TCLC 18**

Morgan, Berry 1919- . . . . **CLC 6**
See also CA 49-52; DLB 6

Morgan, Edwin (George) 1920- . . . . . **CLC 31**
See also CANR 3; CA 7-8R; DLB 27

Morgan, (George) Frederick
1922- . . . . **CLC 23**
See also CANR 21; CA 17-20R

Morgan, Janet 1945- . . . . **CLC 39**
See also CA 65-68

Morgan, Lady 1776?-1859 . . . . **NCLC 29**

Morgan, Robin 1941- . . . . **CLC 2**
See also CA 69-72

Morgan, Seth 1949-1990 . . . . **CLC 65**
See also CA 132

Morgenstern, Christian (Otto Josef Wolfgang)
1871-1914 . . . . **TCLC 8**
See also CA 105

Moricz, Zsigmond 1879-1942 . . . . . **TCLC 33**

Morike, Eduard (Friedrich)
1804-1875 . . . . **NCLC 10**

Mori Ogai 1862-1922 . . . . **TCLC 14**
See also Mori Rintaro

Mori Rintaro 1862-1922
See Mori Ogai
See also CA 110

Moritz, Karl Philipp 1756-1793 . . . . . . **LC 2**

Morris, Julian 1916-
See West, Morris L.

Morris, Steveland Judkins 1950-
See Wonder, Stevie
See also CA 111

Morris, William 1834-1896 . . . . **NCLC 4**
See also DLB 18, 35, 57

Morris, Wright (Marion)
1910- . . . . **CLC 1, 3, 7, 18, 37**
See also CANR 21; CA 9-12R; DLB 2;
DLB-Y 81

Morrison, James Douglas 1943-1971
See Morrison, Jim
See also CA 73-76

Morrison, Jim 1943-1971 . . . . **CLC 17**
See also Morrison, James Douglas

Morrison, Toni 1931- . . . . . **CLC 4, 10, 22, 55**
See also BLC 3; CANR 27; CA 29-32R;
SATA 57; DLB 6, 33; DLB-Y 81;
CDALB 1968-1987; AAYA 1

Morrison, Van 1945- . . . . **CLC 21**
See also CA 116

Mortimer, John (Clifford)
1923- . . . . **CLC 28, 43**
See also CANR 21; CA 13-16R; DLB 13

Mortimer, Penelope (Ruth) 1918- . . . . **CLC 5**
See also CA 57-60

Mosher, Howard Frank 19??- . . . . . . **CLC 62**

Mosley, Nicholas 1923- . . . . **CLC 43, 70**
See also CA 69-72; DLB 14

Moss, Howard
1922-1987 . . . . **CLC 7, 14, 45, 50**
See also CANR 1; CA 1-4R;
obituary CA 123; DLB 5

Motion, Andrew (Peter) 1952- . . . . . . **CLC 47**
See also DLB 40

Motley, Willard (Francis)
1912-1965 . . . . **CLC 18**
See also CA 117; obituary CA 106; DLB 76

Mott, Michael (Charles Alston)
1930- . . . . **CLC 15, 34**
See also CAAS 7; CANR 7, 29; CA 5-8R

Mowat, Farley (McGill) 1921- . . . . . **CLC 26**
See also CLR 20; CANR 4, 24; CA 1-4R;
SATA 3, 55; DLB 68; AAYA 1

Mphahlele, Es'kia 1919-
See Mphahlele, Ezekiel

Mphahlele, Ezekiel 1919- . . . . **CLC 25**
See also BLC 3; CANR 26; CA 81-84

Mqhayi, S(amuel) E(dward) K(rune Loliwe)
1875-1945 . . . . **TCLC 25**
See also BLC 3

Mrozek, Slawomir 1930- . . . . **CLC 3, 13**
See also CAAS 10; CANR 29; CA 13-16R

Mtwa, Percy 19??- . . . . **CLC 47**

Mueller, Lisel 1924- . . . . **CLC 13, 51**
See also CA 93-96

Muir, Edwin 1887-1959 . . . . **TCLC 2**
See also CA 104; DLB 20

Muir, John 1838-1914 . . . . **TCLC 28**

Mujica Lainez, Manuel
1910-1984 . . . . **CLC 31**
See also CA 81-84; obituary CA 112

Mukherjee, Bharati 1940- . . . . **CLC 53**
See also CA 107; DLB 60

Muldoon, Paul 1951- . . . . **CLC 32, 72**
See also CA 113, 129; DLB 40

Mulisch, Harry (Kurt Victor)
1927- . . . . **CLC 42**
See also CANR 6, 26; CA 9-12R

Mull, Martin 1943- . . . . **CLC 17**
See also CA 105

Munford, Robert 1737?-1783 . . . . **LC 5**
See also DLB 31

Mungo, Raymond 1946- . . . . **CLC 72**
See also CANR 2; CA 49-52

Munro, Alice (Laidlaw)
1931- . . . . **CLC 6, 10, 19, 50; SSC 3**
See also CA 33-36R; SATA 29; DLB 53

Munro, H(ector) H(ugh) 1870-1916
See Saki
See also CA 104; DLB 34

Murasaki, Lady c. 11th century- . . . **CMLC 1**

Murdoch, (Jean) Iris
1919- . . . . . . **CLC 1, 2, 3, 4, 6, 8, 11, 15,**
22, 31, 51
See also CANR 8; CA 13-16R; DLB 14

Murphy, Richard 1927- . . . . **CLC 41**
See also CA 29-32R; DLB 40

Murphy, Sylvia 19??- . . . . **CLC 34**

Murphy, Thomas (Bernard) 1935- . . . **CLC 51**
See also CA 101

Murray, Les(lie) A(llan) 1938- . . . . . **CLC 40**
See also CANR 11, 27; CA 21-24R

Murry, John Middleton
1889-1957 . . . . **TCLC 16**
See also CA 118

Musgrave, Susan 1951- . . . . **CLC 13, 54**
See also CA 69-72

Musil, Robert (Edler von)
1880-1942 . . . . **TCLC 12**
See also CA 109; DLB 81

Musset, (Louis Charles) Alfred de
1810-1857 . . . . **NCLC 7**

Myers, Walter Dean 1937- . . . . **CLC 35**
See also BLC 3; CLR 4, 16; CANR 20;
CA 33-36R; SAAS 2; SATA 27, 41;
DLB 33; AAYA 4

Myers, Walter M. 1937-
See Myers, Walter Dean

Nabokov, Vladimir (Vladimirovich)
1899-1977 . . . . **CLC 1, 2, 3, 6, 8, 11, 15,**
23, 44, 46, 64
See also CANR 20; CA 5-8R;
obituary CA 69-72; DLB 2; DLB-Y 80;
DLB-DS 3; CDALB 1941-1968

Nagy, Laszlo 1925-1978 . . . . **CLC 7**
See also CA 129; obituary CA 112

Naipaul, Shiva(dhar Srinivasa)
1945-1985 . . . . **CLC 32, 39**
See also CA 110, 112; obituary CA 116;
DLB-Y 85

Naipaul, V(idiadhar) S(urajprasad)
1932- . . . . **CLC 4, 7, 9, 13, 18, 37**
See also CANR 1; CA 1-4R; DLB-Y 85

Nakos, Ioulia 1899?-
See Nakos, Lilika

Nakos, Lilika 1899?- .... CLC 29

Nakou, Lilika 1899?-
See Nakos, Lilika

Narayan, R(asipuram) K(rishnaswami)
1906- .... CLC 7, 28, 47
See also CA 81-84

Nash, (Frediric) Ogden 1902-1971 .. CLC 23
See also CAP 1; CA 13-14;
obituary CA 29-32R; SATA 2, 46;
DLB 11

Nathan, George Jean 1882-1958 ... TCLC 18
See also CA 114

Natsume, Kinnosuke 1867-1916
See Natsume, Soseki
See also CA 104

Natsume, Soseki 1867-1916..... TCLC 2, 10
See also Natsume, Kinnosuke

Natti, (Mary) Lee 1919-
See Kingman, (Mary) Lee
See also CANR 2; CA 7-8R

Naylor, Gloria 1950- .... CLC 28, 52
See also BLC 3; CANR 27; CA 107;
AAYA 6

Neff, Debra 1972-................ CLC 59

Neihardt, John G(neisenau)
1881-1973 .... CLC 32
See also CAP 1; CA 13-14; DLB 9, 54

Nekrasov, Nikolai Alekseevich
1821-1878 .... NCLC 11

Nelligan, Emile 1879-1941....... TCLC 14
See also CA 114; DLB 92

Nelson, Willie 1933-.............. CLC 17
See also CA 107

Nemerov, Howard 1920- .... CLC 2, 6, 9, 36
See also CANR 1, 27; CA 1-4R; CABS 2;
DLB 5, 6; DLB-Y 83

Neruda, Pablo
1904-1973 .... CLC 1, 2, 5, 7, 9, 28, 62;
PC 4
See also CAP 2; CA 19-20;
obituary CA 45-48

Nerval, Gerard de 1808-1855...... NCLC 1

Nervo, (Jose) Amado (Ruiz de)
1870-1919 .... TCLC 11
See also CA 109

Neufeld, John (Arthur) 1938- ...... CLC 17
See also CANR 11; CA 25-28R; SAAS 3;
SATA 6

Neville, Emily Cheney 1919-....... CLC 12
See also CANR 3; CA 5-8R; SAAS 2;
SATA 1

Newbound, Bernard Slade 1930-
See Slade, Bernard
See also CA 81-84

Newby, P(ercy) H(oward)
1918- .... CLC 2, 13
See also CA 5-8R; DLB 15

Newlove, Donald 1928- .... CLC 6
See also CANR 25; CA 29-32R

Newlove, John (Herbert) 1938-..... CLC 14
See also CANR 9, 25; CA 21-24R

Newman, Charles 1938-.......... CLC 2, 8
See also CA 21-24R

Newman, Edwin (Harold) 1919-.... CLC 14
See also CANR 5; CA 69-72

Newton, Suzanne 1936-.......... CLC 35
See also CANR 14; CA 41-44R; SATA 5

Nexo, Martin Andersen
1869-1954 .... TCLC 43

Nezval, Vitezslav 1900-1958 ...... TCLC 44
See also CA 123

Ngema, Mbongeni 1955- .... CLC 57

Ngugi, James Thiong'o 1938-
See Ngugi wa Thiong'o

Ngugi wa Thiong'o 1938-... CLC 3, 7, 13, 36
See also Ngugi, James (Thiong'o); Wa
Thiong'o, Ngugi
See also BLC 3

Nichol, B(arrie) P(hillip) 1944-..... CLC 18
See also CA 53-56; DLB 53

Nichols, John (Treadwell) 1940-.... CLC 38
See also CAAS 2; CANR 6; CA 9-12R;
DLB-Y 82

Nichols, Peter (Richard)
1927-.................. CLC 5, 36, 65
See also CANR 33; CA 104; DLB 13

Nicolas, F.R.E. 1927-
See Freeling, Nicolas

Niedecker, Lorine 1903-1970.... CLC 10, 42
See also CAP 2; CA 25-28; DLB 48

Nietzsche, Friedrich (Wilhelm)
1844-1900 .... TCLC 10, 18
See also CA 107, 121

Nievo, Ippolito 1831-1861 .... NCLC 22

Nightingale, Anne Redmon 1943-
See Redmon (Nightingale), Anne
See also CA 103

Nin, Anais
1903-1977 ..... CLC 1, 4, 8, 11, 14, 60;
SSC 10
See also CANR 22; CA 13-16R;
obituary CA 69-72; DLB 2, 4

Nissenson, Hugh 1933-.......... CLC 4, 9
See also CANR 27; CA 17-20R; DLB 28

Niven, Larry 1938-................ CLC 8
See also Niven, Laurence Van Cott
See also DLB 8

Niven, Laurence Van Cott 1938-
See Niven, Larry
See also CANR 14; CA 21-24R

Nixon, Agnes Eckhardt 1927-...... CLC 21
See also CA 110

Nizan, Paul 1905-1940........... TCLC 40
See also DLB 72

Nkosi, Lewis 1936-.............. CLC 45
See also BLC 3; CANR 27; CA 65-68

Nodier, (Jean) Charles (Emmanuel)
1780-1844 .... NCLC 19

Nolan, Christopher 1965-.......... CLC 58
See also CA 111

Nordhoff, Charles 1887-1947...... TCLC 23
See also CA 108; SATA 23; DLB 9

Norman, Marsha 1947- .... CLC 28
See also CA 105; CABS 3; DLB-Y 84

Norris, (Benjamin) Frank(lin)
1870-1902 .... TCLC 24
See also CA 110; DLB 12, 71;
CDALB 1865-1917

Norris, Leslie 1921-.............. CLC 14
See also CANR 14; CAP 1; CA 11-12;
DLB 27

North, Andrew 1912-
See Norton, Andre

North, Christopher 1785-1854
See Wilson, John

Norton, Alice Mary 1912-
See Norton, Andre
See also CANR 2; CA 1-4R; SATA 1, 43

Norton, Andre 1912- .... CLC 12
See also Norton, Mary Alice
See also DLB 8, 52

Norway, Nevil Shute 1899-1960
See Shute (Norway), Nevil
See also CA 102; obituary CA 93-96

Norwid, Cyprian Kamil
1821-1883 .... NCLC 17

Nossack, Hans Erich 1901-1978 ..... CLC 6
See also CA 93-96; obituary CA 85-88;
DLB 69

Nova, Craig 1945-................ CLC 7, 31
See also CANR 2; CA 45-48

Novak, Joseph 1933-
See Kosinski, Jerzy (Nikodem)

Novalis 1772-1801 .... NCLC 13

Nowlan, Alden (Albert) 1933-...... CLC 15
See also CANR 5; CA 9-12R; DLB 53

Noyes, Alfred 1880-1958.......... TCLC 7
See also CA 104; DLB 20

Nunn, Kem 19??-................. CLC 34

Nye, Robert 1939- .... CLC 13, 42
See also CANR 29; CA 33-36R; SATA 6;
DLB 14

Nyro, Laura 1947-............... CLC 17

Oates, Joyce Carol
1938-...... CLC 1, 2, 3, 6, 9, 11, 15, 19,
33, 52; SSC 6
See also CANR 25; CA 5-8R; DLB 2, 5;
DLB-Y 81; CDALB 1968-1987

O'Brien, Darcy 1939-............. CLC 11
See also CANR 8; CA 21-24R

O'Brien, Edna
1932-... CLC 3, 5, 8, 13, 36, 65; SSC 10
See also CANR 6; CA 1-4R; DLB 14

O'Brien, Fitz-James 1828?-1862.. NCLC 21
See also DLB 74

O'Brien, Flann
1911-1966 .... CLC 1, 4, 5, 7, 10, 47
See also O Nuallain, Brian

O'Brien, Richard 19??-............ CLC 17
See also CA 124

O'Brien, (William) Tim(othy)
1946-................... CLC 7, 19, 40
See also CA 85-88; DLB-Y 80

Obstfelder, Sigbjorn 1866-1900.... TCLC 23
See also CA 123

O'Casey, Sean
1880-1964 .... CLC 1, 5, 9, 11, 15
See also CA 89-92; DLB 10

Ochs, Phil 1940-1976............. CLC 17
See also obituary CA 65-68

O'Connor, Edwin (Greene)
1918-1968 .... CLC 14
See also CA 93-96; obituary CA 25-28R

O'Connor, (Mary) Flannery
1925-1964 ... CLC 1, 2, 3, 6, 10, 13, 15,
21, 66; SSC 1
See also CANR 3; CA 1-4R; DLB 2;
DLB-Y 80; CDALB 1941-1968

O'Connor, Frank
1903-1966 .... CLC 14, 23; SSC 5
See also O'Donovan, Michael (John)
See also CA 93-96

O'Dell, Scott 1903-................ CLC 30
See also CLR 1, 16; CANR 12; CA 61-64;
SATA 12; DLB 52

Odets, Clifford 1906-1963 .... CLC 2, 28
See also CA 85-88; DLB 7, 26

O'Donovan, Michael (John)
1903-1966 .... CLC 14
See also O'Connor, Frank
See also CA 93-96

Oe, Kenzaburo 1935-.......... CLC 10, 36
See also CA 97-100

O'Faolain, Julia 1932-....... CLC 6, 19, 47
See also CAAS 2; CANR 12; CA 81-84;
DLB 14

O'Faolain, Sean
1900-1991 .... CLC 1, 7, 14, 32, 70
See also CANR 12; CA 61-64;
obituary CA 134; DLB 15

O'Flaherty, Liam
1896-1984 .... CLC 5, 34; SSC 6
See also CA 101; obituary CA 113; DLB 36;
DLB-Y 84

O'Grady, Standish (James)
1846-1928 .... TCLC 5
See also CA 104

O'Grady, Timothy 1951- .... CLC 59

O'Hara, Frank 1926-1966 ..... CLC 2, 5, 13
See also CA 9-12R; obituary CA 25-28R;
DLB 5, 16; CDALB 1929-1941

O'Hara, John (Henry)
1905-1970 ...... CLC 1, 2, 3, 6, 11, 42
See also CA 5-8R; obituary CA 25-28R;
DLB 9; DLB-DS 2; CDALB 1929-1941

O'Hara Family
See Banim, John and Banim, Michael

O'Hehir, Diana 1922-............. CLC 41
See also CA 93-96

Okigbo, Christopher (Ifenayichukwu)
1932-1967 .... CLC 25
See also BLC 3; CA 77-80

Olds, Sharon 1942-........... CLC 32, 39
See also CANR 18; CA 101

Olesha, Yuri (Karlovich)
1899-1960 .... CLC 8
See also CA 85-88

Oliphant, Margaret (Oliphant Wilson)
1828-1897 .... NCLC 11
See also DLB 18

Oliver, Mary 1935-........... CLC 19, 34
See also CANR 9; CA 21-24R; DLB 5

Olivier, (Baron) Laurence (Kerr)
1907- .... CLC 20
See also CA 111, 129

Olsen, Tillie 1913- .... CLC 4, 13
See also CANR 1; CA 1-4R; DLB 28;
DLB-Y 80

Olson, Charles (John)
1910-1970 ..... CLC 1, 2, 5, 6, 9, 11, 29
See also CAP 1; CA 15-16;
obituary CA 25-28R; CABS 2; DLB 5, 16

Olson, Theodore 1937-
See Olson, Toby

Olson, Toby 1937- .... CLC 28
See also CANR 9; CA 65-68

Ondaatje, (Philip) Michael
1943- .... CLC 14, 29, 51
See also CA 77-80; DLB 60

Oneal, Elizabeth 1934-............ CLC 30
See also Oneal, Zibby
See also CLR 13; CA 106; SATA 30

Oneal, Zibby 1934-............... CLC 30
See also Oneal, Elizabeth

O'Neill, Eugene (Gladstone)
1888-1953 .... TCLC 1, 6, 27
See also CA 110; DLB 7;
CDALB 1929-1941

Onetti, Juan Carlos 1909-....... CLC 7, 10
See also CA 85-88

O'Nolan, Brian 1911-1966
See O'Brien, Flann

O Nuallain, Brian 1911-1966
See O'Brien, Flann
See also CAP 2; CA 21-22;
obituary CA 25-28R

Oppen, George 1908-1984 .... CLC 7, 13, 34
See also CANR 8; CA 13-16R;
obituary CA 113; DLB 5

Oppenheim, E. Phillips
1866-1946 .... TCLC 45
See also brief entry CA 111; DLB 70

Orlovitz, Gil 1918-1973 .... CLC 22
See also CA 77-80; obituary CA 45-48;
DLB 2, 5

Ortega y Gasset, Jose 1883-1955 ... TCLC 9
See also CA 106, 130

Ortiz, Simon J. 1941-............ CLC 45

Orton, Joe 1933?-1967 .... CLC 4, 13, 43
See also Orton, John Kingsley
See also DLB 13

Orton, John Kingsley 1933?-1967
See Orton, Joe
See also CA 85-88

Orwell, George
1903-1950 .... TCLC 2, 6, 15, 31
See also Blair, Eric Arthur
See also DLB 15

Osborne, John (James)
1929- .... CLC 1, 2, 5, 11, 45
See also CANR 21; CA 13-16R; DLB 13

Osborne, Lawrence 1958- .... CLC 50

Osceola 1885-1962
See Dinesen, Isak; Blixen, Karen
(Christentze Dinesen)

Oshima, Nagisa 1932- .... CLC 20
See also CA 116

Oskison, John M. 1874-1947...... TCLC 35

Ossoli, Sarah Margaret (Fuller marchesa d')
1810-1850
See Fuller, (Sarah) Margaret
See also SATA 25

Ostrovsky, Alexander
1823-1886 .... NCLC 30

Otero, Blas de 1916- .... CLC 11
See also CA 89-92

Otto, Whitney 1955-.............. CLC 70

Ouida 1839-1908................ TCLC 43
See also de la Ramee, Marie Louise
See also DLB 18

Ousmane, Sembene 1923-
See also BLC 3; CA 125; brief entry CA 117

Ousmane, Sembene 1923- .... CLC 66
See also Sembene, Ousmane
See also CA 125; brief entry CA 117

Ovid 43 B.C.-c. 18 A.D. .... CMLC 7; PC 2

Owen, Wilfred (Edward Salter)
1893-1918 .... TCLC 5, 27
See also CA 104; DLB 20

Owens, Rochelle 1936-............ CLC 8
See also CAAS 2; CA 17-20R

Owl, Sebastian 1939-
See Thompson, Hunter S(tockton)

Oz, Amos 1939- ... CLC 5, 8, 11, 27, 33, 54
See also CANR 27; CA 53-56

Ozick, Cynthia 1928-...... CLC 3, 7, 28, 62
See also CANR 23; CA 17-20R; DLB 28;
DLB-Y 82

Ozu, Yasujiro 1903-1963 .... CLC 16
See also CA 112

P. V. M. 1912-1990
See White, Patrick (Victor Martindale)

Pa Chin 1904-................... CLC 18
See also Li Fei-kan

Pack, Robert 1929-............... CLC 13
See also CANR 3; CA 1-4R; DLB 5

Padgett, Lewis 1915-1958
See Kuttner, Henry

Padilla, Heberto 1932-........... CLC 38
See also CA 123

Page, Jimmy 1944-............... CLC 12

Page, Louise 1955-............... CLC 40

Page, P(atricia) K(athleen)
1916- .... CLC 7, 18
See also CANR 4, 22; CA 53-56; DLB 68

Paget, Violet 1856-1935
See Lee, Vernon
See also CA 104

Paglia, Camille 1947-............ CLC 68

Palamas, Kostes 1859-1943 .... TCLC 5
See also CA 105

Palazzeschi, Aldo 1885-1974....... CLC 11
See also CA 89-92; obituary CA 53-56

Paley, Grace 1922-.... CLC 4, 6, 37; SSC 8
See also CANR 13; CA 25-28R; DLB 28

Palin, Michael 1943- .... CLC 21
See also Monty Python
See also CA 107

Palliser, Charles 1948?-.......... CLC 65

Palma, Ricardo 1833-1919 . . . . **TCLC 29**
See also CANR 123

Pancake, Breece Dexter 1952-1979
See Pancake, Breece D'J

Pancake, Breece D'J 1952-1979 . . . . **CLC 29**
See also obituary CA 109

Papadiamantis, Alexandros
1851-1911 . . . . **TCLC 29**

Papini, Giovanni 1881-1956 . . . . . . **TCLC 22**
See also CA 121

Paracelsus 1493-1541 . . . . **LC 14**

Parini, Jay (Lee) 1948- . . . . **CLC 54**
See also CA 97-100

Parker, Dorothy (Rothschild)
1893-1967 . . . . **CLC 15, 68; SSC 2**
See also CAP 2; CA 19-20;
 obituary CA 25-28R; DLB 11, 45. 86

Parker, Robert B(rown) 1932- . . . . . . **CLC 27**
See also CANR 1, 26; CA 49-52

Parkin, Frank 1940- . . . . **CLC 43**

Parkman, Francis 1823-1893 . . . . . **NCLC 12**
See also DLB 1, 30

Parks, Gordon (Alexander Buchanan)
1912- . . . . **CLC 1, 16**
See also BLC 3; CANR 26; CA 41-44R;
 SATA 8; DLB 33

Parnell, Thomas 1679-1718 . . . . **LC 3**

Parra, Nicanor 1914- . . . . **CLC 2**
See also CA 85-88

Pascoli, Giovanni 1855-1912 . . . . . **TCLC 45**

Pasolini, Pier Paolo
1922-1975 . . . . **CLC 20, 37**
See also CA 93-96; obituary CA 61-64

Pastan, Linda (Olenik) 1932- . . . . . . **CLC 27**
See also CANR 18; CA 61-64; DLB 5

Pasternak, Boris
1890-1960 . . . . **CLC 7, 10, 18, 63**
See also CA 127; obituary CA 116

Patchen, Kenneth 1911-1972 . . . **CLC 1, 2, 18**
See also CANR 3; CA 1-4R;
 obituary CA 33-36R; DLB 16, 48

Pater, Walter (Horatio)
1839-1894 . . . . **NCLC 7**
See also DLB 57

Paterson, Andrew Barton
1864-1941 . . . . **TCLC 32**

Paterson, Katherine (Womeldorf)
1932- . . . . **CLC 12, 30**
See also CLR 7; CANR 28; CA 21-24R;
 SATA 13, 53; DLB 52; AAYA 1

Patmore, Coventry Kersey Dighton
1823-1896 . . . . **NCLC 9**
See also DLB 35

Paton, Alan (Stewart)
1903-1988 . . . . **CLC 4, 10, 25, 55**
See also CANR 22; CAP 1; CA 15-16;
 obituary CA 125; SATA 11

Paulding, James Kirke 1778-1860 . . **NCLC 2**
See also DLB 3, 59, 74

Paulin, Tom 1949- . . . . **CLC 37**
See also CA 123; DLB 40

Paustovsky, Konstantin (Georgievich)
1892-1968 . . . . **CLC 40**
See also CA 93-96; obituary CA 25-28R

Paustowsky, Konstantin (Georgievich)
1892-1968
See Paustovsky, Konstantin (Georgievich)

Pavese, Cesare 1908-1950 . . . . **TCLC 3**
See also CA 104

Pavic, Milorad 1929- . . . . **CLC 60**

Payne, Alan 1932-
See Jakes, John (William)

Paz, Octavio
1914- . . . . . . **CLC 3, 4, 6, 10, 19, 51, 65;**
          PC 1
See also CANR 32; CA 73-76

p'Bitek, Okot 1931-1982
See also BLC 3; CA 124; obituary CA 107

Peacock, Molly 1947- . . . . **CLC 60**
See also CA 103

Peacock, Thomas Love
1785-1886 . . . . **NCLC 22**

Peake, Mervyn 1911-1968 . . . . . . **CLC 7, 54**
See also CANR 3; CA 5-8R;
 obituary CA 25-28R; SATA 23; DLB 15

Pearce, (Ann) Philippa 1920- . . . . . . **CLC 21**
See also Christie, (Ann) Philippa
See also CLR 9; CA 5-8R; SATA 1

Pearl, Eric 1934-
See Elman, Richard

Pearson, T(homas) R(eid) 1956- . . . . **CLC 39**
See also CA 120, 130

Peck, John 1941- . . . . **CLC 3**
See also CANR 3; CA 49-52

Peck, Richard 1934- . . . . **CLC 21**
See also CLR 15; CANR 19; CA 85-88;
 SAAS 2; SATA 18; AAYA 1

Peck, Robert Newton 1928- . . . . **CLC 17**
See also CA 81-84; SAAS 1; SATA 21;
 AAYA 3

Peckinpah, (David) Sam(uel)
1925-1984 . . . . **CLC 20**
See also CA 109; obituary CA 114

Pedersen, Knut 1859-1952
See Hamsun, Knut
See also CA 104, 109, 119

Peguy, Charles (Pierre)
1873-1914 . . . . **TCLC 10**
See also CA 107

Pepys, Samuel 1633-1703 . . . . **LC 11**

Percy, Walker
1916-1990 . . . **CLC 2, 3, 6, 8, 14, 18, 47,**
               65
See also CANR 1, 23; CA 1-4R;
 obituary CA 131; DLB 2; DLB-Y 80

Perec, Georges 1936-1982 . . . . **CLC 56**
See also DLB 83

Pereda, Jose Maria de
1833-1906 . . . . **TCLC 16**

Perelman, S(idney) J(oseph)
1904-1979 . . . **CLC 3, 5, 9, 15, 23, 44, 49**
See also CANR 18; CA 73-76;
 obituary CA 89-92; DLB 11, 44

Peret, Benjamin 1899-1959 . . . . **TCLC 20**
See also CA 117

Peretz, Isaac Leib 1852?-1915 . . . . . **TCLC 16**
See also CA 109

Perez, Galdos Benito 1853-1920 . . . **TCLC 27**
See also CA 125

Perrault, Charles 1628-1703 . . . . **LC 2**
See also SATA 25

Perse, St.-John 1887-1975 . . . . **CLC 4, 11, 46**
See also Leger, (Marie-Rene) Alexis
 Saint-Leger

Pesetsky, Bette 1932- . . . . **CLC 28**

Peshkov, Alexei Maximovich 1868-1936
See Gorky, Maxim
See also CA 105

Pessoa, Fernando (Antonio Nogueira)
1888-1935 . . . . **TCLC 27**
See also CA 125

Peterkin, Julia (Mood) 1880-1961 . . . **CLC 31**
See also CA 102; DLB 9

Peters, Joan K. 1945- . . . . **CLC 39**

Peters, Robert L(ouis) 1924- . . . . **CLC 7**
See also CAAS 8; CA 13-16R

Petofi, Sandor 1823-1849 . . . . **NCLC 21**

Petrakis, Harry Mark 1923- . . . . **CLC 3**
See also CANR 4, 30; CA 9-12R

Petrov, Evgeny 1902-1942 . . . . **TCLC 21**

Petry, Ann (Lane) 1908- . . . . . . **CLC 1, 7, 18**
See also CLR 12; CAAS 6; CANR 4;
 CA 5-8R; SATA 5; DLB 76

Petursson, Halligrimur 1614-1674 . . . . **LC 8**

Philipson, Morris (H.) 1926- . . . . **CLC 53**
See also CANR 4; CA 1-4R

Phillips, David Graham
1867-1911 . . . . **TCLC 44**
See also CA 108; DLB 9, 12

Phillips, Jayne Anne 1952- . . . . . **CLC 15, 33**
See also CANR 24; CA 101; DLB-Y 80

Phillips, Robert (Schaeffer) 1938- . . . **CLC 28**
See also CANR 8; CA 17-20R

Pica, Peter 1925-
See Aldiss, Brian W(ilson)

Piccolo, Lucio 1901-1969 . . . . **CLC 13**
See also CA 97-100

Pickthall, Marjorie (Lowry Christie)
1883-1922 . . . . **TCLC 21**
See also CA 107; DLB 92

Pico della Mirandola, Giovanni
1463-1494 . . . . **LC 15**

Piercy, Marge
1936- . . . . **CLC 3, 6, 14, 18, 27, 62**
See also CAAS 1; CANR 13; CA 21-24R

Pilnyak, Boris 1894-1937? . . . . **TCLC 23**

Pincherle, Alberto 1907- . . . . **CLC 11, 18**
See also Moravia, Alberto
See also CA 25-28R

Pineda, Cecile 1942- . . . . **CLC 39**
See also CA 118

Pinero, Miguel (Gomez)
1946-1988 . . . . **CLC 4, 55**
See also CANR 29; CA 61-64;
 obituary CA 125

Pinero, Sir Arthur Wing
1855-1934 . . . . **TCLC 32**
See also CA 110; DLB 10

Pinget, Robert 1919- . . . . **CLC 7, 13, 37**
See also CA 85-88; DLB 83

Pink Floyd . . . . CLC 35

Pinkney, Edward 1802-1828 . . . . . NCLC 31

Pinkwater, D(aniel) M(anus)
    1941- . . . . CLC 35
    See also Pinkwater, Manus
    See also CLR 4; CANR 12; CA 29-32R;
    SAAS 3; SATA 46; AAYA 1

Pinkwater, Manus 1941-
    See Pinkwater, D(aniel) M(anus)
    See also SATA 8

Pinsky, Robert 1940- . . . . CLC 9, 19, 38
    See also CAAS 4; CA 29-32R; DLB-Y 82

Pinter, Harold
    1930- . . . . . CLC 1, 3, 6, 9, 11, 15, 27, 58
    See also CA 5-8R; DLB 13

Pirandello, Luigi 1867-1936 . . . . . TCLC 4, 29
    See also CA 104

Pirsig, Robert M(aynard) 1928- . . . CLC 4, 6
    See also CA 53-56; SATA 39

Pisarev, Dmitry Ivanovich
    1840-1868 . . . . NCLC 25

Pix, Mary (Griffith) 1666-1709 . . . . LC 8
    See also DLB 80

Plaidy, Jean 1906-
    See Hibbert, Eleanor (Burford)

Plant, Robert 1948- . . . . CLC 12

Plante, David (Robert)
    1940- . . . . CLC 7, 23, 38
    See also CANR 12; CA 37-40R; DLB-Y 83

Plath, Sylvia
    1932-1963 . . . . CLC 1, 2, 3, 5, 9, 11, 14,
                        17, 50, 51, 62; PC 1
    See also CAP 2; CA 19-20; DLB 5, 6;
    CDALB 1941-1968

Plato 428? B.C.-348? B.C. . . . . CMLC 8

Platonov, Andrei (Platonovich)
    1899-1951 . . . . TCLC 14
    See also Klimentov, Andrei Platonovich
    See also CA 108

Platt, Kin 1911- . . . . CLC 26
    See also CANR 11; CA 17-20R; SATA 21

Plimpton, George (Ames) 1927- . . . . . CLC 36
    See also CA 21-24R; SATA 10

Plomer, William (Charles Franklin)
    1903-1973 . . . . CLC 4, 8
    See also CAP 2; CA 21-22; SATA 24;
    DLB 20

Plumly, Stanley (Ross) 1939- . . . . . . CLC 33
    See also CA 108, 110; DLB 5

Poe, Edgar Allan
    1809-1849 . . . NCLC 1, 16; PC 1; SSC 1
    See also SATA 23; DLB 3, 59, 73, 74;
    CDALB 1640-1865

Pohl, Frederik 1919- . . . . CLC 18
    See also CAAS 1; CANR 11; CA 61-64;
    SATA 24; DLB 8

Poirier, Louis 1910-
    See Gracq, Julien
    See also CA 122, 126

Poitier, Sidney 1924?- . . . . CLC 26
    See also CA 117

Polanski, Roman 1933- . . . . CLC 16
    See also CA 77-80

Poliakoff, Stephen 1952- . . . . CLC 38
    See also CA 106; DLB 13

Police, The . . . . CLC 26

Pollitt, Katha 1949- . . . . CLC 28
    See also CA 120, 122

Pollock, Sharon 19??- . . . . CLC 50
    See also DLB 60

Pomerance, Bernard 1940- . . . . CLC 13
    See also CA 101

Ponge, Francis (Jean Gaston Alfred)
    1899- . . . . CLC 6, 18
    See also CA 85-88; obituary CA 126

Pontoppidan, Henrik 1857-1943 . . . TCLC 29
    See also obituary CA 126

Poole, Josephine 1933- . . . . CLC 17
    See also CANR 10; CA 21-24R; SAAS 2;
    SATA 5

Popa, Vasko 1922- . . . . CLC 19
    See also CA 112

Pope, Alexander 1688-1744 . . . . LC 3

Porter, Connie 1960- . . . . CLC 70

Porter, Gene Stratton 1863-1924 . . TCLC 21
    See also CA 112

Porter, Katherine Anne
    1890-1980 . . . . . CLC 1, 3, 7, 10, 13, 15,
                           27; SSC 4
    See also CANR 1; CA 1-4R;
    obituary CA 101; obituary SATA 23, 39;
    DLB 4, 9; DLB-Y 80

Porter, Peter (Neville Frederick)
    1929- . . . . CLC 5, 13, 33
    See also CA 85-88; DLB 40

Porter, William Sydney 1862-1910
    See Henry, O.
    See also YABC 2; CA 104; DLB 12, 78, 79;
    CDALB 1865-1917

Post, Melville D. 1871-1930 . . . . . . TCLC 39
    See also brief entry CA 110

Potok, Chaim 1929- . . . . CLC 2, 7, 14, 26
    See also CANR 19; CA 17-20R; SATA 33;
    DLB 28

Potter, Dennis (Christopher George)
    1935- . . . . CLC 58
    See also CA 107

Pound, Ezra (Loomis)
    1885-1972 . . . . . CLC 1, 2, 3, 4, 5, 7, 10,
                         13, 18, 34, 48, 50; PC 4
    See also CA 5-8R; obituary CA 37-40R;
    DLB 4, 45, 63; CDALB 1917-1929

Povod, Reinaldo 1959- . . . . CLC 44

Powell, Adam Clayton, Jr. 1908-1972
    See also BLC 3; CA 102;
    obituary CA 33-36R

Powell, Anthony (Dymoke)
    1905- . . . . CLC 1, 3, 7, 9, 10, 31
    See also CANR 1; CA 1-4R; DLB 15

Powell, Dawn 1897-1965 . . . . CLC 66
    See also CA 5-8R

Powell, Padgett 1952- . . . . CLC 34
    See also CA 126

Powers, J(ames) F(arl)
    1917- . . . . CLC 1, 4, 8, 57; SSC 4
    See also CANR 2; CA 1-4R

Powers, John J(ames) 1945-
    See Powers, John R.

Powers, John R. 1945- . . . . CLC 66
    See also Powers, John J(ames)
    See also CA 69-72

Pownall, David 1938- . . . . CLC 10
    See also CA 89-92; DLB 14

Powys, John Cowper
    1872-1963 . . . . CLC 7, 9, 15, 46
    See also CA 85-88; DLB 15

Powys, T(heodore) F(rancis)
    1875-1953 . . . . TCLC 9
    See also CA 106; DLB 36

Prager, Emily 1952- . . . . CLC 56

Pratt, E(dwin) J(ohn) 1883-1964 . . . . CLC 19
    See also obituary CA 93-96; DLB 92

Premchand 1880-1936 . . . . TCLC 21

Preussler, Otfried 1923- . . . . CLC 17
    See also CA 77-80; SATA 24

Prevert, Jacques (Henri Marie)
    1900-1977 . . . . CLC 15
    See also CANR 29; CA 77-80;
    obituary CA 69-72; obituary SATA 30

Prevost, Abbe (Antoine Francois)
    1697-1763 . . . . LC 1

Price, (Edward) Reynolds
    1933- . . . . CLC 3, 6, 13, 43, 50, 63
    See also CANR 1; CA 1-4R; DLB 2

Price, Richard 1949- . . . . CLC 6, 12
    See also CANR 3; CA 49-52; DLB-Y 81

Prichard, Katharine Susannah
    1883-1969 . . . . CLC 46
    See also CAP 1; CA 11-12

Priestley, J(ohn) B(oynton)
    1894-1984 . . . . CLC 2, 5, 9, 34
    See also CA 9-12R; obituary CA 113;
    DLB 10, 34, 77; DLB-Y 84

Prince (Rogers Nelson) 1958?- . . . . . CLC 35

Prince, F(rank) T(empleton) 1912- . . CLC 22
    See also CA 101; DLB 20

Prior, Matthew 1664-1721 . . . . LC 4

Pritchard, William H(arrison)
    1932- . . . . CLC 34
    See also CANR 23; CA 65-68

Pritchett, V(ictor) S(awdon)
    1900- . . . . CLC 5, 13, 15, 41
    See also CA 61-64; DLB 15

Probst, Mark 1925- . . . . CLC 59
    See also CA 130

Procaccino, Michael 1946-
    See Cristofer, Michael

Prokosch, Frederic 1908-1989 . . . . CLC 4, 48
    See also CA 73-76; obituary CA 128;
    DLB 48

Prose, Francine 1947- . . . . CLC 45
    See also CA 109, 112

Proust, Marcel 1871-1922 . . TCLC 7, 13, 33
    See also CA 104, 120; DLB 65

Pryor, Richard 1940- . . . . CLC 26
    See also CA 122

Przybyszewski, Stanislaw
    1868-1927 . . . . TCLC 36
    See also DLB 66

Puig, Manuel
1932-1990 . . . . **CLC 3, 5, 10, 28, 65**
See also CANR 2, 32; CA 45-48

Purdy, A(lfred) W(ellington)
1918- . . . . **CLC 3, 6, 14, 50**
See also CA 81-84

Purdy, James (Amos)
1923- . . . . **CLC 2, 4, 10, 28, 52**
See also CAAS 1; CANR 19; CA 33-36R;
DLB 2

Pushkin, Alexander (Sergeyevich)
1799-1837 . . . . **NCLC 3, 27**

P'u Sung-ling 1640-1715 . . . . **LC 3**

Puzo, Mario 1920- . . . . **CLC 1, 2, 6, 36**
See also CANR 4; CA 65-68; DLB 6

Pym, Barbara (Mary Crampton)
1913-1980 . . . . **CLC 13, 19, 37**
See also CANR 13; CAP 1; CA 13-14;
obituary CA 97-100; DLB 14; DLB-Y 87

Pynchon, Thomas (Ruggles, Jr.)
1937- . . **CLC 2, 3, 6, 9, 11, 18, 33, 62, 72**
See also CANR 22; CA 17-20R; DLB 2

Quarrington, Paul 1954?- . . . . **CLC 65**
See also CA 129

Quasimodo, Salvatore 1901-1968 . . . **CLC 10**
See also CAP 1; CA 15-16;
obituary CA 25-28R

Queen, Ellery 1905-1982 . . . . **CLC 3, 11**
See also Dannay, Frederic; Lee, Manfred
B(ennington)

Queneau, Raymond
1903-1976 . . . . **CLC 2, 5, 10, 42**
See also CA 77-80; obituary CA 69-72;
DLB 72

Quin, Ann (Marie) 1936-1973 . . . . **CLC 6**
See also CA 9-12R; obituary CA 45-48;
DLB 14

Quinn, Simon 1942-
See Smith, Martin Cruz
See also CANR 6, 23; CA 85-88

Quiroga, Horacio (Sylvestre)
1878-1937 . . . . **TCLC 20**
See also CA 117

Quoirez, Francoise 1935-
See Sagan, Francoise
See also CANR 6; CA 49-52

Raabe, Wilhelm 1831-1910 . . . . **TCLC 45**

Rabe, David (William) 1940- . . . **CLC 4, 8, 33**
See also CA 85-88; CABS 3; DLB 7

Rabelais, Francois 1494?-1553 . . . . **LC 5**

Rabinovitch, Sholem 1859-1916
See Aleichem, Sholom
See also CA 104

Rachen, Kurt von 1911-1986
See Hubbard, L(afayette) Ron(ald)

Radcliffe, Ann (Ward) 1764-1823 . . **NCLC 6**
See also DLB 39

Radiguet, Raymond 1903-1923 . . . . **TCLC 29**
See also DLB 65

Radnoti, Miklos 1909-1944 . . . . . . **TCLC 16**
See also CA 118

Rado, James 1939- . . . . **CLC 17**
See also CA 105

Radomski, James 1932-
See Rado, James

Radvanyi, Netty Reiling 1900-1983
See Seghers, Anna
See also CA 85-88; obituary CA 110

Rae, Ben 1935-
See Griffiths, Trevor

Raeburn, John 1941- . . . . **CLC 34**
See also CA 57-60

Ragni, Gerome 1942- . . . . **CLC 17**
See also CA 105

Rahv, Philip 1908-1973 . . . . **CLC 24**
See also Greenberg, Ivan

Raine, Craig 1944- . . . . **CLC 32**
See also CANR 29; CA 108; DLB 40

Raine, Kathleen (Jessie) 1908- . . . **CLC 7, 45**
See also CA 85-88; DLB 20

Rainis, Janis 1865-1929 . . . . **TCLC 29**

Rakosi, Carl 1903- . . . . **CLC 47**
See also Rawley, Callman
See also CAAS 5

Ramos, Graciliano 1892-1953 . . . . . **TCLC 32**

Rampersad, Arnold 19??- . . . . **CLC 44**

Ramuz, Charles-Ferdinand
1878-1947 . . . . **TCLC 33**

Rand, Ayn 1905-1982 . . . . **CLC 3, 30, 44**
See also CANR 27; CA 13-16R;
obituary CA 105

Randall, Dudley (Felker) 1914- . . . . . . **CLC 1**
See also BLC 3; CANR 23; CA 25-28R;
DLB 41

Ransom, John Crowe
1888-1974 . . . . **CLC 2, 4, 5, 11, 24**
See also CANR 6; CA 5-8R;
obituary CA 49-52; DLB 45, 63

Rao, Raja 1909- . . . . **CLC 25, 56**
See also CA 73-76

Raphael, Frederic (Michael)
1931- . . . . **CLC 2, 14**
See also CANR 1; CA 1-4R; DLB 14

Rathbone, Julian 1935- . . . . **CLC 41**
See also CA 101

Rattigan, Terence (Mervyn)
1911-1977 . . . . **CLC 7**
See also CA 85-88; obituary CA 73-76;
DLB 13

Ratushinskaya, Irina 1954- . . . . **CLC 54**
See also CA 129

Raven, Simon (Arthur Noel)
1927- . . . . **CLC 14**
See also CA 81-84

Rawley, Callman 1903-
See Rakosi, Carl
See also CANR 12; CA 21-24R

Rawlings, Marjorie Kinnan
1896-1953 . . . . **TCLC 4**
See also YABC 1; CA 104; DLB 9, 22

Ray, Satyajit 1921- . . . . **CLC 16**
See also CA 114

Read, Herbert (Edward) 1893-1968 . . **CLC 4**
See also CA 85-88; obituary CA 25-28R;
DLB 20

Read, Piers Paul 1941- . . . . . . **CLC 4, 10, 25**
See also CA 21-24R; SATA 21; DLB 14

Reade, Charles 1814-1884 . . . . **NCLC 2**
See also DLB 21

Reade, Hamish 1936-
See Gray, Simon (James Holliday)

Reading, Peter 1946- . . . . **CLC 47**
See also CA 103; DLB 40

Reaney, James 1926- . . . . **CLC 13**
See also CA 41-44R; SATA 43; DLB 68

Rebreanu, Liviu 1885-1944 . . . . . . **TCLC 28**

Rechy, John (Francisco)
1934- . . . . **CLC 1, 7, 14, 18**
See also CAAS 4; CANR 6; CA 5-8R;
DLB-Y 82

Redcam, Tom 1870-1933 . . . . **TCLC 25**

Reddin, Keith 1956?- . . . . **CLC 67**

Redgrove, Peter (William)
1932- . . . . **CLC 6, 41**
See also CANR 3; CA 1-4R; DLB 40

Redmon (Nightingale), Anne
1943- . . . . **CLC 22**
See also Nightingale, Anne Redmon
See also DLB-Y 86

Reed, Ishmael
1938- . . . . **CLC 2, 3, 5, 6, 13, 32, 60**
See also BLC 3; CANR 25; CA 21-24R;
DLB 2, 5, 33; DLB-DS 8

Reed, John (Silas) 1887-1920 . . . . . . **TCLC 9**
See also CA 106

Reed, Lou 1944- . . . . **CLC 21**

Reeve, Clara 1729-1807 . . . . **NCLC 19**
See also DLB 39

Reid, Christopher 1949- . . . . **CLC 33**
See also DLB 40

Reid Banks, Lynne 1929-
See Banks, Lynne Reid
See also CANR 6, 22; CA 1-4R; SATA 22

Reiner, Max 1900-
See Caldwell, (Janet Miriam) Taylor
(Holland)

Reizenstein, Elmer Leopold 1892-1967
See Rice, Elmer

Remark, Erich Paul 1898-1970
See Remarque, Erich Maria

Remarque, Erich Maria
1898-1970 . . . . **CLC 21**
See also CA 77-80; obituary CA 29-32R;
DLB 56

Remizov, Alexey (Mikhailovich)
1877-1957 . . . . **TCLC 27**
See also CA 125

Renan, Joseph Ernest
1823-1892 . . . . **NCLC 26**

Renard, Jules 1864-1910 . . . . **TCLC 17**
See also CA 117

Renault, Mary 1905-1983 . . . . **CLC 3, 11, 17**
See also Challans, Mary
See also DLB-Y 83

Rendell, Ruth 1930- . . . . **CLC 28, 48**
See also Vine, Barbara
See also CA 109; DLB 87

Renoir, Jean 1894-1979 . . . . **CLC 20**
See also CA 129; obituary CA 85-88

Resnais, Alain 1922- . . . . **CLC 16**

Reverdy, Pierre 1899-1960 .... CLC 53
See also CA 97-100; obituary CA 89-92

Rexroth, Kenneth
1905-1982 ...... CLC 1, 2, 6, 11, 22, 49
See also CANR 14; CA 5-8R;
obituary CA 107; DLB 16, 48; DLB-Y 82;
CDALB 1941-1968

Reyes, Alfonso 1889-1959 .... TCLC 33

Reyes y Basoalto, Ricardo Eliecer Neftali
1904-1973
See Neruda, Pablo

Reymont, Wladyslaw Stanislaw
1867-1925 .... TCLC 5
See also CA 104

Reynolds, Jonathan 1942?- ...... CLC 6, 38
See also CANR 28; CA 65-68

Reynolds, Michael (Shane) 1937- ... CLC 44
See also CANR 9; CA 65-68

Reynolds, Sir Joshua 1723-1792 ..... LC 15

Reznikoff, Charles 1894-1976 .... CLC 9
See also CAP 2; CA 33-36;
obituary CA 61-64; DLB 28, 45

Rezzori, Gregor von 1914- .... CLC 25
See also CA 122

Rhys, Jean
1890-1979 ...... CLC 2, 4, 6, 14, 19, 51
See also CA 25-28R; obituary CA 85-88;
DLB 36

Ribeiro, Darcy 1922- .... CLC 34
See also CA 33-36R

Ribeiro, Joao Ubaldo (Osorio Pimentel)
1941- .... CLC 10, 67
See also CA 81-84

Ribman, Ronald (Burt) 1932- .... CLC 7
See also CA 21-24R

Ricci, Nino 1959- .... CLC 70

Rice, Anne 1941- .... CLC 41
See also CANR 12; CA 65-68

Rice, Elmer 1892-1967 .... CLC 7, 49
See also CAP 2; CA 21-22;
obituary CA 25-28R; DLB 4, 7

Rice, Tim 1944- .... CLC 21
See also CA 103

Rich, Adrienne (Cecile)
1929- .... CLC 3, 6, 7, 11, 18, 36
See also CANR 20; CA 9-12R; DLB 5, 67

Richard, Keith 1943- .... CLC 17
See also CA 107

Richards, David Adam 1950- .... CLC 59
See also CA 93-96; DLB 53

Richards, I(vor) A(rmstrong)
1893-1979 .... CLC 14, 24
See also CA 41-44R; obituary CA 89-92;
DLB 27

Richards, Keith 1943-
See Richard, Keith
See also CA 107

Richardson, Dorothy (Miller)
1873-1957 .... TCLC 3
See also CA 104; DLB 36

Richardson, Ethel 1870-1946
See Richardson, Henry Handel
See also CA 105

Richardson, Henry Handel
1870-1946 .... TCLC 4
See also Richardson, Ethel

Richardson, Samuel 1689-1761 .... LC 1
See also DLB 39

Richler, Mordecai
1931- .... CLC 3, 5, 9, 13, 18, 46, 70
See also CLR 17; CANR 31; CA 65-68;
SATA 27, 44; DLB 53

Richter, Conrad (Michael)
1890-1968 .... CLC 30
See also CANR 23; CA 5-8R;
obituary CA 25-28R; SATA 3; DLB 9

Richter, Johann Paul Friedrich 1763-1825
See Jean Paul

Riddell, Mrs. J. H. 1832-1906 ..... TCLC 40

Riding, Laura 1901- .... CLC 3, 7
See also Jackson, Laura (Riding)

Riefenstahl, Berta Helene Amalia
1902- .... CLC 16
See also Riefenstahl, Leni
See also CA 108

Riefenstahl, Leni 1902- .... CLC 16
See also Riefenstahl, Berta Helene Amalia
See also CA 108

Rilke, Rainer Maria
1875-1926 .... TCLC 1, 6, 19; PC 2
See also CA 104, 132; DLB 81

Rimbaud, (Jean Nicolas) Arthur
1854-1891 .... NCLC 4, 35; PC 3

Ringwood, Gwen(dolyn Margaret) Pharis
1910-1984 .... CLC 48
See also obituary CA 112

Rio, Michel 19??- .... CLC 43

Ritsos, Yannis 1909- .... CLC 6, 13, 31
See also CA 77-80

Ritter, Erika 1948?- .... CLC 52

Rivera, Jose Eustasio 1889-1928 ... TCLC 35

Rivers, Conrad Kent 1933-1968 ...... CLC 1
See also CA 85-88; DLB 41

Rizal, Jose 1861-1896 .... NCLC 27

Roa Bastos, Augusto 1917- .... CLC 45

Robbe-Grillet, Alain
1922- ...... CLC 1, 2, 4, 6, 8, 10, 14, 43
See also CA 9-12R; DLB 83

Robbins, Harold 1916- .... CLC 5
See also CANR 26; CA 73-76

Robbins, Thomas Eugene 1936-
See Robbins, Tom
See also CA 81-84

Robbins, Tom 1936- .... CLC 9, 32, 64
See also Robbins, Thomas Eugene
See also CANR 29; CA 81-84; DLB-Y 80

Robbins, Trina 1938- .... CLC 21

Roberts, (Sir) Charles G(eorge) D(ouglas)
1860-1943 .... TCLC 8
See also CA 105; SATA 29; DLB 92

Roberts, Kate 1891-1985 .... CLC 15
See also CA 107; obituary CA 116

Roberts, Keith (John Kingston)
1935- .... CLC 14
See also CA 25-28R

Roberts, Kenneth 1885-1957 ...... TCLC 23
See also CA 109; DLB 9

Roberts, Michele (B.) 1949- .... CLC 48
See also CA 115

Robertson, Thomas William
1829-1871 .... NCLC 35

Robinson, Edwin Arlington
1869-1935 .... TCLC 5; PC 1
See also CA 104; DLB 54;
CDALB 1865-1917

Robinson, Henry Crabb
1775-1867 .... NCLC 15

Robinson, Jill 1936- .... CLC 10
See also CA 102

Robinson, Kim Stanley 19??- .... CLC 34
See also CA 126

Robinson, Marilynne 1944- .... CLC 25
See also CA 116

Robinson, Smokey 1940- .... CLC 21

Robinson, William 1940-
See Robinson, Smokey
See also CA 116

Robison, Mary 1949- .... CLC 42
See also CA 113, 116

Roddenberry, Gene 1921- .... CLC 17
See also CANR 110; SATA 45

Rodgers, Mary 1931- .... CLC 12
See also CLR 20; CANR 8; CA 49-52;
SATA 8

Rodgers, W(illiam) R(obert)
1909-1969 .... CLC 7
See also CA 85-88; DLB 20

Rodman, Howard 19??- .... CLC 65

Rodriguez, Claudio 1934- .... CLC 10

Roethke, Theodore (Huebner)
1908-1963 ...... CLC 1, 3, 8, 11, 19, 46
See also CA 81-84; CABS 2; SAAS 1;
DLB 5; CDALB 1941-1968

Rogers, Sam 1943-
See Shepard, Sam

Rogers, Thomas (Hunton) 1931- .... CLC 57
See also CA 89-92

Rogers, Will(iam Penn Adair)
1879-1935 .... TCLC 8
See also CA 105; DLB 11

Rogin, Gilbert 1929- .... CLC 18
See also CANR 15; CA 65-68

Rohan, Koda 1867-1947 .... TCLC 22
See also CA 121

Rohmer, Eric 1920- .... CLC 16
See also Scherer, Jean-Marie Maurice

Rohmer, Sax 1883-1959 .... TCLC 28
See also Ward, Arthur Henry Sarsfield
See also CA 108; DLB 70

Roiphe, Anne (Richardson)
1935- .... CLC 3, 9
See also CA 89-92; DLB-Y 80

Rolfe, Frederick (William Serafino Austin
Lewis Mary) 1860-1913 ...... TCLC 12
See also CA 107; DLB 34

Rolland, Romain 1866-1944 ...... TCLC 23
See also CA 118; DLB 65

Rolvaag, O(le) E(dvart)
1876-1931 .... TCLC 17
See also CA 117; DLB 9

Romains, Jules 1885-1972 .... CLC 7
See also CA 85-88

Romero, Jose Ruben 1890-1952 ... TCLC 14
See also CA 114

Ronsard, Pierre de 1524-1585 .... LC 6

Rooke, Leon 1934- .... CLC 25, 34
See also CANR 23; CA 25-28R

Roper, William 1498-1578 .... LC 10

Rosa, Joao Guimaraes 1908-1967 ... CLC 23
See also obituary CA 89-92

Rosen, Richard (Dean) 1949- .... CLC 39
See also CA 77-80

Rosenberg, Isaac 1890-1918 ...... TCLC 12
See also CA 107; DLB 20

Rosenblatt, Joe 1933- .... CLC 15
See also Rosenblatt, Joseph

Rosenblatt, Joseph 1933-
See Rosenblatt, Joe
See also CA 89-92

Rosenfeld, Samuel 1896-1963
See Tzara, Tristan
See also obituary CA 89-92

Rosenthal, M(acha) L(ouis) 1917-... CLC 28
See also CAAS 6; CANR 4; CA 1-4R;
SATA 59; DLB 5

Ross, (James) Sinclair 1908- .... CLC 13
See also CA 73-76; DLB 88

Rossetti, Christina Georgina
1830-1894 .... NCLC 2
See also SATA 20; DLB 35

Rossetti, Dante Gabriel
1828-1882 .... NCLC 4
See also DLB 35

Rossetti, Gabriel Charles Dante 1828-1882
See Rossetti, Dante Gabriel

Rossner, Judith (Perelman)
1935- .... CLC 6, 9, 29
See also CANR 18; CA 17-20R; DLB 6

Rostand, Edmond (Eugene Alexis)
1868-1918 .... TCLC 6, 37
See also CA 104, 126

Roth, Henry 1906- .... CLC 2, 6, 11
See also CAP 1; CA 11-12; DLB 28

Roth, Joseph 1894-1939 .... TCLC 33
See also DLB 85

Roth, Philip (Milton)
1933- ...... CLC 1, 2, 3, 4, 6, 9, 15, 22,
31, 47, 66
See also CANR 1, 22; CA 1-4R; DLB 2, 28;
DLB-Y 82; CDALB 1968-1988

Rothenberg, James 1931- .... CLC 57

Rothenberg, Jerome 1931- .... CLC 6, 57
See also CANR 1; CA 45-48; DLB 5

Roumain, Jacques 1907-1944 ...... TCLC 19
See also BLC 3; CA 117, 125

Rourke, Constance (Mayfield)
1885-1941 .... TCLC 12
See also YABC 1; CA 107

Rousseau, Jean-Baptiste 1671-1741 ... LC 9

Rousseau, Jean-Jacques 1712-1778 ... LC 14

Roussel, Raymond 1877-1933 ..... TCLC 20
See also CA 117

Rovit, Earl (Herbert) 1927- .... CLC 7
See also CANR 12; CA 5-8R

Rowe, Nicholas 1674-1718 .... LC 8

Rowson, Susanna Haswell
1762-1824 .... NCLC 5
See also DLB 37

Roy, Gabrielle 1909-1983 ...... CLC 10, 14
See also CANR 5; CA 53-56;
obituary CA 110; DLB 68

Rozewicz, Tadeusz 1921- .... CLC 9, 23
See also CA 108

Ruark, Gibbons 1941- .... CLC 3
See also CANR 14; CA 33-36R

Rubens, Bernice 192?- .... CLC 19, 31
See also CA 25-28R; DLB 14

Rubenstein, Gladys 1934-
See Swan, Gladys

Rudkin, (James) David 1936- ...... CLC 14
See also CA 89-92; DLB 13

Rudnik, Raphael 1933- .... CLC 7
See also CA 29-32R

Ruiz, Jose Martinez 1874-1967
See Azorin

Rukeyser, Muriel
1913-1980 .... CLC 6, 10, 15, 27
See also CANR 26; CA 5-8R;
obituary CA 93-96; obituary SATA 22;
DLB 48

Rule, Jane (Vance) 1931- .... CLC 27
See also CANR 12; CA 25-28R; DLB 60

Rulfo, Juan 1918-1986 .... CLC 8
See also CANR 26; CA 85-88;
obituary CA 118

Runyon, (Alfred) Damon
1880-1946 .... TCLC 10
See also CA 107; DLB 11

Rush, Norman 1933- .... CLC 44
See also CA 121, 126

Rushdie, (Ahmed) Salman
1947- .... CLC 23, 31, 55, 59
See also CA 108, 111

Rushforth, Peter (Scott) 1945- ..... CLC 19
See also CA 101

Ruskin, John 1819-1900 .... TCLC 20
See also CA 114; SATA 24; DLB 55

Russ, Joanna 1937- .... CLC 15
See also CANR 11; CA 25-28R; DLB 8

Russell, George William 1867-1935
See A. E.
See also CA 104

Russell, (Henry) Ken(neth Alfred)
1927- .... CLC 16
See also CA 105

Russell, Mary Annette Beauchamp 1866-1941
See Elizabeth

Russell, Willy 1947- .... CLC 60

Rutherford, Mark 1831-1913 ...... TCLC 25
See also CA 121; DLB 18

Ruyslinck, Ward 1929- .... CLC 14

Ryan, Cornelius (John) 1920-1974 ... CLC 7
See also CA 69-72; obituary CA 53-56

Ryan, Michael 1946- .... CLC 65
See also CA 49-52; DLB-Y 82

Rybakov, Anatoli 1911?- .... CLC 23, 53
See also CA 126

Ryder, Jonathan 1927-
See Ludlum, Robert

Ryga, George 1932- .... CLC 14
See also CA 101; obituary CA 124; DLB 60

**Séviné, Marquise de Marie de
Rabutin-Chantal** 1626-1696 ..... LC 11

Saba, Umberto 1883-1957 .... TCLC 33

Sabato, Ernesto 1911- .... CLC 10, 23
See also CA 97-100

Sacher-Masoch, Leopold von
1836?-1895 .... NCLC 31

Sachs, Marilyn (Stickle) 1927- ..... CLC 35
See also CLR 2; CANR 13; CA 17-20R;
SAAS 2; SATA 3, 52

Sachs, Nelly 1891-1970 .... CLC 14
See also CAP 2; CA 17-18;
obituary CA 25-28R

Sackler, Howard (Oliver)
1929-1982 .... CLC 14
See also CA 61-64; obituary CA 108; DLB 7

Sacks, Oliver 1933- .... CLC 67
See also CANR 28; CA 53-56

Sade, Donatien Alphonse Francois, Comte de
1740-1814 .... NCLC 3

Sadoff, Ira 1945- .... CLC 9
See also CANR 5, 21; CA 53-56

Safire, William 1929- .... CLC 10
See also CA 17-20R

Sagan, Carl (Edward) 1934- .... CLC 30
See also CANR 11; CA 25-28R; SATA 58

Sagan, Francoise
1935- .... CLC 3, 6, 9, 17, 36
See also Quoirez, Francoise
See also CANR 6; DLB 83

Sahgal, Nayantara (Pandit) 1927-... CLC 41
See also CANR 11; CA 9-12R

Saint, H(arry) F. 1941- .... CLC 50

Sainte-Beuve, Charles Augustin
1804-1869 .... NCLC 5

Sainte-Marie, Beverly 1941-1972?
See Sainte-Marie, Buffy
See also CA 107

Sainte-Marie, Buffy 1941- .... CLC 17
See also Sainte-Marie, Beverly

**Saint-Exupery, Antoine (Jean Baptiste Marie
Roger) de** 1900-1944 .... TCLC 2
See also CLR 10; CA 108; SATA 20;
DLB 72

Saintsbury, George 1845-1933 ..... TCLC 31
See also DLB 57

Sait Faik (Abasiyanik)
1906-1954 .... TCLC 23

Saki 1870-1916 .... TCLC 3
See also Munro, H(ector) H(ugh)
See also CA 104

Salama, Hannu 1936- .... CLC 18

Salamanca, J(ack) R(ichard)
1922- .... CLC 4, 15
See also CA 25-28R

Sale, Kirkpatrick   1937- . . . . CLC 68
See also CANR 10; CA 13-14R

Salinas, Pedro   1891-1951. . . . . TCLC 17
See also CA 117

Salinger, J(erome) D(avid)
1919- . . . . CLC 1, 3, 8, 12, 56; SSC 2
See also CA 5-8R; DLB 2;
CDALB 1941-1968

Salter, James   1925- . . . . CLC 7, 52, 59
See also CA 73-76

Saltus, Edgar (Evertson)
1855-1921 . . . . TCLC 8
See also CA 105

Saltykov, Mikhail Evgrafovich
1826-1889 . . . . NCLC 16

Samarakis, Antonis   1919- . . . . CLC 5
See also CA 25-28R

Sanchez, Florencio   1875-1910. . . . . TCLC 37

Sanchez, Luis Rafael   1936- . . . . CLC 23

Sanchez, Sonia   1934- . . . . CLC 5
See also BLC 3; CLR 18; CANR 24;
CA 33-36R; SATA 22; DLB 41;
DLB-DS 8

Sand, George   1804-1876. . . . . NCLC 2

Sandburg, Carl (August)
1878-1967 . . . CLC 1, 4, 10, 15, 35; PC 2
See also CA 5-8R; obituary CA 25-28R;
SATA 8; DLB 17, 54; CDALB 1865-1917

Sandburg, Charles August   1878-1967
See Sandburg, Carl (August)

Sanders, (James) Ed(ward)   1939- . . . CLC 53
See also CANR 13; CA 15-16R, 103;
DLB 16

Sanders, Lawrence   1920- . . . . CLC 41
See also CA 81-84

Sandoz, Mari (Susette)   1896-1966 . . CLC 28
See also CANR 17; CA 1-4R;
obituary CA 25-28R; SATA 5; DLB 9

Saner, Reg(inald Anthony)   1931- . . . . CLC 9
See also CA 65-68

Sannazaro, Jacopo   1456?-1530 . . . . LC 8

Sansom, William   1912-1976. . . . . . CLC 2, 6
See also CA 5-8R; obituary CA 65-68

Santayana, George   1863-1952. . . . . TCLC 40
See also CA 115; DLB 54, 71

Santiago, Danny   1911- . . . . CLC 33
See also CA 125

Santmyer, Helen Hooven
1895-1986 . . . . CLC 33
See also CANR 15; CA 1-4R;
obituary CA 118; DLB-Y 84

Santos, Bienvenido N(uqui)   1911- . . . CLC 22
See also CANR 19; CA 101

Sapper   1888-1937 . . . . TCLC 44

Sappho   c. 6th-century B.C.- . . . . CMLC 3

Sarduy, Severo   1937- . . . . CLC 6
See also CA 89-92

Sargeson, Frank   1903-1982 . . . . CLC 31
See also CA 106, 25-28R; obituary CA 106

Sarmiento, Felix Ruben Garcia   1867-1916
See Dario, Ruben
See also CA 104

Saroyan, William
1908-1981 . . . . . CLC 1, 8, 10, 29, 34, 56
See also CA 5-8R; obituary CA 103;
SATA 23; obituary SATA 24; DLB 7, 9;
DLB-Y 81

Sarraute, Nathalie
1902- . . . . CLC 1, 2, 4, 8, 10, 31
See also CANR 23; CA 9-12R; DLB 83

Sarton, Eleanore Marie   1912-
See Sarton, (Eleanor) May

Sarton, (Eleanor) May
1912- . . . . CLC 4, 14, 49
See also CANR 1; CA 1-4R; SATA 36;
DLB 48; DLB-Y 81

Sartre, Jean-Paul (Charles Aymard)
1905-1980 . . . CLC 1, 4, 7, 9, 13, 18, 24,
44, 50, 52
See also CANR 21; CA 9-12R;
obituary CA 97-100; DLB 72

Sassoon, Siegfried (Lorraine)
1886-1967 . . . . CLC 36
See also CA 104; obituary CA 25-28R;
DLB 20

Saul, John (W. III)   1942- . . . . CLC 46
See also CANR 16; CA 81-84

Saura, Carlos   1932- . . . . CLC 20
See also CA 114

Sauser-Hall, Frederic-Louis
1887-1961 . . . . CLC 18
See also Cendrars, Blaise
See also CA 102; obituary CA 93-96

Savage, Thomas   1915- . . . . CLC 40
See also CA 126

Savan, Glenn   19??- . . . . CLC 50

Sayers, Dorothy L(eigh)
1893-1957 . . . . TCLC 2, 15
See also CA 104, 119; DLB 10, 36, 77

Sayers, Valerie   19??- . . . . CLC 50

Sayles, John (Thomas)
1950- . . . . CLC 7, 10, 14
See also CA 57-60; DLB 44

Scammell, Michael   19??- . . . . CLC 34

Scannell, Vernon   1922- . . . . CLC 49
See also CANR 8; CA 5-8R; DLB 27

Schaeffer, Susan Fromberg
1941- . . . . CLC 6, 11, 22
See also CANR 18; CA 49-52; SATA 22;
DLB 28

Schell, Jonathan   1943- . . . . CLC 35
See also CANR 12; CA 73-76

Schelling, Friedrich Wilhelm Joseph von
1775-1854 . . . . NCLC 30
See also DLB 90

Scherer, Jean-Marie Maurice   1920-
See Rohmer, Eric
See also CA 110

Schevill, James (Erwin)   1920- . . . . . . CLC 7
See also CA 5-8R

Schisgal, Murray (Joseph)   1926- . . . . CLC 6
See also CA 21-24R

Schlee, Ann   1934- . . . . CLC 35
See also CA 101; SATA 36, 44

Schlegel, August Wilhelm von
1767-1845 . . . . NCLC 15

Schlegel, Johann Elias (von)
1719?-1749. . . . . LC 5

Schmidt, Arno   1914-1979. . . . . CLC 56
See also obituary CA 109; DLB 69

Schmitz, Ettore   1861-1928
See Svevo, Italo
See also CA 104, 122

Schnackenberg, Gjertrud   1953- . . . . . CLC 40
See also CA 116

Schneider, Leonard Alfred   1925-1966
See Bruce, Lenny
See also CA 89-92

Schnitzler, Arthur   1862-1931 . . . . . . TCLC 4
See also CA 104; DLB 81

Schor, Sandra   1932?-1990 . . . . CLC 65
See also CA 132

Schorer, Mark   1908-1977 . . . . CLC 9
See also CANR 7; CA 5-8R;
obituary CA 73-76

Schrader, Paul (Joseph)   1946- . . . . . . CLC 26
See also CA 37-40R; DLB 44

Schreiner (Cronwright), Olive (Emilie
Albertina)   1855-1920. . . . . TCLC 9
See also CA 105; DLB 18

Schulberg, Budd (Wilson)
1914- . . . . CLC 7, 48
See also CANR 19; CA 25-28R; DLB 6, 26,
28; DLB-Y 81

Schulz, Bruno   1892-1942. . . . . TCLC 5
See also CA 115, 123

Schulz, Charles M(onroe)   1922- . . . . CLC 12
See also CANR 6; CA 9-12R; SATA 10

Schuyler, James (Marcus)
1923- . . . . CLC 5, 23
See also CA 101; DLB 5

Schwartz, Delmore
1913-1966 . . . . CLC 2, 4, 10, 45
See also CAP 2; CA 17-18;
obituary CA 25-28R; DLB 28, 48

Schwartz, John Burnham   1925- . . . . CLC 59

Schwartz, Lynne Sharon   1939- . . . . . CLC 31
See also CA 103

Schwarz-Bart, Andre   1928- . . . . CLC 2, 4
See also CA 89-92

Schwarz-Bart, Simone   1938- . . . . CLC 7
See also CA 97-100

Schwob, (Mayer Andre) Marcel
1867-1905 . . . . TCLC 20
See also CA 117

Sciascia, Leonardo
1921-1989 . . . . CLC 8, 9, 41
See also CA 85-88

Scoppettone, Sandra   1936- . . . . CLC 26
See also CA 5-8R; SATA 9

Scorsese, Martin   1942- . . . . CLC 20
See also CA 110, 114

Scotland, Jay   1932-
See Jakes, John (William)

Scott, Duncan Campbell
1862-1947 . . . . TCLC 6
See also CA 104; DLB 92

Scott, Evelyn   1893-1963. . . . . CLC 43
See also CA 104; obituary CA 112; DLB 9,
48

Author Index

Scott, F(rancis) R(eginald)
    1899-1985 .... CLC 22
    See also CA 101; obituary CA 114; DLB 88

Scott, Joanna   19??- .... CLC 50
    See also CA 126

Scott, Paul (Mark)   1920-1978 .... CLC 9, 60
    See also CA 81-84; obituary CA 77-80;
    DLB 14

Scott, Sir Walter   1771-1832 ..... NCLC 15
    See also YABC 2

Scribe, (Augustin) Eugene
    1791-1861 .... NCLC 16

Scudery, Madeleine de   1607-1701..... LC 2

Sealy, I. Allan   1951- .... CLC 55

Seare, Nicholas   1925-
    See Trevanian; Whitaker, Rodney

Sebestyen, Igen   1924-
    See Sebestyen, Ouida

Sebestyen, Ouida   1924- .... CLC 30
    See also CLR 17; CA 107; SATA 39

Sedgwick, Catharine Maria
    1789-1867 .... NCLC 19
    See also DLB 1, 74

Seelye, John   1931- .... CLC 7
    See also CA 97-100

Seferiades, Giorgos Stylianou   1900-1971
    See Seferis, George
    See also CANR 5; CA 5-8R;
    obituary CA 33-36R

Seferis, George   1900-1971 .... CLC 5, 11
    See also Seferiades, Giorgos Stylianou

Segal, Erich (Wolf)   1937- .... CLC 3, 10
    See also CANR 20; CA 25-28R; DLB-Y 86

Seger, Bob   1945- .... CLC 35

Seger, Robert Clark   1945-
    See Seger, Bob

Seghers, Anna   1900-1983 .... CLC 7, 110
    See also Radvanyi, Netty Reiling
    See also DLB 69

Seidel, Frederick (Lewis)   1936- ..... CLC 18
    See also CANR 8; CA 13-16R; DLB-Y 84

Seifert, Jaroslav   1901-1986 ..... CLC 34, 44
    See also CA 127

Sei Shonagon   c. 966-1017? .... CMLC 6

Selby, Hubert, Jr.   1928- ..... CLC 1, 2, 4, 8
    See also CA 13-16R; DLB 2

Sembene, Ousmane   1923-
    See Ousmane, Sembene

Sembene, Ousmane   1923-
    See Ousmane, Sembene

Senacour, Etienne Pivert de
    1770-1846 .... NCLC 16

Sender, Ramon (Jose)   1902-1982 .... CLC 8
    See also CANR 8; CA 5-8R;
    obituary CA 105

Seneca, Lucius Annaeus
    4 B.C.-65 A.D. .... CMLC 6

Senghor, Leopold Sedar   1906- ...... CLC 54
    See also BLC 3; CA 116, 125

Serling, (Edward) Rod(man)
    1924-1975 .... CLC 30
    See also CA 65-68; obituary CA 57-60;
    DLB 26

Serpieres   1907-
    See Guillevic, (Eugene)

Service, Robert W(illiam)
    1874-1958 .... TCLC 15
    See also CA 115; SATA 20

Seth, Vikram   1952- .... CLC 43
    See also CA 121, 127

Seton, Cynthia Propper
    1926-1982 .... CLC 27
    See also CANR 7; CA 5-8R;
    obituary CA 108

Seton, Ernest (Evan) Thompson
    1860-1946 .... TCLC 31
    See also CA 109; SATA 18; DLB 92

Settle, Mary Lee   1918- .... CLC 19, 61
    See also CAAS 1; CA 89-92; DLB 6

Sevine, Marquise de Marie de
    Rabutin-Chantal   1626-1696..... LC 11

Sexton, Anne (Harvey)
    1928-1974 ... CLC 2, 4, 6, 8, 10, 15, 53;
                                          PC 2
    See also CANR 3; CA 1-4R;
    obituary CA 53-56; CABS 2; SATA 10;
    DLB 5; CDALB 1941-1968

Shaara, Michael (Joseph)   1929- .... CLC 15
    See also CA 102; obituary CA 125;
    DLB-Y 83

Shackleton, C. C.   1925-
    See Aldiss, Brian W(ilson)

Shacochis, Bob   1951- .... CLC 39
    See also CA 119, 124

Shaffer, Anthony   1926- .... CLC 19
    See also CA 110, 116; DLB 13

Shaffer, Peter (Levin)
    1926- .... CLC 5, 14, 18, 37, 60
    See also CANR 25; CA 25-28R; DLB 13

Shalamov, Varlam (Tikhonovich)
    1907?-1982 .... CLC 18
    See also obituary CA 105

Shamlu, Ahmad   1925- .... CLC 10

Shammas, Anton   1951- .... CLC 55

Shange, Ntozake   1948- .... CLC 8, 25, 38
    See also BLC 3; CANR 27; CA 85-88;
    CABS 3; DLB 38

Shapcott, Thomas W(illiam)   1935- .. CLC 38
    See also CA 69-72

Shapiro, Karl (Jay)   1913- .. CLC 4, 8, 15, 53
    See also CAAS 6; CANR 1; CA 1-4R;
    DLB 48

Sharp, William   1855-1905 .... TCLC 39

Sharpe, Tom   1928- .... CLC 36
    See also CA 114; DLB 14

Shaw, (George) Bernard
    1856-1950 .... TCLC 3, 9, 21, 45
    See also CA 128; brief entry CA 104;
    DLB 10, 57

Shaw, Henry Wheeler
    1818-1885 .... NCLC 15
    See also DLB 11

Shaw, Irwin   1913-1984 .... CLC 7, 23, 34
    See also CANR 21; CA 13-16R;
    obituary CA 112; DLB 6; DLB-Y 84;
    CDALB 1941-1968

Shaw, Robert   1927-1978 .... CLC 5
    See also CANR 4; CA 1-4R;
    obituary CA 81-84; DLB 13, 14

Shawn, Wallace   1943- .... CLC 41
    See also CA 112

Sheed, Wilfrid (John Joseph)
    1930- .... CLC 2, 4, 10, 53
    See also CA 65-68; DLB 6

Sheffey, Asa   1913-1980
    See Hayden, Robert (Earl)

Sheldon, Alice (Hastings) B(radley)
    1915-1987
    See Tiptree, James, Jr.
    See also CA 108; obituary CA 122

Shelley, Mary Wollstonecraft Godwin
    1797-1851 .... NCLC 14
    See also SATA 29

Shelley, Percy Bysshe
    1792-1822 .... NCLC 18

Shepard, Jim   19??- .... CLC 36

Shepard, Lucius   19??- .... CLC 34
    See also CA 128

Shepard, Sam
    1943- .... CLC 4, 6, 17, 34, 41, 44
    See also CANR 22; CA 69-72; DLB 7

Shepherd, Michael   1927-
    See Ludlum, Robert

Sherburne, Zoa (Morin)   1912- ...... CLC 30
    See also CANR 3; CA 1-4R; SATA 3

Sheridan, Frances   1724-1766 .... LC 7
    See also DLB 39, 84

Sheridan, Richard Brinsley
    1751-1816 .... NCLC 5; DC 1
    See also DLB 89

Sherman, Jonathan Marc   1970?- .... CLC 55

Sherman, Martin   19??- .... CLC 19
    See also CA 116

Sherwin, Judith Johnson   1936- ... CLC 7, 15
    See also CA 25-28R

Sherwood, Robert E(mmet)
    1896-1955 .... TCLC 3
    See also CA 104; DLB 7, 26

Shiel, M(atthew) P(hipps)
    1865-1947 .... TCLC 8
    See also CA 106

Shiga, Naoya   1883-1971 .... CLC 33
    See also CA 101; obituary CA 33-36R

Shimazaki, Haruki   1872-1943
    See Shimazaki, Toson
    See also CA 105

Shimazaki, Toson   1872-1943 ...... TCLC 5
    See also Shimazaki, Haruki

Sholokhov, Mikhail (Aleksandrovich)
    1905-1984 .... CLC 7, 15
    See also CA 101; obituary CA 112;
    SATA 36

Sholom Aleichem   1859-1916 .... TCLC 1, 35
    See also Rabinovitch, Sholem

Shreve, Susan Richards   1939- ...... CLC 23
    See also CAAS 5; CANR 5; CA 49-52;
    SATA 41, 46

Shue, Larry   1946-1985 .... CLC 52
    See also obituary CA 117

Shulman, Alix Kates   1932- . . . . . . CLC 2, 10
  See also CA 29-32R; SATA 7

Shuster, Joe   1914- . . . . CLC 21

Shute (Norway), Nevil   1899-1960 . . . CLC 30
  See also Norway, Nevil Shute
  See also CA 102; obituary CA 93-96

Shuttle, Penelope (Diane)   1947- . . . . . CLC 7
  See also CA 93-96; DLB 14, 40

Sidney, Mary   1561-1621 . . . . LC 19

Sidney, Sir Philip   1554-1586 . . . . LC 19

Siegel, Jerome   1914- . . . . CLC 21
  See also CA 116

Sienkiewicz, Henryk (Adam Aleksander Pius)
  1846-1916 . . . . TCLC 3
  See also CA 104

Sigal, Clancy   1926- . . . . CLC 7
  See also CA 1-4R

Sigourney, Lydia (Howard Huntley)
  1791-1865 . . . . NCLC 21
  See also DLB 1, 42, 73

Siguenza y Gongora, Carlos de
  1645-1700 . . . . LC 8

Sigurjonsson, Johann   1880-1919 . . . TCLC 27

Sikelianos, Angelos   1884-1951 . . . . TCLC 39

Silkin, Jon   1930- . . . . CLC 2, 6, 43
  See also CAAS 5; CA 5-8R; DLB 27

Silko, Leslie Marmon   1948- . . . . CLC 23
  See also CA 115, 122

Sillanpaa, Franz Eemil   1888-1964 . . . CLC 19
  See also CA 129; obituary CA 93-96

Sillitoe, Alan
  1928- . . . . CLC 1, 3, 6, 10, 19, 57
  See also CAAS 2; CANR 8, 26; CA 9-12R;
  DLB 14

Silone, Ignazio   1900-1978 . . . . CLC 4
  See also CAAS 2; CANR 26; CAP 2;
  CA 25-28, 11-12R,; obituary CA 81-84

Silver, Joan Micklin   1935- . . . . CLC 20
  See also CA 114, 121

Silverberg, Robert   1935- . . . . CLC 7
  See also CAAS 3; CANR 1, 20; CA 1-4R;
  SATA 13; DLB 8

Silverstein, Alvin   1933- . . . . CLC 17
  See also CANR 2; CA 49-52; SATA 8

Silverstein, Virginia B(arbara Opshelor)
  1937- . . . . CLC 17
  See also CANR 2; CA 49-52; SATA 8

Simak, Clifford D(onald)
  1904-1988 . . . . CLC 1, 55
  See also CANR 1; CA 1-4R;
  obituary CA 125; DLB 8

Simenon, Georges (Jacques Christian)
  1903-1989 . . . . CLC 1, 2, 3, 8, 18, 47
  See also CA 85-88; obituary CA 129;
  DLB 72

Simenon, Paul   1956?-
  See The Clash

Simic, Charles   1938- . . . CLC 6, 9, 22, 49, 68
  See also CAAS 4; CANR 12, 33;
  CA 29-32R; DLB 105

Simmons, Charles (Paul)   1924- . . . . . CLC 57
  See also CA 89-92

Simmons, Dan   1948- . . . . CLC 44

Simmons, James (Stewart Alexander)
  1933- . . . . CLC 43
  See also CA 105; DLB 40

Simms, William Gilmore
  1806-1870 . . . . NCLC 3
  See also DLB 3, 30, 59, 73

Simon, Carly   1945- . . . . CLC 26
  See also CA 105

Simon, Claude (Henri Eugene)
  1913- . . . . CLC 4, 9, 15, 39
  See also CA 89-92; DLB 83

Simon, (Marvin) Neil
  1927- . . . . CLC 6, 11, 31, 39, 70
  See also CANR 26; CA 21-24R; DLB 7

Simon, Paul   1941- . . . . CLC 17
  See also CA 116

Simonon, Paul   1956?-
  See The Clash

Simpson, Louis (Aston Marantz)
  1923- . . . . CLC 4, 7, 9, 32
  See also CAAS 4; CANR 1; CA 1-4R;
  DLB 5

Simpson, Mona (Elizabeth)   1957- . . . CLC 44
  See also CA 122

Simpson, N(orman) F(rederick)
  1919- . . . . CLC 29
  See also CA 11-14R; DLB 13

Sinclair, Andrew (Annandale)
  1935- . . . . CLC 2, 14
  See also CAAS 5; CANR 14; CA 9-12R;
  DLB 14

Sinclair, Mary Amelia St. Clair   1865?-1946
  See Sinclair, May
  See also CA 104

Sinclair, May   1865?-1946 . . . . . . TCLC 3, 11
  See also Sinclair, Mary Amelia St. Clair
  See also DLB 36

Sinclair, Upton (Beall)
  1878-1968 . . . . CLC 1, 11, 15, 63
  See also CANR 7; CA 5-8R;
  obituary CA 25-28R; SATA 9; DLB 9

Singer, Isaac Bashevis
  1904-1991 . . . CLC 1, 3, 6, 9, 11, 15, 23,
                       38, 69; SSC 3
  See also CLR 1; CANR 1; CA 1-4R;
  obituary CA 134; SATA 3, 27; DLB 6,
  28, 52; CDALB 1941-1968

Singer, Israel Joshua   1893-1944 . . . TCLC 33

Singh, Khushwant   1915- . . . . CLC 11
  See also CANR 6; CA 9-12R

Sinyavsky, Andrei (Donatevich)
  1925- . . . . CLC 8
  See also CA 85-88

Sirin, V.
  See Nabokov, Vladimir (Vladimirovich)

Sissman, L(ouis) E(dward)
  1928-1976 . . . . CLC 9, 18
  See also CANR 13; CA 21-24R;
  obituary CA 65-68; DLB 5

Sisson, C(harles) H(ubert)   1914- . . . . . CLC 8
  See also CAAS 3; CANR 3; CA 1-4R;
  DLB 27

Sitwell, (Dame) Edith
  1887-1964 . . . . CLC 2, 9, 67; PC 3
  See also CA 11-12R; DLB 20

Sjoewall, Maj   1935-
  See Wahloo, Per
  See also CA 61-64, 65-68

Sjowall, Maj   1935-
  See Wahloo, Per

Skelton, Robin   1925- . . . . CLC 13
  See also CAAS 5; CA 5-8R; DLB 27, 53

Skolimowski, Jerzy   1938- . . . . CLC 20

Skolimowski, Yurek   1938-
  See Skolimowski, Jerzy

Skram, Amalie (Bertha)
  1847-1905 . . . . TCLC 25

Skrine, Mary Nesta   1904-
  See Keane, Molly

Skvorecky, Josef (Vaclav)
  1924- . . . . CLC 15, 39, 69
  See also CAAS 1; CANR 10, 34; CA 61-64

Slade, Bernard   1930- . . . . CLC 11, 46
  See also Newbound, Bernard Slade
  See also DLB 53

Slaughter, Carolyn   1946- . . . . CLC 56
  See also CA 85-88

Slaughter, Frank G(ill)   1908- . . . . . . CLC 29
  See also CANR 5; CA 5-8R

Slavitt, David (R.)   1935- . . . . CLC 5, 14
  See also CAAS 3; CA 21-24R; DLB 5, 6

Slesinger, Tess   1905-1945 . . . . TCLC 10
  See also CA 107

Slessor, Kenneth   1901-1971 . . . . CLC 14
  See also CA 102; obituary CA 89-92

Slowacki, Juliusz   1809-1849 . . . . . NCLC 15

Smart, Christopher   1722-1771 . . . . LC 3

Smart, Elizabeth   1913-1986 . . . . CLC 54
  See also CA 81-84; obituary CA 118;
  DLB 88

Smiley, Jane (Graves)   1949- . . . . CLC 53
  See also CA 104

Smith, A(rthur) J(ames) M(arshall)
  1902-1980 . . . . CLC 15
  See also CANR 4; CA 1-4R;
  obituary CA 102; DLB 88

Smith, Betty (Wehner)   1896-1972 . . . CLC 19
  See also CA 5-8R; obituary CA 33-36R;
  SATA 6; DLB-Y 82

Smith, Cecil Lewis Troughton   1899-1966
  See Forester, C(ecil) S(cott)

Smith, Charlotte (Turner)
  1749-1806 . . . . NCLC 23
  See also DLB 39

Smith, Clark Ashton   1893-1961 . . . . CLC 43

Smith, Dave   1942- . . . . CLC 22, 42
  See also Smith, David (Jeddie)
  See also CAAS 7; CANR 1; DLB 5

Smith, David (Jeddie)   1942-
  See Smith, Dave
  See also CANR 1; CA 49-52

Smith, Florence Margaret   1902-1971
  See Smith, Stevie
  See also CAP 2; CA 17-18;
  obituary CA 29-32R

Smith, Iain Crichton   1928- . . . . CLC 64
  See also DLB 40

Smith, John 1580?-1631............ LC 9
See also DLB 24, 30

Smith, Lee 1944-................. CLC 25
See also CA 114, 119; DLB-Y 83

Smith, Martin Cruz 1942-......... CLC 25
See also CANR 6; CA 85-88

Smith, Martin William 1942-
See Smith, Martin Cruz

Smith, Mary-Ann Tirone 1944-..... CLC 39
See also CA 118

Smith, Patti 1946- .... CLC 12
See also CA 93-96

Smith, Pauline (Urmson)
1882-1959 .... TCLC 25
See also CA 29-32R; SATA 27

Smith, Rosamond 1938-
See Oates, Joyce Carol

Smith, Sara Mahala Redway 1900-1972
See Benson, Sally

Smith, Stevie 1902-1971.... CLC 3, 8, 25, 44
See also Smith, Florence Margaret
See also DLB 20

Smith, Wilbur (Addison) 1933-..... CLC 33
See also CANR 7; CA 13-16R

Smith, William Jay 1918- .... CLC 6
See also CA 5-8R; SATA 2; DLB 5

Smolenskin, Peretz 1842-1885.... NCLC 30

Smollett, Tobias (George) 1721-1771 .. LC 2
See also DLB 39

Snodgrass, W(illiam) D(e Witt)
1926- .... CLC 2, 6, 10, 18, 68
See also CANR 6; CA 1-4R; DLB 5

Snow, C(harles) P(ercy)
1905-1980 .... CLC 1, 4, 6, 9, 13, 19
See also CA 5-8R; obituary CA 101;
DLB 15, 77

Snyder, Gary (Sherman)
1930- .... CLC 1, 2, 5, 9, 32
See also CANR 30; CA 17-20R; DLB 5, 16

Snyder, Zilpha Keatley 1927- ...... CLC 17
See also CA 9-12R; SAAS 2; SATA 1, 28

Sobol, Joshua 19??- .... CLC 60

Soderberg, Hjalmar 1869-1941 .... TCLC 39

Sodergran, Edith 1892-1923...... TCLC 31

Sokolov, Raymond 1941-........... CLC 7
See also CA 85-88

Sologub, Fyodor 1863-1927........ TCLC 9
See also Teternikov, Fyodor Kuzmich
See also CA 104

Solomos, Dionysios 1798-1857 ... NCLC 15

Solwoska, Mara 1929-
See French, Marilyn
See also CANR 3; CA 69-72

Solzhenitsyn, Aleksandr I(sayevich)
1918- ... CLC 1, 2, 4, 7, 9, 10, 18, 26, 34
See also CA 69-72

Somers, Jane 1919-
See Lessing, Doris (May)

Sommer, Scott 1951- .... CLC 25
See also CA 106

Sondheim, Stephen (Joshua)
1930- .... CLC 30, 39
See also CA 103

Sontag, Susan 1933-... CLC 1, 2, 10, 13, 31
See also CA 17-20R; DLB 2, 67

Sophocles
c. 496? B.C.-c. 406? B.C..... CMLC 2;
DC 1

Sorrentino, Gilbert
1929- .... CLC 3, 7, 14, 22, 40
See also CANR 14; CA 77-80; DLB 5;
DLB-Y 80

Soto, Gary 1952-.................. CLC 32
See also CA 119, 125; DLB 82

Soupault, Philippe 1897-1990 ...... CLC 68
See also CA 116; obituary CA 131

Souster, (Holmes) Raymond
1921- .... CLC 5, 14
See also CANR 13; CA 13-16R; DLB 88

Southern, Terry 1926- .... CLC 7
See also CANR 1; CA 1-4R; DLB 2

Southey, Robert 1774-1843 .... NCLC 8
See also SATA 54

Southworth, Emma Dorothy Eliza Nevitte
1819-1899 .... NCLC 26

Soyinka, Wole
1934- .... CLC 3, 5, 14, 36, 44; DC 2
See also BLC 3; CANR 27; CA 13-16R;
DLB-Y 86

Spackman, W(illiam) M(ode)
1905-1990 .... CLC 46
See also CA 81-84

Spacks, Barry 1931-.............. CLC 14
See also CA 29-32R

Spanidou, Irini 1946- .... CLC 44

Spark, Muriel (Sarah)
1918- .... CLC 2, 3, 5, 8, 13, 18, 40;
SSC 10
See also CANR 12; CA 5-8R; DLB 15

Spencer, Elizabeth 1921- .... CLC 22
See also CA 13-16R; SATA 14; DLB 6

Spencer, Scott 1945-.............. CLC 30
See also CA 113; DLB-Y 86

Spender, Stephen (Harold)
1909- .... CLC 1, 2, 5, 10, 41
See also CA 9-12R; DLB 20

Spengler, Oswald 1880-1936 ...... TCLC 25
See also CA 118

Spenser, Edmund 1552?-1599 .... LC 5

Spicer, Jack 1925-1965 ...... CLC 8, 18, 72
See also CA 85-88; DLB 5, 16

Spielberg, Peter 1929- .... CLC 6
See also CANR 4; CA 5-8R; DLB-Y 81

Spielberg, Steven 1947-........... CLC 20
See also CA 77-80; SATA 32

Spillane, Frank Morrison 1918-
See Spillane, Mickey
See also CA 25-28R

Spillane, Mickey 1918- .... CLC 3, 13
See also Spillane, Frank Morrison

Spinoza, Benedictus de 1632-1677 .... LC 9

Spinrad, Norman (Richard) 1940-... CLC 46
See also CANR 20; CA 37-40R; DLB 8

Spitteler, Carl (Friedrich Georg)
1845-1924 .... TCLC 12
See also CA 109

Spivack, Kathleen (Romola Drucker)
1938- .... CLC 6
See also CA 49-52

Spoto, Donald 1941-.............. CLC 39
See also CANR 11; CA 65-68

Springsteen, Bruce 1949-.......... CLC 17
See also CA 111

Spurling, Hilary 1940-............ CLC 34
See also CANR 25; CA 104

Squires, (James) Radcliffe 1917-.... CLC 51
See also CANR 6, 21; CA 1-4R

Stael-Holstein, Anne Louise Germaine Necker,
Baronne de 1766-1817....... NCLC 3

Stafford, Jean 1915-1979... CLC 4, 7, 19, 68
See also CANR 3; CA 1-4R;
obituary CA 85-88; obituary SATA 22;
DLB 2

Stafford, William (Edgar)
1914- .... CLC 4, 7, 29
See also CAAS 3; CANR 5, 22; CA 5-8R;
DLB 5

Stannard, Martin 1947-........... CLC 44

Stanton, Maura 1946- .... CLC 9
See also CANR 15; CA 89-92

Stapledon, (William) Olaf
1886-1950 .... TCLC 22
See also CA 111; DLB 15

Starbuck, George (Edwin) 1931-.... CLC 53
See also CANR 23; CA 21-22R

Stark, Richard 1933-
See Westlake, Donald E(dwin)

Stead, Christina (Ellen)
1902-1983 .... CLC 2, 5, 8, 32
See also CA 13-16R; obituary CA 109

Steele, Sir Richard 1672-1729....... LC 18
See also DLB 84, 101

Steele, Timothy (Reid) 1948-....... CLC 45
See also CANR 16; CA 93-96

Steffens, (Joseph) Lincoln
1866-1936 .... TCLC 20
See also CA 117; SAAS 1

Stegner, Wallace (Earle) 1909-... CLC 9, 49
See also CANR 1, 21; CA 1-4R; DLB 9

Stein, Gertrude 1874-1946... TCLC 1, 6, 28
See also CA 104; DLB 4, 54, 86;
CDALB 1917-1929

Steinbeck, John (Ernst)
1902-1968 ..... CLC 1, 5, 9, 13, 21, 34,
45, 59
See also CANR 1; CA 1-4R;
obituary CA 25-28R; SATA 9; DLB 7, 9;
DLB-DS 2; CDALB 1929-1941

Steinem, Gloria 1934-............. CLC 63
See also CANR 28; CA 53-56

Steiner, George 1929-............. CLC 24
See also CA 73-76; DLB 67

Steiner, Rudolf(us Josephus Laurentius)
1861-1925 .... TCLC 13
See also CA 107

Stendhal 1783-1842............. NCLC 23

Stephen, Leslie 1832-1904 .... TCLC 23
See also CANR 9; CA 21-24R, 123;
DLB 57

Stephens, James 1882?-1950 . . . . **TCLC 4**
See also CA 104; DLB 19

Stephens, Reed
See Donaldson, Stephen R.

Steptoe, Lydia 1892-1982
See Barnes, Djuna

Sterchi, Beat 1949- . . . . **CLC 65**

Sterling, Bruce 1954- . . . . **CLC 72**
See also CA 119

Sterling, George 1869-1926 . . . . **TCLC 20**
See also CA 117; DLB 54

Stern, Gerald 1925- . . . . **CLC 40**
See also CA 81-84

Stern, Richard G(ustave) 1928- . . . **CLC 4, 39**
See also CANR 1, 25; CA 1-4R; DLB 87

Sternberg, Jonas 1894-1969
See Sternberg, Josef von

Sternberg, Josef von 1894-1969 . . . . . **CLC 20**
See also CA 81-84

Sterne, Laurence 1713-1768 . . . . **LC 2**
See also DLB 39

Sternheim, (William Adolf) Carl
1878-1942 . . . . **TCLC 8**
See also CA 105

Stevens, Mark 19??- . . . . **CLC 34**

Stevens, Wallace
1879-1955 . . . . **TCLC 3, 12, 45**
See also CA 124; brief entry CA 104;
DLB 54; CDALB 1929-1941

Stevenson, Anne (Katharine)
1933- . . . . **CLC 7, 33**
See also Elvin, Anne Katharine Stevenson
See also CANR 9; CA 17-18R; DLB 40

Stevenson, Robert Louis
1850-1894 . . . . **NCLC 5, 14**
See also CLR 10, 11; YABC 2; DLB 18, 57

Stewart, J(ohn) I(nnes) M(ackintosh)
1906- . . . . **CLC 7, 14, 32**
See also CAAS 3; CA 85-88

Stewart, Mary (Florence Elinor)
1916- . . . . **CLC 7, 35**
See also CANR 1; CA 1-4R; SATA 12

Stewart, Will 1908-
See Williamson, Jack
See also CANR 23; CA 17-18R

Still, James 1906- . . . . **CLC 49**
See also CANR 10, 26; CA 65-68;
SATA 29; DLB 9

Sting 1951-
See The Police

Stitt, Milan 1941- . . . . **CLC 29**
See also CA 69-72

Stoker, Abraham
See Stoker, Bram
See also CA 105; SATA 29

Stoker, Bram 1847-1912 . . . . **TCLC 8**
See also Stoker, Abraham
See also SATA 29; DLB 36, 70

Stolz, Mary (Slattery) 1920- . . . . **CLC 12**
See also CANR 13; CA 5-8R; SAAS 3;
SATA 10

Stone, Irving 1903-1989 . . . . **CLC 7**
See also CAAS 3; CANR 1; CA 1-4R, 129;
SATA 3

Stone, Robert (Anthony)
1937?- . . . . **CLC 5, 23, 42**
See also CANR 23; CA 85-88

Stoppard, Tom
1937- . . . **CLC 1, 3, 4, 5, 8, 15, 29, 34, 63**
See also CA 81-84; DLB 13; DLB-Y 85

Storey, David (Malcolm)
1933- . . . . **CLC 2, 4, 5, 8**
See also CA 81-84; DLB 13, 14

Storm, Hyemeyohsts 1935- . . . . **CLC 3**
See also CA 81-84

Storm, (Hans) Theodor (Woldsen)
1817-1888 . . . . **NCLC 1**

Storni, Alfonsina 1892-1938 . . . . **TCLC 5**
See also CA 104

Stout, Rex (Todhunter) 1886-1975 . . . **CLC 3**
See also CA 61-64

Stow, (Julian) Randolph 1935- . . **CLC 23, 48**
See also CA 13-16R

Stowe, Harriet (Elizabeth) Beecher
1811-1896 . . . . **NCLC 3**
See also YABC 1; DLB 1, 12, 42, 74;
CDALB 1865-1917

Strachey, (Giles) Lytton
1880-1932 . . . . **TCLC 12**
See also CA 110

Strand, Mark 1934- . . . . . . **CLC 6, 18, 41, 71**
See also CA 21-24R; SATA 41; DLB 5

Straub, Peter (Francis) 1943- . . . . . . **CLC 28**
See also CA 85-88; DLB-Y 84

Strauss, Botho 1944- . . . . **CLC 22**

Straussler, Tomas 1937-
See Stoppard, Tom

Streatfeild, (Mary) Noel 1897- . . . . . **CLC 21**
See also CA 81-84; obituary CA 120;
SATA 20, 48

Stribling, T(homas) S(igismund)
1881-1965 . . . . **CLC 23**
See also obituary CA 107; DLB 9

Strindberg, (Johan) August
1849-1912 . . . . **TCLC 1, 8, 21**
See also CA 104

Stringer, Arthur 1874-1950 . . . . **TCLC 37**
See also DLB 92

Strugatskii, Arkadii (Natanovich)
1925- . . . . **CLC 27**
See also CA 106

Strugatskii, Boris (Natanovich)
1933- . . . . **CLC 27**
See also CA 106

Strummer, Joe 1953?-
See The Clash

Stuart, (Hilton) Jesse
1906-1984 . . . . **CLC 1, 8, 11, 14, 34**
See also CA 5-8R; obituary CA 112;
SATA 2; obituary SATA 36; DLB 9, 48;
DLB-Y 84

Sturgeon, Theodore (Hamilton)
1918-1985 . . . . **CLC 22, 39**
See also CA 81-84; obituary CA 116;
DLB 8; DLB-Y 85

Styron, William
1925- . . . . **CLC 1, 3, 5, 11, 15, 60**
See also CANR 6; CA 5-8R; DLB 2;
DLB-Y 80; CDALB 1968-1987

Sudermann, Hermann 1857-1928 . . **TCLC 15**
See also CA 107

Sue, Eugene 1804-1857 . . . . **NCLC 1**

Sukenick, Ronald 1932- . . . . . **CLC 3, 4, 6, 48**
See also CAAS 8; CA 25-28R; DLB-Y 81

Suknaski, Andrew 1942- . . . . **CLC 19**
See also CA 101; DLB 53

Sully Prudhomme 1839-1907 . . . . . . **TCLC 31**

Su Man-shu 1884-1918 . . . . **TCLC 24**
See also CA 123

Summers, Andrew James 1942-
See The Police

Summers, Andy 1942-
See The Police

Summers, Hollis (Spurgeon, Jr.)
1916- . . . . **CLC 10**
See also CANR 3; CA 5-8R; DLB 6

Summers, (Alphonsus Joseph-Mary Augustus)
Montague 1880-1948 . . . . **TCLC 16**
See also CA 118

Sumner, Gordon Matthew 1951-
See The Police

Surtees, Robert Smith
1805-1864 . . . . **NCLC 14**
See also DLB 21

Susann, Jacqueline 1921-1974 . . . . **CLC 3**
See also CA 65-68; obituary CA 53-56

Suskind, Patrick 1949- . . . . **CLC 44**

Sutcliff, Rosemary 1920- . . . . **CLC 26**
See also CLR 1; CA 5-8R; SATA 6, 44

Sutro, Alfred 1863-1933 . . . . **TCLC 6**
See also CA 105; DLB 10

Sutton, Henry 1935-
See Slavitt, David (R.)

Svevo, Italo 1861-1928 . . . . **TCLC 2, 35**
See also Schmitz, Ettore

Swados, Elizabeth 1951- . . . . **CLC 12**
See also CA 97-100

Swados, Harvey 1920-1972 . . . . **CLC 5**
See also CANR 6; CA 5-8R;
obituary CA 37-40R; DLB 2

Swan, Gladys 1934- . . . . **CLC 69**
See also CANR 17; CA 101

Swarthout, Glendon (Fred) 1918- . . . **CLC 35**
See also CANR 1; CA 1-4R; SATA 26

Swenson, May 1919-1989 . . . . . **CLC 4, 14, 61**
See also CA 5-8R; obituary CA 130;
SATA 15; DLB 5

Swift, Graham 1949- . . . . **CLC 41**
See also CA 117, 122

Swift, Jonathan 1667-1745 . . . . **LC 1**
See also SATA 19; DLB 39

Swinburne, Algernon Charles
1837-1909 . . . . **TCLC 8, 36**
See also CA 105; DLB 35, 57

Swinfen, Ann 19??- . . . . **CLC 34**

Swinnerton, Frank (Arthur)
1884-1982 . . . . **CLC 31**
See also obituary CA 108; DLB 34

Symonds, John Addington
1840-1893 . . . . **NCLC 34**
See also DLB 57

Author Index

Symons, Arthur (William)
1865-1945 .... **TCLC 11**
See also CA 107; DLB 19, 57

Symons, Julian (Gustave)
1912- .... **CLC 2, 14, 32**
See also CAAS 3; CANR 3; CA 49-52;
DLB 87

Synge, (Edmund) John Millington
1871-1909 .... **TCLC 6, 37; DC 2**
See also CA 104; DLB 10, 19

Syruc, J. 1911-
See Milosz, Czeslaw

Szirtes, George 1948- .... **CLC 46**
See also CANR 27; CA 109

Tabori, George 1914- .... **CLC 19**
See also CANR 4; CA 49-52

Tagore, (Sir) Rabindranath
1861-1941 .... **TCLC 3**
See also Thakura, Ravindranatha
See also CA 120

Taine, Hippolyte Adolphe
1828-1893 .... **NCLC 15**

Talese, Gaetano 1932-
See Talese, Gay

Talese, Gay 1932- .... **CLC 37**
See also CANR 9; CA 1-4R

Tallent, Elizabeth (Ann) 1954- ..... **CLC 45**
See also CA 117

Tally, Ted 1952- .... **CLC 42**
See also CA 120, 124

Tamayo y Baus, Manuel
1829-1898 .... **NCLC 1**

Tammsaare, A(nton) H(ansen)
1878-1940 .... **TCLC 27**

Tan, Amy 1952- .... **CLC 59**

Tanizaki, Jun'ichiro
1886-1965 .... **CLC 8, 14, 28**
See also CA 93-96; obituary CA 25-28R

Tarbell, Ida 1857-1944 .... **TCLC 40**
See also CA 122; DLB 47

Tarkington, (Newton) Booth
1869-1946 .... **TCLC 9**
See also CA 110; SATA 17; DLB 9

Tasso, Torquato 1544-1595 .... **LC 5**

Tate, (John Orley) Allen
1899-1979 .... **CLC 2, 4, 6, 9, 11, 14, 24**
See also CA 5-8R; obituary CA 85-88;
DLB 4, 45, 63

Tate, James 1943- .... **CLC 2, 6, 25**
See also CA 21-24R; DLB 5

Tavel, Ronald 1940- .... **CLC 6**
See also CA 21-24R

Taylor, C(ecil) P(hillip) 1929-1981 .. **CLC 27**
See also CA 25-28R; obituary CA 105

Taylor, Edward 1642?-1729 .... **LC 11**
See also DLB 24

Taylor, Eleanor Ross 1920- .... **CLC 5**
See also CA 81-84

Taylor, Elizabeth 1912-1975 ... **CLC 2, 4, 29**
See also CANR 9; CA 13-16R; SATA 13

Taylor, Henry (Splawn) 1917- ...... **CLC 44**
See also CAAS 7; CA 33-36R; DLB 5

Taylor, Kamala (Purnaiya) 1924-
See Markandaya, Kamala
See also CA 77-80

Taylor, Mildred D(elois) 1943- ..... **CLC 21**
See also CLR 9; CANR 25; CA 85-88;
SAAS 5; SATA 15; DLB 52

Taylor, Peter (Hillsman)
1917- ..... **CLC 1, 4, 18, 37, 44, 50, 71;**
SSC 10
See also CANR 9; CA 13-16R; DLB-Y 81

Taylor, Robert Lewis 1912- .... **CLC 14**
See also CANR 3; CA 1-4R; SATA 10

Teasdale, Sara 1884-1933 .... **TCLC 4**
See also CA 104; SATA 32; DLB 45

Tegner, Esaias 1782-1846 .... **NCLC 2**

Teilhard de Chardin, (Marie Joseph) Pierre
1881-1955 .... **TCLC 9**
See also CA 105

Tennant, Emma 1937- .... **CLC 13, 52**
See also CAAS 9; CANR 10; CA 65-68;
DLB 14

Tennyson, Alfred 1809-1892 ..... **NCLC 30**
See also DLB 32

Teran, Lisa St. Aubin de 19??- ..... **CLC 36**

Teresa de Jesus, St. 1515-1582 ...... **LC 18**

Terkel, Louis 1912-
See Terkel, Studs
See also CANR 18; CA 57-60

Terkel, Studs 1912- .... **CLC 38**
See also Terkel, Louis

Terry, Megan 1932- .... **CLC 19**
See also CA 77-80; CABS 3; DLB 7

Tertz, Abram 1925-
See Sinyavsky, Andrei (Donatevich)

Tesich, Steve 1943?- .... **CLC 40, 69**
See also CA 105; DLB-Y 83

Tesich, Stoyan 1943?-
See Tesich, Steve

Teternikov, Fyodor Kuzmich 1863-1927
See Sologub, Fyodor
See also CA 104

Tevis, Walter 1928-1984 .... **CLC 42**
See also CA 113

Tey, Josephine 1897-1952 .... **TCLC 14**
See also Mackintosh, Elizabeth

Thackeray, William Makepeace
1811-1863 .... **NCLC 5, 14, 22**
See also SATA 23; DLB 21, 55

Thakura, Ravindranatha 1861-1941
See Tagore, (Sir) Rabindranath
See also CA 104

Tharoor, Shashi 1956- .... **CLC 70**

Thelwell, Michael (Miles) 1939- .... **CLC 22**
See also CA 101

Theroux, Alexander (Louis)
1939- .... **CLC 2, 25**
See also CANR 20; CA 85-88

Theroux, Paul
1941- .... **CLC 5, 8, 11, 15, 28, 46**
See also CANR 20; CA 33-36R; SATA 44;
DLB 2

Thesen, Sharon 1946- .... **CLC 56**

Thibault, Jacques Anatole Francois
1844-1924
See France, Anatole
See also CA 106

Thiele, Colin (Milton) 1920- .... **CLC 17**
See also CANR 12; CA 29-32R; SAAS 2;
SATA 14

Thomas, Audrey (Grace)
1935- .... **CLC 7, 13, 37**
See also CA 21-24R; DLB 60

Thomas, D(onald) M(ichael)
1935- .... **CLC 13, 22, 31**
See also CANR 17; CA 61-64; DLB 40

Thomas, Dylan (Marlais)
1914-1953 .... **TCLC 1, 8, 45; PC 2;**
SSC 3
See also CA 120; brief entry CA 104;
SATA 60; DLB 13, 20

Thomas, Edward (Philip)
1878-1917 .... **TCLC 10**
See also CA 106; DLB 19

Thomas, John Peter 1928-
See Thomas, Piri

Thomas, Joyce Carol 1938- .... **CLC 35**
See also CLR 19; CA 113, 116; SAAS 7;
SATA 40; DLB 33

Thomas, Lewis 1913- .... **CLC 35**
See also CA 85-88

Thomas, Piri 1928- .... **CLC 17**
See also CA 73-76

Thomas, R(onald) S(tuart)
1913- .... **CLC 6, 13, 48**
See also CAAS 4; CA 89-92; DLB 27

Thomas, Ross (Elmore) 1926- ...... **CLC 39**
See also CANR 22; CA 33-36R

Thompson, Ernest 1860-1946
See Seton, Ernest (Evan) Thompson

Thompson, Francis (Joseph)
1859-1907 .... **TCLC 4**
See also CA 104; DLB 19

Thompson, Hunter S(tockton)
1939- .... **CLC 9, 17, 40**
See also CANR 23; CA 17-20R

Thompson, James Meyers 1906-1976
See Thompson, Jim

Thompson, Jim 1906-1976 .... **CLC 69**

Thompson, Judith 1954- .... **CLC 39**

Thomson, James 1700-1748 .... **LC 16**
See also DLB 95

Thomson, James 1834-1882 ...... **NCLC 18**
See also DLB 35

Thoreau, Henry David
1817-1862 .... **NCLC 7, 21**
See also DLB 1; CDALB 1640-1865

Thurber, James (Grover)
1894-1961 .... **CLC 5, 11, 25; SSC 1**
See also CANR 17; CA 73-76; SATA 13;
DLB 4, 11, 22

Thurman, Wallace 1902-1934 ...... **TCLC 6**
See also BLC 3; CA 104, 124; DLB 51

Tieck, (Johann) Ludwig
1773-1853 .... **NCLC 5**
See also DLB 90

Tilghman, Christopher 1948?- ...... **CLC 65**

Tillinghast, Richard 1940- .... CLC 29
See also CANR 26; CA 29-32R

Timrod, Henry 1828-1867 ...... NCLC 25

Tindall, Gillian 1938- .... CLC 7
See also CANR 11; CA 21-24R

Tiptree, James, Jr. 1915-1987 ... CLC 48, 50
See also Sheldon, Alice (Hastings) B(radley)
See also DLB 8

Tocqueville, Alexis (Charles Henri Maurice
Clerel, Comte) de 1805-1859.. NCLC 7

Tolkien, J(ohn) R(onald) R(euel)
1892-1973 .... CLC 1, 2, 3, 8, 12, 38
See also CAP 2; CA 17-18;
obituary CA 45-48; SATA 2, 24, 32;
obituary SATA 24; DLB 15

Toller, Ernst 1893-1939 .... TCLC 10
See also CA 107

Tolson, Melvin B(eaunorus)
1898?-1966................... CLC 36
See also BLC 3; CA 124;
obituary CA 89-92; DLB 48, 76

Tolstoy, (Count) Alexey Nikolayevich
1883-1945 .... TCLC 18
See also CA 107

Tolstoy, (Count) Leo (Lev Nikolaevich)
1828-1910 ..... TCLC 4, 11, 17, 28, 44;
SSC 9
See also CA 104, 123; SATA 26

Tomlin, Lily 1939- .... CLC 17

Tomlin, Mary Jean 1939-
See Tomlin, Lily
See also CA 117

Tomlinson, (Alfred) Charles
1927- .... CLC 2, 4, 6, 13, 45
See also CA 5-8R; DLB 40

Toole, John Kennedy
1937-1969 .... CLC 19, 64
See also CA 104; DLB-Y 81

Toomer, Jean
1894-1967 ..... CLC 1, 4, 13, 22; SSC 1
See also BLC 3; CA 85-88; DLB 45, 51;
CDALB 1917-1929

Torrey, E. Fuller 19??-............ CLC 34
See also CA 119

Tosei 1644-1694
See Basho, Matsuo

Tournier, Michel 1924- ...... CLC 6, 23, 36
See also CANR 3; CA 49-52; SATA 23;
DLB 83

Townsend, Sue 1946- .... CLC 61
See also CA 119, 127; SATA 48, 55

Townshend, Peter (Dennis Blandford)
1945- .... CLC 17, 42
See also CA 107

Tozzi, Federigo 1883-1920 .... TCLC 31

Traill, Catharine Parr
1802-1899 .... NCLC 31
See also DLB 99

Trakl, Georg 1887-1914 .... TCLC 5
See also CA 104

Transtromer, Tomas (Gosta)
1931- .... CLC 52, 65
See also CA 129; brief entry CA 117

Traven, B. 1890-1969 .... CLC 8, 11
See also CAP 2; CA 19-20;
obituary CA 25-28R; DLB 9, 56

Treitel, Jonathan 1959- .... CLC 70

Tremain, Rose 1943-.............. CLC 42
See also CA 97-100; DLB 14

Tremblay, Michel 1942-........... CLC 29
See also CA 116; DLB 60

Trevanian 1925- .... CLC 29
See also CA 108

Trevor, William 1928- ..... CLC 7, 9, 14, 25
See also Cox, William Trevor
See also DLB 14

Trifonov, Yuri (Valentinovich)
1925-1981 .... CLC 45
See also obituary CA 103, 126

Trilling, Lionel 1905-1975 .... CLC 9, 11, 24
See also CANR 10; CA 9-12R;
obituary CA 61-64; DLB 28, 63

Trogdon, William 1939-
See Heat Moon, William Least
See also CA 115, 119

Trollope, Anthony 1815-1882 .. NCLC 6, 33
See also SATA 22; DLB 21, 57

Trollope, Frances 1780-1863 ..... NCLC 30
See also DLB 21

Trotsky, Leon (Davidovich)
1879-1940 .... TCLC 22
See also CA 118

Trotter (Cockburn), Catharine
1679-1749 .... LC 8
See also DLB 84

Trow, George W. S. 1943-......... CLC 52
See also CA 126

Troyat, Henri 1911-.............. CLC 23
See also CANR 2; CA 45-48

Trudeau, G(arretson) B(eekman) 1948-
See Trudeau, Garry
See also CA 81-84; SATA 35

Trudeau, Garry 1948-............. CLC 12
See also Trudeau, G(arretson) B(eekman)

Truffaut, Francois 1932-1984....... CLC 20
See also CA 81-84; obituary CA 113

Trumbo, Dalton 1905-1976 .... CLC 19
See also CANR 10; CA 21-24R;
obituary CA 69-72; DLB 26

Trumbull, John 1750-1831 .... NCLC 30
See also DLB 31

Tryon, Thomas 1926- .... CLC 3, 11
See also CA 29-32R

Ts'ao Hsueh-ch'in 1715?-1763 .... LC 1

Tse, Isaac 1904-1991
See Singer, Isaac Bashevis

Tsushima Shuji 1909-1948
See Dazai Osamu
See also CA 107

Tsvetaeva (Efron), Marina (Ivanovna)
1892-1941 .... TCLC 7, 35
See also CA 104, 128

Tuck, Lily 1938-................ CLC 70

Tunis, John R(oberts) 1889-1975 ... CLC 12
See also CA 61-64; SATA 30, 37; DLB 22

Tuohy, Frank 1925- .... CLC 37
See also DLB 14

Tuohy, John Francis 1925-
See Tuohy, Frank
See also CANR 3; CA 5-8R

Turco, Lewis (Putnam) 1934- ... CLC 11, 63
See also CANR 24; CA 13-16R; DLB-Y 84

Turgenev, Ivan
1818-1883 .... NCLC 21; SSC 7

Turner, Frederick 1943-........... CLC 48
See also CANR 12; CA 73-76; DLB 40

Tutu, Desmond 1931-
See also BLC 3; CA 125

Tutuola, Amos 1920- .... CLC 5, 14, 29
See also BLC 3; CANR 27; CA 9-12R

Twain, Mark
1835-1910 ... TCLC 6, 12, 19, 36; SSC 6
See also Clemens, Samuel Langhorne
See also YABC 2; DLB 11, 12, 23, 64, 74

Tyler, Anne
1941-........ CLC 7, 11, 18, 28, 44, 59
See also CANR 11; CA 9-12R; SATA 7;
DLB 6; DLB-Y 82

Tyler, Royall 1757-1826......... NCLC 3
See also DLB 37

Tynan (Hinkson), Katharine
1861-1931 .... TCLC 3
See also CA 104

Tytell, John 1939- .... CLC 50
See also CA 29-32R

Tyutchev, Fyodor 1803-1873 ..... NCLC 34

Tzara, Tristan 1896-1963.......... CLC 47
See also Rosenfeld, Samuel

Uhry, Alfred 1947?-.............. CLC 55
See also CA 127

Unamuno (y Jugo), Miguel de
1864-1936 .... TCLC 2, 9
See also CA 104

Underwood, Miles 1909-1981
See Glassco, John

Undset, Sigrid 1882-1949....... TCLC 3
See also CA 104

Ungaretti, Giuseppe
1888-1970 .... CLC 7, 11, 15
See also CAP 2; CA 19-20;
obituary CA 25-28R

Unger, Douglas 1952-............. CLC 34
See also CA 130

Unger, Eva 1932-
See Figes, Eva

Updike, John (Hoyer)
1932- ...... CLC 1, 2, 3, 5, 7, 9, 13, 15,
23, 34, 43, 70
See also CANR 4, 33; CA 1-4R; CABS 1;
DLB 2, 5; DLB-Y 80, 82; DLB-DS 3;
CDALB 1968-1988

Urdang, Constance (Henriette)
1922-...................... CLC 47
See also CANR 9, 24; CA 21-24R

Uris, Leon (Marcus) 1924-....... CLC 7, 32
See also CANR 1; CA 1-4R; SATA 49

Ustinov, Peter (Alexander) 1921- .... CLC 1
See also CANR 25; CA 13-16R; DLB 13

Vaculik, Ludvik 1926- . . . . **CLC 7**
See also CA 53-56

Valenzuela, Luisa 1938- . . . . **CLC 31**
See also CA 101

Valera (y Acala-Galiano), Juan
1824-1905 . . . . **TCLC 10**
See also CA 106

Valery, Paul (Ambroise Toussaint Jules)
1871-1945 . . . . **TCLC 4, 15**
See also CA 104, 122

Valle-Inclan (y Montenegro), Ramon (Maria)
del 1866-1936 . . . . **TCLC 5**
See also CA 106

Vallejo, Cesar (Abraham)
1892-1938 . . . . **TCLC 3**
See also CA 105

Van Ash, Cay 1918- . . . . **CLC 34**

Vance, Jack 1916?- . . . . **CLC 35**
See also DLB 8

Vance, John Holbrook 1916?-
See Vance, Jack
See also CANR 17; CA 29-32R

Van Den Bogarde, Derek (Jules Gaspard
Ulric) Niven 1921-
See Bogarde, Dirk
See also CA 77-80

Vandenburgh, Jane 19??- . . . . **CLC 59**

Vanderhaeghe, Guy 1951- . . . . **CLC 41**
See also CA 113

Van der Post, Laurens (Jan) 1906- . . . **CLC 5**
See also CA 5-8R

Van de Wetering, Janwillem
1931- . . . . **CLC 47**
See also CANR 4; CA 49-52

Van Dine, S. S. 1888-1939 . . . . **TCLC 23**

Van Doren, Carl (Clinton)
1885-1950 . . . . **TCLC 18**
See also CA 111

Van Doren, Mark 1894-1972 . . . . . **CLC 6, 10**
See also CANR 3; CA 1-4R;
obituary CA 37-40R; DLB 45

Van Druten, John (William)
1901-1957 . . . . **TCLC 2**
See also CA 104; DLB 10

Van Duyn, Mona 1921- . . . . **CLC 3, 7, 63**
See also CANR 7; CA 9-12R; DLB 5

Van Itallie, Jean-Claude 1936- . . . . . . **CLC 3**
See also CAAS 2; CANR 1; CA 45-48;
DLB 7

Van Ostaijen, Paul 1896-1928 . . . . . **TCLC 33**

Van Peebles, Melvin 1932- . . . . . . **CLC 2, 20**
See also CA 85-88

Vansittart, Peter 1920- . . . . **CLC 42**
See also CANR 3; CA 1-4R

Van Vechten, Carl 1880-1964 . . . . . . **CLC 33**
See also obituary CA 89-92; DLB 4, 9, 51

Van Vogt, A(lfred) E(lton) 1912- . . . . . **CLC 1**
See also CANR 28; CA 21-24R; SATA 14;
DLB 8

Varda, Agnes 1928- . . . . **CLC 16**
See also CA 116, 122

Vargas Llosa, (Jorge) Mario (Pedro)
1936- . . . . **CLC 3, 6, 9, 10, 15, 31, 42**
See also CANR 18; CA 73-76

Vassa, Gustavus 1745?-1797
See Equiano, Olaudah

Vassilikos, Vassilis 1933- . . . . **CLC 4, 8**
See also CA 81-84

Vaughn, Stephanie 19??- . . . . **CLC 62**

Vazov, Ivan 1850-1921 . . . . **TCLC 25**
See also CA 121

Veblen, Thorstein Bunde
1857-1929 . . . . **TCLC 31**
See also CA 115

Verga, Giovanni 1840-1922 . . . . **TCLC 3**
See also CA 104, 123

Vergil 70 B.C.-19 B.C. . . . . **CMLC 9**

Verhaeren, Emile (Adolphe Gustave)
1855-1916 . . . . **TCLC 12**
See also CA 109

Verlaine, Paul (Marie)
1844-1896 . . . . **NCLC 2; PC 2**

Verne, Jules (Gabriel) 1828-1905 . . . **TCLC 6**
See also CA 110; SATA 21

Very, Jones 1813-1880 . . . . **NCLC 9**
See also DLB 1

Vesaas, Tarjei 1897-1970 . . . . **CLC 48**
See also obituary CA 29-32R

Vian, Boris 1920-1959 . . . . **TCLC 9**
See also CA 106; DLB 72

Viaud, (Louis Marie) Julien 1850-1923
See Loti, Pierre
See also CA 107

Vicker, Angus 1916-
See Felsen, Henry Gregor

Vidal, Eugene Luther, Jr. 1925-
See Vidal, Gore

Vidal, Gore
1925- . . . . . **CLC 2, 4, 6, 8, 10, 22, 33, 72**
See also CANR 13; CA 5-8R; DLB 6

Viereck, Peter (Robert Edwin)
1916- . . . . **CLC 4**
See also CANR 1; CA 1-4R; DLB 5

Vigny, Alfred (Victor) de
1797-1863 . . . . **NCLC 7**

Vilakazi, Benedict Wallet
1905-1947 . . . . **TCLC 37**

Villiers de l'Isle Adam, Jean Marie Mathias
Philippe Auguste, Comte de
1838-1889 . . . . **NCLC 3**

Vinci, Leonardo da 1452-1519 . . . . . . **LC 12**

Vine, Barbara 1930- . . . . **CLC 50**
See also Rendell, Ruth

Vinge, Joan (Carol) D(ennison)
1948- . . . . **CLC 30**
See also CA 93-96; SATA 36

Visconti, Luchino 1906-1976 . . . . **CLC 16**
See also CA 81-84; obituary CA 65-68

Vittorini, Elio 1908-1966 . . . . . . **CLC 6, 9, 14**
See also obituary CA 25-28R

Vizinczey, Stephen 1933- . . . . **CLC 40**

Vliet, R(ussell) G(ordon)
1929-1984 . . . . **CLC 22**
See also CANR 18; CA 37-40R;
obituary CA 112

Voight, Ellen Bryant 1943- . . . . **CLC 54**
See also CANR 11; CA 69-72

Voigt, Cynthia 1942- . . . . **CLC 30**
See also CANR 18; CA 106; SATA 33, 48;
AAYA 3

Voinovich, Vladimir (Nikolaevich)
1932- . . . . **CLC 10, 49**
See also CA 81-84

Voltaire 1694-1778 . . . . **LC 14**

Von Daeniken, Erich 1935-
See Von Daniken, Erich
See also CANR 17; CA 37-40R

Von Daniken, Erich 1935- . . . . **CLC 30**
See also Von Daeniken, Erich

Vonnegut, Kurt, Jr.
1922- . . . . . . **CLC 1, 2, 3, 4, 5, 8, 12, 22,**
40, 60; SSC 8
See also CANR 1, 25; CA 1-4R; DLB 2, 8;
DLB-Y 80; DLB-DS 3;
CDALB 1968-1988; AAYA 6

Vorster, Gordon 1924- . . . . **CLC 34**

Voznesensky, Andrei 1933- . . . **CLC 1, 15, 57**
See also CA 89-92

Waddington, Miriam 1917- . . . . **CLC 28**
See also CANR 12, 30; CA 21-24R;
DLB 68

Wagman, Fredrica 1937- . . . . **CLC 7**
See also CA 97-100

Wagner, Richard 1813-1883 . . . . . . **NCLC 9**

Wagner-Martin, Linda 1936- . . . . **CLC 50**

Wagoner, David (Russell)
1926- . . . . **CLC 3, 5, 15**
See also CAAS 3; CANR 2; CA 1-4R;
SATA 14; DLB 5

Wah, Fred(erick James) 1939- . . . . . . **CLC 44**
See also CA 107; DLB 60

Wahloo, Per 1926-1975 . . . . **CLC 7**
See also CA 61-64

Wahloo, Peter 1926-1975
See Wahloo, Per

Wain, John (Barrington)
1925- . . . . **CLC 2, 11, 15, 46**
See also CAAS 4; CANR 23; CA 5-8R;
DLB 15, 27

Wajda, Andrzej 1926- . . . . **CLC 16**
See also CA 102

Wakefield, Dan 1932- . . . . **CLC 7**
See also CAAS 7; CA 21-24R

Wakoski, Diane
1937- . . . . **CLC 2, 4, 7, 9, 11, 40**
See also CAAS 1; CANR 9; CA 13-16R;
DLB 5

Walcott, Derek (Alton)
1930- . . . . **CLC 2, 4, 9, 14, 25, 42, 67**
See also BLC 3; CANR 26; CA 89-92;
DLB-Y 81

Waldman, Anne 1945- . . . . **CLC 7**
See also CA 37-40R; DLB 16

Waldo, Edward Hamilton 1918-
See Sturgeon, Theodore (Hamilton)

Walker, Alice
1944- . . . . . . **CLC 5, 6, 9, 19, 27, 46, 58;**
SSC 5
See also BLC 3; CANR 9, 27; CA 37-40R;
SATA 31; DLB 6, 33;
CDALB 1968-1988; AAYA 3**

Walker, David Harry 1911- .... **CLC 14**
See also CANR 1; CA 1-4R; SATA 8

Walker, Edward Joseph 1934-
See Walker, Ted
See also CANR 12; CA 21-24R

Walker, George F. 1947- .... **CLC 44, 61**
See also CANR 21; CA 103; DLB 60

Walker, Joseph A. 1935- .... **CLC 19**
See also CANR 26; CA 89-92; DLB 38

Walker, Margaret (Abigail)
1915- .... **CLC 1, 6**
See also BLC 3; CANR 26; CA 73-76;
DLB 76

Walker, Ted 1934- .... **CLC 13**
See also Walker, Edward Joseph
See also DLB 40

Wallace, David Foster 1962- .... **CLC 50**

Wallace, Irving 1916- .... **CLC 7, 13**
See also CAAS 1; CANR 1; CA 1-4R

Wallant, Edward Lewis
1926-1962 .... **CLC 5, 10**
See also CANR 22; CA 1-4R; DLB 2, 28

Walpole, Horace 1717-1797 .... **LC 2**
See also DLB 39

Walpole, (Sir) Hugh (Seymour)
1884-1941 .... **TCLC 5**
See also CA 104; DLB 34

Walser, Martin 1927- .... **CLC 27**
See also CANR 8; CA 57-60; DLB 75

Walser, Robert 1878-1956 .... **TCLC 18**
See also CA 118; DLB 66

Walsh, Gillian Paton 1939-
See Walsh, Jill Paton
See also CA 37-40R; SATA 4

Walsh, Jill Paton 1939- .... **CLC 35**
See also CLR 2; SAAS 3

Wambaugh, Joseph (Aloysius, Jr.)
1937- .... **CLC 3, 18**
See also CA 33-36R; DLB 6; DLB-Y 83

Ward, Arthur Henry Sarsfield 1883-1959
See Rohmer, Sax
See also CA 108

Ward, Douglas Turner 1930- .... **CLC 19**
See also CA 81-84; DLB 7, 38

Warhol, Andy 1928-1987 .... **CLC 20**
See also CA 89-92; obituary CA 121

Warner, Francis (Robert le Plastrier)
1937- .... **CLC 14**
See also CANR 11; CA 53-56

Warner, Marina 1946- .... **CLC 59**
See also CANR 21; CA 65-68

Warner, Rex (Ernest) 1905-1986 .... **CLC 45**
See also CA 89-92; obituary CA 119;
DLB 15

Warner, Susan 1819-1885 .... **NCLC 31**
See also DLB 3, 42

Warner, Sylvia Townsend
1893-1978 .... **CLC 7, 19**
See also CANR 16; CA 61-64;
obituary CA 77-80; DLB 34

Warren, Mercy Otis 1728-1814 ... **NCLC 13**
See also DLB 31

Warren, Robert Penn
1905-1989 ... **CLC 1, 4, 6, 8, 10, 13, 18,
39, 53, 59; SSC 4**
See also CANR 10; CA 13-16R. 129. 130;
SATA 46; DLB 2, 48; DLB-Y 80;
CDALB 1968-1987

Warshofsky, Isaac 1904-1991
See Singer, Isaac Bashevis

Warton, Thomas 1728-1790 .... **LC 15**

Warung, Price 1855-1911 .... **TCLC 45**

Washington, Booker T(aliaferro)
1856-1915 .... **TCLC 10**
See also BLC 3; CA 114, 125; SATA 28

Wassermann, Jakob 1873-1934 ..... **TCLC 6**
See also CA 104; DLB 66

Wasserstein, Wendy 1950- ...... **CLC 32, 59**
See also CA 121; CABS 3

Waterhouse, Keith (Spencer)
1929- .... **CLC 47**
See also CA 5-8R; DLB 13, 15

Waters, Roger 1944-
See Pink Floyd

Wa Thiong'o, Ngugi
1938- .... **CLC 3, 7, 13, 36**
See also Ngugi, James (Thiong'o); Ngugi wa
Thiong'o

Watkins, Paul 1964- .... **CLC 55**

Watkins, Vernon (Phillips)
1906-1967 .... **CLC 43**
See also CAP 1; CA 9-10;
obituary CA 25-28R; DLB 20

Waugh, Auberon (Alexander) 1939- .. **CLC 7**
See also CANR 6, 22; CA 45-48; DLB 14

Waugh, Evelyn (Arthur St. John)
1903-1966 ... **CLC 1, 3, 8, 13, 19, 27, 44**
See also CANR 22; CA 85-88;
obituary CA 25-28R; DLB 15

Waugh, Harriet 1944- .... **CLC 6**
See also CANR 22; CA 85-88

Webb, Beatrice (Potter)
1858-1943 .... **TCLC 22**
See also CA 117

Webb, Charles (Richard) 1939- ...... **CLC 7**
See also CA 25-28R

Webb, James H(enry), Jr. 1946- .... **CLC 22**
See also CA 81-84

Webb, Mary (Gladys Meredith)
1881-1927 .... **TCLC 24**
See also CA 123; DLB 34

Webb, Phyllis 1927- .... **CLC 18**
See also CANR 23; CA 104; DLB 53

Webb, Sidney (James)
1859-1947 .... **TCLC 22**
See also CA 117

Webber, Andrew Lloyd 1948- ...... **CLC 21**

Weber, Lenora Mattingly
1895-1971 .... **CLC 12**
See also CAP 1; CA 19-20;
obituary CA 29-32R; SATA 2;
obituary SATA 26

Webster, John 1580?-1634? .... **DC 2**
See also DLB 58

Webster, Noah 1758-1843 .... **NCLC 30**
See also DLB 1, 37, 42, 43, 73

Wedekind, (Benjamin) Frank(lin)
1864-1918 .... **TCLC 7**
See also CA 104

Weidman, Jerome 1913- .... **CLC 7**
See also CANR 1; CA 1-4R; DLB 28

Weil, Simone 1909-1943 .... **TCLC 23**
See also CA 117

Weinstein, Nathan Wallenstein 1903-1940
See West, Nathanael

Weir, Peter 1944- .... **CLC 20**
See also CA 113, 123

Weiss, Peter (Ulrich)
1916-1982 .... **CLC 3, 15, 51**
See also CANR 3; CA 45-48;
obituary CA 106; DLB 69

Weiss, Theodore (Russell)
1916- .... **CLC 3, 8, 14**
See also CAAS 2; CA 9-12R; DLB 5

Welch, (Maurice) Denton
1915-1948 .... **TCLC 22**
See also CA 121

Welch, James 1940- .... **CLC 6, 14, 52**
See also CA 85-88

Weldon, Fay
1933- .... **CLC 6, 9, 11, 19, 36, 59**
See also CANR 16; CA 21-24R; DLB 14

Wellek, Rene 1903- .... **CLC 28**
See also CAAS 7; CANR 8; CA 5-8R;
DLB 63

Weller, Michael 1942- .... **CLC 10, 53**
See also CA 85-88

Weller, Paul 1958- .... **CLC 26**

Wellershoff, Dieter 1925- .... **CLC 46**
See also CANR 16; CA 89-92

Welles, (George) Orson
1915-1985 .... **CLC 20**
See also CA 93-96; obituary CA 117

Wellman, Mac 1945- .... **CLC 65**

Wellman, Manly Wade 1903-1986 .. **CLC 49**
See also CANR 6, 16; CA 1-4R;
obituary CA 118; SATA 6, 47

Wells, Carolyn 1862-1942 .... **TCLC 35**
See also CA 113; DLB 11

Wells, H(erbert) G(eorge)
1866-1946 ...... **TCLC 6, 12, 19; SSC 6**
See also CA 110, 121; SATA 20; DLB 34,
70

Wells, Rosemary 1943- .... **CLC 12**
See also CLR 16; CA 85-88; SAAS 1;
SATA 18

Welty, Eudora (Alice)
1909- .... **CLC 1, 2, 5, 14, 22, 33; SSC 1**
See also CA 9-12R; CABS 1; DLB 2;
DLB-Y 87; CDALB 1941-1968

Wen I-to 1899-1946 .... **TCLC 28**

Werfel, Franz (V.) 1890-1945 ...... **TCLC 8**
See also CA 104; DLB 81

Wergeland, Henrik Arnold
1808-1845 .... **NCLC 5**

Wersba, Barbara 1932- .... **CLC 30**
See also CLR 3; CANR 16; CA 29-32R;
SAAS 2; SATA 1, 58; DLB 52

Wertmuller, Lina 1928- .... **CLC 16**
See also CA 97-100

Wescott, Glenway 1901-1987...... **CLC 13**
See also CANR 23; CA 13-16R;
obituary CA 121; DLB 4, 9

Wesker, Arnold 1932- .... **CLC 3, 5, 42**
See also CAAS 7; CANR 1; CA 1-4R;
DLB 13

Wesley, Richard (Errol) 1945-...... **CLC 7**
See also CA 57-60; DLB 38

Wessel, Johan Herman 1742-1785 .... **LC 7**

West, Anthony (Panther)
1914-1987 .... **CLC 50**
See also CANR 3, 19; CA 45-48; DLB 15

West, Jessamyn 1907-1984 ...... **CLC 7, 17**
See also CA 9-12R; obituary CA 112;
obituary SATA 37; DLB 6; DLB-Y 84

West, Morris L(anglo) 1916-..... **CLC 6, 33**
See also CA 5-8R; obituary CA 124

West, Nathanael
1903-1940 .... **TCLC 1, 14, 44**
See also CA 104, 125; DLB 4, 9, 28;
CDALB 1929-1941

West, Paul 1930- .... **CLC 7, 14**
See also CAAS 7; CANR 22; CA 13-16R;
DLB 14

West, Rebecca 1892-1983 .. **CLC 7, 9, 31, 50**
See also CANR 19; CA 5-8R;
obituary CA 109; DLB 36; DLB-Y 83

Westall, Robert (Atkinson) 1929-... **CLC 17**
See also CLR 13; CANR 18; CA 69-72;
SAAS 2; SATA 23

Westlake, Donald E(dwin)
1933-..................... **CLC 7, 33**
See also CANR 16; CA 17-20R

Westmacott, Mary 1890-1976
See Christie, (Dame) Agatha (Mary
Clarissa)

Whalen, Philip 1923- .... **CLC 6, 29**
See also CANR 5; CA 9-12R; DLB 16

Wharton, Edith (Newbold Jones)
1862-1937 .... **TCLC 3, 9, 27; SSC 6**
See also CA 104; DLB 4, 9, 12, 78;
CDALB 1865-1917

Wharton, William 1925-........ **CLC 18, 37**
See also CA 93-96; DLB-Y 80

Wheatley (Peters), Phillis
1753?-1784.............. **LC 3; PC 3**
See also BLC 3; DLB 31, 50;
CDALB 1640-1865

Wheelock, John Hall 1886-1978.... **CLC 14**
See also CANR 14; CA 13-16R;
obituary CA 77-80; DLB 45

Whelan, John 1900-
See O'Faolain, Sean

Whitaker, Rodney 1925-
See Trevanian

White, E(lwyn) B(rooks)
1899-1985 .... **CLC 10, 34, 39**
See also CLR 1; CANR 16; CA 13-16R;
obituary CA 116; SATA 2, 29, 44;
obituary SATA 44; DLB 11, 22

White, Edmund III 1940-......... **CLC 27**
See also CANR 3, 19; CA 45-48

White, Patrick (Victor Martindale)
1912-1990 .. **CLC 3, 4, 5, 7, 9, 18, 65, 69**
See also CA 81-84; obituary CA 132

White, T(erence) H(anbury)
1906-1964 .... **CLC 30**
See also CA 73-76; SATA 12

White, Terence de Vere 1912-...... **CLC 49**
See also CANR 3; CA 49-52

White, Walter (Francis)
1893-1955 .... **TCLC 15**
See also BLC 3; CA 115, 124; DLB 51

White, William Hale 1831-1913
See Rutherford, Mark
See also CA 121

Whitehead, E(dward) A(nthony)
1933-....................... **CLC 5**
See also CA 65-68

Whitemore, Hugh 1936-........... **CLC 37**

Whitman, Sarah Helen
1803-1878 .... **NCLC 19**
See also DLB 1

Whitman, Walt
1819-1892 .... **NCLC 4, 31; PC 3**
See also SATA 20; DLB 3, 64;
CDALB 1640-1865

Whitney, Phyllis A(yame) 1903-.... **CLC 42**
See also CANR 3, 25; CA 1-4R; SATA 1,
30

Whittemore, (Edward) Reed (Jr.)
1919-....................... **CLC 4**
See also CAAS 8; CANR 4; CA 9-12R;
DLB 5

Whittier, John Greenleaf
1807-1892 .... **NCLC 8**
See also DLB 1; CDALB 1640-1865

Wicker, Thomas Grey 1926-
See Wicker, Tom
See also CANR 21; CA 65-68

Wicker, Tom 1926-................ **CLC 7**
See also Wicker, Thomas Grey

Wideman, John Edgar
1941-.............. **CLC 5, 34, 36, 67**
See also BLC 3; CANR 14; CA 85-88;
DLB 33

Wiebe, Rudy (H.) 1934-...... **CLC 6, 11, 14**
See also CA 37-40R; DLB 60

Wieland, Christoph Martin
1733-1813 .... **NCLC 17**

Wieners, John 1934-.............. **CLC 7**
See also CA 13-16R; DLB 16

Wiesel, Elie(zer) 1928-..... **CLC 3, 5, 11, 37**
See also CAAS 4; CANR 8; CA 5-8R;
SATA 56; DLB 83; DLB-Y 87

Wiggins, Marianne 1948-.......... **CLC 57**

Wight, James Alfred 1916-
See Herriot, James
See also CA 77-80; SATA 44

Wilbur, Richard (Purdy)
1921-.............. **CLC 3, 6, 9, 14, 53**
See also CANR 2; CA 1-4R; CABS 2;
SATA 9; DLB 5

Wild, Peter 1940-................ **CLC 14**
See also CA 37-40R; DLB 5

Wilde, Oscar (Fingal O'Flahertie Wills)
1854-1900 .... **TCLC 1, 8, 23, 41**
See also CA 119; brief entry CA 104;
SATA 24; DLB 10, 19, 34, 57

Wilder, Billy 1906-.............. **CLC 20**
See also Wilder, Samuel
See also DLB 26

Wilder, Samuel 1906-
See Wilder, Billy
See also CA 89-92

Wilder, Thornton (Niven)
1897-1975 ..... **CLC 1, 5, 6, 10, 15, 35;
DC 1**
See also CA 13-16R; obituary CA 61-64;
DLB 4, 7, 9

Wiley, Richard 1944-............. **CLC 44**
See also CA 121, 129

Wilhelm, Kate 1928-.............. **CLC 7**
See also CAAS 5; CANR 17; CA 37-40R;
DLB 8

Willard, Nancy 1936-........... **CLC 7, 37**
See also CLR 5; CANR 10; CA 89-92;
SATA 30, 37; DLB 5, 52

Williams, C(harles) K(enneth)
1936-.................... **CLC 33, 56**
See also CA 37-40R; DLB 5

Williams, Charles (Walter Stansby)
1886-1945 .... **TCLC 1, 11**
See also CA 104

Williams, Ella Gwendolen Rees 1890-1979
See Rhys, Jean

Williams, (George) Emlyn
1905-1987 .... **CLC 15**
See also CA 104, 123; DLB 10, 77

Williams, Hugo 1942-............. **CLC 42**
See also CA 17-20R; DLB 40

Williams, John A(lfred) 1925-.... **CLC 5, 13**
See also BLC 3; CAAS 3; CANR 6, 26;
CA 53-56; DLB 2, 33

Williams, Jonathan (Chamberlain)
1929-..................... **CLC 13**
See also CANR 8; CA 9-12R; DLB 5

Williams, Joy 1944-.............. **CLC 31**
See also CANR 22; CA 41-44R

Williams, Norman 1952- .... **CLC 39**
See also CA 118

Williams, Paulette 1948-
See Shange, Ntozake

Williams, Sherley Anne 1944-
See also BLC 3; CANR 25; CA 73-76;
DLB 41

Williams, Shirley 1944-
See Williams, Sherley Anne

Williams, Tennessee
1911-1983 .... **CLC 1, 2, 5, 7, 8, 11, 15,
19, 30, 39, 45, 71**
See also CANR 31; CA 5-8R;
obituary CA 108; CABS 3; DLB 7;
DLB-Y 83; DLB-DS 4;
CDALB 1941-1968

Williams, Thomas (Alonzo) 1926-... **CLC 14**
See also CANR 2; CA 1-4R

Williams, Thomas Lanier 1911-1983
See Williams, Tennessee

Williams, William Carlos
1883-1963 ... **CLC 1, 2, 5, 9, 13, 22, 42,
67**
See also CA 89-92; DLB 4, 16, 54, 86;
CDALB 1917-1929

Williamson, David 1932- . . . . **CLC 56**

Williamson, Jack 1908- . . . . **CLC 29**
  See also Williamson, John Stewart
  See also DLB 8

Williamson, John Stewart 1908-
  See Williamson, Jack
  See also CANR 123; CA 17-20R

Willingham, Calder (Baynard, Jr.)
  1922- . . . . **CLC 5, 51**
  See also CANR 3; CA 5-8R; DLB 2, 44

Wilson, A(ndrew) N(orman) 1950- . . **CLC 33**
  See also CA 112, 122; DLB 14

Wilson, Andrew 1948-
  See Wilson, Snoo

Wilson, Angus (Frank Johnstone)
  1913- . . . . **CLC 2, 3, 5, 25, 34**
  See also CANR 21; CA 5-8R; DLB 15

Wilson, August
  1945- . . . . **CLC 39, 50, 63; DC 2**
  See also BLC 3; CA 115, 122

Wilson, Brian 1942- . . . . **CLC 12**

Wilson, Colin 1931- . . . . **CLC 3, 14**
  See also CAAS 5; CANR 1, 122; CA 1-4R;
  DLB 14

Wilson, Edmund
  1895-1972 . . . . **CLC 1, 2, 3, 8, 24**
  See also CANR 1; CA 1-4R;
  obituary CA 37-40R; DLB 63

Wilson, Ethel Davis (Bryant)
  1888-1980 . . . . **CLC 13**
  See also CA 102; DLB 68

Wilson, Harriet 1827?-?
  See also BLC 3; DLB 50

Wilson, John 1785-1854 . . . . **NCLC 5**

Wilson, John (Anthony) Burgess 1917-
  See Burgess, Anthony
  See also CANR 2; CA 1-4R

Wilson, Lanford 1937- . . . . **CLC 7, 14, 36**
  See also CA 17-20R; DLB 7

Wilson, Robert (M.) 1944- . . . . **CLC 7, 9**
  See also CANR 2; CA 49-52

Wilson, Sloan 1920- . . . . **CLC 32**
  See also CANR 1; CA 1-4R

Wilson, Snoo 1948- . . . . **CLC 33**
  See also CA 69-72

Wilson, William S(mith) 1932- . . . . . **CLC 49**
  See also CA 81-84

**Winchilsea, Anne (Kingsmill) Finch, Countess
  of** 1661-1720 . . . . **LC 3**

Wingrove, David 1954- . . . . **CLC 68**
  See also CA 133

Winters, Janet Lewis 1899-
  See Lewis (Winters), Janet
  See also CAP 1; CA 9-10

Winters, (Arthur) Yvor
  1900-1968 . . . . **CLC 4, 8, 32**
  See also CAP 1; CA 11-12;
  obituary CA 25-28R; DLB 48

Winterson, Jeannette 1959- . . . . **CLC 64**

Wiseman, Frederick 1930- . . . . **CLC 20**

Wister, Owen 1860-1938 . . . . **TCLC 21**
  See also CA 108; DLB 9, 78

Witkiewicz, Stanislaw Ignacy
  1885-1939 . . . . **TCLC 8**
  See also CA 105; DLB 83

Wittig, Monique 1935?- . . . . **CLC 22**
  See also CA 116; DLB 83

Wittlin, Joseph 1896-1976 . . . . **CLC 25**
  See also Wittlin, Jozef

Wittlin, Jozef 1896-1976
  See Wittlin, Joseph
  See also CANR 3; CA 49-52;
  obituary CA 65-68

Wodehouse, (Sir) P(elham) G(renville)
  1881-1975 . . . **CLC 1, 2, 5, 10, 22; SSC 2**
  See also CANR 3; CA 45-48;
  obituary CA 57-60; SATA 22; DLB 34

Woiwode, Larry (Alfred) 1941- . . . **CLC 6, 10**
  See also CANR 16; CA 73-76; DLB 6

Wojciechowska, Maia (Teresa)
  1927- . . . . **CLC 26**
  See also CLR 1; CANR 4; CA 9-12R;
  SAAS 1; SATA 1, 28

Wolf, Christa 1929- . . . . **CLC 14, 29, 58**
  See also CA 85-88; DLB 75

Wolfe, Gene (Rodman) 1931- . . . . **CLC 25**
  See also CAAS 9; CANR 6; CA 57-60;
  DLB 8

Wolfe, George C. 1954- . . . . **CLC 49**

Wolfe, Thomas (Clayton)
  1900-1938 . . . . **TCLC 4, 13, 29**
  See also CA 104; DLB 9; DLB-Y 85;
  DLB-DS 2

Wolfe, Thomas Kennerly, Jr. 1931-
  See Wolfe, Tom
  See also CANR 9; CA 13-16R

Wolfe, Tom 1931- . . . **CLC 1, 2, 9, 15, 35, 51**
  See also Wolfe, Thomas Kennerly, Jr.

Wolff, Geoffrey (Ansell) 1937- . . . . . **CLC 41**
  See also CA 29-32R

Wolff, Tobias (Jonathan Ansell)
  1945- . . . . **CLC 39, 64**
  See also CA 114, 117

Wolfram von Eschenbach
  c. 1170-c. 1220 . . . . **CMLC 5**

Wolitzer, Hilma 1930- . . . . **CLC 17**
  See also CANR 18; CA 65-68; SATA 31

Wollstonecraft Godwin, Mary
  1759-1797 . . . . **LC 5**
  See also DLB 39

Wonder, Stevie 1950- . . . . **CLC 12**
  See also Morris, Steveland Judkins

Wong, Jade Snow 1922- . . . . **CLC 17**
  See also CA 109

Woodcott, Keith 1934-
  See Brunner, John (Kilian Houston)

Woolf, (Adeline) Virginia
  1882-1941 . . . . **TCLC 1, 5, 20, 43; SSC 7**
  See also CA 130; brief entry CA 104;
  DLB 36, 100

Woollcott, Alexander (Humphreys)
  1887-1943 . . . . **TCLC 5**
  See also CA 105; DLB 29

Wordsworth, Dorothy
  1771-1855 . . . . **NCLC 25**

Wordsworth, William
  1770-1850 . . . . **NCLC 12; PC 4**
  See also DLB 93, 107

Wouk, Herman 1915- . . . . **CLC 1, 9, 38**
  See also CANR 6; CA 5-8R; DLB-Y 82

Wright, Charles 1935- . . . . **CLC 6, 13, 28**
  See also BLC 3; CAAS 7; CANR 26;
  CA 29-32R; DLB-Y 82

Wright, Charles (Stevenson) 1932- . . **CLC 49**
  See also CA 9-12R; DLB 33

Wright, James (Arlington)
  1927-1980 . . . . **CLC 3, 5, 10, 28**
  See also CANR 4; CA 49-52;
  obituary CA 97-100; DLB 5

Wright, Judith 1915- . . . . **CLC 11, 53**
  See also CA 13-16R; SATA 14

Wright, L(aurali) R. 1939- . . . . **CLC 44**

Wright, Richard (Nathaniel)
  1908-1960 . . . **CLC 1, 3, 4, 9, 14, 21, 48;**
                                              SSC 2
  See also BLC 3; CA 108; DLB 76;
  DLB-DS 2; CDALB 1929-1941; AAYA 5

Wright, Richard B(ruce) 1937- . . . . . . **CLC 6**
  See also CA 85-88; DLB 53

Wright, Rick 1945-
  See Pink Floyd

Wright, Stephen 1946- . . . . **CLC 33**

Wright, Willard Huntington 1888-1939
  See Van Dine, S. S.
  See also CA 115

Wright, William 1930- . . . . **CLC 44**
  See also CANR 7, 23; CA 53-56

Wu Ch'eng-en 1500?-1582? . . . . **LC 7**

Wu Ching-tzu 1701-1754 . . . . **LC 2**

Wurlitzer, Rudolph 1938?- . . . . . **CLC 2, 4, 15**
  See also CA 85-88

Wycherley, William 1640?-1716 . . . . . . **LC 8**
  See also DLB 80

Wylie (Benet), Elinor (Morton Hoyt)
  1885-1928 . . . . **TCLC 8**
  See also CA 105; DLB 9, 45

Wylie, Philip (Gordon) 1902-1971 . . . **CLC 43**
  See also CAP 2; CA 21-22;
  obituary CA 33-36R; DLB 9

Wyndham, John 1903-1969 . . . . **CLC 19**
  See also Harris, John (Wyndham Parkes
  Lucas) Beynon

Wyss, Johann David 1743-1818 . . **NCLC 10**
  See also SATA 27, 29

X, Malcolm 1925-1965
  See Little, Malcolm

Yanovsky, Vassily S(emenovich)
  1906-1989 . . . . **CLC 2, 18**
  See also CA 97-100; obituary CA 129

Yates, Richard 1926- . . . . **CLC 7, 8, 23**
  See also CANR 10; CA 5-8R; DLB 2;
  DLB-Y 81

Yeats, William Butler
  1865-1939 . . . . **TCLC 1, 11, 18, 31**
  See also CANR 10; CA 104; DLB 10, 19

Yehoshua, A(braham) B.
  1936- . . . . **CLC 13, 31**
  See also CA 33-36R

Yep, Laurence (Michael) 1948-..... **CLC 35**
See also CLR 3, 17; CANR 1; CA 49-52;
SATA 7; DLB 52

Yerby, Frank G(arvin) 1916-... **CLC 1, 7, 22**
See also BLC 3; CANR 16; CA 9-12R;
DLB 76

Yevtushenko, Yevgeny (Alexandrovich)
1933-........... **CLC 1, 3, 13, 26, 51**
See also CA 81-84

Yezierska, Anzia 1885?-1970....... **CLC 46**
See also CA 126; obituary CA 89-92;
DLB 28

Yglesias, Helen 1915-........... **CLC 7, 22**
See also CANR 15; CA 37-40R

Yorke, Henry Vincent 1905-1974
See Green, Henry
See also CA 85-88; obituary CA 49-52

Young, Al 1939-................ **CLC 19**
See also BLC 3; CANR 26; CA 29-32R;
DLB 33

Young, Andrew 1885-1971......... **CLC 5**
See also CANR 7; CA 5-8R

Young, Edward 1683-1765.......... **LC 3**

Young, Neil 1945-................ **CLC 17**
See also CA 110

Yourcenar, Marguerite
1903-1987............. **CLC 19, 38, 50**
See also CANR 23; CA 69-72; DLB 72;
DLB-Y 88

Yurick, Sol 1925-................ **CLC 6**
See also CANR 25; CA 13-16R

Zamyatin, Yevgeny Ivanovich
1884-1937................ **TCLC 8, 37**
See also CA 105

Zangwill, Israel 1864-1926....... **TCLC 16**
See also CA 109; DLB 10

Zappa, Francis Vincent, Jr. 1940-
See Zappa, Frank
See also CA 108

Zappa, Frank 1940- .... **CLC 17**
See also Zappa, Francis Vincent, Jr.

Zaturenska, Marya 1902-1982.... **CLC 6, 11**
See also CANR 22; CA 13-16R;
obituary CA 105

Zelazny, Roger 1937-............. **CLC 21**
See also CANR 26; CA 21-24R; SATA 39,
59; DLB 8

Zhdanov, Andrei A(lexandrovich)
1896-1948.................. **TCLC 18**
See also CA 117

Zhukovsky, Vasily 1783-1852.... **NCLC 35**

Ziegenhagen, Eric 1970-.......... **CLC 55**

Zimmerman, Robert 1941-
See Dylan, Bob

Zindel, Paul 1936- .... **CLC 6, 26**
See also CLR 3; CA 73-76; SATA 16, 58;
DLB 7, 52

Zinoviev, Alexander 1922-........ **CLC 19**
See also CAAS 10; CA 116

Zola, Emile 1840-1902... **TCLC 1, 6, 21, 41**
See also brief entry CA 104

Zoline, Pamela 1941-............. **CLC 62**

Zorrilla y Moral, Jose 1817-1893.. **NCLC 6**

Zoshchenko, Mikhail (Mikhailovich)
1895-1958 .... **TCLC 15**
See also CA 115

Zuckmayer, Carl 1896-1977........ **CLC 18**
See also CA 69-72; DLB 56

Zukofsky, Louis
1904-1978 .... **CLC 1, 2, 4, 7, 11, 18**
See also CA 9-12R; obituary CA 77-80;
DLB 5

Zweig, Paul 1935-1984......... **CLC 34, 42**
See also CA 85-88; obituary CA 113

Zweig, Stefan 1881-1942......... **TCLC 17**
See also CA 112; DLB 81

CLC Cumulative Nationality Index

ALBANIAN

Kadare, Ismail 52

ALGERIAN

Camus, Albert 1, 2, 4, 9, 11, 14, 32, 63, 69
Cohen-Solal, Annie 50

AMERICAN

Abbey, Edward 36, 59
Abbott, Lee K., Jr. 48
Abish, Walter 22
Abrahams, Peter 4
Abrams, M. H. 24
Acker, Kathy 45
Adams, Alice 6, 13, 46
Addams, Charles 30
Adler, C. S. 35
Adler, Renata 8, 31
Ai 4, 14, 69
Aiken, Conrad 1, 3, 5, 10, 52
Albee, Edward 1, 2, 3, 5, 9, 11, 13, 25, 53
Alexander, Lloyd 35
Algren, Nelson 4, 10, 33
Allard, Janet 59
Allen, Edward 59
Allen, Woody 16, 52
Alleyne, Carla D. 65
Alta 19
Alter, Robert B. 34
Alther, Lisa 7, 41
Altman, Robert 16
Ammons, A. R. 2, 3, 5, 8, 9, 25, 57
Anaya, Rudolfo A. 23
Anderson, Jon 9
Anderson, Poul 15
Anderson, Robert 23
Angell, Roger 26
Angelou, Maya 12, 35, 64
Anthony, Piers 35

Apple, Max 9, 33
Appleman, Philip 51
Archer, Jules 12
Arendt, Hannah 66
Arnow, Harriette 2, 7, 18
Arrick, Fran 30
Ashbery, John 2, 3, 4, 6, 9, 13, 15, 25, 41
Asimov, Isaac 1, 3, 9, 19, 26
Auchincloss, Louis 4, 6, 9, 18, 45
Auden, W. H. 1, 2, 3, 4, 6, 9, 11, 14, 43
Auel, Jean M. 31
Auster, Paul 47
Bach, Richard 14
Baker, Elliott 8
Baker, Nicholson 61
Baker, Russell 31
Bakshi, Ralph 26
Baldwin, James 1, 2, 3, 4, 5, 8, 13, 15, 17, 42, 50, 67
Bambara, Toni Cade 19
Bandanes, Jerome 59
Banks, Russell 37, 72
Baraka, Imamu Amiri 1, 2, 3, 5, 10, 14, 33
Barbera, Jack 44
Barnard, Mary 48
Barnes, Djuna 3, 4, 8, 11, 29
Barrett, William 27
Barth, John 1, 2, 3, 5, 7, 9, 10, 14, 27, 51
Barthelme, Donald 1, 2, 3, 5, 6, 8, 13, 23, 46, 59
Barthelme, Frederick 36
Barzun, Jacques 51
Baumbach, Jonathan 6, 23
Bausch, Richard 51
Baxter, Charles 45
Beagle, Peter S. 7
Beattie, Ann 8, 13, 18, 40, 63
Becker, Walter 26
Beecher, John 6

Begiebing, Robert J. 70
Behrman, S. N. 40
Belitt, Ben 22
Bell, Madison Smartt 41
Bell, Marvin 8, 31
Bellow, Saul 1, 2, 3, 6, 8, 10, 13, 15, 25, 33, 34, 63
Benary-Isbert, Margot 12
Benchley, Peter 4, 8
Benedikt, Michael 4, 14
Benford, Gregory 52
Bennett, Hal 5
Bennett, Jay 35
Benson, Jackson J. 34
Benson, Sally 17
Bentley, Eric 24
Berger, Melvin 12
Berger, Thomas 3, 5, 8, 11, 18, 38
Bergstein, Eleanor 4
Bernard, April 59
Berriault, Gina 54
Berrigan, Daniel J. 4
Berrigan, Ted 37
Berry, Chuck 17
Berry, Wendell 4, 6, 8, 27, 46
Berryman, John 1, 2, 3, 4, 6, 8, 10, 13, 25, 62
Bessie, Alvah 23
Betts, Doris 3, 6, 28
Bidart, Frank 33
Birch, Allison 65
Bishop, Elizabeth 1, 4, 9, 13, 15, 32
Bishop, John 10
Blackburn, Paul 9, 43
Blackmur, R. P. 2, 24
Blaise, Clark 29
Blatty, William Peter 2
Blessing, Lee 54
Blish, James 14

Bloch, Robert　33
Bloom, Harold　24, 65
Blount, Roy, Jr.　38
Blume, Judy　12, 30
Bly, Robert　1, 2, 5, 10, 15, 38
Bochco, Steven　35
Bogan, Louise　4, 39, 46
Bogosian, Eric　45
Bograd, Larry　35
Bonham, Frank　12
Bontemps, Arna　1, 18
Booth, Philip　23
Booth, Wayne C.　24
Bottoms, David　53
Bourjaily, Vance　8, 62
Bova, Ben　45
Bowers, Edgar　9
Bowles, Jane　3, 68
Bowles, Paul　1, 2, 19, 53
Boyle, Kay　1, 5, 19, 58
Boyle, T. Coraghessan　36, 55
Bradbury, Ray　1, 3, 10, 15, 42
Bradley, David, Jr.　23
Bradley, John Ed　55
Bradley, Marion Zimmer　30
Brammer, William　31
Brancato, Robin F.　35
Brand, Millen　7
Branden, Barbara　44
Branley, Franklyn M.　21
Brautigan, Richard　1, 3, 5, 9, 12, 34, 42
Braverman, Kate　67
Brennan, Maeve　5
Breslin, Jimmy　4, 43
Bridgers, Sue Ellen　26
Brin, David　34
Brodkey, Harold　56
Brodsky, Joseph　4, 6, 13, 36, 50
Brodsky, Michael　19
Bromell, Henry　5
Broner, E. M.　19
Bronk, William　10
Brooks, Cleanth　24
Brooks, Gwendolyn　1, 2, 4, 5, 15, 49
Brooks, Mel　12
Brooks, Peter　34
Brooks, Van Wyck　29
Brosman, Catharine Savage　9
Broughton, T. Alan　19
Broumas, Olga　10
Brown, Claude　30, 59
Brown, Dee　18, 47
Brown, Rita Mae　18, 43
Brown, Rosellen　32
Brown, Sterling A.　1, 23, 59
Browne, Jackson　21
Browning, Tod　16
Bruccoli, Matthew J.　34
Bruce, Lenny　21
Bryan, C. D. B.　29
Buchwald, Art　33
Buck, Pearl S.　7, 11, 18
Buckley, William F., Jr.　7, 18, 37
Buechner, Frederick　2, 4, 6, 9
Bukowski, Charles　2, 5, 9, 41
Bullins, Ed　1, 5, 7
Burke, Kenneth　2, 24
Burnshaw, Stanley　3, 13, 44
Burr, Anne　6
Burroughs, William S.　1, 2, 5, 15, 22, 42
Busch, Frederick　7, 10, 18, 47
Bush, Ronald　34

Butler, Octavia E.　38
Byars, Betsy　35
Byrne, David　26
Cage, John　41
Cain, James M.　3, 11, 28
Caldwell, Erskine　1, 8, 14, 50, 60
Caldwell, Taylor　2, 28, 39
Calisher, Hortense　2, 4, 8, 38
Cameron, Carey　59
Cameron, Peter　44
Campbell, John W., Jr.　32
Campbell, Joseph　69
Canby, Vincent　13
Canin, Ethan　55
Capote, Truman　1, 3, 8, 13, 19, 34, 38, 58
Capra, Frank　16
Caputo, Philip　32
Card, Orson Scott　44, 47, 50
Carey, Ernestine Gilbreth　17
Carlisle, Henry　33
Carlson, Ron　54
Carpenter, Don　41
Carr, John Dickson　3
Carr, Virginia Spencer　34
Carroll, James　38
Carroll, Jim　35
Carruth, Hayden　4, 7, 10, 18
Carson, Rachel　71
Carver, Raymond　22, 36, 53, 55
Casey, John　59
Casey, Michael　2
Casey, Warren　12
Cassavetes, John　20
Cassill, R. V.　4, 23
Cassity, Turner　6, 42
Castedo, Elena　65
Castenada, Carlos　12
Catton, Bruce　35
Caunitz, William　34
Cavanna, Betty　12
Chabon, Michael　55
Chappell, Fred　40
Charyn, Jerome　5, 8, 18
Chase, Mary Ellen　2
Chayefsky, Paddy　23
Cheever, John　3, 7, 8, 11, 15, 25, 64
Cheever, Susan　18, 48
Cherryh, C. J.　35
Chester, Alfred　49
Childress, Alice　12, 15
Chute, Carolyn　39
Ciardi, John　10, 40, 44
Cimino, Michael　16
Cisneros, Sandra　69
Clampitt, Amy　32
Clancy, Tom　45
Clark, Eleanor　5, 19
Clark, Walter Van Tilburg　28
Clarke, Shirley　16
Clavell, James　6, 25
Clayman, Gregory　65
Cleaver, Eldridge　30
Clifton, Lucille　19, 66
Coburn, D. L.　10
Codrescu, Andrei　46
Cohen, Arthur A.　7, 31
Collier, Christopher　30
Collier, James L.　30
Collins, Linda　44
Colter, Cyrus　58
Colum, Padraic　28
Colwin, Laurie　5, 13, 23

Condon, Richard　4, 6, 8, 10, 45
Connell, Evan S., Jr.　4, 6, 45
Connelly, Marc　7
Conroy, Pat　30
Cook, Robin　14
Cooke, Elizabeth　55
Cooper, J. California　56
Coover, Robert　3, 7, 15, 32, 46
Coppola, Francis Ford　16
Corcoran, Barbara　17
Corman, Cid　9
Cormier, Robert　12, 30
Corn, Alfred　33
Corso, Gregory　1, 11
Costain, Thomas B.　30
Cowley, Malcolm　39
Cozzens, James Gould　1, 4, 11
Crace, Douglas　58
Crane, R. S.　27
Creeley, Robert　1, 2, 4, 8, 11, 15, 36
Crews, Harry　6, 23, 49
Crichton, Michael　2, 6, 54
Cristofer, Michael　28
Crowley, John　57
Crumb, Robert　17
Cryer, Gretchen　21
Cudlip, David　34
Cummings, E. E.　1, 3, 8, 12, 15, 68
Cunningham, J. V.　3, 31
Cunningham, Julia　12
Cunningham, Michael　34
Currie, Ellen　44
Dacey, Philip　51
Dahlberg, Edward　1, 7, 14
Daly, Elizabeth　52
Daly, Maureen　17
Danvers, Dennis　70
Danziger, Paula　21
Davenport, Guy　6, 14, 38
Davidson, Donald　2, 13, 19
Davidson, Sara　9
Davis, H. L.　49
Davison, Peter　28
Dawson, Fielding　6
De Ferrari, Gabriella　65
De Man, Paul　55
De Palma, Brian　20
De Vries, Peter　1, 2, 3, 7, 10, 28, 46
Deer, Sandra　45
Del Vecchio, John M.　29
Delany, Samuel R.　8, 14, 38
Delbanco, Nicholas　6, 13
DeLillo, Don　8, 10, 13, 27, 39, 54
Deloria, Vine, Jr.　21
DeMarinis, Rick　54
Demby, William　53
Denby, Edwin　48
Deren, Maya　16
Derleth, August　31
Deutsch, Babette　18
Dexter, Pete　34, 55
Diamond, Neil　30
Dick, Philip K.　10, 30, 72
Dickey, James　1, 2, 4, 7, 10, 15, 47
Dickey, William　3, 28
Dickinson, Charles　49
Didion, Joan　1, 3, 8, 14, 32
Dillard, Annie　9, 60
Dillard, R. H. W.　5
Disch, Thomas M.　7, 36
Dixon, Stephen　52
Dobyns, Stephen　37

Doctorow, E. L.   **6, 11, 15, 18, 37, 44, 65**
Doerr, Harriet   **34**
Donaldson, Stephen R.   **46**
Donleavy, J. P.   **1, 4, 6, 10, 45**
Donovan, John   **35**
Dorn, Ed   **10, 18**
Dos Passos, John   **1, 4, 8, 11, 15, 25, 34**
Dove, Rita   **50**
Drexler, Rosalyn   **2, 6**
Drury, Allen   **37**
Du Bois, W. E. B.   **1, 2, 13, 64**
Duberman, Martin   **8**
Dubie, Norman   **36**
Dubus, André   **13, 36**
Duffy, Bruce   **50**
Dugan, Alan   **2, 6**
Dumas, Henry   **6, 62**
Duncan, Robert   **1, 2, 4, 7, 15, 41, 55**
Duncan Lois   **26**
Dunn, Katherine   **71**
Dunn, Stephen   **36**
Dunne, John Gregory   **28**
Durang, Christopher   **27, 38**
Durban, Pam   **39**
Dworkin, Andrea   **43**
Dylan, Bob   **3, 4, 6, 12**
Eastlake, William   **8**
Eberhart, Richard   **3, 11, 19, 56**
Eberstadt, Fernanda   **39**
Eckert, Allan W.   **17**
Edel, Leon   **29, 34**
Edgerton, Clyde   **39**
Edmonds, Walter D.   **35**
Edson, Russell   **13**
Edwards, Gus   **43**
Ehle, John   **27**
Eigner, Larry   **9**
Eiseley, Loren   **7**
Eisenstadt, Jill   **50**
Eliade, Mircea   **19**
Eliot, T. S.   **1, 2, 3, 6, 9, 10, 13, 15, 24, 34,**
   41, 55, 57
Elkin, Stanley   **4, 6, 9, 14, 27, 51**
Elledge, Scott   **34**
Elliott, George P.   **2**
Ellis, Bret Easton   **39, 71**
Ellis, Trey   **55**
Ellison, Harlan   **1, 13, 42**
Ellison, Ralph   **1, 3, 11, 54**
Ellmann, Lucy   **61**
Ellmann, Richard   **50**
Elman, Richard   **19**
Ephron, Nora   **17, 31**
Epstein, Daniel Mark   **7**
Epstein, Jacob   **19**
Epstein, Joseph   **39**
Epstein, Leslie   **27**
Erdman, Paul E.   **25**
Erdrich, Louise   **39, 54**
Erickson, Steve   **64**
Eshleman, Clayton   **7**
Estleman, Loren D.   **48**
Everett, Percival L.   **57**
Everson, William   **1, 5, 14**
Exley, Frederick   **6, 11**
Ezekiel, Tish O'Dowd   **34**
Fagen, Donald   **26**
Fair, Ronald L.   **18**
Fante, John   **CLC-60**
Fariña, Richard   **9**
Farley, Walter   **17**
Farmer, Philip José   **1, 19**

Farrell, James T.   **1, 4, 8, 11, 66**
Fast, Howard   **23**
Faulkner, William   **1, 3, 6, 8, 9, 11, 14, 18,**
   28, 52, 68
Fauset, Jessie Redmon   **19, 54**
Faust, Irvin   **8**
Fearing, Kenneth   **51**
Federman, Raymond   **6, 47**
Feiffer, Jules   **2, 8, 64**
Feinberg, David B.   **59**
Feke, Gilbert David   **65**
Feldman, Irving   **7**
Felsen, Henry Gregor   **17**
Ferber, Edna   **18**
Ferlinghetti, Lawrence   **2, 6, 10, 27**
Ferrigno, Robert   **65**
Fiedler, Leslie A.   **4, 13, 24**
Field, Andrew   **44**
Fierstein, Harvey   **33**
Fisher, Vardis   **7**
Fitzgerald, Robert   **39**
Flanagan, Thomas   **25, 52**
Fleming, Thomas J.   **37**
Foote, Horton   **51**
Forbes, Esther   **12**
Forché, Carolyn   **25**
Ford, John   **16**
Ford, Richard   **46**
Foreman, Richard   **50**
Forman, James D.   **21**
Fornes, Maria Irene   **39, 61**
Forrest, Leon   **4**
Fosse, Bob   **20**
Fox, Paula   **2, 8**
Fox, William Price   **22**
Francis, Robert   **15**
Frank, Elizabeth   **39**
Fraze, Candida   **50**
Frazier, Ian   **46**
Freeman, Judith   **55**
French, Marilyn   **10, 18, 60**
Friedman, B. H.   **7**
Friedman, Bruce Jay   **3, 5, 56**
Frost, Robert   **1, 3, 4, 9, 10, 13, 15, 26, 34,**
   44
Fuchs, Daniel (1934-)   **34**
Fuchs, Daniel (1909-)   **8, 22**
Fuller, Charles   **25**
Fulton, Alice   **52**
Gaddis, William   **1, 3, 6, 8, 10, 19, 43**
Gaines, Ernest J.   **3, 11, 18**
Gaitskill, Mary   **69**
Gallagher, Tess   **18, 63**
Gallant, Roy A.   **17**
Gallico, Paul   **2**
Galvin, James   **38**
Gann, Ernest K.   **23**
Gardner, Herb   **44**
Gardner, John (Champlin, Jr.)   **2, 3, 5, 7, 8,**
   10, 18, 28, 34
Garrett, George   **3, 11, 51**
Garrigue, Jean   **2, 8**
Gass, William H.   **1, 2, 8, 11, 15, 39**
Gates, Henry Louis, Jr.   **65**
Gaye, Marvin   **26**
Gelbart, Larry   **21, 61**
Gelber, Jack   **1, 6, 14**
Gellhorn, Martha   **14, 60**
Gent, Peter   **29**
George, Jean Craighead   **35**
Gerstler, Amy   **70**
Gertler, T.   **34**

Ghiselin, Brewster   **23**
Gibbons, Kaye   **50**
Gibson, William (1948-)   **39, 63**
Gibson, William (1914-)   **23**
Gifford, Barry   **34**
Gilbreth, Frank B., Jr.   **17**
Gilchrist, Ellen   **34, 48**
Giles, Molly   **39**
Gilroy, Frank D.   **2**
Ginsberg, Allen   **1, 2, 3, 4, 6, 13, 36, 69**
Giovanni, Nikki   **2, 4, 19, 64**
Glasser, Ronald J.   **37**
Glück, Louise   **7, 22, 44**
Godwin, Gail   **5, 8, 22, 31, 69**
Gold, Herbert   **4, 7, 14, 42**
Goldbarth, Albert   **5, 38**
Goldman, William   **1, 48**
Goldsberry, Steven   **34**
Goodman, Paul   **1, 2, 4, 7**
Gordon, Caroline   **6, 13, 29**
Gordon, Mary   **13, 22**
Gordon, Sol   **26**
Gordone, Charles   **1, 4**
Gould, Lois   **4, 10**
Goyen, William   **5, 8, 14, 40**
Graham, Jorie   **48**
Grau, Shirley Ann   **4, 9**
Graver, Elizabeth   **70**
Gray, Amlin   **29**
Gray, Francine du Plessix   **22**
Gray, Spalding   **49**
Grayson, Richard   **38**
Greeley, Andrew M.   **28**
Green, Paul   **25**
Greenberg, Joanne   **3, 7, 30**
Greenberg, Richard   **57**
Greene, Bette   **30**
Greene, Gael   **8**
Gregor, Arthur   **9**
Griffin, John Howard   **68**
Griffin, Peter   **39**
Grumbach, Doris   **13, 22, 64**
Grunwald, Lisa   **44**
Guare, John   **8, 14, 29, 67**
Guest, Barbara   **34**
Guest, Judith   **8, 30**
Guild, Nicholas M.   **33**
Gunn, Bill   **5**
Gurganus, Allan   **70**
Gurney, A. R., Jr.   **32, 50, 54**
Guthrie, A. B., Jr.   **23**
Guthrie, Woody   **35**
Guy, Rosa   **26**
H. D.   **3, 8, 14, 31, 34**
Hacker, Marilyn   **5, 9, 23, 72**
Hailey, Elizabeth Forsythe   **40**
Haines, John   **58**
Haldeman, Joe   **61**
Haley, Alex   **8, 12**
Hall, Donald   **1, 13, 37, 59**
Halpern, Daniel   **14**
Hamill, Pete   **10**
Hamilton, Edmond   **1**
Hamilton, Ian   **55**
Hamilton, Virginia   **26**
Hammett, Dashiell   **3, 5, 10, 19, 47**
Hamner, Earl, Jr.   **12**
Hannah, Barry   **23, 38**
Hansberry, Lorraine   **17, 62**
Hansen, Joseph   **38**
Hanson, Kenneth O.   **13**
Hardwick, Elizabeth   **13**

Harlan, Louis R. 34
Harling, Robert 53
Harmon, William 38
Harper, Michael S. 7, 22
Harris, MacDonald 9
Harris, Mark 19
Harrison, Harry 42
Harrison, Jim 6, 14, 33, 66
Harrison, Kathryn 70
Harriss, Will 34
Hart, Moss 66
Hartman, Geoffrey H. 27
Haruf, Kent 34
Hass, Robert 18, 39
Haviaras, Stratis 33
Hawkes, John 1, 2, 3, 4, 7, 9, 14, 15, 27, 49
Hayden, Robert 5, 9, 14, 37
Hayman, Ronald 44
Hearne, Vicki 56
Hearon, Shelby 63
Heat Moon, William Least 29
Hecht, Anthony 8, 13, 19
Hecht, Ben 8
Heifner, Jack 11
Heilbrun, Carolyn G. 25
Heinemann, Larry 50
Heinlein, Robert A. 1, 3, 8, 14, 26, 55
Heller, Joseph 1, 3, 5, 8, 11, 36, 63
Hellman, Lillian 2, 4, 8, 14, 18, 34, 44, 52
Helprin, Mark 7, 10, 22, 32
Hemingway, Ernest 1, 3, 6, 8, 10, 13, 19, 30, 34, 39, 41, 44, 50, 61
Hempel, Amy 39
Henley, Beth 23
Hentoff, Nat 26
Herbert, Frank 12, 23, 35, 44
Herbst, Josephine 34
Herlihy, James Leo 6
Herrmann, Dorothy 44
Hersey, John 1, 2, 7, 9, 40
Heyen, William 13, 18
Higgins, George V. 4, 7, 10, 18
Highsmith, Patricia 2, 4, 14, 42
Highwater, Jamake 12
Hijuelos, Oscar 65
Hill, George Roy 26
Hillerman, Tony 62
Himes, Chester 2, 4, 7, 18, 58
Hinton, S. E. 30
Hirsch, Edward 31, 50
Hoagland, Edward 28
Hoban, Russell C. 7, 25
Hobson, Laura Z. 7, 25
Hochman, Sandra 3, 8
Hoffman, Alice 51
Hoffman, Daniel 6, 13, 23
Hoffman, Stanley 5
Hoffman, William M. 40
Holland, Isabelle 21
Hollander, John 2, 5, 8, 14
Holleran, Andrew 38
Holmes, John Clellon 56
Honig, Edwin 33
Horgan, Paul 9, 53
Horovitz, Israel 56
Horwitz, Julius 14
Hougan, Carolyn 34
Howard, Maureen 5, 14, 46
Howard, Richard 7, 10, 47
Howe, Fanny 47
Howe, Tina 48
Howe, Susan 72

Howes, Barbara 15
Hubbard, L. Ron 43
Huddle, David 49
Hughart, Barry 39
Hughes, Langston 1, 5, 10, 15, 35, 44
Hugo, Richard F. 6, 18, 32
Humphrey, William 45
Humphreys, Josephine 34, 57
Hunt, E. Howard 3
Hunt, Marsha 70
Hunter, Evan 11, 31
Hunter, Kristin 35
Hurston, Zora Neale 7, 30, 61
Huston, John 20
Hwang, David Henry 55
Hyde, Margaret O. 21
Hynes, James 65
Ian, Janis 21
Ignatow, David 4, 7, 14, 40
Ingalls, Rachel 42
Inge, William 1, 8, 19
Innaurato, Albert 21, 60
Irving, John 13, 23, 38
Isaacs, Susan 32
Ivask, Ivar 14
Jackson, Jesse 12
Jackson, Shirley 11, 60
Jacobs, Jim 12
Jacobsen, Josephine 48
Jakes, John 29
Janowitz, Tama 43
Jarrell, Randall 1, 2, 6, 9, 13, 49
Jeffers, Robinson 2, 3, 11, 15, 54
Jen, Gish 70
Jennings, Waylon 21
Jensen, Laura 37
Joel, Billy 26
Johnson, Charles 7, 51, 65
Johnson, Denis 52
Johnson, Diane 5, 13, 48
Johnson, Joyce 58
Jones, Gayl 6, 9
Jones, James 1, 3, 10, 39
Jones, Louis B. 65
Jones, Madison 4
Jones, Nettie 34
Jones, Preston 10
Jones, Robert F. 7
Jong, Erica 4, 6, 8, 18
Jordan, June 5, 11, 23
Jordan, Pat 37
Just, Ward S. 4, 27
Justice, Donald 6, 19
Kadohata, Cynthia 59
Kahn, Roger 30
Kaletski, Alexander 39
Kallman, Chester 2
Kaminsky, Stuart 59
Kanin, Garson 22
Kantor, MacKinlay 7
Kaplan, David Michael 50
Kaplan, James 59
Karl, Frederick R. 34
Katz, Steve 47
Kauffman, Janet 42
Kaufman, Bob 49
Kaufman, George S. 38
Kaufman, Sue 3, 8
Kazan, Elia 6, 16, 63
Kazin, Alfred 34, 38
Keaton, Buster 20
Keene, Donald 34

Keillor, Garrison 40
Kellerman, Jonathan 44
Kelley, William Melvin 22
Kellogg, Marjorie 2
Kemelman, Harry 2
Kennedy, William 6, 28, 34, 53
Kennedy, X. J. 8, 42
Kerouac, Jack 1, 2, 3, 5, 14, 29, 61
Kerr, Jean 22
Kerr, M. E. 12, 35
Kerr, Robert 55, 59
Kerrigan, Anthony 4, 6
Kesey, Ken 1, 3, 6, 11, 46, 64
Kesselring, Joseph 45
Kessler, Jascha 4
Kettelkamp, Larry 12
Kherdian, David 6, 9
Kienzle, William X. 25
Killens, John Oliver 10
Kincaid, Jamaica 43, 68
King, Stephen 12, 26, 37, 61
Kingman, Lee 17
Kingsley, Sidney 44
Kingsolver, Barbara 55
Kingston, Maxine Hong 12, 19, 58
Kinnell, Galway 1, 2, 3, 5, 13, 29
Kirkwood, James 9
Kizer, Carolyn 15, 39
Klappert, Peter 57
Klein, Norma 30
Klein, T. E. D. 34
Knebel, Fletcher 14
Knight, Etheridge 40
Knowles, John 1, 4, 10, 26
Koch, Kenneth 5, 8, 44
Kopit, Arthur 1, 18, 33
Kosinski, Jerzy 1, 2, 3, 6, 10, 15, 53, 70
Kostelanetz, Richard 28
Kotlowitz, Robert 4
Kotzwinkle, William 5, 14, 35
Kozol, Jonathan 17
Kozoll, Michael 35
Kramer, Kathryn 34
Kramer, Larry 42
Kristofferson, Kris 26
Krumgold, Joseph 12
Krutch, Joseph Wood 24
Kubrick, Stanley 16
Kumin, Maxine 5, 13, 28
Kunitz, Stanley J. 6, 11, 14
Kuzma, Greg 7
L'Amour, Louis 25, 55
Lancaster, Bruce 36
Landis, John 26
Langer, Elinor 34
Lapine, James 39
Larsen, Eric 55
Larsen, Nella 37
Larson, Charles R. 31
Latham, Jean Lee 12
Lattimore, Richmond 3
Laughlin, James 49
Le Guin, Ursula K. 8, 13, 22, 45, 71
Lear, Norman 12
Leavitt, David 34
Lebowitz, Fran 11, 36
Lee, Andrea 36
Lee, Don L. 2
Lee, George Washington 52
Lee, Harper 12, 60
Lee, Lawrence 34
Lee, Stan 17

Leet, Judith 11
Leffland, Ella 19
Leiber, Fritz 25
Leimbach, Marti 65
Leithauser, Brad 27
Lelchuk, Alan 5
Lemann, Nancy 39
L'Engle, Madeleine 12
Lentricchia, Frank 34
Leonard, Elmore 28, 34, 71
Lerman, Eleanor 9
Lerman, Rhoda 56
Lester, Richard 20
Levertov, Denise 1, 2, 3, 5, 8, 15, 28, 66
Levin, Ira 3, 6
Levin, Meyer 7
Levine, Philip 2, 4, 5, 9, 14, 33
Levinson, Deirdre 49
Levitin, Sonia 17
Lewis, Janet 41
L'Heureux, John 52
Lieber, Joel 6
Lieberman, Laurence 4, 36
Lifton, Robert Jay 67
Ligotti, Thomas 44
Linney, Romulus 51
Lipsyte, Robert 21
Lish, Gordon 45
Littell, Robert 42
Loewinsohn, Ron 52
Logan, John 5
Lopate, Phillip 29
Lord, Bette Bao 23
Lorde, Audre 18, 71
Louie, David Wong 70
Lowell, Robert 1, 2, 3, 4, 5, 8, 9, 11, 15, 37
Loy, Mina 28
Lucas, Craig 64
Lucas, George 16
Ludlam, Charles 46, 50
Ludlum, Robert 22, 43
Ludwig, Ken 60
Lurie, Alison 4, 5, 18, 39
Lynch, David 66
Lynn, Kenneth S. 50
Lytle, Andrew 22
Maas, Peter 29
Macdonald, Cynthia 13, 19
MacDonald, John D. 3, 27, 44
Macdonald, Ross 1, 2, 3, 14, 34, 41
MacInnes, Helen 27, 39
MacLeish, Archibald 3, 8, 14, 68
MacShane, Frank 39
Madden, David 5, 15
Madhubuti, Haki R. 6
Mailer, Norman 1, 2, 3, 4, 5, 8, 11, 14, 28, 39
Major, Clarence 3, 19, 48
Malamud, Bernard 1, 2, 3, 5, 8, 9, 11, 18, 27, 44
Maloff, Saul 5
Malone, Michael 43
Malzberg, Barry N. 7
Mamet, David 9, 15, 34, 46
Mamoulian, Rouben 16
Mano, D. Keith 2, 10
Manso, Peter 39
Markfield, Wallace 8
Markson, David 67
Marquand, John P. 2, 10
Marshall, Garry 17
Marshall, Paule 27, 72

Martin, Steve 30
Maso, Carole 44
Mason, Bobbie Ann 28, 43
Masters, Hilary 48
Mastrosimone, William 36
Matheson, Richard 37
Mathews, Harry 6, 52
Matthews, William 40
Matthias, John 9
Matthiessen, Peter 5, 7, 11, 32, 64
Maxwell, William 19
May, Elaine 16
Maynard, Joyce 23
Maysles, Albert 16
Maysles, David 16
Mazer, Norma Fox 26
McBrien, William 44
McCaffrey, Anne 17, 59
McCarthy, Cormac 4, 57, 59
McCarthy, Mary 1, 3, 5, 14, 24, 39
McCauley, Stephen 50
McClure, Michael 6, 10
McCorkle, Jill 51
McCourt, James 5
McCullers, Carson 1, 4, 10, 12, 48
McElroy, Joseph 5, 47
McFarland, Dennis 65
McGinley, Phyllis 14
McGinniss, Joe 32
McGrath, Thomas 28, 59
McGuane, Thomas 3, 7, 18, 45
McHale, Tom 3, 5
McInerney, Jay 34
McIntyre, Vonda N. 18
McKuen, Rod 1, 3
McMillan, Terry 50, 61
McMurtry, Larry 2, 3, 7, 11, 27, 44
McNally, Terrence 4, 7, 41
McNamer, Deirdre 70
McPhee, John 36
McPherson, James Alan 19
McPherson, William 34
Mead, Margaret 37
Medoff, Mark 6, 23
Mehta, Ved 37
Meltzer, Milton 26
Membreno, Alejandro 59
Meredith, William 4, 13, 22, 55
Merkin, Daphne 44
Merrill, James 2, 3, 6, 8, 13, 18, 34
Merton, Thomas 1, 3, 11, 34
Merwin, W. S. 1, 2, 3, 5, 8, 13, 18, 45
Mewshaw, Michael 9
Meyers, Jeffrey 39
Michaels, Leonard 6, 25
Michener, James A. 1, 5, 11, 29, 60
Miles, Josephine 1, 2, 14, 34, 39
Miller, Arthur 1, 2, 6, 10, 15, 26, 47
Miller, Henry 1, 2, 4, 9, 14, 43
Miller, Jason 2
Miller, Sue 44
Miller, Walter M., Jr. 4, 30
Millett, Kate 67
Millhauser, Steven 21, 54
Milner, Ron 56
Miner, Valerie 40
Minot, Susan 44
Minus, Ed 39
Modarressi, Taghi 44
Mohr, Nicholasa 12
Mojtabai, A. G. 5, 9, 15, 29
Momaday, N. Scott 2, 19

Montague, John 46
Montgomery, Marion 7
Mooney, Ted 25
Moore, Lorrie 39, 45, 68
Moore, Marianne 1, 2, 4, 8, 10, 13, 19, 47
Morgan, Berry 6
Morgan, Frederick 23
Morgan, Robin 2
Morgan, Seth 65
Morris, Wright 1, 3, 7, 18, 37
Morrison, Jim 17
Morrison, Toni 4, 10, 22, 55
Mosher, Howard Frank 62
Moss, Howard 7, 14, 45, 50
Motley, Willard 18
Mueller, Lisel 13, 51
Mukherjee, Bharati 53
Mull, Martin 17
Mungo, Raymond 72
Murphy, Sylvia 34
Myers, Walter Dean 35
Nabokov, Vladimir 1, 2, 3, 6, 8, 11, 15, 23, 44, 46, 64
Nash, Ogden 23
Naylor, Gloria 28, 52
Neff, Debra 56
Neihardt, John G. 32
Nelson, Willie 17
Nemerov, Howard 2, 6, 9, 36
Neufeld, John 17
Neville, Emily Cheney 12
Newlove, Donald 6
Newman, Charles 2, 8
Newman, Edwin 14
Newton, Suzanne 35
Nichols, John 38
Niedecker, Lorine 10, 42
Nin, Anaïs 1, 4, 8, 11, 14, 60
Nissenson, Hugh 4, 9
Niven, Larry 8
Nixon, Agnes Eckhardt 21
Norman, Marsha 28
Norton, Andre 12
Nova, Craig 7, 31
Nunn, Kem 34
Nyro, Laura 17
Oates, Joyce Carol 1, 2, 3, 6, 9, 11, 15, 19, 33, 52
O'Brien, Darcy 11
O'Brien, Tim 7, 19, 40
Ochs, Phil 17
O'Connor, Edwin 14
O'Connor, Flannery 1, 2, 3, 6, 10, 13, 15, 21, 66
O'Dell, Scott 30
Odets, Clifford 2, 28
O'Grady, Timothy 59
O'Hara, Frank 2, 5, 13
O'Hara, John 1, 2, 3, 6, 11, 42
O'Hehir, Diana 41
Olds, Sharon 32, 39
Oliver, Mary 19, 34
Olsen, Tillie 4, 13
Olson, Charles 1, 2, 5, 6, 9, 11, 29
Olson, Toby 28
Oneal, Zibby 30
Oppen, George 7, 13, 34
Orlovitz, Gil 22
Ortiz, Simon J. 45
Otto, Whitney 70
Owens, Rochelle 8
Ozick, Cynthia 3, 7, 28, 62

Nationality Index

Pack, Robert   13
Paglia, Camille   68
Paley, Grace   4, 6, 37
Palliser, Charles   65
Pancake, Breece D'J   29
Parini, Jay   54
Parker, Dorothy   15, 68
Parker, Robert B.   27
Parks, Gordon   1, 16
Pastan, Linda   27
Patchen, Kenneth   1, 2, 18
Paterson, Katherine   12, 30
Peacock, Molly   60
Pearson, T. R.   39
Peck, John   3
Peck, Richard   21
Peck, Robert Newton   17
Peckinpah, Sam   20
Percy, Walker   2, 3, 6, 8, 14, 18, 47, 65
Perelman, S. J.   3, 5, 9, 15, 23, 44, 49
Pesetsky, Bette   28
Peterkin, Julia   31
Peters, Joan K.   39
Peters, Robert L.   7
Petrakis, Harry Mark   3
Petry, Ann   1, 7, 18
Philipson, Morris   53
Phillips, Jayne Anne   15, 33
Phillips, Robert   28
Piercy, Marge   3, 6, 14, 18, 27, 62
Pineda, Cecile   39
Pinkwater, D. M.   35
Pinsky, Robert   9, 19, 38
Pirsig, Robert M.   4, 6
Plante, David   7, 23, 38
Plath, Sylvia   1, 2, 3, 5, 9, 11, 14, 17, 50, 51, 62
Platt, Kin   26
Plimpton, George   36
Plumly, Stanley   33
Pohl, Frederik   18
Poitier, Sidney   26
Pollitt, Katha   28
Pomerance, Bernard   13
Porter, Connie   70
Porter, Katherine Anne   1, 3, 7, 10, 13, 15, 27
Potok, Chaim   2, 7, 14, 26
Pound, Ezra   1, 2, 3, 4, 5, 7, 10, 13, 18, 34, 48, 50
Povod, Reinaldo   44
Powell, Dawn   66
Powell, Padgett   34
Powers, J. F.   1, 4, 8, 57
Powers, John R.   66
Prager, Emily   56
Price, Reynolds   3, 6, 13, 43, 50, 63
Price, Richard   6, 12
Prince   35
Pritchard, William H.   34
Probst, Mark   59
Prokosch, Frederic   4, 48
Prose, Francine   45
Pryor, Richard   26
Purdy, James   2, 4, 10, 28, 52
Puzo, Mario   1, 2, 6, 36
Pynchon, Thomas   2, 3, 6, 9, 11, 18, 33, 62, 72
Queen, Ellery   3, 11
Rabe, David   4, 8, 33
Rado, James   17
Raeburn, John   34

Ragni, Gerome   17
Rahv, Philip   24
Rakosi, Carl   47
Rampersad, Arnold   44
Rand, Ayn   3, 30, 44
Randall, Dudley   1
Ransom, John Crowe   2, 4, 5, 11, 24
Raphael, Frederic   2, 14
Rechy, John   1, 7, 14, 18
Reddin, Keith   67
Redmon, Anne   22
Reed, Ishmael   2, 3, 5, 6, 13, 32, 60
Reed, Lou   21
Remarque, Erich Maria   21
Rexroth, Kenneth   1, 2, 6, 11, 22, 49
Reynolds, Jonathan   6, 38
Reynolds, Michael   44
Reznikoff, Charles   9
Ribman, Ronald   7
Rice, Anne   41
Rice, Elmer   7, 49
Rich, Adrienne   3, 6, 7, 11, 18, 36
Richter, Conrad   30
Riding, Laura   3, 7
Ringwood, Gwen Pharis   48
Robbins, Harold   5
Robbins, Tom   9, 32, 64
Robbins, Trina   21
Robinson, Jill   10
Robinson, Kim Stanley   34
Robinson, Marilynne   25
Robinson, Smokey   21
Robison, Mary   42
Roddenberry, Gene   17
Rodgers, Mary   12
Rodman, Howard   65
Roethke, Theodore   1, 3, 8, 11, 19, 46
Rogers, Thomas   57
Rogin, Gilbert   18
Roiphe, Anne   3, 9
Rooke, Leon   25, 34
Rosen, Richard   39
Rosenthal, M. L.   28
Rossner, Judith   6, 9, 29
Roth, Henry   2, 6, 11
Roth, Philip   1, 2, 3, 4, 6, 9, 15, 22, 31, 47, 66
Rothenberg, Jerome   6, 57
Rovit, Earl   7
Ruark, Gibbons   3
Rudnik, Raphael   7
Rukeyser, Muriel   6, 10, 15, 27
Rule, Jane   27
Rush, Norman   44
Russ, Joanna   15
Ryan, Cornelius   7
Ryan, Michael   65
Sachs, Marilyn   35
Sackler, Howard   14
Sadoff, Ira   9
Safire, William   10
Sagan, Carl   30
Saint, H. F.   50
Sainte-Marie, Buffy   17
Salamanca, J. R.   4, 15
Sale, Kirkpatrick   68
Salinger, J. D.   1, 3, 8, 12, 56
Salter, James   7, 52, 59
Sandburg, Carl   1, 4, 10, 15, 35
Sanders, Ed   53
Sanders, Lawrence   41
Sandoz, Mari   28

Saner, Reg   9
Santiago, Danny   33
Santmyer, Helen Hooven   33
Santos, Bienvenido N.   22
Saroyan, William   1, 8, 10, 29, 34, 56
Sarton, May   4, 14, 49
Saul, John   46
Savage, Thomas   40
Savan, Glenn   50
Sayers, Valerie   50
Sayles, John   7, 10, 14
Schaeffer, Susan Fromberg   6, 11, 22
Schell, Jonathan   35
Schevill, James   7
Schisgal, Murray   6
Schnackenberg, Gjertrud   40
Schor, Sandra   65
Schorer, Mark   9
Schrader, Paul   26
Schulberg, Budd   7, 48
Schulz, Charles M.   12
Schuyler, James   5, 23
Schwartz, Delmore   2, 4, 10, 45
Schwartz, John Burnham   59
Schwartz, Lynne Sharon   31
Scoppettone, Sandra   26
Scorsese, Martin   20
Scott, Evelyn   43
Scott, Joanna   50
Sebestyen, Ouida   30
Seelye, John   7
Segal, Erich   3, 10
Seger, Bob   35
Seidel, Frederick   18
Selby, Hubert, Jr.   1, 2, 4, 8
Serling, Rod   30
Seton, Cynthia Propper   27
Settle, Mary Lee   19, 61
Sexton, Anne   2, 4, 6, 8, 10, 15, 53
Shaara, Michael   15
Shacochis, Bob   39
Shange, Ntozake   8, 25, 38
Shapiro, Karl   4, 8, 15, 53
Shaw, Irwin   7, 23, 34
Shawn, Wallace   41
Sheed, Wilfrid   2, 4, 10, 53
Shepard, Jim   36
Shepard, Lucius   34
Shepard, Sam   4, 6, 17, 34, 41, 44
Sherburne, Zoa   30
Sherman, Jonathan Marc   55
Sherman, Martin   19
Sherwin, Judith Johnson   7, 15
Shreve, Susan Richards   23
Shue, Larry   52
Shulman, Alix Kates   2, 10
Shuster, Joe   21
Siegel, Jerome   21
Sigal, Clancy   7
Silko, Leslie Marmon   23
Silver, Joan Micklin   20
Silverberg, Robert   7
Silverstein, Alvin   17
Silverstein, Virginia B.   17
Simak, Clifford   55
Simic, Charles   6, 9, 22, 49, 68
Simmons, Charles   57
Simmons, Dan   44
Simon, Carly   26
Simon, Neil   6, 11, 31, 39, 70
Simon, Paul   17
Simpson, Louis   4, 7, 9, 32

Simpson, Mona 44
Sinclair, Upton 1, 11, 15, 63
Singer, Isaac Bashevis 1, 3, 6, 9, 11, 15, 23, 38, 69
Sissman, L. E. 9, 18
Slade, Bernard 11, 46
Slaughter, Frank G. 29
Slavitt, David 5, 14
Smiley, Jane 53
Smith, Betty 19
Smith, Clark Ashton 43
Smith, Dave 22, 42
Smith, Lee 25
Smith, Martin Cruz 25
Smith, Mary-Ann Tirone 39
Smith, Patti 12
Smith, William Jay 6
Snodgrass, W. D. 2, 6, 10, 18, 68
Snyder, Gary 1, 2, 5, 9, 32
Snyder, Zilpha Keatley 17
Sokolov, Raymond 7
Sommer, Scott 25
Sondheim, Stephen 30, 39
Sontag, Susan 1, 2, 10, 13, 31
Sorrentino, Gilbert 3, 7, 14, 22, 40
Soto, Gary 32
Southern, Terry 7
Spackman, W. M. 46
Spacks, Barry 14
Spanidou, Irini 44
Spencer, Elizabeth 22
Spencer, Scott 30
Spicer, Jack 8, 18, 72
Spielberg, Peter 6
Spielberg, Steven 20
Spillane, Mickey 3, 13
Spinrad, Norman 46
Spivack, Kathleen 6
Spoto, Donald 39
Springsteen, Bruce 17
Squires, Radcliffe 51
Stafford, Jean 4, 7, 19, 68
Stafford, William 4, 7, 29
Stanton, Maura 9
Starbuck, George 53
Steele, Timothy 45
Stegner, Wallace 9, 49
Steinbeck, John 1, 5, 9, 13, 21, 34, 45, 59
Steinem, Gloria 63
Steiner, George 24
Sterling, Bruce 72
Stern, Gerald 40
Stern, Richard G. 4, 39
Sternberg, Josef von 20
Stevens, Mark 34
Stevenson, Anne 7, 33
Still, James 49
Stitt, Milan 29
Stolz, Mary 12
Stone, Irving 7
Stone, Robert 5, 23, 42
Storm, Hyemeyohsts 3
Stout, Rex 3
Strand, Mark 6, 18, 41, 71
Straub, Peter 28
Stribling, T. S. 23
Stuart, Jesse 1, 8, 11, 14, 34
Sturgeon, Theodore 22, 39
Styron, William 1, 3, 5, 11, 15, 60
Sukenick, Ronald 3, 4, 6, 48
Summers, Hollis 10
Susann, Jacqueline 3

Swados, Elizabeth 12
Swados, Harvey 5
Swan, Gladys 69
Swarthout, Glendon 35
Swenson, May 4, 14, 61
Talese, Gay 37
Tallent, Elizabeth 45
Tally, Ted 42
Tan, Amy 59
Tate, Allen 2, 4, 6, 9, 11, 14, 24
Tate, James 2, 6, 25
Tavel, Ronald 6
Taylor, Eleanor Ross 5
Taylor, Henry 44
Taylor, Mildred D. 21
Taylor, Peter 1, 4, 18, 37, 44, 50, 71
Taylor, Robert Lewis 14
Terkel, Studs 38
Terry, Megan 19
Tesich, Steve 40, 69
Tevis, Walter 42
Theroux, Alexander 2, 25
Theroux, Paul 5, 8, 11, 15, 28, 46
Thomas, Audrey 7, 13, 37
Thomas, Joyce Carol 35
Thomas, Lewis 35
Thomas, Piri 17
Thomas, Ross 39
Thompson, Hunter S. 9, 17, 40
Thompson, Jim 69
Thurber, James 5, 11, 25
Tilghman, Christopher 65
Tillinghast, Richard 29
Tiptree, James, Jr. 48, 50
Tolson, Melvin B. 36
Tomlin, Lily 17
Toole, John Kennedy 19, 64
Toomer, Jean 1, 4, 13, 22
Torrey, E. Fuller 34
Traven, B. 8, 11
Trevanian 29
Trilling, Lionel 9, 11, 24
Trow, George W. S. 52
Trudeau, Garry 12
Trumbo, Dalton 19
Tryon, Thomas 3, 11
Tuck, Lily 70
Tunis, John R. 12
Turco, Lewis 11, 63
Tyler, Anne 7, 11, 18, 28, 44, 59
Tytell, John 50
Uhry, Alfred 55
Unger, Douglas 34
Updike, John 1, 2, 3, 5, 7, 9, 13, 15, 23, 34, 43, 70
Urdang, Constance 47
Uris, Leon 7, 32
Van Ash, Cay 34
Van Doren, Mark 6, 10
Van Duyn, Mona 3, 7, 63
Van Peebles, Melvin 2, 20
Van Vechten, Carl 33
Vance, Jack 35
Vandenburgh, Jane 59
Vaughn, Stephanie 62
Vidal, Gore 2, 4, 6, 8, 10, 22, 33, 72
Viereck, Peter 4
Vinge, Joan D. 30
Vliet, R. G. 22
Voigt, Cynthia 30
Voigt, Ellen Bryant 54

Vonnegut, Kurt, Jr. 1, 2, 3, 4, 5, 8, 12, 22, 40, 60
Wagman, Frederica 7
Wagner-Martin, Linda 50
Wagoner, David 3, 5, 15
Wakefield, Dan 7
Wakoski, Diane 2, 4, 7, 9, 11, 40
Waldman, Anne 7
Walker, Alice 5, 6, 9, 19, 27, 46, 58
Walker, Joseph A. 19
Walker, Margaret 1, 6
Wallace, David Foster 50
Wallace, Irving 7, 13
Wallant, Edward Lewis 5, 10
Wambaugh, Joseph 3, 18
Ward, Douglas Turner 19
Warhol, Andy 20
Warren, Robert Penn 1, 4, 6, 8, 10, 13, 18, 39, 53, 59
Wasserstein, Wendy 32, 59
Watkins, Paul 55
Webb, Charles 7
Webb, James H., Jr. 22
Weber, Lenora Mattingly 12
Weidman, Jerome 7
Weiss, Theodore 3, 8, 14
Welch, James 6, 14, 52
Wellek, René 28
Weller, Michael 10, 53
Welles, Orson 20
Wellman, Mac 65
Wellman, Manly Wade 49
Wells, Rosemary 12
Welty, Eudora 1, 2, 5, 14, 22, 33
Wersba, Barbara 30
Wescott, Glenway 13
Wesley, Richard 7
West, Jessamyn 7, 17
West, Paul 7, 14
Westlake, Donald E. 7, 33
Whalen, Philip 6, 29
Wharton, William 18, 37
Wheelock, John Hall 14
White, E. B. 10, 34, 39
White, Edmund III 27
Whitney, Phyllis A. 42
Whittemore, Reed 4
Wicker, Tom 7
Wideman, John Edgar 5, 34, 36, 67
Wieners, John 7
Wiesel, Elie 3, 5, 11, 37
Wiggins, Marianne 57
Wilbur, Richard 3, 6, 9, 14, 53
Wild, Peter 14
Wilder, Billy 20
Wilder, Thornton 1, 5, 6, 10, 15, 35
Wiley, Richard 44
Wilhelm, Kate 7
Willard, Nancy 7, 37
Williams, C. K. 33, 56
Williams, John A. 5, 13
Williams, Jonathan 13
Williams, Joy 31
Williams, Norman 39
Williams, Tennessee 1, 2, 5, 7, 8, 11, 15, 19, 30, 39, 45, 71
Williams, Thomas 14
Williams, William Carlos 1, 2, 5, 9, 13, 22, 42, 67
Williamson, Jack 29
Willingham, Calder 5, 51
Wilson, August 39, 50, 63

Nationality Index

Wilson, Brian 12
Wilson, Edmund 1, 2, 3, 8, 24
Wilson, Lanford 7, 14, 36
Wilson, Robert 7, 9
Wilson, Sloan 32
Wilson, William S. 49
Winters, Yvor 4, 8, 32
Wiseman, Frederick 20
Wodehouse, P. G. 1, 2, 5, 10, 22
Woiwode, Larry 6, 10
Wojciechowska, Maia 26
Wolfe, Gene 25
Wolfe, George C. 49
Wolfe, Tom 1, 2, 9, 15, 35, 51
Wolff, Geoffrey 41
Wolff, Tobias 39, 64
Wolitzer, Hilma 17
Wonder, Stevie 12
Wong, Jade Snow 17
Wouk, Herman 1, 9, 38
Wright, Charles 6, 13, 28
Wright, Charles (Stevenson) 49
Wright, James 3, 5, 10, 28
Wright, Richard 1, 3, 4, 9, 14, 21, 48
Wright, Stephen 33
Wright, William 44
Wurlitzer, Rudolph 2, 4, 15
Wylie, Philip 43
Yates, Richard 7, 8, 23
Yep, Laurence 35
Yerby, Frank G. 1, 7, 22
Yglesias, Helen 7, 22
Young, Al 19
Yurick, Sol 6
Zappa, Frank 17
Zaturenska, Marya 6, 11
Zelazny, Roger 21
Ziegenhagen, Eric 55
Zindel, Paul 6, 26
Zoline, Pamela 62
Zukofsky, Louis 1, 2, 4, 7, 11, 18
Zweig, Paul 34, 42

ARGENTINE
Bioy Casares, Adolfo 4, 8, 13
Borges, Jorge Luis 1, 2, 3, 4, 6, 8, 9, 10,
    13, 19, 44, 48
Cortázar, Julio 2, 3, 5, 10, 13, 15, 33, 34
Costantini, Humberto 49
Mujica Láinez, Manuel 31
Puig, Manuel 3, 5, 10, 28, 65
Sabato, Ernesto 10, 23
Valenzuela, Luisa 31

ARMENIAN
Mamoulian, Rouben 16

AUSTRALIAN
Anderson, Jessica 37
Astley, Thea 41
Brinsmead, H. F. 21
Buckley, Vincent 57
Buzo, Alexander 61
Carey, Peter 40, 55
Clark, Mavis Thorpe 12
Courtenay, Bryce 59
Davison, Frank Dalby 15
Elliott, Sumner Locke 38
FitzGerald, Robert D. 19
Frame, Janet 2, 3, 6, 22, 66
Grenville, Kate 61
Hall, Rodney 51

Hazzard, Shirley 18
Hope, A. D. 3, 51
Hospital, Janette Turner 42
Jolley, Elizabeth 46
Jones, Rod 50
Keneally, Thomas 5, 8, 10, 14, 19, 27, 43
Koch, C. J. 42
Lawler, Raymond (Evenor) 58
Malouf, David 28
Matthews, Greg 45
McAuley, James 45
McCullough, Colleen 27
Murray, Les A. 40
Porter, Peter 5, 13, 33
Prichard, Katharine Susannah 46
Shapcott, Thomas W. 38
Slessor, Kenneth 14
Stead, Christina 2, 5, 8, 32
Stow, Randolph 23, 48
Thiele, Colin 17
Weir, Peter 20
West, Morris L. 6, 33
White, Patrick 3, 4, 5, 7, 9, 18, 65, 69
Williamson, David 56
Wright, Judith 11, 53

AUSTRIAN
Adamson, Joy 17
Bachmann, Ingeborg 69
Bernhard, Thomas 3, 32, 61
Canetti, Elias 3, 14, 25
Gregor, Arthur 9
Handke, Peter 5, 8, 10, 15, 38
Hochwälder, Fritz 36
Jandl, Ernst 34
Lang, Fritz 20
Lind, Jakov 1, 2, 4, 27
Sternberg, Josef von 20
Wellek, René 28
Wilder, Billy 20

BARBADIAN
Kennedy, Adrienne 66
Lamming, George 2, 4, 66

BELGIAN
Ghelderode, Michel de 6, 11
Lévi-Strauss, Claude 38
Mallet-Joris, Françoise 11
Michaux, Henri 8, 19
Sarton, May 4, 14, 49
Simenon, Georges 1, 2, 3, 8, 18, 47
Tytell, John 50
Van Itallie, Jean-Claude 3
Yourcenar, Marguerite 19, 38, 50

BRAZILIAN
Amado, Jorge 13, 40
Andrade, Carlos Drummond de 18
Dourado, Autran 23, 60
Lispector, Clarice 43
Ribeiro, Darcy 34
Ribeiro, João Ubaldo 10, 67
Rosa, João Guimarães 23

BULGARIAN
Bagryana, Elisaveta 10

CAMEROONIAN
Beti, Mongo 27

CANADIAN
Acorn, Milton 15
Aquin, Hubert 15
Atwood, Margaret 2, 3, 4, 8, 13, 15, 25, 44
Avison, Margaret 2, 4
Barfoot, Joan 18
Bellow, Saul 1, 2, 3, 6, 8, 10, 13, 15, 25,
    33, 34
Birney, Earle 1, 4, 6, 11
Bissett, Bill 18
Blais, Marie-Claire 2, 4, 6, 13, 22
Blaise, Clark 29
Bowering, George 15, 47
Bowering, Marilyn R. 32
Buckler, Ernest 13
Buell, John 10
Callaghan, Morley 3, 14, 41, 65
Carrier, Roch 13
Child, Philip 19
Chislett, Anne 34
Cohen, Leonard 3, 38
Cohen, Matt 19
Coles, Don 46
Cook, Michael 58
Craven, Margaret 17
Davies, Robertson 2, 7, 13, 25, 42
De la Roche, Mazo 14
Donnell, David 34
Dudek, Louis 11, 19
Engel, Marian 36
Everson, Ronald G. 27
Faludy, George 42
Finch, Robert 18
Findley, Timothy 27
Fraser, Sylvia 64
Frye, Northrop 24, 70
Gallant, Mavis 7, 18, 38
Garner, Hugh 13
Glassco, John 9
Gotlieb, Phyllis 18
Govier, Katherine 51
Gunnars, Kristjana 69
Gustafson, Ralph 36
Haig-Brown, Roderick L. 21
Hailey, Arthur 5
Harris, Christie 12
Hébert, Anne 4, 13, 29
Hillis, Rick 66
Hine, Daryl 15
Hodgins, Jack 23
Hood, Hugh 15, 28
Hospital, Janette Turner 42
Hyde, Anthony 42
Jacobsen, Josephine 48
Jiles, Paulette 13, 58
Johnston, George 51
Jones, D. G. 10
Kelly, M. T. 55
Kinsella, W. P. 27, 43
Klein, A. M. 19
Krizanc, John 57
Kroetsch, Robert 5, 23, 57
Lane, Patrick 25
Laurence, Margaret 3, 6, 13, 50, 62
Layton, Irving 2, 15
Levine, Norman 54
Lightfoot, Gordon 26
Livesay, Dorothy 4, 15
Mac Ewen, Gwendolyn 13, 55
Mac Leod, Alistair 56
MacLennan, Hugh 2, 14
Macpherson, Jay 14

Maillet, Antonine 54
Major, Kevin 26
McFadden, David 48
McLuhan, Marshall 37
Metcalf, John 37
Mitchell, Joni 12
Mitchell, W. O. 25
Moore, Brian 1, 3, 5, 7, 8, 19, 32
Morgan, Janet 39
Mowat, Farley 26
Munro, Alice 6, 10, 19, 50
Musgrave, Susan 13, 54
Newlove, John 14
Nichol, B. P. 18
Nowlan, Alden 15
Ondaatje, Michael 14, 29, 51
Page, P. K. 7, 18
Pollack, Sharon 50
Pratt, E. J. 19
Purdy, A. W. 3, 6, 14, 50
Quarrington, Paul 65
Reaney, James 13
Ricci, Nino 70
Richards, David Adam 59
Richler, Mordecai 3, 5, 9, 13, 18, 46, 70
Ringwood, Gwen Pharis 48
Ritter, Erika 52
Rooke, Leon 25, 34
Rosenblatt, Joe 15
Ross, Sinclair 13
Roy, Gabrielle 10, 14
Rule, Jane 27
Ryga, George 14
Scott, F. R. 22
Skelton, Robin 13
Škvorecký, Josef 15, 39, 69
Slade, Bernard 11, 46
Smart, Elizabeth 54
Smith, A. J. M. 15
Souster, Raymond 5, 14
Suknaski, Andrew 19
Thesen, Sharon 56
Thomas, Audrey 7, 13, 37
Thompson, Judith 39
Tremblay, Michel 29
Vanderhaeghe, Guy 41
Vizinczey, Stephen 40
Waddington, Miriam 28
Wah, Fred 44
Walker, David Harry 14
Walker, George F. 44, 61
Webb, Phyllis 18
Wiebe, Rudy 6, 11, 14
Wilson, Ethel Davis 13
Wright, L. R. 44
Wright, Richard B. 6
Young, Neil 17

CHILEAN
Alegria, Fernando 57
Allende, Isabel 39, 57
Donoso, José 4, 8, 11, 32
Dorfman, Ariel 48
Neruda, Pablo 1, 2, 5, 7, 9, 28, 62
Parra, Nicanor 2

CHINESE
Ch'ien Chung-shu 22
Ding Ling 68
Jung Chang 71
Lord, Bette Bao 23
Mo, Timothy 46

Pa Chin 18
Peake, Mervyn 7
Wong, Jade Snow 17

COLOMBIAN
García Márquez, Gabriel 2, 3, 8, 10, 15, 27, 47, 55, 68

CUBAN
Arenas, Reinaldo 41
Cabrera Infante, G. 5, 25, 45
Carpentier, Alejo 8, 11, 38
Fornes, Maria Irene 39
Guillén, Nicolás 48
Lezama Lima, José 4, 10
Padilla, Heberto 38
Sarduy, Severo 6

CZECHOSLOVAKIAN
Havel, Václav 25, 58, 65
Hrabal, Bohumil 13, 67
Klima, Ivan 56
Kohout, Pavel 13
Kundera, Milan 4, 9, 19, 32, 68
Lustig, Arnost 56
Seifert, Jaroslav 34, 44
Škvorecký, Josef 15, 39, 69
Vaculík, Ludvík 7

DANISH
Abell, Kjeld 15
Bødker, Cecil 21
Dinesen, Isak 10, 29
Dreyer, Carl Theodor 16

DUTCH
De Hartog, Jan 19
Mulisch, Harry 42
Ruyslinck, Ward 14
Van de Wetering, Janwillem 47

EGYPTIAN
Chedid, Andrée 47
Mahfūz, Najīb 52, 55

ENGLISH
Ackroyd, Peter 34, 52
Adams, Douglas 27, 60
Adams, Richard 4, 5, 18
Adcock, Fleur 41
Aickman, Robert 57
Aiken, Joan 35
Aldington, Richard 49
Aldiss, Brian W. 5, 14, 40
Allingham, Margery 19
Almedingen, E. M. 12
Alvarez, A. 5, 13
Ambler, Eric 4, 6, 9
Amis, Kingsley 1, 2, 3, 5, 8, 13, 40, 44
Amis, Martin 4, 9, 38, 62
Anderson, Lindsay 20
Anthony, Piers 35
Archer, Jeffrey 28
Arden, John 6, 13, 15
Armatrading, Joan 17
Arthur, Ruth M. 12
Arundel, Honor 17
Auden, W. H. 1, 2, 3, 4, 6, 9, 11, 14, 43
Ayckbourn, Alan 5, 8, 18, 33
Ayrton, Michael 7
Bagnold, Enid 25
Bailey, Paul 45

Bainbridge, Beryl 4, 5, 8, 10, 14, 18, 22, 62
Ballard, J. G. 3, 6, 14, 36
Banks, Lynne Reid 23
Barker, Clive 52
Barker, George 8, 48
Barker, Howard 37
Barker, Pat 32
Barnes, Julian 42
Barnes, Peter 5, 56
Bates, H. E. 46
Beer, Patricia 58
Bennett, Alan 45
Berger, John 2, 19
Berkoff, Steven 56
Bermant, Chaim 40
Betjeman, John 2, 6, 10, 34, 43
Billington, Rachel 43
Binyon, T. J. 34
Blunden, Edmund 2, 56
Bogarde, Dirk 19
Bolt, Robert 14
Bond, Edward 4, 6, 13, 23
Booth, Martin 13
Bowen, Elizabeth 1, 3, 6, 11, 15, 22
Bowie, David 17
Boyd, William 28, 53, 70
Bradbury, Malcolm 32, 61
Bragg, Melvyn 10
Braine, John 1, 3, 41
Brenton, Howard 31
Brittain, Vera 23
Brooke-Rose, Christine 40
Brophy, Brigid 6, 11, 29
Brunner, John 8, 10
Bryce, Courtenay 59
Bunting, Basil 10, 39, 47
Burgess, Anthony 1, 2, 4, 5, 8, 10, 13, 15, 22, 40, 62
Byatt, A. S. 19, 65
Caldwell, Taylor 2, 28, 39
Campbell, Ramsey 42
Carter, Angela 5, 41
Causley, Charles 7
Caute, David 29
Chambers, Aidan 35
Chaplin, Charles 16
Chatwin, Bruce 28, 57, 59
Christie, Agatha 1, 6, 8, 12, 39, 48
Churchill, Caryl 31, 55
Clark, Brian 29
Clarke, Arthur C. 1, 4, 13, 18, 35
Clash, The 30
Clavell, James 6, 25
Colegate, Isabel 36
Comfort, Alex 7
Compton-Burnett, Ivy 1, 3, 10, 15, 34
Cooney, Ray 62
Costello, Elvis 21
Coward, Noël 1, 9, 29, 51
Creasey, John 11
Crispin, Edmund 22
Dahl, Roald 1, 6, 18
Daryush, Elizabeth 6, 19
Davie, Donald 5, 8, 10, 31
Davies, Ray 21
Davies, Rhys 23
Day Lewis, C. 1, 6, 10
Deighton, Len 4, 7, 22, 46
Delaney, Shelagh 29
Dennis, Nigel 8
Dickinson, Peter 12, 35
Drabble, Margaret 2, 3, 5, 8, 10, 22, 53

Nationality Index

du Maurier, Daphne 6, 11, 59
Duffy, Maureen 37
Durrell, Lawrence 1, 4, 6, 8, 13, 27, 41
Eagleton, Terry 63
Edgar, David 42
Edwards, G. B. 25
Eliot, T. S. 1, 2, 3, 6, 9, 10, 13, 15, 24, 34,
   41, 55, 57
Elliott, Janice 47
Ellis, A. E. 7
Ellis, Alice Thomas 40
Empson, William 3, 8, 19, 33, 34
Enright, D. J. 4, 8, 31
Ewart, Gavin 13, 46
Fairbairns, Zoë 32
Farrell, J. G. 6
Feinstein, Elaine 36
Fenton, James 32
Figes, Eva 31
Fisher, Roy 25
Fitzgerald, Penelope 19, 51, 61
Fleming, Ian 3, 30
Follett, Ken 18
Forester, C. S. 35
Forster, E. M. 1, 2, 3, 4, 9, 10, 13, 15, 22,
   45
Forsyth, Frederick 2, 5, 36
Fowles, John 1, 2, 3, 4, 6, 9, 10, 15, 33
Francis, Dick 2, 22, 42
Fraser, Antonia 32
Fraser, George MacDonald 7
Frayn, Michael 3, 7, 31, 47
Freeling, Nicolas 38
Fry, Christopher 2, 10, 14
Fugard, Sheila 48
Fuller, John 62
Fuller, Roy 4, 28
Gardam, Jane 43
Gardner, John (Edmund) 30
Garfield, Leon 12
Garner, Alan 17
Garnett, David 3
Gascoyne, David 45
Gee, Maggie 57
Gerhardie, William 5
Gilliatt, Penelope 2, 10, 13, 53
Glanville, Brian 6
Glendinning, Victoria 50
Gloag, Julian 40
Godden, Rumer 53
Golding, William 1, 2, 3, 8, 10, 17, 27, 58
Graham, Winston 23
Graves, Richard P. 44
Graves, Robert 1, 2, 6, 11, 39, 44, 45
Gray, Simon 9, 14, 36
Green, Henry 2, 13
Greene, Graham 1, 3, 6, 9, 14, 18, 27, 37,
   70, 72
Griffiths, Trevor 13, 52
Grigson, Geoffrey 7, 39
Gunn, Thom 3, 6, 18, 32
Haig-Brown, Roderick L. 21
Hailey, Arthur 5
Hall, Rodney 51
Hamburger, Michael 5, 14
Hamilton, Patrick 51
Hampton, Christopher 4
Hare, David 29, 58
Harrison, Tony 43
Hartley, L. P. 2, 22
Harwood, Ronald 32
Hastings, Selina 44

Hawking, Stephen 63
Heppenstall, Rayner 10
Herriot, James 12
Hibbert, Eleanor 7
Hill, Geoffrey 5, 8, 18, 45
Hill, Susan B. 4
Hinde, Thomas 6, 11
Hitchcock, Alfred 16
Hocking, Mary 13
Holden, Ursula 18
Holdstock, Robert 39
Hollinghurst, Alan 55
Hooker, Jeremy 43
Hopkins, John 4
Household, Geoffrey 11
Howard, Elizabeth Jane 7, 29
Hughes, Richard 1, 11
Hughes, Ted 2, 4, 9, 14, 37
Huxley, Aldous 1, 3, 4, 5, 8, 11, 18, 35
Ingalls, Rachel 42
Isherwood, Christopher 1, 9, 11, 14, 44
Ishiguro, Kazuo 27, 56, 59
Jacobson, Dan 4, 14
Jagger, Mick 17
James, P. D. 18, 46
Jellicoe, Ann 27
Jennings, Elizabeth 5, 14
Jhabvala, Ruth Prawer 4, 8, 29
Johnson, B. S. 6, 9
Johnson, Pamela Hansford 1, 7, 27
Jolley, Elizabeth 46
Jones, David 2, 4, 7, 13, 42
Jones, Diana Wynne 26
Jones, Mervyn 10, 52
Josipovici, Gabriel 6, 43
Kavan, Anna 5, 13
Kaye, M. M. 28
Keates, Jonathan 34
King, Francis 8, 53
Koestler, Arthur 1, 3, 6, 8, 15, 33
Kops, Bernard 4
Kureishi, Hanif 64
Larkin, Philip 3, 5, 8, 9, 13, 18, 33, 39, 64
Le Carré, John 3, 5, 9, 15, 28
Leavis, F. R. 24
Lee, Tanith 46
Lehmann, Rosamond 5
Lennon, John 12, 35
Lessing, Doris 1, 2, 3, 6, 10, 15, 22, 40
Levertov, Denise 1, 2, 3, 5, 8, 15, 28
Levi, Peter 41
Lewis, C. S. 1, 3, 6, 14, 27
Lively, Penelope 32, 50
Lodge, David 36
Loy, Mina 28
Luke, Peter 38
MacInnes, Colin 4, 23
Mackenzie, Compton 18
Macpherson, Jay 14
Maitland, Sara 49
Manning, Olivia 5, 19
Markandaya, Kamala 8, 38
Masefield, John 11, 47
Maugham, W. Somerset 1, 11, 15, 67
Mayne, William 12
McCartney, Paul 12, 35
McEwan, Ian 13, 66
McGrath, Patrick 55
Mercer, David 5
Metcalf, John 37
Middleton, Christopher 13
Middleton, Stanley 7, 38

Mitford, Nancy 44
Mo, Timothy 46
Monty Python 21
Moorcock, Michael 5, 27, 58
Mortimer, John 28, 43
Mortimer, Penelope 5
Mosley, Nicholas 43, 70
Motion, Andrew 47
Mott, Michael 15, 34
Murdoch, Iris 1, 2, 3, 4, 6, 8, 11, 15, 22,
   31, 51
Naipaul, V. S. 4, 7, 9, 13, 18, 37
Newby, P. H. 2, 13
Nichols, Peter 5, 36, 65
Nye, Robert 13, 42
O'Brien, Richard 17
O'Faolain, Julia 6, 19, 47
Olivier, Laurence 20
Orton, Joe 4, 13, 43
Osborne, John 1, 2, 5, 11, 45
Osborne, Lawrence 50
Page, Jimmy 12
Page, Louise 40
Parkin, Frank 43
Paulin, Tom 37
Peake, Mervyn 7, 54
Pearce, Philippa 21
Pink Floyd 35
Pinter, Harold 1, 3, 6, 9, 11, 15, 27, 58
Plant, Robert 12
Poliakoff, Stephen 38
Police, The 26
Poole, Josephine 17
Potter, Dennis 58
Powell, Anthony 1, 3, 7, 9, 10, 31
Pownall, David 10
Powys, John Cowper 7, 9, 15, 46
Priestley, J. B. 2, 5, 9, 34
Prince, F. T. 22
Pritchett, V. S. 5, 13, 15, 41
Pym, Barbara 13, 19, 37
Quin, Ann 6
Raine, Craig 32
Raine, Kathleen 7, 45
Rathbone, Julian 41
Rattigan, Terence 7
Raven, Simon 14
Read, Herbert 4
Read, Piers Paul 4, 10, 25
Reading, Peter 47
Redgrove, Peter 6, 41
Reid, Christopher 33
Renault, Mary 3, 11, 17
Rendell, Ruth 28, 48, 50
Rhys, Jean 2, 4, 6, 14, 19, 51
Rice, Tim 21
Richard, Keith 17
Richards, I. A. 14, 24
Roberts, Keith 14
Roberts, Michèle 48
Rudkin, David 14
Rushdie, Salman 23, 31, 55, 59
Rushforth, Peter 19
Russell, Ken 16
Russell, Willy 60
Sacks, Oliver 67
Sansom, William 2, 6
Sassoon, Siegfried 36
Scammell, Michael 34
Scannell, Vernon 49
Schlee, Ann 35
Scott, Paul 9, 60

Shaffer, Anthony 19
Shaffer, Peter 5, 14, 18, 37, 60
Sharpe, Tom 36
Shaw, Robert 5
Sheed, Wilfrid 2, 4, 10, 53
Shute, Nevil 30
Shuttle, Penelope 7
Silkin, Jon 2, 6, 43
Sillitoe, Alan 1, 3, 6, 10, 19, 57
Simpson, N. F. 29
Sinclair, Andrew 2, 14
Sisson, C. H. 8
Sitwell, Edith 2, 9, 67
Slaughter, Carolyn 56
Smith, Stevie 3, 8, 25, 44
Snow, C. P. 1, 4, 6, 9, 13, 19
Spender, Stephen 1, 2, 5, 10, 41
Spurling, Hilary 34
Stannard, Martin 44
Stewart, J. I. M. 7, 14, 32
Stewart, Mary 7, 35
Stoppard, Tom 1, 3, 4, 5, 8, 15, 29, 34, 63
Storey, David 2, 4, 5, 8
Streatfeild, Noel 21
Sutcliff, Rosemary 26
Swift, Graham 41
Swinfen, Ann 34
Swinnerton, Frank 31
Symons, Julian 2, 14, 32
Szirtes, George 46
Taylor, Elizabeth 2, 4, 29
Tennant, Emma 13, 52
Teran, Lisa St. Aubin de 36
Thomas, D. M. 13, 22, 31
Tindall, Gillian 7
Tolkien, J. R. R. 1, 2, 3, 8, 12, 38
Tomlinson, Charles 2, 4, 6, 13, 45
Townsend, Sue 61
Townshend, Peter 17, 42
Treitel, Jonathan 70
Tremain, Rose 42
Tuohy, Frank 37
Ustinov, Peter 1
Vansittart, Peter 42
Wain, John 2, 11, 15, 46
Walker, Ted 13
Walsh, Jill Paton 35
Warner, Francis 14
Warner, Marina 59
Warner, Rex 45
Warner, Sylvia Townsend 7, 19
Waterhouse, Keith 47
Waugh, Auberon 7
Waugh, Evelyn 1, 3, 8, 13, 19, 27, 44
Waugh, Harriet 6
Webber, Andrew Lloyd 21
Weldon, Fay 6, 9, 11, 19, 36, 59
Weller, Paul 26
Wesker, Arnold 3, 5, 42
West, Anthony 50
West, Paul 7, 14
West, Rebecca 7, 9, 31, 50
Westall, Robert 17
White, Patrick 3, 4, 5, 7, 9, 18, 65, 69
White, T. H. 30
Whitehead, E. A. 5
Whitemore, Hugh 37
Williams, Hugo 42
Wilson, A. N. 33
Wilson, Angus 2, 3, 5, 25, 34
Wilson, Colin 3, 14
Wilson, Snoo 33

Wingrove, David 68
Winterson, Jeannette 64
Wodehouse, P. G. 1, 2, 5, 10, 22
Wyndham, John 19
Young, Andrew 5

ESTONIAN
Ivask, Ivar 14

FIJIAN
Prichard, Katharine Susannah 46

FINNISH
Haavikko, Paavo 18, 34
Salama, Hannu 18
Sillanpää, Franz Eemil 19

FRENCH
Adamov, Arthur 4, 25
Anouilh, Jean 1, 3, 8, 13, 40, 50
Aragon, Louis 3, 22
Arrabal, Fernando 2, 9, 18
Audiberti, Jacques 38
Aymé, Marcel 11
Barthes, Roland 24
Bataille, Georges 29
Baudrillard, Jean CLC-60
Beauvoir, Simone de 1, 2, 4, 8, 14, 31, 44, 50, 71
Beckett, Samuel 1, 2, 3, 4, 6, 9, 10, 11, 14, 18, 29, 57
Bonnefoy, Yves 9, 15, 58
Bresson, Robert 16
Breton, André 2, 9, 15, 54
Butor, Michel 1, 3, 8, 11, 15
Camus, Albert 1, 2, 4, 9, 11, 14, 32, 63, 69
Cayrol, Jean 11
Céline, Louis-Ferdinand 1, 3, 4, 7, 9, 15, 47
Cendrars, Blaise 18
Chabrol, Claude 16
Char, René 9, 11, 14, 55
Chedid, Andrée 47
Clair, René 20
Cocteau, Jean 1, 8, 15, 16, 43
Cousteau, Jacques-Yves 30
Del Castillo, Michel 38
Derrida, Jacques 24
Duhamel, Georges 8
Duras, Marguerite 3, 6, 11, 20, 34, 40, 68
Federman, Raymond 6, 47
Foucault, Michel 31, 34, 69
Francis, Claude 50
Gary, Romain 25
Gascar, Pierre 11
Genet, Jean 1, 2, 5, 10, 14, 44, 46
Giono, Jean 4, 11
Godard, Jean-Luc 20
Goldmann, Lucien 24
Gontier, Fernande 50
Gracq, Julien 11, 48
Gray, Francine du Plessix 22
Green, Julien 3, 11
Guillevic 33
Ionesco, Eugène 1, 4, 6, 9, 11, 15, 41
Jouve, Pierre Jean 47
Laurent, Antoine 50
Le Clézio, J. M. G. 31
Leduc, Violette 22
Leiris, Michel 61
Lévi-Strauss, Claude 38
Mallet-Joris, Françoise 11

Malraux, André 1, 4, 9, 13, 15, 57
Mandiargues, André Pieyre de 41
Marcel, Gabriel 15
Mauriac, Claude 9
Mauriac, François 4, 9, 56
Merton, Thomas 1, 3, 11, 34
Modiano, Patrick 18
Montherlant, Henri de 8, 19
Morand, Paul 41
Perec, Georges 56
Perse, St.-John 4, 11, 46
Pinget, Robert 7, 13, 37
Ponge, Francis 6, 18
Prévert, Jacques 15
Queneau, Raymond 2, 5, 10, 42
Renoir, Jean 20
Resnais, Alain 16
Reverdy, Pierre 53
Rio, Michel 43
Robbe-Grillet, Alain 1, 2, 4, 6, 8, 10, 14, 43
Rohmer, Eric 16
Romains, Jules 7
Sagan, Françoise 3, 6, 9, 17, 36
Sarduy, Severo 6
Sarraute, Nathalie 1, 2, 4, 8, 10, 31
Sartre, Jean-Paul 1, 4, 7, 9, 13, 18, 24, 44, 50, 52
Schwarz-Bart, André 2, 4
Schwarz-Bart, Simone 7
Simenon, Georges 1, 2, 3, 8, 18, 47
Simon, Claude 4, 9, 15, 39
Soupault, Philippe 68
Steiner, George 24
Tournier, Michel 6, 23, 36
Troyat, Henri 23
Truffaut, François 20
Tuck, Lily 70
Tzara, Tristan 47
Varda, Agnès 16
Wittig, Monique 22
Yourcenar, Marguerite 19, 38, 50

GERMAN
Becker, Jurek 7, 19
Benary-Isbert, Margot 12
Bienek, Horst 7, 11
Böll, Heinrich 2, 3, 6, 9, 11, 15, 27, 39, 72
Buchheim, Lothar-Günther 6
Dürrenmatt, Friedrich 1, 4, 8, 11, 15, 43
Eich, Günter 15
Ende, Michael 31
Enzensberger, Hans Magnus 43
Fassbinder, Rainer Werner 20
Figes, Eva 31
Grass, Günter 1, 2, 4, 6, 11, 15, 22, 32, 49
Hamburger, Michael 5, 14
Heidegger, Martin 24
Herzog, Werner 16
Hesse, Hermann 1, 2, 3, 6, 11, 17, 25, 69
Heym, Stefan 41
Hildesheimer, Wolfgang 49
Hochhuth, Rolf 4, 11, 18
Hofmann, Gert 54
Johnson, Uwe 5, 10, 15, 40
Kroetz, Franz Xaver 41
Kunze, Reiner 10
Lenz, Siegfried 27
Levitin, Sonia 17
Mueller, Lisel 13, 51
Nossack, Hans Erich 6
Preussler, Otfried 17

Nationality Index

Remarque, Erich Maria 21
Riefenstahl, Leni 16
Sachs, Nelly 14
Schmidt, Arno 56
Seghers, Anna 7
Strauss, Botho 22
Süskind, Patrick 44
Walser, Martin 27
Weiss, Peter 3, 15, 51
Wellershoff, Dieter 46
Wolf, Christa 14, 29, 58
Zuckmayer, Carl 18

GHANAIAN
Armah, Ayi Kwei 5, 33

GREEK
Broumas, Olga 10
Elytis, Odysseus 15, 49
Haviaras, Stratis 33
Karapánou, Margaríta 13
Nakos, Lilika 29
Ritsos, Yannis 6, 13, 31
Samarakis, Antonis 5
Seferis, George 5, 11
Spanidou, Irini 44
Vassilikos, Vassilis 4, 8

GUADELOUPEAN
Condé, Maryse 52
Schwarz-Bart, Simone 7

GUATEMALAN
Asturias, Miguel Ángel 3, 8, 13

GUINEAN
Laye, Camara 4, 38

GUYANESE
Harris, Wilson 25

HUNGARIAN
Faludy, George 42
Koestler, Arthur 1, 3, 6, 8, 15, 33
Konrád, György 4, 10
Lengyel, József 7
Lukács, Georg 24
Nagy, László 7
Szirtes, George 46
Tabori, George 19
Vizinczey, Stephen 40
Wiesel, Elie 3, 5, 11, 37

ICELANDIC
Gunnars, Kristjana 69
Laxness, Halldór 25

INDIAN
Ali, Ahmed 69
Anand, Mulk Raj 23
Desai, Anita 19, 37
Ezekiel, Nissim 61
Ghosh, Amitav 44
Mahapatra, Jayanta 33
Markandaya, Kamala 8, 38
Mehta, Ved 37,
Mistry, Rohinton 71
Mukherjee, Bharati 53
Narayan, R. K. 7, 28, 47
Rao, Raja 25, 56
Ray, Satyajit 16
Rushdie, Salman 23, 31, 55, 59

Sahgal, Nayantara 41
Sealy, I. Allan 55
Seth, Vikram 43
Singh, Khushwant 11
Tharoor, Shashi 70

IRANIAN
Modarressi, Taghi 44
Shamlu, Ahmad 10

IRISH
Banville, John 46
Beckett, Samuel 1, 2, 3, 4, 6, 9, 10, 11, 14, 18, 29, 57
Behan, Brendan 1, 8, 11, 15
Blackwood, Caroline 6, 9
Boland, Eavan 40, 67
Bowen, Elizabeth 1, 3, 6, 11, 15, 22
Boyle, Patrick 19
Brennan, Maeve 5
Brown, Christy 63
Carroll, Paul Vincent 10
Clarke, Austin 6, 9
Dillon, Eilís 17
Donleavy, J. P. 1, 4, 6, 10, 45
Durcan, Paul 43, 70
Friel, Brian 5, 42, 59
Gébler, Carlo 39
Hanley, James 3, 5, 8, 13
Hart, Josephine 70
Heaney, Seamus 5, 7, 14, 25, 37
Johnston, Jennifer 7
Kavanagh, Patrick 22
Keane, Molly 31
Kiely, Benedict 23, 43
Kinsella, Thomas 4, 19
Lavin, Mary 4, 18
Leonard, Hugh 19
Longley, Michael 29
Mac Laverty, Bernard 31
MacNeice, Louis 1, 4, 10, 53
Mahon, Derek 27
McGahern, John 5, 9
McGinley, Patrick 41
McGuckian, Medbh 48
Montague, John 13, 46
Moore, Brian 1, 3, 5, 7, 8, 19, 32
Morrison, Van 21
Muldoon, Paul 32, 72
Murphy, Richard 41
Murphy, Thomas 51
Nolan, Christopher 58
O'Brien, Edna 3, 5, 8, 13, 36, 65
O'Brien, Flann 1, 4, 5, 7, 10, 47
O'Casey, Sean 1, 5, 9, 11, 15
O'Connor, Frank 14, 23
O'Faolain, Julia 6, 19, 47
O'Faoláin, Seán 1, 7, 14, 32, 70
O'Flaherty, Liam 5, 34
Paulin, Tom 37
Rodgers, W. R. 7
Simmons, James 43
Trevor, William 7, 9, 14, 25, 71
White, Terence de Vere 49

ISRAELI
Agnon, S. Y. 4, 8, 14
Amichai, Yehuda 9, 22, 57
Appelfeld, Aharon 23, 47
Grossman, David 67
Kaniuk, Yoram 19

Levin, Meyer 7
Megged, Aharon 9
Oz, Amos 5, 8, 11, 27, 33, 54
Shamas, Anton 55
Sobol, Joshua 60
Yehoshua, A. B. 13, 31

ITALIAN
Antonioni, Michelangelo 20
Bacchelli, Riccardo 19
Bassani, Giorgio 9
Bertolucci, Bernardo 16
Buzzati, Dino 36
Calvino, Italo 5, 8, 11, 22, 33, 39
De Sica, Vittorio 20
Eco, Umberto 28, 60
Fallaci, Oriana 11
Fellini, Federico 16
Fo, Dario 32
Gadda, Carlo Emilio 11
Ginzburg, Natalia 5, 11, 54, 70
Giovene, Andrea 7
Landolfi, Tommaso 11, 49
Levi, Primo 37, 50
Luzi, Mario 13
Montale, Eugenio 7, 9, 18
Morante, Elsa 8, 47
Moravia, Alberto 2, 7, 11, 18, 27, 46
Palazzeschi, Aldo 11
Pasolini, Pier Paolo 20, 37
Piccolo, Lucio 13
Quasimodo, Salvatore 10
Ricci, Nino 70
Silone, Ignazio 4
Ungaretti, Giuseppe 7, 11, 15
Visconti, Luchino 16
Vittorini, Elio 6, 9, 14
Wertmüller, Lina 16

JAMAICAN
Bennett, Louise 28
Cliff, Jimmy 21
Marley, Bob 17
Thelwell, Michael 22

JAPANESE
Abé, Kōbō 8, 22, 53
Enchi, Fumiko 31
Endo, Shusaku 7, 14, 19, 54
Ibuse, Masuji 22
Ichikawa, Kon 20
Ishiguro, Kazuo 56
Kawabata, Yasunari 2, 5, 9, 18
Kurosawa, Akira 16
Mishima, Yukio 2, 4, 6, 9, 27
Ōe, Kenzaburō 10, 36
Oshima, Nagisa 20
Ozu, Yasujiro 16
Shiga, Naoya 33
Tanizaki, Jun'ichirō 8, 14, 28

KENYAN
Ngugi wa Thiong'o 3, 7, 13, 36

MEXICAN
Castellanos, Rosario 66
Fuentes, Carlos 3, 8, 10, 13, 22, 41, 60
Ibargüengoitia, Jorge 37
López Portillo, José 46
López y Fuentes, Gregorio 32
Paz, Octavio 3, 4, 6, 10, 19, 51, 65
Rulfo, Juan 8

MOROCCAN
Arrabal, Fernando   2, 9, 18, 58

NEW ZEALAND
Adcock, Fleur   41
Ashton-Warner, Sylvia   19
Baxter, James K.   14
Frame, Janet   2, 3, 6, 22
Gee, Maurice   29
Grace, Patricia   56
Hilliard, Noel   15
Hulme, Keri   39
Ihimaera, Witi   46
Marsh, Ngaio   7, 53
Sargeson, Frank   31

NICARAGUAN
Cardenal, Ernesto   31

NIGERIAN
Achebe, Chinua   1, 3, 5, 7, 11, 26, 51
Clark, John Pepper   38
Ekwensi, Cyprian   4
Emecheta, Buchi   14, 48
Okigbo, Christopher   25
Soyinka, Wole   3, 5, 14, 36, 44
Tutuola, Amos   5, 14, 29

NORWEGIAN
Friis-Baastad, Babbis   12
Heyerdahl, Thor   26

PAKISTANI
Ali, Ahmed   69
Ghose, Zulfikar   42

PALESTINIAN
Bakshi, Ralph   26

PARAGUAYAN
Roa Bastos, Augusto   45

PERUVIAN
Arguedas, José María   10, 18
Goldemberg, Isaac   52
Vargas Llosa, Mario   3, 6, 9, 10, 15, 31, 42

POLISH
Agnon, S. Y.   4, 8, 14
Becker, Jurek   7, 19
Bermant, Chaim   40
Bienek, Horst   7, 11
Brandys, Kazimierz   62
Dąbrowska, Maria   15
Gombrowicz, Witold   4, 7, 11, 49
Herbert, Zbigniew   9, 43
Konwicki, Tadeusz   8, 28, 54
Kosinski, Jerzy   1, 2, 3, 6, 10, 15, 53, 70
Lem, Stanislaw   8, 15, 40
Miłosz, Czesław   5, 11, 22, 31, 56
Mrożek, Sławomir   3, 13
Polanski, Roman   16
Różewicz, Tadeusz   9, 23
Singer, Isaac Bashevis   1, 3, 6, 9, 11, 15, 23, 38, 69
Skolimowski, Jerzy   20
Wajda, Andrzej   16
Wittlin, Joseph   25
Wojciechowska, Maia   26

PORTUGUESE
Miguéis, José Rodrigues   10

PUERTO RICAN
Piñero, Miguel   4, 55
Sánchez, Luis Rafael   23

RUMANIAN
Appelfeld, Aharon   23, 47
Celan, Paul   10, 19, 53
Cioran, E. M.   64
Codrescu, Andrei   46
Ionesco, Eugène   1, 4, 6, 9, 11, 15, 41
Rezzori, Gregor von   25
Tzara, Tristan   47

RUSSIAN
Aitmatov, Chingiz   71
Akhmadulina, Bella   53
Akhmatova, Anna   11, 25, 64
Aksyonov, Vasily   22, 37
Aleshkovsky, Yuz   44
Almedingen, E. M.   12
Bitov, Andrei   57
Brodsky, Joseph   4, 6, 13, 36, 50
Ehrenburg, Ilya   18, 34, 62
Eliade, Mircea   19
Gary, Romain   25
Goldberg, Anatol   34
Grade, Chaim   10
Grossman, Vasily   41
Iskander, Fazil   47
Kaletski, Alexander   39
Krotkov, Yuri   19
Limonov, Eduard   67
Nabokov, Vladimir   1, 2, 3, 6, 8, 11, 15, 23, 44, 46, 64
Olesha, Yuri   8
Pasternak, Boris   7, 10, 18, 63
Paustovsky, Konstantin   40
Rahv, Philip   24
Rand, Ayn   3, 30, 44
Ratushinskaya, Irina   54
Rybakov, Anatoli   23, 53
Shalamov, Varlam   18
Sholokhov, Mikhail   7, 15
Sinyavsky, Andrei   8
Solzhenitsyn, Aleksandr I.   1, 2, 4, 7, 9, 10, 18, 24, 26, 34
Strugatskii, Arkadii   27
Strugatskii, Boris   27
Trifonov, Yuri   45
Troyat, Henri   23
Voinovich, Vladimir   10, 49
Voznesensky, Andrei   1, 15, 57
Yanovsky, Vassily S.   2, 18
Yevtushenko, Yevgeny   1, 3, 13, 26, 51
Yezierska, Anzia   46
Zaturenska, Marya   6, 11
Zinoviev, Alexander   19

SALVADORAN
Argueta, Manlio   31

SCOTTISH
Banks, Iain   34
Brown, George Mackay   5, 48
Cronin, A. J.   32
Dunn, Douglas   6, 40
Graham, W. S.   29
Gray, Alasdair   41
Hunter, Mollie   21
Jenkins, Robin   52
Kelman, James   58
MacBeth, George   2, 5, 9

MacCaig, Norman   36
MacDiarmid, Hugh   2, 4, 11, 19, 63
MacInnes, Helen   27, 39
MacLean, Alistair   3, 13, 50, 63
McIlvanney, William   42
Morgan, Edwin   31
Smith, Iain Crichton   64
Spark, Muriel   2, 3, 5, 8, 13, 18, 40
Taylor, C. P.   27
Walker, David Harry   14
Young, Andrew   5

SENEGALESE
Ousmane, Sembène   66

SENGALESE
Senghor, Léopold Sédar   54

SICILIAN
Sciascia, Leonardo   8, 9, 41

SOMALIAN
Farah, Nuruddin   53

SOUTH AFRICAN
Breytenbach, Breyten   23, 37
Brink, André   18, 36
Brutus, Dennis   43
Coetzee, J. M.   23, 33, 66
Fugard, Athol   5, 9, 14, 25, 40
Fugard, Sheila   48
Gordimer, Nadine   3, 5, 7, 10, 18, 33, 51, 70
Harwood, Ronald   32
Head, Bessie   25, 67
Hope, Christopher   52
La Guma, Alex   19
Millin, Sarah Gertrude   49
Mphahlele, Ezekiel   25
Mtwa, Percy   47
Ngema, Mbongeni   57
Nkosi, Lewis   45
Paton, Alan   4, 10, 25, 55
Plomer, William   4, 8
Prince, F. T.   22
Smith, Wilbur   33
Van der Post, Laurens   5
Vorster, Gordon   34

SPANISH
Alberti, Rafael   7
Aleixandre, Vicente   9, 36
Alfau, Felipe   66
Alonso, Dámaso   14
Azorín   11
Benet, Juan   28
Buero Vallejo, Antonio   15, 46
Buñuel, Luis   16
Casona, Alejandro   49
Cela, Camilo José   4, 13, 59
Cernuda, Luis   54
Del Castillo, Michel   38
Delibes, Miguel   8, 18
Donoso, José   4, 8, 11, 32
Espriu, Salvador   9
Gironella, José María   11
Gómez de la Serna, Ramón   9
Goytisolo, Juan   5, 10, 23
Guillén, Jorge   11
Matute, Ana María   11
Otero, Blas de   11
Rodríguez, Claudio   10

Nationality Index

Saura, Carlos   20
Sender, Ramón   8

SWEDISH
Beckman, Gunnel   26
Bergman, Ingmar   16, 72
Ekelöf, Gunnar   27
Johnson, Eyvind   14
Lagerkvist, Pär   7, 10, 13, 54
Martinson, Harry   14
Tranströmer, Tomas   52, 65
Wahlöö, Per   7
Weiss, Peter   3, 15, 51

SWISS
Cendrars, Blaise   18
Dürrenmatt, Friedrich   1, 4, 8, 11, 15, 43
Federspiel, J. F.   42
Frisch, Max   3, 9, 14, 18, 32, 44
Hesse, Hermann   1, 2, 3, 6, 11, 17, 25, 69
Pinget, Robert   7, 13, 37
Sterchi, Beat   65
Von Däniken, Erich   30

TURKISH
Hikmet, Nâzim   40
Kemal, Yashar   14, 29

URUGUAYAN
Galeano, Eduardo   72
Onetti, Juan Carlos   7, 10

WELSH
Abse, Dannie   7, 29
Clarke, Gillian   61
Dahl, Roald   1, 6, 18
Davies, Rhys   23
Francis, Dick   2, 22, 42
Hughes, Richard   1, 11
Humphreys, Emyr   47
Jones, David   2, 4, 7, 13, 42
Levinson, Deirdre   49
Llewellyn, Richard   7
Mathias, Roland   45
Norris, Leslie   14
Roberts, Kate   15
Rubens, Bernice   19, 31
Thomas, R. S.   6, 13, 48
Watkins, Vernon   43
Williams, Emlyn   15

WEST INDIAN
Armatrading, Joan   17
Césaire, Aimé   19, 32
Dabydeen, David   34
Edwards, Gus   43
Glissant, Édouard   10, 68
Guy, Rosa   26
James, C. L. R.   33
Kincaid, Jamaica   43, 68
Lovelace, Earl   51
Naipaul, Shiva   32, 39
Naipaul, V. S.   4, 7, 9, 13, 18, 37
Rhys, Jean   2, 4, 6, 14, 19, 51
Walcott, Derek   2, 4, 9, 14, 25, 42, 67

YUGOSLAVIAN
Andrić, Ivo   8
Ćosić, Dobrica   14
Kiš, Danilo   57
Krleža, Miroslav   8
Pavic, Milorad   60

Popa, Vasko   19
Simic, Charles   6, 9, 22, 49, 68
Tesich, Steve   40, 69

CLC-72 Title Index

"Das Abenteuer" (Böll) **72**:71, 77

"Abschied" (Böll) **72**:70, 73

Absent without Leave (Böll)
See *Entfernung von der Truppe*

Adam, Where Art Thou? (Böll)
See *Wo warst du, Adam?*

"Adultery" (Banks) **72**:5, 9

"Adventures of a Haversack" (Böll) **72**:100

Affliction (Banks) **72**:11-19, 22

After Lorca (Spicer) **72**:348, 352-57, 359-65

After the Rehearsal (Bergman) **72**:59, 61

"Against Silence" (Hacker) **72**:191

"The Air and the Wind" (Galeano) **72**:139

"Alba" (Spicer) **72**:364

All These Women (Bergman)
See *For att ente tala om alla dessa kvinnor*

"Almost Aubade" (Hacker) **72**:184

Als der Krieg ausbrach (*Enter and Exit; When the War Began; When the War Started*) (Böll) **72**:79

Als der Krieg zu Ende war (*When the War Ended; When the War Was Over*) (Böll) **72**:78, 80

And Where Were You, Adam? (Böll)
See *Wo warst du, Adam?*

"The Android and the Human" (Dick) **72**:107

"Anseo" (Muldoon) **72**:266

Ansichten eines Clowns (*The Clown*) (Böll) **72**:68, 73

Ansikte mot ansikte (*Face to Face*) (Bergman) **72**:53-7, 59, 61

Ansiktet (*The Face; The Magician*) (Bergman) **72**:31, 33, 40-1, 50

"Armageddon, Armageddon" (Muldoon) **72**:265-66

Armageddon?: Essays 1983-1987 (*At Home: Essays*) (Vidal) **72**:398, 400

Articulation of Sound Forms in Time (Howe) **72**:202-05, 207, 209

The Artificial Kid (Sterling) **72**:372

"Asra" (Muldoon) **72**:281

Assumptions (Hacker) **72**:182-84, 189-90

At Home: Essays (Vidal)
See *Armageddon?: Essays 1983-1987*

"Aufenthalt in X" ("Sojourn in X") (Böll) **72**:69, 79

Aus dem Leben der Marionetten (*From the Life of the Marionettes*) (Bergman) **72**:59, 61

"Autumn 1980" (Hacker) **72**:183-84

Autumn Sonata (Bergman)
See *Höstsonaten*

"The Balek Scales" (Böll)
See "Die Waage der Baleks"

"Ballad of Ladies Lost and Found" (Hacker) **72**:182-85, 190

"Barbados" (Marshall) **72**:227, 248

"The Beautiful and the Sublime" (Sterling) **72**:372

"Bechbretha" (Muldoon) **72**:273

Berichte zur Gesinnungslage der Nation (*Reports on the Ideological Situation of the Nation*) (Böll) **72**:85

Beröringen (*The Touch*) (Bergman) **72**:47, 50, 53-5, 57, 59

"Beyond Lies the Wub" ("The Wub") (Dick) **72**:113

Beyond the Revolution: My Life and Times Since :Famous Long Ago: (Mungo) **72**:292

A Bibliography of the King's Book or, Eikon Basilike (Howe) **72**:208

"The Big House" (Muldoon) **72**:264-65

"Bigfoot" (Muldoon) **72**:270

Billard um Halblzehn (*Billiards at Half-past Nine*) (Böll) **72**:68, 72-3, 85

Billiards at Half-past Nine (Böll)
See *Billard um Halblzehn*

"Blowing Eggs" (Muldoon) **72**:265

"Bonn Diary" (Böll) **72**:68

The Book of Embraces (Galeano) **72**:138-41, 143-44

The Book of Jamaica (Banks) **72**:4, 14

Book of Magazine Verse (Spicer) **72**:345-46, 351, 358

"Die Botschaft" ("Breaking the News"; "The Message") (Böll) **72**:69, 73, 78

"The Boundary Commission" (Muldoon) **72**:268

"Brazil" (Marshall) **72**:230

"Breaking the News" (Böll)
See "Die Botschaft"

"The Briefcase" (Muldoon) **72**:281

Brighton Rock (Greene) **72**:149-51, 155, 157-59, 161-63, 165, 178

The British Dramatists (Greene) **72**:153

"British Guiana" (Marshall) **72**:229

"Brock" (Muldoon) **72**:273

Brown Girl, Brownstones (Marshall) **72**:212, 222-23, 226-27, 231-32, 243, 248-50, 252, 254-55

"Buffalo. 12.7.41" (Howe) **72**:202

A Burnt-Out Case (Greene) **72**:177

Burr (Vidal) **72**:377, 379-80, 382, 384-85, 387, 389, 391-92, 394-95, 398, 400-02, 404

"Business is Business" (Böll)
See "Geschäft ist Geschäft"

"Callings" (Galeano) **72**:139

The Captain and the Enemy (Greene) **72**:177

"Les carabosses" (Hacker) **72**:188

"Cass and Me" (Muldoon) **72**:272

"Celles" (Hacker) **72**:192

"The Child Screams and Looks Back at You" (Banks) **72**:4

Children Are Civilians, Too (Böll) **72**:73

"Chinook" (Muldoon) **72**:275

The Chosen Place, the Timeless People
(Marshall) **72**:212-13, 216, 219, 231, 233,
235, 247-48, 250-51, 254
"Christmas Every Day" (Böll)
See "Nicht nur zur Weihnachtzeit"
"Christo's" ("Cristo's") (Muldoon) **72**:273-
74, 277
"Cicada Queen" (Sterling) **72**:368
The City and the Pillar (Vidal) **72**:378, 387
Clans of the Alphane Moon (Dick) **72**:109,
121
The Clown (Böll)
See *Ansichten eines Clowns*
The Collected Books of Jack Spicer (Spicer)
72:345, 348, 352
"Colony" (Dick) **72**:108
"Come into My Parlour" (Muldoon) **72**:267
The Comedians (Greene) **72**:156-57, 163, 165
The Communicants (Bergman)
See *Nattvardsgästerna*
"The Coney" (Muldoon) **72**:273, 277
*Confessions from Left Field: A Baseball
Pilgrimage* (Mungo) **72**:291-92
The Confidential Agent (Greene) **72**:148, 151,
155, 169, 171-72, 176, 179
Continental Drift (Banks) **72**:2-5, 7, 9, 11-12,
14, 16-18, 22
"Conversation in the Park" (Hacker) **72**:188
*Cosmic Profit: How to Make Money without
Doing Time* (Mungo) **72**:291
Counter-Clock World (Dick) **72**:121-22
"Country & Western I" (Hacker) **72**:192
"Country & Western II" (Hacker) **72**:192
"The Country Club" (Muldoon) **72**:265
The Crack in Space (Dick) **72**:121
Creation (Vidal) **72**:385, 387
Cries and Whispers (Bergman)
See *Viskningar och rop*
Crisis (Bergman)
See *Kris*
"Cristo's" (Muldoon)
See "Christo's"
"Crossing the Line" (Muldoon) **72**:273
The Crying of Lot 49 (Pynchon) **72**:294-342
Crystal Express (Sterling) **72**:372
"Cuba" (Muldoon) **72**:266
"Cuckoo Corn" (Muldoon) **72**:265
"Cultural Exchanges" (Hacker) **72**:192
"Damals in Odessa" ("That Time in Odessa")
(Böll) **72**:69, 79
"Dancers at the Moy" (Muldoon) **72**:264
Daughters (Marshall) **72**:254-60
Days and Nights of Love and War (Galeano)
72:129-31, 143-44
"Dear Jool, I Miss You in Saint-Saturnin"
(Hacker) **72**:192
"The Death of Elsa Baskoleit" (Böll)
See "Der Tod der Elsa Baskoleit"
Defenestration of Prague (Howe) **72**:195, 197-
98, 208
"The Defenseman" (Banks) **72**:4
"An der Angel" (Böll) **72**:70-1
"An der Brücke" (Böll) **72**:69
Deus Irae (Dick) **72**:108
The Devil's Eye (Bergman)
See *Djävulens öga*
The Devil's Wanton (Bergman)
See *Fängelse*
The Difference Engine (Sterling) **72**:372-73
"Dinner in Audoghast" (Sterling) **72**:372
The Divine Invasion (Dick) **72**:113, 119-20

Djävulens öga (*The Devil's Eye*) (Bergman)
72:40
Do Androids Dream of Electric Sheep? (Dick)
72:104, 108, 110, 113, 117-24
*Dr. Bloodmoney, or How We Got Along After
the Bomb* (Dick) **72**:107, 110, 114, 121
Dr. Futurity (Dick) **72**:120
Dr. Murke's Collected Silences (Böll)
See *Doktor Murkes gesammeltes Schweigen,
und andere Satiren*
*Doktor Murkes gesammeltes Schweigen, und
andere Satiren* (*Dr. Murke's Collected
Silences; Murke's Collected Silences*) (Böll)
72:72, 80
Dreams (Bergman)
See *Kvinnodröm*
"Dreams" (Galeano) **72**:130
"The Ducking Stool" (Muldoon) **72**:265
"Duffy's Circus" (Muldoon) **72**:275
Duluth (Vidal) **72**:384-87, 389
1876: A Novel (Vidal) **72**:377, 382-85, 387,
389, 391-93, 395-96, 399-402, 404
18 Stories (Böll) **72**:67, 73
"Elizabeth" (Muldoon) **72**:265-66
Empire (Vidal) **72**:391-404
En lektion i kärlek (*A Lesson in Love*)
(Bergman) **72**:40-1, 48, 52, 62
En Passion (*The Passion of Anna; A Passion*)
(Bergman) **72**:49-50, 53, 57, 59
End of a Mission (Böll)
See *Ende einer Dienstfahrt*
The End of the Affair (Greene) **72**:155, 167,
169, 177-78
Ende einer Dienstfahrt (*End of a Mission*)
(Böll) **72**:89, 93
England Made Me (Greene) **72**:148, 150-51,
161
Enter and Exit (Böll)
See *Als der Krieg ausbrach*
Entfernung von der Truppe (*Absent without
Leave*) (Böll) **72**:68, 93
"Entropy" (Pynchon) **72**:302-04
"Epilog zu Stifters 'Nachsommer'" (Böll)
72:77
"Er kam als Bierfahrer" (Böll) **72**:77
Erzählungen, 1950-1970 (Böll) **72**:76
"Es wird etwas geschehen" (Böll) **72**:72
"Die Essenholer" (Böll) **72**:69
The Europe of Trusts (Howe) **72**:208
Eye in the Sky (Dick) **72**:104, 108, 120, 122
The Face (Bergman)
See *Ansiktet*
Face to Face (Bergman)
See *Ansikte mot ansikte*
The Fallen Idol (Greene) **72**:165
Family Life (Banks) **72**:14
*Famous Long Ago: My Life and Hard Times
with Liberation News Service* (Mungo)
72:285-89, 291
Fängelse (*The Devil's Wanton; Prison*)
(Bergman) **72**:39, 52
Fanny and Alexander (Bergman)
See *Fanny och Alexander*
Fanny och Alexander (*Fanny and Alexander*)
(Bergman) **72**:57-61
"Firewood" (Banks) **72**:5
"The Fish" (Banks) **72**:3, 5
"Five Meals" (Hacker) **72**:192
Flow My Tears, the Policeman Said (Dick)
72:104, 106
"Flowers of Edo" (Sterling) **72**:372

For att ente tala om alla dessa kvinnor (*Now
about These Women; All These Women*)
(Bergman) **72**:40
"For K. J., Leaving and Coming Back"
(Hacker) **72**:192
Four Screenplays of Ingmar Bergman
(Bergman) **72**:31, 33, 35
"Fourteen" (Hacker) **72**:182
"The Fox" (Muldoon) **72**:276
"Fragments of a Liquidation" (Howe) **72**:195
Frenzy (Bergman)
See *Hets*
"From Orient Point" (Hacker) **72**:192
From the Life of the Marionettes (Bergman)
See *Aus dem Leben der Marionetten*
Galactic Pot-Healer (Dick) **72**:121
"Gathering Mushrooms" ("Mushroom
Gathering") (Muldoon) **72**:282
"Gerda in the Eyrie" (Hacker) **72**:182
"Geschäft ist Geschäft" ("Business is
Business") (Böll) **72**:70, 101
Getting to Know the General (Greene) **72**:177
Going Back to the River (Hacker) **72**:191-92
"Gold" (Muldoon) **72**:272
"Good Friday 1971. Riding Westward"
(Muldoon) **72**:264-65
"Graffiti from the Gare Saint-Manqué"
(Hacker) **72**:182-84, 190
Gravity's Rainbow (Pynchon) **72**:332, 335-36,
340
"Green Days in Brunei" (Sterling) **72**:372
"Grief" (Muldoon) **72**:267, 269
Group Portrait with Lady (Böll)
See *Gruppenbild mit Dame*
Gruppenbild mit Dame (*Group Portrait with
Lady*) (Böll) **72**:78, 85, 89, 100
Guatemala: Occupied Country (Galeano)
72:129
"The Gully" (Banks) **72**:5
A Gun for Sale (*This Gun for Hire*) (Greene)
72:148
Gycklarnas afton (*The Naked Night; Sawdust
and Tinsel; The Sunset of a Clown*)
(Bergman) **72**:29-30, 40-1, 48, 62
Hamilton Stark (Banks) **72**:4-5
Hamnstad (*Port of Call*) (Bergman) **72**:52, 62
"Haupstädtisches Journal" (Böll) **72**:72
Haus ohne Hüter (*Tomorrow and Yesterday;
The Unguarded House*) (Böll) **72**:72
The Heads of the Town up to the Aether
(Spicer) **72**:348, 350, 357
The Heart of the Matter (Greene) **72**:148-49,
151-52, 155, 177-78
"Heroes are Made in Childhood" (Greene)
72:151
Hets (*Frenzy; Torment*) (Bergman) **72**:51, 61
"Hier ist Tibten" (Böll) **72**:72
"The Hint of an Explanation" (Greene)
72:148
"Hisperica Famina" (Spicer) **72**:357-58
Hollywood: A Novel of America in the 1920s
(Vidal) **72**:400-04, 406
The Holy Grail (Spicer) **72**:351
"Holy Thursday" (Muldoon) **72**:275
"Hope Atherton's Wanderings" (Howe)
72:204
"Hostages" (Banks) **72**:3, 5
Höstsonaten (*Autumn Sonata*) (Bergman)
72:57, 59
Hour of the Wolf (Bergman)
See *Vargtimmen*

"How to Play Championship Tennis"
(Muldoon) **72**:265
The Human Factor (Greene) **72**:177
"Identities" (Muldoon) **72**:265
Illicit Interlude (Bergman)
See *Sommarlek*
"Im Lande der Rujuks" ("In the Land of the
Rujuks") (Böll) **72**:72
"Immram" (Muldoon) **72**:267-68, 270, 273-
74, 280
"Immrama" (Muldoon) **72**:278
"In Defense of the Word" (Galeano) **72**:130
"In der Finsternis" (Böll) **72**:69
"In the Land of the Rujuks" (Böll)
See "Im Lande der Rujuks"
"Inheritances" (Hacker) **72**:184
"Introduction to History" (Galeano) **72**:130
"Ireland" (Muldoon) **72**:266, 268
Islands in the Net (Sterling) **72**:370-71, 373
It's a Battlefield (Greene) **72**:148-49, 152-53,
158, 160-61
Journey into Autumn (Bergman)
See *Kvinnodröm*
"Journey into the Mind of Watts" (Pynchon)
72:332, 335
Journey without Maps (Greene) **72**:149-50,
152, 161
Julian (*Julian the Apostate*) (Vidal) **72**:386-
87, 389, 399, 406
Julian the Apostate (Vidal)
See *Julian*
Kalki (Vidal) **72**:386-87
"Kerzen für Maria" (Böll) **72**:70
"The Key" (Muldoon) **72**:282
"Die Kirche im Dorf" (Böll) **72**:77
"The Knife-Thrower" (Böll)
See "Der Mann mit den Messern"
Kris (*Crisis*) (Bergman) **72**:51
"Kumpel mit dem langen Haar" (Böll) **72**:69
Kvinnodröm (*Dreams*; *Journey into Autumn*)
(Bergman) **72**:41, 62
Kvinnors väntan (*Secrets of Women*; *Waiting
Women*) (Bergman) **72**:40, 62
Language (Spicer) **72**:346, 348, 351
Lanterna Magica (*The Magic Lantern*)
(Bergman) **72**:60-2
"Largesse" (Muldoon) **72**:265
"The Lass of Aughrim" (Muldoon) **72**:277
"The Last of the Masters" (Dick) **72**:113
"Late August" (Hacker) **72**:192
The Lawless Roads (Greene) **72**:150-51, 155,
160
A Lesson in Love (Bergman)
See *En lektion i kärlek*
"Letter from the Alpes-Maritimes" (Hacker)
72:189
"Letter on August 15" (Hacker) **72**:188, 190
The Liberties (Howe) **72**:208
Lincoln: A Novel (Vidal) **72**:386-87, 389-93,
395-400, 402-04, 406
"The Little Black Box" (Dick) **72**:113
"The Little Robber Girl Considers Some
Options" (Hacker) **72**:190
"Lohengrin's Tod" (Böll) **72**:70
*The Lost Honor of Katharina Blum: How
Violence Develops and Where It Can Lead*
(Böll)
See *Die verlorene Ehre der Katharina Blum:
oder, Wie Gewalt entstehen und wohin sie
führen kann*
Love, Death, and the Changing of the Seasons
(Hacker) **72**:185, 187-88, 191-92

"Lull" (Muldoon) **72**:266
"Lunch with Pancho Villa" (Muldoon)
72:265-66, 268
"Madoc: A Mystery" (Muldoon) **72**:279-82
Madoc: A Mystery (Muldoon) **72**:279, 281-83
The Magic Flute (Bergman)
See *Trollflöjten*
The Magic Lantern (Bergman)
See *Lanterna Magica*
The Magician (Bergman)
See *Ansiktet*
The Man in the High Castle (Dick) **72**:105,
107, 117-22
The Man Within (Greene) **72**:148-50, 177
"Der Mann mit den Messern" ("The Knife-
Thrower") (Böll) **72**:69, 76
"Market Day" (Hacker) **72**:192
"The Marriage of Strongbow and Aoife"
(Muldoon) **72**:279
Martian Time-Slip (Dick) **72**:108, 114, 119,
121-22
A Maze of Death (Dick) **72**:121-22
"Meeting the British" (Muldoon) **72**:276
Meeting the British (Muldoon) **72**:273-74,
277-79
"Mein Onkel Fred" (Böll) **72**:72
"Mein trauriges Gesicht" (Böll) **72**:70-1
Memory of Fire (Galeano) **72**:131, 133-37,
139-41, 143-44
Memory of Fire: Century of the Wind
(Galeano) **72**:135-38, 140
Memory of Fire: Faces and Masks (Galeano)
72:132-37
Memory of Fire: Genesis (Galeano) **72**:131-38
"The Merman" (Muldoon) **72**:264
"The Message" (Böll)
See "Die Botschaft"
Messiah (Vidal) **72**:387
The Ministry of Fear (Greene) **72**:148-50,
169-72
Mirrorshades: The Cyberpunk Anthology
(Sterling) **72**:370
"The Mist Net" (Muldoon) **72**:277
Monsignor Quixote (Greene) **72**:163-64
"The More a Man Has, the More a Man
Wants" (Muldoon) **72**:270, 274, 279, 282
"Mother" (Hacker) **72**:182
Mules (Muldoon) **72**:264-65, 273-74, 276
"Murke's Collected Silences" (Böll) **72**:73,
101
Murke's Collected Silences (Böll)
See *Doktor Murkes gesammeltes Schweigen,
und andere Satiren*
"Mushroom Gathering" (Muldoon)
See "Gathering Mushrooms"
My Emily Dickinson (Howe) **72**:195-201, 203,
209
"My Grandfather's Wake" (Muldoon) **72**:273
"My Life" (Howe) **72**:198, 200
Myra Breckinridge (Vidal) **72**:386-87, 389
Myron (Vidal) **72**:387
The Naked Night (Bergman)
See *Gycklarnas afton*
The Name of Action (Greene) **72**:158-59, 161
"Nanny" (Dick) **72**:118
Nattvardsgästerna (*The Communicants*; *Winter
Light*) (Bergman) **72**:33, 38-41, 46-7, 49,
52, 54 5, 59
"Ned Skinner" (Muldoon) **72**:276
New Weather (Muldoon) **72**:264-65, 276, 279
The New World (Banks) **72**:4, 12, 14

Nicht nur zur Weihnachtzeit (Böll) **72**:72,
90-4
"Nicht nur zur Weihnachtzeit" ("Christmas
Every Day") (Böll) **72**:90
"The Night / 1" (Galeano) **72**:139
"Nights of 1964-1966: The Old Reliable"
(Hacker) **72**:191
"1901: In All Latin America" (Galeano)
72:138
Now about These Women (Bergman)
See *For att ente tala om alla dessa kvinnor*
Now Wait for Last Year (Dick) **72**:121
"October 1950" (Muldoon) **72**:265
"The One Desire" (Muldoon) **72**:267
One Night Stand, and Other Poems (Spicer)
72:352, 363
"Ontario" (Muldoon) **72**:273
*The Open Veins of Latin America: Five
Centuries of the Pillage of a Continent*
(Galeano) **72**:127-29, 131, 136, 143
"Open Windows" (Hacker) **72**:182
Orient Express (Greene)
See *Stamboul Train*
Ormen's ägg (*The Serpent's Egg*) (Bergman)
72:55, 57, 59
"The Other Side of the Border" (Greene)
72:149
Our Friends from Frolix-8 (Dick) **72**:121-22
"Our Lady of Ardboe" (Muldoon) **72**:266
Our Man in Havana (Greene) **72**:163-65, 169,
171-72
"Palm Sunday" (Muldoon) **72**:267-68
"Paris" (Muldoon) **72**:266
"Party Piece" (Muldoon) **72**:265
"Pascal" (Muldoon) **72**:280
A Passion (Bergman)
See *En Passion*
The Passion of Anna (Bergman)
See *En Passion*
The Penultimate Truth (Dick) **72**:108, 123-24
Persona (Bergman) **72**:40, 46, 48-52, 55, 57,
59
Pink Triangle and Yellow Star (Vidal)
See *The Second American Revolution, and
Other Essays, 1976-1982*
"Poems 1946-56" (Spicer) **72**:362
Port of Call (Bergman)
See *Hamnstad*
"Die Postkarte" (Böll) **72**:71
The Power and the Glory (Greene) **72**:148,
151-55, 157, 178-79
Praisesong for the Widow (Marshall) **72**:231-
32, 236-37, 242-46, 248-50, 252-54
Presentation Piece (Hacker) **72**:182, 184, 192
"The Princess and the Pea" (Muldoon)
72:278
Prison (Bergman)
See *Fängelse*
"Profumo" (Muldoon) **72**:277
"Promises, Promises" (Muldoon) **72**:268
"Pythagoras in America" (Muldoon) **72**:281
Pythagorean Silence (Howe) **72**:195, 202, 207-
08
"Queen for a Day" (Banks) **72**:5
The Quiet American (Greene) **72**:155-56, 173,
177
Quoof (Muldoon) **72**:270, 272-74, 276, 282
"Radar" (Spicer) **72**:361-63
"Reena" (Marshall) **72**:222
"Regent's Park Sonnets" (Hacker) **72**:182
The Relation Of My Imprisonment (Banks)
72:8

Reports on the Ideological Situation of the Nation (Böll)
See *Berichte zur Gesinnungslage der Nation*
Return to Sender or, When the Fish in the Water Was Thirsty (Mungo) 72:290
"Reunion in the Avenue" (Böll)
See "Wiedersehen in der Allee"
"Reunion on the Avenue" (Böll)
See "Wiedersehen in der Allee"
"The Revolver in the Corner Cupboard" (Greene) 72:151-52
"The Right Arm" (Muldoon) 72:272
"Riposte" (Hacker) 72:191
The Rite (Bergman)
See *Riten*
Riten (*The Rite*; *The Ritual*) (Bergman) 72:46-7, 56, 61
The Ritual (Bergman)
See *Riten*
"Roog" (Dick) 72:113
Rumour at Nightfall (Greene) 72:148, 158-59, 161
"Runaways Café I" (Hacker) 72:187
"Runaways Café II" (Hacker) 72:187
"Sarah Cole: A Type of Love Story" (Banks) 72:3-5
Såsom i en spegel (*Through A Glass Darkly*) (Bergman) 72:33, 37-41, 47, 50, 52, 54-5, 57, 59, 62
Sawdust and Tinsel (Bergman)
See *Gycklarnas afton*
A Scanner Darkly (Dick) 72:110
Scener ur ett äktenskap (*Scenes from a Marriage*) (Bergman) 72:57, 59-61
Scenes from a Marriage (Bergman)
See *Scener ur ett äktenskap*
Schismatrix (Sterling) 72:368, 370
Searching for Survivors (Banks) 72:4-5, 12, 14
The Second American Revolution, and Other Essays, 1976-1982 (*Pink Triangle and Yellow Star*) (Vidal) 72:386
Secrets of Women (Bergman)
See *Kvinnors väntan*
Selected Poems: 1968-86 (Muldoon) 72:275-76
"Self" (Hacker) 72:191
Separations (Hacker) 72:188
The Serpent's Egg (Bergman)
See *Ormen's ägg*
"7, Middagh Street" (Muldoon) 72:274, 277, 280, 282
The Seventh Seal (Bergman)
See *Det sjunde inseglet*
Shame (Bergman)
See *Skammen*
"Shaping the World of My Art" (Marshall) 72:249
"Sheep Trails Are Fateful to Strangers" (Spicer) 72:349
"Shell Game" (Dick) 72:109
The Silence (Bergman)
See *Tystnaden*
The Simulacra (Dick) 72:104, 121
Singularities (Howe) 72:209
Det sjunde inseglet (*The Seventh Seal*) (Bergman) 72:27-40, 52, 54-6, 59-60
Skammen (*Shame*) (Bergman) 72:40, 49-50, 52, 54, 57, 59
Smiles of a Summer Night (Bergman)
See *Sommarnattens leende*
Smultronstället (*Wild Strawberries*) (Bergman) 72:31-7, 39-41, 52
"So ein Rummel" (Böll) 72:69

So ward Abend und Morgen (Böll) 72:71, 74
"The Soap-Pig" (Muldoon) 72:273
"Sojourn in X" (Böll)
See "Aufenthalt in X"
Solar Lottery (Dick) 72:120
"Some Get Wasted" (Marshall) 72:248
Sommarlek (*Illicit Interlude*; *Summer Interlude*; *Summerplay*) (Bergman) 72:40-1, 62
Sommarnattens leende (*Smiles of a Summer Night*) (Bergman) 72:30-1, 40, 52, 54-5, 60-2
A Sort of Life (Greene) 72:160, 179
Soul Clap Hands and Sing (Marshall) 72:212, 227, 231, 248, 254
"Speeches at the Barriers" (Howe) 72:195
"Spider Rose" (Sterling) 72:368
"The Staech Affair" (Böll)
See "Veränderungen in Staech"
Stamboul Train (*Orient Express*) (Greene) 72:159, 169, 171, 176
"Steh auf, steh doch auf" (Böll) 72:69
The Stories of Heinrich Böll (Böll) 72:99
"Stranger, Bear Words to the Spartans We..." (Böll)
See "Wanderer, kommst du nach Spa..."
Success Stories (Banks) 72:2-5, 9, 11
Summer Interlude (Bergman)
See *Sommarlek*
Summerplay (Bergman)
See *Sommarlek*
The Sunset of a Clown (Bergman)
See *Gycklarnas afton*
"Sushi" (Muldoon) 72:273-74, 277
"Swarm" (Sterling) 72:368, 372
The Sweet Hereafter (Banks) 72:19-24
"Sword" (Hacker) 72:184
"The System" (Galeano) 72:130
Taking Notice (Hacker) 72:182-83
"The Territory Is Not the Map" (Spicer) 72:349
"That Time in Odessa" (Böll)
See "Damals in Odessa"
"Then" (Hacker) 72:191
The Third Man (Greene) 72:165-66, 168, 173-76
Thirst (Bergman)
See *Törst*
This Gun for Hire (Greene)
See *A Gun for Sale*
"Thorow" (Howe) 72:205, 209
The Three Stigmata of Palmer Eldritch (Dick) 72:113, 117-19, 121-22
Through A Glass Darkly (Bergman)
See *Såsom i en spegel*
"The Thrower-Away" (Böll)
See "Der Wegwerfer"
Till glädje (*To Joy*) (Bergman) 72:62
Time Out of Joint (Dick) 72:110
Timothy Archer (Dick)
See *The Transmigration of Timothy Archer*
To Joy (Bergman)
See *Till glädje*
"Der Tod der Elsa Baskoleit" ("The Death of Elsa Baskoleit") (Böll) 72:68, 71
"The Toe-Tag" (Muldoon) 72:273
Tomorrow and Yesterday (Böll)
See *Haus ohne Hüter*
Torment (Bergman)
See *Hets*
Törst (*Thirst*) (Bergman) 72:40, 52

Total Loss Farm: A Year in the Life (Mungo) 72:288-92
The Touch (Bergman)
See *Beröringen*
"Towards Autumn" (Hacker) 72:182
Trailerpark (Banks) 72:4, 9, 11, 14, 17
The Train Was on Time (Böll)
See *Der Zug war pünktlich*
The Transmigration of Timothy Archer (*Timothy Archer*) (Dick) 72:114, 119-20
Traveller, If You Come to Spa (Böll)
See *Wanderer, kommst du nach Spa...*
"Traveller, If You Come to the Spa" (Böll)
See "Wanderer, kommst du nach Spa..."
"Traveller, If You Go to Spa" (Böll)
See "Wanderer, kommst du nach Spa..."
Travels with My Aunt (Greene) 72:164
Trollflöjten (*The Magic Flute*) (Bergman) 72:61
"Truce" (Muldoon) 72:266
"Trunk in Petöcki" (Böll) 72:69
Two Sisters (Vidal) 72:387
Tystnaden (*The Silence*) (Bergman) 72:39-41, 52, 54-5, 59, 62
"Über die Brücke" (Böll) 72:69
Ubik (Dick) 72:104, 108, 110-12, 117, 119, 121-22
Unberechenbare Gäste (Böll) 72:71
The Unguarded House (Böll)
See *Haus ohne Hüter*
"The Universe as Seen Through a Keyhole" (Galeano) 72:130
"Unsere gute, alte Renée" (Böll) 72:70
The Unteleported Man (Dick) 72:110, 121
V. (Pynchon) 72:296-99, 301-02, 308-09, 311, 325, 339
VALIS (Dick) 72:109, 116-20
"The Valley Between" (Marshall) 72:254
"Vampire" (Muldoon) 72:265
"Vaquero" (Muldoon) 72:264
Vargtimmen (*Hour of the Wolf*) (Bergman) 72:40-1, 50, 52, 55, 62
"Veränderungen in Staech" ("The Staech Affair") (Böll) 72:77, 101
Die verlorene Ehre der Katharina Blum: oder, Wie Gewalt entstehen und wohin sie führen kann (*The Lost Honor of Katharina Blum: How Violence Develops and Where It Can Lead*) (Böll) 72:85-6, 88, 90
Viskningar och rop (*Cries and Whispers*) (Bergman) 72:52, 54-5, 57, 59, 62
"Die Waage der Baleks" ("The Balek Scales") (Böll) 72:71, 74-6
Waiting Women (Bergman)
See *Kvinnors väntan*
"Wanderer, kommst du nach Spa..." ("Stranger, Bear Words to the Spartans We..."; "Traveller, If You Come to the Spa"; "Traveller, If You Go to Spa") (Böll) 72:70, 73, 79-84, 94, 98, 100
Wanderer, kommst du nach Spa... (*Traveller, If You Come to Spa*) (Böll) 72:69, 76, 78
Was soll aus dem Jungen bloß werden?: oder, Irgendwas mit Büchern (*What's to Become of the Boy? or, Something to Do with Books*) (Böll) 72:101
Washington, D.C. (Vidal) 72:377-79, 382-84, 389, 391-93, 395-97, 400-03
Ways of Escape (Greene) 72:179
We Can Build You (Dick) 72:104
"We Can Remember It for You Wholesale" (Dick) 72:123-24

"Der Wegwerfer" ("The Thrower-Away")
(Böll)   **72**:67, 72-3, 101
*Werke: Essayistiche Schriften und Reden I,
1952-1956* (Böll)   **72**:97
The Western Borders (Howe)   **72**:202
*What's to Become of the Boy? or, Something to
Do with Books* (Böll)
See *Was soll aus dem Jungen bloß werden?:
oder, Irgendwas mit Büchern*
When the War Began (Böll)
See *Als der Krieg ausbrach*
When the War Ended (Böll)
See *Als der Krieg zu Ende war*
When the War Started (Böll)
See *Als der Krieg ausbrach*
When the War Was Over (Böll)
See *Als der Krieg zu Ende war*
"Who is an SF Writer?" (Dick)   **72**:106
"Why Brownlee Left" (Muldoon)   **72**:267, 272
Why Brownlee Left (Muldoon)   **72**:365-66,
268-69, 273-74, 276-78
"Wie das Gesetz es befahl" (Böll)   **72**:98
"Wiedersehen in der Allee" ("Reunion in the
Avenue"; "Reunion on the Avenue") (Böll)
72:69, 101
"Wiedersehen mit Drüng" (Böll)   **72**:69
Wild Strawberries (Bergman)
See *Smultronstället*
Williwaw (Vidal)   **72**:387
Winter Light (Bergman)
See *Nattvardsgästerna*
"Wir Besenbinder" (Böll)   **72**:69
"The Wishbone" (Muldoon)   **72**:277, 279
*Wo warst du, Adam? (Adam, Where Art Thou?;
And Where Were You, Adam?)* (Böll)
72:78-80, 100
The Woman without a Face (Bergman)   **72**:51
"The World (This One), the Flesh (Mrs.
Oedipa Maas), and the Testament of Pierce
Inverarity" (Pynchon)   **72**:309, 323, 333
"The Wub" (Dick)
See "Beyond Lies the Wub"
"The Year of the Sloes, for Ishi" (Muldoon)
72:279
The Zap Gun (Dick)   **72**:110, 121-22
*Der Zug war pünktlich (The Train Was on
Time)* (Böll)   **72**:78-80, 100

ISBN 0-8103-4976-0

90000